Shooter's Bible

Shooter's Bible

No. 71
1980 Edition

EDITOR:
Robert F. Scott

MANAGING EDITOR:
Linda E. S. Heimburg

ASSISTANT MANAGING EDITOR:
Maureen Lyons

EDITORIAL ASSISTANTS:
Bryna Bloomberg
Sarah Harnick
Florence McCoy

ARTISTS:
Cheryl Greenwald
Thomas J. McGrory, Jr.

CONSULTANTS:
Frank Ercolino
Frank Gologorsky
Hermann Koelling

TYPOGRAPHER:
Emil P. Popp & Sons

COVER PHOTOGRAPHER:
Deaton, Wells & Koumjian

Stoeger Publishing Company

Copyright © 1979 by Stoeger Publishing Company

All rights reserved

Published by Stoeger Publishing Company
55 Ruta Court, South Hackensack, New Jersey 07606

Library of Congress Catalog Card No.: 63-6200

International Standard Book No.: 0-88317-093-0

Manufactured in the United States of America

Distributed to the book trade by Follett Publishing Company, 1010 West Washington Boulevard, Chicago, Illinois 60607 and to the sporting goods trade by Stoeger Industries, 55 Ruta Court, South Hackensack, New Jersey 07606

In Canada, distributed to the book trade and to the sporting goods trade by Stoeger Trading Company, 2020R 32nd Avenue, Northeast, Calgary, Alberta T2E 6T4

Contents

Foreword

I do not recall that any writer has ever remarked on the curious coincidence that the invention of gunpowder and printing took place at the same time. Thus, the gun and the book are contemporaries, and both have a distinguished history.

In assembling the lineup of articles for the SHOOTER'S BIBLE, we use no formula. In addition to timeliness in our articles, there is one thing, however, we do look for in our authors and that is expertise. It is no exaggeration to say that every article in this SHOOTER'S BIBLE has been written by *the recognized authority* on the subject.

Our cover article is a significant contribution to the history of technology by someone whose name will be familiar to SHOOTER'S BIBLE readers. In *The Great Equalizer*, George M. Horn has encapsulated the highlights of the history of the revolver in a delightful contribution to the history of this fascinating weapon. Readers will no doubt be surprised to discover just how ancient the lineage of the revolver really is, with antecedents going back to the sixteenth century.

Chuck Adams, rising California outdoor writer and hunter extraordinary, next debunks some myths and misrepresentations about the difficulties associated with hunting various types of North American big game. If you have never tried your hand at big game, this illuminating article will enable you to plan a hunting trip that can be both challenging and rewarding.

The year 1980 will be dominated by a series of news events that will take place in Russia—The XXII Olympiad at Moscow. The time-honored track and field events will be the focus of interest as always, but shooters everywhere will be watching the seven shooting events with special attention. To bring readers up-to-date on Who's Who and What's What in the shooting sports at the Olympics, we have asked Robert Hunnicutt of the National Rifle Association to describe the separate events and to single out individual competitors in the several events. His article is an indispensable *vade mecum* for anyone who would follow Olympic shooting.

James F. Brady is no stranger to SHOOTER'S BIBLE readers. This retired Treasury agent just happens to be one of America's best-known turkey hunters, and author of a standard work on the subject, *Modern Turkey Hunting.* In this year's SHOOTER'S BIBLE, he has contributed an informative and highly useful article on equipment for the varmint hunter.

"As American as apple pie," is an often-heard expression, but anyone who has ever attended the *Grand American Handicap* which is conducted each year in the quaint Ohio town of Vandalia would want to change it to, "As American as the Grand American." John M. Bahret, editor of the prestigious magazine *Trap & Field* has captured in *The Grand Old Grand* the sights, sounds and excitement of this traditional American event.

No name is more respected in the field of replica guns than that of Val Forgett, President of Navy Arms, Inc. The explosion of interest in black powder weapons—in fact, in guns of all kinds as collectors' items for pleasure and investment—has caused a rash of fakes to be turned loose on an unsuspecting public. In *How to Detect Counterfeit Guns,* this respected expert gives readers tips on how to spot the genuine from the fake. His revealing illustrations alone are worth the price of admission.

Don Lewis is the owner of Lewis Gun Shop of Kittanning, Pennsylvania, where hunters and shooters gather from all parts of the country to benefit from his wide-ranging knowledge. No stranger to SHOOTER'S BIBLE readers, in *How to Sight-in Your Rifle,* Don Lewis offers invaluable tips that will ensure hitting the ten ring of the target or the quarry every time.

Eleven times New Jersey skeet champion (in 1952, he won every individual and team event statewide, a never-duplicated feat) and now outdoor columnist for the *Newark Star-Ledger*, Howard Brant is exceptionally well qualified to advise on *Selecting a Shotgun*, which offers solid advice to enable you to tailor your shotgun to your shooting style.

Frank T. Hanenkrat's name will be recognized from one of the first volumes published in the Stoeger Sportsman's Library series, POSITION RIFLE SHOOTING, which he wrote with Bill Pullum. Since the role of vision in target shooting is so critical, it is surprising that standard works on shooting never cover it. Mr. Hanenkrat now remedies that deficiency in his authoritative article.

Oregon-based Tom Roster has achieved a wide reputation as a shotgunner. In his timely article on the steel-shot controversy, he cuts through the fog of misinformation that has sprung up around this contentious subject.

Last but not least, British gun writer John Walter concludes his two-part article on the military models of Browning Blowback Pistols, a truly significant contribution to the documentation of these important guns.

Of course, mention must be made, too, of the other half of the SHOOTER'S BIBLE: the authoritative descriptions, specifications and illustrations of every gun—handgun, rifle or shotgun—plus air guns, black powder guns, reloading tools and accessories, and ballistics tables. For more than a half-century, the SHOOTER'S BIBLE has been the book of choice of every hunter, shooter, gun collector or gun fancier.

For 500 years, guns and books and books about guns have had a distinguished history. Taken together, all the parts of the SHOOTER'S BIBLE make a fitting tribute to the gun and the book.

—ROBERT F. SCOTT

Articles

Inventor and gun manufacturer Samuel Colt. His genius in designing a simple and reliable gun, his relentless and flamboyant efforts to promote his invention, and his introduction of machine tools and interchangeable parts into gun manufacture made him one of the most significant contributors to revolver development.

The Great Equalizer
A Short History of the Revolver

by George M. Horn

We know the identity of the inventors of many modern miracles — the radio, the electric light, the automobile, the airplane. But it is unlikely that the inventor of the revolver will ever be identified.

A revolver is a firearm in which a rotating carrier — a series of barrels or a cylinder with a number of chambers — turns around a central axis parallel to the bore and by a partial revolution each barrel or chamber comes under the firing mechanism in succession.

A revolver can be a handgun, long gun or even a machine gun. The famous Gatling gun is an example of the latter. Today, the term "revolver" is restricted to guns with a revolving cylinder. Guns whose barrels revolve are called "pepperboxes"; other forms of revolvers have included radial cylinder, or turret guns, whose chambers radiate from the center of the cylinder like the spokes of a wheel.

The principle of the revolving-cylinder/revolving-barrel gun developed around the beginning of the sixteenth century. In Venice, Italy, a matchlock pistol with three revolving barrels was listed in a 1548 inventory. Another three-barreled German revolver that once belonged to the Emperor Charles V is in the Armeria Reale in Turin. Other matchlock and wheellock revolving-cylinder guns were made in Germany in the middle and late sixteenth century.

The problems that faced the unidentified inventor of the revolver were twofold: Firstly, each chamber in turn had to be capable of separate ignition. Secondly, each chamber had to line up with the breech of the barrel and be able to be locked in that position until it was fired, yet the cylinder had to revolve freely to bring a new round into position for firing.

Understandably, early revolver ignition systems were identical with those used for ordinary firearms. In the most primitive revolvers, it was necessary to have a separate priming pan for each chamber and, in flintlocks, complete frizzens were also needed. These made such guns awkward to carry. Consequently, many gunsmiths retained the snaphance with a stationary steel on the barrel of the revolver. In order to keep the powder from falling out when it was on the underside of the barrel and to prevent the flash in one pan from igniting others, pan covers had to be tightly fitted.

It was not until after the invention of the percussion system of ignition by the Rev. Alexander Forsyth in 1807 that reasonably effective ignition could be assured without clumsy protuberances or the danger of powder spillage. Safety still had to await the metal-cased cartridge, which was perfected in the middle of the nineteenth century and overcame the possibility of one round setting off others.

The problem of lining up the chamber and the barrel should not be minimized, for it was not easily solved. At first, various locking levers and springs were used. One enterprising London gunsmith, the French Huguenot Jacques Gorgo, attempted to solve the alignment problem in the late seventeenth century by attaching a funnel to the barrel to catch the bullet as it emerged from the cylinder and guide it into the bore.

Two Artemus Wheeler revolving-cylinder flintlocks. Top: 7-chambered cylinder smoothbore musket. Bottom: 7-barrel "pepperbox" smoothbore carbine. Both approximately 52 caliber.

In 1718, James Puckle patented a "portable gun, or machine called a defence" that solved the problem of alignment. This was a large revolver mounted on a tripod and with interchangeable cylinders turned by hand. A crank at the back enabled the shooter to screw the coned mouth of each cylinder tightly against the barrel, which was countersunk to receive it. The result was a reasonably tight fit and an aligned joint. Examples of Puckle's invention — a matchlock and two flintlocks — survive in the Armouries of the Tower of London.

One unusual feature of Puckle's 1718 patent called for changing the shape of the chambers and bullets: some "for shooting square bullets against Turks," others "for shooting round bullets against Christians."

Despite Puckle's advanced design (it resembled nothing more than a modern machine gun) and diligent attempts to get his gun adopted by the British Army, his company failed. Nevertheless, we must pay tribute to this gun as being well ahead of its time. In a demonstration in 1722, Puckle's gun was fired 63 times in seven minutes during a rainstorm!

For a hundred years thereafter, gunsmiths continued to produce clumsy flintlock revolvers. It was an American, Captain Artemus Wheeler, who introduced the first *practical* revolving firearm. Wheeler patented his gun on June 10, 1818; it has the honor of being the first rotating-cylinder firearm to have been tested by the fledgling American government — two Wheeler pepperboxes and two

Wheeler muskets were tried by the U.S. Navy in 1821.

Wheeler's gun was a 7-shot flintlock of about 52 caliber, with a fixed frizzen and a priming magazine that filled each pan automatically before closing to fire a shot. Although the rotating mechanism is missing from the surviving examples in the U.S. National Museum, the cylinders were probably rotated by hand.

Unfortunately, the U.S. Navy decided that it wasn't interested in Wheeler's gun and he stopped promoting his invention, which became the basis for the better-known Collier Revolving Flintlock.

Shortly after Wheeler's patent had been granted, Elisha Haydon Collier, of Boston, sailed for England with a sample gun and obtained a British patent on November 24, 1818. Similarly, another Bostonian, Cornelius Coolidge, set out for France, where he received a patent in 1819 on a gun identical with Collier's. Historians are at a loss to explain why Collier in his British patent application claimed that the device had been described to him in part "by a foreigner living abroad," but did not name Wheeler. Collier modified Wheeler's design somewhat and made improvements, including a better fit at the junction of the chambers and the barrel. (This was actually James Puckle's system in reverse, with the barrel-breech lipped and the chambers countersunk.)

Collier's guns were manufactured for him in England both as handguns and shoulder arms. As pistols, his guns had 6⅛-inch smoothbored barrels and an overall length of about 14 inches. Between 1819 and 1824, Collier unsuccessfully tried to secure British Army adoption of his guns; his failure to do this drove him out of business in London in 1827.

Collier later testified that he had sold rifles, shotguns and pistols employing his invention to the value of $456,000. This was probably an exaggeration, but there is no doubt that Collier's modification of Wheeler's invention deserves recognition as the first revolving gun produced and sold in considerable quantities.

It was percussion ignition that made the revolver a genuinely practicable firearm. The Rev. Forsyth's loose "scent bottle" detonating powders (so called because the container of fulminate was shaped like a perfume bottle) gave way eventually to cones or nipples and finally to the modern cartridge, with primer, propellant and projectile all in one case, usually of metal.

Gone was the clumsy pan and its priming powder that could fall out or explode at the slightest accidental spark. Without the protuberances of the past and with a silhouette closely resembling the handguns of today, a revolver could be concealed in a waistband or pocket and be drawn quickly. The day of the handgun had indeed dawned.

In every country, gunsmiths quickly adapted to the new technology. Pepperboxes and cylinder revolvers made their appearance in a variety of forms.

The first percussion pepperboxes were probably made in the 1820s, with barrels revolved by hand. Later these were made to turn automatically as the hammer was cocked. Since such a system had been used by British gunsmith John Dafte on his flintlock revolver in the seventeenth century, no one ever attempted to obtain a British patent on it, and so it is impossible to date its introduction exactly.

Two Americans, Barton and Benjamin M. Darling, obtained a patent on their pepperbox pistol in 1836. Their 6-shot guns are now among the rarest and most sought after American production-type pepperbox firearms.

The following year, Ethan Allen, of Grafton, Massachusetts (no relation to the fabled Revolutionary War hero), obtained a patent for a double-action mechanism, making his pepperbox pistols the fastest-firing handguns of their time — in fact, they were far better known and more popular than Colt revolvers for many years.

Among American pepperboxes, the best known are those made by Ethan Allen (also Allen & Thurber and Allen & Wheelock), Blunt & Syms, Robbins & Lawrence, Stocking & Company, W.W. Marston (as Marston & Knox or Sprague & Marston), Thomas K. Bacon, and the Manhattan Firearms Manufacturing Company.

American pepperboxes were usually made with four to six barrels, but in Europe as many as 24 barrels have been found. Among the famous European makers were Joseph Lang, J.R. Cooper and James Purdy in England, and the Rigbys in Dublin. On the Continent the Mariette system, patented by a Liège gunsmith in 1857, was widely employed.

Although multibarreled weapons gave the user a measure of security, they were difficult to aim accurately because the trigger pull was hard and the entire barrel was rotating as the gun was being fired. Furthermore, in the larger calibers, they had a tendency to be muzzle heavy. For all these reasons, the stage was set for the appearance of the true revolver.

A few makers later produced pepperboxes designed to take rimfire cartridges in the 1860s and 1870s. These included the Bacon Arms Company, Jacob Rupertus and the Continental Arms Company. During this period, James Reid, of Catskill, New York, produced his *My Friend* knuckle-duster pistol in brass or steel and which could also be used for striking a blow.

Thus, the concept of a revolving-cylinder handgun was hardly a new one when young Samuel Colt made improvements and perfected an innovative design. With the assistance of gunsmith Anson Chase of Hartford, Connecticut, who made the working drawings and patent models, the 21-year-old Colt first applied for a British patent, which was granted to him on October 22, 1835. This was done to establish priority of invention. Colt's U.S. patent was issued on February 25, 1836. It covered such patentable features as the indexing and locking of the cylinder, the isolation of the nipples of each percussion chamber, the lifter and ratchet mechanism, and — in that phrase beloved by copywriters —"much, much more."

Gone was the hand-rotated cylinder. Upon bringing the hammer to full cock, Colt's 5-shot cylinder revolved simultaneously on an arbor and was locked in the correct alignment for firing.

The main feature of Colt's patent lay in the *automatic* rotation of the cylinder when the hammer was cocked, yet even this was by no means a new concept. The Milwaukee Public Museum has an eighteenth-century revolving-flintlock carbine

UNITED STATES PATENT OFFICE.

SAMUEL COLT, OF HARTFORD, CONNECTICUT.

IMPROVEMENT IN FIRE-ARMS.

Specification forming part of Letters Patent dated February 25, 1836.

To all whom it may concern:

Be it known that I, SAMUEL COLT, of Hartford, in the county of Hartford and State of Connecticut, have invented a new and useful Improvement in Fire-Arms; and I hereby declare that the following, with the accompanying drawings, is a full and exact description of the construction and operation of the said improvements as invented by me.

Division 1 of the drawings represents a pistol. Division 2 represents Division 1 in four sections, as 1, 2, 3, and 4. Division 3 represents all the parts in Section 1 of Division 2. Division 4 represents all the parts of Section 2 of Division 2. Division 5 represents the mechanical combination of the entire instrument.

Figure 1 of Division 3 represents the hammer which discharges the percussion-caps. It acts upon a fulcrum at *a*. *b* is a pin projecting from the hammer, which serves to operate the key that locks the cylinder when its respective chambers are brought directly opposite the barrel. C represents the hole which receives the lower arm of the lifter that turns the cylinder. *a* represents the part of the hammer where the mainspring acts upon it. *e* is a projection by which the hammer is drawn back.

Fig. 2 is the mainspring.

Fig. 3 is the key that holds the cylinder in its place by the arm *a* when each chamber is brought opposite the barrel. *b* is a spring, which is attached to the part *c*, which has a lateral motion to the right by means of a hinge at *d*, and serves to allow the pin *b* in Fig. 1 to pass it. The fulcrum of the key is at *e*. *f* is the fulcrum-pin. *g* is the spring which forces the key into the wards of the cylinder.

Fig. 4 is the lifter or hand, with a spring on the left side to allow it to move laterally to the left when acted on *a* by each tooth of the ratchet. At *b* is a joint, which connects it with the pin *c*, which acts in the hole *e* in Fig. 1.

Fig. 5 is the connecting-rod. The end *a* serves as a catch to the hammer when the lock is set, and when the hammer is pulled back the rod moves forward horizontally in consequence of the hammer's coming in contact with it, and the end *b* operates upon the trigger, Fig. 6, at the catch *a* and throws down the end *b*, by which means the claw *c* hooks into the end *b* of Fig. 5, and is held in its place by the spring, Fig. 7, acting upon it at the pin *d*.

Fig. 8 is the pin which holds in their places the spring, Fig. 7, at *a* and the connecting-rod, Fig. 5, at *c*. Fig. 6 moves on the pin *c* at *f*.

Fig. 9 is a spring, which holds the rod, Fig. 5, toward the hammer, that the connecting-rod may catch in a notch at the bottom of the hammer to hold it when set.

Division 4 is a dissection of Section 2.

Fig. 1 is the arbor on which the cylinder revolves. *a a'* are the bearings on which the cylinder rests. *b* is the slot through which a key enters to connect Section 4 with it. The part C passes through the shackle, Fig. 2, which is keyed to the cylinder, Section 3, Fig. 1, at the groove *a* by means of the tongue or projections A on the shackle. *c* is the part which receives the nut, Fig. 3, when it is connected with the shackle, Fig. 4, as seen at *a*, Section 2 in Division 2.

Fig. 5 is the ratchet, which is placed in the middle of the shield at *a*, and receives the shackle, to which it is connected by the tongue or projection *b*. The arbor is prevented from turning in the shield by means of a pin or key in the shield, which enters the groove *d* on the arbor.

Fig. 2, Section 3 of Division 2, represents the fore part of the cylinder. The holes *a a*, &c., represent the ends of the chambers for the charges. *b* is the hole through which the arbor (on which the cylinder revolves) passes. C C, &c., represent the wards to receive the end *a* of the key, Fig. 3, Division 3, to prevent the cylinder from turning when a charge is brought opposite the barrel.

b b, &c., Fig. 1, represent the tubes on which are placed the percussion-caps. C C, &c., are partitions which, when embraced in the shield, as in Division 1, prevent the communication of fire or smoke from one cap to the other.

In Division 2, Section 4, *a* represents the hole through which the arbor passes, and *b* a mortise for the key *c* to connect this section with the arbor. At *d* the ball enters the barrel from the chamber. At *e* the barrel is fastened to the plate. At *f* is a groove in the plate to receive the end *a* of the lock-plate of Section 1, which serves to steady it. *g* represents the bayonet hung on a pin at *h*, *i* being a catch to hold it in its place when it is thrown out. In Division 5 the hammer is hung at the fulcrum *a*. The key which holds the cylinder

Samuel Colt's historic master patent was issued on February 25, 1836. On the strength of this, young Colt obtained support from investors and opened his Patent Arms Manufacturing Company in Paterson, New Jersey, that same year. With a proposed capital of $230,000, the company was probably undercapitalized; apparently only about $150,000 in stock was sold. Before it closed permanently in 1842, the Colt factory manufactured several thousand guns embodying the principles of Colt's patent, including pistols, rifles, carbines, shotguns, and a few muskets, all featuring a "rotating-chambered breech," or revolving cylinder, as it is known today. Most of the factory's output was 5-shot repeating pistols.

which does this in principle. Some Collier revolvers also rotated automatically. The difference was that Colt had made his design simpler, stronger and surer.

The fact that Colt's invention was much copied and that his British and American master patents were defended successfully until their expiration in 1857 is a tribute to young **Sam Colt's** inventive genius.

The introduction of rapid-firing, easily-concealed weapons made great changes in the methods and odds of personal combat. One early Colt revolver is reputed to have had the following verse engraved on it:

> *"Fear no man,*
> *No matter what his size;*
> *When trouble threatens, call on me*
> *And I will equalize.".*

Shortly after his U.S. patent was issued, Colt's Patent Arms Manufacturing Company, of Paterson, New Jersey, was chartered on March 5, 1836, with a capitalization of $230,000. Colt produced his Paterson model 5-shot revolver in calibers 28, 31, 34 and 36, with octagonal barrel lengths ranging from 3 to 9 inches.

By 1839, Colt had taken steps to meet some of the objections to his new guns. In that year, he perfected and patented an attached loading lever, which made it unnecessary to disassemble a weapon for loading, and he worked on a waterproof foil cartridge which would be consumed as the weapon was fired.

Paterson Colts were single action (a design feature that was to continue on Colt guns until 1877) with a folding trigger that flipped out of a slot in the frame as the hammer was drawn back.

Then, as now, a gun manufacturer needed government contracts in order to survive. Despite the excellence of Colt's product, orders from the military were not forthcoming. A small order for 50 Paterson revolving rifles (Colt's guns were made both as long guns and handguns) was received in 1838 for use in the Seminole Indian War, and the Texas Navy (yes, Texas had one) ordered a small quantity of Paterson revolvers, but neither order was substantial enough to keep the infant firm afloat. Operations in Paterson ended in 1842 in a bitter dispute between Colt and his plant manager, John Ehlers.

Ironically, with the firm out of business, the fame of Colt's revolvers began to spread. Along the frontier, Indians who were accustomed to charging troops while they were reloading after the first volley, were cut down in a hail of bullets from Colt-equipped dragoons.

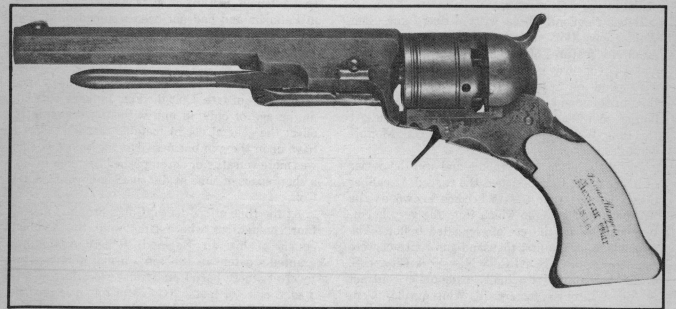

West Point Museum Collection

Between 1836 and 1842, Samuel Colt produced a total of about 2000 Paterson models (so called because they were manufactured in Paterson, New Jersey). The Paterson model first saw military service in the Seminole Indian War and was the first practical combat revolver. Note the folding trigger which appeared when the hammer was cocked and the attached loading lever, patented by Colt in 1839. This 36-caliber gun is marked on the grips to indicate that it was used in the Mexican War.

West Point Museum Collection

Because the largest caliber available in Colt Paterson models was only 36, Colt designed large heavy dragoon pistols (the word "revolver" was not yet current), suitable for horse-mounted troops. Manufacture of the so-called Walker Model began in 1847 by Eli Whitney in his factory in Whitneyville, Connecticut, under contract. Eventually, Samuel Colt took over manufacture of the Walker Model in his own factory in Hartford, Connecticut.

In the now-famous battle of the Pedernales in 1844, 15 Texas Rangers were attacked by 80 mounted Comanches. When the smoke of battle had cleared, 42 Indians lay dead and those remaining had beat a disorganized retreat. One of the participants in this battle was Samuel H. Walker, whose name was later to be associated with another model of the Colt revolver.

It has frequently been written that Capt. Sam Walker gave Colt advice about the improvements which are features of Colt's 1839 patent. The evidence is conclusive that Walker and Colt did not correspond or meet until Gen. Zachary Taylor, then in command of U.S. troops along the Mexican border, sent Walker north in 1846 to buy guns. At this time, Walker was serving with the U.S. Mounted Rifles.

In collaboration with Walker, and still the owner of his patents, Colt designed the rugged 44-caliber 6-shot weapon that was to become known as the "Walker Colt"— a gun which from the very beginning anticipated the use of elongated bullets. The guns made for the first thousand-gun contract were marked "Address Sam'l Colt, New York City, U.S. 1847," but they were actually made under contract in Eli Whitney's factory in Whitneyville, Connecticut.

Within a year, Samuel Colt was back in the gun business and prospering as never before — thanks to the Mexican War. He soon established his own shop on Pearl Street in Hartford, later moving to the South Meadow site along the Connecticut River in 1855.

By 1848, Colt had become worried about the impending termination of his 1836 patent, whose 14-year term was scheduled to expire in 1850. Consequently, he sought an extension, citing the fact that all manufacture of guns had ceased in 1842 in Paterson and had not been resumed until 1847. A generous seven-year extension was granted in 1849, carrying Colt's patent protection forward until 1857.

Wealth and success followed, but in one of those cruel twists of fate, Colt died on January 10, 1862, at the age of only 48 and without witnessing the effect the general use of metallic cartridges was to have upon the gun business. No one before or since was more versatile or accomplished so much in such a short space of time as did the flamboyant Samuel Colt.

At the time of his death, Colt's firm had at least four competitors whose guns were the technical equals of his. In England, Robert Adams was granted a patent in 1851 on a 5-shot double-action revolver whose barrel and frame were forged from a solid piece of metal. (Colt's pistols had separate barrels and frames held together by a key.) In addition, the larger calibers of Adams revolvers (up to 50 caliber) gave them much greater stopping power.

THE SHOOTER'S BIBLE

R. WHITE.
REPEATING FIREARM.

No. 12,648.   Patented Apr. 3, 1855.

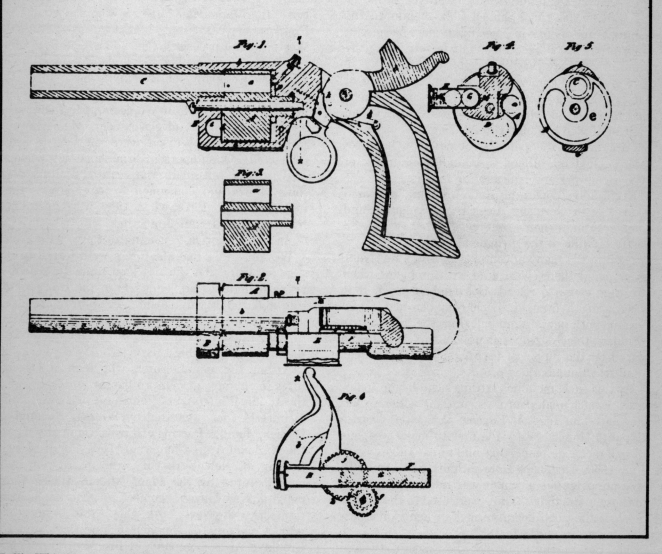

Rollin White's patent, No. 12,648, was issued on April 3, 1855, covering the use of a cylinder bored through from front to back, making it possible to utilize the newly-patented rimfire cartridges of Horace Smith and Daniel B. Wesson. In order to avoid infringing on White's patent rights, many gun manufacturers attempted to develop other cartridges and cylinder systems without noteworthy success. Lacking the ability to insert and extract a cartridge from the rear of the cylinder, these systems were little better than the awkward cap and ball revolver. Ironically, before his invention was acquired by Smith & Wesson, White had unsuccessfully tried to interest Samuel Colt in it. The first Smith & Wesson revolver was put on the market in 1857 as Model No. 1 in 22 caliber.

Adams and Colt both exhibited their guns at London's famous Crystal Palace Exhibition in 1851. Subsequently, Colt set up a London factory in the hope of securing British Army contracts.

Other manufacturers of high-quality revolvers included the London Armoury Company and its Beaumont-Adams pistol and Kerr revolver. In the United States, competition for the Colt came from revolvers made by a rifle manufacturer, E. Remington & Sons, of Ilion, New York. Upon the expiration of Colt's master patent in 1857, Remington began production of a 5-shot single-action pocket revolver under patents issued to Fordyce Beals.

At about this time, Samuel Colt abandoned the manufacture of guns in England, in part because of labor problems; his recently-built factory along the Connecticut River easily took up the slack.

It is said that imitation is the sincerest form of flattery. During the time that Colt's master patents remained in force, imitators were restricted in their ability to copy his guns and had to find ways to circumvent the patents. Some kept hand-rotated cylinders; others tried radial cylinders or even clockwork mechanisms for rotation.

Eventually, copies of Colt revolvers appeared abroad — in Germany, Russia and Belgium, and some even in his home country — but they were all vastly inferior to the genuine article.

Despite the many advantages of Colt's revolvers, users found themselves faced with problems when the time came to reload. Heaven help them if it was during a firefight. Each chamber had to be charged with powder and ball from the front of the cylinder, then a tiny percussion cap had to be placed on the nipple of each chamber at the rear — all in all, a laborious process.

By this time, metallic cartridges had begun to appear. French manufacturers, initially Casimir Lefaucheux and his son Eugène, and later Charles Hypolite Houiller, were the first to make weapons on a large scale employing pinfire cartridges.

In 1860, Americans Horace Smith and Daniel B. Wesson patented a rimfire cartridge very similar to those in use today. These were used in the pocket revolver they had begun to make when Colt's patent protection ended in 1857.

The noteworthy feature of the Smith & Wesson revolver was its cylinder with holes bored completely through — an innovation that had been patented in 1855 by Rollin White, at one time a Colt subcontractor — which enabled the cylinder to be loaded at the breech.

Paradoxically, Colt had first been offered White's invention and had turned it down. White received a royalty of 25 cents for each pistol manufactured under his patent; by the time it expired in 1869, he collected nearly $70,000 from Smith & Wesson.

For a dozen years, White's invention gave Smith & Wesson a virtual monopoly on the manufacture of breech-loading revolvers using metallic cartridges, not unlike the one enjoyed previously by Colt's mechanically rotated cylinders.

But such a monopoly did not come easily. White's agreement with Smith & Wesson called for him to contest any infringement, and there were many. However, with the defeat of two powerful firms, the Manhattan Firearms Company and E.A. Prescott, of Worcester, Massachusetts, Smith & Wesson found it easier to get other makers to come to terms with them. These included Moore's Patent Firearms Company, of Brooklyn, New York; the Bacon Manufacturing Company, of Norwich, Connecticut; L.W. Pond, of Worcester, Massachusetts; and James Warner, of Springfield, Massachusetts (where Smith & Wesson were themselves headquartered). One important firm, Allen & Wheelock, of Worcester, Massachusetts, resisted Smith & Wesson's efforts and continued to manufacture their revolvers until 1863, when they were restrained from doing so by an injunction.

As an alternative to coming to terms with Smith & Wesson, other manufacturers were forced to design revolvers that did not load from the rear, devising cylinders that loaded from the front or the side and that used teat-fire or lip-fire cartridges. Others employed divided cylinders and sliding tubes. Although most of these expedients worked, there were no notable successes.

Among the manufacturers who took other measures to circumvent White's patent protection were the Rollin White Arms Company, of Lowell Massachusetts (not organized by White); Remington; Daniel Moore's Patent Firearms Company (later the National Arms Company); L.W. Pond; Merwin & Bray, of New York City, who distributed guns manufactured by the Plant Manufacturing Company, of New Haven, Connecticut; the Eagle Arms Company, of New York City; the Connecticut Arms Company, of Norwich, Connecticut; and the Brooklyn Arms Company, of Brooklyn, New York.

Because there was no British equivalent to Rollin White's master patent, many English revolver makers produced rimfire revolvers without interference.

It is curious that the Civil War was fought largely with percussion-type weapons. Smith &

The Civil War might have been ended sooner had hidebound Brig. Gen. James Wolfe Ripley not been Chief of Ordnance from 1861 to 1863. Ripley was suspicious of breech-loading and repeating guns, so the Union forces were largely equipped with percussion weapons. In 1863, President Abraham Lincoln overruled him and ordered the purchase of breechloaders for the special corps of Sharpshooters organized by Col. Hiram Berdan. Retired in 1863, he continued to serve as inspector of armaments until 1869. This venerable officer had the distinction of having served his country continuously for over 55 years and in four wars.

Wesson, who enjoyed a virtual monopoly on the cartridge revolver from 1857 to 1869, built nothing larger than a 32-caliber model during the war. In part, the backwardness of Union materiel was the fault of the Chief of Ordnance from 1861 to 1863, Brig. Gen. James Wolfe Ripley, who had commanded the Springfield Armory and who was suspicious of the new breech-loading and repeating weapons that had appeared. Many of these were, in fact, dangerous; the trouble was General Ripley couldn't distinguish the good from the bad, the practical from the impractical.

In 1869, with the denial of Rollin White's application for an extension of his patent, manufacturers rushed to bring out single-action rimfire revolvers, loosing a flood of what have been called "suicide specials"— a term synonymous with "Saturday night specials." (The term "suicide special" was apparently first applied to these guns by Duncan McConnell in an article in *The American Rifleman* in February, 1948.)

A few manufacturers, such as the American Standard Tool Company, of Newark, New Jersey (successor to the Manhattan Firearms Company), the Marlin Company, of New Haven, Connecticut, and I.J. Clark, of Philadelphia, all used the Smith & Wesson tip-up barrel design. Most of these cheap revolvers were solid frame, however, and invariably nickel plated. More than 200 trade names of "suicide specials" have been identified so far.

Prices were amazingly low, and guns were widely available through mail-order sources. For example, in 1888 Merwin, Hulbert & Company, of New York City, offered their *Robin Hood* revolver free with the purchase of one of their 44-caliber army revolvers. Two years later they were offering their *Liberty* revolver for only $1.10. In 1887, they offered their *Blue Jacket* for 60 cents, and Sears, Roebuck & Company offered a 68-cent *Defender* revolver in their catalog. Prices for engraved guns with better grips could go as high as ten dollars — ivory or pearl grips often cost more than the guns themselves.

Understandably, quality suffered. Although false rifling appeared as three deep notches visible at the muzzle, the *Robin Hood* revolver had a smoothbore barrel.

In 1872, Colt brought out its famous Single Action Army revolver, variously called the Peacemaker, Frontier Model or Single Six. This was to become the most famous revolver in the history of the American West. Its other claim to fame is that

West Point Museum Collection

This Navy Model 36-caliber double-action revolver with its distinctive figure-eight trigger and lever guard was produced under U.S. government contracts during the Civil War by the Savage Revolving Fire-Arms Company of Middletown, Connecticut. A pull on the lower ring cocked the action and rotated the cylinder; the hammer was released by light pressure on the conventional trigger above.

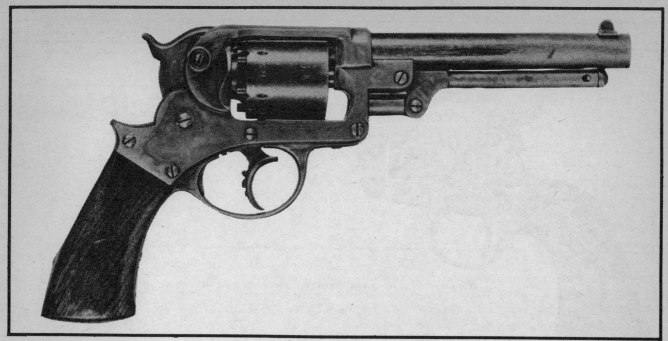

The Starr Arms Company of New York City made this 6-shot double-action Army Revolver in 44 caliber with 6-inch barrel for Union forces during the Civil War. It fired a self-consuming, combustible cartridge and could be loaded with loose powder and ball. Later, a single-action version with 8-inch barrel was produced between 1863 and 1865. Starr handguns ranked third after Colts and Remingtons in the number purchased by the North.

it was manufactured for a longer time than any other revolver — production was maintained continuously from 1872 to 1940, and was resumed after the Second World War, in response to tremendous popular demand.

For some reason, the single-action revolver remained the gun of choice in the United States long after other countries had adopted the faster-firing double action. Robert Adams' 1851 double-action revolver in England has already been mentioned. His brother John made a double-action revolver in 1867 that was adopted by the British Army. French double-action revolvers included some Lefaucheux models, as well as the Perrin and Raphaël cartridge revolvers. An Austrian, Leopold Gasser, developed a double-action revolver in 1870, which was adopted by Austria-Hungary for its officers. By 1882, a double-action sidearm had become the standard for every European nation.

Acceptance of the double-action mechanism came much more slowly in the United States. Many American marksmen still maintain that greater accuracy can be achieved by firing a pistol single action rather than double action. Some percussion revolvers during the Civil War, notably the Savage Revolving Fire-Arms Company's Navy Model in

36 caliber, with its unusual figure-eight trigger guard, and the Starr Arms Company's Army revolver in 44 caliber used double-action, but never became popular. Colt did not introduce a double-action cartridge revolver until 1877; Smith & Wesson followed suit three years later.

From time to time, attempts have been made to design revolvers in which the hammer or striker could be cocked by trigger pull and released by a second pull of the trigger. Other devices attempted to compensate for the disturbance in aiming that inevitably occurs when a double-action trigger is pulled, often because of the abrupt loss of tension between trigger and hammer or because the trigger travels a different distance in double action than in thumb cocking.

With the almost universal proliferation of double-action models, it can be said that revolvers reached the peak of their technical development. Few major improvements were possible. In 1895, Col. G.V. Fosbery, a much-decorated British army officer, obtained a patent on a pistol that utilized the recoil of the discharge to rotate the cylinder and cock the hammer. Called the Webley-Fosbery Automatic Revolver, this gun was made by Webley & Scott, of Birmingham, England, beginning in 1901,

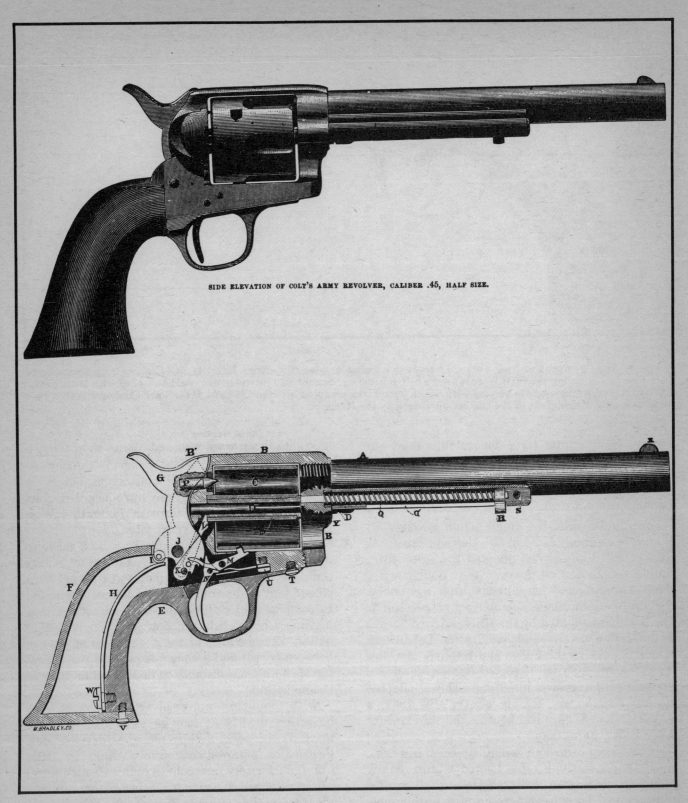

SIDE ELEVATION OF COLT'S ARMY REVOLVER, CALIBER .45, HALF SIZE.

A. Barrel B. Frame C. Cylinder D. Center-pin bushing DD. Center pin E. Guard F. Backstrap G. Hammer H. Main-spring I. Hammer roll and hammer-roll rivet J. Hammer screw K. Hammer cam L. Hand and handspring M. Bolt and bolt screw N. Trigger and trigger screw P. Firing pin and firing-pin rivet Q. Ejector rod, spring and tube R. Ejector head S. Ejector-tube screw T. Guard screw, short U. Sear and bolt spring and sear and bolt-spring screw W. Main spring screw X. Front sight Y. Center-pin screw.

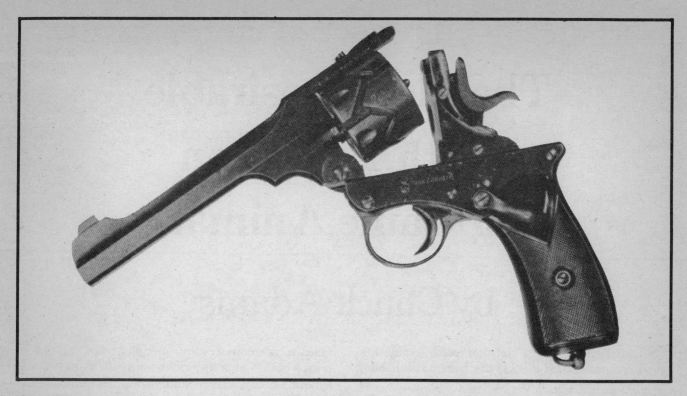

Col. G. Vincent Fosbery, who was awarded the Victoria Cross for valor, patented his ingenious but cumbersome "automatic" revolver in 1895. A top-break pistol operated by mechanical recoil and manufactured by the Webley & Scott Revolver & Arms Company, Ltd., of Birmingham, England, the Webley-Fosbery was made in two calibers, a 455 6-chambered revolver designed for the British 455 cordite cartridge and an 8-chambered version which took the 38 Colt ACP cartridge. Components of the Webley revolver, official British sidearm for many years, were used wherever possible. A target version of the Webley-Fosbery was highly successful in competitive shooting matches at Bisley, England.

and it was not discontinued until the Second World War. Trivia experts may recall that in Dashiell Hammett's *The Maltese Falcon*, a Webley-Fosbery automatic revolver was the gun employed to kill Sam Spade's partner, the private detective Miles Archer.

An American firm, the Union Firearms Company, of Toledo, Ohio, also made a 32-caliber 6-shot recoil-operated revolver early in the twentieth century. Although it used a similar zigzag rotation system, it was not a copy of the Webley-Fosbery, but was manufactured under a 1909 patent issued to C.F. Lefever. Other automatic revolvers dating from the same period include the Spanish 22 Zulaika and the Belgian van der Haegen.

Changes came over the years, mostly in ammunition. Smokeless powder marked the last great advance in ammunition, but it was not without its problems. Smokeless powders required stronger primers and created higher pressures within a gun. When mercury fulminate ignites, however, free metallic mercury is released which combines with cartridge brass to form an amalgam that weakens the case, making it less desirable for reloading. For this reason, the U.S. government did not employ mercury in small-arms primers after 1900.

Also, the hot gases generated by smokeless powders melted and eroded the sides of the bullet, causing inaccurate flight patterns, loss of velocity, and an accumulation of lead in the bore. The addition of tin to the powder helped to reduce fouling, but is was not until the 1920s that a copper-zinc alloy — called a gilding metal — was adopted as jacket material to overcome this.

Today's revolvers stand at the head of a long line of succession dating back over the past four centuries, and the new Llama 44 Magnum shown on the cover of this SHOOTER'S BIBLE is a direct descendant of every revolver-type weapon that has gone before. That the revolver has changed so little in basic design and usage is a tribute to its very practical beginnings. If form follows function, there is no reason why many of today's revolvers should not be considered for the awards given each year for good design by the prestigious Museum of Modern Art.

The Most Desirable North American Big-Game Animals

by Chuck Adams

The primary factors to consider when evaluating any big-game animal include the terrain it inhabits, its intelligence and alertness, the hunting methods employed to bag it, the quality of its meat, and the beauty of its antlers, horns, and pelt. These factors determine exactly how difficult an animal will be to hunt, how a hunter must proceed to bag that animal, and how desirable that animal will be once it has been bagged. A hunter who studies the traits of various North American big game and hunting methods needed to take these animals can intelligently plan his hunting trips without fear of unpleasant surprises later on. He'll know well beforehand whether or not a hunt for a particular species can satisfy his particular hunting needs.

Few outdoor writers have had enough practical field experience to make realistic evaluations about these animals. As a result, the average hunter entertains misconceptions about which animals are most elusive, most desirable, and most difficult to drop with a high-powered rifle. To make matters worse, these misconceptions are often reinforced by special-interest groups that wish to sell guided hunts or trespass rights on land where certain species abound. Such groups often inflate the hunting difficulty and desirability of these species in order to line their own pockets with sportsmen's dollars.

Every North American big-game animal has something to offer the serious hunter, but the various species do not offer equivalent challenges. For example, a whitetail deer is a cagey customer, slippery as soap and alert as the town gossip. In contrast, a big bull moose is clumsy and slow-witted. The moose pro-vides a gorgeous trophy and plenty of top-notch meat, but even a beginning nimrod with limited shooting ability can generally score. By comparison, a trophy whitetail deer can completely frustrate an adept hunter — hiding like a rooster pheasant, slipping away like a puff of fog, or exploding from cover like a runaway freight train. Both the moose and the whitetail deer can provide hunting interest, but they certainly don't offer identical hunting rewards.

By all odds, the bison is one of the easiest big-game animals to hunt. This wild bovine isn't terribly bright which is the main reason it was able to be slaughtered by the millions during the late 1800s. Today, bison may be shot on many so-called "game preserves" across the country; bison may also be hunted on a few public lands in Canada and Alaska. Such hunting does nothing to endanger existing bison populations.

Shooting a bison is easy, involving a close-range, open-country shooting exercise which is neither exciting nor difficult for most hunters. A bison does provide a gorgeous hide, an impressive trophy head, and some of the best meat available on the entire continent. If you are after the trophy or the meat, or if you simply want to shoot a bison as a sort of kinship rite with your ancestors, the experience might be worthwhile. However, most of us who have shot these hulking, 2500-pound beasts have come away somewhat less than satisfied with the experience.

The muskox runs a close second to the bison in hunting ease. This shaggy North Country creature has become fairly popular with trophy hunters dur-

Mountain sheep have been much overrated, in the author's opinion. They are pretty and taste good, but bagging a full-curl trophy like this Alaskan Dall is almost a cinch for anyone in good health.

ing the past few years, mainly because the open tundra flats where muskoxen stay have become accessible by modern aircraft. Muskoxen are on the increase in some parts of the remote North, so sport hunting does not endanger this species. However, like the bison, they offer something less than an exciting challenge.

Finding a muskox to shoot is the main difficulty. These animals wander over vast, open areas, making muskoxen as difficult to locate as hen's teeth. However, muskoxen mill around in confusion or close up in a tight group when danger threatens, making it easy for a hunter with a high-powered rifle to approach within 100 yards and knock one down. Even though many feel that a muskox is not the most attractive of big-game animals, it does present an off-beat hunting challenge.

A bit more difficult to hunt are the so-called "exotic" animals — non-native species originally introduced to suitable habitats by sportsmen's groups and/or state fish and game officials. Some of the more widely hunted exotic animals include the Spanish goat, merino sheep, mouflon sheep, Corsican sheep, fallow deer, axis deer, sika deer, and Indian blackbuck antelope. Each type of exotic game has its unique characteristics, but most creatures possess no better than average intelligence or senses. One exception to this is the axis deer, which has a definite knack for eluding hunters.

Some exotics provide good meat, most provide an attractive trophy, and all provide off-season shooting action. However, a hunter should not head for Texas or another "exotic" state with illusions of difficult stalks and equally difficult shooting.

Because such animals make interesting trophies, exotics have been played up by some hunters. The fallacy has been promoted that exotic animals are extremely difficult to bag. Sportsmen travel hundreds of miles each year to hunt exotics, thrilled at the chance to take a trophy with big horns and antlers and to enjoy a superb shooting challenge. However, most exotic animals can be shot at fairly close range without much challenge. This is even true of the Indian blackbuck, touted for years as a desirable trophy, quick of brain and fleet of foot. Misrepresentation of the blackbuck as a worthy game animal is a blatant hoax. The blackbuck is a beautiful animal, but doesn't require much hunting skill to bag.

Moose are popular North Country animals, especially with hunters who can afford to have these huge creatures mounted and have half a ton of meat shipped home. The moose's main claim to fame is a beautiful rack and excellent meat. It is neither intelligent, alert, nor too tough to hit with a reasonably accurate rifle. A moose can be difficult to find in heavy cover, however, once found, it's relatively easy to bag. During the September and October rutting period, the moose is so preoccupied that it becomes an even easier target for hunters. The moose's strategy is to head for cover thick enough to choke a chipmunk, but a good hunter with some tracking ability can follow a moose through the thickest lodgepole pine and eventually find it.

The pronghorn antelope is consistently overrated by outdoor writers with inadequate field experience. Because pronghorn prefer the wide-open western prairies, the inexperienced conclude that this animal is difficult to approach within decent rifle range. The truth is that the pronghorn is one of the easiest animals to hunt, mainly because of its limited intelligence and insatiable curiosity. A pronghorn's primary defenses are razor-sharp eyesight, comparable to eight-power binoculars, and an incredible ability to run at speeds which are surpassed only by the African cheetah. A pronghorn can spot danger several miles away and can race across open country at speeds approaching 70 mph when thoroughly spooked. However, curiosity makes the pronghorn a sucker for almost any moving object, and this behavior often allows a hunter to score. An expert rifle shot can often hit a running antelope in spite of its speed because the animal moves with such an even, fluid gait that it is fairly easy to swing on and hit. In some flat regions of the West, pronghorn hunting requires accurate, long-range shooting ability. However, in top pronghorn states like Wyoming and Montana, it is reported that hunters have almost total success hunting pronghorn antelope, which shows that these animals are not too difficult to bag.

The caribou is similar to the pronghorn in temperament — and just about as easy to bag. Moving rapidly, this big-racked animal wanders the wilderness in herds as small as 20 or as large as 200. Caribou are not as fleet of foot as pronghorn, but are more difficult to locate within their vast northern range. Like pronghorn, caribou have keen eyes, but, also like pronghorn, are not as intelligent as other big-game animals. In fact, caribou can be less bright than pronghorn, and perhaps even more curious about strange objects; often a caribou will allow a hunter to approach within range over even the flattest of terrain. The beauty of caribou country and the animals' splendid antlers make the hunt worthwhile. Caribou meat is also on a par with the best beef. However, a person who wants a hunting and shoot-

The author enjoys hunting caribou, but admits these gorgeous trophies are usually easy enough to bag. Part of the fun in caribou hunting is the wilderness experience that results — complete with pack horses and invigorating hikes.

ing challenge should go after another species.

An equally interesting open-country animal is the Rocky Mountain goat, which inhabits the high and rugged crags of the northern ranges that make up the Rocky Mountains. This "goat" is really not a true goat, being closely related to the antelope-like serow and goral of Asia and the chamois of Europe. The Rocky Mountain goat is similar to the pronghorn antelope and caribou in its traits except that it inhabits steep terrain. It has excellent vision, a limited intelligence and, like the caribou and pronghorn, insatiable curiosity. However, the goat is more

The Spanish goat is one of the many "exotics" available in North America. These animals are generally not too difficult to bag, but the author finds them worthwhile off-season trophies, especially when a handgun or black powder gun is used.

difficult to hunt than the pronghorn or the caribou because of its habitat. A hunter must be in tip-top condition to scale the slopes and cliffs found in goat terrain.

The Rocky Mountain goat is not popular with trophy hunters because of its relatively small horns. However, goat hunting is on the upswing as more nimrods discover the challenge of goat terrain. Inveterate riflemen also favor goat hunting because the shooting is seldom easy. Even when shots are short, they are likely to be sharply up or down from awkward positions — a test of any shooter's skill.

Wild mountain sheep have been touted for years by hunters who don't know better. Without a doubt, Dall, Stone, and bighorn sheep are beautiful animals, sporting heavy, symmetrical horns which curl exotically. The mystique of sheep hunting has been captured by writers and professional guides over the years. All but a few experienced big-game hunters have accepted the sheep myth.

The fact is, a sheep is easy to hunt. Its sight is keen, but its hearing and sense of smell are only fair. Because a sheep is not particularly bright and does not inhabit steep terrain (despite the exaggerated claims to the contrary), a hunter can often approach to within sure-kill rifle range. Hunter success on sheep in the better parts of Canada and Alaska approaches 90 percent, proof of sheep-hunting ease. Sheep are handsome animals, good to eat, and easy for any competent rifleman to bag. But hunters who believe the sheep myth are likely to find it to be just that.

Bears are worth hunting for many reasons. For one, they provide the spine-tingling excitement of hunting a dangerous species. For another, they provide absolutely unexcelled trophy hides with their long, luxuriant hair. Brown and grizzly bears are the most dangerous, being big, mean, and unpredictable. Black bears are less dangerous but more intelligent and cagey, providing a different challenge. All bears are very near-sighted, but have good hearing and an excellent sense of smell.

Browns and grizzlies are not difficult to take once they are found, provided a hunter uses a large-caliber rifle in the 300 Weatherby class. However, these 600 to 800-pound brutes cover a lot of ground and are few and far between, making them difficult to locate unless they are lured to a smelly bait. Black bears are generally more plentiful than browns and grizzlies, but tend to be more nocturnal which makes them harder to find. The easiest ways to hunt a black bear are finding its tracks and chasing it with hounds, or sitting near a heap of pungent meat or

fruit and waiting for it to come to the feast. Both methods can be exciting, and usually result in easy shots at point-blank ranges.

The wild pig is similar to the bear in habits and hunting difficulty. However, a porker is more intelligent than a bear, which makes it more difficult to hunt under average conditions. Like the bear, sense of smell is its strong point and vision its weak point. Feral hogs (domestics gone wild) and European hogs introduced by sportsmen abound in the warmer parts of the continent and provide excellent sport, attractive trophies and first-rate meat. Wild pigs can be baited or chased with dogs in similar fashion to bear hunting, but the most satisfying way to hunt them is still-hunting or waiting patiently on stand in terrain they inhabit.

One of the most difficult North American animals to hunt is the elk. This large, big-racked forest-dweller combines the attributes experienced hunters admire: intelligence, keen senses, an innate sense of caution, a large and beautiful rack of antlers, and

Wild hogs make spectacular trophies and present an interesting hunting challenge.

The author is shown with some of the beautiful antlers collected during one of his hunting expeditions.

NORTH AMERICAN BIG-GAME ANIMALS		DIFFICULTY POSED BY TERRAIN	DIFFICULTY IN LOCATING ANIMAL	ANIMAL CUNNING	Meat	DESIRABLE PORTIONS OF ANIMAL Antlers/Horns	Tusks	Hide	HUNTING SKILL REQUIRED TO BAG
Bison		Little	Little	Little	X	X		X	Little
Muskox		Moderate	Moderate	Little		X		X	Little
Exotics		Moderate	Moderate	Little	X	X		X	Little
Moose		Moderate	Moderate	Little	X	X		X	Little
Pronghorn Antelope		Little	Little	Moderate	X	X		X	Moderate
Caribou		Moderate	Moderate	Little	X	X		X	Moderate
Rocky Mountain Goat		Very	Moderate	Moderate		X		X	Moderate
Sheep		Moderate	Moderate	Moderate	X	X		X	Moderate
Bear		Moderate	Very	Moderate	X			X	Moderate
Wild Pig		Moderate	Moderate	Moderate	X		X	X	Moderate
Elk		Very	Very	Very	X	X		X	Very
Deer	Mule	Very	Moderate	Moderate	X	X		X	Moderate
	Blacktail	Very	Very	Very	X	X		X	Very
	Whitetail	Very	Very	Very	X	X		X	Very

succulent, tasty meat. The elk, especially a wise old trophy bull, provides a challenge for any hunter. The exception to this occurs during the September rutting season, when bull elk bugle and crash, preoccupied with mating. At that time of year, elk meat tastes like mud and elk seldom provide much of a challenge for a rifleman. For this reason, the best trophies are usually taken during the rut.

During the balance of the fall, a successful elk hunter usually must cover miles of steep terrain at a snail's pace, either making a well-timed snapshot as an elk runs off through heavy timber or dropping the animal at long range across a big canyon. The elk will satisfy any hunter or shooter who is in good condition and thrives on challenging situations.

The most widely hunted animals in North America are deer. These animals provide some of the best sport this continent has to offer. They far surpass "glamour animals" like sheep, moose and caribou in terms of hunting challenge, and also carry antlers which are every bit as impressive as any other kind of North American trophy. Besides, they are readily accessible to most hunters, providing first-rate sport without exorbitant outlays of time and money.

The mule deer is generally acknowledged to be the easiest of the deer to hunt, mainly because it prefers open terrain and seems to have a more docile nature. However, big mulie bucks seldom are easily hunted what with their keen eyesight and super-sensitive ears and noses to detect and avoid danger. Because of their open habitat, taking mule deer often requires pinpoint accuracy at ranges past 200 yards.

The mule deer boasts the largest antlers of the North American deer, making it the favorite of many trophy hunters. These antlers often spread more than 25 inches, and sometimes exceed 30. Like all deer, the mule deer's meat is tasty unless it's taken during the November rutting period. Its stocky, 200-pound body provides plenty of steaks for the freezer.

The blacktail deer is without a doubt the most underrated deer in North America. This Pacific Coast animal is the smallest of the deer in terms of body and antlers, seldom weighing over 120 pounds and seldom sporting a rack of more than 20 inches. However, it is perhaps the most challenging deer to hunt because of its nervous nature, its preference for heavy cover, and its total unpredictability. A blacktail makes a hard-earned prize, the result of careful still-hunting in thick cover and pinpoint snap-shooting as it dashes away through heavy brush and trees.

The whitetail deer is by far the most widely hunted big-game species in North America, and many feel this slippery customer is the most challenging quarry our continent has to offer. Undeniably, the whitetail is the most nervous and most alert of the deer, which tends to support the views of his fans. The whitetail's preference for heavy cover also supports the idea that this deer is king. However, the whitetail has one flaw — a very predictable nature. A hunter who studies a whitetail's movement patterns prior to hunting season can usually ambush the animal later on from a well-placed tree stand or ground blind. Whitetail deer tend to be easier targets during the late-fall rut, spending more time in the open and becoming susceptible to calling techniques such as those made by rattling antlers together to simulate the sound of two bucks fighting over a doe. Obviously, the whitetail is not as invincible as it is often cracked up to be. However, it is fully capable of giving any good hunter a run for his money, and its tasty meat and well-formed rack nicely complement the challenge.

All North American big-game animals are worth hunting. When planning a trip for any species, the key is knowing something about what that species has to offer. The result can be realistic expectations and a satisfying adventure without disappointments.

The little blacktail deer is probably the most underrated animal in North America. What he lacks in size he more than makes up for in cunning and good looks.

The Shooting Sports in the 1980 Olympic Games

by Robert W. Hunnicutt

On Saturday, July 19, 1980, the entire world will take two weeks off from other concerns and turn its attention to the most grandiose and costly athletic event in human history — the Games of the XXII Olympiad.

For two weeks, Americans, like sports fans in every corner of the globe, will be glued to their radios and televisions, waiting to hear and see how their athletes perform in Moscow.

The first gold medal presented will be awarded in a sport many Americans don't even associate with the Olympics — pistol shooting.

Yet shooting, which ranks fourth highest of the Olympic sports in participation, has been one of the best medal-producers for United States teams, with a total of 104 gold, 31 silver and 30 bronze medallions won by American shooters.

Three of the matches fired at the 1948 Olympics — the English match, free pistol and rapid-fire pistol — are still part of the Olympic program. The 300-meter rifle event was dropped after the 1972 Games, while the running deer event was fired only in 1952 and 1956. Four matches have been added: small-bore free rifle and clay pigeon in 1952, skeet in 1968 and running game target (running boar) in 1972. These seven events will form the program for the 1980 Games, and for future Olympics as well, although the ISU is campaigning for the inclusion of air gun events at the 1984 Games and for the establishment of a separate category for women.

The first gold medal awarded in Moscow will hang from the neck of the winner in free pistol, a match first fired at the 1900 Games in Paris.

As the name "free" implies, there are very few restrictions placed on the firearm used in the match. Regulations require only that it be a 22-caliber rimfire pistol with metallic sights. The match is customarily fired on the same range used for the 50-meter rifle events. The bullseye target has a 5.08-centimeter 10-ring inside a 20-centimeter black. Shooters fire one shot at a time until all 60 shots have been fired for a possible 600 score. The time limit of 2½ hours encourages a leisurely competitive pace, and free-pistol shooters often sit down to rest and even leave the line during the course of a match.

The leeway which the rules grant in the design of the free pistol has encouraged the most arcane developments in firearm technology. U.S. shooters have for several years been using the Green Electroarm, a bolt-action pistol with a solenoid-actuated trigger. Europeans are now getting into electronics with the Walther FP, probably the first factory-made firearm equipped with a pilot light!

Whether free pistols use exotic electronic triggers or more conventional mechanisms, they are all equipped with hand-fitting orthopedic grips, usually adjustable for tightness, and with accurately adjustable sights. Free pistols are invariably single-shot arms, often with Martini-type falling-block actions.

Perhaps the strangest variation on the free pistol was used by Moritz Minder, who fired a new world record of 577 to take the free pistol gold medal at the 42nd World Shooting Championships at Seoul,

Uwe Potteck, 1976 Olympic winner, is the East German hopeful in the free-pistol competition.

Korea, in 1978.

Minder, a Swiss switchboard manufacturer, rotated the sights on his Russian-made TOZ-35 pistol almost 90 degrees counter-clockwise, allowing him to grip the gun with his palm facing upward. The unorthodox grip allows him to lock up his elbow for a steadier hold.

If Minder can keep firing such scores (he tallied a 578 in national competition) he might be able to break the stranglehold that Russian and East German shooters have held on the free-pistol awards.

Minder's competition at the 1980 Games should come from East Germans Uwe Potteck, the 1976 Olympic champ, and Harald Vollmar, 1975 Euro-

pean champion and holder of the current world air-pistol record. The Soviets will be counting on Sergei Psychanov, winner of the 1978 European junior championships, while Sweden will have two experienced and multi-talented pistoleers in Ragnar Skanaker and Ove Gunnarson. Skanaker was 1972 Olympic champion and finished second at the 42nd World Championships, where he set a new world mark of 582 in standard pistol. Gunnarson was 1977 European champion in free pistol and world champion in rapid-fire.

Free pistol was the only event in which no individual U.S. shooters placed at the II Confederation of the Americas Championships in 1977, and the top U.S. finisher at the 42nd World Champion-

A strong contender representing the United States in free pistol is Steve Reiter from California, 1978 U.S. champion and top American finisher at the 42nd World Championships.

ships was 12th, posting a 552 — 25 points off the winning score.

Few U.S. pistol shooters concentrate on free-pistol competition except in Olympic years, since they can make World Championship, Confederation of the Americas Championship and Pan-American Games teams in less-demanding disciplines like centerfire and air pistol.

The retirement of Hershel Anderson from international competition left a vacuum at the top of U.S. free-pistol shooting which has yet to be filled by a new figure. Darius Young, a college professor from Winterburn, Alberta, Canada, (he retains U.S. citizenship) was 1977 national champion and finished fourth at the II Confederation Championships and 33rd at the 42nd World Championships.

Steve Reiter, a plumber from Daly City, California, was 1978 U.S. champ and top American finisher at the 42nd World Championships, while Don Hamilton of Kingston, Massachusetts, a veteran of two world championships and the 1968 Olympics, placed 31st in Korea.

The match is fired with 22-caliber (almost invariably 22-short) pistols from a range of 25 meters at a bank of five coffin-shaped targets having 10 scoring zones. Firing is divided into two courses

of 30 shots each, for a maximum score of 600 points. Each course is subdivided into six series of five shots. The entire bank of five targets turns to face the shooter simultaneously.

The shooter fires two series of five shots while the targets face him for eight seconds per series. The process is repeated, but this time the shooter must fire within six seconds. Finally, the shooter has only four seconds to squeeze off each series of five shots. The competitor must begin each series with the pistol lowered at an angle of 45 degress or less, and may raise the gun only when the targets begin to turn.

The rapid-fire target has evolved from a humanoid silhouette to a more abstract shape over the years. The 10-point zone is a lozenge-shaped area 10 centimeters wide and 15 centimeters high. The other zones retain the same shape — the dimensions are simply increased by 10 centimeters of width and 15 centimeters of height for each zone. Needless to say, very few shots hit the "feet" of the target, though every rapid-fire shooter seems to have a funny story about a "foot shot."

The targets are scored on the line by a team of officials who call out the value of each shot, record the score and then paste the target in a well-oiled

Terry Anderson, lauded as the best rapid-fire shooter in America, boosts his energy with V8 before a meet.

ritual.

Pistols used in the rapid-fire event are every bit as specialized as free pistols, but are, literally, boxed in by the rules. The pistol must fit into a rectangular box with maximum inside measurements of 300x150x50 mm. The pistol may weigh no more than 1260 grams, and the height of the barrel and sights may not exceed 40 millimeters.

To reduce recoil to a bare minimum, rapid-fire pistols use 22-caliber short ammunition and have a series of vents drilled in the top of the barrel to bleed off gas. Gas escaping from the vents pushes the barrel downward, making it easier to keep the gun on target.

Thoroughbred pistols are often finicky about the ammo they're fed, so shooters test lot after lot of Eley Short Pistol Match, RWS R-25 and other hard-to-get brands to find the perfect match cartridge.

Initially, rapid-fire pistols were simply modifications of standard automatics, equipped with extra weights, muzzle brakes and vented barrels. But the rapid-fire gun has evolved into being exotic and often bulky, unlike other pistols. The breed is typified by imports like the Domino, Unique, Walther OSP and Hammerli 230 — firearms which are almost devoid of recoil but which require constant tuning to perform to their full potential, which is high, indeed. The world record is 598, fired by Italy's Giovanni Liverzani at the 40th World Championships in 1970 with a Walther OSP.

Liverzani's record was matched at the 1977 European championships by a man to be reckoned with at the 1980 Olympics, Romania's Ion Corneliu. Corneliu's 598 is the highest mark fired in recent world-level competition, eclipsing the 597 of East Germany's Norbert Klaar at the 1976 Olympics. Klaar's teammate Jurgen Wiefel could be a threat, as could two Germans from the other side of the Wall, Heinz Weissenburger and Werner Beier. Sweden's Gunnarson, current world champion, could be part of the picture, as could Afanasy Kuzmin and Vavim Vysoschon of the Soviet host team.

Rapid-fire is an unpredictable event, as two of America's top shooters found during 1978. One of them, Bill McMillan of Del Mar, California, was performing well in the 42nd World Championships when a late shot went through the edge of a target, knocking him out of contention. McMillan, a deputy sheriff in San Diego, has been a member of 14 U.S. international teams, including six Olympic squads. He won the last U.S. gold medal in rapid-fire at the 1960 Games in Rome. At 50, he shows little sign of slowing down and should be quite capable of making his seventh Olympic team.

The man who may be the best rapid-fire shooter in the nation never made it to the plane for the 42nd World Championships. Terry Anderson, a contractor from New Orleans, suffered a trigger malfunction during his first four-second string and

Sixth-place winner at the 42nd World Championships, Mel Makin is another United States rapid-fire rising star.

wound up finishing 17th. Anderson, orginally from Australia, was the 1977 national champion and a gold medalist at the II Confederation Championships at Mexico City, firing a 590. He is a colorful (some might say eccentric) character who has made a minor science of rapid-fire shooting. He has been known to take samples of his blood during the course of matches to analyze the blood-sugar level, and likes to knock back a can of V-8 juice before an important string of shots.

Mel Makin, the nation's other rising rapid-fire star, is as taciturn as Anderson is outspoken. The Aunsville, Oregon, engineer's sixth-place finish at the 42nd World Championships was the best showing of any U.S. male pistol shooter, and his 591 score was just four points back from the winning mark.

The English match, or some slight variation on it, has been a part of the Olympic program since 1912. It is a match in which precision counts for everything. The slightest error can cost a medal more quickly in this event than in any other. Shooters fire on the same 50-meter range used for free pistol at a target having a 10-ring 12 millimeters in diameter — about the width of a 45-caliber pistol slug. A match includes 60 shots from the prone position for a possible 600 score; firing must be completed in two hours or less.

The rifle used in English match shooting may weigh as much as eight kilos and must fire 22-caliber rimfire ammunition. It is otherwise free of restrictions, which means that a top competitor's rifle can be equipped with a spirit level, adjustable butt plate and cheekpiece or any other device the shooter feels he needs.

Shooters also wear special clothing, including shooting coats, boots, shooting pants and gloves, adjustable shooting glasses and other accoutrements, all of which are subject to stringent rules limitation.

Since the shooter cannot tolerate anything less than tack-driving accuracy, the rifles used for the English match must be of the highest quality. The Anschutz action predominates, though there are those who prefer the Walther. Finnish Lion, Winchester and Soviet rifles are occasionally encountered.

Eley Tenex ammunition dominates world-level competition, almost to the exclusion of other brands, although Finnish Lapua ammo can sometimes be spotted. Soviet competitors have been known to pack Eley in Russian boxes at big meets

The third place slot in the most recent world championship in English match was taken by Lanny Bassham of the United States.

to save national face.

American shooters almost always select custom-made stainless barrels for their rifles, but many European and Asian shooters use the factory tubes and seem to suffer no ill effect.

The most recent world championship in English match was won, appropriately enough, by an Englishman, Alistair Allan. Allan had warmed up for his victory by winning both the British and Commonwealth Championships, and made the most of the calm morning air in Korea. Following Allan were two Americans whose names are so well known in rifle shooting that the ISU magazine *International Shooting Sport* referred to them as "Emperor and King." Lt. Col. Lones W. Wigger of the U.S. Army Marksmanship Unit, Ft. Benning, Georgia, and Lanny Bassham of New Braunfels, Texas, both tallied 598s, with Wigger taking the silver medal on a tie breaker.

Neither Wigger nor Bassham thinks of himself as a "prone shooter," but each has the ability to capitalize on good conditions and the experience to accept the pressure of world championship competition.

Other top English match competitors include Karlheinz Smieszek, of West Germany, the defending Olympic champ, who finished seventh in Korea; Ulrich Lind, another West German; Gennady Luschikov, the "free spirit" of the Soviet team; the USSR's Alexander Pasternak, 1978 Europeon junior champ; and farther afield, Asian champion Kyung Ho Kim of North Korea.

Lt. Col. Lones W. Wigger of the U.S. Army Marksmanship Unit came home with the silver after the world championship in English match.

Karlheinz Smieszek (right) of West Germany will defend his world title in the English match competition.

The small-bore free-rifle match, first fired at Helsinki in 1952, was developed from the classic 300-meter free-rifle match. The rules are the same, except for the distance and the rifle used.

The match includes 120 shots from three positions—prone, standing and kneeling—for a possible score of 1200. The range, target and rifle are the same as those used in the English match, but several accessories are added to the rifle in three-position shooting, including the butt hook and palm-rest.

The free-rifle match is a grueling affair lasting up to 5½ hours. Not only does the shooter have to deal with fatigue, but there are inevitably numerous wind changes during such a lengthy match. Shooters formerly overcame this by juggling the order of the three positions, but the rules now require the stages to be fired in succession, with 1½ hours allowed for prone, two hours for standing and 1¾ hours for kneeling.

To fire a score like Wigger's world-record 1167, a free-rifle shooter must drop no more than a point or two prone, score in the high 370s standing and around 390 kneeling. It's a strain that few shooters are up to, physically and mentally. The constantly-changing conditions of wind, light and mirage require an attention to detail that few shooters can maintain for most of a day.

Many of those shooters are Americans. In *International Shooting Sport's* listing of the top ten scores fired in small-bore free rifle, five were carded by U.S. shooters. Quite simply, U.S. shooters have dominated free-rifle shooting for more than a decade. The late 1960s and 1970s saw a parade of greats, including Gary Anderson, D. I. Boyd, Jack Foster, David Kimes, Margaret Murdock, Jack Writer and, of course, Lones Wigger and Lanny Bassham.

The question is whether a new generation of American riflemen can carry on that tradition of dominance. Anderson has gone on to become NRA Executive Director of General Operations. Murdock and Writer have retired, while Foster and Boyd have become team officials. Kimes, Wigger and Bassham seem to regard 1980 as, possibly, a last hurrah.

The last three, of course, are far from over the hill. Each returned from the 42nd World Championships with suitcases full of medals and golden crowns for Kimes and Wigger, who set new world records in 300-meter standard and 300-meter free rifle, respectively. Bassham will start 1980 as defending Olympic and world champion in small-bore free rifle.

The younger generation of rifle shooters must contend with invidious comparisons with these titans, but there are several of the new generation who have the talent to win big.

Ed Etzel, coach of the West Virginia University team, came within a point of Wigger's record at the II Confederation Championships as he carded an 1166, tying scores fired in earlier years by Writer and Murdock.

Two shooters in an even younger age group, the Fitz-Randolph brothers of Palm Bay, Florida, have already tasted world-level competition while still students at Tennessee Tech University. Rod, now a junior, was a member of the II Confederation team, while brother Kurt, a sophomore, was on the U.S. World Championship squad.

There are distaff shooters working to inherit Murdock's mantle, too.

The U.S. Army Marksmanship Unit is home base for Wanda Jewell, the only shooter at the 42nd World Championships to take two individual gold medals, and Karen Monez, who took an individual award in every event she entered.

Jewell gave a sparkling performance in both air rifle and standard rifle, three position, winning both events.

Monez put on a similar show at the II Confederation Championships, winning both air rifle and standard rifle, three position.

The nation's top woman prone shooter is a doctoral student at Columbia University, Sue Ann Sandusky. Sandusky, an expert in the field of

David Kimes was a member of the U.S. shooting team that dominated free-rifle shooting events during the 60s and 70s.

Talented newcomers to the shooting sports merit watching. Rod Fitz-Randolph of Palm Bay, Florida, tasted world-level competition while still a college student.

As a sophomore at Tennessee Tech University, Rod's brother Kurt Fitz-Randolph was a member of the U.S. World Championship Squad.

Wanda Jewell, only shooter at the 42nd World Championships to take two individual gold medals, calls the U.S. Army Marksmanship Unit home base.

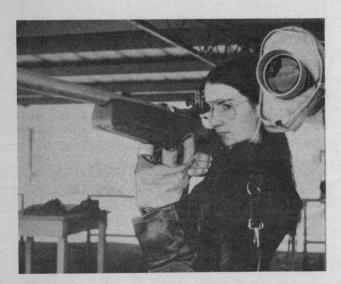

A U.S. woman shooter who garnered an individual award in every event she entered at the 42nd World Championships was Karen Monez. At the II Confederation Championships, she took air rifle and standard rifle, three position.

The title of top U.S. woman prone shooter belongs to Sue Ann Sandusky. She won gold medals in standard rifle, prone at both the II Confederation and World Championships.

Balkan politics, won the standard rifle, prone, gold medals at both the II Confederation and World Championships.

Running-game target, or running boar, as it's commonly known, is the newest Olympic shooting event. It was first fired in world-level competition at the 39th World Shooting Championships at Wiesbaden, West Germany, in 1966. Shooters use specialized 22-caliber rifles equipped with telescopic sights.

The target is a lithograph of a wild boar charging at right angles to the shooter, over which is superimposed a set of rings with a 10-ring 10 centimeters in diameter. The targets (one for each direction) are mounted on a dolly which rolls on a steel track across a 10-meter wide opening. The shooter sees the target for five seconds in slow runs and 2.5 seconds in fast runs. A match includes 30 slow-run shots and 30 fast-run shots for a possible score of 600.

A firearms fancier could probably go a lifetime without seeing a running-boar rifle — there probably aren't more than 100 in the United States. Most are made by Anschutz or Walther, though some beginners build their own using Winchester 52, Remington 40X or other actions. All have some features in common, including a short, thick barrel, often with a muzzle weight; a fat, stippled forend; a thumbhole stock, often with adjustable cheekpiece, and an adjustable butt plate with a small hook.

Running boar is the only international shooting event in which telescopic sights are allowed, and the sights are as specialized as the rifles. Most are 3-9X variables with custom-made reticles, usually with two or three dots located along the horizontal center line of the scope. The shooter places one of the outside dots on the boar's eye or tusk to measure the proper lead. The power setting is varied to regulate the amount of lead required for slow or fast runs. The power setting also allows the shooter to compensate for different types of ammunition. "Pig shooters" use a wide variety of ammo, ranging from Eley HV Moving Target to familiar over-the-counter brands like Remington High Velocity.

With the exception of Colombian Helmut Bellingrodt's win at the 41st World Championships, running boar has been dominated from the start by the Soviets and East Germans. The current world record of 581 is held by East Germany's Thomas Pfeffer, who fired the score at the 1978 European Championships. The host Soviets will field a strong team, probably including defending Olympic champ Aleksandr Gazov, 1976 silver medalist Aleksandr Kediarov and European junior champion Igor Solokov.

Pfeffer and the Russians could get some competition either from world champion Juha Rannikko of Finland or mixed-runs record-holder Giovanni Mezzanni of Italy.

United States running-boar shooters have shown steady and encouraging improvement over the past couple of years, but are still a few years away from an Olympic medal.

One of the United States' most capable entrants in the event is 52-year-old Charles Davis of Ft. Benning, a durable competitor who started his career as a high-power rifleman in the late 1950s. Davis has competed in the Olympics, two World Championships, both Confederation Championships and the 1975 World Moving Target Championships. He anchored the U.S. quartet to a silver-medal team finish at the 42nd World Championships.

Mike Theimer of Iowa Park, Texas, was a member of the 1976 Olympic squad and has fired in the 41st and 42nd World Championship teams, as well as both Confederation Championships.

Running boar was strictly a military affair in this country until Jack Anderson of Phoenix, Arizona, arrived on the scene. Anderson, an aerospace machinist, started his competitive career in metallic silhouette shooting, but got interested in the running boar event at Phoenix's Black Canyon

The silver medal in the running boar event at the II Confederation Championships went to Jack Anderson. This U.S. aerospace machinist began his competitive career in metallic silhouette shooting.

Range, part of the facilities left over from the 40th World Championships. A few years of practice on the old range led Anderson to a silver-medal finish at the II Confederation championships and a place on last year's World Championships squad.

Anderson also was responsible for getting the nation's top junior, Todd Bensley of Lordsburg, New Mexico, hooked on the sport. Bensley followed his 1977 junior championship in metallic silhouette with the 1978 junior boar title.

International clay pigeon is a shooting sport only slightly more familiar than running boar to most Americans. It resembles American trapshooting in that the shooter fires a shotgun at a clay target flying away from him, but there the similarity ends.

The clay pigeon field (and there are but a handful in this country) is built around a 20-meter long bunker sunk into the ground 15 meters in front of the five firing points. In the bunker are five sets of traps, three for each firing point. The traps are set to throw the targets at random angles and elevations a minimum of 75 meters. The targets, 110 millimeters in diameter, emerge from the bunker at speeds of up to 130 miles-per-hour, at angles of up to 45 degrees and at elevations which can seem to verge on the vertical. The traps are actuated by the shooter's own voice and are selected by a mechanical device which ensures that each shooter gets a random sample of possible targets. The gun is held at shoulder level as the target is called for, and the shooter may fire twice at each target. An international course includes eight rounds of 25 for a total of 200 targets, and only two shooters have broken all but one in world-level competition.

The shotguns used in international clay pigeon shooting are a far cry from the scatterguns most shooters use to hunt ducks or quail. The over-and-under is an expensive favorite, and the most costly brands are the ones best-liked by world champions. Perazzi, Krieghoff, FN, Franchi, Beretta and Belgian-made Brownings are the predominant choices. Long barrels and tight chokes are the rule, with release triggers being a popular option.

The ammunition used is always 12 gauge, with a 32-gram load of shot, usually nickel-plated No. 7½. U.S. shooters usually choose Federal or Winchester AA International Trap, while shooters from Europe use Eley, Fiocchi, Gevelot, Gyttorp, Rottweil or other local brands. Reloads are not allowed.

Latins excel in clay pigeon, with shooters from France, Italy and Spain holding many of the records.

The current world title holder is Spain's Elladio Vallduvi, who edged out world record co-holder Michel Carrega of France and Italy's Silviano Basagni for the gold. Canada is home for two other top contenders, John Primrose, winner at the 1975 World Moving Target Championships, and Susan Nattrass, the world's best woman trapshooter and holder of the world ladies' record of 195.

The United States, despite the dearth of ranges, is quite capable of a strong showing in clay pigeon at the 1980 Olympics. The defending Olympic champ is Don Haldeman of Souderton, Pennsylvania, who also was a member of the U.S. quartet which established the world team record of 586 at the II Confederation Championships.

But Haldeman's toughest job could be earning a spot on the team. There will be at least a half-dozen U.S. trapshooters who will have a good chance of making the journey to Moscow.

International skeet uses the same field as the domestic variety, but the rules make it a much tougher competition. Shooters move through a series of eight stations set in a semicircle between two buildings which house the traps. The flight of the targets is the same throughout a match, but the several positions of the shooter present him with a variety of shots.

The shooter must call for the target with the shotgun held at hip level until the clay bird emerges from the house. A three-second variable delay is built into the throwing mechanism, which propels the target a distance of 65 meters at a speed of nearly 100 miles-per-hour. The difficulty is further increased by the addition of doubles at stations 3 and 5, and the elimination of the "option shot" used in domestic skeet. As in clay pigeon, the international course includes eight rounds of 25 targets for a total of 200.

The equipment used in skeet is similar to that in clay pigeon, except that the shotguns have short barrels and open chokes. Over-and-unders are again most common, though some shooters, like Dan Carlisle, prefer the Remington 1100 autoloader. The Perazzi Mirage and MT-6, the Krieghoff Model 32, the Rottweil Olympia '72, the Soviet-made Baikal, the Remington 3200, and the ubiquitous Browning are among the other common choices.

Most U.S. shooters prefer Winchester AA International Skeet or Federal T123 shells with 2-mm shot, while Europeans stick to their national brands.

The U.S. team should be strong in skeet at

Bill Clemmons of the U.S. Army Marksmanship Unit set a new one-man record of 199 in the skeet event at the II Confederation Championships.

Moscow. American skeet shooters had a banner year in 1977, setting new world individual and team records at the II Confederation Championships. Bill Clemmons of the U.S. Army Marksmanship Unit at Ft. Benning, set the new one-man mark at 199, and he was joined by Carlisle, Alger Mullins of USAMU and Dean Clark (then a high school senior, but now a USAMU team member) in setting a new team record of 586.

Hopes were high for a similar performance at the 42nd World Championships, but U.S. skeeters came up empty-handed. Carlisle and Clark were replaced by Matt Dryke of USAMU and Jeff Sizemore of Corpus Christi, Texas, both talented but inexperienced shooters. More seasoning could make all of these shooters promising Olympic contenders.

The host team's hopes will ride on shooters like Alik Aliev, 1977 European champion, while Czechoslovakia will send defending gold medalist Josef Panacek. Italy will have a powerful squad, probably including world champion Luciano Brunetti and co-silver medalist Romano Garagnani. Smaller nations like Argentina, Denmark and the Netherlands will weigh in with Firmo Roberti, Benny Seiffert and Eric Swinkels.

The Soviets are planning to make available the most lavish and up-to-date facilities for all sports on the Olympic calendar, and shooting is no exception. They have completely renovated the Dynamo Sports Club ranges at Mytischtschi, 37 kilometers northwest of Moscow, the site of the 37th World Championships in 1958.

Michael Tipa, Chairman of the ISU Technical Committee and Assistant Director for International Activities of NRA's Competitions Division, says the Olympic facilities should even surpass those at Seoul.

The 90-point 50-meter range will be equipped with German-made Spieth electric target boxes, which will be mounted on elevators extending into an underground chamber. Using the elevators, match personnel can quickly replace an inoperative target box and can unload the targets of a shooter who finishes early. The targets will be scored in the underground chamber, ensuring both speed and close supervision of the scoring procedure.

Running-boar shooters will have three ranges on which to compete, all equipped with closed-circuit television so that spectators can watch the targets being scored.

Rapid-fire pistol and the pistol phase of the modern pentathlon will be fired on a 12-position 25-meter range with an extra function-testing position.

Clay pigeon and skeet will be fired on four fields equipped with Spieth traps.

Administration, press and equipment storage areas, a cafe and an assembly plaza for awards ceremonies complete with complex.

As U.S. national governing body for the shooting sports, the National Rifle Association has taken several important steps in the past few years to ensure that American shooters can compete with the best.

The NRA has established the National Shooting Sports Coach Certification Program to develop coaches qualified to help promising shooters become international champions.

To help the shooters themselves, the NRA Board of Directors established the International Shooter Development Fund, a tax-exempt foundation designed to assist in the development of world-class shooting champions.

With a growing number of young shooters becoming more interested in international competition and increasing aid from organizations such as the NRA, U.S. shooters may be able to dominate world competition in the 1980s.

Equipping the Varmint Hunter
by James F. Brady

The term "varmint hunting" was originally applied to the pursuit of mostly inedible animals and birds classified generally as pests and vermin and unprotected by law. Many of these species have now been recognized as offering fine sport and have some economic value as furbearers. Closed seasons on foxes, coyotes and bobcats have been set in many jurisdictions. Even the much-disparaged crow is now protected by state and federal laws.

The art of calling predators is an ancient one that has been employed for centuries. The calling of foxes was practiced in Europe, and the Indians of Central and South America call jaguars by imitating the big cat's coughing roar with an ingenious calling device.

The author called in his first fox by using the simple handsqueak. The handsqueak is accomplished by sucking on the forefinger or palm of the hand with a kissing action. The result is a high-pitched squealing similar to that made by a rabbit or small rodent in the clutches of a predator.

While squirrel hunting on a late fall afternoon, I spotted a fox trotting along a hillside some 200 yards away. I had heard that foxes and other predators could be called in with the handsqueak and decided to give it a try. At the first squeak, the fox stopped, poised and alert, one front foot raised and with head and ears pointed in my direction. As I continued to squeal and squeak, he broke into a dead run toward me and stopped when he was about 75 yards from my position. I was using a reduced load in my 22 Hornet rifle for squirrels, but the 45-grain bullet dropped the fox where he stood. I had nothing with me on that long-ago day that could be classified as varmint-hunting equipment, except perhaps the rifle. The intervening years have witnessed a gradual accumulation of gear for use in this exciting sport.

Unlike children, the varmint hunter, especially if calling, should be heard but not seen. Proper outer clothing will do much to further the search for invisibility, but it must be chosen with an eye to the background against which the hunter will be operating. Headgear, pants and jackets made of camouflage material are available and ideal for the hunter operating in brush and woodlands, although camouflage trousers are not absolutely necessary. The varmint hunter will usually be sitting, squatting or kneeling, and any dull-colored trousers will blend in with earth, rocks and stumps. Attention to background is all-important. Bowhunters present one of the most comical sights in the woods when they perch in trees which are entirely bare of foliage. Each hunter resplendent in complete camouflage in leaf patterns resembles nothing so much as an elongated squirrel nest that stands out like the proverbial sore thumb.

When snow covers the hunting grounds, white clothing from head to foot will enable the hunter to play the "Invisible Man." However, you should be aware that on bright sunny days in snow-covered terrain, your outlined shadow can give you away to sharp-eyed varmints such as foxes. Try to position yourself so that your shadow blends in with that of a bush, rock outcrop or snowdrift. Some varmint hunters even go to the trouble of painting their guns with white water-based paints when in snow-

Varmint hunters who operate in heavy cover and brush and those who hunt at night prefer to carry a shotgun for the fast action often encountered under these conditions. This hunter is equipped with complete camouflage including a face mask.

covered landscapes.

The human face and hands stand out starkly against most outdoor backgrounds, and an effort should be made to mask these telltale signs from view. Various types of face masks and gloves in camouflage patterns are available. Some varmint hunters prefer to use the various camouflage make-up paints on the market for this purpose, while others rely on burnt cork or charcoal to do the job.

Camouflage will help to hide the hunter's visual presence, but will do nothing to hide his scent from the keen noses with which most varmints are endowed. Taking a position downwind or crosswind from the direction in which game is expected to appear is standard operating procedure for experienced hunters, but vagrant breezes will sometimes carry human scent to an approaching animal and spoil the stand. This happens quite frequently on those days when there is no prevailing wind but gentle air currents are flowing in all directions.

Masking scents are of great value in such situations. There are many brands and types of such scents available. Perhaps the most useful are those containing skunk essence. The odor of skunks is one that is familiar to most animals, and may in fact attract rather than repel them. The main use of these scents, however, is to mask the hunter's own scent. The double-bottle technique will prevent the hunter's clothing, gear and vehicle from being permeated by this socially unacceptable odor. In this method, the skunk essence is poured into a small bottle or vial stuffed with cotton to prevent the essence from running and spilling. This bottle is closed and placed inside a larger bottle or jar that is also closed. In use, both bottles are opened and placed on the ground.

Some of the best varmint-hunting opportunities occur after the sun has set. Although foxes can be successfully stalked and called during daylight hours, the hours between dusk and dawn are prime

The bobcat is a favorite quarry of dedicated varmint hunters. It comes slowly to the hunter's calling, but once in, the cat tends to stay around longer than foxes or coyotes.

The double-bottle technique will prevent strong masking scents such as skunk essence from permeating the user's clothing and vehicle. Cotton in inner jar is soaked with enough scent to prevent running or spilling. Both jars are capped when transporting scent and opened and placed on the ground when ready to use.

time for fox hunting and also for calling bobcats to the gun. It has long been known that the use of lights at night does not seem to particularly bother these animals, especially when the light is indirect. For many years, varmint hunters have used headlamps with the beams directed upward so that the eyes of incoming animals are illuminated by the outer edge of the beam. These lamps are battery operated and held by an elastic band that passes around the user's head. When the varmint is within range, the lamp is brought to bear fully on the animal and the shot is made.

Of late, it has been found that lights with red filters are even less disturbing to the animals than lights throwing a clear beam. Various lamps are available with clamping devices to hold them on scope sights or shotgun barrels. The author has sometimes used an ordinary flashlight with built-in magnets fastened to the left side of the receiver of a Remington 1100 shotgun. Lighting equipment for the night varmint hunter is growing quite sophisticated. For example, there are lights available with mercury switches that fasten to scopes or gun barrels. When the gun is tilted to the side, the light remains off. When the gun is brought to the shoulder and leveled, the light goes on.

Varmint-calling devices are designed to reproduce the sounds of prey species in mortal agony. Most are breath operated, but a few utilize a small rubber bulb or are of the friction type. The author has had

foxes come charging in when using a crow call and once had a big red dog fox come in while using a turkey call. Since no turkeys had answered my calling in that area, I opted for the fox and walked off with $45-worth of fur over my shoulder.

Varmint hunters should carry at least three calls into the field on every hunt. If you should lose your only call, or if its reed should break, you will be out of business on that particular stand. Another reason for carrying more than one type of call is that at times a change of tone will be the deciding factor as to whether or not varmints will come in. When an animal approaches closely, the squeaker or coaxer types of calls will often bring it those last few steps necessary for a clear and successful shot.

Always carry extra reeds for your calls. These replacement reeds are available from many call makers and will keep you going throughout the season. If you do much calling, you will break reeds, so stock up on these inexpensive but indispensable items. The call can be suspended on a cord or thong that passes around the neck; the others can be wrapped in plastic sandwich bags to keep them clean and free of debris, and carried in the pocket.

Guns for the varmint hunter can be almost anything that shoots. They range from those chambered for the ubiquitous 22 Long Rifle cartridge to the

For night varmint hunting, a battery-operated headlamp should be standard equipment. Battery case at left clips to belt and lamp is held by elastic band around the head.

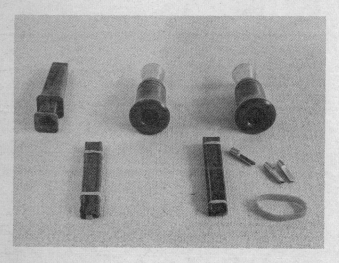

Every varmint hunter should carry at least three calls. If a call is lost or a reed breaks, you will still be able to continue. At the top are breath-operated reed-type calls. The two lower calls are of the squeaker or coaxer type for use when the varmint has approached close to the calling stand. At the lower right are replacement reeds for both types.

flat-shooting and heavy-barreled rifles so dear to the hearts of woodchuck hunters. I've seen everything in between pressed into service including a muzzle-loading shotgun. Handguns are regularly used by those who prefer these short and handy tools. The reasons for this wide choice of armament can be appreciated when we examine the various and devious ways in which the varmint hunter plies his craft.

Hunters who call foxes, bobcats and coyotes in open country, pastures and hayfields, most fre-

quently choose a rifle chambered for a cartridge delivering a flat trajectory. Shots are usually long and at unknown ranges over such terrain, and a flat-shooting cartridge helps in placing the shot. Those hunters who use the spotting and stalking method without calling have even more reason to choose one of the hotshot cartridges. The 222 Remington is the minimum cartridge for this use and is an excellent choice where ranges are not likely to be much more than 200 yards. It combines a fairly flat trajectory with outstanding accuracy.

Since the price of furs has gone through the ceiling in the past few years, many varmint hunters are wary of using a cartridge that does too much damage to pelts. It does not pay to use a cartridge such as the 7mm Remington Magnum for such game as most fur buyers would not be interested in bidding on two halves of a fox pelt. Considering that four good fox skins will bring the price of a fine rifle on today's market, a little attention to what you stuff in that chamber will pay off. The 222 Remington is good on lightly-built animals, such as foxes and bobcats up to 200 yards, but coyotes require a little more zap.

The 222 will take coyotes cleanly most of the time — but most of the time is not good enough. A better choice for these larger varmints would be the 22-250 cartridge or one of the 6mm's. These cartridges are also good choices for foxes where shots are likely to be taken at well over 200 yards by hunters using the spotting and stalking method. Hunters operating in brushy and wooded country will at times team up, one man carrying a shotgun for the close and sudden shots while the other carries a rifle for the infrequent long tries. Here again, the 222 is a good choice but the dependable 22 Hornet is even better for those shots just out of shotgun range. Again, avoiding pelt damage is the name of the game. Some hunters use the 22 Magnum Rimfire for these shots. The Hornet is a better choice as it delivers more power; if you reload your own, it is much cheaper to shoot.

The shotgun is by far the better tool for those varmint hunters who operate in heavy cover and call their quarry in close to the gun. Gray foxes and bobcats are partial to this type of habitat, especially the former, which bear the colloquial name of "brushpoppers" in recognition of their preferred territory. Although the red fox generally prefers open fields and pastures for both his denning and hunting areas, many reds spend their lives in wooded country.

Some expert fox hunters use the 20-gauge gun,

Some varmint hunters prefer the handgun for use in rough terrain or jungle-like growth. Ranges are usually short; when used by a good shot, a pistol or revolver can be an efficient tool. Revolver being used by this hunter is a 357 Magnum.

THE SHOOTER'S BIBLE

Three of the most useful rifle cartridges for hunting varmints, from left: the 22 Hornet, 222 Remington and the 243 Winchester. These three rounds will cover just about every varmint-hunting situation calling for the use of a rifle.

but the 12 gauge is a better all around choice. A full-choked 12-gauge pump or autoloader or a double gun bored modified/full is hard to beat for use on called foxes and bobcats when hunting at night. Ranges are often short and the animals may appear anywhere in a full circle surrounding the stand. Two hunters sitting back-to-back and armed with shotguns make an efficient and deadly team under these circumstances. There is nothing wrong with a shotgun chambered for the 3-inch magnum, 12-gauge shell for this work, but a 1½-ounce load of No. 4s in the 2¾-inch shell will take down most foxes and bobcats with precision.

If coyotes are the expected visitors, No. 2 shot is a better choice for these larger and more heavily built varmints. No. 6 shot is preferred by those hunters who believe that pattern density is more important than penetration. Smaller-size shot might be the better choice for those, using 20-gauge guns with their lighter-shot charges.

When most 20-gauge guns are loaded with shot larger than No. 6 they do not pattern very well. Tests with buckshot show that even the best of these loads are not suitable for use on varmints.

Quite a few varmint hunters use handguns when the animals can be called in close enough to make such guns practical. There is no handier implement than the handgun for carrying over rough country and operating in thickets and jungle-like growth.

A revolver or pistol with adjustable target-type sights is most efficient. This type of sighting equipment allows the user to make certain that his shots will strike exactly where the front sight rests on the target.

Handguns chambered for the 22 Long Rifle cartridge do not deliver enough energy for use on foxes, bobcats or coyotes, and should not be considered for this use. Revolvers for the 22 Rimfire Magnum are the lightest handguns artillery that can be depended upon for clean kills and then only at the shorter handgun ranges. The 357 Magnum is an excellent cartridge for the handgun varmint hunter. Bullets in this caliber are available for 110 grains to 170 grains, and handloads can be tailored to fit particular circumstances. In view of prices being paid for fur today, it might not be wise to use the 41 Magnum or 44 Magnum on valuable furbearers. The bigger the hole, even if sewed, the less valuable the pelt.

One item of handgun equipment that is particularly useful is the orange or red front-sight insert. These bright but nonreflecting sights show up plainly under almost all conditions and make precise shot placement easier. Combined with a white outline rear sight, they are the ultimate in sighting equipment for the handgun hunter.

Choice of sighting equipment for the varmint hunter's rifle should be given careful thought. Straight single-power scopes on hunting rifles can be used for both large and small game. These simple and trouble-free instruments generally give complete satisfaction. Variable-power scopes on dual-purpose rifles can also be used on both varmints and medium-sized game such as deer. Rifles chambered for the 243 Winchester, 6mm Remington, 257 Roberts, 250 Savage, and the 25-06 can utilize variable-power scopes to best advantage, and such sighting equipment is probably the best choice for use on these rifles. However, when a particular rifle is intended for use on one class of game, the single-power scope is more suitable.

On varmint rifles in the 22 Hornet-222 Remington class, scopes of 6X to 8X will take full advantage of these cartridges to the limits of their useable ranges. The more powerful 22 caliber centerfires such as the 220 Swift and the 22-250 and the 6mm's and 257 calibers that will be used at extended ranges beyond 200 yards are, in my opinion, best fitted with a scope of about 12X. Anything more powerful brings a reduced field of view that makes picking up the target a slow process and also causes a reduction in image brightness. Varmint

The spotting and stalking method of hunting varmints calls for a flat-shooting rifle. Here is the author's 22-250 with a 12X Leupold scope.

hunters who use rifles chambered for the 22 Magnum Rimfire are well fitted with a 4X scope.

Anything that makes long-range rifle shooting easier is appreciated when the mark is the comparatively small one presented by most varmints. Their vital areas are small compared to those of big-game animals; on a fox, for instance, this area is about the size of a football. For the long-range spotter and stalker, various rifle rests are available although many hunters make their own. One example is a bipod-type rest that fastens to the rifle by means of the sling-swivel studs. This is a fine and steady rest whose only fault might be that it is difficult to use on uneven or sloping ground, where it is often almost impossible to level the crosshairs in the scope because of the rigid attachment of the rest to the rifle.

The author has been field testing the prototype of a new commercial rest that uses the old principle of the single-shooting stick but with many refinements. It is not quite as steady as a bipod rest, but during the past summer I made successful shots at woodchucks at distances from 300 yards to just over 400 yards.

Carrying too much equipment into the field can cause a hunter to become bogged down and almost immobilized. However, careful selection of equipment based on the particular varmint being hunted, the season, terrain, method of hunting, and whether it is to be a day or night venture will do much to ensure success in this fascinating sport of varmint hunting.

The Grand Old Grand
by John M. Bahret

A quiet tension pervades the atmosphere. The men, the women, the young people—all with their trap guns—mill around the grounds late Thursday. Some have been there a week; others have recently arrived. They have come from Arizona and Alaska, Maine and California, even from as far away as Australia, jamming their cars, trucks and campers into the parking lot of the homegrounds of the Amateur Trapshooting Association in Vandalia, Ohio. They are there to take part in the single largest participation sporting event in the world—the Grand American. And on Friday they will shoot 100 clay targets in the most prestigious competition of the week—the Grand American Handicap.

Seventy-four shooters gathered at Interstate Park in Queens (a borough of New York City), for the first Grand American Handicap, featured at a four-day shoot in June of 1900. Rolla (Pop) Heikes, recognized as one of the nation's top trapshooters, hit 91 of the 100 clay birds to win the event by two targets over his nearest competitor.

In August of 1978, more than 4000 shooters took to the line in that one event. Like the summoning of the Grand Army of the Republic, they took the trap fields in squads of five, until at the end of the day, one would emerge as champion. And what a champion he was. Reg Jachimowski from Illinois became the 79th winner of the Grand American Handicap with a history-making 100 straight from 27 yards— the first to attain the crown from the maximum handicap yardage in the Amateur Trapshooting Association.

What is so grand about this Grand American?

These ten days in August are a mini-section of American history. It is a small part of the great American mosaic as doctors and farmers, housewives and schoolboys, pilots and school teachers stand side-by-side vying for the elusive championships in singles, doubles and handicap events. The Grand means challenge, the same challenge experienced by the early frontiersmen who gathered in the forest clearings to test their shooting skills. It is the challenge of split-second timing, of endurance, concentration and coordination. It is a culmination of effort where nothing matters but the ability of the individual shooter to smash a speeding clay disc.

The Grand American was a natural outgrowth of the increasing interest in trapshooting at the turn of the century. The sport in North America had begun with the "trapping" of live birds in the 1830s and had progressed to the use of glass balls in the search of a consistently stable inanimate target. Captain Adam Bogardus, a familiar name to trapshooters, stimulated interest in glass-ball targets by his exhibition shooting in the 1860s. He also developed a trap to throw the targets in a more consistent flight path. The perfection of a flat-disc clay target by George Ligowsky, a Cincinnati machinist, was the most significant turning point in trapshooting history. In 1881 he produced an improved trap for throwing his clay birds. An Englishman named McCaskey further improved the baked ground-clay-and-water targets by using river silt and pitch to make a disc easier to break. Later, limestone replaced river silt. With standardized targets and consistent, reliable traps, trapshooting took off as a

Aerial view of the American Trap Association's spacious and well-laid-out homegrounds in Vandalia, Ohio.

Reg Jachimowski receiving congratulations after winning the 1978 Grand American Handicap with 100 straight from 27 yards, a history-making achievement.

sport, and by 1890 the greatest target shooters of the times were competing throughout the country.

The first Grand American Handicap Target Tournament in 1900 was an experiment. The idea of handicapping was, of course, to make the competition as equitable as possible. Early handicap systems allowed extra targets to the weaker shots, or to permit an allowance of "misses as breaks" to those less skilled than their opponents. However, at the first Grand, the handicapping was by distance only. The Association felt this method was the fairest and most adjustable. A Handicap Committee would have personal knowledge of the scores and records of the majority of shooters, and they could perform the arduous task of assigning the yardage at which each competitor would shoot. Maximum yardage has changed through the years—from 23 to 25, then in 1955, to the present "back fence" mark of 27 yards.

Any time you see a bunch of shooters together, it won't be long until someone asks, "Who was the greatest shooter you ever saw?" This question was asked in 1921 of Mark Arie, the Olympic champion;

Since 1924, Vandalia, Ohio, has been the permanent home of the Grand American.

George McCarty, who had recently won the championship at the New York Athletic Club, and Neaf Apgar, who saw the first clay target thrown. The consensus of opinion was that Frank Brewer was the greatest. However, if you look through the records from the Grand American Handicap through the years, Brewer's name is not mentioned, thus giving some credence to the tradition that the stars of trapshooting succeed at 16-yard events, but the unknowns win the Grand American Handicap. And since the feat was accomplished by Rolla (Pop) Heikes in 1900, there have been few times the winners have come from among the ranks of the "hotshots."

The Grand American Handicap has been won by men in their 60s and by boys in their teens. The winners have been farmers, a former baseball pitcher, railroad conductors and postmen. Some have gone

on to accomplish other feats in the sport; others have etched their names on just that one winner's plaque. (No one has won the Grand American Handicap more than one time.) The Grand American Handicap continues to be the premier event of the Grand, and, on any given day, if the circumstances are right and lady luck is smiling, any shooter entered has his chance at that glory.

In 1905, the wife of R. R. Barber glued a four-leaf clover to his gunstock, and Barber went out and broke all previous records with a 99 in the Grand American Handicap.

In 1910, Riley (Farmer) Thompson posted the first 100 straight in the 10-year history of the Grand.

Alfred Rufus King's father did not want him to shoot in the 1930 Grand American Handicap. But the 14-year-old Texan prevailed and ended in a tie for the championship. He had originally come to the

Grand to watch his father shoot, but at the end of the day, all eyes were upon the youngster as he demolished 24 shootoff clays to emerge victorious over his seniors.

An Ohio minister, the Reverend Garrison Roebuck, who had not shot a single registered target until the Preliminary Handicap at the 1931 Grand and had never taken part in a tournament, wound up winning a shootoff between two more experienced shooters for the 32nd Grand American Handicap crown.

The handicap was indeed the major event at the early Grands, but through the years other events also took on added importance. In 1906 the Clay Target Championship of America was added, and the illustrious names of Guy Dering, Frank Troeh, Mark Arie, Phil Miller, Ned Lilly, Joe Hiestand, Rudy Etchen, Dan Orlich, Gene Sears, and other trapshooting greats have been numbered among the winners.

The Doubles Championship of America became a feature at the Grand in 1912, and in 1918 the Women's Clay Target Championship of America came into being. In subsequent years there were categories for juniors, subjuniors and veterans. At present-day Grands there have been more than 200 individual trophies awarded during the days of competition. But the granddaddy of them all, the Grand American Handicap, still draws the greatest number of entrants.

In 1914, Woolfolk Henderson, the "yellow-haired lad from Kentucky," accomplished the nearly impossible feat of winning three major races at the Grand. He captured the Grand American Handicap with 98 from 22 yards, and he also won the Clay Target Championship of America with 99 out of 100 and the Doubles Championship with 90.

Mark Arie, "the little Dutchman from Illinois," finally garnered Grand American Handicap laurels in 1923 after years of trapshooting success in other races. He was the first Grand Doubles champ in 1912. He was a member of the gold medal U.S. Olympic team in 1920, winning an individual gold medal in Antwerp, Belgium. He almost won the elusive Grand American Handicap title in 1917, with a tie at 98, but he lost the shootoff. In the many Grands he attended, Arie won the High-Over-All championship seven times from 1912 through 1932.

In 1926, one of the most colorful trapshooters of all time snatched the Grand American Handicap crown with 100 straight from the then long-yardage mark of 23 yards. Charles (Sparrow) Young began shooting in 1884 and was one of the crack shots of

the era. Besides being a marksman, he was also a gunsmith and inventor, one of the originators of the release trigger.

Captain Jack Wulf was so confident that he was going to win the 1916 Grand American Handicap, held that year in St. Louis, Missouri, he gave his picture to the sports editor of the *St. Louis Dispatch* the day before so they would have it ready for printing. Dressed in a Palm Beach suit and wearing a Mexican sombrero, Wulf made his way down the line with his beaded-shell bag and smashed 99 out of the 100 targets from 19 yards for the victory.

Walter Beaver was also a well-known shooter who grabbed the GAH title. And he did it with a history-making 98 from the then maximum distance of 25 yards in 1933. However, it was not easy going for Beaver as his competition came from a 17-year-old from Michigan who also posted a 98. In the shootoff, Beaver broke 25 to Ned Lilly's 24.

Roy Foxworthy, who was an outstanding teenage shooter in 1942 and 1943, captured the 1960 Grand American Handicap with 100 straight targets.

Trapshooting, like any other sport, has its legendary greats. Records are made; records are broken. The great Dan Orlich of Reno, Nevada, won his first major victory at the 1956 Grand American. His 199

Captain Jack Wulf, self-confident winner of the 1916 Grand American Handicap, was noted for his colorful attire as well as his trapshooting technique.

in the North American Clay Target Championship tied with Bob Allen and Walter Ostrom, but Orlich prevailed in shootoff by demolishing 150 straight clays. In 1961, he, George Snellenberger, and Ohmer Webb tied with five others in Monday's Men's Champion of Champions race (in which only state singles champions of that year compete). The trio had broken 100 in the main race and another 100 extra when Snellenberger received news of his mother's death. Rather than have George forfeit, the two opponents (the only other ones left at that point), insisted the shootoff continue after his return. The following Friday the three started firing again at the extra birds. Webb dropped out after the first 25 to settle for third place, but Orlich and Snellenberger fired at another 275 and were still tied. They tried again on Saturday, the last day of the Grand, when each broke an additional 100 straight. Finally, Amateur Trapshooting Association officials resolved the deadlock by declaring them to be co-champions— 100 straight in the program and 500-out-of-500 in shootoff, a shootoff record which still stands. Orlich, a former Green Bay Packer, also holds the record for the most 200 straights at the Grand—21. That record may continue to stand, but each year there are competitors like Leo Harrison III, Dan Bonillas and Brad Dysinger, as well as a new generation of young shooters who will be gunning for their places in history.

The name of Annie Oakley is synonymous with the most famous woman shooter in America. She and her husband, famed marksman Frank Butler, made an appearance at the third Grand American in 1902, but she did not compete. There was, however, one woman who took to the line in that competition—Mrs. Parkes—and she started a long procession of women shooters at the Grand.

Mrs. Ad (Plinky) Topperwein was a pioneer woman trapshooter and was one of the best shots in the country. At the 1910 Grand, Mrs. Topperwein finished with a 96. Again the only feminine competitor in 1913, she broke 94 from 20 yards in the Grand American Handicap, just three targets below the winner. It was during her early shooting lessons from her husband that she earned the name Plinky. After several misses firing at a tin can, she met with success and "plinked it." The name stuck, and through the years the Topperweins became a famous professional husband and wife shooting team, giving exhibitions all over the world. Annie Oakley once called her the greatest shooter of all time.

The woman who would dominate shooting in the '30s and '40s was Lela Hall. Between 1935 and 1940, Lela won five out of six Women's Clay Target Cham-

Shootoffs can last until well after dark at the Grand when the "World Series" of trapshooting draws thousands of entries.

Annie Oakley, the most famous woman shooter of all time, attended the 1902 Grand American, but did not compete.

pionships, missing the race because of illness in 1939. She came back to win once more in '45, and after a move to California and marrying Dave Frank, she captured the women's title in 1947, with 100 straight, and again in 1948. In the 1934 Grand American Handicap she finished third in the entire field after a shootoff of 97s.

Lela Hall Frank is an embodiment of the determination of the trapshooter. Her triumph in the 1945 Grand came after a fight with a near-fatal illness. After 31 years as an active shooter, she retired because of losing center vision in her right eye to spend her time painting in the desert of the Southwest. Each year at successive Grands she donated an original oil to the winner of the women's All-Around title. However, in 1978, true grit showed itself again as Lela registered her first targets in 11 years in a preliminary singles race, using a custom-made offset gun stock. (She mounts the gun on her right shoulder, but the stock curves so that her left eye sights down the rib of the gun.)

The Grands of the '50s saw such women stars as Joan Pflueger, who defeated four of the top men shooters to win the 1950 Champion of Champions race. Joan blasted 74 out of 75 in the shootoff to earn the unique victory. In 1956, Iva Pembridge (Jarvis) of Kansas became the first woman to break 200 straight clays at the Grand American, thus winning the women's title in the Class Championships.

In 1946, Frances and Clyde King captured the husband-and-wife championship at the Grand with a score of 190, while Frances ended third among the women in the Champion of Champions event. The next year she captured the victory as woman champ of the Grand American Handicap with a 97. Ten years later she duplicated this victory, and, at her last Grand in 1962, she finally captured the top spot for women in the Champion of Champions after tieing for it six times.

Who can forget the exploits of Punkin Flock who won 30 trophies at the Grand beginning in 1953? Or the shooting skills of Loral I Delaney of Anoka, Minnesota, who began her string of five consecutive High-Over-All victories at the 1966 Grand and who has led the High-Over-All among the women the last two years? Or the long run of Nadine Ljutic,

Frances King (Garlington), on the right, was the woman victor in the Grand American Handicap in 1957. She presented the Frances and Clyde King trophy to Lela Hall Frank for her win in the women's High-Over-All competition.

Out of the past: Some of the best women shooters in North America joined in the Champion of Champions race in 1956.

who went 360 straight in 1972, becoming the only woman to enter 200 in the Clay Target championship? Or Susan Nattrass, Barbara Yochem and Nora Martin? The list can go on and on. They are a part of a great tradition of feminine competitors.

Since 1924, Vandalia, Ohio, has been the home of the Grand American. Until that time the Interstate Association, controlled by the shooting industry, moved the tournament from place to place including Chicago, Dayton, Indianapolis, Kansas City, and New York. However, in 1923, the 24th Grand was the first under amateur management, and after years of talk about the need for a permanent home, the dream became a reality when the 25th handicap took place at the newly-built permanent home just north of Dayton in 1924.

For almost 50 years the residents of Vandalia have looked forward to this peaceful invasion. Each round of firing is welcomed because it represents millions of dollars poured into the city's economy each year. There is a carnival atmosphere as families gather on the grounds and in the surrounding hotels and motels. And the people who call Vandalia home cannot help but be impressed as these thousands of gun-toting visitors continue a heritage of respect for property and respect for themselves and others.

To accommodate this horde of competitors, family members and spectators takes planning and organization. Through the years Amateur Trapshooting Association officials have added to the facilities, and the grounds boast permanent buildings for entering and classifying, scorekeeping, storage of targets and shells, locker room, cafeteria, the original clubhouse (which is now the Hall of Fame Museum), and buildings for purveyors of shooting clothes, glasses, guns and souvenirs.

The Trapshooting Hall of Fame and Museum contains the artifacts, the records and the nostalgia of this competitive sport. At the 1979 Grand American this repository of trapshooting's history will take on a new look. Two floors of memorabilia enable the visitor to return to yesteryear and make the acquaintance of the greats of trapshooting.

Every Grand has its own stories, its own human drama. There is the air of gaiety, yet there is a serious intensity created by the desire to win. It is a postscript to the 4th of July, which, according to John Adams, should be commemorated with "shows, games, sports, guns" and all the pomp derived of freedom. To believe it you have to see it—it's the grand old Grand living on in the future.

How to Detect Counterfeit Guns
by Val Forgett, Jr.

Fake: 1. to prepare or make something specious, deceptve or fraudulent 2. to conceal the defects of or make appear more attractive, interesting, valuable, etc., usually in order to deceive 3. to pretend; simulate 4. designed to deceive or cheat 5. anything made to appear otherwise than it actually is. (According to Random House Dictionary.)

Replica: 1. a copy or reproduction produced by the maker of the original or under his supervision 2. an open, frank reproduction of an original.

Ever since men have collected arms there have been people making fakes. Read some early arms books and you will discover that faking and forging of armor was done as early as 1800. For example, Samuel Pratt of England became famous for his attempts at creating medieval armor; most notable are his helmets, which feature eye slots so misplaced that it is nearly impossible to see through them. The then-antique wheellock pistols also were faked at that time. It is usually quite difficult to tell whether these are contemporaneous antique fakes or modern fakes; many of the antique fakes are as good if not better than the originals. With the advent of the replica firearms, faking has been made simpler for the unscrupulous.

There are basically two types of fakes: The fake which is created by alteration of a replica firearm or the completely manufactured fake produced from scratch, often from another gun of the same period. In recent years, the guns faked in the second fashion have been the Colt Paterson and the Colt Walkers, as well as a few extremely fine flintlock pistols. The 45/70 single-shot pistol made from the Trapdoor 45/70 rifle is a classic example of a fake made from an original firearm.

Another type of faking is the conversion of a relatively inexpensive antique firearm into a valuable firearm by altering its markings. The addition of military inspectors' marks or military usage marks greatly enhances a gun's value.

Another way of increasing value is by faking evidence of state ownership or police usage. These marks are relatively easy to make because they were originally done with crude dies. A classic example would be the addition of "NJ" (for New Jersey) on a Civil War musket or the addition of some famous unit markings such as "Seventh Cavalry" on a 45/70 Springfield or a Colt Frontier. The author knows of many Smith & Wesson and Colt revolvers that were upgraded in value by stamping an "MP" (for Royal Canadian Mounted Police), on the side of the guns.

No one will ever know how many old shotguns were marked by unscrupulous dealers "Wells Fargo & Co." Be careful of any markings on a gun unless you can authenticate them. Even slight alterations of some characteristic of a gun can produce a convincing fake. Many 45/70 rifles were sold as surplus and then reamed out to 20-gauge smoothbore, and cut down to make low-priced shotguns. These were later sold as original military foragers' shotguns. (The seller was unaware, however, that none of the original shotguns had serial numbers.)

Original Colt Walker (top). Bottom gun is an Italian reproduction Walker altered by aging and restamping markings. Note the half-moon-type cut (caused by rotary milling-cutter used to cut loading-lever channel under barrel) where barrel enters barrel boss.

Standard arms are often encountered that have been shortened and lightened, as the seller will tell you, for "cavalry or naval use." Verify that such a model existed. There have been literally hundreds of 45/70 rifles that have been cut down and altered to carbines because carbine sights and saddle bars were available on the surplus market for years. Inspect the forend carefully to make sure a small piece of wood has not been inletted in the ramrod hole.

The addition of a few lines of engraving can raise the value of a fake or antique gun considerably. Refinishing a good original is another method of raising value. In addition to converting and reconverting, fakers often change parts of a gun. Replica firearms are sometimes antiqued by aging to create fake "antiques." Verify the markings to ascertain that they are what an original would have had. (See the photograph of the fake Walker; here markings on top of the barrel go the wrong way.)

Look at every gun for what can be called "honest" wear and perhaps abuse. Be wary of a gun that is evenly pitted all over. (This is often a sign of acid aging. Antique guns never pit evenly all over unless they have been buried — then the damage is usually so complete that the gun has no value as a collector's item.) Next, all the parts should be carefully cleaned so that the collector can detect what may have been changed; look for "dishonest" wear, which could have been done with a small hammer to peen the metal which is then pitted and acid "aged".

To determine whether the antique you are considering is genuine, you should also know as much as you can about the faking of specific models and how to detect such faking. The Colt 1849 can be converted to a Baby

Dragoon by changing the trigger guard from a round to a square one, removing the loading lever, and carefully plugging the holes. Different colors in the brass are the telltale signs on a Colt Navy whose guard has been altered from round to square. Once the brass has aged slightly, slight discoloration of the two different brasses will show where they have been welded or altered. Also, look for slight blow holes in the brass caused by brazing or welding. If there is any pitting where two pieces of brass may have been joined, be careful.

The serial numbers on a gun are a valuable aid in ascertaining authenticity. Changed serial numbers can result in a good fake. Counterfeiters will sometimes take a gun with mixed serial numbers and change the numbers so that they all will match. Look at the serial numbers carefully on a gun to make sure that they all have the same type of stamping and all have the same amount of wear. Check also to see whether the gun falls in the proper serial-number range. Square-back Navys with serial numbers too high to be original have been encountered. Check the other markings to make sure that they match the time of apparent manufacture. Remember, markings on many guns changed over the years and the serial numbers should conform with the markings.

To change mixed serial numbers on parts of an original gun to correspond with the original numbers raises the value of the gun. A careful scrutiny of all serial numbers should be made to make sure that they are all of the same type and age. This is a key overlooked by many fakers of Colts. Checking the markings a particular model should have and then checking the serial numbers found on all parts will provide a good indication of whether a gun is genuine or has been altered.

Another way to increase the value of a gun is by adding an inscription stating that it was presented to some public figure, or even better, to someone not so well known, such as a soldier in the Civil War. Unscrupulous dealers do not hesitate to look up the service records of Civil War soldiers and then engrave the name on the back of a gun. It's difficult to detect this type of faking; always attempt to get a pedi-

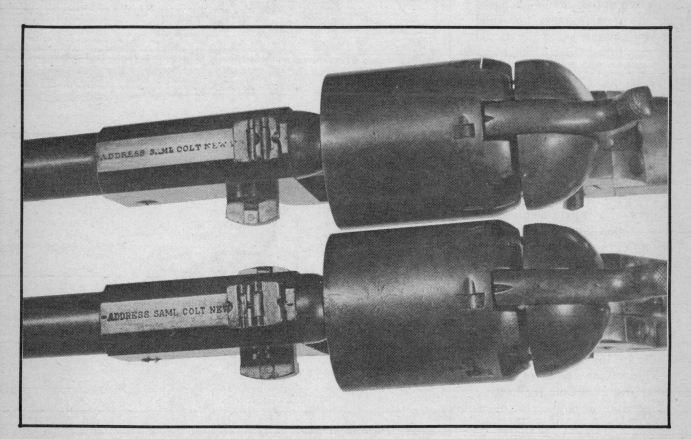

Original Colt Third Model Dragoon pistol cut for shoulder stock with rifle sights (top). Altered Italian reproduction (bottom). Note difference in styles of lettering, rear sights, checkering on hammers and cylinder slots, which are on reproduction.

gree on a gun from the seller. A few lines of engraving cost almost nothing but can sometimes raise the value many hundreds of dollars. Many Smith & Wessons have been engraved by Italian engravers, for example, copying the work of the famous engraver Nimschke. (The author has seen several double-action Frontiers — exact copies of the guns that Nimschke engraved. It would be difficult to tell them from the originals.) Many Henry and Model 66 Winchesters as well as Colt Frontiers and other guns popular with collectors have been subsequently engraved to raise their value. To verify most Colt Frontiers and Bisleys, as well as other cartridge models and many of the Winchesters, collectors can write to the factory. Colt charges $15 to furnish a description of any gun based on the serial number furnished and information about any special features it had (such as engraving and finish) before it left the factory. Smith & Wesson also has many early records, and if you have a fine collector's item, write to Roy Jinks, in care of Smith & Wesson, P.O. Box 2208, Springfield, Massachusetts 01101, for the background of your gun.

There are many other reputable dealers who will authenticate a rare weapon for a fee, giving the history of the gun and their opinion as to its authenticity. To name a few: Larry Wilson, Box 68, Manchester, Connecticut 06040; Herb Glass, Bullville, New York 10915, and Red Jackson of Jackson Arms, 6292 Crest Avenue, Dallas, Texas 75216.

The author knows of a very finely engraved Colt 1849 with a presentation inscription to a member of Lincoln's Cabinet that was refinished and sold as being in original condition by a prominent collector who knew that it had

been refinished. The gun itself was correct, the refinish was not.

An early fake was the conversion of the Aston Model 1842 pistol made by Henry Aston of Middletown, Connecticut, to the Palmetto pistol. Palmetto pistols were originally manufactured by William Glaze & Co., Columbia, South Carolina, a private armory which began production about

1853 and made approximately 1000 pistols. The conversion was done by carefully grinding off the original Aston marks and marking the guns from a new die with S.C. markings. This gun was detected to be a fake by several well-known dealers. You can tell the difference by comparing the markings with those of a genuine Palmetto pistol. One of the branches of the

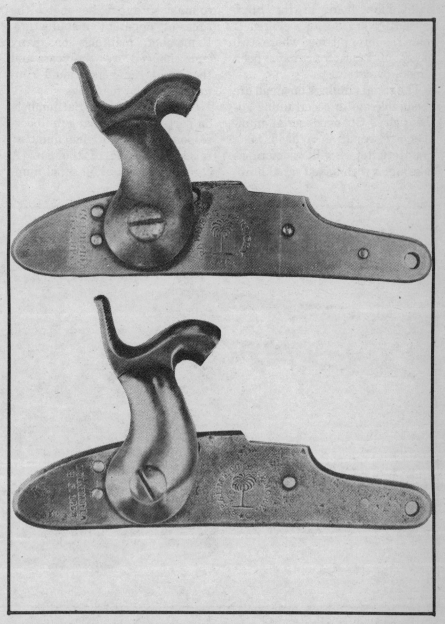

Two versions of the Palmetto pistol. Top gun is a fake — branch does not touch the trunk of the tree. Bottom gun is the original with branch touching the trunk of tree. Note also difference in palm fronds.

fake's palmtree differs slightly from the original. (This is the only mistake the faker made.) By itself, it is hardly detectable yet, laid next to the real thing, is unmistakably a forgery.

Many Colt replicas as well as modern Colts are being aged and sold as originals, especially the valuable ones such as the Dragoon series. The difference between the antique and the modern guns is easily seen in the rifling and barrel-loading lever cut. On all modern-made Colts as well as replicas, the rifling differs from the original. The original has a gain twist while all replicas and present-day Colts have a constant twist. In the originals a reciprocal cutter was used to give the barrel-loading lever opening a square cut. Today a round milling-cutter is used. The small half-moon cut is easily discernible and distinguishes the original from the fake or reproduction. Another giveaway on many replica guns made into originals is the size of the chambers, which vary greatly from the originals. A little knowledge of metallurgy will show you that virtually all the internal parts such as hammers, frame and loading levers of the reproduction guns are investment castings and the brass work is diecast.

One of the most lucrative fields for faking is Confederate arms, which represent a special challenge for collectors. Because the South needed weapons so desper-

Reproduction Third Model Dragoon (top). Original Colt Third Model Dragoon with rifle sights cut for stock (center). Fake Third Model Dragoon (bottom). Note half-moon cut in bottom of barrel boss. Also, note variations in loading port in barrel and also angle of grip.

ately, they used whatever guns were available — everything from European-made models to primitive homemade ones. True Confederate-made guns are scarce and since most were used extensively, the majority are not in good condition. The major Confederate manufacturers include Richmond Armory (Richmond, Virginia), Fayetteville Armory (Fayetteville, North Carolina), and Griswold & Gunnison (Griswoldville, Georgia.)

During the Civil War Centennial, unscrupulous dealers stamped "CSA" on every gun they could get. (This "Confederate States of America" stamping was supposed to indicate Confederate usage.) Others would take the lock from a damaged Confederate gun and insert it into a well-preserved gun or any gun from the period, claiming the gun was of Confederate manufacture completely. This was done with the Palmetto arms lock, which was

often inserted into a Mississippi rifle. The giveaway is the patchbox. If it is drilled and tapped to take a spare nipple inside, it was a Mississippi rifle; a Palmetto rifle never had a spare nipple in the patchbox. Also, many Dixon-Nelsons were put into Mississippies. Unfortunately, what the faker did not realize is the Dixon-Nelson had no patchbox.

Probably the most faked of all arms has been the Confederate Griswold & Gunnison revolver.

Reproduction Griswold & Gunnison (top). Original Griswold & Gunnison (center). Fake Griswold & Gunnison (bottom). Note half-moon cut in barrel for loading lever where barrel meets barrel boss on reproduction and fake versus original. Note angle of grip and cut in barrel-loading port on original versus reproduction and fake.

Samuel Griswold's factory was the pre-eminent Southern revolver manufacturer in terms of both quantity and quality. Although production ceased with the factory's destruction by Union forces in November of 1864, a large number of these revolvers are extant. (Occasionally, early collectors identified Griswold & Gunnison revolvers as Griswold & Grier.) The reproductions can be so close to the originals that it is hard to tell the difference. With a little bit of aging, removal of the marks and restamping some serial numbers, the gun can be turned into a rather good fake. What will give it away is the rifling in the barrel, the metal used in the cylinder, and the wood used in the grips. The original cylinders were made from bar iron that had been heated and twisted for strength. This twisting is evident in the twist lines on the cylinders of all of the original guns. Moreover, the replicas are usually of excellent workmanship whereas the originals were crude and poorly fitted. The angle of the grip will also give away the fake. On the original the grip is bent back slightly; the replica has grips similar to those on the Colt Navy. Check the serial numbers against those of an original gun. Original-style dies are rather hard to come by and many of the casual fakers do not even bother to copy the original type of stamping. Also, markings on the barrels and patent dates, must be carefully scrutinized. The wear should be uniform on the gun. If one section of the gun looks different from another, be careful!

Exercise caution in the purchase of flintlocks that have been converted or reconverted from percussion. An unscrupulous dealer can often double the value of a fine gun in this way. Work-manship can vary from amateurish to that of master craftsmen and be not easily detectable. There are, however, certain signs to look for. The flashpan should be used and corroded and basically should have the same wear as the rest of the gun. Open the lock and look inside; often you can see where a new flashpan has been fixed to the old lock plate. The most telltale sign of any reconversion of a flintlock is around the touchhole area. When the gun is reconverted, the old nipple, drum, etc., must be removed, the hole plugged and new touchhole drilled. On an original flintlock you will always find natural wear and pitting around the touchhole. This is very had to duplicate except possibly on a reconverted gun or one that had very little use.

Also, if you remove the breech-plug and check the inside of the barrel you may see signs of welding—it is difficult to rerifle the bore and finish it off as it should be. With an excellent reconversion that will have been polished brightly, it is sometimes a good idea to rub a little cold blue around the touchhole area. Because the two metals (the original barrel steel and the new weld material) will have different chemical compositions, they will take the blueing differently. This will reveal the telltale edges of welding. The blueing can be buffed off later, but this test can answer a lot of questions.

Sometimes fakers will go to great lengths to produce fine antique fakes. Several years ago six pairs of Dutch pistols were sold. These should have been fashioned by different makers over a period of ninety years. The workmanship on the guns was flawless — they supposedly came from a castle in Europe. Several experts examined them and pronounced them to be fine original guns in mint condition. The buyer still had doubts and eventually had them examined by yet another expert, who carefully disassembled the guns, photographed their parts, and then enlarged the photographs. Comparisons were carefully made and a pattern was picked up on the inletting of the inside of the locks. The chisel that had been used to make several of the small cuts had a minor imperfection on the blade. The chisel cuts supposedly made by different manufacturers over a ninety year span were identical.

Two famous European fakers were Frederic Spitzer, a Parisian art dealer, and a Dresden locksmith named Konrad. Many of their fakes found their way into the collections of wealthy Americans, among them William Randolph Hearst.

To be safe, a collector should buy from a reputable dealer. Be wary of the little old lady who found a Confederate gun in her attic. This ruse has been used many times to trick collectors. Know from whom you are buying. A reputable dealer will always stand behind what he sells. This is not to say that he himself might not have been fooled by a fake, but if the gun is proved to be a fake, he should refund your money and take the gun back. Should you find a gun that you believe to be a fine antique, buy it with a three-day inspection privilege. Any legitimate dealer should permit you to do this. Bring it to an acknowledged expert in the field, especially if it is a gun such as the Colt Walker or an engraved presentation Winchester. Finally, get a letter of authenticity which can ensure that you got what you paid for. Remember that for every faker there is someone who can spot his fakes.

How to Sight-in Your Rifle
by Don Lewis

The prime requisite for a hunting rifle is accuracy. It doesn't make any difference what name a gun carries, its caliber, or even what it costs; if it isn't accurate, it will never perform satisfactorily in the field. It might be said that a good rifle is an accurate one.

In another sense of the word, no matter how great a rifle's accuracy potential, it will never serve the hunter's purpose unless it is sighted-in properly. The hunter must know where his rifle is placing its bullets at various ranges, or success will be more a product of luck than good shooting.

It is a fact that literally hundreds of rifles carried afield have not been sighted-in. In many cases, the hunter is not even remotely aware of the distance for which his rifle is zeroed, if it is zeroed-in at all. This may be a sad commentary, but it happens to be true. For some strange reason, checking a rifle's zero point doesn't rank high on the hunter's priority list.

There are several misconceptions about a rifle's sighting arrangement. First, the belief that iron or open sights cannot get out of adjustment is false. This type of sight set-up gives the impression of being immovable, but all sights are susceptible to accidents from a variety of sources. The rifle scope is causing a reduction in the number of open sights in use, but new scope converts are often leery of the scope's ability to stay on zero. Many feel the slightest jar or bump will knock a scope out of commission—but that is also a falsehood.

Another myth that has been around for decades claims that the factory precisely zeroes-in every rifle prior to shipment. It is true that the factory checks every rifle for safety by live firing, but the sighting arrangement is aligned on a target only at close range. The hunter is still responsible for checking out his rifle on a 100-yard range.

Because most hunters are unfamiliar with the idiosyncrasies of the various sight set-ups, adjusting scopes and open sights can be confusing. Unnecessary ammunition is wasted, and the shooter can reach a point of frustration while trying to get the rifle sighted-in. Seeking professional help is a step in the right direction. However, the person using the rifle should always be the last to check its performance from a rest. Hunters who know what they can do with a rifle from a benchrest will have more assurance in the woods. Good results on the range will produce good results in the field.

Accuracy is not a product of sheer luck or good fortune. Accuracy is made. It's the end result of many things including good ammo, a well-tuned rifle, and the shooter's ability to get the very best from his rifle. Most rifles have a higher accuracy potential than the hunter can achieve in the field under normal hunting conditions. Therefore, it is vital that a hunter completely understands his rifle's sighting arrangement, and it's just as imperative that he knows where the rifle is placing its shots at 100 yards. Even some understanding of the flight of the bullet will also be beneficial when sighting-in the hunting rifle.

In simple terms, sighting-in a hunting rifle requires certain procedures. Firing several shots from a makeshift rest at a large boulder across a valley

This Pennsylvania antlerless deer is proof that author's wife Helen had her LSA 65 Ithaca 25-06 properly sighted-in.

is not what is meant by "certain procedures." There are definite guidelines to follow in advance, during the actual firing, and after the rifle is zeroed. The paramount objective is to have the rifle placing its shots dead center at a predetermined distance. In other words, the ram hunter may want his outfit zeroed for 500 yards, while the hunter of black bear may settle for a dead-on-zero at 200 yards.

Strange as it may seem, both the long distance varmint shooter and the 22 rimfire squirrel-hunting buff need to know not only the accuracy potential of their outfits, but where their rifles place the first shot from a cold barrel. Impact points can change as a barrel warms, hence the importance of determining the first shot where the targets are extremely small or at long ranges.

Any rifle should be thoroughly checked prior to the actual sighting-in. Loose screws head the list of reasons why most sighting arrangements get out of alignment. Usually, it's the screws directly related to the open sight or scope that cause a problem, but stock screws also have a definite bearing on how a rifle shoots. Checking the screw that goes through the forearm into the recoil lug on the rifle's action is extremely important. All the recoil is absorbed at this point, and if the recoil lug screw is loose, the stock will eventually be damaged and the rifle can lose its accuracy potential. Rifles with metal bands around their forearms can suffer impact changes as a result of the band screw being loose.

A rifle scope is more susceptible to loose screws than regular open sights. The scope has more

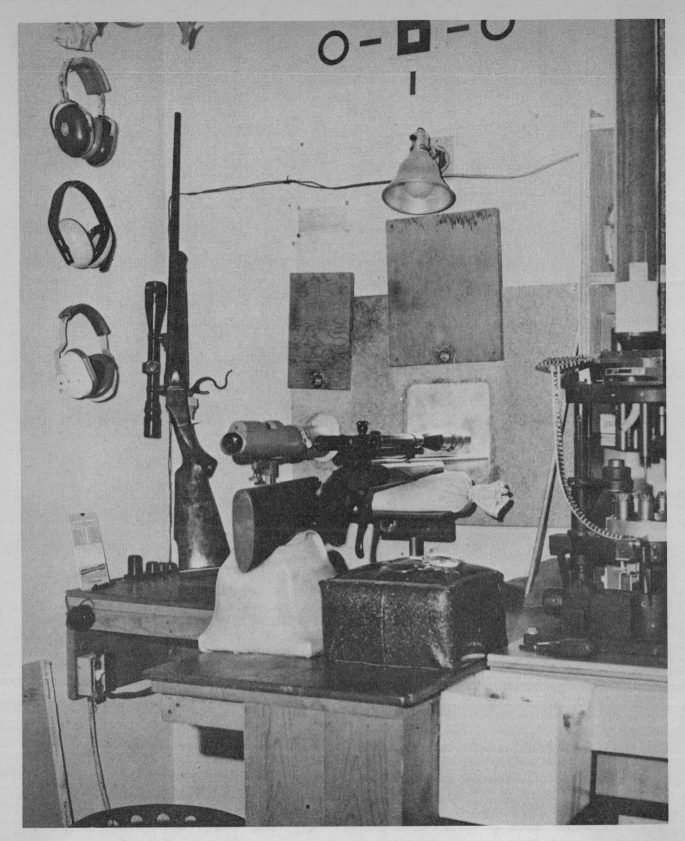

Author's benchrest inside his testing shop has a fully adjustable seat and front rest. A switch on the rest electrically controls targets 100 yards away.

bulk and weight, so inevitably it is subjected to more abuse. Every screw in the scope set-up is important and should be checked. This includes not only the ring screws but the base screws as well. After the reticle is squared and the eye relief has been set for the person using the scope, the ring screws should be pulled down evenly. They must be very tight to prevent the scope from moving forward in the rings when the rifle is fired.

It's questionable whether tightening agents such as shellac or nail polish are needed to aid in holding base screws. It is advisable to seat each base screw after the initial tightening. This is done by tapping the screwdriver handle sharply with a hammer after the screw has been tightened. The sharp blow loosens the screw's grip somewhat, and it can be reseated by as much as a quarter turn.

Once the rifle has been checked to assure that everything is tight and functioning properly, the actual firing process can begin. The equipment needed is neither expensive nor complex. If regular range facilities aren't available, a simple folding ironing board and several sacks of sand or sawdust will serve the purpose. If the shooting isn't being done on a range, a place with a safe backstop is imperative. About the only tool needed for the scoped rifle is a small screwdriver for turning the adjustment wheels, if they are slotted. For open sights, a hammer and small brass rod will be needed to tap the rear sight for windage adjustment. A brass rod or punch is better than steel since it won't mar or scratch the barrel.

At this point many shooters use a collimator commonly called a bore-sighting device. It's an excellent tool for any shooter, but it's also often misunderstood and improperly used. The collimator is merely a guide or an aid for the initial alignment of the sights or scope. When the scope's reticle is superimposed on the collimator's reticle, the bullet theoretically should be on center. At 100 yards, the bullet would strike on center but would be low. To raise the point of impact, the scope's horizontal crosswire must be below the horizontal crosswire in the collimator.

There are so many technical factors involved that it's best to use the collimator only as a starter. Contrary to a growing belief, it is next to impossible to zero a rifle without firing it. Many hunters are misled into thinking their scopes were "machine" zeroed. Many retail outlets use the collimator as a sight-in device. In some cases, the hunter is told his scope has been machine zeroed for an exact yardage. This is impossible with any type of bore-sight-

A screwdriver will make most scope adjustments. Best results will be obtained by metering a few clicks at a time and then firing.

ing device. Nothing beats using a solidrest and a set of sandbags for sighting-in a rifle.

Instead of placing a target at a great distance from the muzzle, fire the first few shots at a large square of paper with a two-inch bullseye at 25 yards. It will only take a few rounds to get the shots in the black. The rifle should be shot dead-on at this distance before moving the target out to 100 yards.

It is much easier to shoot a tight group at 25 yards than at 100. When the distance gets longer, the shooter must be acutely aware of his hold and trigger squeeze. Take a deep breath, release some of it, and while the reticle or sights freeze on the bullseye, squeeze the trigger in one smooth motion. Repeat this several more times without touching the sights. It should then be apparent where the rifle is placing its shots. For instance, if the three-shot group formed low and to the left, the impact point will have to be raised and moved to the right. This can be done all at once, but it is wiser to go in one direction at a time.

With open sights, there's more trial and error in-

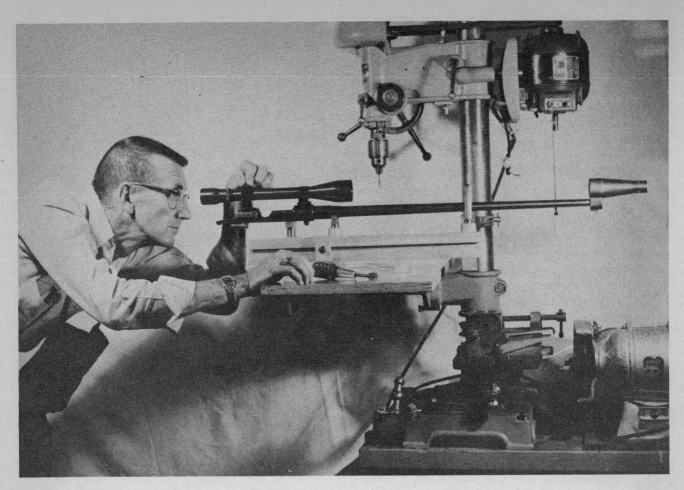

Gunsmith Blair Hooks aligns scope after drilling and tapping on a collimator. A bore-sighting device is a must for gunsmiths.

volved than precise metering or adjusting. The rifle scope's metering adjustments are marked with an arrow showing which way to turn to move the impact point up or down or left or right. Also, the scope's instruction sheet will indicate how far the point of impact will change at 100 yards with each click. If the bullet moves a half inch with each click and the group is three inches to the left, it should take six clicks to the right to bring the bullet on center.

Most scope adjustments are accurate, but adjusting the scope several clicks at a time and firing several rounds after each adjustment will show whether the scope adjustments are precise. Shooting one or even two boxes of ammo during a sight-in session is not wasteful. The shooter will be getting familar with his outfit, and he will be learning how to adjust his scope. His only concern during the shooting should be not to overheat the rifle. Fire several three-shot groups, and then allow the rifle to cool.

With open sights, the rear sight should always be moved in the direction of the bullet's path. If the group is high, the rear sight must be lowered. If the group is to the right, the rear sight must be moved to the left. The front sight is moved in the opposite direction. In those cases where the rear sight is down as far as it will go and the rifle is still shooting high, a higher front sight will have to be installed.

All rifles should be zeroed on a vertical line through the center of the target. The height of the impact point is a matter for the shooter to decide. For close-range shooting in dense cover, dead-on at 100 yards is adequate. For longer ranges, the point of impact at 100 yards will have to be above the horizontal center line of the bullseye. To know exactly how high to zero at 100 yards for a particular distance requires that the shooter understand to some extent the flight or arc of the bullet.

It is not true that a bullet sails to 100 yards and then begins its downward curve. The 100-yard point is often mistaken for what is termed "midrange" trajectory. Also, there is a misunderstanding about

Serious target shooters can reap greater benefits from a precision rest such as the Cravener Micro Benchrest, manufactured in Ford City, Pennsylvania. This rest is fully adjustable for elevation and windage, and is one-piece, incorporating both front and rear V-Forks.

Author zeroes-in a Ruger M-77. Note ear protectors, a good investment for shooters.

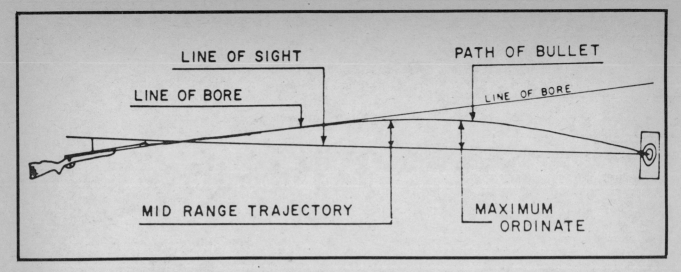

LINE OF SIGHT

PATH OF BULLET

LINE OF BORE

LINE OF BORE

MID RANGE TRAJECTORY

MAXIMUM ORDINATE

Trajectory chart shows it's impossible for bullet to rise above bore. Note highest point of flight is well beyond the midrange point.

the relationship between the line of sight and the line of bore. For years a myth existed that high-speed bullets would rise above the line of bore. This violates the laws of physics; this old myth stems from confusion of the line of sight with the line of bore.

The bullet's flight even today is not too well understood, and it is not difficult to understand why. A bullet is seldom seen, and it is impossible for the naked eye to trace its flight—consequently, there's plenty of room for conjecture and myths. All that can be relied upon is that the fact of gravity is a constant, never-changing force that subjects the speeding bullet to the same downward pull as a falling apple. Nothing heavier than air can rise of its own accord, and this goes for the unseen bullet no matter how fast it is moving.

A bullet fired parallel to the ground begins to fall the instant it is free from the confines of the bore. Its speed has nothing to do with whether it will fall a little or a lot, but the quicker it gets to the target, the less time is spend in the grasp of gravity. A good comparision is between the 150-grain, 30-30 slug traveling at a slow 2150 feet-per-second, and a bullet of the same weight fired from a 30-06 at 3000 feet-per-second. The velocity difference is 850 fps; on a close 50-yard shot, this would not be significant, but at 300 yards, the faster bullet would have a much lower trajectory arc.

The line of sight is always a straight line from the eye through the sights to the target. The line of bore is also a straight line from the rifle's chamber through the bore to infinity. Here it can be

seen that both lines are straight, but it's common to confuse the bullet's path, which is always a curved line, with the line of bore.

However, the path of the bullet is a down-curving line from the rifle's muzzle; it falls faster as the bullet moves forward. If the sights were aligned with the bore line, it would be impossible for them to ever intersect the path of the bullet, which is falling below the line of bore all the time. If this were the case, the hunter would have to hold high and hope his estimate was correct.

Fortunately, this problem can be overcome by adjusting the sights in such a way that the line of sight intersects the bore line instead of being parallel to it. What actually happens when the sights are adjusted for more elevation is that the rifle's muzzle is tipped upward when the sights are aligned on the target. This causes the bullet to pass through the line of sight a few yards in front of the muzzle, travel in a curved line above the line of sight, and then fall through the line of sight at whatever distance the rifle is sighted-in for. *Note that the bullet never once rises above the bore line.* Technically, the rifle is sighted-in for two places, one a few yards from the muzzle, and another where the bullet comes through the line of sight the second time.

The actual flight of the bullet is not a true arc of a circle; rather, it can be characterized as an elongated arc. The reason it is not a true curve is that the highest point of the bullet's flight occurs about two thirds of the distance to the sight in point. Technically, the highest point of the bullet's flight is called the "maximum ordinate." For example, a

L. James Bashline, left, host of TV's *Outdoorsman*, and Bob Bell, center, editor of *Pennsylvania Game News*, watch custom gunsmith Al Wardrop zero a bench rifle. Note the folding benchrest and variety of rifles being zeroed.

130-grain, 270 Winchester bullet leaving the muzzle at 3140 feet-per-second and zeroed for 250 yards will be ¾ inches high at 50 yards, 2½ inches high at 100 yards, 3 inches high at 165 yards (⅔rds of 250), down to 2 inches high at 200, and on zero at the 250 mark. The bullet was not at its highest point at the midrange distance of 125 yards.

Many shooters don't understand what the midrange trajectory figures given in published tables really mean. A 150-grain bullet fired from a 30-06 at 2970 feet-per-second at the muzzle will serve as an example. Midrange trajectory figures read 0.6 inch at 100 yards, 2.4 inches at 200 yards, and 6.1 inches at 300 yards, giving the impression that the total drop of the bullet is a mere 6.1 inches at 300 yards. The actual drop of this particular load would be 2.1 inches at 100 yards, 8.9 inches at 200 yards, and 22 inches at 300 yards.

To put it in simple terms, the tables show that if the rifle is zeroed dead-on at 300 yards, the bullet will not be more than 6.1 inches high at intermediate distances, and that the highest point of the flight or the maximum ordinate is 6.1 inches.

A folding ironing board can be used as shooting bench.

Table 1 shows representative drop figures for a variety of calibers and bullet weights. Exact drop values depend on the ballistic coefficient of each bullet. Since this will vary slightly with bullet manufacturers because of changes in bullet profile, the table uses average values whenever possible. With normal variations from rifle to rifle (despite the uniformity of ammunition), no table is likely to exactly agree with individual results. However, the values shown in Table 1 will serve as a reliable guide.

Table 2 gives the point-of-aim height in inches at 100 yards at which the center of the group must be above in order for a rifle to be sighted-in at the ranges indicated. It also represents the sight correction needed in minutes of angle (MOA) to rezero from 100 yards. If a 30-06 is sighted-in at 100 yards with the 150-grain spitzer hitting 2970 fps at the muzzle, the sights will have to be elevated 4½ MOA to be rezeroed at 300 yards. This will put the group 4½ inches high at 100 yards.

Table 2 can serve only to give general guidelines since there are many variables that can cause individual results to vary. Each rifle's zero should be confirmed and corrected by range firing. The values in Table 2 should be fairly accurate though, and are much better guides than raising the sights by an unknown amount and watching for a puff of dust in the distance.

Today's big-game rifle is more accurate than those built prior to World War II. Still, it has its limitations. The minute-of-angle syndrome (roughly one inch at 100 yards) is very much in vogue today. Many good rifles are discarded because they do not produce the MOA result. Although this level of accuracy is desirable, that type of action is ridiculous. The big-game rifle doesn't need the accuracy potential of a varmint or competitive outfit. Any rifle that will put its first three shots in two inches at 100 yards is more than adequate.

The paramount reason for sighting-in a rifle is to make a clean, one-shot kill when the moment of truth arrives. This makes sighting-in a big-game rifle that much more important and necessary. It was a wise hunter who claimed if he had but four shells, he would use three of them to sight-in his rifle.

TABLE 1

Inches of Drop from Muzzle

Cartridge	WT.	Bullet B.C.	M.V.	100 yards	200 yards	300 yards	400 yards	500 yards
222 Rem	50	.202	3200	1.9"	8.5"	22"	46"	83"
22-250	55	.229	3810	1.3	5.8	14.4	29	52
243 Win	80	.278	3450	1.5	6.8	17.0	33	57
243 Win	100	.376	2960	2.1	8.9	21	42	69
250-3000	87	.313	3030	2.0	8.7	21	42	67
250-3000	100	.357	2820	2.3	10.0	24	46	79
25-06 Rem	87	.313	3500	1.5	6.5	15.9	31	53
25-06 Rem	120	.414	3120	1.9	8.0	18.9	36	60
264 Win Mag	140	.441	3200	1.7	7.5	17.6	33	55
270 Win	100	.261	3480	1.5	6.7	17.3	32	56
270 Win	130	.392	3110	1.9	8.4	19.3	36	61
270 Win	150	.438	2900	2.1	9.1	22	41	68
7mm R-Mag	125	.323	3430	1.5	6.8	16.2	32	55
7mm R-Mag	150	.357	3110	1.9	8.2	19.7	38	63
7mm R-Mag	175	.447	3070	1.9	8.1	19.3	37	60
30-30 Win	150	.210	2410	3.3	14.8	36	77	130
30-30 Win	170	.204	2220	3.9	16.9	41	82	142
30-40 Krag	200	.431	2200	3.7	16.2	38	74	124
308 Win	150	.359	2860	2.2	9.6	23	44	75
308 Win	180	.482	2610	2.7	11.3	27	51	85
30-06	150	.359	2970	2.1	8.9	22	41	69
30-06	180	.482	2700	2.5	10.5	25	47	80
30-06	220	.290	2400	3.2	14.3	35	70	123
300 W-Mag	150	.359	3400	1.5	6.7	16	31	51
300 W-Mag	180	.482	3070	1.9	8.0	19.1	37	61
8mm R-Mag	185	.303	3080	1.9	8.5	21	41	70
8mm R-Mag	220	.325	2830	2.3	10.0	25	48	80
338 W-Mag	200	.384	3000	2.0	8.6	21	40	67
338 W-Mag	250	.280	2700	2.5	11.3	28	56	97
375 W-Mag	270	.264	2740	2.5	11.1	28	56	98
375 W-Mag	300	.263	2550	2.9	12.7	32	63	111

Note: All drop figures above 20 inches rounded to nearest inch.
Ballistic coefficients of bullets vary due to changes in bullet profile. Above table indicates BC averages or calculated figures.

TABLE 2

Sight Adjustments in Minutes of Angle — 100 Yard Zero

Cartridge	Bullet Wt.	Velocity	200 yards	300 yards	400 yards	500 yards
222 Rem	50	3200	1.6"	4.3"	7.9"	12.5"
22-250 Rem	55	3810	0.8	2.5	4.7	7.4
243 Win	80	3450	1.2	3.3	6.0	9.3
243 Win	100	2960	1.8	4.4	7.6	11.2
250-3000	87	3030	1.7	4.3	7.5	11.5
250-3000	100	2820	2.0	4.9	8.5	12.7
25-06 Rem	87	3500	1.0	2.8	5.1	7.8
25-06 Rem	120	3120	1.4	3.6	6.2	9.3
264 Win Mag	140	3200	1.2	3.2	5.6	8.3
270 Win	100	3480	1.2	3.3	6.1	9.5
270 Win	130	3110	1.5	3.7	6.4	9.5
270 Win	150	2900	1.7	4.2	7.3	10.6
7mm Rem Mag	125	3430	1.1	3.1	5.5	8.4
7mm Rem Mag	150	3110	1.5	3.8	6.6	10.0
7mm Rem Mag	175	3070	1.6	3.9	6.6	9.8
30-30 Win	150	2410	3.5	8.4	14.8	22.8
30-30 Win	170	2220	4.6	9.4	16.1	24.2
30-40 Krag	200	2200	3.7	8.3	13.9	20.2
308 Win	150	2860	2.0	4.9	8.4	12.6
308 Win	180	2610	2.3	5.5	9.2	13.3
30-06	150	2970	1.8	4.5	7.8	11.6
30-06	180	2700	2.1	5.0	8.4	12.2
30-06	220	2400	3.3	7.7	13.4	20.3
300 Win Mag	150	3400	1.1	2.9	5.2	7.9
300 Win Mag	180	3070	1.5	3.8	6.5	9.5
8mm Rem Mag	185	3080	1.8	4.4	7.8	11.9
8mm Rem Mag	220	2830	2.1	5.2	9.0	13.7
338 Win Mag	200	3000	1.6	4.1	7.1	10.5
338 Win Mag	350	2700	2.4	5.9	10.4	15.8
375 Win Mag	270	2740	2.0	4.9	8.3	12.1
375 Win Mag	300	2550	3.0	7.4	12.9	19.8

Note: Sight adjustment figures based on scope mounted 1½-inches over bore. A slight variation in scope height will not make a significant difference.

Selecting a Shotgun
by Howard Brant

Choosing your first shotgun can be a difficult but rather pleasant task. You can spend countless hours perusing the gun racks at your favorite sporting goods emporium and pleasurable hours mulling over the latest SHOOTER'S BIBLE, but when it comes to making that final decision you must always consider your primary shooting interests.

Are you basically an upland bird hunter who prefers to stalk the hillside thickets for ruffed grouse or the hedgerow coverts for ringneck pheasant?

Perhaps your interest tends to waterfowl hunting or busting claybirds on the trap or skeet field?

Or do you hunt in a state that mandates only the use of scatterguns for deer hunting?

Such questions must be carefully answered when purchasing your first scattergun. Cost is another important factor. The average weekend hunter doesn't need a delicately engraved smoothbore which can cost upwards of several thousands of dollars, nor does he require buttstocks and forearms of selected fancy wood. Although such features surely enhance any firearm and equally swell the pride of its owner, such arms really have no place afield. However, they do have a niche in the competitive shooting world, not because they shoot better, but because they enhance the aura of the competition firearm. Additionally, raised matted or ventilated ribs, also far from essential for field work, are important to the competitive trap or skeet gunner.

So let's say you have given serious thought to your future shooting activities and have ultimately decided that upland hunting will be your bag. You have a pair of good pointing dogs in your backyard kennel and after feeding and caring for them throughout the year, you plan to spend as much time as possible during the relatively short upland bird seasons pursuing game such as pheasant, grouse, quail, chukar, and Hungarian partridge or little migratory targets like dove and woodcock.

Upland bird hunting is also a hiking sport. You'll spend many an hour trudging the swales, hedgerows and uplands seeking game birds. Let's be honest: Most upland sport is highly competitive —covers are hard-pressed and birds are at a premium. For these reasons the upland bird gun should be lightweight; you will be carrying the scattergun far more than you will be shooting it. In addition, a rather large-bore gun is preferable because it affords every advantage when that occasional game bird does flush.

There's no question that a great number of upland gunners today utilize the 20 gauge, and, with "beefed-up" magnum loadings, the little 20 is closely comparable to the 12. Nevertheless, the author still personally turns to the 12 gauge as his favorite selection for all field work. It's universal. Shells can be obtained most everywhere, even in remote back-country areas, and, above all, 12-gauge hulls are manufactured in a diversity of loadings which can be tailored to meet the exacting demands of both hunters and shooting conditions.

Most upland bird shooting is relatively short range and most upland birds present rising targets. The average ruffed grouse or woodcock in dense New England coverts, for example, is usually

The all-around shotgun for that occasional quail or grouse, as well as for ringnecks and wildfowl, is the 12-gauge autoloader sporting a barrel not more than 28 inches in length with variable choking device attached.

bagged at distances not greater than 15-20 yards, while ringneck pheasants are generally tumbled at not more than 30 yards. Even in the West, with the wide-ranging chukar or Hungarian partridge, most are tagged at under 30 yards.

For such relatively close-range work the upland gun should boast rather short barrels. Ideally, lightweight short-barreled upland smoothbores should also feature twin tubes because of the advantage of choke selection. The best choice for an upland gun, therefore, would be either a side-by-side double gun or an over-and-under for one prime reason: The scattergun in question should feature an open-bored tube for extreme close-range shooting plus a more tightly choked tube for the occasional 30-yard-plus shot. The most effective boring for upland guns should have either a cylinder or improved cylinder bored tube plus a modified or improved modified tube for the longer-range requirement.

The optimum upland bird gun? If one selection had to be made, the author would unquestionably turn to the traditional side-by-side double or the over-and-under with a barrel length of 26 inches and bored improved cylinder and modified chokes. The author continues to display a fondness for the 12 gauge because of its universal attributes, but such a selection would be equally fitting for a 20- or 28-gauge upland gun as well,

A lightweight side-by-side double or over-and-under is the optimum smoothbore for the uplands.

especially if you consider overall weight a factor. Such upland scattergun possibilities would include over-and-under models like the Beretta S55B and S56E, Browning Superposed and Citori, Galef Silver Snipe, Ruger over-and-under, Savage 330 and 333, SKB 500 and 600, and Winchester 101. Side-by-side double models include Beretta 424 and M426E, Browning B-SS, Fox BSE and Model B, and Winchester Model 23.

The selection of a waterfowl scattergun is quite another matter. Although decoying fowl offer targets at less than 30 yards' distance, pass shooting at high-flying waterfowl is often accomplished at maximum yardage. As a consequence, the waterfowler looks for a shotgun capable of tumbling wildlife at greater ranges.

Today a large segment of the duck- and goose-hunting fraternity has turned to the magnum, especially the three-inch chambered magnum 12, because of its pattern attributes at extreme yardage.

The waterfowl gun should also be fairly heavy in overall weight to help dampen the excessive recoil produced by the magnum loadings. The waterfowl shotgun should also be capable of firing three shells, not only to conform to federal regulations, but to increase the chances of bringing birds home. Ducks and geese present difficult targets, particularly heavy-feathered geese, and are hard to bring down, making it necessary for the waterfowler to select either an autoloading or pump-action shotgun in order to take advantage of the extra hulls.

The waterfowl smoothbore should feature a long barrel, not less than 28 inches in length. If you are pass shooting exclusively, the 30-inch tube is even more advantageous because long barrels offer the shooter a better sighting plane. The scattergun should be further bored not less than modified choke, with full choke favored.

While the pump and autoloading shotgun are preferred for waterfowl hunting, the individual hunter should examine the attributes of each before making a purchase. A pump-action shotgun can be difficult for some hunters to master, especially when trying to shuck out a shell in a cramped duck blind or goose pit. Consequently, the average waterfowl hunter should choose the autoloading shotgun for his waterfowl activities simply because of its convenience and ease of loading.

Thus the preferred shotgun for waterfowl would be either a pump or autoloader in conventional 12 gauge or three-inch magnum 12 and sporting a 28- or 30-inch barrel, bored either modified or full choke. In pump action you could select from Ithaca Model 37, Marlin 120, Mossberg 500 ALDR, Remington 870, Smith & Wesson 916, and Winchester 1300 XTR and 1200. In autoloaders, they would include Browning 2000, Franchi 520 and 500, Ithaca 51, Remington 1100, Smith & Wesson 1000, and Winchester 1400, Super X Model 1, and 1500 XTR.

Even more consideration should be given to the selection of a trap or skeet gun because such clay-bird games are competitive and optimum gun performance is a must.

Although skeet and trap are target shooting sports, both are different and require different smoothbores. Skeet shooting is performed on a semi-circular layout and such targets are usually falling. Thus, the skeet gun must be constructed to produce the best performance at comparatively short range with falling targets.

The game of skeet had its inception back in the early 1920s when a group of New England bird-hunting enthusiasts developed the sport to enhance their wing-shooting ability. The course was laid out to simulate the flight of their favorite game bird, the ruffed grouse. At that time, most such bird hunters employed side-by-side double guns, and in the beginning, the side-by-side double was widely employed. Today, one will rarely see a double gun on the skeet field since the game has become highly competitive, and the gun-pointing specialists who shoot skeet regularly have become far more demanding in the selection of tournament guns.

The most popular skeet gun in use today is unquestionably the autoloader, followed by the over-and-under and the pump. All skeet-grade guns now manufactured today incorporate the necessary attributes for the consistent breaking of clay targets. Skeet guns have considerably more drop in the stock compared to trap guns, to compensate for shooting at falling targets.

Such guns should also boast ventilated ribs, must be open bored, and have a barrel length of not more than 28 inches. During my early days on the competitive skeet circuit, I selected a pump gun, but today my preference tends to the over-and-under. However, the beginner and even the recoil-shy veteran would be wise to select a skeet grade gas-operated autoloader if he hopes to pursue the sport.

Competitive skeet shooting also necessitates the use of .410 bore as well as 12-, 20- and 28-gauge guns; for this reason, most avid skeet enthusiasts select guns of different gauges with identical stocking and balance. Many over-and-under skeet guns are available

The most popular smoothbore for waterfowl hunting is the pump or autoloader in standard 12 gauge or three-inch magnum 12, featuring a 28- or 30-inch barrel bored with either modified or full choke.

The gas-operated autoloader with its associated reduced recoil has brought women and the younger set into the shooting sports.

with added sets of barrels, while some autoloader models are usually stocked similarly for all four gauges. The popular Remington Model 1100 tournament-grade skeet gun in all four gauges, for example, is identically stocked and even provides higher vent ribs in its 20 gauge and .410 bore models to duplicate the exact pointing advantages of the 12-gauge model.

Trap shooting is one of the oldest shooting games and is keenly contested, often for large amounts of prize money. Understandably, trap guns can cost a tidy sum. The clay target presented on the trap layout is a rising one and generally shot at maximum range, so the universal gauge for the trap gun is 12. Trap guns are stocked with a much straighter stock as compared to the skeet gun. They have

longer barrels — 30 and even 32 inches — for better pointing and also feature a ventilated rib of sorts.

A trap model scattergun should weigh approximately 7½ to 8 pounds to aid in absorbing recoil because trap gunners usually shoot at many targets in the course of a tournament. Modern trap guns are manufactured in four basic versions: single barrel, over-

The rifled slug-loaded smoothbore is a highly efficient deer weapon, but a telescopic sight should be attached for optimum results.

and-under, pump and autoloader. The single-barrel trap model is the oldest, but the autoloader and over-and-under are the most popular today among trap shooters. The over-and-under has its proponents simply because many doubles shooters like the idea of the two barrels offering two different choke borings. Ideally, trap model over-and-unders are bored improved modified and full choke.

While the pump gun has un-doubtedly produced more championships and prize money for its owners than all other trap guns combined, the touted "corn shucker," as it is sometimes called, is taking a back seat to the autoloader because modern gas-operated autoloaders produce less recoil than other actions. It is a fine trap gun for the younger set and for women shooters, and its autoloading capabilities makes it a logical selection for doubles events as well.

The ideal trap gun? For the beginner and even the recoil-shy veteran, the gas-operated autoloader is a wise selection. Trap model autoloaders have conventional trap stock dimensions and ventilated ribs. They are also usually bored either improved modified or full choke and have 30-inch barrels. Again, the Remington 1100 trap gun would be a wise choice, as well as the Franchi 530, Winchester Super X Model 1, and Browning 2000.

Big-game hunting for animals the size of deer is generally associated with the high-powered rifle. But in states such as Delaware, Maryland, New Jersey, and Massachusetts, deer hunters are required to use only shotguns and some states have stipulations regarding loads.

When we mention loading stipulations we mean that some areas permit only buckshot loads and others the rifled slug. For many years New Jersey hunters were required to use only buckshot loadings for deer hunting; recently the use of the rifled slug was also legalized. Paradoxically, elsewhere buckshot is outlawed and the rifled slug is considered the only legal big-game load.

Several arms manufacturers currently offer scatterguns designed purely to handle the rifled slug: Franchi with Slug Barrel, Ithaca Model 37 or 51, Marlin 120 Slug Gun, Mossberg 500 ALS, SKB 900 Slug Gun, and Remington 870R and 1100 Deer Gun. Such arms generally boast relatively short barrel lengths — not more than 24 inches — and further feature open or cylinder-bored tubes. Most basic rifled-slug arms are available in either pump or autoloader actions. Some even offer slings for convenience in carrying.

Above all, when considering the purchase of a rifled-slug gun, consider sights. Most slug guns are available with buckhorn-type rear sights and blade or bead front sights. However, the rifled-slug arm can be efficient even at 100 yards provided the arm is fitted with a telescopic sight—e.g., scopes of about 1½ to 2 power — or a receiver-type sight. Many states which mandate the use of shotguns for big-game hunting also

permit the use of 16- and 20-gauge guns, as well as the conventional 12 and with good results. But arms primarily used for deer hunting should be limited to 12 gauge, preferably in the magnum versions as well. Properly scoped, a rifled-slug arm produces relatively good accuracy at 50 yards; generally three- to four-inch groups can be expected, and respectable groups can also be obtained at the 100-yard butt as well. The slug is a powerhouse at short range and a 12-gauge scope-fitted slug gun can cause mayhem in deer country.

On the other hand, in areas where scatterguns loaded only with buckshot are mandated, the deer hunter should turn again to either the pump-action or autoloading smoothbore with a 28-inch barrel bored either modified or full choke. Some years ago, prior to the development of plastic wads and shot cup protectors, the heavy buck pellets were actually crushed when pushed through the choking cone of a modified or full choke scattergun barrel. For this reason, hunters of yesteryear turned to open-bored scatterguns in an attempt to eliminate deformation of the large pellets.

However, it's another story today, with modern buckshot loadings complete with poly-fill and plastic shot protectors. The heavy pellets are protected from deformation and move through the choking cone with relative ease. Hence, today's buckshot loadings require a modified or full choke tube to produce optimum performance. Don't scoff at buckshot either. At close range — for example, under 45 yards — it can be a totally efficient load for tumbling big-game animals the size of whitetailed deer.

Last but not least, we have the versatile autoloader shotgun.

When considering the purchase of only one gun, the autoloader is the logical choice. I'm sure such a statement will invoke the wrath of the over-and-under advocate and the dedicated pump-gun enthusiast and will further cause the staunch uplander with his favored side-by-side double to snarl in anger. Nevertheless, when every aspect is considered, the gas-operated autoloading shotgun is most suited to the average gunner and his basic all-around shooting requirements.

The field-grade gas-operated autoloader may not stand up to the competition performance of the masterfully constructed trap or skeet gun, but most field-grade autoloaders will produce surprisingly fine scores when it comes to claybird busting. Additionally, it can be employed with equal success under demanding field conditions. However, autoloading shotguns ideally should be fitted with some sort of variable choke device.

Your selection depends on your pocketbook, but such autoloaders would include Browning 2000, Franchi 520, Ithaca 51, Remington 1100, SKB 300 and 900, Smith & Wesson 1000, and Winchester 1400 and Super X Model 1.

If you want a shotgun for hunting ringneck pheasant or ruffed grouse and perhaps, on occasion, dove, wild turkey and waterfowl, then the autoloader is the most logical choice. Gas-operated autoloaders should be bought in 12 gauge and feature a barrel not more than 28 inches long with a variable choke attached. With this scattergun you may not become a skeet or trap champion or be the "hot-shot" grouse hunter in your club, but the average gun-pointer will produce more than his share of success under various field conditions with it.

Vision in Target Shooting
by Frank T. Hanenkrat

"Sunshine almost always makes me high," says a popular song. Indeed, something like a state of inebriation may afflict a shooter who, sober as a judge, begins to suffer various forms of illusions, mirages and failures of vision. These experiences are fairly common and often are unrecognized by the shooter himself, though, of course, they seriously affect performance. The more you know about vision problems in shooting and how to cope with them, the better your performance can be.

Most of us take vision for granted, assuming that it is a straightforward, reliable process. Actually it is not. Seeing is a complex process involving the often peculiar behavior of light and a still-mysterious chemical reaction to light that occurs in the back of the eye. One of the most important considerations in shooting is visual clarity. Almost everyone knows that when we look at an object we "see" the light rays emanating or reflecting from it. For an object to be seen clearly, the light rays must be brought into sharp focus on the back of the eye, a task accomplished primarily by the cornea and the lens. Many people have defective corneas or lenses and cannot achieve completely sharp focus without the aid of glasses; however, many such defects can be corrected and clear vision obtained. Even with the best of vision, there is a problem inherent in focus that affects all shooters: The eye cannot bring both near and far objects into focus simultaneously. This means, of course, that if you're using mechanical sights, you can't have the sights and the distant target in *sharp* focus at the same time.

For example, look through a window at a distant object and hold one finger up in front of your eyes. Close one eye. Now focus on the distant object, and your finger will appear blurred; focus on your finger, and the distant object will be blurred. This illustrates the problem of focus with monocular (one-eyed) vision. Now repeat the experiment with both eyes open; the out-of-focus part of the image will appear not only blurred, but doubled, which is an additional problem in binocular vision.

Another experiment will illustrate the concept of depth of field. Depth of field refers to the distance between the farthest and closest points at which objects are clearly visible when the eye is focused on a given point. For example, if the eye is focused on an object 24 inches away and can see clearly objects in the line of sight between 28 and 20 inches away, the depth of field is 8 inches. The farther away the point of focus, the greater the depth of field.

Depth of field can be increased by looking through a small aperture held close to the eye. Repeat the earlier experiment with one eye, but this time look through a 1/16-inch-diameter hole punched in a piece of paper held before the eye. You should find that although you cannot bring both your finger and the distant object into perfect focus at the same time, at least you have reduced the degree of blurring of the out-of-focus part of the image.

Keeping these principles in mind, let's now examine the proper way of dealing with focusing problems in target shooting. You will find that the solutions differ as you change from handgun to shotgun to rifle. Furthermore, many of

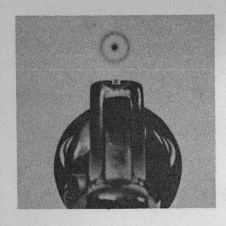

The unaided eye cannot focus on both near and far objects at the same time. Focus (top) is on the sights, and the target appears blurred; focus (center) is on the target, and the sights appear blurred; focus (bottom) is still on the sights, but the target has been brought into sharper focus by photographing through a small aperture. This effect can be somewhat duplicated by looking through a small aperture placed close to the eye. Because sight alignment is critical in rifle and handgun shooting, focus should be on the sights; in shotgunning, focus should be on the moving target.

the old admonitions such as, "Always keep both eyes open," and "Always focus on the front sight," are not correct in all situations.

Handgunning

The critical factor in handgunning is sight alignment. Held in a firing position, the gun is gripped in a hand that connects to the body through a pivoting wrist-joint, a hinged elbow-joint, and a ball-and-socket shoulder joint. Obviously there is a great deal of movement potential in this structure to cause errors both in aim and sight alignment. Of the two, sight alignment is the more important because of the extremely short sight-radius of the gun. A small error in aim may direct the bullet away from the 10-ring to the 8-ring, but a comparably small error in sight alignment might send the bullet off at an angle that would take it completely outside the bull. To ensure good sight alignment then, the point of focus must be the sights. As a result, the distant target will appear somewhat blurred; even so, good aim

can be attained with this method, although beginners may have to practice before feeling comfortable with it.

There are several things a handgunner can do to help vision while shooting. Many people are bothered by seeing two targets when they keep both eyes open, and prefer to shut one eye. If holding one eye closed is difficult or distracting, it is possible to put tape on one lens of the shooting glasses (or on one lens of flip-down sunglasses) and block vision in one eye.

Also, many people feel that they get a better sight picture with less blurring of the target if they cut a small aperture in a piece of tape and affix it to the aiming lens of the shooting glasses. Some experimentation is necessary to find the correct placement of the tape and the right aperture size. If prescription glasses are worn, the aperture must be centered on the visual axis of the lens, or its corrective powers will be lost.

An alternative method of improving the sight picture is to have

Some handgun shooters like to tape the lens glass of the non-aiming eye to prevent seeing a double target, and to tape the lens of the aiming eye and cut a small aperture in the tape to improve depth of field. Experimentation is necessary to find the correct aperture size and placement. If prescription lenses are worn, the aperture must be on the visual axis of the lens or the corrective power of the lens will be affected.

Handgun shooter with taped glasses.

a small plus lens ground into, or cemented onto the aiming lens of shooting glasses. This is best done by an ophthamologist.

Shotgunning

The critical factor in shotgunning is precise visual tracking of the moving target. Thus, the eyes should focus on the target; the sighting plane and front bead of the gun will appear blurred. Precision sight alignment is less crucial in a gun that shoots an expanding pattern of pellets instead of a single bullet. (Most shotguns, in fact, have no rear sight.) However, something like sight alignment is employed in shotgunning, and it is best achieved by a gun

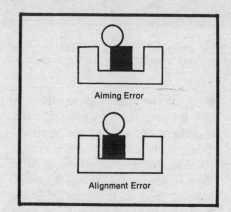

While approximately the same degree of error is apparent in both of these sight pictures, the alignment error is much more serious than the aiming error. The aiming error would still place the shot in the target at 3 o'clock; the alignment error would place the shot completely outside the target at 9 o'clock.

that provides a natural fit to the shooter's aiming stance. The length, drop and pitch of the stock should be such that when the individual brings the gun to his shoulder, his aiming eye is centered behind the sighting plane and the front bead centers in his natural line of sight. A gun that fits properly will give this result every time it is brought to the shoulder, requiring no adjustments of the shooter to the gun. An improperly fitting gun will cause the shooter to make some adjustment or produce some strain in the arms or neck to obtain a good sight picture, a situation almost certain to result in an incon-

Protective lenses should always be worn when shooting to avoid eye damage from flying bits of lead, metal, burning powder, and other debris. Glasses also protect the eye from windblown particles, excessive drying and strong sunlight.

sistency of eye/gun alignment serious enough to angle the expanding pattern of pellets away from the target.

It is desirable to keep both eyes open in shotgunning, for it is with binocular vision that we are best able to judge the speed, distance and direction of a moving target. Some people, however, have a problem when they shoot right-handed yet have a dominant left eye, or vice versa. With both eyes focused on the target, as is proper,

they see two front sights, which is also proper, but they aim with the dominant or "wrong" eye, a situation guaranteed to produce a miss. Shooters with this problem who cannot teach themselves to overcome it through practice drills are best advised to shoot with one eye closed, despite the problems of depth perception that this creates.

Riflery

Riflery poses more complex visual problems than does handgun or shotgun shooting. As in hand-

gunning, sight alignment is of paramount importance, and in competitions requiring open sights (such as moving-target or Service Rifle events), focus should be fixed near the front sight to ensure good alignment. The precise point of focus may be on the front sight or it may be slightly forward or behind the front sight — the exact point is unimportant so long as the shooter uses the same method consistently, can detect errors in sight alignment and can see the

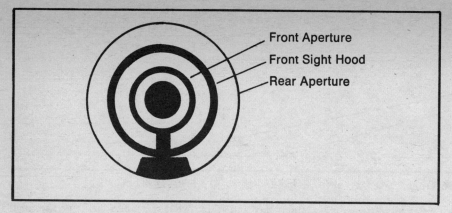

Labels: Front Aperture, Front Sight Hood, Rear Aperture

Patterning aperture sights with a round bullseye yields a series of concentric circles which make it easy to see errors in aim and alignment. As a rule of thumb, each element of the pattern should appear 1.5X the diameter of the next smaller element.

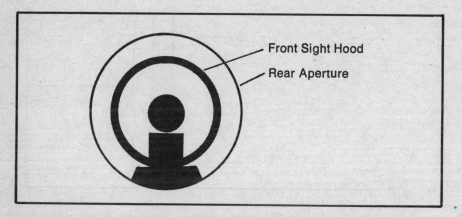

Labels: Front Sight Hood, Rear Aperture

Patterning a post front sight with a round bullseye provides smaller elements and places greater demands upon visual acuity, or sharpness. If a post is used, its width should appear equal to that of the bull. The top of the post should not cut into the bull; it should just touch the bottom, or display a thin line of white below the bull.

Ghost images that interfere with vision can occur as a result of staring fixedly at a sight picture. Stare at the center of the ringed target for 30 or more seconds; then stare at the center of the black dot. In a short time a white ghost image of the ringed target should appear on or behind the black dot. Ghost images can be avoided by darting the eye constantly around the areas of a sight picture.

target clearly enough to aim with precision.

Competitive shooters, however, are involved in events that allow for the use of an aperture sight system, which introduces significant advantages as well as additional problems. One advantage is that a small rear aperture will usually improve depth of field and will reduce the blurring of the target when the front sight is in focus. Another advantage is that the round rear aperture allows for excellent readings of sight alignment if the front sight is covered by a round hood; the gain is increased even further if the front sight itself is a round aperture. In this situation the visual pattern under observation consists of a series of concentric circles formed by the bull, the front aperture, the front sight hood, and the field of view proscribed by the rear aperture. In such a system, errors in both aim and sight alignment are easily and quickly detectable.

Some people prefer a post rather than an aperture front sight and a frequent question is: Which is better, aperture or post? For most people an aperture is clearly the best choice. If for some reason a person cannot get accustomed to an aperture, then obviously a post should be used. But anyone making this decision should be aware that patterning a post with the bull makes a greater demand upon the eye than patterning with an aperture.

What size should the aperture be? A rule of thumb used by world-class shooters is that the diameter of the front aperture should appear to be 1.5 times the diameter of the bull and that of the rear aperture 1.5 times the diameter of the front sight hood. However, there may be strong exceptions to this rule, especially when the shooter experiences the pheno-

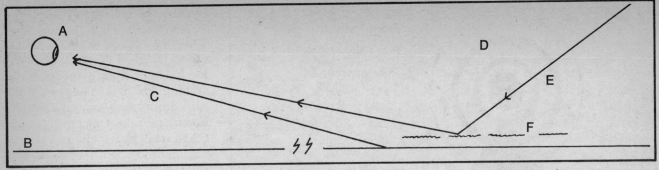

A. Observer's eye: B. Road;   C. Light from road;   D. Cool air;   E. Light   F. Layer of hot air.

Most people have experienced looking down a flat highway on a hot, sunny day and seeing what resembles a lake on the road ahead, only to have it disappear when the area is seen from a closer distance. The "lake" is actually a piece of blue sky, a mirage created by the bending of light rays as they enter layers of hot air near the surface of the road.

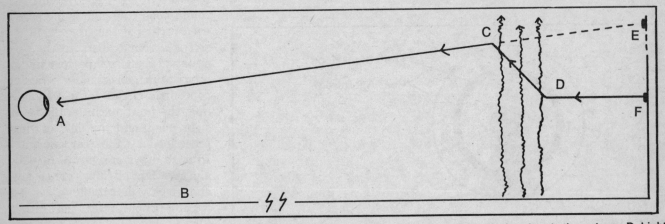

A. Shooter's eye; B. Shooting range; C. Rising, turbulent hot air bends light rays up; cool air then bends them down; D. Light from target; E. Apparent target; F. Actual target.

Mirages can appear on shooting ranges, particularly at long distances. Light traveling from the target strikes rising, turbulent hot air, is bent upwards, then down again when it enters cooler air. As a result, the target appears higher than it actually is. Anyone shooting at the apparent target would shoot completely above the actual target. If winds are blowing across the zone of hot air, the illusion can cause the target to appear right or left of its actual position.

menon known as "graying out," in which the bull appears as a dull, indistinct gray. (The cause of this phenomenon is understood, but too complex to explain here.) The solution is to vary the size of either or both the front or rear aperture. Not everyone experiences this problem; for those who do, variable-aperture sights are a good investment.

For good results, the rear aperture must be centered directly in front of the pupil of the eye. Failure to achieve centering will result in yet another phenomenon

known as "flattening" of the bull. This can be illustrated by looking through an aperture system and moving your head to the left; the right side of the bull will appear flat. Move your head down and the top of the bull will appear flat. The solution to this problem is always to position the head to achieve accurate centering.

Staring fixedly at one point in the sight picture can affect the eye and produce ghost images that interfere with accurate perception. This problem is easily avoided by darting the eye around the sight

picture instead of staring steadily at one part of it.

Where is the point of focus when using aperture sights? World-class shooters disagree. Some insist that you should focus on the front sight; some on the bull; and others at some point in between. Whatever allows you to achieve the optimum in sight alignment and aim is right for you.

Various kinds of optical sight systems are available for various types of guns, although, except in riflery, they are rarely used in formal competition. The advantages of these systems are that they may offer some degree of magnification, they may diminish the problem of sight alignment and they eliminate the problem of depth of field by bringing the target and the aiming device (crosshair, dot or post) into the same plane of focus. If a magnifying system is used the disadvantages are that any movement of the gun also appears magnified and the target may appear to jump around so much as to offer insurmountable distractions to some shooters. Another problem is parallax, which can be serious if the scope is improperly adjusted for the user's eyes. To make proper adjustments, consult the owner's manual.

Under certain conditions, rifle shooters using either scopes or iron sights are forced to deal with the optical illusion known as "mirage." Mirage results from the bending or refracting of light as it passes through air layers of different temperatures and densities. The bending may be severe enough to make the target appear to be several feet away from its actual location. Anyone shooting at the apparent target would miss the actual target altogether. Even when less extreme, it can seriously affect scores. Mirage conditions can be observed with the unaided eye, but are best observed through a telescope focused just short of the target. The condition appears as a shimmering or wavering effect in the atmosphere. The direction of motion may be to either side as

a result of wind, or upward in windless conditions. Over a long-distance course, mirage may run in two or three different directions between the firing line and the targets, creating an extremely difficult situation for the shooter. Only experience and careful analysis will enable a person to cope with this troublesome illusion by making changes in the sight setting or in the point of aim.

Eye Care

Good vision is obviously of great value to a shooter. You can help preserve it by maintaining good general health and having annual or bi-annual eye examinations. You should always wear protective glasses when shooting; if you wear prescription glasses, you should use a protective cover or lens. Had I not been wearing them several years ago, I would now be blind in one eye as a result of a 308 cartridge case rupturing and sending burning powder and metal fragments back through the bolt and directly toward my right eye. Protective glasses unquestionably saved my vision.

Experienced shooters soon learn to rest their eyes. In strong sunlight, gray or green tinted sunglasses help reduce glare and consequent eyestrain. In conditions of haze or fog, amber glasses may provide some reduction in target haziness for some people, though not all. Exercise the eyes each day by spending a few moments directing the eyes up, down, right, left, and rolling them in a circle in order

to stretch and strengthen the muscles that control the eyes. And when the eyes feel tired or strained, rest them by cupping the palms over the eyes to shut out all light. A minute or two of palming provides rest and refreshment for tired eyes and may help restore the sharpness that diminishes with fatigue.

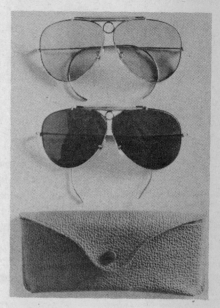

Excellent eye protection is provided by these glasses designed especially for shooters by Bausch & Lomb. The lenses are made of safety glass and can withstand the impact of a $\frac{5}{8}$-inch steel ball dropped from 50 inches without shattering. Commercially available with non-prescription lenses or prescription lenses; the latter should be ground with the optical axis at the point where the eyes look through the lenses while aiming in the common shooting position. (Some rifle shooters may want two or more pairs with different axes.) Most shooters like to have a clear pair for normal conditions, a dark pair (gray or green) for strong sunlight, and an amber pair for hazy conditions.

The Steel-Shot Controversy
by Tom Roster

Steel shot and its mandatory use for waterfowl hunting in certain areas of the four flyways continues to be controversial. Basically, the controversy boils down to three issues: biology, ballistics and cost. Since no expertise in biology is claimed by the author, lead poisoning will be left to the various federal and state game agencies to resolve. What will be examined are the relative ballistics and cost of steel versus lead shot.

Lead-Shot Substitutes

Many hunters still seem to be confused about why steel shot has won acceptance as the only non-toxic substitute for lead, rather than some other metal, or plated-lead pellet. Others keep waiting for the "big breakthrough" in which another non-toxic type shot will be developed that will offer improved ballistics over steel. The trouble is that any substitute must meet three criteria: It must be non-toxic; it must offer acceptable ballistics, and it must be economically feasible to manufacture so that the resulting pellet type is cost-competitive with lead shot. To date, virtually every conceivable metal substitute, non-metal substitute, metal/lead mixture, metal-plating substance, and various thicknesses of plating of lead pellets have been tried. Without citing precise historical development, research and chronology of non-toxic lead-shot substitute attempts, all except steel have failed to meet the three requirements. No known substance holds promise as a replacement for steel shot. Nor is the arms and ammunition industry pretending there ever will be one. Steel shot remains the only non-toxic substitute for lead shot.

Steel-Shot Load Efficiency

Despite research and field data to the contrary, the belief that steel-shot loads are not an effective substitute for lead-shot loads persists. The truth is that all available research tends to indicate that there is no significant difference in the ability of 12-gauge steel-shot loads vs. 12-gauge lead-shot loads to bag ducks and geese under similar field circumstances and conditions.

In controlled tests Bellrose found that steel shot performed as well as lead shot of the same size out to 40 yards. At 50 and 60 yards lead proved more lethal than steel (Bellrose, 1959). At Nilo in 1964, Mikula found that 1-ounce loads of No. 2 steel shot exceeded the performance of 1¼-ounce loads of No. 4 lead shot at all ranges. The Bureau of Sport Fisheries and Wildlife tests and questionnaires on federal refuges in 1963-75 where 1⅛-ounces of No. 1 or No. 4 steel-shot loads were compared for effectiveness against 1¼-ounce lead loads of No. 2, 4 or 6, revealed the two load types were very similar with respect to effectiveness and loss rate. The semi-controlled field test at the the McGraw Foundation in 1971-72 showed no significant differences in bagging or crippling rates between the 1¼-ounce load of No. 6 lead vs. the 1⅛-ounce load of No. 4 steel at distances of 40 to

60 yards (Nicklaus, 1976). The same was found at Shiawassee in 1973, when the effectiveness of 1⅛-ounce loads of No. 4 steel were compared to 1¼-ounce loads of No. 4 lead (Mikula et al, 1977). Recently, in 1978-79, the Illinois Department of Conservation released preliminary results of a controlled field test to determine the efficiency of steel shot for hunting Canada geese in southern Illinois. William L. Anderson, the biologist in charge, reported 3-inch, 12-gauge, 1¼-ounce loads of No. BB steel, when shot by volunteer goose hunters, produced a higher bagging rate and lower crippling rate than 3-inch, 12-gauge, 1⅞-ounce magnum loads of No. 2 lead. In the same test, 3-inch, 12-gauge, 1¼-ounce loads of No. 1 steel produced a lower bagging rate than either of the other two loads, but still produced a lower crippling rate than the No. 2 lead load.

Damage to Gun Barrels

The fear that steel shot will damage shotgun barrels continues to linger despite all indications that it will not. In the six years of usage and field tests of steel shot on state game management areas and federal refuges involving the hunting public, the fact remains that not a single documented case exists of barrel damage or choke erosion directly attributable to steel shot. In addition, the three major arms and ammunition manufacturers have issued public statements and statistics in the USFWS final EIS on steel shot that currently available steel-shot loads containing steel shot of no greater hardness than 95 diamond pyramid hardness (DPH) would cause no significant reduction in the life of most American full-choke shotguns. Their statements and statistics supported the conclusion that only superficial damage to full-choked shotguns, such as minor choke expansion, might occur, that such expansion might actually improve pattern values, and that only owners of thin-walled, soft-steel shotguns, some Brownings of early serial number vintage, or shotguns with sharp-angled or swedged full chokes need worry at all. After 40,000 rounds were expended by hunters during the Tulelake NWR steel vs. lead-shot goose-shooting test in 1977-78, there were no reports of barrel damage.

Popular Attitudes Toward Steel

While fears of barrel damage from steel shot may be waning, the belief that steel shot is an inefficient projectile that will increase crippling losses continues to linger. This is despite the aforementioned research which indicates steel shot can be as efficient as lead in bagging ducks and geese.

The most frequently cited basis for the belief that steel shot must necessarily increase crippling losses is the "laboratory" study of Winchester-Western done at Nilo. Unfortunately, those who look to Nilo for support of their belief that steel shot is inefficient beyond 40 yards fail to recognize that the Nilo test was in many ways an unfair comparison. First, the Nilo test was not a field test using real hunters, nor were wild ducks and geese shot at under actual field conditions, (such as was the case in the above tests with the exception that Mikula used game farm mallards). Rather, it was a laboratory test on game farm mallards in which a mechanical "robot" fired at tethered ducks.

Secondly, the Nilo test compared the very best available 2¾-inch lead-shot loads — the Super-X Double X Magnum, a 1½-ounce load of very hard No. 4 lead shot buffered with a granulated plastic filler, which results in abnormally high pattern performance above 90 percent in most full-choke shotguns — against a quite primitive 1⅛-ounce load of No. 4 steel and another of No. 6 steel. Ballistically, the No. 6 steel load never had a chance, and while the No. 4 steel load contained nearly the same number of pellets as the No. 4 lead load (that is, they were volumetrically equivalent), the steel load did not pattern as well, nor could the size of steel pellets compare to the size of lead pellets in terms of retained energy. Ballistically, a steel pellet must be nearly two sizes larger than a lead pellet to retain similar energy over distance. Thus, a fair ballistic comparison can occur only when No. 4 lead is tested against No. 2 steel, but No. 2 steel was omitted from the Nilo test.

In addition, the XX Magnum load tested at Nilo is not one that is frequently used by the public for the majority of this nation's duck hunting. The standard 1¼-ounce lead load, together with the "baby magnum," 1½-ounce, non-buffered lead load easily comprises 95 percent of all the 2¾-inch, 12-gauge lead-shot loads used to hunt ducks. Thus, the Nilo project tested the Cadillac of lead loads, used at that time by no more than five percent of this country's waterfowlers, against a mediocre steel load, loaded with a shot size that could never compare ballistically to the lead shot of the size and quality loaded in the "Cadillac" load.

Current field research tends to indicate no significant differences in the ability of steel shot to bag ducks and geese when compared to lead shot.

If the Nilo project had compared a 1¼-ounce load of No. 4 lead (possessing a lower antimony level which renders a softer pellet more closely approximating the quality of lead shot found in many of the 1¼-ounce and 1½-ounce lead loads used by most waterfowlers), against a ballistically equivalent No. 2 steel pellet in a 1⅛-ounce steel load which had been tested, altered and refined for as long as the decades-old 1¼-ounce and 1½-ounce loads, results would have been much different. In fact, results might have been very similar to what Mikula found in 1964 — that a steel-shot load truly equivalent to a given lead-shot load,

cannot only hold its own, but oftentimes can exceed lead-shot performance.

Understanding Steel Shot

Size for size, steel shot is lighter than lead shot. This does not necessarily mean, however, that it cannot be loaded in such a manner as to compensate for its lightness so that steel can serve as an acceptable, even desirable, ballistic projectile for waterfowl hunting. To understand steel shot, one must first recognize and admit the instrinsic deficiences in lead shot and lead-shot loads. Secondly, one must recognize that steel shot inherently overcomes lead shot's major ballistic flaw. Thirdly, attention must be paid to the fact that steel shot's only ballistic problem is its light weight, but that projectile weight is not the sole factor in determining the ballistic merits of a shotshell load.

Lead-Shot Load Problems

Since for centuries lead shot has been used almost exclusively for waterfowl hunting, and since many millions of waterfowl have been successfully bagged wtih lead shot, there is a tendency to believe that only lead shot can successfully bag waterfowl. While lead shot is ballistically desirable from the standpoint of its pellet density, lead shot suffers from its inability to remain round under the forces of combustion in shot-shell loads, and during forcing cone, bore and choke passage. Thus, de-

pending upon the load and loading technique, a high percentage of the pellets in any given lead-shot load are deformed before they leave the muzzle. Deformed pellets expose more surface area to air resistance (drag) than round pellets, and therefore diverge from the point of aim as flyer shot, reducing pattern values. In addition, deformed shot does not retain as much energy over distance as round shot, and tends to fall behind round shot, excessively lengthening the shot string. Deformed lead-shot pellets and excessive shot stringing increase crippling losses. (Roster, 1976, 1977; Brister, 1976)

The hardness of lead pellets in unbuffered lead-shot loads is the principal factor in their ability to pattern well. It is a common myth among hunters that shot quality in all factory loads and even reloads is the same. In fact, this is not true. As price goes down for a given load of factory lead-shot ammunition for a given gauge, usually so does the amount of antimony added to the shot. Since anti-

Steel stars more perfectly round and possesses a superior ability to stay round, which makes it a much more efficient projectile than lead. This becomes more obvious when comparing lead pellets (above) to steel pellets of the same size (below) recovered from bagged ducks and geese.

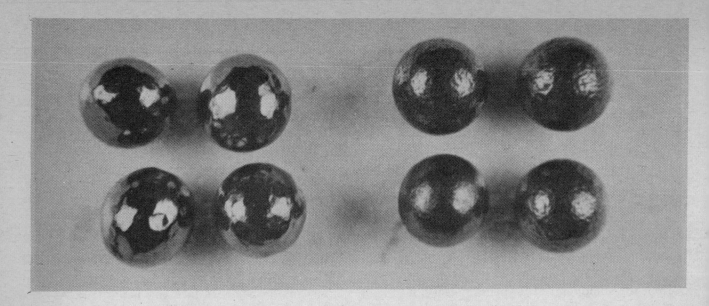

Due to differences in manufacturing technique, lead shot (left) can never be made as round as steel shot (right). This factor plus lead's proclivity to deform during bore and choke passage accounts for steel's ability to deliver significantly improved patterns over lead, especially at long range.

mony is the chief hardening agent in lead shot, shot hardness will decrease when less antimony is added. Thus, the least expensive factory loads and the least expensive bagged shot sold to reloaders tend to contain the softest shot.

Lead-Shot Load Patterning Performance

The ammunition industry has traditionally attempted to overcome lead shot's proclivity for deformation and low pattern values by loading larger shot charges per gauge, popularly called "magnum loads." Hunters commonly believe that magnum loads pattern the best of all shotshell loads and are the most lethal of all loads, especially for goose hunting. This accounts for the currently unbuffered 1½-ounce "baby magnum" 12-gauge load comprising the largest percentage of goose loads sold by the three leading ammunition manufacturers. In reality, both Brister and the author have found that when subjected to arduous pattern testing, unbuffered magnum lead-shot loads consistently pattern the poorest of all shot shell loads in current use, and that lighter, less popular loads actually produce better patterns at long range.

Steel-Shot's Form Factor

Unlike lead, steel shot of 75 DPH or harder tends to be extremely resistant to deformation, emerging from the barrel in an essentially spherical shape. Currently manufactured steel-shot loads contain pellets at or near the 90 DPH level of hardness. While working on the Nilo project, E.D. Lowry (1973), who had participated in the Patuxent test and played a major role in developing the Nilo lethality formula, found, during the course of a Sporting Arms and Ammunition Manufacturers' Institute (SAAMI) grant to Winchester-Western in 1969, that steel shot maintains a minimum of a 12 percent higher form factor than lead shot. In other words, a lead pellet would have to be at least 12 percent heavier than a steel pellet of the same size to match the steel pellet for actual delivered pellet energy, due to the deformation (and thus energy loss) the lead pellet would suffer because it is softer than steel. A projectile's form is one of three major factors used to rate the ballistic effectiveness of shotshell pellets, the other two being the density of the pellet and its original velocity. Thus steel pellets, due to their high form factor, are capable of traveling through atmostpheric resistance at a higher degree of efficiency than their density would indicate.

A brief examination of Table 1, which compares the "new" tables developed by Lowry for SAAMI in 1970 at Winchester-Western, to the "old" tables, helps explain why Mikula (1974) found No. 2 steel outperforming No. 4 lead. The same comparison shows why the primitive 1-ounce steel load used at

Table 1

Partial comparison among the SAAMI shotshell ballistics for lead (Old); the SAAMI ballistics completed and submitted in 1970 (New), and the steel-shot ballistics compiled by Roster in 1978.

Pellet Type	Ballistic Table	Pellet Size	Instrumental Velocity	Velocity (fps)		Energy Per Pellet (ft/lbs.)		Time in Flight (sec.)	
				40 yds.	60 yds.	40 yds.	60 yds.	40 yds.	60 yds.
Lead	Old	4	1330	815	685	4.77	3.35	.1187	.1993
Lead	New	4	1330	740	590	3.91	2.49	.1235	.2147
Lead	Old	2	1330	860	730	7.98	5.76	.1148	.1908
Lead	New	2	1330	770	630	6.39	4.28	.1204	.2071
Lead	Old	BB	1330	915	790	16.27	12.23	.1107	.1815
Lead	New	BB	1330	815	675	12.89	8.84	.1167	.1980
Lead	Old	6	1330	765	630	2.50	1.70	.1238	.2108
Lead	New	6	1330	700	550	2.11	1.30	.1278	.2252
Lead	Old	66	1255	740	610	2.34	1.61	.1292	.2189
Lead	New	6	1255	680	535	1.99	1.23	.1327	.2328
Lead	Old	4	1255	785	665	4.45	3.16	.1240	.2074
Lead	New	4	1255	715	575	3.65	2.36	.1288	.2228
Lead	Old	2	1255	830	705	7.43	5.36	.1201	.1994
Lead	New	2	1255	745	610	5.98	4.01	.1255	.2148
Lead	Old	BB	1255	880	765	15.05	11.37	.1160	.1894
Lead	New	BB	1255	785	655	11.96	8.33	.1219	.2059
Lead	Old	6	1185	715	595	2.18	1.52	.1348	.2274
Lead	Old	4	1185	760	645	4.13	2.97	.1297	.2159
Lead	Old	2	1185	795	685	6.81	5.06	.1259	.2073
Steel	—	4	1500	700	532	2.48	1.43	.1216	.2204
Steel	—	2	1500	739	575	4.25	2.57	.1175	.2100
Steel	—	1	1500	769	602	5.58	3.42	.1133	.2021
Steel	—	BB	1500	790	628	8.39	5.31	.1128	.1985
Steel	—	4	1450	689	601	2.40	1.40	.1242	.2243
Steel	—	2	1450	728	567	4.12	2.50	.1201	.2139
Steel	—	1	1450	745	586	5.24	3.24	.1183	.2096
Steel	—	BB	1450	777	620	8.11	5.16	.1154	.2024
Steel	—	4	1400	679	517	2.33	1.35	.1269	.2285
Steel	—	2	1400	716	559	3.98	2.43	.1228	.2181
Steel	—	1	1400	732	577	5.06	3.14	.1211	.2138
Steel	—	BB	1400	763	610	7.83	5.00	.1182	.2066
Steel	—	4	1365	671	512	2.28	1.33	.1290	.2317
Steel	—	2	1365	707	552	3.88	2.37	.1249	.2213
Steel	—	1	1365	723	571	4.94	3.07	.1232	.2170
Steel	—	BB	1365	753	603	7.62	4.69	.1203	.2098
Steel	—	4	1300	656	500	2.18	1.27	.1330	.2381
Steel	—	2	1300	690	540	3.70	2.27	.1290	.2276
Steel	—	1	1300	706	558	4.70	2.94	.1273	.2233
Steel	—	BB	1300	734	590	7.24	4.68	.1245	.2160
Steel	—	4	1250	644	491	2.10	1.22	.1365	.2435
Steel	—	2	1250	677	530	3.56	2.19	.1324	.2329
Steel	—	1	1250	692	548	4.51	2.83	.1308	.2286
Steel	—	BB	1250	719	579	6.94	4.50	.1280	.2213
Steel	—	4	1200	631	482	2.02	1.17	.1402	.2494
Steel	—	2	1200	663	520	3.41	2.10	.1362	.2387
Steel	—	1	1200	677	537	4.32	2.72	.1345	.2343
Steel	—	BB	1200	703	567	6.63	4.32	.1318	.2271
Steel	—	4	1100	603	460	1.84	1.07	.1486	.2629
Steel	—	2	1100	633	496	3.11	1.91	.1447	.2520
Steel	—	1	1100	646	512	3.94	2.48	.1431	.2476
Steel	—	BB	1100	669	541	6.01	3.94	.1404	.2403

This hunter had no trouble bagging his limit of mallards and gadwall with 1⅛ oz. loads of No. 4 steel. To improve his ability to hit with tight-patterning steel, he chose an improved cylinder choke.

Patuxent (Andrews et al., 1969) was capable of bagging ducks as effectively at 40 yards and nearly as effectively at 60 yards as the 1¼-ounce lead load.

Steel-Shot Retained Energy

Of the three major factors used to determine a pellet's ballistic effectiveness, steel shot is inferior to lead in only one way — pellet density or weight. Steel is only 68 percent as heavy as lead. The popular belief is that this factor alone makes steel inferior to lead, and therefore, never as effective as lead. This is true, however, only when comparing steel and lead pellets *of the same size*.

But what hard and fast rule requires that the same size pellets of steel be used for the same tasks required of lead pellets? While 6s and 5s have traditionally been popular with duck hunters, and 4s and 2s with goose hunters, for example, what

Table 2.

Standard American steel and lead-shot size designations by diameter.

Shot-Size Designation (American)	Diameter (Inches)
BB	.180
Air Rifle	.175
B	.170
1	.160
2	.150
3	.140
4	.130
5	.120
6	.110

law or constraint prevents the use of No. 4s or 2s for ducks or No. 1s or BB's for geese? (Table 2). There is no ballistic reason. Shot-size choice is largely a matter of preference governed to a certain extent by desired pattern density. The currently popular lead-shot sizes are used as a matter of habit more than ballistic logic.

A steel-shot pellet two sizes larger than a lead-shot pellet performs in a similar ballistic manner and is therefore ballistically comparable. The simple switch from a given lead-shot pellet size to a steel-shot pellet two sizes larger immediately compensates for steel's lightness (Table 3). With steel, then, replacement-shot sizes for ducks could be 4s, 3s or even 2s. Replacement steel shot sizes for geese could 2s, 1s Bs or BBs.

Since retained energy is a function of mass and velocity ($KE = \frac{1}{2} MV^2$), steel's lighter mass can also be compensated for by increasing velocity. A 1365 fps steel-shot load (average instrumental velocity of currently available commercial 1⅛ ounce, 2¾-inches, 12-gauge steel shot loads) of No. 2 steel retains almost identical per-pellet energy at 60 yards (2.37 ft/lbs.) as a 1255 fps (average instrumental velocity of currently available commercial 2¾-inch, 1½-ounce lead loads) of No. 4 lead (2.36 ft/lbs.). For geese, the 2¾-inch, 12-gauge, 1⅛-ounce load of steel 1s retains 3.07 ft/lbs. of energy per pellet at 60 yards and steel BBs in the same loading would retain 4.69 ft/lbs. per pellet at the same range. This slightly exceeds the per-pellet retained energy values of the most popular American goose load, the 2¾-inch, 12-gauge "baby magnum" load (1255 fps average instrumental velocity) of lead 4s which retain 2.36 ft/lbs. of energy-per-pellet and lead 2s which retain 4.01 ft/lbs. of energy-

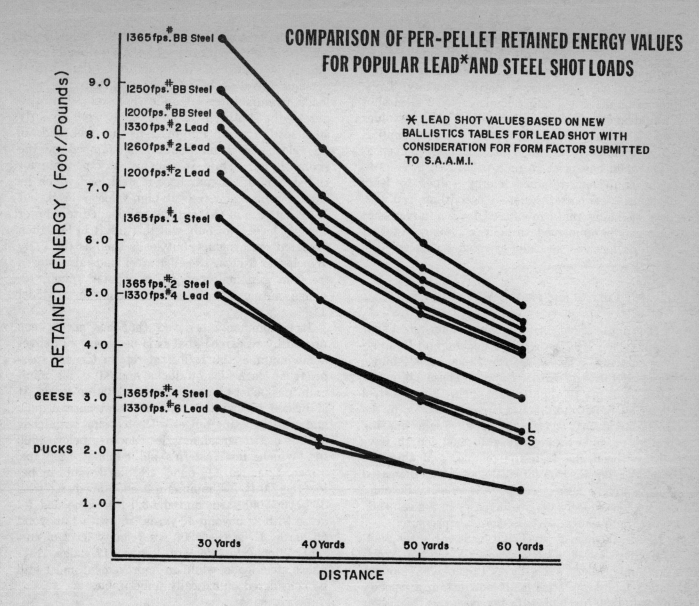

COMPARISON OF PER-PELLET RETAINED ENERGY VALUES FOR POPULAR LEAD*AND STEEL SHOT LOADS

✱ LEAD SHOT VALUES BASED ON NEW BALLISTICS TABLES FOR LEAD SHOT WITH CONSIDERATION FOR FORM FACTOR SUBMITTED TO S.A.A.M.I.

RETAINED ENERGY (Foot/Pounds)

1365 fps. BB Steel
1250 fps. BB Steel
1200 fps. BB Steel
1330 fps. #2 Lead
1260 fps. #2 Lead
1200 fps. #2 Lead
1365 fps. #1 Steel
1365 fps. #2 Steel
1330 fps. #4 Lead
GEESE — 1365 fps. #4 Steel
1330 fps. #6 Lead
DUCKS

9.0 · 8.0 · 7.0 · 6.0 · 5.0 · 4.0 · 3.0 · 2.0 · 1.0

L
S

DISTANCE

30 Yards · 40 Yards · 50 Yards · 60 Yards

---

per-pellet at the same distances. Steel shot's ability to retain energy in a manner equivalent to lead shot (given proper shot-size selection and velocity compensations) enables steel shot to be as efficient in bagging waterfowl as lead shot up to size No. 2.

Steel Patterning-Performance

A direct result of steel's higher form factor is its tendency to pattern better than lead shot. While most unbuffered-lead loads struggle to achieve 70 percent patterns at 40 yards and 30-35 percent patterns at 60 yards through full-choke guns, current steel-shot loads typically pattern 80-92 percent at 40 yards and 45-60 percent at 60 yards,

depending on shot size, load and gun used. Thus, current steel-shot loads, even though they are in the infancy of their development, consistently pattern as well as the most modern of lead loads—those buffered with a filler material added to the shot column. Typical steel-shot loads, then, outpattern by a wide margin the popular lead-shot loads used for the majority of waterfowl hunting.

In addition, steel-shot load shot strings are much shorter than lead-shot load strings. Brister (1976) found during moving pattern tests to measure shot-stringing at speeds equivalent to flighted waterfowl —40-50 mph—that steel-shot loads produced shot strings significantly shorter than non-buffered (popular) lead-shot loads at ranges of 40 to 60 yards.

Since steel loads tend to pattern more densely than lead-shot loads, a steel load volumetrically equivalent to a lead-shot load of the same shot size would produce a superior pattern density. Thus, for example, a 1⅛-ounce load of No. 2 steel shot would be expected to produce higher pattern values and a shorter-shot string than a 1½-ounce unbuffered load of No. 2 lead. This also offers compensation when having to go up a pellet size in steel to gain equivalent retained energy values to lead. Because steel patterns more densely than lead with less stringing than unbuffered lead, a larger shot size can be employed to deliver similar on-target pattern density, especially as range increases.

Current and Past Steel-Shot Loads

To date, three manufacturers offer steel-shot ammunition in 12 gauge only. Federal and Remington currently offer a 2¾-inch, 12-gauge, 1⅛-ounce steel load in sizes No. 1, 2 and 4. These 1⅛-ounce steel loads are the lightest 2¾-inch, 12-gauge steel loads available and are also currently loaded to the highest velocity levels (1365 fps). Light hunting loads for any given gauge and shell length have always been the fastest available, and this will probably remain true for steel-shot loads. Increased ejecta weight always compounds velocity development, for as ejecta weight increases in a given shell length and gauge, so does chamber pressure.

Thus, the heavier steel-shot loads currently available have lower velocity levels. Winchester-Western and Federal's 2¾-inch, 12-gauge, 1¼-ounce latest fold-crimp steel loads now attain a velocity of over 1330 fps. This is faster, however, than their earlier fold-crimp 1¼-ounce loads which traveled at about 1260 fps. Winchester's newest 3-inch, 12-gauge, 1½-ounce steel load attains an instrumental velocity of 1200 fps. This is significantly better than its old, now discontinued, 3-inch, 12-gauge, 1½-ounce steel load which traveled at only slightly better than 1100 fps. In the fall of 1978, Remington made available on a limited basis a 3-inch, 12-gauge, 1¼-oz. steel load in 1s, 2s and 4s with a nominal velocity of 1375 fps. This was the load in size BB and 1s that was tested for effectiveness on Canada geese by the Illinois Department of Conservation. Federal has increased the velocity of its 3-inch, 12-gauge, 1⅜-ounce steel load (available in shot sizes BB, 1, 2, and 4) from a nominal 1210 fps to 1280 fps.

Of the steel loads available, the fastest steel loads tend to be the most desirable ballistically. The trouble is that many of the steel loads have undergone changes in manufacture, so that current versions travel at higher velocities than the same loads manufactured at an earlier date. Unfortunately, the shotshell consumer cannot tell an early steel load from an improved recent steel load, as no velocity-level information is stamped on the shotshell box. Thus, it remains very possible for the shotgunner to purchase a steel load which he thinks is of a new, recent high-velocity level, but in actuality is of old vintage, and loaded to a lower velocity level. Not only will this result in less than expected performance, but loads such as the early Winchester 3-inch, 12-gauge steel loads also caused frequent gun malfunctions in popular 3-inch, 12-gauge autoloaders such as Remington's Model 1100.

It is commonly believed (but has never been proven by research) that it is necessary to deliver a minimum of 2.0 ft/lbs. of retained energy-per-pellet for clean kills on ducks, and 3.0 ft/lbs. minimum per-pellet-energy for clean kills on geese. It is difficult to maintain these levels at normal duck and goose shooting ranges with steel shot with loads having instrumental muzzle velocities below 1300 fps. Winchester-Western's old nominal 1100 fps, 3-inch, 12-gauge, 1½-ounce steel load would be below the 2.0 ft/lbs. minimum needed for ducks with 4s beyond 40 yards and the 3.0 ft/lbs. needed for geese with 2s beyond 40 yards, and with 1s beyond 50 yards. Even the 1200 fps velocity level of current Winchester-Western 3-inch, 12-gauge, 1½-ounce steel loads, while an improvement, must still be considered ballistically undesirable.

Plans for New Steel Loads

Remington Arms Co. hopes to market a heavier fold-crimp, 2¾-inch 12-gauge steel load by the fall of 1979. The Remington steel load will be 1¼ ounces in weight and available in No. BB, 1, 2 and 4 with a targeted minimum velocity level of 1350 fps. The steel-shot load development picture remains a constantly changing one, with velocity levels being ever increased, new shot charge weights added, and new pellet sizes offered. With the exception of Federal in its 3-inch offering, size BB steel has been conspicuously absent in commercial offerings for goose hunting. For a comparison of steel-shot load and lead-shot weights and pellet counts, see Table 4. No steel loads have been an-

Table 4

Comparison of volumetrically equivalent steel and lead-shot loads of the same shot size.

STEEL VS. LEAD

PELLET COUNT/SHOT CHARGE WEIGHT

	1⅛ Oz. Steel (492.2 grs.)	1½ Oz. Lead (656.3 grs.)	1¼ Oz. Steel (546.9 grs.)	1¾ Oz. Lead (765.6 grs.)	1⅜ Oz. Steel (601.6 grs.)	1⅞ Oz. Lead (820.3 grs.)	1½ Oz. Steel (656.3 grs.)	2⅛ Oz. Lead (929.7 grs.)	1⅝ Oz. Steel (710.9 grs.)	2¼ Oz. Lead (984.4 grs.)
				Approximate Number of Pellets Per Load						
#BB .180"	80	75	93	88	99	94	107	106	119	113
#1 .160"	116 Federal 119 Roster	—	133	—	146	—	159	—	172	—
#2 .150"	140 Federal 137 Roster	132	153	154	168	165	189	187	199	198
#4 .130"	216	204	241	238	267	259	291	289	315	307

nounced for sale to the public by any company for 16 and 20 gauges as of this writing. The U.S. Fish and Wildlife Service, however, intends to field test 2¾-inch and 3-inch, 20-gauge steel-shot ammunition during the 1979 waterfowl hunting season.

Cost

Current manufacturer suggested retail price for steel-shot ammunition ranges from approximately $10 per box for 12-gauge, 2¾-inch, 1⅛-ounce loads, to approximately $12.50 a box for 1¼-ounce loads, to a whopping $14 a box for 3-inch, 12-gauge loads. Suggested retail price is usually undercut in the shotshell marketplace, but due to high demand and limited supplies, the price of steel shot in many areas is held close to suggested retail. These prices may seem excessive insofar as the only component significantly more expensive in loading steel than lead is the steel shot itself. Current cost of steel shot to ammunition manufacturers is approximately 70 cents a pound, versus about approximately 40-45 cents a pound for lead shot. Therefore, the retail differential between a box of steel and a box of volumetrically equivalent lead does not reflect this manufacturing differential.

The high cost of steel shot is one of the major factors alienating hunters from using it. In addition, no reloading data nor components are as yet available to allow hunters to reload steel shot. Nor are there signs the ammunition manufacturers intend to make either available in the near future. As a consequence, the U.S. Fish and Wildlife Serv-

ice is seriously considering making steel shot reloading data available to the public. Perhaps, the public demand will cause steel-shot reloading components to be sold to reloaders. It may be that reloading is the only means waterfowl hunters have of reducing the current high cost of steel-shot ammunition.

Conclusions

Steel shot remains the only ballistically acceptable and economically feasible non-toxic substitute for lead shot. Current field research tends to indicate no significant differences in the ability of steel to bag ducks and geese when compared to lead. Current data indicate that steel shot will not harm the majority of shotguns and that the possibility of choke erosion exists only for a very limited number of full-choke guns.

Steel shot is lighter than lead, but maintains a higher form factor. Compensations can be made for steel's light weight by employing pellets two sizes larger than lead, and by driving steel at higher velocity levels than lead. When this is done, steel-shot loads become ballistically similar to lead-shot loads, and are capable of performing as well as lead-shot loads in bagging waterfowl at ranges of 70 yards.

Some old commercial steel-shot loads have been dropped. Improved factory steel-shot loads and reloading data for steel-shot loads may be forthcoming in 1979. Those steel-shot loads possessing the highest muzzle velocities tend to be the most desirable ballistically.

Fabrique Nationale's Browning Blowback Pistols
The Military Models 1899-1945, Part II

by John Walter

Editor's note: Part I of this two-part article on Fabrique Nationale's Blowback Pistols, Military Models, appeared in the 1979 SHOOTER'S BIBLE, No. 70, pp. 63-68.

The Pistols

Early in 1897, the commercial manager of Fabrique Nationale—who rejoined in the somewhat unlikely name of Hart O. Berg—was sent to the United States to discover if any improvements were being made in bicycle manufacture. During his travels in North America, Berg met the Browning brothers—one of whom, John M., had attained notoriety as the inventor of a variety of rifles and shotguns being marketed by the Winchester Repeating Arms Company, and a gas-operated machine gun being developed by Colt's Patent Fire Arms Manufacturing Company. Colt was also contemplating exploiting a number of pistols patented by Browning in 1895-7, as a result of an agreement signed on 24th July 1896. But though Browning had licensed US Patent 580923 —protecting an early blowback pistol design—to Colt, the latter had not proceeded with work on the grounds that no suitable American market existed and the rights to license the patent had reverted to the inventor.

Browning mentioned to Berg that he was interested in using the patent granted on the blowback pistol "dont le verrouillage était opéré par la masse" (in which the lock was operated by the weight), and Berg subsequently approached the FN Conseil d'Administration in June 1897. An agreement with Browning was signed in 17th July by Baron Charles de Marmol, the President of Fabrique Nationale. The company history pictures a receipt of money, dated 26th July 1897 and reading *Received of the Fabrique Nationale d'Armes de Guerre, Two thousand dollars ($2000⁰⁰). In payment on Automatic Pistol as per contract.* It is signed by the Browning brothers, John M. and Matthew S.

Though it took many months to perfect production methods—the first guns were not made in Belgium until 1898—the superiority of the perfected Browning blowback design was clearly evident from the start. It was adopted by the Belgian army in 1900, one of the first of its type to be officially adopted anywhere,[11] and the success of FN's pistol business was ensured.

Pistolets Automatiques Browning, Modèle 1899 and Modèle 1900.

On 10th July 1897, Colt's Patent Fire Arms Manufacturing Company was granted a British patent protecting the design of five different pistols. Four have been identified as Browning's work while the fifth, an aberrant "blow forward" pistol, has been credited to Carl J. Ehbets. The Brownings included the prototype of the later locked-breech designs, a gas-operated weapon based on the "Potato Digger" machine gun, and a simple blowback.

The blowback weapon was designed in 1894-5 and application for the corresponding US. Patent (590923) was made on 14th September 1895, though the grant of Letters Patent did not occur

The FN-Browning Mle 1903 9mm military blowback pistol was sold to Belgium, Sweden (as the m/07), Russia, Turkey, Paraguay and elsewhere. This example has a special tangentleaf back sight and was usually supplied with a holster-stock.

until 20th April 1897. By the time the printed patent specifications had appeared, Browning had refined the original design—with its internal bolt and "hinge-crank" recoil unit—until the bolt was carried inside a full-length one-piece slide, shown on U.S. Patent 590,926. A single example of each pistol is known to have been made,[1 2] and the gun sent to Fabrique Nationale in July 1897 was probably an additional "improved" example. Browning and FN undertook further improvement of the "1896" design and sought more patents in Europe in 1898. The application for the relevant British patent, 22,455/98, was made on 25th October by the patent agent Sidney Pitt, though the grant was delayed until 1st July 1899. However, a comparable German patent—DRP 101,077—dates from 6th February 1898.

The illustrations accompanying the patent specifications show a simple blowback of a type generally associated with the later Mle 1900 Browning —which, after all, was little more than a refinement of the later experimental models (1898-9) suited to mass production. The recoil spring was housed in a chamber above the barrel while the mechanism was extremely simple, contained very few parts and was easily made on uncomplicated machine tools.

Fabrique Nationale's records indicate that 3,900 pistols were made in 1899, most of which, after the production of a handful of experimental guns, were of what has come to be called the "Modèle 1899." This can be easily distinguished from the Mle 1900, though the external appearances are essentially similar, as it is larger and heavier. Cormack[13] records that the Mle 1899 was 183mm long, had a barrel measuring 122mm and weighed about 765gm —compared to 162mm, 102mm and 625gm for the smaller Mle 1900. The Mle 1899 also had a plain (rather than panelled) frame and lacked the lanyard ring inevitably found on the bottom left side of the Mle 1900 butt. Its grips were also much smaller than the "production pattern" of the Mle 1900.

The FN-Browning's success was greatly accelerated by the results of the Belgian army trials, in which it had been pitted against pistols such as the Mauser, the Bergmann Nr. 5, the Roth, the Borchardt and the Borchardt-Luger (Parabellum).[14] The Département de la Guerre decided to retain the "large and small Brownings",[15] the Borchardt-Luger and a Mannlicher for further tests, from which the smaller of the Brownings emerged the victor. The prototype form of the Mle 1900, therefore, was adopted on 3rd July 1900. Manufacture was naturally entrusted to Fabrique Nationale, and the guns were inspected and accepted by personnel of the Manufacture d'Armes de l'Etat.

Issues of the first Mle 1900 pistols—the initial contracts having apparently been for 20,000—were made to army officers, though their use was subsequently extended on several occasions. In October 1901, the pistols were issued to the gendarmerie and some mounted artillerymen; on 6th May 1905, to the non-commissioned officers of the élite cavalry. In October 1910, all the personnel still armed with the old Mle 76 and Mle 83 Nagant revolvers were ordered to exchange them for Browning pistols and issue was completed. Even the officers of the Garde Civique (civil guard) had received semi-automatic pistols by the beginning of the First World War.

Against such a background of official Belgian orders, the pistols sold very widely; in 1904, an article in the *Revue de l'Armée Belge* stated that *"Ce succes est dû à l'adoption de cette arme, par beaucoup de pays; pour des services publics, gendarmerie, police ou autres, et en outre par des milliers d'officiers de toutes nationalities."* (The success (of the FN-Browning) is due to its adoption by many countries; for the public services, the gendarmerie, police and others, and, furthermore, by many officers of all nationalities.)

Many countries tested the FN-Browning with a view to adopting it, including Britain and Sweden. In early October 1900, the British military attaché in Brussels reported that the Belgian army had adopted the Browning pistol; subsequently, the Small Arms Committee asked the attaché whether it was possible to increase the caliber of the gun to 10.2mm (0.40in), which was reckoned to meet

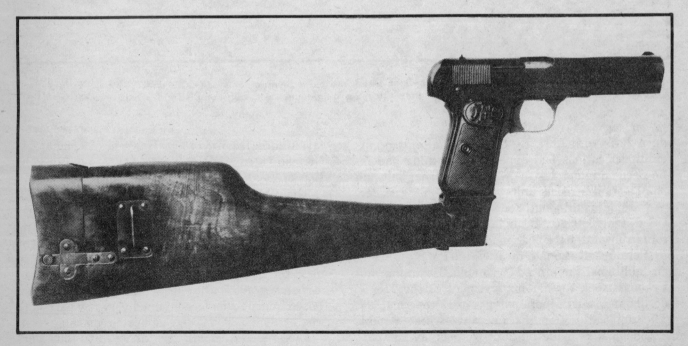

A Mle 1903 fitted with its wooden holster-stock.

the then-current British specification for a gun firing a 200gr bullet of 0.40in diameter at 1,200 fps. On 24th October, his enquiries complete, the attaché reported to the Director-General of Ordnance that FN's technicians doubted that the caliber of the Browning pistol could safely exceed 9mm. He also noted that the Belgian army experts, too, had been initially suspicious of a caliber as small as 7.65mm but had overcome their objections and acquired 4,500 (sic) for issue.

Ultimately, one example of the Mle 1899 and the Mle 1900, together with five hundred 7.65mm cartridges, arrived in Britain for trials. The pistols and their ammunition were given to the Chief Inspector of Small Arms (CISA) and a short trial of the Mle 1899 was undertaken in December 1900. Though only 80 rounds had been expended, the pistol was criticized for its poor penetration (only six or seven half-inch boards at 25yd), the light weight of its bullet—a miserable 4.8gm or 75gr—and its complicated field-stripping procedure. The CISA also recorded his opinion that the caliber was much too small for military use and that blowback principles could not be safely adapted to more powerful loads. No further action was taken.

The Mle 1900 pistol was subsequently tested by the Captain of the Naval School of Gunnery, HMS *Excellent*, in 1901 in comparison with the Mauser C 96, the service-pattern Webley revolver and the Borchardt pistol. (The last named was actually the 7.65mm 1900-model Parabellum, but the pre-1914 Small Arms Committee minutes persistently refer to it incorrectly.) The report from *Excellent*, which was contained in WO Paper 77/19/1459 and discussed in committee on 7th October 1901, noted the advantages of the FN-Browning as *Light and compact. Mechanism simple,* and its disadvantages as *Poor grip owing to handle being too close to trigger. Sighting arrangements require improvement. Pull-off rather heavy. Very small charge.* The Small Arms Committee noted *Excellent*'s report but decided that it did not ... *consider the Browning ... suitable for the Service, and recommends that no further action be taken.* These brief words ended the trials history of the Mle 1899 and Mle 1900 in Britain.

The character of the Swedish trials differed considerably. Held at the Infanteriskjutskolan—or infantry musketry school—in Rosersberg in 1903-4,[16] they became a straightforward contest in which two FN-Brownings were pitted against an assortment of other pistols, including Mannlichers, the Parabellum, a Frommer, a Swedish Hamilton and a

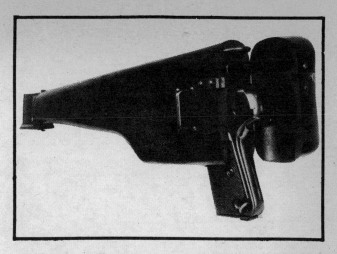

The holster-stock sold with the Mle 1903 pistol contained, as can be seen in this photograph, a compartment for a spare magazine and another for the cleaning rod.

Colt-Browning. The Mle 1900 Browning stood virtually no chance of adoption, since Fabrique Nationale had also submitted an example of the much-improved "försoksmödell 03" "fm/03"—or Mle 1903 FN-Browning. These trials ended when the Swedes adopted the fm/03 in 1907 and are described in greater detail in the section devoted to the Mle 1903.

Fabrique Nationale made the 100,000th Mle 1900 pistol in August 1904,[17] half a million had been made by 1909, and production was discontinued in 1910/11 at gun number 724,450. On Monday 2nd February 1914, the Liège newspaper *La Meuse* reported that the millionth Browning had been made on 10th June 1910[18]—most of which had been Mle 1900 specimens, though appreciable quantities of Mle 1903 and Mle 1906 guns were also included. The total aptly illustrates the amazing impact of the simple and reliable blowbacks.

The markings on the earliest Mle 1900 specimens included FABRIQUE NATIONALE HERSTAL LIEGE in a single line on the left side of the slide, immediately above a small cartouche containing a pistol and a scriptic FN monogram. The latter, together with BREVETE S.G.D.G. ("Sans Garantie de Gouvernement," without government guarantee), was struck into the raised panel milled on the left side of the frame. The serial numbers (most of those observed contained only three digits) appeared on the right side of the slide above the ejection port, on the right side of the backsight base, and on the right side of the frame directly in front of the ejection port. There was no internal duplication or repetition of all or even parts of the numbers. Proof

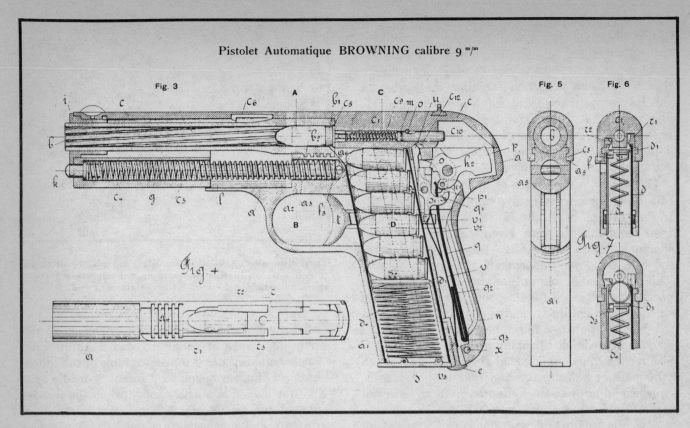

A longitudinal section of the Mle 1903, from the *Revue de l'Armée Belge*.

marks applied by the Liège house were struck into the left side of the frame, slide and backsight; while the words FEU (fire) and SÛR (safe) appeared alongside the safety lever, which rotated downwards to the "fire" position.

These initial revisions were quickly made to the external appearance of the FN-Browning pistol. These included a notable enlargement of the milled panels on the frame sides, which, instead of running backwards as far as the mid-point of the trigger guard bow, reach the *rear* of the guard. The grips were enlarged, the slide retraction grooves were widened and reduced in number from six to five, and the pattern on the head of the small safety lever was altered from concentric circles to conventional crosshatching. A lanyard loop was added to the base of the butt on the left side.

The markings were also revised; FABRIQUE NATIONALE D'ARMES de GUERRE HERSTAL BELGIQUE lay on the left side of the slide, above the cartouche (containing FN and a pistol) stamped into the raised panel on the left side of the frame above BROWNING'S-PATENT/BREVETE S.G.D.G. The safety and proof marks, together with the style and positioning of the serial numbers, remained unchanged.

Two types of grips have been identified. The earlier had a small molded-in cartouche depicting the Mle 1900 pistol and the company monogram, but was replaced by a simple monogram–only design somewhere in the region of gun number 625000-650000.[19]

A catalogue distributed by Manufacture Française d'Armes et Cycles of Saint-Etienne, dating from 1905-6, offered the standard Mle 1900 for 45 Francs, the same with engraved parts for 60 Francs, with pearl grips for 70, and engraved and inlaid—the "Modèle de Luxe"—for 100. A box of 25 cartridges was 2 Francs 75, spare magazines were 2 Francs 50, and two types of cases were available: "toile grenat, satin" and "beau cuir, velours" (red cloth-covered with a satin lining, or plush-lined with a leather covering). Each gun came with a screwdriver, a cleaning rod and three dummy cartridges. In comparison, MFAC was selling the 1900-model Parabellum for 110 Francs.

The 1911 catalogue distributed by A.L. Frank Exportgesellschaft of Hamburg ("ALFA") advertised the Mle 1900 for 60.80 Marks, the nickel-plated version for 63.13 Marks, the standard gun with pearl grips for 91.20, an engraved version with pearl grips for 106.40, and a nickel-finished gun with pearl grips for 93.53. The "Luxusmodell"—nickel-plated, engraved and pearl gripped—cost 108.73 Marks. The spare magazines were 2 Marks each, and the 1906-model Parabellum was 122 Marks.

Pistolet Automatique Browning, Modèle de 9mm or Modèle 1903.

Despite the outstanding success of the Mle 1900, it was clear that its design was not especially suited to military service and contained some features that could be improved. The position of the recoil spring above the barrel was one, and its use to actuate the striker was another.

Prototypes of the new gun had been made by June 1902, when the British military attaché in Brussels sent the Small Arms Committee a photograph, together with details of its cartridge—the so-called "9mm Browning Long"—which propelled a bullet of 110gr at 1100fs (7.1gm at 335m/sec). The development of the Mle 1903, as the gun came to be called, seems to have proceeded slowly: the specimen tested by the Swedish army in 1903-4 was, for example, entered as the "försöksmodell 03" or "experimental model 03." Towards the end of 1903, the *Revue de l'Armée Belge* reviewed the new FN-Browning. The article—"Le Pistolet Automatique Browning, Caliber 9mm"—opened by saying, *The question of the caliber of pistols, and also that of rifles, has long been the subject of controversy. The greatest difference of viewpoint is shown among the most distinguished and competent officers and technicians. The question is not resolved . . . and each side has taken viewpoints that are completely different. The caliber* [requirement] *naturally varies according to the special circumstances in which an arm is used, and it is for this reason that the English, for example, who are often required to fight uncivilized peoples, prefer to sacrifice—in a certain measure—the advantages of small-caliber weapons in sole favour of "stopping power"* [pouvoir d'arrêt]. *It is a response to these special conditions that the Fabrique Nationale d'Armes de Guerre, at Herstal-lèz-Liège, has decided to devise a large-model automatic pistol* ["pistolet automatique grand modèle"] *in 9mm caliber.*

The gun described by the *Revue*, from which the sectional drawings pictured here were taken, differed in many ways from the Mle 1899 and the Mle 1900. Apart from the radical external alterations—the Mle 1903 being the neater and of far more modern appearance—the recoil spring was moved from above to beneath the barrel, where it was compressed against the standing frame by the spring housing attached to the lower part of the slide. The recoil spring was guided by a half-length rod seated in a short tunnel cut into the standing frame below the chamber, and the barrel was anchored in the frame by five radial lugs. The trigger mechanism was radically altered to operate an internal hammer rather than a striker, though the hammer struck a spring-loaded firing pin protruding from the breechblock forged integrally with the slide. The Mle 1903[20] was a more powerful weapon than its FN-Browning predecessors, although sharing simple blowback operation. The *Revue de l'Armée Belge* notes the muzzle velocity as 340m/sec, which gave a muzzle energy of slightly under 44kpm (ie: 1,115fs and 320fp).

The mere fact that the Mle 1903 was a blowback caused its rejection by several armies—notably the British, who had refused even to entertain in its submission until the caliber had been increased to more than 0.40in and the bullet weight all but doubled. Many European countries, however, saw the semi-automatic pistol purely as a close-range defensive weapon and consequently favored simplicity at the expense of power. Sweden, Belgium, the Netherlands and others were among this group.

The Mle 1903, together with the obsolescent Mle 1900, was submitted to the Swedes in the autumn of 1903 and was tested at the Infanteriskjutskolan in Rosersberg (1903-4). Its rivals included the Parabellum, the Colt-Browning, a Mannlicher and a Mannlicher Karbin-Pistol, a Swedish Hamilton and the Frommer. All except the FN-Browning designs—which were known as the No. 1 and No. 2, or m/00 and fm/03—and the Hamilton were recoil operated and had breech locking systems. The extensive trials program contained accuracy, penetration, rust, sand and endurance experiments, and the FN-Browning No. 2 (or fm/03) emerged with much credit.

The Mle 1903 was also purchased in quantity by Belgium, by the Royal Netherlands army (as the Pistool M/1911[21]), by Russia and by Turkey. Small numbers are also said to have been purchased by the Danish army prior to the adoption of the Pistol m/1910, but, though small numbers were acquired for trials, any bulk purchases would have been intended for the police. Many private sales were made to military personnel—especially officers—in many European nations. In 1911, the Mle 1903 could be purchased in Germany, according to the contemporary ALFA catalogue, for 98.80 Marks. The price included a spare magazine, a screwdriver, a cleaning rod, three dummy cartridges and a cardboard box. Spare magazines each cost 4.80 Marks, while 114 bought the pistol complete with its detachable wooden holster-stock. The 1906 model Parabellum, by comparison, was then selling for 122 Marks. The pistol was sold under a number of different names; originally, at least, as the "Pistolet Automatique Browning, Grande Modèle," the "Pistolet Automatique Browning, Modèle de Guerre," or the "Pistolet Automatique Browning, Calibre 9mm." The Mle 1903 designation was added firstly by the Belgian army and then by some sections of the commercial market after the introduction of the Mle 1910 (qv). The 1911 ALFA catalogue makes no mention of the model date, but does not mention the Mle 1910 at all.

The standard Belgian FN-Browning Mle 1903 pistols bore FABRIQUE NATIONALE D'ARMES de GUERRE HERSTAL BELGIQUE/BROWNING'S-PATENT DEPOSE on the left side of the slide, together with Liège proof marks on the mid-point of the slide and the frame. The proofs were repeated on the right side of the barrel, being visible through the ejection port, and the master serial number lay on the right side of the frame above the trigger guard. It was repeated inside both grips, on the underside of the barrel beneath the breech, inside the hammer recess in the top rear of the slide, and on the left side of the barrel bushing. Small factory inspectors' marks appeared on some of the parts—Ⅴ and '6' on the trigger guard, for example.

The first Swedish m/07 pistols were purchased from Fabrique Nationale, but will often be found with Swedish government inspectors' marks (tiny crowns) on many of their parts and Swedish unit markings on the left side of the frame above the grip.[22] Later guns were made by Husqvarna, where 94,731 were made between 1917 and about 1941[23]: 88,586 for the army and 6,145 for export and private sale. Production began in Sweden because the Germans, occupying Belgium in the First World War, had cut off supplies of pistols to the Swedish army. Pistols were made for the army in every year except 1925, 1927-32 and 1934-7, the peaks being in 1918 and 1940. Small scale assembly continued until 1944. Their serial numbers ran from 1 to 102960, though about eight thousand numbers have yet to be accounted for. It seems likely that small batches of numbers were omitted, but research has still to be done to ascertain where these occurred. All Husqvarna-Brownings, with the exception of 80931-80945 which were unsuccessfully adapted for the 9mm Parabellum, chambered the 9mm Brown-

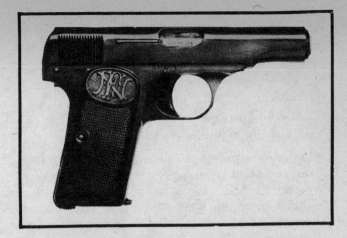
The FN-Browning Mle 1910 personal defense pistol, showing its clean lines.

ing Long round. The first guns were marked HUSQVARNA VAPENFABRIKS AKTIEBOLAG on the left side of the slide, though later guns added SYSTEM BROWNING below the company name. The serial numbers were placed similarly to the original Belgian type and unit markings are invariably found on the frame. The grips of Husqvarna-made guns have a "crowned h" moulding rather than an FN monogram, but the Swedish and Belgian products are otherwise very similar.

The Swedish m/07 pistols, whether made by Fabrique Nationale or Husqvarana, were issued with a lanyard ring, a lanyard (Pistolsnodd), a cleaning rod (Läskstång), three spare magazines, a leather holster (Pistolfodral) and a double-chambered oil bottle (Oljedosa).

Guns sold to Turkey bear the full Fabrique Nationale company marks and standard Liège proofs, but most also have an inscription in old Turkish script on the right side of the slide which, it is believed, translates as an army property mark. A "Russian" version has been reported with crossed Mosin-Nagant rifles on top of the slide, but its authenticity awaits verification even though Browning & Gentry [24] state that five thousand guns were sold to Russia in 1904. Small quantities were also sold to the Paraguayan army in about 1908, the pistols bearing an enrayed five-point star in a wreath and the legend REPUBLICA DEL PARAGUAY.[25] The encircled mark apparently lay on the top of the slide.

A special wooden holster-stock was sometimes provided for the Mle 1903. Its body had a hinged lid which, when opened, revealed compartments for a spare magazine and the cleaning rod; and which was closed by a checkered-head spring steel bar that locked over a second bar inlet in the stock body. The photographs show its position and construction more clearly. The steel stock tip slid onto rails machined along the bottom edge of the butt and was locked in place by a spring catch. To capitalize on the better accuracy obtainable from stock-fitted pistols, Fabrique Nationale made some tangent-leaf back sights to be mounted on top of the Mle 1903 slide. Needless to say, these, graduated from 200 to 1,000 metres in 100m increments, were of very little value on a low powered blowback pistol[26] and very few were produced.

The production total of Mle 1903 pistols seems to have been 153,173, since 94,731 were made by Husqvarna and 58,422[27] by Fabrique Nationale. Manufacture is believed to have ceased in Belgium in 1909—though Browning & Gentry record the date as 1939, which may be a misprint. Husqvarna, however, continued to make m/07 Brownings for the Swedish army until the 1940s.

Pistolet Automatique Browning, Modèle 1910.

By 1908-9, Browning and Fabrique Nationale had realized that not only was their basic pocket pistol capable of improvement but also that the then-current market conditions (and the introduction of "improved" competitors) demanded a new design if FN was to remain a world leader in blowback semi-automatic pistol technology. The result was the Mle 1910, patented in 1909[28] to become another in a long line of outstanding successes—as a million had been sold by 1936, according to the company's prewar sales literature.

The Mle 1910 differed considerably from its FN-Browning predecessors in its external appearance and internal layout. The old recoil spring assembly, which had lain parallel to the axis of the bore (above the barrel in the Mle 1899 and Mle 1900, beneath it in the Mle 1903 and Mle 1906) was replaced by a coil spring concentric with the barrel itself. The barrel acted as the spring guide, compression being obtained by a special bushing held in the front of the slide by a bayonet joint. This pushed the spring back against the barrel shoulder. The striker firing system and the basic Mle 1906 trigger mechanism were retained, though the parts were redesigned to make their movement smoother and shorten the lock time. A new magazine safety —always a feature of questionable utility—was developed and the grip safety was retained.

The lines of the pistol were refined until they resulted in one of the cleanest and most elegant guns of its class ever to be introduced.[29] The basic design of the Mle 1910 was such that the caliber could be changed from 7.65mm ACP to 9mm ACP simply by replacing the barrel, the recoil spring, and the magazine. As the gun was very easily dismantled, and as the barrels were retained in the frame by a series of simple transverse ribs, the change from one caliber to the other could be accomplished quite literally in seconds.

Markings included FABRIQUE NATIONALE D'ARMES de GUERRE, HERSTAL-BELGIQUE over BROWNING'S-PATENT DEPOSE in two lines of serifed type on the left side of the slide, and a master serial number struck into the right side of the frame above the trigger. The latter was repeated on the underside of the slide alongside the striker channel, on the left side of the barrel by the breech and on the inner surface of the grip safety lever. Liège proof marks appeared on the mid-point of the left side of the frame and slide, and on the right side of the barrel(where they were visible through the ejection port) together with the caliber designation CAL $7^m/_m65$ or CAL $9^m/_m00$. Small inspectors' letters —M, J, etc.—were to be found on the major parts and the company monogram was molded into the plastic grips.

Several variations in the style and content of the slide legend have been noted, though work has yet to be done to establish their significance and chronology. The earliest type, as has been mentioned, made use of serified type with "de" in the upper line and a space between the words PATENT and DEPOSE in the lower. However, several pistols which apparently[30] date to the mid 1920s have been seen with wide inscriptions in sans-serif type[31]; these, assumed to be a "second" pattern, read FABRIQUE NATIONALE D'ARMES DE GUERRE S.A. HERSTAL BELGIQUE over the patent note. The top line ran for virtually the entire length of the slide from muzzle to retraction grooves. This style seems to have been replaced by a similar but narrower sans-serif inscription reading FABRIQUE NATIONALE D'ARMES DE GUERRE-HERSTAL-BELGIQUE over BROWNING'S PATENT DEPOSE; this was approximately the same width as the original (from the front of the frame to some way short of the retraction grooves), but replaced "de" with "DE" and eliminated the space between PATENT and DEPOSE. There may also be other variations.

The Modèle 1910, later known simply as the "Mle 10", remained in production until the Germans invaded Belgium in 1940 and reappeared in the mid 1950s. The slide markings on the modern guns include a mid-width FABRIQUE NATIONALE D'ARMES DE

GUERRE HERSTAL-BELGIQUE over the patent mark. In 1966, the Mle 10 imported into the USA by the Browning Arms Company[32] cost $54.75, while the "Renaissance" engraved version was $149.75. A 9mm ACP Llama then cost $48.00, and the Beretta Cougar was $52.95.

Browning & Gentry record that 572,590 Mle 1910 and Mle 10 had been sold by 1961, but it is assumed that this figure excludes any weapons assembled under German supervision.

Pistolet Automatique Browning, Modele 1910/22 (or 10/22).

The Mle 10/22 was a minor variant of the Mle 1910, from which it differed principally in the length of its barrel and the depth of its grip. It had been designed in response to an order for sixty thousand 9mm ACP pistols, and six million suitable cartridges, which had been placed with FN by the government "du royaume des Serbes, Croates et Slovenes"[33] on 23rd February 1923. The Mle 10/22 honored the contract requirements so far as barrel length and cartridge capacity were concerned, while using as many Mle 1910 parts and as much of the Mle 1910 production line as possible. The 1923 order was insufficient to justify developing an entirely new gun.

Fabrique Nationale's Bureau d'Etudes (design office) solved the problems in an ingenious way: the Mle 1910 barrel was lengthened and the slide was extended by a light sheet-steel shroud, attached to the muzzle by a bayonet joint and locked by a sliding springloaded catch on the lower left side of the slide/extension joint. The butt was lengthened to accomodate a longer magazine, a blade pattern front sight was attached to the slide extension, a standing V-notch open back sight was added to the rear of the slide and a lanyard ring to the bottom left side of the butt.

The contract for the Kingdom of Serbs, Croats and Slovenes was fulfilled by 1925, and orders were subsequently obtained from the Royal Netherlands army in about 1926-8[34] and Yugoslavia in the early 1930s.[35] The Mle 10/22 pistol was also marketed commercially in 7.65mm ACP and 9mm ACP chamberings; several hundred thousand were made, and production continued under German control after the invasion of Belgium in 1940—until the Allies reoccupied the Herstal factory in September 1944. Belgian production recommenced in the 1950s but finally ceased in about 1959. The earliest examples of Mle 10/22 had slides with the oldstyle serifed inscription FABRIQUE NATIONALE D'ARMES DE GUERRE HERSTAL BELGIQUE over BROWNING'S DEPOSE on the left side. The old Liège proof marks were to be found on the mid-point of the left side of the slide and frame, and sometimes on the side of the barrel above the serial number and caliber designation CAL $7^m/_m65$ or CAL $9^m/_m$. However, the smaller caliber mark seems to have been used very rarely; unmarked 7.65mm guns seem to have been the rule rather than the exception, since the 9mm variety was much scarcer. Factory inspectors' marks, such as FN over M, were to be found on parts such as the trigger-guard bow.

The master serial number initially appeared on the right side of the frame above the trigger and was repeated in full on the right side of the barrel shroud, inside the upper rear of the slide and often on the right side of the barrel above the caliber mark. Consequently, the serial number and the caliber designation were usually visible through the ejection port.

Pistols made after the early 1930s bore a revised sans-serif inscription FABRIQUE NATIONALE D'ARMES DE GUERRE-HERSTAL-BELGIQUE over the usual patent mark; though it occupied much the same width as its predecessor, the space between the words PATENT and DEPOSE was eliminated.

The pistols made for Yugoslavia bore the standard FN marks and Belgian proofs, but the majority of those examined bore Cyrillic markings on the right side of the receiver. These, which included a repetition of the master serial number, usually translate as "Officers" or "State Troops", but Mathews[36] illustrates one bearing property marks applied by the Split police department. It has been suggested that the first sixty thousand pistols sent to the Yugoslavs—apparently numbered from 1—were made with special grips, though those examined, their numbers ranging from 5778 to 49356, all had the standard FN monogram pattern. However, pistol 62420, pictured by Smith & Smith in *Small Arms of The World* does have grips displaying three encircled pictograms—from top to bottom, a double-headed eagle (from the Serbian coat of arms), a crown and a "wild man" carrying a club. Unfortunately, no other examples of this grip have yet been reported; it seems plausible that a few thousand guns could have been so altered for élite units—though the slide markings on the "Smith" gun is quite standard. But it seems from the photograph that the frame number does not match the slide number, which in turn differs from those on the barrel and muzzle extension; which resolves none of the problems. The grips may not have been made by FN, but added in Yugoslavia for special (but still unkown) purposes.

The second Yugoslav contract consisted of standard FN guns in the low 200,000s (227,033 and 231,260, for example), all of which had standard FN monogram grips. They were supplied at random from commercial production [37] The marks FN and S appeared in the trigger guards, in addition to other inspectors' marks.

The pistols acquired by the Koninklijke Nederlandse Leger during the 1920s and 1930s bore standard Fabrique Nationale marks and Belgian proofs. Most bore a large crowned 'W' cipher of the Belgian Queen of the Netherlands, Wilhelmina, on the slide or frame.

Production of the Mle 10/22 continued under German control between 1940 and August 1944, when the Germans, under pressure from the approaching Allies, withdrew from Herstal. During the occupation, 363,200 pistols were accepted by the Heereswaffenamt. Yearly production, according to Whittington, [38] amounted to 200 in 1940, 45,000 in 1941, 69,000 in 1942, 166,000 in 1943 and 83,000 in 1944. The Mle 10/22 was given the Fremdengeräte[39] designations Pistole 626(b), in 7.65mm ACP caliber, or Pistole 641(b) in 9mm ACP. Their slides were marked FABRIQUE NATIONALE D'ARMES DE GUERRE HERSTAL BELGIQUE/BROWNING'S PATENT DEPOSE on the left side, while the inspectors' marks of the Heerewaffenamt sub-bureaus 103, 140 or 613 were struck into various parts such as slide, frame and barrel. Whittington states that . . . serial numbers were a continuation of those numbers of the Belgian weapons, which had approached 70,000. Use of digits continued above 100,000 and even 200,000 without a letter. The majority of the numbers were reduced to a maximum of five digits with a small letter added—a with the second 100,000, b with the third 100,000, and c when production exceeded 300,000. Examples of tabulated numbers with and without letters are as follows:

WITHOUT LETTERS	WITH LETTERS
73041	9985a (actually 109985)
156295	328b (actually 200328)
204337	19924c (actually 319924)

Despite this claim, it will be seen that a disparity exists. The total number of guns that could have been made under the "Whittington system", even assuming the serial numbers run as high as 99999c, [40] could scarcely have exceeded 330,000—that is, the remaining 30,000 in the 'Belgian serial number block' below 100,000, and three completed blocks of a hundred thousand each (a, b and c suffixes). This does not tally with the official HWaA procurement figures of 363,200; and Fabrique Nationale had made at least two hundred thousand Mle 10/22 pistols prior to the German invasion, since guns delivered to Yugoslavia in the early 1930s have been seen with numbers as high as 231,260. It is believed, therefore, that the Germans recommenced production at number 1 and ran onwards to about 63,200c (ie: 363,200). It is true that the serial suffix letters were not applied consistently and that some guns in the second block, for instance, were numbered in the form '165,437' while others in the same group were '65,437a'.

The HWaA procured many more 7.65mm than 9mm Mle 10/22 pistols, the latter being made only until the supplies of existing parts were exhausted. The quality of guns made in the early years of German control was generally quite good, but deteriorated rapidly after 1942. Many guns from this era exhibit rough machining marks and coarsely checkered wooden grips.

Browning & Gentry state that by 1961, 396,865 Mle 10/22 pistols had been made, but this clearly excludes the several hundred thousand made during the Second World War under German supervision.

Acknowledgments

This article could not have been written without the co-operation of Fabrique Nationale, from whom most of the illustrations were obtained. In addi-

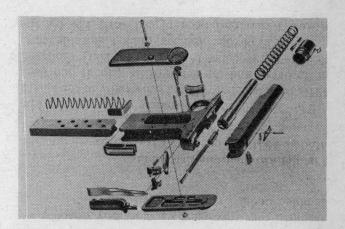

The FN-Browning Mle 10/22 was a derivative of the Mle 1910, achieved by lengthening the barrel and fitting an extension to the slide. It was used by several armies — including those of the Netherlands and Yugoslavia — and production was continued under German control during the Second World War.

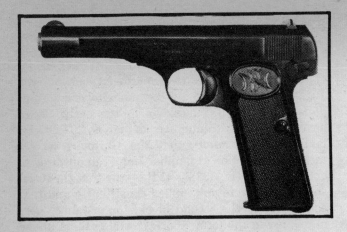

The Mle 10/22.

tion, Eric Claëssen, once of FFV Sport AB (successors to Husqvarna Våpenfabrik), supplied as much information as he could concerning the production history of the Swedish m/07 Browning pistol. However, in no sense has the work been officially sanctioned by FN or any other interested parties, and the opinions remain substantially my own: mistakes, therefore, are also my responsibility.

© John Walter and The Lyon Press, 1977.

Footnotes

11. The Italian *navy* adopted the Mauser in 1899. The Belgians accepted the Browning on 3rd July 1900; but the Swiss had taken the Parabellum on 4th May.

12. These are pictured in Donald B. Brady's *Colt Automatic Pistols, 1896-1955*, p. 270.

13. A.J.R. Cormack, 'Browning Pistols and the Hi-Power', in *Small Arms in Profile*, vol. 1, p. 22.

14. The results of which may be found summarized in John Walter, *Luger*, p. 52. See also contemporary issues of the *Revue de l'Armée Belge*.

15. Presumed to have been one example of the Mle 1899 and one of the Mle 1900.

16. The results are summarized in the *Artilleri Tidskrift*, 1904, pp. 195-207; and in John Walter, *Luger*, pp. 65-7.

17. John Browning and Curt Gentry, *John M. Browning, American Gunmaker*, p. 289.

18. A.J.R. Cormack, *Small Arms in Profile*, vol. 1, p. 22, wrongly states that the millionth Mle 1900 pistol was made in June 1912 — by which time production had ceased.

19. Guns 550542 and 623747 have old grips; 650342 and 703712 the new. But there may well have been an overlap.

20. It had, however, been developed and patented in 1902.

21. The Dutch also tentatively adopted the Parabellum in 1911, though the intended purchases never took place. It is believed that the Parabellum would have been issued as the "Pistol M/1911 No. 1", and the Browning as the "Pistol M/1911 No. 2".

22. These take the form 'I15 N° 779' — the 779th gun issued to the 15th infantry regiment (Alvsborgs Regemente).

23. These figures appear through the kindness of Eric Claëssen, but should be considered as unofficial. Most of the original records have been lost.

24. John Browning & Curt Gentry, *John M. Browning, American Gunmaker*, p. 291.

25. J. Howard Mathews, *Firearms Identification*, vol. 3, p. 711.

26. Compare the accuracy figures obtained from a rest during the 1903-4 Swedish trials (qv) with the chances of hitting a man at 1,000m!

27. *John M. Browning, American Gunmaker*, p. 292.

28. The Belgian patent was granted on 20th July 1909.

29. This, of course, is a purely personal opinion. The title may be shared with the Pedersen-designed Remington Model 51 and a few others.

30. According to their serial numbers.

31. That is to say, letters such as R rather than R.

32. These have grips marked BROWNING, slides marked BROWNING ARMS COMPANY ST LOUIS Mo. & MONTREAL P.Q. over MADE IN BELGIUM, and are sold as "Browning .380 Automatic Pistols".

33. The 'Kingdom of Serbs, Croats and Slovenes', which became Yugoslavia in 1929.

34. This is assumed to have been placed at about the same time the Netherlands sought Parabellums from DWM in 1928. The FN-Brownings were issued as 'M25 No. 2' pistols.

35. The FN company history notes that the second Yugoslav and the Dutch orders totalled 40,000 guns.

36. A. J. Howard Mathews, *Firearms Identification*, vol. 3, p. 279.

37. Since pistol number 227048 was a standard commercial example.

38. R. D. Whittington, *German Pistols and Holsters, 1933/1945*, p. 120.

39. A list of foreign military equipment, drawn up by German military intelligence before the Second World War and numbered to a master sequence.

40. The highest number reported during research has been 54851c.

Reference

Where to Hunt What in the U.S. and Canada: A Guide for All Who Hunt with Gun or Camera

(The name of an animal in italics indicates that it is one of the most popular species sought in that state or province.)

United States

Alabama
Deer, rabbit, squirrel, *bobwhite quail*, *mourning dove* and waterfowl.

Alaska
Moose, *caribou*, *Dall sheep*, mountain goat, grizzly bear, brown bear, black bear, polar bear, deer, elk, bison, musk ox, wolf, snowshoe hare, arctic hare, seal, walrus, ptarmigan, grouse and waterfowl.

Arizona
Mule deer, *white-tailed deer*, elk, pronghorn antelope, *javelina*, black bear, cougar, quail, *white-winged dove*, wild turkey, band-tailed pigeon and waterfowl.

Arkansas
Deer, rabbit, *squirrel*, duck, wild turkey, *mourning dove* and *bobwhite quail*.

California
Mule deer, elk, pronghorn antelope, black bear, wild boar, rabbit, squirrel, *dove*, *waterfowl*, *quail*, *pheasant*, chukar, Hungarian partridge, grouse, wild turkey and pigeon.

Colorado
Elk, *mule deer*, bighorn sheep, pronghorn antelope, black bear, cougar, waterfowl, pheasant, chukar, grouse, quail and mourning dove.

Connecticut
Rabbit, squirrel, raccoon, *ruffed grouse* and woodcock.

Delaware
Deer, rabbit, squirrel, *waterfowl*, bobwhite quail, mourning dove and woodcock.

Florida
Deer, wild hog, cottontail rabbit, marsh rabbit, *gray squirrel*, fox squirrel, *bobwhite quail*, wild turkey, *waterfowl* and *mourning dove*.

Georgia
Deer, rabbit, squirrel, *bobwhite quail*, mourning dove, ruffed grouse, woodcock, wild turkey and waterfowl.

Hawaii
Feral sheep, wild goat, wild pig, deer, barred dove, lace-necked dove, mourning dove, ring-necked pheasant, chukar, francolin and quail.

Idaho
Mule deer, white-tailed deer, elk, mountain sheep, mountain goat, moose, pronghorn antelope, black bear, cottontail rabbit, snowshoe hare, jack rabbit, *pheasant*, Hungarian partridge, chukar, quail, grouse, dove, wild turkey and waterfowl.

Illinois
Rabbit, squirrel, deer, *mourning dove*, *quail*, pheasant, *duck* and *goose*.

Indiana
Rabbit, *squirrel*, deer, pheasant and quail.

Iowa
Squirrel, *cottontail rabbit*, deer, *pheasant*, *quail*, Hungarian partridge, ruffed grouse and waterfowl.

Kansas
Cottontail rabbit, jack rabbit, fox squirrel, gray squirrel, *waterfowl*, *pheasant*, *prairie chicken* and *quail*.

Kentucky
Deer, *gray squirrel*, rabbit, red fox, *mourning dove*, quail, wild turkey, ruffed grouse and goose.

Louisiana
White-tailed deer, fox squirrel, gray squirrel, swamp rabbit, cottontail rabbit, *mourning dove*, *bobwhite quail*, *waterfowl* and wild turkey.

Maine
White-tailed deer, *black bear*, snowshoe hare, squirrel, ruffed grouse, pheasant, *woodcock*, snipe, rail and *black duck*.

Maryland
Deer, *squirrel*, *rabbit*, *waterfowl*, *mourning dove*, quail and ruffed grouse.

Massachusetts
Deer, squirrel, rabbit, *pheasant*, ruffed grouse, quail, waterfowl, snipe, rail and woodcock.

Michigan
Deer, bear, squirrel, rabbit, *ruffed grouse*, woodcock, waterfowl, *pheasant* and quail.

Minnesota
Deer, moose, black bear, squirrel, snowshoe hare, rabbit, *pheasant*, *ruffed grouse*, *waterfowl*, sharp-tailed grouse and woodcock.

Mississippi
White-tailed deer, *gray squirrel*, fox squirrel, cottontail rabbit, swamp rabbit, *bobwhite quail*, *mourning dove*, *wild turkey* and waterfowl.

Missouri
Deer, *squirrel*, *cottontail rabbit*, swamp rabbit, *bobwhite quail*, dove, wild turkey and waterfowl.

Montana
Elk, *mule deer*, white-tailed deer, pronghorn antelope, mountain goat, mountain sheep, moose, black bear, pheasant, grouse, Hungarian partridge, chukar, wild turkey and waterfowl.

Nebraska
White-tailed deer, mule deer, pronghorn antelope, cottontail rabbit, squirrel, *ring-necked pheasant*, bobwhite quail, sharp-tailed grouse, prairie chicken, *waterfowl* and *wild turkey*.

Nevada
Mule deer, elk, pronghorn antelope, desert bighorn sheep, cougar, cottontail rabbit, jack rabbit, mourning dove, chukar, quail, grouse and waterfowl.

New Hampshire
Deer, *black bear*, rabbit, snowshoe hare, gray squirrel, raccoon, *ruffed grouse* and *woodcock*.

New Jersey
Deer, squirrel, *cottontail rabbit*, quail, pheasant, ruffed grouse, woodcock, *waterfowl* and rail.

New Mexico
Mule deer, white-tailed deer, elk, pronghorn antelope, javelina, black bear, cougar, squirrel, cottontail rabbit, wild turkey, quail, mourning dove, sandhill crane and waterfowl.

New York
Deer, black bear, rabbit, snowshoe hare, squirrel, *ruffed grouse*, *pheasant*, wild turkey, woodcock and waterfowl.

North Carolina
Deer, black bear, wild boar, rabbit, *squirrel*, *mourning dove*, quail, ruffed grouse, wild turkey and *waterfowl*.

North Dakota
White-tailed deer, mule deer, pronghorn antelope, fox squirrel, gray squirrel, cottontail rabbit, jack rabbit, *sharp-tailed grouse*, duck, Hungarian partridge, sage grouse, ruffed grouse, pheasant and wild turkey.

Ohio
Deer, *rabbit*, *squirrel*, raccoon, ruffed grouse, *pheasant*, Hungarian partridge, quail, waterfowl and wild turkey.

Oklahoma
White-tailed deer, mule deer, fox squirrel, gray squirrel, cottontail rabbit, jack rabbit, *bobwhite quail*, mourning dove, prairie chicken, *wild turkey* and waterfowl.

Oregon
Black-tailed deer, *mule deer*, *elk*, black bear, rabbit, squirrel, *waterfowl*, *pheasant*, *chukar*, Hungarian partridge, quail, grouse, wild turkey, *band-tailed pigeon* and mourning dove.

Pennsylvania
Deer, *black bear*, squirrel, rabbit, woodcock, mourning dove, *wild turkey*, waterfowl, ruffed grouse, quail and pheasant.

Rhode Island
Deer, *cottontail rabbit*, snowshoe hare, *squirrel*, pheasant, quail, ruffed grouse and waterfowl.

South Carolina
Deer, rabbit, squirrel, *quail*, *mourning dove*, wild turkey and waterfowl.

South Dakota
White-tailed deer, mule deer, pronghorn antelope, mountain goat, cottontail rabbit, fox squirrel, gray squirrel, *ring-necked pheasant*, sharp-tailed grouse, bobwhite quail, Hungarian partridge, mourning dove, jacksnipe, prairie chicken, sage grouse, Hungarian partridge, wild turkey and waterfowl.

Tennessee
Deer, wild boar, *squirrel*, *rabbit*, *mourning dove*, ruffed grouse, *quail* and waterfowl.

Texas
White-tailed deer, *mule deer*, javelina, cottontail rabbit, jack rabbit, squirrel, *mourning dove*, *bobwhite quail*, *scaled quail*, ring-necked pheasant, wild turkey, prairie chicken, prairie grouse and waterfowl.

Utah
Mule deer, elk, moose, pronghorn antelope, desert bighorn sheep, cougar, squirrel, snowshoe hare, jack rabbit, cottontail rabbit, *pheasant*, mourning dove, chukar, grouse, quail and *waterfowl*.

Vermont
White-tailed deer, black bear, cottontail rabbit, snowshoe hare, raccoon, gray squirrel, *ruffed grouse*, woodcock and waterfowl.

Virginia
Deer, black bear, *squirrel*, *rabbit*, *bobwhite quail*, *mourning dove*, ruffed grouse, wild turkey and waterfowl.

Washington
Deer, elk, mountain goat, black bear, cougar, rabbit, *pheasant*, quail, chukar, Hungarian partridge, grouse, dove, band-tailed pigeon, wild turkey and *waterfowl*.

West Virginia
Deer, rabbit, squirrel, *ruffed grouse*, woodcock, mourning dove and *quail*.

Wisconsin
Deer, black bear, rabbit, squirrel, fox, *ruffed grouse*, sharp-tailed grouse, Hungarian partridge, pheasant and woodcock.

Wyoming
Mule deer, *white-tailed deer*, *elk*, antelope, moose, mountain sheep, mountain goat, bear, *pheasant*, *chukar*, Hungarian partridge, *sage grouse*, wild turkey and waterfowl.

Canada
Alberta
Mule deer, white-tailed deer, *moose*, elk, mountain sheep, caribou, mountain goat, antelope, grizzly bear, black bear, cottontail rabbit, snowshoe hare, jack rabbit, *waterfowl*, pheasant. Hungarian partridge, *sharp-tailed grouse*, *ruffed grouse*, blue grouse, spruce grouse and ptarmigan.

British Columbia
Mule deer, *black-tailed deer*, white-tailed deer, *moose*, mountain goat, Dall sheep, Stone sheep, bighorn sheep, elk, caribou, grizzly bear, black bear, cougar, wolf, coyote, wolverine, fox, snowshoe hare, grouse, ptarmigan, *waterfowl*, mourning dove, pheasant, California quail, Hungarian partridge and chukar.

Manitoba
White-tailed deer, *moose*, elk, woodland caribou, black bear, snowshoe hare, fox, wolf, lynx, wolverine, *sharp-tailed grouse*, spruce grouse, ruffed grouse, ptarmigan grouse, Hungarian partridge, pheasant, wild turkey and *waterfowl*.

New Brunswick
White-tailed deer, moose, black bear, snowshoe hare, ruffed grouse, spruce grouse, *woodcock* and waterfowl.

Newfoundland and Labrador
Moose, *caribou*, black bear, snowshoe hare, arctic hare, *ptarmigan*, spruce grouse, ruffed grouse and waterfowl.

Northwest Territories
Black bear, grizzly bear, *moose*, *caribou*, Dall sheep, mountain goat, wolf, wolverine, *waterfowl*, *ptarmigan* and *grouse*.

Nova Scotia
White-tailed deer, black bear, moose, *snowshoe hare*, *ruffed grouse*, pheasant, Hungarian partridge, woodcock and *waterfowl*.

Ontario
White-tailed deer, *moose*, black bear, cottontail rabbit, snowshoe hare, *ruffed grouse*, spruce grouse, sharp-tailed grouse, ptarmigan, Hungarian partridge, pheasant, bobwhite quail, *waterfowl* and woodcock.

Prince Edward Island
Snowshoe hare, red fox, woodcock, Wilson's snipe, ruffed grouse, Hungarian partridge, ring-necked pheasant and *waterfowl*.

Quebec
White-tailed deer, *moose*, caribou, black bear, snowshoe hare, *ruffed grouse*, spruce grouse, sharp-tailed grouse, ptarmigan, Hungarian partridge and *waterfowl*.

Saskatchewan
Mule deer, white-tailed deer, *moose*, elk, caribou, antelope, black bear, cottontail rabbit, snowshoe hare, jack rabbit, fox, coyote, *waterfowl*, *sharp-tailed grouse*, ruffed grouse, spruce grouse, *Hungarian partridge*, pheasant and ptarmigan.

Yukon Territory
Black bear, grizzly bear, polar bear, *moose*, *caribou*, Dall sheep, Stone sheep, snowshoe hare, arctic hare, *grouse*, ptarmigan and waterfowl.

Federal, State and Provincial Agencies Concerned with Wildlife Protection and Exploitation

FEDERAL GOVERNMENT

Bureau of Sport Fisheries and Wildlife
Fish and Wildlife Service
Department of the Interior
18th and C Streets, N.W.
Washington, D.C. 20240

Environmental Protection Agency
401 M Street, S.W.
Washington, D.C. 20460

Forest Service
Department of Agriculture
Building E
Rosslyn Plaza
Rosslyn, Virginia 22209

Migratory Bird Conservation
    Commission
Department of the Interior Building
Washington, D.C. 20240

National Zoological Park
Smithsonian Institution
Adams Mill Rd.
Washington, D.C. 20009

STATE GOVERNMENTS

ALABAMA
Game and Fish Division
Department of Conservation and
    Natural Resources
64 North Union Street
Montgomery, Alabama 36104

ALASKA
Department of Fish and Game
Subport Building
Juneau, Alaska 99801

ARIZONA
Game and Fish Department
2222 West Greenway Road
Phoenix, Arizona 85023

ARKANSAS
Game and Fish Commission
Game and Fish Commission Building
Little Rock, Arkansas 72201

CALIFORNIA
Department of Fish and Game
Resources Agency
1416 Ninth Street
Sacramento, California 95814

Wildlife Conservation Board
Resources Agency
1416 Ninth Street
Sacramento, California 95814

COLORADO
Division of Wildlife
Department of Natural Resources
6060 Broadway
Denver, Colorado 80216

CONNECTICUT
Fish and Wildlife Unit
Department of Environmental
    Protection
State Office Building
165 Capitol Avenue
Hartford, Connecticut 06115

DELAWARE
Division of Fish and Wildlife
Department of Natural Resources and
    Environmental Control
Tatnall Building
Legislative Avenue and D Street
Dover, Delaware 19901

DISTRICT OF COLUMBIA
Department of Environmental Services
1875 Connecticut Avenue, N.W.
Washington, D.C. 20009

FLORIDA
Game and Fresh Water Fish
    Commission
Farris Bryant Building
620 South Meridian Street
Tallahassee, Florida 32304

GEORGIA
Game and Fish Division
Department of Natural Resources
270 Washington Street, S.W.
Atlanta, Georgia 30334

HAWAII
Fish and Game Division
Department of Land and Natural
    Resources
1179 Punchbowl Street
Honolulu, Hawaii 96813

IDAHO
Fish and Game Department
600 South Walnut
P.O. Box 25
Boise, Idaho 83707

ILLINOIS
Wildlife Resources Division
Department of Conservation
605 State Office Building
400 South Spring Street
Springfield, Illinois 62706

INDIANA
Fish and Wildlife Division
Department of Natural Resources
State Office Building
Indianapolis, Indiana 46204

Land, Forests, and Wildlife
Resources Advisory Council
Department of Natural Resources
State Office Building
Indianapolis, Indiana 46204

IOWA
Fish and Wildlife Division
Conservation Commission
300 Fourth Street
Des Moines, Iowa 50319

KANSAS
Forestry, Fish and Game Commission
P.O. Box 1028
Pratt, Kansas 67124

KENTUCKY
Department of Fish and Wildlife
    Resources
State Office Building Annex
Frankfort, Kentucky 40601

LOUISIANA
Game Division
Wildlife and Fisheries Commission
Box 44095
Capitol Station
Baton Rouge, Louisiana 70804

MAINE
Department of Inland Fisheries
    and Game
284 State Street
Augusta, Maine 04330

MARYLAND
Wildlife Administration
Department of Natural Resources
Tawes State Office Building
580 Taylor Avenue
Annapolis, Maryland 21401

MASSACHUSETTS
Department of Natural Resources
Leverett Saltonstall Building
100 Cambridge Street
Boston, Massachusetts 02202

MICHIGAN
Wildlife Division
Department of Natural Resources
Mason Building
Lansing, Michigan 48926

MINNESOTA
Game and Fish Division
Department of Natural Resources
Centennial Office Building
St. Paul, Minnesota 55155

MISSISSIPPI
Game and Fish Commission
Game and Fish Building
402 High Street
P.O. Box 451
Jackson, Mississippi 39205

MISSOURI
Game Division
Department of Conservation
2901 North Ten Mile Drive
P.O. Box 180
Jefferson City, Missouri 65101

MONTANA
Game Management Division
Department of Fish and Game
Helena, Montana 59601

NEBRASKA
Game and Parks Commission
2200 North 33rd Street
P.O. Box 30370
Lincoln, Nebraska 68503

NEVADA
Department of Fish and Game
P.O. Box 10678
Reno, Nevada 89510

NEW HAMPSHIRE
Game Management and Research
    Division
Department of Fish and Game
34 Bridge Street
Concord, New Hampshire 03301

NEW JERSEY
Wildlife Management Bureau
Fish, Game and Shellfisheries Division
Department of Environmental
    Protection
Labor and Industry Building
P.O. Box 1809
Trenton, New Jersey 08625

NEW MEXICO
Game Management Division
Department of Game and Fish
State Capitol
Sante Fe, New Mexico 87503

NEW YORK
Division of Fish and Wildlife
Department of Environmental
    Conservation
50 Wolf Road
Albany, New York 12233

NORTH CAROLINA
Wildlife Resources Commission
Albermarle Building
325 North Salisbury Street
P.O. Box 27687
Raleigh, North Carolina 27611

NORTH DAKOTA
Department of Game and Fish
2121 Lovett Avenue
Bismarck, North Dakota 58505

OHIO
Wildlife Division
Department of Natural Resources
1500 Dublin Road
Columbus, Ohio 43224

OKLAHOMA
Department of Wildlife Conservation
1801 North Lincoln Boulevard
P.O. Box 53465
Oklahoma City, Oklahoma 73105

OREGON
Wildlife Commission
1634 Southwest Alder Street
P.O. Box 3503
Portland, Oregon 97208

PENNSYLVANIA
Game Commission
P.O. Box 1567
Harrisburg, Pennsylvania 17120

RHODE ISLAND
Division of Fish and Wildlife
Department of Natural Resources
83 Park Street
Providence, Rhode Island 02903

SOUTH CAROLINA
Department of Wildlife Resources
1015 Main Street
P.O. Box 167
Columbia, South Carolina 29202

SOUTH DAKOTA
Department of Game, Fish and Parks
State Office Building No. 1
Pierre, South Dakota 57501

TENNESSEE
Game and Fish Commission
Ellington Agricultural Center
P.O. Box 40747
Nashville, Tennessee 37220

TEXAS
Fish and Wildlife Division
Parks and Wildlife Department
John H. Reagan State Office Building
Austin, Texas 78701

UTAH
Division of Wildlife Resources
Department of Natural Resources
1596 West North Temple
Salt Lake City, Utah 84116

VERMONT
Department of Fish and Game
Agency of Environmental Conservation
Montpelier, Vermont 05602

VIRGINIA
Commission of Game and Inland
    Fisheries
4010 West Broad Street
P.O. Box 11104
Richmond, Virginia 23230

WASHINGTON
Department of Game
600 North Capitol Way
Olympia, Washington 98501

WEST VIRGINIA
Division of Wildlife Resources
Department of Natural Resources
1800 Washington Street, East
Charleston, West Virginia 25305

WISCONSIN
Game Management Bureau
Forestry, Wildlife and Recreation
    Division
Department of Natural Resources
P.O. Box 450
Madison, Wisconsin 53701

WYOMING
Game and Fish Division
P.O. Box 1589
Cheyenne, Wyoming 82001

CANADA

ALBERTA
Alberta Fish and Wildlife Division
Natural Resources Building
9833 - 109th Street
Edmonton, Alberta T5K 2E1

BRITISH COLUMBIA
Environment and Land Use
    Commission
Parliament Building
Victoria, British Columbia V8V 1X4

Department of Land, Forest and
    Water Resources
Parliament Building
Victoria, British Columbia V8V 1X4

MANITOBA
Department of Lands, Forests and
    Wildlife Resources
9-989 Century Street
Winnipeg, Manitoba R3H 0W4

NEWFOUNDLAND
Canadian Wildlife Service
Sir Humphrey Gilbert Building
Duckworth St.
St. John's, Newfoundland A1C 1G4

Department of Tourism
Wildlife Division
Confederation Building, 5th Floor
St. John's, Newfoundland

NORTHWEST TERRITORIES
Game Management Branch
Government of the Northwest
    Territories
Yellowknife, Northwest Territories

NOVA SCOTIA
Department of Environment
Box 2107
Halifax, Nova Scotia

Department of Land and Forests
Dennis Building
Granville Street
Halifax, Nova Scotia

ONTARIO
Wildlife Branch
Ministry of Natural Resources
Whitney Block
Toronto, Ontario M7A 1W3

PRINCE EDWARD ISLAND
Department of Fish and Wildlife
Environmental Control Commission
Box 2000
Charlottetown, Prince Edward Island
    C1A 7N8

Department of Environment and
    Tourism
Box 2000
Charlottetown, Prince Edward Island
    C1A 7N8

QUEBEC
Department of Tourism, Fish and
    Game
150 St. Cyrille East - 15th Floor
Quebec, Quebec G1R 4Y3

SASKATCHEWAN
Department of Natural Resources
Fisheries and Wildlife Branch
Administrative Building
Regina, Saskatchewan S4S 0B1

YUKON TERRITORY
Game Branch
Government of the Yukon Territory
Whitehorse, Yukon Territory

Organizations and Associations of Interest to the Hunter and Shooter

AMATEUR TRAPSHOOTING ASSOCIATION
P.O. Box 456, West National Road   Phone: (513) 898-4638
Vandalia, Ohio 45377
David D. Bopp, General Manager
Founded: 1923
Members: 70,000
Persons interested in the sport of trapshooting. Sanctions and determines rules governing shoots held by local, state, and provincial trapshooting associations: maintains permanent records for each shooter participating in 16 yard, handicap and doubles classifications in registered class competitions in state and provincial meets. Sponsor of Grand American Trapshooting Tournament held annually at Vandalia, Ohio, where historical exhibit and Hall of Fame are maintained. Publications: (1) *Trap and Field Magazine,* monthly; (2) *Official Trapshooting Rules,* annual; (3) *Trap and Field Official ATA Averages,* annual.

AMERICAN ASSOCIATION FOR CONSERVATION INFORMATION
c/o George Feltner, Editor   Phone: (303) 934-6734
458 Lowell Boulevard
Denver, Colorado 80204
Chuck Post, President
Founded: 1938
Members: 52
Professional society of officials of state and provincial conservation agencies. Sponsors annual awards program whereby winners in various categories of conservation education work are selected by a panel of judges. Publications: (1) *Balance Wheel,* bimonthly; (2) *Yearbook.* Convention/Meeting: Annual — always June.

AMERICAN COMMITTEE FOR INTERNATIONAL CONSERVATION
917 15th Street, N.W.   Phone: (202) 737-5000
Washington, D.C. 20005
Thomas B. Stoel, Secretary-Treasurer
Founded: 1930
Affiliates: 20
A council of organizations concerned with international conservation of species and habitats. Serves as a national committee of the International Union for Conservation of Nature and Natural Resources (IUCN).

AMERICAN CONSERVATION ASSOCIATION
30 Rockefeller Plaza
New York, N.Y. 10020
George R. Lamb, Executive Vice-President
Founded: 1958
Trustees: 11
Not a membership group. A private foundation established "to advance knowledge and understanding of conservation and to preserve and develop natural and living resources for public use, either directly or in cooperation with federal, state, local and private conservation agencies."

AMERICAN COON HUNTERS ASSOCIATION
Box 30   Phone: (618) 752-6691
Ingraham, Illinois 62434
Floyd E. Butler, Sec.
Founded: 1948
Members: 500
Persons interested in coon hunting. To promote and encourage the great sport of coon hunting; to seek to encourage proper practices of conservation of our raccoons and their natural habitats; to encourage the propagation of raccoons; to encourage liberation of live raccoons so that their numbers will increase rather than decrease; to promote and maintain friendly relations between land-owners and coon hunters, everywhere; to seek to restore decency and fairness in the sale of coonhounds, placing the ability to hunt, strike, trail and tree raccoons and stay treed, above all other qualities; to discourage the breeding of worthless ones; and so far as possible, place the coon-hunting fraternity upon the highest standard of sportsmanship so that it can pass on to posterity a sport unsurpassed in wholesome recreation, enjoyment, pleasure and delight. Convention/Meetings: World Championship for coon hounds held each year in October. Meeting held first day of World Championship.

AMERICAN DEFENSE PREPAREDNESS ASSOCIATION
740 15 St. N.W.   Phone: (202) 347-7250
Suite 819 Union Trust Bldg.
Washington, D.C. 20005
Henry A. Miley, Jr., Exec. V. Pres.
Founded: 1919
Members: 3,000
Staff: 22
Local groups: 53
Manufacturers, military personnel and engineers interested in industrial preparedness for the national defense of the United States. Divisions: Air Armament; Artillery; Chemical-Biological; Combat and Surface Mobility; Electronics; Fire Control; Management; Materials; Missiles and Astronautics; Packaging, Handling, and Transportability; Research; Small Arms Systems; Standards and Metrology; Technical Documentation; Underwater Ordnance; Cost and Value Management. Publications: (1) *Common Defense,* monthly newsletter; (2) *National Defense,* bimonthly magazine. Formerly: American Ordnance Association. Absorbed: (1965) Armed Forces Chemical Association; (1974) Armed Forces Management Association. Convention/Meeting: Annual—during May in Washington, D.C.

AMERICAN INSTITUTE OF BIOLOGICAL SCIENCES
1401 Wilson Boulevard   Phone: (703) 527-6776
Arlington, Virginia 22209
Aunther Gentile, Executive Director
Founded: 1948
Members: 10,000
Federation of professional biological associations and individuals with an interest in the life sciences. To promote unity and effectiveness of effort among persons engaged in biological research, teaching or application of biological data; to further the relationships of biological sciences to other sciences, the arts, and industries. Conducts symposium series; arranges for prominent biologists to lecture at small liberal arts colleges and radiation biologists to visit certain medical schools; provides advisory committees and other services to the Atomic Energy Commission, Office of Naval Research, and National Aeronautics and Space Administration. Created in 1966 on Office of Biological Education which serves as a clearing-house for information and conducts programs relative to several facets of biological education. Maintains placement service. Committees: Education; Environmental Biology; Exobiology; Hydrobiology; Microbiology; Oceanic Biology; Physiology; Public Responsibilities. Publications: Scientific Manpower Commission. Publications: (1) *Bio-Science,* monthly; (2) *Directory of Bioscience Departments and Facilities in the U.S. and Canada.*

AMERICAN PHEASANT AND WATERFOWL SOCIETY
Route 1   Phone: (205) 648-5301
Granton, Wisconsin 54436
Charles Siveile, President
Founded: 1936
Members: 1900
Hobbyists, aviculturists, zoos. To perpetuate all varieties of up-

land game, ornamental birds and waterfowl. Publications: (1) *Bulletin,* bimonthly; (2) *Membership Roster,* annual. Formerly: (1962) American Pheasant Society. Convention/Meeting: Annual.

AMERICAN PISTOL AND REVOLVER ASSOCIATION, INC.
512 East Wilson Avenue, Suite 301   Phone: (213) 247-1100
Glendale, California 91206
Elliott Stone Graham, Pres.
Founded: 1975
Members: 4500
Staff: 3
Officers and directors: 50
Regional groups: 3
Collectors of firearms, target shooters and individuals concerned about preserving the constitutional right to keep and bear arms. To inform and alert citizens on current anti-gun legislation, particularly owners of pistols and revolvers. To oppose legislation that would in any way infringe upon the ownership of handguns (pistols) and to oppose any candidate favoring such restrictions. Urges repeal of Federal Firearms Act of 1968. Publications: *Hot Pistol News* and *The Pistol Owners Legislative Handbook.* Convention/meeting: Biennial.

AMERICAN SECURITY COUNCIL
Washington Communications Center   Phone: (703) 825-8336
Boston, Virginia 22713
John M. Fisher, Pres.
Founded: 1955
Members: 200,000
Staff: 200
Corporations and individuals from all walks of life. Research and education in the field of national security. Publications: Monthly newsletter, *The Washington Report; American Security Council and Council Foundation,* quarterly journal.

ASSOCIATION OF AMERICAN ROD AND GUN CLUBS, EUROPE OCPA,
Headquarters USAREUR/7A
APO New York, N.Y. 09403
James W. Hirzel, LTC, GS, Exec.-Sec. Custodian
Founded: 1952
Members: 65,000
Local groups: 70
Federation of rod and gun clubs connected with American military forces in Europe, North Africa and the Near East. To encourage hunting, fishing, archery and allied sports; to promote the principles of sportsmanship and game conservation. Maintains library on conservation and European wildlife, with majority of books in German language. Publication: *Rod and Gun,* monthly. Convention/Meeting: Annual.

ASSOCIATION OF MIDWEST FISH AND GAME COMMISSIONERS
c/o Fred Warders   Phone: (316) 672-5911
Kansas Fish and Game Commission
P.O. Box 54A, R.R. 2
Pratt, Kansas 67124
Fred Warders, Treas.
Founded: 1934
Members: 18
Fish and game commissioners and directors of 15 midwestern states and 3 Canadian provinces. Promotes conservation of wildlife and outdoor recreation. Sponsors Midwest Pheasant Council; Dove Committee. Committees: Federal-State Relations; Federal Aid; Legislation; Federal Farm Program; Wetlands. Publication: *Proceedings,* annual. Convention/Meeting: Annual.

BIG THICKET ASSOCIATION
Box 198   Phone: (713) 838-8313
Saratoga, Tex. 77585
Gene Fiegelson, President
Founded: 1964
Members: 1400
Conservationists and others interested in preserving the wilderness area of southeast Texas known as the "Big Thicket." The Thicket is one of the major resting places along the Gulf Coast for migratory birds; in addition, at least 300 species live there permanently, many of them endangered species. Members of the Association have succeeded in having parts of the area declared a national biological preserve. Other activities include assisting scientists with research projects, operating a tourguide service, helping to maintain a Big Thicket Museum at Saratoga, Texas, a Big Thicket collection at the Lamar University Library in Beaumont, Tex., and coordinating programs aimed at preserving the area with other conservation organizations. Publication: *Big Thicket Bulletin,* quarterly; also publishes informational pamphlets, a bibliography and other materials. Convention/Meeting: Annual—always May or June, Saratoga, Tex.

BOUNTY INFORMATION SERVICE
c/o Stephens College Post Office   Phone: (314) 442-2211
Columbia, Mo. 65201   x473
H. Charles Laun, Dir.
Founded: 1965
Members: 2000
Individuals interested in the removal of wildlife bounties in the U.S. and Canada. Organizes bounty removal programs, publishes literature on the bounty system and methods for removal, compiles yearly summary of bounties in North America and executes individual studies of areas (i.e. cougar bounty in Texas). Maintains library. Publications: *Bounty News,* 1-3/year; has also published "*Guide for the Removal of Bounties*" and "*A Decade of Bounties.*" Convention/Meeting: Annual or Biennial.

BRIGADE OF THE AMERICAN REVOLUTION
The New Windsor Cantonment   Phone: (914) 561-1765
P.O. Box 207
Vails Gate, New York 12584
Robert Showalter, Commander
Founded: 1962
Members: 1000
Staff: 9
Units: 80
The men and women of the Brigade are dedicated to the authentic re-creation of soldier life during the period of the American Revolution. The Brigade fosters and encourages the exhibition and display of crafts and skills of the 18th century in general and specifically those closely relating to the life of the armies of the time. Each member regiment assumes the identity and organization of an original unit known to have participated in the Revolutionary War. All clothing, arms and equipment are researched for historical accuracy and no substitutions or modern materials are permitted. Various performances of a pageant-like nature are staged, usually at some historic site, involving military drills and exercises and demonstrations of camp life and craft skills designed to educate and entertain. Publications: Quarterly journal, *The Brigade Dispatch;* Monthly newsletter. Convention/Meeting: Brigade events commence in March and generally take place every other weekend through November.

CITIZENS COMMITTEE FOR THE RIGHT TO KEEP AND BEAR ARMS
1601 114th S.E.   Phone: (206) 454-4911
Bellevue, Washington 98004
Alan M. Gottlieb, Chairman
Founded: 1971
Members: 305,000
Staff: 5

A national independent non-profit mass membership organization concerned solely with preserving the right to keep and bear arms. The committee also maintains a public affairs office in the nation's capital (600 Pennsylvania Avenue, S.E., Suite 205). The Committee's National Advisory Council, made up of businessmen, educators, legislators, religious leaders, and includes 90 members of the U.S. Congress. Issues action bulletins, pro-gun rights brochures, bumper strips, decals, buttons and patches, and legislative action materials. Supported by membership fees and voluntary contributions. Publication: *Point Blank,* monthly.

CITIZENS COMMITTEE ON NATURAL RESOUURCES
1000 Vermont Ave., N.W.   Phone: (202) 638-3396
Washington, D.C. 20005
Spencer M. Smith, Jr., Executive Director
Founded: 1954
Staff: 2
Individuals interested in lobbying in behalf of conservation program dealing with government departments.

COMPANY OF MILITARY HISTORIANS
North Main Street   Phone: (203) 399-9460
Westbrook, Connecticut 06498
Major Wm. Reid, Admin.
Founded: 1951
Members: 2800
Staff: 4
Professional society of military historians, museologists, artists, writers, and private collectors interested in the history of American military units, organization, tactics, uniforms, arms, and equipment. Publications: (1) *Military Collector and Historian,* quarterly; (2) *Military Uniforms in America,* quarterly; (3) *Military Music in America* (records), irregular. Formerly: (1962) Company of Military Collectors and Historians. Convention/Meeting: Annual. Open to the public Mon.-Fri., 9-4.

CONSERVATION EDUCATION ASSOCIATION
c/o Richard W. Presnell
University of Wisconsin — Green Bay
Green Bay, Wisconsin 54302
Richard W. Presnell, Secretary-Treasurer
Founded: 1947
Members: 950
Conservationists, educators and others interested in improving conservation education in public schools, teacher training institutions, and organization programs. Outstanding state, local and organizational conservation publications, especially those of normally limited distribution, are circulated bimonthly to members. Publications: (1) *Newsletter,* bimonthly; (2) *Proceedings,* annual. Formerly: (1953) National Committee on Policies in Conservation Education. Convention/Meeting: Annual — always August.

CONSERVATION FOUNDATION
1717 Massachusetts Ave., N.W.   Phone: (202) 797-4300
Washington, D.C. 20036
William K. Reilly, Pres.
Founded: 1948
Staff: 46
Not a membership organization. Conducts research, education and information programs to develop knowledge, improve techniques, and stimulate public and private decision-making and action to improve the quality of the environment. Carries out environmental studies, demonstration planning programs, and offers a variety of conservation services at home and abroad. Publication: *CF Letter,* monthly; also publishes books, pamphlets, studies, guides, reports, and reprints.

CONSERVATION AND RESEARCH FOUNDATION
Department of Botany   Phone: (203) 442-5391 x306
Connecticut College
New London, Conn. 06320
Richard H. Goodwin, Pres.
Founded: 1953
Not a membership organization. To encourage biological research and promote conservation of renewable natural resources. Makes research grants; offers Jeanette Siron Pelton Award for outstanding published contributions in experimental plant morphology. Publishes *A Five Year Report* (last one in 1978). Convention/Meeting: Annual.

CONSERVATION SERVICES
South Great Road
Lincoln, Mass. 01773
Allen H. Morgan, Exec. Dir.
Founded: 1965
Members: 5
Staff: 5
Small Audubon and conservation groups, comprising 34,000 individual members. Purpose is to publish magazines, newsletters and environmental brochures for New England conservation organizations, and to develop television, radio and audiovisual materials that can be used in New England. Maintains extensive source files. Publications: (1) *Massachusetts Audubon Society Newsletter,* 10/year; (2) *Man and Nature Yearbook,* quarterly. Formerly: Conservation Services Center.

DEFENDERS OF WILDLIFE
1244 19th Street, N.W.   Phone: (202) 659-9510
Washington, D.C. 20036
John W. Grandy, Executive Vice-President
Founded: 1925
Members: 40,000
Persons interested in wildlife and conservation. To promote, through education and research, the protection and humane treatment of all mammals, birds, fish and other wildlife, and the elimination of painful methods of trapping, capturing and killing wildlife. Publication: *Defenders of Wildlife News,* bi-monthly. Formerly: Anti-Steel-Trap League; Defenders of Furbearers. Convention/Meeting: Semi-annual.

DESERT PROTECTIVE COUNCIL
P.O. Box 4294   Phone: (714) 397-4264
Palm Springs, California 92262
Glenn Vargas, Executive Director
Founded: 1954
Members: 700
Persons interested in safeguarding desert areas that are of unique scenic, scientific, historical, spiritual, and recreational value. Seeks to educate children and adults to a better understanding of the desert. Works to bring about establishment of wildlife sanctuaries for protection of indigenous plants and animals. The Desert Protective Council Education Foundation, a subdivision of the Council formed in 1960, handles educational activities and distributes reprints of desert and wildlife conservation articles. Publication: *El Paisano* (by Foundation), quarterly, and a yearly publication on a special topic. Convention/Meeting: Annual—Oct.

DUCKS UNLIMITED
P.O. Box 66300   Phone: (312) 299-3334
Chicago, Ill. 60666
Dale E. Whitesell, Exec. V. Pres.
Founded: 1937
Members: 300,000
Staff: 20
State groups: 1300
Conservationists in the United States and Canada interested in migratory waterfowl conservation. To restore or build natural

breeding habitats for migratory waterfowl primarily in the prairie provinces of Canada, which provides 80% of North America's wild geese and ducks. The American group raises funds for this construction and rehabilitation work, carried on by the field operating unit in Canada. Publications: (1) *Ducks Unlimited Magazine*, bi-monthly; (2) *Annual Report;* also publishes *The Ducks Unlimited Story*. Affiliated with: Ducks Unlimited (Canada). Absorbed: (1936) More Game Birds in America. Convention/Meeting: Annual.

FEDERATION OF WESTERN OUTDOOR CLUBS

512½ Boylston East, No. 106   Phone: (206) 322-3041
Seattle, Washington 98102
Hazel A Wolf, President
Founded: 1932
Members: 1341
Outdoor clubs (41) in western United States with combined membership of 48,000, associate members 1300. Promotes conservation of forests, wildlife, and natural features. Publication: *Western Outdoor,* semi-annually. Convention/Meeting: Annual — always late August.

FIREARMS LOBBY OF AMERICA

325 Pennsylvania Avenue S.E.   Phone: (202) 547-1670
Washington, D.C. 20003
Morgan Norval, National Director
Founded: 1968
Members: 18,000
A national, independent, voluntary, non-profit association of American citizens concerned with preserving their right to keep and bear arms. Publication: Quarterly newsletter, *Aim & Fire.*

FRIENDS OF THE EARTH

124 Spear Street   Phone: (415) 495-4770
San Francisco, California 94105
David Brower, Founder, President
Founded: 1969
International conservation organization which concentrates on legislative and political activities in this field. Publications: *Not Man Apart,* monthly newspaper.

FRIENDS OF NATURE, INC.

Martin R. Haase, Exec. Sec.
Brooksville, Me. 04617
Founded: 1953
Conservationists "dedicated to maintaining the balance of nature for the mutual benefit of man and his plant and animal friends." Carries on educational work and maintains several nature sanctuaries. Holds annual meeting.

FRIENDS OF THE WILDERNESS

3515 East Fourth St.   Phone: (218) 724-7227
Duluth, Minn. 55804
William H. Magie, Exec. Sec.
Founded: 1949
Members: 17,364
Persons interested in preservation of the Boundary Water Canoe Area of Minnesota, the wilderness canoe country of the Superior National Forest. Maintains library of 400 volumes pertaining to the area. Holds annual meeting.

GAME CONSERVATION INTERNATIONAL

900 N.E. Loop 410, Suite D-211   Phone: (512) 824-7509
San Antonio, Texas 78209
Bob Hollerton, Executive Director
Founded: 1967
Members: 900
Staff: 3
Individuals interested in wildlife conservation. Administers Hunters' Legal Defense Fund. Publications: *Hook n' Bullet,*

quarterly. Convention/Meeting: Biennial Hunters and Fishermen's Conservation Conference.

INTERNATIONAL ASSOCIATION OF WILDLIFE AGENCIES

1412 16th Street, N.W.   Phone: (202) 232-1652
Washington, D.C. 20036
Jack H. Berryman, Executive Vice-President
Founded: 1902
Members: 384
State and provincial game, fish and conservation departments (61) and officials (316). To educate the public to the economic importance of conserving natural resources and managing wildlife properly as a source of recreation and a food supply; to seek better conservation legislation, administration and enforcement. Publications: (1) *Proceedings,* annual; (2) *Newsletter,* bimonthly. Formerly: (1917) National Association of Game Commissioners and Wardens. Convention/Meeting: Annual — always second Monday in September.

INTERNATIONAL BENCHREST SHOOTERS

411 North Wilbur Avenue   Phone: (717) 882-5795
Sayre, Pennsylvania 18840
James A. Stekl, President
Founded: 1970
Members: 1150
Staff: 7
Gunsmiths, research engineers, gun writers, other interested persons. "To develop the ultimate in gun accuracy." Sponsors tournaments with demonstrations of new inventions or idea developments in the field. Also sponsors seminars. Publication: *Precision Shooting Magazine,* monthly. Convention/Meeting: Annual.

INTERNATIONAL UNION FOR CONSERVATION OF NATURE AND NATURAL RESOURCES

Secretariat: 1110 Morques   Phone: (703) 280-4086
Switzerland
U.S. Address: P.O. Box 19347
Washington, D.C. 20036
Harold J. Coolidge, Pres.
Founded: 1948
Members: 266
International federation of national governments (39) and national and international organizations (393) in 97 countries. For the preservation of the natural environment of man and the conservation of the world's natural resources. Serves as a forum for discussion of conservation problems and studies; sponsors international youth camps; intercedes with governments on conservation matters; maintains Van Tienhoven Library. Conducts research on measures to promote and protect national parks, nature reserves, wildlife and its habitat. Provides advisory field missions. International headquarters located in Morges, Switzerland. Technical Commissions: Conservation Education; Ecology; Environmental Policy, Law and Administration; Landscape Planning; Law and Administration; National Parks and protected areas; Survival Service. Publications (must be ordered from Switzerland: (1) *IUCN Bulletin,* monthly; (2) *Proceedings* (of conferences); also publishes *Red Data Book* (endangered species), technical reports and a UN List of National Parks and Equivalent Reserves. Formerly: (1956) International Union for the Protection of Nature. General Assembly/Technical Meeting: Triennial.

INTERNATIONAL WILD WATERFOWL ASSOCIATION (IWWA)

c/o Carl E. Strutz   Phone: (701) 252-1239
Box 1075
Jamestown, N.D. 58401
Carl E. Strutz, Sec.
Founded: 1958
Members: 500

Persons concerned with conservation and the preservation of wild waterfowl. Works toward protection, conservation and reproduction of any species considered in danger of eventual extinction; encourages the breeding of well known and rare species in captivity so that more people may learn about them by observation and enjoy them in the natural habitats created for this purpose. Has established Avicultural Hall of Fame. Publications: (1) *Bulletin,* bimonthly; (2) *Membership list,* annual; has published books on keeping cranes, wild geese, and wild ducks in captivity. Convention/Meeting: Annual

IZAAK WALTON LEAGUE OF AMERICA
1800 N. Kent St., Suite 806   Phone: (703) 528-1818
Arlington, Va. 22209
Jack Lorenz, Exec. Dir.
Founded: 1922
Members: 50,000
Staff: 16
State divisions: 22
Local chapters: 600
Promotes means and opportunities for educating the public to conserve, maintain, protect and restore the soil, forest, water and other natural resources of the U.S. and promotes the enjoyment and wholesome utilization of those resources. Committees: Energy Resources, Environmental Education, Fish and Wildlife, Public Lands, Urban Environment, Water and Wetlands, Water Quality, and Youth. Publication: *Outdoor America.* Absorbed: (1962) Friends of the Land. Convention/Meeting: Annual — always July.

J. N. "DING" DARLING FOUNDATION
c/o S. R. Fisher   Phone: (515) 255-9860
3663 Grand, Suite 608
Des Moines, Iowa 50312
Mr. Sherry R. Fisher, Chm.
Founded: 1962
Trustees: 33
"To initiate plans and to coordinate, guide and expedite programs, research and education which will bring about conservation and sound management of water, woods and soil; to restore and preserve historical sites; to create and assist in wildlife management plans; to improve and assure outdoor recreational opportunities for present and future generations." Established 1700-acre wildlife and waterfowl sanctuary on Sanibel Island, off the west coast of Florida. Awards scholarships at Iowa State University for wildlife management students. Named for the late J. N. "Ding" Darling, a professional cartoonist long active in conservation activities. Holds annual meeting.

LEAGUE TO SAVE LAKE TAHOE
1176 Emerson St.   Phone: (415) 328-5313
Palo Alto, California 94301
Steven C. Brandt, Pres.
Staff: 1
Membership comprised of individuals and organizations who give financial support to the League. Purpose is to "do all things and to perform all acts necessary to keep Lake Tahoe blue and to protect and preserve the natural beauty and grandeur of the Lake Tahoe area of California and Nevada; to promote and encourage the concept that all developments, improvements and man-made changes of any kind, which may be required to accommodate the proper and desirable growth of the area and provide the maximum recreational values, should place primary emphasis on preserving the natural beauty of the lake." Publication: *Newsletter,* quarterly. Convention/Meeting: Annual.

NATIONAL AUDUBON SOCIETY
950 Third Ave.   Phone: (212) 832-3200
New York, N.Y. 10022
Elvis J. Stahr, Pres.
Founded: 1905

Membrs: 370,000
Staff: 225
Chapters: 398
Affiliated groups: 162
Persons interested in conservation and restoration of natural resources, with emphasis on wildlife, wildlife habitats, soil, water, and forests. Sponsors four Audubon camps for teachers and youth leaders; nature lectures; and wildlife tours. Supports a force of 18 wardens to patrol wildlife refuge areas and sanctuaries; produces teaching materials for schools. Divisions: Educational Services; Lecture; Nature Centers; Research; Sanctuary; Service. Publications: (1) *Audubon Leader,* semimonthly; (2) *Audubon Magazine,* bimonthly; (3) *American Birds,* bimonthly; (4) *Nature Bulletins,* quarterly. Formerly: (1935) National Association of Aububon Societies for the Protection of Wild Birds and Animals, Inc. Convention/Meeting: Biennial.

NATIONAL BENCHREST SHOOTERS ASSOCIATION
5735 Sherwood Forest Drive   Phone: (216) 882-6877
Akron, Ohio 44319
Stella Buchtel, Secretary-Treasurer
Founded: 1951
Rifle enthusiasts interested in precision shooting. Conducts registered shoots and certifies records. Sections: Bench Rest Rifle; Heavy Varmint; Light Varmint; Sporter Classes. Publication: *Rifle,* bimonthly. Holds annual directors' meeting.

NATIONAL BOARD FOR THE PROMOTION OF RIFLE PRACTICE
Forrestal Bldg. (West) Room 1E053   Phone: (202) 693-6460
Washington, D.C. 20314
Col. Jack R. Rollinger, Exec. Off.
Founded: 1903
Members: 25
Staff: 14
Local clubs: 2000
Civilian shooting clubs and marksmanship clubs in high schools and colleges. An agency of the U.S. Department of the Army, "to promote marksmanship training with rifled arms among able bodied citizens of the U.S. and to provide citizens outside the active services of the Armed Forces with means whereby they may become proficient with such arms." Provides arms and ammunition to member clubs; exhibits national marksmanship trophies; maintains records and distributes awards for national and international marksmanship competitions. Publication: *National Board Directory.* Convention/Meeting: Annual—always Washington, D.C.

NATIONAL MUZZLE LOADING RIFLE ASSOCIATION
Friendship, Ind. 47021   Phone: (812) 667-5131
Mrs. Maxine Moss, Office Mgr.-Editor
Founded: 1933
Members: 23,000
Local clubs: 250
Persons interested in black powder shooting. To preserve the heritage left to us by our forefathers, and to promote safety in the use of arms. Maintains National Range located at Friendship, Ind. Sponsors Beef Shoot in Jan., Spring Shoot, National Shoot in the fall, and Turkey Shoot in Oct. Committees: Long Range Planning; Property; Fund Raising; Range Officers; Grounds; Commercial Row; Traffic; Safety; Camping; Memorial; Public Relations; Scoring; Award. *Muzzle Blasts,* monthly. Convention/Meeting: Annual.

NATIONAL PRAIRIE GROUSE TECHNICAL COUNCIL
College Natural Resources   Phone: (715) 346-3665
University of Wisconsin
Stevens Point, Wisconsin 55461
Raymond K. Anderson, Chairman
Founded: 1952

Sponsors biennial meeting for technical personnel and administrators of state, provincial and federal agencies, and individuals from private groups involved in preservation, research, and management of the prairie chicken and sharp-tailed grouse. Conference makes possible exchange of information on current research and management of these species and reviews local and national legislation affecting the prairie grouse resource. Publications: (1) *P.G. News*, semiannual; (2) *Proceedings*, biennial. Formerly: (1956) National Committee on the Prairie Chicken; (1961) Prairie Chicken Technical Committee. Conference: Biennial.

NATIONAL RIFLE ASSOCIATION OF AMERICA

1600 Rhode Island Ave., N.W.   Phone: (202) 783-6505
Washington, D.C. 20036
Harlan B. Carter, Executive Vice-President
Founded: 1871
Members: 1,057,000
Staff: 317
State groups: 53
Local groups: 9000
Target shooters, hunters, gun collectors, gunsmiths, police officers, and others interested in firearms. Promotes rifle, pistol, and shotgun shooting, hunting, gun collecting, hunter and home firearms safety, conservation, etc. Encourages civilian marksmanship in interests of national defense. Maintains national records of shooting competitions; sponors teams to compete in the Olympic Games and other world championships. Committees: Twenty-nine standing committees and four standing committees all with a charter of responsibilities to cover every phase of the shooting sport. Publications: (1) *The American Rifleman*, monthly; (2) *The American Hunter*, monthly; (3) *The American Marksman*, monthly. Other publications include a large variety of training, educational, and informational pamphlets, brochures, and pamphlets. Meeting. Annual—always April.

NATIONAL SHOOTING SPORTS FOUNDATION

1075 Post Road   Phone: (203) 637-3618
Riverside, Conn. 06878
Arnold H. Rohlfing, Executive Director
Founded: 1961
Members: 103
Staff: 11
Chartered to promote in the American public a better understanding and more active participation in the recreational shooting sports. Organizes the annual observance of National Hunting and Fishing Day. Prints and distributes over 3 million copies of various shooting and hunting/conservation publications. Write for catalog of publications.

NATIONAL SKEET SHOOTING ASSOCIATION

P.O. Box 28188   Phone: (512) 688-3371
San Antonio, Tex. 78228
Carroll E. Bobo, Exec. Dir.
Founded: 1935
Members: 19,000
Staff: 17
State groups: 54
Locla groups: 715
Amateur skeet shooters. Registers competitive shoots and supervises them through formulation and enforcement of rules. Publication: *Skeet Shooting Review*, monthly. Convention/Meeting (World Championship Shoot): Annual.

NATIONAL SPORTING GOODS ASSOCIATION

717 North Michigan Avenue   Phone: (312) 944-0205
Chicago, Illinois 60611
G. Marvin Shutt, Executive Director
Founded: 1929

Members: 5000
Staff: 40
Manufacturers, wholesalers, retailers, and importers of athletic equipment, sporting goods, and supplies. Provides data on cost-of-doing-business, store modernization, etc. Sponsors annual Gold Medal Award Program of the Sports Foundation for excellence in park and recreation management and in pollution control. Divisions: Athletic Goods Team Distributors; Awards Specialists; Outdoor Sports Stores; Ski Retailers International. Publications: (1) *Selling Sporting Goods*, monthly; (2) *Memo to Management*, monthly; (3) *NSGA Buying Guide*, annual; also publishes research and statistical studies. Convention/Meeting: Annual.

NATIONAL TRAPPERS ASSOCIATION

c/o Don Hoyt, Sr.   Phone: (616) 781-3472
15412 Tau Road
Marshall, Michigan 49068
Don Hoyt, Sr., President
Founded: 1959
Members: 5900
State groups: 31
Trappers of animals for the purpose of selling skins and furs; fur dealers, outdoorsmen. Researches animal control techniques; compiles statistics. Committees: Conservation. Publications: *Voice of the Trapper*, quarterly. Convention/Meeting: Annual.

NATIONAL WATERFOWL COUNCIL

c/o Jack Crockfort, Director   (404) 656-3500
Game and Fish Division
Department of Natural Resources
270 Washington Street
Atlanta, Georgia 30334
Members: 50
State and provincial fish and game departments. To coordinate waterfowl planning, research, and management. Convention/Meeting: Semiannual—Mar. and Aug., held in conjunction with conventions of North American Wildlife Conference and Bureau of Sport Fish and Wildlife Service Waterfowl Regulations.

NATIONAL WILDLIFE FEDERATION

1412 16th St., N.W.   Phone: (202) 797-6800
Washington, D.C. 20036
Thomas L. Kimball, Exec. V. Pres.
Founded: 1936
State affiliated members: 1,400,000
Staff: 20
Local chapters: 6500
Federation of 53 state conservation organizations and 1.1 million associate members, plus individual conservationist-contributors. Represents in its structure 3.6 million supporters. To encourage the intelligent management of the life-sustaining resources of the earth, and to promote a greater appreciation of these resources, their community relationship and wise use. Gives organizational and financial help to local conservation projects; annually awards fellowships for graduate study of conservation; publishes conservation-education teaching materials. Compiles and distributes annual survey of compensation in the fields of fish and wildlife management. Maintains library of conservation publications. Sponsors National Wildlife Week; many public service television and radio announcements. Activities are financed by sales of Wildlife Conservation Stamps and nature-related materials. Publications: (1) *Conservation Report*, weekly; (2) *Conservation News*, semimonthly; (3) *Ranger Rick's Nature Magazine*, 10/year; (4) *National Wildlife Magazine*, bimonthly; (5) *International Wildlife Magazine*, bimonthly; (6) *Conservation Directory*, annual; also publishes numerous free and lowcost conservation materials. Convention/Meeting: Annual.

NATURAL RESOURCES COUNCIL OF AMERICA

1025 Connecticut Ave., N.W.   Phone: (202) 293-3200
Suite 914
Washington, D.C. 20036
Hamilton K. Pyles, Exec. Sec.
Founded: 1946
Members: 47

Federation of national and regional conservation organizations and scientific societies interested in conservation of natural resources. Sponsors special natural resource studies and surveys. Committee: Scientific Advisory. Publications: (1) *Legislative News Service* (actions taken by Congress on natural resources), weekly; (2) *Executive News Service* (actions taken by Executive Branch on natural resources), weekly; also publishes books on selected natural resource topics. Convention/Meeting: Semi-annual—always held with North American Wildlife and Natural Resources Conference.

NEW ENGLAND ADVISORY BOARD
FOR FISH AND GAME PROBLEMS

115 Summit Avenue   Phone: (401) 821-9096
West Warwick, Rhode Island 02839
Theodore Boyer, Sec.
Founded: 1951
Members: 102

Sportsmen. To promote and improve conservation, hunting, fishing and recreation in New England. All New England states affiliated. Convention/Meeting: 3/year.

NORTH AMERICAN WILDLIFE FOUNDATION

709 Wire Bldg.   Phone: (202) 347-1774
1000 Vermont Avenue, N.W.
Washington, D.C. 20005
L. R. Jahn, Sec.
Founded: 1911
Contributing members: 400
Trustees: 30

"To insure, through financial support, the continuity of practical and systematic investigation into management practices and techniques throughout North America, to the end that the latest, most effective local, national, and international programs for wildlife and other natural resources will be adopted in the public interest." Foundation is not an action organization and does not attempt the actual mechanics of wildlife restoration; works through cooperating agencies, organizations, institutions. Owns Delta Waterfowl Research Station in Manitoba, Canada. Maintains library of 450 volumes on natural science subjects and wildlife restoration and management. Formerly: (1935) American Game Protective Association; (1946) American Wildlife Institute; (1951) American Wildlife Foundation.

NORTH-SOUTH SKIRMISH ASSOCIATION, INC.

Route 2, Box 245A   (703) 888-3335
Winchester, Virginia 22601
John L. Rawls, Executive Secretary
Founded: 1950
Members: 3000
Local groups: 186

"To preserve the history and spirit of the Civil War soldier, and to promote marksmanship with the small arms and artillery of the Civil War era, fired in the original manner." Sponsors semi-annual national skirmishes at Ft. Shenandoah, Virginia and some 40 regional skirmishes throughout the eastern United States, in which competitors, dressed as were Union and Confederate soldiers, compete. Skirmishes feature: individual matches with muskets, carbines, and revolvers; 6-man artillery matches; 5-man team carbine matches; and 8-man musket matches. Publication: *The Skirmish Line,* bimonthly. Affiliated with: National Rifle Association of America. Convention/Meeting: Semi-annual.

OUTDOOR WRITERS ASSOCIATION OF AMERICA

4141 W. Bradley Rd.   Phone: (414) 354-9690
Milwaukee, Wis. 53209
Edwin W. Hanson, Exec. Dir.
Founded: 1927
Members: 1500
Staff: 3

Professional organization of newspaper, magazine, radio, television, and motion picture writers and photographers (both staff and free-lance) on outdoor recreation and conservation. Gives awards for outstanding writing and films in the field; conducts surveys for educational and industrial organizations; compiles market data for writer members, and offers liaison aid in writer assignments. Committees: Awards; Educational and Scholarship; Ethics; Youth Program. Publications: (1) *Outdoors Unlimited,* monthly; (2) *Spotlight,* quarterly; (3) *Outdoor Writers' Association of America Directory;* also publishes *Communicating the Outdoor Experience.*

PACIFIC INTERNATIONAL TRAPSHOOTING
ASSOCIATION

3847 Glenwood Loop, S.E.   Phone: (503) 364-1042
Salem, Ore. 97301
Gordon E. Hull, Sec.-Mgr.
Founded: 1928
Members: 6000

Sponsors state, provincial, international and individual registered trapshoots. "Grand Pacific Trapshoot"/Meeting: Annual, Reno, Nevada, mid July.

PHEASANT TRUST

Great Witchingham
Norwich, Norfolk, England
Philip Wayre, Hon. Dir.
Founded: 1959
Members: 500
Staff: 3

Purposes are: to breed rare and threatened species of game birds for release in suitable reserves in their native lands; to maintain the world's largest collection of rare pheasants for education and scientific research; to promote the conservation of rare game birds throughout the world. Has received several first breeding awards from Agricultural Society of Great Britain. Publication: Annual report. Formerly: Ornamental Pheasant Trust.

PRAIRIE CHICKEN FOUNDATION

4122 Mineral Point Rd.   Phone: (608) 233-5474
Madison, Wis. 53705
Paul J. Olson, Pres.
Founded: 1958

Persons dedicated to preservation of the prairie chicken in Wisconsin. Raises funds and acquires land to develop prairie chicken habitat in the state. Owns some 5000 acres, at a cost of $200,000; makes some purchases cooperatively with the Society Tympanuchus Cupido Pinnatus. Publication: *Prairie Chicken,* irregular.

RUFFED GROUSE SOCIETY

1314 Fourth Avenue   Phone: (412) 262-4044
Corapolis, Pennsylvania 15108
Samuel R. Pursglove, Jr., Executive Director
Founded: 1961
Members: 3500
State chapters: 12

Ruffed grouse hunters; game biologists; conservationists. Actively supports ruffed grouse and woodcock research and habitat improvement. Cooperates with state conservation departments, paper and pulp industries, and strip mining companies in habitat improvement and encourages conservation measures. Endows research into ecological aspects of the ruffed grouse and woodcock. Publications: *The Drummer,* semi-monthly. Convention/Meeting: Annual.

SAFARI CLUB INTERNATIONAL

515 East Broadway Phone: (602) 747-0260
Suite 1680
Tucson, Arizona 85711
C. J. McElroy, Chm. of Board
Seymour H. Levy, Administrative Director
Founded: 1972
Members: Regular, 2200; associate, 4700; affiliate, 500,000
Staff: 9
Regional groups: 39
To promote good fellowship among those who love the outdoors and the sport of hunting. To promote the conservation of the wildlife of the world through selective trophy hunting of aged and infirm animals, leaving prime animals to procreate. To educate youth in the safe and proper use of firearms and to interest them in the conservation and preservation of forests and animals, our natural heritage. Publication: *Safari* magazine. Convention/Meetings: Annual convention in Las Vegas; quarterly director's meetings; monthly chapter meetings.

SAINT HUBERT SOCIETY OF AMERICA

Henry C. Neville Phone: (212) 986-3180
P.O. Box 626
Montauk, New York 11954
Henry C. Neville, President
Founded: 1958
Members: 100
Individuals interested in wildlife, conservation, hunting, and the lore of the outdoors. "Dedicated to the promulgation of conservation, hunting, fishing, and the preservation of the great American heritage of the outdoors and those traditions of sportsmanship and fair play which have become associated with the American way of life." Sponsors outings for members including shoots, hunts, and fishing expeditions. Named in honor of the patron saint of hunters who was born in Belgium in the middle of the seventh century. Similar organizations have been in existence in Europe since the eighth century. Meet bimonthly.

SHOOTERS CLUB OF AMERICA

591 Camino de la Reina, Suite 200
San Diego, California 92108
Founded: 1963
Hunters, shooters, gun dealers, collectors, industry personnel, and others interested in "protecting the fundamental right of citizens to keep and bear arms and in combatting restrictive anti-gun legislation on local, state, and national levels." Conducts educational and public relations program on behalf of gun sportsmen and in support of "pro-gun" legislation.

SIERRA CLUB

530 Bush Street Phone: (415) 981-8634
San Francisco, California 94104
Michael McCloskey, Executive Director
Members: 140,000
Staff: 130
Regional chapters 300
All who feel the need to know more of nature, and know that this need is basic to man. "To protect and conserve the natural resources of the Sierra Nevada, the United States and the World; to undertake and publish scientific and educational studies concerning all aspects of man's environment and the natural ecosystems of the World; and to educate the people of the United States and the World to the need to preserve and restore the quality of that environment and the integrity of those ecosystems." Works on urgent campaigns to save threatened areas, wildlife, and resources; conducts annual environmental workshops for educators; schedules wilderness outings; presents awards; main-

tains library. Chapters and committees schedule talks, films, exhibits, and conferences. Committees: Economics; Energy; Environmental Education; Environmental Research; Forest Practices; International Environment; Mountaineering; National Land Use; National Water Resources; Native American Issues; Outings; Population; Wilderness; Wildlife and Endangered Species. Departments: Conservation; Outings. Publications: (1) *National News Report,* weekly; (2) *Sierra Club Bulletin,* monthly; (3) *Ascent,* Sierra Club mountaineering journal, annual; also publishes books and produces films, posters, and exhibits. Member of: United Nations (with non-government organization status). Convention/Meeting (Wilderness Conference): Biennial.

SOCIETY FOR THE PRESERVATION OF BIRDS OF PREY

Pacific Palisades, Calif. 90272
J. Richard Hilton, Pres.
Founded: 1966
Members: 210
Staff: 1
Professional ornithologists, bird watchers, and raptor enthusiasts. Seeks to stress the value of birds of prey (raptors) and to encourage their protection; disseminates information and promotes communication among members; discourages harvesting of raptorial birds for purposes of falconry and research; denounces caging, selling and trading, display, or exhibition of the birds; urges reasonable and biologically sound pest control measures and supports abolition of accumulative, wide-target insecticides. Publications: *The Raptor Report,* 3/year; also publishes numerous bulletins and pamphlets. Formerly: (1966) Palisades Hawking Club.

SOCIETY OF TYMPANUCHUS CUPIDO PINNATUS

c/o Robert T. Foote Phone: (414) 271-6755
433 East Michigan
Milwaukee, Wisconsin 53202
Robert T. Foote, Pres.
Founded: 1960
Sportsmen dedicated to preserving the prairie chicken and to "doing so with humor, excellent taste, and efficiency—at the same time having a bit of fun along the way." (The prairie chicken or prairie hen, also called a pinneated grouse, is a game bird of the northern hemisphere, related to the pheasant and having mottled plumage. The Society calls itself by the scientific name for the prairie chicken.) Members' contributions are used to buy land for prairie chicken habitat, specifically to add acres to the Buena Vista Reservation in Portage County, Wisconsin. As of June, 1971, the Society had bought over 6300 acres of land, which is leased to the Wisconsin Conservation Department for clearing, restoration, and maintenance on chicken range. Only other organized activity is an annual cocktail party and business meeting held in December in Milwaukee where many of the members live. Publications: (1) *Boom,* quarterly; (2) *Membership Roll.*

SOUTHEASTERN ASSOCIATION OF
FISH AND WILDLIFE AGENCIES

c/o Gary T. Myers, Secretary-Treasurer Phone: (502) 564-3400
P.O. Box 40747
Nashville, Tennessee 37204
James A. Timmerman, Jr., President
Founded: 1947
Members: 17
Directors of state game and fish commissions in 16 southern states. To protect the right of jurisdiction of southeastern states over their wildlife resources on public and private lands; study state and federal wildlife legislation and regulations as they affect the area; consult with and make recommendations to federal wildlife and public land agencies on federal management programs and programs involving federal aid to southeastern states; serve as a clearing house for exchange of ideas on wildlife management and research techniques. Sponsors statistical studies at North Carolina.

SPORTING ARMS AND AMMUNITION MANUFACTURERS' INSTITUTE, INC.

420 Lexington Ave.   Phone: (212) 986-6920
New York, N.Y. 10017
Harry L. Hampton, Jr., Exec. Dir.
Founded: 1926
Members: 11
Staff: 9
Manufacturers of sporting firearms, ammunition and powder. Promotes shooting sports, safe handling of firearms, technical research, etc. Committees: Legislative and Legal Affairs; Promotional Guidance; Internat'l Trade; Traffic; Technical. Meeting: Semi-annual.

UNITED STATES REVOLVER ASSOCIATION

59 Alvin St.   Phone: (413) 734-5725
Springfield, Mass. 01104
Stanley A. Sprague, Exec. Sec.
Founded: 1900
Members: 1200
Staff: 2
To foster and develop revolver and pistol shooting; to establish and preserve records; and to encourage and conduct pistol matches between members and clubs of this country as well as marksmen of other countries. Publication: *U.S. Handgunner,* bimonthly. Convention/Meeting: Annual—always Springfield, Mass.

WATERFOWL ADVISORY COMMITTEE

Group of thirteen national organizations interested in waterfowl management. Meets each Aug. in Washington, D.C. to hear reports on the status of waterfowl, and to recommend annual hunting regulations to the director of Bureau of Sports Fisheries and Wildlife of U.S. Department of the Interior.

WESTERN ASSOCIATION OF STATE GAME AND FISH COMMISSIONERS

c/o Robert L. Salter   Phone: (208) 344-3772
Box 25
600 S. Walnut St.
Boise, Idaho 83707
Robert L. Salter, Sec.-Treas.
Founded: 1920
Members: 16
Officials of state and provincial game and fish agencies of western states and provinces. Promotes fish and game conservation in West. Publication: *Proceedings of WASGFC,* annual. Convention/Meeting: Annual.

WILDERNESS SOCIETY

1901 Pennsylvania Avenue, N.W.   Phone: (202) 293-2732
Washington, D.C. 20006
James G. Deane, Editor
Founded: 1935
Members: 70,000
Staff: 35
Persons interested in preserving wilderness through educational programs, scientific studies, and cooperation with local and state citizen organizations in resisting the destruction of wildland resources and wildlife. Conducts leadership training programs for citizen conservationists. Sponsors book award program for young people. Sponsors "A Way to the Wilderness" trip program. Publication: *Living Wilderness,* quarterly; also publishes *Wilderness Reports,* notices, and conservation alerts on critical conservation issues. Convention/Meeting: Semi-annual.

WILDLIFE MANAGEMENT INSTITUTE

709 Wire Bldg.   Phone: (202) 347-1774
Washington, D.C. 20005
Daniel A. Poole, Pres.
Founded: 1946
Staff: 22
To promote better management and wise utilization of all renewable natural resources in the public interest. Publications: (1) *Outdoor News Bulletin, biweekly;* (2) *Transactions of Annual North American Wildlife and Natural Resources Conference* (and cumulative index); also publishes various books and monographs. Holds annual conference.

WILDLIFE SOCIETY

7101 Wisconsin Avenue N.W., Suite 611 Phone: (301) 986-8700
Washington, D.C. 20014
Richard N. Denney, Executive Director
Founded: 1937
Members: 10,000
Sectional groups: 7
Professional society of wildlife biologists and others interested in resource conservation and wildlife management on a sound biological basis. Publications: (1) *Journal of Wildlife Management,* quarterly; (2) *Wildlife Society Bulletin,* quarterly; (3) *Wildlife Monographs,* irregular. Formerly: (1937) Society of Wildlife Specialists. Convention/Meeting: Annual—held with North American Wildlife and Natural Resources Conference.

WORLD WILDLIFE FUND

1319 Eighteenth St. N.W.   Phone: (202) 466-2160
Washington, D.C. 20036
Godfrey A. Rockefeller, Exec. Dir.
Founded: 1961
Staff: 15
Supported by contributions from individuals, funds, corporations, and foundations with a concern for conservation of wildlife and its habitat. Emphasizes preservation of endangered and vanishing species of wildlife, plants, and natural areas anywhere in the world. Makes grants for land acquisition, habitat protection and maintenance and scientific ecological research around the globe. Support is given existing conservation societies, agencies, and governments to carry out projects and services. Maintains small library. Committee: Scientific Advisory. Affiliated with: World Wildlife Fund International, and International Union for Conservation of Nature and Natural Resources, both headquartered at Morges, Switzerland. Holds quarterly board meetings. WWF includes 26 national affiliates.

(NOTE: Organizations and associations which are national in scope and who desire to be listed in this directory should send detailed information about themselves in the format shown here. Address: The Editor, SHOOTER'S BIBLE, 55 Ruta Court, South Hackensack, N.J. 07606.)

Ammunition

Amber, John T., ed. **Handloader's Digest.** 7th ed. 1975. pap. 7.95. DBI.

Central Intelligence Agency. **CIA Ammunition & Explosives Supply Catalog.** (Illus.). 1975. pap. 7.95. Paladin Pr.

——**CIA Explosives for Sabotage Manual.** (Illus.). 1975. pap. 5.95. Paladin Pr.

Parkerson, Codman. **A Brief History of Bullet Moulds.** 1.75. Pioneer Pr.

Sears & Roebuck Ammunition Catalog. (Illus.). pap. 1.50. Sand Pond.

Steindler, R. A. **Reloader's Guide.** 3rd ed. (Illus.). 1975. softbound. 6.95. Stoeger.

Suydam, Charles R. **U.S. Cartridges & Their Handguns: 1795-1975.** (Illus.). 1978. 14.95; pap. 9.95. Beinfeld.

Williams, Mason. **The Law Enforcement Book of Weapons, Ammunition & Training Procedures: Handguns, Rifles & Shotguns.** (Illus.). 1977. 32.50. C C Thomas.

Wooters, John. **The Complete Book of Practical Handloading.** (Illus.). 1977. softbound. 5.95. Stoeger.

Antelopes

Bere, Rennie. **Antelopes.** (Illus.). 1971. 3.95. Arco.

Bronson, Wilfrid S. **Horns & Antlers.** (Illus.). 1942. 4.95. HarBraceJ.

Caton, John D. **The Antelope & Deer of America: A Scientific Treatise Upon the Natural History, Habits, Affinities & Capacity for Domestication of the Antilocapra & Cervidae of North America.** (Illus.). 1974. Repr. 22.00. Arno.

Anti-Tank Guns

Chamberlain, Peter & Gander, Terry. **Anti-Tank Weapons.** (Illus.). 1975. 5.95; pap. 3.95. Arco.

——**Self-Propelled Anti-Tank & Anti-Aircraft Guns.** (Illus.). 1975. pap. 3.95. Arco.

Hoffschmidt, Edward J. & Tantum, William H. **German Tank & Antitank of World War Two.** 1968. 10.00. We Inc.

Archery

American Alliance for Health, Physical Education & Recreation. **Archery: A Planning Guide for Group & Individual Instruction.** 1972. pap. 4.25. AAHPER.

——**Archery Selected Articles, 1971.** pap. 1.25. AAHPER.

Annarino, A. **Archery: Individualized Instructional Program.** 1973. pap. 2.75. P-H.

Archery. 1976. pap. 2.50. British Bk Ctr.

Archery-Fencing Guide 1978-80. 1978. pap. 2.50. AAHPER.

Ascham, Roger. **Toxophilus, the Schole of Shootinge,** 2 bks. 1969. Repr. of 1545 ed. 25.00. W J Johnson.

——**Toxophilus, 1545.** Arber, Edward, ed. 1971. Repr. of 1895 ed. 8.50. Scholarly.

Barrett, Jean A. **Archery.** 2nd ed. 1973. pap. 3.95. Goodyear.

Bear, Fred. **Archer's Bible.** (Illus.). 1968. pap. 2.95. Doubleday.

Burke, Edmund. **Archery.** (Illus.). 1963. pap. 1.75. Arc Bks.

Burke, Edmund H. **Archery Handbook.** (Illus.). 1954. 4.95. Arco

——**Archery Handbook.** 1976. pap. 2.95. Arco.

——**Field & Target Archery.** (Illus.). 1961. 4.00. Arco.

——**History of Archery.** 1971. Repr. of 1957 ed. 14.75. Greenwood.

Butler, David F. **The New Archery.** rev. ed. (Illus.). 1973. 6.95. A S Barnes.

Campbell, Donald W. **Archery.** 1970. pap. 2.50. P-H.

Ford, Horace A. **Archery, Its Theory & Practice.** 1971. Repr. of 1856 ed. 8.00. Shumway.

Foy, Tom. **Archery.** 1976. pap. 2.50. Charles River Bks.

——**Beginner's Guide to Archery.** 8.75. Transatlantic.

Gillelan, G. Howard. **Complete Book of the Bow & Arrow.** rev. ed. 1977. 9.95. Stackpole.

Heath, E. G. **Archery. The Modern Approach.** rev. 2nd ed. (Illus.). 1978. 11.95; pap. 5.95. Faber & Faber.

——**A History of Target Archery.** (Illus.). 1974. 9.95. A S Barnes.

Helgeland, Glenn, ed. **Archery World's Complete Guide to Bowhunting.** (Illus.). 1975. 8.95. P-H.

Herrigel, Eugen. **Zen in the Art of Archery.** 1971. pap. 1.95. Random.

Hochman, Louis. **Complete Archery Book.** (Illus.). 1957. 4.95. Arco.

Hougham, Paul. **Encyclopedia of Archery.** (Illus.). 1957. 5.00. A S Barnes.

Klann, Margaret L. **Target Archery.** 1970. pap. 5.50. A-W.

Latham, J. D., ed. **Saracen Archery.** (Illus.). 25.00. Saifer.

Laubin, Reginald & Laubin, Gladys. **American Indian Archery.** (Illus.). 1978. 12.50. U of Okla Pr.

Laycock, George & Bauer, Erwin. **Hunting with Bow & Arrow.** 1965. 3.95. Arco.

Learn, C. R. **Bowhunter's Digest.** 1974. pap. 6.95. DBI.

Lewis, Jack, ed. **Archer's Digest.** 2nd ed. (Illus.). 1977. pap. 7.95. DBI.

McKinney, Wayne C. **Archery.** 3rd ed. 1975. pap. 2.50. Wm C Brown.

Markham, Gervase. **The Art of Archerie.** facs. ed. 1968. Repr. of 1634 ed. 12.00. Shumway.

Mosely, Walter M. **An Essay on Archery.** 1976. 17.50. Charles River Bks.

Neade, William. **The Double Armed Man.** facs. ed. (Illus.). 1971. 8.00. Shumway.

Niemeyer, Roy K. & Zabik, Roger. **Beginning Archery.** 3rd. ed. 1978. pap. 3.95. Wadsworth Pub.

Pszczola, Lorraine. **Archery.** 2nd ed. (Illus.). 1976. pap. 3.50. Saunders.

Reichart, N. & Keasey, G. **Archery.** 3rd ed. (Illus.). 1961. 5.95. Ronald.

Richardson, M. E. **Archery.** 1975. pap. 2.95. McKay.

Roberts, Daniel. **Archery for All.** 1976. 4.95. David & Charles.

Smith, Mike. **Archery.** 1978. 6.95. Arco.

Stamp, Don. **Archery—an Expert's Guide.** pap. 2.00. Wilshire.

——**Archery: An Expert's Guide.** pap. 2.00. Borden.

——**Challenge of Archery.** (Illus.). 1971. 10.00. Intl Pubns Serv.

Tinsley, Russell. **Bow Hunter's Guide.** (Illus.). 1975. softbound. 4.95. Stoeger.

Williams, John. **Archery for Beginners.** (Illus.). 1976. pap. 4.95. Contemp Bks.

With Stick & String: Adventures with Bow & Arrow. (Illus.). 4.95. Avery Color.

Wood. Sir William. **The Bowman's Glory or Archery Revived.** 1976. 7.50. Charles River Bks.

Arms and Armor

Albion, Robert G. **Introduction to Military History.** (Illus.). 1971. Repr. of 1929 ed. 22.50. AMS Pr.

American Machine & Foundry Co. **Acoustic Study Program.** (Illus.). 1972. pap. 7.95. Paladin Pr.

Archer, Denis, ed. **Jane's Infantry Weapons 1977.** 1977. 72.50. Watts.

——**Jane's Infantry Weapons 1978.** 1978. 72.50. Watts.

Ashdown, Charles H. **Armour & Weapons in the Middle Ages.** (Illus.). 10.00. Saifer.

——**British & Continental Arms & Armour.** (Illus.). 6.00. Peter Smith.

——**British & Continental Arms & Armour.** (Illus.). 1970. pap. 4.00. Dover.

Barker, A. J. **Russian Infantry Weapons of World War Two.** 1971. 3.50. Arco.

Bearse, Ray. **Sporting Arms of the World.** 1977. 15.95. Har-Row.

Birla Institute of Scientific Research, Economic Research Division & Agarwal, R. J. **Defense Production & Development.** 1978. 7.50. Verry.

Brassey's Infantry Weapons of the World. 2nd ed. 1978. 39.50. Crane-Russak Co.

Brodie, Bernard & Brodie, Fawn M. **From Crossbow to H-Bomb.** rev. ed. (Illus.). 1973. 10.00. pap. 2.95. Ind U Pr.

Chappelear, Louis E. **Japanese Armor Makers.** 1978. 25.00. Hawley.

Cowper, H. S. **The Art of Attack: Being a Study in the Development of Weapons & Appliances of Offense, from the Earliest Times to the Age of Gunpowder.** (Illus.). 1977. Repr. of 1906 ed. 16.00. Rowman.

Curtis, Howard M. **European Helmets, 800 B.C. – 1700 A.D.** (Illus.). 1978. 19.95. Beinfeld.

Daniel, Larry J. & Gunter, Riley W. **Confederate Canon Foundries.** Pioneer Press, ed. 17.95. Pioneer Pr.

De Gheyn, Jacob. **The Exercise of Arms.** (Illus.). 1976. Repr. of 1607 ed. 65.00. Arma Pr.

Draeger, Donn F. **The Weapons & Fighting Arts of the Indonesian Archipelago.** (Illus.). 1972. 12.50. C E Tuttle.

Featherstone, Donald. **Weapons & Equipment of the Victorian Soldier.** (Illus.). 1978. 12.95. Blandford Pr.

Ffoulkes, Charles & Hopkinson, E. C. **Sword, Lance & Bayonet.** (Illus.). 1967. 7.50. Arco.

Ffoulkes, Charles J. **Armourer & His Craft.** (Illus.). 1967. Repr. of 1912 ed. 18.50 Arno.

Finlay, Ian H. & Bann, Stephen. **Heroic Emblems.** (Illus.). 1978. pap. 3.50. Z Pr.

Foss, Christopher. **Infantry Weapons of the World.** 1977. 7.95. Scribner.

Frost, H. Gordon. **Blades & Barrels: Six Centuries of Combination Weapons.** 16.95; deluxe ed. 25.00; presentation ed. 50.00. Walloon Pr.

Funcken, Liliane & Funcken, Fred. **Arms & Uniforms: Lace Wars, Pt. 1.** 1978. 17.95. Hippocrene Bks.

——**Arms & Uniforms: Lace Wars, Pt. 2.** 1978. 17.95. Hippocrene Bks.

——**Arms & Uniforms—Ancient Egypt to the Eighteenth Century.** 11.95. Hippocrene Bks.

——**Arms & Uniforms—Late Eighteenth Century to the Present Day.** 11.95. Hippocrene Bks.

——**Arms & Uniforms—the First World War, Pt. 1.** 11.95. Hippocrene Bks.

——**Arms & Uniforms—the First World War, Pt. 2.** 11.95. Hippocrene Bks.

——**Arms & Uniforms—the Napoleonic Wars, Pt. 1.** 11.95. Hippocrene Bks.

——**Arms & Uniforms—The Napoleonic Wars, Pt. 2.** 11.95. Hippocrene Bks.

——**Arms & Uniforms—the Second World War, Pt. 1.** 11.95. Hippocrene Bks.

——**Arms & Uniforms—the Second World War, Pt. 2.** 11.95. Hippocrene Bks.

——**Arms & Uniforms—the Second World War, Pt. 3.** 11.95. Hippocrene Bks.

——**Arms & Uniforms—the Second World War, Pt. 4.** 11.95. Hippocrene Bks.

——**British Infantry Uniforms from Marlborough to Wellington.** (Arms & Uniforms Ser.). (Illus.). 1977. pap. 4.95. Hippocrene Bks.

——**First World War, 2 pts.** (Illus.). 1974. 12.50. Intl Pubns Serv.

——**The Lace Wars, Pt. 1.** (Illus.). 1977. 17.50. Intl Pubns Serv.

——**The Lace Wars, Pt. 2.** (Illus.). 1977. 17.50. Intl Pubns Serv.

Gettens, Rutherford J., et al. **Two Early Chinese Bronze Weapons with Meteoritic Iron Blades.** (Illus.). 1971. pap. 5.00. Freer.

Grancsay, Steven V. **Catalog of the John Woodman Higgins Armory Museum.** (Illus.). 10.00. Mowbray Co.

Gruzanski, C. V. **Spike & Chain.** 5.25. Wehman.

Hamilton, T. M. **Firearms on the Frontier: Guns at Fort Michilimackinac 1715-1781.** Armour, David A., ed. (Illus.). 1976. pap. 3.00. Mackinac Island.

Hart, Harold H., ed. **Weapons & Armor.** 1977. 23.95; pap. 7.95. Hart.

Hawley, W. M. **Introduction to Japanese Swords.** 1973. pap. 2.00. Hawley.

Held, Robert, ed. **Arms & Armor Annual.** 1973. pap. 9.95. DBI.

Hoff, Arne. **Feuerwaffen.** 2 vols. (Illus.). 1976. Set 75.00. Arma Pr.

Hogg, Ian. **Military Small Arms of the Twentieth Century.** 1973. pap. 7.95. Follett.

Hughes, B. P. **Firepower: Weapon Effectiveness on the Battlefield, 1630-1815.** (Illus.). 1974. 12.50 Scribner.

Hulton, A. **Sword & the Centuries.** 8.50. Wehman.

Johnson, Thomas M. **Collecting the Edged Weapons of the Third Reich,** 2 vols. Bradach, Wilfrid, tr. (Illus.). Vol. 1: 16.50; pap. 8.75. Vol. 2: 18.50. T M Johnson.

——**Collecting the Edged Weapons of the Third Reich.** Vol. 3. Bradach, Wilfrid, tr. (Illus.). 1978. 20.00. T M Johnson.

——**Wearing the Edged Weapons of the Third Reich.** Bradach, Wilfred, tr. (Illus.). 1977. pap. 8.50. T M Johnson.

Johnson, Thomas M. & Bradach, Wilfrid. **Third Reich Edged Weapons Accouterments.** (Illus.). 1978. pap. 10.00. T M Johnson.

Joly, H. L. **Naunton Collection of Japanese Sword Fitting.** 1973. Repr. of 1912 ed. 50.00. Hawley.

Journal of the Arms & Armour Society, Vol. 1. (Illus.). 1970. 10.00. Shumway.

Keller, May L. **The Anglo-Saxon Weapon Names, Treated Archaeologically & Etymologically.** 1967. Repr. of 1906 ed. 30.00. Intl Pubns Serv.

Kelly, Francis M. & Schwabe, Randolph. **Short History of Costume & Armour, Chiefly in England 1066-1800,** 2 vols. in 1. (Illus.). 1968. Repr. of 1931 ed. 16.00. Arno.

——**A Short History of Costume & Armour 1066-1800,** 2 vols. in 1. (Illus.). 1972. 12.50. Arco.

Lindsay, Merrill. **The Lure of Antique Arms.** (Illus.). 1978. softbound. 5.95. Stoeger.

——**Miniature Arms.** (Illus.). 1976. 7.95. Arma Pr.

——**Twenty Great American Guns.** (Illus.). 1976. pap. 1.75. Arma Pr.

Mason, Richard O. **Use of the Long Bow with the Pike.** 1970. limited ed. 8.00. Shumway.

Mavrodin, Valentin, compiled by. **Fine Arms from Tula.** (Illus.). 1978. 25.00. Abrams.

Milton, Roger. **Heralds & History.** (Illus.). 1978. 14.95. Hipprocrene Bks.

Mowbray, E. Andrew, ed. **Arms-Armor: From the Atelier of Ernst Schmidt, Munich.** (Illus.). 1967. 15.00. Mowbray Co.

Moyer, Frank A. **Special Forces Foreign Weapons Handbook.** (Illus.). 1970 15.95. Paladin Pr.

Neal, W. Keith & Back, D. H. **Great British Gunmakers 1740-1790: The History of John Twigg & the Packington Guns.** (Illus.). 1975. 70.00. S P Bernet.

Norman, A. V. & Pottinger, Don. **History of War & Weapons 449-1660: English Warfare from the Anglo-Saxons to Cromwell.** Orig. Title: **Warrior to Soldier: 449-1660.** 1967. 7.95. T Y Crowell.

Owen, J. I. ed. **Brassey's Infantry Weapons of the World 1975.** (Illus.). 1975. 39.50. Westview.

——**Brassey's NATO Infantry and Its Weapons.** 1976. 14.50. Westview.

——**Brassey's Warsaw Pact Infantry & Its Weapons: Defence Publications.** 1976. 12.00. Westview.

Pretty, Ronald T., ed. **Jane's Weapon Systems.** 1976. 72.50. Watts.

——**Jane's Weapon Systems 1977-78.** (Illus.). 1977. 72.50. Watts.

Reid, William. **Arms Through the Ages.** (Illus.). 1976. 35.00. Har-Row.

Robinson, H. Russell. **The Armour of Imperial Rome.** (Illus.). 1974. 17.50. Scribner.

Rusi & Brassey's Defense Yearbook. 1978/79. 89th ed. 1979. 27.50. Crane-Russak Co.

Sampson, Anthony. **The Arms Bazaar: From Lebanon to Lockheed.** 1978. pap. 2.95. Bantam.

Schreir, Konrad F., Jr. **Marble Knives and Axes.** (Illus.). 1978. pap. 4.95. Beinfeld.

Schroeder, Joseph J., Jr., ed. **Arms of the World: 1911.** pap. 5.95. DBI.

Schuyler-Hartley-Graham Military Furnishers. **Illustrated Catalog Arms & Military Goods.** facs. ed. (Illus.). 1864. 9.50. Flayderman.

Seitz, Heribert. **Blankwaffen,** 2 vols. (Illus.). 1976. set. 75.00 Arma Pr.

Shepperd, G. A. **A History of War & Weapons, 1660-1918.** (Illus.). 1972. 7.95. T Y Crowell.

Snodgrass, A. M. **Arms & Armour of the Greeks.** (Illus.). 1967. 17.50. Cornell U Pr.

Stephens, Frederick J. **Edged Weapons, a Collector's Guide.** (Illus.). 1977. 14.95. Hippocrene Bks.

Thomas, Donald G. **U.S. Silencer Patents,** 2 vols. new ed. Brown, Robert K. & Lund, Peder C., eds. Incl. Vol. 1. 1888-1935. 15.95. Vol. 2. 1936-1972. 15.95. (Illus.). 1973. Set. 29.95. Paladin Pr.

Truby, J. David. **Silencers, Snipers & Assassins.** Brown, Robert K. & Lund, Peder C., ed. (Illus.). 1972. 15.95. Paladin Pr.

——**Quiet Killers.** (Illus.). 1972. 6.95; pap. 4.00. Paladin Pr.

U.S. Army Foreign Science & Technology Center, Washington, D.C. **Typical Foreign Unconventional Warfare Weapons.** 1976. pap. 3.00. Paladin Pr.

U.S. Army Munitions Command. **Silencers: 1896.** (Illus.). 1971. 10.95; pap. 6.95. Paladin Pr.

U.S. Army Sniper Training Manual. (Illus.). 1975. 12.95; pap. 8.95. Paladin Pr.

Vangen, Roland D. **Indian Weapons.** (Illus.). 1972. 4.50; pap. 1.50. Filter.

Von Mellenthin, F. W. **Panzer Battles: A Study of the Employment of Armor in the Second World War.** Turner, L. C., ed. Betzler, H., tr. (Illus.). 1971. 14.50. U of Okla Pr.

Werner, E. T. **Chinese Weapons.** 3.50. Wehman.

——**Chinese Weapons.** Alston, Pat, ed. (Illus.). 1972. pap. 3.50. Ohara Pubns.

Wilkinson-Latham, Robert. **Swords & Other Edged Weapons.** (Illus.). 1978. 8.95; pap. 5.95. Arco.

Williams, John. **Atlas of Weapons & War.** 1976. 12.95. John Day.

Wintringham, Thomas H. **Story of Weapons & Tactics.** facs. ed. 1943. 13.50. Arno.

Yumoto, J. M. **Samurai Sword.** 7.25. Wehman.

Artillery

Archer, Denis, ed. **Jane's Pocket Book of Naval Armament.** (Illus.). 1976. pap. 5.95. Macmillan.

Batchelor, John. **Artillery.** 1973. pap. 4.95. Ballantine.

Behrend, Arthur. **As from Kemmel Hill.** (Illus.). 1975. Repr. of 1963 ed. 13.00. Greenwood.

Bidwell, R. G., ed. **Brassey's Artillery of the World: Defence Publications.** 1977. 39.50. Westview.

Bourne, William. **The Arte of Shooting in Great Ordnaunce.** 1969. Repr. of 1587 ed. 13.00. W J Johnson.

Chamberlain, Peter & Gander, Terry. **Heavy Artillery.** (Illus.). 1975. pap. 3.95. Arco.

Foss, Christopher. **Artillery of the World.** 2nd ed. (Illus.). 1976. 7.95. Scribner.

Gibbon, John, ed. **Artillerist's Manual.** Repr. of 1860 ed. 29.50. Greenwood.

Hogg, Ian. **Guns, 1939-45.** 1976. pap. 2.50. Ballantine.

Hogg, O. F. **Artillery: Its Origin, Heyday, & Decline.** (Illus.). 1970. 13.50. Shoe String.

Hughes B. P. **Firepower: Weapon Effectiveness on the Battlefield, 1630-1815.** (Illus.). 1974. 12.50. Scribner.

Macchiavelli, Niccolo. **The Arte of Warre (Certain Waies of the Orderyng of Souldiours).** Whitehorne, P., tr. 1969. Repr. of 1562 ed. 42.00. W J Johnson.

Marsden, E. W. **Greek & Roman Artillery: Technical Treatises.** 1971. 18.95. Oxford U Pr.

Norton, Robert. **The Gunner, Showing the Whole Practise of Artillerie.** 1973. Repr. of 1628 ed. 40.00. W J Johnson.

Patrick, John M. **Artillery & Warfare During the Thirteenth & Fourteenth Centuries.** 1961. pap. 2.00. Utah St U Pr.

Rogers, H. B. **A History of Artillery.** (Illus.). 1974. 7.95. Citadel Pr.

Rogers, H. C. **A History of Artillery.** 1977. pap. 4.95. Citadel Pr.

Simienowicz, Casimir. **The Great Art of Artillery. 1976.** 20.00. Charles River Bks.

——**The Great Art of Artillery.** Chevlet, George, tr. from Fr. 1973. Repr. of 1729 ed. 17.95. British Bk Ctr.

Tousard, Louis De. **American Artillerists Companion.** 3 vols. 1809-1813. Repr. Set. 106.00. Greenwood.

Ballistics

Wilber, Charles G. **Ballistic Science for the Law Enforcement Officer.** (Illus.). 1977. 23.50. C C Thomas.

——**Forensic Biology for the Law Enforcement Officer.** (Illus.). 1974. 19.00. C C Thomas.

Bayonets

Carter, J. Anthony. **Allied Bayonets of World War Two.** (Illus.). 1969. 3.50. Arco.

Hardin, Albert N. **The American Bayonet: 1776-1964.** (Illus.). 1977. 24.50. Hardin.

Stephens, Frederick J. **A Collector's Pictorial Book of Bayonets.** (Illus.). 1976. pap. 3.95. Hippocrene Bks.

Bird Dogs

Brown, William F. **National Field Trial Champions, 1956-1966.** (Illus.). 1966. 12.00. A S Barnes.

Davis, Henry P. **Training Your Own Bird Dog.** rev. ed. (Illus.). 1970. 6.95. Putnam.

Evans, George Bird. **Troubles with Bird Dogs & What to Do About Them: Training Experiences with Actual Dogs Under the Gun.** (Illus.). 1975. 10.00. Winchester Pr.

Falk, John R. **The Complete Guide to Bird Dog Training.** 1976. 10.00. Winchester Pr.

——**The Practical Hunter's Dog Book.** (Illus.). 1975. softbound. 5.95. Stoeger.

Long, Paul. **All the Answers to All Your Questions About Training Pointing Dogs.** (Illus.). 1974. pap. 4.35. Capital Bird.

Mueller, Larry. **Bird Dog Guide.** rev. ed. (Illus.). 1976. softbound. 6.95 Stoeger.

Seminatore, Mike & Rosenburg, John M. **Your Bird Dog & You.** (Illus.). 1977. 9.95. A S Barnes.

Webb, Sherman. **Practical Pointer Training.** (Illus.). 1974. 6.95. Winchester Pr.

Black Powder Guns

Buchele, William & Shumway, George. **Recreating The American Longrifle.** Orig. Title: Recreating The Kentucky Rifle. (Illus.). 1973. pap. 7.50. Shumway.

Lauber, George. **How to Build Your Own Flintlock Rifle or Pistol.** Seaton, Lionel, tr. from Ger. (Illus.). 1976. pap. 6.95. Jolex.

——**How to Build Your Own Percussion Rifle or Pistol.** Seaton, Lionel, tr. from Ger. (Illus.). 1976. pap. 6.95. Jolex.

——**How to Build Your Own Wheellock Rifle or Pistol.** Seaton, Lionel, tr. from Ger. (Illus.). 1976. 6.95. Jolex.

Lewis, Jack & Springer, Robert, eds. **Black Powder Gun Digest,** 2nd ed. (Illus.). 1977. ppa. 7.95. DBI.

National Muzzle Loading Rifle Association. **Muzzle Blasts: Early Years Plus Vol. I & II. 1939-41.** 1974. pap. 15.00. Shumway.

Nonte, George C., Jr. **Black Powder Guide.** 2nd ed. (Illus.). 1976. softbound. 6.95. Stoeger.

——**Home Guide to Muzzle Loaders.** (Illus.). 1974. pap. 6.95. Stackpole.

Steindler, R. A., ed. & illus. **Shooting the Muzzle Loaders.** (Illus.). 1975. 11.95; pap. 6.95. Jolex.

Bow and Arrow

Barwick, Humphrey. **Concerning the Force & Effect of Manuall Weapons of Fire.** 1974. Repr. of 1594 ed. 8.00. W J Johnson.

Hamilton, T. M. **Native American Bows: Their Types & Relationships.** (Illus.). 1972. 10.00. Shumway.

Hardy, Robert. **Longbow: A Social & Military History.** (Illus.). 1977. 19.95. Arco.

Mason, Richard O. **Use of the Long Bow with the Pike.** 1970. limited ed. 8.00. Shumway.

Murdoch, John. **Study of the Eskimo Bows in the U.S. National Museum.** facs. ed. (Illus.). Repr. of 1884 ed. pap. 2.00. Shorey.

A New Invention of Shooting Fireshafts in Long-Bowes. 1974. Repr. of 1628 ed. 3.50. W J Johnson.

Pope, Saxton T. **Bows & Arrows.** 1974. 10.00. U of Cal Pr.

Smythe, John. **Bow Versus Gun.** 1974. Repr. of 1590 ed. text ed. 17.50. British Bk Ctr.

Tinsley, Russell. **Bow Hunter's Guide.** (Illus.). 1975. softbound. 5.95. Stoeger.

Caribou

Georgeson, C. C. **Reindeer & Caribou.** facs. ed. (Illus.). Repr. of 1904 ed. pap. 1.50. Shorey.

Murie, Olaus J. **Alaska Yukon Caribou.** facs. ed. (Illus.). 1935. pap. 10.00. Shorey.

Cartridges

Barnes, Frank. **Cartridges of the World.** 3rd ed. 1972. pap. 7.95. DBI.

Bartlett, W. A. & Gallatin, D. B. **B & G Cartridge Manual.** 2.00. Pioneer Pr.

Datig, Fred A. **Cartridges for Collectors,** 3 vols. 7.50 ea. Borden.

Steindler, R. A. **Reloader's Guide.** 3rd ed. (Illus.). 1975. softbound. 6.95. Stoeger.

Suydam. **American Cartridge.** 8.50. Borden.

Suydam, Charles R. **U.S. Cartridges & Their Handguns: 1795-1975.** (Illus.). 1978. 14.95; pap. 9.95. Follett.

Thomas, Gough. **Shotguns & Cartridges for Game & Clays.** 3rd ed. (Illus.). 1976. 15.00. Transatlantic.

Treadwell. **Cartridges, Regulation & Experimental.** 2.00. Pioneer Pr.

Whelen, Townsend. **Why Not Load Your Own?** (Illus.). 7.95. A S Barnes.

Collecting

Chapel, Charles E. **The Gun Collector's Handbook of Values: 1977-78.** rev. ed. 1977. 17.95. Coward.

Liu, Allan J., ed. **The American Sporting Collector's Handbook.** (Illus.). 1977. softbound. 5.95. Stoeger.

Colt Revolvers

Bady, Donald B. **Colt Automatic Pistols.** rev. ed. 1973. 12.50. Borden.

Barnard, Henry. **Armsmear: The Samuel Colt Biography.** (Illus.). 1978. 24.95. Beinfeld.

Keating, Bern. **The Flamboyant Mr. Colt & His Deadly Six-Shooter.** 1978. 9.95. Doubleday.

Larson, E. Dixon. **Colt Tips.** 3.95. Pioneer Pr.

McClernan, John B. **Slade's Wells Fargo Colt.** (Illus.). 1977. 5.00. Exposition.

Shumaker, P. L. **Colt's Variations of the Old Model Pocket Pistol.** 1957. 6.00. Borden.

Swayze, Nathan L. **Fifty One Colt Navies.** (Illus.). 1967. 15.00. Gun Hill.

Virgines, George. **Saga of the Colt Six Shooter: And the Famous Men Who Used It.** 1969. 7.95. Fell.

Wilson, R. L. **The Book of Colt Engraving.** 1978. 39.95. Follett.

Crossbows

Bilsom, Frank. **Crossbows.** (Illus.). 1975. 8.95. Hippocrene Bks.

Payne-Gallwey, R. **Crossbow.** 27.50. Newbury Bks Inc.

Payne-Gallwey, Ralph. **Cross-Bow, Medieval & Modern.** 25.00. Saifer.

Wilbur, C. Martin. **History of the Crossbow.** (Illus.). Repr. of 1936 ed. pap. 1.50. Shorey.

Decoys

Barber, Joel. **Wild Fowl Decoys.** (Illus.). pap. 5.00. Dover.

——**Wild Fowl Decoys.** (Illus.). 9.00. Peter Smith.

Becker, A. C., Jr. **Decoying Waterfowl.** (Illus.). 1973. 12.00. A S Barnes.

Berkey, Barry R., et al. **Pioneer Decoy Carvers: A Biography of Lemuel & Stephen Ward.** (Illus.). 1977. 17.50. Cornell Maritime.

Brown, Ercil. **Thrills of the Duck Hunt for the Officebound.** (Illus.). 1973. 2.50. Dorrance.

Casson, Paul W. **Decoy-Collecting Primer.** (Illus.). pap. 5.95. Eriksson.

Connett, Eugene. **Duck Decoys.** 1954. 9.50. Durrell.

Coykendall, Ralf. **Duck Decoys & How to Rig Them.** (Illus.). 1965. 7.95. HR&W.

Decoys. (Illus.). 1974. 1.50. Applied Arts.

Frank, Charles W., Jr. **Louisiana Duck Decoys.** 1978. 19.95. Pelican.

Johnsgard, Paul A., ed. **The Bird Decoy: an American Art Form, A Catalog of Carvings Exhibited at the Sheldon Memorial Art Gallery, Lincoln Nebraska.** (Illus.). 1976. 17.95. U of Nebr Pr.

Starr, George. **Decoys of the Atlantic Flyway.** (Illus.). 1974. 17.95. Winchester Pr.

Starr, George R., Jr. **How to Make Working Decoys.** (Illus.). 1978. 15.00. Winchester Pr.

Wilson, Loring D. **The Handy Sportsman.** (Illus.). 1976. softbound. 5.95. Stoeger.

Deer Hunting

Anderson, Luther A. **Hunting The Uplands with Rifle & Shotgun.** (Illus.). 1977. 10.00. Winchester Pr.

Cartier, John O. **The Modern Deer Hunter.** (Illus.). 1977. 10.95. Funk & W.

Conway, Bryant W. **Successful Hints on Hunting White Tail Deer.** 2nd ed. 1967. pap. 1.98. Claitors.

Dalrymple, Byron W. **Complete Book of Deer Hunting.** (Illus.). 1975. softbound. 5.95. Stoeger.

Dickey, Charley. **Charley Dickey's Deer Hunting.** (Illus.). 1977. pap. 3.95. Oxmoor Hse.

Donovan, Robert E. **Hunting Whitetail Deer.** (Illus.). 1978. 12.50. Winchester Pr.

Elman, Robert, ed. **All About Deer Hunting in America.** 1976. 10.00. Winchester Pr.

Hayes, Tom. **How to Hunt the White Tail Deer.** rev. ed. 8.95; pap. 4.95. A S Barnes.

Hewitt, H. P. **Fairest Hunting: Hunting & Watching Exmoor Deer.** 1974. 4.95. British Bk Ctr.

——**The Fairest Hunting.** (Illus.). 3.25. J A Allen.

James, M. R. **Bowhunting: For Whitetail & Mule Deer.** 1976. 10.95; pap. 6.96. Jolex.

Kittredge, Doug & Wambold, H. R. **Bowhunting for Deer.** rev. ed. 1978. 8.95. Stackpole.

Koller, Lawrence R. **Shots at Whitetails.** rev. ed. (Illus.). 1970. 12.50. Knopf.

Laycock, George. **Deer Hunter's Bible.** rev. ed. (Illus.). 1971. pap. 2.50. Doubleday.

——**The Deer Hunter's Bible.** 2nd rev. ed. (Illus.). 1977. pap. 2.95. Doubleday.

McNair, Jack. **Shooting for the Skipper: Memories of a Veteran Deerstalker.** (Illus.). 1971. 6.75. Reed.

Outdoor Life Editors. **Outdoor Life's Deer Hunting Book.** (Illus.). 1975. 8.95. Har-Row.

Sisley, Nick. **Deer Hunting Across North America.** (Illus.). 1975. 12.95. Freshet Pr.

Smith, Richard P. **Deer Hunting.** 1978. 9.95. Stackpole.

Strung, Norman. **Deer Hunting.** (Illus.). 1973. 7.95. Lippincott.

Tillett, Paul. **Doe Day: The Antlerless Deer Controversy in New Jersey.** 1963. pap. 3.25. Rutgers U Pr.

Tinsley, Russell. **Hunting the Whitetail Deer.** (Illus.). 1974. pap. 1.95. B&N.

——**Hunting the Whitetail Deer.** rev. ed. (Illus.). 1977. 7.95; pap. 4.95. Funk & W.

Wootters, John. **Hunting Trophy Deer.** 1977. 13.95. Winchester Pr.

Duck Shooting

Barber, Joel. **Wild Fowl Decoys.** (Illus.). 9.00. Peter Smith.

——**Wild Fowl Decoys** (Illus.). pap. 5.00. Dover.

Coykendall, Ralf. **Duck Decoys & How to Rig Them.** (Illus.). 1965. 7.95. HR&W.

Gresham, Grits. **The Complete Wildfowler.** (Illus.). 1975. softbound. 5.95. Stoeger.

Hinman, Bob. **The Duck Hunter's Handbook.** (Illus.). 1976. softbound. 5.95. Stoeger.

Ducks

Dethier, Vincent G. **Fairweather Duck.** 1970. 4.95. Walker & Co.

Ellis, Melvin R. **Peg Leg Pete.** 1973. 5.95. HR&W.

Hyde, Dayton. **Raising Wild Ducks in Captivity.** 1974. 15.00. Dutton.

Jaques, Florence P. **Geese Fly High.** (Illus.). 1964. Repr. of 1939 ed. 6.95. U of Minn Pr.

Kortright, E. H. **Ducks, Geese & Swans of North America,** rev. ed. Bellrose, Frank C., rev. by. (Illus.). 1975. 15.00. Stackpole.

McKane, John G. **Ducks of the Mississippi Flyway.** (Illus.). 1969. pap. 2.98. North Star.

Ogilvie, M. A. **Ducks of Britain & Europe.** 1975. 14.50. R Curtis Bks.

——**Ducks of Britain & Europe.** (Illus.). 1975. 15.00. Bueto.

Ripley, Dillon. **Paddling of Ducks.** (Illus.). 1969. 6.95. Smithsonian.

Romashko, Sandra D. **Wild Ducks & Geese of North America.** (Illus.). 1978. pap. 2.95. Windward Pub.

Sowls, Lyle K. **Prairie Ducks: A Study of Their Behavior, Ecology & Management.** (Illus.). 1978. 11.50; pap. 3.50. U of Nebr Pr.

Dueling

Bacon, Francis. **The Charge of Sir F. Bacon Touching Duells.** Repr. of 1614 ed. 8.00. W J Johnson.

Bennetton, Norman A. **Social Significance of the Duel in Seventeenth Century Drama.** Repr. of 1938 ed. 15.50. Greenwood.

Coleman, J. Winston. **Famous Kentucky Duels.** (Illus.). 1969. 3.95. Henry Clay.

Douglas, William. **Duelling Days in the Army.** 1977. 30.00. Scholarly.

Gamble, Thomas. **Savannah Duels & Duellists: 1733-1877.** (Illus.). 1974. Repr. of 1923 ed. 15.00. Reprint.

Hutton, Alfred. **The Sword & the Centuries; or, Old Sword Days & Old Sword Ways.** (Illus.). 1973. Repr. of 1901 ed. 8.50. C E Tuttle.

McCarty, Clara S. **Duels in Virginia & Nearby Bladenburg.** 1976. 8.50. Dietz.

Melville, Lewis & Hargreaves, Reginald. **Famous Duels & Assassinations.** (Illus.). 1974. Repr. of 1929 ed. 14.00. Gale.

Risher, James F. **Interview with Honor.** 1975. 6.95. Dorrance.

Seitz, Don C. **Famous American Duels.** facs. ed. 1929. 15.25. Arno.

Thimm, Carl A. **Complete Bibliography of Fencing & Dueling.** (Illus.). 1968 Repr. of 1846 ed. 20.00. Arno.

Falconry

Ap Evans, Humphrey. **Falconry.** (Illus.). 1974. 15.00. Arco.

——**Falconry for You.** 6.50. Branford.

Beebe, F. L. **Hawks, Falcons & Falconry.** (Illus.). 1976. 25.00. Hancock Hse.

Beebe, Frank L. & Webster, Harold M., eds. **North American Falconry & Hunting Hawks.** 4th ed. (Illus.). 1976. 30.00. North Am Fal Hunt.

Berners, Juliana. **The Boke of Saint Albans Containing Treatises on Hawking, Hunting & Cote Armour.** 1976. Repr. of 1881 ed. 15.00. Scholarly.

——**The Book of Hawking, Hunting & Blasing of Arms.** 1969. Repr. of 1486 ed. 42.00. W J Johnson.

Bert, Edmund. **An Approved Treatise of Hawkes & Hawking Divided into Three Bookes.** 1968. Repr. of 1619 ed. 16.00. W J Johnson.

Brander, Michael. **Dictionary of Sporting Terms.** (Illus.). 1968. 7.00. Humanities.

Burton, Richard F. **Falconry in the Valley of the Indus.** 1971. 13.50. Falcon Head Pr.

Danielsson, Bror, ed. **Middle English Falconry Treatises, Pt. 1.** 1978. pap. Humanities.

Falconer's Club of America Journals: 1941-1961. 1974. 32.50. Falcon Head Pr.

Fisher, Charles H. **Falconry Reminiscences.** 1972. 15.00; deluxe ed. 25.00. Falcon Head Pr.

Fleming, Arnold. **Falconry & Falcons: Sport of Flight.** (Illus.). 1976. Repr. of 1934 ed. 20.00. Charles River Bks.

——**Falconry & Falcons: Sport of Flight.** (Illus.). Repr. text ed. 20.00. Charles River Bks.

Frederick Second of Hohenstaufen. **The Art of Falconry.** Wood, Casey A. & Fyfe, F. Marjorie, eds. (Illus.). 1943. 25.00. Stanford U Pr.

Freeman, Gage E. & Salvin, Francis H. **Falconry: Its Claims, History & Practice.** 1972. 12.50; deluxe ed. 25.00. Falcon Head Pr.

Gryndall, William. **Hawking, Hunting, Fouling & Fishing;** Newly Corrected by W. Gryndall Faulkener. 1972. Repr. of 1596 ed. 13.00. W J Johnson.

Hands, Rachel, ed. **English Hawking & Hunting in the Boke of St. Albans.** facs. ed. (Illus.). 1975. 48.00. Oxford U Pr.

Illingworth, Frank. **Falcons & Falconry.** 3rd rev. ed. 1964. 8.95. British Bk Ctr.

Jameson, E.W. Jr. & Peeters, Hans J. **Introduction to Hawking.** 2nd ed. (Illus.). 1977. pap. 6.95. Jameson & Peeters.

Jameson, Everett W., Jr. **The Hawking of Japan, the History & Development of Japanese Falconry.** (Illus.). Repr. of 1962 ed. 24.50. Jameson & Peeters.

Lascelles, Gerald. **Art of Falconry.** (Illus.). 1971. Repr. of 1895 ed. 7.25. Branford.

Latham, Simon. **Lathams Falconry,** 2 pts. 1977. Repr. of 1615 ed. 32.50. W J Johnson.

Madden, D. H. **Chapter of Mediaeval History.** 1969. Repr. of 1924 ed. 12.50. Kennikat.

Mellor, J. E. **Falconry Notes by Mellor.** 1972. 8.50. Falcon Head Pr.

Michell, E. B. **Art & Practice of Hawking.** 8.50. Bradford.

Phillott, D. C. & Harcourt, E. S., trs. from Persian Urdu. **Falconry—Two Treatises.** 1968. text ed. 30.00. Falcon Head Pr.

Salvin, Francis H. & Broderick, William. **Falconry in the British Isles.** 1970. Repr. of 1855 ed. 22.50. North Am Fal Hunt.

Samson, Jack. **Falconry Today.** (Illus.). 1975. 8.95. Walck.

Schlegel, H. & Wulverhorst, A. H. **Traite De Fauconnerie: Treatise of Falconry.** Hanlon, Thomas, tr. (Illus.). 1973. 32.50. Chasse Pubns.

Summers, Gerald. **The Lure of the Falcon.** 1973. 7.95. S&S.

Turberville, George. **The Books of Faulconrie or Hawking.** 1969. Repr. of 1575 ed. 44.00. W J Johnson.

Woodford, Michael H. **Manual of Falconry.** 12.00. Branford.

Firearms

Ackley, Parker O. **Home Gun Care & Repair.** (Illus.). 1974. pap. 4.95. Stackpole.

Amber, John T. **Gun Digest Treasury.** 5th ed. 1977. pap. 7.95. DBI.

——**Gun Digest 1979.** 33rd ed. (Illus.). 1978. pap. 9.95. DBI.

Amber, John T., ed. **Handloader's Digest.** 1978. pap. 7.95. DBI.

——**Handloader's Digest,** 7th ed. 1975. pap. 7.95. DBI.

Baer, L. R. **The Parker Gun: An Immortal American Classic.** (Illus.). 1978. 24.95. Beinfeld.

Barker, A. J. **Principles of Small Arms.** (Illus.). 1977. pap. 4.00. Paladin Pr.

Barwick, Humphrey. **Concerning the Force & Effect of Manuall Weapons of Fire.** 1974. Repr. of 1594 ed. 8.00. W J Johnson.

Bearse, Ray. **Sporting Arms of the World.** (Illus.). 1977. 15.95. Har-Row.

Bianchi, John. **Blue Steel & Gunleather.** 1978. 9.95. Follett.

Bowman, Hank W. **Famous Guns from the Winchester Collection.** (Illus.). 1958. 3.50. Arco.

Bristow, Allen P. **The Search for an Effective Police Handgun.** (Illus.). 1973. 15.75. C C Thomas.

Brophy, William S. **Krag Rifles.** (Illus.). Beinfeld.

Browne, Bellmore H. **Guns & Gunning.** (Illus.). Repr. of 1908 ed. pap. 6.00. Shorey.

Burch, Monte **Gun Care & Repair.** 1978. 10.95. Winchester Pr.

Cadiou, Yves & Richard, Alphonse. **Modern Firearms.** (Illus.). 1977. 19.95. Morrow.

Carmichel, Jim. **The Modern Rifle.** (Illus.). 1976. softbound. 5.95. Stoeger.

Chapel, Charles E. **Complete Guide to Gunsmithing: Gun Care & Repair.** rev. ed. (Illus.). 1962. 9.95. A S Barnes.

Consumer Guide. **The Consumer Guide: Guns.** 1972. pap. 1.95. PB.

Cromwell, Giles. **The Virginia Manufactory of Arms.** 1975. 20.00. U Pr of Va.

Daenhardt, Rainer, ed. **Espingarda Perfeyta; or The Perfect Gun: Rules for Its Use Together with Necessary Instructions for Its Construction & Precepts for Good Aiming.** Daenhardt, Rainer & Neal, W. Keith, trs. from Port. (Illus., Eng. & Port.). 1975. 28.50. Biblio Dist.

Davis, John E. **Introduction to Tool Marks, Firearms & the Striagraph.** (Illus.). 1958. 8.50. C C Thomas.

Dunlap, Roy. **The Gunowner's Book of Care, Repair & Maintenance.** (Illus.). 1974. 12.95. Har-Row.

Durham, Douglass. **Taking Aim.** 1977. 7.95. Seventy Six.

Edsall, James. **The Story of Firearm Ignition.** 3.50. Pioneer Pr.

——**Volcanic Firearms & Their Successors.** 2.50. Pioneer Pr.

Educational Research Council of America. **Firearms Examiner.** Ferris, Theodore N. & Marchak, John P., eds. (Illus.). 1977. 1.95. Changing Times.

Ezell, Edward C., rev. by. **Small Arms of the World.** 11th ed. 1977. 20.00 Stackpole.

Fairbairn, W. E. & Sykes, E. A. **Shooting to Live.** 1974. Repr. of 1942 ed. 5.95. Paladin Pr.

Flayderman, Norm. **Flayderman's Guide to Antique Firearms & Their Values.** 1977. pap. 12.95. DBI.

George, John N. **English Pistols & Revolvers.** 10.00. Saifer.

Grennell, Dean A. **ABC's of Reloading.** 1974. pap. 6.95. DBI.

Grennell, Dean A., ed. **Law Enforcement Handgun Digest.** 2nd rev. ed. 1976. pap. 6.95. DBI.

Hanauer, Elsie. **Guns of the Wild West.** (Illus.). 12.00. A S Barnes.

Hatcher, et al. **Firearms Investigation, Identification & Evidence.** 1977. Repr. 22.50. Stackpole.

Hatcher, Julian S. **Hatcher's Notebook.** rev. ed. (Illus.). 1962. 12.95. Stackpole.

Held, Robert. **Age of Firearms.** (Illus.). 2nd rev. ed. pap. 4.95. DBI.

Helmer, William J. **The Gun That Made the Twenties Roar.** (Illus.). rev. and enl. ed. 1977. 16.95. Gun Room Pr.

Hertzberg, Robert. **The Modern Handgun.** 1977. 4.95; pap. 2.50. Arco.

Hoff, Arne. **Dutch Firearms.** Stryker, Walter A., ed. (Illus.). 1978. 70.00 S B Bernet.

Hoffschmidt, Edward J. **Know Your Gun.** Incl. **Know Your .45 Auto Pistols; Know Your Walther P. 38 Pistols; Know Your Walther P.P. & P.P.K. Pistols; Know Your M1 Garand Rifles; Know Your Mauser Broomhandle Pistol; Know Your Anti-Tank Rifle.** 1976. pap. 3.95 ea. Borden.

Hogg, Brig., fwrd. by. **The Compleat Gunner.** (Illus.). 1976. Repr. 10.50. Charles River Bks

Hogg, Ian V. **The Complete Illustrated Encyclopedia of the World's Firearms.** (Illus.). 1978. 24.95. A & W Pubs.

Hogg, Ian V. & Weeks, John **Military Small Arms of the Twentieth Century.** 3rd ed. (Illus.). 1977. 19.95. Hippocrene Bks.

Howe, James V. **Amateur Guncraftsman.** (Illus.). 1967. pap. 1.95. Funk & W.

Howe, Walter J. **Professional Gunsmithing.** (Illus.). 1946. 14.95. Stackpole.

Huebner, Siegfried. **Silencers for Hand Firearms.** Schreier, Konrad & Lund, Peder C., eds. 1976. pap. 9.95. Paladin Pr.

Huntington, R. T. **Hall's Breechloaders: John H. Hall's Invention & Development of a Breechloading Rifle with Precision-Made Interchangeable Parts, & Its Introduction into the United States Service.** (Illus.). 1972. pap. 15.00. Shumway.

Ingram, M V. **The Bellwitch.** 3.00. Pioneer Pr.

Jackson. & Whitelaw. **European Hand Firearms.** 1978. 22.50. Saifer.

James, Garry, ed. **Guns for Home Defense.** (Illus.). 1975. pap. 3.95. Petersen Pub.

——**Guns of the Gunfighters.** (Illus.). 1975. pap. 4.95. Petersen Pub.

Journal of the Historical Firearms Society of South Africa. Vol. 1. (Illus.). 1964. Repr. of 1958 ed. 7.50. Verry.

Kennedy, Monty. **Checkering & Carving of Gunstocks.** rev. ed. (Illus.). 1952. 14.95. Stackpole.

Koller, Larry. **How to Shoot: A Complete Guide to the Use of Sporting Firearms— Rifles, Shotguns & Handguns—on the Range & in the Field.** rev. ed. Elman, Robert, ed. (Illus.). 1976. 9.95. Doubleday.

Larson, E. Dixon. **Remington Tips.** 4.95. Pioneer Pr.

Lauber, George. **How to Build Your Own Flintlock Rifle or Pistol.** Seaton, Lionel, tr. from Ger. (Illus.). 1976. pap. 6.95. Jolex.

——**How to Build Your Own Percussion Rifle or Pistol.** Seaton, Lionel, tr. from Ger. (Illus.). 1976. pap. 6.95. Jolex.

——**How to Build Your Own Wheellock Rifle or Pistol.** Seaton, Lionel, tr. from Ger. (Illus.). 1976. pap. 6.95. Jolex.

Lenk, Torsten. **Flintlock: Its Origin & Development.** 30.00. Saifer.

The Lewis Gun. 1976. 17.95. Paladin Pr.

Lewis, Jack. **Gun Digest Book of Modern Gun Values.** 1976. pap. 7.95. DBI.

Lewis, Jack & Springer, Robert, eds. **Black Powder Gun Digest,** 2nd ed. (Illus.). 1977. pap. 7.95. DBI.

Lindsay, Merrill. **Twenty Great American Guns.** (Illus.). 1976. Repr. pap. 1.75. Arma Pr.

——**The Lure of Antique Arms.** (Illus.). 1978. softbound. 5.95. Stoeger.

Liu, Allan, J **The American Sporting Collector's Handbook.** 1977. softbound. 5.95. Stoeger.

Miller, Martin. **Collector's Illustrated Guide to Firearms.** (Illus.). 1978. 24.95. Mayflower Bks.

Murtz, Harold A. **Guns Illustrated 1978.** 10th ed., (Illus.). 1977. pap. 6.95. DBI.

Murtz, Harold A., ed. **Gun Digest Book of Exploded Firearms Drawings.** 2nd ed. 1977. pap. 7.95. DBI.

National Muzzle Loading Rifle Association. **Muzzle Blasts: Early Years Plus Vol. I & II 1939-41.** 1974. pap. 15.00. Shumway.

Nonte, George. **Firearms Encyclopedia.** (Illus.). 1973. 15.00. Har-Row.

Nonte, George C. **Handgun Competition.** (Illus.). 1978. 12.95. Winchester Pr.

——**Handloading for Handgunners.** 1978. pap. 7.95 DBI.

Nonte, George C., Jr. **Black Powder Guide.** 2nd ed. (Illus.). 1976. softbound. 6.95. Stoeger.

——**Home Guide to Muzzle Loaders.** (Illus.). 1975. pap. 6.95. Stackpole.

——**Pistol & Revolver Guide.** 3rd ed. (Illus.). 1967. softbound. 6.95. Stoeger.

Nonte, George C., Jr., & Juras Lee. **Handgun Hunting.** (Illus.). 1976. softbound. 5.95. Stoeger.

Owen, J.I., ed. **Brassey's Infantry Weapons of the World, 1975.** (Illus.). 1975. 39.50. Westview.

Page, Warren. **The Accurate Rifle.** 1975. softbound. 5.95. Stoeger.

Peterson & Elman. **The Great Guns.** 1977. 9.95. G & O.

Peterson, Harold L. **Encyclopedia of Firearms.** (Illus.). 1964. 16.95. Dutton.

Pollard, Hugh B. **The History of Firearms.** 1974. 25.50; pap. 8.95. B Franklin.

R. W. Norton Art Gallery. **E. C. Prudhomme: Master Gun Engraver.** (Illus.). 1973. pap. 3.00. Norton Art.

Reese, Michael, II. **Nineteen Hundred Luger— U.S. Test Trials.** 2nd rev. ed. Pioneer Press, ed. (Illus.). pap. 4.95. Pioneer Pr.

Rice, F. Philip. **Outdoor Life Gun Data Book.** (Illus.). 1975. 10.95. Har-Row.

Richardson, H.L. & Wood, Wallis W. **Firearms & Freedom.** Seventy Six.

Riviere, Bill. **The Gunner's Bible.** rev. ed. 1973. pap. 2.50. Doubleday.

Roberts, Willis J. & Bristow, Allen P. **Introduction to Modern Police Firearms.** Gourley, Douglas, ed. (Illus.). 1969. text ed. 10.95. Glencoe.

Russell, Carl. **Firearms, Traps & Tools of the Mountain Men.** (Illus.). 1977. pap. 6.50. U of NM Pr.

Schroeder, Joseph J., Jr., ed. **Gun Collector's Digest.** 2nd ed. 1976. pap. 7.95. DBI.

Scott, Robert F., ed. **Shooter's Bible, 1980, No. 71.** (Illus.). 1979. softbound. 8.95. Stoeger.

Sell. **Handguns Americana.** 1973. 8.50. Borden.

Sherrill, Robert. **The Saturday Night Special.** 1975. pap. 2.75. Penguin.

Shotgun Shooting. 4th ed. (Illus.). 1974. pap. 2.50. Charles River Bks.

Smythe, John & Barwick, Humphrey. **Bow vs. Gun.** 1976. Repr. 15.00. Charles River Bks.

Smith, W. H. B. **Small Arms of the World.** (Illus.). 1975. pap. 9.95. A & W Visual Library.

Stack, Robert. **Shotgun Digest.** 1974. pap. 6.95. DBI.

Stanford, J. K. **Complex Gun.** 12.50. Soccer.

Steindler, R.A. **Firearms Dictionary.** (Illus.). 1975. pap. 6.95. Paladin Pr.

——**Reloader's Guide.** (Illus.). 3rd ed. 1975. softbound. 6.95. Stoeger.

——**Rifle Guide.** (Illus.). 1978. softbound. 7.95. Stoeger.

Steindler, R.A., ed. & illus. **Shooting the Muzzle Loaders.** (Illus.). 1975. 11.95; pap. 6.95. Jolex.

Stockbridge, V. D. **Digest of U.S. Patents Relating to Breech-Loading & Magazine Small Arms, 1836-1873.** (Illus.). 1963. 12.50. Flayderman.

Suydam, Charles R. **U.S. Cartridges & Their Handguns: 1795-1975.** (Illus.). 1978. 14.95; pap. 9.95. Follett.

Tappen, Mel. **Survival Guns.** 1978. 12.95. Janus Pr.

——**Survival Guns.** 1977. pap. 7.95. Janus Pr.

Thomas, Donald G. **Silencer Patents, Vol. III: European Patents 1901-1978.** (Illus.). 1978. 15.00. Paladin Pr.

Truby, J. David. **The Lewis Gun.** (Illus.). 1977. 17.95. Sycamore Island.

Truby, J. David & Minnery, John. **Improvised Modified Firearms,** 2 vols. Lund, Peder C., ed. (Illus.). 1975. 9.95 each. Paladin Pr.

Truby, J. David, et al. **Improvised Modified Firearms,** 2 vols. 1975. 17.95 set. Paladin Pr.

U.S. Army. **Forty-MM Grenade Launcher: M79.** (Illus.). pap. 4.00. Paladin Pr.

U.S. Cartridge Company. **U.S. Cartridge Company Collection of Firearms.** (Illus.). 6.00. Sycamore Island.

Van Rensselaer, S. **American Firearms.** (Illus.) 1978. 16.00. Century Hse.

Wahl, Paul. **Gun Trader's Guide.** (Illus.). 8th ed. 1978. softbound. 7.95. Stoeger.

Waite, M.D. & Ernst, Bernard. **The Trapdoor Springfield.** 1979. 19.95. Beinfeld.

West, Bill. **Know Your Winchesters: General Use, All Models & Types, 1849-1969.** (Illus.). 12.00. B West.

——**Winchester, Cartridges, & History.** (Illus.). 25.00. B West.

——**Winchester-Complete: All Wins & Forerunners, 1849-1970.** (Illus.). 1975. 28.00. B West.

——**Winchester Encyclopedia.** (Illus.). 12.00. B West.

——**Winchester Lever-Action Handbook.** (Illus.). 25.00. B West.

——**The Winchester Single Shot.** (Illus.). 12.00. B West.

Willett, Roderick. **Gun Safety.** (Illus.). 1967. 5.25. Intl Pubns Serv.

Williams, Mason. **The Law Enforcement Book of Weapons, Ammunition & Training Procedures: Handguns, Rifles & Shotguns.** (Illus.). 1977. 32.50. C C Thomas.

Wirnsberger, Gerhard. **Standard Directory of Proof Marks.** Steindler, R. A. tr. from Ger. (Illus.). 1976. pap. 5.95. Jolex.

Wood, J. B. **Trouble-shooting Your Handgun.** 1978. pap. 5.95. DBI.

Wootters, John. **The Complete Book of Practical Handloading.** (Illus.). 1977. softbound. 5.95. Stoeger.

Wycoff, James. **Famous Guns That Won the West.** (Illus.). 1975. pap. 2.00. Arco.

Firearms—Catalogs

Amber, John T. **Gun Digest, 1979.** 33rd ed. 1978. pap. 9.95. DBI.

Byron, D. **The Firearms Price Guide.** (Illus.). 1977. pap. 9.95. Crown.

Chapel, Charles E. **Gun Collector's Handbook of Values: 1977-78.** rev. ed. (Illus.). 1977. 17.95. Coward.

Eighteen-Sixty Two Ordnance Manual. 1.50. Pioneer Pr.

Hoxie Bullet Catalog. 0.75. Pioneer Pr.

Lewis, Jack. **Gun Digest Book of Modern Gun Values.** (Illus.). 1978. pap. 7.95. DBI.

Murtz, Harold A., ed. **Guns Illustrated, 1979.** 11th ed. 1978. pap. 6.95. DBI.

Owen, J. I., ed. **Brassey's Infantry Weapons of the World, 1974-75: Infantry Weapons and Combat Aids in Current Use by the Regular & Reserve Forces of All Nations.** (Illus.). 1974. text ed. 49.00. British Bk Ctr.

Remington Gun Catalog 1877. 1.50. Pioneer Pr.

Schroeder, Joseph J., ed. **Gun Collector's Digest.** 2nd ed. 1976. pap. 7.95. DBI.

Scott, Robert F., ed. **Shooter's Bible. 1980, No. 71.** (Illus.). 1979. softbound. 8.95. Stoeger.

Sears & Roebuck Amunition Catalog. (Illus.). pap. 1.50. Sand Pond.

Sellers, Frank. **Sharps Firearms.** (Illus.). 1978. 34.95. Follett.

Smith Brothers-Boston Mass. 3.00. Sand Pond.

Tarassuk, L. **Antique European & American Firearms at the Hermitage Museum.** Drapkin, R., tr. (Illus., Eng. & Rus.). 1973. 20.00. Arco.

——**Antique European & American Firearms at the Hermitage Museum.** 1973. 15.00. State Mutual Bk.

Tarassuk, Leonid, ed. **Antique European & American Firearms at the Hermitage Museum.** (Illus., Eng. & Rus.). 1976. 30.00. Arma Pr.

United States Cartridge Co.-Lowell, Mass. 2.50. Sand Pond.

U.S. Cartridge Company's Collection of Firearms. 1971. 6.00. We Inc.

Wahl, Paul. **Gun Trader's Guide.** (Illus.). 8th ed. 1978. softbound. 7.95. Stoeger.

West, Bill. **Remington Arms Catalogues, 1877-1899.** 1st ed. (Illus.). 1971. 10.00. B West.

——**Stevens Arms Catalogues, 1877-1899.** 1st ed. (Illus.). 1971. 12.00. B West.

Wilson, Loring D. **The Handy Sportsman.** 1977. softbound. 5.95. Stoeger.

Winchester Shotshell Catalog 1897. (Illus.). pap. 1.25. Sand Pond.

Firearms—Collectors and Collecting

Akehurst, Richard. **Antique Weapons.** (Illus.). 1969. 5.95. Arco.

Amber, John T. **Gun Digest Treasury.** 5th ed. 1977. pap. 7.95. DBI.

——**Gun Digest 1978.** 32nd ed. pap. 8.95. DBI.

Bowman, Hank W. **Antique Guns from the Stagecoach Collection.** (Illus.). 1964. lib. bdg. 3.50. Arco.

Chapel, Charles E. **Gun Collector's Handbook of Values: 1975-76 Values.** 11th rev. ed. (Illus.). 1975. 17.50. Coward.

Di Carpengna, N. **Firearms in the Princes Odescalchi Collection in Rome.** (Illus.). 1976. Repr. of 1969 ed. 20.00. Arma Pr.

Dixie Gun Works Antique Arms Catalog. 10.00. Pioneer Pr.

Early Firearms of Great Britain & Ireland from the Collection of Clay P. Bedford. (Illus.). 1971. 17.50; pap. 4.95. Metro Mus Art.

Flayderman, Norm. **Norm Flayderman's Book of Antique Gun Values.** 1977. pap. 12.95. DBI.

Gusler, Wallace B & Lavin, James D. **Decorated Firearms, 1540-1870, from the Collection of Clay P. Bedford.** 1977. 25.00. University Press of Virginia.

Hake, Ted. **Six Gun Hero Collectibles.** 1976. 7.95. Wallace-Homestead.

Kennard, A. M. **French Pistols & Sporting Guns.** 1972. 2.95. Transatlantic.

Lindsay, Merrill. **The Lure of Antique Arms.** (Illus.). 1978. softbound. 5.95. Stoeger.

Liu, Allan J. **The American Sporting Collector's Handbook.** (Illus.). 1977. softbound. 5.95. Stoeger.

Murtz, Harold A., ed. **Guns Illustrated 1978.** 10th ed. (Illus.). 1977. pap. 6.95. DBI.

Neal, Robert J. & Jinks, Roy G. **Smith & Wesson, 1857-1945.** rev. ed. 1975. 25.00. A S Barnes.

Quertermous, Russell & Quertermous, Steve. **Modern Guns, Identification & Values.** 1978. pap. 11.95. Collector Bks.

Schroeder, Joseph J., Jr. ed. **Gun Collector's Digest.** 2nd ed. 1976. pap. 7.95. DBI.

Schroeder, Joseph J. **Gun Collector's Digest,** 1974. pap. 6.95. DBI.

Serven, James. **Rare & Valuable Antique Arms.** 1976. 4.95. Pioneer Pr.

Shumaker, P. L. **Colt's Variations of the Old Model Pocket Pistol.** 1957. 6.00. Borden.

Steinwedel, Louis W. **Gun Collector's Fact Book.** 1975. 10.00; pap. 5.95. Arco.

Tarassuk, L. **Antique European & American Firearms at the Hermitage Museum.** Drapkin, R., tr. (Illus., Eng. & Rus.). 1973. 20.00. Arco.

U.S. Cartridge Company's Collection of Firearms. 1971. 6.00. We Inc.

Wahl, Paul. **Gun Trader's Guide.** 8th ed. (Illus.). 1978. softbound. 7.95. Stoeger.

Wilkinson-Latham, Robert. **Antique Guns in Color: 1750-1865.** (Illus.). 1978. 8.95; pap. 6.95. Arco.

Wilson, R.L. **The Book of Colt Engraving.** (Illus.). 1978. 39.95. Follett.

Firearms—History

Ayalon, David. **Gunpowder & Firearms in the Mamluk Kingdom: A Challenge to Midaeval Society.** 2nd ed. 1978. Biblio Dist.

Baer, L.R. **The Parker Gun: An Immortal American Classic.** (Illus.). 1978. 24.95. Beinfeld.

Blanch, H.J.A. **A Century of Guns: A Sketch of the Leading Types of Sporting & Military Small Arms.** (Illus.). 1977. Repr. of 1909 ed. 25.00. Charles River Bks.

Bowman, Hank W. **Famous Guns from the Smithsonian Collection.** (Illus.). 1966. lib. bdg. 3.50. Arco.

Bowman, Hank W. & Cary, Lucian. **Antique Guns.** (Illus.). 1953. 3.50. Arco.

Brophy, William S. **Krag Rifles.** (Illus.). 1978. 19.95. Beinfeld.

——**L. C. Smith Shotguns.** (Illus.). 1978. 24.95. Beinfeld.

Buchele, W. & Shumway, G. **Recreating the American Longrifle.** Orig. Title: **Recreating the Kentucky Rifle.** (Illus.). 1973. pap. 7.50. Shumway.

Burrell, Brian. **Combat Weapons: Handguns & Shoulder Arms of World War 2.** (Illus.). 1974. 9.50. Transatlantic.

Campbell, Hugh B. **The History of Firearms.** (Illus.). 1977. pap. 8.95. B. Franklin.

DuMont, John S. **Custer Battle Guns.** (Illus.). 1974. 10.00. Old Army.

Editors of Outdoor Life, ed. **The Story of American Hunting & Fire Arms.** 1976. 12.95. Dutton.

Fuller, Claud E. **Breech-Loader in the Service 1816-1917.** (Illus.). 1965. 14.50. Flayderman.

Gaier, Claude. **Four Centuries of Liege Gunmaking.** (Illus.). 1977. 80.00. Arma Pr.

Grancsay, Stephen V. & Lindsay, Merrill. **Master French Gunsmith's Designs from the XVII to the XIX Centuries.** (Illus.). 1976. Ltd. ed. (1000 copies). 89.00. Arma Pr.

Greener, William W. **The Gun & Its Development: With Notes on Shooting.** 1975. Repr. of 1881 ed. 26.00. Gale.

Hartzler, Daniel D. **Arms Makers of Maryland.** (Illus.). 1976. 29.50. Shumway.

Held, Robert. **Age of Firearms.** (Illus.). 2nd ed. rev. pap. 4.95. DBI.

Hetrick, Calvin. **The Bedford County Rifle & Its Makers.** (Illus.). 1975. pap. 5.00. Shumway.

Jackson, Melvin H. & De Beer, Charles. **Eighteenth Century Gunfounding.** (Illus.). 1974. 19.95. Smithsonian.

Jinks, Roy G. **History of Smith & Wesson.** (Illus.). 1978. Follett.

Kennet, Lee & Anderson, James L. **The Gun in America.** (Illus., Orig.). 1975. 12.95; pap. text ed. 3.95. Greenwood.

Kindig, Joe Jr. **Thoughts on the Kentucky Rifle in Its Golden Age.** 1976. casebound. 39.50. Shumway.

Lindsay, Merrill. **The New England Gun: The First 200 Years.** (Illus.). 1976. 20.00; pap. 12.50. Arma Pr.

——**One Hundred Great Guns.** (Illus.). 1967. 25.00. Walker & Co.

Neal, Keith W. & Back, D. H. **Great British Gunmakers 1740-1790: The History of John Twigg & the Packington Guns.** (Illus.). 1975. 70.00. S P Bernet.

Peterson, Harold. **Historical Treasury of American Guns.** 4.95; pap. 2.95. Benjamin Co.

Pollard, Hugh B. **History of Firearms.** (Illus.). 1974. 25.50. B Franklin.

Reese, Michaell II. **Nineteen-Hundred Luger-U.S. Test Trials.** 2nd rev. ed. (Illus.). pap. 4.95. Pioneer Pr.

Rosebush, Waldo E. **American Firearms & the Changing Frontier.** 1962. pap. 3.00. Eastern Wash.

Rywell, Martin. **American Antique Pistols.** 2.00. Pioneer Pr.

——**Confederate Guns.** 2.00. Pioneer Pr.

Schreier, Konrad F., Jr. **Remington Rolling Block Firearms.** (Illus.). pap. 3.95. Pioneer Pr.

Schroeder, Joseph J., Jr. **Arms of the World—Nineteen Hundred & Eleven.** 1972. pap. 5.95. DBI.

Serven, James. **Two hundred Years of American Firearms.** (Illus., Orig.). 1975. pap. 7.95. Follett.

——**Colt Firearms from 1836.** 1974. 19.95. Foun Pr.

——**Conquering the Frontiers.** 1974. 19.95. Foun Pr.

SIPRI. **Anti-Personnel Weapons.** 1978. 22.95. Crane-Russak Co.

Smythe, John & Barwick, Humphrey. **Bow Versus Gun: Certain Discourses, & a Breefe Discourse.** 1974. 10.00. Shumway.

Suydam, Charles R. **U.S. Cartridges & Their Handguns: 1795-1975.** (Illus.). 1978. 14.95; pap. 9.95. Beinfeld.

Tarassuk, Leonid. **Antique European & American Firearms at the Hermitage Museum.** limited ed. (Illus., Eng. & Rus.). 1973. 30.00. Arma Pr.

Tout, Thomas F. **Firearms in England in the Fourteenth Century.** (Illus.). 1969. pap. 5.00. Shumway.

West, Bill. **Browning Arms & History, 1847-1973.** (Illus.). 1972. 20.00. B West.

——**Marlin & Ballard, Arms & History, 1861-1971.** (Illus.). 1972. 22.00. B West.

——**Remington Arms & History, 1816-1971.** (Illus.). 1972. 22.00. B West.

——**Savage Stevens, Arms & History, 1849-1971.** (Illus.). 1971. 22.00. B West.

——**Winchester-Complete: All Wins & Forerunners, 1849-1970.** (Illus.). 1975. 28.00. B West.

Wilkinson, Frederick. **Antique Firearms.** 1978. Repr. 14.95. Presidio Press.

Wilkinson-Latham, Robert. **Antique Guns in Color: 1250-1865.** 1978. 8.95; pap. 6.95. Arco.

Williamson, Harry F. **Winchester: The Gun That Won the West.** (Illus.). 7.98. A S Barnes.

Wycoff, James. **Famous Guns That Won the West.** (Illus.). 1975. pap. 2.00. Arco.

Firearms—Identification

Ahern, Jerry & Hart, Dave. **Peace Officer's Guide to Concealed Handguns.** 1978. pap. 7.95. Follett.

Grancsay, Stephen V. & Lindsay, Merrill. **Illustrated British Firearms Patents, 1718-1853.** (Illus.). 1976. boxed, ltd. ed. 75.00. Arma Pr.

Mathews, J. Howard. **Firearms Indentification: Original Photographs & Other Illustrations of Hand Guns, Vol. 2.** 1973. Repr. of 1962 ed. 44.75. C C Thomas.

——**Firearms Indentification: Original Photographs & Other Illustrations of Hand Guns, Data on Rifling Characteristics of Hand Guns & Rifles, Vol. 3.** Wilimovsky, Allan E., ed. (Illus.). 1973. 69.50. C C Thomas.

——**Firearms Indentification: The Laboratory Examination of Small Arms, Rifling Characteristics in Hand Guns, & Notes on Automatic Pistols, Vol. 1.** 1973. Repr. of 1962 ed. 44.75. C C Thomas.

Wilber, Charles G. **Ballistic Science for the Law Enforcement Officer.** (Illus.). 1977. 23.50. C C Thomas.

Firearms—Industry and Trade

Farley, Philip J., et al. **Arms Across the Sea.** 1978. 8.95. Brookings.

Gervasi, Tom. **Arsenal of Democracy: American Weapons Available for Export.** (Illus.). 1978. 19.50. Grove.

Grancsay, Stephen V. & Lindsay, Merrill. **Illustrated British Firearms Patents 1718-1853.** limited ed. (Illus.). 75.00. Arma Pr.

Hanifhen, Frank C. & Engelbrecht, Helmuth C. **Merchants of Death: A Study of the International Armaments Industry.** 33.00. Garland Pub.

Hartzler, Daniel D. **Arms Makers of Maryland.** 1975. 29.50. Shumway.

Kennett, Lee & Anderson, James L. **The Gun in America.** (Illus.). pap. 3.95. Greenwood.

Kirkland, Turner. **Southern Derringers of the Mississippi Valley.** 2.00. Pioneer Pr.

Lindsay, Merrill. **One Hundred Great Guns.** (Illus.). 1967. 25.00. Walker & Co.

Noel-Baker, Philip. **Private Manufacture of Armaments.** 1971. pap. 6.00. Dover.

Smith, Merritt R. **Harper's Ferry Armory and the New Technology: The Challenge of Change.** (Illus.). 1977. 17.50. Cornell University Press.

Stockholm International Peace Research Institute (SIPRI). **The Arms Trade Registers.** 1975. 14.95. MIT Pr.

——**Arms Trade with the 3rd World.** rev. ed. (Illus.). 1975. 17.50. Holmes & Meier.

West, Bill. **Browning Arms & History, Eighteen Forty-Two to Nineteen Seventy-Three.** (Illus.). 1972. 25.00. B West.

Firearms—Laws and Regulations

Dolan, Edward F. Jr. **Gun Control: A Decision for Americans.** (Illus.). 1978. 4.90. Watts.

Gottlieb, Alan B. **The Gun Owner's Political Manual.** 1976. pap. 1.95. Green Hill.

Gun Control. 1976. pap. 2.00. AM Enterprise.

Gun Control Means People Control. 1974. 1.75. Ind American.

Kates, Don B., Jr. **Gun Control: The Liberal Skeptic's Point of View.** 1979. price not set. North River.

Kennet, Lee & Anderson James L. **The Gun in America.** (Illus.). text ed. pap. 3.95. Greenwood.

Krema, Vaclav. **Identification & Registration of Firearms.** (Illus.). 1971. 14.50. C C Thomas.

Kukla, Robert J. **Gun Control: A Written Record of Efforts to Eliminate the Private Possession of Firearms in America.** Orig. Title: Other Side of Gun Control. 1973. pap. 4.95. Stackpole.

Scanlon Robert A. ed. **Law Enforcement Bible.** (Illus.). 1978. softbound. 7.95. Stoeger.

Sherrill Robert. **The Saturday Night Special.** 1975. pap. 2.75. Penguin.

Fowling

Bauer, Erwin A. **Duck Hunter's Bible.** pap. 2.95. Doubleday.

Becker, A. C., Jr. **Waterfowl in the Marshes.** (Illus.). 1969. 9.95. A S Barnes.

Bell, Bob. **Hunting the Long Tailed Bird.** (Illus.). 1975. 14.95. Freshet Pr.

Bourjaily, Vance. **Unnatural Enemy.** (Illus.). 1963. 6.95. Dial.

Carroll, Hanson, et al. **The Wildfowler's World.** 1973. 12.95. Winchester Pr.

Day, J. Wentworth. **The Modern Fowler.** 1973. Repr. of 1934 ed. 18.50. British Bk Ctr.

Dickey, Charley. **Quail Hunting.** (Illus.). 1975. softbound. 3.95. Stoeger.

Gresham, Grits. **The Complete Wildfowler.** (Illus.). 1975. softbound. 5.95. Stoeger.

Gryndall, William. **Hawking, Hunting, Fouling & Fishing; Newly Corrected by W. Gryndall Faulkner.** 1972. Repr. of 1596 ed. 13.00. W J Johnson.

Hastings, Macdonald. **Shooting—Why We Miss: Questions and Answers on the Successful Use of the Shotgun.** 1977. 6.95. pap. 3.95. McKay.

Hinman, Bob. **The Duck Hunter's Handbook.** (Illus.). 1976. softbound. 5.95. Stoeger.

Knap, Jerome, ed. **All About Wildfowling in America.** 1976. 10.00. Winchester Pr.

Petzal, David E., ed. **The Expert's Book of Upland Bird & Water-Fowl Hunting.** 1975. 9.95. S&S.

Rice, F. Philip & Dahl, John. **Game Bird Hunting.** 1965. pap. 4.95. Funk & Wagnalls.

Russell, Dan M. **Dove Shooter's Handbook.** 1974. 6.95. Winchester Pr.

Waterman, Charles F. **Hunting Upland Birds.** (Illus.). 1975. softbound. 5.95. Stoeger.

Wood, Shirley E. Jr. **Gunning for Upland Birds & Wildfowl.** 1976. 10.00. Winchester Pr.

Youel, Milo A. **Cook the Wild Bird.** (Illus.). 1976. 17.50. A S Barnes.

Game and Game Birds

Anderson. Luther A. **Hunting the Uplands with Rifle & Shotgun.** (Illus.). 1977. 10.00. Winchester Pr.

Becker, A. C., Jr. **Game & Bird Calling.** (Illus.). 1972. 7.95. A S Barnes.

Brakefield, Tom. **The Sportsman's Complete Book of Trophy & Meat Care.** (Illus.). 1975. 8.95. Stackpole.

Bucher, Ruth & Gelb, Norman. **The Book of Hunting.** (Illus.). 1977. 60.00. Paddington Pr.

Burk, Bruce. **Game Bird Carving.** (Illus.). 1972. 12.50. Winchester Pr.

Colby, C. B. **Big Game: Animals of the Americas, Africa & Asia.** (Illus.). 1967. 4.69. Coward.

Cone, Arthur L. Jr., **The Complete Guide to Hunting.** (Illus.). 1978. softbound. 5.95. Stoeger.

Dalrymple, Byron. **How to Call Wildlife.** (Illus.). 1975. 7.50. Funk & W.

——**North American Big Game Hunting.** (Illus.). 1978. softbound. 5.95. Stoeger.

Dasmann, Raymond F. **Wildlife Biology.** (Illus.). 1964. 13.50. Wiley.

Dickey, Charley. **Dove Hunting.** (Illus.). 1976. 2.95. Oxmoor House.

——**Quail Hunting.** (Illus.). 1974. softbound. 3.95. Stoeger.

Elliott, Charles. **Care of Game Meat & Trophies.** (Illus.). 1975. 7.50; pap. 4.50. Funk & W.

Gooch, B. **Squirrels & Squirrel Hunting.** 6.00. Cornell Maritime.

Gresham, Grits. **The Complete Wildfowler.** (Illus.). 1975. softbound. 5.95. Stoeger.

Hagerbaumer, David. **Selected American Game Birds.** 1972. 30.00. Caxton.

Hinman, Bob. **The Duck Hunter's Handbook.** (Illus.). 1976. softbound. 5.95. Stoeger.

McCristal, Vic. **Top End Safari.** 10.00. Soccer.

Ormond, Clyde. **Small Game Hunting.** (Illus.). 1974. pap. 1.95. B&N.

——**How to Track and Find Game.** (Illus.). 1975. 7.50; pap. 4.50. Funk & W.

Rue, Leonard L. **Sportsman's Guide to Game Animals.** (Illus.). 1968. 12.95. Har-Row.

Rue, Leonard L., III. **Game Birds of North America.** (Illus.). 1973. 12.50. Times Mirror Mag.

Scheid, D. **Raising Game Birds.** 1974. 2.50. Scribner.

Scott, P. **Coloured Key to the Wildfowl of the World.** rev. ed. (Illus.). 1972. 8.50. Heinman.

Scott, Peter. **A Coloured Key to the Wildfowl of the World.** rev. ed. (Illus.). 1972. 8.50. Intl Pubns Serv.

Waterman, Charles F. **Hunting Upland Birds.** (Illus.). 1975. softbound. 5.95. Stoeger.

Youel, Milo A. **Cook the Wild Bird.** (Illus.). 1976. 17.50. A. S. Barnes.

Game and Game Birds—France

Villenave, G. M. **Chasse.** (Illus., Fr.) 21.75. Larousse.

Game and Game Birds—Mexico

Tinker, Ben. **Mexican Wilderness and Wildlife,** (Illus.). 1978. 9.95. University of Texas Press.

Game and Game Birds— New Zealand

Poole, A. L. **Wild Animals in New Zealand.** (Illus.). 1969. 14.50. Reed.

Game and Game Birds— North America

Alaska Magazine Editors. **Alaska Hunting Guide.** (Illus.). 1976. pap. 3.95. Alaska Northwest.

Bromhall & Grundle. **British Columbia Game Fish.** pap. 9.95. International School Book Service.

Dalrymple, Byron. **North American Big Game Hunting.** (Illus.). 1974. softbound. 5.95. Stoeger.

Dickey, Charley. **Quail Hunting.** (Illus.). 1974. softbound. 3.95. Stoeger.

Elman, Robert. **The Hunter's Field Guide.** 1974. 12.50. Knopf.

Gresham, Grits. **The Complete Wildfowler.** (Illus.). 1975. softbound. 5.95. Stoeger.

Hinman, Bob. **The Duck Hunter's Handbook.** (Illus.). 1976. softbound. 5.95. Stoeger.

Holland, Dan. **Upland Game Hunter's Bible.** (Illus.). pap. 3.50. Doubleday.

Jaques, Florence P. **Geese Fly High.** (Illus.). 1964. Repr. of 1939 ed. 6.95. U. of Minn Pr.

Johnsgard, Paul A. **North American Game Birds of Upland & Shoreline.** (Illus.). 1975. 11.95; pap. 6.95. U of Nebr Pr.

Knap, Jerome. **All About Wildfowling in America.** 1976. 10.00. Winchester Pr.

Leopold, A. Starker & Darling, F. Fraser. **Wildlife in Alaska.** 1973. Repr. of 1953 ed. 11.25. Greenwood.

Mullin, John M., ed. **Game Bird Propagation.** 1978. 12.95. North American Game Breeders & Shooting Preserves Association, Inc.

Phillips, John C. **American Game Mammals & Birds: A Catalog of Books, Sports, Natural History & Conservation, 1582-1925.** 1978. Repr. of 1930 ed. 37.00. Arno.

Rice, F. Philip & Dahl, John I. **Game Bird Hunting.** (Illus.). 1974. pap. 1.95. B&N.

Rue, Leonard L. **Game Birds of North America.** 1973. 13.50. Har-Row.

Tinsley, Russell, ed. **Small-Game Hunting.** 1977. softbound. 5.95. Stoeger.

Walsh, H. M. **Outlaw Gunner.** 1971. 8.50. Cornell Maritime.

Walsh, Roy. **Gunning the Chesapeake.** 1960. 7.00. Cornell Maritime.

Waterman, Charles F. **Hunting Upland Birds.** (Illus.). 1975. softbound. 5.95. Stoeger.

Zim, Herbert S. & Sprunt, Alexander, 4th. **Game Birds.** 1961. 5.50; pap. 1.95. Western Pub.

Gatling Guns

Wahl, Paul & Toppel, Donald R. **Gatling Gun.** (Illus.). 1978. 5.95. Arco.

Guns

Carmichel, Jim. **The Modern Rifle.** (Illus.). 1976. softbound. 5.95. Stoeger.

Daenhardt, Rainer. **Espingarda Perfeyta: or the Perfect Gun: Rules of Its Use Together with Necessary Instructions for Its Construction & Precepts for Good Aiming.** Daenhardt, Rainer, tr. from Port. (Illus., Eng. & Port.). 1975. 27.50. S P Bernet.

George, John N. **English Pistols & Revolvers.** 10.00. Saifer.

Lindsay, Merrill. **The Lure of Antique Arms.** (Illus.). 1978. softbound. 5.95. Stoeger.

Liu, Allan J., ed. **The American Sporting Collector's Handbook.** (Illus.). 1977. softbound. 5.95. Stoeger.

Luger Manual. (Reprint of original English-language edition). 1967. softbound. 1.95. Stoeger.

Mauser Manual. (Facs. ed. of early English language Mauser Catalog and Manual.). 1974. softbound. 1.95. Stoeger.

Nonte, George C., Jr. **Black Powder Guide.** 2nd ed. (Illus.). 1976. softbound. 6.95. Stoeger.

——**Pistol and Revolver Guide.** 3rd ed. (Illus.). 1975. softbound. 6.95. Stoeger.

O'Connor, Jack. **The Hunting Rifle.** (Illus.). 1975. softbound. 5.95. Stoeger.

Page, Warren. **The Accurate Rifle.** (Illus.). 1975. softbound. 5.95. Stoeger.

Peterson, Harold. **Historical Treasury of American Guns.** 4.95; pap. 2.95. Benjamin Co.

Scott, Robert F., ed. **Shooter's Bible 1980, No. 71.** (Illus.). 1979. softbound. 8.95. Stoeger.

Steindler, R. A. **Rifle Guide.** (Illus.). 1978. softbound. 7.95. Stoeger.

Wahl, Paul. **Gun Trader's Guide.** 8th ed. (Illus.). 1978. softbound. 7.95. Stoeger.

Gunsmithing

Ackley, Parker O. **Home Gun Care & Repair.** (Illus.). 1974. 3.95. Stackpole.

Angier, R. H. **Firearms Blueing & Browning.** 1936. 6.95. Stackpole.

Bailey, De Witt & Nic, Douglas A. **English Gunmakers: The Birmingham & Provincial Guntrade in the 18th & 19th Century.** (Illus.). 1978. 18.95. Arco.

Carmichel, Jim. **Do-It-Yourself-Gunsmithing.** (Illus.). 1978. 13.95. Har-Row.

Demeritt, Dwight B., Jr. **Maine Made Guns & Their Makers.** (Illus.). 22.00. Maine St Mus.

Dunlap, Roy F. **Gunsmithing.** 1963. 14.95. Stackpole.

Gaier, Claude. **Four Centuries of Liège Gunmaking.** (Illus.). 1977. 80.00. Biblio. Dist.

Gill, Harold B., Jr. **Gunsmith in Colonial Virginia.** (Illus.). 1974. 7.50; pap. 4.50. U Pr of Va.

Grancsay, Stephen A. & Lindsay, Merrill. **Master French Gunsmith's Designs: From the Twelfth to Fourteenth Century.** limited ed. (Illus.). 89.00. Arma Pr.

Hartzler, Daniel D. **Arms Makers of Maryland.** (Illus.). 1976. 29.50. Shumway.

Howe, James V. **Amateur Guncraftsman.** (Illus.). 1967. pap. 1.95. Funk & W.

Howe, Walter J. **Professional Gunsmithing.** (Illus.). 1946. 14.95. Stackpole.

Hutslar, Donald A. **Gunsmiths of Ohio: 18th & 19th Centuries.** (Illus.). 1973. 29.50. Shumway.

Lindsay, Merrill. **The New England Gun: The First 200 Years.** (Illus.). 1976. 20.00; pap. 12.50. McKay.

MacFarland, Harold E. **Gunsmithing Simplified.** (Illus.). 12.00. A S Barnes.

——**Introduction to Modern Gunsmithing.** (Illus.). 1975. pap. 2.95. B&N.

Newell, A. Donald. **Gunstock Finishing & Care.** (Illus.). 1949. 12.95. Stackpole.

Norton Art Gallery. **Artistry in Arms: The Art of Gunsmithing & Gun Engraving.** (Illus.). 1971. pap. 2.50. Norton Art.

Steindler, R. A. **Home Gunsmithing Digest.** 2nd ed. 1978. pap. 7.95. DBI.

Walker, Ralph. **Hobby Gunsmithing.** (Illus.). 1972. pap. 5.95. DBI.

——**Black Powder Gunsmithing.** 1978. pap. 7.95. DBI.

Gunstocks

Arthur, Robert. **Shotgun Stock: Design, Construction & Embellishment.** (Illus.). 1970. 17.50. A S Barnes.

Hawken Rifles

Baird, John D. **Fifteen Years in the Hawken Lode.** (Illus.). 1971. 10.00. Buckskin Pr.

——**Hawken Rifles. The Mountain Man's Choice.** 1968. 10.00. Buckskin Pr.

Hunting

Amory, Cleveland. **Man Kind? Our Incredible War on Wildlife.** 1974. 12.50. Har-Row.

Ardrey, Robert. **The Hunting Hypothesis.** 1977. pap. 2.25. Bantam.

Babcock, Havilah. **Jaybirds Go to Hell on Friday.** 1964. 4.95. HR&W.

Bashline, L. James, ed. **The Eastern Trail.** (Illus.). 1972. 8.95. Freshet Pr.

——**Hunter's Digest.** 1973. 6.95. Follett.

Beckford, Peter. **Thoughts on Hunting.** (Illus.). Repr. price not set. British Bk Ctr.

Berners, Juliana. **The Boke of St. Albans Containing Treatises on Hawking, Hunting & Cote Armour.** 1976. Repr. of 1881 ed. 15.00. Scholarly.

——**The Book of Hawking, Hunting & Blasing of Arms.** 1969. Repr. of 1486 ed. 42.00. W J Johnson.

Bourjaily, Vance. **Country Matters: Collected Reports from the Fields & Streams of Iowa & Other Places.** 1973. 8.95. Dial.

——**Unnatural Enemy.** (Illus.). 1963. 6.95. Dial.

Bowring, Dave. **How to Hunt.** (Illus.). 1978. 10.95. Winchester Pr.

Brakefield, Tom. **Small Game Hunting.** (Illus.). 1978. 10.00. Lippincott.

Brister, Bob. **Shotgunning: The Art & The Science.** 1976. 10.00. Winchester Pr.

Bucker, Ruth & Gelb, Norman. **The Book of Hunting.** (Illus.). 1977. 60.00. Paddington Pr.

Buckle, Esme. **Dams of National Hunt Winners.** Supplement 1. 1963-1964. 4.50. Supplement 2: 1966-1973. 1972. 18.95. British Bk Ctr.

Cadman, Arthur. **A Guide to Rough Shooting.** (Illus.). 1975. 9.95. David & Charles.

Clarke, I. A. **An Introduction to Beagling.** (Illus.). 1974. 4.95. British Bk Ctr.

Clayton, Michael. **A-Hunting We Will Go.** 1972. 8.50. British Bk Ctr.

Cone, Arthur L., Jr. **The Complete Guide to Hunting.** (Illus.). 1978. softbound. 5.95. Stoeger.

Coon, Carleton S. **The Hunting Peoples.** 1972. 10.00. Rowman.

Dalrymple, Byron W. **The Complete Book of Deer Hunting.** (Illus.). 1976. softbound. 5.95. Stoeger.

——**North American Big Game Hunting.** (Illus.). 1975. softbound. 5.95. Stoeger.

DeRuttie, Andrew. **Hunting on a Budget—for Food & Profit.** 1975. pap. 1.25. Major Bks.

Dickey, Charley. **Quail Hunting.** (Illus.). 1974. softbound. 3.95. Stoeger.

Dodd, Ed. **Mark Trail's Hunting Tips.** (Illus.). 1969. pap. 1.00. Essandess.

Dougherty, Jim. **Varmint Hunter's Digest.** 1977. pap. 6.95. DBI.

East, Ben. **The Ben East Hunting Book.** (Illus.). 1974. 13.95. Har-Row.

Eggert, Richard. **Fish & Hunt the Back Country.** 1978. 9.95. Stackpole.

Elliott, William. **Carolina Sports by Land & Water: Incidents of Devil-Fishing. Wild-Cat, Deer & Bear Hunting.** (Illus.). 1978. Repr. of 1859 ed. 10.00. Attic Pr.

Elman, Robert. **The Hunter's Field Guide** 1974. 12.50. Knopf.

Fadala, Sam. **Blackpowder Hunting.** 1978. 10.95. Stackpole.

Ferber, Steve, ed. **All About Rifle Hunting & Shooting in America.** 1977. 10.00. Winchester Pr.

Field & Stream. **Field & Stream Reader.** facs. ed. 1946 17.95. Bks for Libs.

Frankenstein, Alfred. **After the Hunt.** (Illus.). 1975. 35.00. U. of Cal Pr.

Gilsvik, Bob. **All-Season Hunting.** (Illus.). 1977. 5.95. softbound. Stoeger.

——**The Guide to Good Cheap Hunting.** (Illus.). 10.95. Stein & Day.

Gresham, Grits. **The Complete Wildfowler.** (Illus.). 1975. softbound. 5.95. Stoeger.

Grey, Hugh, ed. **Field & Stream Treasury.** 1971. 12.95. HR&W.

Grey, Zane. **Zane Grey, Outdoorsman: Zane Grey's Best Hunting & Fishing Tales.** Reiger, George, ed. (Illus.). 1972. 9.95. P-H.

Grinnel, George B. & Sheldon, Charles, eds. **Hunting & Conservation.** 1970. Repr. of 1925 ed. 25.00. Arno.

Gryndall, William. **Hawking, Hunting, Fouling & Fishing: Newly Corrected by W. Gryndall Faulkener.** 1972. Repr. of 1596 ed. 13.00. W J Johnson.

Hagel, Bob. **Game Loads & Practical Ballistics for the American Hunter.** (Illus.). 1978. 12.95. Knopf.

Hanenkrat, William F. **The Education of a Turkey Hunter.** 1974. 8.95. Winchester Pr.

Harbour, Dave. **Hunting the American Wild Turkey.** (Illus.). 1975. 8.95. Stackpole.

Harker, Peter & Eunson, Keith. **Hunting with Harker.** (Illus.). 1976. 9.75. Reed.

Hill, Gene. **A Hunter's Fireside Book: Tales of Dogs, Ducks, Birds & Guns.** (Illus.). 1972. 8.95. Winchester Pr.

——**Mostly Tailfeathers.** 1975. 8.95. limited ed. 20.00. Winchester Pr.

Hinman, Bob. **The Duck Hunter's Handbook.** (Illus.). 1976. softbound. 5.95. Stoeger.

Holden, Philip. **Hunter by Profession.** (Illus.). 1974. 9.90. Intl Pubns Serv.

James, Davis & Stephens, Wilson, eds. **In Praise of Hunting.** (Illus.). 1961. 10.00. Devin.

Janes, Edward C. **Boy & His Gun.** (Illus.). 1951. 6.95. A S Barnes.

——**Ringneck! Pheasants & Pheasant Hunting.** (Illus.). 1975. 8.95. Crown.

Johnson, et al. **Outdoor Tips.** pap. 2.95. Benjamin Co.

Klineburger, Bert & Hurst, Vernon W. **Big Game Hunting Around the World.** (Illus.). 1969. 15.00. Exposition.

Knap, Jerome J. **Complete Hunter's Almanac: A Guide to Everything the Hunter Needs to Know About Guns, Game, Tracking & Gear with a Special Section on Hunting Locations in North America.** (Illus.). 1978. Pagurian.

Laycock, George. **Shotgunner's Bible.** (Illus.). 1969. pap. 2.50. Doubleday.

Lindner, Kurt. **The Second Hunting Book of Wolfgang Birkner.** (Illus.). 1976. with case 175.00. Arma Pr.

McNair, Paul C. **The Sportsman's Crafts Book.** 1978. 10.95. Winchester Pr.

Madden, D. H. **Chapter of Mediaeval History.** 1969. Repr. of 1924 ed. 12.50. Kennikat.

Madden, Dodgson H. **Diary of Master William Silence: A Study of Shakespeare & Elizabethan Sport.** 1970. Repr. of 1897 ed. 21.95. Haskell.

Merrill, William K. **Hunter's Bible.** (Illus.). 1968. 2.95. Doubleday.

Mosher, John A. **The Shooter's Workbench.** 1977. 10.95. Winchester Pr.

Mueller, Larry. **Bird Dog Guide.** (Illus.). 1976. softbound. 6.95. Stoeger.

Needwood. **The Hunting Quiz Book.** pap. 2.95. British Bk Ctr.

Nonte, George C., Jr. & Jurras, Lee E. **Handgun Hunting.** (Illus.). 1976. softbound. 5.95. Stoeger.

O'Connor, Jack. **The Hunting Rifle.** (Illus.). 1975. softbound. 5.95. Stoeger.

——**Shotgun Book.** (Illus.). 1978. 15.00; pap. 8.95. Knopf.

Ormond, Clyde. **Complete Book of Hunting.** rev. ed. (Illus.). 1972. 10.95. Har-Row.

——**Small Game Hunting.** 1970. 4.95. Dutton.

——**Outdoorsman's Handbook.** 1975. pap. 1.95. Berkeley Pub.

Page, Warren. **One Man's Wilderness.** 1973. 8.95. HR&W.

Petzal, David E., ed. **Experts' Book of the Shooting Sports.** 9.95. S&S.

Pollard, Hugh B. **The Mystery of Scent.** 1972. 4.95. British Bk Ctr.

Pollard, Jack. **Straight Shooting.** 12.50. Soccer.

Pryce, Dick. **Hunting for Beginners.** (Illus.). 1978. softbound. 5.95. Stoeger.

Pulling, Pierre. **Game & the Gunner: Common-Sense Observations on the Practice of Game Conservation & Sport Hunting.** 1973. 8.95. Winchester Pr.

Randolph, J. W. **World of Wood, Field & Stream.** 1962. 3.95. HR&W.

Robinson, Jerome B. **Hunt Close!** (Illus.). 1978. 10.00. Winchester Pr.

Scharff, Robert. **Hunter's Game, Gun & Dog Guide.** 1963. pap. 1.95. Macmillan.

Schwenk, Sigrid, et al, eds. **Multum et Multa: Beitraege zur Literatur, Geschichte und Kultur der Jagd.** (Illus.). 1971. 53.30. De Gruyter.

Scott, Robert F. **Shooters Bible 1980 No. 71.** (Illus.). 1979. softbound. 8.95. Stoeger.

Sell, Francis. **Art of Small Game Hunting.** 1973. pap. 3.95. Stackpole.

Sparano, Vin T. **The Complete Outdoors Encyclopedia.** (Illus.). 1973. 18.95. Har-Row.

Spiller, Burton. **Grouse Feathers.** (Sportsmen's Classics Ser.). (Illus.). 1972. 8.95. Crown.

Spiller, Burton L. **More Grouse Feathers.** (Illus.). 1972. 7.50. Crown.

Stehsel, Donald L. **Hunting the California Black Bear.** (Illus.). pap. 4.95. Stehsel.

Strung, N. **Complete Hunter's Catalog.** (Illus.). 1978. pap. 8.95. Lippincott.

Tapply, Horace G. **Sportsman's Notebook.** 1964. 7.95. HR&W.

Taylor, Zack. **Successful Waterfowling.** (Illus.). 1974. 8.95. Crown.

Tinsley, Russell. **Bow Hunter's Guide.** (Illus.). 1975. softbound. 5.95. Stoeger.

——**Small-Game Hunting.** (Illus.). 1977. softbound. 5.95. Stoeger.

Trueblood, Ted. **The Ted Trueblood Hunting Treasury.** (Illus.). 1978. 14.95. McKay.

Washburn, O. A. **General Red.** (Illus.). 5.50. Jenkins.

Waterman, Charles F. **Hunter's World.** (Illus.). 1970. 15.00. Random.

——**Hunting Upland Birds.** (Illus.). 1975. softbound. 5.95. Stoeger.

——**The Part I Remember.** (Illus.). 1974. 8.95. Winchester Pr.

Wehle, Robert G. **Wing & Shot.** (Illus.). 1971. 8.50; deluxe ed. 20.00. Country Pr.

Willett, Roderick. **Gun Safety.** (Illus.). 1967. 5.25. Intl Pubns Serv.

Wilson, James. **The Rod & The Gun.** (Illus.). 1973. Repr. of 1844 ed. 16.95. British Bk Ctr.

Wilson, Loring. **The Handy Sportsman.** (Illus.). 1977. softbound. 5.95. Stoeger.

Woodcock, E. N. **Fifty Years a Hunter & Trapper.** pap. 2.50. Fur-Fish-Game.

Woolner, Frank. **Timberdoodle: A Thorough Guide to Woodcock Hunting.** (Illus.). 1974. 7.95. Crown.

Woolner, Lionel. **Hunting of the Hare.** 1972. 7.50. British Bk Ctr.

Zutz, Don. **Handloading for Hunters.** 1977. 12.50. Winchester Pr.

Hunting—Dictionaries

Brander, Michael. **Dictionary of Sporting Terms.** (Illus.). 1968. text ed. 7.00. Humanities.

Burnand, Tony. **Dictionnaire Chasse.** (Fr.). 1970. 5.95. Larousse.

Wisconsin Hunting Encyclopedia. 1976. pap. 2.95. Wisconsin Sptm.

Hunting—History

Butler, Alfred J. **Sport in Classic Times.** (Illus.). 1975. 11.95. W Kaufman.

Cheney, Roberta & Erskine, Clyde. **Music, Saddles & Flapjacks: Dudes at the Oto Ranch.** 1978. 12.95. Mountain Pr.

Danielsson, Bror, ed. **William Twiti's the Art of Hunting, Vol. 1.** (Illus.). 1977. pap. ed. 30.00. Humanities.

Greene, Robert. **The Third & Last Part of Conny-Catching.** 1923. 12.50. Arden Lib.

Hunting—Primitive

Clarke, Grahame. **Stone Age Hunters.** 1967. 5.50; pap. 2.95. McGraw.

Coon, Carleton. **The Hunting Peoples.** 1971. 10.00; pap. 3.95. Little.

Frison, George C. **Prehistoric Hunter's of the High Plains.** 1978. 29.50. Acad Pr.

Gerstacker, Friedrich. **Wild Sports in the Far West.** Steeves, Edna L. & Steeves, Harrison R., eds. 1968. 8.75. Duke.

Lee, Richard B. & De Vore, Irven, eds. **Man the Hunter.** 1968. pap. 7.95. Aldine.

Marks, Stuart A. **Large Mammals & a Brave People: Subsistence Hunters in Zambia.** (Illus.). 1976. 15.00. U of Wash Pr.

Sergeant, R. B. **South Arabian Hunt.** 1976. text ed. 20.00. Verry.

Service, Elman R. **Hunters.** (Illus.). 1966. pap. 3.95. P-H.

Hunting—Africa

Capstick, Peter H. **Death in the Long Grass.** (Illus.). 1978. 10.00. St. Martin.

Cloudsley-Thompson, J. L. **Animal Twilight, Man & Game in Eastern Africa.** (Illus.). 1967. 7.95. Dufour.

Findlay, Frederick R. N. & Cronwright-Schreiner, S. C. **Big Game Shooting and Travel in Southeast Africa: Account of Shooting Trips in the Cheringoma & Gorongoza Divisions of Portuguese South-East Africa & in Zululand.** Repr. of 1903 ed. 40.25. Bks for Libs.

Gillmore, Parker. **Days & Nights by the Desert.** Repr. of 1888 ed. 20.50. Bks for Libs.

Haardt, Georges M. & Audouin-Dubreuil, Louis. **Black Journey: Across Central Africa with Citroen Expedition.** (Illus.). Repr. of 1927 ed. 18.25. Negro U Pr.

Hemingway, Ernest. **Green Hills of Africa.** 1935. 7.95; pap. 3.95. Scribner.

Holub, Emil. **Seven Years in South Africa,** 2 vols. 1881. Set. 43.50. Scholarly.

——**Seven Years in South Africa: Travels, Researches, & Hunting Adventures Between the Diamond Fields & the Zambesi, 1827-79.** 2 vols. 1971. Repr. of 1881 ed. 51.75. Johnson Repr.

MacQueen, Peter. **In Wildest Africa.** 1909. 23.00. Scholarly.

Mazet, Horace S. **Wild Ivory.** 1971. 6.95. Galloway.

Mohr, Jack. **Hyenas in My Bedroom.** (Illus.). 1969. 5.95. A S Barnes.

Nassau, Robert H. **In an Elephant Corral: And Other Tales of West African Experiences.** Repr. of 1912 ed. 8.00. Negro U Pr.

Pohl, Victor. **Farewell the Little People.** (Illus.). 1968. pap. 3.75. Oxford U Pr.

Hunting—Alaska

Alaska Hunting Guide: (Illus.). 1976. pap. 3.95. Alaska Northwest.

Alaska Hunting Guide 1978-79. rev. ed. (Illus.). pap. 5.95. Alaska Northwest.

Alaska Magazine Editors. **Selected Alaska Hunting & Fishing Tales, Vol. 4.** 1976. pap. 3.95. Alaska Northwest.

Hubback, T. R. **Ten Thousand Miles to Alaska for Moose & Sheep.** facs. ed. 1921. 4.00. Shorey.

Keim, Charles J. **Alaska Game Trails with a Master Guide.** pap. Alaska Northwest.

Waugh, Hal & Keim, Charles J. **Fair Chase with Alaskan Guides.** (Illus.). 1972. pap. 3.95. Alaska Northwest.

Hunting—Arctic Regions

Nelson, Richard K. **Hunters of the Northern Ice.** 1969. 14.00. U of Chicago Pr.

Stefansson, Vilhjalmur. **Hunters of the Great North.** 1922. 22.00. AMS Pr.

Hunting—Australia

Byrne, Jack. **Duck Hunting in Australia & New Zealand.** (Illus.). 1974. 9.25. Reed.

Stewart, Allan. **The Green Eyes Are Buffaloes.** 13.25. Soccer.

Hunting—France

Villenave, G. M. **Chasse.** (Illus., Fr.). 19.75. Larousse.

Hunting—Great Britain

Danielsson, Bror, ed. **William Twiti's the Art of Hunting, Vol. 1.** (Illus.). 1977. pap. text ed. 30.00. Humanities.

Edward of Norwich. **Master of Game: Oldest English Book on Hunting.** Baillie-Grohman, William A. & Baillie-Grohman, F., eds. (Illus.). Repr. of 1904 ed. 45.00. AMS Pr.

Hands, Rachel, ed. **English Hawking & Hunting in the Boke of St. Albans.** facs. ed. (Illus.). 1975. 48.00. Oxford U Pr.

Hewitt, H. P. **Fairest Hunting: Hunting & Watching Exmoor Deer.** 1974. 4.95. British Bk Ctr.

Hunting—Greece

Butler, Alfred J. **Sport in Classic Times.** (Illus.). 1975. 11.95. W Kaufmann.

Hull, Denison B. **Hounds & Hunting in Ancient Greece.** (Illus.). 1964. 15.00. U of Chicago Pr.

Hunting—New Zealand

Byrne, Jack. **Duck Hunting in Australia & New Zealand.** (Illus.). 1974. 9.25. Reed.

Forrester, Rex & Illingworth, Neil. **Hunting in New Zealand.** (Illus.). 1967. 8.25. Reed.

Joll, Gary. **Big Game Hunting in New Zealand.** (Illus.). 1968. 9.00. Intl Pubns Service.

Roberts, Gordon. **Game Animals in New Zealand.** (Illus.). 1968. 7.50. Reed.

Hunting—North America

Anderson, Luther A. **How to Hunt American Small Game.** (Illus.). 1969. 5.95. Funk & W.

Dalrymple, Byron W. **North American Big Game Hunting.** (Illus.). 1975. softbound. 5.95. Stoeger.

Elman, Robert. **The Hunter's Field Guide.** 1974. 12.50. Knopf.

Elman, Robert & Peper, George, eds. **Hunting America's Game Animals & Birds.** (Illus.). 1975. 12.95. Winchester Pr.

Holland, Dan. **Upland Game Hunter's Bible.** (Illus.). pap. 3.50. Doubleday.

Knap, Jerome. **Where to Fish & Hunt in North Amercia: A Complete Sportsman's Guide.** (Illus.). 8.95. Pagurian.

Leopold, Luna B., ed. **Round River: From The Journals of Aldo Leopold.** (Illus.). 1972. pap. 2.50. Oxford U Pr.

O'Connor, Jack. **The Art of Big Game Hunting in North America.** 2nd ed. 1977. 13.95. Knopf.

Ormond, Clyde. **Small Game Hunting.** rev. ed. (Illus.). 1977. pap. 4.95. Funk & W.

Petzal, David E. **The Expert's Book of Big Game Hunting in North America.** (Illus.). 1976. 10.95. S&S.

Hunting—U.S.

Babcock, H. **My Health Is Better In November.** (Illus.). 1960. 5.95. HR&W.

Bailey's Hunting Directory. 1977-78. (Illus.). 1977. 23.25. J A Allen.

Cadbury, Warder, intro. by. **Journal of a Hunting Excursion to Louis Lake. 1851.** (Illus.). 1961. 4.95. Syracuse U Pr.

Cone, Arthur L. **The Complete Guide to Hunting.** (Illus.). 1978. softbound. 5.95. Stoeger.

Cory, Charles B. **Hunting & Fishing in Florida, Including a Key to the Water Birds.** 1970. Repr. of 1896 ed. 14.00. Arno.

Dalrymple, Bryon W. **The Complete Book of Deer Hunting.** (Illus.). 1975. softbound. 5.95. Stoeger.

——**North American Big Game Hunting.** (Illus.). 1975. softbound. 5.95. Stoeger.

Duffy, M. **Hunting and Fishing in Louisiana.** 1969. 4.95. Pelican.

Gilsvik, Bob. **All-Season Hunting.** (Illus.). 1976. softbound. 5.95. Stoeger.

Gohdes, Clarence, ed. **Hunting in the Old South: Original Narratives of the Hunters.** (Illus.). 1967. 7.50. La State U Pr.

Kaplan, Meyer A. **Varmint Hunting.** 1977. pap. 2.95. Monarch Pr.

Lang, Varley. **Follow the Water.** (Illus.). 1961. 4.50. Blair.

McTeer, Ed. **Adventures in the Woods & Waters of the Low Country.** 5.95. Beaufort.

Murray, William H. **Adventures in the Wilderness.** Verner, William K., ed. (Illus.). 1970. Repr. 10.50. Syracuse U Pr.

O'Connor, Jack. **The Hunting Rifle.** (Illus.). 1975. softbound. 5.95. Stoeger.

Palliser, John. **Solitary Rambles & Adventures of a Hunter in the Prairies.** (Illus.). 1969. Repr. of 1853 ed. 5.00. C E Tuttle.

Pryce, Dick. **Hunting for Beginners.** (Illus.). 1978. softbound. 5.95. Stoeger.

Roosevelt, Theodore. **Hunting Trips of a Ranchman.** 1970. Repr. of 1885 ed. 12.50. Gregg.

——**Outdoor Pastimes of an American Hunter.** 1970. Repr. of 1905 ed. 16.00. Arno.

——**Ranch Life & the Hunting-Trail.** 1970. Repr. of 1901 ed. 8.00. Arno.

——**Ranch Life & the Hunting-Trail.** 1966. Repr. of 1899 ed. 8.95. Univ Microfilms.

——**Ranch Life in the Far West.** (Illus.). 1968. 6.00. Northland.

——**Theodore Roosevelt's America.** Wiley, Farida, ed. (Illus.). 1955. 7.50. Devin.

——**Wilderness Hunter.** 1970. Repr. of 1900 ed. 16.00. Irvington.

Sandoz, Mari. **The Buffalo-Hunter's: The Story of the Hide Men.** 1978. pap. 4.50. UU of Nebr Pr.

Tillett, Paul. **Doe Day: the Antlerless Deer Controversy in New Jersey.** 1963. 6.00; pap. 3.25. Rutgers U Pr.

Tome, Philip. **Pioneer Life or Thirty Years a Hunter: Being Scenes & Adventures in the Life of Philip Tome.** (Illus.). 1971. Repr. of 1854 ed. 10.00. Arno.

Hunting Dogs

Baily's Hunting Directory 1974-1975. 1975. 22.50. British Bk Ctr.

Bernard, Art. **Dog Days.** 1969. 5.95. Caxton.

Duffey, Dave. **Hunting Dog Know-How.** (Illus.). 1972. 6.95. Winchester Pr.

——**Hunting Hounds: How to Choose, Train & Handle America's Trail & Tree Hounds.** (Illus.). 1972. 6.95. Winchester Pr.

Duffey, David M. **Dave Duffey Trains Gun Dogs.** (Illus.). 1974. 7.95. Dreenan Pr.

Falk, John R. **The Practical Hunter's Dog Book.** (Illus.). 1975. softbound. 8.95. Stoeger.

Hartley, Oliver. **Hunting Dogs.** pap. 2.50. Fur-Fish-Game.

Henschel, Stan. **How to Raise & Train a Chesapeake Bay Retriever.** 1965. pap. 1.50. TFH Pubns.

——**How to Raise & Train a Coonhound.** pap. 1.50. TFH Pubns.

——**How to Raise & Train a Labrador Retriever.** (Illus.). pap. 1.29. TFH Pubns.

Lent, Patricia A. **Sport with Terriers.** (Illus.). 1973. 7.50. Arner Pubns.

Mueller, Larry. **Bird Dog Guide.** 1976. softbound. 6.95. Stoeger.

Rice, F. Philip & Dahl, John. **Hunting Dogs.** 1967. 10.95. Har-Row.

Stetson, Joe. **Hunting with Scenthounds.** 1965. pap. 1.50. TFH Pubns.

——**Handbook of Gundogs.** 1965. pap. 1.50. TFH Pubns.

——**Hunting with Flushing Dogs.** 1965. pap. 1.50. TFH Pubns.

Whitney, Leon F. & Underwood, Acil B. **Coon Hunter's Handbook.** Hart, Ernest, ed. (Illus.). 1952. 5.95. HR&W.

Wolters, Richard A. **Gun Dog. Revolutionary Rapid Training Method.** (Illus.). 1961. 8.95. Dutton.

Hunting Dogs—Pointers

Hart, Ernest H. **How to Raise & Train a Pointer.** (Illus.). 1966. 1.29. TFH Pubns.

Pet Library Ltd. **Know Your Setters & Pointers.** (Illus.). pap. 1.50. Doubleday.

Spirer, L. Z. & Spirer, H. F. **German Short-Haired Pointer.** 1970. 5.95. TFH Pubns.

Steinfeldt, Cecilia. **The Onderdonks: A Family of Texas Pointers.** 1975. 25.00. Trinity U Pr.

Stetson, Joe. **Hunting with Pointing Dogs.** 1965. pap. 1.50. TFH Pubns.

Hunting Dogs—Retrievers

Coykendall, Ralph W., Jr. **You & Your Retriever.** (Illus.). 1963. 5.95. Doubleday.

Fowler, Ann & Walters, D.K., eds. **Charles Morgan on Retrievers.** (Illus.). 1968. 17.50. October.

Free, James L. **Training Your Retriever.** 5th rev. ed. (Illus.). 1974. 8.95. Coward.

Kersley, J. A. **Training the Retriever: A Manual.** (Illus.). 1971. 9.95. Howell Bk.

Leclerc, Maurice J. **Retriever Trainer's Manual.** (Illus.). 1962. 8.50. Ronald.

Pet Library Ltd. **Know Your Retriever.** (Illus.). pap. 1.50. Doubleday.

Stetson, Joe. **Hunting with Retrievers.** pap. 1.50. TFH Pubns.

Wolters, Richard A. **Water Dog.** (Illus.). 8.95. Dutton.

Hunting Dogs—Setters

Pet Library Ltd. **Know Your Setters & Pointers.** (Illus.). pap. 1.50. Doubleday.

Hunting Stories

Alaska Magazine Editors. **Selected Alaska Hunting & Fishing Tales.** Vol. 3. 1974. pap. 3.95. Alaska Northwest.

Bear. Fred. **Fred Bear's Field Notes.** 8.95. Doubleday.

Brister, Bob. **Moss, Mallards & Mules: And Other Hunting & Fishing Stories.** 1973. 8.95. Winchester Pr.

Hill, Gene. **Hill Country: Stories About Hunting & Fishing & Dogs & Such.** (Illus.). 1978. 9.95. Dutton.

Holden, Philip. **Backblocks.** (Illus.). 1974. 9.25. Intl Pubns Serv.

Neasham, V. Aubrey. **Wild Legacy: California Hunting & Fishing Tales.** (Illus.). 1973. 6.50. Howell-North.

Hunting with Bow and Arrow

Bear, Fred. **Archer's Bible.** (Illus.). 1968. pap. 2.95. Doubleday.

Conaster, Dean. **Bowhunting the White-Tailed Deer.** (Illus.). 1977. 10.00. Winchester Pr.

Gillelan, G. Howard. **Complete Book of the Bow & Arrow.** rev. ed. 1977. 9.95. Stackpole.

Helgeland, Glenn. **Archery World's Complete Guide to Bowhunting.** 1977. pap. 3.95. P-H.

James, M. R. **Bowhunting for Whitetail & Mule Deer.** (Illus.). 1976. 10.95; pap. 6.96. Jolex.

Kittredge, Doug & Wambold, H. R. **Bowhunting for Deer.** rev. ed. 1978. 8.95. Stackpole.

Laycock, George & Bauer, Erwin. **Hunting with Bow & Arrow.** 1965. 3.95. Arco.

Learn, C. R. **Bow Hunter's Digest.** 1974. pap. 6.95. DBI.

Schuyler, Keith C. **Bow Hunting for Big Game.** (Illus.). 1974. 5.95. Stackpole.

Smyth, John & Barwick, Humphrey. **Bow Vs. Gun.** 1976. Repr. 15.00. Charles River Bks.

Tinsley, Russell. **Bow Hunter's Guide.** (Illus.). 1975. softbound. 5.95. Stoeger.

Knife Throwing

McEvoy, Harry K. **Knife Throwing: A Practical Guide.** (Illus.). 1973. 3.25. C E Tuttle.

Knives

Barney, Richard W., and Loveless, Robert W. **How to Make Knives.** 1977. pap. 9.95. Beinfeld Publ.

Boye, David. **Step-by-Step Knifemaking.** 1977. softbound. 7.95. Stoeger.

Cassidy, William. **Knife Digest.** Peterson, Harold L., et al. eds. (Illus.). 1974. 15.00; pap. 5.95. Knife Digest.

Cassidy, William L. **The Complete Book of Knife Fighting.** Lund, Peder C., ed. 1975. 10.95. Paladin Pr.

Ehrhardt, Roy. **Encyclopedia of Pocket Knives: Book Three Price Guide.** (Illus.). 6.95. Heart Am Pr.

——**Encyclopedia of Pocket Knives: Book One & Book Two Combined.** (Illus.). 6.95. Heart Am Pr.

Hughes, B. R. **American Hand-Made Knives of Today.** 2.95. Pioneer Pr.

Hughes, B. R. & Lewis, Jack. **Gun Digest Book of Knives,** pap. 7.95. DBI.

Latham, Sid. **Knives & Knifemakers.** (Illus.). 1974. pap. 5.95. Macmillan.

——**Knives & Knifemakers.** 1973. 15.00. Winchester Pr.

Parker, James F. **Official Guide to Collectible Pocket Knives.** (Illus.). 1976. pap. 5.95. Hse of Collectibles.

Peterson, Harold L. **American Knives.** (Illus.). 1958. 5.95. Scribner.

——**American Knives.** 1975. pap. 4.95. Scribner.

——**History of Knives.** (Illus.). 1966. 5.95. Scribner.

Schreir, Konrad F., Jr. **Marble Knives and Axes.** (Illus.). 1978. pap. 4.50. Beinfeld.

Schroeder, William. **A Collector's Illustrated Price Guide to Pocket Knives.** 1977. pap. 2.95. Collector Bks.

Strung, Norman. **The Encyclopedia of Knives.** (Illus.). 1976. 12.50. Lippincott.

Wallace George B. **Knife Handling for Self Defense.** 1973. pap. 5.00. Walmac Bks.

Warner, Ken. **Practical Book of Knives.** (Illus.). 1976. softbound. 5.95. Stoeger.

Lee-Enfield Rifles

Chamberlain, Peter & Gander, Terry. **Machine Guns.** (Illus.). 1975. 5.95; pap. 3.95. Arco.

Mauser Pistols

Belford & Dunlap. **Mauser Self-Loading Pistol.** 12.50. Borden.

Holland, Claude V. **The Military Four.** 4.95; pap. 2.98. C V Holland.

Mauser Manual. (Facs. ed. of early English language Mauser Catalog and Manual). 1974. softbound. 1.95. Stoeger.

Pender. **Mauser Pocket Pistols: 1910-1946.** 14.50. Borden.

Moose

Berry, William D. **Deneki: An Alaskan Moose.** 1965. 4.50. Macmillan.

Mason, George F. **Moose Group.** (Illus.). 1968. pap. 2.25. Hastings.

Peterson, Randolph L. **North American Moose.** 1955. 19.00. U of Toronto Pr.

Van Wormer, Joe. **The World of the Moose.** (Illus.). 1972. 6.95. Lippincott.

Natural History—Outdoor Books

Bedichek, Roy. **Adventures with a Texas Naturalist.** (Illus.). 1961. 11.95. U of Tex Pr.

Beston, Henry. **Outermost House.** 1977. pap. 2.95. Penguin.

Borland, Hal. **Beyond Your Doorstep.** (Illus.). 1962. 6.95. Knopf.

Borland, Hal G. **This Hill, This Valley.** 1963. 10.00. Lippincott.

Brown, Vinson. **How to Explore the Secret Worlds of Nature.** (Illus.). 1962. 4.95. Little.

——**Knowing the Outdoors in the Dark.** (Illus.). 1973. pap. 2.95. Macmillan.

Burroughs, John. **Under the Apple-Trees.** 1916. 15.00. Folcroft.

——**Wake-Robin.** 1896. 15.00. Folcroft.

——**Winter Sunshine.** 1879. 15.00. Folcroft.

——**A Year in the Fields.** 1901. 15.00. Folcroft.

Cooper, Susan F. **Rural Hours.** (Illus.). 1968. Repr. of 1887 ed. 5.50. Syracuse U Pr.

Davids, Richard C. **How to Talk to Birds & Other Uncommon Ways of Enjoying Nature the Year Round.** (Illus.). 1972. 7.95. Knopf.

Errington, Paul L. **The Red Gods Call.** (Illus.). 1973. 5.95. Iowa St U Pr.

Fuller, Raymond T. **Now That We Have to Walk: Exploring the Out-of-Doors.** facs. ed. Repr. of 1943 ed. 12.00. Bks for Libs.

Gibbons, Euell. **Euell Gibbons' Beachcombers Handbook: Field Guide Edition.** 1967. pap. 2.95. McKay.

Halle, Louis J. **Spring in Washington.** 5.00. Peter Smith.

——**Spring in Washington.** (Illus.). 1963. pap. 1.25. Atheneum.

Harrison, Hal H. **Outdoor Adventures.** (Illus.). 5.95. Vanguard.

Jefferies, Richard. **Old House at Coate.** 1948. 14.00. Bks for Libs.

Kieran, John F. **Nature Notes.** facs. ed. 1941. 12.50. Bks for Libs.

Leopold, Aldo. **Sand County Almanac: With Other Essays on Conservation from Round River.** (Illus.). 1966. 10.00. Oxford U Pr.

O'Kane, Walter C. **Beyond the Cabin Door.** 1957. 4.50. Bauhan.

Olson, Sigurd F. **Listening Point.** (Illus.). 1958. 7.95. Knopf.

——**Open Horizons.** (Illus.). 1969. 6.95. Knopf.

——**Singing Wilderness.** (Illus.). 1956. 6.95. Knopf.

Ormond, Clyde. **Complete Book of Outdoor Lore.** (Illus.). 1964. 8.95. Times Mirror Mag.

Pearson, Haydn S. **Sea Flavor.** facs. ed. 1948. 13.00. Bks for Libs.

Quinn, John R. **The Winter Woods.** (Illus.). 1976. 8.95. Chatham Pr.

Rood, Ronald, et. al. **Vermont Life Book of Nature.** Hard, Walter, Jr., ed. (Illus.). 1967. 7.95. Greene.

Rowlands, John J. **Cache Lake County.** (Illus.). 1959. 8.95. Norton.

Sharp, Dallas L. **Face of the Fields.** facs. ed. 1911. 10.50. Bks for Libs.

——**Sanctuary! Sanctuary!** facs. ed. 1926. 11.25. Bks for Libs.

Sharp, William. **Where the Forest Murmurs.** 1906. 17.00. Bks for Libs.

Shepard, Odell. **Harvest of a Quiet Eye: A Book of Digressions.** facs. ed. Repr. of 1927 ed. 14.50. Bks for Libs.

Teale, Edwin W. **American Seasons.** 4 vols. (Illus.). 1966. Set. 40.00; 10.00 ea. Dodd.

——**Autumn Across America.** (Illus.). 1956. 10.00. Dodd.

——**Journey into Summer.** (Illus.). 1960. 10.00; pap. 2.25. Dodd.

——**North with the Spring.** (Illus.). 1951. 10.00. Dodd.

——**Wandering Through Winter.** (Illus.). 1965. 10.00; pap. 2.25. Dodd.

Wiley, Farida, ed. **John Burroughs' America.** (Illus.) 7.50; pap. 5.25. Devin.

Wood, Robert S. **Mountain Cabin.** (Illus.). 1977. pap. 4.95. Chronicle Bks.

Working from Nature. (Color Crafts Ser.) 1975. 6.95. Watts.

Ordnance

Bruce, Robert V. **Lincoln & the Tools of War.** (Illus.). 1974. Repr. of 1956 ed. 17.25. Greenwood.

Carman, W. Y. **History of Firearms from Earliest Times to 1914.** 1955. 6.50. St Martin.

Chamberlain, Peter & Gander, Terry. **Infantry, Mountain & Airborne Guns.** 1975. 5.95; pap. 3.95. Arco.

——**Light & Medium Artillery.** (Illus.). 1975. 5.95; pap. 3.95. Arco.

——**Mortars & Rockets.** 1975. 5.95; pap. 3.95. Arco.

Cipolla, Carlo M. **Guns, Sails & Empires: Technological Innovation & the Early Phases of European Expansion 1400-1700.** pap. 2.25. Funk & W.

Colby, C. B. **Civil War Weapons: Small Arms & Artillery of the Blue & Gray.** (Illus.). 1962. 4.69. Coward.

Ffoulkes, Charles. **The Gun Founders of England.** (Illus.). 1969. 20.00. Shumway.

Hoffschmidt, Edward J. & Tantum, William H. **Second World War Combat Weapons: Japanese Combat Weapons, Vol. 2.** (Illus.). 10.00. We Inc.

Norton, Robert. **The Gunner, Shewing the Whole Practise of Artillerie.** 1973. Repr. of 1628 ed. 35.00. W J Johnson.

Office Strategic Services. **OSS Sabotage & Demolition Manual.** (Illus.) 1973. pap. 12.95. Paladin Pr.

Simon, Leslie E. **Secret Weapons of the Third Reich: German Research in World War II.** (Illus.). 1970. 10.00. We Inc.

Orientation

Burton, Maurice. **The Sixth Sense of Animals.** (Illus.). 1973. 7.95. Taplinger.

Corballis, M. C. and Beak, I. L. **The Psychology of Left and Right.** 1976. 14.95. Halsted Pr.

Disley, John. **Orienteering.** (Illus.). 1973. pap. 3.95. Stackpole.

Henley, B. M. **Orienteering.** (Illus.). 1976. 6.95. Charles River Bks.

Hill, Everett W. and Ponder, Purvis. **Orientation & Mobility Techniques: A Guide for the Practitioner.** 1976. 4.50. Am Foun Blind.

Howard, I. P. & Templeton, W. B. **Human Spatial Orientation.** 1966. 16.25. Wiley.

Kjellstrom, Bjorn. **Be Expert with Map & Compass: The Orienteering Handbook.** 1972. pap. 3.95. Scribner.

Knapp, Robert R. **Handbook for the Personal Orientation Inventory.** 12.95. EDITS.

Kreitler, Hans & Kreitler, Shulamith. **Cognitive Orientation & Behavior.** 1976. 27.50. Springer Pub.

Mooers, Robert L., Jr. **Finding Your Way in the Outdoors.** 1972. 6.95. Dutton.

Orienteering. 1976. pap. 2.50. British Bk Ctr.

Rand, Jim & Walker, Tony. **This Is Orienteering.** (Illus.). 1977. 12.50. Transatlantic.

Ratliff, Donald E. **Map, Compass & Campfire.** (Illus.). 1970. pap. 2.00. Binford.

Rutstrum, Calvin. **Wilderness Route Finder.** 1967. 4.95. Macmillan.

Outdoor Cookery

Allen, Gale & Allen, Robert F. **The Complete Recreational Vehicle Cookbook: For Campers, Motor Homes, RV's & Vans.** Moulton, Jocelyn, ed. 1977. pap. 4.95. Celesial Arts.

Ames, Mark & Ames, Roberta. **Barbecues.** 1973. pap. 0.95. Warner Bks.

Anderson, Ken. **The Stereo Outdoor Living Book.** 1977. 5.95. Dorison Hse.

Angier, Bradford. **Food-from-the-Woods-Cooking.** (Illus.). 1973. pap. 1.50. Macmillan.

——**Wilderness Cookery.** (Illus.). 1970. pap. 3.95. Stackpole.

Banks, James E. **Alferd Packer's Wilderness Cookbook.** (Illus.). 1969. 4.50; pap. 1.00. Filter.

Barker, Harriett. **One Burner Gourmet.** 1975. pap. 4.95. Greatlakes Liv.

Bartmess, Marilyn A., ed. **Woodall's Campsite Cookbook.** 1971. pap. 2.95. S&S.

Bates, Joseph D., Jr. **Outdoor Cook's Bible.** (Illus.). 1964. pap. 2.95. Doubleday.

Beard, James A. **Fireside Cookbook.** (Illus.). 1969. 14.95. S&S.

Berglund, Berndt & Bolsby, Clare. **Wilderness Cooking.** 1973. 4.95. Scribner.

Better Homes & Gardens Editors. **The Better Homes & Gardens Barbecue Book.** 1974. pap. 1.25. Bantam.

Blanchard, Marjorie P. **The Outdoor Cookbook.** (Illus.). 1977. 5.90. Watts.

Bock, Richard. **Camper Cookery.** 1977. pap. 5.95. Lorenz Pr.

Bond, Jules. **The Outdoor Cookbook.** 1976. pap. 1.95. PB.

Brent, Carol D., ed. **Barbecue: The Fine Art of Charcoal, Gas & Hibachi Outdoor Cooking.** (Illus.). 1971. 4.95. Doubleday.

Bultmann, Phyllis. **Two Burners & an Ice Chest: The Art of Relaxed Cooking in Boats, in Campers & Under the Stars.** (Illus.). 1978. 11.95. pap. 5.95. H-R.

Bunnelle, Hasse. **Food for Knapsackers: And Other Trail Travelers.** 1971. pap. 4.95. Sierra.

Bunnelle, Hasse & Sarvis, Shirley. **Cooking for Camp & Trail.** 1972. pap. 3.95. Sierra.

Carhart, Arthur H. **Outdoorsman's Cookbook.** rev. ed 1962. pap. 0.95. Macmillan.

Crocker, Betty. **Betty Crocker's New Outdoor Cookbook.** (Illus.). 1967. 3.95. Western Pub.

Cross, Margaret & Fiske, Jean. **Backpacker's Cookbook.** 1973. 3.00. Ten Speed Pr.

Culinary Arts Institute Editorial Staff. **The Master Chef's Outdoor Grill Cookbook.** 1975. pap. 2.95. G&D.

Dawson, Charlotte. **Recreational Vehicle Cookbook.** (Illus., Orig.). 1970. 3.95. Trail-R.

——**Trailerists Cookbook.** 2.95. Trail-R.

Dodd, Ed. **Mark Trail's Cooking Tips.** 1971. pap. 1.00. Essandess.

Douglas, Luther A. & Douglas, Conda E. **The Explorers Cookbook.** (Illus.). 1971. 14.95. Caxton.

Drew, Edwin P. **The Complete Light-Pack Camping & Trail-Food Cookbook.** 1977. 3.95. McGraw.

Farmer, Charles J. & Farmer, Kathy, eds. **Campground Cooking.** 1974. pap. 6.95. DBI.

Fitzgerald. **Easy to Bar-B-Q Cook Book: A Guide to Better Barbecuing.** pap. 2.95. Pacifica.

Fleming, June. **The Well-Fed Backpacker.** 1976. pap. 4.50. Victoria Hse.

Hemingway, Joan & Maricich, Connie. **The Picnic Gourmet.** (Illus.). 1977. 12.95. Random.

Holm, Don. **Old-Fashioned Dutch Oven Cookbook.** 1969. pap. 3.95. Caxton.

Hughes, Stella. **Chuck Wagon Cookin'.** 1974. pap. 4.95. U of Ariz Pr.

Hunter, Rob. **Camping & Backpacking Cookbook.** (Illus.). 1978. pap. 2.95. Hippocrene Bks.

Jones, Phil. **Cooking over Wood.** 1976. pap. 4.95. Drake Pubs.

Kaatz, Van. **The Thrifty Gourmet's Chopped Meat Book.** (Illus.). 1976. pap. 1.50. Major Bks.

Kamins, James. **The Cookout Conspiracy.** Young, Billie, ed. 1974. 7.95. Ashley Bks.

Kinmont, Vikki, & Axcell, Claudia. **Simple Foods for the Pack.** (Illus.). 1976. pap. 4.95. Sierra.

Kitchin, Frances. **Cook-Out.** (Illus.). 1978. 7.95. David & Charles.

Knap, Alyson. **The Outdoorsman's Guide to Edible Wild Plants of North America: an Illustrated Manual.** (Illus.). 1975. 8.95. Pagurian.

MacDonald, Barbara & Culinary Arts Institute Staff. **Outdoor Cookbook.** (Illus.). 1975. pap. 2.45. Consolidated Bk.

McElfresh, Beth. **Chuck Wagon Cookbook.** pap. 1.95. Swallow.

Macklin, Harvey: **Backpacker's Cookbook: A Complete Manual & Handbook for Cooking Freeze-Dried & Wild Foods on the Trail & in the Wilderness.** (Illus.). 1978. Price not set. Pagurian.

Macmillan, Diane D. **The Portable Feast.** (Illus.). 1973. 7.95; pap. 4.95. One Hund One Prods.

McMorris, Bill & McMorris, Jo. **The All Outdoors Cookbook.** (Illus.). 1974. 9.95. McKay.

Marshall, Mel. **Cooking Over Coals.** 1975. softbound. 5.95. Stoeger.

——The Family Cookout Cookbook. 1973. pap. 0.95. Ace Bks.

Martin, George W. The Complete Book of Outdoor Cooking. (Illus). 1975. 7.95. A S Barnes.

Mendenhall, Ruth D. Backpack Cookery. (Illus.). 1974. pap. 1.50. La Siesta.

Messner, Yvonne. Campfire Cooking. (Illus., Orig.). 1973. pap. 1.95. Cook.

Miller, Dorcas S. The Healthy Trail Food Book. (Illus.). 1976. 3.95. Fast & McMillan.

Mohney, Russ. Trailside Cooking. (Illus.). 1976. pap. 2.95. Stackpole.

Morris, Dan & Morris, Inez. The Complete Fish Cookbook. (Illus.). 1978. softbound. 5.95. Stoeger.

——Complete Outdoor Cookbook. 1970. 9.95. Hawthorn.

Nagy, Jean. Brown Bagging it: a Guide to Fresh Food Cooking in the Wilderness. 1976. pap. 2.50. Marty-Nagy.

——The Outdoor Cookbook. (Illus.). 1976. 5.95. Oxmoor Hse.

Powledge, Fred. The Budget Backpacker's Food Book: How to Select & Prepare Your Provision from Supermarket Shelves with Over 50 Trail-Tested Recipes. 1977. pap. 3.95. McKay.

Raup, Lucy G. Camper's Cookbook. 1967. pap. 3.75. Tuttle.

Reimers, Emil. Cooking for Camp & Caravan. 1976. 5.95. British Bk Ctr.

Riviere, William A. Family Campers' Cookbook. (Illus.). 1965. 4.95. HR&W.

Schubert, Ruth L. The Camper's Cookbook. 1974. pap. 3.50. Little.

Steindler, Geraldine. Game Cookbook. (Illus.). 1965. softbound. 5.95. Stoeger.

Strom, Arlene. Cooking on Wheels. (Illus.). 1970. 4.95; pap. 2.95. Wheelwright.

Tarr, Yvonne Y. The Complete Outdoor Cookbook. (Illus.). 1973. 8.95. Quadrangle.

Thomas, Dian. Roughing It Easy: A Unique Ideabook on Camping & Cooking. (Illus.). 1974. 7.95; pap. 4.95. Brigham.

Tonn, Maryjane H., ed. Ideals Outdoor Cookbook. 1975. pap. 2.25. Ideals.

Wallace Aubrey. Natural Foods for the Trail. 1977. 3.95. Vogelsang Pr.

Western Publishing Editors, ed. Betty Crocker's New Outdoor Cookbook. No. 10. 1976. pap. 1.50. Bantam.

Wood, Jane. Elegant Fare from the Weber Kettle. (Illus.). 1977. 6.95. Western Pub.

Woodall's Campside Cookbook. pap. 2.95. Woodall.

Outdoor Life

Acerrano, Anthony J. The Outdoorsman's Emergency Manuel. 1976. softbound. 5.95. Stoeger.

Allison, Linda. The Sierra Club Summer Book. (Illus.). 1977. 4.95. Sierra.

Andreson, Steve. The Orienteering Book. (Illus.). 1977. pap. 3.50. World Pubns.

Angier, Bradford. Food-from-the-Woods-Cooking. (Illus.). 1973. pap. 1.50. Macmillan.

——How to Stay Alive in the Woods. Orig. Title. Living off the Country. 1962. pap. 1.25. Macmillan.

——One Acre & Security: How to Live off the Earth Without Ruining It. 1972. 7.95. Stackpole.

——Skills for Taming the Wilds: A Handbook of Woodcraft Wisdom. 1972. pap. 1.50. PB.

——Survival with Style. (Illus.). 1972. 6.95. Stackpole.

——Wilderness Gear You Can Make Yourself. (Illus.). 1973. pap. 2.95. Macmillan.

Angier, Bradford & Angier, Vena. Wilderness Wife. (Illus.). 1976. 7.95. Chilton.

Bourjaily, Vance. Country Matters: Collected Reports from the Fields & Streams of Iowa & Other Places. 1973. 8.95. Dial.

Bradford, William. Survival Outdoors. 1977. pap. 2.95. Macmillan.

Brittain, William Survival Outdoors. (Illus.). 1977. pap. 2.95. Monarch.

Brown, Vinson. Knowing the Outdoors in the Dark. (Illus.). 1973. pap. 2.95. Macmillan.

——Knowing the Outdoors in the Dark. 1972. 7.95. Stackpole.

Carrighar, Sally. Home to the Wilderness. (Illus.). 1973. 7.95. HM.

Cartier, John O. The Modern Deer Hunter. (Illus.). 1977. 10.95. Funk & W.

Colby, C. B. Camper's and Backpacker's Bible. (Illus.). 1977. softbound. 7.95. Stoeger.

Eastman, P. F. Advanced First Aid for All Outdoors. 1976. pap. 6.00. Cornell Maritime.

Explorers Limited, compiled by. Explorers Ltd. Source Book. (Illus.). 1973. pap. 5.95. Har-Row.

Fear, Daniel E., ed. Surviving the Unexpected: A Curriculum Guide for Wilderness Survival & Survival from Natural & Man Made Disasters. (Illus.). 1974. 2.50. Survival Ed Assoc.

Frederickson, Olive A. & East, Ben. The Silence of the North. 1973. pap. 1.50. Warner Bks.

Gearing, Catherine. Field Guide to Wilderness Living. 1973. pap. 3.95. Southern Pub.

Gregory, Mark. The Good Earth Almanac. 1973. pap. 4.95. G&D.

Hall, Bill. A Year in the Forest. (Illus.). 1975. 6.95. McGraw.

Hamper, Stanley R. Wilderness Survival. 3rd ed. 1975. Repr. of 1963 ed. 1.79. Peddlers Wagon.

Heacox, Cecil E. The Education of an Outdoorsman. 1976. 8.95. Winchester Pr.

Henderson, Luis M. Campers' Guide to Woodcraft & Outdoor Life. Orig. Title: Outdoor Guide. 1972. pap. 3.50. Dover.

Hickin Norman. Beachcombing for Beginners. 1976. pap. 2.00. Wilshire.

Hollatz, Tom. The White Earth Snowshoe Handbook. (Illus.). 1973. pap. 3.50. North Star.

Hunter, Rodello. Wyoming Wife. 1969. 7.95. Knopf.

Jeneid, Michael. The Outdoors Adventure Book. (Illus.). 1975. 8.95. Walck.

Johnson, et al. Outdoor Tips: A Remington Sportsmen's Library Bk. pap. 2.95. Wheelwright.

Jones, James C., ed. The National Outdoor Living Directory, No. 2. (Illus.). 1975. price not set. Live Free.

Kephart, Horace. Camping & Woodcraft. (Illus.). 1948. 8.95. Macmillan.

Kodet, E. Russel & Angier, Bradford. Being Your Own Wilderness Doctor. (Illus.). 1975. 3.95. Stackpole.

Labostille, Anne. Woodswoman. (Illus.). 1978. pap. 3.95. Dutton.

Lamoreaux, Bob & Lamoreaux, Marcia. Outdoor Gear You Can Make Yourself. (Illus.). 1976. pap. 3.95. Stackpole.

Lueders, Edward. The Clam Lake Papers: A Winter in the North Woods. 1977. 7.95. Har-Row.

McGuire, Thomas. Ninety-Nine Days on the Yukon: An Account of What Was Seen & Heard in the Company of Charles A. Wolf, Gentleman Canoeist. 1977. pap. 7.95. Alaska-Northwest.

McPhee Gribble Publishers. Out in the Wilds. (Illus.). 1977. pap. 1.50. Penguin.

Merrill, W. K. The Survival Handbook. (Illus.). 1972. 6.95. Winchester Pr.

Mitchell, Jim. Fundamentals of Outdoor Enjoyment: Text or Teaching Guide for Coping with Outdoor Environments, All Seasons. (Illus.). 1976. pap. 3.95. Survival Ed Assoc.

Mohney, Russ. Wintering: The Outdoor Book for Cold-Weather Ventures. 1976. pap. 2.95. Stackpole.

Nickols, Maggie. Wild, Wild Woman. 1978. pap. 4.95. Berkeley Pub.

Olsen, Larry D. Outdoor Survival Skills. rev. ed. 1973. 8.95; pap. 4.95. Brigham.

Ormond, Clyde. Complete Book of Outdoor Lore. (Illus.). 1965. 9.95. Har-Row.

——Outdoorsman's Handbook. 1971. 6.95. Dutton.

Owings, Loren C., ed. Environmental Values, 1860-1972: A Guide to Information Sources. 1976. 18.00. Gale.

Patmore, J. Allan. Land & Leisure in England & Wales. 1971. 18.00. Fairleigh Dickinson.

Petzoldt, Paul. The Wilderness Handbook. (Illus.). 1977. pap. 4.95. Norton.

Rae, William E. Treasury of Outdoor Life. (Illus.). 1975. 11.95. Har-Row.

Rawick, George P. From Sundown to Sunup. 1972. 11.00; pap. 2.95. Greenwood.

Robinson, David. The Complete Homesteading Book: Proven Methods for Self-Sufficient Living. 1974. 8.95; pap. 5.95. Garden Way Pub.

Rood, Ronald. It's Going to Sting Me: A Coward's Guide to the Great Outdoors. 1977 pap. 3.95. McGraw.

Rutstrum, Calvin. New Way of the Wildnerness. (Illus.). 1966. 4.95; pap. 2.95. Macmillan.

——Once Upon a Wilderness (Illus.). 1973. 6.95. Macmillan.

Ruxton, George F. Adventures in Mexico & the Rocky Mountains. 10.00. Rio Grande.

Van Der Smissen, Betty, et al. Leader's Guide to Nature-Oriented Activities. 2nd ed. (Illus.). 1968. pap. 4.95. Iowa St U Pr.

Vogt, Bill. How to Build a Better Outdoors: The Action Manual for Fishermen, Hunters, Backpackers, Hikers, Canoeists, Riders, & All Other Outdoor Lovers. (Illus.). 1978. pap. 4.95. McKay.

Waterman, Charles F. The Part I Remember. (Illus.). 1974. 8.95. Winchester Pr.

Woolner, Frank. My New England. (Illus.). 1972. 6.50. Stone Wall Pr.

Wurman, Richard S. et. al. The Nature of Recreation: A Handbook in Honor of Frederick Law Olmstead. 1972. pap. 4.95. MIT Pr.

Pistols

Archer, Denis, ed. Jane's Pocketbook of Pistols & Submachine Guns. 1977. pap. 6.95. Macmillan.

Best, Charles W. Cast Iron Toy Pistols, 1870-1940: A Collector's Guide. (Illus.). 1973. 15.00. Rocky Mtn Arms.

Bianchi, John. Blue Steel and Gun Leather. 1978. 9.95. Beinfeld.

Blair, Claude. Pistols of the World. (Illus.). 1969. 30.00. Viking Pr.

Chamberlain, Peter & Gander, Terry. Allied Pistols, Rifles, & Grenades. 1976. pap. 3.95. Arco.

Datig, Fred A. Luger Pistol. rev. ed. 9.50. Borden.

Dixon, Norman. Georgian Pistols: The Art & Craft of the Flintlock Pistol, 1715-1840. 1972. 18.00. Shumway.

Dunlap, H. J. American, British & Continental Pepperbox Firearms. (Illus.). 1967. Repr. of 1964 ed. 17.95. Pacific Bks.

Dyke, S. E. Thoughts on the American Flintlock Pistol. (Illus.). 1974. 5.00. Shumway.

Grennell, Dean A. A Pistol & Revolver Digest. 1976. pap. 6.95. DBI.

Hertzberg, Robert. Modern Handguns. (Illus.). 1965. 3.50. Arco.

Hogg, I. V. Military Pistols & Revolvers. (Illus.). 1970. 3.50; pap. 1.95. Arco.

Holland, Claude V. The Military Four. 4.95; pap. 2.98. C V Holland.

Horlacher, R., ed. The Famous Automatic Pistols of Europe. Seaton, L. & Steindler, R.A., trs. from Ger. (Illus.). 1976. pap. 6.95. Jolex.

Jinks, Roy G. History of Smith & Wesson. (Illus.). 1978. 15.95. Beinfeld.

Kirkland, Turner. **Southern Derringers of the Mississippi Valley.** 2.00. Pioneer Pr.

Koch, R. W. **The FP-45 Liberato-Pistol 1942-45.** (Illus.). 1977. 10.00. Research.

Leithe. **Japanese Hand Pistols.** 8.50. Borden.

Luger Manual. (Reprint of original English-language edition). 1967. softbound. 1.95. Stoeger.

Mauser Manual (Facs. ed. of early English language **Mauser Catalog and Manual.**). 1974. softbound. 1.95. Stoeger.

Millard, J. T. **A Handbook on the Primary Identification of Revolvers & Semi-Automatic Pistols.** (Illus.). 1974. 10.50; pap. 7.95. C C Thomas.

Neal, Robert J. & Jinks, Roy G. **Smith & Wesson** 1857-1945. 1972. 25.00. A S Barnes.

Nonte, George C., Jr. **Pistol & Revolver Guide.** 3rd ed. (Illus.). 1975. softbound. 6.95. Stoeger.

——**Pistolsmithing.** (Illus.). 1974. 14.95. Stackpole.

Nonte, George C., Jr. & Jurras, Lee E. **Handgun Hunting.** (Illus.). 1976. softbound 5.95. Stoeger.

Olson, John, compiled by. **The Famous Automatic Pistols of Europe.** (Illus.). 1975. 9.95; pap. 6.95. Jolex.

Pollard, H. B. **Automatic Pistols.** (Illus.). 1970. Repr. of 1921 ed. 6.00. We Inc.

Reese, Michael. **Collector's Guide to Luger Values.** 1972. pap. 1.00. Pelican.

——**Luger Tips.** 1976. 6.95. Pioneer Pr.

Sawyer, Charles W. **United States Single Shot Martial Pistols.** 1971. 5.00. We Inc.

Van Der Mark, Kist & Van Der Sloot, Puype. **Dutch Muskets & Pistols.** (Illus.). 1974. 24.00. Shumway.

Wallack, L. R. **American Pistol & Revolver Design & Performance.** 1978. 13.95. Winchester Pr.

Wilkerson, Frederick. **British & American Flintlocks.** 1972. 2.95. Transatlantic.

Wilkinson, F. J. **Flintlock Pistols.** 1976. pap. 2.95. Hippocrene Bks.

Reloading

Scott, Robert F., ed. **Shooter's Bible 1980, No. 71.** (Illus.). 1979. softbound. 8.95. Stoeger.

Steindler, R. A. **Reloader's Guide.** 3rd ed. (Illus.). 1975. softbound. 6.95. Stoeger.

Wootters, John. **The Complete Book of Practical Handloading.** (Illus.). 1977. softbound. 5.95. Stoeger.

Revolvers

Bianchi, John. **Blue Steel and Gun Leather.** 1978. 9.95. Beinfeld.

Chamberlain, W. H. & Taylorson, A. W. **Adam's Revolvers.** 1978. 29.95. Barrie & Jenkins.

Grennell, Dean A. **Pistol & Revolver Digest.** (Illus.). 1976. pap. 7.95. DBI.

Hertzberg, Robert. **Modern Handgun.** (Illus.). 1965. 3.50. Arco.

Hogg, I. V. **Military Pistols & Revolvers.** (Illus.). 1970. 3.50; pap. 1.95. Arco.

James, Garry, ed. **Guns of the Gunfighters.** (Illus.). 1975. pap. 4.95. Petersen Pub.

Jinks, Roy G. **History of Smith & Wesson.** (Illus.). 1978. 15.95. Beinfeld.

Millard, J. T. **A Handbook on the Primary Identification of Revolvers & Semi-Automatic Pistols.** (Illus.). 1974. 10.50; pap. 7.95. C C Thomas.

Neal, Robert J. & Jinks, Roy G. **Smith & Wesson, 1857-1945.** 1975. 25.00. A S Barnes.

Nonte, George C., Jr. **Pistol & Revolver Guide.** 3rd ed. (Illus.). 1975. softbound. 6.95. Stoeger.

Nonte, George C., Jr. & Jurras, Lee E. **Handgun Hunting.** (Illus.). 1976. softbound. 5.95. Stoeger.

Report of Board on Tests of Revolvers & Automatic Pistols 1907. (Illus.). 3.00. Sand Pond.

Rifles

Archer, Denis. **Jane's Pocket Book of Rifles & Light Machine Guns.** 1977. pap. 6.95. Macmillan.

Beard, Ross E., Jr. **Carbine: The Story of David Marshall Williams.** 1977. 12.50; ltd. ed., signed 25.00. Sandlapper Store.

Brophy, William S. **Krag Rifles.** (Illus.). 1978. 19.95. Beinfeld.

Buchele, William & Shumway, George. **Recreating the American Longrifle.** Orig. Title: **Recreating the Kentucky Rifle.** (Illus.). 1973. pap. 7.50. Shumway.

Carmichel, Jim. **The Modern Rifle.** (Illus.). 1976. softbound. 5.95. Stoeger.

Chamberlain, Peter & Gander, Terry. **Allied Pistols, Rifles & Grenades.** 1976. pap. 3.95. Arco.

——**Axis Pistols, Rifles, & Grenades.** 1977. pap. 4.95. Arco.

——**Submachine Guns & Automatic Rifles: World War II Facts.** 1976. pap. 3.95. Arco.

Chapman, John R. **Improved American Rifle.** (Illus.). 1978. 5.95. Beinfeld.

Colby, C. B. **First Rifle: How to Shoot It Straight & Use It Safely.** (Illus.). 1954. 4.29. Coward.

De Haas, Frank. **Bolt Action Rifles.** Amber, John T., ed. 1971. pap. 7.95. DBI.

——**Bolt Action Rifles.** Amber, John T., ed. pap. 6.95. DBI.

——**Single Shot Rifles & Actions.** (Illus.). 1976. pap. 8.95. DBI.

Dillin, John G. **The Kentucky Rifle.** 5th ed. (Illus.). 1967. deluxe limited ed. 35.00. Shumway.

Editors of Gun Digest. **NRA Collector's Series: 1885-1888-1906-1923.** pap. 2.95. DBI.

Edsall, James. **The Golden Age of Single Shot Rifles.** 2.75. Pioneer Pr.

——**The Revolver Rifles.** 2.50. Pioneer Pr.

Huddleston, Joe D. & Shumway, George. **Rifles in the American Revolution.** 1978. Shumway.

Huddleston, Joe D. **Colonial Riflemen in the American Revolution.** (Illus.). 1978. 15.00. Shumway.

Kindig, Joe, Jr. **Thoughts on the Kentucky Rifle in Its Golden Age.** (Illus.). 1971. 39.50. Shumway.

Lachuk, John. **The Gun Digest Book of the .22 Rimfire.** 1978. pap. 6.95. DBI.

Lindsay, Merrill. **The Kentucky Rifle.** (Illus.). 1972. 15.00. Arma Pr.

Mauser Manual (Facs. ed. of early English language **Mauser Catalog and Manual.**). 1974. softbound. 1.95. Stoeger.

O'Connor, Jack, et al. **Complete Book of Shooting: Rifles, Shotguns and Handguns.** 1966. 10.95. Har-Row.

——**Complete Book of Rifles & Shotguns.** rev. ed. (Illus.). 1966. 11.95. Har-Row.

——**The Hunting Rifle.** (Illus.). 1975. softbound. 5.95. Stoeger.

——**Rifle Book.** 3rd ed. (Illus.). 1978. 13.95. Knopf.

Olson, John. **John Olson's Book of the Rifle.** (Illus.). 1974. 9.95; pap. 5.95. Jolex.

Otteson, Stuart. **The Bolt Action: A Design Analysis.** 1976. 12.95. Winchester Pr.

Page, Warren. **The Accurate Rifle.** (Illus.). 1975. softbound. 5.95. Stoeger.

Petzal, David. **Twenty-Two Caliber Rifle.** (Illus.). 1973. 6.95. Winchester Pr.

Pullum, Bill & Hanenkrat, Frank T. **Position Rifle Shooting.** (Illus.). 1975. softbound. 5.95. Stoeger.

Rywell, Martin. **American Antique Rifles.** 2.00. Pioneer Pr.

——**U.S. Muskets, Rifles & Carbines.** 2.00. Pioneer Pr.

Schedelman, Hans. **Vienna Kunsthistorisches Die Grossen Buchsenmacher.** (Illus.). 1976. 155.00. Arma Pr.

Steindler, R. A. **Rifle Guide.** (Illus.). 1978. softbound. 7.95. Stoeger.

U.S. Rifle Caliber .30 Model 1903. 2.00. Pioneer Pr.

U.S. Rifle Model 1866 Springfield. 0.75. Pioneer Pr.

U.S. Rifle Model 1870 Remington. 0.75. Pioneer Pr.

Wahl, Paul. **Carbine Handbook.** (Illus.). 1964. 6.00; pap. 4.95. Arco.

Waite, M.D. & Ernst, Bernard. **The Trapdoor Springfield.** 1979. 19.95. Beinfeld.

Wallack, L. R. **American Rifle Design & Performance.** 1977. 12.95. Winchester Pr.

Wood, J. B. **Troubleshooting Your Rifle & Shotgun.** (Illus.). 1978. pap. 5.95. DBI.

Sharps Rifles

Manual of Arms for the Sharps Rifle. 1.50. Pioneer Pr.

Rywell, Martin. **Sharps Rifle: The Gun That Shaped American Destiny.** 2.95. Pioneer Pr.

Sellers, Frank. **Sharps Firearms.** (Illus.). 1978. 34.95. Beinfeld.

Shields

Davison, Betsy. **Shields of Ancient Rome.** (Illus.). 1969. pap. 2.00. Westerfield. Malter-Westerfield.

Wright, Barton. **Pueblo Shields.** (Illus.). 1976. 9.50. Northland.

Shooting

Anderson, Gary. **Marksmanship.** 1972. pap. 2.95. S&S.

Arnold, Richard. **Clay Pigeon Shooting.** (Illus.). 1974. 9.00. Intl Pubns Serv.

——**Clay Pigeon Shooting.** (Illus.). 1974. text. ed. 14.50. Soccer.

Brister, Bob. **Shotgunning: The Art & the Science.** (Illus.). 1976. 10.00. Winchester Pr.

Carmichel, Jim. **The Modern Rifle.** (Illus.). 1976. softbound. 5.95. Stoeger.

Chapman, John R. **Improved American Rifle Instructions to Young Marksmen.** (Illus.). 1978. pap. 5.95. Follett.

Cogwell & Harrison. **Shooting.** 1973. pap. 2.95. McKay.

Day, J. Wentworth. **The Modern Shooter.** 1976. Repr. of 1952 ed. 15.00. Charles River Bks.

——**The Modern Shooter.** 1976. Repr. 15.00. Dynamic Learn Corp.

Ferber, Steve, ed. **All About Rifle Hunting & Shooting in America.** 1977. 10.00. Winchester Pr.

Fuller, W. H. **Small-Bore Target Shooting.** rev. ed. Palmer, A. J., ed. 1978. 11.95. Barrie & Jenkins.

Grennell, Dean A. **ABC's of Reloading.** 1974. pap. 6.95. DBI.

Hastings, MacDonald. **Shooting—Why We Miss: Questions & Answers on the Successful Use of the Shotgun.** 1977. pap. 3.95. McKay.

Janes, Edward C. **Boy & His Gun.** (Illus.). 1951. 6.95. A S Barnes.

Koller, Larry. **How to Shoot: A Complete Guide to the Use of Sporting Firearms—Rifles, Shotguns, & Handguns—on the Range & in the Field.** (Illus.). 1976. 9.95. Doubleday.

Lind, Ernie. **Complete Book of Trick & Fancy Shooting.** (Illus.). 1972. 6.95. Winchester Pr.

——**Complete Book of Trick & Fancy Shooting.** (Illus.). 1972. 6.95. Winchester Pr.

McCawley, E. S. **Shotguns & Shooting.** 1976. pap. 4.95. Van Nos Reinhold.

McGivern, Ed. **Ed McGivern's Book on Fast & Fancy Revolver Shooting, Centennial Edition.** (Illus.). 1975. 10.00. Follett.

Mason, James D. **Combat Handgun Shooting.** (Illus.). 1976. C C Thomas.

Missildine, Fred & Karas, Nick. **Score Better at Trap and Skeet.** (Illus.). 1977. softbound. 5.95. Stoeger.

Montague, Andrew A. **Successful Shotgun Shooting.** (Illus.). 1971. 6.95. Winchester Pr.

Mosher, John A. **The Shooter's Workbench.** (Illus.). 1977. 10.95. Winchester Pr.

O'Connor, Jack. **Complete Book of Shooting: Rifles, Shotguns, Handguns.** (Illus.). 1966. 9.95. Har-Row.

——**Rifle Book.** 2nd rev. ed. (Illus.). 1978. 13.95. Random Hse.

——**Shotgun Book.** (Illus.). 1965. 15.00. Knopf.

O'Connor, Jack, et al. **Complete Book of Shooting: Rifles, Shotguns, Handguns.** (Illus.). 1975. 8.95. Times Mirror Mag.

Page, Warren. **The Accurate Rifle.** (Illus.). 1975. softbound. 5.95. Stoeger.

Petzal, David E., ed. **Experts' Book of the Shooting Sports.** 9.95. S&S.

Pryce, Dick. **Hunting for Beginners.** 1978. softbound. 5.95. Stoeger.

Pullum, Bill & Hanenkrat, Frank T. **Position Rifle Shooting.** (Illus.). 1975. softbound. 5.95. Stoeger.

Riviere, Bill. **Gunner's Bible.** 1973. pap. 2.50. Doubleday.

Rees, Clair F. **Beginner's Guide to Guns & Shooting.** 1978. 6.95. Follett.

Reynolds, E. G. & Fulton, Robin. **Target Rifle Shooting.** 1978. 11.95. Barrie & Jenkins.

Roberts, Willis J. & Bristow, Allen P. **Introduction to Modern Police Firearms.** Gourley, Douglas, ed. (Illus.). 1969. 9.95. Glencoe.

Ruffer, J. E. **The Art of Good Shooting.** (Illus.). 1976. 4.95. David & Charles.

Scott, Robert F., ed. **Shooter's Bible, 1980, No. 71.** (Illus.). 1979. softbound. 8.95. Stoeger.

Sherrod, Blackie. **Blackie Sherrod . . . Scattershooting.** 1975. 6.95. Strode.

Shotgun Shooting. 1976. pap. 2.50. British Bk Ctr.

Stanbury, Percy & Carlisle, G. L. **Shotgun Marksmanship.** rev. ed. (Illus.). 1971. 8.95. A S Barnes.

Steindler, R. A. ed. **Shooting the Muzzleloaders.** (Illus.). 1975. 11.95; pap. 6.95. Jolex.

Weston, Paul B. **Combat Shooting for Police.** 2nd ed. (Illus.). 1978. 10.75. C C Thomas.

Shotguns

Arthur, Robert. **Shotgun Stock: Design, Construction & Embellishment.** (Illus.). 1970. 17.50. A S Barnes.

Baer, L. R. **The Parker Gun: An Immortal American Classic.** (Illus.). 1978. 24.95. Beinfeld.

Barker, A. J. **Shotguns & Shooting.** Brown, Robert K. & Lund, Peder C., eds. (Illus.). 1973. 4.95; pap. 2.50. Paladin Pr.

Boy Scouts of America. **Rifle & Shotgun Shooting.** (Illus.). 1967. pap. 0.55. BSA.

Brister, Bob. **Shotgunning: The Art and the Science.** (Illus.). 1976. 10.00. Winchester Pr.

Brophy, William S. **L. C. Smith Shotguns.** (Illus.). 1978. 24.95. Beinfeld.

Crudgington, I. M. & Baker, D. J. **The British Shotgun: 1850-1870.** Vol. 1. (Illus.). 1978. 21.95. Barrie & Jenkins.

Garwood, G. T. **Gough Thomas's Gun Book.** (Illus.). 1970. 8.95. Winchester Pr.

——**Gough Thomas's Second Gun Book.** (Illus.). 1972. 8.95. Winchester Pr.

Hastings, Macdonald. **Shooting—Why We Miss: Questions & Answers on the Successful Use of the Shotgun.** 1977. pap. 3.95. McKay.

Hinman, Bob. **Golden Age of Shotgunning.** (Illus.). 1972. 8.95. Winchester Pr.

Jinks, Roy G. **History of Smith & Wesson.** (Illus.). 1978. 15.95. Beinfeld.

Knight, Richard A. **Mastering the Shotgun.** (Illus.). 1975. 7.95. Dutton.

Laycock, George. **Shotgunner's Bible.** (Illus.). 1969. pap. 2.50. Doubleday.

McCawley, E. S. **Shotguns & Shooting.** 1976. pap. 4.95. Van Nos Reinhold.

O'Connor, Jack. **Shotgun Book.** (Illus.). 1965. 15.00. Knopf.

Olson, John. **John Olson's Book of the Shotgun.** (Illus.). 1975. 9.95; pap. 6.95. Jolex.

Robinson, Roger H. **The Police Shotgun Manual.** (Illus.). 1973. 10.50. C C Thomas.

Stanbury, Percy & Carlisle, G. L. **Shotgun Marksmanship.** (Illus.). 1971. 8.95. A S Barnes.

Thomas, Gough. **Shotguns & Cartridges for Game & Clays.** 3rd ed. (Illus.). 1976. 15.00. Transatlantic.

Wallack, L. R. **American Shotgun Design & Performance.** 1977. 13.95. Winchester Pr.

Williams, Mason. **The Defensive Use of the Handgun: For the Novice.** rev. ed. (Illus.). pap. 6.95. C C Thomas.

Woods, J. B. **Troubleshooting Your Rifle & Shotgun.** (Illus.). 1978. pap. 5.95. DBI.

Survival

Acerrano, Anthony J. **The Outdoorsman's Emergency Manual.** (Illus.). 1977. softbound. 5.95. Stoeger.

Allaby, Michael. **The Survival Handbook.** Tension, Marika H., ed. (Illus.). 1977. 14.95. State Mutual Bk.

Angier, Bradford. **How to Stay Alive in the Woods.** Orig. Title: **Living off the Country.** 1966. pap. 1.25. Macmillan.

——**Survival with Style.** (Illus.). 1972. 6.95. Stackpole.

Belisle, David A. **The American Family Robinson: The Adventures of a Family Lost in the Great Desert of the West.** 1976. Repr. of 1854 ed. 25.00. Scholarly.

Biggs, Don. **Survival Afloat.** (Illus.). 1976. 9.95; pap. 5.95. McKay.

Brown, Terry & Hunter, Rob. **The Concise Book of Survival & Rescue.** 1978. pap. 2.95. Vanguard.

Colby, C. B. **Survival: Training in Our Armed Services.** (Illus.). 1965. 4.29. Coward.

Dalrymple, Byron. **Survival in the Outdoors.** 1972. 6.95. Dutton.

Dennis, Lawrence. **Operational Thinking for Survival.** 1969. 5.95. R Myles.

Fear, Daniel E., ed. **Surviving the Unexpected: A Curriculum Guide for Wilderness Survival & Survival from Natural & Man Made Disasters.** (Illus.). rev. ed. 1974. 3.50. Survival Ed Assoc.

Fear, Eugene H. **Surviving the Unexpected Wilderness Emergency.** rev. ed. (Illus.). 1974. pap. 3.95. Survival Ed Assoc.

Fear, Gene. **Where Am I: A Text & Workbook for Personal Navigation Anywhere.** 1974. pap. 4.50. Survival Ed Assoc.

Gibbons, Euell. **Stalking the Good Life.** 1971. 8.95. McKay.

Graves, Richard. **Bushcraft: A Serious Guide to Survival & Camping.** (Illus.). 1972. 10.00; pap. 3.95. Schocken.

Greenbank, Anthony. **A Handbook for Emergencies: Coming Out Alive.** (Illus.). 1976. 5.95; pap. 3.95. Doubleday.

Hal, Betty L. **Survival Education.** 1976. pap. 4.50. Binford.

Hersey, John R. **Here to Stay.** 1963. 6.95. Knopf.

Jones, Tristan. **Ice!** 1978. 8.95. Sheed, Andrews & McMeel.

Koller, James, ed. **The Best of Live Free.** (Illus.). 1977. pap. 3.95. Live Free.

LaValla, Rick. **Survival Teaching Aids.** 1974. pap. 2.00. Survival Ed Assoc.

Lee, E. C. & Lee, Kenneth. **Safety & Survival at Sea.** (Illus.). 1972. 10.00. Norton.

Merrill, Bill. **The Survival Handbook.** 1974. pap. 1.95. Arc Bks.

Nelson, Dick & Nelson, Sharon. **Desert Survival.** (Illus.). 1976. pap. 2.95. Tecolote Pr.

Nesbitt, Paul, et al. **Survival Book.** (Illus.). 1969. pap. 1.95. Funk & W.

Olsen, Larry D. **Outdoor Survival Skills.** rev. ed. 1973. 8.95; pap. 5.95. Brigham.

Platt, Charles. **Outdoor Survival.** (Illus.). 1976. 4.33. Watts.

Read, Piers Paul. **Alive: The Story of the Andes Survivors.** (Illus.). 1974. 12.50; pap. 1.95. Lippincott.

Stoeffel, Skip. **Disaster-Survival Education Lesson Plans.** 1974. pap. 2.50. Survival Ed Assoc.

Szczelkun, Stefan A. **Survival Scrapbook 1: Shelter.** (Illus.). 1974. pap. 3.95. Schocken. 1963. 4.95. Naturegraph.

Troebst, Cord-Christian. **Art of Survival.** Coburn, Oliver, (tr. from Ger). (Illus.). pap. 2.95. Doubleday.

Vignes, Jacques. **The Rage to Survive.** Voukitchevitch, Mihailo, tr. (Illus.). 1976. 6.95. Morrow.

Western Electric. **Survival in the North.** 7.50. Wehman.

Swords

Akehurst, Richard. **Antique Weapons.** (Illus.). 1969. 5.95. Arco.

Campbell, Archibald. **Scottish Swords from the Battlefield at Culloden.** Mowbray, E. Andrew, ed. (Illus.). 5.00. Mowbray Co.

Castle, Egerton. **Schools & Masters of Fence from the Middle Ages to the Eighteenth Century.** (Illus.). 1969. casebound. 20.00. Shumway.

Dobree, Alfred. **Japanese Sword Blades.** 3rd ed. (Illus.). 1971. pap. 5.00. Shumway.

Ffoulkes, Charles & Hopkinson, E. C. **Sword, Lance & Bayonet.** (Illus.). 1967. 7.50. Arco.

Gunsaulus, H. C. **Japanese Sword-Mounts.** (Illus.). 1923. pap. 16.00. Kraus Repr.

Hamilton, John. **Collection of Japanese Sword Guards with Selected Pieces of Sword Furniture.** 1975. pap. 9.75. Peabody Mus Salem.

Hawley, Willis M. **Japanese Swordsmiths.** 2 vols. 1966-67. Vol. 1. 15.00; Vol. 2. 10.00. Hawley.

Hutton, Alfred. **The Sword & the Centuries; or, Old Sword Days & Old Sword Ways.** (Illus.). 1973. Repr. of 1901 ed. 8.50. C E Tuttle.

Johnson, Thomas M. **Collecting the Edged Weapons of the Third Reich.** Vol. 3. Bradach, Wilfred, tr. (Illus.). 1978. 20.00. T M Johnson.

Joly, Henri. **Shosankenshu: Japanese Sword Mounts.** 18.00. Saifer.

Kammer, Reinhard, ed. **Zen & Confucius in the Art of Swordsmanship.** Fitzgerald, Betty, tr. (Illus.). 1978. 9.75. Routledge & Kegan.

Ogasawara, Nobuo. **Japanese Swords.** Kenny, Don, tr. from Jap. (Illus.). 1976. pap. 3.95. Japan Pubns.

Rankin, Robert H. **Small Arms of the Sea Services: A History of the Firearms & Edged Weapons of the U.S. Navy, Marine Corps & Coast Guard from the Revolution to the Present.** (Illus.). 1972. 14.50. Flayderman.

Rawson, Philip S. **Indian Sword.** (Illus.). 1967. 8.50. Arco.

Sasano, Mesayki. **Early Japanese Sword Guards: Sukashi Tsuba. (Pierced Work).** (Illus.). 1972. 15.00. Japan Pubns.

Schnorr, Emil. **Japanese Sword Guards.** (Illus.). 1976. pap. 5.00. C E Tuttle.

Silver, George. **Paradoxes of Defence, Wherein Is Proved the True Grounds of Fight to Be in the Short Ancient Weapons.** 1968. Repr. of 1599 ed. 8.00. Walter J Johnson.

Tsuba, Sukashi. **Early Japanese Sword Guards.** 15.00. Wehman.

Wilkinson, Latham, Robert. **Swords & Other Edged Weapons.** 1978. pap. 5.95. Arco.

Yumoto, John M. **Samurai Sword: A Handbook.** (Illus.). 1958. 7.25. C E Tuttle.

Taxidermy

Brakefield, Tom. **The Sportsman's Complete Book of Trophy & Meat Care.** (Illus.). 1975. 8.95. Stackpole.

Cappel, Leo J. **A Guide to Model Making & Taxidermy.** (Illus.). 1973. pap. 5.95. Reed.

Farnham, Albert B. **Home Taxidermy for Pleasure & Profit.** (Illus.). pap. 2.50. Fur-Fish-Game.

Grantz, Gerald J. **Home Book of Taxidermy & Tanning.** (Illus.). 1970. 8.95. Stackpole.

Hardin, Cleo. **How to Preserve Animal & Other Specimens in Clear Plastic.** (Illus.).

Harrison, James M. **Bird Taxidermy.** (Illus.). 1977. 7.95. David & Charles.

Labrie, Jean. **The Amateur Taxidermist.** (Illus.). 1972. 7.50; pap. 4.95. Hart.

McFall, Waddy F. **Taxidermy Step by Step.** (Illus.). 1975. 8.95. Winchester Pr.

Maurice, Michael. **Complete Taxidermist's Guide to Books, Instructions & Supplies.** 1975. pap. 1.00. Reel Trophy.

Migdalski, Edward C. **How to Make Fish Mounts & Other Fish Trophies.** 1960. 8.00. Ronald.

Moyer, John W. **Practical Taxidermy: A Working Guide.** (Illus.). 1953. 9.50. Ronald.

Pray, Leon L. **Taxidermy.** (Illus.). 1943. 4.95. Macmillan.

Tinsley, Russell. **Taxidermy Guide.** (Illus.). 1977. softbound. 6.95. Stoeger.

Trap and Skeet Shooting

Campbell, Robert, ed. **Skeet Shooting with D. Lee Braun.** 5.95; pap. 3.95. Benjamin Co.

——**Trapshooting with D. Lee Braun & the Remington Pros.** 5.95; pap. 2.95. Benjamin Co.

Chapel, C. E. **Field, Skeet & Trapshooting.** pap. 2.95. Funk & W.

Hartman, Barney. **Hartman on Skeet.** (Illus.). 1973. 8.95. Stackpole.

Missildine, Fred with Nick Karas. **Score Better at Trap & Skeet.** (Illus.). 1977. softbound. 5.95. Stoeger.

Sports Illustrated Staff. **Sports Illustrated Book of Shotgun.** (Illus.). 4.95. Lippincott.

Trapping

Argus Archives. **Traps & Trapping: Furs & Fashion.** 1977. pap. 2.50. Argus Archives.

Bateman, James A. **Animal Traps & Trapping.** (Illus.). 1971. 8.50. Stackpole.

Chansler, Walter S. **Successful Trapping Methods: A Guide to Good Trapping.** 2nd ed. (Illus.). 1968. pap. 3.95. Van Nos Reinhold.

Clawson, George. **Trapping & Tracking.** (Illus.). 1977. 8.95. Winchester Pr.

Dearborn, Ned. **Trapping on the Farm.** Repr. of 1910 ed. pap. 2.00. Shorey.

Errington, Paul L. **Muskrats & Marsh Management.** (Illus.). 1978. pap. 3.25. U of Nebr Pr.

Finnerty, Edward W. **Trappers, Traps & Trapping.** (Illus.). 1976. 9.95. A S Barnes.

Gilsvik, Bob. **The Complete Book of Trapping.** 1976. 12.50. Chilton.

Glendinning, Richard. **When Mountain Men Trapped Beaver.** (Illus.). 1967. 3.68. Garrard.

Harbottle, Jeanne & Credeur, Fern. **Woman in the Bush.** 6.00. Pelican.

Harding, A. R. **Deadfalls & Snares.** (Illus.). pap. 2.00. A R Harding Pub.

——**Fox Trapping.** (Illus.). pap. 2.00. A R Harding Pub.

——**Mink Trapping.** (Illus.). pap. 2.00. A R Harding Pub.

——**Steel Traps.** (Illus.). pap. 2.00. A R Harding Pub.

——**Wolf & Coyote Trapping.** (Illus.). pap. 2.00. A R Harding Pub.

Karras, A. L. **North to Cree Lake.** (Illus.). 1971. 7.95. Trident.

Kreps, E. **Science of Trapping.** (Illus.). pap. 2.00. Fur-Fish-Game.

Lindsay, Neil M. **Tales of a Wilderness Trapper.** 1973. pap. 1.00. A R Harding Pub.

Lynch, V. E. **Trails to Successful Trapping.** pap. 2.00. A R Harding Pub.

McCracken, Harold & Van Cleve, Harry. **Trapping.** (Illus.). 1974. 8.95. A S Barnes.

Mascall, Leonard. **A Booke of Fishing with Hooke & Line.** 1973. Repr. of 1590 ed. 9.50. Walter J Johnson.

Mason, Otis T. **Traps of the American Indians.** facs. ed. (Illus.). 1901. pap. 1.25. Shorey.

Russell, Andy. **Trails of a Wilderness Wanderer.** 1975. 7.95. Knopf.

Russell, Carl. **Firearms, Traps & Tools of the Mountain Men.** (Illus.). 1967. 15.00. Knopf.

Russell, Osborne. **Journal of a Trapper.** Haines, Aubrey L., ed. (Illus.). 1976. 9.50. U of Nebr Pr.

Ruxton, George F. **Mountain Men.** Rounds, Glen, ed. & illus. (Illus.). 1966. 3.95. Holiday.

Sandoz, Mari. **The Beaver Men: Spearheads of Empire.** (Illus.). 1978. pap. 4.50. U of Nebr Pr.

Speck, F. G. et al. **Rappahannock Taking Devices: Traps, Hunting & Fishing.** (Illus.). 1946. 1.00. Univ Mus of U PA.

The Trapper's Companion. (Illus.). pap. 2.00. A R Harding Pub.

Woodcock, E. N. **Fifty Years a Hunter & Trapper.** pap. 2.00. Fur-Fish-Game.

White-Tailed Deer

Conaster, Dean. **Bowhunting the White-Tailed Deer.** (Illus.). 1977. 10.00 Winchester Pr.

Conway, Bryant W. **Successful Hints on Hunting White Tail Deer.** 2nd ed. 1967. pap. 1.98. Claitors.

Hayes, Tom. **How to Hunt the Whitetail Deer.** new & rev ed. pap. 4.95. A S Barnes.

Koller, Lawrence R. **Shots at Whitetails.** rev. ed. (Illus.). 1970. 12.50. Knopf.

La Bastille, Anne. **White-Tailed Deer.** Bourne, Russell & Lawrence, Bonnie S., eds. (Illus.). 1973. 2.50. Natl Wildlife.

Rue, Leonard L. **World of the White-Tailed Deer.** 1962. 8.95. Lippincott.

Stadtfeld, Curtis K. **The Whitetail Deer: A Year's Cycle.** (Illus.). 1975. 7.95. Dial.

Tinsley, Russell. **Hunting the Whitetail Deer.** (Illus.). 1974. pap. 1.95. B&N.

Winchester Rifles

Butler, David F. **Winchester Eighteen Seventy-Three & Seventy-Six: The First Repeating Centerfire Rifles.** (Illus.). 1970. 11.95. Winchester Pr.

Colby, C. B. **Firearms by Winchester: A Part of U.S. History.** (Illus.). 1957. 4.69. Coward.

Madis, George. **Winchester Book.** 3rd ed. (Illus.). 1971. 35.00. Art & Ref.

Parsons, John E. **First Winchester Story of the 1866 Repeating Rifle.** rev. ed. 1955. Repr. of 1955 ed. 14.95. Winchester Pr.

Watrous, George R. **History of Winchester Firearms 1866-1966.** 1975. 15.00. Winchester Pr.

West, Bill. **Know Your Winchester: General Use, All Models & Types, 1849-1969.** (Illus.). 12.00. B West.

——**Winchester-Complete: All Wins & Forerunners, 1849-1976.** (Illus.). 1975. 29.00. B West.

——**Winchester Encyclopedia.** (Illus.). 12.00. B West.

——**Winchester Lever-Action Handbook.** (Illus.). 25.00. B West.

——**The Winchester, Single Shot.** (Illus.). 12.00. B West.

——**Winchester, Cartridge & History.** (Illus.). 25.00. B West.

Williamson, Harry F. **Winchester: The Gun That Won the West.** (Illus.). 8.95. A S Barnes.

Magazines and Periodicals of Interest
to the Hunter and Shooter

Alaska (M)
Established 1935
Circulation: 182,000
Robert A. Henning, Editor and Publisher
Alaska Northwest Publishing Company
Box 4-EEE
Anchorage, Alaska 99509
(907) 274-0521

Alaska Geographic (Q)
Established 1972
Circulation: 8000
Robert A. Henning, Editor
The Alaska Geographic Society
Box 4-EEE
Anchorage, Alaska 99509
(907) 274-0521

The American Blade (BM)
Established 1973
Circulation: 20,000
Wallace Beinfeld, Editor and Publisher
Beinfeld Publishing, Inc.
12767 Saticoy Street
North Hollywood, California 91605
(213) 982-3700

American Field (W)
Established 1874
Circulation: 15,000
W. F. Brown, Editor
American Field Publishing Company
222 West Adams Street
Chicago, Illinois 60606
(312) 372-1383

American Firearms Industry (11 x yr.)
Established 1972
Circulation: 23,000
John Cahill, Editor and Publisher
National Association of Federally
   Licensed Firearms Dealers
7001 North Clark Street
Chicago, Illinois 60626
(312) 338-7600

American Handgunner (BM)
Established 1976
Circulation: 107,000
Jerome Rakusan, Editor
Publishers' Development Corporation
591 Camino de la Reina, Suite 200
San Diego, California 92108
(714) 297-5350

The American Hunter (M)
Established 1973
Circulation: 185,000
Earl Shelsby, Managing Editor
National Rifle Association of America
1600 Rhode Island Avenue, N.W.
Washington, D.C. 20036
(202) 783-6505

The American Rifleman (M)
Established 1871
Circulation: 1,129,000
William F. Parkerson, III, Editor
National Rifle Association of America
1600 Rhode Island Avenue, N.W.
Washington, D.C. 20036
(202) 783-6505

The American Shotgunner (M)
Established 1973
Circulation: 180,000
Bob Thruston, Editor
Celebrity Sports
P.O. Box 3351
Reno, Nevada 89505
(702) 329-2521

The American West (BM)
Established 1964
Circulation: 22,000
Ed Holm, Editor
American West Publishing Company
Suite 160
20380 Town Center Lane
Cupertino, California 95014
(408) 996-7786

Archery World (BM)
Established 1952
Circulation: 96,000
Glenn Helgeland, Editor
Market Communications, Inc.
225 E. Michigan Ave.
Milwaukee, Wisconsin 53202
(414) 276-6600

Argosy (M)
Established 1882
Circulation: 1,000,000
Lou Sahadi, Editor
Popular Publications, Inc.
150 East 58th Street
New York, N.Y. 10022
(212) 935-7160

Arms Gazette (M)
Established 1973
Circulation: 15,000
Wallace Beinfeld, Editor and Publisher
12767 Saticoy Street
North Hollywood, California 91605
(213) 982-3700

Army (M)
Established 1904
Circulation: 12,000
L. James Binder, Editor
Association of the U.S. Army
2421 Wilson Boulevard
Arlington, Virginia 22201
(703) 841-4300

Bow & Arrow (BM)
Established 1963
Circulation: 87,000
Cheri Elliott, Editor
Gallant Publishing Company, Inc.
34249 Camino Capistrano
Capistrano Beach, California 92624
(714) 493-2101

Bowhunter (BM)
Established 1971
Circulation: 105,000
M. R. James, Editor
Bowhunter
9715 Saratoga Road
Fort Wayne, Indiana 46804
(219) 744-1373

Chase Magazine (M)
Established 1920
Circulation: 3,000
Jo Brandenburg, Editor
The Chase Publishing Co., Inc.
1150 Industry Road
Lexington, Kentucky 40555
(606) 254-4262

Ducks Unlimited Magazine (BM)
Established 1937
Circulation: 325,000
Lee D. Salber
Ducks Unlimited, Inc.
P.O. Box 66300
Chicago, Illinois 60666
(312) 299-3334

Enforcement Journal (Q)
Established 1962
Circulation: 43,000
Frank J. Schira, Editor
National Police Officers Association of
   America
239 South Fifth Avenue, Suite 602
Louisville, Kentucky 40202
(502) 845-4141

Field & Stream (M)
Established 1895
Circulation: 2,000,000
Jack Samson, Editor
CBS Consumer Publishing
1515 Broadway
New York, N.Y. 10036
(212) 975-7435

Fins & Feathers (M)
Established 1972
Circulation: 110,000
Steve Grooms, Editor
Fins & Feathers
318 West Franklin Avenue
Minneapolis, Minnesota 55404
(612) 874-8404

Fishing and Hunting News (W)
Established 1944
Circulation: 140,000
Vence Malernee, Editor
Outdoor Empire Publishing, Inc.
511 Eastlake Avenue E.
Seattle, Washington 98109
(206) 624-3845

Florida Sportsman (M)
Established 1969
Circulation: 75,500
Vic Dunaway, Editor
Wickstrom Publishers, Inc.
2701 S. Bayshore Dr.
Miami, Florida 33133
(305) 858-3546

Fur-Fish-Game (Harding's Magazine) (M)
Established 1905
Circulation: 190,000
A. R. Harding, Editor
A. R. Harding Publishing Co.
2878 East Main Street
Columbus, Ohio 43209
(614) 231-9585

Gray's Sporting Journal (7 x yr.)
Established 1975
Circulation: 60,000
Edward E. Gray, Editor and Publisher
Gray's Sporting Journal Company
1330 Beacon Street
Brookline, Massachusetts 02146
(617) 731-8691

Grit and Steel (M)
Established 1899
Circulation: 6,000
Mary M. Hodge, Editor
DeCamp Publishing Company
Drawer 208
Gaffney, South Carolina 29340
(803) 489-2324

The Gun Report (M)
Established 1955
Circulation: 8000
Kenneth W. Liggett, Editor
World-Wide Gun Report, Inc.
110 South College Avenue
Aledo, Illinois 61231
(309) 582-5311

Gun Week (W)
Established 1966
Circulation: 35,000
James C. Schneider, Editor
Amos Press, Inc.
911 Vandemark Road
Sidney, Ohio 43537
(513) 492-4141

Gun World (M)
Established 1960
Circulation: 126,000
Jack Lewis, Editor
Gallant Publishing Company, Inc.
34249 Camino Capistrano
Capistrano Beach, California 92624
(714) 493-2101

Guns (M)
Established 1954
Circulation: 128,000
Jerome Rakusan, Editor
Publishers' Development Corporation
591 Camino de la Reina, Suite 200
San Diego, California 92108
(714) 297-5350

Guns and Ammo (M)
Established 1958
Circulation: 475,000
Howard French, Editor
Petersen Publishing Company
8490 Sunset Boulevard
Los Angeles, California 90069
(213) 657-5100

**Handloader: The Journal of Ammunition
Reloading (BM)**
Established 1966
Circulation: 36,000
David R. Wolfe, Editor
Wolfe Publishing Company, Inc.
138 North Montezuma Street
Prescott, Arizona 86301
(602) 445-7810

Hobbies, The Magazine for Collectors (M)
Established 1931
Circulation: 46,000
Pearl Ann Reeder, Editor
Lightner Publishing Company
1006 South Michigan Avenue
Chicago, Illinois 60605
(312) 939-4767

Hounds & Hunting (M)
Established 1903
Circulation: 14,000
R. F. Slike, Editor
Hounds & Hunting
Box 372
Bradford, Pennsylvania 16701
(814) 368-6154

Hunter Safety News (BM)
Established 1972
Circulation: 20,000
Leslie Hunter, Editor
Outdoor Empire Publishing, Inc.
511 Eastlake Avenue East
Seattle, Washington 98109
(206) 624-3845

Hunter's Horn (M)
Established 1921
Circulation: 10,000
George Slankard, Editor
The Hunter's Horn Publishing
    Company, Inc.
P.O. Box 426
Sand Springs, Oklahoma 74063
(918) 245-9571

Law and Order (M)
Established 1953
Circulation: 25,000
Frank G. MacAloon, Editor
Copp Organization, Inc.
37 West 38th Street
New York, N.Y. 10018
(212) 840-0740

Michigan Out-of-Doors (M)
Established 1947
Circulation: 110,000
Kenneth Lowe, Editor
Michigan United Conservation Clubs, Inc.
P.O. Box 30235
Lansing, Michigan 48909
(517) 371-1041

Michigan Sportsman (BM)
Established 1976
Circulation: 20,000
Thomas Petrie, Editor
Michigan Sportsman, Inc.
P.O. Box 2483
Oshkosh, Wisconsin 54903
(414) 231-9338

Minnesota Sportsman (BM)
Established 1977
Circulation: 12,000
Bob Gilsvik, Editor
Minnesota Sportsman, Inc.
P.O. Box 3003
Oshkosh, Wisconsin 54903
(414) 231-8160

Muzzle Blasts (M)
Established 1932
Circulation: 23,000
Maxine Moss, Editor
National Muzzle Loading Rifle Association
P.O. Box 67
Friendship, Indiana 47021
(812) 667-5131

The Muzzleloader (BM)
Established 1974
Circulation: 7500
B. R. Hughes, Editor
Rebel Publishing Company, Inc.
P.O. Box 6072
Texarkana, Texas 75501
(214) 832-4726

Mzuri Drumbeat (Q)
Established 1972
Circulation: 30,000
Bob Dill, Editor and Publisher
Dill & Associates
41 East Taylor
Reno, Nevada 89501
(702) 323-0779

National Defense (BM)
Established 1920
Circulation: 31,000
R. E. Lewis, Editor
American Defense Preparedness
    Association
819 Union Trust Building
740 15th Street, N.W.
Washington, D.C. 20005
(202) 347-7250

Outdoor Arizona (M)
Established 1928
Circulation: 65,000
Manya Winsted, Editor
Phoenix Publishing, Inc.
4707 N. 12th Street
Phoenix, Arizona 85014
(602) 248-8900

Outdoor Life (M)
Established 1897
Circulation: 1,700,000
Lamar Underwood, Editor
Times Mirror Magazines, Inc.
380 Madison Avenue
New York, N.Y. 10017
(212) 687-3000

Outdoor Press (W)
Established 1966
Circulation: 6,000
Fred L. Peterson, Editor and Publisher
The Outdoor Press, Inc.
N. 2012 Ruby Street
Spokane, Washington 99207
(509) 328-9392

Outdoors Today (50 x yr.)
Established 1970
Circulation: n.s.
Gary Dotson, Editor
Outdoors Today, Inc.
P.O. Box 6852
St. Louis, Missouri 63144
(314) 727-2722

Pennsylvania's Outdoor People (M)
Established 1959
Circulation: 70,000
Tom Price, Editor
Dardanell Publications, Inc.
610 Beatty Road
Monroeville, Pennsylvania 15146
(412) 373-7900

Petersen's Hunting (M)
Established 1973
Circulation: 200,000
Ken Elliott, Editor
Petersen Publishing Company
8490 Sunset Boulevard
Los Angeles, California 90069
(213) 657-5100

Point Blank (M)
Established 1971
Circulation: 209,000
John M. Snyder, Editor
Citizens Committee for the Right
   to Keep and Bear Arms
1601 114th S.E.,
Bellevue, Washington 98004
(206) 454-4911

The Police Marksman (Q)
Established 1975
Circulation: 19,000
James Collins, Editor
Police Marksman Association
217 South Court Street
Montgomery, Alabama 36140
(205) 262-5761

Police Times (M)
Established 1964
Circulation: 97,000
Donald Anderson, Editor
American Law Enforcement Officers'
   Association
1100 N.E. 125th Street
North Miami, Florida 33161
(305) 891-1700

Popular Guns (BM)
Established 1969
Circulation: 150,000
Herbert Bradford, Editor
Country Wide Publications, Inc.
257 Park Avenue South
New York, New York 10010
(212) 777-4200

Popular Mechanics (M)
Established 1902
Circulation: 1,670,000
John A. Linkletter, Editor
The Hearst Corporation
224 West 57th Street
New York, N.Y. 10019
(212) 262-4282

Popular Science (M)
Established 1872
Circulation: 1,833,000
Hubert P. Luckett, Editor
Times Mirror Magazines, Inc.
380 Madison Avenue
New York, N.Y. 10017
(212) 687-3000

Precision Shooting (M)
Established 1956
Circulation: 2500
Ritchie Moorhead, Editor
Precision Shooting, Inc.
P.O. Box 6
Athens, Pennsylvania 18810
(717) 888-7801

Rifle: The Magazine for Shooters (BM)
Established 1969
Circulation: 27,000
David R. Wolfe, Editor
Wolfe Publishing Company, Inc.
138 North Montezuma Street
Prescott, Arizona 86301
(602) 445-7810

Saga (M)
Established 1950
Circulation: 209,000
David J. Elrich, Editor
Gambi Publishing Corporation
333 Johnson Avenue
Brooklyn, N.Y. 11206
(212) 456-8600

The Shooting Industry (M)
Established 1956
Circulation: 24,000
Jerome Rakusan, Editor
Publishers' Development Corporation
591 Camino de la Reina, Suite 200
San Diego, California 92108
(714) 297-5350

Shooting Times (M)
Established 1960
Circulation: 179,000
Alex Bartimo, Editor
P J S Publications, Inc.
P.O. Box 1790
Peoria, Illinois 61656
(309) 682-6626

Shotgun News (SM)
Established 1946
Circulation: 120,000
Jim Weaver, Editor
Snell Publishing Company
P.O. Box 669
Hastings, Nebraska 68901
(402) 463-4589

Skeet Shooting Review (M)
Established 1946
Circulation: 18,000
Patricia A. Oliver, Editor
National Skeet Shooting Association
P.O. Box 28188
San Antonio, Texas 78228
(512) 688-3560

Soldier of Fortune (BM)
Established 1975
Circulation: 80,000
Robert K. Brown, Editor and Publisher
Omega Group, Ltd.
P.O. Box 693
Boulder, Colorado 80302
(303) 449-3750

Southern Outdoors (8 x yr.)
Established 1953
Circulation: 200,000
Dave Ellison, Editor
Bass Anglers Sportsman Society
P.O. Box 17915
Montgomery, Alabama 36117
(205) 272-9530

Sporting Goods Business (M)
Established 1968
Circulation: 23,000
Robert Carr, Editor
Gralla Publications
1515 Broadway
New York, N.Y. 10036
(212) 869-1300

Sporting Goods Dealer (M)
Established 1899
Circulation: 16,000
C. C. Johnson Spink, Editor
Sporting Goods Publishing Co.
1212 North Lindbergh Boulevard
St. Louis, Missouri 63166
(314) 997-7111

Sports Afield (M)
Established 1887
Circulation: 500,000
Tom Paugh, Editor
The Hearst Corporation
250 W. 55th Street
New York, N.Y. 10019
(212) 262-8852

Sports and Recreation (BM)
Established 1946
Circulation: 35,000
Robert Bushnell, Editor
Nystrom Publishing Co.
9100 Cottonwood Lane
Maple Grove, Minnesota 55369
(612) 425-7900

Sports Merchandizer (M)
Established 1968
Circulation: 24,000
Eugene R. Marnell, Editor
1760 Peachtree Road, Northwest
Atlanta, Georgia 30357
(404) 874-4462

Sports Illustrated (W)
Established 1954
Circulation: 2,250,000
Roy Terrell, Editor
Time, Inc.
Time-Life Bldg.
New York, N.Y. 10020
(212) 586-1212

Texas Sportsman Magazine (BM)
Established 1971
Circulation: 25,000
R. Allan Charles, Editor and Publisher
Neptune Publications
P.O. Box 10411
San Antonio, Texas 78210
(512) 533-8991

Trap and Field (M)
Established 1890
Circulation: 24,000
John M. Bahret, Editor
Curtis Publishing Company
1100 Waterway Boulevard
Indianapolis, Indiana 46206
(317) 634-1100

Turkey Call (BM)
Established 1973
Circulation: 31,000
Gene Smith, Editor
The National Wild Turkey Federation
P.O. Box 467
Edgefield, South Carolina 29824
(803) 637-3106

West Virginia Hills and Streams (M)
Established 1970
Circulation: 1400
Julia P. Young, Editor
West Virginia Hills and Streams, Inc.
Box 38
Durbin, West Virginia 26264
(304) 456-4789

Western Outdoor News (W)
Established 1953
Circulation: 80,000
Bill Rice, Editor
Western Outdoors Publications
3197 East Airport Loop Drive
Costa Mesa, California 92626
(714) 546-4370

Western Outdoors (M)
Established 1960
Circulation: 128,000
Burt Twiligar, Editor
Western Outdoors Publications
3197 East Airport Loop Drive
Costa Mesa, California 92626
(714) 546-4370

Wildlife Harvest (M)
Established 1973
Circulation: 1,000
John M. Mullin, Editor
North American Game Breeders &
  Shooting Preserves Association, Inc.
Goose Lake, Iowa 52750
(319) 577-2267

Wildlife Review (Q)
Established 1935
Circulation: 5,000
Kenneth J. Chiavetta, Editor
Aylesworth Hall, Room 263
Colorado State University
Fort Collins, Colorado 80523
(303) 491-7002

Wisconsin Sportsman (BM)
Established 1972
Circulation: 48,000
Thomas C. Petrie, Editor and Publisher
Wisconsin Sportsman, Inc.
P.O. Box 2266
Oshkosh, Wisconsin 54903
(414) 233-1327

Canadian Periodicals
B.C. Outdoors (M)
Established 1945
Circulation: 30,000
Donald Stainsby, Editor
S.I.P. Division of MacLean-Hunter, Ltd.
#202-1132 Hamilton Street
Vancouver, British Columbia V6B 2S2
(604) 687-1581

Canada Gunsport (M)
Established 1975
Circulation: 20,000
Canada Gun Sports
G. N. Dentay, Editor
P.O. Box 201
Willowdale, Ontario M2N 5S8
(416) 881-8446

**The Canadian Journal of
  Arms Collecting (Q)**
Established: 1962
Circulation: 1300
S. J. Gooding, Editor
Museum Restoration Service
P.O. Box 390
Bloomfield, Ontario K0K 1G0
(613) 393-2980

Fish and Game Sportsman (Q)
Established 1969
Circulation: 18,000
J. B. Wilkinson, Editor
Nimrod Publications, Ltd.
P.O. Box 737
Regina, Saskatchewan S4P 3A8
(306) 523-8384

Northwest Sportsman (6 x yr.)
Established 1946
Circulation: 10,000
Jim Railton, Editor
Railton Publications, Ltd.
125 Talisman Avenue
Vancouver, British Columbia V5Y 2L6
(604) 876-3535

Ontario Fisherman & Hunter (M)
Established 1967
Circulation: 32,000
Burton J. Myers, Editor
Ontario Fisherman and Hunter
5 Guardsman Road
Thornhill, Ontario L3T 2A1
(416) 881-1033

Québec Chasse et Pêche (M) (French)
Established 1971
Circulation: 64,000
André Y. Croteau, Editor
Les Publications Plein Air, Inc.
3580 Masson Street
Montreal, Quebec H1X 1S2
(514) 376-5910

Sporting Goods Canada (8 x yr.)
Established 1973
Circulation: 9300
Dan Wilton, Editor and Publisher
Maclean-Hunter, Ltd.
481 University Avenue
Toronto, Ontario M5W 1V5
(416) 595-1811

Sporting Goods Trade (7 x yr.)
Established 1973
Circulation: 9,000
Gordon Bagley, Editor
Page Publications
380 Wellington Street West
Toronto, Ontario M5V 1E3
(416) 366-4608

Western Angling (BM)
Established 1965
Circulation: 14,000
J. L. Grundle, Editor and Publisher
Western Fish & Game Magazine, Ltd.
205-1591 Bowser Street
Vancouver, British Columbia V7P 2Y2
(604) 980-5821

Wildlife Crusader (M)
Established 1944
Circulation: 36,000
Paul F. Murphy, Editor
Stovel Advocate Press
365 Bannatyne Avenue
Winnipeg, Manitoba R3A 0E5
(204) 774-2926

Explanation of Symbols: (M) Monthly; (BM) Bi-monthly; (SM) Semi-monthly; (W) Weekly; (Q) Quarterly

THE SHOOTER'S BIBLE

Firearms, Ammunition and Accessory Manufacturers

Air Rifle Headquarters
247 Court Street
Grantsville, West Virginia 26147

Anschutz Rifles
(see Savage Arms)

Anschutz Air Guns
(see Air Rifle Headquarters, Beeman's
Precision Air Guns or Savage Arms)

Astra
(see Interarms)

BSA
(see Air Rifle Headquarters, Beeman's
Precision Air Guns or Ithaca Gun
Company)

Bauer Firearms Corporation
34750 Klein Avenue
Fraser, Michigan 48026

Bausch & Lomb, Inc.
(see Bushnell Optical Company)

Bear Reloaders, Inc.
57 Glendale Avenue
Akron, Ohio 44305

Beeman's Precision Air Guns
47 Paul Drive
San Rafael, California 94903

Benjamin Air Rifle Company
1525 South 8th Street
St. Louis, Missouri 63104

The Beretta Arms Company, Inc.
P.O. Box 2000
Ridgefield, Connecticut 06877

Bernardelli Pistols
(see Interarms)

Bernardelli Shotguns
(see Sloan's Sporting Goods Co., Inc.)

Bersa
(see Interarms)

Bonanza Sports Manufacturing Co.
412 Western Avenue
Faribault, Minnesota 55021

Browning
Route 1
Morgan, Utah 84050

Maynard P. Buehler, Inc.
17 Orinda Highway
Orinda, California 94563

Bushnell Optical Company
2828 East Foothill Boulevard
Pasadena, California 91107

CCI
(see Omark Industries)

CVA
(see Connecticut Valley Arms, Inc.)

C-H Tool & Die Corporation
P.O. Box L
Owen, Wisconsin 54460

Charter Arms Corporation
430 Sniffens Lane
Stratford, Connecticut 06497

Colt Industries, Firearms Division
150 Huyshope Avenue
Hartford, Connecticut 06102

Connecticut Valley Arms, Inc.
Saybrook Road
Haddam, Connecticut 06438

Crosman Air Guns
980 Turk Hill Road
Fairport, New York 14450

Daisy
P.O. Box 220
Rogers, Arkansas 72756

Dakota
(see EMF Company, Inc.)

Darne
(see Firearms Center, Inc.)

Dixie Gun Works, Inc.
Gunpowder Lane
Union City, Tennessee 38261

E. I. DuPont de Nemours & Co., Inc.
Explosives Department
1007 Market Street
Wilmington, Delaware 19898

EMF Company, Inc.
2911 West Olive Avenue
Burbank, California 91505

Eastern Sports International
Savage Road
Milford, New Hampshire 03055

Euroarms of America
14 West Monmouth Street
Winchester, Virginia 22601

Federal Cartridge Corporation
2700 Foshay Tower
Minneapolis, Minnesota 55402

Feinwerkbau
(see Air Rifle Headquarters, Beeman's
Precision Air Guns or Daisy)

Fias
(see Kassnar Imports)

Fiocchi
Guilio Fiocchi, S.p.A.
Via Santa Barbara, 4
22053 Lecco
Italy

Firearms Center, Inc.
113 Spokane
Victoria, Texas 77901

(FIE) Firearms Import & Export Corp.
2470 N. W. 21st Street
Miami, Florida 33142

Fox
(see Savage Arms)

Franchi
(see Stoeger Industries)

Freedom Arms
1 Freedom Lane
Freedom, Wyoming 83120

J. L. Galef & Son, Inc.
85 Chambers Street
New York, New York 10007

Golden Eagle Firearms, Inc.
5750 Ranchester
Houston, Texas 77042

Griffin & Howe, Inc.
589 Broadway
New York, New York 10012

Harrington & Richardson, Inc.
Industrial Rowe
Gardner, Massachusetts 01440

Hawes Firearms
15424 Cabrito Road
Van Nuys, California 91406

Healthways
233 East Manville Street
Compton, California 90220

Heckler & Koch
Suite 218
933 North Kenmore Street
Arlington, Virginia 22201

Hercules, Inc.
910 Market Street
Wilmington, Delaware 19899

High Standard Sporting Firearms
31 Prestige Park Circle
East Hartford, Connecticut 06108

B. E. Hodgdon, Inc.
7710 West 50 Highway
Shawnee Mission, Kansas 66202

Hopkins & Allen
1 Melnick Road
Monsey, New York 10952

Hornady Manufacturing Company
P.O. Box 1848
Grand Island, Nebraska 68801

Hy-Score Arms Corporation
200 Tillary Street
Brooklyn, New York 11201

Interarms
10 Prince Street
Alexandria, Virginia 22313

International Distributors, Inc.
7290 S.W. 42nd Street
Miami, Florida 33155

Ithaca Gun Company, Inc.
123 Lake Street
Ithaca, New York 14850

Paul Jaeger, Inc.
209-11 Leedom Street
Jenkintown, Pennsylvania 19046

Jana International Company
P.O. Box 1107
Denver, Colorado 80201

Iver Johnson's Arms, Inc.
P.O. Box 251
Middlesex, New Jersey 08846

Kassnar Imports
P.O. Box 6097
Harrisburg, Pennsylvania 17112

Krieghoff Gun Company
5900 N.W. 36th Street
Miami, Florida 33152

Leupold & Stevens, Inc.
P.O. Box 688
Beaverton, Oregon 97005

Llama
(see Stoeger Industries)

London Guns
1528 20th Street
Santa Monica, California 90404

Luger
(see Stoeger Industries)

Lyman Products Corporation
Route 147
Middlefield, Connecticut 06455

MEC, Inc.
Mayville Engineering Company, Inc.
715 South Street
Mayville, Wisconsin 53050

MTM Molded Products Company
5680 Webster Street
Dayton, Ohio 45414

Mannlicher
80 Field Point Road
Greenwich, Connecticut 06830

Marksman Products, Inc.
2133 Dominguez Street
Torrance, California 90509

Marlin Firearms Company
100 Kenna Drive
North Haven, Connecticut 06473

Mauser Pistols
(see Interarms)

Merit Gunsight Company
318 Sunnyside North
Sequim, Washington 98382

The Merrill Company
704 East Commonwealth
Fullerton, California 92631

Micro Sight Company
242 Harbor Boulevard
Belmont, California 94002

O. F. Mossberg & Sons, Inc.
7 Grasso Avenue
North Haven, Connecticut 06473

Navy Arms Company
689 Bergen Boulevard
Ridgefield, New Jersey 07657

Norma Precision
P.O. Box E
Lansing, New York 14882

Nosler Bullets, Inc.
(see Leupold & Stevens, Inc.)

Numrich Arms Corporation
Williams Lane
West Hurley, New York 12491

Omark Industries
605 Oro Dam Boulevard
Oroville, California 95965

Pachmayr Gun Works, Inc.
1220 South Grand Avenue
Los Angeles, California 90015

Pacific Tool Company
P.O. Box 2048
Grand Island, Nebraska 68801

Parker-Hale
(see Jana International Company)

Peters
(see Remington)

Ponsness-Warren, Inc.
P.O. Box 8
Rathdrum, Idaho 83858

RCBS, Inc.
(see Omark Industries)

Redding-Hunter, Inc.
114 Starr Road
Cortland, New York 13045

Redfield
5800 East Jewell Avenue
Denver, Colorado 80224

Remington Arms Company, Inc.
939 Barnum Avenue
Bridgeport, Connecticut 06602

Rossi
(see Interarms)

Rottweil
(see Eastern Sports International)

Ruger
(see Sturm, Ruger & Company, Inc.)

SKB Sports, Inc.
190 Shepard Avenue
Wheeling, Illinois 60090

Sako
(see Stoeger Industries)

Savage Arms
Springdale Road
Westfield, Massachusetts 01085

Sheridan Products, Inc.
3205 Sheridan Road
Racine, Wisconsin 53403

Shiloh Products, Inc.
37 Potter Street
Farmingdale, New York 11735

Sierra Bullets
10532 South Painter Avenue
Santa Fe Springs, California 90670

Sloan's Sporting Goods Company, Inc.
10 South Street
Ridgefield, Connecticut 06877

Smith & Wesson Ammunition Company
2399 Forman Road
Rock Creek, Ohio 44084

Smith & Wesson Company
2100 Roosevelt Avenue
Springfield, Massachusetts 01101

Snap Caps
(see Stoeger Industries)

Speer, Inc.
(see Omark Industries)

Springfield Armory
111 East Exchange
Genesco, Illinois 61254

Star
(see Interarms)

Sterling Arms Corporation
211 Grand Street
Lockport, New York 14094

Stevens
(see Savage Arms)

Stoeger Industries
55 Ruta Court
South Hackensack, New Jersey 07606

Sturm, Ruger & Company, Inc.
Lacey Place
Southport, Connecticut 06490

Taurus
(see International Distributors, Inc.)

Texan Reloaders, Inc.
444 Cips Street
Watseka, Illinois 60970

Thompson/Center Arms
Farmington Road
Rochester, New Hampshire 03867

Ventura Imports
P.O. Box 2782
Seal Beach, California 90740

Virginian
(see Interarms)

Walther Air Guns
(see Air Rifle Headquarters, Beeman's
Precision Air Guns or Interarms)

Walther Pistols
(see Interarms)

Weatherby, Inc.
2781 Firestone Boulevard
South Gate, California 90280

W. R. Weaver Company
7125 Industrial Avenue
El Paso, Texas 79915

Webley
(see Air Rifle Headquarters or Beeman's
Precision Air Guns)

Webley & Scott
(see Navy Arms Company)

Weihrauch
(see Air Rifle Headquarters or Beeman's
Precision Air Guns)

Dan Wesson Arms, Inc.
293 Main Street
Monson, Massachusetts 01057

Western
(see Winchester-Western)

Williams Gun Sight Company
7389 Lapeer Road
Davison, Michigan 48423

Winchester-Western
275 Winchester Avenue
New Haven, Connecticut 06504

Winslow Arms Company
P.O. Box 783
Camden, South Carolina 29020

Wischo
(see Air Rifle Headquarters or Beeman's
Precision Air Guns)

Handguns

ASTRA PISTOLS & REVOLVERS

ASTRA 357, 357 MAG. & 38 SPECIAL

3" barrel

6" barrel

4" barrel

Potent, powerful and smooth as silk: the Astra 357. Chambered for the hot 357 Magnum cartridge, this large-frame revolver also handles the popular 38 Special, making it equally suitable for the serious target shooter and for the sportsman.

All forged steel and highly polished to a rich blue, the Astra 357 has a heavyweight barrel with integral rib and ejector shroud. The rear sight is click-adjustable for windage and elevation. The hammer is of the wide-spur target type, and the trigger is grooved. The grips are of checkered hardwood. The cylinder is recessed, and the gun utilizes a spring-loaded, floating firing pin for additional safety.

The internal lockwork of the Astra 357 is as finely fitted and finished as the exterior, giving it a smoothness second to none. There's even a four-stage adjustment to control spring tension on the hammer.

The Astra 357 is available with 3", 4", 6" and 8½" barrel. The 4" and longer-barreled models have square butts and are supplied with comfortable, hand-filling oversized grips. The 3" version has the more compact round butt with magna-style grips. Length overall with 6" barrel is 11¼".

Barrel Length	Finish	Caliber	Weight	
3"	Blue	357 Mag.	37 oz.	**$235.00**
4"	Blue	357 Mag.	38 oz.	235.00
4"	Chrome	357 Mag.	38 oz.	**Price Not Set**
6"	Blue	357 Mag.	39 oz.	235.00
8½"	Blue	357 Mag.	41 oz.	245.00

ASTRA CONSTABLE 22 L.R. 380 ACP

The Astra Constable is a double-action, all steel small-frame auto, so you can safely carry it fully loaded with a round in the chamber and the safety off. A single pull of the trigger then cocks and fires the pistol without the necessity of cocking the hammer manually, as is necessary with most autos. The thumb safety completely blocks the hammer and actually locks the firing pin in place until released. The barrel is rigidly mounted in the frame for greater accuracy and the gun features quick, no-tool takedown, integral non-glare rib on the slide, push-button magazine release and a round, non-snagging hammer spur.

22 L.R. & 380 ACP Blue	**$205.00**
22 L.R. & 380 ACP Chrome	220.00
22 L.R. & 380 ACP Blue Engraved	310.00
22 L.R. & 380 ACP Silver Engraved	330.00

BERETTA PISTOLS

MODEL 70S PISTOL

This pistol is available in 22 Auto and 380 Auto and has a frame of steel alloy. Longer barrel guide; safety lever blocking the hammer; push button magazine release; sloping grip; sight and rear sight blade fixed on the breech block.

SPECIFICATIONS:
Total Length: 6.5". **Barrel Length:** 3.5". **Height:** 4.8". **Weight (mag. empty):** 1 lb. 7 ozs. **Magazine Capacity, 380 Auto:** 7 rounds. **Magazine Capacity, 22 Auto:** 8 rounds.

Model 70S **$213.00**

MODEL 81/84 PISTOLS

These pistols are pocket size with a large magazine capacity. The lockwork is of double-action type. The first shot (with hammer down, chamber loaded) can be fired by a double-action pull on the trigger without cocking the hammer manually.

The pistols also feature a favorable grip angle for natural pointing, positive thumb safety (uniquely designed for both right- and left-handed operation), quick take-down (by means of special take-down button) and a conveniently located magazine release. The magazine capacity is 13 rounds in 380 caliber (Model 84) and 12 rounds in the 32 auto caliber (Model 81). Black plastic grips. Wood grips available at extra cost.

SPECIFICATIONS — Model M-81
Caliber: 32 Auto (7.65mm). **Weight:** 1 lb. 8 oz. **Barrel Length:** 3¾" (Approx.). **Overall Length:** 6½" (Approx.). **Sights:** Fixed - Front and Rear. **Magazine Capacity:** 12 Rounds. **Height, overall:** 4¼" (Approx.).

SPECIFICATIONS — Model M-84
Caliber: 380 Auto (9mm Short). **Weight:** 1 lb. 7 oz. (Approx.). **Barrel Length:** 3¾" (Approx.). **Overall Length:** 6½" (Approx.). **Sights:** Fixed - Front and Rear. **Magazine Capacity:** 13 Rounds. **Height, overall:** 4¼" (Approx.).

Model 81 (with plastic grips)	**$307.00**
Model 81 (with wood grips)	**329.00**
Model 84 (with plastic grips)	**307.00**
Model 84 (with wood grips)	**329.00**

MODEL 76 PISTOL

Designed for target shooting the M-76 features built-in, fixed counterweight for correct balance and control of recoil; raised, matted rib on which both front and rear sights are solidly mounted; rear sight fully adjustable for windage and elevation; front sight supplied in three interchangeable widths. Trigger pull is factory adjusted to a weight between 3 lbs. 5 oz. and 3 lbs. 12 oz.

Grips are plastic, shaped and checkered to give a firm hold. Pistols are equipped with a positive thumb safety. All metal parts are finished in blue-black. Wood grips available at extra cost.

SPECIFICATIONS:
Caliber: 22 LR. **Magazine Capacity:** 10 Rounds. **Overall Length:** 8.8" (223mm). **Barrel Length:** 6" (150mm). **Sight Radius:** 6.9" (176mm). **Weight (mag. empty):** 2 lbs. 1 oz. (930 grams). **Height:** 5.6" (143mm). **Rifling:** 6 lands & grooves, R.H. pitch.

Model 76 (with plastic grips)	**$259.00**
Model 76 (with wood grips)	**287.00**

MODEL 92 PISTOL

A heavy-duty handgun, chambered for the high velocity 9mm Parabellum (Luger) cartridge. Double-action lockwork — pistol may be fired by a double-action pull on the trigger (with hammer down), as well as in the regular single-action mode. Magazine has extra-large capacity of 15 rounds, although of standard length (another cartridge may be carried in the chamber). Pistol is fully locked at time of firing. Extractor acts as loaded chamber indicator, visually and by feel. Both front and rear sights are mounted on the slide. All metal parts are finished in blue-black. Grips are black plastic, checkered and grooved. Wood grips available at extra cost.

SPECIFICATIONS:
Caliber: 9mm Parabellum (Luger). **Magazine Capacity:** 15 Rounds. **Overall Length:** 8.54" (217mm). **Barrel Length:** 4.92" (125mm). **Sight Radius:** 6.1" (155mm). **Weight (mag. empty):** 2 lbs. 1½ oz. (950 grams). **Height:** 5.39" (137mm). **Width:** 1.45" (37mm). **Rifling:** 6 lands & grooves, R.H. pitch.

Model 92 (with plastic grips)	**$410.00**
Model 92 (with wood grips)	**436.00**

BERNARDELLI PISTOLS

MODEL 80

Caliber: .22 L.R.-10 Shot; 380 ACP-7 Shot. **Barrel:** 3.54". **O.A. Length:** 6.45". **Weight:** 26.8 oz. **Stock:** Checkered plastic w/thumb rest (Wrap Around). **Sights:** Adjustable. **Features:** Hammer-blocking slide safety which locks firing pin to permit loading or clearing of chamber w/safety engaged. Loaded round indicator, adjustable rear sight. White outline rear sight and white dot front sight. Dual recoil buffer springs. Serrated trigger. Inertia type firing pin. Magazine follower interlock holds slide open after last round is fired.

Model 80 .... **$163.00**

MODEL 100

Caliber: .22 L.R. only—10 shot. **Barrel:** 5.9". **O.A. Length:** 9.00". **Weight:** 37.75 oz. **Features:** Target barrel weight included. Heavy sighting rib with interchangeable front sight. Rear sight adjustable for elevation and windage. Serrated trigger, inertia type firing pin. Comfortable checkered walnut grips with thumb rest. Accessories include cleaning equipment and assembly tools. Case included.

Model 100 .... **$285.00**

BERSA PISTOLS

MODEL M85

Caliber: 380 ACP.
Barrel Length: 3¾".
Overall Length: 6⅝".
Height: 4½".
Magazine Capacity: 13 rounds.
Empty Weight: 27 oz.

Model M85 .... **$225.00**
    extra 380 ACP magazine 15.00

MODEL 644

Caliber: 22 L.R.
Barrel Length: 3½".
Overall Length: 6½".
Height: 4¼".
Magazine Capacity: 7 rounds.
Empty Weight: 26½ oz.

Model 644 with extra magazine .. **$135.00**
    extra 22 L.R. magazine 12.00

BROWNING AUTOMATIC PISTOLS

22 CHALLENGER II

The 22 Challenger II has a unique wedge locking system (patent pending) that prevents the slightest instability or loosening. The screw adjustable rear sight is recoil-proof. It does not move with the operating slide, so the Challenger remains sighted in, shot after shot. The 6¾" barrel is cleanly rifled, and the muzzle is recessed. This barrel length also offers a long sighting plane, which contributes to accuracy.

The Challenger II's frame is all steel, deeply blued. All the parts are machined and hand fitted for long wear. The wide, gold-plated trigger has a positive, crisp action.

The grips are made of tough impregnated hardwood that resist scarring and scraping. After you fire the last cartridge, the slide stays open, a convenience in determining the pistol's safety status and in facilitating safe reloading.

The Challenger II's spring-loaded magazine stores 10 Long Rifle 22 cartridges. A magazine follower button allows you to depress the magazine spring to make the loading fast and easy.

Challenger II **$169.95**
Extra magazine **11.50**

SPECIFICATIONS:
Magazine Capacity: 10. **Overall length:** 10⅞". **Barrel length:** 6¾". **Height:** 5¼". **Weight:** 38 oz. **Sight radius:** 9⅛". **Ammunition:** 22 L.R. **Grips:** Impregnated hardwood. **Front sights:** ⅛" wide. **Rear sights:** Screw adjustable for vertical correction. Drift adjustable for windage. **Grades available:** Standard.

9mm HI-POWER

The Browning 9mm Parabellum, also known as the 9mm Browning Hi-Power has a 14-cartridge capacity and weighs two pounds. The push-button magazine release permits swift, convenient withdrawal of the magazine.

The 9mm is available with either a fixed blade front sight and a windage adjustable rear sight or a non-glare rear sight, screw adjustable for both windage and elevation. The front sight is a ⅛-inch wide blade mounted on a ramp. The rear surface of the blade is serrated to prevent glare.

In addition to the manual safety, the firing mechanism includes an external hammer so it is easy to ascertain whether the pistol is cocked.

Standard **$359.95**
Standard with adjustable sights **389.95**
Extra magazine **29.50**

BDA-45 and BDA-380. A high-powered, double-action pistol with fixed sights in 45 or 380 caliber.

BDA-45 .... **$349.95** BDA-380 .... **$262.50**
Extra magazine .... **11.00** Extra magazine **16.50**

RENAISSANCE ENGRAVED MODEL is finished with silver-grey, leaf-scroll metal frame, pure-white Nacrolac pearl grips and a gold-plated trigger. It is available with either fixed or adjustable sights.

Renaissance **$1400.00**
Renaissance with adjustable sights **1450.00**
Extra magazine **54.50**

AUTOMATIC PISTOL SPECIFICATIONS

		9 mm Hi-Power		BDA-380	BDA-45
	22 Challenger II	Fixed Sights	Adjustable Sights	(Double Action)	(Double Action)
Capacity of Magazine	10	13	13	12	7
Overall Length	10⅞"	7¾"	7¾"	6¾"	8 1/16"
Barrel Length	6¾"	4 21/32"	4 21/32"	3 13/16"	4¼"
Height	5¼"	5"	5"	4¾"	5½"
Weight (Empty)	39 oz.	32 oz.	32-1/5 oz.	23 oz.	29 oz.
Sight Radius	9⅛"	6 5/16"	6⅜"	4 15/16"	6¼"
Ammunition	22LR	9 mm Luger	9 mm Luger	380 Auto	45 Auto
Grips	Impregnated hardwood	Checkered walnut [1]	Checkered walnut [1]	Walnut	Black checkered plastic
Front Sights	⅛" wide	Fixed blade	⅛" wide blade on ramp	Fixed blade with white dot	Fixed blade with white dot
Rear Sights	Screw adjustable for vertical correction. Drift adjustable for windage.	Drift adjustable for windage.	Screw adjustable horizontal and vertical.	White outlined square notch. Drift adjustable for windage.	White outlined square notch. Drift adjustable for windage.
Grades Available	Standard	Standard [2] and Renaissance [3]	Standard [2] and Renaissance [3]	Standard	Standard

[1] Renaissance models come with Nacrolac pearl grips. [2] The Standard 9 mm caliber pistol comes in lined, padded vinyl, flexible, zipper case. [3] The Renaissance 9 mm caliber is encased in a deluxe black vinyl pistol case.

BAUER PISTOLS

25 CALIBER AUTOMATIC
$104.85

SPECIFICATIONS:
Caliber: 25 automatic
Capacity: 6 shot
Barrel length(s): 2¼"
Weight: 10 oz.
Overall length: 4"
Safety: Positive manual
Grips: Pearl or genuine walnut
Finish: Neutral Satin Stainless

CHARTER ARMS REVOLVERS

POLICE BULLDOG
38 SPECIAL 6-SHOT REVOLVER

SPECIFICATIONS:
Caliber: 38 Special. **Type of Action:** 6-shot single and double action. **Barrel length:** 4 inches. **Overall length:** 9 inches. **Height:** 5⅛ inches. **Weight:** 20½ ounces. **Grips:** Square butt, American walnut hand-checkered. **Sights:** Full-length ramp front; fully adjustable combat rear. **Finish:** High-luster Police Blue **$149.00**

TARGET BULLDOG 357 MAG.
44 SPECIAL

SPECIFICATIONS:
Caliber: 357 Mag., 44 spl. **Type of action:** 5 shot, single and double action. **Barrel length:** 4 inches. **Overall length:** 9 inches. **Height:** 5⅛ inches. **Weight:** 20½ ounces. **Grips:** American walnut square butt. **Sights:** Full length ramp front sight; fully adjustable, milled channel, square notch rear sight. **Finish:** High-luster Police Blue. Blue finish with Square butt grips **$165.00**

PATHFINDER
22 MAGNUM

SPECIFICATIONS:
Caliber: 22 Magnum. **Type of action:** 6 shot, single and double action. **Barrel length:** 3 or 6 inches. **Overall length:** 7¾" (3" bbl.), 10⅝" (6" bbl.). **Height:** 4¾" (3" bbl.), 5" (6" bbl.). **Weight:** 20 oz. (3" bbl.), 22½ oz. (6" bbl.). **Grips:** Hand-checkered Bulldog grips or square butt grips. Hand-checkered Bulldog grips or square butt grips. **Sights:** Patridge-type ramp front sight, fully adjustable notch rear sight. **Finish:** High-luster Police Blue. Blue finish with Bulldog grips or square butt grips.

With 3" barrel **$158.00**
With 6" barrel **158.00**

CHARTER ARMS REVOLVERS

UNDERCOVER   32 S & W Long
Blue finish with Regular grips $130.00

SPECIFICATIONS:
Caliber: 32 S & W Long. **Type of Action:** 6 Shot, single and double action. **Barrel Length:** 2". **Overall Length:** 6¼". **Height:** 4⅛". **Weight:** 16 ounces. **Grips:** Smooth American walnut, uncheckered. **Sights:** Wide Patridge type front; notch rear 9/64". **Rifling:** One turn in 17", right hand twist. **Finish:** High luster Police Blue.

UNDERCOVER   38 Special

2" barrel Blue finish with Regular grips
.... $130.00

2" barrel Nickel finish with Regular grips
.... 142.00

3" barrel Blue finish with Square Butt grips 139.00

SPECIFICATIONS:
Caliber: 38 Special (Mid-Range & Standard). **Type of Action:** 5 shots, single and double action. **Barrel Length:** 2" or 3". **Overall Length:** 6¼" (2" bbl.), 8" (3" bbl.). **Height:** 4¼" (2" bbl.), 4¾" (3" bbl.). **Weight:** 16 oz. (2" bbl.), 17½ oz. (3" bbl.). **Grips:** Smooth American walnut. **Sights:** Patridge type ramp front, square-notched rear. **Finish:** High-luster Police Blue or Nickel.

PATHFINDER   .22 L.R.

Blue finish with Regular grips
3" barrel $144.00
Blue finish with Square Butt grips
6" barrel 153.00

SPECIFICATIONS:
Caliber: 22 Long Rifle. **Type of Action:** 6 shot, single and double action. **Barrel Length:** 3 or 6 inches. **Overall Length:** 7⅛" (3" bbl.), 10⅝" (6" bbl.). **Height:** 4¼" (3" bbl.), 5" (6" bbl.). **Weight:** 19 oz. (3" bbl.), 22½ oz. (6" bbl.). **Grips:** Smooth American walnut, uncheckered. Optional: Bulldog grips American walnut hand-checkered. **Sights:** Fully adjustable rear; Patridge-type ramp front. **Rifling:** One turn in 16 inches, right hand twist. **Finish:** High luster Police Blue.

**BULLDOG 357 MAG.
44 SPECIAL**

Blue finish with Bulldog grips 3" 44 SPL   **$150.00**
Blue finish with square-butt grips 6" 357 MAG   **150.00**

SPECIFICATIONS:
Caliber: 44 SPL, 357 MAG. **Type of Action:** 5 shot, single and double action. **Barrel length:** 3 or 6 inches. **Overall Length:** 7¾" (3" bbl.), 11" (6" bbl.). **Height:** 4¾" (3" bbl.), 5⅛" (6" bbl.). **Weight:** 19 oz. (3" bbl.), 25 oz. (6" bbl.). **Grips:** American walnut hand-checkered bulldog grips, or square butt grips. **Sights:** Patridge-type, 9/64-inch wide front; square-notched rear. **Finish:** High luster Police Blue.

Government Model MK IV/Series '70

Full-size automatic with 5″ barrel. Available in 45 ACP, 9 mm Parabellum, 38 Super, and 22 LR.

Features:
Fixed military sights, grip and thumb safeties, grooved trigger, sand-blasted walnut stocks and Accurizor barrel and bushing. Colt Blue or Polished Nickel finishes.

Weight: 38 oz. in 45 ACP
Overall Length: 8½″
Magazine Capacity: 45 ACP-7 rounds, 38 Super and 9 mm -9 rounds

Government Model
45 A.C.P. & 9mm, blue finish	$276.95
45 A.C.P., polished nickel	292.95
38 Super, blue finish	282.95
22 LR, blue finish	292.95

**MK IV/Series '70
GOVERNMENT
MODEL**
45 Automatic, 38 Super Automatic
9 mm Luger and 22 LR
(With Accurizor barrel and bushing)

Lightweight Commander

This lightweight, shorter version of the Government Model offers increased ease of carrying with the firepower of 45 ACP.

Features:
Alloy frame, fixed style sights, grooved trigger, and lanyard style hammer. Colt Blue with Walnut stocks.

Weight: 27 oz.
Overall Length: 7⅞″
Magazine Capacity: 7 rounds in 45 ACP

Lightweight Commander
Blue	$268.95

**LIGHTWEIGHT
COMMANDER**
(Alloy Frame)
45 Automatic

Combat Commander

An all-steel frame gives the stocky Combat Commander extra heft and stability. Genuine walnut sand-blasted stocks embedded with the Colt medallion. Available in 45 ACP, 9mm Parabellum and 38 Super cartridges.

Features:
Fixed style sights, thumb safety and grip safety. In Colt Blue or Satin Nickel finishes.

Weight: 37 oz. in 45 ACP ; 36 oz. in 38 Super and 9mm
Overall Length: 7⅞″
Magazine Capacity: 45 ACP-7 rounds, 38 Super and 9 mm -9 rounds

Combat Commander
Blue	$276.95
Satin Nickel	287.95

**COMBAT
COMMANDER**
(All Steel)
45 Automatic
38 Super Auto
9mm Luger

COLT PISTOLS & REVOLVERS

TROOPER MK III
357 Mag., 22 Win. Mag. RF, 22 LR, Barrels: 4″, 6″

Tremendous penetrating power in the Magnum caliber makes this handgun suitable for hunters of big game or for police officers. Its quick draw type, ramp-style front sight and adjustable rear sight makes this a target-sighted general purpose revolver. Features include: wide target trigger; wide serrated hammer; full checkered walnut stocks. Trooper MKIII, 357 Magnum, 22 Win. Mag. Rimfire, 22 Long Rifle. 4″ or 6″ barrel.

4″ barrel, blue finish	**$264.95**
4″ barrel, nickel finish	**280.95**
6″ barrel, blue finish	**265.95**
6″ barrel, nickel finish	**286.50**
6″ barrel, blue finish, 22 Win. Mag. RF or 22 LR only	**265.95**

Trooper Specifications: Caliber: 357 Magnum, 22 Win. Mag. RF, 22 LR. **Barrel Length:** 4″, 6″. With target stocks: 1/8″ longer. **Weight (Oz.):** 39 oz. with 4″ bbl. 42 oz. with 6″ bbl. **Sights:** Fixed ramp-type front sight with 1/8″ blade. Rear sight adjustable for windage and elevation. **Trigger:** Wide target trigger. **Hammer:** Wide checkered spur on target hammer. **Target—**case hardened finish. **Stocks:** Target stocks, checkered walnut. **Finish:** Colt blue and polished nickel finishes. **Cylinder Capacity:** 6 shot counterbored. **Overall Length:** 9 1/2″ with 4″ barrel.

POLICE POSITIVE

Blue Finish **$225.00**

The same basic design as the Detective Special, but with a four-inch barrel for longer sight radius and reduced muzzle jump. The walnut grips are redesigned to conform to a wider variety of hand sizes. The tops are tapered and the bottom is rounded for a comfortable grip. Target-style ramp sight in front and notched rear sight.

SPECIFICATIONS:
Caliber: 38 Special
Barrel length(s): 4″
Weight: 26 1/2 oz.
Overall length: 9″
Sights: Fixed square notch rear, ramp-style front
Stock: Checkered walnut
Finish: Colt blue or nickel

GOLD CUP NATIONAL MATCH MK IV SERIES '70
45 A.C.P.
$370.95

SPECIFICATIONS:
Caliber: 45 A.C.P.
Capacity: 7 rounds
Barrel length(s): 5″
Weight: 38 1/2 oz.
Overall length: 8 3/8″
Sights: Undercut front; Colt-Elliason adjustable rear
Hammer: Serrated target hammer
Stock: Checkered walnut
Finish: Colt blue

BALLISTICS PERFORMANCE

CARTRIDGES	BULLET		VELOCITY— FEET PER SECOND			ENERGY— FOOT POUNDS			MID-RANGE TRAJECTORY		TEST BARREL LGTH.
	WGT.-GRS.	STYLE	MUZZLE	50 YDS.	100 YDS.	MUZZLE	50 YDS.	100 YDS.	50 YDS.	100 YDS.	
45 AUTOMATIC	230	Metal Case	850	810	775	370	335	305	1.6″	6.5″	5″
	185*	Metal Case Wad Cutter	775	695	625	245	200	160	2.0″	9.0″	5″
	230	Metal Case, Targetmaster	850	810	775	370	335	305	1.6″	6.5″	5″

*45 Automatic

COLT REVOLVERS

COLT DIAMONDBACK

**22 L.R., 6″ bbl.,
blue** **$265.00**

**38 Spec., 4″ bbl.,
blue** **261.00**

The Colt Diamondback all-steel revolver was designed along the lines of the Python and includes the features of the bigger Python on a medium-size frame. These features include the ventilated rib, which dissipates barrel heat, reduces mirage effect and provides the preferred flat sighting plane . . . the wide spur target hammer which has a new cross-cut design which assures non-slip cocking . . . a grooved trigger and shrouded ejector rod, which protects the ejector rod and minimizes "barrel bounce."

The Diamondback is equipped with a fully adjustable rear sight for windage and elevation. The front sight is an integral ramp type.

SPECIFICATIONS:
Calibers: 22 L.R. and 38 Special.
Barrel lengths: 2½″ and 4″.
Sights: Adjustable rear sight, ramp-type front.
Trigger: Smooth.
Hammer: Wide-spur, checkered.
Stocks: Checkered walnut target stock.
Weights: 2½″ bbl. 38 Spec. (24 ozs.);
4″ bbl. 38 Spec. (27 oz.); 4″ bbl. 22 L.R. (31¾ oz.).
Finish: Colt Blue. Polished nickel. (38 only).

COLT DETECTIVE SPECIAL IN 38 SPECIAL WITH 2″ BARREL (All Steel)

Blue Finish **$225.00**

SPECIFICATIONS:
Caliber: 38 Special. **Barrel Length:** 2″ barrel.
Overall Length: 6⅞″. **Weight:** 21½ ounces. **Sights:** Fixed-type ramp-style, glare proofed. **Trigger:** Smooth. **Stocks:** Full checkered walnut, round butt.
Finish: Colt Blue. Polished Nickel.

COLT LAWMAN MK III
357 MAGNUM REVOLVER
Barrel: 2″, 4″

SPECIFICATIONS:
Caliber: 357 Magnum
Barrel length(s): 2″ & 4″
Weight: 2″ barrel 32 oz.; 4″ barrel 35 oz.
Overall length: 2″ barrel 7¼″; 4″ barrel 9⅜″
Sights: Fixed blade front; fixed square notch rear
Hammer: Target
Stock: 2″ barrel round-butt checkered walnut only; 4″ barrel square-butt checkered walnut
Finish: Colt blue or polished nickel

Blue Finish **$215.95**
Polished Nickel **229.95**

COLT SINGLE ACTION REVOLVERS

NEW FRONTIER SINGLE ACTION ARMY

The Colt New Frontier Single Action Army Revolver is made in two calibers, 44-Special and 45 Colt, both with 7½-inch barrels. It features an adjustable rear sight, with flat top frame and ramp front sight. The sighting radius with the 5½-barrel is 6⅝″ and 8⅝″ with the 7½-inch barrel. Additional features include smooth trigger, knurled hammer spur and walnut stocks.

NEW FRONTIER SINGLE ACTION ARMY, 44-Special, 45 Colt $431.95

SPECIFICATIONS

CALIBERS: 44-Special, 45 Colt.
LENGTH OF BARREL: 7½″ in above calibers.
LENGTH OVERALL: 12⅞″ with 7½″ bbl.
WEIGHT: 39½ oz.

SIGHTS: Ramp front. Adjustable rear.
SIGHT RADIUS: With 7½″ barrel—8⅝″

FINISH: Case hardened frame; blued barrel, cylinder, trigger guard & backstrap.
STOCKS: Walnut.

SINGLE ACTION ARMY

The Colt Single Action Army, also known as the original "Peacemaker" is in 44-Special, 45 Colt and 357 Magnum calibers. The 45 Colt and 357 Magnum models come in 4¾″, 5½″ and 7½″ barrel lengths. The sights are fixed type with a 5¾″ sighting radius for the 4¾″ barrel, 6⅜″ for the 5½″ barrel and 8⅜″ for the 7½″ barrel. With color case-hardened frame, blued barrel, cylinder, trigger guard and backstrap. The Colt Single Action Army is also available with a polished nickel finish in .45 caliber and comes with walnut stocks. The 44 Special comes in 7½″ barrel length.

S.A. Army 45 Colt or 357 Mag., w/7½″ bbl., Blue **$374.50**
S.A. Army 45 Colt, w/7½″ bbl., Polished Nickel **431.95**
S.A. Army 44 Special, 45 Colt, w/4¾″ or 5½″ bbl., Blue **367.95**
1860 Army 44-Special, w/8″ bbl., Blue .... **Price not available.**

SPECIFICATIONS

Caliber: 45 Colt, 357 Magnum, 44-Special
Barrel length(s): 4¾″, 5½″, 7½″
Weight: 45 caliber w/5½″ barrel, 37 oz.; 357 caliber w/ 5½″ barrel, 41½ oz.
Overall length: 4¾″ barrel, 10⅛″; 5½″ barrel, 10⅞″; 7½″ barrel, 12⅞″

Sights: Fixed front blade; fixed rear square notch
Stock: Black composite rubber or walnut (7½″ barrel nickel finish only)
Finish: Colt blue or polished nickel (7½″ barrel only)

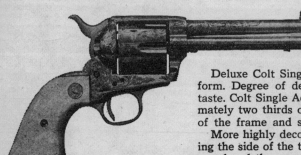

COLT SINGLE ACTION REVOLVERS

Deluxe Colt Single Action revolvers are also available in highly decorated form. Degree of decoration is dependent only on the individual customer's taste. Colt Single Action Army illustrated at left provides coverage of approximately two thirds of the barrel, portions of the cylinder and partial coverage of the frame and sideplate.

More highly decorated models provide larger coverage of engraving, including the side of the top strap, the backstrap down to the stock, the butt, trigger guard and the crane.

COLT REVOLVERS

PYTHON 357 MAGNUM

357 Magnum—Barrels: 2½″, 4″, 6″

**PYTHON
6-INCH BARREL**

The Colt Python revolver is chambered for the powerful 357 Magnum cartridge, suitable for hunting, target shooting and police use. Made in 2½″, 4″ and 6″ barrel lengths, every contact part is hand honed, hand-fitted. Features include: ventilated rib; fast-cocking, wide-spur hammer; shrouded ejector rod; target hammer, trigger and grips; adjustable rear and ramp-type front sights. Shoots both 357 Mag. and 38 Spec. loads.

Sights consist of an adjustable rear sight, and ramp-type front sight, ⅛″ wide. The sighting radius with 2½″ barrel is 4.4″; 4″ barrel—5.7″; and 6″ barrel—7.65″. The Python comes fitted with full-checkered walnut, square butt, target stocks. Length overall with 2½″ barrel—7¾″; 4″ barrel—9¼″; and 6″ barrel—11¼″. Weights: with 2½″ barrel—33 ounces; 4″ barrel—38 ounces; and 6″ barrel—43½ ounces. Finish—Colt royal blue or polished nickel.

Python with 2½″ barrel, blue finish	**$407.50**
Python with 4″ barrel, blue finish	**416.95**
nickel	**433.95**
Python with 6″ barrel, blue finish	**422.95**
nickel	**435.95**

IVER JOHNSON PISTOLS

X300 PONY

X300 PONY

All-steel, the X300 Pony is chambered for 380 ACP. The magazine holds six rounds and one in the chamber. **Length:** 6″. **Height:** 4″. For maximum security it has an inertia firing pin, and the large thumb safety cams the hammer out of contact with the sear. The windage-adjustable rear sight is rounded on its outer dimensions so it won't snag on clothing. Grips are of solid walnut, and the backstop is extra long to protect a hand from being bitten by the hammer.

Walnut, Blue finish	**$170.00**
Walnut, Military finish	**170.00**
Walnut, Nickel finish	**180.25**

EMF DAKOTA REVOLVERS

DAKOTA SINGLE-ACTION REVOLVERS

MODEL SA511E
1873 ARMY REVOLVER

$395.00

Custom engraved single-action revolver. Custom blue finish, one-piece walnut grips. Available with 4⅝", 5½" and 7½" barrels, in 357 Mag., 44/40, and 45 L.C.

MODEL SA511

$179.00

Genuine Dakota fast-draw single-action revolver with 4⅝" barrel. Exact shooting copy of the original Colt Single Action Revolver. Colt-type hammer with firing pin, beautiful blue finish, case-hardened frame, one-piece walnut grips and solid brass back strap and trigger guard. Available in 22 L.R., 357 Mag., 30 MI, 44/40, 45 L.C. Optional barrels available in 5½" and 7½" barrels.

MODEL SA511T

$199.00

Modern version of the Old Single Action Revolver. It is available with a ramp front blade target sight and adjustable rear sight. Polished blue finish with case-hardened frame, brass back and trigger guard, one-piece walnut grips. Available in 357 Mag., 44/40, and 45 L.C. with 5½" or 7½" barrels.

MODEL SA511-16¼
BUCKHORN

$209.00

Dakota Buckhorn shown with shoulder stock. Equipped with 16¼" barrel for precision shooting. Can be obtained without the shoulder stock, or with, which transforms it to a revolving carbine. Available in either 357 Mag. or 45 L.C.

HAWES REVOLVERS

SILVER CITY MARSHAL

The dress and show piece of the Marshal series with nickeled frame, solid-brass back-strap and trigger guard, blued cylinder and barrel, and white pearlite grips.

Model 6357S — 357 Mag.
Model 644S — 44 Mag.
Model 645S — 45 L.C.

Model 6357S	$201.95
Model 645S	201.95
Model 644S	211.95

HAWES SAUER WESTERN MARSHAL

This single-action six-shooter is made with chrome-molybdenum steel with all milled parts, all hand honed, custom blued. Modern floating firing pin. Hand-rubbed rosewood grips.
Weight 46 oz.; Overall length 11¾"; Barrel length 6".

Model 6357 — 357 Mag.
Model 644 — 44 Mag.
Model 645 — 45 L.C.

Model 6357	$166.70
Model 645	166.70
Model 644	174.50

MONTANA MARSHAL

A deluxe version of the Western Marshal featuring solid-brass back-strap and trigger guard with hand rubbed rosewood grips.

Model 6357B — 357 Mag.
Model 644B — 44 Mag.
Model 645B — 45 L.C.

Model 6357B	$189.70
Model 645B	189.70
Model 644B	198.95

TEXAS MARSHAL

This fully nickeled six-shooter has white pearlite grips. The Texas Marshal is designed for show and exhibition shooting.

Model 6357T — 357 Mag.
Model 644T — 44 Mag.
Model 645T — 45 L.C.

Model 6357T	$193.65
Model 645T	193.65
Model 644T	203.35

CHIEF MARSHAL

The precision target model six-shooter with massive frame, over-sized rosewood target grips, and fully adjustable target sights.

Model 6357CM — 357 Mag.
Model 644CM — 44 Mag.
Model 645CM — 45 L.C.

Model 6357CM	$200.90
Model 645CM	200.90
Model 644CM	210.95

HAWES REVOLVERS

FEDERAL MARSHAL

This version of the Marshal line has color case-hardened frame, solid-brass back-strap and trigger guard. One piece walnut grip.

Model 6357H — 357 Mag.
Model 644H — 44 Mag.
Model 645H — 45 L.C.

Model 6357H	$203.35
Model 645H	203.35
Model 644H	212.95

HAWES DEPUTY MONTANA MARSHAL

A deluxe version of the original Deputy Marshal. This new model has customized features including brass finish back-strap and trigger guard with solid walnut grips. Also features adjustable rear sight and floating firing pin. Barrel 5½"; Overall length 11"; Weight 34 oz.

Model 621B — 22 Long Rifle
Model 621BC — Combination
Same as above plus both
22 L.R. and 22 Mag. cylinders

Model 621B	$83.90
Model 621BC	96.55

HAWES DEPUTY SILVER CITY MARSHAL

This model has chrome frame set off by brass finish back-strap and trigger guard. Barrel and cylinder are blued, with molded white stag grips and adjustable rear sight and floating firing pin. Barrel 5½"; Overall length 11"; Weight 34 oz.

Model 621S — 22 L.R.
Model 621SC — Combination
22 L.R. w/extra 22 Mag. Cyl.
Model 621SW — Same as 621S w/Wood Grips
Model 621SCW — Same as 621SC w/Wood Grips

Model 621S	$ 83.90
Model 621SC	96.55
Model 621SW	91.55
Model 621SCW	104.20

HAWES DEPUTY TEXAS MARSHAL

This fully chromed six-shooter has molded white-stag grips and features adjustable rear sight and floating firing pin. Barrel 5½"; Overall length 11"; Weight 34 oz.

Model 621T — 22 L.R.
Model 621TC — Combination
22 L.R. w/extra 22 Mag. Cyl.
Model 621TW — Same as 621T w/Wood Grips
Model 621TCW — Same as 621TC w/Wood Grips

Model 621T	$ 83.90
Model 621TC	98.85
Model 621TW	91.55
Model 621TCW	106.50

HAWES DEPUTY DENVER MARSHAL

The blue finish and solid walnut grips are accented by the polished solid brass frame which also meets highest heat-treat and tensile strength requirements. Features adjustable rear sight and floating firing pin. Barrel 5½"; Overall length 11"; Weight 34 oz.

Model 621D — 22 L.R.
Model 621DC — Combination
22 L.R. w/extra 22 Mag. Cyl.
Model 621DM — Same as 621D
w/Black Molded Grips
Model 621DCM — Same as 621DC
w/Black Molded Grips

Model 621D	$ 93.85
Model 621DC	106.50
Model 621DM	86.20
Model 621DCM	98.85

HAWES DEPUTY MARSHAL

A reproduction of the "Scout" size version of the single action western six-shooter. Features adjustable rear sight, floating firing pin, blued finish and molded grips. Barrel, 5½"; Overall length, 11"; Weight 34 oz.

Model 621 — 22 L.R.
Model 621C — Combination
22 L.R. w/extra 22 Mag. Cyl.
Model 621W — Same as 621 w/Wood Grips
Model 621 CW — Same as 621C w/Wood Grips

Model 621	$68.95
Model 621C	81.60
Model 621W	76.60
Model 621CW	89.25

HAWES AUTOMATIC PISTOLS

SIG-SAUER P230

The new compact size double-action auto with all the same design and safety features of the P220. Non-locking blow back slide and stationary barrel.

Model 738 — 380 ACP

SPECIFICATIONS:	380 ACP
Overall Length	6½"
Height	4¾"
Breadth	1¼"
Barrel Length	3¾"
Weight	16 oz.
Magazine Capacity	7

Model 738 .... **$299.95**

SIG-SAUER P220

The decocking lever permits hazardless lowering of the hammer into the safety notch. A loaded pistol can be carried without danger, since the firing pin is automatically locked. Quick readiness for firing, as there are no safety devices to be manipulated manually. An automatic firing pin lock guarantees absolute safety, even if the weapon is dropped. Rapid aiming, contrast sights. Closed construction affords protection against dirt. Slide remains held in open position after last shot has been fired.

Model 745 — 45 ACP
Model 790 — 9mm Para.
Model 795 — 38 Super

SPECIFICATIONS:	45 ACP	38 Super 9MM Para.
Overall Length	7¾"	7¾"
Height	5¾"	5¾"
Breadth	1-1/3"	1-1/3"
Barrel Length	4-3/8"	4-3/8"
Weight	28¼ oz.	29¼ oz.
Magazine Capacity	7	9

Model 745 .... **$349.95**
Model 790 .... **349.95**
Model 795 .... **349.95**

HECKLER & KOCH PISTOLS

MODEL P9S COMPETITION PISTOL

This model is fitted with two barrel configurations: first, the standard 4" barrel for medium and combat ranges; second, it can be converted to a competition or long-range pistol with a special barrel kit. This kit is fitted to each pistol at the factory and bears the same serial number as the gun. The standard 4" barrel P9S Competition Model consists of one P9S with 4" barrel (102 mm), one recoil spring, trigger stop, adjustable trigger and adjustable sights. One 5½" barrel kit consists of one 5½" barrel, one recoil spring and one barrel weight.

SPECIFICATIONS:
Barrel Length: 5.5"
Pistol Length: 9.1"
Pistol Weight, without magazine: 32 oz.
Barrel Weight for 5.5" barrel: 6.7 oz.
Pistol with barrel weight and full magazine: 39 oz.
Sight Radius with adjustable sight: 5.9 in.

Model P9S Competition w/Walnut Wrap-around Competition Grip ......
$599.00

HECKLER & KOCH PISTOLS

MODEL P9S Cal. 45 ACP PISTOL

The P9S double action 45 ACP embodies the same features of the P9S 9mm—Polygonal rifling and the delayed roller-locked bolt system in the slide.

SPECIFICATIONS:

Caliber: 45 ACP
Magazine: 7 rounds (plus 1 in chamber)
Barrel Length: 4"
Length of Pistol: 7.6 in.
Height of Pistol: 5.4 in.
Sight radius: 5.8 in.
Weight without Magazine: approx. 30 oz.
Weight of Magazines Empty: 2.6 oz.

Model P9S Caliber 45 (w/Combat Sight)	**$384.00**
Also available in 45 Target Model	**436.00**
8" Hunting Barrel	**87.00**

HECKLER & KOCH PISTOLS
MODEL P9S AUTOMATIC PISTOL

The P9S is an automatic pistol with a stationary barrel and sliding delayed roller-locked system which reduces recoil. The polygonal twist barrel affords 5% to 6% increase in muzzle velocity.

SPECIFICATIONS:

Caliber: 9 mm parabellum (9 mm Luger)
Weight: 32 oz.
Barrel Length: 4"
Overall Length: 7⅝"
Magazine Capacity: 9 rounds
Sights: Fixed, square-blade quick-draw front; square-notch rear
Sights Radius: 5¾"
Rifling: Polygonal, right twist

Model P9S (w/combat sights)	**$384.00**
Also available in Target pistol as Model P9S Target	**436.00**
30 Luger cal. Conversion Kit (w/barrel and 2 magazines), must be ordered with P9S 9mm	**95.00**

HK4 AUTOMATIC PISTOL

The HK4 provides the choice of 380, 32, 25 ACP or 22 LR. A dust-proof self-sealed auto with multiple safety features and double-action trigger.

SPECIFICATIONS:

Calibers: 380 - 22 LR - 32 - 25
Length: 6³⁄₁₆" (157 mm)
Height: 4²¹⁄₆₄" (110 mm)
Width at Butt: 1¹⁷⁄₆₄" (32 mm)
Barrel Length: 3¹¹⁄₃₂" (85 mm)
Sight Radius: 4⁴⁹⁄₆₄" (121 mm)
Weight of Pistol: 16,9 oz (480 g)
Weight of Magazine: 1,4 oz (40 g)
Magazine Capacity: 7   8   8   8

Model HK4 (380 cal.)	**$265.00**
Model HK4 380 caliber with 22 caliber conversion kit	**285.00**
Model HK4 380 caliber with set of 3 conversion kits in 22LR, 25, and 32	**340.00**

MODEL VP702 DOUBLE-ACTION
AUTOMATIC PISTOL

The VP70 Automatic Pistol is recoil operated, with an inertia bolt and stationary barrel. The receiver is of solid plastic material. The parallel-type revolver trigger (double-action trigger only) and the direct **firing pin ignition** ensure constant **readiness to fire** and permit the weapon to be safely carried while **loaded and** uncocked until the trigger is pulled. The cartridges are fed from an 18-round magazine.

The sights on the VP70 are based on the light-and-shadow principle. Targets can be aimed at even under unfavorable lighting and vision conditions.

SPECIFICATIONS:

Magazine: 18 rounds
Caliber: 9 mm x 19 (Parabellum)
Sight, Front: Ramp type, channelled
Length of Pistol: 8.03 in.
Height of Pistol: 5.67 in.
Length of Barrel: 4.57 in.
Sight Radius: 6.89 in.
Pistol, without Magazine: 29 oz.
Weight of Magazine Empty: 3.5 oz.

Model VP70Z (w/Combat Sights & 18-Round Magazine)	**$268.00**

H&R Model 922

9-Shot Revolver

9-Shot 22 Short, Long & Long Rifle—Barrel: 2½", 4", & 6"

The H&R Model 922 is a 9-shot single and double action .22 caliber revolver which handles 22 short, long, and long rifle, standard or high velocity, and features a safety rim cylinder. Available in 2½", 4", and 6" barrel lengths. Blue finish. 2½" .... **$67.50** 4" and 6" **$67.50**
Available with nickel finish as Model 923, 2½" ...... **$69.50** 4" 69.50

FEATURES AND SPECIFICATIONS

Caliber: 22 short, long, and long rifle; standard or high velocity.

Capacity: 9 shots.

Grips: Black Cycolac.

Barrel Length: 2½", 4", and 6".

Weight: 20 oz., 24 oz., and 26 oz.

Action: Single and double. Pull pin cylinder.

Sights: Blade front sight.

Finish: H&R Crown-Lustre Blue barrel Satin finish frame

H&R Model 732

6-Shot Revolver

32 S&W Long—Barrel: 2½", 4"

The H&R Model 732 features an easy-loading swing-out cylinder and comes with either 2½ or 4-inch barrel in blue finish.

2½" **$79.50**
4" 79.50

FEATURES AND SPECIFICATIONS

Caliber: 32 S&W long.

Capacity: 6 shots.

Grips: Black Cycolac.

Barrel Length: 2½" and 4".

Action: Single and double. Swing-out cylinder.

Sights: 4" barrels have windage adjustment on rear sight.

Finish: H&R Crown-Lustre Blue.

Weight: 23½ oz., and 26 oz.

H&R Model 733

6-Shot Revolver

32 S&W Long—Barrel: 2½", 4"

Model 733: Offering the same features as the Model 732, this revolver is finished in a high-lustre, protective nickel. With

2½" **$84.50**
4" 84.50

FEATURES AND SPECIFICATIONS

Caliber: 32 S&W long.

Capacity: 6 shots.

Grips: Black Cycolac.

Barrel Length: 2½", 4".

Action: Single and double. Swing-out cylinder.

Sights: Blade front sight.

Finish: Nickel.

Weight: 23½ oz.; 26 oz.

H&R REVOLVERS

H&R Model 999

9-Shot 22 Short, Long & Long Rifle
Also available in 6-Shot 32 S&W Long

H&R's Model 999 is a break-open type 9-shot revolver featuring a wide hammer spur for fast and easy cocking. Made with unbreakable coil springs throughout.
With 6" ventilated rib barrel. **$125.00**
With 4" barrel **120.00**

FEATURES AND SPECIFICATIONS

Caliber: 22 short, long, and long rifle.
Capacity: 9 shots.
Grips: Checkered walnut.
Barrel Length: 6" ventilated.
Weight: 30 oz.

Action: Single and double. Top break-open.
Sights: Adjustable front and rear.
Finish: H&R Crown-Lustre Blue.

H&R Model 949

9-Shot 22 Short, Long & Long Rifle—Barrel: 5½"

H&R's Model 949 is a modern 9-shot 22 caliber revolver with frontier features. With automatic rebound hammer, wide cocking spur and unbreakable coil spring construction. **$79.50**

FEATURES AND SPECIFICATIONS

Caliber: 22 short, long, and long rifle.
Capacity: 9 shots.
Grips: One-piece walnut grip.
Barrel Length: 5½".
Weight: 31 oz.

Action: Single and double. Side loading and ejection.
Sights: Adjustable rear sight; Western type front blade sight.
Finish: H&R Crown-Lustre Blue; (or nickel—Model 950 $84.50 .

Available with color-cased frame, 7½" barrel as Model 976.
$89.50

H&R Model 929

9-Shot Revolver

9-Shot 22 Short, Long & Long Rifle—Barrel: 2½", 4", & 6"

H&R's Model 929 revolver features a 9-shot swing-out cylinder. Made in 22 caliber, it is available with 2½", 4" and 6" barrel lengths. The 4" and 6" barrels have windage adjustment on rear sight. Blue finish. 2½" **$79.50** 4" and 6" **$79.50**. **Model 930** has identical features, but is finished in durable, protective nickel, and comes with 2½" or 4" barrel. Matte finish on top frame. 2"½ **$84.50**. 4" **$84.50**

FEATURES AND SPECIFICATIONS

Caliber: .22 short, long, and long rifle:
Capacity: 9 shots.
Grips: Black Cycolac.
Barrel Length: 2½", 4", and 6".
Weight: 22 oz., 26 oz., and 28 oz.

Action: Single and double. Swing-out cylinder.
Sights: 4" and 6" barrels have windage adjustment on rear sight.
Finish: H&R Crown-Lustre Blue.

H&R REVOLVERS

H&R Model 939
9-Shot 22 Short, Long & Long Rifle—Barrel: 6"

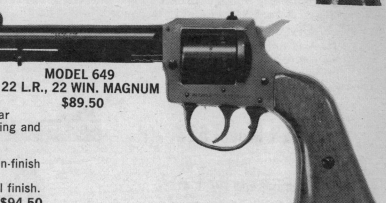

The **H&R Model 939** revolver comes equipped with a precision adjustable rear sight and ventilated rib barrel. Features include a safety lock device which prevents unauthorized persons from firing your revolver. **$99.50**

Caliber: 22 short, long, and long rifle.
Capacity: 9 shots.
Grips: Checkered walnut with contoured thumb rest.
Barrel Length: 6" target weight; ventilated rib.
Weight: 33 oz.

Action: Single and double. Swing-out cylinder.
Sights: Fixed front. Rear sight adjustable for windage and elevation.
Finish: H&R Crown-Lustre Blue.

SPECIFICATIONS:
Caliber: 22 Long rifle; 22 Win. Magnum
Capacity: 6 shot
Barrel length(s): 5½"
Weight: 32 oz.
Sights: Western-type front blade sight; adjustable rear
Action: Single action and double action side loading and ejecting
Grips: One piece wrap around genuine walnut
Finish: H&R Crown Lustre Blue barrel, blue satin-finish frame
Model 650: Same as Model 649 except with nickel finish.
$94.50

MODEL 649
22 L.R., 22 WIN. MAGNUM
$89.50

SPECIFICATIONS:
Caliber: 22 Long rifle; 22 Win. Magnum
Capacity: 6 shot
Barrel length(s): 6"
Weight: 28 oz.
Sights: Blade front sight
Action: Single and double pull pin
Grips: Black Cycolac
Finish: H&R Crown Lustre Blue

MODEL 666
22 L.R., 22 WIN. MAGNUM
$74.50

MODEL 676
22 L.R., 22 WIN. MAGNUM
4½", 5½" & 7½" BARREL $99.50
12" BARREL $125.00

SPECIFICATIONS:
Caliber: 22 Long rifle, 22 Win. Magnum
Capacity: 6 shot
Barrel length(s): 4½"; 5½"; 7½"; 12"
Weight: 31 oz.; 32 oz.; 36 oz.; 41 oz.
Sights: Western-type front blade sight; adjustable rear
Action: Single action and double action side loading and ejecting
Grips: One piece wrap around genuine walnut
Finish: H&R Crown Lustre Blue barrel and cylinder guard; Antique color-cased frame, ejector tube, trigger

H&R REVOLVERS

H&R Model STR 022

9-Shot 22 Blank—Barrel: 2½"

For use as a signaling device for all types of athletic events, or for realism in theatrical use, the Model 970 fires rimfire, blank ammunition. **$57.50**

FEATURES AND SPECIFICATIONS
Caliber: .22 blank. **Capacity:** 9 shots. **Grips:** Black Cycolac. **Barrel Length:** 2½". **Weight:** 19 oz. **Action:** Single and double. Pull pin cylinder. **Finish:** Blue satin finished frame

Available with nickel finish as Model STR 122 .... **$62.50**

NOTE: *If a louder report is required, the 6-shot Model STR 032 is available at the same price, and with features identical to those of the Model STR 022. It is chambered for 32 caliber S&W center-fire, blank cartridges* **$57.50**

Available with nickel finish as Model STR 132. .... 62.50

H&R Model 622

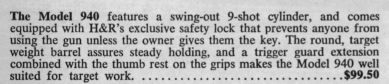

6-Shot 22 Long Rifle—Barrel: 2½" & 4"

The H&R Model 622 is a 6-shot single and double action 22 caliber revolver which handles 22 long rifle and features a safety rim cylinder. Available in 2½" and 4" barrel lengths. Blue finish. **$59.50**
Available with nickel finish as Model 623. .... 64.50

FEATURES AND SPECIFICATIONS

Caliber: 22 long rifle.	**Action:** Single and double.
Capacity: 6 shots.	Pull pin cylinder.
Grips: Black Cycolac. Round Butt.	**Sights:** Blade front sight.
Barrel Length: 2½" and 4".	**Finish:** Satin finished frame. H&R
Weight: 20 oz. and 26 oz.	Crown-Lustre Blue barrel.

> Also in 32 S&W Long as Model 632
> 2½" & 4". Blue Finish **$67.50**
> Model 633, 2½" nickel finish
> **$72.50**

Model 940
9-Shot Revolver

The **Model 940** features a swing-out 9-shot cylinder, and comes equipped with H&R's exclusive safety lock that prevents anyone from using the gun unless the owner gives them the key. The round, target weight barrel assures steady holding, and a trigger guard extension combined with the thumb rest on the grips makes the Model 940 well suited for target work. **$99.50**

FEATURES AND SPECIFICATIONS

Caliber: 22 short, long, and long rifle;	**Action:** Single and double.
Capacity: 9 shots.	Swing-out cylinder.
Grips: Checkered walnut with	**Sights:** Fixed front sight. Rear sight
contoured thumb rest.	adjustable for windage and
Barrel Length: 6" target weight; ventilated rib.	elevation.
Weight: 33 oz.	**Finish:** H&R Crown-Lustre Blue.

HIGH STANDARD AUTO PISTOLS

VICTOR MILITARY MODEL TARGET PISTOL

10-Shot 22 Long Rifle—Barrel: 4½", 5½"

High Standard's Victor is available with a restyled rib, and an interchangeable front sight. The rib, which reduces the overall weight of the 5½" Victor by three ounces is vented. The 5½" Victor, less barrel weight, is now ISU qualified. All models feature push button barrel takedown. The wide target trigger can be adjusted for travel and weight of pull. The rear sight is stationary (mounted on rib), and is micro adjustable for elevation and windage—adjustment screws are positive click spring loaded. The Victor comes fitted with checkered American walnut military grips with thumb rest. Front and backstrap are stippled for a positive grip. Equipped with positive double-action safety, and automatic slide lock, holding the action open after the last round has been fired. Additional features include 24 carat gold-plated trigger, safety and magazine release, with identifying roll marks gold-filled. Available with 4½" or 5½" barrel, in blue finish **$270.50**

FEATURES AND SPECIFICATIONS: Caliber: 22 L.R. **Capacity:** 10 rounds. **Barrel:** 4½ inch and 5½ inch, specially molded and contoured barrels. **Sights:** Adjustable micrometer rear sight mounted on rib. **Trigger:** Wide target trigger—2-2¼ lb. pull. **Grips:** Checkered walnut military. **Weight:** 48 oz. for 4½ inch model; 52 oz. for 5½ inch model. **Overall Length:** 8¾" for 4½ inch model; 9¾" for 5½ inch model. **Finish:** Blue.

TROPHY GRADE—MILITARY MODEL AUTOMATICS

MILITARY TROPHY
10 Shot 22 L.R.
5½" Bull Barrel
$236.25

MILITARY TROPHY
10 Shot 22 L.R.
7¼" Fluted Barrel
$251.00

The High-Standard "Trophy" grade automatics come in military models only with a choice of a 5½" bull barrel, or a 7¼" fluted barrel. They differ only in length and style of barrel. The trigger pull is 2 to 2¼ lbs. and has a trigger travel adjustment, enabling the shooter to limit the amount of backward travel of trigger to a minute distance beyond the firing point. Also, there is a trigger-pull adjustment (a positive, click-stop adjusting screw) which adjusts the degree of tension on Trophy and Citation model triggers. A uniform trigger pull is achieved because the sear engages the hammer on the outside periphery, making the engaging surfaces further away from the hammer pivot point. The Trophy models are ground, polished, buffed and blued and come with a gold, target-size trigger

and gold identification. The back and front strap are stippled and the mechanical parts are machined and hand-honed. The rear sight is new in that the bracket is rigidly fixed to the frame—the slide moves through the yoke, making it completely vibration and shock free. The fixed ramp type front sight, dovetail slots in the barrel. The military grip is a faithful duplicate of the Military 45 and comes with thumbrest in checkered American walnut (also available with left hand design—right hand with thumb rest is standard). Automatic slide lock holds action open after last shot is fired. When the safety is in position, the sear is blocked and the sear bar is disconnected, thereby completely disconnecting the firing mechanism. It cannot discharge.

SPECIFICATIONS FOR MILITARY TROPHY MODELS (5½" & 7¼" BARRELS)

CALIBER: 22 Long Rifle.
CAPACITY: 10 shot.
BARREL: 5½" bull barrel; 7¼" fluted barrel.
SIGHTS: Stationary bracket type, deep notched rear; fixed ramp type dovetail front sight.
SIGHT RADIUS: With 5½" barrel—8¾"; with 7¼" barrel—10".

TRIGGER: Wide target trigger, with trigger travel adjustment and trigger-pull adjustment (2-2¼ lbs.).
SAFETY: Double acting safety. Automatic side lock.
LENGTH OVERALL: With 5½" bbl.—9¾"; with 7¼" bbl.—11½".
WEIGHT: 44.5 ounces for both models.
FINISH: Ground, polished, buffed and blued.

HIGH STANDARD AUTO PISTOLS

CITATION MILITARY MODEL AUTOMATICS

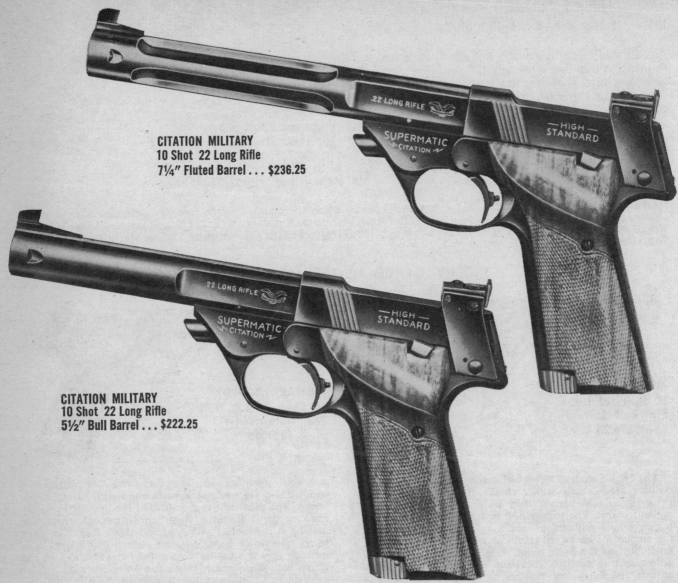

CITATION MILITARY
10 Shot 22 Long Rifle
7¼" Fluted Barrel . . . $236.25

CITATION MILITARY
10 Shot 22 Long Rifle
5½" Bull Barrel . . . $222.25

The Supermatic "Citation" grade military models are available in two barrel lengths—5½" bull barrel, and 7¼" fluted barrel. The trigger pull and trigger travel adjustment are standard on all Citation models. The military models have a stationary type near sight with a dovetail, fixed ramp type front sight. Back and front straps are stippled. The grips are checkered American walnut and come with thumb rest, in right or left hand design. All Citation models come with positive double-action safety and side lock features. Barrel interchangeability is also standard with all Citation models. Mechanical parts are machined and hand-honed.

SPECIFICATIONS

CALIBER: 22 Long Rifle.
CAPACITY: 10 shot.
BARREL: 5½" bull barrel; 7¼" fluted barrel.
SIGHTS: Stationary bracket type, deep notched rear; fixed ramp type dovetail front sight.
SIGHT RADIUS: With 5½" barrel—8¾"; with 7¼" barrel—10".
TRIGGER: Wide target trigger, with trigger travel adjustment and trigger-pull adjustment (2-2¼ lbs.).
SAFETY: Positive, double action. Side lock.
GRIPS: Military type checkered American walnut with thumb rest.
LENGTH OVERALL: With 5½" barrel—9¾"; with 7¼" barrel—11½".
WEIGHT: 44.5 ounces for both models.
FINISH: Ground, polished, blued.

SHARPSHOOTER
10-Shot 22 Long Rifle
w/5½" Bull Barrel
$179.50

Model: 9210
Caliber: 22 LR
Rounds: 10
Barrel: 5½" Bull
Weight: 42 oz.
Overall Length: 10¼"
Overall Height: 5¼"

Sights: Front—⅛" Blade Serrated Ramp; Rear—Adjustable—Micrometer Click—Windage & Elevation
Grips: Walnut—Checkered with Thumbrest
Finish: Blue
Features: Wide Serrated Target Trigger; Military Grip; Pushbutton Barrel Takedown.

SPORT KING
10-Shot 22 Long Rifle
w/4½" or 6¾" Barrel
Blue $148.75

Model: 9258/9259
Caliber: 22 L.R.
Rounds: 10
Barrel: 9258—4½"
9259—6¾"
Weight: 9258—39 oz.
9259—42 oz.
Overall Length: 9258— 9¼"
9259—11½"

Overall Height: 5"
Sights: Front—⅛" Blade; Rear—⅛" Square Notch—Adjustable for Windage
Grips: Walnut—Checkered
Finish: Blue
Features: Wide Serrated Target Trigger; Military Grip; Pushbutton Barrel Takedown.

DERRINGERS
22 R. F. Magnum
w/3½" 2-Shot Dual Barrels

The Derringers from High Standard offer the traditional look of the old, with the safety design features of the new. They feature hammerless design.

Their double action is safety-engineered—the High Standard Derringer cannot ever fire accidentally—even if dropped.

They're available in either onyx black with black grips or polished nickel with black grips. These derringers have an overall width of less than 1" and weigh 11 oz. Chambered to fire 22 magnum.

NO. 9306 MAGNUM DERRINGER							
9194	22 Mag.	2	Blue	Black	3½"	5"	11	$ 94.50
9306	22 Mag.	2	Nickel	Black	3½"	5"	11	109.50

HIGH STANDARD REVOLVERS

Camp Gun

SPECIFICATIONS:
Caliber: 22 L.R.; 22 Magnum
Capacity: 9 round
Barrel length(s): 6"
Sights: Adjustable
Grips: Checkered walnut target grips
Finish: Blue

22 L R $156.00
22 MAGNUM $156.00

Sentinel
22L.R./22 Mag.
2" Fixed Sights   **$159.25**
4" Adjustable Rear Sight   **168.50**

Model: 9390/9392
Caliber: 22L.R./22 Mag.
Rounds: 9
Barrel: 9390—2"
         9392—4"
Weight: 9390—22 oz.
         9392—27 oz.
Overall Length: 9390—7⅛"
                 9392—9⅛"
Overall Height: 5¼"
Sights: Front—⅛" Serrated Ramp; Rear—9390; Square Notch
   —9392—Adjustable—Windage & Elevation
Grips: Walnut—Checkered
Finish: Trophy Blue

Features: Steel Frame; Dual Cylinder; Swing-Out Cylinder;
         Multiple Ejection; Double Action

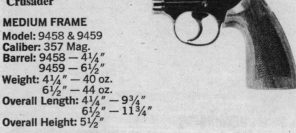

Crusader

MEDIUM FRAME
Model: 9458 & 9459
Caliber: 357 Mag.
Barrel: 9458 — 4¼"
         9459 — 6½"
Weight: 4¼" — 40 oz.
         6½" — 44 oz.
Overall Length: 4¼" — 9¾"
                 6½" — 11¾"
Overall Height: 5½"

Crusader

LARGE FRAME
Model: 9452, 9453 & 9454
Caliber: 44 Mag.
Model: 9455, 9456 & 9457
Caliber: 45 Colt
Barrel: 9452 & 9455 — 4¼"
         9453 & 9456 — 6½"
         9454 & 9457 — 8⅜"
Weight: 4¼" — 43 oz.
         6½" — 48 oz.
         8⅜" — 52 oz.
Overall Length: 4¼" — 9⅞"
                 6½" — 12⅛"
                 8⅜" — 14"
Overall Height: 6"
Sights: Front—Blade on Ramp; Rear—Adjustable—Windage &
   Elevation
Grips: Walnut—44 Smooth, 45 Checkered
Finish: Blue

Crusader			
44 Mag.	4¼"		$335.50
	6½"		340.00
	8⅜"		345.00
45 Colt	4¼"		335.00
	6½"		340.00
	8⅜"		345.00
357 Mag.	4¼"		330.00
	6½"		335.00

HIGH STANDARD REVOLVERS

HIGH SIERRA DELUXE
9-SHOT 22 LONG RIFLE
7" OCTAGONAL BARREL

The High Sierra Western-style revolver features a steel frame and comes with a 7" octagonal barrel with a custom blue finish, complemented by hand-rubbed walnut grips. Trigger guard and backstraps are gold-plated. Available with dual cylinders (22L.R./22 Magnum). High Sierra deluxe comes equipped with an adjustable rear sight. Price: High Sierra with adjustable rear sight and two cylinders (22LR/mag), **$176.75**.

The Double Nine with steel frame and 5½" barrel, comes with interchangeable cylinders for standard 22 L.R. and 22 Magnum ammunition. Features include nine-shot capacity, double action and swing out cylinders. With fixed sights, the Double Nine sells for **$159.50** in blue finish. Also available with adjustable rear sight in blue finish, priced at **$173.25**

The Longhorn Deluxe: Same as Double Nine except with 9½" "Buntline" barrel. Available in trophy blue with dual cylinders with adjustable rear sights **$176.75**

Western Revolvers (9-shot) Double Action

MODEL NO.	NAME	FEATURES	FINISH	CAL.	BBL. LGTH.
9320	Double Nine	Fixed Sights	Trophy Blue	2 Cyl 22 LR/mag	5½"
9324	Double Nine Deluxe	Adj. Rear Sight	Trophy Blue	2 Cyl 22 LR/mag	5½"
9328	Longhorn Deluxe	Adj. Rear Sight	Trophy Blue	2 Cyl 22 LR/mag	9½"
9375	High Sierra Deluxe	Adj. Rear Sight	Trophy Blue	2 Cyl 22 LR/mag	7" Oct

LLAMA AUTOMATIC PISTOLS

**LLAMA LARGE FRAME
AUTOMATIC PISTOL IN
BLUE ENGRAVED FINISH**
45 Auto Caliber
$299.95

**LLAMA SMALL FRAME
AUTOMATIC PISTOL IN
BLUE ENGRAVED FINISH**
380 Caliber
$241.95

Llama's time-proven design, enhanced by individual hand-fitting and hand-honing of all moving parts, has resulted in handguns that provide smooth operation, pin-point accuracy, and rugged reliability under the toughest conditions.

Deluxe features, all indicative of the extra care lavished on each gun, are found in all Llama handguns.

The small-frame Llama models, available in 22 L.R., 32 Auto. and 380 Auto., are impressively compact handguns. All frames are precision machined of high strength steel, yet weigh a featherlight 23 ounces. A full complement of safeties . . . side lever, half-cock, and grip . . . is incorporated.

Every small-frame Llama is complete with ventilated rib, wide-spur serrated target-type hammer and adjustable rear sight.

The large-frame Llama models, available in potent 45 ACP, 38 Super and 9mm Parabellum, are completely crafted of high strength

**LLAMA LARGE FRAME
AUTOMATIC WITH
DEEP BLUE FINISH**
9mm, 38 Super & 45 Auto
$249.95

**LLAMA SMALL FRAME
AUTOMATIC WITH
DEEP BLUE FINISH**
22, 32 & 380 Caliber
$182.95

LLAMA AUTOMATIC PISTOLS

steel, machined and polished to perfection. Complete with ventilated rib for maximum heat dissipation, wide-spur checkered target-type hammer, adjustable rear sight and genuine walnut grips, make these truly magnificent firearms.

In addition to High Polished Deep Blue, these superb handguns are available in deluxe fancy finishes:

- High Polished Deep Blue Engraved (380 Auto., 45 ACP).
- Handsome Satin Chrome (22 L.R., 380 Auto., 45 ACP).
- Satin Chrome Engraved (380 Auto., 45 ACP).
- Gold Damascened. (380 Auto.). Richly engraved Spanish Gold for those who will be satisfied with nothing but the best.

Extra Magazines: 22, 32, 380 calibers . . **$13.50**
Extra Magazines: 9mm, 38 super, 45 . . **14.95**

LLAMA LARGE FRAME AUTOMATIC IN SATIN CHROME ENGRAVED FINISH
45 Auto Caliber
$316.95

LLAMA SMALL FRAME AUTOMATIC WITH SATIN CHROME ENGRAVED FINISH
380 Caliber
$249.95

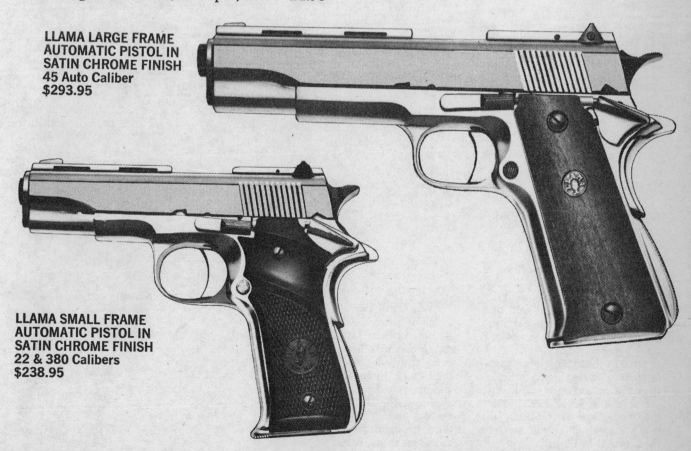

LLAMA LARGE FRAME AUTOMATIC PISTOL IN SATIN CHROME FINISH
45 Auto Caliber
$293.95

LLAMA SMALL FRAME AUTOMATIC PISTOL IN SATIN CHROME FINISH
22 & 380 Calibers
$238.95

LLAMA AUTOMATIC PISTOLS

LLAMA 45 DOUBLE ACTION AUTOMATIC

NEW FOR 1980

LLAMA Automatic Pistol Specifications

TYPE:	Small Frame Auto Pistols			Large Frame Auto Pistols		
CALIBERS:	.22 L.R.	.32 Auto.	.380 Auto.	.38 Super	9mm	.45 Auto.
FRAME:	Precision machined from high strength steel. Serrated front strap, checkered (curved) backstrap.			Precision machined from high strength steel. Plain front strap, checkered (curved) backstrap.		
TRIGGER:	Serrated.			Serrated.		
HAMMER:	External. Wide spur, serrated.			External. Wide spur, serrated.		
OPERATION:	Straight blow-back.			Locked breech.		
LOADED CHAMBER INDICATOR: No	Yes	Yes	Yes	Yes	Yes	
SAFETIES:	Side lever thumb safety, half-cock safety. Note: .22 L.R. with additional magazine safety (gun will not fire with magazine removed).			Side lever thumb safety, half-cock safety.		
GRIPS:	Modified thumb-rest black plastic grips.			Genuine walnut on blue models. Genuine teakwood on satin chrome, satin chrome engraved and blue engraved models.		
SIGHTS:	Square notch rear, and Patridge-type front; screw adjustable rear sight for windage.			Square notch rear, and Patridge-type front; screw adjustable rear sight for windage.		
SIGHT RADIUS:	4¼"			6¼"		
MAGAZINE CAPACITY:	8-shot	7-shot	7-shot	9-shot	9-shot	7-shot
WEIGHT:	23 ounces			2 lbs., 8 ozs.		
BARREL LENGTH:	3¹¹/₁₆ inches			5 inches		
OVER-ALL LENGTH:	6½"			8½"		
HEIGHT:	4⅜"			5¼"		
FINISH:	Std. models: High-polished, deep blue. Deluxe models: satin chrome (.22, .380, .45); satin chrome engraved (.380, .45); blue engraved (.380, .45); Gold Damascened with simulated pearl grips (.380, .45).					

GOLD DAMASCENED FINISH
380 Caliber
$1250.00

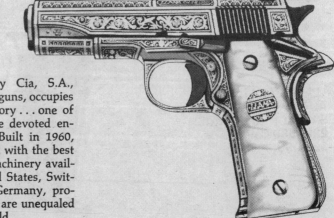

In the centuries-old tradition of Toledo steel, this superb example of a nearly lost art ... Gold Damascened. Rich Spanish gold, magnificently engraved by old world craftsmen to create true works of art.

Crafted in the mountainous Basque Region of Spain, Llama handguns have enjoyed a reputation of rugged dependability since 1910. This is the same ageless tradition that made blades of Toledo steel the most prized in Europe.

Today, Gabilondo y Cia, S.A., maker of Llama handguns, occupies a huge, modern factory ... one of the largest in Europe devoted entirely to handguns. Built in 1960, the factory, equipped with the best and most modern machinery available from the United States, Switzerland and West Germany, produces handguns that are unequaled anywhere in the world.

LLAMA REVOLVERS

**LLAMA SUPER COMANCHE IV
IN HIGH POLISHED DEEP BLUE FINISH
44 Magnum 6" Barrel
$349.95**

SUPER COMANCHE, LLAMA'S ALL-NEW 44 MAGNUM DOUBLE ACTION . . . THE MOST RUGGED, ACCURATE AND SAFEST REVOLVER BUILT.

Three years of intensive product development and generations of prototypes evolved before final specifications were set for this all-new Super Comanche. If ever a handgun was conceived, designed and built to fit the exacting requirements of big-bore handgunners, this one is it.

Take the frame for example: it's massive. The most solid, most rugged of any other double-action revolver. Its weight and balance are such that the heavy recoil generated by the powerful 44 Magnum cartridge is easily and comfortably controlled, even when rapid firing in the double-action mode. In the single-action mode, the broad, serrated hammer-spur makes cocking easy and fast.

Instead of a single cylinder latch, the new Llama has two. In addition to the conventional center pin at the rear of the ratchet, there's a second latch up front which locks the crane to the frame at the underside of the barrel ring. Using this two-lock system, the cylinder and crane are locked in a more positive manner than can be achieved using the common detent/ball arrangement found on other revolvers.

Only coil springs are used throughout. Not only does this provide added strength in a critical area, but the added rigidity raises the gun's accuracy potential as well. Also aiding accuracy is the heavyweight barrel measuring .815" in diameter. A matte-finish rib reduces glare and helps get on target faster.

But building the strongest and most accurate revolver were only two of the three basic goals Llama engineers set for themselves; they also wanted to build the safest. To that end, the hammer is mounted on an eccentric cam, the position of which is controlled by the trigger. Only when the latter is fully depressed can the firing pin contact the primer. Accidental discharge is virtually impossible.

LLAMA REVOLVERS

IN REVOLVERS TODAY, THERE'S A NEW NAME IN EXCELLENCE. IT'S THE LLAMA COMANCHE® SERIES. Designed for you and incorporating every feature worth having to make these Llamas the finest revolvers made today . . . at any price.

All the Comanche models — 22 L.R., 38 Special, and the sledgehammer 357 Magnum caliber utilize massively forged solid–steel frames for tremendous strength and enduring reliability.

Up front, Llama added a precision-bored heavyweight barrel of target quality, complete with a solid shroud to protect the ejector rod, and a raised ventilated-rib that dissipates heat from the barrel to give you a clear, sharp sight image even when the action gets hot.

The sights are fully adjustable, with a square notch, rear sight and a quick-draw ramp front.

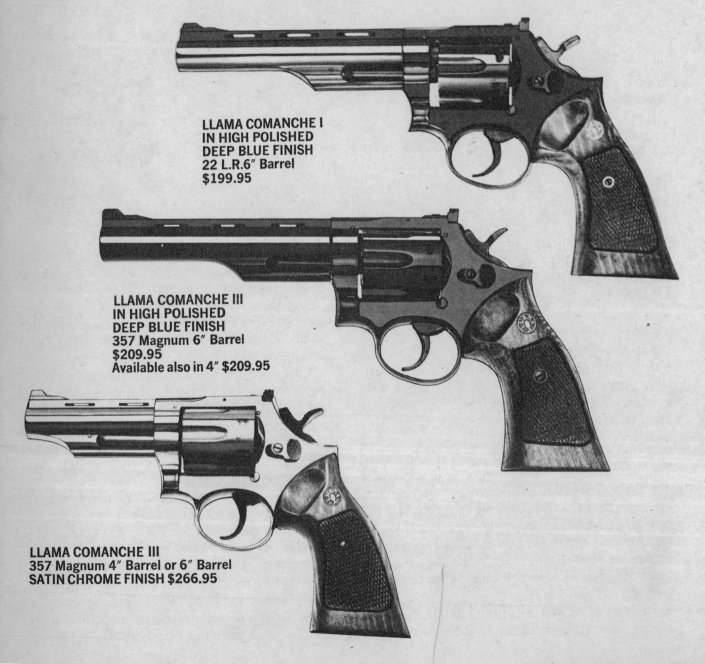

**LLAMA COMANCHE I
IN HIGH POLISHED
DEEP BLUE FINISH
22 L.R.6" Barrel
$199.95**

**LLAMA COMANCHE III
IN HIGH POLISHED
DEEP BLUE FINISH
357 Magnum 6" Barrel
$209.95
Available also in 4" $209.95**

**LLAMA COMANCHE III
357 Magnum 4" Barrel or 6" Barrel
SATIN CHROME FINISH $266.95**

LLAMA REVOLVERS

The frame topstrap and the integral ventilated-rib are matte finished to eliminate glare along the sight plane.

The deeply-colored, case-hardened hammer and trigger are target quality. Both the wide spur on the hammer and the wide trigger itself are cleanly serrated for greater ease in cocking and firing.

On the inside, everything is finely fitted and polished, for a double action that's slick and smooth, and a single-action trigger-pull that's light, crisp and clean. Llama gave all Comanches a floating firing pin, for greater safety and dependability...a feature you'll find only on the finest handguns.

Every Llama revolver is hand fitted with generously over-sized target grips of deeply-checkered genuine walnut. As you would expect on a revolver of this quality, the finish is superb...flawlessly polished and richly blued.

LLAMA COMANCHE II IN HIGH POLISHED DEEP BLUE FINISH
38 Special 6" Barrel
$199.95

LLAMA COMANCHE II IN HIGH POLISHED DEEP BLUE FINISH
38 Special 4" Barrel
$199.95

LLAMA "Comanche"® Revolver Specifications

	.44 Magnum	.357 Magnum	.38 Special (Hi-speed or Mid-range)	.22 L.R.
CALIBERS:	.44 Magnum	.357 Magnum	.38 Special (Hi-speed or Mid-range)	.22 L.R.
BARREL LENGTH:	6-inch	4 and 6-inch	4 and 6-inch	6-inch
NUMBER OF SHOTS:	6-shots	6 shots	6 shots	6 shots
FRAME:	Forged high tensile strength steel. Serrated front and back strap.			
ACTION:	Conventional double-action. Floating firing pin.			
TRIGGER:	Wide grooved target trigger. Case-hardened.			
HAMMER:	Wide spur target hammer with serrated gripping surface. Case-hardened.			
SIGHTS:	Square notch rear sight with windage and elevation adjustments; serrated quick-draw front sight on ramp.			
SIGHT RADIUS:	With 4-inch barrel — 5¾"; with 6-inch barrel — 7¾".			
GRIPS:	Oversized target, walnut. Checkered.			
WEIGHT:	3 lbs., 2 ozs.	w/4" bbl. — 2 lbs., 4 ozs. w/6" bbl. — 2 lbs., 7 ozs.	w/4" bbl. — 2 lbs., 1 ozs w/6" bbl. — 2 lbs., 4 ozs.	2 lbs., 8 ozs.
OVER-ALL LENGTH:	11¾"	With 4-inch barrel — 9¼"; with 6-inch barrel — 11".		
FINISH:	High-polished, deep blue. Deluxe models: satin chrome (.357 w/4" and 6" bbl.); Gold Damascened with simulated pearl grips (.357 w/4" bbl.).			

LUGER 22 AUTOMATIC PISTOLS

**LUGER STANDARD MODEL
22 LR 4½" Barrel**

Luger Standard:
STLR-4— 22 L.R., w/4½" barrel
No. 4 Luger Kit, w/STLR-4
(includes Luger, holster, charger)
No. 4 Luger Combo (includes Luger,
holster, charger, & carrying case)

Luger Target:
TLR-4— 22 L.R., w/target sights,
4½" barrel
TLR-5— 22 L.R., w/target sights,
5½" barrel

Luger Accessories:
Extra Luger Magazines
Luger Magazine Charger
Standard Luger Holster
Basket-weave Luger Holster
Carrying Case

**THE TARGET LUGER: With
checkered walnut grips, square
blade front sight and a square
notch fully adjustable
micrometer rear sight with
special quick view aiming
stripes.**

MAUSER PISTOLS

The Mauser Parabellum auto pistol is available in 9mm Luger, and 30 Luger calibers. The 9mm comes in 4" barrel length; the 30 Luger comes in 6" barrel length. All parts of the Mauser Parabellum are forged and precision-machined from special high-carbon steel. The finish is of highly polished blue/black finish, and is complemented with checkered walnut grips. There are two positive safety devices: the positive standard manual thumb safety, plus the positive grip safety. The magazine release, takedown lever, trigger safety and ejectors are finished in the traditional "straw" color. Additional features include an American eagle over the chamber. Price with spare magazine, cleaning brush and combination tool: Imported by Interarms **$625.00**

MAUSER PARABELLUM w/6" BARREL

MODEL HSc AUTOMATIC PISTOL

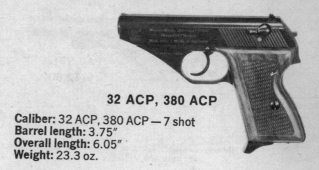

Bright blue finish. Checkered walnut grips. Open, fixed recessed sights. Positive thumb safety, magazine safety, exposed hammer for added safety. Matted, non-glare sight channel. Safe, inertia firing pin. Constructed of high alloy steel. Final Mauser production of this double-action pistol. A limited edition to mark the final chapter in the long history of Mauser craftsmen in Germany. Each pistol is distinctly engraved with the American Eagle and specially numbered to identify each piece as one of a kind, and last of the Mauser HSc line. Consecutive serial numbers available while they last. All are specially boxed in a uniquely imprinted case, with extra magazine, cleaning brush and factory test target. Imported by Interarms. **$250.00**

Standard HSc 32 ACP only **$250.00**
American Eagle Model one of 5000 32 ACP & 380 ACP
$275.00

32 ACP, 380 ACP

Caliber: 32 ACP, 380 ACP — 7 shot
Barrel length: 3.75"
Overall length: 6.05"
Weight: 23.3 oz.

MERRILL

MERRILL PISTOL

This pistol features a full-length, raised, matted and vented rib barrel for the open-sight target and varmint shooter. The barrel is grooved to accommodate a scope without additional drilling or tapping. Cocking indicator visible from rear of gun. Features a precision spring loaded barrel lock.

SPECIFICATIONS:
Caliber: 22 LR; 22 W.M.R., 22 Hornet; 22 Jet; 256 Mag.; 357 Mag., 357/44 B&D, 30 Herrett, 35 Herrett; 44 Mag.; and 30-30 Winchester. Others upon request.
Action: Break-open single-shot
Barrel: 9" semi-octagonal. .400" wide vented rib, matted to prevent glare.
Sights: Front .125" blade rear square notched, adjusted for elevation and windage.

Overall Length: 10½" with 9" barrel; 13½" with 12" barrel.
Trigger: 1 Piece, grooved, well shaped and ¼" wide.
Finish: Polished blue finish.
Stock: Smooth walnut with thumb and heelrest.
Scope Mounts available from manufacturer.

Merrill Pistol 9" (with Micro Sight)	**$269.50**
Merrill Pistol 12" (with Micro Sight)	**289.50**
Extra Barrels 9"	**79.50**
Extra Barrels 12"	**99.50**

FREEDOM ARMS

454 CASULL REVOLVER
Price Not Set

Caliber: 454 Casull or 45 Long Colt
Action: Single action
Cylinder capacity: 5 rounds
Construction: All-stainless steel
Finish: Polished
Barrel length: 7½"
Overall length: 14"
Weight: 3 lbs. 2 oz.
Sights: Blade front, notched rear
Grips: Genuine hardwood
Safety: Hammer down

FA-S 22 LR
$109.50

Caliber	22 Short, Long and Long Rifle—High Speed or Standard Velocity
Action	Single
Cylinder	5 Shot—Fluted Design
Construction	All Stainless Steel
Finish	Semi-Matte
Barrel length	1¾ inches
Overall length	4¾ inches
Weight	4¼ oz.
Sights	Blade Front, Notched Rear
Safety	Notch on Hammer

These mini-revolvers feature a serrated hammer spur, new patented cylinder locking system, a "birds head" grip frame with black ebonite grips, blade front sight, sheathed trigger, luxurious semi-matte finish, and more. Included is also a fully lined presentation case.

FA-L 22 LR
$112.80

Caliber	22 Short, Long or Long Rifle—High Speed or Standard Velocity
Action	Single
Cylinder	5 Shot—Fluted Design
Construction	All Stainless Steel
Finish	Semi-Matte
Barrel length	1 inch
Overall length	4 inches
Weight	4 oz.
Sights	Blade Front, Notched Rear
Safety	Notch on Hammer

STAR AUTOMATIC PISTOLS

STAR PD
45 ACP BLUE $255.00

STAR BKM & BM
9mm LUGER BLUE
9mm LUGER CHROME

Overall Length: 7.17". Barrel Length: 3.9".
Magazine Capacity: 8 rounds.
Model BM Blue   34.06 oz..........$215.00
Model BM Chrome 34.06 oz...........230.00
Model BKM Blue   25.59 oz...........215.00

Chambered for the sledgehammer 45 ACP, the PD has the same capacity— 7 rounds —as the U.S. Government Model, yet it weighs nearly a pound less, as well as being smaller in every dimension. Just a fraction over 7" long, it weighs only 25 ounces.
45 ACP Blue **$255.00**

The Model BM offers all steel construction and the BKM offers a high strength, weight-saving duraluminum frame. An improved thumb safety locks both the slide and hammer with hammer cocked or uncocked; further, an automatic magazine safety locks the sear when the magazine is removed.

ROSSI REVOLVERS

MODEL 31
$105.00

Caliber: 38 Special
Bbl. Length: 4"
Weight: 22 ozs.
Mag. Capacity: 5 rds.
Finish: Nickel
Features: Solidly built to meet the demands of military and police service. Swing out 5-shot cylinder. Target trigger and wide-spur target hammer. Medium weight 4" barrel w/ramp front sight. Checkered wood grips. Crisp double-action and exceptional balance.

MODEL 51 SPORTSMAN
$110.00

Caliber: 22 LR
Bbl. Length: 6"
Finish: Deep blue
Features: Checkered wood grips. Rear sight fully adjustable.

MODELS 68, 69 & 70
$105.00

Caliber: 22 short—mod. 70
  32 S&W—mod. 69
  38 special—mod. 68
Bbl. Length: 3"
Weight: 22 ozs.
Mag. Capacity: 6 rds.—22 L.R. & 32 S&W; 5 rds.—38 spec.
Finish: Nickel
Features: Rugged, all-steel small frame. Smooth double-action pull and combat styling. Ramp front sight and low profile adjustable rear sight. Thumb-latch operated swingout cylinder. Checkered wood grips.

RUGER REVOLVERS

POLICE SERVICE-SIX
357 Mag. & 38 Special
2¾" & 4" barrels

The Ruger Police Service-Six has all of the basic features built into the Ruger Security-Six revolvers. The grip of both the Police Service-Six and the Security-Six has been subtly redesigned to permit rapid, accurate double-action firing without any tendency for the revolver to shift during operation. The new Police Service-Six differs from the Security-Six in that it has fixed (non-adjustable) sights to eliminate any potential for accidental sight misalignment with resulting error in aim, and comes in 2¾" and 4" barrel lengths but not in 6" length. 357 Mag. w/2¾" & 4" barrel, blue finish **$140.00**; 357 Mag. w/4" barrel, stainless steel **$154.00**; 38 Special w/2¾" & 4" barrel, blue finish **$140.00**; 38 Special w/4" barrel, stainless steel **$154.00**;

SECURITY-SIX
357 Mag. 2¾", 4" & 6" barrels

SPECIFICATIONS: Six Shots. Calibers: 357 Magnum caliber (handles 38 Spec.), 38 Special. **Barrel:** 2¾", 4", 6", five-groove-rifling 18¾" right twist. **Weight:** 33½ ounces (4" barrel). **Overall Length:** 9¼" (4" barrel). **Sights:** Ruger adjustable rear (elevation and windage adjustments). Front sight is ⅛" wide, serrated. **Grips:** Checkered walnut, semi-target style. **Finish:** Polished all over and blued. Stainless steel models have brushed satin finish.
357 Mag. w/ 2¾", 4" & 6" barrel, blue finish . . **$177.50**
357 Mag. w/ 2¾", 4" & 6" barrel, stainless steel   **192.00**

RUGER 22 AUTOMATIC PISTOLS

STANDARD MODEL AUTO PISTOL
(With 4¾" & 6" Barrel)

CALIBER: 22 Long Rifle only
BARREL: Length, 4¾" or 6" medium weight, 6 groove rifling, 14" twist.
SPRINGS: Music wire springs.
WEIGHTS: 36 ozs. for 4¾" barrel; 38 ozs. for 6" barrel.
OVERALL LENGTH: 8¾" or 10" depending on barrel length.
SIGHTS: Front fixed; rear adjustable.
MAGAZINE: Detachable, 9-shot capacity.
TRIGGER: Grooved, curved finger surface, ⅜" wide. Two stage pull.
SAFETY: Locks sear and bolt. Cannot be put in safe position unless gun is cocked.
GRIPS: Hard rubber.
RST4—4¾" Barrel, equipped with hard rubber panels **$92.00**
RST6—6" Barrel, equipped with hard rubber panels **92.00**
Checkered walnut panels (available as spare parts only) **10.00**

MARK I
TARGET PISTOL
(With 6⅞" Barrel)

CALIBER: 22 Long Rifle only.
BARREL: Length, 6⅞" heavy weight, burnish reamed.
SPRINGS: Music wire springs.
WEIGHT: 42 ounces.
OVERALL LENGTH: 10⅞".
SIGHTS: Patridge style, front blade, .125" wide, undercut to prevent glare. Micro rear sight, click adjustment for windage and elevation. Sight radius, 9⅜".
MAGAZINE: Detachable, 9-shot capacity.
TRIGGER: Light crisp pull, no backlash.
SAFETY: Locks sear and bolt. Cannot be put in safe position unless gun is cocked.
GRIPS: Hard rubber.
T678—6⅞" Barrel, equipped with hard rubber panels **$118.00**
Checkered walnut grips with left thumb rest (available as spare parts only) **15.00**

MARK I
BULL BARREL TARGET PISTOL
(With 5½" Barrel)

CALIBER: 22 Long Rifle only
BARREL: 5½" heavyweight bull barrel.
OVERALL LENGTH: 9½".
SIGHTS: Patridge style, front blade, .125" wide, undercut Micro rear sight, click adjustments for windage and elevation.
MAGAZINE: Detachable, 9-shot capacity.
TRIGGER: Light crisp pull, no backlash.
GRIPS: Hard rubber.
T-512—5½" Bull Barrel. **$118.00**

RUGER BLACKHAWK

RUGER "BLACKHAWK"
357 Magnum Caliber

CALIBER: 357 Magnum; 38 Special interchangeably.

BARREL: 4⅝" and 6½", 8 groove rifling, 16" twist.

FRAME: Chrome molybdenum steel with bridge reinforcement and rear-sight guard.

SPRINGS: Music wire springs throughout.

WEIGHT: 40 ounces with 4⅝" barrel and 42 ounces with 6½" barrel.

SIGHTS: Patridge style, ramp front matted blade ⅛" wide. Rear sight click adjustable for windage and elevation.

GRIPS: Genuine walnut.

FINISH: Polished and blued; or stainless steel.

BN34—4⅝" Barrel, 357 Magnum caliber ....**$179.75**; Stainless Steel **$195.80**

BN36—6½" Barrel, 357 Magnum caliber ....**179.75**; Stainless Steel **195.80**

BN34-X—4⅝" Barrel ⎫ fitted with 9mm Parabellum extra

BN36-X—6½" Barrel ⎭ cylinder. Walnut panels **$196.90**

9mm Parabellum Cylinder and fitting for 357 Magnum Blackhawks now in service **$34.00**

Note: (Convertible model not available in Stainless Steel)

Also handles 38 Special interchangeably

RUGER "BLACKHAWK"
41 Magnum Caliber

CALIBER: 41 Magnum.

BARREL: 4⅝ and 6½", Buttoned rifling 1 turn in 20" twist.

FRAME: Chrome molybdenum steel with bridge reinforcement and rear-sight guard.

SPRINGS: Music wire springs throughout.

WEIGHT: 38 ounces with 4⅝" barrel and 40 ounces with 6½" barrel.

SIGHTS: Patridge style, ramp front matted blade ⅛ wide. Rear sight click adjustment for windage and elevation.

GRIPS: Genuine walnut.

OVERALL LENGTH: 12⅛" (6½" bbl.); 10¼" (4⅝" bbl.).

FINISH: Polished and blued.

BN-41—4⅝" Barrel **$179.75**

BN-42—6½" Barrel **179.75**

RUGER "SUPER BLACKHAWK"
44 Magnum Caliber

CALIBER: 44 Magnum; 44 Special interchangeably.

BARREL: 6 groove rifling, 20" twist.

FRAME: Chrome molybdenum steel with bridge reinforcement and rear sight guard.

SPRINGS: Music wire springs throughout.

WEIGHT: 48 ounces.

SIGHTS: Patridge style, ramp front matted blade ⅛" wide. Rear sight click adjustable for windage and elevation.

GRIP FRAME: Chrome molybdenum steel enlarged and contoured to minimize recoil effect.

TRIGGER: Wide spur, low contour, sharply serrated for convenient cocking with minimum disturbance of grip.

OVERALL LENGTH: 13⅜".

FINISH: Polished and blued.

S47N—7½" Barrel, with Steel grip frame **$207.00**

S410N—10" Barrel, with Steel grip frame **207.00**

Also handles 44 Special interchangeably

RUGER BLACKHAWK

45 Caliber and 45 / 45 ACP Convertible BLACKHAWK

Blackhawk 45 caliber:
4⅝" & 7½" barrel $179.75
Blackhawk 45 caliber convertible:
(fitted with 45 ACP extra cylinder)
4⅝" & 7½" barrel 196.90

CALIBER 45 & 45/45 ACP
For almost a century the caliber 45 Colt cartridge has been a favorite of hunters and outdoorsmen. At 50 yards the 250 grain factory loaded bullet has a velocity of 820 feet per second and remaining energy of 375 foot pounds. The convertible model comes with an extra, interchangeable cylinder chambered for the popular and readily available 45 Automatic (ACP) cartridge.

SPECIFICATIONS: (45 Colt caliber): **Barrel:** 4⅝" and 7½" lengths, 6 groove rifling, 16" twist. **Weight:** 38 ounces (4⅝"), and 40 ounces (7½") **Overall Length:** 13⅛" (with 7½" barrel). Specifications for **Sights, Grips, Ignition Mechanism, Springs, Screws, Cylinder Frame** the same as for the 44 Magnum Blackhawk. **No. BN-44** (4⅝" bbl.) **No. BN-45** (7½" bbl.)— $179.75 Convertible model—(includes extra cylinder For 45 ACP cartridge) **No. BN-44X** (4⅝"), **No. BN-45X** (7½")— **$196.90**

**"BLACKHAWK" SINGLE-ACTION
(IN 30 CARBINE CALIBER)
$179.75**

(IN 30 CARBINE CALIBER)

This Ruger Blackhawk provides the many owners of M-1 Carbines with a companion revolver. With the 7½" barrel, the 30 carbine caliber cartridge develops an energy of over 600 foot-pounds with a muzzle velocity approaching 1600 fps.

SPECIFICATIONS

Caliber: 30 Carbine.
Barrel Length: 7½" only, 6 groove rifling 20" twist.
Springs: Unbreakable music wire springs used throughout. No leaf springs.
Screws: For security, Nylok® screws are used at all 5 locations that might be affected by recoil.
Weight: 44 ounces.
Overall Length: 13⅛".
Sights: Patridge style, ramp front sight with ⅛" wide blade, matted to eliminate glare. Rear sight adjustable for windage and elevation.
Ignition System: Independent alloy steel firing pin, mounted in frame, transfer-bar.
Frame: Same cylinder frame as 44 mag. Super Blackhawk.
Grips: Genuine walnut.
Finish: Polished, blued and anodized.

RUGER SINGLE-ACTION

"SUPER SINGLE-SIX" CONVERTIBLE
(With two cylinders— 22 L.R. & 22 WMR)

Features: Ruger single action mechanism. Transfer bar ignition. Interlocked gate, transfer-bar, cylinder latch functions. Gate controlled loading. All stressed components hardened chrome-molybdenum steel. Music wire springs throughout. Improved patridge front sight. **Calibers:** 22 Short, Long, Long Rifle and 22 WMR. **Barrel:** 6 groove, 14" twist. **Cylinders:** 2-interchangeable. **Ignition mechanism:** transfer-bar. Independent-alloy steel firing pin mounted in frame.

Sights: Adjustable rear and ramp front blade sight. **Grips:** Genuine walnut. **Finish:** Polished and blued or stainless steel.

NR4-4⅝" Barrel (with interchangeable 22WMR cyl.)	**$141.50**	stainless steel	not available
NR5-5½" Barrel (with interchangeable 22WMR cyl.)	141.50	stainless steel	**$174.50**
NR6-6½" Barrel (with interchangeable 22WMR cyl.)	141.50	stainless steel	174.50
NR9-9½" Barrel (with interchangeable 22WMR cyl.)	141.50	stainless steel	not available

RUGER REVOLVERS

SPEED-SIX

Double Action, Round Butt
(Checkered Walnut Grip Panels)

The **Speed-Six** is a round butt lightened version of the Security-Six, designed for the use by off-duty and plainclothes officers where weight and concealability are essential. The Speed-Six is available on special order with a spurless hammer. The mechanism and construction are identical to the Security-Six. (Models 207 and 208 can be had with a spurless hammer.)

Model 208— 38 Spec. Caliber-Fixed Sights
2¾" barrel $140.00
4" barrel 140.00

Model 207— 357 Mag. Caliber-Fixed Sights
2¾" barrel $140.00
4" barrel 140.00

Stainless Steel
Model 737—357 Mag. Caliber-Fixed Sights
2¾" barrel $154.00
4" barrel 154.00

Model 738—38 Spec. Caliber-Fixed Sights
2¾" barrel $154.00

SMITH & WESSON AUTO PISTOLS

9MM AUTOMATIC PISTOL
DOUBLE ACTION
(MODEL NO. 39)

BLUE
$210.50

NICKEL
$232.00

CALIBER:	9mm Luger (Parabellum)
MAGAZINE CAPACITY:	8 (2-eight round magazines furnished)
BARREL:	4 inches
LENGTH OVER ALL:	7⁷/₁₆ inches
WEIGHT:	26½ ounces without magazine
SIGHTS:	Fixed, ⅛-inch serrated ramp front; Patridge type rear adjustable for windage only
STOCKS:	Checked walnut with S & W monograms
FINISH:	S & W Blue or Nickel

22 CAL. AUTOMATIC PISTOL
(MODEL NO. 41)

BLUE ONLY
(7⅜″ BARREL)
WITH MUZZLE BRAKE
$252.00

CALIBER:	22 Long Rifle
MAGAZINE CAPACITY:	10 rounds
BARREL:	7⅜ inches
LENGTH OVERALL:	With 7⅜″ barrel, 12 inches
SIGHT RADIUS:	With 7⅜″ barrel, 9 5/16 inches
WEIGHT:	With 7⅜″ barrel, 43½ ounces
SIGHTS:	Front: ⅛-inch Patridge undercut. Rear: S & W Micrometer Click Sight, adjustable for windage and elevation
STOCKS:	Checked walnut with modified thumb rest, equally adaptable to right- or left-handed shooters
FINISH:	S & W Bright Blue
TRIGGER:	⅜-inch width, with S & W grooving and an adjustable trigger stop
MUZZLE BRAKE:	Detachable (7⅜″ barrel only)

NOTE: Model 41 is also available in 22 Short caliber for international shooting

22 AUTOMATIC PISTOL (HEAVY BARREL)
(MODEL NO. 41)

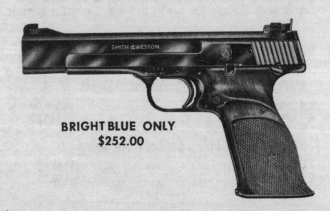

BRIGHT BLUE ONLY
$252.00

CALIBER:	22 Long Rifle
MAGAZINE CAPACITY:	10 rounds
BARREL:	5½, 7⅜ inches
LENGTH OVERALL:	9 inches
SIGHT RADIUS:	8 inches
WEIGHT:	44½ oz
SIGHTS:	Front: ⅛″ Patridge on ramp base. Rear: New S & W Micrometer Click Sight with wide ⅞″ sight slide
STOCKS:	Checked walnut with modified thumb rest, equally adaptable to right- or left-handed shooters
FINISH:	S & W Bright Blue
TRIGGER:	⅜-inch width, with S & W grooving and an adjustable trigger stop

SMITH & WESSON AUTO PISTOLS & REVOLVERS

38 MASTER
(MODEL NO. 52)

BRIGHT BLUE ONLY
$411.50

CALIBER:	38 S & W Special for Mid Range Wad Cutter only
MAGAZINE CAPACITY:	5 rounds (2-five round magazines furnished)
BARREL:	5 inches
LENGTH OVERALL:	8⅝ inches
SIGHT RADIUS:	6¹⁵⁄₁₆ inches
WEIGHT:	41 oz. with empty magazine
SIGHTS:	Front: ⅛" Partridge on ramp base. Rear: New S & W Micrometer Click Sight with wide ⅞" sight slide
STOCKS:	Checked walnut with S & W monograms
FINISH:	S & W Bright Blue with sandblast stippling around sighting area to break up light reflection
TRIGGER:	⅜-inch width with S & W grooving and an adjustable trigger stop

9MM AUTOMATIC PISTOL DOUBLE ACTION
(MODEL NO. 59)

BLUE
$252.00

NICKEL
$275.00

CALIBER:	9mm Luger (Parabellum)
MAGAZINE CAPACITY:	2-14 round magazines furnished
BARREL:	4 inches
LENGTH OVERALL:	7⁷⁄₁₆ inches
WEIGHT:	27 oz. without magazine
SIGHTS:	Front: ⅛-inch serrated ramp. Rear: Square notch with Micrometer Click adjustment for windage only.
STOCKS:	Checked high impact molded nylon
FINISH:	S & W Blue or Nickel

38 MILITARY & POLICE
(MODEL NO. 10)

BLUE
$125.00

NICKEL
$137.00

CALIBER:	38 S & W Special
NUMBER OF SHOTS:	6
BARREL:	2, 4, 5, 6 inches
LENGTH OVERALL:	With 4-inch barrel, 9¼ inches
WEIGHT:	With 4-inch barrel, 30½ oz
SIGHTS:	Front: Fixed, ⅛-inch serrated ramp. Rear: Square notch
STOCKS:	Checked walnut Service with S & W monograms, round or square butt
FINISH:	S & W Blue or Nickel

SMITH & WESSON REVOLVERS

38 MILITARY & POLICE (HEAVY BARREL)
(MODEL NO. 10)

CALIBER: 38 S & W Special.
NUMBER OF SHOTS: 6.
BARREL: 4 inches.
LENGTH OVERALL: 9¼ inches.
WEIGHT: 34 oz.
SIGHTS: Front: ⅛-inch serrated ramp. Rear: Square notch
STOCKS: Checked walnut Service with S & W monograms, square butt.
FINISH: S & W Blue or Nickel.

BLUE
$125.50

NICKEL
$137.00

38 MILITARY & POLICE (AIRWEIGHT)
(MODEL NO. 12)

CALIBER: 38 S & W Special.
NUMBER OF SHOTS: 6.
BARREL: 2 or 4 inches.
LENGTH OVERALL: With 2-inch barrel and round butt, 6⅞ inches.
WEIGHT: With 2-inch barrel and round butt, 18 oz.
SIGHTS: Front: Fixed, ⅛-inch serrated ramp. Rear: Square notch.
STOCKS: Checked walnut Service with S & W monograms, round or square butt.
FINISH: S & W Blue or Nickel.

BLUE
$166.00

NICKEL
$188.50

(Illus. with round butt)

357 MILITARY & POLICE (HEAVY BARREL)
(MODEL NO. 13)

CALIBER: 357 Magnum and 38 S&W Special.
ROUNDS: 6-shot cylinder capacity.
BARREL: 4 inches.
LENGTH OVERALL: 9¼ inches.
WEIGHT: 34 oz.
SIGHTS: Front: ⅛-inch serrated ramp. Rear: Square notch.
STOCKS: Checked walnut Service with S&W monograms, square butt.
FINISH: S&W Blue or Nickel.

BLUE
$139.00

NICKEL
$152.00

K-38 MASTERPIECE
(MODEL NO. 14)

CALIBER: 38 S & W Special.
NUMBER OF SHOTS: 6.
BARREL: 6, 8⅜ inches.
LENGTH OVERALL: With 6-inch barrel, 11⅛ inches.
WEIGHT LOADED: With 6-inch barrel, 38½ oz.; 8⅜-inch, 42½ oz.
SIGHTS: Front: ⅛-inch plain Patridge. Rear: S & W Micrometer Click Sight, adjustable for windage and elevation.
STOCKS: Checked walnut Service with S & W monograms.
FINISH: S & W Blue.

BLUE ONLY
6" **$195.50**
8⅜" 205.00

SMITH & WESSON REVOLVERS

K-38 MASTERPIECE SINGLE ACTION
(MODEL NO. 14)

CALIBER:	38 S & W Special
NUMBER OF SHOTS:	6
BARREL:	6
LENGTH OVERALL:	11 1/8 inches.
WEIGHT LOADED:	38 1/2 oz.
SIGHTS:	Front: 1/8-inch plain Patridge. Rear: S & W Micrometer Click Sight, adjustable for windage and elevation.
STOCKS:	Checked walnut Service with S & W monograms.
HAMMER:	Checked target type.
TRIGGER:	Grooved target type.
FINISH:	S & W Blue.

BLUE ONLY
6" $244.50

.38 COMBAT MASTERPIECE
WITH 4-INCH BARREL
(MODEL NO. 15)

CALIBER:	38 S & W Special
NUMBER OF SHOTS:	6
BARREL:	2 & 4 inches.
LENGTH OVERALL:	9 1/8 inches
WEIGHT LOADED:	with 4-inch barrel, 34 oz.
SIGHTS:	Front: 1/8-inch Baughman Quick Draw on plain ramp. Rear: S & W Micrometer Click Sight, adjustable for windage and elevation
STOCKS:	Checked walnut Service with S & W monograms
FINISH:	S & W Blue or Nickel

BLUE
$149.50
NICKEL
$161.00

K-22 MASTERPIECE
(MODEL NO. 17)

CALIBER:	22 Long Rifle
NUMBER OF SHOTS:	6.
BARREL:	6, 8 3/8 inches.
LENGTH OVERALL:	With 6-inch barrel, 11 1/8 inches.
WEIGHT LOADED:	With 6-inch barrel, 38 1/2 oz.; 8 3/8-inch, 42 1/2 oz.
SIGHTS:	Front: 1/8-inch plain Patridge. Rear: S & W Micrometer Click Sight, adjustable for windage and elevation.
STOCKS:	Checked walnut Service with S & W monograms.
FINISH:	S & W Blue.

BLUE ONLY
6" $194.00
8 3/8" 204.00

SMITH & WESSON REVOLVERS

22 COMBAT MASTERPIECE
WITH 4-INCH BARREL
(MODEL NO. 18)

BLUE ONLY
$181.00

CALIBER:	22 Long Rifle
NUMBER OF SHOTS:	6
BARREL:	4 inches
LENGTH OVERALL:	9⅛ inches
WEIGHT LOADED:	36½ oz.
SIGHTS:	Front: ⅛-inch Baughman Quick Draw on plain ramp. Rear: S & W Micrometer Click Sight, adjustable for windage and elevation
STOCKS:	Checked walnut Service with S & W monograms
FINISH:	S & W Blue

"357" COMBAT MAGNUM
(MODEL NO. 19)

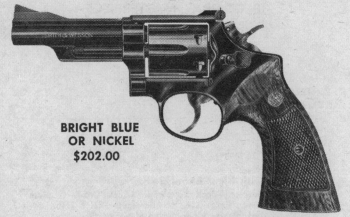

BRIGHT BLUE OR NICKEL
$202.00

CALIBER:	357 Magnum (Actual bullet dia. 38 S & W Spec.)
NUMBER OF SHOTS:	6
BARREL:	2½, 4, 6 inches
LENGTH OVERALL:	9½ inches with 4" barrel; 7½ inches with 2½" barrel; 11½ inches with 6" barrel
WEIGHT:	35 oz. (2½" model weighs 31 oz.)
SIGHTS:	Front: ⅛" Baughman Quick Draw on 2½" or 4" barrel, ⅛" Patridge on 6" barrel. Rear: S & W Micrometer Click Sight, adjustable for windage and elevation
STOCKS:	Checked Goncalo Alves Target with S & W monograms. (2½" barrel model comes with round butt; Service type stocks)
FINISH:	S & W Bright Blue or Nickel

1955 45 TARGET
(MODEL No. 25)

BLUE ONLY
$331.50

CALIBER:	45 A. C. P.
NUMBER OF SHOTS:	6
BARREL:	6½ inches
LENGTH OVERALL:	11⅞ inches
WEIGHT:	45 oz.
SIGHTS:	Front: ⅛-inch plain Patridge. Rear: S & W Micrometer Click Sight, adjustable for windage and elevation
STOCKS:	Checked walnut Target with S & W monograms
HAMMER:	Checked target type
TRIGGER:	Grooved target type
FINISH:	S & W Blue

SMITH & WESSON REVOLVERS

"357" MAGNUM

(MODEL NO. 27)

CALIBER:	357 Magnum (Actual bullet dia. 38 S & W Spec.)
NUMBER OF SHOTS:	6
BARREL:	3½, 5, 6, 8⅜ inches
LENGTH OVERALL:	With 6-inch barrel, 11¼ inches.
WEIGHT:	With 3½-inch barrel, 41 oz.; 5-inch, 42½ oz.; 6-inch, 44 oz.; 8⅜-inch, 47 oz.
SIGHTS:	Front: Choice of any S & W target sight. Rear: S & W Micrometer Click Sight, adjustable for windage and elevation.
STOCKS:	Checked walnut Service with S & W monograms.
FRAME:	Finely checked top strap and barrel rib.
FINISH:	S & W Bright Blue or Nickel.

**BRIGHT BLUE
OR NICKEL
With Presentation box**
3½", 5", 6" $331.50
8⅜" 342.00
Without Presentation box
3½", 5", 6" $303.00
8⅜" 314.00

HIGHWAY PATROLMAN

(MODEL NO. 28)

CALIBER:	357 Magnum (Actual bullet dia. 38 S & W Spec.)
NUMBER OF SHOTS:	6
BARREL:	4, 6 inches
LENGTH OVERALL:	With 6-inch barrel, 11¼ inches.
WEIGHT:	With 4-inch barrel, 41¾ oz.; 6-inch, 44 oz.
SIGHTS:	Front: ⅛-inch Baughman Quick Draw on plain ramp. Rear: S & W Micrometer Click Sight, adjustable for windage and elevation.
STOCKS:	Checked walnut Service with S & W monograms (Walnut Target stocks at additional cost).
FINISH:	S & W Satin Blue with sandblast stippling or barrel rib and frame edging.

**BLUE ONLY
$190.50
with Target stocks (Illus.)
$205.50**

44 MAGNUM

(MODEL NO. 29)

CALIBER:	44 Magnum
NUMBER OF SHOTS:	6
BARREL:	4, 6½, 8⅜ inches
LENGTH OVERALL:	With 6½-inch barrel, 11⅞ inches.
WEIGHT:	With 4-inch barrel, 43 oz.; 6½-inch, 47 oz.; 8⅜-inch, 51½ oz.
SIGHTS:	Front: ⅛-inch S & W Red Ramp. Rear: S & W Micrometer Click Sight adjustable for windage and elevation. White Outline notch.
STOCKS:	Special oversize Target type of checked Goncalo Alves, with S & W monograms.
HAMMER:	Checked target type.
TRIGGER:	Grooved target type.
FINISH:	S & W Bright Blue or Nickel.

**BRIGHT BLUE
OR NICKEL
4", 6½" $331.50
8⅜" 342.00**

SMITH & WESSON REVOLVERS

41 MAGNUM
(MODEL NO. 57)

CALIBER:	.41 Magnum.
NUMBER OF SHOTS:	6.
BARREL:	4, 6, 8⅜ inches.
LENGTH OVERALL:	With 6-inch barrel, 11⅜ inches.
WEIGHT:	With 6-inch barrel, 48 oz.
SIGHTS:	Front: ⅛-inch S & W Red Ramp. Rear: S & W Micrometer Click Sight adjustable for windage and elevation. White Outline notch.
STOCKS:	Special oversize Target type of checked Goncalo Alves, with S & W monograms.
HAMMER:	Checked target type.
TRIGGER:	Grooved target type.
FINISH:	S & W Bright Blue or Nickel.

BRIGHT BLUE OR NICKEL
4", 6" $331.50
8⅜" 342.00

1953 22/32 KIT GUN
(MODEL NO. 34)

CALIBER:	22 Long Rifle
NUMBER OF SHOTS:	6
BARREL:	2, 4 inches
LENGTH OVERALL:	With 4-inch barrel and round butt, 8 inches
WEIGHT:	With 4-inch barrel and round butt, 22¼ oz.
SIGHTS:	Front: ¹⁄₁₀-inch serrated ramp. Rear: S & W Micrometer Click Sight, adjustable for windage and elevation.
STOCKS:	Checked walnut Service with S & W monograms, round or square butt
FINISH:	S & W Blue or Nickel

BLUE $159.00

NICKEL $172.50

STAINLESS STEEL MODELS

1977 22/32 KIT GUN
(MODEL NO. 63)

SPECIFICATIONS: Caliber: 22 Long Rifle. **Number of shots:** 6. **Barrel Length:** 4 inches. **Weight:** 24½ oz. (empty). **Sights:** ⅛-inch red ramp front sight. Rear sight is the black stainless steel S&W Micrometer Click square-notch, adjustable for windage and elevation. **Stocks:** Square butt. **Finish:** Satin.

STAINLESS STEEL $187.00

38 CHIEFS SPECIAL STAINLESS
MODEL NO. 60

SPECIFICATIONS: Caliber: 38 S&W Special. **Number of shots:** 5. **Barrel:** 2 Inch. **Length Overall:** 6½ inches. **Weight:** 19 oz. **Sights:** Front Fixed, 1/10-inch serrated ramp. Rear: Square notch. **Stocks:** Checked walnut Service with S&W monograms. **Finish:** Satin

Stainless Steel $181.50

SMITH & WESSON REVOLVERS

38 MILITARY & POLICE STAINLESS
MODEL NO. 64

SPECIFICATIONS: Caliber: 38 S&W Special. **Number of Shots:** 6. **Barrel:** 4 Inch heavy barrel, square butt. 2-inch regular barrel, round butt. **Length Overall:** With 4-inch barrel, 9¼ inches 2-inch barrel, 6⅞ inches. **Weight:** With 4-inch barrel, 34 ounces. **Sights:** Fixed, ⅛-inch serrated ramp front; square notch rear. **Stocks:** Checked walnut Service with S&W monograms. **Finish:** Satin. **Ammunition—** 38 S&W Special, 38 S&W Special Mid Range.

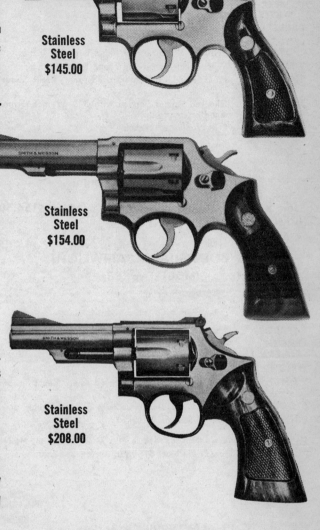

Stainless Steel
$145.00

357 Military & Police Stainless
Heavy Barrel
MODEL NO. 65

SPECIFICATIONS: Caliber: 357 Magnum and 38 S&W Special. **Rounds:** 6-shot cylinder capacity. **Barrel:** 4-inch heavy barrel. **Length Overall:** With 4-inch barrel, 9¼ inches. **Weight:** With 4-inch barrel, 34 oz. **Sights:** Fixed, ⅛-inch serrated ramp front; square notch rear. **Stocks:** Checked walnut Service with S&W monograms, square butt. **Finish:** Satin.

Stainless Steel
$154.00

357 COMBAT MAGNUM REVOLVER
MODEL NO. 66

SPECIFICATIONS: Caliber: 357 Magnum (Actual bullet diam. 38 S&W Spec.). **Number of shots:** 6. **Barrel:** 6 or 4 Inch with square butt; 2½ inches with round butt. **Length Overall:** 9½" with 4" barrel; 7½ inches with 2½-inch barrel. **Weight:** 35 ounces with 4" barrel. **Sights:** Front: ⅛" Rear: S&W Red Ramp on ramp base, S&W Micrometer Click Sight, adjustable for windage and elevation. **Stocks:** Checked Goncalo Alves target with square butt with S&W monograms. **Finish:** Satin. **Trigger:** S&W grooving with an adjustable trigger stop. **Ammunition:** 357 S&W Magnum, 38 S&W Special Hi-Speed, 38 S&W Special, 38 S&W Special Mid Range.

Stainless Steel
$208.00

K-38 COMBAT MASTERPIECE REVOLVER
MODEL NO. 67

SPECIFICATIONS: Caliber: 38 S&W Special. **Number of shots:** 6. **Barrel:** 4 Inch. **Length Overall:** 9⅛" with 4" barrell. **Weight Loaded:** 34 oz. with 4" barrel. **Sights:** Front: ⅛" Rear: S&W Red Ramp on ramp base, S&W Micrometer Click Sights, adjustable for windage and elevation. **Stocks:** Checked walnut Service with S&W Monograms square butt. **Finish:** Satin. **Trigger:** S&W grooving with an adjustable trigger stop. **Ammunition:** 38 S&W Special, 38 S&W Special Mid Range.

Stainless Steel
$187.50

SMITH & WESSON REVOLVERS

38 CHIEFS SPECIAL
(MODEL No. 36)

CALIBER:	38 S & W Special
NUMBER OF SHOTS:	5.
BARREL:	2 or 3 inches.
LENGTH OVERALL:	With 2-inch barrel and round butt, 6½ inches.
WEIGHT:	With 2-inch barrel and round butt, 19 oz.
SIGHTS:	Front: Fixed, ¹/₁₀-inch serrated ramp. Rear: Square notch.
STOCKS:	Checked walnut Service with S & W monograms, round or square butt.
FINISH:	S & W Blue or Nickel.

BLUE
$147.50

NICKEL
$160.00

MODEL NO. 37
38 Chief's Special Airweight

Same as Model 36 except: weight 14 oz. **Blue $154.50**
Nickel $175.00

38 BODYGUARD "AIRWEIGHT"
(MODEL No. 38)

CALIBER:	38 S & W Special.
NUMBER OF SHOTS:	5.
BARREL:	2 inches.
LENGTH OVERALL:	6⅜ inches.
WEIGHT:	14 ½ oz.
SIGHTS:	Front: Fixed, ¹/₁₀-inch serrated ramp. Rear: Square notch.
STOCKS:	Checked walnut Service with S & W monograms,
FINISH:	S & W Blue or Nickel.

NOTE: The Bodyguard also supplied in all-steel construction, Model 49, weighing 20½ oz. Price: Blue, **$150.00**; Nickel, **$162.50**.

BLUE
$171.00

NICKEL
$193.00

K-22 MASTERPIECE M.R.F.
(MODEL NO. 48)

CALIBER:	22 Magnum Rim Fire.
NUMBER OF SHOTS:	6.
BARREL:	4, 6, 8⅜ inches.
LENGTH OVERALL:	With 6-inch barrel, 11⅛ inches.
WEIGHT:	With 6-inch barrel, 39 oz.
SIGHTS:	Front: ⅛-inch plain Patridge. Rear: S & W Micrometer Click Sight, adjustable for windage and elevation.
STOCKS:	Checked walnut Service with S & W monograms.
FINISH:	S & W Blue.

BLUE ONLY
4", 6" **$209.00**
8⅜"   218.50

Auxiliary cylinder available in 22 LR.

SMITH & WESSON REVOLVERS

32 REGULATION POLICE
(MODEL NO. 31)

CALIBER:	32 S & W Long.
NUMBER OF SHOTS:	6.
BARREL:	2, 3, or 4 inches.
LENGTH OVERALL:	With 4-inch barrel, 8½ inches.
WEIGHT:	With 4-inch barrel, 18¾ oz.
SIGHTS:	Front: Fixed, 1/10-inch serrated ramp. Rear: Square notch.
STOCKS:	Checked walnut Service with S & W monograms.
FINISH:	S & W Blue or Nickel.

**BLUE
$156.00
NICKEL
$170.00**

SAKO PISTOL

SAKO 22-32 CONVERSION PISTOL/OLYMPIC MATCH PISTOL

The Sako pistol is available either in one caliber, or with one or two additional conversion sets, complete in a plastic carrying case with space for ammunition and other equipment. Additional conversion sets can be obtained later with guarantee of positive fitting into the frame.

Three different weapons by only changing the conversion set and magazine.

MATCH PISTOL
Caliber: 22 L.R.
Sight radius: 220mm
Weight: 1250 grams
Trigger: fully adjustable
5-shot magazine

RAPID-FIRE PISTOL
Caliber: 22 Short
Sight radius: 225mm
Weight: 1215 grams
Trigger: fully adjustable
Barrel length: 110mm
5-shot magazine

CENTERFIRE PISTOL
Caliber: 32 S&W Long
Functions with Wadcutter bullets only
Sight radius: 220mm
Weight: 1320 grams
Trigger: fully adjustable
Barrel length: 150mm
5-shot magazine

STERLING AUTOMATIC PISTOLS

The 45 double-action 9-shot automatic pistol was designed by Sterling Arms to the specifications of law enforcement officers, military personnel, and competition shooters. It was designed by experts for experts.

- **SIZE:** 7½" x 5"
- **WEIGHT:** 36 oz.
- **MAGAZINE CAPACITY:** 8 shots
- **CALIBER:** 45ACP
- **GRIPS:** Handcrafted walnut
- **FINISH:** Blue
- **PRICE:** $269.95

**Sterling 45 Auto
Model 450
Double Action**

STERLING AUTOMATIC PISTOLS

STERLING
25 AUTO
MODEL 300

STERLING ARMS introduces the *dependable* MODEL 300, a personal sized automatic, constructed of ordnance steel, featuring indestructable Cycolac grips.

- **SIZE:** 4½" x 3½"
- **WEIGHT:** 13 oz.
- **CAPACITY:** 6 shots
- **CALIBER:** 25 A.C.P.
- **CONSTRUCTION:** All steel
- **GRIPS:** Cycolac—Black
- **FINISH:** Blue or Stainless Steel

Model 300S: Same as Model 300 except has stainless steel construction and finish. **$108.95**

BLUE $89.95

STERLING
380 AUTO
MODEL 400 MK II
DOUBLE ACTION

BLUE $199.95

Your *security* is assured with the MODEL 400 featuring both double and single action, combined with the powerful 380 cartridge.

- **SIZE:** 6½" x 4¾"'
- **WEIGHT:** 26 oz.
- **CAPACITY:** 7 shots
- **CALIBER:** 380
- **CONSTRUCTION:** All ordnance steel
- **GRIPS:** Walnut hand checkered
- **FINISH:** Blue

Model 400S: Same as Model 400 except has stainless steel construction and finish. **$249.95**

STERLING 22 AUTO
MODEL 302

Performance and standards of the potent little MODEL 302, chambered for the 22 LR cartridge, provides companionship above the ordinary.

- **SIZE:** 4½" x 3½"
- **WEIGHT:** 13 oz.
- **CAPACITY:** 6 shots
- **CALIBER:** 22 Long Rifle
- **CONSTRUCTION:** All steel
- **GRIPS:** Cycolac—Black
- **FINISH:** Blue

Model 302S: Same as Model 302 except has stainless steel construction and finish **$108.95**

BLUE $89.95

TAURUS REVOLVERS

MODEL 84
Target Grade
Price not set

SPECIFICATIONS:
Caliber: 38 Special
Capacity: 6 shot
Barrel length(s): 4″
Weight: 34 oz.
Sights: 2/8″ on ramp front; micrometer click adjustable rear for windage and elevation.
Action: Double
Stock: Checkered walnut
Finish: Blue and nickel

MODEL 86
Target Master
Price not set

SPECIFICATIONS:
Caliber: 38 Special
Capacity: 6 shot
Barrel length(s): 6″
Weight: 35 oz.
Sights: Patridge-type front; micrometer click adjustable rear for windage and elevation
Stock: Checkered-walnut target
Finish: Bright royal blue

Model 96 Target Scout: Same as Model 86 Target Master except 22 L.R. caliber. Blue.

MODEL 83
Price not set

SPECIFICATIONS:
Caliber: 38 Special
Action: Double
Number of Shots: 6
Barrel Length: 4″ only
Weight: 34½ oz.
Sights: 2/8″ on Ramp, Front. Rear Micrometer Click Adjustable for Windage and Elevation
Finish: Blue or Nickel
Stocks: Checkered Walnut Target

TAURUS REVOLVERS

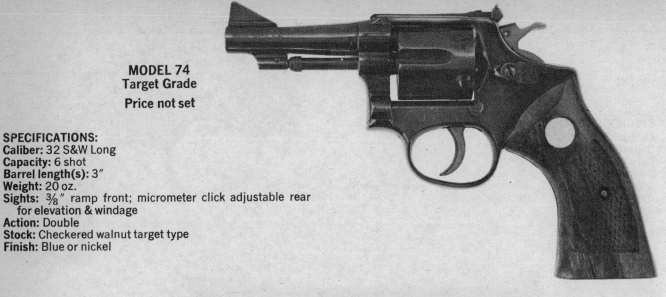

MODEL 74
Target Grade
Price not set

SPECIFICATIONS:
Caliber: 32 S&W Long
Capacity: 6 shot
Barrel length(s): 3″
Weight: 20 oz.
Sights: 3/8″ ramp front; micrometer click adjustable rear for elevation & windage
Action: Double
Stock: Checkered walnut target type
Finish: Blue or nickel

MODEL 80
Price not set

SPECIFICATIONS:
Caliber: 38 Special
Capacity: 6 shot
Barrel length(s): 3″, 4″
Weight: 33 oz.
Action: Double
Stock: Checkered walnut
Finish: Blue or nickel

MODEL 82
Heavy Barrel
Price not set

SPECIFICATIONS:
Caliber: 38 Special
Capacity: 6 shot
Barrel length(s): 3″, 4″
Weight: 33 oz.
Action: Double
Stock: Checkered walnut
Finish: Blue and nickel

TAURUS REVOLVERS

MODEL 65
Price not set

SPECIFICATIONS:
Caliber: 357 Magnum
Capacity: 6 shot
Barrel Length: 4"
Weight: 34 oz.
Sights: Rear—square notch, front ramp
Action: Double
Stock: Checkered walnut target
Finish: Royal blue

MODEL 66
Price not set

SPECIFICATIONS:
Caliber: 357 Magnum
Capacity: 6 shot
Barrel Length: 3", 4", 6"
Weight: 35 oz.
Sights: Serrated ramp, front. Rear Micrometer Click adjustable for windage and elevation
Action: Double
Stock: Checkered walnut magna grips (3"); checkered walnut target grips (4" & 6")
Finish: Royal blue

VIRGINIAN REVOLVER

THE VIRGINIAN DRAGOON REVOLVER

Precision-machined from rugged 4140 steel throughout. Rich, traditional color case-treated frame, lock-fitted, spring-loaded floating firing pin. Durable, heavy-duty coiled main spring. Standard model features classic frontier field sights. Fully adjustable rear sight and ramp-type patridge front blade w/white dot for fast targeting in low-light-level conditions are optional. Manufactured by Interarms Industries, Inc. Calibers: 44 Magnum; 45 Colt; 357 Magnum. Barrel Lengths: 6", 7½", 8⅜"—44 Magnum; 5", 6", 7½"—45 Colt & 357 Magnum. Overall Length: 5"—10⅞"; 6"—11⅞"; 7½"—13⅜"; 8⅜"—14¾". Weight: 5"—47 oz.; 6"—48 oz.: 7½"—50 oz.; 8⅜"—52 oz. Price: Adjustable Sights **$229.00**
Buntline Model, 44 Mag. 357 Mag., 12" BBL. **319.00**

WALTHER PISTOLS

DOUBLE ACTION AUTOMATIC PISTOLS

The Walther double action system combines the principles of the double action revolver with the advantages of the modern pistol . . . without the disadvantages inherent in either design. Published reports from independent testing laboratories have cited Walther superiority in rugged durability, positive performance and reliability. Special built-in safety design and a simple disassembly procedure combine to make these one of the safest and most easily maintained handguns.

Models PP and PPK/S differ only in the overall length of the barrel and slide. Both models offer the same features, including compact form, light weight, easy handling and absolute safety—both models can be carried with a loaded chamber and closed hammer, but ready to fire either single or double action. Both models in calibers 32 ACP and 380 ACP are provided with a live round indicator pin to signal a loaded chamber. An automatic internal safety blocks the hammer to prevent accidental striking of the firing pin, except with a deliberate pull of the trigger. Sights are provided with white markings for high visibility in poor light.

Rich Walther blue/black finish is standard and each pistol is complete with extra magazine with finger rest extension. Available in calibers 22 L.R., 32 ACP and 380 ACP.

The Walther P-38 is a double action, locked breech, semi-automatic pistol with an external hammer. Its compact form, light weight and easy handling is combined with the superb performance of the 9mm Luger Parabellum cartridge.

The P-38 is equipped with both a manual and automatic safety, which allows it to be safely carried while the chamber is loaded.

Available in calibers 9mm Luger Parabellum, 30 Luger and 22 L.R. with either a rugged non-reflective black finish or in a polished blued finish.

Overall length: model PP (6.7"); PPK/S (6.1"); P-38 (8½") P-38IV (8"); P-38K (6⅜"). Height: models PP, PPK/S (4.28"); P-38 (5.39") P-38IV (5.39); P-38K (5.39). Weight: model PP (23.5 oz.); PPK/S (23 oz.); P-38 (28 oz.) P-38IV (29 oz.); P-38K (26 oz.).

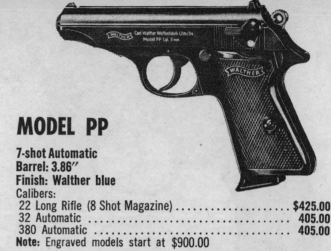

MODEL PP

7-shot Automatic
Barrel: 3.86"
Finish: Walther blue
Calibers:
22 Long Rifle (8 Shot Magazine) $425.00
32 Automatic 405.00
380 Automatic 405.00
Note: Engraved models start at $900.00

MODEL PPK/S

7-shot Automatic
Barrel: 3.27"
Finish: Walther blue
Calibers:

Model PPK/S American, 380ACP $235.00
.22 Long Rifle (8 Shot Magazine) 415.00
32 Automatic 395.00
380 Automatic 395.00
Note: Engraved models start at $900.00

MODEL P-38

8-shot Automatic
Barrel: 4¹⁵/₁₆" (9mm & 30 Luger)
5¹/₁₆" (.22 L.R.)
Finish: matte
Calibers:
22 Long Rifle $690.00
30 Luger 600.00
9mm Luger 600.00
Note: Engraved models start at $1025.00

P-38IV AUTO-PISTOL

8-shot Automatic
Barrel: 4½"
Finish: Matte
Caliber:
9mm Luger $650.00
Same as the P-38K except for longer barrel, O.A. length and weight. Sights are non-adjustable. Imported by Interarms.

MODEL P-38K

8-shot Automatic
Barrel: 2¾"
Finish: matte

Calibers:
9mm Luger $650.00
Same as Model P-38 except for slide mounted front sight and rear sight adjustable for windage.

WALTHER PISTOLS

WALTHER GSP MATCH PISTOL

Calibers: 22 L.R. & 32 S&W wadcutter

WALTHER OSP

22 Short only
$990.00

Models:

GSP—22 Long Rifle w/carrying case	$ 990.00
GSP-C—32 S&W wadcutter w/carrying case	1180.00
22 caliber L.R. conversion unit for GSP-C	650.00
22 Short Cal. Conversion Unit for GSP-C	690.00

Walther match pistols are built to conform to ISU and NRA match target pistol regulations. The model GSP, caliber 22 L. R. is available with either 2.2 lb. (1000 gm) or 3.0 lb. (1360 gm) trigger, and comes with 4½" barrel and special hand-fitting design walnut stock. Sights consist of fixed front, and adjustable rear sight. The

GSP-C 32 S&W wadcutter center fire pistol is factory tested with a 3.0 lb. trigger. The 22 L. R. conversion unit for the model GSP-C consists of an interchangeable barrel, a slide assembly and two magazines. The 22 caliber model weighs 44.8 oz; 32 S&W weighs 49.4 oz. Overall length is 11.8". Magazine capacity is 5-shot.

DAN WESSON REVOLVERS

FEATURE INTERCHANGEABLE BARREL CAPABILITY WITHIN CALIBER

The Dan Wesson 38 special and 357 Magnum revolver features interchangeable barrel capability. It may be had with a choice of 2½", 4", 6" & 8" barrel lengths, and comes equipped with Sacramento-, Combat- or Target-type walnut grips. Extra interchangeable barrel assemblies (includes barrel shroud) are available. To change barrel one simply removes the barrel nut with wrench (supplied), slip off barrel shroud and unscrew barrel from frame. Screw new barrel to clearance gauge (supplied), slip corresponding

shroud over barrel, screw on barrel nut and tighten with wrench. Sight adjustment remains constant when changing barrel lengths.

Shown are two handguns designed and developed by Wesson Arms. Each gun can accommodate three different sizes of interchangeable barrels in both 357 Magnum and 38 caliber size. Engraved designs can also be provided and alternate grips in three styles are available—each handcarved in genuine walnut.

Model 8— 38 Special   Model 14— 357 Magnum   (with fixed sights)

SPECIFICATIONS:

Caliber: 357 Magnum (Standard)
38 Special (Optional)

Ammunition: 357 Magnum, 38 Special, Hi-Speed, 38 Special Mid-Range.

Number of Shots: 6 (Double Action & Single Action)

Barrel Lengths: 2½", 4", 6" & 8" (Optional & Interchangeable)

Weight: 2½", 30 oz.; 4", 34 oz.; 6", 38 oz.; 8", 42 oz.
Dimensions: 4"—9¼" x 5⅜"

Sights: Front — ⅛" Serrated Blade
Rear — Integral with frame
Trigger: Wide Tang (⅜") with adjustable overtravel stop.

Hammer: Wide Spur (⅜") with short double action travel.

Plate Screws: Socket head high torque.

Grips: Walnut, interchangeable and optional.

Finish: Satin Blue

Model 8 (38 Special) & Model 14 (357 Magnum):	
2½", 4" & 5" barrel	$176.65
8" barrel	182.75

DAN WESSON REVOLVERS

SPECIFICATIONS:

Caliber: 357 Magnum (Standard)
38 Special (Optional)

Ammunition: 357 Magnum, 38 Special, Hi-Speed, 38 Special Mid-Range.

Number of Shots: 6 (Double Action & Single Action)

Barrel Lengths: 2½", 4", 6", 8", 10", 12", 15" (Optional & Interchangeable)

Weight: 2½", 32 oz.; 4", 36 oz.; 6", 40 oz.; 8", 44 oz.

Dimensions: 4" — 9¼" x 5½"

Sights: Front — ⅛" Serrated Interchangeable Blade
Rear — Adjustable for Windage & Elevation Click graduated — 1 click — ⅜" at 25 Yds.

Trigger: Wide Tang (⅜") with adjustable overtravel stop.

Hammer: Wide Spur (⅜") with short double action travel.

Plate Screws: Socket head high torque

Grips: Walnut, interchangeable and optional.

Finish: Brite Blue

Model 9— 38 Special
Model 15— 357 Magnum
(with adjustable rear sights)

Model 9 (38 Special) & Model 15 (357 Magnum):	
2", 4" & 6" barrel	$227.45
8" barrel	235.35

NAVY ARMS PISTOL

SPECIFICATIONS:

CALIBER: 9mm parabellum.

CAPACITY: 15 rounds; optional magazines with 20, 25, 35 and 40 rounds.

BARREL LENGTH: 5".

WEIGHT: 42 oz.

FINISH: Stainless steel. Standard version with matte finish. Deluxe version with polished sides.

The Mamba is a double action as well as a single action and can be carried in the cocked and locked position. Designed to be durable, this pistol also features an adjustable trigger stop and a self-cleaning rifling system.

MAMBA 9MM PARABELLUM
$295.00

Rifles

BROWNING RIFLES

Browning 78
SINGLE SHOT RIFLE

BROWNING 78, SINGLE SHOT RIFLE — A superbly accurate rifle, closely resembling the famous Model 1885 High Wall designed by John M. Browning in 1878 (his first invention). Classic falling block action with automatic ejector and exposed hammer. Choose either an Octagon or a Round barrel. Either is a good, husky barrel without iron sights . . . a nice, clean taper the full 26 inches. The 45-70 Govt. caliber is fitted only with an octagon bull barrel 24" long. Furnished with specially designed scope mounts and rings.

22/250, 6mm, 243 Win., 25/06, 30/06, 7mm Rem. Mag. and 45-70 Govt. calibers **$399.95**

**BROWNING 78
45-70 GOVT.**

BROWNING 22 L.R. AUTOMATIC RIFLES

Grade I 22 Long Rifle

Barrels on all models drilled and tapped to accommodate barrel mount base.

Grade III 22 Long Rifle

Grade I Long Rifle	$199.95
Grade II Long Rifle	289.95
Grade III Long Rifle	699.95
Grade I Short	199.95

The Browning 22 automatic rifle is unique in that the barrel and stock separate to a length of 19 inches, by depressing a small latch on the underside of the receiver and giving the barrel section a quarter turn. This facility provides a compact unit for carrying or storage. All moving parts are contained in a solid steel receiver which is completely closed on the top and both sides, and features downward ejection. It is a non-mechanically locked semi-automatic rifle in which the recoil is used to activate the breechblock in such a way that, when the bullet has left the barrel and no harmful gas remains in it, the mechanism ejects the empty shell, cocks the firing pin, and introduces a fresh cartridge into the barrel. The location of the magazine with the loading port on the right face of the stock simplifies loading. Fitted with a new folding leaf rear sight, it folds flush to the barrel when a scope is mounted, and is adjustable for elevation. The front sight is a 1/16 inch gold bead on a slender base.

SPECIFICATIONS

Caliber: 22 Long Rifle in Grades I, II, III; 22 Short in Grade I only. **Action:** Semi-automatic, double extractors with bottom ejection. **Barrel length:** 22 LR, 19¼"; 22 Short, 22". **Magazine:** Tubular with loading port in stock. **Capacity:** 22 LR, 11 rounds; 22 Short, 16 rounds. **Sights:** Gold bead front. Adjustable, folding leaf rear. **Length of pull:** 13¾". **Overall length:** Long Rifle, 37". Short, 40". **Weight:** Long Rifle, 4 lbs. 12 oz.; Short, 4 lbs. 15 oz. **Grade II**—(not illus.) Chrome plated receiver in satin finish with small game scenes engraved on all surfaces. Select walnut and forearm, hand checkered in diamond design.

BROWNING RIFLES

MODEL BL-22 LEVER ACTION RIFLE
GRADE I $169.95

MODEL BL-22 LEVER ACTION RIFLE
GRADE II $194.95

BL-22 SPECIFICATIONS

ACTION — Short throw lever action. Lever travels through an arc of only 33 degrees and carries the trigger with it, preventing finger pinch between lever and trigger on the upward swing. The lever cycle ejects the fired shell, cocks the hammer, and feeds a fresh round into the chamber.

MAGAZINE — Rifle is designed to handle 22 caliber ammunition *in any combination* from tubular magazine. Magazine capacity is 15 Long Rifles, 17 Longs, and 22 Shorts. The positive magazine latch opens and closes easily from any position.

SAFETY — A unique disconnect system prevents firing until the lever and breech are fully closed and pressure is released from and reapplied to the trigger. An inertia firing pin and an exposed hammer with a half-cock position are other safety features.

RECEIVER — Forged and milled steel. Grooved. All parts are machine finished and hand fitted.

TRIGGER — Clean and crisp without creep. Average pull 5 pounds. Trigger gold-plated on Grade II model.

STOCK AND FOREARM — Forearm and straight grip butt stock are shaped from select, polished walnut. Hand checkered on Grade II model. Stock dimensions:

Length of Pull......................13½"
Drop at Comb......................1⅝"
Drop at Heel........................2¼"

SIGHTS — Precision, adjustable folding leaf rear sight. Raised bead front sight.

SCOPES — Grooved receiver will accept the Browning 22 riflescope (Model 1217) and two-piece ring mount (Model 9417) as well as most other groove or tip-off type mounts or receiver sights.

ENGRAVING — Grade II receiver and trigger guard are hand-engraved with tasteful scroll designs.

BARREL — Recessed muzzle. Barrel length: 20 inches.

OVERALL LENGTH — 36¾ inches.

WEIGHT — 5 pounds.

BLR RIFLE
243 Winchester, 308 Winchester & 358 Winchester
$299.95

BLR SPECIFICATIONS

CALIBERS: 243 Win., 308 Win. and 358 Win.

APPROXIMATE WEIGHT: 6 pounds, 15 ounces.

OVERALL LENGTH: 39¾ inches.

ACTION: Lever action with rotating head, multiple lug breech bolt with recessed bolt face. Side ejection.

BARREL: Individually machined from forged, heat treated chrome-moly steel. Length: 20 inches. Crowned muzzle. Rifling: 243 Win.—one turn in 10 inches. 308 and 358 Win.—one turn in 12 inches.

MAGAZINE: Detachable, 4-round capacity.

TRIGGER: Wide, grooved finger piece. Short crisp pull of 4½ pounds. Travels with lever.

RECEIVER: Non-glare top. Drilled and tapped to accept most top scope mounts. Forged and milled steel. All parts are machine-finished, and hand-fitted. Surface deeply polished.

SIGHTS: Low profile, square notch, screw adjustable rear sight. Gold bead on a hooded raised ramp front sight. Sight radius: 17¾ inches.

SAFETY: Exposed, 3-position hammer. Trigger disconnect system. Inertia firing pin.

STOCK AND FOREARM: Select walnut with tough oil finish and sure-grip checkering, contoured for use with either open sights or scope. Straight grip stock. Deluxe recoil pad installed.

Length of pull ....13¾ inches
Drop at comb ....1¾ inches
Drop at heel ....2⅜ inches

ACCESSORIES: Extra magazines are available as well as sling swivel attachment for forearm bolt and butt-stock eyelet for sling mounting.. $15.00

BROWNING AUTOMATIC RIFLES

Browning Arms Company has added a center fire (semi) Rifle to their line of sporting arms. Called simply the Browning Automatic Rifle, it is gas operated, and has the strong, precision locking principle of a bolt action rifle. It weighs less than 7⅜ pounds and is offered in 30-06 Sprg., 308 Win., 270 Win., 243 Win., 7mm Rem. Mag. and 300 Win. Mag. calibers.

The Browning Automatic is a magazine-fed rifle with a new "trap door" design, box type magazine that is attached to the hinged floor plate. The magazine may be loaded while attached to the gun or is easily detached for conventional loading.

The receiver is machined from a solid bar of steel and is completely free of exposed screws, pins or holes, except provisions for scope mountings. A multiple head breech bolt locks directly into the barrel, engaging 7 sturdy lugs.

The stock and forearm are of select French walnut, sharply checkered and hand finished. Sights consist of: a gold bead on a hooded ramp front sight, and a folding leaf-type rear sight adjustable for windage and elevation.

GRADE I—Quiet Browning quality. The receiver is deeply blued and left smooth as silk. Stock and forearm are carved from dense-grained French walnut, sharply checkered on the pistol grip and forearm for a good steady hold.

30/06 Sprg., .270 Win., .308 Win. & 243 Win. **$429.95**
7mm Rem. Mag. & 300 Win. Mag. **479.95**

GRADE III—Features beautiful scrollwork.
30/06 Sprg., 270 Win., 308 Win. & 243 Win. **$819.95**
7mm Rem. Mag. & 300 Win. Mag. **869.95**

GRADE IV—The ultimate big-game rifle. The Grade IV's receiver is grayed steel with intricate hand-engraved game scenes. Standard calibers have running deer on one side, running antelope on the other. Magnum calibers have moose on one side, elk on the other. The floor plate and trigger guard are covered with intricate hand engraving too.

The stock on this rifle is the very finest, highly figured French walnut. Flawless hand-checkering covers the pistol grip and forearm, bordered by ornate hand carving. As a final touch, the trigger is gold-plated.

30/06 Sprg., .270 Win., 308 Win. & 243 Win. ... **$1345.00**
7mm Rem. Mag. & 300 Win. Mag. **1395.00**

Extra Magazines
Grade I **$15.75**
Grade III **23.75**
Grade IV **23.75**

BAR-22 22 Caliber Automatic Rifle
grade I **$199.95**

BPR-22 22 Caliber Pump Rimfire Rifle
grade I 22 Long Rifle **$199.95**
grade I 22 Magnum **209.95**

BAR-22 SPECIFICATIONS

MODELS: 22 Long Rifle, Grade I.

ACTION: Self-loading and ejecting. Shoots as rapidly as trigger is pulled. Side ejection.

BARREL: Recessed muzzle — 20¼″.

OVERALL LENGTH: 38¼″.

MAGAZINE: Tubular. Latch closes from any position.

MAGAZINE CAPACITY: 22 Long Rifle — 15.

STOCK: French walnut. Pistol grip and forearm cut checkering.

STOCK DIMENSIONS: Length of pull 13¾″. Drop at comb 1½″. Drop at heel 2¼″.

SAFETY: Cross-bolt safety on rear of trigger guard.

SIGHTS: Front: Gold bead. Rear: Folding leaf with calibrated adjustments.

SIGHT RADIUS: 16″.

APPROXIMATE WEIGHT: 6 lbs. 4 oz.

TRIGGER: Black anodized. Average pull 5 lbs.

RECOMMENDED SCOPE & MOUNTS: 4x 22 rifle scope. Receiver grooved to accept scope mount base.

BPR-22 SPECIFICATIONS

MODELS: BPR-22, Grade I only. BPR-22 Magnum, Grade I only.

ACTION: Short, positive pump stroke. Finger must be released and re-applied to trigger at end of stroke. Side ejection.

BARREL: Recessed muzzle, both models: 20¼″.

OVERALL LENGTH: Both Models: 38¼″.

MAGAZINE: Tubular. Latch closes from any position.

MAGAZINE CAPACITY: BPR-22—22 Long Rifle: 15. BPR-22 Magnum—22 Magnum: 11.

STOCK: French walnut. Pistol grip and forearm—cut checkering.

STOCK DIMENSIONS: Length of pull 13¾″. Drop at comb 1½″. Drop at heel 2¼″.

SAFETY: Cross bolt safety on rear of trigger guard.

SIGHTS: Front: Gold bead. Rear: Folding leaf with calibrated adjustments.

SIGHT RADIUS: 16″

APPROXIMATE WEIGHT: 6 lbs. 4 oz.

TRIGGER: Black anodized. Average pull 5 lbs.

RECOMMENDED SCOPE AND MOUNTS: 4x 22 Riflescope. Receiver grooved to accept scope mount base.

BROWNING RIFLES

BBR BOLT ACTION RIFLE
Calibers — 25-06 Rem., 270 Win., 30-06 Sprg., 7mm Rem. Mag., 300 Win. Mag.
$354.95

SPECIFICATIONS:

ACTION: Short throw bolt of 60-degrees. The large diameter bolt and fluted surface reduce wobble and friction. The rotary bolt head has 9 engaging locking lugs and a recessed bolt face. Plunger-type ejector.
MAGAZINE: Detachable. Depress the magazine latch and the hinged floorplate swings down. The magazine can be removed from the floorplate for reloading or safety reasons.
TRIGGER: Adjustable within the average range of 3 to 6 pounds. Also grooved to provide sure finger control.
STOCK AND FOREARM: Anti-warp inlays of structural aluminum ⅛" thick and 8" long in the barrel channel.

Stock is select grade American walnut cut to the lines of a Monte Carlo sporter with a full pistol grip and high cheek piece. Stock dimensions:
Length of Pull .... 13⅜"
Drop at Comb .... 1⅝"
Drop at Heel .... 2⅛"
SCOPES: Closed. Clean tapered barrel. Receiver is drilled and tapped for a scope mount.
BARREL: Hammer forged rifling where a precision machined mandrel is inserted into the bore. The mandrel is a reproduction of the rifling in reverse. As hammer forces are applied to the exterior of the barrel, the barrel is actually molded around the mandrel to produce flawless rifling and to guarantee a straight bore. 24" long.
OVERALL LENGTH: 44½" **WEIGHT:** 8 pounds.

BROWNING 92
44 Rem. Magnum Grade I $249.95

SPECIFICATIONS:

ACTION: Lever operated with double verticle locks. Exposed 3 position hammer with half cock position. Top ejection.
RECEIVER: Forged and milled from high strength steel.
BARRELS: Machined from forged, heat-treated billets of steel. Chambered and rifled for 44 Rem. Magnum caliber. Rifling twist 1 turn in 38". Barrel length 20".
SIGHTS: Classic cloverleaf rear with notched elevation ramp. Steel post front. Sight radius 16⅝".

TRIGGER: Gold plated. Trigger pull approximately 5½ lbs.
MAGAZINE: Tubular. Loading port in right side of receiver. Magazine capacity 11 rounds.
STOCK AND FOREARM: Seasoned French walnut with high gloss finish. Straight grip stock and classic forearm style. Steel modified crescent butt plate.
      Length of pull—12¾"
      Drop at comb—2"
      Drop at heel—2⅞"
OVERALL LENGTH: 37½"
APPROXIMATE WEIGHT: 5½ lbs.
HAND ENGRAVED RECEIVER: Hand engraved scrollwork on both receiver sides.

CHARTER AR-7 EXPLORER RIFLE

MODEL AR-7 EXPLORER RIFLE
(22 Long Rifle Caliber)
$89.00

The AR-7 survival weapon is a semiautomatic 22 Long Rifle caliber with a 16" barrel and is fitted with a plastic stock which floats if accidentally dropped in water. For transport, the AR-7 compacts into its own stock, measuring 16½" overall. The rear sight is a hooded peep with the aperature adjustable for elevation changes. Windage may be accomplished by moving the front sight back and forth.

SPECIFICATIONS:

CALIBER: 22 Long Rifle. **ACTION:** Semi-automatic. **LOAD:** Detachable box, magazine fed. **SIGHTS:** Square blade front, adjusting rear peep. **CAPACITY:** 8 rounds. **BARREL:** High test alloy with rifled steel liner. **STOCK:** Full pistol grip, recessed to carry barrel and action. **WEIGHT:** 2¾ pounds. **OVERALL LENGTH:** 34½". **LENGTH WHEN STOWED:** 16½".

COLT HIGH POWER RIFLES

COLT SAUER SPORTING RIFLE
standard calibers **$719.95**
magnum calibers **739.95**

SPECIFICATIONS:

Caliber: 25-06, 270, 30-06, 7mm Rem. Mag., 300 Win. Mag., 300 Weatherby Mag.
Capacity: 3 round with detachable magazines
Barrel length(s): 24"
Weight: Standard 8 lb.; mag. 8 lbs. 10 oz.
Overall length: 43¾"
Sights: Drilled and tapped for scope mounts

Action: Bolt action
Safety: Tang-type safety that mechanically locks the sear
Stock: American walnut, cast-off Monte Carlo design with cheek piece; fore-end tip and pistol-grip cap are rosewood with white line spacers, hand checkering and black recoil pad
Features: Unique barrel/receiver union, non-rotating bolt with 3 internal articulating locking lugs.

COLT SAUER SHORT ACTION
$719.95

Caliber:	22-250, 243 and 308 (7.62mm NATO)
Barrel Length:	24"
Overall Length:	43¾"
Barrel Type:	Krupp Special Steel, hammer forged
Stock:	American walnut, Monte Carlo cheek piece with rosewood fore-end tip and pistol grip cap
Weight (empty):	7 lbs. 8 oz.
Safety:	Tang
Sights:	Drilled and tapped for scope mounts

Magazine Capacity: 3 rounds in detachable magazine
Finish: Colt Blue with polyurethane

FEATURES:

Now the Colt Sauer Rifle is available in 22-250, 243 and 308. Features the same revolutionary non-rotating bolt with three large locking lugs. American walnut stock with high-gloss finish, 18-line-per-inch checkering, rosewood forend tip and grip cap, black recoil pad. Cocking indicator, loaded chamber indicator, and Safety-on bolt opening capability.

COLT SAUER GRAND AFRICAN
$839.95

SPECIFICATIONS:
Caliber: 458 Win. Mag. **Capacity:** 3 rounds with detachable magazines. **Barrel length(s):** 24" round tapered. **Weight:** 10 lbs. without sights. **Overall length:** 44½". **Sights:** Hooded ramp style front; fully adjustable rear. **Action:** Bolt action. **Safety:** Tang type that mechanically locks the sear.

Stock: Solid African bubinga wood, cast-off Monte Carlo design with cheek piece, contrasting rosewood, forend tip and pistol-grip cap with white line spacers, and checkering on the forend and pistol grip. **Features:** Unique barrel/receiver union, non-rotating bolt with 3 internal articulating locking lugs.

COLT RIFLES

COLT SAUER GRAND ALASKAN
$759.95

SPECIFICATIONS:

Caliber: 375 H&H. **Capacity:** 3 rounds with detachable magazine. **Barrel length:** 24″. **Weight:** 8 lbs. 10 oz. **Overall length:** 43¾″. **Sights:** Drilled and tapped for scope mounts.

Safety: Tang. **Stock:** American walnut, Monte Carlo cheek piece with rosewood fore-end tip and pistol grip cap and black recoil pad.

COLT SAUER DRILLING
THREE-BARREL SHOTGUN-RIFLE
$2295.00

The Colt Sauer Drilling is a three-barrel combination side-by-side 12-gauge shotgun available in .30-06 Springfield or .243 calibers. This addition to the Colt Sauer line is 41¾-inches overall. Its 25-inch barrels are mounted on a selected, oil-finish, American walnut stock. The barrels are made from fine steel, finished in traditional Colt Blue, as are other metal parts, with an engraved rib that reduces glare and a brass-bead front sight. The left shotgun barrel is bored with modified choke and the right barrel with full choke. The barrel has four-groove rifling with a right hand twist. A thumb activated device on the tang raises or lowers the rear sight for firing of the rifle barrel. A system of double triggers fires the two shotgun and one rifle barrels. The safety is located on the left side of the stock for convenient thumb operation. When the safety button is moved, a red dot indicates "fire" position. Checkering on the stock at forend and pistol grip is 16-lines per inch. Each Colt Sauer Drilling is individually engraved at the receiver with game scenes. The recoil pad and pistol grip cap are black composition.

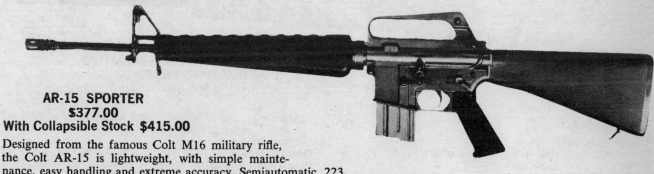

AR-15 SPORTER
$377.00
With Collapsible Stock $415.00

Designed from the famous Colt M16 military rifle, the Colt AR-15 is lightweight, with simple maintenance, easy handling and extreme accuracy. Semiautomatic 223 (5.56 mm) with 5-round magazine capacity. Front sight post adjustable for elevation. Quick flip rear sight assembly with short-range and long-range tangs, adjustable for windage. Weight: 7½ lbs. Overall Length: 39″
Barrel Length: 20″; with collapsible stock 16″

GOLDEN EAGLE RIFLES

MODEL 7000 BIG BORE RIFLE

All model 7000 rifles are drilled and tapped for scope mounts and also feature a shotgun tang-type safety. Plus the bolt can be opened while the safety is engaged. Hinged floor plate, five hefty locking lugs. The barrel is hammer-forged and the stock is checkered hand-bedded American walnut.

Grade I Big Bore Rifle **$449.00**
(all standard & mag. calibers)
Grade I Big Bore Rifle
(African calibers furnished with sights) **485.00**

GOLDEN EAGLE RIFLES

MODEL 7000 SPECIFICATIONS

RIFLE GRADE I SPECIFICATIONS

Caliber	Mag. Capacity	Barrel Length	Twist RH 1 Turn In	Overall Length	Length of Trigger Pull	Approximate Weight
22/250	4	24"-26"	14"	43½-45½	13½"	7 lbs.
243	4	24"-26"	10"	43½-45½	13½"	7 lbs. 12 oz.
25/06	4	24"-26"	10"	43½-45½	13½"	7 lbs. 12 oz.
270 WIN	4	24"-26"	10"	43½-45½	13½"	7 lbs. 12 oz.
270 WBY MAG	3	24"-26"	12"	43½-45½	13½"	7 lbs. 12 oz.
7mm REM MAG	3	24"-26"	9"	43½-45½	13½"	7 lbs. 12 oz.
30/06	4	24"-26"	10"	43½-45½	13½"	7 lbs. 12 oz.
300 WIN MAG	3	24"-26"	10"	43½-45½	13½"	7 lbs. 12 oz.
300 WBY MAG	3	24"-26"	12"	43½-45½	13½"	7 lbs. 12 oz.
338 WIN MAG	3	26"	10"	45½	13½"	8 lbs. 12 oz.
375 H & H	3	26"	12"	45½	13½"	8 lbs. 12 oz.
458 WIN MAG	3	26"	14"	45¾	13¾"	10 lbs. 8 oz.

H&R COMMEMORATIVE CARBINES

MODEL 174
LITTLE BIG HORN COMMEMORATIVE
SPRINGFIELD CARBINE
$300.00

Sights: Tang mounted aperture sight adjustable for windage and elevation. Blade front sight.
Weight: 7 lbs. 8 oz.
Overall Length: 41"
Metal Finish: Barrel—Blue-Black
Action—Color case hardened

SPECIFICATIONS
Caliber: 45-70 GOVT.
Stock: American Walnut with metal grip adapter
Action: Trap door, single shot
Barrel Length: 22"

MODEL 171 STD., 171 DEL.
SPRINGFIELD CAVALRY CARBINE
standard $275.00
deluxe   300.00

Weight: 7 lbs.
Overall Length: 41"
Metal Finish: Blue-Black

NOTE: Deluxe version, as illustrated, available at extra cost. Standard model has open rear sight adjustable for windage and elevation, and is finished in blue-black without engraving.

SPECIFICATIONS
Caliber: 45-70 GOVT.
Stock: American Walnut with saddle ring and bridle
Action: Trap door, single shot
Barrel Length: 22"
Sights: Barrel mounted leaf sight adjustable for elevation. Blade front sight.

H&R COMMEMORATIVE CARBINES

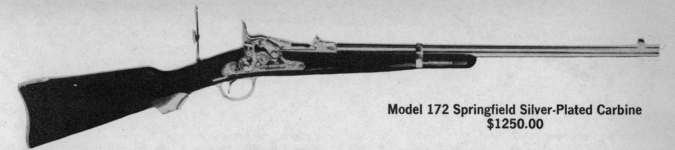

Model 172 Springfield Silver-Plated Carbine
$1250.00

SPECIFICATIONS :
Caliber: 45-70 Govt.
Barrel Length: 22".
Capacity: Single shot.

Overall Length: 41".
Sights: Tang mounted aperture sight. Blade front sight.
Weight: 7¼ lbs.
Finish: Silver plated barrel. Stock American walnut.

H&R RIFLES

H&R RIFLE
MODELS 750, 865

Models 750 and 865

A pair of economically priced 22 caliber rifles including single shot Model 750 with "fluid feed" platform for quick, easy loading; double extractors for dependable ejection; "Bulls-Eye" broach rifling for accuracy. Model 865 repeater has double extractors; 5-shot magazine; cocking indicator; side thumb safety.

22 CAL. RIFLES

Model 750 single shot **$59.50**
Model 865 5-shot clip **69.50**

MODEL 750

Caliber: 22 long rifle; standard and high velocity cartridge.
Capacity: Single shot.
Stock: Walnut finished American hardwood. Hard rubber butt plate, white liner.
Action: Self-cocking bolt action.
Safety: Side thumb lever.
Barrel Length: 22" tapered.
Sights: Blade front. Open rear sight with elevator. Grooved for tip-off scope mounts.
Weight: 5 lbs.
Overall Length: 39".

MODEL 865

Caliber: 22 long rifle; standard and high velocity cartridge.
Capacity: 5-round magazine.
Stock: Walnut finished American hardwood. Hard rubber butt plate, white liner.
Action: Self-cocking bolt action.
Safety: Side thumb lever.
Barrel Length: 22" tapered.
Sights: Blade front. Open rear sight with elevator. Grooved for tip-off scope mounts.
Weight: 5 lbs.
Overall Length: 39".

MODEL 058 COMBO GUN
30-30 Win. and 20 gauge
22 Hornet and 20 gauge

$99.50

SPECIFICATIONS:

Gauge: 20 gauge modified choke shotgun
Barrel length(s): 26" mod. Rifle 22"
Weight: 5¼ lbs., 6 lbs. with rifle barrel
Overall length: Shotgun barrel, 41½"; rifle barrel, 37½"
Sights: Front bead on shotgun barrel; blade front, folding leaf rear on rifle barrel
Action: Single shot
Stock: Walnut–finished hardwood with hard-rubber butt plate
Finish: Blue-black; color cased frame
Accessories: 30-30 Win. or 22 Hornet 22" barrels

H&R RIFLES

MODEL 155
44 Rem. Mag., 45-70 Govt.
$99.50

SPECIFICATIONS:

Caliber: 44 Rem. Mag., 45-70 Govt.
Barrel length(s): 44 Rem. Mag., 24"; 45-70 Govt., 24", 28"
Weight: 44 Rem. Mag., 7 lbs.; 45-70 Govt., 7 lbs., 7½ lbs.
Overall length: 44 Rem. Mag., 39"; 45-70 Govt., 39", 43"
Sights: Blade front with ramp; folding leaf rear

Action: Single shot
Stock: Walnut–finished hardwood with hard-rubber butt plate
Finish: Blue-black barrel with color-cased frame
Accessories: Brass cleaning rod

MODEL 173
SPRINGFIELD OFFICER'S MODEL
$315.00

SPECIFICATIONS:

Caliber: 45-70 Govt.
Barrel length(s): 26"
Weight: 8 lbs.
Overall length: 45"

Sights: Blade front; tang mounted aperature rear
Action: Trap door, single shot
Stock: American walnut with hand checkering
Finish: Blue-black; color cased receiver

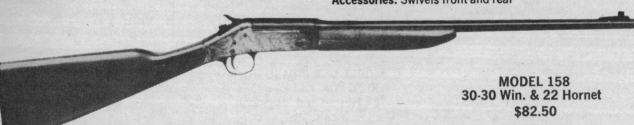

MODEL 157
30-30 Win., 22 Hornet
22 WMRF $89.50

SPECIFICATIONS:

Caliber: 30-30 Win., 22 Hornet, 22 WMRF
Barrel length(s): 22"
Weight: 6¼ lbs.
Overall length: 37"

Sights: Blade front; folding leaf rear; drilled and tapped for scope bases
Action: Single shot
Stock: Walnut-finished hardwood with hard-rubber butt plate
Finish: Blue-black barrel with color-cased frame
Accessories: Swivels front and rear

MODEL 158
30-30 Win. & 22 Hornet
$82.50

SPECIFICATIONS:

Caliber: 30-30 Win., 22 Hornet
Barrel length(s): 22"
Weight: 6 lbs.
Overall length: 37"

Sights: Blade front with ramp; folding leaf rear; drilled and tapped for scope bases
Action: Single shot
Stock: Walnut finished hardwood with a hard-rubber butt plate
Finish: Blue-black barrel with color case-hardened frame

H&R CENTERFIRE RIFLES

MODEL 300
$375.00

Caliber: 22-250 Rem., 243 Win., 25-06 Rem., 270 Win., 30-06, 308 Win., 7mm Rem. Mag., 300 Win. Mag.

Capacity: 7mm Rem., Mag. and 300 Win. Mag. calibers have 3 round magazine. All others have 5 round magazine.

Stock: One piece genuine American walnut stock with roll-over cheek piece, and pistol grip. Hand checkered, contrasting wood on forearm tip and pistol grip cap. Rifle recoil pad.

Action: Mauser type bolt action with hinged floor plate and adjustable trigger.

Barrel Length: 22" tapered.

Weight: 7¾ lbs.

Sights: Fully adjustable rear sight drilled and tapped for scope mounts and receiver sight. Gold bead front sight grooved for hood.

Overall Length: 42½"

Safety: Sliding safety.

Also Available: Model 301 carbine with full length Mannlicher style stock and 18 inch barrel. Available in most of the above calibers. $450.00

H&R RIFLES

MODEL 700
22 WMR
$159.50

Model 700 Deluxe 22 caliber WMRF 22 inch barrel   250.00

SPECIFICATIONS:

Caliber: 22 WMRF
Capacity: 5-round clip
Barrel length(s): 22"
Weight: 6½ lbs.

Overall length: 43¼"
Sights: Blade front; folding leaf rear; drilled and tapped for scope bases
Stock: Walnut stock
Finish: Blue-black barrel and receiver

HECKLER & KOCH RIFLES

SEMI-AUTOMATIC HUNTING RIFLES
MODEL 770

Caliber: 6.5mmx57, 7mmx57, 243, 308
Weight: 7.7 lbs. (cal. 308)
Barrel: Hammer forged, standard or polygonal profile.
Overall Length: 42.5"
Magazine: 4 rounds
Sights: Telescopic sight
Trigger: Single stage
Action: Delayed Roller locked

Stock: European walnut with Monte Carlo cheek rest
Model 770 (308 cal. w/scope and 3-round magazine) **$405.00**
Model 630 same as **Model 770** except:
Caliber: 22 Hornet, 221, 222, 223
Weight: 7.26 lbs. (cal. 223)
Overall Length: 39.7"
Model 630 ....**Price not set**

HECKLER & KOCH RIFLES

SEMI-AUTOMATIC VARMINT RIFLES
MODEL HK 300

The Model HK 300 features a European walnut checkered stock. All metal parts are finished in a high luster custom blue. The receiver is fitted with special bases for a HK 05 quick snap-on clamp mount with 1" rings that will fit all standard scopes. The positive locking action of the HK 05 provides for instant scope mounting with no change in zero, even after hundreds of repetitions. The rifle has a V-notch rear sight, adjustable for windage, and a front sight adjustable for elevation. Scope mounts are available as an additional accessory.

Caliber: 22 Winchester Magnum.
Weight: 5.7 lbs.

Barrel: Hammer forged, polygonal profile.
Overall length: 39.4".
Magazine: Box type, 5 and 15 rounds capacity.
Sights: V-notch rear, adjustable for windage; post front, adjustable for elevation.
Trigger: Single stage, 3½ lb. pull.
Action: Straight blow-back inertia bolt.
Stock: Top-grade European walnut, Monte Carlo style with cheek rest, checkered pistol grip and forearm.
Accessories: HK 05 clamp mount with 1" rings to fit most U.S. made telescopic sights............................**$260.00**

H&K SEMI-AUTOMATIC RIFLES

HK93 SEMI-AUTOMATIC RIFLES
223 Caliber

HK93 SPECIFICATIONS:	A-2	A-3
Length of rifle:	37.0 in.	29.94 in.
Length of barrel:	16.13 in.	16.13 in.
Sight radius:	18.89 in.	18.89 in.
Weight of rifle without magazine:	7.60 lbs.	8.42 lbs.

Weight of magazine filled with 5 cartridges:	4.93 oz.	4.93 oz.
Sight adjustments:	100, 200, 300, 400 meters	
Telescopic sight:	As specified by buyer	
Telescopic sight mount:	HK special mount	

Model HK93 (w/20-round magazine & sling) **$425.00**
With retractable metal stock **495.00**

HK91 SEMI-AUTOMATIC RIFLES
308 Caliber

HK91 SPECIFICATIONS:	A-2	A-3
Length of rifle:	40.25 in.	32.94 in.
Length of barrel:	19.0 in.	19.0 in.
Sight radius:	22.52 in.	22.52 in.
Weight of rifle without magazine:	9.37 lbs.	10.56 lbs.

Weight of magazine with 5 cartridges:	10.08 oz.	10.08 oz.
Sight adjustments:	100, 200, 300, 400 meters	
Telescopic sight:	As specified by buyer	
Telescopic sight mount:	HK special mount	

Model HK91 (w/20-round magazine & sling) **$428.00**
With retractable metal stock **515.00**

IVER JOHNSON RIFLES

**PLAINFIELD MODEL M-1 CARBINES
PM 30P
PRICE: $181.00**

Telescoping American walnut stock permits packing in back pack or saddle bag for campers or hunters. Adjustable sights. Available in 30 caliber. **Barrel:** 18″. **Weight:** 5½ lbs. Blue finish.

**PM 30G & PM 30S
PRICE: $149.50**
New military and military sporter version of PM 30P.

**PP 30 SUPER ENFORCER
PRICE: $193.00**
The Enforcer is a pistol based on a carbine action. The stock is made of American walnut. The Enforcer can accommodate a 30, 15, or 5 round magazine. Available in 30 caliber. **Barrel:** 9½″. Adjustable sights.

**PM 5.7 SPITFIRE
PRICE: $181.00**

The Spitfire is a high velocity, small-caliber plinking rifle. **Caliber:** 5.7. **Barrel:** 18″. Readily uses 224 bullets.

BEEMAN RIFLES

BEEMAN/FWB 2000
$800.00

22-caliber long rifle. Micrometer match aperture sights. Fore-sight with interchangeable inserts. Meets ISU standard rifle specifications. Short lock time. Precision match trigger adjustable for weight, release point, finger length, lateral position, etc. Barrel length: 22" and 26¼". Length: 39" and 43¾". Weight: 9⅛ lbs. and 9¾ lbs.

KASSNAR RIFLES

MODEL M-16 SEMI-AUTOMATIC
$99.95

SPECIFICATIONS:
Caliber: 22 L.R.
Barrel Length(s): 16½"
Weight: 6 lbs. 12 oz.

Sights: Ramp front; adjustable peep rear sight
Stock: Black painted mahogany
Features: Sling and sling swivels included

MODEL M-14S BOLT ACTION
$79.95

SPECIFICATIONS:
Caliber: 22 L.R.
Barrel: Tapered sporter weight barrel
Weight: 6 lbs.
Sights: Hooded ramp front sight; open rear sporter-type
Action: Bolt

Safety: Positive sliding thumb safety
Stock: Hand-checkered nato wood, with Monte Carlo comb. Receiver grooved for tip-off scope mount.

MODEL M-15S BOLT ACTION

$94.95

SPECIFICATIONS:
Caliber: 22 mag.
Barrel: Tapered sporter-weight barrel
Weight: 6½ lbs.
Sights: Open sight sporter-type

Action: Bolt
Safety: Positive sliding thumb safety
Stock: Nato wood, with Monte Carlo comb. Receiver grooved for tip-off scope mount.

KASSNAR RIFLES

MODEL M-20S SEMI-AUTOMATIC
$79.95

Weight: 5 lbs., 14 oz.
Sights: Open sights sporter-type
Safety: Positive sliding thumb safety
Stock: Nato wood, receiver grooved for tip-off scope mount. Hand checkered.

SPECIFICATIONS:
Caliber: 22 L.R.
Capacity: 15-round clip
Barrel Length(s): 19½"

PARKER-HALE RIFLES

PARKER-HALE SUPER

SPECIFICATIONS:
Caliber: 22/250, 243, 6mm, 25/06, 270, 30/06, 308, 7mm Mag., 300 Mag.
Capacity: 5 shot, magnum 4 shot
Barrel Length(s): 24"
Overall Length: 45"
Sights: Hooded bead front sight; folding adjustable rear sight
Action: Bolt action. Receiver drilled and tapped for standard scope mounts
Safety: Slide thumb safety, locks trigger, bolt and sear
Stock: Two-tone walnut stock with a rollover Monte Carlo cheek piece, skip-line checkering and rosewood at forend and grip cap
Standard calibers **$299.95**
Magnum calibers **312.50**

PARKER-HALE VARMINT

SPECIFICATIONS:
Caliber: 22/250, 243, 6mm, 25/06
Capacity: 5 shot
Barrel Length(s): 24"
Overall Length: 45"
Action: Glass-bedded, bolt action. Receiver drilled and tapped for standard scope mounts
Safety: Slide thumb safety, locks trigger, bolt and sear
Stock: Two-tone European walnut stock has high comb with rollover cheek piece, skip checkering, Wundhammer grip and ventilated recoil pad
Price **$312.50**

MARLIN LEVER ACTION CARBINES

IN 22 CALIBER

Marlin Golden 39A
(less scope) $151.95

Marlin Golden 39M $151.95
(less scope)

Marlin Golden 39A

The Marlin lever action 22 is the oldest (since 1891) shoulder gun still being manufactured. In fact, the only older gun design still being manufactured is Colt's 1873 Single Action Army revolver.

Solid Receiver Top. You can easily mount a scope on your Marlin 39 by screwing on the machined scope adapter base provided. The screw-on base is a neater, more versatile method of mounting a scope on a .22 sporting rifle. The solid top receiver and scope adapter base provide a maximum in eye relief adjustment. If you prefer iron sights, you'll find the 39 receiver clean, flat and sand-blasted to prevent glare.

Exclusive Brass Magazine Tube. A small point perhaps, but not if you've ever had a steel tube rust.

Micro-Groove® Barrel. Marlin's famous rifling system of multi-grooving has consistently produced fine accuracy because the system grips the bullet more securely, minimizes distortion, and provides a better gas seal.

And the Model 39 maximizes accuracy with the heaviest barrels available on any lever action .22.

Marlin Golden 39A Specifications

Caliber .22 Short, Long and Long Rifle

Capacity: Tubular magazine holds 26 Short, 21 Long and 19 Long Rifle Cartridges

Action: Lever action; solid top receiver; side ejection; gold plated steel trigger; one-step take-down; deeply blued metal surfaces; receiver top sand-blasted to prevent glare.

Stock: Two-piece genuine American black walnut with fluted comb; full pistol grip and forend. Blued-steel forend cap; sling swivels; grip cap; white butt plate and pistol-grip spacers; tough Mar-Shield® finish.

Barrel: 24″ with Micro-Groove® rifling (16 grooves)

Sights: Adjustable folding semi-buckhorn rear, ramp front sight with new Wide-Scan™ hood. Solid top receiver tapped for scope mount or receiver sight; scope adapter base; offset hammer spur for scope use—works right or left.

Overall Length: 40″

Weight: About 6½ lbs.

Marlin Golden 39M Specifications

Caliber: .22 Short, Long and Long Rifle.

Capacity: Tubular magazine holds 21 Short, 16 Long or 15 Long Rifle Cartridges.

Action: Lever action with square finger lever; solid top receiver; side ejection; gold-plated steel trigger; one-step take-down; deeply blued-metal surfaces; receiver top sandblasted to prevent glare.

Stock: Two-piece straight-grip genuine American black walnut with full forend. Blued steel forend cap; sling swivels; white butt plate spacer; tough Mar-Shield® finish.

Barrel: 20″ with Micro-Groove® rifling (16 grooves).

Sights: Adjustable folding semi-buckhorn rear, ramp front sight and new Wide-Scan™ hood. Solid top receiver tapped for scope mount or receiver sight; scope adapter base; offset hammer spur for scope use—works right or left.

Overall Length: 36″

Weight: About 6 lbs.

MARLIN BOLT ACTION RIFLES

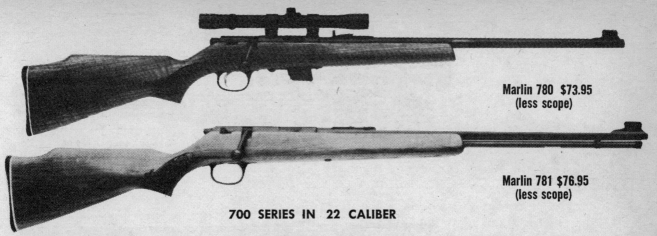

Marlin 780 $73.95
(less scope)

Marlin 781 $76.95
(less scope)

700 SERIES IN 22 CALIBER

Marlin 780 Specifications
Caliber: .22 Short, Long or Long Rifle
Capacity: Clip magazine holds 7 Short, Long or Long Rifle Cartridges.

Action: Bolt action; serrated, anti-glare receiver top; gold-plated steel trigger; positive thumb safety; red cocking indicator.
Stock: Monte Carlo genuine American

black walnut with full pistol grip; checkering on pistol grip and underside of fore-end; white butt plate spacer; tough Mar-Shield® finish.
Barrel: 22″ with Micro-Groove® rifling (16 grooves)
Sights: Adjustable folding semi-buckhorn rear, ramp front, Wide-Scan™ front sight hood; receiver

grooved for tip-off scope mount.

Overall Length: 41″
Weight: About 5½ lbs.
  Marlin 781. Specifications same as Marlin 780, except with tubular magazine that holds 25 Short, 19 Long or 17 Long Rifle Cartridges. Weight: About 6 lbs.

700 SERIES IN 22 MAGNUM

Marlin 783 Magnum $84.95 (less scope)

Marlin 783 Magnum Specifications
Caliber: .22 Win. Magnum Rimfire (Not interchangeable with any other .22 cartridge)

Capacity: 12-shot tubular magazine with patented closure system

Action: Bolt action; serrated, anti-glare receiver top; gold-plated steel trigger; positive thumb safety; red cocking indicator.
Stock: Monte Carlo genuine American black walnut with full pistol grip; checkering on pistol grip and underside of fore-end; white butt

plate spacer; sling swivels and handsome leather carrying strap; tough Mar-Shield® finish.
Barrel: 22″ with Micro-Groove rifling (20 grooves)
Sights: Adjustable folding semi-buckhorn rear, ramp front with new Wide-Scan™ hood; receiver grooved for tip-off scope mount.
Overall Length: 41″
Weight: About 6 lbs.

Marlin 782 Magnum $81.00 (less scope)

Marlin 782 Magnum Specifications
Same as 783 Magnum, except with 7-shot clip magazine.

MARLIN LEVER ACTION CARBINES

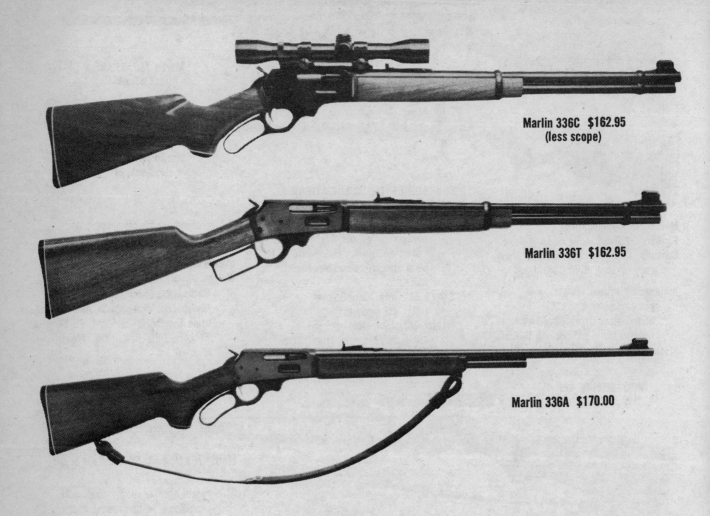

Marlin 336C $162.95
(less scope)

Marlin 336T $162.95

Marlin 336A $170.00

Now you have three models to choose from. The 336C with full pistol grip, the 336T saddle gun, or the 336A, a rifle model with 24" barrel and half magazine. All three models feature side-ejecting, solid top receivers, heat-treated machined steel forgings, American black-walnut stock with Mar-shield® finish, Micro-Groove® rifling, and folding semi-buckhorn rear sights.

Marlin 336C Specifications
Caliber: .30/30 Win., or .35 Rem.
Capacity: 6-shot tubular magazine
Action: Lever action; solid top receiver; side ejection; gold-plated steel trigger; deeply blued metal surfaces; receiver top sand-blasted to prevent glare
Stock: Two-piece genuine American black walnut with fluted comb and full pistol grip. Grip cap; white butt plate and pistol-grip spacers; tough Mar-Shield® finish
Barrel: 20" with Micro-Groove® rifling (12 grooves)
Sights: Adjustable semi-buckhorn folding rear, ramp front sight with brass bead and Wide-Scan™ front sight hood. Solid top receiver tapped for scope mount or receiver sight; offset hammer spur for scope use—works right or left.
Overall Length: 38½"
Weight: About 7 lbs.

Marlin 336T Specifications
Same action as 336C, available in .30/30 Win. only, with straight-grip stock and squared finger lever. Approx. 6¾ lbs.

Marlin 336A Specifications
Same action as 336C, with 24" barrel, ½ magazine tube with 5-shot capacity, blued steel fore-end cap and sling swivels with leather carrying strap. Approx. 7 lbs.
Available in .30/30 Win. only.

Forgings. Marlin uses six forged parts in the manufacture of all high power rifles: receiver, lever, trigger plate, carrier, hammer, and locking bolt.

MARLIN LEVER ACTION CARBINES

Marlin 1895 gun $234.00

Caliber: .45/70 Government
Capacity: 4-shot tubular magazine
Action: Lever action; solid top receiver; side ejection; blued steel trigger; honed chamber; deeply blued metal surfaces; receiver top sand-blasted to prevent glare.
Stock: Two-piece straight-grip genuine American black walnut; traditional hard-rubber rifle butt plate, blued-steel forend cap; tough Mar-Shield® finish.
Barrel: 22″, with rifling designed to give maximum performance with both lead and jacketed bullets (12 grooves.) Honed chamber.
Sights: Adjustable semi-buckhorn folding rear, brass bead front sights; solid top receiver tapped for scope mount or receiver sight; offset hammer spur for scope use —works right or left.
Overall Length: 40½″
Weight: About 7 lbs.

Marlin 1894 $162.95

Caliber: .44 Rem. Magnum
Capacity: 10-shot tubular magazine
Action: Lever action with traditional squared finger lever; solid top receiver; side ejection; gold-plated steel trigger; deeply blued metal surfaces; receiver top sand-blasted to prevent glare.
Stock: Two-piece straight-grip genuine American black-walnut butt plate white spacer; blue-steel forend cap; tough Mar-Shield® finish.
Barrel: 20″ with Micro-Groove® rifling (12 grooves). Honed chamber.
Sights: Adjustable semi-buckhorn folding rear, hooded-ramp front sights; solid top receiver tapped for scope mount or receiver sight; offset hammer spur for scope use—works right or left.
Overall Length: 37½″
Weight: About 6 lbs.

Marlin 1894 357 Magnum $234.00

Caliber: 357 Magnum
Capacity: 9-shot tubular magazine
Action: Lever action; side ejection; solid top receiver; gold-plated steel trigger; deeply blued metal surfaces; receiver top sandblasted to prevent glare.
Stock: Straight-grip two-piece genuine American black walnut with white butt plate spacer.
Barrel: 18½″ with modified Micro-Groove® rifling (12 grooves)
Sights: Adjustable semi-buckhorn folding rear, bead front. Solid top receiver tapped for scope mount or receiver sight; offset hammer spur for scope use—adjustable for right or left hand use.
Overall Length: 36″
Weight: 6 lbs.

Marlin 444 Sporter $182.95

Caliber: .444 Marlin
Capacity: 4-shot tubular magazine
Action: Lever-action; solid top receiver; side ejection; gold plated steel trigger; deeply blued metal surfaces; receiver top sand-blasted to prevent glare.
Stock: Two-piece genuine American black walnut with fluted comb; recoil pad; full pistol grip; white butt plate and pistol grip spacers; tough Mar-Shield finish.
Barrel: 22″ with Micro-Groove® rifling (12 grooves)
Sights: Adjustable folding semi-buckhorn rear, hooded-ramp front sight with brass bead and Wide-Scan™ front sight hood; solid top receiver tapped for scope mount or receiver sight; offset hammer spur for scope use—works right or left.
Overall Length: 40½″

MARLIN 22 AUTOLOADER

Marlin 990 $81.00

Stock: Monte Carlo genuine American black walnut with fluted comb and full pistol grip.
Sights: Adjustable folding semi-buckhorn rear, ramp front sight with brass bead; Wide-Scan™ hood.
Overall Length: 40¾"
Weight: About 5½ lbs.
Features: Receiver grooved tip-off scope; bolt hold-open device; cross-bolt safety.

Specifications
Caliber: 22 Long Rifle
Capacity: 18-shot tubular magazine
Barrel: 22" with Micro-Groove® rifling (16 grooves)

Marlin 995 $75.95

walnut with full pistol grip.
Sights: Adjustable folding semi-buckhorn rear; ramp front sight with brass bead; Wide-Scan™ front sight hood.
Overall Length: 36¾"
Weight: About 5½ lbs.
Features: Receiver grooved for tip-off scope mount; bolt hold-open device; cross-bolt safety.

Specifications
Caliber: 22 Long Rifle
Capacity: 7-shot clip magazine
Barrel: 18" with Micro-Groove® rifling (16 grooves)
Stock: Monte Carlo genuine American black

MARLIN RIFLES
GLENFIELD SERIES

**MARLIN GLENFIELD 15
$57.95**

sight
Features: Receiver grooved for tip-off scope mount; checkering on pistol grip; sling swivels; thumb safety; bolt hold-open device
Stock: One-piece walnut finished hardwood Monte Carlo stock with full pistol grip

Capacity: Single shot
Barrel Length: 22" (16 grooves)
Weight: 5½ lbs.
Overall Length: 41"
Sights: Adjustable open rear, ramp front

SPECIFICATIONS:
Caliber: 22 Short, Long or Long Rifle

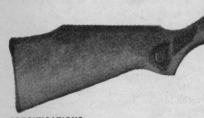

GLENFIELD 20 (less scope) $61.95

Action: Bolt action; serrated anti-glare receiver top; chrome-plated steel trigger; positive thumb safety; red cocking indicator
Stock: One-piece walnut-finished hardwood stock with full pistol grip; checkering on pistol grip
Shown here with Glenfield 200C, 4X scope

Long or Long Rifle cartridges
Barrel Length(s): 22"
Weight: 5½ lbs.
Overall Length: 41"
Sights: Ramp front sight; adjustable open rear; receiver grooved for tip-off scope mount

SPECIFICATIONS:
Caliber: 22 Short, Long or Long Rifle
Capacity: Clip magazine holds 7 Short,

MARLIN RIFLES
GLENFIELD SERIES

GLENFIELD 60 SPECIFICATIONS:
Caliber: 22 Long Rifle
Capacity: 18-shot tubular magazine with patented closure system
Barrel Length: 22"
Weight: 5½ lbs.
Overall Length: 40½"
Sights: Ramp front sight; adjustable open rear. Receiver grooved for tip-off scope mount
Action: Semi-automatic; side ejection;

bolt hold-open device; receiver top has serrated, non-glare finish; cross-bolt safety
Stock: One-piece walnut-finished

GLENFIELD 60
$66.00 (less scope)

hardwood Monte Carlo stock with full pistol grip; checkering on pistol grip and forend
Shown here with Glenfield 200C, 4X scope

GLENFIELD 30A SPECIFICATIONS:
Caliber: 30/30 Win.
Capacity: 6-shot tubular magazine
Barrel Length: 20"
Weight: 7 lbs.
Overall Length: 38¼"
Sights: Ramp front sight; adjustable open rear. Solid top receiver tapped for scope mount or receiver sight; offset hammer spur for scope use—adaptable

for right- or left-handed use
Action: Lever action; solid top receiver; side ejection; deeply blued metal

GLENFIELD 30A
(less scope) $152.95

surfaces; blued steel trigger; receiver top sandblasted to prevent glare
Stock: Two-piece walnut-finished hardwood stock with full pistol grip; checkering on pistol grip and forend
Shown here with Glenfield 400 A, 4X scope

GLENFIELD 70
$66.00

magazine
Barrel Length: 18"
Weight: 5½ lbs.
Overall Length: 36½"
Sights: Adjustable open rear, ramp front sight. Receiver grooved for tip-off scope mount

Action: Semiautomatic; side ejection; bolt hold-open device; receiver top has serrated, non-glare finish; chrome-plated trigger; cross-bolt safety
Stock: One-piece walnut finished hardwood Monte Carlo stock with full pistol grip; checkering on pistol grip and fore-end; sling swivels

SPECIFICATIONS:
Caliber: 22 Long Rifle
Capacity: Chrome-plated 7-shot clip

MARLIN GLENFIELD
30GT $152.95

SPECIFICATIONS:
Caliber: 30/30 Win.
Capacity: 6-shot tubular magazine

Barrel Length: 18½" (12 grooves)
Weight: 7 lbs.
Overall Length: 36¾"
Sights: Adjustable rear, brass bead front sight

Features: Checkering on butt stock and fore-end; receiver sand blasted to prevent glare
Stock: Two-piece straight grip walnut finished hardwood stock

MARLIN GLENFIELD 40
$84.00

SPECIFICATIONS:
Caliber: 22 Long Rifle only
Capacity: 18-shot tubular

Barrel Length: 22"
Weight: 5½ lbs.
Overall Length: 40½"
Sights: Adjustable open rear, ramp front sight

Features: Patented closure system; bolt hold-open device; checkering on pistol grip
Stock: Two-piece Monte Carlo walnut finished hardwood with full pistol grip

MOSSBERG CENTERFIRE RIFLES

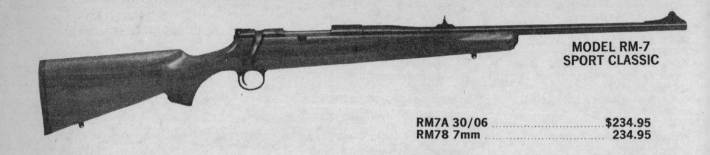

**MODEL RM-7
SPORT CLASSIC**

RM7A 30/06 .... $234.95
RM78 7mm 234.95

RM-7 bolt-action centerfire rifles

CENTER-FIRE BOLT ACTION RIFLES

Model No.	RM7A	RM7B
CALIBER	30/06	7mm Rem. Mag.
CAPACITY	5 SHOT*	4 SHOT*
BARREL LENGTH	22"	24"
APPROX. WEIGHT	7.5 lbs.	7.5 lbs.
OVERALL LENGTH	43¼	45¼"
LENGTH OF PULL	13¾"	13¾"
DROP AT COMB	⅝"	⅝"
DROP AT MONTE CARLO	—	—
DROP AT HEEL	1"	1"
RATE OF TWIST (R. H.) 1 TURN IN	10"	9½"

*Includes 1 in chamber
Specifications subject to change without notice.

MODEL 479PCA

479PCA pistol-grip carbine 30/30 Win. 20" barrel **$154.50**
479PCB pistol-grip carbine 35 Rem. 20" barrel 154.50
479SCA straight-grip carbine 30/30 Win. 20" barrel 154.50
479SCB straight-grip carbine 35 Rem. 20" barrel 154.50

MODEL 479 LEVER-ACTION RIFLES

Model	479PCA	479PCB	479SCA	479SCB
CALIBER	30/30 WIN.	.35 REM.	30/30 WIN.	.35 REM.
R. H. TWIST	12" (30.5cm)	16" (40.6cm)	12" (30.5cm)	16" (40.6cm)
LENGTH OF PULL	13¾" (4.4cm)	13¾" (34.9cm)	13½" (34.3cm)	13½" (34.3cm)
DROP AT COMB	1¾" (4.4cm)	1¾" (4.4cm)	1¾" (4.4cm)	1¾" (4.4cm)
DROP AT HEEL	2½" (6.4cm)	2½" (6.4cm)	2½" (6.4cm)	2½" (6.4cm)
OVERALL LENGTH	38½" (97.8cm)	38½" (97.8cm)	38½" (97.8cm)	38½" (97.8cm)
APPROX. WEIGHT*	7 lbs. (3.2kg)	7 lbs. (3.2kg)	6¾ lbs. (3.1kg)	6¾ lbs. (3.1kg)

*Varies slightly due to wood density. Specifications subject to change without notice.

22 caliber rimfire rifles

MODEL 377 PLINKSTER 22 cal. **Price $74.95**
Action—Semi-automatic. **Caliber**—22 Long Rifle. **Capacity**—15 Long Rifle Cartridges. Brass tubular magazine through buttstock; bright orange follower. **Barrel**—20" tapered with AC-KRO-GRUV rifling; ordnance steel. **Stock**—Straight-line, molded one-piece thumb hole of modified polystyrene foam, Monte Carlo comb and roll-over cheek piece. Sling swivel studs and fore-end checkering. Serrated, non-slip butt plate. **Color**—Walnut finish with blued barrel and receiver. Black butt plate and trigger guard. **Sight**—4 power scope with cross hair reticle. **Safety**—Positive, thumb operated; bolt locks in open position. **Receiver**—Milled ordnance steel, complete with scope mount base. Shell deflector included. **Length**—4". **Weight**—About 6.25 lbs. with scope.

MODEL 321K 22 cal. single-shot. **Price $68.50**
Action—Hammerless single-shot bolt-action with drop-in loading platform and automatic safety. The safety goes on when the action is open. Won't fire until the action is locked and safety moved to "off" position. **Stock**—Walnut-finish stock with cheekpiece; checkered pistol grip and forend; black buttplate and sling swivels. **Barrel**—24" barrel. Shoots all short, long, and long-rifle cartridges. **Sights**—Ramp front sight and adjustable rear sight. **Weight**—About 6½ lbs. Length overall, 43½".

MODEL 353 22 cal. "Auto" Carbine. **Price $87.50**
With exclusive two-position, extension forend of black Tenite for steady firing from the prone position, up to 7 shots in less than 2 seconds. **Action**—Shoots 22 cal. Long Rifle, regular or High Speed cartridges. Automatic self loading action from 7-shot clip. Receiver grooved for scope mounting.

Stock—Genuine American walnut with Monte Carlo. Checkered at forend and pistol grip. Sling swivels and web strap on left of stock. Butt plate with white liner. **Barrel**—18" AC-KRO-GRUV® 8-groove rifled barrel. **Sights**—Open rear with "U" notch, adjustable for windage and elevation; ramp front with bead. **Weight**—About 5 lbs. Length overall 38".

MODEL 341 22 cal. Bolt-Action Sporter. **Price $77.95**
Action—Hammerless bolt rifle action with Mossberg's "Magic 3-Way" 7-shot clip magazine which adjusts instantly to load, Short, Long or Long Rifle cartridges. Positive safety at side of receiver. Receiver grooved for scope mounting, tapped and drilled for peep sights. (Mossberg No. S330 receiver peep sight.) **Stock**—Genuine American walnut with Monte Carlo and cheek piece. Custom checkering on pistol grip and forend. Sling swivels. Butt plate with white line spacer. **Barrel**—24" AC-KRO-GRUV® 8-groove rifled barrel. **Sights**—Open rear with "U" notch, adjustable for windage and elevation; ramp front with bead. **Weight**—About 6½ lbs. Length overall 43½".

MODEL 353   MODEL 341   MODEL 377 PLINKSTER

MOSSBERG RIFLES

22 caliber magnum

MODEL 640K 22 Win. Magnum. **Price $89.95** Especially designed for the powerful and accurate .22 WMRF Magnum cartridge. Our exclusive Mossberg AC-KRO-GRUV® rifling assures your long range shots. **Action**—Hammerless, bolt action, with extra-heavy receiver and bolt. (Caution: Do not use any other .22 RF cartridge.) Double shell extractors, grooved trigger and 5-shot detachable clip. Thumb operated safety on right hand side of receiver. Receiver grooved for scope mounting, tapped and drilled for Mossberg S330 peep sight. **Stock**—Genuine American walnut with Monte Carlo and cheek piece. Sling swivels. Custom checkered at pistol grip and forend. Butt plate and pistol grip cap with white spacers. **Barrel**—24″ special gun quality steel. **Sights**—Fully adjustable, folding leaf rear sight. Ramp front with bead. **Weight**—About 6 lbs. Length overall 44¾″.

Magnum   22LR

APPROXIMATE MUZZLE VELOCITIES

Magnum — 2,000 ft./sec.
22LR — 1,335 ft./sec.

target rifles

MODEL 340B

MODEL 144

MODEL 340B .22 cal. Target Sporter. Price **$83.95** **Action**—Hammerless bolt action rifle with Mossberg's "Magic 3-Way" 7 shot clip magazine that adjusts instantly to load Short, Long, or Long Rifle cartridges. Positive safety at side of receiver. Receiver grooved for scope mounting. **Stock**—Walnut finish with pistol grip. Monte Carlo and cheek piece. Sling swivels. **Barrel**—24″ AC-KRO-GRUV® 8-groove rifled barrel. **Sights**—Furnished Mossberg S331 receiver peep sight has ¼-minute adjustments for windage and elevation. S320 Mossberg hooded ramp front sight. **Weight**—About 6 lbs. Length overall 43½″.

MODEL 144 .22 cal. Super Target Rifle. Price **$119.95** **Action**—Hammerless bolt action with 7 shot clip magazine; also loads as single shot. Features adjustable trigger pull, grooved trigger and thumb safety with red and green safety buttons inlaid in stock. Receiver grooved for scope mounting. Furnished with Mossberg S331 receiver peep sight. **Stock**—Genuine American walnut, target type with beavertail forend, cheek piece, high thick comb, adjustable hand stop, pistol grip and special 1¼″ target sling swivels. Butt plate, with white liner. **Barrel**—26″ heavy target barrel, 15/16″ round. Chambered for .22 Long Rifle, regular or High Speed cartridges. **Sights**—Lyman 17A hooded front sight with 7 interchangeable inserts. **Weight**—About 8 lbs. Length overall 43″.

S330. Receiver Peep Sight has ¼-minute click adjustments. No backlash. Bracket removable for scope mounting. On Models 320B, 340B and 346B. Same features on S331 Sight for Model 144

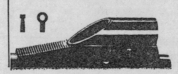

S320. Hooded Ramp Front Sight offers instant choice of post or aperture, both contained within the sight. On Models 320B, 340B and 346B. Lyman Hooded Sight 17A with 7 interchangeable inserts on Model 144

MOSSBERG RIFLES

22 CALIBER RIMFIRE RIFLES

NEW HAVEN BRAND

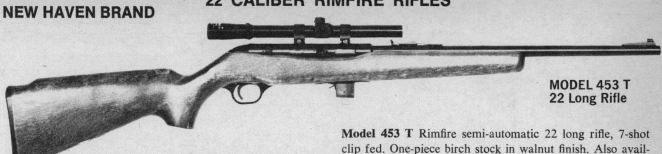

MODEL 453 T
22 Long Rifle

Model 453 T Rimfire semi-automatic 22 long rifle, 7-shot clip fed. One-piece birch stock in walnut finish. Also available with 4x scope and mounts (Model 453 TS).

MODEL 740 T
22 Mag.

Model 740 T Bolt-action rimfire 22 Mag. rifle. 5-shot clip fed, 26" heavy barrel, chambered for 22 WMR cartridge. Walnut-finished birch stock.   Also available with 4x scope and mounts (Model 740TS)

Model No.	Description	Price
453 T	Semi-Auto 22 L.R.	Not set
453 TS	Semi-Auto 22 L.R. w/4X Scope	Not set
740T	22 Win. R.F. Magnum	Not set
740TS	22 Win. R.F. Magnum w/4x scope	Not set

MANNLICHER RIFLES

MANNLICHER SSG MARKSMAN, shown with synthetic stock and optional Kahles scope.

SPECIFICATIONS:
Caliber: 308 Win. (7.62x51)
Barrel: 25.6"
Weight: 8.6 lbs. (9.9 lbs. with Kahles scope)
Overall Length: 44.5"
Stock: Choice of synthetic half stock of ABS "CYCOLAC" or walnut. Removable spacers in butt section adjusts length of pull from 12¾" to 14".
Sights: Hooded blade front; folding rear leaf sight.

Features: Parkerized finish. Choice of interchangeable single or double set triggers. Detachable 5-shot rotary straight-line feed magazine of "Makrolon." 10-shot magazine optional. Heavy duty receiver drilled and tapped for scope mounting. 6 rear locking lugs.

Cycolac half stock	$ 557.45
Walnut half stock	612.50
Cycolac half stock, with mounted Kahles sniper scope	1225.00
Optional 10-shot magazine	57.75
Spare 5-shot magazine	18.00

MANNLICHER SSG MATCH

SPECIFICATIONS:

Same as the Model SSG MARKSMAN, except with Walther target peep sights, and adjustable rail in forend to adjust sling travel. Weight: 11 lbs.

Cycolac half stock	$753.50
Walnut half stock	804.65
Spare magazine	18.00

MANNLICHER RIFLES

MANNLICHER ML 79

SPECIFICATIONS:
Caliber: 7x57, 7x64, 270 Win., 30-06 Spr. (Optional calibers—6.5x57, 6.5x55, 7.5x55)
Barrel: 20" (full stock); 23.6" (half stock)
Weight: 6.8 lbs. (full stock); 6.9 lbs. (half stock)
Overall Length: 39" (full stock); 43" (half stock)
Stock: Hand-checkered walnut with Monte Carlo cheekpiece. Either full Mannlicher or half stock. European hand-rubbed oil finish or high gloss lacquer finish.
Sights: Ramp front—adjustable for elevation; open U-notch rear— adjustable for windage.
Features: Single combination trigger (becomes hair trigger when moved forward before firing). Detachable 3-shot steel straight-line feed magazine (6-shot optional). 6 rear locking lugs. Drilled and tapped for scope mounts.

Full stock	$780.00
Half stock	730.00
Optional calibers	add 32.00
Spare 3-shot magazine	29.30
Spare 6-shot magazine	57.75

MANNLICHER Model L, shown with full stock

MANNLICHER Model L, VARMINT

SPECIFICATIONS:
Caliber: Model SL—222 Rem., 222 Rem. Mag., 223 Rem.
   Model SL Varmint—222 Rem.
   Model L—22-250 Rem., 6mm Rem., 243 Win., 308 Win.
   Model L Varmint—22-250 Rem., 243 Win., 308 Win.
   Model L (Optional caliber)—5.6x57
Barrel: 20" (full stock); 23.6" (half stock); 25.6" (Varmint)
Weight: 5.95 lbs. (full stock); 6.05 lbs. (half stock); 7.92 lbs. (Varmint)
Overall Length: 38.25"/SL, 38.5"/L (full stock); 41.75"/SL, 42"/L (half stock); 43.75"/SL, 44"/L (Varmint)
Sights: Ramp front, open U-notch rear.
Features: Choice of interchangeable single or double set triggers. 5-shot detachable "Makrolon" rotary magazine. 6 rear locking lugs. Drilled and tapped for scope mounts.

Full stock	$602.70
Half stock	554.00
Varmint	575.75
Optional caliber	add 32.00
Spare magazine	18.00

MANNLICHER RIFLES

MANNLICHER Model M,
shown with half stock

MANNLICHER Model M
"PROFESSIONAL"

SPECIFICATIONS:
Caliber: 7x64, 7x57, 270 Win., 30-06 Spr. (left-handed action calibers —7x64, 270 Win., 30-06 Spr.); (Optional calibers—6.5x57, 8x57JS, 9.3x62, 6.5x55, 7.5x55)
Barrel: 20" (full stock); 23.6", 25.5" opt. (half stock)
Weight: 6.8 lbs. (full stock); 6.9 lbs. (half stock); 7.5 lbs. (Professional)
Overall Length: 39" (full stock); 43" (half stock)
Stock: Full Mannlicher or standard half stock with Monte Carlo cheekpiece and rubber recoil pad. Hand-checkered walnut in skip-line pattern. The Model M with half stock is also available in a "Professional" version with a parkerized finish and synthetic stock made of ABS "CYCOLAC" (made with right-handed action

only). Note: Model M is available with left-handed action in full stock and half stock.
Features: Choice of interchangeable single or double set triggers. Detachable 5-shot rotary magazine of "Makrolon." 6 rear locking lugs. Drilled and tapped for scope mounting.

Full stock	$663.56
Full stock, with left-handed action	717.35
Half stock	613.75
Half stock, with left-handed action	667.00
Professional	440.95
Optional calibers	add 32.00
Spare magazine	18.00

MANNLICHER Model S/T Magnum, with heavy barrel
(shown with optional butt magazine inletted in stock)

SPECIFICATIONS:
Caliber: Model S—300 Win. Mag., 338 Win. Mag., 7mm Rem. Mag., 300 H&H Mag., 375 H&H Mag.
Model S (Optional calibers)—6.5x68, 8x68S, 9.3x64
Model S/T (Heavy barrel)—375 H&H Mag., 458 Win. Mag.
Model S/T (Optional caliber)—9.3x64
Barrel: 25.6"
Weight: 8.4 lbs. (Model S); 9.02 lbs. (Model S/T); add .66 lbs. for butt mag. opt.
Overall Length: 45"

Stock: Half stock with Monte Carlo cheekpiece and rubber recoil pad. Hand-checkered walnut in skip-line pattern. Available with optional spare magazine inletted in butt stock.
Features: Choice of interchangeable single or double set triggers. Detachable 4-shot rotary magazine of "Makrolon." 6 rear locking lugs. Drilled and tapped for scope mounting.

Model S or S/T	$715.35
Model S or S/T, with opt. butt magazine	764.25
Optional calibers	add 32.00
Spare magazine	18.00

VOERE 22LR

Model 2115	$168.00
Model 2117	210.00
Model 2117 Deluxe	244.00

MANNLICHER RIFLES AND CARBINES

THE MUSTANG

The Mustang is a break-open rifle with side locks of the Holland & Holland type and fitted with set trigger. The barrel is of monoblock design from Boehler Blitz steel, with right-handed rifling. The frame is made of heat-treated high-alloy steel, and the locking is of Triple Greener design, equipped with a double safety. Stock and forend are of walnut with hand-checkering. Stock has a pistol grip and cheekpiece. Forend is of the Schnabel style. The Mustang is hand engraved and available in a choice of 243 Win., 6.5x57R, 270 Win. calibers.

Standard $7420.00
With Engraving 7900.00

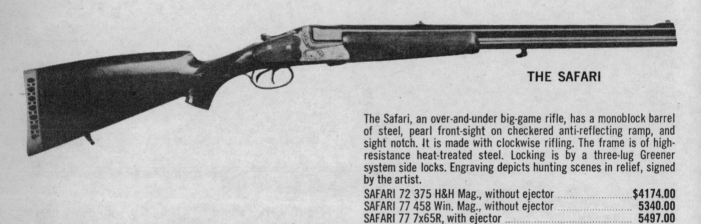

THE SAFARI

The Safari, an over-and-under big-game rifle, has a monoblock barrel of steel, pearl front-sight on checkered anti-reflecting ramp, and sight notch. It is made with clockwise rifling. The frame is of high-resistance heat-treated steel. Locking is by a three-lug Greener system side locks. Engraving depicts hunting scenes in relief, signed by the artist.

SAFARI 72 375 H&H Mag., without ejector $4174.00
SAFARI 77 458 Win. Mag., without ejector 5340.00
SAFARI 77 7x65R, with ejector 5497.00

FN FAL MODEL COMPETITION

Available only through Mannlicher dealers. $2000.00. Consecutive serial numbered pairs available at additional cost. Optional accessories also available.

SPECIFICATIONS:
Caliber: 308 Win. Match Gas-Operated Semiautomatic.
Weight: 9 lbs., 7 ozs., without magazine. Comes with 10-shot magazine (20-shot optional).
Overall Length: 44¼"
Barrel Length: 21" (24" with flash hider). Rear sight adjustable from 200 to 600 yards.

REMINGTON BOLT ACTION RIFLES

MODEL 788 CLIP REPEATER

**Calibers: 222 Remington, 223 Rem., 22-250
Remington, 6mm Rem., 243 Win., 308 Win.**

$186.95

MODEL 788 LEFT HAND
Calibers: 6mm Rem. & 308 Win.

$191.95

The Model 788 bolt action rifle is also available in a left hand version chambered for 6mm Rem. and 308 Win. calibers only. Has all the features of the regular Model 788 but left hand bolt handle is tailored for the left handed shooter. The artillery type bolt has nine extra heavy locking lugs that engage grooves in the solid steel receiver. Rear bolt cover provides extra protection and streamlining. The clip magazine slips in or out of the receiver with one hand. Tapered barrel is of ordnance steel and is crowned at muzzle. Elevated barrel provides a solid, positive scope back-up. Round receiver permits accurate wood-to-metal bedding. Receiver is also drilled and tapped for 'scope mounts and receiver sight at left rear. Blade front sight on serrated ramp is detachable and U notch rear sight is lock-screw adjustable for windage

Model 788 Sling Strap and Swivels	$ 9.50
Extra clip	6.95
Model 788 with 4x Scope	211.95

and elevation. Rear sight barrel holes are correct for target scope block. Serrated safety is positioned at rear of receiver. The American walnut Monte Carlo type stock is designed for use with scope or open sights. Stock dimensions are: 13⅝" length of pull; 2⅝" drop at heel; 1⅞" drop at comb (from open sight line).

Calibers	Clip Mag. Cap.	Barrel Length	Overall Length	Av. Wt. Lbs.
Model 788				
222 Remington	4	24"	43⅝"	7½
223 Remington	4	24"	43⅝"	7½
22-250 Remington	3	24"	43⅝"	7½
6mm Rem.	3	22"	42"	7¼
243 Win.	3	22"	42"	7¼
308 Win.	3	22"	42"	7¼

MODEL 700 BDL
HEAVY BARREL "VARMINT SPECIAL"

**Calibers: 222 Rem., 223 Rem., 22-250 Rem.,
25-06 Rem., 6mm Rem., 243 Win. & 308 Win.**

$329.95

The Model 700 BDL heavy barrel "Varmint Special" version comes equipped with a 24" heavy target-type barrel with target-rifle (Remington 40XB) scope bases. The "Varmint Special" is available in a wide range of popular high velocity, varmint calibers which include the 222 Rem., 223 Rem., 22-250 Rem., 25-06 Rem., 6mm Rem., 308 Win. and 243 Win. calibers. The "Vermint Special" was designed for minimum-target, maximum-range precision shooting—suitable for chucks, 'cats, foxes and other pests. Features include hinged floor plate; quick release swivels and strap; crisp trigger pull; American walnut stock, Monte Carlo style with cheek piece, positive cut skip-line checkering on grip and all three sides of fore end, grip cap with white line spacer and butt plate; DuPont developed RK-W wood finish. Stock dimensions are as follows: 13⅜" length

of pull; 1⅜" drop at heel; ½" drop at comb (from open sight line). The safety is a thumb-lever type and is serrated. The bolt knob is oval shaped, serrated top and bottom. As in the Model 700 BDL the cartridge head is completely encased by the bolt face and is supported by three rings of steel when the action is closed.

SPECIFICATIONS

Calibers	Clip Mag. Cap.	Barrel Length	Overall Length	Av. Wt. Lbs.
22-250 Rem.	5	24"	43½"	9
222 Rem.	6	24"	43½"	9
223 Rem.	6	24"	43½"	9
25-06 Rem.	5	24"	44½"	9
6 mm Rem.	5	24"	43½"	9
243 Win.	5	24"	43½"	9
308 Win.	5	24"	43½"	9

REMINGTON AUTOLOADING RIFLES

The Model 742 "Woodsmaster" is a gas-operated automatic rifle available in 30-06, 280 Rem., 308 Win., 243 Win., and 6mm Rem. calibers. The "Woodsmaster" automatic comes in both rifle and carbine models with fleur-de-lis checkering and all-purpose stock (for use with either scope or open sights). The rifle model is also available with basket-weave checkering, Monte-Carlo stock with cheekpiece, RK-W wood finish, and step receiver, in 30-06 and 308 Winchester calibers only. The rifle models are equipped with 22-inch barrels, come in all five calibers, and measure 42-inches overall in length. The carbine model comes with an 18½-inch barrel, and is made in 30-06 and 308 Winchester calibers only. The overall length for the carbine model—38½ inches. The solid-steel receiver houses a rotary multiple-lug breech bolt, which locks bolt and barrel together when action is closed, ensuring strength and constant headspace. The bolt face is recessed which completely encases the cartridge. The receiver is drilled and tapped for scope mounts. Comes with one 4-shot detachable clip magazine (extra 4-shot clip costs $7.95).

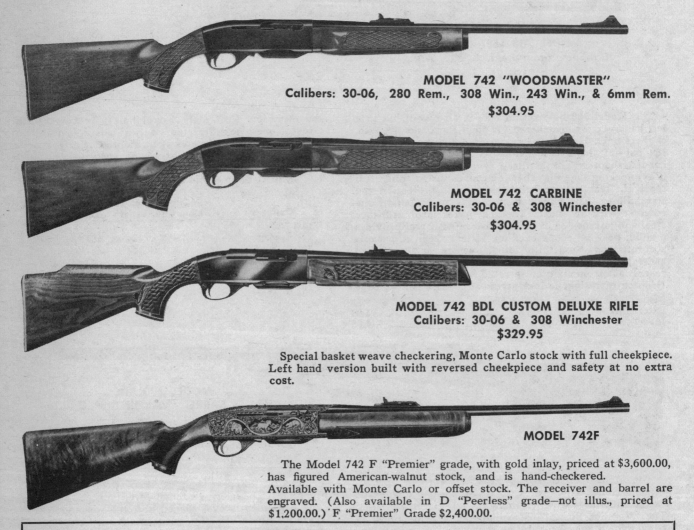

MODEL 742 "WOODSMASTER"
Calibers: 30-06, 280 Rem., 308 Win., 243 Win., & 6mm Rem.
$304.95

MODEL 742 CARBINE
Calibers: 30-06 & 308 Winchester
$304.95

MODEL 742 BDL CUSTOM DELUXE RIFLE
Calibers: 30-06 & 308 Winchester
$329.95

Special basket weave checkering, Monte Carlo stock with full cheekpiece. Left hand version built with reversed cheekpiece and safety at no extra cost.

MODEL 742F

The Model 742 F "Premier" grade, with gold inlay, priced at $3,600.00, has figured American-walnut stock, and is hand-checkered.
Available with Monte Carlo or offset stock. The receiver and barrel are engraved. (Also available in D "Peerless" grade—not illus., priced at $1,200.00.) F "Premier" Grade $2,400.00.

MODEL 742 SPECIFICATIONS

Sling Strap and Swivels Installed	$15.75
Extra 4-shot clip	8.95

CALIBERS: Regular Model: 6mm Rem., 243 Win., .280 Rem., 30/06, .308 Win. Carbine: 30/06 and .308 Win. Deluxe: 30/06, 308 Win.

CAPACITY: 4 in clip magazine plus one in chamber.

BARREL LENGTH: 22"—Carbine 18½".

OVER-ALL LENGTH: 42"—Carbine 38½".

STANDARD STOCK DIMENSIONS: Stock and fore-end: rich American Walnut. 13¼" length of pull, 2¼" drop at heel, 1⅝" drop at comb.
Deluxe Model: 13¼" length of pull, 2½" drop at heel, 1⅝" drop at comb, 1⅝" drop at Monte Carlo.

RECEIVER: Drilled and tapped for scope mounts. Removable clip magazine.

SIGHTS: Flat faced gold bead with ramp front sight. Step adjustable rear sight with windage adjustment screw.

AVERAGE WEIGHT: 7½ lbs.—Carbine 7¼ lbs.

REMINGTON BOLT ACTION RIFLES

MODELS 581 & 582 IN 22 L. R. CALIBER

The 581 series 22 Long Rifle rimfire bolt-action rifles feature the look, feel and balance of big-game center-fire rifles. They are available in three styles—a single shot; a clip repeater; and a tubular-magazine repeater. The single shot also comes in a smoothbore model. The bolt is an artillery type with rear lock-up and has six extra-heavy, rotary locking lugs at the back that engage grooves in the solid-steel receiver. A bolt cover at rear keeps dirt and bad weather outside. Two extractors are standard on this series of 22 rifles. Hunting-type trigger is wide and the trigger guard is roomy enough to accommodate a gloved finger. The stock is Monte Carlo style with pistol grip suitable for use with or without a scope. Sights consist of a bead front sight and U-notch lock-screw adjustable rear. Precise bedding into the stock is achieved by a new round receiver. The receiver is also grooved for tip-off scope mounts. There are no slots or notches cut into the receiver and the bolt handle isn't used as lock-up lugs. The barrel is of ordnance steel, crowned at the muzzle, polished and blued. The non-slip thumb safety is located at the right rear of the receiver. With positive safety.

MODEL 581 "BOYS' RIFLE" $99.95

**MODEL 581 CLIP REPEATER
WITH SINGLE SHOT ADAPTER
$99.95**

Model 581
Sling Strap and Swivels Installed $9.50
Model 581
Extra 5-shot clip 4.50
Extra 10-shot clip 5.50

**MODEL 581 LEFT HAND
CLIP REPEATER WITH
SINGLE SHOT ADAPTER $104.95**

**MODEL 582 TUBULAR REPEATER
$114.95**

Model 582
Sling Strap and Swivels Installed $9.50

MODEL 581 & MODEL 582

Specifications:

Stock & Fore-end: Walnut-finished hardwood with Monte Carlo, full size, black butt plate. Single-screw takedown.
Receiver: Round, ordnance steel, grooved for scope mounts.
Capacity: M/581 6-shot clip repeater with single-shot adapter. M/582 20 Short, 15 Long, 14 Long Rifle cartridges.

Sights: Front: bead, dovetail adjustable. Rear: U-notch type, lock-screw adjustable.
Safety: Positive, serrated thumb-type. Left-hand safety on left-hand model.
Weight: M/581 4¾ lbs.; M/582 5 lbs.
Overall Length: 42⅜"

REMINGTON BOLT ACTION RIFLES

MODEL 700ADL

MODEL 700 ADL "Deluxe": Calibers— 222 Remington, 22-250 Remington, 6mm Remington, 243 Winchester, 25-06 Remington, 270 Winchester, 30-06, 308 Winchester, 7mm Express Remington $259.95
MODEL 700 ADL "Deluxe" MAGNUM: Caliber—7mm Rem. Mag..... 274.95

MODEL 700BDL

MODEL 700 BDL "Custom Deluxe": Calibers— 222 Remington, 22-250 Remington, 6mm Remington, 243 Winchester, 25-06 Remington, 270 Winchester, 30-06, 308 Winchester, 7mm Express Remington $309.95
17 Remington caliber 324.95
Left-Hand Model in 270 Win. & 30-06 .... 319.95
MODEL 700 BDL "Custom Deluxe" MAGNUM: Calibers—7mm Remington Mag., 8mm Rem. Mag. 17 Rem., 300 Winchester Mag. $324.95
Left-Hand Model in 7mm Rem. Magnum 334.95
MODEL 700 SAFARI in 375 H&H Mag., 458 Win. Mag. 500.00

MODEL 700 Classic: Calibers—22-250 Remington, 6mm Remington, 243 Winchester, 270 Winchester, 30-06 and 30-06 Accelerator $289.95
7mm Rem. Mag. 304.95

MODEL 700 C • "Custom"

CALIBERS: Same as Model 700 BDL except 17 Remington, 264 Win. Mag., 375 H&H Mag. and 458 Win. Mag. **CAPACITY:** Same as Model 700 BDL. **BARREL:** Choice of 20", 22", or 24" length in Remington high-proof ordnance steel. With or without sights. Not available with stainless-steel barrel. **BOLT:** Jeweled with shrouded firing pin. **RECEIVER:** Drilled and tapped for scope mounts. Fixed magazine with or without hinged floor plate. **STOCK:** Hand-checkered selected American walnut with quick detachable sling swivels installed. Recoil pad standard equipment on Magnum rifles. Installed at extra charge on others.

Model 700 C "Custom" $575.00

REMINGTON PUMP ACTION RIFLES

The Model 760 "Gamemaster" pump action rifle is available in both rifle and carbine models. The regular rifle model 760 is made in 6mm Rem., 243 Win., 270 Win., 30-06 and 308 Win. calibers and comes with a 22-inch barrel. The rifle model is also available in a custom deluxe version with basket weave checkering, black fore end tip and pistol grip cap with white line spacer, full cheek piece (right or left), with Monte-Carlo, RK-W wood finish, and step receiver, in 30-06, 270 Win. and 308 Win. calibers only.

The carbine model comes with an 18½-inch barrel, in 30-06, and 308 Win. calibers only. Overall length for the carbine model—38½ inches.

The trigger must be released and squeezed for each shot—can't fire unless action is completely closed. With positive cross-bolt safety, free floating barrel, double action slide handle bars, rotary multiple-lug breech bolt, recessed bolt face and detachable 4-shot clip magazine.

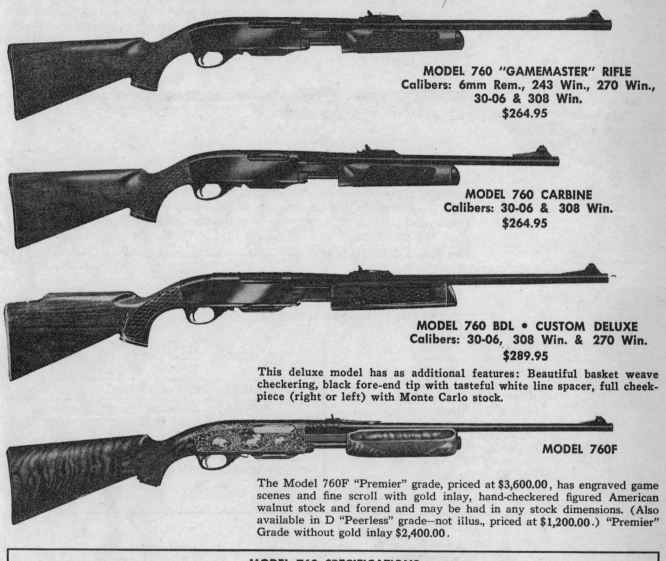

MODEL 760 "GAMEMASTER" RIFLE
Calibers: 6mm Rem., 243 Win., 270 Win.,
30-06 & 308 Win.
$264.95

MODEL 760 CARBINE
Calibers: 30-06 & 308 Win.
$264.95

MODEL 760 BDL • CUSTOM DELUXE
Calibers: 30-06, 308 Win. & 270 Win.
$289.95

This deluxe model has as additional features: Beautiful basket weave checkering, black fore-end tip with tasteful white line spacer, full cheekpiece (right or left) with Monte Carlo stock.

MODEL 760F

The Model 760F "Premier" grade, priced at $3,600.00, has engraved game scenes and fine scroll with gold inlay, hand-checkered figured American walnut stock and forend and may be had in any stock dimensions. (Also available in D "Peerless" grade—not illus., priced at $1,200.00.) "Premier" Grade without gold inlay $2,400.00.

MODEL 760 SPECIFICATIONS

CALIBERS: Regular Model: 6mm Rem., 243 Win., 270 Win., 30/06, 308 Win. Carbine: 30/06, 308 Win. Deluxe: 30/06, 270 Win., 308 Win.

CAPACITY: 4 in clip magazine plus one in chamber

BARREL LENGTH: 22"—760 Carbine 18½".

OVER-ALL LENGTH: 42"—760 Carbine 38½".

STANDARD STOCK DIMENSIONS: Stock and fore-end; American Walnut. 13¼" length of pull, 2⅛" drop at heel, 1⅝" drop at comb. Deluxe Model: 13⁵⁄₁₆" length of pull, 2½" drop at heel, 1⅝" drop at comb, 1⅝" drop at Monte Carlo.

RECEIVER: Drilled and tapped for scope mounts. Removable clip magazine.

SIGHTS: Flat faced gold bead with ramp front sight. Step adjustable rear sight with windage adjustment screw.

AVERAGE WEIGHT: 7½ lbs.—760 Carbine 7¼ lbs.

REMINGTON PUMP ACTION RIFLES

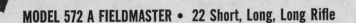

MODEL 572 A FIELDMASTER • 22 Short, Long, Long Rifle

Exclusive cartridge-feeding design prevents jamming, permits easy single loading. By simply removing the inner magazine tube, parent or instructor can convert the Model 572 into a single-shot rifle for the beginning shooter; when shooter is experienced, magazine tube can be put back again to make the Model 572 a repeater. **$114.95**

MODEL 572 BDL Deluxe • 22 Short, Long, Long Rifle

Features of this rifle with big-game feel and appearance are: DuPont beautiful but tough RK-W finish, center-fire-rifle-type rear sight fully adjustable for both vertical and horizontal sight alignment, big-game style ramp front sight, beautiful Remington impressed checkering on both stock and forend.

Model 572 BDL DELUXE **$129.95**
Sling Strap & Swivels installed 13.25

SPECIFICATIONS • MODELS 572A & 572 BDL DELUXE

ACTION:	Pump repeater.		**SIGHTS:**	A—Adjustable rear, bead front. BDL—Fully adjustable rear, ramp front. Screw removable.
CALIBER:	22 Short, Long and Long Rifle rim fire.		**SAFETY:**	Positive cross bolt.
CAPACITY:	Tubular magazine holds 20 Short, 17 Long, 14 Long Rifle cartridges.		**RECEIVER:**	Grooved for "tip-off" scope mounts.
			OVER-ALL LENGTH:	40".
STOCK AND FORE-END:	A—American Walnut. BDL—American Walnut with DuPont RK-W tough lustrous finish and fine line custom checkering.		**BARREL LENGTH:**	21".
			AVERAGE WEIGHT:	5½ lbs.

REMINGTON MODEL XP-100 LONG RANGE PISTOL.
Bolt Action • Single Shot • Center Fire

$239.95

221 REMINGTON "FIREBALL" CALIBER
Rotating Thumb-Safety. Ventilated Rib. Custom-Style Checkering. Internal Fore-End Cavities for Addition of Weights. Match Type Trigger. Scientifically Balanced to give minimum whip, jump and recoil. One-Piece Stock of Du Pont "Zytel" Nylon. Rifle-Type Rear Sight. Universal Grip fits either left or right hand. Weight 3¾ lbs. Price Includes Zippered Carrying Case

REMINGTON AUTOLOADING 22 RIFLES

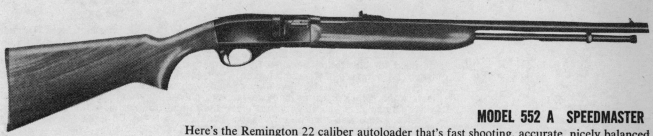

MODEL 552 A SPEEDMASTER

Here's the Remington 22 caliber autoloader that's fast shooting, accurate, nicely balanced ... the rifle you'll want for small game hunting, controlling crop-destroying and marauding pests, or for just plain fun-shooting. The Model 552 has every feature the shooter wants, such as: twenty shots as fast as you can squeeze the trigger, rich walnut stock, cross bolt safety, receiver grooved for "tip-off" scope mounts. **$109.95**

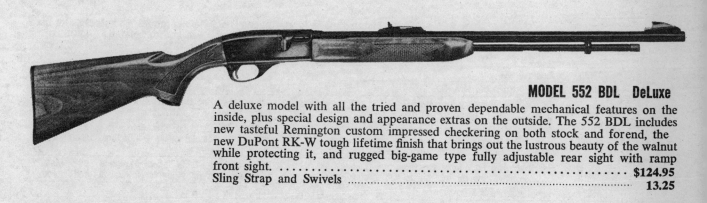

MODEL 552 BDL DeLuxe

A deluxe model with all the tried and proven dependable mechanical features on the inside, plus special design and appearance extras on the outside. The 552 BDL includes new tasteful Remington custom impressed checkering on both stock and forend, the new DuPont RK-W tough lifetime finish that brings out the lustrous beauty of the walnut while protecting it, and rugged big-game type fully adjustable rear sight with ramp front sight. **$124.95**
Sling Strap and Swivels **13.25**

SPECIFICATIONS FOR MODELS 552A, 552BDL

ACTION:	Autoloading. Tubular Magazine.
CALIBER:	22 Short, Long and Long Rifle rim fire.
CAPACITY:	Holds 20 Short, 17 Long, 15 Long Rifle cartridges.
STOCK:	American Walnut. DuPont RK-W tough lustrous finish and fine-line custom checkering on BDL Model.
SIGHTS:	552 A —Adjustable rear, bead front. 552 BDL—Fully adjustable rear, ramp front. Screw removable.
SAFETY:	Positive cross bolt.
RECEIVER:	Grooved for "tip-off" scope mounts.
OVER-ALL LENGTH:	40"
BARREL LENGTH:	21"
AVERAGE WEIGHT:	5¾ lbs.

REMINGTON AUTOLOADING 22 RIFLES

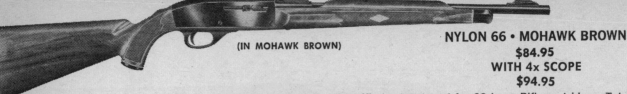

(IN MOHAWK BROWN)

NYLON 66 • MOHAWK BROWN
$84.95
WITH 4x SCOPE
$94.95

The Nylon 66 Autoloading rifle is chambered for 22 Long Rifle cartridges. Tubular magazine thru butt stock holds 14 long rifle cartridges. Remington's Nylon 66 receiver parts, stock and barrel are interlocked with steel and structural nylon. There's no need for lubrication because friction-free parts glide on greaseless bearings of nylon. Barrel made of Remington proof steel. Stock is made of DuPont "Zytel" nylon, a new gunstock material. Resembles wood, weighs less than wood, outwears, outlasts wood. Stock features fine-line non-slip checkering, white diamond inlays and white line spacers at grip cap, butt plate and forend tip and has a lifetime warranty. Receiver is grooved for "tip-off" scope mounts. The Nylon 66 is also available in a "Gallery Special" (22 Shorts only) as Model 66-GS. $99.95.

(IN APACHE BLACK)

Nylon 66 Black Diamond	$89.95
Nylon 66 Black Diamond w/4x Scope	94.95
Sling Strap and Swivels Installed	9.25

The Nylon 66 is also made in an Apache Black deluxe model. The stock is jet black nylon and both the barrel and the receiver cover are chrome plated. $94.95.

	NYLON 66 "MOHAWK BROWN"	NYLON 66 "APACHE BLACK"
ACTION	Autoloading.	Autoloading.
CALIBER	22 Long Rifle Rim Fire.	22 Long Rifle Rim Fire.
CAPACITY	Tubular magazine thru butt stock. Holds 14 long rifle cartridges.	Tubular magazine thru butt stock. Holds 14 long rifle cartridges.
STOCK	DuPont "ZYTEL" nylon, checkered grip & fore-end with white diamond inlays, white line spacers on butt plate, grip cap & fore-end. Black fore-end tip.	DuPont "ZYTEL" nylon, checkered grip & fore-end with white diamond inlays, white line spacers on butt plate, grip & fore-end.
SIGHTS	Rear sight adjustable for windage and range, blade front, common sight line for iron sights and scope.	Rear sight adjustable for windage and range, blade front, common sight line for iron sights and scope.
SAFETY	Top-of-grip, Positive.	Top-of-grip, Positive.
RECEIVER	Grooved for "tip-off" scope mounts. Double extractors.	Grooved for "tip-off" scope mounts. Double extractors. Chrome Plated Receiver and Barrel.
OVER-ALL LENGTH	38½".	38½".
WEIGHT	4 lbs.	4 lbs.

MODEL 541-S "CUSTOM" SPORTER • Clip Repeater

Remington Model 541-S "Custom" Sporter	$250.00
Extra 5-Shot Clip Magazine	4.50
Extra 10-Shot Clip Magazine	5.50
Sling Strap and Quick Release Swivels Installed	14.00

A customized .22 rim fire rifle. Combines the match rifle accuracy of the Model 540-X with the features of a custom rifle. American walnut stock with fine-line cut checkering in an attractive, raised diamond pattern, and protected by DuPont's rugged RK-W finish. Receiver and bowed trigger guard handsomely scroll engraved. Matching rosewood-colored fore-end tip, pistol grip cap and checkered butt plate fitted with white line spacers.

Hand polished exterior metal surfaces richly blued to a tasteful, medium high lustre. Receiver is drilled and tapped for regular scope mounts or receiver sights as well as grooved for "tip-off" type mounts. Barrel also drilled and tapped for open sights. Supplied with a 5-shot clip magazine. 5 and 10-shot extra magazines are available.

REMINGTON TARGET RIFLES

MODEL 540-XR
Rim Fire Position Rifle

An extremely accurate 22 caliber single shot match rifle. Extra fast lock time contributes to this fine accuracy. Specially designed stock has deep fore-end and 5 way adjustable butt plate for added comfort and better scores in all positions.

Pistol grip designed to eliminate wrist-twisting and assures straight-back trigger pull. Adjustable match trigger. Match style sling strap with adjustable front swivel block and set sight available as accessories at extra charge. $229.95

MODEL 540-XR, 540-XRJR
Front Swivel Block and Sling Strap Assembly (Optional Accessory at Extra Charge). 12.00

MODEL 540-XRJR • Junior Rim Fire Position Rifle

A match rifle with all the features of the Model 540-XR but fitted with 1¾" shorter stock to fit the junior shooter. $229.95

MODEL 40-XR
Rim Fire Position Rifle

Stock designed with deep fore-end for more comfortable shooting in all positions. Butt plate vertically adjustable. Exclusive loading platform provides straight line feeding with no shaved bullets. Crisp, wide, adjustable match trigger. Meets all International Shooting Union standard rifle specifications. $420.00

MODEL 40-XC National Match Course Rifle

Chambered for the 7.62mm NATO cartridge solely, this match rifle was designed to meet the needs of competitive shooters firing the national match courses. Position style stock, five shot repeater with top loading magazine, anti-bind bolt and receiver and in the bright stainless steel barrel. Meets all International Shooting Union Army Rifle specifications. $600.00

	MODEL 540-XR, 540-XRJR RIM FIRE POSITION RIFLE	**MODEL 40-XR RIM FIRE POSITION RIFLE**
ACTION	Bolt action single shot.	Bolt action single shot.
CALIBER	22 Long Rifle rim fire.	22 Long Rifle rim fire.
CAPACITY	Single loading.	Single loading.
SIGHTS	Optional at extra cost. Williams Receiver No. FPTK and Redfield Globe front match sight.	Optional at extra cost. Williams Receiver No. FPTK and Redfield Globe front match sight.
SAFETY	Positive serrated thumb safety	Positive thumb safety.
LENGTH OF PULL	540-XR—Adjustable from 12¾" to 16". 540-XRJR—Adjustable from 11" to 14¼".	13½".
RECEIVER	Drilled and tapped for receiver sight.	Drilled and tapped for receiver sight or target scope blocks.
BARREL	26" medium weight target barrel countersunk at muzzle. Drilled and tapped for target scope blocks. Fitted with front sight base.	24" heavy barrel.
BOLT	Artillery style with lock-up at rear. 6 locking lugs, double extractors.	Heavy, oversized locking lugs and double extractors.
TRIGGER	Adjustable from 1 to 5 lbs.	Adjustable from 2 to 4 lbs.
STOCK	Position style with Monte Carlo, cheekpiece and thumb groove. 5-way adjustable butt plate and full length guide rail.	Position style with front swivel block on fore-end guide rail.
OVER-ALL LENGTH	540-XR—Adjustable from 42½" to 46¾". 540-XRJR—Adjustable from 41¾" to 45".	42½".
AVERAGE WEIGHT	8 lbs. 13 oz. without sights. Add 9 oz. for sights.	10 lbs. 2 oz.

REMINGTON TARGET RIFLES

MODEL 40-XB "RANGEMASTER"
Center Fire

MODEL 40-XB "RANGEMASTER" • Center Fire Rifle

Barrels are unblued stainless steel. Choice of either standard weight or heavy barrel. Comb grooved for easy bolt removal. Mershon White Line non-slip rubber butt plate supplied. See below for complete specifications and prices.

MODEL 40XB-BR • Bench Rest Center Fire Rifle

Built with all the features of the extremely accurate Model 40-XB-CF but modified to give the competitive bench rest shooter a standardized rifle that provides the inherent accuracy advantages of a short, heavy, extremely stiff barrel. Wider, squared off fore-end gives a more stable rest on sandbags or other supports and meets weight limitations for the sporter and light-varmint classes of National Bench Rest Shooters Association competition.

	MODEL 40-XB CENTER FIRE	**MODEL 40XB-BR CENTER FIRE**
ACTION	Bolt—Single shot in either standard or heavy barrel versions. Repeater in heavy barrel only. Receiver bedded to stock. Barrel is free floating.	Bolt, single shot only.
CALIBERS	See listing below.	222 Rem., 22 Bench Rest Rem., 7.62 NATO (308 Win.), 6mm Bench Rest Rem.
SIGHTS	No sights supplied. Target scope blocks installed.	Supplied with target 'scope blocks.
SAFETY	Positive thumb operated.	Positive thumb operated.
RECEIVER	Drilled and tapped for scope block and receiver sights.	Drilled and tapped for target scope blocks.
BARREL	Drilled and tapped for scope block and front target iron sight. Muzzle diameter S2—approx. ¾", H2—approx. ⅞". Length: 27¼". Unblued stainless steel only.	Unblued stainless steel only. 20" barrel for Light Varmint Class. 24" barrel for Heavy Varmint Class.
TRIGGER	Adjustable from 2 to 4 lbs. pull. Special 2 oz. trigger available at extra cost. Single shot models only.	Adjustable from 1½ to 3½ lbs. Special 2 oz. trigger available at extra cost.
STOCK	American Walnut. Adjustable front swivel block on rail. Rubber non-slip butt plate.	Selected American Walnut. Length of pull—12".
OVER-ALL LENGTH	Approx. 47".	38" with 20" barrel. 42" with 24" barrel.
AVERAGE WEIGHT	S2—9¼ lbs. H2—11¼ lbs.	Light Varmint Class (20" barrel) 9¼ lbs. Heavy Varmint Class (24" barrel) 12 lbs.

MODEL 40-XB CENTER FIRE	**PRICES**
40XB-CF-S2 Stainless steel, standard weight barrel.	$550.00
40XB-CF-H2 Stainless steel, heavy barrel.	

CALIBERS: Single-shot: 222 Rem., 22-250 Rem., 6mm Rem., 243 Win., 7.62mm NATO (308 Win.), 30-06, 30-338 (30-7mm Mag.), 300 Win. Mag.

MODEL 40-XB CENTER FIRE	**PRICES**
Extra for repeating models. Heavy barrel version only.	$37.00
CALIBERS: 222 Rem., 22-250 Rem., 6mm Rem., 243 Win., 7.62mm NATO (308 Win.).	
Extra for two ounce trigger. Single shot version only.	$63.00

MODEL 40XB-BR CENTER FIRE	**PRICES**
40XB-BR Heavy barrel without sights.	$580.00
Extra for two-ounce trigger.	$63.00

RUGER No. 1 SINGLE-SHOT RIFLES

These five illustrations show the variations which are currently offered in the Ruger No. 1 Single-Shot Rifle. Orders for variations or calibers other than those listed are not available from Ruger. The Ruger No. 1 rifles come fitted with selected American walnut stocks. Pistol grip and forearm are hand-checkered to a borderless design. Price for any listed model is $308.00 Barreled action is $189.50

RUGER Number One Light Sporter
Calibers: 243 Win., 30/06, 270 Win. 7x57mm **Sights:** Open.
Barrel: 22 inches. **Weight:** 7¼ pounds.

RUGER Number One Medium Sporter
Calibers: 7mm Rem. Mag., 300 Win. Mag. **Weight:** 8 pounds (7¼ in 45/70).
45/70, 338 Mag.
Barrel: 26 inches. (22" in 45/70).
Sights: Open.

RUGER Number One Standard Rifle
Calibers: 22/250, 243 Win., 6mm Rem., 25/06, 270 Win., 30/06, 7mm Rem. Mag., 300 Win. Mag., 220 Swift, 333 Mag.
Barrel: 26 inches.
Sights: Ruger steel tip-off scope rings, 1".
Weight: 8 pounds.

RUGER Number One Special Varminter
Caliber: 22/250, 25/06, 220 Swift
Barrel: 24 inches.
Sights: Ruger Steel blocks and Tip-off scope rings, 1"
Weight: 9 pounds.

RUGER Number One Tropical Rifle
Calibers: 375 H & H Mag., 458 Win., Mag.
Barrel: 24 inches.
Sights: Open.
Weight: 8¼ pounds for 375, 9 pounds for 458.

RUGER No. 1 SINGLE-SHOT RIFLES

RUGER NUMBER ONE STANDARD RIFLE

General Description

The RUGER No. 1 SINGLE-SHOT action belongs in the under-lever, falling-block category and follows in many characteristics the Farquharson design. In all mechanical details, however, the RUGER No. 1 action is completely new and is in no sense a replica of any older action. The action has been engineered to use the most powerful of the modern magnum cartridges with safety and reliability.

Receiver Design.

The heart of the design is the massive receiver which forms a rigid connection between the barrel and butt stock. The butt stock is mortised into the receiver in such a way as to reinforce the grip section against splitting or cracking. A longitudinal bolt which passes through the butt stock binds the butt stock and receiver together into a solid, rigid structure. Projecting forward from the main part of the receiver and lying directly below the barrel is a heavy steel extension formed integrally with the receiver to facilitate forearm attachment. Because of this forearm hanger, it is possible to arrange the forearm to be completely clear of the barrel or to have any desired pressure on the barrel. The side walls of the receiver are .218" thick; these side walls are joined behind the breech block by a massive solid section. It is in this area that the RUGER No. 1 receiver represents the major improvement over the Farquharson type. In these older actions, there is only a thin web of steel effectively joining the side walls behind the breech block.

Firing Pin Hammer Design.

The advantages of the No. 1 hammer-firing pin design are:
1. The mainspring located in the forearm, is in an area where ample space is available for a large, lightly stressed spring.
2. Mounting of the hammer on the lever pivot simplifies the mechanism.
3. Hammer notch located on the periphery of the hammer greatly reduces the pressure on the sear.
4. The swinging transfer block, located in the upper interior of the breech block, functions to virtually lock the firing pin in its forward position against gas pressure during firing.
5. The ignition mechanism requires no openings in the rear of the breech block and, accordingly, no gas can issue in the direction of the shooter's face as it might in some older designs where some leakage can pass along the sides of the firing pin and exit at the rear surface of the breech block.
6. The hammer is retracted upon the first opening motion of the lever and can never actuate the firing pin unless the breech block is fully elevated into firing position.

Ejector Design.

The provisions for removal of fired cartridge cases from the chamber are particularly complete. The action readily handles any type of cartridge case i.e., rimmed, semi-rimmed, belted, rimless, etc. The extractor-ejector mechanism is designed to provide great leverage between the hand-lever and the point where the ejector actually engages the rim or groove of the cartridge case. It is so powerful, in fact, that if the case does not come out, the extractor will usually pull through the rim by use of a moderate force on the lever. With this mechanism, the shells will be thrown clear of the gun when the action is opened and the mechanism is in effect, a powerful spring-actuated automatic ejector. However, if the auto ejector feature is not desired, the ejector spring may be removed.

Trigger and Safety.

The trigger mechanism is adjustable for sear engagement, over travel, and weight of pull. The minimum pull at the present time is slightly under three pounds. The mechanism is free of take-up motion and trigger release is notably crisp. The crispness of this pull is attained by simply establishing leverages which greatly multiply, at the point of sear engagement, the movement of the trigger finger. The safety engages both the sear and the hammer directly to provide an absolute maximum of real security. The safety cannot be put on if the hammer is not cocked, but the action may be opened and closed whether the safety is on or off. The safety is of the sliding shotgun type.

Sights.

The mounting of telescopic sights has been carefully studied in connection with the RUGER No. 1 Single Shot. The rifle is sold complete with scope mounts of RUGER design, made particularly for this rifle. These mounts are split horizontally and fit 1" diameter scope tubes. They are the tip-off type, made entirely of steel. RUGER No. 1 rifles are equipped with ¼ rib scope mount only, unless open sights are also ordered. This ¼ rib functions primarily as a base for the RUGER scope mounts and may also be used for mounting open sights which are optional.

Two forearms are available: a semi beaver-tail modern type of forearm and a short slender design patterned after the typical designs of Alexander Henry.

When the short Henry type forearm is used, the front sling swivel is mounted on a barrel band and a sling in this event would be regarded as primarily a carrying sling. The front swivel is mounted in the forearm.

Both pistol grip and forearm are hand-checkered in an ample area to a borderless design. The finish completely reveals the character and grain of the carefully selected American walnut from which the stocks and forearms are made.

RUGER M-77 BOLT ACTION RIFLE

MODEL No. M77R (TELESCOPE NOT INCLUDED) COMPLETE WITH 1" STEEL RUGER RINGS (NO SIGHTS)

MODEL No. M77RS COMPLETE WITH 1" STEEL RUGER RINGS AND OPEN SIGHTS

Calibers: 22-250 Remington, 243 Winchester, 6mm Remington, 25-06 Remington, 220 Swift, 257 Roberts 250-3000, 7x57mm, 270 Winchester, 30-06, 7mm Remington Magnum, 300 Winchester Mag., 338 Winchester Mag., and 458 Win. Magnum.

Action. The M-77 is available in two action lengths—the Short Stroke and the Magnum.

The Short Stroke action is designed to take advantage of the accuracy and ballistic efficiency of the modern short series of cartridges. (Magazine box length: 2.920")

The Magnum action—about ½" longer than the Short Stroke—assures smooth and faultless feeding of the versatile long series of cartridges. (Magazine box length: 3.340")

The M-77 short stroke is available in calibers 22-250, 243, 6mm, 220 Swift, and 308. The M-77 Magnum is chambered for 270, 25-06, 7x57mm 30-06, 7mm Rem. Magnum, 300. Win. Mag., 338 Win. Mag. and 458 Win. Magnum. Also available in calibers 22-250, 220 Swift, 243 Win., 6mm Remington, 25-06, and 308 with a heavy 24" barrel, drilled and tapped for target-scope blocks, and supplied with 1" Ruger steel rings. 26" barrel in 220 Swift.

The M-77 Round top (Magnum Action only) is equipped with open sights. The receiver is shaped and tapped to accommodate standard commercial scope mount bases. The Round top is not milled for Ruger scope rings. Available only in 25/06, 270, 30-06, 7mm Rem. Mag., and 300 Win. Mag.

In the rare event of a cartridge case failure, the mechanism of the Model 77 has been provided with numerous vents to minimize the effect of escaping gas. A vent of the usual type is provided on the right side of the receiver. Gas which flows along the locking lug channel is largely diverted by the rugged bolt stop and vented through a special opening. In addition, the substantial flange on the bolt sleeve is designed to deflect gas away from the shooter. The one-piece bolt of the Model 77 avoids the brazed joints which are now commonly used as an economy measure. Two massive front locking lugs and a positive long extractor, combined with one-piece construction, result in extraordinary strength and reliability.

The external bolt stop, held in position by a strong hidden spring, is conveniently located on the left rear of the receiver. No tools are needed to open the bolt stop and remove the bolt.

The serrated steel-trigger is adjustable to a minimum pull of 3½ pounds. Trigger action is smooth, crisp and free from creep at all adjustments.

The safety, which is securely mounted in the heavy metal of the tang, is of the desired shotgun type; positive and readily accessible.

For added safety and convenience, the magazine floor plate is hinged to allow emptying of the magazine without having to work the cartridges through the action. The floor plate can be easily opened by pressing the release lever located at the inside front of the trigger guard.

Specifications:

ACTION: Short-stroke or magnum lengths. **BOLT:** One-piece construction, with two massive locking lugs. **EXTRACTOR:** Long external type. **BOLT STOP:** Left side of receiver, coil spring action. **TRIGGER:** Serrated steel, adjustable for weight of pull. **SPRINGS:** Music wire coil springs throughout (except for special magazine follower spring). **MAGAZINE:** Staggered box type with stainless steel follower and quick release hinged floor plate. Capacity: five rounds (plus one in chamber), three rounds in Magnum calibers. **BARREL:** 22", Chrome-molybdenum alloy steel. Except calibers 25/06, 300 Win. Mag., 338 Win. Mag., 458 Win. Magnum and 7mm Remington Magnum and all M77V which are 24". **SAFETY:** Sliding shotgun-type, mounted on receiver tang. **STOCK:** Genuine American Walnut, thoroughly seasoned, hand-checkered, and hand rubbed. Pistol grip cap with Ruger medallion. Swivel studs. Live rubber recoil pad. **STOCK DIMENSIONS:** Drop at heel: 2⅛". Drop at comb: 1⅝". **LENGTH OF PULL:** 13¾". **STOCK BEDDING:** Ruger diagonal-front-mounting-screw system (Patented) insures consistent bedding of receiver barrel assembly in stock. **LENGTH OVERALL:** 42 inches. **WEIGHT:** Approximately 6½ pounds without scope. (M77V 9 lbs.) and 458 mag. model, approx. 8¾ lbs.

MODELS AND PRICES

M77R—with scope rings only	$277.50
M77ST—(Round Top) with open sights	277.50
M77R — 338 Mag.	293.75
M77RS—with rings and sights	293.75
M77RS—338 Win. Mag.	310.00
M77RS— 458 Win. Mag.,	382.00
M77V—with 24" heavy barrel	277.50
M77B/A—Barreled actions	$215.00 to 310.00
D-71—Ruger 1" Steel Extra Rings (pr.)	19.50

RUGER AUTOLOADING CARBINES
IN 22 LONG RIFLE AND 44 MAGNUM CALIBERS

10-Shot Rotary Magazine

STANDARD CARBINE

10/22 Carbine (22 L. R. cal.) $87.50

STANDARD CARBINE

44 Carbine (44 Mag. cal.) $198.00

DELUXE SPORTER (Illustrated)

10/22 Deluxe Sporter (22 L. R. cal.) $102.50

Model 10/22 Carbine
22 LONG RIFLE CALIBER

Identical in size, balance and style to the Ruger 44 Magnum Carbine and nearly the same in weight, the 10/22 is a companion to its high-power counterpart. Construction of the 10/22 Carbine is rugged and follows the Ruger design practice of building a firearm from integrated sub-assemblies. For example, the trigger housing assembly contains the entire ignition system, which employs a high-speed, swinging hammer to insure the shortest possible lock time. The barrel is assembled to the receiver by a unique dual-screw dove-tail system that provides unusual rigidity and strength—and accounts, in part, for the exceptional accuracy of the 10/22.

Specifications: Caliber: 22 long rifle, high-speed or standard velocity loads. **Barrel:** 18½" length. Barrel is assembled to the receiver by unique dual-screw dove-tail mounting for added strength and rigidity. **Weight:** 5 pounds. **Overall Length:** 37". **Sights:** 1/16" gold bead front sight. Single folding leaf rear sight, adjustable for elevation. Receiver drilled and tapped for scope blocks or tip-off mount adapter. **Magazine:** 10-shot capacity, exclusive Ruger rotary design. Fits flush into stock. **Trigger:** Curved finger surface, 3/8" wide. **Safety:** Sliding cross-button type. Safety locks both sear and hammer and cannot be put in safe position unless gun is cocked. **Stocks:** Solid American walnut, oil finished. Available in 2 styles. The Standard Carbine and The Sporter. **Finish:** Polished all over and blued or anodized.

Model 44 Carbine
44 MAGNUM CALIBER

The carbine is gas-operated, with the slide energized by a short-stroke piston driven by a very small quantity of gas tapped from the barrel during firing. The mechanism is exceptionally smooth in operation, strong, reliable and safe; the breech remains locked until it is opened automatically *after* the bullet has left the barrel. The receiver is machined from a solid block of hot-rolled chrome molybdenum steel. The tubular magazine is located in the fore-end, capacity is 4 shots, with an additional shot in the chamber. When the last shot has been fired, the breech remains open until it is released by operating the latch located just ahead of the trigger guard.

Specifications: Caliber: 44 Magnum only, using all factory loads. The use of jacketed bullets is recommended to insure optimum accuracy and maximum stopping power. **Barrel:** 18½" long, 12 groove rifling, 38" twist. Barrel is permanently assembled to the receiver by 20 pitch screw threads. **Weight:** 5 pounds, 12 ounces. **Overall Length:** 36¾". **Sights:** 1/16" gold bead front sight. Single folding leaf rear sight, adjustable for elevation. Receiver drilled and tapped. **Magazine:** Fixed, tubular type located in fore-end. **Capacity:** 4 rounds plus 1 round in chamber. **Trigger:** Two stage pull. Curved finger surface 3/8" wide. **Safety:** Sliding cross-button type. Safety locks both sear and hammer and cannot be put in safe position unless gun is cocked. **Stock:** Genuine American walnut.

RUGER No. 3 CARBINE

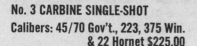

No. 3 CARBINE SINGLE-SHOT

Calibers: 45/70 Gov't., 223, 375 Win.
& 22 Hornet $225.00

The Same Strong, Rugged Action as the
Ruger No. 1 Rifle, with an American Style Lever

A mechanism of power and precision. Receiver and all action parts are made of heat treated alloy steel.

SPECIFICATIONS

Caliber—45/70, 223, 22 Hornet, 375 Win., Single-shot.
Barrel—22 inches.
Weight—6 pounds.
Overall Length—38½ inches.
Rear Sight—Folding leaf adjustable.
Front Sight—Gold bead.
Safety—Sliding tang.
Stock and Forearm—Solid American Walnut.

RUGER MINI-14 223 CARBINE

RUGER MINI-14
223 (5.56mm)
Blued $217.50
Stainless Steel $267.50

General:

MATERIALS—Heat–treated Chrome molybdenum and other alloy steels, as well as music wire coil springs, are used throughout the mechanism to ensure reliability under field operating conditions.

SAFETY—The safety blocks both the hammer and sear. The slide can be cycled when the safety is on. The safety is mounted in the front of the trigger guard so that it may be set to Fire position without removing finger from trigger guard.

FIRING PIN—The firing pin is retracted mechanically during the first part of the unlocking of the bolt. The rifle can only be fired when the bolt is safely locked.

STOCK—One-piece American hardwood reinforced with steel liner at stressed areas. Handguard and forearm separated by air space from barrel to promote cooling under rapid-fire conditions.

FIELD STRIPPING—The Carbine can be field stripped to its eight (8) basic subassemblies in a matter of seconds and without the use of tools. All of these subassemblies are significant in size and not subject to loss. Further disassembly can be accomplished, if desired, without the use of special tools. This should, however, not be necessary for cleaning or field maintenance.

SPECIFICATIONS—CALIBER: 223 (5.56mm). **LENGTH:** 37¼" **WEIGHT:** 6 lbs. 4 oz. **MAGAZINE:** 5 round, detachable box magazine. 10-shot and 20-shot magazines available from Ruger dealers. **BARREL LENGTH:** 18½".

STERLING RIFLES

MODEL BP-22

THE BACKPACKER

$49.95

Single shot rifle, available in 22 short, long or long rifle calibers. A lightweight, take-down model convenient for small game. Equipped with ramp sights and a cross bolt safety. Woodtone plastic stock and forearm; deep blued finish. Length assembled: 34". Length knocked down: 19". Weight: 3¼ lbs.

ROSSI RIFLES

ROSSI SLIDE-ACTION GALLERY MODEL
Standard or Carbine
Blue $125.00

The tubular magazine holds 20 short, 16 long, and 13 long rifle 22 rimfire cartridges interchangeably. Available in blue finish.

Model	Finish	Weight	Barrel Length	Price
Standard	Blue	5¾	23"	$139.00
Carbine	Blue	5½	16¼"	125.00

ROSSI SADDLE-RING LEVER ACTION CARBINE
357 Mag. or 38 Special

Model	Finish	Weight	Barrel Length	Price
Carbine	Blue	5¾ lbs.	20"	$209.00

SPRINGFIELD ARMORY

SPRINGFIELD ARMORY 7.62MM M1A
Standard Rifle M1A $420.00
Match Grade M1A $540.50
Super Match M1A Rifle
with heavy premium bbl. $650.00

Specifications: Mechanism Type: Gas-operated, semi-automatic, clip-loaded, detachable box magazine. **Grade:** Standard "Issue-Grade" w/walnut stock. **Caliber:** 7.62 mm. NATO (308 Winchester). **Weight:** 8 lbs. 15 ozs. **Barrel Length:** 25-1/16" w/flash suppressor. **Over-All Length:** 44¼".

Magazine Capacity: 20 rounds. **Stock Dimensions:** Length of pull, 13¼"; drop at comb, 2⅜"; drop at heel, 2¾". **Sights:** Military. Square blade front; full click-adjustable aperture rear. **Sight Radius:** 26-1/16". **Accessories:** 1 magazine.

M1 GARAND RIFLE
Standard $420.00
National Match 564.00

Specifications: Mechanism Type: Gas operated, semi-automatic, clip-fed. **Grade:** Standard "Issue-Grade" w/walnut stock. **Caliber:** 30M2, (30-06). **Weight:** 9 lbs., 8 ozs. **Barrel Length:** 24". **Over-All Length:** 43½". **Magazine Capacity:** 8 rounds. **Stock Dimensions:** Length of pull, 13"; drop at comb, 2"; drop at heel, 2½". **Sights:** Front, military square blade; Rear, full click-adjustable aperture.

SAKO RIFLES

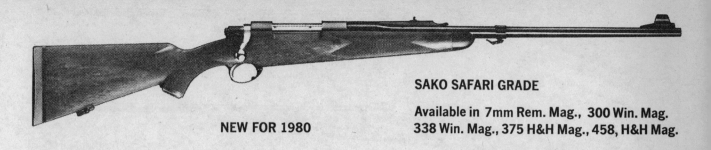

SAKO SAFARI GRADE

NEW FOR 1980

Available in 7mm Rem. Mag., 300 Win. Mag.
338 Win. Mag., 375 H&H Mag., 458, H&H Mag.

SAKO SUPER DELUXE

NEW FOR 1980

Available in AIII Calibers (Long action)
25-06 Rem., 270 Win., 30-06, 7mm Rem. Mag.,
300 Win. Mag., 338 Win., 375 H&H.

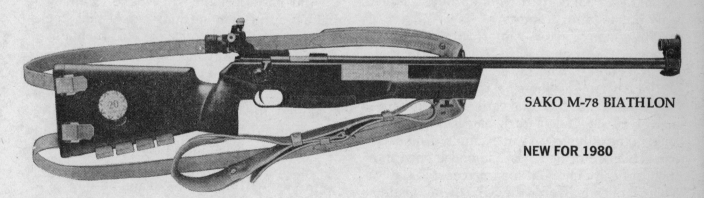

SAKO M-78 BIATHLON

NEW FOR 1980

- Caliber: 22 L.R.
- Total weight: (with all balance weights) 4.7 kg
- Barrel length: 660 mm
- Total length: 1115 mm
- Stock: strong polyurethane
- Weight: 0.75 kg + balance weights 0.5 kg
- Trigger pressure: adjustable between 0.3 — 1.1 kg without any disassembly of weapon

- Action: M-78 action and trigger mechanism
- Sights: micrometric with snow cover
- Function and grouping tested at various degrees down to —20°C.
- Includes carrying harnesses, shooting sling and 5 magazines of 5 rounds each + 2 casettes of 3 rounds, for relay

SAKO RIFLES

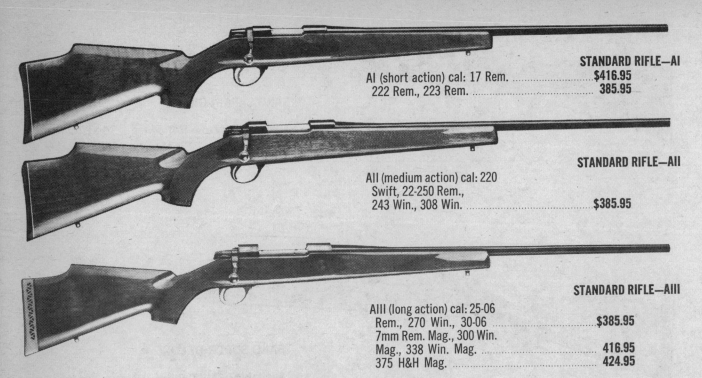

STANDARD RIFLE—AI

AI (short action) cal: 17 Rem. $416.95
222 Rem., 223 Rem. 385.95

STANDARD RIFLE—AII

AII (medium action) cal: 220
Swift, 22-250 Rem.,
243 Win., 308 Win. $385.95

STANDARD RIFLE—AIII

AIII (long action) cal: 25-06
Rem., 270 Win., 30-06 .... $385.95
7mm Rem. Mag., 300 Win.
Mag., 338 Win. Mag. 416.95
375 H&H Mag. 424.95

THE SAKO TRIGGER IS A RIFLEMAN'S DELIGHT ... SMOOTH, CRISP AND FULLY ADJUSTABLE.

If these were the only Sako features, it would still be the best rifle available. But the real quality that sets Sako apart from all others is its truly outstanding accuracy.

While many factors can affect a rifle's accuracy, 90% of any rifle's accuracy potential lies in its barrel. And the creation of superbly accurate barrels is where Sako is unique.

The care that Sako takes in the cold-hammering processing of each barrel is unparalleled in the industry. As an example, after each barrel blank is drilled, it is diamond-lapped and then optically checked for microscopic flaws. This extra care affords the Sako owner lasting accuracy and a finish that will stay "new" season after season.

You can't buy an unfired Sako. Every gun is test fired using special overloaded proof cartridges. This ensures the Sako owner total safety and uncompromising accuracy. Every barrel must group within Sako specifications or it's scrapped. Not recycled. Not adjusted.

Scrapped. Either a Sako barrel delivers Sako accuracy, or it never leaves the factory.

And hand-in-hand with Sako accuracy is Sako beauty. Genuine European walnut stocks, flawlessly finished and checkered by hand.

Sako rifles are available in the following:

- Standard, with AI, AII and AIII actions.
- Deluxe, with AI, AII and AIII actions. Varmint, with heavy-barrel and Varminter forend in AI, AII and AIII (25-06 Rem. and 7mm Rem. Mag. only) actions.
- Carbine — with full length stock. AII action in 243. AIII action in 270 and 30-06.
- Model 78, with lightweight action in 22 L.R., 22 Hornet, 22 L.R. Heavy Barrel, and 22 Magnum.

Sako rifles. Whichever you choose, you'll be buying a superbly accurate, outstandingly beautiful rifle.

Because that's the only kind of rifle that Sako makes.

SAKO RIFLES

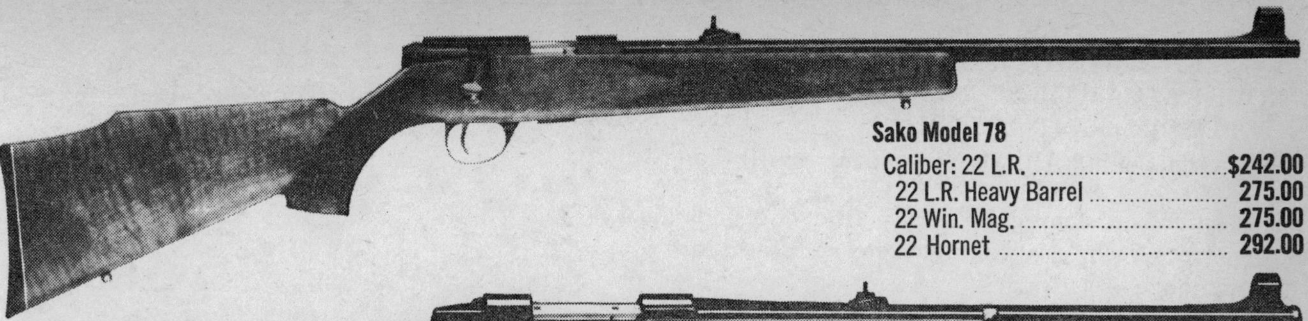

Sako Model 78

Caliber: 22 L.R. $242.00
22 L.R. Heavy Barrel 275.00
22 Win. Mag. 275.00
22 Hornet 292.00

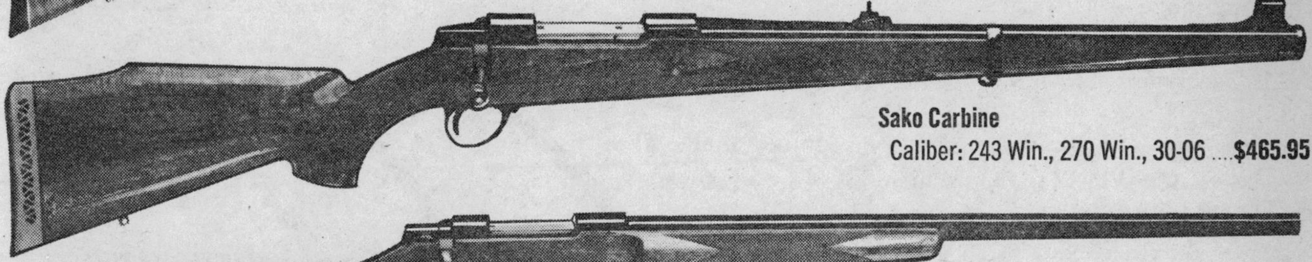

Sako Carbine

Caliber: 243 Win., 270 Win., 30-06 .... $465.95

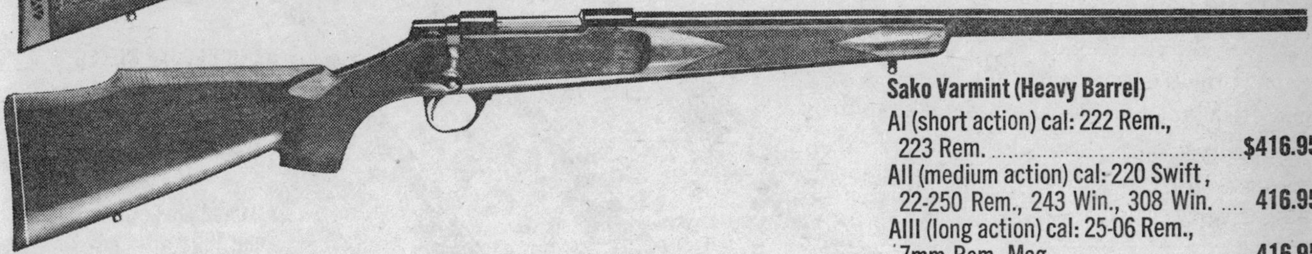

Sako Varmint (Heavy Barrel)

AI (short action) cal: 222 Rem., 223 Rem. $416.95
AII (medium action) cal: 220 Swift, 22-250 Rem., 243 Win., 308 Win. 416.95
AIII (long action) cal: 25-06 Rem., 7mm Rem. Mag. 416.95

FINLAND sako Specifications

1) COMPLETE RIFLES:

CALIBERS	AVAILABLE MODELS	ACTIONS TYPE	MAGAZINE CAPACITY	BARREL LENGTH	APPROX. WEIGHT (STD. & DELUXE)	APPROX. WEIGHT (VARMINT & CARBINE)	TWIST: R.H. 1-TURN-IN	LENGTH OF PULL
.22 L.R.	78	78	5	22½"	6¾ lbs.		16½"	13½"
.22 L.R. Heavy Barrel	78	78	5	22½"	7¼ lbs.		16"	13½"
.22 Hornet	78	78	4	22½"	6¾ lbs.		14"	13½"
.22 Magnum	78	78	4	22½"	6¾ lbs.		16"	13½"
.17 Rem.	Standard	AI$_1$	5	23½"	6½ lbs.		9"	13½"
.222	Standard/Deluxe/Varmint	AI$_1$	5	23½"	6½ lbs.	8¼ lbs.	14"	13½"
.223	Standard/Deluxe/Varmint	AI$_1$	5	23½"	6½ lbs.	8¼ lbs.	13"	13½"
.220 Swift	Standard/Deluxe/Varmint	AII$_2$	5	23½"	7¼ lbs.	8½ lbs.	14"	13½"
.22-250	Standard/Deluxe/Varmint	AII$_3$	5	23½"	7¼ lbs.	8½ lbs.	14"	13½"
.243	Standard/Deluxe/Varmint/Carbine	AII$_1$	5	23" (20" Carbine)	7¼ lbs.	8½ lbs.	10"	13½"
.308	Standard/Deluxe/Varmint	AII$_1$	5	23"	7¼ lbs.	8½ lbs.	12"	13½"
.25-06	Standard/Deluxe/Varmint	AIII$_1$	5	24"	8 lbs.	8¾ lbs.	10"	13½"
.270	Standard/Deluxe/Carbine	AIII$_1$	5	24" (20" Carbine)	8 lbs.	8¾ lbs.	10"	13½"
.30-06	Standard/Deluxe/Carbine	AIII$_1$	5	24" (20" Carbine)	8 lbs.	7½ lbs.	10"	13½"
7mm Rem. Mag.	Standard/Deluxe/Varmint	AIII$_2$	4	24"	8 lbs.	8¾ lbs.	9½"	13½"
.300 Win. Mag.	Standard/Deluxe	AIII$_3$	4	24"	8 lbs.		10"	13½"
.338 Win. Mag.	Standard/Deluxe	AIII$_3$	4	24"	8 lbs.		10"	13½"
.375 H&H Mag.	Standard/Deluxe	AIII$_4$	4	24"	8 lbs.		12"	13½"

STOCK: Mod. 78: European walnut, oil-type finish, hand-checkered 20-lines to the inch. Carbine: Full length stock, European walnut, high gloss finish, hand-checkered 20-lines to the inch. Varmint: European walnut, high gloss finish, hand-checkered 20 lines to the inch, full beavertail forend. Standard: European walnut, high gloss finish, hand-checkered 20-lines to the inch. Deluxe: European walnut, high gloss finish, French-type hand-checkered 22-lines to the inch, rosewood grip cap and forend tip, semi-beavertail forend.

METAL FINISH: Mod. 78, Carbine, Varmint and Standard: Satin finish. Deluxe Models: Super high-polished deep blue.

2) BARRELLED ACTIONS:

Are available for all calibers and models with exclusion of Model 78 and Carbine.

3) SAKO ACTIONS:

ACTION TYPE	CALIBERS	BARREL THREAD	OVER-ALL LENGTH	APPOX. WEIGHT	MAGAZINE LENGTH
AI$_1$	.17, .222, .222 Rem. Mag., .223	.866 x 16w	6½"	2½ lbs.	2.32"
AII$_1$	.243, .308	1 x 16 unified	7⅜"	2½ lbs.	2.85"
AII$_2$	.220 Swift	1 x 16 unified	7⅜"	2½ lbs.	2.85" (backside inclined)
AII$_3$	.22-250	1 x 16 unified	7⅜"	2½ lbs.	2.72"
AIII$_1$	.25-06, .270, .30-06	1 1/64 x 16 unified	8⅜"	2¾ lbs.	3.64"
AIII$_2$	7mm Rem. Mag.	1 1/64 x 16 unified	8⅜"	2¾ lbs.	3.64"
AIII$_3$	.300 Win. Mag., .338 Win. Mag.	1 1/64 x 16 unified	8⅜"	2¾ lbs.	3.64"
AIII$_4$	.375 H&H Mag.	1 1/64 x 16 unified	8⅜"	2¾ lbs.	3.64"

SAKO RIFLES

SAKO HIGH-POWERED RIFLES ARE UNIQUE IN THAT THEY ARE MADE IN THREE DIFFERENT ACTIONS.

• AI (Short action) • AII (Medium action) • AIII (Long action)

Each action is customized to fit a specific set of individual hunting needs, each designed, engineered and scaled for a specific range of cartridges:

• AI (Short action) 222 Rem., 223 Rem.

• AII (Medium action) 22-250 Rem., 220 Swift, 243 Win., 308 Win.

• AIII (Long action) 25-06 Rem., 270 Win., 30-06, 7mm Rem. Mag., 300 Win. Mag., 338 Win. Mag., 375 H&H Mag.

Every Sako rifle, regardless of caliber, is built on an action with no unnecessary bulk or excess weight and with a bolt action as short as it is smooth.

Not only is the action scaled to the cartridge, the entire rifle is beautifully proportioned and perfectly scaled.

SAKO DELUXE RIFLES

AI (short action)
cal: 222 Rem., 223 Rem. **$545.00**

AII (medium action)
cal: 220 Swift, 22-250 Rem., 243 Win., 308 Win. **$545.00**

AIII (long action)
cal: 25-06 Rem., 270 Win., 30-06 .. **$545.00**
7mm Rem. Mag. ... **$575.00**
300 Win Mag. **575.00**
338 Win Mag. **575.00**
375 H&H Mag. **600.00**

• The Sako AI, (Short action) chambered for 222 Rem., will weigh an easy-to-carry 6½ lbs.

• The Sako AII (Medium action), chambered for 220 Swift, comes in at 7¼ lbs.

• The Sako AIII (Long action), chambered for the big 375 H&H Mag., will tip the scales at a recoil-absorbing 8 lbs.

As a result, every Sako delivers better handling, faster swing and less fatigue.

The scope mounting system on these Sakos is among the strongest in the world. Instead of using separate bases, a tapered dovetail is milled right into the receiver, to which the scope rings are mounted. A beautifully simple system that's been proven by over twenty years of use. Sako scope rings are available in: low (2½ to 3-power scopes); medium (4-power scopes) and high (6-power scopes). In either 1" or 26mm rings.

SAKO RIFLES

SAKO BARRELLED ACTIONS:

FOR THE PRIVATE OR PROFESSIONAL GUNSMITH WHO WISHES TO
BUILD HIS OWN CUSTOM RIFLE, SAKO OFFERS BARRELLED
ACTIONS IN STANDARD DEEP BLUE AND DELUXE MIRROR-POLISHED
DEEP BLUE FINISH. AVAILABLE IN AI (SHORT ACTION), AII (MEDIUM
ACTION) AND AIII (LONG ACTION).

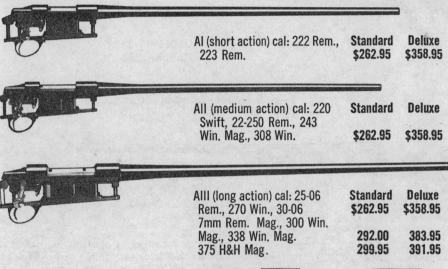

	Standard	Deluxe
AI (short action) cal: 222 Rem., 223 Rem.	$262.95	$358.95

	Standard	Deluxe
AII (medium action) cal: 220 Swift, 22-250 Rem., 243 Win. Mag., 308 Win.	$262.95	$358.95

	Standard	Deluxe
AIII (long action) cal: 25-06 Rem., 270 Win., 30-06	$262.95	$358.95
7mm Rem. Mag., 300 Win. Mag., 338 Win. Mag.	292.00	383.95
375 H&H Mag.	299.95	391.95

SAKO ACTIONS: ONLY WHEN
YOU BUY A SAKO RIFLE DO
YOU HAVE THE CHOICE OF
THREE DISTINCT ACTIONS.
EACH CUSTOMIZED TO FIT
A SPECIFIC SET OF INDIVID-
UAL HUNTING NEEDS. EACH
DESIGNED, ENGINEERED AND
SCALED FOR A SPECIFIC
RANGE OF CARTRIDGES. AS
A RESULT, SAKO DELIVERS
BETTER HANDLING, FASTER
SWING AND LESS FATIGUE.
SAKO ALSO OFFERS THESE
ACTIONS ALONE IN AI
(SHORT ACTION), AII (MED-
IUM ACTION) AND AIII (LONG
ACTION). AVAILABLE IN THE
WHITE ONLY.

**AI (SHORT ACTION)
CALIBERS:**
17 Rem.
222 Rem.
222 Rem. Mag.
223 Rem.
In the white only $186.95

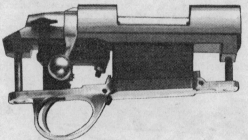

**AII (MEDIUM ACTION)
CALIBERS:**
22-250 Rem.
220 Swift
243 Win.
308 Win.
In the white only $186.95

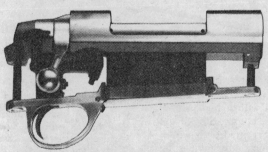
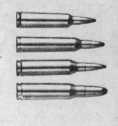

**AIII (LONG ACTION)
CALIBERS:**
25-06 Rem.
270 Win.
30-06
7mm Rem. Mag.
300 Win. Mag.
338 Win.
375 H&H Mag.
In the white only $186.95

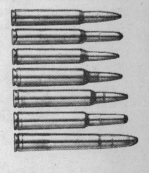

SAVAGE CENTER FIRE RIFLES

MODEL 99-358
Caliber: 358

A fast-handling rotary magazine rifle with straight stock with recoil pad, grooved fore-end for firmer control, fitted with swivel studs. **$256.68**

MODEL 99-C RIFLE
WITH CLIP MAGAZINE
Calibers: 22-250 243 & 308 Win.

Caliber: 22-250, 243 & 308 Win. **Barrel:** Tapered, lightweight, chrome-moly steel, proof-tested. Length, 22". **Action:** Hammerless, solid breech, lever action. Damascened bolt, case-hardened lever, blued steel receiver. Gold plated trigger, improved sear mechanism for crisp pull. Indicator on top tang shows when action is cocked. Safety on top tang locks trigger and lever. **Magazine:** Detachable clip magazine. Handy release and ejection push-button re-cessed in receiver. Holds 4 cartridges plus one in chamber. Extra clip magazines available at $6.50 each. **Stock:** Selected walnut, checkered. Capped pistol grip; fluted comb. Checkered fore-end. Dimensions: length 13½"; drop 1½" at comb, 2½" at heel. Corrugated steel butt plate. **Sights:** Front, gold bead on raised ramp; rear, semi-buckhorn with step elevator, folds flat for scope use, returns to same elevation setting. Tapped for top-mount scopes. **Weight:** About 7 pounds. Length overall, 41¾". . . **$254.39**

MODEL 99-CD
Calibers: 250 Savage
308 & 243 Winchester

99-CD The North American Classic—Calibers: 250 Savage; 308 and 243 Winchester.
Features: Select walnut stock designed with a high Monte Carlo, cheekpiece and deeply fluted comb. Stock and grooved forend hand-checkered. Stock is fitted with white-line recoil pad and pistol-grip cap. Quick adjustable sling with swivels. Detachable hooded ramp front sight, rear sight adjustable for elevation and windage. **$284.91**

The 99-E lever-action carbine (not illustrated) comes with a 22" barrel and is made in 300 Savage, 243 and 308 Winchester calibers. The fully enclosed box type magazine with rotary carrier has a 5-shot capacity; plus one in chamber. With blued steel lever, grooved trigger and corrugated butt plate. Walnut finished stock has tapered fore-end. Finger tip safety on right side of trigger locks trigger and lever **$217.25**

MODEL 99-A
Calibers: 250 Savage 243 & 308 Winchester

99-A Calibers: 250 Savage; 243 and 308 Winchester. The 99-A features a straight (saddle) stock with schnabel forend **$249.87**

SPECIFICATIONS—FEATURES

MODEL	Barrel Length	Barrel Steel	Steel Receiver	Tapped For Top Mount Scope	Sights		Cocking Indicator	Magazine Type	Cartridge Counter	Capacity	Safety	Stock and Fore-end	Checkered	Flut. Comb.	Capped Grip	Butt Plate	Avg. Wgt. (Lbs.)
					Front	Rear											
99-CD	22″	Chrome Moly	Blued	X	Removable Hooded Ramp	Removable -Adjustable	X	Clip		5	Top Tang	Select Walnut	X	X	X	White-Line Recoil Pad	8¼
99-C	22″	Chrome Moly	Blued	X	Removable Ramp	Folding Leaf	X	Clip		5	Top Tang	Select Walnut	X	X	X	Hard Rubber	7
99-A	22″	Chrome Moly	Blued	X	Removable Ramp	Folding Leaf	X	Rotary	X	6	Top Tang	Select Walnut		X		Steel	7
99-E	22″	Chrome Moly	Blued	X	Removable Ramp	Folding Leaf	X	Rotary		6	Slide Safety	Wal. Fin. Hardwood	X	X		Hard Rubber	7
99-358	22″	Chrome Moly	Blued	X	Removable Ramp	Folding Leaf	X	Rotary	X	6	Top Tang	Select Walnut				White-Line Recoil Pad	7

MODELS 99-CD Stock: Length 13½″; drop 1⅝″ at comb, at Monte Carlo 1½″, at heel 2½″.
99-C, A and E Stock: Length 13½″; drop 1½″ at comb. 2½″ at heel.
Length over-all: 41¾″.
99-358 Stock: Length 13½″; drop 1⅝″ at comb, at heel 2½″.

RATE OF TWIST (R.H.) 1 turn in 10″ 250 Savage, 243 and 12″ 300 Savage, 308. & 358 and 14″ 22-250.

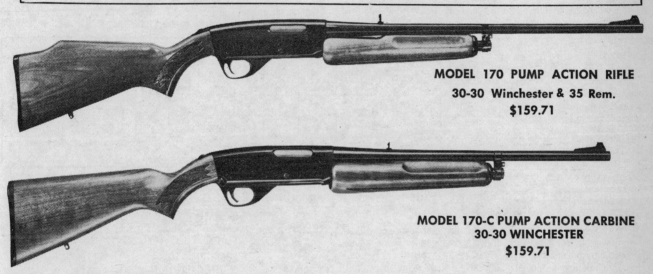

MODEL 170 PUMP ACTION RIFLE
30-30 Winchester & 35 Rem.
$159.71

MODEL 170-C PUMP ACTION CARBINE
30-30 WINCHESTER
$159.71

The Model 170 pump-action rifle was designed to handle the 30-30 Winchester and 35 Rem. cartridge. The 170 pump stroke is 3-¾″. Savage claims to have reduced friction in the action by an automatic vibrating process. It's Savage's answer to what hand-honing is meant to do. It includes the slide, bolt and sear. All locking surfaces between receiver and bolt are heat hardened. The receiver is machined from 8.9 pounds of solid tempered steel. The receiver is drilled and tapped for scope mounts.

Features include a top tang safety (under the shooter's thumb). The 170 comes with a selected walnut Monte Carlo style stock with checkered pistol grip and slide handle. Savage designed the slide handle of the 170 to slightly overlap the receiver while in the forward position. The action is hammerless, and the trigger must be released and squeezed for each shot. With 22″ barrel, the 170 weighs 6¾ lbs.

170-C (Carbine) 30-30.

The 170 is offered in a carbine variation. Shorter barrel (18½″). Sporter stock and Silent-Lok feature.

SPECIFICATIONS — FEATURES

MODEL	Barrel Length	Tapped For Top Mount Scope	Sights		Safety Fire Control	Magazine Type	Capacity	Top Tang Safety	Stock and Slide Handle	Silent -Lok	Checkered	Monte Carlo	Sling Studs	Stock Finish	Butt Plate	Avg. Wgt. (Lbs.)
			Front	Rear												
170	22″	X	Removable Ramp	Folding Leaf	X	Tubular	4	X	Select Walnut	X	X	X	X	Electro -Cote	Hard Rubber	6¾
170-C	18½″	X	Removable Ramp	Folding Leaf	X	Tubular	4	X	Select Walnut	X	X		X	Electro -Cote	Hard Rubber	6

MODEL 170   Stock: Length 14″; drop 1½″ at comb, 1½″ at Monte Carlo, 2½″ at heel.
Length over-all 41½″.
170-C   Stock: Length 14″; drop at comb 1½″, 2½″ at heel.
Length over-all 38″. Models proof-tested.

RATE OF TWIST (R.H.) 1 turn in 12″ for 30-30 & 35.

SAVAGE CENTER FIRE RIFLES

MODEL 110 BOLT ACTION CENTER FIRE RIFLES (Right & Left-Hand)

110-C (right hand)
110-CL (left hand)
Std. Calibers: 30-06 Sprg., 270 Win. & 243
Mag. Caliber: 7mm Rem. Mag.

110-C (right hand) 110-CL (left hand) Calibers: Standard—30-06 and 270 Win. & 243 (110-C only). Magnum—7mm Rem. Mag. The solid features of the 110 plus the ejector clip magazine for convenient loading and unloading. To unload, press the recessed button and out pops the clip with the shells neatly held and tips protected. An extra loaded clip in a jacket pocket provides additional fire power.

Exclusive twin gas ports in receiver, gas baffle lugs on bolt and bolt end cap give most complete protection.

Standard calibers: .... **right-hand** **$234.65**
" .... **left-hand** **243.00**
Magnum caliber: .... **right-hand** **252.15**
extra clip, $8.10 (specify caliber) **left-hand** **260.00**

SPECIFICATIONS — FEATURES

MODEL	Free Floating Barrel: Barrel Length	Free Floating Barrel: Barrel Steel	Steel Receiver	Gas Ports	Tapped For Top Mount Scope	Sights: Front	Sights: Rear	Satin Slide Bolt	Recessed Bolt Face	Safety Gas Baffles	Cocking Indicator	Magazine	Capacity	Top Tang Safety	Checkered Stock	Cheek Piece	Butt Plate	Avg. Wgt. (Lbs.)
110-C,CL	22″	Chrome Moly	Blued	2	X	Removable Ramp	Folding Leaf	X	X	3	X	Clip	5	X	Select Walnut	X	Hard Rubber	7
110-C,CL (Mag)	24″	Chrome Moly	Blued	2	X	Removable Ramp	Folding Leaf	X	X	3	X	Clip	4	X	Select Walnut	X	Recoil Pad	7¾

LEFT-HAND rifles built to same specifications, except with left-hand stock and action.
ALL MODELS Stock: Length 13½″; drop 1⅝″ at comb, 1½″ at Monte Carlo. 2¼″ at heel. Length over-all: 42½″-45″.
RATE OF TWIST (R.H.): 1 turn in 10″ for 243, 30-06, 270 and 9½″ for 7mm Rem. Mag.

MODEL 110-S Silhouette Rifle
Caliber: 308

Features: A heavy 22″ tapered barrel, ⅞″ diameter at muzzle, allows for greater accuracy. Receiver is drilled and tapped for scope mounting, satin blue finish on receiver to reduce light reflection. The barrel is free floating in special "Silhouette" stock of select walnut, has high fluted comb, hard filling, Wundhammer swell pistol grip for both right and left-hand use. Anschutz style stippled checkering on pistol grip and under fore-end. Stock is fitted with rifle recoil pad. **$229.00**

SPECIFICATIONS

MODEL		110-S
LENGTH	OVERALL	43″
	BARREL	22″
	STOCK	13½″
DROP AT	COMB	1⅜″
	MONTE CARLO	1¼″
	HEEL	2¼″
AVERAGE WEIGHT (LBS.)		(MAX. 8 lbs. 10 oz.)
CARTRIDGE CAPACITY		5

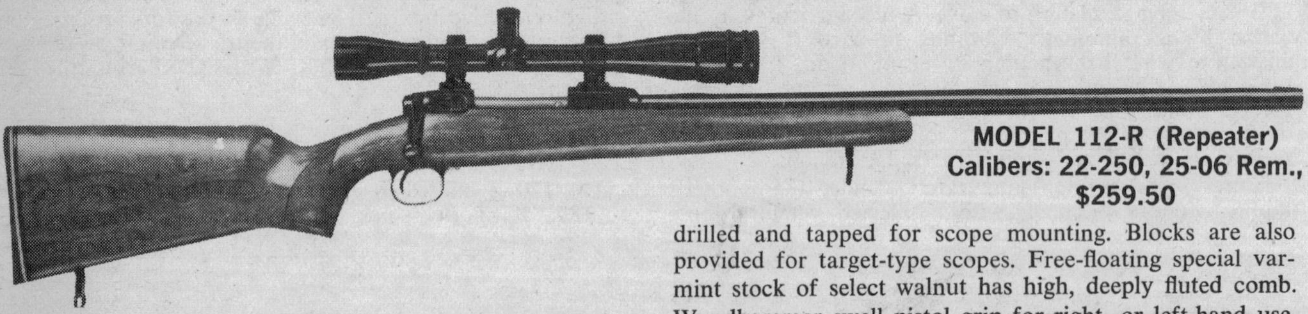

MODEL 112-R (Repeater)
Calibers: 22-250, 25-06 Rem.,
$259.50

Features: Solid, single-shot action (no magazine cuts in receiver) for rugged strength. A 26″ tapered barrel (13⁄16″ diameter at muzzle) for greater accuracy. Receiver is drilled and tapped for scope mounting. Blocks are also provided for target-type scopes. Free-floating special varmint stock of select walnut has high, deeply fluted comb. Wundhammer swell pistol grip for right- or left-hand use. Five-shot capacity. Stock is fitted with white-line recoil pad and 1¼″ quick detachable swivel loops.

SPECIFICATIONS—FEATURES

MODEL	Free Floating Barrel: Barrel Length	Free Floating Barrel: Barrel Steel	Gas Ports	Tapped For Top Mount Scope	Sights: Front	Sights: Rear	Satin Slide Bolt	Recessed Bolt Face	Safety Gas Baffles	Magazine	Capacity	Top Tang Safety	Hand Checkered Stock	Checkpiece	Swivels-Adj. Sling	Grip Cap Butt Plate	Avg. Wgt. (Lbs.)
112-R	26″	Chrome Moly	2	X Plus Blocks			X	X	3		1 In Chamber	X	Select Walnut		Swivels Only	White-Line Recoil Pad	9¼

MODEL 112-R Stock: Length 13½″; drop at comb and heel 9⁄16″ (measured from barrel center line). Length over-all: 47″.
RATE OF TWIST (R.H.): 1 turn in 10″ for 25-06, 243, 30-06, 270 and 14″ for 222, 223, 22-250, 220 Swift; 9½″ for 7mm Rem. Mag., 7 x 57.

SAVAGE & STEVENS RIFLES
MODEL 340 BOLT ACTION RIFLES

MODEL 340
Calibers: 30-30 Win., 22 Hornet, 222 and 223 Rem.
$149.06

The Savage 340 bolt-action center-fire rifle comes in calibers 30-30 Win., 22 Hornet, 222 and 223 Remington. The bolt locks up in front, assuring strength and accuracy. The barrel is precision-rifled and the muzzle is crowned.

The bolt handle is curved. Features include a Monte Carlo style stock of American walnut; checkering; pistol-grip cap and white-line spacers. Other features include detachable clip magazine (the clip pops out when the release lever is pushed) and metal open sights.

SPECIFICATIONS—FEATURES

MODEL	Barrel Length	Tapped for Scope Mount	Sights Front	Sights Rear	Thumb Safety	Clip Maga-zine	Ca-pacity	Checkered Stock Select Walnut	Checkered Stock Fluted Comb.	White Line Butt Plate	White Line Grip Cap	Monte Carlo Stock	Roll-Over Cheek Piece	Butt Plate	Avg. Wgt. (Lbs.)
340	22 Hornet, 223, 222:24"	Side Mount	Removable Ramp	Folding Leaf	X	X	5	X	X	X	X	X		Hard Rubber	7½
	30-30 22"	Side Mount	Removable Ramp	Folding Leaf	X	X	4	X	X	X	X	X		Hard Rubber	7¼

MODEL 340 Stock: Length 13½"; drop 1¾" at comb, 1¾" at Monte Carlo, 2½" at heel.
RATE OF TWIST (R.H.) 1 turn in 12" for 30-30 and 14" for 222, 223; 16" for 22 Hornet.

FALLING BLOCK MODEL SINGLE SHOT IN 22 LONG RIFLE CALIBER

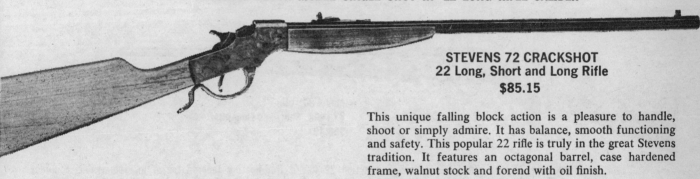

STEVENS 72 CRACKSHOT
22 Long, Short and Long Rifle
$85.15

This unique falling block action is a pleasure to handle, shoot or simply admire. It has balance, smooth functioning and safety. This popular 22 rifle is truly in the great Stevens tradition. It features an octagonal barrel, case hardened frame, walnut stock and forend with oil finish.

STEVENS 89
22 Short, Long and Long Rifle
$59.15

This little single shot has the balance and feel of a traditional western carbine. Featuring western-style lever action with a rugged Martini-type breech block, automatic ejection. Hammer must be cocked by hand independent of the lever prior to firing. Ideal for that young beginner.

SAVAGE & STEVENS 22 RIFLES

Model 73, single shot
22 Long , Short and Long Rifle

Stevens 73 22 long rifle. For the man or boy choosing his first gun—for anyone who wants a safe, dependable rifle. The safety goes on automatically when the bolt is operated—an ideal design for a first-rifle. Dependable—the bolt action is sturdy. Accurate—the free floating barrel is precision rifled. With a handsome stock and a streamlined receiver that has a satin finish. **$48.50**
Stevens 73-Y Youth model 22 long rifle (not illustrated). The 73-Y is designed for the younger shooter. The same design as the 73, but stock and barrel are shorter. Weight is only 4¼ pounds, making the 73-Y a good choice for a youngster's first gun. **$48.50**

SPECIFICATIONS — FEATURES

| MODEL | Barrel Length | Action | | | Single Shot | Frame Finish | Visible Hammer | Manually Cocking | Automatic Safety | Sights | | Stock—Fore-end | Butte Plate | Length Overall | Average Weight (Lbs.) |
		Bolt	Lever	Falling Block						Front	Rear				
89	18½″		X		X	Satin Black	X	X		Sporting	Open	Walnut Finished Hardwood	Hard Rubber	35″	5
72	22″			X	X	Case Hardened	X	X		Sporting	Open	Select Walnut	Hard Rubber	37″	4½
73	20″	X			X	Satin Black			X	Sporting	Open	Walnut Finished Hardwood	Hard Rubber	38½″	4¾
73-Y	18″	X			X	Satin Black			X	Sporting	Open	Walnut Finished Hardwood	Hard Rubber	35″	4½

Note: Chambered for 22 long rifle, long or short cartridges.
MODELS 89 and 72 Stock: Length 14″; drop 1¾″ at comb, 2¾″ at heel.
    73 and 73-Y Stock: Length 14″ (73-Y 12½″); drop 1½″ at comb, 2½″ at heel.
RATE OF TWIST (R.H.) 1 turn in 16″ for 22 L.R.

Model 34, clip
22 Long , Short and Long Rifle
$66.40

34 (extra clips): 5 shot **$4.80**
             10 shot **5.95**

Stevens 34 22 long rifle. This Stevens bolt action 22 has a free-floating tapered barrel for remarkable accuracy. Convenient thumb safety at rear of receiver. Walnut finish hardwood stock has fluted comb. Receiver is grooved for scope mount.

Model 65-M, Clip
22 Magnum
$80.45

65-M (extra clips): 5 shot **$4.80**

65-M 22 magnum. The Savage 65M, with select walnut, Monte Carlo stock, is patterned after a high power rifle. The solid steel receiver houses a smooth, fast action with a crisp trigger pull. Action is safe and dependable, with bolt encased in the receiver, a recessed bolt face, and double extractors. The free-floating barrel means accuracy.
The 65-M offers accurate shooting at ranges up to 100-125 yards for the varmint and small game hunter. Exceptionally strong lock-up and free-floating barrel make the 65-M a good choice for the magnum cartridge.

SAVAGE/STEVENS/ANSCHUTZ RIFLES

SAVAGE 80
22 Long Rifle
$84.85

This deluxe autoloader has the style and the feel of a high-power rifle. It features checkering, Monte Carlo stock, white-line pistol-grip cap and butt plate. The tubular magazine holds 15 22 long rifle cartridges. Grooved receiver for instant scope mounting.

SPECIFICATIONS — FEATURES

MODEL	Barrel Length	Grvd. For Scope	Sights Front	Sights Rear	Bolt Action	Auto-matic	Maga-zine Type	Ca-pacity	Side Safety	Stock Check-ered	Stock Monte-Carlo	Select Walnut	Walnut Fin. Hard-wood	Fluted Comb.	White Line Butt Plate	Butt Plate	Length Overall	Avg. Wgt. (Lbs.)
80	20"	X	Sporting	Open		X	Tubular	16*	X	X	X	X		X	X	Hard Rubber	40"	6
34	20"	X	Sporting	Open	X		Clip	6**	X	X	X		X	X		Hard Rubber	39"	5½
65-M	22"	X	Remove-able Ramp	Open	X		Clip	6	X	X	X	X		X	X	Hard Rubber	41"	5¾

Note: 65-M chambered for 22 WMR ONLY.
*80 chambered for 22 L.R. only. Table includes one in chamber.
**Chambered for 22 long rifle, long or short cartridges. Table includes one in chamber.
MODELS 80, 65M and 34 Stock: Length 14"; drop 1½" at comb, 1⅝" at Monte Carlo, 2½" at heel.

RATE OF TWIST (R.H.) 1 turn in 16" for 22 L.R. and 22 Mag.

ANSCHUTZ 1432
CUSTOM SPORTER

Anschutz 1432 Caliber: 22 Hornet. Anschutz has introduced this handsome sporter featuring a custom Monte Carlo stock with roll over cheek piece, contoured pistol grip and schnabel forend. Grip and forend are lavishly hand-checkered in a skip-line pattern. The stock is of fine French walnut. Receiver is grooved for scope mount and drilled and tapped for scope bases. **$510.28**

SPECIFICATIONS — FEATURES

MODEL	Barrel Length	Grooved for Scope	Tapped for Scope Mount	Sights Front	Sights Rear	Thumb Safety	Clip Maga-zine	Ca-pacity	Checkered Stock Select Walnut	Checkered Stock Fluted Comb.	White Line Butt Plate	White Line Grip Cap	Monte Carlo Stock	Roll-Over Cheek Piece	Butt Plate	Avg. Wgt. (Lbs.)
1432	22 Hornet, 24"	X	Top Mount	Hooded Ramp	Folding Leaf	Wing	X	5	X	X	X	X	X	X	Hard Rubber	6¾

1432 Stock: Length 14"; drop 1¼" at comb, 1¼" at Monte Carlo, 1¼" at heel.
RATE OF TWIST (R.H.) 1 turn in 14" for 222; 16" for 22 Hornet.

SAVAGE/ANSCHUTZ 22 SPORTERS

1418

54 SPORTER (22 L.R. or 22 Mag.)

164

CUSTOM GRADE 22 SPORTERS

164 22 long rifle, 164-M 22 magnum. The action of the 164—is the same one used on the Savage/Anschutz model 64 target rifle. The barrel is precision bored for pinpoint accuracy. Receiver is grooved for instant scope mounting. The select European walnut stock has all the custom grade features,—Monte Carlo with cheek-piece, Wundhammer swell pistol grip, schnabel fore-end and checkering. $263.06
The 164-M is chambered for the 22 magnum cartridge for those longer range shots. $269.10

54 Sporter 22 long rifle, 54-M 22 Magnum. The model 54 Sporter combines the smallbore action with a handsome sporting Monte Carlo stock of fine French walnut. Strictly custom grade from the hand-carved roll-over cheek-piece and contoured pistol grip to the graceful schnabel fore-end. Both fore-end and pistol grip are hand checkered in a skip-line pattern.

The action is the Anschutz Match 54 that has dominated smallbore rifle shooting in recent years. Receiver is grooved for scope mount and drilled and tapped for scope bases. 54 Sporter, 22 L. R. $464.22

The 54-M magnum offers Anschutz - accurate shooting up to 100-125 yards for the varmint and small game hunter. 54-M, 22 Magnum. $476.35

Anschutz 1418 22 Long Rifle, 1518 22 Win. Mag. The action is the same as the model 164 but the stock is completely European. This compact Mannlicher sporter has features such as a choice of double-set or single-stage triggers, hand-cut skip-line checkering, stock inlays and European-style Monte Carlo stock with cheek piece.
1418 22 L.R. **$373.32**
1518 22 Mag. **379.38**

SPECIFICATIONS — FEATURES

MODEL	Barrel Length	Groov-ed for Scope	Tapped For Scope Mount	Sights Front	Sights Rear	Trigger Factory set for crisp trigger pull.	Clip Maga-zine	Capa-city	Safety	Checkered Stock Cheek-piece	Checkered Stock Monte Carlo	Checkered Stock Wal-nut	Fluted Comb.	White Liner	Butt Plate	Length Overall	Average Weight (Lbs.)
54, 54-M	24″	X	X	Hooded Ramp	Folding Leaf	X	X	6*,5†	Wing	X	X	X	X	X	Hard Rubber	43″	6¾
164, 164-M	23″	X		Hooded Ramp	Folding Leaf	X	X	6*,5†	Slide	X	X	X	X	X	Hard Rubber	40¼″	6
1418 1518	19¾″	X		Hooded Ramp	Folding Leaf	X	X	6*,5†	Slide	X	X	X	X	X	Hard Rubber	37⅝″	5½

Models 54, 164 and 1418 are chambered for 22 long rifle ONLY. †Models: 1518, 164-M and 54-M chambered for 22 W.M.R. ONLY. Clip capacity 4.
MODELS 164   Stock: Length 14″; drop 1½″ at comb, 1½″ at Monte Carlo, 2¼″ at heel.
            54   Stock: Length 14″; drop 1¼″ at comb, 1¼″ at Monte Carlo, 1¼″ at heel. RATE OF TWIST (R.H.) 1 turn in 16″ for 22 L.R., 22 Mag.
      1418, 1518   Stock: Length 13½″; drop 1⅝″ at comb, 2⅛″ at Monte Carlo, 2⅜″ at heel.

Anschutz and Savage/Anschutz Target Rifles

With Adjustable Cheek Piece, Combination Hand Stop / Sling Swivel and Variable Angle Hook Butt Plate

1413 Super Match 54.

You can have the Super Match 54 in three models (1413, 1407, 1411).

Model 1413 Super Match 54. The free-style international target rifle that dominates international competition for these reasons: a new superb Match 54 bolt design that is satin smooth; very short firing pin travel for extremely fast lock time; new conveniently located side safety. The new model 5071 Match Two-Stage Triggers are faster, more precise and more reliable. The mechanism reaction time is reduced. Other features include combination hand-stop/sling swivel, hook butt plate for right- and left-hand use, adjustable palm-rest, butt plate and cheek piece. **1413 Super Match 54 $874.75 1413-L,** left-hand stock **$898.38.**

Model 1407 Match 54. Meets all International Shooting Union requirements and is suitable for all N.R.A. matches. Has new satin smooth Match 54 bolt design, new Match Two-Stage for precise and reliable adjustments and new convenient side safety. The whole stock and pistol grip are sculptured to fit the shooter in either a prone or standing position match. Hand-stop/sling swivel is included. **1407 ISU Match 54 $529.71 1407-L,** left-hand stock **$549.07.**

Model 1411 Match 54. The famous Anschutz prone rifle with the new Match 54 bolt design. Very short firing pin travel for extremely fast lock time. New conveniently located side safety, new single stage triggers are even faster, even more precise and reliable. The mechanism reaction time is reduced. Other features include adjustable cheek piece, combination hand-stop/sling swivel and adjutable butt plate. **1411 Match 54,** prone stock **$575.75 1411-L,** left-hand stock **$593.94**

1407 Match 54

1411 Match 54.

SPECIFICATIONS—FEATURES

	64	Mark 12
BARREL	Precision rifled. 22 long rifle only.	
LENGTH	26″ Medium heavy 1¹⁄₁₆″ diameter.	26″ ⅞″ diameter.
ACTION	Single shot. Large loading platform.	
TRIGGER	3 lbs. Single stage, adjustable for weight of pull, take-up, over-travel.	Factory set for crisp trigger pull.
SAFETY	Slide safety locks sear and bolt.	Slide safety locks trigger.
STOCK	Walnut finished hardwood Cheek-piece. Swivel rail.	Walnut finished hardwood.
SIGHTS	Receiver grooved for Anschutz sights. Scope blocks. Front sight base. 64-S models are equipped with Anschutz 6723 match sight set.	Front—Insert type globesight. Rear—(Micrometer click adjustments)
LENGTH	44″	43″
WEIGHT (avg.)	7¾ lbs.	8 lbs.

Left hand rifles built to same specifications, except with left-hand stock, cast-off.

RATE OF TWIST (RH) 1 turn in 16″ for 22 LR.

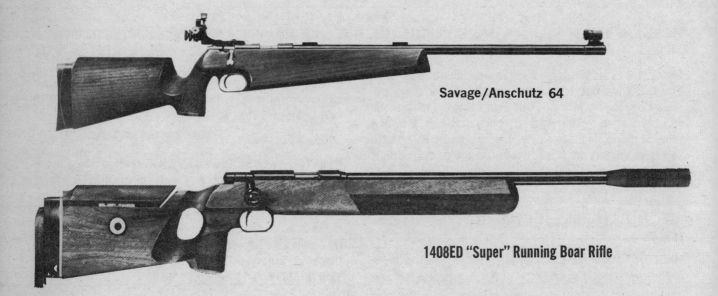

Savage/Anschutz 64

1408ED "Super" Running Boar Rifle

1408ED "Super" Running Boar Rifle.

Available on special order only. **$644.85**

SAVAGE/ANSCHUTZ 64. The 64 offers shooters a superior but moderately priced, medium weight entry into the world of international champions. Target stock has checkered pistol grip, contoured thumb groove, Wundhammer swell, beavertail fore-end and adjustable butt plate with new blackline spacer—allows you to adjust length of trigger pull to your own specifications. Three-pound single stage trigger is adjustable for weight of pull, take-up and over-travel. 64-S models are equipped with the Anschutz 6723 Match Sight Set. 64 right-hand **$260.60** 64-L left-hand **$272.72** 64-S right-hand (with sights) **$335.96** 64-SL left-hand (with sights) **$348.07.**

Savage/Anschutz Mark 12. A target rifle with true target rifle features designed in the Anschutz tradition. Action is similar to Model 64. The heavy ⅞″ diameter 26″ long barrel is precision rifled. Other features include an authentic target rifle stock with cheekpiece, thumb groove and Wundhammer swell pistol grip, adjustable hand stop and sling swivel. Comes fully equipped with front and rear target sights. The rear micrometer sight has click adjustments for windage and elevation. The globe front sight has seven aperture and post inserts for various shooting conditions and individual preferences. **$132.45.** Target sling, for right or left hand **$15.30.**

WEATHERBY RIFLES

VARMINTMASTER
Calibers: 22-250 Rem. & 224 W. Mag.
$639.95 (without sights)

Mark V VARMINTMASTER—Calibers: 22-250 Rem. and 224 Weatherby Magnum. **Action:** Mark V bolt action scaled down, six locking lugs, enclosed cartridge case head, three gas ports. **Sights:** shown with 3X to 9X Weatherby Variable Scope on Buehler Mount. **Stock:** Monte Carlo with cheek piece and hand checkering. Fore-end tip, pistol grip and rubber butt pad. $639.95 without sights.

CALIBERS: 240 W.M., 257 W.M., 270 W.M.
7 M/M W.M., 300 W.M., 340 W.M.,
378 W.M., 460 WEATHERBY MAGNUM & 30-06

MARK V
DELUXE RIFLE

MARK V DELUXE RIFLE—Calibers: 257, 270, 7m/m, 300, 340, 378 and 460 Weatherby Magnum and 30-06 calibers. **Action:** Weatherby Mark V with recessed bolt face, nine locking lugs, three gas escape ports. 54° bolt lift. **Sights:** shown with hooded ramp front sight and receiver peep sight. **Stock:** Monte Carlo with cheek piece and checkering, fore-end tip, pistol grip cap, fitted rubber recoil pad.

Mark V Deluxe Rifle, less sights, in 240, 257, 270, 7m/m, 300 W.M. and 30-06 calibers $659.95 In 340 W.M., less sights $669.95; 378 W.M. less sights $799.95; and in 460 W.M. caliber less sights $919.95. Rifles with factory-mounted scopes at extra cost. (Left hand deluxe model, $10.00 additional without sights)

MARK V CUSTOM RIFLE
(Priced from $1000.00 to $3000.00)

MARK V CUSTOM RIFLE—Specifications same as Deluxe rifle except with fancy grade walnut stock and full metal engraving. Prices range from $1000.00 to $3000.00 depending upon degree of decoration and sights desired by the shooter. Mark V Custom rifle shown is equipped with 3X to 9X Weatherby Variable scope on Buehler mount. Customs require approximately 18 months to produce.

RIFLE SPECIFICATIONS

CALIBER	224	22/250	240	257	270	7mm	30-06	300	340	378	460
Model	Right hand 24" or 26" bbl. Left hand model not available.		Right or left hand 24" bbl. Right hand 26" bbl. Left hand 26" bbl. **available in 300 cal. only**						Right or left hand 26" bbl. only.	Right or left hand 26" bbl. only.	Right or left hand 26" bbl. only.
Weight w/o sights	6½ lbs.		7¼ lbs.						8½ lbs.		10½ lbs.
Overall length	43¼" or 45¼" dependent on barrel length		44½" or 46½" dependent on barrel length						46½"		
Capacity	5 shots: 4 in magazine; 1 in chamber	4 shots: 3 in mag.; 1 in chamber	6 shots: 5 in mag.; 1 in chamber	4 shots: 3 in magazine; 1 in chamber			5 shots: 4 in mag.; 1 in chamber	4 shots: 3 in magazine; 1 in chamber		3 shots: 2 in magazine; 1 in chamber	
Barrel	24" standard or 26" semi-target		24" standard or 26" #2 contour						26" #2 contour	26" #3 contour	26" #4* contour
Rifling	1-14" twist		1-10" twist		1-10" twist		1-10" twist	1-10" twist	1-10" twist	1-12" twist	1-16" twist
Sights	Scope or iron sights extra										
Stock	American walnut, individually hand-bedded to assure precision accuracy. High-lustre, durable stock finish. Quick detachable sling swivels. Basket weave checkering. Monte Carlo style with cheek piece, especially designed for both scope and iron sighted rifles. Length of pull 13½". Length of pull of 460-13⅞".										French walnut only.
Action	A scaled-down version of the popular Mark V action with 6 precision locking lugs in place of 9.		Featuring the Mark V action. The nine locking lugs have almost double the shear area of the lugs found on conventional bolt rifles. The cartridge case head is completely enclosed in the bolt and barrel. 460 action includes hand honing, bolt knob fully checkered, bolt and follower damascened, custom engraved floor plate.								
Safety	Forward moving release accessible and positive										

BARRELED ACTION SPECIFICATIONS

CALIBER	224	22/250	240	257	270	7mm	30-06	300	340	378	460
Model	Right hand 24" or 26" bbl. Left hand model not available.		Right or left hand 24" bbl. Right hand 26" bbl. Left hand 26" bbl. **available in 300 cal. only**						Right or left hand 26" bbl. only.	Right or left hand 26" bbl. only.	Right or left hand 26" bbl. only.

*Pendleton Dekicker is an integral part of the barrel.
Prices for barreled action models
22-250 and 224 Varmintmaster calibers $400.00 240 W.M., 257 W.M., 270 W.M., 7mm W.M., 300 W.M., and 30-06 calibers $415.00. 340 W.M. $425.00 378 W.M. $495.00. 460 W.M. $555.00

WEATHERBY RIFLES

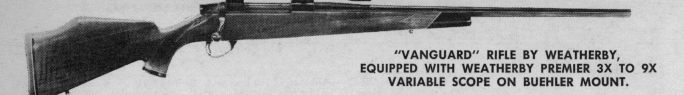

"VANGUARD" RIFLE BY WEATHERBY, EQUIPPED WITH WEATHERBY PREMIER 3X TO 9X VARIABLE SCOPE ON BUEHLER MOUNT.

The Vanguard by Weatherby is now available in the following calibers: 243 Win., 25-06, 270 WCF 7mm Rem. Mag., 30-06, and 300 Win. Mag.

The "hammer-forging" method of barrel manufacture, guarantees a glass-smooth bore with optimum dimensional stability from breech to muzzle. It is this "hammer-forging" technique which gives the Vanguard rifle its accuracy and long life.

The Vanguard action is based on one of the most highly acclaimed designs in the gun industry, yet sports many of the modern safety advancements. The bolt face is recessed and it in turn is recessed into the barrel forming 3 concentric bands of steel around the cartridge case head. In addition to this case support, the Vanguard also features a completely enclosed bolt sleeve to prevent escaping gases from flowing back through the bolt into the shooter's face. Other safety features include a gas ejection port, two massive bolt lugs, and side operated safety lever. The action

has a knurled bolt knob for a better grip, a hinged floor plate for easy removal of loaded cartridges from the magazine, and a drilled and tapped receiver for simplified scope installation. The action is forged out of high strength chrome moly steel, polished and blued to a rich deep hue. The trigger guard and floor plate are black chromed for maximum durability.

The Vanguard has a fully adjustable trigger mechanism providing a crisp and clean pull down to 3 pounds.

The Vanguard stock is made of select American walnut and bedded for accuracy, it sports a Weatherby butt pad, 45° rosewood fore-end tip and pistol grip cap, white line spacers, and the traditional Weatherby diamond inlay. The finish of the Vanguard stock is the same high luster type found on the Mark V . . . scratch resistant and impervious to water, perspiration, or solvents. The Vanguard stock has a 13½" pull and just the right amount of cast-off and drop for the average shooter.

SPECIFICATIONS
Vanguard Rifles available in right-hand models only

Calibers	243 Win.	25-06 Rem.	270 WCF	7mm Rem. Mag.	30-06	300 Win. Mag.
Price	$439.95	$439.95	$439.95	$439.95	$439.95	$439.95
Weight (approximate)	7 lb. 14 oz.	7 lb. 14 oz.	7 lb. 14 oz.	7 lb. 14 oz.	7 lb. 14 oz.	7 lb. 14 oz.
Overall Length	44 "	44½"	44½"	44½"	44½"	44½"
Magazine Capacity	5 rds.	5 rds.	5 rds.	3 rds.	5 rds.	3 rds.
Barrel Length	24"	24"	24"	24"	24"	24"
Rifling	1-10"	1-10"	1-10"	1-10"	1-10"	1-10"
Sights	Scope or iron sights at extra cost.					
Stocks	American Walnut, 13½" pull, fore-end tip & pistol grip cap					
Action	Vanguard action of the improved Mauser type					
Safety	Side operated, forward moving release, accessible & positive					
Scope Mounts	The Vanguard accepts any Mark V scope mount					

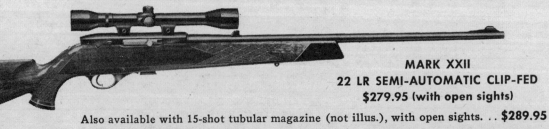

MARK XXII
22 LR SEMI-AUTOMATIC CLIP-FED
$279.95 (with open sights)

Also available with 15-shot tubular magazine (not illus.), with open sights. . . $289.95

MARK XXII RIMFIRE RIFLE—Caliber: 22 Long Rifle Rimfire. **Action:** semi-automatic, clip magazine (5 and 10 shot). Single shot selector. Bolt stays open after last shot. Shotgun-type tang safety. Receiver grooves for scope mounting. **Sights:** folding rear leaf and ramp front sight. **Stock:** Monte Carlo with cheek piece and hand checkering. Rosewood pistol grip cap and fore-end tip, and a "non-skid" rubber butt plate. Sling swivels. **Overall length:** 42¼". **Weight:** approximately 6 lbs.

WINCHESTER MODEL 70 XTR

- Classic stock design and finish • Real, cut checkering • Pistol grip contour
- Machined chrome molybdenum steel barrel and action • Hinged floor plate

Model 70 XTR Standard
$320.00

Calibers: 22-250, 243 Win., 270 Win.,
30-06, 308 Win., 222 Rem. & 25-06 Rem.

Model 70A XTR
Bolt Action Rifle
Standard calibers $283.00
Magnum calibers 301.00
70A Police 272.00

Model 70 XTR

Model 70 XTR advantages: Versatility and broad selection of calibers. Inherent accuracy due to barrel construction and precise chambering. High strength and durability from machined steel components. Dependable, smooth operation because of anti-bind bolt; fully machined and polished internal surfaces. Three-position safety; easy removal of firing pin assembly from bolt.

Features include Monte Carlo stock of American walnut with cheek-piece. Fine cut checkering. Tough, high-luster finish on wood. Black fore-end tip and pistol grip cap with white spacers. Black serrated butt plate. Hooded ramp front sight; new adjustable rear sight. Receiver drilled and tapped for scope. High polish and blueing. Engine-turned bolt. Detachable sling swivels. Hinged floor plate for fast unloading. Crisp trigger pull. Swaged rifling for accuracy.

Sets the standard for accuracy, ruggedness and dependability for hunters on seven continents.

22 in. barrel, right hand twist, 1 turn in 10 in., except 308 caliber which is 1 turn in 12 in., and 222 Rem., and 22-250 calibers which is 1 turn in 14 in.

Hooded front bead and adjustable rear sights. Stock dimensions: length of pull 13½ in., drop at comb 1¾ in., drop at heel 2⅛ in., drop at Monte Carlo 1½ in.; with cheek piece. Magazine holds 5 cartridges plus 1 in chamber.

Calibers: 22-250, 222 Rem., 243 Win., 25-06 Rem., 270 Win., 30-06, 308 Win.
$320.00

Model 70 XTR Magnum

In a range of calibers for knocking over hyenas and other predators to large game animals such as elk, moose, caribou or Kodiak bear.

24 in. barrel except the 375 H & H Magnum which has a heavyweight barrel. Hooded bead front and adjustable rear sights except for 375 H & H Magnum which is furnished with a shallow V-notch adjustable rear sight. Stock dimensions: length of pull 13½ in., drop at comb 1¾ in.; with cheek piece. Winchester rubber recoil pad. Magazine holds 3 cartridges plus 1 in chamber.

Calibers: 264 Win. Mag., 7mm Rem. Mag., 300 Win. Mag., 338 Win. Mag. **$338.00**
375 H & H Mag **495.00**

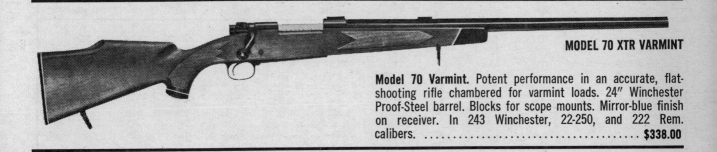

MODEL 70 XTR VARMINT

Model 70 Varmint. Potent performance in an accurate, flat-shooting rifle chambered for varmint loads. 24″ Winchester Proof-Steel barrel. Blocks for scope mounts. Mirror-blue finish on receiver. In 243 Winchester, 22-250, and 222 Rem. calibers. **$338.00**

WINCHESTER RIFLES

1. Model 70 XTR Magnum $338.00
in 375 H&H Mag. $495.00

Magnum calibers: 264 Win. Mag., 7mm Rem. Mag., 300 Win. Mag., 338 Win. Mag. & 375 H&H Mag.

2. Model 70 African
.458 Win. Magnum
$549.00

Known the world over as "The Rifleman's Rifle", today's Winchester Model 70 XTRs are quality sporting arms perfectly suited to the needs and desires of the shooter. The Model 70 XTR and the 70A XTR improvements and modifications—from all-weather stock finish and cut checkering to steel barrel and action—give every sportsman all he's ever looked for in a bolt action big game rifle.

1. Model 70 XTR Magnum. Knock-down punch for the biggest North American game . . . and then some. Black rubber recoil pad with white spacer. Twin stock reinforcing bolts. In 264, 300, and 338 Winchester Magnums, 7mm Rem. 375 H & H Magnum.

2. Model 70 African—458 Winchester Magnum. More than five thousand foot-pounds of crushing muzzle energy placed on target with superb Model 70 XTR accuracy. Special African open rear sight. Rubber recoil pad. Hand checkering. Detachable sling swivels. Carrying strap. Twin steel stock reinforcing bolts. Ebony fore-end tip.

Model 70 XTR Specifications

Caliber	222 Rem.	222 Rem. Varmint	22-250	22-250 Varmint	243 Win.	243 Win. Varmint	25-06 Rem.	264 Win. Mag.	270 Win.	7mm Rem. Mag.	30-06 Springfield	30-06 Springfield Target	308 Win.	308 Target	308 Int'l Army Match	300 Win. Mag.	338 Win. Mag.	375 H & H Mag.	458 Win. Mag. African
Mag. Capacity (a)	5	5	5	5	5	5	5	5	5	5	5	5	5	5	5	3	3	3	3
Overall Length	42½"	44½"	42½"	44½"	42½"	44½"	44½"	44½"	42½"	44½"	42½"	46½"	42½"	46½"	43¼"	44½"	44½"	44½"	42½"
Barrel Length	22"	24"	22"	24"	22"	24"	24"	24"	22"	24"	22"	26"	22"	26"	24"	24"	24"	24"	22"
Length of Pull	13½"	13½"	13½"	13½"	13½"	13½"	13½"	13½"	13½"	13½"	13½"	13¾"	13½"	13¾"	12"	13¼"	13½"	13½"	13½"
Drop at Comb	1¾"	*9/16"	1¾"	*9/16"	1¾"	*9/16"	1¾"	1¾"	1¾"	1¾"	1¾"	*½"	1¾"	*½"	1¼"	1¾"	1¾"	1¾"	1⅜"
Drop at Heel	2⅛"	*15/16"	2⅛"	*15/16"	2⅛"	*15/16"	2⅛"	2⅛"	2⅛"	2⅛"	2⅛"	*⅞"	2⅛"	*⅞"	1¼"	2⅛"	2⅛"	2⅛"	2⅜"
Drop at Monte Carlo	1½"	*⅜"	1½"	*⅜"	1½"	*⅜"	1½"	1½"	1½"	1½"	1½"	—	1½"	—	—	1½"	1½"	1½"	2⅜" / 1¾"
Weight (lbs.)	7½	9¾	7½	9¾	7½	9¾	7½	7¾	7½	7¾	7½	10½"	7½	10½"	11	7¾	7¾	8½	8½
Rate of Twist (R.H.) 1 turn in	14"	14"	14"	14"	10"	10"	10"	9"	10"	9½"	10"	10"	12"	12"	12"	10"	10"	12"	14"

(a) Add one round for cartridge in chamber   *From center line of bore. All others from line of sight.

Model 70A XTR Specifications

Caliber	222 Rem.	22-250	243 Win.	25-06 Rem.	264 Win. Magnum	270 Win.	7mm Rem. Magnum	30-06 Springfield	308 Win.	300 Win. Magnum
Magazine capacity (a)	4	4	4	4	3	4	3	4	4	3
Overall Length	42½"	42½"	42½"	44½"	44½"	42½"	44½"	42½"	42½"	44½"
Barrel Length	22"	22"	22"	24"	24"	22"	24"	22"	22"	24"
Length of Pull	13½"	13½"	13½"	13½"	13½"	13½"	13½"	13½"	13½"	13½"
Drop at Comb	1¾"	1¾"	1¾"	1¾"	1¾"	1¾"	1¾"	1¾"	1¾"	1¾"
Drop at Heel	2⅛"	2⅛"	2⅛"	2⅛"	2⅛"	2⅛"	2⅛"	2⅛"	2⅛"	2⅛"
Drop at Monte Carlo	1½"	1½"	1½"	1½"	1½"	1½"	1½"	1½"	1½"	1½"
Weight (lbs.)		7⅛	7⅛	7½	7¼	7⅛	7¼	7⅛	7⅛	7¼
Rate of Twist (R.H.) 1 turn in	14"	14"	10"	10"	9"	10"	9½"	10"	12"	10"

(a) Add one round for cartridge in chamber.

WINCHESTER RIFLES & CARBINES

MODEL 70 TARGET
CALIBERS: 30-06, 308 Winchester

The Model 70 Target rifle is available in 30-06 and 308 Win. calibers and equipped with a 26" free-floating target weight barrel; twist: 1 turn in 10", right hand. Furnished with a high comb Marksman stock for both iron and telescopic sights, full pistol grip, and wide checkered steel butt plate. Stock dimensions are listed at right. Drop dimensions are taken from center line of bore. It's also drilled and tapped for standard micrometer sights. Fitted with telescope blocks for target type mounts. Slotted for clip loading. Over-all length, 44½". Weight, 11 lbs. **$538.00**

SPECIFICATIONS
Caliber: 30-06 Springfield, 308 Winchester.
Capacity: 6 cartridges, magazine holds 5.
Sights: None; telescope blocks attached for target type mounts. Barrel tapped for front sight base.
Receiver: Tapped for popular scope mounts and receiver sights; clip slot.
Safety: 3-position type—located at rear of bolt.
Barrel: 26" Free-Floating heavyweight; twist: 30-06 1 turn in 10", 308 1 turn in 12", right hand.
Overall Length: 44½"
Stock Dimensions: Pull—30-06 13½", 308 13¼"; drop at comb—½"*; heel—⅞"*
Weight: 11 lbs.
*From center line of bore.

1. Model 94 Regular $153.00
30-30 Winchester

1. **Model 94 Lever Action Carbine.** Straight tang-to-toe lines of the American West. Hooded front sight. Sporting rear sight. Barrel band. Half-cock safety. In 30-30 Winchester, 32 Winchester Special.

2. Model 94 Antique $164.00
30-30 Winchester

2. **Model 94 Antique Lever Action Carbine.** Handsome scrollwork on marbled, case-hardened receiver. Brass-plated loading gate. Saddle ring. 30-30 Winchester.

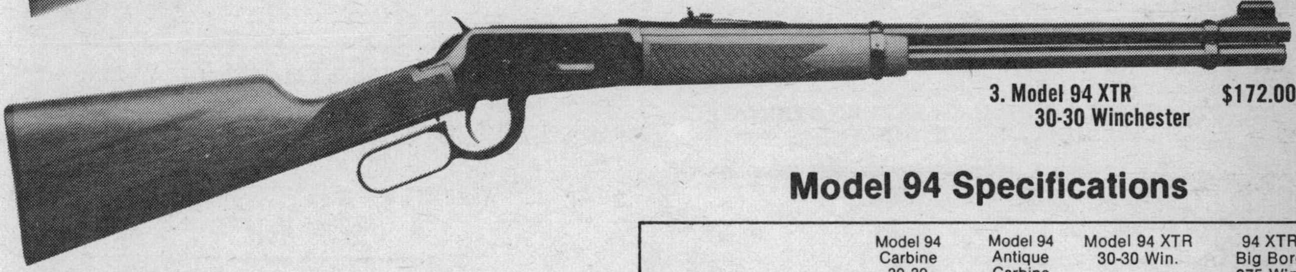

3. Model 94 XTR $172.00
30-30 Winchester

3. **Model 94 XTR.** Exposed hammer with half-cock safety. Receiver accepts several scope mounts without drilling or tapping. Black serrated butt plate. Hooded blade front sight; semibuckhorn rear sight. Barrel of chromium molybdenum steel. Improved slot in lever for smooth, fast action and feeding. 30-30 Winchester.

4. **Model 94 XTR Big Bore.** Non-glare finish on walnut; fine cut checkering on forearm and butt stock; high polish and deep blueing on the metal; beefed-up side panels; rubber butt pad reduces recoil. 375 Winchester. **$220.00**

Model 94 Specifications

	Model 94 Carbine 30-30 Win.	Model 94 Antique Carbine 30-30 Win.	Model 94 XTR 30-30 Win.	94 XTR Big Bore 375 Win.
Mag. Capacity (a)	6	6	6	6
Overall Length	37¾"	37¾"	37¾"	37¾"
Barrel Length	20"	20"	20"	20"
Length of Pull	13"	13"	13"	13¼"
Drop at Comb	1¾"	1¾"	1¾"	1¾"
Drop at Heel	2½"	2½"	2½"	2½"
Weight (lbs.)	6½	6½	6½	6⅛
Rate of Twist (R.H.) 1 turn in	12"	12"	12"	12"

(a) Add one round for cartridge in chamber

WINCHESTER Model 9422 XTR & 9422M XTR

LEVER-ACTION XTR RIM FIRE
1. Model 9422 XTR Standard $200.00
2. Model 9422M XTR Magnum 206.00

The Model 9422 XTRs have been designed with a lever action that operates quickly and smoothly, with superior control during cartridge feeding. Both the Standard and Magnum rifles are grooved for scope mounting and include these most-wanted features: a front ramp sight with dovetail bead and hood. An adjustable semi-buckhorn rear sight. Simplified takedown. Scalloped tangs. And a solid American walnut stock and forearm. All important features when you buy a sporting arm.

1. Model 9422 XTR Standard. Magazine tube holds 21 Shorts, 17 Longs, or 15 Long Rifles interchangeably.
2. Model 9422M XTR Magnum. Magazine tube holds 11 22 W.M.R. cartridges.

A choice of 22 rim fire Standard or Magnum cartridge capability.

- Coldformed Winchester Proof-Steel Barrel
- Forged steel receiver, frame, and finger lever
- Solid American walnut stock and forearm
- Side ejection
- Receiver grooved for scope mounting

Specifications

	9422 XTR	9422M XTR Magnum
Caliber	22 Rim Fire	22 Win. Mag.
Magazine Capacity	21 Shorts, or 17 Longs, or 15 Long Rifles	11 W.M.R.
Overall Length	37⅛"	37⅛"
Barrel Length	20½"	20½"
Length of Pull	13½"	13½"
Drop at Comb	1¾"	1¾"
Drop at Heel	2½"	2½"
Weight (lbs.)	6¼	6¼
Rate of Twist (R.H.) 1 turn in	16	16

WINCHESTER MODEL 70 INTERNATIONAL ARMY MATCH RIFLE

Model 70 performance and dependability in a big-bore match rifle that's accepted in International Army Match competition. Built with the same quality-engineered precision as the famed Model 70 Target. Heavy contour 24 in. barrel bedded to special stock for ultimate stability and accuracy. Receiver drilled and tapped for all standard target sights. Clip slot in receiver bridge. Counterbore protects muzzle crown. External trigger adjustment. Special stock conforms to International Shooting Union dimensions. Military oil finish on stock. Serrations on sides and bottom. Forearm rail fits all standard accessories. "Standard Rifle" type butt plate with 3 centimeters vertical adjustment. Special non-glare finish on barrel and receiver.

Bolt Action Rifle, 6 Shot

24 in. barrel; twist 1 turn in 12 in., right hand. Stock dimensions: length of pull 12 in., drop at comb 1¼ in., drop at heel 1¼ in. Magazine holds 5 cartridges plus 1 in chamber. Weight, 11 lbs.

G7041 308 Winchester $670.00

(7-62 mm Nato)

WINCHESTER MODEL 70 ULTRA MATCH
Bolt Action, 6 Shot

(not illustrated) Externally adjustable trigger provides quick, positive trigger adjustments without removing action from the stock. New glass bedding to insure perfect fit and rigidity for greater accuracy. In 308 Win. and 30-06 Springfield.

26 in. barrel. Overall length 46½ in. Magazine holds 5 cartridges plus 1 in chamber. Stock dimensions: length of pull 13¼ in., drop at comb ½ in., drop at heel ⅞ in. Rate of twist: one R.H. turn in 12 in. Weight, 12 lbs.

308 Win. $670.00
30-06 Springfield 670.00

WINCHESTER RIFLES

**LEGENDARY FRONTIERSMAN MODEL 94
$425.00**

Nickel-silver medallion is inlaid in stock. Antique silver-plated receiver engraved with scenes of the old frontier. Chambered for 38-55 Winchester caliber cartridge. Barrel is 24" round, tapered. Walnut stock. Checkered forearm.

WINCHESTER RIM-FIRE RIFLES

22 LONG RIFLE CALIBER SEMI-AUTOMATIC

**MODEL 190 WITH 4-POWER SCOPE
$88.00**

This autoloading rim-fire rifle is designed for small game or varmint hunting and plinking. The Model 190 has checkering on stock and forearm; rounded cocking handle; open blade front sight. It is furnished with a Weaver® 4x Marksman® Scope as a combination economy package. Adjustable semi-buckhorn rear sights. Semi-automatic action for rapid fire. Easy disassembly and cleaning due to one-piece trigger assembly. Holds 17 Long or 15 Long Rifle cartridges.

Model 190 Semi-Automatic Specifications

Caliber	Magazine Capacity	Barrel Length	Overall Length	Length of Pull	Drop at Comb	Drop at Heel	Drop at Monte Carlo	Weight (lbs.)	Rate of Twist (R.H.) 1 turn in
Model 190 with Scope									
22 Rim Fire Long, Long Rifle	17 Longs, or 15 Long Rifles	20½"	39"	13⅝"	1¾"	2¾"	2¼"	5	16"

WINCHESTER 22 TARGET RIFLES

MODEL 52 INTERNATIONAL MATCH RIFLE
22 L.R. Special Order

This entry from Winchester is designed and styled to offer serious competitive shooters the finest in match rifles. Features include international style laminated stock with thumbhole. International butt plate assembly complete with hook and rubber butt plate. Fully adjustable for cant, horizontal and vertical movement. Full length, black modified aluminum accessory track. Polished aluminum trigger guard with trigger adjustment holes. International palm rest assembly. Aluminum fore-end stop assembly with felt base, detachable swivel, clamping bar. Heavyweight 28″ barrel with special Winchester counterbore. Supplied with steel telescopic blocks.

$744.00

Available with Kenyon Trigger or I.S.U. Trigger **937.00**

MODEL 52D TARGET RIFLE
22 Long Rifle only
(Single Shot)

The Model 52D single-shot target rifle is made in 22 Long Rifle only. Available with 28″ heavy weight barrel; comes without sights. With free-floating barrel, adjustable bedding device and squared bright finished muzzle. Receiver, bolt and firing pin are carburized. American Walnut stock with non-slip rubber butt pad and adjustable hand-stop in full length channel.

G5225 Target Rifle (Heavy Wt. Barrel) **$393.00**

Capacity—Single shot.
Sights—None.
Receiver—Tapped for popular receiver sights.
Barrel—28″, tapped for front sight base; twist 1 turn in 16″. Right hand.
Overall Length—46″.
Stock Dimensions—
Standard Weight—Pull—13⅝″; drop at comb—¼″; drop at heel—¾″. Heavy Weight—Pull—13⅝″; drop at comb—¼″; drop at heel—none (drop dimensions taken from center line of bore.)
Weight—Heavy Weight barrel—11 lbs.

MODEL 52 INTERNATIONAL PRONE TARGET RIFLE
22 Long Rifle
(Single Shot)

With bolt action and ultra-modern styled prone stock, the Winchester Model 52 International Prone Target Rifle features a full rollover cheek piece easily removable for bore cleaning—plus all the features of the Model 52 International barrelled action. Available on special order only. 28 in. barrel, twist 1 turn in 16 in. Length of pull 13⅝ in., drop at heel ¼ in.; 46 in. lengths over all.

For 22 caliber long rifle cartridges. Weight is 11½ lbs. **$634.00**

Rim Fire Rifle Specifications

	Model	Caliber	Magazine Capacity	Over-all Length	Barrel Length	Length of Pull	Drop at Comb	Drop at Heel	Drop at M.C.	Weight (lbs.)	Rate of Twist
Lever	9422	22 Rim Fire Short, Long, Long Rifle	21 Shorts or 17 Longs or 15 Long Rifles	37⅛"	20½"	13½"	1¾"	2½"	—	6¼	16"
	9422M	22 Win. Mag.	11 W.M.R.	37⅛"	20½"	13½"	1¾"	2½"	—	6¼	16"
Target	52D Hvy. Wt.	22 Long Rifle Only	Single Shot	46"	28"	13⅝"	¼"††	None	—	11	16"
	52 Int'l. Match	22 Long Rifle Only	Single Shot	44½"	28"	12⅛₆" 14₁₆" ♦	⅛₆"††	⅜₆"	⅛₆"	13½	16"
	52 Int'l Prone	22 Long Rifle Only	Single Shot	46"	28"	13⅝"	—	¼"††	No drop at center cheek piece	11½	16"

♦Spread of adjustment   ††Drop dimensions taken from center line of bore

WINSLOW RIFLES

Standard specifications for all Winslow Rifles

Stock: Hand rubbed black walnut. Length of pull—13½ inches. Plainsmaster ⅜ inch castoff. Bushmaster 3/16 inch castoff. All rifles are drilled and tapped to incorporate the use of telescopic sights. Rifles with receiver or open sights are available on special order. All rifles are equipped with quick detachable sling swivel studs and white line recoil pad. Choice of two standard stock models; Plainsmaster stock, and Bushmaster stock. **Magazine:** Staggered box type, four shot. (Blind in the stock has no floor plate.) **Action:** Mauser Mark x Action. **Overall Length:** 43 inches (Standard Model); 45 inches (Magnum). All Winslow rifles have company name and serial number and grade engraved on the action and caliber engraved on barrel. **Barrel:** Douglas barrel premium grade, chrome moly-type steel. All barrels 20 caliber through 35 caliber have six lands and grooves. All barrels larger than 35 caliber have eight lands and grooves.

All barrels are finished to (.2 to .4) micro inches inside the lands and grooves. **Total Weight (without scope):** 24 inch barrel—Standard calibers 243, 308, 270, etc. 7 to 7½ lbs. 26 inch barrel—Magnum calibers 264 Win., 300 Wby., 458 Win., etc. 8 to 9 lbs.

Winslow rifles are made in the following calibers:

Standard cartridges—22-250, 243 Win., 244 Rem., 257 Roberts, 308 Win., 30-06, 280 Rem., 270 Win., 25-06, 284 Win., 358 Win. and 7mm (7x57).

Magnum Cartridges—300 Weatherby, 300 Win., 338 Win., 358 Norma, 375 H.H., 458 Win., 257 Weatherby, 264 Win., 270 Weatherby, 7mm Weatherby, 7mm Rem., 300 H.H., 308 Norma.

Left-handed models available in most calibers.

The Winslow rifle can be fitted to suit your needs through choice of two models of stock. The Plainsmaster—Pinpoint accuracy in open country with full curl pistol grip and flat forearm. The Bushmaster—Lighter weight for bush country. Slender pistol with palm swell. Beavertail forend for light hand comfort.

All Winslow stocks incorporate a slight castoff to deflect recoil, minimizing flinch and muzzle jump.

WINSLOW BASIC RIFLE

The Basic Rifle, available in the Bushmaster stock, features one ivory diamond inlay in a rosewood grip cap and ivory trademark in bottom of forearm. Grade 'A' walnut jewelled bolt and follower **$550.00.** Plainsmaster stock **$75.00** extra. Left hand model **$650.00.**

WINSLOW RIFLES

WINSLOW GRADE CROWN

In addition to the foregoing features, the Crown includes basket weave carving, both sides and under forearm, also on each side of and to the rear of pistol grip. It also includes two eightpoint ivory and ebony inlays, one on each side of magazine box, two large triangle ivory and ebony inlays, one on each side of buttstock, one large animal ivory and ebony inlay (engraved) in buttstock. **$1630.00**

WINSLOW VARMINT

This 17 caliber is available in the Bushmaster stock and the Plainsmaster stock, which is a miniature of the original high roll-over cheek piece and a round leading edge on the forearm, modified spoon billed pistol grip. Available in 17/222, 17/222 mag. 17/233, 222 Rem. and 223. Regent grade shown. **$950.00**

WINSLOW GRADE ROYAL

In addition to foregoing features, the Winslow Royal includes carving under forearm tip, carving on each side of magazine box, carving grip cap, carving belly behind pistol grip, carving in front of and in back of cheek piece, carving on each side of buttstock. **Price upon request**

WINSLOW GRADE IMPERIAL

In addition to foregoing features, the Winslow Imperial includes barrel engraved from receiver to point eleven inches forward of receiver, engraving on the forward receiver ring, engraving on rear receiver ring, engraving on bolt handle and trigger guard, engraving on scope mounts and rings. **Price upon request**

WINSLOW GRADE EMPEROR

In addition to the foregoing features, the Winslow Emperor is engraved in gold raised relief from receiver to point six inches forward of receiver and on tip of barrel, 1 animal on each side of front receiver, 1 animal on rear receiver, 1 animal head top each scope ring, 1 animal head on bolt handle and 1 animal head on trigger guard. **Price upon request**

shotguns

Note: Gun weights may vary due to different stock wood densities, etc.

Model S55B (12 & 20 ga.) **$626.00**
Model S56E (12 & 20 ga.) **734.00**

MODEL S55B & S56E
DOUBLE BARREL OVER/UNDER SHOTGUNS

The Model S55B is made of alloy steel and European walnut. The barrels are of "Mono Bloc" construction, fitted with ventilated ribs, and have chrome-lined bores. Action bodies are made of solid, forged steel with a rich blue-black finish. All guns of this model are equipped with a single selective trigger—inertia block type (selector in safety), plain extractors, and automatic safety. Receivers and barrels are finished in rich blue-black. Stocks are of pistol grip (capped) style, while forearms are of fluted beavertail design. The wood is European walnut, hand-checkered and finished. 12 gauge, 3" magnum guns are fitted with recoil pads. The S56E model is basically the same as the fine Model S55B, but is, in addition, decorated on the receiver with **light scroll engraving**. Further, these guns are fitted with **selective automatic ejectors.**

SPECIFICATIONS—S55B & S56E

Ga.	Length	Chamber	Description	Approx. Weight
12	26"	2¾"	Imp. Cyl/Mod.	7 lbs. 3 oz.
12	28"	2¾"	Mod./Full	7 lbs. 3 oz.
12	30"	3"	Mod./Full, Mag. w/recoil pad	7 lbs. 8 oz.
12	30"	3"	Full/Full, Mag. w/recoil pad	7 lbs. 8 oz.
20	26"	3"	Imp. Cyl./Mod., Magnum	5 lbs. 8 oz.
20	28"	3"	Mod./Full, Magnum	5 lbs. 8 oz.

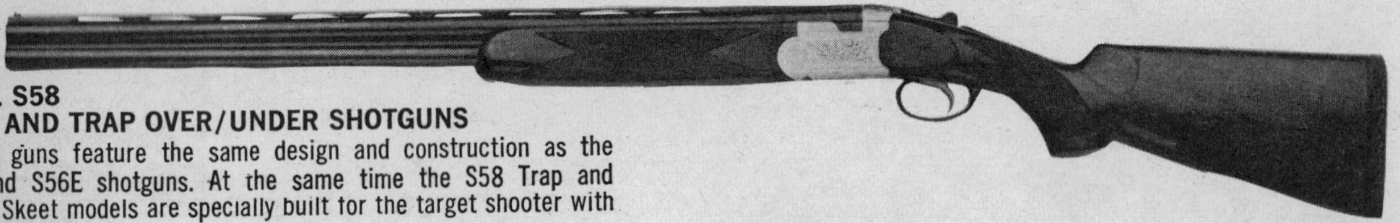

MODEL S58
SKEET AND TRAP OVER/UNDER SHOTGUNS

These guns feature the same design and construction as the S55B and S56E shotguns. At the same time the S58 Trap and the S58 Skeet models are specially built for the target shooter with the following features:

S58 Trap guns have light trigger pulls. Barrels are made of Boehler "Antinit Anticorro" steel, and fitted with a ventilated rib 0.4" (10mm) wide, knurled against glare. Safety is manual.

S58 Skeet guns are as above, except that their chokes and stock dimensions are suitable for skeet shooting.

The above S58 models are decorated like the S56E models, but actions are in silver-gray finish.

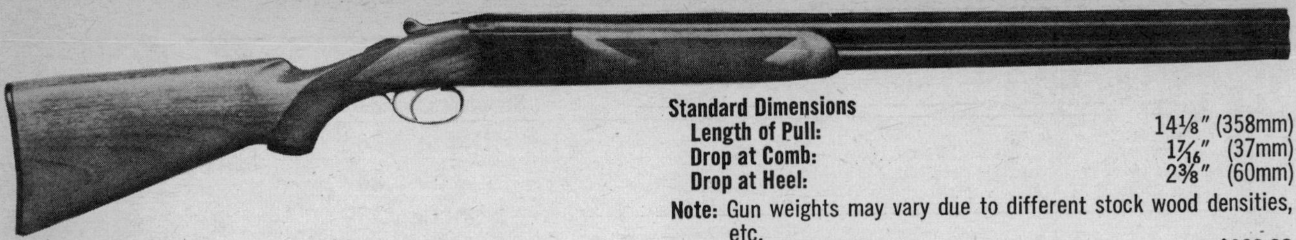

Standard Dimensions

Length of Pull (Skeet):		14¼" (362mm)
Drop at Comb (Skeet):		1½" (38mm)
Drop at Heel (Skeet):		2⁹⁄₁₆" (65mm)

Length of Pull (Trap):		14¼" (362mm)
Drop at Monte Carlo (Trap):		1⅜" (35mm)
Drop at Heel (Trap):		1⅝" (40mm)

Model S58 (12 ga.) **$829.00**

SPECIFICATIONS—S58

Ga.	Length	Chamber	Description	Approx. Weight
12	26"	2¾"	Skeet/Skeet	7 lbs. 8 oz.
12	30"	2¾"	Imp. Mod./Full Trap	7 lbs. 10 oz.

(Trap gun has Monte Carlo stock and recoil pad.)

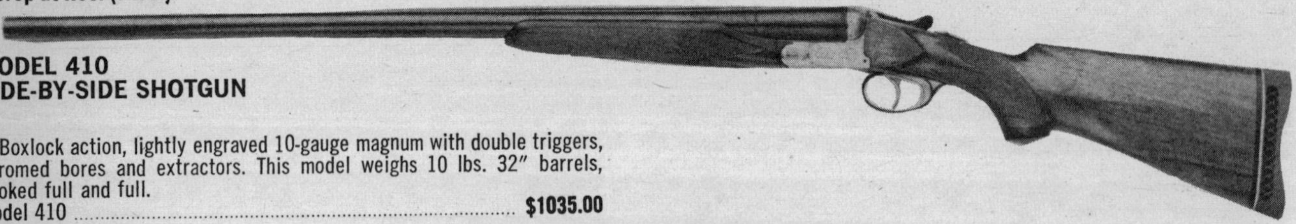

MODEL 410
SIDE-BY-SIDE SHOTGUN

Boxlock action, lightly engraved 10-gauge magnum with double triggers, chromed bores and extractors. This model weighs 10 lbs. 32" barrels, choked full and full.
Model 410 .... **$1035.00**

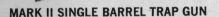

MARK II SINGLE BARREL TRAP GUN

Specifications:
12GA. 32" or 34" BBL. Full Choke (2¾" chambers. Wt. approx. 8 lbs. Auto ejector. Recoil pad. Monte Carlo type stock made of fine European walnut, hand finished and hand checkered. Fore-end is special hand filling design. Length of pull 14⅜". Drop at Monte Carlo comb 1⅜". Drop at heel 1⅝".
Mark II **$530.00**

BERETTA SHOTGUNS

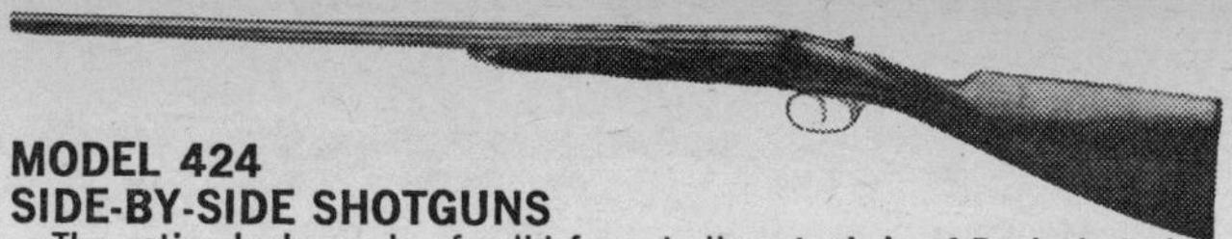

MODEL 424
SIDE-BY-SIDE SHOTGUNS

The action body, made of solid forged alloy steel, is of Boxlock design (Beretta patent) with coil springs throughout, and is nicely finished with light border engraving. Lockup is by means of double underlugs and bolts.

Barrels of steel "S" (chrome-moly) are joined on the "Mono Bloc" system giving alignment and rigidity. They are finished in a rich blue-black and are chrome lined. A hollow, matted rib is fitted to the barrels.

Model 424 shotguns are equipped with double triggers (front trigger hinged), automatic safety and plain, positive extractors.

Stocks are of the "English" straight grip type, fore-ends and stocks are made of fine, seasoned European walnut and hand-checkered.

STANDARD DIMENSIONS

Length of Pull:	14⅛" (358mm)
Drop at Comb:	1⁹⁄₁₆" (40mm)
Drop at Heel:	2⁹⁄₁₆" (65mm)

Note: Gun weights may vary due to different stock wood densities. etc.

Model 424 (12 & 20 ga.) **$757.00**

SPECIFICATIONS—Model 424

Ga.	Length	Chamber	Description	Approx. Weight
12	26"	2¾"	Imp Cyl./Mod.	6 lbs. 10 oz.
12	28"	2¾"	Mod./Full	6 lbs. 10 oz.
20	26"	3"	Imp. Cyl./Mod.	5 lbs. 14 oz.
20	28"	3"	Mod./Full	5 lbs. 14 oz.

MODEL A-301
GAS-OPERATED, SEMIAUTOMATIC SHOTGUNS

The gas system absorbs a considerable part of the recoil. All parts in contact with the powder gases are made of stainless steel. The gas piston allows the use of all 2¾" (70mm) shotshells, loaded to all standard pressure levels, without any adjustment to the gun. Those models chambered for 3" (76mm) magnum shells need no adjustment for the various 3" loads and will fire any 2¾" shotshells as well. The breech bolt is locked into the steel barrel extension at time of firing. Barrels are made of steel "S" (chrome-moly) and have chrome-lined bores. The lightweight receivers are decorated with scroll pattern and finished in blue-black, as are the barrels. Stocks and forearms are of choice European walnut, hand-checkered and richly finished.

Standard Dimensions

Length of Pull, Field Guns:	14⅛" (358mm)
Drop at Comb:	1⅜" (35mm)
Drop at Heel:	2⅜" (60mm)
Magazine Capacity:	3 Rounds

All barrels fitted with ventilated ribs, except for "Slug" barrels which have adjustable rifle sights.

All stocks are of pistol grip (capped) style, fore-ends are shaped for a firm grip. Trap gun and 3" Magnum gun stocks are fitted with recoil pads.

Safety is push button type, in trigger guard.

Model A301 Automatic w/VR (12 & 20 ga.)	**$445.00**
Model A301 Mag. Automatic w/VR (12 & 20 ga.)	**487.00**
Model A301 Automatic Slug Gun (12 ga.)	**445.00**

SPECIFICATIONS—Model A-301

Ga.	Length	Chamber	Description	Approx. Weight
12	22"	2¾"	Slug choke w/rifle sights	6 lbs. 14 oz.
12	26"	2¾"	Imp. Cyl.	6 lbs. 14 oz.
12	28"	2¾"	Mod.	6 lbs. 14 oz.
12	28"	2¾"	Full	6 lbs. 14 oz.
12	30"	2¾"	Full	7 lbs.
20	28"	3"	Full, Magnum	6 lbs. 8 oz.
20	28"	2¾"	Mod.	6 lbs. 5 oz.
20	28"	2¾"	Full	6 lbs. 5 oz.

MODEL 426E
SIDE-BY-SIDE SHOTGUNS

The 426E is basically the same as the 424, with the following added features:

The action body is decorated with fine engraving. A silver pigeon is inlaid into the top lever. The action is fitted with a selective single trigger (selector button on safety slide) and the gun has selective automatic ejectors. A hollow matted rib is joined to the barrels. The pistol-grip style stock and fore-end are of select European walnut, hand-checkered and richly finished.

Standard Dimensions

Length of Pull:	14⅛" (358mm)
Drop at Comb:	1⁹⁄₁₆" (40mm)
Drop at Heel:	2⁹⁄₁₆" (65mm)

Note: Gun weights may vary due to different stock wood densities, etc.

Model 426E (12 & 20 ga.) **$986.00**

SPECIFICATIONS—Model 426E

Ga.	Length	Chamber	Description	Approx. Weight
12	26"	2¾"	Imp. Cyl./Mod.	6 lbs. 10 oz.
12	28"	2¾"	Mod./Full	6 lbs. 10 oz.
20	26"	3"	Imp. Cyl./Mod.	5 lbs. 14 oz.
20	28"	3"	Mod./Full	5 lbs. 14 oz.

MODEL A-301
SKEET AND TRAP SHOTGUNS

These guns incorporate the same design features and materials as the A-301 field guns but are crafted for target shooting. The Trap gun has a Monte Carlo stock, fitted with recoil pad, and is choked for trap shooting The trigger is gold plated. The Skeet gun has choke and stock dimensions suitable for skeet shooting. The trigger is gold plated.

SPECIFICATIONS—TRAP GUN MODEL A-301

Ga.	Length	Chamber	Description	Approx. Weight
12	30"	2¾"	Full Choke	7 lbs. 10 oz.

Standard Dimensions

Length of Pull:	14⅜" (362mm)
Drop at M.C.:	1⅜" (35mm) to 1⁹⁄₁₆" (40mm)
Drop at Heel:	1⅝" (40mm)

SPECIFICATIONS—SKEET GUN MODEL A-301

Ga.	Length	Chamber	Description	Approx. Weight
12	26"	2¾"	Skeet Choke	7 lbs., 8 oz.

Standard Dimensions

Length of Pull:	14¼" (362mm)
Drop at Comb:	1⅜" (35mm)
Drop at Heel:	2⅜" (60mm) to 2⁹⁄₁₆" (65mm)

Model A-301 SKEET (12 & 20 ga.)	**$445.00**
Model A-301 TRAP (12 ga.)	**462.00**

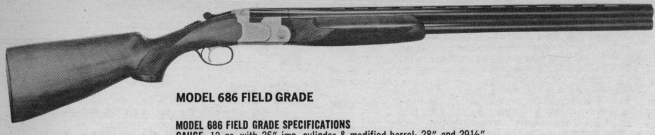

MODEL 686 FIELD GRADE

MODEL 686 FIELD GRADE SPECIFICATIONS
GAUGE: 12 ga. with 26" imp. cylinder & modified barrel; 28" and 29½"
modified & full barrel; 29½" full barrel.
ACTION: Thick side walls, with Beretta's famous low profile and high
security lockup.
TRIGGER: Selective single trigger.
STOCK: Choice European walnut, hand checkered and hand finished with
a tough gloss finish.
WEIGHT: 7 lbs. 2 oz.
PRICE: $786.00

MODEL 685 FIELD GRADE
MODEL 685 FIELD GRADE SPECIFICATIONS
GAUGE: 12 ga. with 26" imp. cylinder & modified barrel; 28" and 29½"
modified & full barrel; 29½" full barrel.
ACTION: Matte, silver-gray finished sides with reinforced receiver.
TRIGGER: Selective single trigger.
STOCK: Fine European walnut, hand checkered and finished.
WEIGHT: 7 lbs. 2 oz.
PRICE: $664.00

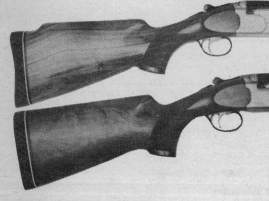

SERIES 680 TRAP & SKEET

SERIES 680 TRAP & SKEET SPECIFICATIONS
GAUGE:
   TRAP: 12 ga. with 29½" barrel, 2¾" chamber. Choked imp mod/full.
   SKEET: 12 ga. with 28" barrel, 2¾" chamber. Choked skeet/skeet.
ACTION: Thick walled and heat treated for durability and strength, with
Beretta's low profile.
TRIGGER: Selective gold-plated trigger.
STOCK: Hand-finished select figured European walnut. Dimensions are:
1¼"-1½" drop at comb. 2⅛" drop at heel and 14⅜" length of pull.
WEIGHT:
   TRAP: 8⅛ lbs.
   SKEET: 8 lbs.
PRICE: $1214.00

Beretta makes the 680 Series Trap and Skeet guns with competition features such as true box-locks and a patented firing mechanism to give the shortest possible firing time. A specially designed trigger prevents slipping. The finely sculpted receiver is reinforced with thick walls and a high security lockup—eliminating much of the kick. The technology and quality of the Beretta 680 Series makes for an ideal competition shotgun.

BERNARDELLI

DOUBLE BARREL SHOTGUNS

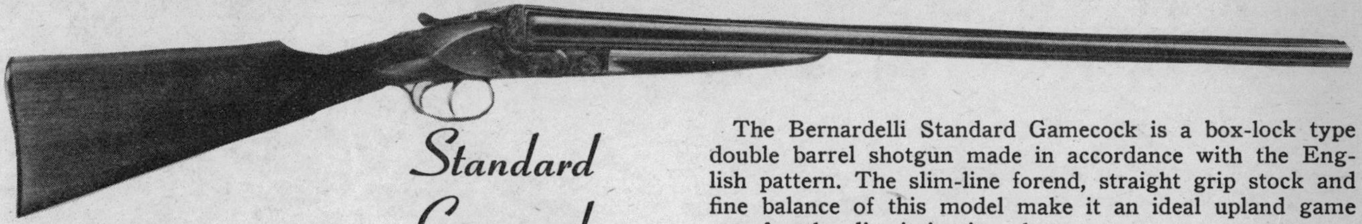

Standard Gamecock

12 OR 20 GAUGE

SPECIFICATIONS

GAUGES: Standard 12 gauge with 2¾-inch chamber or 20 gauge with 3-inch chamber.

ACTION: Box-lock type with scalloped receiver, color case-hardened with light engraving. With plain extractors and double trigger.

SAFETY: Automatic, sliding tang safety.

BARRELS: Precision bored and highly polished, inside and out. Equipped with double underlugs and Purdey-type lock.

STOCK: Selected walnut with high gloss hand finish and fine line hand checkering at pistol grip. Dimensions are: 1½" drop at comb. 2½" drop at heel and 14" length of pull. Forearm is slim field type, cut from same blank as stock and attractively hand-checkered.

WEIGHTS: (Approximate because of varying densities of wood components) 12 gauge—about 6 lbs. 6 ozs., 20 gauge —about 5 lbs. 12 ozs.

The Bernardelli Standard Gamecock is a box-lock type double barrel shotgun made in accordance with the English pattern. The slim-line forend, straight grip stock and fine balance of this model make it an ideal upland game gun for the discriminating shotgunner.

The quality of materials and workmanship in this model are particularly outstanding; barrels are highly polished and finished in a lustrous blue-black, the receiver is elegantly color case-hardened and the selected walnut stock is beautifully hand-finished to a durable, high-gloss.

Internal parts, too, are superbly fitted and finished.

For quail, pheasant, grouse, dove or woodcock hunting, the Bernardelli Standard Gamecock is an ideal shotgun. Because of its slim lines and light weight the overall balance is perfectly suited to fast, smooth gun handling. Price, Standard Gamecock in 12 or 20 gauge .. **$725.00**

AVAILABLE GAUGES, BARREL LENGTHS AND CHOKES

GAUGE	BARREL LENGTH	CHOKE COMBINATIONS	WEIGHT (approximate)
12	25½"	Improved Cylinder Modified	6¾ lbs.–7 lbs.
12	27½"	Modified & Full	6¾ lbs.–7 lbs.
20	25½"	Improved Cylinder Modified	5¾ lbs.–5 lbs. 14 oz.
20	27½"	Modified & Full	5¾ lbs.–5 lbs. 14 oz.

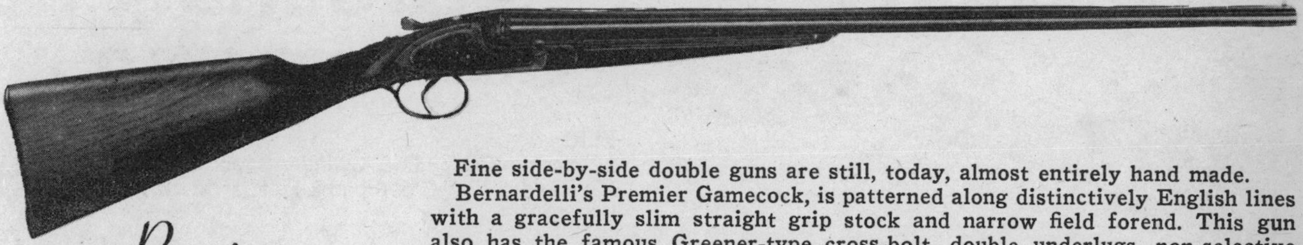

Premier Gamecock

12 or 20 GAUGE

SPECIFICATIONS

GAUGES: 12 or 20 (all 20 gauge models with 3 inch chambers).

ACTION: Box lock with dummy side plates, with light scroll engraving and beautiful color case-hardened finish. Automatic ejectors. Automatic safety. Greener-type cross bolt. Double underlugs.

TRIGGER: Non-selective single trigger.

STOCK: English style with straight grip. 1⁵⁄₁₆" drop at comb, 2⅜" drop at heel and 14³⁄₁₆" length of pull. Hand checkered.

BARRELS: Hard chrome lined with matted rib. (See chokes and weights below).

Fine side-by-side double guns are still, today, almost entirely hand made.

Bernardelli's Premier Gamecock, is patterned along distinctively English lines with a gracefully slim straight grip stock and narrow field forend. This gun also has the famous Greener-type cross-bolt, double underlugs, non-selective single trigger, automatic ejectors, box lock with dummy side plates and automatic safety.

Wood components are of finely grained Italian Walnut, exactingly hand checkered and finished in a double high-gloss epoxy.

In 12 or 20 gauge, the Premier Gamecock is a very smooth, aristocratic upland game gun. Quail, pheasant, partridge and dove hunters will thrill to its light weight, exquisite balance and smooth handling qualities.

For the shooter who wants a truly outstanding side-by-side—a gun that he can one day pass on to his son, the Bernardelli Premier Gamecock is the ideal choice. **$990.00**

AVAILABLE GAUGES, BARREL LENGTHS & CHOKES

GAUGE	BARREL LENGTH	CHOKE COMBINATIONS	(Approximate) Weight
12	25½"	Improved Cylinder & Modified	6¾ lbs.–7 lbs.
12	27½"	Modified & Full	6¾ lbs.–7 lbs.
20	25½"	Improved Cylinder & Modified	5¾ lbs.–5 lbs. 14 oz.
20	27½"	Modified & Full	5¾ lbs.–5 lbs. 14 oz.

BERNARDELLI HAMMER SHOTGUNS

Italia

Double Barrel
HAMMER MODEL

With
Half-Cock Safety

The Italia Gun is a hammer-type shotgun made from modern steels and designed for use with either standard or high-velocity 2¾ inch shells.

This model is exceptionally finished and is unusually attractive. Mechanical features include: Greener-type cross bolt, double triggers, purdy-type forend catch, slim, English style forend and stock of extra fancy walnut, elaborately hand-engraved side plates, side-wings, double underlugs, fine-line hand checkering, half-cock safety, and hard chrome lined barrels.

Available in the following choices of gauges and barrel lengths:

12 gauge, 29½-inch, modified & full chokes
12 gauge, 27½-inch, modified & full chokes
Weight: 6¾ lbs.–7 lbs.
Price, Italia Model, all variations, each **$935.00**

Brescia

Double Barrel
HAMMER MODEL

With
Half-Cock Safety

The hammer shotgun has enjoyed a revival of interest in recent years and the Bernardelli firm, in acknowledging this renewed interest, has released a new line of hammer models constructed of modern steels for modern high-velocity shells.

The Brescia Model, shown here, has Greener-type locks, cross bolt, case-hardened action, English-style select walnut stock and forend, and light engraving.

In 12 gauge this model may be had in choice of 29½-inch (M & F), or 27½-inch (M & F) barrels and chokes.
Weights: 12 gauge—6¾ lbs.–7 lbs.
20 gauge—5¾ lbs.–5 lbs. 14 oz.

In 20 gauge this model is made only with 25½-inch barrels bored improved cylinder and modified. The Brescia Model cannot be had in any other gauges or with any other barrel lengths or chokes **$795.00**

BERNARDELLI SHOTGUNS

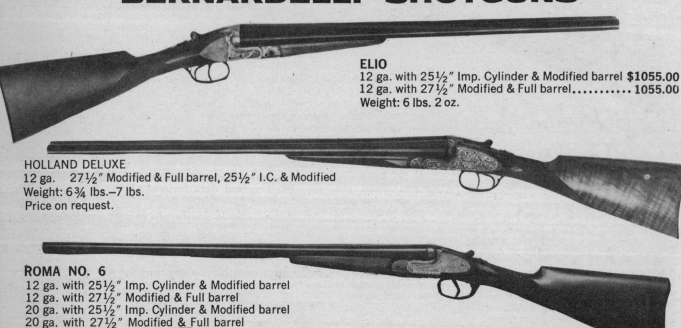

ELIO
12 ga. with 25½" Imp. Cylinder & Modified barrel **$1055.00**
12 ga. with 27½" Modified & Full barrel............ 1055.00
Weight: 6 lbs. 2 oz.

HOLLAND DELUXE
12 ga.   27½" Modified & Full barrel, 25½" I.C. & Modified
Weight: 6¾ lbs.–7 lbs.
Price on request.

ROMA NO. 6
12 ga. with 25½" Imp. Cylinder & Modified barrel
12 ga. with 27½" Modified & Full barrel
20 ga. with 25½" Imp. Cylinder & Modified barrel
20 ga. with 27½" Modified & Full barrel
Weight: 12 gauge 6¾ lbs.-7 lbs.
        20 gauge 5¾ lbs.-5 lbs. 14 oz.
Roma No. 6 with double trigger and straight grip **$1295.00**

BROWNING PRESENTATION SUPERPOSED SHOTGUNS

TWO GUNS IN ONE — The Superposed is a two-barreled shotgun with one barrel positioned directly over the other, rather than side by side. The first shot causes little disturbance to aim, since the veritcal barrel positioning reduces muzzle jump to the minimum and since the under barrel, containing the more open choke, is usually fired first, delivering recoil to the lower, steadier portion of the shoulder.

SINGLE SELECTIVE TRIGGER — You may fire either the tighter choked over barrel or the more open choked under barrel first by the quick movement of the "barrel selector button" to the right or to the left. This selector button is located on the top tang just behind the receiver, where the thumb naturally rests in the shooting position. After the first shot, the gun's mechanism automatically readies the second barrel for firing.

SAFETY — The manual safety operates off the "barrel selector button" described above. With the "barrel selector" forward, the gun is "off-safe." In its rearward position the gun is "on safe."

AUTOMATIC EJECTORS — Fired shells are automatically ejected by an ejection system upon each opening of the breech. Unfired shells remain in the chamber or chambers upon opening but are lifted above the level of the chamber so that they can be lifted out by hand.

TAKEDOWN SYSTEM — The barrels and forearm portion of the gun may be separated from the receiver and stock portion. A latch in the forearm unlocks the two sections after which they need only be unhinged. The forearm does not separate from the barrels in this maneuver.

FINISH — The stock and forearm are made from seasoned walnut individually hand-adjusted to each gun. The checkering of the stock and forearm not only adds to the gun's beauty but affords a sure grip. The receiver is hand engraved.

SUPERPOSED MODELS — Twelve and 20 gauge models are available in two weights: Lightning and the Super-Light. The 28 and .410 gauge models are provided in one weight.

The 12 gauge 3-inch Magnum Superposed will handle the lightest available 2¾-inch loads or the big 3-inch, carrying 1⅞ ounces of shot. For extra shooting comfort, the Magnum is fitted with a deluxe recoil pad. The Super-Light Model is an ultra light field gun with the classic straight grip stock favored by many upland bird hunters. It weighs only 6 lbs. 8 ounces in 12 gauge and 6 lbs. in 20 gauge.

A special feature of all Browning 20 gauge Superposed hunting models, except in the fast-handling Super-Light model, is 3-inch chamber boring.

SUPERPOSED SKEET — The Superposed Skeet models come in 12, 20, 28 and .410 gauge with a short over-all length. Each model features a special skeet stock complete with a full pistol grip and comfortable recoil pad, hand-filling beavertail forearm, plus front and center ivory sight beads. Available with 26½- or 28-inch barrels, all have special Skeet chokes. Browning's Skeet Set has 4 sets of barrels all perfectly matched in 12, 20, 28 and .410 gauge. Each barrel is hand fitted to a single 12-gauge frame and a single removable beavertail forearm. All Browning Superposed target guns may be ordered with one or more extra sets of barrels fitted to the same receiver, each with its own forearm. They may be of the same gauge with different barrel lengths and chokes, or in any combination of 12 and 20 gauge, or 20, 28, and .410 gauge. A fitted luggage type gun case is provided.

SUPERPOSED TRAP — Both Broadway and Lightning Models have a reliable mechanical trigger. The special trap stock with full pistol grip affords good control of the gun and assists consistent face alignment. The contoured trap recoil pad aids identical gun positioning with each shot and adds comfort over a long shoot. The long beavertail forearm places the hands in the same horizontal plane for natural pointing. Front and center ivory sights quickly show any error in pointing. *Broadway Trap:* Its unusually wide ⅝-inch sighting plane quickly aligns eye to target and, without effort, facilitates holding a true bearing on the target during flight. *Lightning Trap:* The Lightning model carries carefully proportioned 30-inch barrels and a ⁵⁄₁₆-inch-wide full ventilated rib.

PRESENTATION GRADE — The Presentation Series in Superposed Shotguns offers a choice of four basic receiver engraving styles and engraved animal or bird scenes. *Presentation One (P-1):* A combination of oak leaf engraving with scrollwork covering the outer edges of the silver grey receiver. The bottom of the receiver sports an oak leaf cluster. The scrollwork extends along the trigger guard, with an oak leaf cluster in the center. One of six animal scenes may be chosen for the receiver. Also available is the P-1 Superposed with gold inlaid birds or dogs and choice of blued or grey finish receiver.

Presentation Two (P-2): The P-2 offers a fleur-de-lis engraving with a choice from three sets of game scenes on both sides and the bottom of the receiver, plus a higher grade of walnut and more elaborate checkering than the P-1 series. Any of these animal scenes are available in gold inlay on either the regular silver grey receiver or a satin blued finish.

Presentation Three (P-3): The P-3 Superposed is offered in three bird and dog scene combinations. All birds and dogs are inlaid with gold on a grey or blue receiver.

Presentation Four (P-4): The basic motif of the P-4's grey receiver is the fleur-de-lis engraving. The deep floral carving covers the sides, top, bottom, forearm, latch and trigger guard. One engraving motif is available. Also available are gold inlaid game birds and dog's head.

BROWNING PRESENTATION SUPERPOSED SHOTGUNS

OVER/UNDER SUPERPOSED SPECIFICATIONS

STOCK—

	12 Gauge Hunting	20, 28 and .410 Gauge Hunting
Length of Pull	14¼"	14¼"
Drop at Comb	1⅝"	1½"
Drop at Heel	2½"	2⅜"

EXTRA SET OF BARRELS — Presentation Series Superposed in any of the specifications listed below are available in gauge combinations of 12 & 12, 12 & 20, 20 & 20, 20 & 28, and/or .410, 28 & .410. A choice of either Hunting, Skeet or Trap stock.

SIGHTS — Medium raised steel bead. Trap and Skeet models: Ivory Front and Center sights.

CHOKE — On all models any combination of Full — Improved-Modified — Modified — Improved-Cylinder — Skeet — Cylinder.

TRIGGER — Gold plated on all models except the Super Light. Fast, crisp, positive.

Model and Gauge HUNTING	Barrel Length	Average Weight (1)	Rib
Lightning 12	28"	7 lbs. 8 oz.	5⁄16" Vent
Lightning 12	26½"	7 lbs. 6 oz.	5⁄16" Vent
Super Light 12	26½"	6 lbs. 8 oz.	5⁄16" Vent
Magnum 12 (2)	30"	8 lbs. 1 oz.	5⁄16" Vent
Magnum 12 (2)	28"	7 lbs. 15 oz.	5⁄16" Vent
Lightning 20	28"	6 lbs. 6 oz.	¼" Vent
Lightning 20	26½"	6 lbs. 4 oz.	¼" Vent
Super Light 20	26½"	6 lbs.	¼" Vent
Lightning 28	28"	6 lbs. 10 oz.	¼" Vent
Lightning 28	26½"	6 lbs. 7 oz.	¼" Vent
Lightning .410	28"	6 lbs. 14 oz.	¼" Vent
Lightning .410	26½"	6 lbs. 10 oz.	¼" Vent

TARGET GUN SPECIFICATIONS

SKEET MODELS

SUPERPOSED	Barrel Length (in.)	Approx. Weight (lbs.-oz.)	Vent. Rib (width, in.)	Length of Pull (in.)	Drop at Comb (in.)	Drop at Heel (in.)	Chokes	Grades Available
Lightning 12	26½	7 lbs. 9 oz.	5⁄16	14⅜	1½	2	S-S	All
Lightning 12	28	7 lbs. 11 oz.	5⁄16	14⅜	1½	2	S-S	All
Lightning 20	26½	6 lbs. 8 oz.	¼	14⅜	1½	2	S-S	All
Lightning 20	28	6 lbs. 12 oz.	¼	14⅜	1½	2	S-S	All
Lightning 28	26½	6 lbs. 11 oz.	¼	14⅜	1½	2	S-S	All
Lightning 28	28	6 lbs. 14 oz.	¼	14⅜	1½	2	S-S	All
Lightning .410	26½	6 lbs. 13 oz.	¼	14⅜	1½	2	S-S	All
Lightning .410	28	7 lbs.	¼	14⅜	1½	2	S-S	All
Skeet Set 12, 20, 28, .410	26½	7 lbs. 10 oz.	¼	14⅜	1½	2	S-S	All
Skeet Set 12, 20, 28, .410	28	7 lbs. 12 oz.	¼	14⅜	1½	2	S-S	All

TRAP MODELS

SUPERPOSED	Barrel Length (in.)	Approx. Weight (lbs.-oz.)	Vent. Rib (width, in.)	Length of Pull (in.)	Drop at Comb (in.)	Drop at Monte Carlo (in.)	Drop at Heel (in.)	Chokes	Grades Available
Lightning 12*	30	7 lbs. 13 oz.	5⁄16	14⅜	1 7⁄16		1⅝	F-F, IM-F, M-F	All
Broadway 12*	30	7 lbs. 15 oz.	⅝	14⅜	1 7⁄16		1⅝	F-F, IM-F, M-F	All
Broadway 12*	32	8 lbs.	⅝	14⅜	1 7⁄16		1⅝	F-F, IM-F, M-F	All!
*These models also available with Monte Carlo comb				14⅜	1⅜	1⅜	2		

BROWNING PRESENTATION SUPERPOSED SHOTGUNS

HUNTING MODELS

Lightning 12 and 20, 3″ Magnum 12 gauges

Presentation 1 Engraved	$3380.00
Presentation 1 Gold Inlay	3740.00
Presentation 2 Engraved	3990.00
Presentation 2 Gold Inlay	4790.00
Presentation 3 Gold Inlay	6020.00
Presentation 4 Engraved	6840.00
Presentation 4 Gold Inlay	7750.00

Super-Light 12 and 20 gauges

Presentation 1 Engraved	$3410.00
Presentation 1 Gold Inlay	3770.00
Presentation 2 Engraved	4020.00
Presentation 2 Gold Inlay	4820.00
Presentation 3 Gold Inlay	6050.00
Presentation 4 Engraved	6870.00
Presentation 4 Gold Inlay	7780.00

Lightning 28 gauge and .410 bore

Presentation 1 Engraved	$3480.00
Presentation 1 Gold Inlay	3840.00
Presentation 2 Engraved	4090.00
Presentation 2 Gold Inlay	4890.00
Presentation 3 Gold Inlay	6120.00
Presentation 4 Engraved	6940.00
Presentation 4 Gold Inlay	7850.00

TRAP MODELS

Lightning 12 gauge

Presentation 1 Engraved	$3430.00
Presentation 1 Gold Inlay	3790.00
Presentation 2 Engraved	4040.00
Presentation 2 Gold Inlay	4840.00
Presentation 3 Gold Inlay	6070.00
Presentation 4 Engraved	6890.00
Presentation 4 Gold Inlay	7800.00

BROADway 12 gauge

Presentation 1 Engraved	$3500.00
Presentation 1 Gold Inlay	3860.00
Presentation 2 Engraved	4110.00
Presentation 2 Gold Inlay	4910.00
Presentation 3 Gold Inlay	6140.00
Presentation 4 Engraved	6960.00
Presentation 4 Gold Inlay	7870.00

SKEET MODELS

Lightning 12 and 20 gauges

Presentation 1 Engraved	$3430.00
Presentation 1 Gold Inlay	3790.00
Presentation 2 Engraved	4040.00
Presentation 2 Gold Inlay	4840.00
Presentation 3 Gold Inlay	6070.00
Presentation 4 Engraved	6890.00
Presentation 4 Gold Inlay	7800.00

Lightning 28 gauge and .410 bore

Presentation 1 Engraved	$3520.00
Presentation 1 Gold Inlay	3880.00
Presentation 2 Engraved	4130.00
Presentation 2 Gold Inlay	4930.00
Presentation 3 Gold Inlay	6160.00
Presentation 4 Engraved	6980.00
Presentation 4 Gold Inlay	7890.00

BROWNING PRESENTATION ONE

BROWNING PRESENTATION THREE

BROWNING PRESENTATION TWO

BROWNING PRESENTATION FOUR

BROWNING SHOTGUNS

SUPERPOSED CONTINENTAL
20 GAUGE

SPECIFICATIONS:

ACTION: Superposed 20 gauge action, engineered to function with extra set of 30-06 Sprg. over and under rifle barrels.

SHOTGUN BARRELS: 20 gauge, 26½". Choked, modified and full with 3-inch chambers. Engine turned ventilated rib with medium raised German nickel silver sight bead.

RIFLE BARRELS: 30-06 Springfield caliber, 24". Right hand rifling twist, 1 turn in 10 inches. Crowned muzzles. Folding leaf rear sight finely calibrated for elevation. Flat face gold bead front sight mounted on matted ramp. Sight radius — 16¹⁵⁄₁₆". Maximum distance between centers of impact of a 2 shot group from each barrel, using commercially available 150 grain 30-06 ammunition, is 1½ inches at 100 yards.

TRIGGER: Single, selective, inertia. Gold plated, fast and crisp. Let off approximately 4½ lbs.

AUTOMATIC SELECTIVE EJECTORS: Fired shells ejected from chambers upon opening of action. Unfired shells elevated for easy removal.

SAFETY: Manual thumb safety on top tang incorporated with barrel selector mechanism. Either over or under barrel can be selected to fire first.

STOCK AND FOREARM: Select high grade American walnut with deluxe oil finish. Straight grip stock and Schnabel forearm with 25 line hand checkering.

	With Shotgun Barrels Installed	With Rifle Barrels Installed
Length of pull	14¼"	14¼"
Drop at comb	1½"	1¹¹⁄₁₆"
Drop at heel	2⁷⁄₃₂"	2½"

OVERALL LENGTH: With 20 gauge shotgun barrels—43½"
With 30-06 rifle barrels—41"

APPROXIMATE WEIGHT: With 20 gauge shotgun barrels—5 lbs. 14 oz.
With 30-06 rifle barrels—6 lbs. 14 oz.

SUPERPOSED CONTINENTAL MODEL: 20 Gauge Over/Under Shotgun with extra set of 30-06 Over/Under Rifle barrels, including fitted luggage.
$4650.00

BPS PUMP SHOTGUN
12 GAUGE

BPS SPECIFICATIONS:

GAUGE: 12 gauge only.

BARRELS: Choice of 26", 28", or 30" with high post ventilated rib. Trap model has front and center ivory sight beads. Hunting model has German nickel sight bead.

ACTION: Pump action with double-action bars. Bottom loading and ejection. Magazine cut-off to switch loads in chamber without disturbing shells in magazine and to convert gun from repeating to single shot operation.

CHOKE: Your choice of full, modified, or improved cylinder.

TRIGGER: Crisp and positive.

CHAMBER: Hunting model: All 2¾", 2¾" magnum and 3" magnum shells, Target models: 2¾" shells only.

SAFETY: Convenient top receiver safety. Slide forward to shoot.

APPROXIMATE WEIGHT: 28" barrel model weighs 7 lbs. 12 oz.

OVERALL LENGTH: 26" barrel 46¾". 28" barrel 48¾". 30" barrel 50¾".

STOCK AND FOREARM: Select walnut, weather resistant finish, sharp 20-line checkering. Full pistol grip. Semi-beavertail forearm with finger grooves, Length of pull — 14¼". Drop at comb — 1½". Drop at heel — 2½".

Grade I, Hunting, 12 ga., Ventilated Rib	$289.95
Grade I, Trap, 12 ga., Ventilated Rib	299.95
Grade I, Buck Special, 12 ga., no accessories	299.95
Grade I, Buck Special, 12 ga., with accessories	314.95

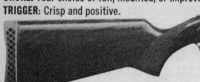

SPECIFICATIONS:

RECEIVER: Grade I blued steel hand engraved with ST-100 insignia in laurel background.

BARRELS: 30 inch. Five position impact adjustment device allows points of impact adjustment. Fluting under barrel expands and contracts naturally during heated shooting.

CHOKES: Choice of Full-Full, Improved Modified-Full, or Modified-Full.

CHAMBERS: 12 gauge. 2¾" shells only.

TRIGGER: Single selective. Mechanical with deep contour for sure control. Fast, crisp, positive.

ST-100 SUPERPOSED TRAP SPECIAL $3025.00

SIGHTS: Front and center ivory sight beads.

RIB: ½" rib with full length and transverse serrations to break up reflection. Full floating, high post design.

RECOIL PAD: Deluxe contoured trap style.

AUTOMATIC EJECTION: Fired shells ejected automatically on opening action. Unfired shells elevated from chamber for convenient removal.

STOCK AND FOREARM: Select walnut, high gloss finish with hand checkering for sure grip. Full pistol-grip stock; semi-beavertail forearm.

Length of pull: 14⅜"
Drop at comb: 1⁷⁄₁₆"
Drop at heel: 1⅝"

APPROXIMATE WEIGHT: 8 pounds.

BROWNING AUTOMATIC SHOTGUNS

**LIGHT 12 AND LIGHT 20 GAUGE
WITH VENT. RIB $444.95
3" MAGNUM 12 AND MAGNUM 20 GAUGE
WITH VENT. RIB $449.95**

AUTOMATIC-5 MODELS—The Browning Automatic-5 Shotgun is offered in an unusually wide variety of models and specifications. The Browning 12-gauge 3-inch Magnum accepts up to and including the 3-inch, 1⅞ ounce, 12-gauge Magnum load, which contains only ⅛ ounces of shot less than the maximum 3½-inch 10-gauge load. The 2¾-inch Magnums and 2¾-inch high-velocity shells may be used with equal pattern efficiency. Standard features include a special shock absorber and a hunting-style recoil pad. The kick is not unpleasant with even the heaviest 3-inch loads.

Browning also offers the 20 gauge in a 3-inch Magnum model. This powerful, light heavyweight offers maximum versatility to 20-gauge advocates. It handles the 20-gauge, 2¾-inch high velocity and Magnums, but it literally thrives on the 3-inch, 1¼ ounce load which delivers real 12-gauge performance in a 20-gauge package.

The 12-gauge Automatic-5, chambered for regular 2¾-inch shells handles all 12-gauge, 2¾-inch shells, from the very lightest 1 ounce field load to the heavy 1½ ounce Magnums. The Browning 20-gauge Automatic is lightweight and a top performer for the upland hunter. Yet, with 2¾-inch high velocity or 2¾-inch Magnums, it does a fine job in the duck blind.

All models and gauges of the Automatic-5 are available in the Buck Special version, which is designed to accurately fire the rifled slug or buckshot loads. In addition, its specially bored 24-inch barrel will deliver nice open patterns with standard field loads.

SKEET MODELS—Special 26-inch skeet barrels fit all Browning Automatic-5's of like gauge and model so an owner may easily convert his favorite hunting gun to a skeet gun by a quick change of barrels. **$444.95**

AUTOMATIC-5 MODEL

All models and gauges of the Automatic-5 are available in the Buck Special version, which is designed to fire the rifled slug or buckshot loads. It's bored 24" barrel will deliver open patterns with standard field loads. Adjustable rifle sights and 24" barrel.

Buck Special with accessories*
Light 12, and Light 20 gauge	**$469.95**
3" magnum 12 gauge and magnum 20 gauge	474.95

Buck Special without accessories
Light 12, and Light 20 gauge	**$454.95**
3" magnum 12 gauge and magnum 20 gauge	459.95

*Accessories include carrying strap, detachable swivels and swivel attachments.

2000 GAS OPERATED AUTOMATIC SHOTGUN

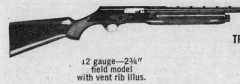

12 gauge—2¾"
field model
with vent rib illus.

TRAP AND SKEET MODELS

12 Ga. 2¾" Trap and Skeet (with receiver rib and high post vent rib)	**$444.95**
12 and 20 Ga. 2¾" Skeet (with standard receiver and standard target rib)	**$399.95**

HUNTING MODELS

12 and 20 Ga. 2¼" Field Model Ventilated Rib	**$399.95**
12 and 20 Ga. 3" Mag. Model Ventilated Rib	**$399.95**

2000 Specifications

Gauge—12 gauge.

Barrel—Choice of 26", 28" or 30" barrel in 2¾" Field models. 28", 30" or 32" in 3" Magnum models. Plain or ventilated rib. Plain barrels have matted sighting surface. All barrels are completely interchangeable within the same gauge.

Chamber—All 2¾" standard and 2¾" Magnum loads with 2¾" chambered barrel. 3" Magnum loads with Magnum barrel.

Choke—Choice of Full, Modified, Improved Cylinder or Cylinder in 2¾" models. Full of Modified in 3" Magnum models.

Capacity—Five 2¾" loads; Four 3" Magnum loads. Reduced to three 2¾" or 3" Magnum

loads with magazine plug.

Trigger—Crisp. Positive.

Safety—Cross bolt. Red warning band visible when in "fire" position. Easily reversible by gunsmith for left hand shooter.

Receiver—Engraved with handsome scroll designs. Machined and forged from high grade steel.

Sight—Medium raised bead. German nickel silver.

Stock and Forearm—French walnut, skillfully checkered. Full pistol grip. No recoil pad.

Length of pull—14¼"
Drop at comb—1⅝"
Drop at heel—2½"

Overall Length—
26" Barrel—45⅜"
28" Barrel—47⅜"
30" Barrel—49⅜"
32" Barrel—51⅜"

Approximate Weight—Ventilated Rib Models. (Plain barrel models weigh 3 oz. less.)
26" Barrel—7 lbs. 10 oz.
28" Barrel—7 lbs. 11 oz.
30" Barrel—7 lbs. 12 oz.
32" Barrel—7 lbs. 13 oz.

Also available in Buck Special: 12 & 20 gauge 2¾", 12 gauge 3" Magnum with 24" barrel. With accessories $414.95, without accessories $399.95.

2000 20 Gauge Specifications

Barrel—Ventilated Rib only. Front and center ivory sight beads on skeet barrel. Available in 26" & 28" lengths.

Chamber—All 2¾" standard and 2¾" Magnum loads with 2¾" chambered barrel. 3" Magnum loads only with Magnum barrel.

Capacity—Five 2¾" loads; four 3" loads. Reduced to three 2¾"

or 3" Magnum loads with magazine plug provided.

Trigger—Crisp, positive.

Safety—Cross bolt. Red warning band. Easily reversible.

Receiver—Engraved with scroll designs. Cold forged and machined from high-grade steel.

BROWNING SHOTGUNS

CITORI STANDARD

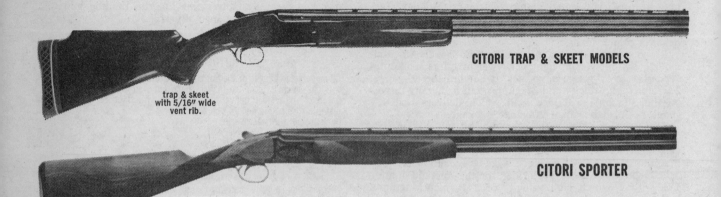

CITORI TRAP & SKEET MODELS

trap & skeet
with 5/16" wide
vent rib.

CITORI SPORTER

FIELD GRADE CITORI SPECIFICATIONS

Gauge—12, 20, 28 and 410 gauge.
Barrels—Choice of 30", 28" or 26" in 12 gauge. 28" or 26" in 20 gauge. Ventilated rib with matted sighting plane. Medium raised German nickel silver sight bead. 26" or 28" in 28 gauge. 26" or 28" in 410 gauge.

Overall Length—12, 20, 28 and 410 gauge.
With 26" barrels—43"
With 28" barrels—45"
With 30" barrels—47"

Chokes—Choice of Full-Full or Mod-Full in 30" barrels; choice of Mod-Full or Imp Cyl-Mod in 28" and 26" barrels.
Trigger—Single selective. Gold plated. Fast and crisp.
Chamber—All 20 gauge Field models and all 12 gauge Field models accept all 3" magnum loads, as well as 2¾" loads. 28 gauge accepts 2¾" loads. 410 gauge accepts 2½", 3" or 3" mag. loads.
Safety—Manual thumb safety. Combined with barrel selector mechanism.
Automatic Ejectors—Fired shells thrown out of gun; unfired shells are elevated for easy removal.

APPROXIMATE WEIGHT—

	12 gauge	20 gauge
With 26" barrels —	7 lbs. 9 oz.	6 lbs. 11 oz.
With 28" barrels —	7 lbs. 11 oz.	6 lbs. 13 oz.
With 30" barrels —	7 lbs. 13 oz.	

Stock and Forearm—Dense walnut. Skillfully checkered. Full pistol grip. Hunting Beavertail forearm. Field type recoil pad installed on 12 gauge models.

	12 gauge	20 gauge
Length of pull—	14¼"	14¼"
Drop at comb—	1⅝"	1½"
Drop at heel—	2½"	2⅜"

HUNTING MODELS

Standard 12 and 20 Ga.

Grade I	$ 574.95
Grade II	1025.00
Grade V	1525.00

Sporter 12 and 20 Ga.

Grade I	574.95
Grade II	1025.00
Grade V	1525.00

Standard 28 Ga. and 410 Bore

Grade I	599.95
Grade II	1025.00
Grade V	1525.00

Sporter 28 Ga. and 410 Bore

Grade I	599.95
Grade II	1025.00
Grade V	1525.00

TRAP MODELS

Standard 12 Ga.

Grade I (High Post Target Rib)	$ 649.95
Grade II (High Post Target Rib)	1095.00
Grade V (High Post Target Rib)	1600.00

COMBO TRAP SET

(Furnished with fitted luggage case for gun and extra barrel.)

Standard 12 Guage with 32" Over/Under barrels and 34" single barrel. One removable forearm supplied.

Grade I (High Post Target Rib)	$1075.00

SKEET MODELS

Standard 12 and 20 Ga.

Grade I (Conventional Target Rib-20 gauge only.)	$ 499.95
Grade I (High Post Target Rib)	649.95
Grade II (High Post Target Rib)	1095.00
Grade V (High Post Target Rib)	1600.00

Standard 28 Ga. and 410 Bore

Grade I (High Post Target Rib)	$ 674.95
Grade II (High Post Target Rib)	1095.00
Grade V (High Post Target Rib)	1600.00

(Furnished with fitted luggage case for gun and extra barrel.)

BROWNING SHOTGUNS

BT-99
BROWNING TRAP SPECIAL

BT-99 SPECIFICATIONS: RECEIVER—Machined steel, tastefully hand-engraved and richly blued. **BARREL**—Choice of 32 inch or 34 inch. **CHOKE**—Choice of Full, Improved Modified or Modified. **CHAMBER**—for 12 gauge, 2¾″ shells only. **TRIGGER**—Gold plated, crisp, positive, pull approximately 3½ pounds.

STOCK AND FOREARM—Select French walnut, hand-rubbed finish, sharp 20-line hand-checkering. Monte Carlo or Conventional Stock available.
Stock: Full pistol grip.
   Length of Pull: 14⅜″
   Drop at Comb: 1⅜″
   Drop at Heel: 2″
Forearm: Full beavertail.

SAFETY—No manual safety, a feature preferred by trap shooters.
SIGHTS—Ivory front and center sight beads.
RIB—High post, ventilated, full floating, matted, 11/32 inch wide.
RECOIL PAD—Deluxe, contoured trap style.
WEIGHT—32 inch barrel 8 lbs., 34 inch barrel 8 lbs. 3 oz.
AUTOMATIC EJECTION—Fired shell ejected automatically on opening action, unfired shell elevated from chamber for convenient removal.

GRADE I COMPETITION: 32″ & 34″ barrel ... **$ 589.95**
   With extra barrel (includes case) **839.95**
PIGEON GRADE COMPETITION **1275.00**

SIDE-BY-SIDE SHOTGUN

BROWNING "B-SS"
12 & 20 GAUGE

12 GAUGE
B-SS SPECIFICATIONS:

GAUGE: 12 and 20 gauge.
BARRELS: Choice of 26″, 28″ or 30″ barrels. Solid rib with matted top. Sight bead is German nickel silver.
CHOKE: 30″ barrels chocked full or modified and full. 28″ barrel model chocked modified and full. 26″ barrels choked, modified and full, or improved cylinder and modified.
TRIGGER: Single mechanical trigger fires right barrel first (the more open choke). Gold plated on all models.
CHAMBER: All 12 and 20 gauge 2¾″, 2¾″ mag. and 3″ mag.
AUTOMATIC SAFETY: Goes on safe when breech is opened and remains there until manually moved to off safe.
AUTOMATIC EJECTORS: Fired shells are thrown out of gun. Unfired shells are elevated for easy removal.
WEIGHT: With 30″ barrels approx. 7 lbs. 7 oz., with 26″ barrels approx. 7 lbs. 3 oz., with 28″ barrels approx. 7 lbs. 5 oz.
OVERALL LENGTH: 26″ barrels 43″. 28″ barrels 45″. 30″ barrels 47″.

STOCK AND FOREARM: Select walnut, hand-rubbed finish, sharp 20-line hand checkering. Full pistol grip. Full grip beavertail forearm.
   Length of pull: 14¼″.
   Drop at comb: 1⅝″.
   Drop at heel: 2½″.

The Browning Side by Side has a "mechanical" trigger which differs from the "inertia" trigger found on many two barreled guns in that the recoil of the first shot is not used to set up the mechanism for the second shot. The first pull of the trigger fires the right barrel. The next pull fires the left barrel. The positive linkage of the B-SS mechanical trigger prevents doubling (both barrels firing at the same instant) or balking. The chromed trigger lets off crisply at about 4½ pounds.

B-SS SIDE BY SIDE SHOTGUN
Modified/Full Imp.-Cylinder Modified

Grade I Standard 12 & 20 ga. without Barrel Selector	**$349.95**
Grade I Standard 12 & 20 ga. with Barrel Selector	**419.95**
Grade II Standard 12 & 20 ga. with Barrel Selector	**735.00**
Grade I Sporter 12 & 20 ga. with Barrel Selector	**419.95**
Grade II Sporter 12 & 20 ga. with Barrel Selector	**735.00**

DARNE SHOTGUNS

Darne is a side-by-side sliding breech shotgun, used for birds, quail, dove and live pigeon shooting. All models are guaranteed for five years from date of purchase.
Calibers: 12, 16, 20, 28 and 12 gauge magnum.
Chokes: Full, modified, improved cylinder, cylinder.
Stocks: English or semi pistol grip.
Ribs: Raised or plume.
Barrels: 27½ standard (25½ on request).
Chambers: 2¾", magnum 3" only.

The R10 and the V19 in **12 and 20** gauge, English stock, choked improved and modified, plume rib, standard barrel length and weighing 5½ lbs. are our regular stock items.

R10 Bird Hunter	12 & 20 ga.		**$750.00**
R15 Quail Hunter	12, 20 & 28 ga.		**1031.00**
R16	12, 20, 3" mag.	Spec Order	**1250.00**
V19	12, 16, 20 ga.	Spec Order	**1590.00**
V22	12, 16, 20 ga.	Spec Order	**3500.00**
Honor I	12, 16, 20	Spec Order	**4600.00**
Honor II	12, 16, 20	Spec Order	On request less 25%

KASSNAR–FIAS SHOTGUNS

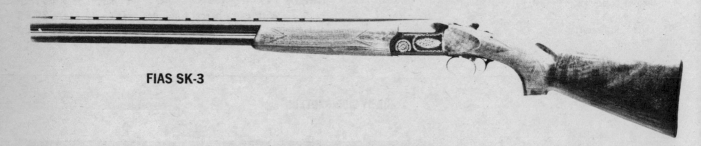

FIAS SK-3

Brescia, the firearms capital of Italy and maybe of all Europe, is the home of the Fias line of over-and-unders. Featured in three grades, 12 and 20 gauge and all popular barrel lengths and chokes. Weight 6-6½ lbs.
SK-1 Series: Featuring double triggers, European walnut stock and forend, chrome lined Breda steel barrels, hand checkered, hand fitted, with Anson and Deely lock mechanism. **$399.95**
SK-3 Series: Features all of the above with a single selective trigger and standard extractors. **$419.95**
SK-4D: Deluxe engraved, beavertail fore-end, automatic ejectors, ventilated rib and single selective trigger. **$499.95**

KASSNAR–ZABALA SHOTGUNS

KASSNAR SIDE BY SIDE SHOTGUNS

The Kassnar-Zabala side by side shotguns offer the sportsman as complete a line of doubles as is available. Zabalas are available in 10, 12, 20 and .410 gauge in all popular chokes and barrel lengths. Of added interest is the 20 gauge, 24" M-F which affords the young beginner a light weight and shorter stock piece which is easy to handle and carry.
12, 20 and .410 gauge **$350.00**
10 gauge **410.00**

KASSNAR FOX SHOTGUN

KASSNAR FOX SHOTGUN

Kassnar Fox 12 ga. semiautomatic shotgun. This gas-operated deluxe shotgun is supplied with ventilated rib barrel and hand-checkered buttstock and fore-end. Available in: 30 in. full choke; 28 in. modified; 28 in. full choke; 26 in. modified; 26 in. improved cylinder; 26 in. skeet. **$314.95**

FIE SHOTGUNS

THE S.O.B.

Gauge	BBL	Overall Length	Price
12	18"	27½"	$74.95
20	18"	27½"	74.95
.410	18"	27½"	74.95

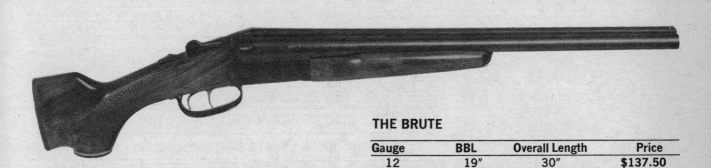

THE BRUTE

Gauge	BBL	Overall Length	Price
12	19"	30"	$137.50
20	19"	30"	137.50
.410	19"	30"	137.50

FIE SHOTGUNS

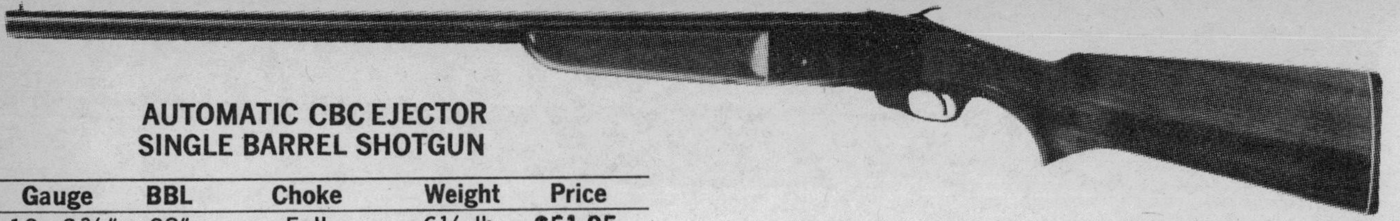

AUTOMATIC CBC EJECTOR SINGLE BARREL SHOTGUN

Gauge	BBL	Choke	Weight	Price
12—2¾"	28"	Full	6¼ lb.	$51.95
20—2¾"	28"	Full	6 lbs.	51.95
410—3"	26"	Full	5½ lb.	51.95
12—2¾"	28"	Hammerless Full	6½ lb.	63.95
20—2¾"	28"	Hammerless Full	6½ lb.	63.95
20—2¾"	26"	Youth Model Full	5¾ lb.	54.95
410—3"	26"	Youth Model Full	5¼ lb.	54.95

HAMMERLESS RIFLE/SHOTGUN COMBO
20 GAUGE/30-30 CALIBER
$86.95

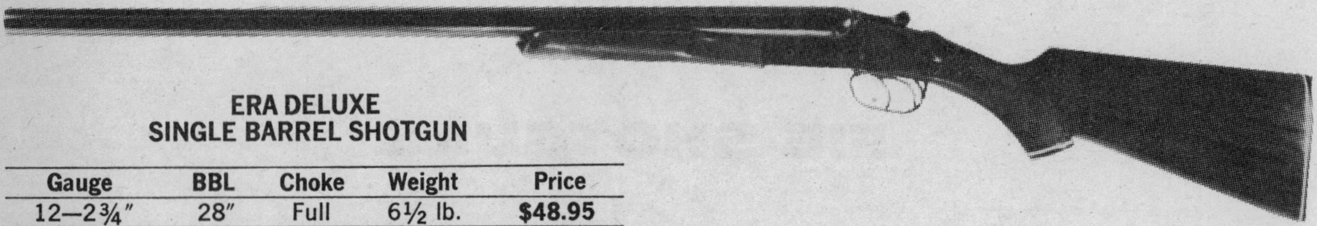

ERA DELUXE SINGLE BARREL SHOTGUN

Gauge	BBL	Choke	Weight	Price
12—2¾"	28"	Full	6½ lb.	$48.95
12—2¾"	30"	Full	6½ lb.	48.95
20—2¾"	28"	Full	6½ lb.	48.95
410—3"	26"	Full	6½ lb.	48.95
16—2¾"	28"	Full	6½ lb.	48.95
20—2¾"	26"	Full	6 lb.	51.95
410—3"	26"	Full	6 lb.	51.95

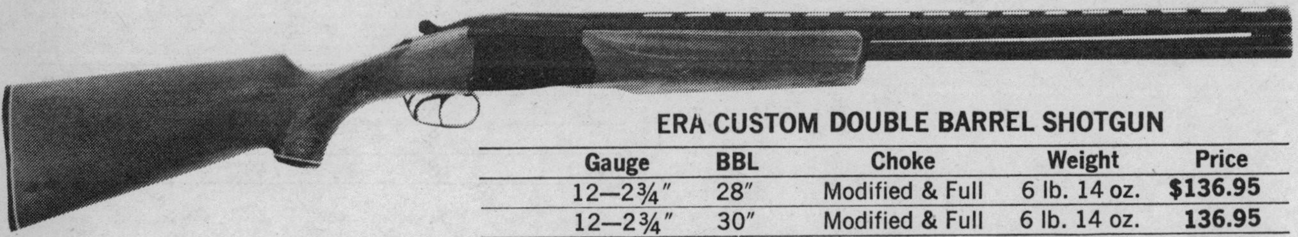

ERA CUSTOM DOUBLE BARREL SHOTGUN

	Gauge	BBL	Choke	Weight	Price
	12—2¾"	28"	Modified & Full	6 lb. 14 oz.	$136.95
	12—2¾"	30"	Modified & Full	6 lb. 14 oz.	136.95
	16—2¾"	28"	Modified & Full	6 lb. 11 oz.	136.95
	20—2¾"	28"	Modified & Full	6 lb. 11 oz.	136.95
	410—3"	26"	Modified & Full	6 lb. 4 oz.	136.95
Riot	12—2¾"	18" or 20"	Cylinder Bore	6 lb. 6 oz.	152.95
Riot	20—2¾"	18" or 20"	Cylinder Bore	6 lb. 3 oz.	152.95
Riot	16—2¾"	18" or 20"	Cylinder Bore	6 lb. 3 oz.	152.95

ERA DELUXE OVER AND UNDER SHOTGUN

Gauge	BBL	Choke	Weight	Price
12—2¾"	28"	Modified & Full	9.8 lb.	$199.95
12—2¾" Trap	30"	Full & Full	9.14 lb.	218.00
12—2¾" Skeet	26"	Skeet & Skeet	9.6 lb.	218.00
20—2¾"	28"	Modified & Full	9.8 lb.	199.95
20—2¾" Skeet	26"	Skeet & Skeet	9.3 lb.	218.00

KRIEGHOFF O&U SHOTGUNS

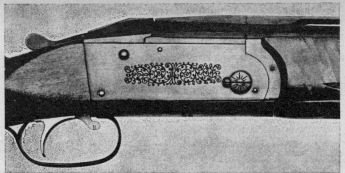

Standard

Features unique Krieghoff split barrel design, simplified construction. Internal parts are specially hardened, heat-treated steel. Single trigger is mechanical, dependable. Selected European stocks and forends.

Standard Grade Trap	$2495.00
Standard Grade Hunting	2995.00
Standard Grade Skeet	2995.00
Standard Vandalia Rib Trap	2995.00
Standard Low Rib 2 Barrel Trap Combo Set	3995.00
Standard Vandalia Rib 2 Barrel Trap Combo Set	4995.00
Standard Grade 4 Barrel Skeet Set	6995.00

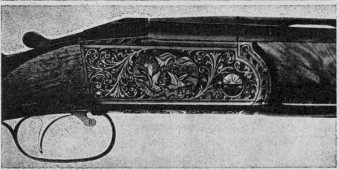

San Remo (Vandalia Grade only)

Fine American walnut wood. Relief engraving meticulously insculpted. Polished mechanism. Krieghoff weight is between the hands for perfect balance, fast pointing. All Krieghoffs have special short hammer fall for instant response.

San Remo Grade 4 Barrel Skeet Set	$9995.00
San Remo Vandalia Trap	4995.00
San Remo Vandalia Combo Trap Set	5995.00
San Remo Low Rib Combo Trap Set	5495.00
San Remo Low Rib Trap	3995.00

Monte Carlo

Superb relief engraving, silver inlaid figurines. Fancy grade walnut. All Krieghoffs have light recoil, straight back, no barrel whip, better position for second shot. In Monte Carlo grade.

Monte Carlo Grade 4 Barrel Skeet Set	$18,495.00
Monte Carlo Trap	9995.00
Monte Carlo or Crown Combo Trap	12,495.00

Crown

The finest Krieghoff. Gold inlaid figurines. Superbly grained, polished, epoxy-finished woods. Polished mechanism. Double and triple checking of every Krieghoff assures matchless quality.

Crown Grade 4 Barrel Skeet Set	$19,495.00
Crown Trap	10,995.00

Super Crown

The ultimate version of the Crown Krieghoff. Relief engraving with gold and silver inlaid figurines. Polished mechanism. Epoxy-finished woods, superbly grained and polished. Peerless performance.

Super Crown Grade 4 Barrel Skeet Set	$21,995.00

München

The München is hand-forged from Böhler ordnance steel. The stock is handrubbed American Claro walnut. And, like all Krieghoffs, the München has an interchangeable barrel system that comes boxed in a leather case.

München Grade 4 Barrel Skeet Set	$7995.00

EXTRA BARRELS:

Skeet, Hunting, Vandalia (High Rib Trap)	$1295.00
Low Rib Trap	1095.00

FRANCHI TRAP 2000 SERIES

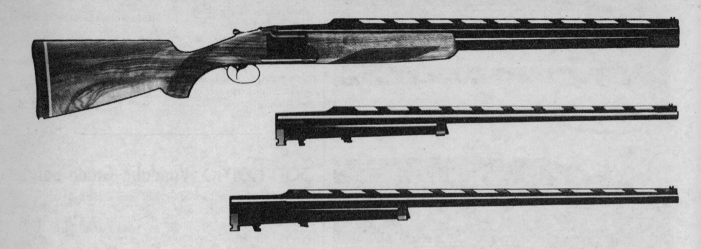

FRANCHI 2005/3 TRAP COMBINATION
$2200.00

**FRANCHI DESIGNED THE 2000 TRAP SERIES
IN COLLABORATION WITH THE FINEST TRAP
SHOOTERS IN AMERICA TODAY**

Franchi started with the frame. Every one machined in a single piece from a solid steel forging for incredible strength. Next, Franchi anatomically designed a special trigger which brings your shooting finger to the same exact position shot after shot. Franchi calls it the "ceiling-swell"® trigger, and after using it, you'll wonder why someone didn't think of it before.

Franchi created trigger mechanisms that are crisp and clean, without slack. And to make sure they stay that way, Franchi mounts them all directly to the solid steel receivers.

To cut down on wind resistance and for maximum heat dissipation, Franchi separated the barrels from forend to muzzle. Franchi then added the exclusive steel muzzle collar that lets either barrel expand independently,

without affecting the alignment of the other.

To give you a definite bird-breaking advantage, Franchi designed the exclusive "hi-loft"® rib. Machined from solid bar stock, this higher non-glare sighting plane provides you with the clearest sight picture yet achieved.

The stocks and the broad forends on these magnificent competition guns are hand crafted from specially selected European walnut. Matched for density and grain structure, each is generously hand checkered, and protected by a hand-applied oil finish for a classic elegance. Stocks are also drilled for a recoil reducer.

For perfect fit and pattern, you can customize any of Franchi's 2000 Series with six different stocks; standard with cast-off (for right-handed shooters).

FRANCHI TRAP 2000 SERIES

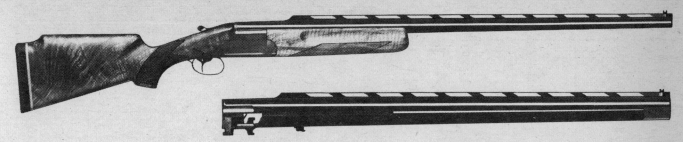

FRANCHI 2005/2 TRAP COMBINATION
$1650.00

Franchi's unique cast-off (or cast-on) stock places your sighting eye in a more natural position along the sighting plane for more accurate bird-breaking ability with less fatigue.

All Franchi 2000 Series competition guns have chrome-lined chambers and bores for freedom from rust and leading . . . all except for the choke area near the muzzle.

EXCLUSIVE "HI-LOFT"® RIB

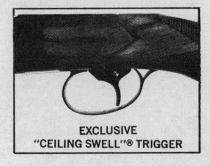

EXCLUSIVE
"CEILING SWELL"® TRIGGER

EXCLUSIVE STEEL MUZZLE COLLAR

EXCLUSIVE ONE PIECE FORGED
STEEL MONOBLOCK RECEIVERS

FRANCHI TRAP 2000 SERIES

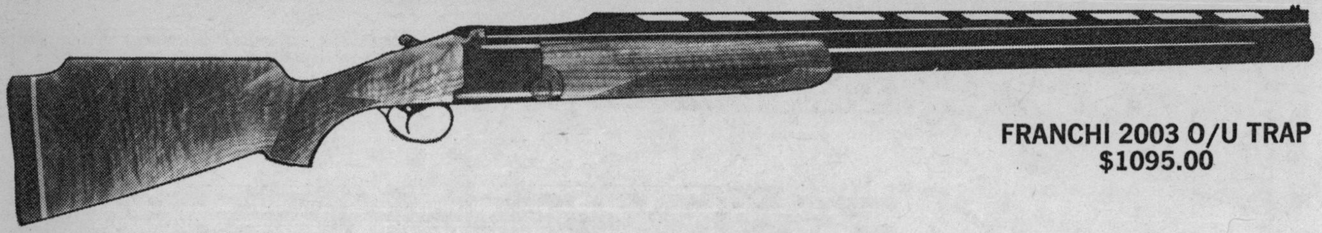

FRANCHI 2003 O/U TRAP
$1095.00

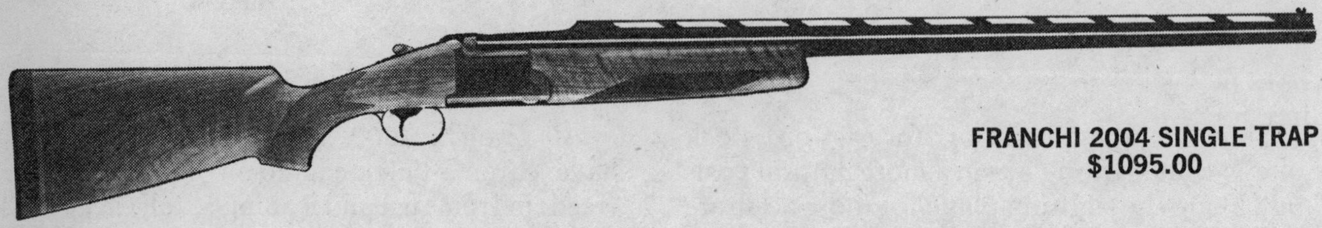

FRANCHI 2004 SINGLE TRAP
$1095.00

AN ELEGANT FITTED CASE IS SUPPLIED WITH EVERY 2000 SERIES FRANCHI TRAP AND SKEET

FRANCHI Trap Guns Specifications

STYLE:	O/U, single barrel, undergun combination set with interchangeable chokes, and combination set, trap guns.
GAUGE:	12 gauge (chambered for all 2¾" shells).
BARRELS:	Made from chrome-molybdenum steel. The bores are chromed only to the beginning of the choke cone, making possible any eventual choke modification.
VENTILATED-RIB:	"Hi-loft"® special trap rib.
SIGHTS:	Raised steel middle bead, with 7/16" long translucent red front sight.
SAFETY:	Manual thumb safety located on the tang (independent of any other function).
TRIGGER:	"Ceiling-swell"®, trap trigger anatomically designed. O/U barrel selector is located on the trigger.
STOCKS:	Selected European walnut oil finished. All Franchi stocks are interchangeable and the buttstocks are drilled for a recoil reducer. All stocks are compound cast-off to align the right-handed shooter's eye with the sighting plane. Compound cast-on stocks for the left-handed shooter and straight stocks are available on special order. Generously applied hand-checkering in a classical pattern. A deep, soft Franchi trap pad for consistent shouldering is standard on every model.

1) TRAP SERIES – 12 GAUGE:

MODEL	GRADE	GAUGE	CHAMBER	BARREL LENGTH	CHOKE	WEIGHT (lbs.)
2003	Trap O/U	12	2¾"	30"	Imp Mod & Full Full & Full	8 lbs., 4 ozs.
		12	2¾"	32"	Imp Mod & Full Full & Full	8 lbs., 6 ozs.
2004	Trap Single Barrel	12 12	2¾" 2¾"	32" 34"	Full Full	8 lbs., 4 ozs. 8 lbs., 6 ozs.
2005/2	Trap Combination	12	2¾"	30" O/U 32" Single	Imp Mod & Full Full	8 lbs., 4 ozs.
		12	2¾"	32" O/U 34" Single	Imp Mod & Full Full	8 lbs., 6 ozs.
	Special Order Only	12	2¾"	30" O/U 34" Single	Please Specify	
2005/3	Trap Combination	12	2¾"	30" or 32" O/U 32" or 34" Single Any Combination	Please Specify	

STOCK CODE:	A	B	C	D*	E	F*
Drop at Comb	1½"	1 7/16"	1 7/16"	1 7/16"	1⅜"	1⅜"
Drop at Monte Carlo	—	—	—	1 7/16"	—	1⅜"
Drop at Heel	1⅞"	1 9/16"	1 7/16"	2 1/16"	1⅜"	2 1/16"
Length of Pull	14½"	14½"	14½"	14½"	14½"	14½"

* Monte Carlo Stock

FRANCHI TRAP 3000 SERIES

FRANCHI 3000 UNDERCOMBO TRAP

Featured in this all new Undercombo Trap set are:

- The all–new underbarrel unit with high-trestle rib for singles and handicap event.
- The conventional O/U barrel set for doubles.
- The 3000 comes complete with three choke tubes, fully interchangeable within either barrel set for total pattern control.

With typical Franchi innovative engineering, the underbarrel unit is built around the bottom barrel rather than the top for three important reasons:

**FRANCHI 3000/2
TRAP UNDERGUN COMBINATION
$2495.00**

1. Apparent recoil sensation is reduced because, by utilizing the bottom barrel, recoil forces are closer to the centerline of the butt. This means less muzzle jump and cheek slap, the latter being especially important in long, grueling competition.
2. Firing the bottom barrel puts less strain on the hinge pin and locking mechanism than does the top barrel thus assuring dependable performance and a "tightness" to the action, even after tens of thousands of rounds.
3. The sighting plane is substantially higher than the barrel surface thereby reducing heat-wave distortion to an absolute minimum.

The Undercombo is also available in your choice of six different cast-off butt stocks.

FRANCHI'S REVOLUTIONARY 3000 UNDER-COMBO TRAP . . . THE ULTIMATE CLAY-BUSTING MACHINE.

THIS EXCLUSIVE 3000 UNDERCOMBO TRAP MAKES THE DIFFERENCE BETWEEN BRINGING HOME THE GOLD OR BEING AN ALSO-RAN. AND BRINGING HOME THE GOLD IS WHAT FRANCHI TRAP GUNS ARE ALL ABOUT.

FRANCHI Trap Guns Specifications

3000	Undergun	12	2¾"	30" O/U 32" Underbarrel	(3 interchangeable chokes)	8 lbs., 4 ozs.
	Trap Combination	12	2¾"	32" O/U 34" Underbarrel	Full, Imp Mod, Mod	8 lbs., 6 ozs.

FRANCHI AUTOMATIC SHOTGUNS

IN FIELD GUNS, FRANCHI OFFERS A SUPERLATIVE SELECTION ENCOMPASSING A SUPER NEW GAS-OPERATED AUTOLOADER AND TIME-PROVEN LONG RECOIL AUTO LOADERS.

Whichever type appeals to you, you'll find that each offers unsurpassed balance, crisp handling and outstanding quality.

One of the most significant advantages of Franchi Automatics is the complete interchangeability of barrels within a given gauge. No factory fitting is required.

To give you the light weight you want in a field gun, the receivers of the autoloaders are made of an incredibly tough alloy. So tough, in fact, that we back the receiver with a lifetime guarantee. The bores and chambers are chrome lined for freedom from rust and corrosion. And yet, for all the modern features, Franchi continues the tradition of old-fashioned craftsmanship and excellence.

Like fine checkering. A rare feature these days. But something that we feel very strongly about at Franchi.

As well as generous, handsome engraving on the Hunter and 520.

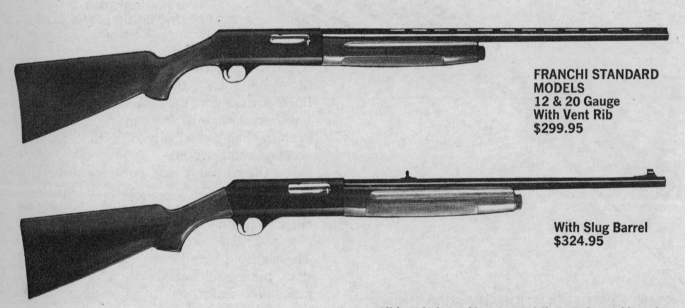

FRANCHI STANDARD MODELS
12 & 20 Gauge
With Vent Rib
$299.95

With Slug Barrel
$324.95

The Franchi Automatic Shotgun is made in 12 and 20 gauges chambered for all 2¾-inch shells.

All models are with chrome-lined barrels, automatic cut-off, five-shot capacity, stock and forend with fully checkered pistol grip and fore-grip.

In a wide selection of barrel lengths and chokes, the Franchi is the world's lightest automatic shotgun: The 12-gauge model weighs only 6 lbs. 4 ozs. and the 20 gauge weighs about 5 lbs. 2 ozs.

Adjustable friction piece controls recoil action, permitting specific settings for standard or high velocity loads. Effects of recoil are therefore greatly minimized.

All barrels for each gauge are fully interchangeable without factory fitting; this is a particularly desirable feature because a gun purchased with both a 30-inch full choke barrel and a 26-inch improved cylinder barrel could be used for anything from quail to ducks, (and skeet and trap too, if the shooter is so inclined).

In addition to its extreme light weight, the Franchi automatic shotgun has two exclusive and unique features: hard chrome-lined barrels and simplified take-down.

The smooth chrome lining not only adds greatly to the life of the barrel by preventing rust and corrosion, but improves patterning at all ranges by reducing pellet deformation. Removal of two lateral pins, located through the receiver immediately above the trigger guard, permits the trigger-safety-lifter mechanism to be removed as a single unit. For cleaning purposes this can then be rinsed in a kerosene bath, oiled lightly and re-installed simply and easily.

FRANCHI AUTOMATIC SHOTGUNS

FRANCHI STANDARD MODELS
12 & 20 Gauge Magnum
With Vent Rib
$324.95

The Franchi Magnum Automatic in 12 or 20 gauge is a shotgun designed specifically for 3-inch Magnum shells. With factory-fitted recoil pad, automatic cut-off and long, full-choke barrels, these Magnum models are considerably heavier than the standard field guns; 12 gauge Magnum weighs 8 lbs. 4 ozs. and the 20 gauge Magnum weighs 6 lbs. These weights, coupled with the recoil-operated design common to all Franchis, greatly reduce the effects of recoil felt by the shooter.

All models are regularly furnished with 3-shot plug to conform with Federal Migratory Bird Laws. Normal capacity is four in the magazine and one in the chamber for a total of five shots.

Barrel lengths: 12 gauge—32-inch with full choke and 20 gauge—28-inch with full choke. Hard-chrome lining—an exclusive Franchi feature—greatly reduces deformation of pellets and facilitates smooth, even patterns at all ranges. Furthermore, this chrome lining resists rust and corrosion and lengthens barrel life.

FRANCHI DELUXE AUTOMATIC SHOTGUNS

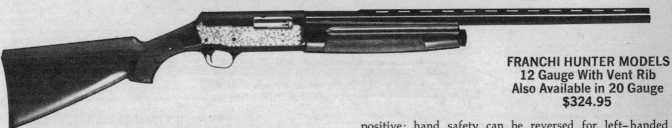

FRANCHI HUNTER MODELS
12 Gauge With Vent Rib
Also Available in 20 Gauge
$324.95

Franchi Hunter features include: specially selected European stock, forend; fully engraved million-dollar lightweight receiver covered by a lifetime guarantee; the automatic safety, which securely locks the hammer, is silent and positive; hand safety can be reversed for left–handed shooters; chrome-lined barrel for light weight and maximum strength; checkered pistol grip; reliable recoil action requiring no maintenance and no cleaning. Chambered for 2¾ shells.

FRANCHI Field Guns Specifications

1) STANDARD RECOIL OPERATED SHOTGUNS – 12 and 20 GAUGES: **(2) DELUXE HUNTER RECOIL SHOTGUNS – 12 and 20 GAUGES:**

STYLE:	5-shot recoil operated automatic shotgun.
GAUGES:	12 and 20 gauges (chambered for all 2¾ shells). 12 and 20 gauge Magnum (chambered for 3" Magnum shells).
BARREL:	Made from chrome-molybdenum steel with cold forged chokes and chrome-lined bores. Extra barrels are interchangeable within gauge except Magnum. Slug gun barrel comes equipped with fully adjustable rifle-type sights. All models are equipped with ventilated-rib except slug gun.

BARREL LENGTHS & CHOKES:

Ventilated-rib Barrel	22" (cyl) Slug	24" Cyl.	26" **** I.C.	26" *** Mod.	28" *** Mod.	28" * Full	30" * Full	32" * Full
Standard 12	X	X	X	X	X	X	X	
Standard 20	X	X	X	X	X			
Magnum 12								X
Magnum 20						X		

OVER-ALL LENGTH:	47½" with 28-inch barrel.
SAFETY:	Lateral push button safety. Removal of two lateral pins, located through the receiver, permits the trigger-safety-lifter mechanism to be removed as a single unit.
STOCK:	Stock and forend with fully machine cut checkered pistol grip and fore-grip. Magnum models equipped with factory fitted recoil pad (optional on other 12 gauge models).
STANDARD STOCK DIMENSIONS:	14" length of pull; 1½" drop at comb; 2¼" drop at heel.
AVERAGE WEIGHT:	12 gauge—6 lbs., 4 ozs.; 20 gauge—5 lbs., 2 ozs.; 12 gauge Magnum—8 lbs., 4 ozs.; 20 gauge Magnum—6 lbs. Weight may vary depending on wood density.

Note: All Franchi automatic shotguns are supplied with 3-shot plug to conform with migratory bird laws, where applicable.

2) GAS OPERATED SHOTGUNS—12 GAUGE:

STYLE:	5-shot gas operated automatic shotgun.
GAUGE:	12 gauge (chambered for all 2¾" shells).
BARREL:	Made from chrome-molybdenum steel with cold forged chokes and chrome-lined bores. All models are equipped with ventilated-rib.

FRANCHI GAS OPERATED SHOTGUNS

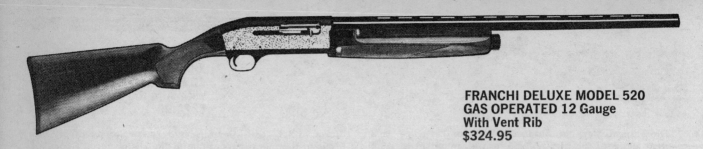

**FRANCHI DELUXE MODEL 520
GAS OPERATED 12 Gauge
With Vent Rib
$324.95**

There are four main units in the Franchi 520: Stock-receiver, barrel, breechbolt-cocking rod, and forend. The gun can be easily disassembled into these four units without any tools in less than 15 seconds.

Fixed barrel: the reloading operation is entirely carried out by the gas-piston breech-bolt system.

Fast cycling time: It fires, ejects and reloads in less than 120 thousandths of a second!

The only shotgun with its magazine completely isolated from the gas, thus preventing carbon deposits which could affect functioning.

Can accommodate five 2¾-inch shotshells when not in conflict with state or area regulations.

Easy ejection and extremely smooth cocking. Removable plug converts four-round magazine capacity to two to comply with Federal regulations on the hunting of waterfowl.

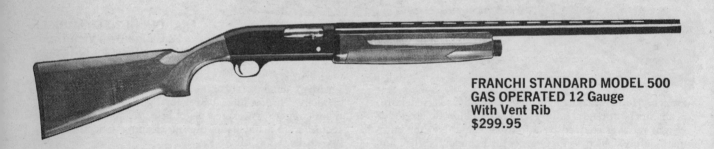

**FRANCHI STANDARD MODEL 500
GAS OPERATED 12 Gauge
With Vent Rib
$299.95**

Franchi 500: Same as Franchi 520 except Standard model.

FEATURES: Stock Finish: semi-gloss. **Drop at heel:** 2" - 2⅛" - 2¼". **Barrels:** 26, 28, and 30 inches with ventilated rib. **Gauge:** 12. **Chamber:** 2¾". **Weight:** Approx. 7 pounds.

Chokes: 26 inch. Imp., Cyl., 28 inch Mod or Full and 30 inch Full

500 Gas Operated **$299.95**

Field Guns Specifications (cont.)

BARREL LENGTHS & CHOKES: Ventilated-rib Barrel	26" **** I.C.	26" (sk) Skeet	28" *** Mod.	28" * Full	30" * Full
Std. Model 500	X	X	X	X	X
Deluxe Model 520	X	X	X	X	X
OVER-ALL LENGTH:	47½" with 28-inch barrel.				
SAFETY:	Lateral push button safety. Removal of two lateral pins, located through the receiver, permits the trigger-safety-lifter mechanism to be removed as a single unit.				
STOCK:	Stock and forend with fully machine cut checkered pistol grip and fore-grip.				
STANDARD STOCK DIMENSIONS:	14" length of pull; 1½" drop at comb; 2¼" drop at heel.				
AVERAGE WEIGHT:	7 lbs. Over-all weight may vary slightly depending on density of wood.				

Note: All Franchi automatic shotguns are supplied with 3-shot plug to conform with migratory bird laws, where applicable.

GALEF SHOTGUNS

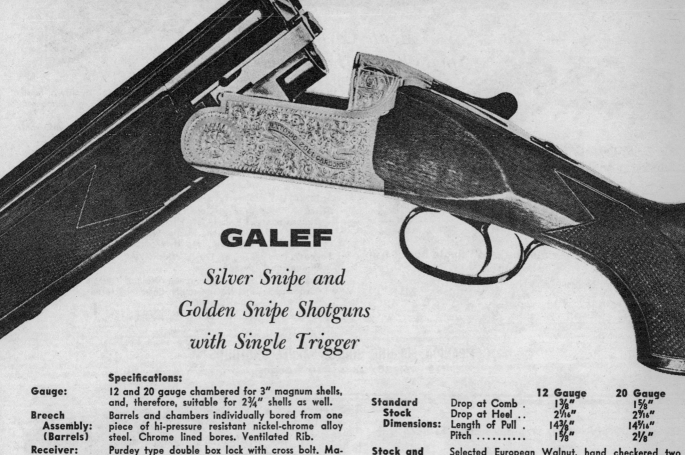

GALEF

Silver Snipe and Golden Snipe Shotguns with Single Trigger

Specifications:

			12 Gauge	**20 Gauge**

Gauge: 12 and 20 gauge chambered for 3" magnum shells, and, therefore, suitable for 2¾" shells as well.

Breech Assembly: (Barrels) Barrels and chambers individually bored from one piece of hi-pressure resistant nickel-chrome alloy steel. Chrome lined bores. Ventilated Rib.

Receiver: Purdey type double box lock with cross bolt. Machined from solid stock and handsomely engraved in satin chrome.

Safety: Automatic.

Extractors: Silver Snipe—Plain
Golden Snipe—Selective Automatic Ejectors

Trigger: Single Trigger

Standard Stock Dimensions:

		12 Gauge	**20 Gauge**
Drop at Comb	.	1⅜"	1⅝"
Drop at Heel	..	2⁵⁄₁₆"	2⁹⁄₁₆"
Length of Pull	.	14⅜"	14⁵⁄₁₆"
Pitch	....	1⅝"	2⅛"

Stock and Forearm: Selected European Walnut, hand checkered two point panel design. Full pistol grip with hard plastic butt plate.

Sights: Gold bead on field models. Ivory bead on Trap and Skeet models.

Approximate Weights:
12 gauge 28" barrels ....6 lbs. 8 ounces
20 gauge 28" barrels ....6 lbs. 4 ounces

Silver Snipe—Ventilated Rib

Gauge:	Barrel-Chokes:		
12	30"	Modified & Full	
12	28"	Modified & Full	
12	26"	IC-Modified	**$416.75**
20	28"	Modified & Full	
20	26"	IC-Modified	

Golden Snipe—Ventilated Rib with Automatic Ejectors

Gauge:	Barrel-Chokes:		
12	30"	Modified & Full	
12	28"	Modified & Full	**$489.00**
12	26"	IC-Modified	

**SILVER SNIPE
OVER & UNDER SHOTGUN
WITH SINGLE TRIGGER
(12 & 20 Gauge)**

GALEF SHOTGUNS

Monte Carlo —
Single Barrel Trap Shotgun

**MONTE CARLO
SINGLE BARREL TRAP GUN
$317.00**

**Barrel
Assembly:** Monobloc. Barrel tubes of superior quality hi-tensil chromoly steel with extra heavy walls. Chambered for 2¾" shells.

Rib: 5/16" tapered wide track Ventilated Rib with front and rear bead sights.

Action: Monte Carlo design with release forward of trigger guard. Handsomely engraved and finished in a non-glare blue. Automatic type extractor. Gold plated trigger and forend screw.

Safety: Slide type mounted on upper tang.

**Stock
Dimensions:** Drop at Comb: 1⅛", Drop at Heel: 1⅝", Length of Pull: 14½", Pitch: ½". Straight without cast-off or cast-on. Monte Carlo comb. Full pistol grip with cap. Trap style recoil pad.

**Forearm
Dimensions:** Length: 12½", Width: 2⅝". Beavertail semi-pear shaped.

**Stock And
Forearm:** Selected European Walnut. Custom finished and fitted. Generously hand checkered in two point panel design.

Weight: Approximately 8¼ pounds.

Specifications of the "Monte Carlo" single barrel trap shotgun

Gauge: 12 gauge only

Barrel Length: 32 inches

Choke: Trap

COMPANION FOLDING SINGLE BARREL SHOTGUNS
(12, 16, 20, 28 & 410 Gauges)

COMPANION, w/plain barrel $100.75

COMPANION w/vent rib barrel $107.50

Specifications:

Gauge: 12, 16, 20, 28, and 410 gauge, 12 and 20 gauge chambered for 3" magnum shells. 16 and 28 gauge are chambered for 2¾" shells. 410 with 3 inch chamber.

Style: Single barrel, folding shotgun.

**Breech
Assemby:
(Barrel)** Monobloc. Special alloy steel drawn from a single block including the rib extension and locking lug. Greatest elasticity and strength are thus obtained, especially as the barrel tubes are completely inserted to coincide with the breech face. Also available in Ventilated Rib Barrel with specifications same throughout.

Receiver: Machined from solid stock and handsomely engraved in satin chrome.

Safety: Non-automatic shotgun type, positioned at upper tang.

**Standard
Stock
Dimensions:** Drop at Comb ..... 1½" } Approximate for all gauges and lengths
Drop at Heel ...... 2⅝"
Length of Pull ......14"
Pitch .... 3"

Sights: Gold bead front. Receiver notched for alignment in pointing.

**Stock and
Forearm:** Selected European Walnut, hand checkered two point panel design. Full pistol grip with cap and hard plastic butt plate.

**Approximate
Weights:** 12 gauge 30" barrel ....5 lbs. 9 ounces
410 gauge 28" barrel ....4 lbs. 8 ounces

	Gauge:	Barrel-Chokes:
Barrel Length	12	30" Full—Magnum
& Choke	12	28" Full—Magnum
Combin-	16	28" Full
ations:	20	28" Full—Magnum
	28	28" Full
	410	26" Full

GOLDEN EAGLE SHOTGUNS

MODEL 5000 SPECIFICATIONS		Gauge	Chamber Length	Barrel Length and Choke	Rib Width	Length of Trigger Pull	Approximate Weight
GRADE I FIELD MODELS*		12 ga.	2¾"	28" F/M	8mm	14"	7 lbs. 4 oz.
		12 ga.	2¾"	28" M/IC	8mm	14"	7 lbs. 4 oz.
		12 ga.	2¾"	26" M/IC	8mm	14"	7 lbs. 4 oz.
		12 ga.	3"	30" F/M (MG)	11mm	14"	8 lbs. 0 oz.
		20 ga.	3"	28" F/M	8mm	14"	6 lbs. 4 oz.
		20 ga.	3"	28"M/IC	8mm	14"	6 lbs. 4 oz.
		20 ga.	3"	26" M/IC	8mm	14"	6 lbs. 4 oz.
GRADE I SKEET MODELS*		12 ga.	2¾"	28" S/S	11mm	14"	7 lbs. 4 oz.
		12 ga.	2¾"	26" S/S	11mm	14"	7 lbs. 4 oz.
		20 ga.	3"	28" S/S	11mm	14"	6 lbs. 4 oz.
		20 ga.	3"	26" S/S	11mm	14"	6 lbs. 4 oz.
GRADE I TRAP MODELS*		12 ga.	2¾"	32" F/F	11mm	14⅜"	8 lbs. 0 oz.
		12 ga.	2¾"	32" F/IM	11mm	14⅜"	8 lbs. 0 oz.
		12 ga.	2¾"	32" F/M	11mm	14⅜"	8 lbs. 0 oz.
		12 ga.	2¾"	30" F/F	11mm	14⅜"	8 lbs. 0 oz.
		12 ga.	2¾"	30" F/IM	11mm	14⅜"	8 lbs. 0 oz.
		12 ga.	2¾"	30" F/M	11mm	14⅜"	8 lbs. 0 oz.

*Trap models are furnished with recoil pads;
Skeet and Field models are furnished with contoured butt plates.

Grade I Field (all standard barrels & chokes) **$699.00**
Grade I Trap (all standard barrels & chokes) **799.00**
Grade I Skeet (all standard barrels & chokes) **749.00**

GOLDEN EAGLE MODEL 5000 GRADE I

Each Golden Eagle Grade I is hand finished with receiver engravings consisting of 14kt. gold eagle head overlay surrounded by a scroll engraving pattern. Modern boxlock receiver mechanism, precision barrels with hard chrome plated bores and chambers, rapid heat dispersing ventilated ribs, anti-balk gold-plated single selective trigger, tang safety and barrel selector, automatic ejectors, 20-line-to-the-inch hand-checkered stock and forearm.
Available in Field, Skeet Models in 12 or 20 guage and Trap Models in 12 gauge.

MODEL 5000 SPECIFICATIONS		Gauge	Chamber Length	Barrel Length and Choke	Rib Width	Length of Trigger Pull	Approximate Weight
GRADE II FIELD MODELS		12 ga.	3"	30" F/M (MG)	11mm	14"	8 lbs. 0 oz.
		12 ga.	2¾"	28" F/M	8mm	14"	7 lbs. 4 oz.
		12 ga.	2¾"	28" M/IC	8mm	14"	7 lbs. 4 oz.
		12 ga.	2¾"	26" M/IC	8mm	14"	7 lbs. 4 oz.
		20 ga.	3"	28" F/M	8mm	14"	6 lbs. 4 oz.
		20 ga.	3"	28" M/IC	8mm	14"	6 lbs. 4 oz.
		20 ga.	3"	26" M/IC	8mm	14"	6 lbs. 4 oz.
		28 ga.	2¾"	28" F/M	8mm	14"	6 lbs. 0 oz.
		28 ga.	2¾"	26" M/IC	8mm	14"	6 lbs. 0 oz.
		410 ga.	3"	28" F/M	8mm	14"	6 lbs. 0 oz.
		410 ga.	3"	28" M/IC	8mm	14"	6 lbs. 0 oz.
GRADE II SKEET MODELS		12 ga.	2¾"	28" S/S	15mm	14"	7 lbs. 4 oz.
		12 ga.	2¾"	26" S/S	15mm	14"	7 lbs. 4 oz.
		20 ga.	3"	28" S/S	11mm	14"	6 lbs. 4 oz.
		20 ga.	3"	26" S/S	11mm	14"	6 lbs. 4 oz.
		28 ga.	2¾"	28" S/S	8mm	14"	6 lbs. 10 oz.
		28 ga.	2¾"	26" S/S	8mm	14"	6 lbs. 9 oz.
		410 ga.	3"	28" S/S	8mm	14"	6 lbs. 10 oz.
		410 ga.	3"	26" S/S	8mm	14"	6 lbs. 9 oz.
GRADE II TRAP MODELS*		12 ga.	2¾"	32" F/F	15mm	14⅜"	8 lbs. 0 oz.
		12 ga.	2¾"	32" F/IM	15mm	14⅜"	8 lbs. 0 oz.
		12 ga.	2¾"	32" F/M	15mm	14⅜"	8 lbs. 0 oz.
		12 ga.	2¾"	30" F/F	15mm	14⅜"	8 lbs. 0 oz.
		12 ga.	2¾"	30" F/IM	15mm	14⅜"	8 lbs. 0 oz.
		12 ga.	2¾"	30" F/M	15mm	14⅜"	8 lbs. 0 oz.

GOLDEN EAGLE MODEL 5000 GRADE II

*Trap models are furnished with recoil pads, skeet and field models are furnished with contoured butt plates.

Grade II Field, 12 & 20 gauge .... **$ 799.00**
           28 gauge & .410 bore **1259.00**
Grade II Skeet, 12 & 20 gauge **849.00**
           28 gauge & .410 bore **1349.00**
           3 barrel set, 20, 28 gauge & .410 bore **2749.00**
Grade II Trap, 12 & 20 gauge **949.00**

The Golden Eagle Grade II is set off by an eagle 14kt. gold overlay. The receiver is engraved. Trap and Skeet versions have inertia triggers and ventilated side ribs. Available in Field, Skeet Models in 12, 20, 28 or 410 gauge and Trap Models in 12 gauge.

GOLDEN EAGLE SHOTGUNS

MODEL 5000 SPECIFICATIONS		Gauge	Chamber Length	Barrel Length and Choke	Rib Width	Length of Trigger Pull	Approximate Weight
GRADE III FIELD MODELS*		12 ga.	2¾"	28" F/M	8mm	14"	7 lbs. 8 oz.
		12 ga.	2¾"	26" M/IC	8mm	14"	7 lbs. 8 oz.
		20 ga.	2¾"	28" F/M	8mm	14"	7 lbs. 8 oz.
		20 ga.	2¾"	26" M/IC	8mm	14"	7 lbs. 8 oz.
GRADE III SKEET MODELS*		12 ga.	2¾"	26" S/S	11mm	14"	7 lbs. 8 oz.
		20 ga.	3"	28" S/S	9.5mm	14"	6 lbs. 4 oz.
		20 ga.	3"	26" S/S	9.5mm	14"	6 lbs. 4 oz.
GRADE III TRAP MODELS*		12 ga.	2¾"	30" F/IM	11mm	14⅜"	8 lbs. 0 oz.

GOLDEN EAGLE "GRANDEE"
MODEL 5000 GRADE III

Grandee combines metal work, engraving, fancy walnut and checkering. Available in Field and Skeet Models in 12 and 20 gauge and Trap Model in 12 gauge. Hard-luggage type gun case included.

*Trap models are furnished with recoil pads; skeet and field models are furnished with contoured butt plates.

Grade III Grandee Field (all standard barrel lengths & chokes) $2999.00
Grade III Grandee Trap (all standard barrel lengths & chokes) 2999.00
Grade III Grandee Skeet (26" and 28") 2999.00

HECKLER & KOCH BENELLI SHOTGUN

MODEL SL121
AUTOMATIC SHOTGUN
SPECIFICATIONS:

Gauge: 12 (5-shot); 3-shot plug furnished 20 (4-shot); 3-shot plug furnished.
Action: Tubular steel receiver, bolt group and alloy trigger group.

Barrel: 26".
Stock: Walnut. Hand checkered pistol grip and forearm.
Weight: 12 gauge, 6¾ lbs.; 20 gauge, 5¾ lbs.
Features: Quick interchangeable barrel within gauge. Cross-bolt safety.

Model SL121V 12 ga. standard with modified choke $316.00
     with full choke 316.00
Model SL123V 12 ga. with engraved receiver, modified choke 399.50
     with full choke 399.50
Model SL201 20 ga. with improved modified choke 354.00
Model 121V slug 458.00

H&R SINGLE BARREL SHOTGUNS

H&R MODEL 162

Model 162, 12-and 20-gauge, single shot shotgun with cylinder bore barrel, fires rifled slugs for deer hunting. Also can be used for birds and small game.

Model 162 12/24" Cyl. Bore $82.50

MODEL 162
Gauge: 12 and 20 chambered for 3" shells.
Capacity: Single shot
Stock: Walnut finished American hardwood.

Overall Length: 40"
Weight: 5½ lbs.
Barrel Length: 24" with fully adjustable rear sight and dovetail front sight.

H&R MODEL 088 and 088JR

$59.50

Gauge: Model 088 available in 12, 16, 20, and .410; Model 088JR available in 20 and .410.
Capacity: Single shot
Stock: Semi-pistol grip walnut finished hardwood. Semi-beavertail forend.

Overall Length: Model 088, 40 to 43 inches; Model 088JR, 39 inches.
Weight: 5½ lbs.
Barrel Length: 25 inches (Model 088, .410 ga., Model 088JR, 20 and .410 ga.); 26 inches (Model 088, 20 ga.); 28 inches (Model 088, 12 and 16 ga.).

H&R SHOTGUNS

OVER AND UNDER SHOTGUNS

**MODEL 1212
THE WATERFOWL GUN
12 GAUGE
$450.00**

SPECIFICATIONS:
Gauge: 12
Barrel length(s): 28″ ventilated rib, 2¾″ chambers, improved cylinder & improved modified chokes.

Trigger: Single, selective
Safety: Automatic
Stock & forend: Hand-checkered walnut
Butt plate: Hard rubber

**MODEL 1212
THE FIELD GUN
12 GAUGE
$465.00**

SPECIFICATIONS:
Gauge: 12
Barrel length(s): 30″ ventilated rib, 3″ Magnum full & modified choke

Trigger: Single, selective
Safety: Automatic
Stock & forend: Hand-checkered walnut
Butt plate: Recoil pad

SINGLE SHOT SHOTGUNS

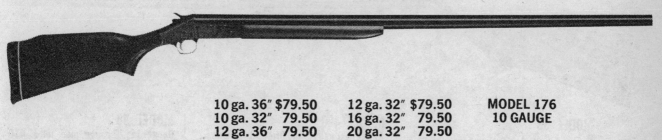

10 ga. 36″ $79.50	12 ga. 32″ $79.50	**MODEL 176**
10 ga. 32″ 79.50	16 ga. 32″ 79.50	**10 GAUGE**
12 ga. 36″ 79.50	20 ga. 32″ 79.50	

Stock dimensions - Length 13¼″, Drop at comb 1½″, Drop at heel 2½″.

Gauge: 10 full, 12 full, 16 full, 20 full
Chamber: 10 Ga. - 3½ inch Magnum
   12 Ga. - 3 inch Magnum
   16 Ga. - 12¾ inch Magnum
   20 Ga. - 3 inch Magnum
Stock: Walnut finished hardwood with recoil pad
Metal Finish: Blue-black barrel.
   Color cased frame

Ave. Weight: 10 ga. 36″ bbl. 10 lbs.
   10 ga. 32″ bbl. 9½ lbs.
   12 ga. 36″ bbl. 9 lbs.
   12 ga. 32″ bbl. 8½ lbs.
   16 ga. 32″ bbl. 8¼ lbs.
   20 ga. 32″ bbl. 8½ lbs.
Sights: Brass bead front.
Overall Length: 47-51″

H&R SINGLE BARREL SHOTGUNS

H&R SHOTGUN MODELS 58, 490, 98

Model 58 has self-adjusting barrel lock, positive shell ejection, rebounding hammer.
Model 490, with identical features, is designed for young shooters and overall length is 3″ shorter. **Model 98,** available in .410 and 20 gauge, features a rich ebony-finished stock and distinctive chrome frame.

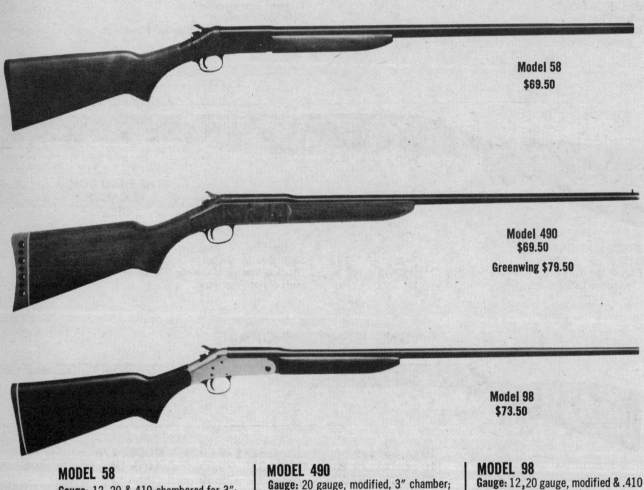

Model 58
$69.50

Model 490
$69.50

Greenwing $79.50

Model 98
$73.50

MODEL 58

Gauge: 12, 20 & 410 chambered for 3″; 16 & 28 chambered for 2¾″.

Capacity: Single shot.

Stock: Walnut-finished hardwood.

Overall length: 12/36″-51″; 12/32″-47″; 12/30″-45″; 12/28″-43″; 16/28″-43″; 20/28″-43″; 28/26″-41″; 410/26″-41″.

Weight: 5½ -6 lbs.

Choke combinations: 12/30″ full; 12/28″ full; 12/28″ mod.; 16/28″ mod.; 20/28″ full; 20/28″ mod.; 28/26″ mod.; 410/26″ full.

MODEL 490

Gauge: 20 gauge, modified, 3″ chamber; .410 gauge, full, 3″ chamber; 28 gauge, modified, 2¾″ chamber.

Capacity: Single shot.

Stock: Walnut finished American hardwood with recoil pad.

Overall Length: 40″.

Weight: 5 lbs.

Barrel Length: 26″ barrel.

MODEL 98

Gauge: 12, 20 gauge, modified & .410 gauge, full chambered for 6-3″.

Capacity: Single shot.

Stock: Ebony finished American hardwood with recoil pad.

Overall Length: 41″.

Weight: 5½ lbs.

Barrel Length: 26″ with brass bead front sight.

MANNLICHER SHOTGUNS

AMBASSADOR SIDE-BY-SIDE
SPECIFICATIONS:

Gauges: 12 and 20 chambered for 2¾" shells

Barrels: Chrome-lined demi-block barrels of Boehler steel

Barrel Length: 27½" and 28½", (other barrel lengths available on request)

Chokes: Any combination on request

Trigger: Single or double trigger

Action: Side-locks based on the Holland & Holland system with double safety and three-lug Purdey locking system

Ejectors: Automatic

Receiver: Chrome-nickel molybdenum, heat-treated steel frame

Stock: European walnut with hand-checkered straight grip. Checkered butt for non-slip surface. Oil finish

Forend: European walnut, hand-checkered. Slim English style with Anson type pushbutton release. 18 carat gold shield inlaid in forend

Stock Dimensions: Length of pull — 14½"; drop at comb — 1½"; drop at heel — 2½"

Weights (Approx.): Depending on density of wood, gauge and barrel length. 12 gauge — 6 lbs. 8 ozs.; 20 gauge — 5 lbs. 10 ozs.

Executive: Special order, customer specification **$19,500.00**

Golden Black: Blued steel with 24-carat gold decorative border **12,975.00**

Extra: Engraving combining a floral design with hunting scenes **9865.00**

English: Engraving on external surface of the actions, side-locks, trigger guard, forend iron and top lever **9865.00**

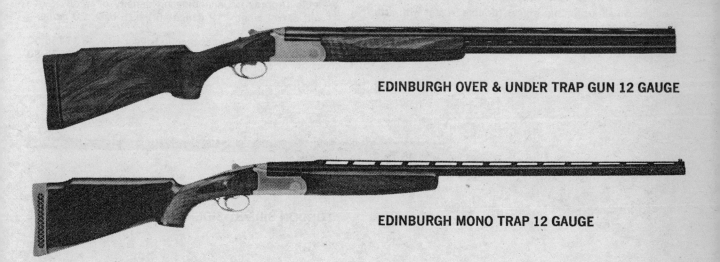

EDINBURGH OVER & UNDER TRAP GUN 12 GAUGE

EDINBURGH MONO TRAP 12 GAUGE

SPECIFICATIONS:

Gauge: 12 chambered for 2¾" shells

Barrels: Chrome-lined demi-block barrels of special Boehler steel with double ventilated ribs (file cut top rib and ventilated mid rib)

Barrel Length & O/U Trap—30", 32" (Trap chokes)

Choke   O/U Skeet—26.5" (Skeet chokes)

Combinations: Mono Trap—32", 34" (Trap choke)

Trigger: Shaped single trigger (selective available)

Action: Patented Anson system

Ejectors: Automatic ejectors

Receiver: Chrome-nickel molybdenum heat-treated steel

Stock & Forend: Selected walnut with Monte Carlo design trap stock with shaped pistol grip and ventilated rubber recoil pad. Hand checkering and European oil finish on trap models. Skeet model comes with high gloss lacquer finish stock and skeet pad.

Stock Dimensions:	TRAP	SKEET
Length of pull:	14½"	14"
Drop at comb:	1½"	1¼"
Drop at heel:	2¼"	2"
Drop at Monte Carlo:	2"	N/A

Weights (Approx.): Trap—7¾ lbs.; Skeet—7¼ lbs.

O/U TRAP	$1699.50
O/U SKEET	1699.50
MONO TRAP	1699.50

MANNLICHER SHOTGUNS

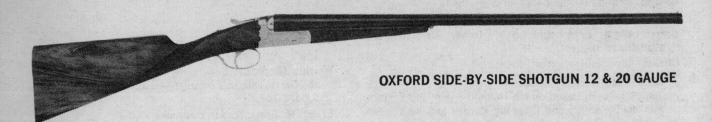

OXFORD SIDE-BY-SIDE SHOTGUN 12 & 20 GAUGE

Grade: Field model with receiver hand engraved in English scroll

Gauges: 12 gauge chambered for 2¾" shells; 20 gauge available with 2¾" or 3" chambers

Barrels: Chrome-lined demi-block barrels of Boehler steel

Barrell Length & 26.5" Imp. Cyl. & Modified

Choke Combinations: 27.5" Modified & Full (other combinations available on request)

Trigger: Single or double trigger (double trigger with articulated front trigger)

Action: Box-lock based on the Anson and Deeley system

Ejectors: Automatic

Receiver: Chrome-nickel molybdenum, heat-treated steel frame

Stock: European walnut with hand-checkered straight grip. Checkered butt for non-slip surface. European oil finish

Forend: European walnut, hand-checkered. English style with Anson type pushbutton release

Stock Dimensions: Length of pull—14½"; drop at comb—1½"; drop at heel—2½"

Weights (Approx.): Depending on density of wood, gauge and barrel length. 12 gauge—6 lbs. 8 ozs.; 20 gauge—5 lbs. 10 ozs.

OXFORD 12 or 20 gauge double trigger $1455.00
OXFORD 12 or 20 gauge single trigger 1575.00

LONDON SIDE-BY-SIDE SHOTGUNS 12 & 20 GAUGE

Grade: Field model with bright or case-hardened receiver. Hand engraved in rose bouquet and scroll work

Gauges: 12 & 20 chambered for 2¾" shells only

Barrels: Chrome-lined demi-block barrels of Boehler steel

Barrel Length & Choke Combinations: 26.5" Imp. Cyl. & Modified. 27.5" Modified & Full (other combinations available on request)

Trigger: Single or double trigger

Action: Side-locks based on the Holland & Holland system with double safety, and three-lug Purdey locking system

Ejectors: Automatic ejectors

Receiver: Chrome-nickle molybdenum heat-treated steel frame

Stock: European walnut with hand-checkered straight grip, and butt inlaid gold oval. Checkered butt for non-slip surface. Hand-rubbed European oil finish

Forend: European walnut, hand checkered. Slim English style with Anson-type pushbutton release

Stock Dimensions: Length of pull — 14½"; drop at comb — 1½"; drop at heel — 2½"

Weights (Approx.): Depending on density of wood, gauge and barrel length. 12 gauge, 6 lbs. 8 ozs.; 20 gauge, 5 lbs. 10 ozs.

LONDON 12 or 20 gauge, with leather case
double trigger $3130.00

LONDON 12 or 20 gauge, with leather case
single trigger 3280.00

MARLIN SHOTGUNS
MARLIN MODEL 120 12-GAUGE MAGNUM PUMP-ACTION SHOTGUN

(12 GAUGE ONLY)

**MARLIN 120 MAGNUM PUMP SHOTGUN
WITH VENTILATED RIB
$217.95
(extra barrels $74.95)**

After years of design study, Marlin has introduced a pump action shotgun that is designed to fill the demand for a solid, reliable, pump action gun. An all-steel receiver is made from a solid block of high tensile steel. New-design, exclusive slide lock release lets you open the action to remove unfired sheel even with gloved hands. All-steel floating concave ventilated rib, serrated on top, provides clean sighting, reduces mirage when trap and skeet shooting. Front and middle sights help the eye align barrel and target. Handsomely engine turned bolt, shell carrier and bolt slide add elegance and double action bars provide smoothest possible operation with no binding or twisting. Matte finish, grooved receiver top eliminates glare, aids natural gun pointing and sighting. Big reversible safety button—serrated and located where it belongs, in front of the trigger—operates the cross-bolt safety that positively blocks the trigger. Choice of barrels—26″ improved cylinder choke, 28″ modified choke, 30″ full choke, 20″

slug barrel (with rifle sights), and 40″ full choke barrel. Select the length and boring of your choice. Extra barrels are completely interchangeable. 5-shot magazine capacity (4 with 3″ shells) 3-shot plug furnished. Stainless steel, non-jamming shell follower. Like all Marlins, the 120 Magnum has a genuine American walnut stock and fore-end. The buttstock design is made to fit American shooters with its full dimensions. Semi-beavertail fore-end is full and fits a full range of hands. Both stock and fore-end are checkered with a handsome pattern and feature Mar-Shield® finish. Deluxe recoil pad is standard.

MARLIN 120 MAGNUM SPECIFICATIONS: 12 gauge, 2¾″ or 3″ Magnum or regular shells interchangeably; 5 shots in magazine (4 with 3″ shells), 3-shot plug furnished; approx. 7¾″ #; 20″, 26″, 28″ or 30″ barrels with steel ventilated ribs, front and middle sights; recoil pad; grip cap; white butt and grip spacers; stock dimensions: 14″ long including recoil pad, 1½″ drop at comb, 2⅜″ drop at heel; genuine American walnut stock and fore-end are finely checkered and Mar-Shield™ finished; all-steel receiver; cross bolt safety.

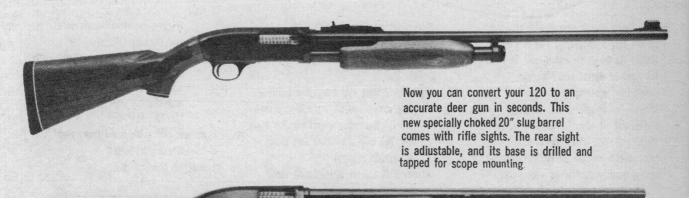

Now you can convert your 120 to an accurate deer gun in seconds. This new specially choked 20″ slug barrel comes with rifle sights. The rear sight is adjustable, and its base is drilled and tapped for scope mounting.

**MARLIN GLENFIELD 778
12 GAUGE PUMP
Plain $150.00   Vent. Rib $169.29**

778 SPECIFICATIONS:

Gauge: 12 gauge; handles 2¾″ Magnum, 3″ Magnum, or 2¾″ Regular shells interchangeably.

Choke: Modified

Capacity: 5-shot tubular magazine (4-shot with 3″ shells); 3-shot plug furnished.

Stock: Two-piece walnut finish hardwood with full pistol grip; semi-beavertail fore-end. Ventilated recoil pad; checkering on pistol grip.

Action: Pump; engine-turned bolt, shell carrier and bolt slide; double action bars; slide lock release; stainless steel shell follower; reversible crossbolt safety; blued steel trigger; deeply blued metal surfaces.

Barrel: 26″ Improved Cylinder, with or without vent rib. 28″ Modified Choke, with or without vent rib. 30″ Full Choke, with or without vent rib. 40″ MXR, Full Choke, without rib. 20″ Slug Barrel (Improved Cylinder), with semi-buckhorn rear, ramp front sight with brass bead and Wide-Scan™ hood. Drilled and tapped for scope mount.

Approx. Weight: 7¾ lbs.

MARLIN SHOTGUNS

MARLIN SUPERGOOSE 10
$177.90

SPECIFICATIONS:
Gauge: 10, 3½" Magnum or 2⅞" reg shells
Capacity: 2-shot clip magazine
Barrel length: 34"
Weight: 10½ lbs.

Overall length: 55½"
Sights: Bead front sight
Action: Bolt action
Trigger: Gold-plated steel
Safety: Positive thumb
Stock: Extra long genuine American black

walnut with pistol grip and Pachmayr® ventilated recoil pad; white butt spacer, quick-detachable steel swivels and deluxe leather carrying strap; Mar-Shield® finish.

MARLIN GLENFIELD 50
$89.95

GLENFIELD 50 SPECIFICATIONS:
Gauge: 12; handles 3" Magnum, 2¾" Magnum and 2¾ shells
Barrel: 28" Full Choke

Weight: 7½ lbs.
Length: 49"
Stock: Walnut finished hardwood with

pistol grip and ventilated recoil pad
Sights: Brass bead front sight
Features: Thumb safety; red cocking indicator

ORIGINAL GOOSE GUN
12 GAUGE 3" MAGNUM—36" BARREL
(FULL CHOKE ONLY)
$96.95

High-flying ducks and geese are the Goose Gun's specialty. The Marlin Goose Gun has an extra-long 36" full-choked barrel and Magnum capability, making it the perfect choice for tough shots at wary waterfowl. It also features a quick-loading 2-shot clip magazine, a convenient leather carrying strap and a quality ventilated recoil pad.

Marlin Goose Gun Specifications
Gauge: 12 gauge; 2¾" Magnum 3" Magnum or 2¾" Regular shells
Choke: Full
Capacity: 2-shot clip magazine (with the exception of some No. 2 and 00 Buck shells, which are too long for the clip magazine and must be single loaded).
Action: Bolt action; gold-plated steel

trigger; positive thumb safety; red cocking indicator.
Stock: Genuine American walnut with pistol grip and ventilated recoil pad; white butt spacer; swivels and leather carrying strap; tough Mar-Shield® finish.
Barrel: 36" with bead front sight.
Overall Length: 56¾"
Weight: About 8 lbs.

Marlin Slug Gun Model 55S
$103.95

Marlin Slug Gun
Based on the Goose Gun bolt action system, the Model 55S is a

heavy cover deer gun. Its short 20" barrel gets into action fast. It comes with iron sights—rear sight is adjustable.

2¾" and 3" shells, the 55S is also equipped with swivels, a handy leather carrying strap and a quality recoil pad. 2-shot clip magazine. About 7½ lbs. Overall length 40¾".

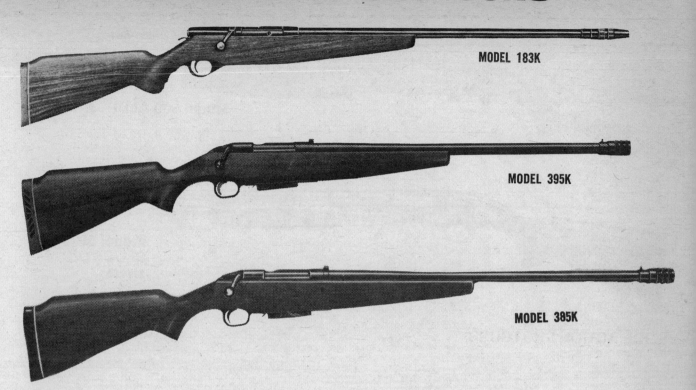

MODEL 183K

MODEL 395K

MODEL 385K

bolt-action shotguns

The most popular bolt action shotguns are those made by Mossberg, in 12 and 20 gauge and 410 bore. Proof tested in our factory and chambered for all standard and Magnum factory loads. A modern streamline designed self-cocking action with **positive safety on top—right under your thumb.** The design and dimensions of these guns make them ideal for fast shooting. All Mossberg shotguns shoot rifled slugs accurately for deer or other big game.

Model 183K 410 bore bolt-action with C-LECT-CHOKE **$79.95**

The only 410 bore shotgun that gives you the advantage of finger-operated adjustable choke. **Action**—Fixed-type top loading magazine holds two shells, plus one in chamber. Chambered for all 2½" and 3" factory loaded shells. Convenient thumb-operated safety.
Stock—Walnut finish Monte Carlo design. Rubber recoil pad with white liner. Molded trigger guard. **Barrel**—25" tapered blued steel barrel, including C-LECT-CHOKE. Mossberg's exclusive factory installed adjustable choke lets you instantly choose Full Choke, Modified Choke, Improved Cylinder Bore or points in between. Gold bead front sight. **Weight**—About 5¾ lbs. Length overall 45¼".

Model 395K 12 ga. bolt-action with C-LECT-CHOKE **$91.95**

With 3" Magnum shells and number 2 shot this becomes a great goose gun. **Action**—Strong bolt action chambered for 3" Magnum as well as 2¾" factory loaded shells.

Double locking lugs for added strength. Quick removable bolt with double extractors. Detachable clip magazine. Magazine holds two shells plus one in chamber. Positive Safety on Top—"Right Under Your Thumb". **Stock**—Walnut finish, modern Monte Carlo design, pistol grip and cushion rubber recoil pad. **Barrel**—26" including C-LECT-CHOKE. **Sights**—Grooved rear sight for accurate alignment. Shotgun bead front. **Weight**—About 7½ lbs. Length overall 45¾".

Model 385K 20 ga. bolt action with C-LECT-CHOKE **$86.95**
Identical to Model 395K except that it is a 20 gauge shotgun with 26" barrel, including C-LECT-CHOKE. Chambered for 3" Magnum as well as 2¾" factory loaded shells. **Weight**—About 6¼ lbs. Length overall 45½".

MOSSBERG SHOTGUNS

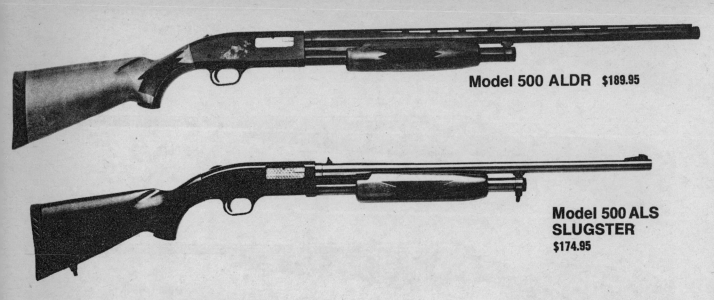

Model 500 ALDR $189.95

Model 500 ALS SLUGSTER $174.95

SLIDE ACTION SHOTGUNS

MODEL 500 SERIES
Slide-Action Shotguns
12 and 20 gauges; .410 bore

All Mossberg 500 12-gauge and 20-gauge shotguns are designed to operate with both 2¾″ and 3″ Magnum shotshells. The .410 will shoot 2½″ and 3″ shells.

SPECIFICATIONS:
Fast slide action feeds shells into chamber quickly. All 12-gauge models have double slide bars for smoother operation. Straight-line feeding aligns shell with chamber before chambering for better functioning. Bolt locks into barrel extension, and action must be locked before gun will fire. Extra-large double extractors for positive ejection; double shell releases assure smooth feeding into carrier and chamber. Action is easily disassembled without special tools.

Positive slide-safety on top of receiver is "right under your thumb." Disconnecting trigger is an added safety feature. Trigger must be released after each shot before the next round will fire. This prevents accidental doubling.

Bolt and carrier have chrome-damascened finish. All other metal parts are deep-blue finished.

Stock—Walnut with filled finish; fluted comb and pistol grip with black spacer and cap. Cushion-rubber recoil pad with black spacer. Checkered on both beavertail forend and pistol grip.

Barrel—All Model 500 barrels are made of selected gun-quality steel machined from solid-bar stock with deep-blue finish. All Model 500 field guns are available with a variety of barrel lengths and chokes. All barrels are easily interchangeable within gauge.

Shell capacity—All Model 500's have six-shot capacity (2¾″)—five in the magazine and one in the chamber. Hold five magnum shells (3″).

500-HI-RIB TRAP
Model 500-AHTD 12 ga. 28″ ACCU-CHOKE w/Imp., Mod., Mod. & Full choke tubes $274.95

Model 500-AHT 12 ga. 30″ Full choke 266.95

500-COMBO PACK w/EXTRA SLUGSTER BAR
Model 500 ALDRX 12 ga. 28″ ACCU-CHOKE, Vent. rib & 24″ Slugster **$222.65**

500—VENT. RIB
Model 500ALDR 12 ga. w/Vent. Rib. 3 interchangeable choke tubes: full; modified; improved cylinder. Chambered for 2¾″ and 3″ factory loaded shells. Barrel length—28″.
....**$189.95**

Model 500CLDR 20 ga. Same as model 500ALDR. **$189.95**

Model 500ELR .410 Bore. Full choke w/Vent. Rib. Chambered for 2½″ and 3″ factory loaded shells. Barrel length—26″. **$181.95**

MOSSBERG SHOTGUNS

ALMR30   12 Ga. 30″ Full w/Vent. Rib 3″ Mag

500ELR   .410 Bore 26″ Full w/Vent. Rib 2½″ & 3″ Chbr.

SLUGSTER
Model 500 ALS24 12 ga. 24″ barrel length, 2¾″ & 3″ chamber
$174.95

Model 500 ALS18½ 12 ga. 18½″ barrel length, 2¾″ & 3″ chamber **$131.21**

Model 500 CLS24 20 ga. 24″ barrel length, 2¾″ & 3″ chamber
$131.21

HEAVY DUCK GUN
Model 500 ALMR30 12 ga. full choke w/vent. barrel length is 30″ and 3″ magnum **$192.50**

Model 500 ALMR32 12 ga. same as model 500 ALMR30 except: barrel length is 32″ **$192.50**

LAW ENFORCEMENT SHOTGUNS:

Model 500 ATP-8 8-shot 20″ barrel **$162.95**
Model 500 ATP-8S 8-shot 20″ barrel w/sights **168.95**
Special firepower, 12 gauge, 8-shot, pump action shotgun in Cylinder Bore. 20″ Barrel. Magazine tubes hold seven standard 2¾″ shells, plus one in the chamber for 8-shot capacity (capacity is one less with 3″ mag.). Lustre-deep bluing. Walnut stained stock and forearm. Deluxe recoil pad. Drilled and tapped for scope and factory installed sling swivels.

Model 500 ATP-6 6-shot 18½″ barrel **$154.95**
Model 500 ATP-6S 6-shot 18½″ barrel **160.95**
Special 12 gauge, 6-shot pump action shotgun in Cylinder Bore. 18½″ Barrel. Magazine tube holds five standard 2¾″ shells, plus one in the chamber for 6-shot capacity. (Capacity is one less with 3″ mag.). Lustre-deep bluing. Walnut-stained stock and forearm. Deluxe recoil pad.

Model 500 ATP-8SP 8-shot 20″ barrel Special Defense/ Enforcement Shotgun **$182.95**
Special 12 gauge, 8-shot pump action shotgun in Cylinder Bore Choke. 20″ Barrel. Magazine tube holds seven standard 2¾″ shells, plus one in the chamber (capacity is one less with 3″ mag.) non-glare, military-style metal finish. Stock and forearm oil finished. Equipped with bayonet lug for U.S. M-7 Bayonet.

MOSSBERG SHOTGUNS

NEW HAVEN BRAND

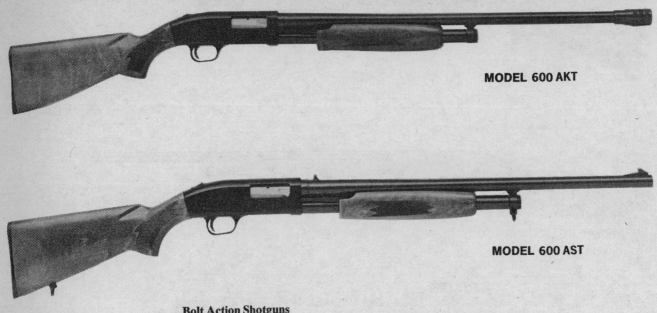

MODEL 600 AKT

MODEL 600 AST

Bolt Action Shotguns

Model 283 T .410 bore bolt-action repeater, Standard Grade. Full choke. Chambered for all 2½" and 3" factory loaded shells. **Barrel**—24". **Stock**—Walnut finish Monte Carlo design. **Weight**—About 6¾ lbs. Length overall 43½". Price not set.

Model 495 T 12 ga. bolt action repeater, Standard Grade. Full choke. Chambered for all 2½" and 3" factory loaded shells. **Barrel**—28". Price not set.

Model 485 T 20 ga. bolt action repeater, Standard Grade. Full choke. Chambered for all 2½" and 3" factory loaded shells. **Barrel**—26". Price not set.

SLIDE ACTION SHOTGUNS PLAIN BARRELS AND VENTILATED RIB

Slide Action 600 "T" offers a lightweight action, high tensile strength alloy. It also features the famous Mossberg "Safety on Top" and a full range of interchangeable barrels. The stock is walnut-finished birch with serrated buttplate and has a fluted comb and grooved beavertail forend.

Model 600 AT: 12 ga. Std. grade, 30" full or 28" mod., plain barrel. 26" Imp. Cyl. .... **Price not set**

Model 600 CT: 20 ga. Std. grade, 28" full or 28" mod., plain barrel. 26" Imp. Cyl. .... **Price not set**

Model 600 ET: .410 Std. grade, 26" full, plain barrel.

Model 600 ATV: 12 ga. Std. grade, 30" full or 28" mod., vent. rib barrel. 26" Imp. Cyl. .... **Price not set**

Model 600 CTV: 20 ga. Std. grade, 28" full or 28" mod., vent. rib barrel. 26" Imp. Cyl. .... **Price not set**

Model 600 ETV: .410 Bore, Std. grade, 26" Full, vent. rib barrel. .... **Price not set**

Model 600 AKT: 12 ga. Std. grade, 28" C-LECT-CHOKE, plain barrel. .... **Price not set**

Model 600 CKT: 20 ga. Std. grade, 28" C-LECT-CHOKE, plain barrel. .... **Price not set**

Model 600 AKTV: 12 ga. Std. grade, 28" C-LECT-CHOKE, vent. rib barrel. .... **Price not set**

Model 600 CKTV: 20 ga. Std. grade, 28" C-LECT-CHOKE, vent. rib barrel. .... **Price not set**

Model 600 AST: 12 ga. Std. grade, 28" Slugster barrel with rifle sights. .... **Price not set**

PARKER-HALE SHOTGUNS

MODEL 900 SEMIAUTOMATIC GAS-OPERATED SHOTGUNS

Specifications—Features:

- 4-shot capacity in 2¾″ chambered guns, the easy-to-remove magazine plug reduces capacity to 3 shots.
- Ventilated rib barrels.
- Patented floating gas piston is self cleaning, needs no adjustment to accommodate different shell loads.
- Gentle recoil. Most of the punch is absorbed by the gas system.
- Cross-bolt safety.
- Lightweight alloy receiver.
- Polished barrel with deep blue lustre and non-glare receiver.
- Hand-checkered, high gloss walnut stock and fore-end with solid rosewood grip cap and white diamond inlay.
- Magnum guns are fitted with rubber recoil pad.

Model 900 12 Gauge: **$287.95**
        26″ Improved Cylinder
        28″ Modified
        28″ Full
        30″ Full
        26″ Skeet

Model 900 12 Gauge Magnum: **$307.95**
        28″ Modified
        30″ Full

ROTTWEIL SHOTGUNS

Rottweil Supreme Field Over/Under Shotgun

SPECIFICATIONS:
Gauge: 12 ga. only
Action: Boxlock
Barrel: 28″ (Mod. & Full, Imp. Cyl. & Imp. Mod. & Full), vent. rib.
Weight: 7¼ lbs.
Length: 47″ overall
Stock: European walnut, hand-checkered and rubbed

Sight: Metal bead front
Features: Removable single trigger assembly with button selector; retracting spring mounted firing pins; engraved action. Extra barrels available.
Price: 28″ Mod. & Full $2750.00
28″ Imp. Cyl. & Imp. Mod. 2750.00
28″ Live Pigeon, Mod. & Full, overall length 45½″ 2750.00

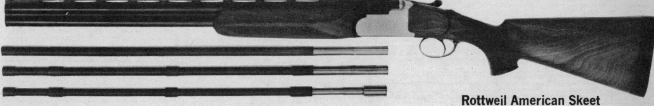

**Rottweil American Skeet
(designed for tube sets) $2750.00**

SPECIFICATIONS:
Gauge: 12 ga.
Action: Boxlock, Skeet and Skeet choke
Barrel: 27″ Skeet and Skeet, vent rib
Weight: 7½ lbs.
Length: 44½″ overall
Stock: Selected European walnut, hand-checkered, modified forend

Sights: Plastic front housed in metallic sleeve with additional center bead
Features: Interchangeable inertia-type trigger group. Receiver milled from solid block of special gun steel. Retracting firing pins are spring mounted. All coil springs. This was the first shotgun specially designed for tube sets.

ROTTWEIL SHOTGUNS

Rottweil Montreal Trap $2750.00

SPECIFICATIONS:
Gauge: 12 ga. only
Action: Boxlock
Barrel: 30″ Imp. Mod. & Full
Weight: 8 lbs.
Length: 48½″ overall

Stock: European walnut, hand-checkered
Sights: Metal bead front
Features: Inertia-type trigger, interchangeable for any system. Frame and lock milled from solid-steel block. Retracting firing pins are spring mounted. All coil springs. Selective single trigger. Action engraved. Extra barrels available.

Rottweil American Trap Combo $3495.00

SPECIFICATIONS:
Gauge: 12 ga. only
Action: Boxlock ¾ & 1/1 choke
Barrels: O/U 32″ separated, ¾ & 1/1 choke. Single 34″, high vent rib, 1/1 choke.
Weight: O/U 8½ lbs. Single 8½ lbs.
Stock: European walnut, hand-checkered and rubbed. (Unfinished stocks available.)

Sights: Plastic front housed in metallic sleeve with additional center bead.
Features: Interchangeable inertia-type trigger groups, 2 standard. Lower tang surface milled to accommodate fast change. Receiver milled from solid block of special gun steel. Barrel locking lugs are recessed into breech face. Chokes are hand-honed, test-fired and then reworked until each shoots flawless patterns. Retracting firing pins spring mounted. All coil springs. Action engraved.

Rottweil Olympia '72 Skeet Shotgun $2750.00

SPECIFICATIONS:
Gauge: 12 ga. only
Action: Boxlock
Barrel: 27″ (special skeet choke), vent. rib.
Weight: 7¼ lbs.
Length: 44½″ overall

Stock: European walnut, hand-checkered, modified beaver-tail fore-end.
Sights: Metal bead front
Features: Inertia-type trigger, interchangeable for any system. Frame and lock milled from solid-steel block. Retracting firing pins are spring mounted. All coil springs. Selective single trigger. Action engraved. Extra barrels available.

Rottweil Adjustable American Trap Combo $4495.00
SPECIFICATIONS: Available single barrel only: $2795.00
Gauge: 12 ga.   Available double barrel only: $2795.00
Action: Rebounding lock, ejector
Barrels: Double barrel, 12 ga., length 32″, improved modified and full choke, exposed lower barrel, muzzle-collar-fitted
Weight: 8½ lbs.
Stock: European Walnut, hand checkered and rubbed

Sights: Plastic front housed in metallic sleeve with additional center bead
Features: The trap shooter adjusts the point of impact of the barrel with an L-wrench. Solid-block, special gun steel receiver. Recessed barrel-locking lugs. Interchangeable stocks, firing pins and bolts. Double-vented recoil pad. Sandblasted receiver.

REMINGTON AUTOLOADING SHOTGUNS

The Remington Model 1100 is a 5-shot gas operated autoloading shotgun with a gas metering system designed to reduce recoil-effect. This design enables the shooter to use all 2¾" standard velocity, "Express," and 2¾" magnum loads without any gun adjustments. Barrels, within gauge and versions, are interchangeable. The 1100 is made in 12, 16, 20, 28 and .410 gauge, with a choice of different chokes, barrel lengths, and gauge combinations. The solid-steel receiver features decorative scroll work. Stocks come with fine-line checkering in a fleur-de-lis design combined with American walnut and a scratch-resistant finish developed by DuPont called RK-W. Features include decorative receiver scrolls, white-diamond inlay in pistol-grip cap, white-line spacers, full beavertail forend, fluted-comb cuts and chrome-plated bolt.

Model 1100 D Tournament with vent. rib barrel **$1200.00**
Model 1100 F Premier vent. rib barrel **2400.00**
Model 1100 F Premier with gold inlay **3600.00**

MODEL 1100 FIELD GUN
(12 and 16 Gauges)
with plain barrel **$291.95**
with ventilated rib **328.95**

REMINGTON MODEL 1100 TB AUTOLOADING TRAP GUN LEFT HAND ACTION — 12 GAUGE (SHOWN WITH OPTIONAL MONTE CARLO STOCK)

MODEL 1100 LEFT HAND

A complete mirror image of the regular Model 1100, these left hand shotguns put an end to the bothersome flying hulls that left-handed shooters had to face. Ejection is on the left side—all other specifications are the same as the regular Model 1100, 12 and 20 gauge. Left hand Monte Carlo stock available on trap model.

Model	Barrel length, in.	Choke	
1100LH with Vent. Rib Barrel	30	Full	$339.95
	28	Mod.	339.95
	26	I.C.	339.95
1100LH Mag. with Vent. Rib Barrel	30	Full	$371.95
1100LH SA Skeet with Vent. Rib Barrel	26	Skeet	$349.95

(12 & Lightweight-20 Gauges)
For 3" & 2¾" Magnum Shells Only

MODEL 1100 MAGNUM
with plain barrel **$322.95**
with ventilated rib **359.95**

Designed for 3" and 2¾" Magnum shells but accepts and functions with any 1100 standard 2¾" chambered barrel. Available in 30" plain and 30" ventilated-rib full or modified choke in 12 gauge, and 28" full or modified choke in 20 gauge, plain or ventilated rib barrels. Stock dimensions: 14" long including pad, 1½" drop at comb. Furnished with recoil pad. Weight: about 8 lbs.

MODEL 1100 DEER GUN
(12 & Lightweight-20 Gauges)

22" barrel, improved cylinder choke. Rifle sights adjustable for windage and elevation. Recoil pad. Weight: about 7¼ lbs. Choked for both rifled slugs and buck shot. **$326.95**

REMINGTON TRAP & SKEET GUNS

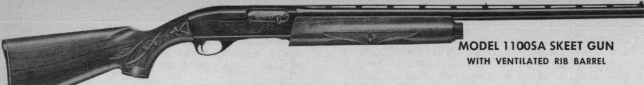

MODEL 1100SA SKEET GUN
WITH VENTILATED RIB BARREL

Model 1100SA Skeet Gun: is made in 12, 20, LT-20, 28 gauge and .410 bore. It comes with 26″ barrel, skeet boring, ventilated rib, ivory bead front sight and white metal rear sight. Stock dimensions are 14″ long, 2½″ drop at heel, 1½″ drop at comb. Weight, about 7½ lbs.

Model 1100 SA Skeet, with ventilated rib barrel	**$338.95**
Model 1100 Tournament Skeet 12 and LT-20 gauge	**400.00**
Model 1100 Tournament Skeet small bore version .410 and 28 gauge	**405.00**

BARREL LENGTH & CHOKE COMBINATIONS

26″	Rem. Skeet

Model 1100TA Trap Gun: is made in 12 gauge only and is equipped with rubber recoil pad and ventilated rib barrel. Stock is of selected grade wood and features fine-line fleur-de-lis design checkering and white spacers on butt plate and grip cap. Fore-end has swept back design and fluting to give secure gripping area. Trap stock dimensions: 14⅜″ long including recoil pad, 1¾″ drop at heel, 1⅜″ drop at comb. Weight: about 8 lbs. Available in 30″ full choke and 30″ modified choke only. Ivory bead front sight, white metal rear sight. Also available with Monte Carlo stock $10.00 extra.

Model 1100 TB Trap, w/vent rib barrel	**$344.95**
Model 1100 TB Trap, w/vent rib & Monte Carlo stock	**354.95**
Model 1100 Tournament Trap 30″ barrel Mod. Full	**410.00**
Model 1100 Tournament Trap 30″ barrel Monte Carlo stock Mod. Full	**420.00**

BARREL LENGTH & CHOKE COMBINATIONS

30″	Full Choke
30″	Modified Trap

(Shown with Monte Carlo stock)

12 GAUGE ONLY

MODEL 1100 TA • Left Hand Trap Gun

The Model 1100 TA is the first autoloading shotgun to achieve serious acceptance by the trap shooting fraternity. Now this famous trap gun is offered in a true "mirror-image" left hand version featuring left hand feeding and ejection. Produced in 30″ full choke ventilated rib barrels with either regular or Monte Carlo stocks. Other specifications same as above. With regular stock **$356.95** with Monte Carlo stock **$366.95.**

SPECIFICATIONS: Model 1100 (12, 16 & LT-20 Gauges):

SPECIFICATIONS: STYLE — 5 shot gas operated shotgun. 3 shot plug furnished. **GAUGE** — Made in 12, 16 and 20 gauge. **BARREL** — Special Remington ordnance steel. Extra barrel is interchangeable within gauge. **OVER-ALL LENGTH** — 48″ (with 28″ Barrel). **SAFETY** — Convenient cross-bolt type. **RECEIVER** — Made from solid steel, top matted, scroll work on bolt and both sides of receiver. **STANDARD STOCK DIMENSIONS** — Stock and fore-end: Rich American walnut. 14″ long, 2½″ drop at heel, 1½″ drop at comb. Trap reg., 14⅜″ long, 1¾″ drop at heel, 1⅜″ drop at comb. Monte Carlo, 14⅜″ long, 1¾″ drop at heel, 1¼″ drop at comb, 1¼″ drop at M.C. **AVERAGE WEIGHT** — 12 ga. - 7½ lbs., 16 ga. - 7⅜ lbs., 20 ga. - 6½ lbs.

MODEL 1100 12, 16 & LT-20 Gauges BARREL LENGTH & CHOKE COMBINATIONS

30″	Full Choke
28″	Full Choke
28″	Modified Choke
26″	Imp. Cyl. Choke

Note: (16 & 20 gauge models are not available in 30″ barrel length).

REMINGTON AUTOLOADING SHOTGUNS

MODEL 1100 LT-20 • LIGHTWEIGHT
(in 20 Gauge only)

with plain barrel $291.95
with ventilated rib 328.95

Model 1100 SA Skeet 20 gauge lightweight LT-20, with ventilated rib barrel. $338.95
Barrel length and choke combinations for the Model 1100 lightweight in 20 gauge: 28" full; 28" modified; and 26" improved Cylinder. Weight, 6½ pounds.

MODEL 1100 • SMALL GAUGES
(28 & 410 Gauges)

with plain barrel $296.95
with ventilated rib 333.95
SA Skeet Ventilated Rib,
 28 & .410 ga., 25" skeet bbl. 343.95

The Remington Model 1100 Autoloading shotguns in 28 and .410 gauges are scaled-down models of the 12 and 16 gauge versions. Built on its own receiver and frame, these small gauge shotguns are available in a wide selection of chokes with either plain or ventilated rib barrels. The .410 gauge field grade will handle 2½" and 3" shotgun shells, while the .410 Skeet gun is supplied with a 2½" chambered barrel. Extra barrels are interchangeable within gauge regardless of chamber length of original barrel. .410 gauge guns are designed for the exclusive use of plastic shells. The model 1100 field grade 28 and .410 gauge guns are equipped with American walnut stocks and forends and feature a scratch resistant RK-W wood finish.

**MODEL 1100
28 & 410 GAUGES
BARREL LENGTH
& CHOKE COMBINATIONS**

25" Full Choke
25" Modified Choke
25" Imp. Cyl. Choke

SPECIFICATIONS: STYLE — Gas operated. 5 shot capacity with 28 ga. shells — 4 shot capacity with 3" - 410 ga. shells. 3 shot plug furnished. **BARREL** — Special Remington ordnance steel. Extra barrels interchangeable within gauge **CHAMBER** — 2½" in .410 ga. skeet; 3" in field grades; 2¾" in 28 ga. field and skeet models. **OVER-ALL LENGTH** — 45½". **SAFETY** — Convenient cross-bolt type. **RECEIVER** — Made from solid steel, top matted, scroll work on bolt and both sides of receiver. **STOCK DIMENSIONS,** walnut in .410, 28 ga., and 20 ga. — 14" long, 2½" drop at heel, 1½" drop at comb. **AVERAGE WEIGHT** — 28 ga. skeet-6¾ lbs.; .410 ga. skeet-7¼ lbs.; 28 ga. plain barrel-6¼ lbs.; .410 ga. plain barrel-6¾ lbs.; 28 ga. vent. rib-6½ lbs.; .410 ga. vent. rib-7 lbs.

3200 LIVE BIRD GUN

3200 LIVE BIRD GUN
12 GAUGE
Price Not Set

The 3200 Pigeon gun is a modified competition grade with 28" barrel, choked improved modified and full. Stocked to competition skeet dimensions. Satin-finished in high grade American walnut.

REMINGTON O&U SHOTGUNS

Remington 3200 Competition Skeet
(In 12 Gauge only)

Remington 3200 Competition Trap
(In 12 Gauge only)

3200 OVER/UNDER SHOTGUNS

SPECIFICATIONS:

Stock and Fore-end: Specially selected fancy walnut stock and fore-end. (Special Trap select but not fancy grade.) Cut checkering, 20 lines to the inch. Full beavertail fore-end. Satin finish standard on Competition grade guns. Optional 1⅜" or 1½" drop on Monte Carlo stocks in Competition grade guns. All with recoil pad.

Frame: Machined steel with sliding top lock. Shield-covered breech. Hammers cock on opening. Sides richly embellished.

Ejection: Automatic. Fired shells eject on opening. Unfired shells remain in chamber but are raised above chamber level for easy manual extraction.

Safety and Barrel Selector: Combination manual safety and barrel selector mounted on top tang. Left for bottom barrel; right for top barrel; middle position for safety on.

Trigger: Single selective. ⁵⁄₁₆" wide. Crisp with extra-fast lock time.

Sights: Ivory bead front, white-metal middle.

3200 Trap

Nominal Stock Dimensions: 14⅜" long. 2" drop at heel. 1½" drop at comb. 1⅜" drop at comb.

Over-all Length: 48" with 30" barrels and recoil pad.

Average Weight: 8¼ lbs. for guns with 30" barrels.

3200 Skeet

Nominal Stock Dimensions: 14" long, 2⅛" drop at heel. 1½" drop at comb.

Over-all Length: Skeet—44¼" with 26" barrels. Competition Skeet—43" with 26" barrels.

Average Weight: 7¾ lbs. with 26" barrels.

3200 Models	Barrel Length	Type of Choke	
Skeet	28"	Skeet & Skeet	
	26"	Skeet & Skeet	
Competition Skeet	28"	Skeet & Skeet	
	26"	Skeet & Skeet	
Special Trap Ventilated Rib	32"	Improved Modified & Full	
Special Trap Ventilated Rib	30"	Improved Modified & Full	Prices not set for any Trap and Skeet Models.
Special Trap Ventilated Rib with Monte Carlo Stock	32"	Improved Modified & Full	
Special Trap Ventilated Rib with Monte Carlo Stock	30"	Improved Modified & Full	
Competition Trap	32"	Imp. Modified & Full	
	30"	Full & Full	
	30"	Imp. Modified & Full	
Competition Trap with Monte Carlo Stock	32"	Imp. Modified & Full	
	32"	Imp. Modified & Full	
	30"	Full & Full	
	30"	Imp. Modified & Full	
	30"	Imp. Modified & Full	
Pigeon	28"	Imp. Modified & Full	

REMINGTON PUMP SHOTGUNS

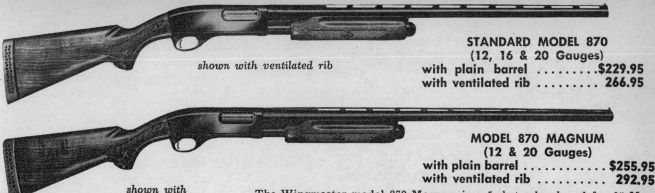

shown with ventilated rib

STANDARD MODEL 870
(12, 16 & 20 Gauges)
with plain barrel $229.95
with ventilated rib 266.95

shown with ventilated rib

MODEL 870 MAGNUM
(12 & 20 Gauges)
with plain barrel $255.95
with ventilated rib 292.95

The Wingmaster model 870 Magnum is a 5 shot; chambered for 3" Magnum shells—will also handle 2¾" shells with 3-shot plug. 12 gauge with 28" and 30" full choke, plain or ventilated rib barrel. Steel-bead front sight, rubber recoil pad. Stock: 14" long including pad, 2½" drop at heel, 1⅝" drop at comb. 20 gauge furnished in 28" full and modified choke ventilated rib and plain barrels. Weight: 12 gauge about 8 lbs., 20 gauge about 7 lbs.

MODEL 870 DEER GUN
(12 & 20 Gauges)
Brushmaster Deluxe (illus.) $249.95
Standard Deer Gun 234.95
Brushmaster 20 ga. Lightweight 254.95

*deluxe "Brushmaster" shown
with rifle sight barrel*

The Model 870 Brushmaster is made to handle rifled slugs and buck shot. With 20" barrel and fully adjustable rifle-type sights. Stock fitted with rubber recoil pad and white line spacer. Other specifications same as standard 870. Also available in standard model. Same as Deluxe Brushmaster above, but with lacquer finish; no checkering, recoil pad, grip cap; special handy short fore-end. The Lightweight 20 ga. Brushmaster includes rifle sights and has a 20" barrel.

The Wingmaster Model 870SA skeet gun comes with 26" barrel, special skeet boring, ventilated rib with ivory-bead front and white-metal middle sight. Also available in 28 & 410 gauge .

12 ga. about 7 lbs., 20 ga. about 6½ lbs. Also available in SC grade with selected wood and hand checkering.

**MODEL 870 SA SKEET GUN
WITH VENTILATED RIB BARREL
(12, 20, 28 Gauges and .410 bore)**

870 SA Skeet gun, with ventilated rib, Rem. Skeet choke (12 & 20 gauges) **$271.95**
870 SA Skeet gun, with vent rib, Rem Skeet choke (28 & .410 gauges). **276.95**
870 SC Skeet gun, with vent rib, Rem Skeet choke (select wood and cut checkering).
440.00

MODEL 870 12, 16 & 20 GAUGE BARREL LENGTH & CHOKE COMBINATIONS	
30"	Full Choke
28"	Full Choke
28"	Modified Choke
26"	Imp. Cyl. Choke
Deer Gun 20" Imp. Cyl.	

SPECIFICATIONS: STYLE — 5 shot pump action shotgun. Take down. 3 shot plug furnished. **GAUGES** — 12, 16 and 20. **BARREL** — Special Remington ordnance steel. Extra barrel is interchangeable within gauge. **OVER-ALL LENGTH** — 48½" with 28" barrel. **SAFETY** — Convenient cross-bolt type, positive. **RECEIVER** — Made from solid steel, top matted. **STANDARD STOCK DIMENSIONS** — Stock and fore-end: Rich American walnut. Beautiful checkering. 14" long, 2½" drop at heel, 1⅝" drop at comb. Trap reg., 14⅜" long, 1⅞" drop at heel, 1½" drop at comb. Monte Carlo; 14⅜" long, 1⅞" drop at heel, 1⅜" drop at comb, 1⅜" drop at M.C. **AVERAGE WEIGHT** — 12 ga. - 7 lbs.; 16 ga. - 6¾ lbs.; 20 ga. - 6½ lbs.

REMINGTON PUMP SHOTGUNS
MODEL 870 PUMP ACTION SHOTGUNS—TRAP MODELS

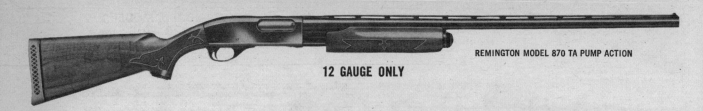

12 GAUGE ONLY

REMINGTON MODEL 870 TA PUMP ACTION

MODEL 870 TA • Trap Gun 12 ga.

SPECIFICATIONS:

TA Trap Ventilated Rib 30" barrel Full	$276.95
TA Trap Ventilated Rib with Monte Carlo stock 30" barrel Mod. Trap	286.95
TB Trap Ventilated Rib 30" barrel Mod. Full	306.95
TB Trap Ventilated Rib 30" barrel with Monte Carlo stock, Mod. Full	316.95
TC Trap Ventilated Rib 30" barrel Full	470.00
TC Trap Ventilated Rib 30" barrel with Monte Carlo stock Full	470.00

Monte Carlo stock shown

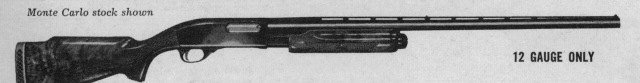

12 GAUGE ONLY

MODEL 870 TB • Trap Gun

SPECIFICATIONS: Available with 30" full or modified trap, ventilated rib barrel. Ivory bead front and white metal rear sight. Recoil pad. Special target grade hammer, sear and trigger assembly. Beautiful "B" grade walnut stock with lustrous DuPont RK-W finish, fleur-de-lis checkering, special small pistol grip with cap. Regular stock dimensions: drop at comb 1½", drop at heel 1⅞", length of pull 14⅜". Monte Carlo stock dimensions: drop at comb 1⅜", drop at Monte Carlo 1⅜", drop at heel 1⅞", length of pull 14⅜" ... Extra 34" full choke trap gun barrels available.

Model	Barrel length, in.	Choke	
870TB with Vent. Rib Barrel	30 30	Mod. Full	$306.95 306.95
870TB with Vent. Rib Barrel & Monte Carlo Stock	30 30	Mod. Full	$316.95 316.95
870TBLH with Vent. Rib Barrel	30	Full	$316.95
870LH with Monte Carlo Stock	30	Full	$326.95

MODEL 870 TB • Left Hand Trap Gun

The only pump action trap gun built specifically for the left handed shooter. True "mirror image" design offers left hand feeding and ejection. Produced in 30" full choke ventilated rib barrels with either regular or Monte Carlo stocks. Other specifications same as above.

12 GAUGE ONLY

MODEL 870 TC • Trap Gun

SPECIFICATIONS: Same as 870 TB except: Rich, highly figured, hand-rubbed walnut stock with beautiful hand-checkering. Special hand-polished parts.

Model	Barrel length, in	Choke	
870TC with Vent. Rib Barrel	30"	Full	$470.00

Model	Barrel length, in.	Choke	
870TC with Vent. Rib Barrel & Monte Carlo Stock	30"	Full	$470.00

REMINGTON MODEL 870
PUMP ACTION SHOTGUNS

12 and 20 Gauges

MODEL 870 LEFT HAND • Field Gun "WINGMASTER"

A complete mirror image of the regular Model 870, these left hand shotguns put an end to the bothersome flying hulls that left-handed shooters had to face. Ejection is on the left side—all other specifications are the same as the regular Model 870, 12 and 20 gauge. Left hand Monte Carlo stock available on trap model.

Model	Barrel length, in.	Choke	
870LH	30	Full	$281.95
With Vent.	28	Full	281.95
Rib Barrel	28	Mod.	281.95
	26	I.C.	281.95
870LH Mag. with Vent. Rib Barrel	30	Full	$307.95

SPECIFICATIONS

STYLE	5 shot pump action shotgun.
GAUGES	Right hand versions: 12,16 and 20. Left hand versions: 12 and 20.
BARREL	Special Remington proof steel. Extra barrels are interchangeable within version (reg. or left hand) and gauge without fitting.
OVER-ALL LENGTH	48½" with 28" barrel.
SAFETY	Convenient positive cross-bolt type. Reversed on left hand models.
RECEIVER	Made from solid steel, top matted.
STANDARD STOCK DIMENSIONS	Stock and fore-end: Rich American walnut. Beautiful checkering. 14" long including recoil pad, 2½" drop at heel, 1⅝" drop at comb.
AVERAGE WEIGHT	20 ga.-6½ lbs.; 16 ga.-6¾ lbs.; 12 ga.-7 lbs.

20 GAUGE LIGHTWEIGHT SHOWN

MODEL 870 • 20 Gauge Lightweight
MODEL 870 • 20 Gauge Lightweight Magnum

**20 Gauge Lightweight
20 Gauge Lightweight 3 Inch Magnum**

This is the pump action designed for the upland game hunter who wants enough power to stop fast flying game birds but light enough to be comfortable on all day hunting. The 20 gauge Lightweight handles all 20 gauge 2¾ in. shells. The magnum version handles all 20 gauge shells including the powerful 3 in. shells. American walnut stock and forend.

Model	Barrel length, in.	Choke	
870L,W.	28	Full	$234.95
With Plain	28	Mod.	234.95
Barrel	26	I.C.	234.95
870L,W.	28	Full	$271.95
With Vent.	28	Mod.	271.95
Rib Barrel	26	I.C.	271.95
870L.W. Mag. With Plain Barrel	28	Full	$260.95
870L.W. Mag. With Vent. Rib Barrel	28	Full	$297.95

MODEL 870 • 28 & .410 Gauges

These small gauges are scale models of the famous Model 870 "Wingmaster" in the larger gauges. Built on their own receiver and frame, they give the shooter unique handling and pointing characteristics. Beautiful fleur-de-lis fine line checkering, white line spacers at butt plate and grip cap, chrome plated bolt, and steel bead front sight are bonus features.

Model	Barrel length, in.	Choke	
870 with Plain Barrel	25	Full	$234.95
	25	Mod.	234.95
	25	I.C.	234.95
870 with Vent. Rib Barrel	25	Full	$271.95
	25	Mod.	271.95
	25	I.C.	271.95

REMINGTON SHOTGUNS

MODEL 870 HIGH GRADE

D Tournament Ventilated Rib, all gauges and versions $1200.00
F Premier Ventilated Rib, all gauges and versions 2400.00
F Premier Ventilated Rib with Gold Inlay, all gauges and versions 3600.00

RUGER SHOTGUNS

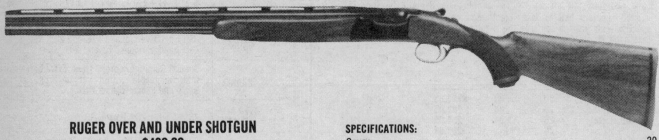

RUGER OVER AND UNDER SHOTGUN
$480.00

Hardened 4140 chrome molybdenom and other alloy steels and music wire coil springs are used throughout the frame. Single selective trigger. Automatic top safety serves as the selector that determines which of the two barrels will be fired first. Standard gold bead front sight. Stock and semi-beavertail forearm are shaped from American walnut with hand cut checkering. Pistol grip cap and rubber recoil pad are standard and all wood surfaces are polished and weatherproof-sealed.

SPECIFICATIONS:

Gauge	20
Chambers	3"
Barrel Lengths	26", 28"
Overall Length (26" Barrels)	43"
Chokes	Skeet & Skeet, Improved Cylinder & Modified
Length of Pull	14"
Drop at Comb	1½"
Drop at Heel	2½"
Weight	Approximately 7 lbs.

ROSSI SHOTGUNS

OVERLAND MODEL II

SQUIRE MODEL 14

MODEL 11 12 or 20 GAUGE

OVERLAND MODEL II: Available in a 410 bore and 12 or 20 gauge for both standard 2¾-inch shells or 3-inch magnum. The 12 and 20 gauges are offered in the Coach Gun version with abbreviated 20 inch-barrels with improved and modified chokes. Overlands feature a raised rib with matted sight surface, hardwood stocks, rounded semi-pistol grips, color case-hardened hammers, triggers and locking lever.

Gauge	Barrel Length	Choke	Price
12	20" 28"	IC&M M&F	$189.00
20	20" 28"	IC&M	189.00
410	26"	F&F	196.00

SQUIRE MODEL 14: Available in 410 bore or 12 or 20 gauge, the Squire has 3-inch chambers to handle the full range of shotgun loads. Features double triggers, raised matted rib, beavertail forend and pistol grip. Twin underlugs mesh with synchronized sliding bolts for double-safe solid lockup.

Gauge	Barrel Length	Choke	Price
12	26" 28"	IC&M M&F	$199.00
20	28"	M&F	199.00
410	26"	F&F	216.00

SAVAGE STEVENS SHOTGUN

STEVENS .410 GAUGE BOLT-ACTION SHOTGUN

**STEVENS MODEL 58—.410 BORE
BOLT ACTION—CLIP MAGAZINE
(.410 Bore, $64.95-69.95)**

Stevens 58 .410 gauge. The 58 in .410 gauge has a three-shot detachable clip magazine. A shell in the chamber makes it a four-shot repeater. The electro-cote stock finish seals the stock for longer protection. It comes equipped with a 24″ full choke barrel, chambered for 2½″ and 3″ shells. Length overall, 43″. Weight, 5½ lbs.

SAVAGE
FOX AND STEVENS SHOTGUNS

(DOUBLE BARREL SHOTGUNS IN 12, 16, 20 & .410 Gauges)

**STEVENS MODEL 311
(12, 16, 20 & .410 Gauges)
$173.60**

The Stevens 311 Gauges: 12, 16, 20 &.410.

(12 and 20 gauge now in 3″ magnum.) This double barrel shotgun has many refinements usually found only in higher priced guns. It offers sturdy construction, solid lockup, excellent balance and superior shooting qualities.

SAVAGE
FOX AND STEVENS SHOTGUNS

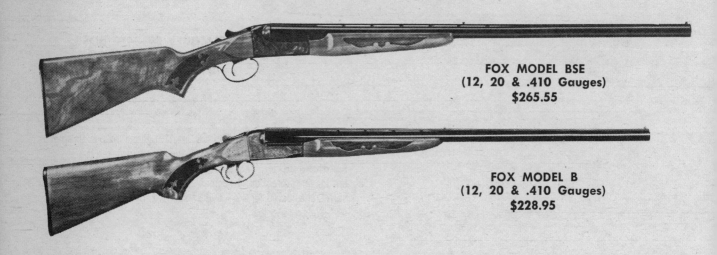

FOX MODEL BSE
(12, 20 & .410 Gauges)
$265.55

FOX MODEL B
(12, 20 & .410 Gauges)
$228.95

Fox B-SE Gauges 12, 20 and 410. Automatic ejectors are standard equipment on the Fox B-SE. Other fine gun features are the single trigger and ventilated rib. The B-SE has the lines found only in a double gun, enriched with materials and finishes typical of expensive custom guns. Its selected walnut stock has a deeply fluted comb and checkering on pistol grip. The gracefully tapered beavertail fore-end is also attractively checkered. The frame has color case hardened finish with decoration on bottom. Convenient top tang safety.

24" Fox B 12 and 20 Gauge. With 24" barrels this Fox B is ideal for grouse, woodcock, quail—any game bird at closer range or in thick cover. Impossible shots made possible with this short, light-barreled, fast-swing Fox shotgun. Other specifications are the same as Fox-B above.

Fox-B Gauges: 12, 20 & 410.

(12 and 20 gauge now in 3" magnum.) For sheer beauty of design, fine balance and fast handling, nothing equals a double—the traditional sporting gun. The Fox B standard equipment includes ventilated rib, select walnut stock with fluted comb, beavertail fore-end and checkering. Two triggers give the shooter instant command of two shots—the split second choice of two chokes.

Fox B Gauges: 12, 20 & .410.
Fox B E Gauges: 12, 20 & .410.
(12 and 20 gauge in 3" magnum.) Same as Fox B but with automatic ejectors. The two triggers give you instant choice of two chokes. **$265.55**

SPECIFICATIONS — FEATURES

MODEL	Vent Rib	Solid Rib	Bead Sights	Automatic Top Tang Safety	Extractors	Selective Ejectors	Trigger Single	Trigger Double	Frame Case Hardened	Frame Decorated	Coil Springs	Checkered Stock Select Walnut	Checkered Stock Walnut Finished Hardwood	White Line Butt Plate	Average Weight (Lbs.)
B-SE	X		2	X		X	X		X	X	X	X			7–8
B or B-E	X		2	X	X			X	X	X	X	X			6½–8
311		X	1	X	X			X	X		X		X	X	7¼–8
ALL MODELS															

ALL MODELS Stock: Length 14"; drop 1½" at comb, 2½" at heel.
Length over-all 41¾"–45¾"; take down 24"–30". All Models proof-tested.

SAVAGE RIFLE/SHOTGUNS

MODEL 24-D

MODEL 24 FIELD GRADE

24-C Campers Companion Combination: 22 long rifle/20 gauge. At 5¾ pounds, it's a pound lighter and five inches shorter than other 24's. When stored in special case, it measures just 5″ x 22″. The case has handles for carrying, thongs for tieing to pack or saddle. Recess in stock holds extra shells. **$122.65**

24-D Deluxe Combinations: 22 long rifle/20 or .410 gauge; 22 magnum/20 gauge. A breech and separated barrels on this handsome deluxe model means lighter weight and better balance. Two-way top opening lever swings either way for right- or left-hand use. The checkered walnut stock and fore-end are protected for lasting beauty with our new electro-cote finish. The decorated receiver adds a final deluxe touch. This combination gun is ideal for small game, pests and varmints as well as plinking. A 20 gauge slug can be used for larger game; the 22 magnum adds extra power and range for bobcat, fox, turkey **$131.00**

24 Field Grade Combinations: 22 long rifle/20 or .410 gauge; 22 magnum/20 or .410 gauge. A combination gun at a field grade price makes this model an ideal first gun—combines the ever popular 22 cartridge with either of two popular shotgun gauges. New top lever opening. Walnut finished hardwood stock and fore-end receives our new electro-cote finish. **$110.80**

CHOKE—BARREL—CHAMBER

MODEL	Caliber Gauge	23½″ F	24″ F	20″ C	Chambered For
2400	308, 12 222, 12	X X			2¾″ 2¾″
24-V	30-30, 20 222, 20		X X		2¾″ & 3″ 2¾″ & 3″
24-D	22 L.R., 20 22 L.R., 410 22 Mag., 20		X X X		2¾″ & 3″ 2½″ & 3″ 2¾″ & 3″
24-F.G.	22 L.R., 20 22 L.R., 410 22 Mag., 20		X X X		2¾″ & 3″ 2½″ & 3″ 2¾″ & 3″
24-C	22 L.R., 20			X	2¾″

F—Full C—Cylinder

SPECIFICATIONS—FEATURES

MODELS	Barrels Length	Scope Mounting	Grooved For Scope	Sights		Color Case Hardened Frame	Rebounding Hammer	Hammer Selector	Top Lever Opening	Takedown	Stock		Checkered Stock	Monte Carlo	White Line Butt Plate	White Line Grip Cap	Length Over-all	Avg. Wgt. (Lbs.)
				Front	Rear						Select Walnut	Walnut Finished Hardwood						
2400	23½″	Dovetailed		Blade	Folding Leaf	Blued		Trigger Selector	X	X	X		Cut Checked	X	X		40½″	7½
24-V	24″	Tapped		Ramp	Folding Leaf	X	X	X	X	X	X		X	X	X	X	40″	6¾–7½
24-D	24″		X	Ramp	Sporting	X	X	X	X	X	X		X	X	X	X	40″	7½
24-F.G.	24″		X	Ramp	Sporting	X	X	X	X	X		X					40″	6½
24-C	20″		X	Ramp	Sporting	X	X	X	X	X		X					36″	5¾

MODELS 2400 Stock: Length 14″; drop 1½″ at comb, 1¾″ at Monte Carlo, 2½″ at heel; taken down 23½″.
24-V, 24-D Stock: Length 14″; drop 2″ at comb, 1¾″ at Monte Carlo, 2⅝″ at heel; taken down 24″.
24-C Stock: Length 13½″; drop 1¾″ at comb, 2¾″ at heel; taken down 20″.
24-F.G. Stock: Length 14″; drop 1¾″ at comb, 2¾″ at heel; taken down 24″.

RATE OF TWIST (R.H.) 1 turn in 12″ for 30-30, 308; 14″ for 222; 16″ for 22 Mag., for 22 L.R.

SAVAGE STEVENS SHOTGUNS

94-C
(12, 16, 20, & .410 Gauge)
$64.85-$69.00

Stevens 94-C: Single barrel shotgun with hammer style action. Opening lever on top tang swings either way, automatic ejectors, checkered walnut finished hardwood stock and forend. Available with 36″ "Long Tom" barrel in 12 gauge .... **$64.85-$69.00**

94-Y Youth Model: 20 & 410 gauges, top lever opening. Has shooter stock with rubber recoil pad, 26″ barrel. **$69.00**

Model 9478: A single barrel shotgun in 10, 12, 20, or 410 gauges. Features manual cocking, visible hammer, unbreakable coil springs. Automatic ejection and bottom-opening lever. Color, case-hardened finish.

Model 9478 10 gauge Waterfowl: With 36-in. barrel, stock is fitted with rubber recoil pad, and fore-end is grooved.

Model 9478-Y Youth Model. With 20 and 410 gauges. Bottom opening lever, shorter stock with hard rubber butt plate, 26-in. barrel. 20 ga. modified or 410 full choke.

Price: 9478, 9478 Waterfowl and 9478-Y .... **Price Not Set**

242 Shotgun: .410 gauge over .410. Has two-way opening lever, swings either way for right- or left-hand use. The 242 has separated barrels; select walnut stock with checkering; beavertail fore-end, grooved for a surer grip. Color casehardened receiver, positive extraction and a hand-operated hammer. **$140.58**

SPECIFICATIONS: BARREL—CHOKE—CHAMBER

MODEL		242
CALIBER & GAUGE		.410 ONLY
BARREL LENGTHS & CHOKES	24″ FULL	•
	20″ CYL.	
CHAMBERED FOR		2½″ or 3″
LENGTH	OVERALL	40″
	TAKEN DOWN	24″
	STOCK	14″
DROP AT	COMB	1¾″
	MONTE CARLO	
	HEEL	2¾″
AVERAGE WEIGHT (LBS.)		7

FEATURES

MODEL		242
GROOVED FOR SCOPE		
TOP LEVER OPENING		•
BARREL SELECTOR ON HAMMER		•
STOCK	SELECT WALNUT	•
	WAL. FIN. HARDWOOD	
SIGHTS	FRONT: RAMP	BEAD
	REAR: SPORTING	

SPECIFICATIONS: BARREL—CHOKE—CHAMBER

MODEL			9478*—94-C					9476-Y—94-Y	
GAUGE		10	12	16	20	410	20	410
BARREL LENGTHS & CHOKES	26″ F					•		•
	26″ M						•	
	28″ F		•	•	•			
	30″ F		•	•	•			
	32″ F		•					
	36″ F	•	•					
CHAMBERED FOR		2⅞″ & 3½″	2¼″ & 3″	2¼″	2¼″ & 3″	2½″ & 3″	2¼″ & 3″	2½″ & 3″
LENGTH	OVERALL			42″–52″			40½″	
	TAKEN DOWN			26″–36″			26″	
	STOCK			14″			12½″	
DROP AT	COMB			1½″			1½″	
	HEEL			2½″			2½″	
AVERAGE WEIGHT (LBS.)		9½		6–6¼			5½	

*MODEL 9478 NOT AVAILABLE IN 16 GAUGE OR 12 GAUGE 32″ F

FEATURES

MODEL	94-C—94-Y	9478—9478-Y
REBOUNDING HAMMER	•	
2-WAY TOP LEVER OPENING	•	
BOTTOM OPENING LEVER		•
AUTO EJECTOR	•	•
POSITIVE EXTRACTION	•	•
STOCK WAL. FIN. HARDWOOD	•	•
FORE-END WAL. FIN. HARDWOOD	•	•

24-V
20 gauge
357 Mag.; 30-30 Win.; 222 Rem.

24-V Combinations: 30-30 Win./20 ga.; 222 Rem./20 ga.; 357 Mag./20 ga.; Takes regular 3″ magnum shells for small game, use a 20-gauge slug for larger game. **$155.48**

Features: Select European walnut stock, semi-beavertail forend with cut checkering, white-line rubber recoil pad and sling swivels. Selective single trigger, solid matted rib blade front sight and folding leaf rear. Metal is highly polished blue lustre.

SKB OVER & UNDER SHOTGUNS

TARGET MODELS

600 Grade
- **Frame :** Hunting scene and black finish.
- **Barrel :** Black finish, chrome-lined inside.
- **Action :** Single selective trigger, non-automatic safety and automatic selective ejector.
- **Stock and Fore-end :** Hand-checkered French walnut available either oil or dull-urethane finish.
- **Locking :** Cross-bolt locking plus extra barrel lug. Silver-plated frame with deeply etched scroll work.

700 Grade Additional scroll work design on frame enhances appearance. The extra wide ventilated rib creates a perfect sighting plane on trap and skeet.

800 Grade The supreme grade of SKB over and under with all the features of 700 Grade.

880 Grade The only SKB gun with side plate. Richly etched scroll work on frame and perfect functioning.

MODELS 500, 600, 700, 800 & 880 SKEET AND TRAP

Model 500 Skeet 12 and 20 gauge	$610.00
Model 500 Trap 12 gauge	620.00
Model 600 Skeet 12 and 20 gauge	740.00
28 and 410 gauge	765.00
Model 600 Skeet 3bbl combination 20, 28 and 410 gauge (case included)	2260.00
Model 600 Trap 12 gauge	750.00
Model 700 Skeet 12 and 20 gauge	970.00
Model 700 Trap 12 gauge	970.00
Model 800 Skeet 12 and 20 gauge	1510.00
Model 800 Trap 12 gauge	1510.00
Model 880 Skeet 12 and 20 gauge	2710.00
Model 880 Trap 12 gauge	2710.00

Standard specifications for SKB Over-and-Under Shotguns/Target Models

GAUGE (Chamber)	RIB	MODEL	BARREL LENGTH	AVAILABLE CHOKES	STOCK LENGTH	COMB	HEEL	MONTE CARLO	OVERALL WT. (Approx.)
12 (2¾")	Regular Ventilated Rib (9.5mm)	Trap	30" 30"	Full & Full Imp. Modified & Full	14"	1½"	2"	1½"	3.6 kgs. (8 lbs.)
		Skeet	28" or 26"	SPR. & SPR.	14"	1½"	2⅝"		3.2 kgs. (7 lbs.)
	Wide-Rib (16mm) Semi Wide-Rib (12mm)	Trap	30" 30"	Full & Full Imp. Modified & Full	14"	1½"	2"	1½"	3.7 kgs. (8¼ lbs.)
		Skeet	26"	SPR. & SPR.	14"	1½"	2⅝"		3.3 kgs. (7¼ lbs.)
20 (3")	Regular Ventilated Rib (8.5mm)	Skeet	26"	SPR. & SPR.	14"	1½"	2⅝"		2.8 kgs. (6¼ lbs.)

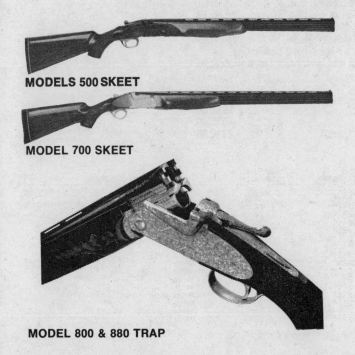

MODELS 500 SKEET

MODEL 700 SKEET

MODEL 800 & 880 TRAP

MODEL 600 TRAP

MODEL 800 & 880 SKEET

SKB OVER & UNDER SHOTGUNS

FIELD MODELS

Box lock type action.
Selective automatic ejectors.

Selective single trigger mechanism with the selector located on the trigger. Smooth pull for both barrels. Firing is always in sequence.

Non-automatic safety.
Roto-forged barrel of high-tensile alloy steel, with ventilated rib.
Hand-checkered, pistol-grip stocks and fore-ends are made from finished walnut.
Inside of barrels is chrome-lined.
All major action components are fitted to minute tolerances.
All the mechanisms as well as etching on receiver of each Grade are same as the Target Models.

Model 500 12 and 20 gauge	$599.00
Model 500 Mag. 12 gauge	615.00
Model 600 12 and 20 gauge	719.00
Model 600 Mag. 12 gauge	735.00
Model 680 12 and 20 gauge (English)	785.00

(Specialized for field hunting, having English grip stock.)

SMALL GAUGE OVER-AND-UNDER-SHOTGUNS/FIELD MODELS

FIELD MODEL 500

Model 500 28 and 410 gauge	$625.00
Model 600 28 and 410 gauge	745.00

Standard specifications for SKB Over-and-Under Shotguns/Field Models

GAUGE (CHAMBER)	BARREL LENGTH	AVAILABLE CHOKES	STOCK LENGTH	STOCK COMB	STOCK HEEL	OVERALL WT. (Approx.)
12 (2¾″)	30″ 28″ 26″	Modified & Full Modified & Full Imp. Cylinder & Modified	14″	1½″	2⅜″	3.2 kgs (7 lbs.)
20 (3″)	28″ 26″	Modified & Full Imp. Cylinder & Modified	14″	1½″	2⅝″	2.9 kgs (6¼ lbs.)

MODELS 5600, 5700, 5800 TARGET

Available in both trap and skeet versions. Automatic selective ejectors, mechanical trigger. Semi-beavertail forend. Hand-checkered, non-slip design, wide and semi-wide raised ribs: 16 mm wide rib on trap; 16 mm and 12 mm for skeet, Model 5600. Hand-polished, blued frame and barrel Model 5700. Same as Model 5600 except finer grade walnut. Case-hardened frame. More hand checkering. Model 5800. Hand engraved frame and barrel top. Ivory grip cap in addition to other features.

SPECIFICATIONS:

Model 5600 Skeet and Trap	$995.00
Model 5700 Skeet and Trap	1510.00
Model 5800 Skeet and Trap	2310.00

SPECIFICATIONS:

MODEL	GAUGE	CHOKE	CHAMBER	BARREL LENGTH	RIB	STOCK
	12	SK-SK	2¾″	28″	Semi-wide	*
5600	12	SK-SK	2¾″	28″	Wide	*
Skeet	12	SK-SK	2¾″	26″	Semi-wide	*
	12	SK-SK	2¾″	26″	Wide	*
5600	12	F-IM	2¾″	30″	Wide	**
Trap	12	F-IM	2¾″	30″	Wide	*
	12	SK-SK	2¾″	28″	Semi-wide	*
5700	12	SK-SK	2¾″	28″	Wide	*
Skeet	12	SK-SK	2¾″	26″	Semi-wide	*
	12	SK-SK	2¾″	26″	Wide	*
5700	12	F-IM	2¾″	30″	Wide	**
Trap	12	F-IM	2¾″	30″	Wide	*
	12	SK-SK	2¾″	28″	Wide	*
5800	12	SK-SK	2¾″	26″	Semi-wide	*
Skeet	12	SK-SK	2¾″	26″	Wide	**
5800	12	F-IM	2¾″	30″	Wide	**
Trap	12	F-IM	2¾″	30″	Wide	*

*Semi-Wide: 12mm (approx. ½″)   Wide: 16mm (approx. ⅝″)   **Monte Carlo

SKB SIDE-BY-SIDE SHOTGUNS

100 Grade

Frame : Simple design of hand engraving and black finish.

Barrel : Black chrome finish, chrome-lined inside.

Action : Single selective trigger, automatic safety and non-automatic extractor.

Stock and Fore-end : Hand-checkered French walnut. Available either oil or dull-urethane finish.

200 Grade Has automatic selective ejector and pure silver plated frame, fore-end iron and trigger guard.

280 Grade Excellent hunting gun for quail and pheasant with classic stock. All other features are same as 200 Grade.

300 Grade Deluxe grade of field gun with finer work. All silver plated frame in addition to all features of 200 Grade.

400 Grade Highest grade of SKB side-by-side with all features of 300 Grade.

Model 100 12 and 20 gauge	$425.00
Model 100 Mag. 12 gauge	435.00
Model 200 12 and 20 gauge	589.00
Model 200 Mag. 12 gauge	599.00
Model 200 Skeet 12 and 20 gauge	595.00
Model 280 English 12 and 20 gauge	609.00
Model 300 12 and 20 gauge	795.00
Model 400 12 and 20 gauge	1069.00
Model 400 Skeet 12 and 20 gauge	1069.00
Model 480 English 20 gauge	1069.00

Standard specifications for SKB Side-by-Side Shotguns

MODEL	GAUGE (CHAMBER)	BARREL LENGTH	AVAILABLE CHOKES	STOCK LENGTH	STOCK COMB	STOCK HEEL	OVERALL WT. (Approx.)
Field	12 (2¾")	30" 28" 26"	Modified & Full Modified & Full Imp. Cylinder & Modified	14"	1½"	2⅝"	3.2 kgs. (7 lbs.)
	20 (3")	28" 25"	Modified & Full Imp. Cylinder & Modified	14"	1½"	2⅝"	2.8 kgs. (6¼ lbs.)

ENGLISH MODEL 280

MODEL 100 MAGNUM

SKB SLIDE-ACTION PUMP SHOTGUNS

MODEL 7900 TRAP 12 GAUGE

MODEL 7900 SKEET 12 AND 20 GAUGE

Model 7300 Vent Rib 12 and 20 gauge **$279.00**
Model 7900 Skeet 12 and 20 gauge **289.00**
Model 7900 Trap 12 gauge **305.00**
Model 7300 Slug 12 and 20 gauge **279.00**

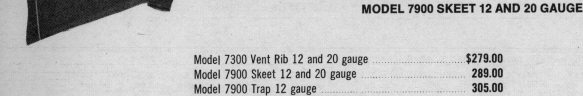

Specifications

MODEL	GAUGE	BARREL LENGTH	CHOKE	CHAMBER	STOCK DIMENSIONS LENGTH	DROP AT COMB	DROP AT HEEL	WEIGHT (lbs.)
7300 Field	12	30″	F	3″	14″	1½″	2½″	7¼
		28″	F or M	3″	14″	1½″	2½″	7¼
		26″	IC	3″	14″	1½″	2½″	7¼
	20	28″	F or M	3″	14″	1½″	2½″	6¼
		26″	IC	3″	14″	1½″	2½″	6¼
7900 Skeet	12	26″	SK	2¾″	14″	1½″	2¼″	7½
	20	26″	SK	2¾″	14″	1½″	2¼″	6½
7900 Trap	12	30″	F or IM	2¾″	14½″	1½″	1⅞″	8
	12	30″	F or IM	2¾″	14½″	1½″	2″	8
7300 Slug	12	24″	Cyl	2¾″	14″	1½″	2½″	7
	20	24″	Cyl	3″	14″	1½″	2½″	6¼

GAS-AUTOMATIC SHOTGUNS

5-shot capacity (4 in magazine, 1 in chamber). 3-shot plug available.

Roto-forged barrel of high-tensile alloy steel, with ventilated rib or plain. Completely interchangeable.

Press-checkered pistol-grip stocks and fore-ends are made from beautifully finished walnut.

Expertly balanced light weight permits easy carrying.

Features positive cross-bolt type trigger safety.

Automatic safety keeps the gun from firing until the bolt is completely closed.

Chrome-plated inside of bore.

Attractive chemical etching on receiver. Both hunting scene and scroll available for 900 Grade.

300 Grade: Plain barrel. Ventilated rib barrel also available (300 V Grade).

900 Grade: Ventilated rib barrel. Receiver deep etched. Gold plate trigger. Gold color square nameplate. White spacers at pistol grip cap and at butt plate.

MODEL XL 900 VENT RIB

SKB SHOTGUNS

Specifications

MODEL	GAUGE	BARREL LENGTH	CHOKE	CHAMBER	STOCK DIMENSIONS			WEIGHT (lbs.)
					LENGTH	DROP AT COMB	DROP AT HEEL	
XL900		30″	F	2¾″	14″	1½″	2½″	7¼
XL900MR*	12	28″	F or M	2¾″	14″	1½″	2½″	7¼
		26″	IC	2¾″	14″	1½″	2½″	7¼
XL900MR*		30″	F	3″	14″	1½″	2½″	7¼
MAGNUM	12	28″	F or M	3″	14″	1½″	2½″	7¼
		26″	IC	3″	14″	1½″	2½″	7¼
XL900	20	28″	F or M	3″	14″	1½″	2½″	6¼
		26″	IC	3″	14″	1½″	2½″	6¼
XL900*	12	26″	SK	2¾″	14″	1½″	2¼″	7½
XL900MR SKEET	20	26″	SK	2¾″	14″	1½″	2¼″	6½
XL900	12	30″	F or IM	2¾″	14½″	1½″	1⅞″	8
XL900MR TRAP*	12	30″	F or IM	2¾″	14½″	1½″	2″	8
XL900	12	24″	Cyl	2¾″	14″	1½″	2½″	7
XL900MR SLUG†	20	24″	Cyl	3″	14″	1½″	2½″	6¼
XL100 SLUG†	12	20″	Cyl	2¾″	14″	1½″	2½″	7

*Recoil Pad Standard.   Monte Carlo drop 1½″.   †Sling Swivels Included.

MODEL XL 900 SKEET

MODEL XL 900 TRAP

Model XL 100 Plain 12 gauge	$275.00
Model XL 900 Vent Rib 12 and 20 gauge	324.00
Model XL 900 Skeet 12 and 20 gauge	336.00
Model XL 900 Trap 12 gauge	352.00
Model XL 900 Slug 12 and 20 gauge	324.00
Model XL 900MR 12 and 20 gauge	359.00
Model XL 900MR Skeet 12 and 20 gauge	369.00
Model XL 900MR Trap 12 gauge	395.00
Model XL 900MR Slug 12 and 20 gauge	352.00

MODEL XL 900 SLUG

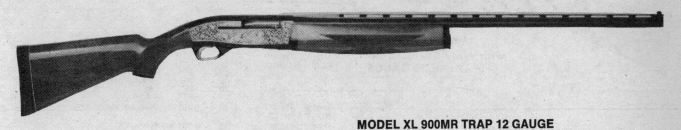

MODEL XL 900MR TRAP 12 GAUGE

MODEL XL 900MR SLUG 12 AND 20 GAUGE

SMITH & WESSON SHOTGUNS

AUTOLOADING SHOTGUN MODEL 1000

MODEL 1000 AUTO SHOTGUN
12 Gauge, w/vent. rib and
3" Magnum chamber
$359.95

MODEL 1000 AUTO SHOTGUN
12 & 20 Gauge, w/vent. rib and 2¾" chamber
$328.95

MODEL 1000 SPECIFICATIONS

STYLE: 4-Shot (Plugged for 2 Shots) Autoloading gas-operated shotgun with pressure compensator and floating piston for light recoil.

GAUGE: 12 & 20 (2¾" Chamber) ; 12 3" Magnum Chamber

BARREL: Smith & Wesson Proof-Tested Chrome Molybdenum Steel.

RECEIVER: Light Weight High Tensile Strength Alloy, Scroll Engraved both sides ; 12 gauge 3" magnum has steel receiver.

LENGTH: 48" Over-all (with 28" Barrel).

SAFETY: Positive Cross-Bolt Type, Interchangeable left or right hand.

STOCK: Selected American Walnut: Length of Pull 14", Drop at Comb 1½", Drop at Heel 2⅜".

WEIGHT: 7½ lbs. with 28" barrel (12 gauge, 2¾" chamber); 6½ lbs. with 28" barrel (20 gauge, 2¾" chamber); 8 lbs. with 30" barrel (12 gauge, 3"chamber)

The S&W Model 1000 auto shotgun comes in 12 & 20 gauge. Features include high-luster blue steel finish; genuine American walnut, specially selected for superior grain, lustrously finished and sure grip hand-checkered; cross-hatched, smooth flowing ventilated sighting rib; double sighting beads; broad comfort-contoured hard-chromed trigger; handsomely designed and executed scroll engraving on both sides of the receiver and the unique inset Smith & Wesson logo in the pistol-grip cap.

Additional features include right or left handed safety; cold hammer-forged chrome molybdenum steel barrel hard chromed bolt, bolt carrier, pressure compensator valve and piston; and an all new patent pending gas operating system which features a unique gas pressure compensator valve (to stabilize variations in gas port pressures) and an oversized gas expansion chamber with a piston actuated gas port cutoff. Virtual self-cleaning of the gas cylinder wall is achieved by the sharp edge of the piston which expels carbon residue with every stroke. The S & W Model 1000 will shoot thousands of rounds without cleaning.

26"	Skeet	
26"	Improved Cylinder	with
28"	Modified	Vent.
28"	Full	Rib and 2¾"
30"	Full	Chamber
30"	Modified	with Vent.
30"	Full	Rib and 3" Chamber

PUMP SHOTGUN MODEL 916

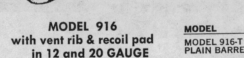

MODEL 916
with vent rib & recoil pad
in 12 and 20 GAUGE

MODEL 916 SPECIFICATIONS

STYLE: 6 Shot Pump Action Shotgun, Plugged for 3 shots.

GAUGE 12 and 20 gauge chambered to accept both 2¾" and 3" magnum shells

BARREL: (Model 916-T offers interchangeable barrel capacity.)

RECEIVER: From Solid Chrome Molybdenum Steel with Hardened Lock Areas, Satin, Non-Glare Top.

LENGTH: 48" Over-All with 28" Barrel.

SAFETY: Convenient Top Tang Type.

STOCK: Genuine American Walnut with Fluted Comb and Finger Grooved Walnut Fore-End. 14" Length of Pull, 2½" Drop at Heel, 1⅝" Drop at Comb.

WEIGHT: 7¼ lbs. (with a 28" Plain Barrel).

MODEL	GAUGE	BARREL LENGTH	CHOKE	
MODEL 916-T PLAIN BARREL	12	30"	Full	
	12	28"	Modified	
	12	26"	Imp. Cylinder	$152.00
	20	26"	Imp. Cylinder	
	20	28"	Full	
	20	28"	Modified	
MODEL 916-T RIFLE SIGHTS	12	20"	Cylinder (recoil pad)	179.50
MODEL 916 PLAIN BARREL	12	30"	Full	
	12	28"	Modified	
	12	26"	Imp. Cylinder	146.50
	12	20"	Cylinder	
	12	18"	Cylinder	
	20	28"	Full	
	20	28"	Modified	
	20	26"	Imp. Cylinder	
MODEL 916-T VENTILATED RIB AND VENTILATED RECOIL PAD	12	30"	Full	
	12	28"	Modified	
	12	26"	Imp. Cylinder	180.50
	20	28"	Full	
	20	28"	Modified	
	20	26"	Imp. Cylinder	
MODEL 916 VENTILATED RIB AND VENTILATED RECOIL PAD	12	30"	Full	
	12	28"	Modified	
	12	26"	Imp. Cylinder	
	20	28"	Full	175.00
	20	28"	Modified	
	20	26"	Imp. Cylinder	
MODEL 916 RIFLE SIGHTS	12	20"	Cylinder (8 shot)	168.00
	12	20"	Cylinder (8 shot, recoil pad)	174.00

VENTURA SHOTGUNS

CONTENTO OVER-AND-UNDER TRAP SHOTGUNS
Gauge: 12.

Action: Box lock with Woodward side-lugs and double internal bolts.

Barrels: 32″ with high "Mexico" sighting rib, and ventilated side ribs choking, modified and improved modified or option of screw-in chokes in both O/U barrels and single interchangeable barrels.

Stocks: Hand checkered European walnut. Monte Carlo, 14½ x 1 5/16, recoil pad included for individual fitting.

Features: Single selective triggers, auto ejectors, MK3 Model has fancy walnut and extensive Florentine engraving. Both MK2 (shown) and MK3 Models available with O/U and single barrels. Combination sets with O/U and single barrels and screw-in chokes are supplied in leather trunk case.

MK2 O/U Trap	$ 940.00
MK2 combination set	1633.00
MK3 O/U Trap	1445.00
MK3 combination set	2373.00

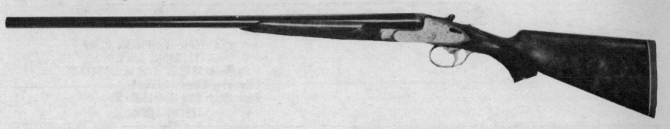

VENTURA MODEL 51 DOUBLE-BARREL SHOTGUN
Gauges: 12 & 20.

Action: Anson & Deeley boxlock with double under lugs.

Barrels: 25-26-28-30″, lengths and chokes according to gauge and use.

Stocks: Select European walnut, finely hand checkered with either English or pistol grip.

Features: All models have beavertail forend, and optional single selective triggers; interchangeable parts; engraving.

Model 51	$540.00

VENTURA MODELS 62 & 64 DOUBLE-BARREL SHOTGUNS
Gauges: 12 (2¾″) & 20 (3″).

Action: Holland & Holland sidelock with treble locks.

Barrels: 25-26-28 30″, with chokes according to gauge and use.

Stocks: European walnut, hand checkered, straight English or pistol grip with slender beavertail forends.

Features: Single selective triggers or double triggers; automatic ejectors; Model 62 has Purdey style and Model 64 has Florentine style hand engraving. Both models have cocking indicators, gas escape valves, intercepting safeties and side clips.

Models 62 & 64	**Prices from $925.00**

PIOTTI SIDE-BY-SIDE SHOTGUNS
Gauges: 12, 20, 28 & .410.

Action: Valtrompia Crown, Holland & Holland sidelock; Gardone, Anson & Deeley boxlock.

Barrels: 25″ to 30″ with chokes as required.

Weight: From 4 lbs. 9 oz.

Stocks: English or pistol grip dimensions as required in highly figured European walnuts; forends small or beavertail.

Features: Hand engraving, automatic ejectors; single selective triggers or double triggers.

Sidelocks	**Prices from $4860.00**
Boxlocks	**Prices from 2410.00**

VERNEY-CARRON OVER-AND-UNDER SHOTGUNS
Gauge: 12.

Action: Lightweight boxlock with double internal bolts.

Barrels: Field 26″ & 28″; Skeet 28″.

Weight: 6 lbs. 7 ozs in 26″ barrel Field.

Stock: French walnut, hand checkered, English or pistol grip.

Features: Self-opener, automatic ejectors, single selective triggers. Engraved; two higher grades available—Dyane & Supreme.

Field Grade	$ 995.00
Skeet Grade	1045.00

WEATHERBY SHOTGUNS

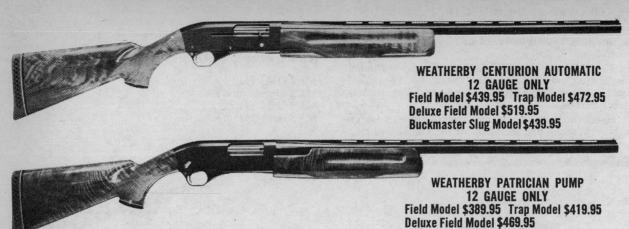

WEATHERBY CENTURION AUTOMATIC
12 GAUGE ONLY
Field Model $439.95   Trap Model $472.95
Deluxe Field Model $519.95
Buckmaster Slug Model $439.95

WEATHERBY PATRICIAN PUMP
12 GAUGE ONLY
Field Model $389.95   Trap Model $419.95
Deluxe Field Model $469.95
Buckmaster Slug Model $389.95

SPECIFICATIONS
for
PATRICIAN and CENTURION SHOTGUNS

WEATHERBY CENTURION AUTOMATIC

Gas operated means no friction rings and collars to adjust for different loads. The barrel holds stationary instead of plunging backward with every shot.

To these natural advantages of the gas-operated automatic, Weatherby has added revolutionary "Floating Piston" action. In the Weatherby Centurion, the piston "floats" freely on the magazine tube completely independent of every other part of the action. Nothing to get out of alignment. Nothing to cause drag or friction.

WEATHERBY PATRICIAN PUMP

The super-fast slide action operates on double rails for precision and reliability. No twists, no binds, no hang-ups.

To remove a loaded round, push the gold-plated forearm release lever to its forward position. Now the forearm is unlocked and the action can be opened.

	Field	Trap
Gauges:	12 ga. only	
Chamber length:	2¾" chamber and 3" Mag.	
Barrel lengths & chokes:	30" Full 28" Mod 26" Imp Cyl 30" Full 3" Mag	
	28" Full 26" Mod 26" Skeet 30" Full Trap	
Stock dimensions		
Length of pull:	14¼"	14¾"
Drop at comb:	1⅜"	1⅜"
Drop at heel:	2¼"	1¾"
Approx. weight:		
Patrician pump shotguns:	30" bbl — 7 lb. 9 oz.	
	28" bbl — 7 lb. 7 oz.	
	26" bbl — 7 lb. 5¼ oz.	
Centurion auto shotguns:	30" bbl — 7 lb. 11¾ oz.	
	28" bbl — 7 lb. 10½ oz.	
	26" bbl — 7 lb. 9¼ oz.	
Safety:	Cross bolt type, right or left hand	
Stock:	Figured American walnut, fine line hand checkering.	
Interchangeable barrels:	Available in above lengths and chokes.	
Price of extra barrels:	Patrician pump — $164.95	
	Centurion auto — 164.95	

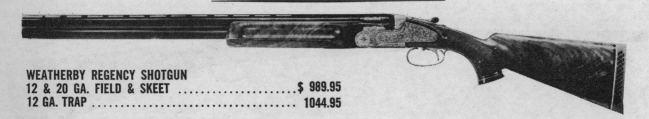

WEATHERBY REGENCY SHOTGUN
12 & 20 GA. FIELD & SKEET .... **$ 989.95**
12 GA. TRAP **1044.95**

RECEIVER . . . The Regency receiver houses a strong, reliable box lock action, yet it features side lock type plates to carry through the fine floral engraving. The hinge pivots, are made of a special high strength steel alloy. The locking system employs the time-tested Greener cross bolt design.

SINGLE SELECTIVE TRIGGER . . . It is mechanically rather than recoil operated. This provides a fully automatic switch-over, allowing the second barrel to be fired on a subsequent trigger pull, even in the event of a misfire.

The Regency trigger is selective, as well. A flick of the trigger finger and the selector lever, located just in front of the trigger, is all the way to the left enabling you to fire the lower barrel first, or to the right for the upper barrel.

SELECTIVE AUTOMATIC EJECTORS . . . The Regency contains ejectors that are fully automatic both in selection and action. **SLIDE SAFETY** . . . The safety is the traditional slide type located conveniently on the upper tang on top of the pistol grip **BARRELS** . . . The breech block is hand fitted to the receiver, providing closest possible tolerances. Every Regency is equipped with a matted, ventilated rib and bead front sight.

REGENCY SHOTGUN SPECIFICATIONS

	Field and Skeet Models		Trap Models
Gauges	12 ga.	20 ga.	12 ga. (20 ga. not avail.)
Chamber Length	2¾" chamber	3" chamber	2¾" chamber
Barrel Lengths & Chokes	26" M/IC. S/S	26" F/M M/IC. S/S	30" F/F. F/IM. F/M
	28" F/M. M/IC. S/S	28" F/M M/IC. S/S	32" F/F. F/IM. F/M
	30" F/M		
Stock Dimensions			
Length of pull	14¼"	14¼"	14⅜"
Drop at comb	1½"	1½"	1⅜"
Drop at heel	2½"	2½"	1⅞"
Approx. Weight	26" 7 lbs. 3 oz.	26" 6 lbs. 11 oz.	30" 7 lbs. 12 oz.
	28" 7 lbs. 6 oz.	28" 6 lbs. 14 oz.	32" 8 lbs.
	30" 7 lbs. 9 oz.		

Safety on all models—Slide operated rear tang
Stock on all models—Select American Walnut

WEATHERBY SHOTGUNS

WEATHERBY OLYMPIAN OVER/UNDER

Field Grade 12 & 20 ga. $899.95   Trap Grade 12 ga. only $999.95

Specifications	Field and Skeet Models		Trap Models
Gauges	12 ga.	20 ga.	12 ga. (20 ga. not avail.)
Chamber Length	2¾" chamber 3" chamber (for 30" barrel only)	3" chamber	2¾" chamber
Barrel Lengths & Chokes	30" F/M 28" F/M, M/IC, S/S 26" M/IC, S/S	28" F/M, M/IC, S/S 26" F/M, M/IC, S/S	32" F/M, F/IM 30" F/M, F/IM

Stock Dimensions			
Length of pull	14³⁄₁₆"	14"	14⅜"
Drop at Comb	1½"	1½"	1⁷⁄₁₆"
Drop at heel	2½"	2½"	1¹⁵⁄₁₆"
(Monte Carlo)*			1¹¹⁄₁₆"
Approx. Weight	28" 7 lbs. 12 oz.	28" 7 lbs. 1 oz.	30" 8 lbs.
	26" 7 lbs. 8 oz.	26" 6 lbs. 14 oz.	

Safety on all models—Tang' thumb operated and combined with automatic barrel selector.
Stocks on all models—American Walnut.

*Trap models only.

WEBLEY & SCOTT

MODEL 712, 720 & 728

These Webley & Scott shotguns have English-style straight stock and slim fore-end of figured French walnut, hand checkered. The stock has an inlayed gold oval suitable for engraving with the owner's initials. The action, trigger guard and top lever are hand engraved with delicate English scroll.

RIBS: Concave, English-style game rib.
ACTION: Hammerless boxlock, top lever, automatic selective ejectors, solid tumblers, automatic safety, double triggers.
STOCK: Figured selected French walnut. Hand-checkered straight grip, and butt. Inlayed gold oval.
STOCK DIMENSIONS: Length of pull, 14⅝". Drop at comb, 1½". Drop at heel, 2¼". Cast-off, 3/16".

FORE-END: Select French walnut, hand-checkered. Slim English style with "Anson"-type push button release.
ENGRAVING: Hand engraved with fine English scroll as illustrated.
FINISH: Superior quality finish throughout. Color case-hardened action, blued barrels and furniture.
WEIGHTS (Approx.): Model 712, 6½ lbs. Model 720, 5¾ lbs. Model 728, 5½ lbs.
ACCESSORIES: Guns come complete with fitted case, cleaning implements, oil bottle and snap caps

Model 712	**Price Not Set**
Model 720	**Price Not Set**
Model 728	**Price Not Set**

SPECIFICATIONS:
MODELS 712 (12 Ga.) 720 (20 Ga.) 728 (28 Ga.)

All models are identical except for gauge, barrel and chamber lengths.

BARRELS:

MODEL	GAUGE	CHAMBER	BARREL LENGTH	CHOKES
712	12	2¾"	26"	Imp. Cyl. & Mod.
720	20	3"	26"	Imp. Cyl. & Mod.
728	28	2¾"	25"	Imp. Cyl. & Mod.

WINCHESTER CUSTOM SHOTGUNS

MODEL 12 SLIDE-ACTION SHOTGUNS IN 12 GAUGE ONLY

Literally brought back by popular demand, the Model 12 remains the standard of the slide action shotgun world. Many years ago we said that a lifetime of shooting wouldn't wear out a Model 12. It is still true with today's new Model 12 . . . a sporting arm made the same uncompromising way from machined chrome molybdenum steel and choice walnut by craftsmen in Connecticut who enthusiastically welcome a chance to turn this old favorite out again.

Standard Trap Model With ventilated rib and recoil pad. Hand checkered. Full-fancy walnut stock and slide handle. Engine-turned bolt and carrier. Length of pull 14⅜", drop at comb 1⅜", drop at heel 1⅞". Overall length 49¾" with 30" full choke barrel **$854.00**

Trap Model With Monte Carlo Same specifications as Standard model with drop at comb 1½ in., drop at heel 2⅛ in., drop at Monte Carlo 1½ in. with 30" full-choke-barrel **$854.00**

Model 12 Specifications

Type	Trap Standard	Trap Monte Carlo
Gauge	12	12
Magazine Capacity	6 (a)	6 (a)
Barrel Length	30"	30"
Overall Length	49¾"	49¾"
Length of Pull	14⅜"	14⅜"
Drop at Comb	1⅜"	1½"
Drop at Heel	1⅞"	2⅛"
Drop at M.C.	—	1½"
Weight (lbs.)	8¼	8¼

(a) Add one round for shell in chamber. Model 12s have factory-installed plug, which, when removed, increases magazine capacity to six shells.
(b) All guns have ventilated ribs.

DOUBLE BARREL SHOTGUNS
WINCHESTER MODEL No. 21

Custom Grade

Choice of gauge—12, 16 or 20 gauge; choice of barrel lengths—

      12 gauge—32, 30, 28 and 26 in.
      16 gauge—30, 28 and 26 in.
      20 gauge—30, 28 and 26 in.

Choice of choke combination; matted rib barrel, 2¾ in. chamber, rounded frame. Stock and beavertail forearm of Grade AA full-fancy American walnut. Stock built to individual specifications (within manufacturing limits). Straight or pistol grip—includes cheek piece, Monte Carlo and/or offset. Choice of forearm—field, skeet or trap; black insert in forearm tip. Fancy checkering on stock and forearm; steel pistol grip cap. Choice of composition butt plate, recoil pad or checkered butt. Panel in top rib inscribed "Custom built by Winchester for (Customer's Name)." Automatic or non-automatic safety (optional). Choice of front and middle bead sights.

Engine turned standing breech, frame, barrel flats, barrel lug, extractors, barrel breech, forearm retainer and inside upper surfaces of forearm shoe. Custom style ornamentation. Gold plated trigger. Gold oval name plate (optional). Choice of three initials engraved on name plate or trigger guard.

Custom Grade .... Special Order

Pigeon Grade

Carries all features of the Custom Grade plus the following added refinements: Matted rib or ventilated rib. 2¾ or 3 in. chamber (3 in. chamber not available in 16 gauge). Full leather covering on recoil pad (optional). Style "A" carving on stock and beavertail forearm. No. 6 engraving on frame and barrels. Gold inlaid pistol grip cap. Gold oval name plate or three initials gold inlaid on trigger guard.

Pigeon Grade .... Special Order

Grand American

Carries all features of the Custom and Pigeon Grades plus the following: Style "B" carving on stock and beavertail forearm. No. 6 engraving with all figures gold inlaid. Set of interchangeable barrels complete with extra beavertail forearm suitably engraved and carved to match balance of gun. Leather trunk gun case with canvas cover—both case and cover embossed with three initials in gold or black.

Grand American .... Special Order

WINCHESTER AUTOMATIC SHOTGUNS

Winchoke 1400s

The Winchester Model 1400 with the Winchoke feature. It offers fully interchangeable precision-machined steel choke units to make three guns out of one.

Winchester Model 1400 automatic shotguns with Winchoke feature are offered in 12 and 20 gauges, featuring a push-button carrier release for loading ease. There's a unique, self-compensating gas system that automatically adjusts for standard and 2-¾" magnum loads. Plus frontlocking, rotating steel bolthead that locks into a steel barrel breech. Rustproof aluminum receiver. Engine-turned bolt. Crossbolt safety.

Winchester Winchokes are actually three, 2-inch interchangeable choke tubes, precision-bored to a specific choke. The lightweight tubes are machined from chrome molybdenum steel. One is an Improved Cylinder; the second is a Modified choke and the third is a Full choke. Together, they amount to three guns in one.

Shotgunners know that most shotgun barrels are slightly constricted or "choked" at the muzzle to achieve a particular type of shot pattern. For close-in shooting you want an open-bored gun with little or no choke. You have to pick up another gun for best performance in moderate range hunting. You'd want another with a full-choked barrel for long range shooting of larger game or high-flying wildfowl.

Winchoke lets you change chokes freely and quickly without altering either the gun's point of impact or the shooter's sight picture. Winchokes are lightweight, 2"-long, threaded choke tubes that simply screw into the muzzle of the specially adapted gun barrel . . . without changing the streamlined appearance of the shotgun. There's no bulge and the tube of your choice fits snugly and won't shoot loose. In effect, the Winchoke is a two-inch interchangeable barrel . . . without changing the entire barrel.

For Winchester Model 1200 and 1400 field guns, three Winchoke tubes are offered, including Improved Cylinder for close-in shooting, Modified choke for medium-range patterns, and Full choke for long-range hunting. All three are packed with each gun, with the Modified choke tube installed and a handy spanner wrench included. Together, they amount to a cabinet-full of shotguns you can carry in your pocket, allowing you to change your pattern to suit your changing sport . . . with the same gun.

Winchoke available in 12 or 20 gauge 2¾" chamber only, ventilated rib or plain barrel.

Winchoke Model 1400 Mark II Field Gun with Plain Barrel. In 12 or 20 gauge with 28" barrel, modified, full & improved cylinder $239.00

Winchoke Model 1400 Field Grade with Plain Barrel

Winchoke Model 1400 Mark II Field Gun with Ventilated Rib. In 12 or 20 gauge with 28" barrel, modified, full & improved cylinder $260.00

Winchoke Model 1400 Field Grade with Ventilated Rib

Extra Barrels:
Field with Winchoke $73.95
Field, ventilated rib with Winchoke 93.95
Deer Barrel 80.95

WINCHESTER AUTOMATIC SHOTGUNS

SUPER-X MODEL 1 XTR GAS-OPERATED AUTOMATIC SHOTGUN

SUPER-X MODEL 1 XTR

Receiver and all other metal parts machined steel.

All Ventilated Rib models have a mid-rib sight.

1. Super-X Model 1 Field Gun. With ventilated rib barrel and bead front sight. 12 gauge chambering 2¾″ shells available in 26″ improved cylinder, 28″ with modified or full choke, and 30″ full choke.

2. Super-X Model 1 Trap Gun. 12 gauge. 30″ ventilated rib barrel Full choke. Selected walnut regular or Monte Carlo stock and wide forearm. Engraved receiver. Black-rubber recoil pad with white spacer. Red-bead front sight.

3. Super-X Model 1 Skeet Gun. 12 gauge with 26″ ventilated rib barrel. Skeet choke. Selected walnut stock with wide forearm. Engraved receiver.

Super-X Model 1 XTR

Field Gun, w/vent rib **$396.00**
Trap Gun, w/reg. trap stock & vent rib **521.00**
Trap Gun, w/Monte Carlo trap stock & vent rib **533.00**
Skeet Gun, w/vent rib **521.00**

Extra Barrels:

Field, plain **84.95**
Field, vent rib **118.95**
Trap or Skeet **123.95**

Super-X Model 1 XTR Specifications

					Length			Drop at		
Model	Gauge	Chamber	Mag. Cap*	Choke	Barrel	Overall	Length Pull	Comb	Heel/ Monte Carlo	Sights
Field V.R.	12	2¾″	4	IC, M, F	26″-			1½″	2½″	
					28″-30″	46¼″-50¼″	14¼″	1⅜″	2½″	MB, F & M
Trap	12	2¾″	4	IM, F	30″	50⅝″	14⅝″	1⅜″	1⅞″	WB, F; MB, M
Trap MC	12	2¾″	4	IM, F	30″	50⅝″	14⅝″	1$^5/_{16}$″	2⅛″-1⅜″	WB, F; MB, M
Skeet V.R.	12	2¾″	4	S	26″	46½″	14¼″	1½″	2″	WB, F; MB, M

*Add one round for shell in chamber. Super X Model 1 has a five-round capacity with factory-installed plug removed and one round in chamber.
MBF — Metal Bead Front; MB, F & M — Metal Bead, Front & Middle; RTFR — Rifle Type, Front & Rear; IC — Improved Cylinder; M — Modified; F — Full; S — Skeet.
WB, F — White Bead Front; MB, M — Metal Bead Middle

MODEL 37A SINGLE SHOT SHOTGUN

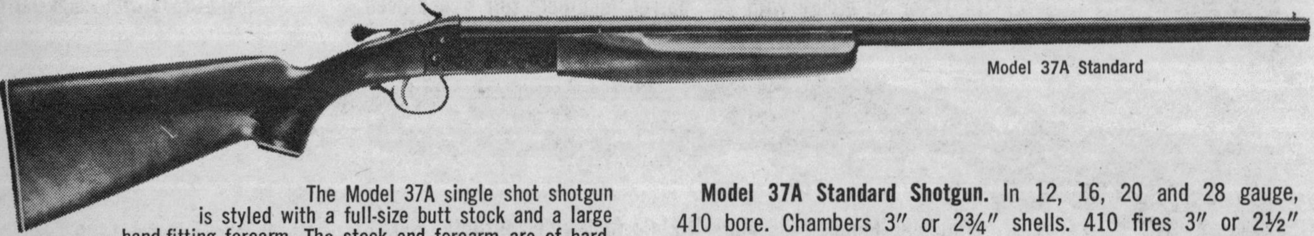

Model 37A Standard

The Model 37A single shot shotgun is styled with a full-size butt stock and a large hand-fitting forearm. The stock and forearm are of hardwood with a dark finish. Checkering on the bottom of the forearm and on the pistol grip.

Features include a gold-plated trigger and engraved receiver; a concave hammer spur for non-slip cocking; a pistol grip cap with white spacer and a white spacer between the buttplate and stock.

There's a Winchester Proof-Steel barrel. Positive lock forearm. Automatic ejector. Top level that opens either right or left and a brass bead front sight.

Model 37A Standard Shotgun. In 12, 16, 20 and 28 gauge, 410 bore. Chambers 3″ or 2¾″ shells. 410 fires 3″ or 2½″ shells. Full choke only **$69.00**
12 gauge available with extra-long 36″ barrel **74.00**

Model 37A Youth Shotgun. (not illus.) Shorter 26″ barrel and youth-size stock. 20 gauge with Improved Modified choke. 410 bore with Full choke. Rubber recoil pad **$74.00**

WINCHESTER
SLIDE ACTION SHOTGUNS

MODEL 1300 XTR
12 and 20 GAUGE

All Model 1300 XTR 12 and 20 gauge field guns are chambered for 3" shells. They will chamber 3" Magnum, 2¾" Magnum and Standard 2¾" shot shells interchangeably. This eliminates the need to buy a separate Magnum field gun.

The hunter can select an interchangeable barrel or the Winchoke system. Extra interchangeable field barrels in popular lengths and chokes are also available at additional charge.

Model 1300 XTR Winchoke is available with a plain or ventilated rib barrel specially adapted for the Winchoke systems. Improved Cylinder, Modified, and Full Winchoke tubes are supplied with the gun. Three interchangeable chokes on one shotgun to cover a broad range of game and shooting situations.

It has a shortened, tapered forearm, cut-checkered on the underside for sure gripping. Nickel-plated carrier. High-luster finish on wood. Hight polish and blueing.

Front-locking, rotating bolt of machined steel locks precisely into the barrel to form one unit.

Model 1300 XTR Specifications:

Model	Gauge	Mag.* Cap.	Choke	Chamber	Barrel Length	Overall Length	Length of Pull	Drop at Comb	Drop at Heel	Sights	Weight [lbs.]	
Field Gun												
G13001 *XTR*	12	5	Full	3"	30"	50⅝"	14"	1⅜"	2⅜"	MB, F	6¾	
G13003 *XTR*	12	5	Modified	3"	28"	48⅝"	14"	1⅜"	2⅜"	MB, F	6⅝	
G13005 *XTR*	12	5	Imp. Cyl.	3"	26"	46⅝"	14"	1⅜"	2⅜"	MB, F	6½	
G13021 *XTR*	20	5	Full	3"	28"	48⅝"	14"	1⅜"	2⅜"	MB, F	6⅜	$219.00
G13023 *XTR*	20	5	Modified	3"	28"	48⅝"	14"	1⅜"	2⅜"	MB, F	6⅜	
G13025 *XTR*	20	5	Imp. Cyl.	3"	26"	46⅝"	14"	1⅜"	2⅜"	MB, F	6¼	
Field with V.R.												
G13051 *XTR*	12	5	Full	3"	30"	50⅝"	14"	1½"	2½"	MB, F	6⅞	
G13053 *XTR*	12	5	Modified	3"	28"	48⅝"	14"	1½"	2½"	MB, F	6⅞	
G13055 *XTR*	12	5	Imp. Cyl.	3"	26"	46⅝"	14"	1½"	2½"	MB, F	5¾	244.00
G13071 *XTR*	20	5	Full	3"	28"	48⅝"	14"	1½"	2½"	MB, F	6⅝	
G13073 *XTR*	20	5	Modified	3"	28"	48⅝"	14"	1½"	2½"	MB, F	6⅝	
G13075 *XTR*	20	5	Imp. Cyl.	3"	26"	46⅝"	14"	1½"	2½"	MB, F	6½	
†Extra Barrels												
Field												71.95
Field w/V.R.												96.95

Model 1300 *XTR* with Winchoke

Model	Gauge	Mag.* Cap.	Choke	Chamber	Barrel Length	Overall Length	Length of Pull	Drop at Comb	Drop at Heel	Sights	Weight [lbs.]	
Field												
G13081 *XTR*	12	5	Mod., Full	3"	28"	48⅝"	14"	1⅜"	2⅜"	MB, F	7	$233.00
G13083 *XTR*	20	5	& Imp. Cyl.	3"	28"	48⅝"	14"	1⅜"	2⅜"	MB, F	7	
Field with V.R.												
G13085 *XTR*	12	5	Mod., Full	3"	28"	48⅝"	14"	1½"	2½"	MB, F	7¼	258.00
G13087 *XTR*	20	5	& Imp. Cyl.	3"	28"	48⅝"	14"	1½"	2½"	MB, F	7¼	
†Extra Barrels												
Field w/Winchoke (Full, Mod., & Imp. Cyl.)												85.95
Field V.R. with Winchoke (Full, Mod., & Imp. Cyl.)												110.95

WINCHESTER
SEMI-AUTOMATIC SHOTGUNS

MODEL 1500 XTR
12 and 20 GAUGE

The Winchester Model 1500XTR gives you a gas-operated, semi-automatic field gun with the option of interchangeable barrels or with the Winchoke® system. This shotgun comes supplied with plain or ventilated rib barrel. Extra interchangeable field barrels in popular lengths and chokes are available at an additional charge. Metal bead front sight.

Model 1500 XTR Winchoke. This shotgun is available with a special barrel adapted for the Winchoke system. Improved Cylinder, Modified, and Full Winchoke tubes are supplied with the gun. One winchoke tube on the gun and two ready in your pocket.

The Model 1500 XTR features a streamlined forearm design, fluted and cut-checkered.

This semi-automatic shotgun delivers reliable performance with reduced recoil. Front-locking, rotating bolt of machined steel locks precisely into the barrel to form one unit.

WINCHESTER SEMI-AUTOMATIC SHOTGUNS

Model 1500 XTR Specifications:

Model Symbol	Gauge	Mag.* Cap.	Choke	Chamber	Barrel Length	Overall Length	Length of Pull	Drop at Comb	Drop at Heel	Sights	Weight [lbs.]	
Field Gun												
G15001 *XTR*	12	3	Full	2¾"	30"	50⅝"	14"	1⅜"	2⅜"	MB, F	7	
G15003 *XTR*	12	3	Modified	2¾"	28"	48⅝"	14"	1⅜"	2⅜"	MB, F	6⅞	
G15005 *XTR*	12	3	Imp. Cyl.	2¾"	26"	46⅝"	14"	1⅜"	2⅜"	MB, F	6¾	$275.00
G15021 *XTR*	20	3	Full	2¾"	28"	48⅝"	14"	1⅜"	2⅜"	MB, F	6⅝	
G15023 *XTR*	20	3	Modified	2¾"	28"	48⅝"	14"	1⅜"	2⅜"	MB, F	6⅝	
G15025 *XTR*	20	3	Imp. Cyl.	2¾"	26"	46⅝"	14"	1⅜"	2⅜"	MB, F	6½	
Field with V.R.												
G15051 *XTR*	12	3	Full	2¾"	30"	50⅝"	14"	1½"	2½"	MB, F	7¼	
G15053 *XTR*	12	3	Modified	2¾"	28"	48⅝"	14"	1½"	2½"	MB, F	7⅛	
G15055 *XTR*	12	3	Imp. Cyl.	2¾"	26"	46⅝"	14"	1½"	2½"	MB, F	7	300.00
G15071 *XTR*	20	3	Full	2¾"	28"	48⅝"	14"	1½"	2½"	MB, F	6⅞	
G15073 *XTR*	20	3	Modified	2¾"	28"	48⅝"	14"	1½"	2½"	MB, F	6⅞	
G15075 *XTR*	20	3	Imp. Cyl.	2¾"	26"	46⅝"	14"	1½"	2½"	MB, F	6¾	
†Extra Barrels												
Field												74.95
Field w/V.R.												99.95

Model 1500 *XTR* Semi-Automatic with Winchoke

Model Symbol	Gauge	Mag.* Cap.	Choke	Chamber	Barrel Length	Overall Length	Length of Pull	Drop at Comb	Drop at Heel	Sights	Weight [lbs.]	
Field												
G15081 *XTR*	12	3	Mod., Full & Imp. Cyl.	2¾"	28"	48⅝"	14"	1⅜"	2⅜"	MB, F	7	$289.00
G15083 *XTR*	20	3	& Imp. Cyl.	2¾"	28"	48⅝"	14"	1⅜"	2⅜"	MB, F	6½	
Field with V.R.												
G15085 *XTR*	12	3	Mod., Full & Imp. Cyl.	2¾"	28"	48⅝"	14"	1½"	2½"	MB, F	7¼	
G15087 *XTR*	20	3	& Imp. Cyl.	2¾"	28"	48⅝"	14"	1½"	2½"	MB, F	6¾	314.00
†Extra Barrels												
Field with Winchoke (Full, Mod., & Imp. Cyl.)												88.95
Field V.R. with Winchoke (Full, Mod., & Imp. Cyl.)												113.95

*Includes one round in chamber. Model 1300s have factory installed plug which, when removed, increases magazine capacity to four shells.   V.R. — Ventilated Rib   MBF — Metal Bead Front
•Winchoke in 12 or 20 gauge Models; supplied with Full and Improved Cylinder Winchoke tubes, with Modified unit installed.

WINCHESTER PUMP SHOTGUNS
MODEL 1200 IN 12 & 20 GAUGES

Hunters and shooters know that they've got to have a reliable shotgun that practically points by itself. They want a gun light enough to carry through a long day but just heavy enough to swing smoothly and surely when the chance comes. That's why more and more sportsmen are turning to a Model 1200—a shotgun that's lightweight, versatile, and troublefree.

The Winchester Model 1200 slide action shotguns blend fit, feel and performance with advanced engineering. Twin action slide bars give the Model 1200s a self-starting action designed to move back in a quick, effortless motion. Exclusive front-locking, rotating bolthead locks the steel bolt securely into the steel breech for superb strength and safety. High-strength rustproof forged aluminum receiver. Crossbolt safety. Extended beavertail fore-end. Positive checkering. Weather-resistant stock finish. Engine turned steel bolt. American walnut stock and forearm. Fluted comb.

WINCHESTER PUMP SHOTGUNS

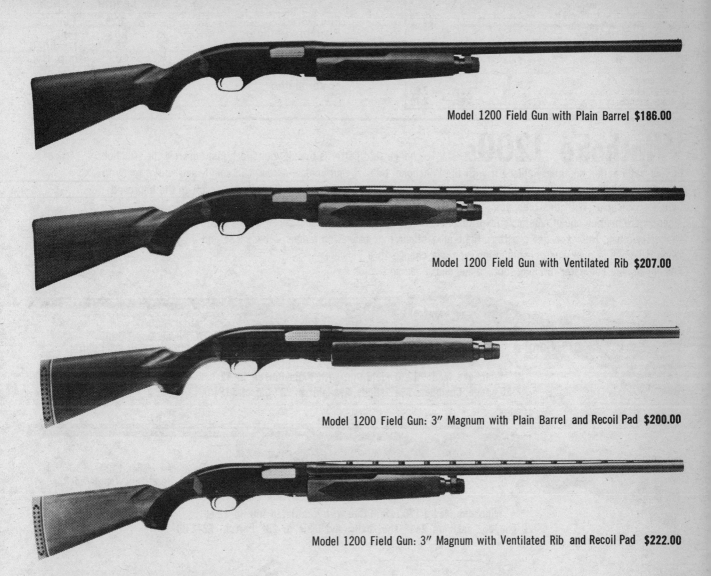

Model 1200 Field Gun with Plain Barrel **$186.00**

Model 1200 Field Gun with Ventilated Rib **$207.00**

Model 1200 Field Gun: 3″ Magnum with Plain Barrel and Recoil Pad **$200.00**

Model 1200 Field Gun: 3″ Magnum with Ventilated Rib and Recoil Pad **$222.00**

Model 1200 Specifications

Type	Field Plain Barrel	Field V.R.		Magnum Field Available only in Model 1200 with 3″ chamber Plain Barrel		V.R.	
				12	20	12	20
Gauge	12-20	12-20		12	20	12	20
Magazine Capacity*	5	5		5	5	5	5
Barrel Length	26″-28″-30″	26″-28″-30″		30″	28″	30″	28″
Overall Length	46⅝″-50⅝″	46⅝″-50⅝″		50⅝″	48⅝″	50⅝″	48⅝″
Length of Pull	14″	14″		14″	14″	14″	14″
Drop at Comb	1⅜″	1½″		1⅜″	1⅜″	1½″	1½″
Drop at Heel	2⅜″	2½″		2⅜″	2⅜″	2½″	2½″
Weight (lbs.)	6½-7	6½-7¼		7¾	7⅜	7⅞	7⅝
Sights	MBF	MBF		MBF	MBF	MBF	MBF

*Includes one round in chamber. Model 1200s have factory installed plug which limits total capacity to three shells.
V.R. — Ventilated Rib   MBF — Metal Bead Front

WINCHESTER PUMP SHOTGUNS

Model 1200 Extra barrels:	
1200—Field	$66.95
1200—Field, w/winchoke (full, mod., & imp. cyl.)	70.95
1200—Field, w/vent rib	85.95
1200—Field, vent rib, w/winchoke (full, mod. & imp. cyl.)	90.95
Deer Barrel	77.95
Winchoke:	
Extra tube	7.95
Tube wrench	2.10

Model 1200	12 Ga.	20 Ga.	Barrel Length	Type of Choke
Field Grade Plain or Ventilated Rib	x	—	30"	Full
	—	x	28"	Full
	x	x	28"	Modified
	x	x	26"	Imp. Cyl.
3" Magnum Plain or Ventilated Rib	x	—	30"	Full
	—	x	28"	Full

Winchoke 1200s

To change shot patterns to suit your sport, just unscrew the Winchoke in your slide action shotgun. Replace it with the Winchoke tube of your choice, screw it in snugly and you're ready to swing . . . with the same gun. If quail is your game . . . bobwhite, mountain or valley quail . . . pick up the Improved Cylinder Winchoke. With this tube, you get an open pattern that's most effective up to 30 yards.

When you're hunting one of America's favorite game birds—the pheasant—Just screw on the Modified choke tube with the spanner wrench. Here you get a pattern-tightening effect that's best on ranges between 25 and 45 yards.

When it comes to duck and goose hunting, you can change to a Winchoke.

Full choke unit. For waterfowl long shots a Full choke can do the job.

Winchoke Model 1200
Field Grade with Plain Barrel

Winchoke Model 1200 Field Gun with Plain Barrel. In 12 or 20 gauge. Chambers 2¾" shells. Available in 28" barrel $191.00

Winchoke Model 1200
Field Grade with Ventilated Rib

Winchoke Model 1200 Field Gun with Ventilated Rib. In 12 or 20 gauge. Chambers 2¾" shotshells. Available in 28" barrel. $212.00

Chokes:
12 ga., 28", mod., full & imp. cyl.
20 ga., 28", mod., full & imp. cyl.

Winchoke Model Specifications

Type	Field Plain Barrel	Field V.R.
Gauge	12-20●	12-20●
Magazine Capacity M/1200 ★	5	5
Magazine Capacity M/1400 ★★	3	3
Barrel Length	28"	28"
Overall Length	48⅝"	48⅝"
Length of Pull	14"	14"
Drop at Comb	1⅜"	1½"
Drop at Heel	2⅜"	2½"
Weight (lbs.)	6½-7	6½-7¼
Sights	MBF	MBF

WINCHOKE TUBES & WRENCH

●Winchoke in 12 or 20 gauge Models; supplied with Full and Improved Cylinder Winchoke tubes, with Modified unit installed.
★Includes one round in chamber. Model 1200s have factory installed plug which limits total capacity to three shells.
V.R. — Ventilated Rib   MBF — Metal Bead Front
★★ Includes one round in chamber.

WINCHESTER O&U SHOTGUNS

Model 101 Field Gun

Model 101 Field Gun. Engine-turned breech. Crisp, narrow border hand-checkering. In 12 or 20 gauge. 20 gauge with 3" chambers **$820.00**

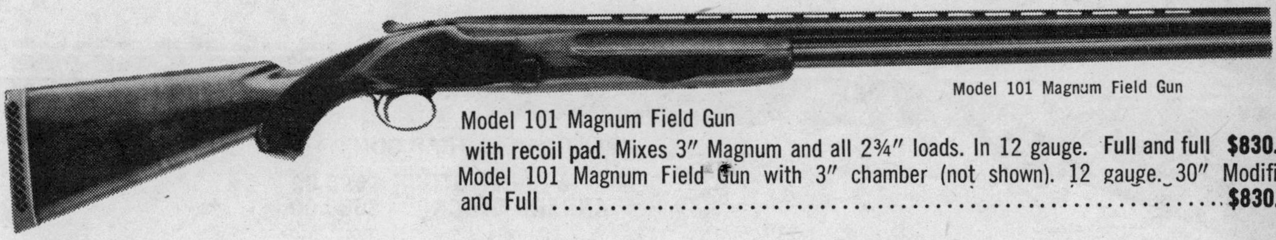

Model 101 Magnum Field Gun

Model 101 Magnum Field Gun

with recoil pad. Mixes 3" Magnum and all 2¾" loads. In 12 gauge. Full and full **$830.00**
Model 101 Magnum Field Gun with 3" chamber (not shown). 12 gauge. 30" Modified and Full **$830.00**

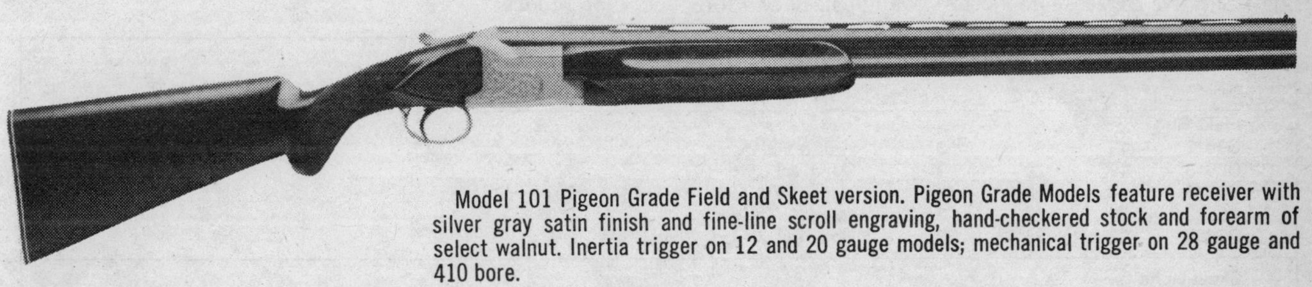

Model 101 Pigeon Grade Field and Skeet version. Pigeon Grade Models feature receiver with silver gray satin finish and fine-line scroll engraving, hand-checkered stock and forearm of select walnut. Inertia trigger on 12 and 20 gauge models; mechanical trigger on 28 gauge and 410 bore.

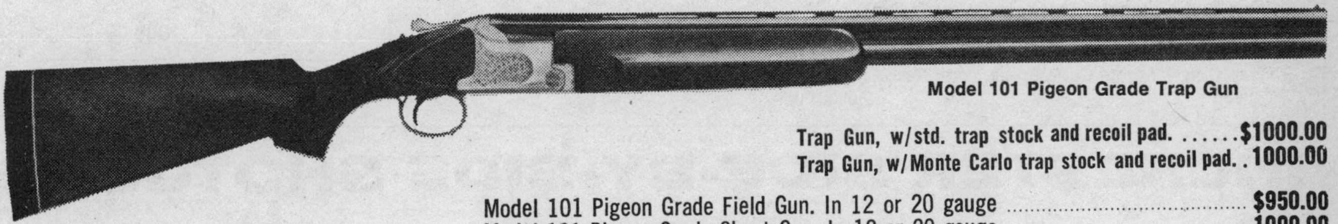

Model 101 Pigeon Grade Trap Gun

Trap Gun, w/std. trap stock and recoil pad. **$1000.00**
Trap Gun, w/Monte Carlo trap stock and recoil pad. . **1000.00**

Model 101 Pigeon Grade Field Gun. In 12 or 20 gauge **$950.00**
Model 101 Pigeon Grade Skeet Gun. In 12 or 20 gauge **1000.00**
Model 101 Pigeon Grade Skeet Gun in 28 or 410 gauge **1000.00**

Model 101 Specifications

	Field	Magnum Field	Trap M.C. STock	Pigeon Grade Trap Reg. Stock	Pigeon Grade Trap M.C. Stock	Pigeon Grade Field	Pigeon Grade Skeet
Gauge	12-20-28-410	12	12 only	12 only	12 only	12-20	12-20
Overall Length	42¾"	46¾"	46⅜"	47⅛"	47⅛"	42¾"-44¾"	43¾"
Barrel Length	(26" barrels)	(30" barrels)		(30" barrels)	(30" barrels)	26"-28"	27"
Length of Pull	14"	14"	14"	14⅜"	14⅜"	14"	14"
Drop at Comb	1½"	1½"	1½"	1¹³/₃₂"	1¹³/₃₂"	1½"	1½"
Drop at Heel	2½"	2½"	2½"	1¾"	2⅛"	2½"	2½"
Drop at Monte Carlo	—	—	1⅜"	—	1¹³/₃₂"	—	—
Pitch Down	2"	2"	1¼"	1"	1"	2"	2"
Recoil Pad	None	12 ga. only	Yes	Yes	Yes	None	None
Sights	Metal Bead Front	Metal Bead Front	Metal Bead Front & Middle	White Bead Front & Middle	White Bead Front & Middle	WB, F	WB, F&M

WINCHESTER SHOTGUNS

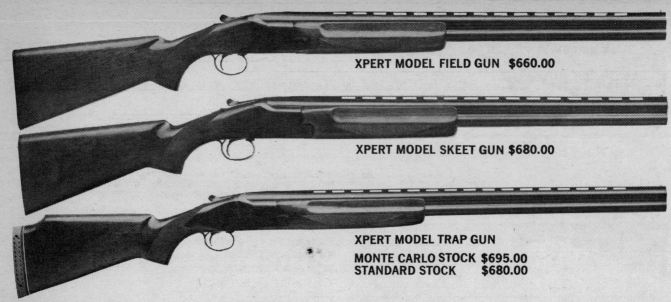

XPERT MODEL FIELD GUN $660.00

XPERT MODEL SKEET GUN $680.00

XPERT MODEL TRAP GUN
MONTE CARLO STOCK $695.00
STANDARD STOCK $680.00

The Xpert Model over-and-under features ventilated rib, single selective trigger, auto ejectors, walnut stock and fore- arm. It is available in 12 and 20 gauge in Field, Skeet and Trap Models.

Symbol	Gauge	Barrel Length	Chamber	Choke	Weight (lbs.)	Suggested Retail Each
Field Gun						
G9612	12	30″	3″	Full & Full	7¾	
G9613	12	28″	3″	Mod. & Full	7¾	
G9615	12	26″	3″	Imp. Cyl. & Mod.	7¾	$660.00
G9623	20	28″	3″	Mod. & Full	6½	
G9625	20	26″	3″	Imp. Cyl. & Mod.	6½	
Skeet Guns						
G9617	12	27″	2¾″	Skeet & Skeet	7¼	680.00
G9627	20	27″	2¾″	Skeet & Skeet	6¼	
Trap Gun — Regular Stock (with Recoil Pad)						
G9635	12	30″	2¾″	Full & Full	8¼	680.00
Trap Gun — Monte Carlo Stock (with Recoil Pad)						
G9636	12	30″	2¾″	Full & Full	8¼	695.00

WINCHESTER SIDE-BY-SIDE SHOTGUNS

MODEL 23 XTR PIGEON GRADE $830.00

Side-by-side; selective single trigger; tapered ventilated rib with serrated sighting plane; white bead front sight and black butt plate with white spacers; chrome-lined bores; automatic ejectors.

MODEL 23 XTR PIGEON GRADE SPECIFICATIONS

Model	Gauge	Chamber	Choke	Barrel Length	Overall Length	Length of Pull	Drop at Comb	Drop at Heel	Sights	Weight
Field	12-20*	3″	M & F	28″	44¾″	14″	1½″	2½″	WBF	6½-7 lbs.
Field	12-20*	3″	IC & M	26″	42¾″	14″	1½″	2½″	WBF	6½-7 lbs.

*20 gauge available in mid 1979.

Black Powder Guns

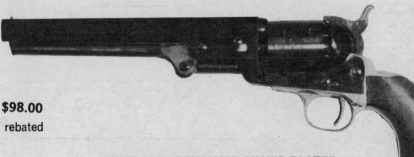

SCHNEIDER & GLASSICK CONFEDERATE REVOLVER
36 CALIBER MODEL 1050 .... $80.00

A modern replica of a Confederate Percussion Army Revolver. Polished brass frame, rifled high-luster blued round barrel and polished walnut grips.
Weight: 41 oz.
Barrel Length: 7½ in.
Overall Length: 13 in.
Finish: Brass frame, back strap and trigger guard, blued round rifled barrel, case-hardened hammer and loading lever, engraved cylinder with battle scene.

SHERIFF REVOLVER
36 CALIBER MODEL 1170 .... $94.95
44 CALIBER MODEL 1180 .... 98.00

Shortened version of the Navy Revolver with a 5" octagonal barrel.
Weight: 39 oz.
Barrel Length: 5 in.
Overall Length: 11½ in.
Finish: Brass frame, back strap and trigger guard, blued octagon rifled barrel, case-hardened hammer and loading lever, engraved cylinder with battle scene.
36 caliber available with steel frame **$104.95**

SCHNEIDER & GLASSICK CONFEDERATE REVOLVER
44 CALIBER MODEL 1060 .... $82.00

Weight: 39 oz.
Barrel Length: 7½ in.
Overall Length: 13 in.

ARMY 1860 REVOLVER
44 CALIBER MODEL 1210 ......$110.00

The historic Army Model 1860 needs no introduction to shooter and collector. The cylinder is authentically roll engraved with a highly polished brass trigger guard and steel frame cut for shoulder stock. The frame, loading lever and hammer are beautifully finished in color case hardening.
Weight: 41 oz.
Barrel Length: 8 in.
Overall Length: 13⅝ in.
Caliber: 44
Finish: Brass trigger guard, steel back strap, round barrel, rebated cylinder engraved battle scene. Frame cut for shoulder stock.

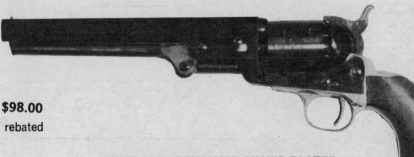

NAVY 1851 REVOLVER
44 CALIBER MODEL 1130 .... $98.00

A 44 caliber Navy Revolver with rebated cylinder.
Weight: 40 oz.
Barrel Length: 7½ in.
Overall Length: 13 in.
Finish: Steel frame, brass back strap and trigger guard, octagon rifled barrel, case-hardened hammer and loading lever, engraved cylinder with battle scene.

NAVY 1851 REVOLVER
36 CALIBER MODEL 1120 .... $95.00

Weight: 43 oz.
Barrel Length: 7½ in.
Overall Length: 13 in.
Finish: Brass frame, back strap and trigger guard, blued octagon rifled barrel. Case-hardened hammer and loading lever, engraved cylinder with battle scene.

NAVY 1851 REVOLVER SILVER PLATED
36 CALIBER MODEL 1150 ...... $105.00

Weight: 42 oz.
Barrel Length: 7½ in.
Overall Length: 13 in.
Finish: Silver Plated back strap and trigger guard, octagon rifled barrel, case-hardened hammer and loading lever.

NAVY 1851 REVOLVER SILVER PLATED
44 CALIBER MODEL 1160 .... $110.00

Weight: 40 oz.
Barrel Length: 7½ in.
Overall Length: 13 in.
Finish: Silver Plated back strap and trigger guard, octagon rifled barrel, case-hardened hammer and loading lever.

EUROARMS OF AMERICA

MODEL 1190
$105.00

Police, 36 caliber, fluted cylinder, steel frame, 5-in. octagonal barrel.
Weight: 38 oz.
Barrel Length: 5 in.
Overall Length: 10½ in.
Finish: Deep luster blue rifled octagon barrel

Model 1190
Navy 1851 Police

MODEL 1200
$105.00

Same as Model 1190 except with 7½-in. octagonal barrel.
Weight: 41 oz.
Barrel Length: 7½ in.
Overall Length: 13 in.

MODEL 1250
$116.00

Police revolver with a steel frame, engraved cylinder and 5-inch barrel in 36 caliber.
Weight: 39 oz.
Barrel Length: 5 in.
Overall Length: 10½ in.
Finish: Deep luster blue rifled octagon barrel

Model 1250
Police 1862

NEW MODEL ARMY
MODEL 1030
$128.00

New Model Army Revolver, caliber 44 in a target version. Fully adjustable for windage and elevation. Rear sight and ramp front sight.
Weight: 41 oz.
Barrel Length: 8-in. octagonal
Overall Length: 14¾ in.
Finish: Deep luster blue rifled barrel, polished walnut stock, brass trigger guard.

NEW MODEL ARMY REVOLVER
MODEL 1020
$110.00

This model is equipped with blued steel frame, brass trigger guard in 44 caliber.
Weight: 41 oz.
Barrel Length: 8 in.
Overall Length: 14¾ in.
Finish: Deep luster blue rifled barrel, polished walnut stock, brass trigger guard.

New Model Army

NAVY MODEL REVOLVER
MODEL 1010
$110.00

The Navy Model Remington Revolver in 36 caliber with a 6½-inch barrel. Always a popular companion to the Remington Army Model.
Weight: 40 oz.
Barrel Length: 6½ in.
Overall Length: 13¼ in.
Finish: Deep luster blue rifled barrel, polished walnut stock, brass trigger guard.

Navy Model Revolver

EUROARMS OF AMERICA

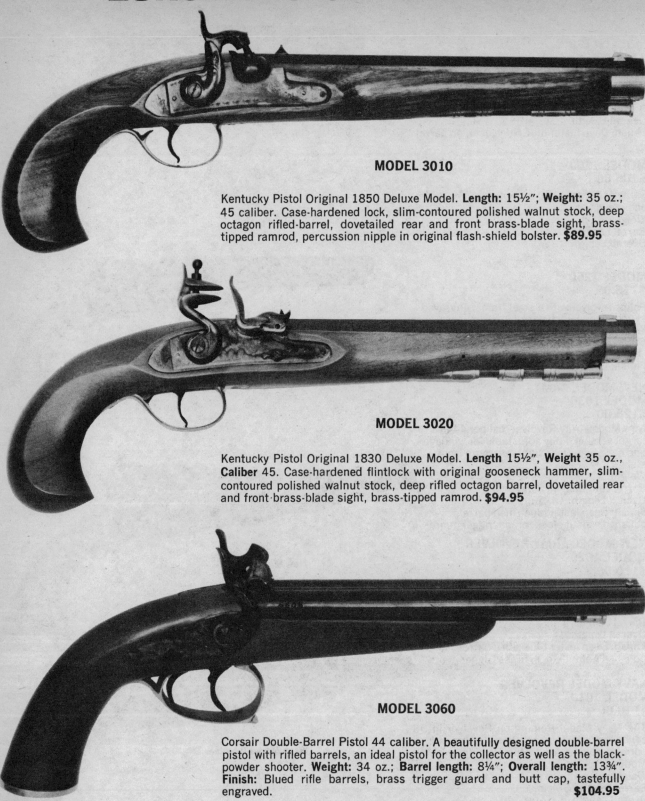

MODEL 3010

Kentucky Pistol Original 1850 Deluxe Model. **Length:** 15½"; **Weight:** 35 oz.; 45 caliber. Case-hardened lock, slim-contoured polished walnut stock, deep octagon rifled-barrel, dovetailed rear and front brass-blade sight, brass-tipped ramrod, percussion nipple in original flash-shield bolster. **$89.95**

MODEL 3020

Kentucky Pistol Original 1830 Deluxe Model. **Length** 15½", **Weight** 35 oz., **Caliber** 45. Case-hardened flintlock with original gooseneck hammer, slim-contoured polished walnut stock, deep rifled octagon barrel, dovetailed rear and front·brass-blade sight, brass-tipped ramrod. **$94.95**

MODEL 3060

Corsair Double-Barrel Pistol 44 caliber. A beautifully designed double-barrel pistol with rifled barrels, an ideal pistol for the collector as well as the black-powder shooter. **Weight:** 34 oz.; **Barrel length:** 8¼"; **Overall length:** 13¾". **Finish:** Blued rifle barrels, brass trigger guard and butt cap, tastefully engraved. **$104.95**

EUROARMS OF AMERICA

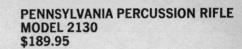

PENNSYLVANIA PERCUSSION RIFLE
MODEL 2130
$189.95

SPECIFICATIONS:

Caliber: 45 (actual bore size .453) Deep rifling.
Barrel: Octagonal 13/16″ across flats, length of barrel 36″.
Lock Plate: Flint or Percussion. Case-hardened with flash shield on percussion guns.
Stock: Full-length one-piece walnut stock.
Ramrod: Made in a single piece, brass tipped at both ends and threaded at bottom end.
Mountings: Polished brass, including a large original-type patch box. Light engraving on lock plate.
Overall Length: 50″.
Weight: 6½ to 7 lbs., depending on density of walnut stock.

LONDON ARMORY COMPANY
ENFIELD MUSKETOON
MODEL 2280
$189.95

SPECIFICATIONS:

Caliber: 58. Minie ball.
Barrel Length: 24″.
Overall Length: 40¼″.
Weight: 7 to 7½ lbs., depending on density of wood.
Barrel: Round high-luster blue barrel.
Stock: Seasoned walnut stock, with sling swivels.
Ignition: Heavy-duty percussion lock.
Sights: Graduated military-leaf sight.
Furniture: Brass furniture.

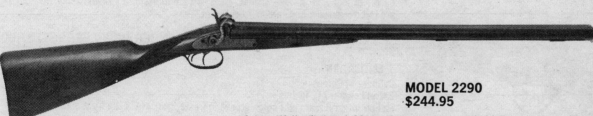

MODEL 2290
$244.95

A beautifully designed 12-gauge percussion muzzle-loading shotgun with modified and full choke. Tastefully engraved side locks and English-browned barrels. A wooden ramrod, brass tipped, capable of taking a brush or worm (worm is included with each shotgun). The weight is approximately 6 lbs. making it an easy-to-handle lightweight field gun.

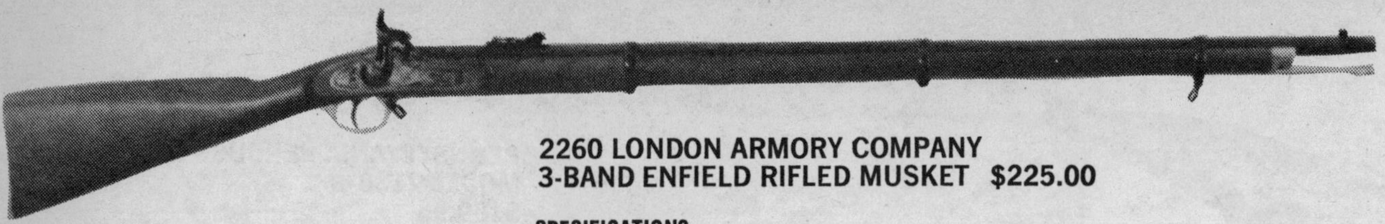

2260 LONDON ARMORY COMPANY
3-BAND ENFIELD RIFLED MUSKET $225.00

SPECIFICATIONS:
Caliber: 58
Barrel Length: 39″
Overall Length: 54″
Weight: 9½ lbs.
Stock: One-piece walnut. Polished "bright" brass butt plate, trigger guard and nose cap.
Sights: Inverted 'V' front sight; Enfield folding ladder rear.

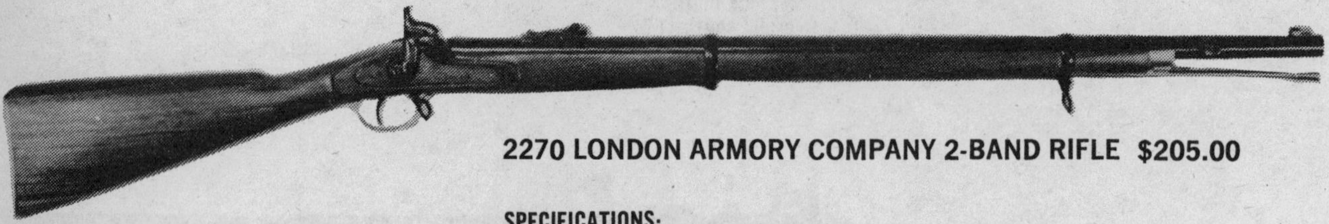

2270 LONDON ARMORY COMPANY 2-BAND RIFLE $205.00

SPECIFICATIONS:
Caliber: 58
Barrel Length: 33″
Overall Length: 50″
Weight: 9½ lbs.
Stock: One-piece walnut.
Sights: Inverted 'V' front sight; Enfield folding ladder rear.

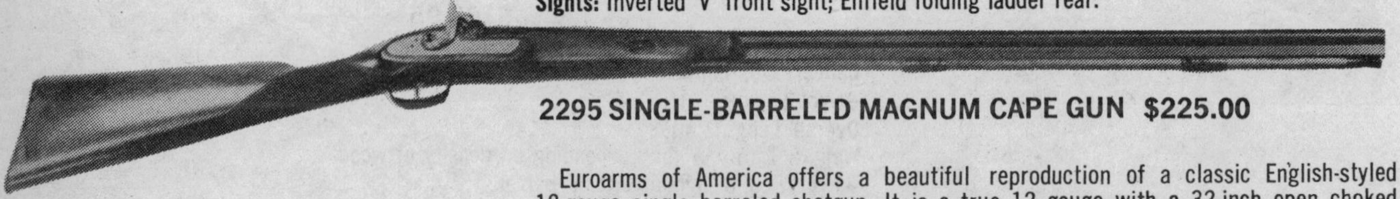

2295 SINGLE-BARRELED MAGNUM CAPE GUN $225.00

Euroarms of America offers a beautiful reproduction of a classic English-styled 12-gauge single barreled shotgun. It is a true 12 gauge with a 32-inch open choked barrel. Although the single barrel muzzleloader weighs only 7½ pounds, the English-styled stock is well proportioned and recoil with even relatively heavy powder charges is moderate. The stock is of European walnut with a satin oil finish. The barrel, underrib, thimbles, nose cap, trigger guard and butt plate are finished with EOA deep, rich blue. The lock is left in the white and displays a scroll engraving, as does the bow of the trigger guard and the top of the barrel just forward of the tang. Overall length of the single barreled shot gun is 47½ inches. Uses #11 percussion caps and recommended wads are felt overpowder and cardboard overshot.

1005 ROGERS & SPENCER REVOLVERS $127.00

SPECIFICATIONS:
Caliber: 44 Percussion.
Barrel Length: 7½ inches.
Sights: Integral rear sight notch groove in frame, truncated cone front sight of brass.
Overall Length: 13¾ inches.
Weight: 47 ounces.
Recommended Ball Diameter: 451 round or conical, pure lead.
Percussion Cap Size: Number 11.

1009   Nickel Plated Rogers & Spencer Revolver
Revolver is the same as Model 1005, except for finish, which is nickel, polished to a brilliant, rust-resistant shine. Recommended same ball size and percussion caps.

EUROARMS OF AMERICA

REMINGTON 1862 RIFLE MODEL 2255
$200.00

SPECIFICATIONS:
Caliber: 58
Ignition: Case-hardened percussion lock
Barrel: 32½" rifled
Overall length: 48½"
Weight: 9½ lbs.
Finish: High-polished round barrel, polished brass mountings and cap box
Sights: Original 3-leaf rear sight, blade front sight
Ramrod: Heavy one-piece steel

KENTUCKY RIFLE
MODELS 2010 and 2060 $179.95

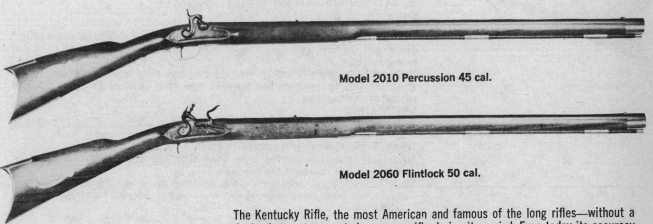

Model 2010 Percussion 45 cal.

Model 2060 Flintlock 50 cal.

The Kentucky Rifle, the most American and famous of the long rifles—without a doubt the most accurate long-range rifle during its period. Even today its accuracy will often equal or even exceed many modern rifles. Here is an accurate replica of this most famous of American rifles, made with a one-piece walnut stock.

SPECIFICATIONS:
Calibers: 45 and 50
Ignition: Case-hardened—flintlock or percussion lock with bolster
Barrel length: 36" rifled
Overall length: 50"
Weight: 7 lbs.
Finish: High polish blue octagon barrel, polished brass mountings and cap box with engraving
Sights: Dovetailed open-type rear, Kentucky style blade front
Stock: Full length one-piece walnut stock
Ramrod: Wood, brass tipped at both ends, threaded at bottom end

EUROARMS OF AMERICA

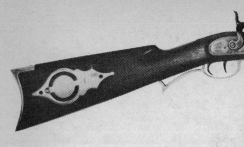

HAWKEN RIFLE MODEL 2190
$199.95

SPECIFICATIONS:
Caliber: 45, 50, 54, 58
Ignition: Double set triggers, heavy-duty percussion lock
Barrel length(s): 29"
Weight: 8¾-9 lbs.
Overall length: 45¾"
Sights: Dovetail front sight, fully adjustable rear sight
Furniture: Brass end inletted patch box
Stock: Walnut
Finish: Highly polished

BROWNING

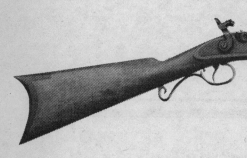

JONATHAN BROWNING MOUNTAIN RIFLE
$373.50

Models: Browned steel model has tinned forend tip and natural-finished wedge plates. Barrel, lock, hammer, butt plate, trigger guard and other metal parts are traditional browned steel.
Brass model has brass forend tip, wedge plates, lock plate screw escutcheon, trigger guard, thimbles, toe plate and butt plate. All other parts including the barrel, lock, and hammer are browned steel.
SPECIFICATIONS:
Barrel: 30" octagonal. 1 inch across the flats. Twist is 1 turn in 56" on 45 caliber, 1 turn in 62" on 50 caliber and 1 turn in 66" on 54 caliber. Hooked breech.
Trigger: Single set design with roller bearing sear.
Sights: Traditional buck horn rear sight, screw adjustable for elevation, drift adjustable for windage. Blade front sight. Sight radius is 21⅞".
Stock: Half stock with semi-cheek piece. Seasoned stock with oil finish. Traditional curved butt plate. Hickory ramrod with brass fittings threaded for cleaning jag and patch retriever.
Stock Dimensions: Length of pull—13½", Drop at comb—2½", Drop at heel—4".
Overall Length: 47"
Approximate Weight: 9 lbs. 10 oz.

COLT

BABY DRAGOON

SPECIFICATIONS:
Caliber: 31
Barrel: 4", 7 groove, right-hand twist
Cylinder: 5-shot unfluted, straight with ranger and Indian scene, oval bolt cuts
Sight: Brass pin
Finish: Color case-hardened frame and hammer, blue barrel, trigger, wedge, cylinder and screws; silver backstrap and trigger guard and varnished grips.
Price: $257.65

COLT

1851 NAVY REVOLVER

SPECIFICATIONS:
Caliber: 36
Barrel: 7½", 7 groove, left-hand twist
Weight: 42 oz.
Cylinder: 6 chambers with Naval scene
Sights: Brass front sight
Finish: Color case-hardened frame, loading lever, plunger, hammer and latch. Blue cylinder, trigger, barrel, screws and wedge. Silver-plated trigger guard and backstrap. Varnished one-piece walnut grips.
Price: $266.89

1861 NAVY REVOLVER

SPECIFICATIONS:
Same as 1851 Navy Revolver except:
Sights: German silver front
Price: $266.89

1862 POCKET NAVY REVOLVER

SPECIFICATIONS:
Caliber: 36
Barrel: 5½", octagonal, 7 groove, left-hand twist
Weight: 27 oz.
Cylinder: 5 chambers, round-rebated with stage coach scene, 1³⁄₁₆" overall, rebated ³⁄₁₆"
Sights: Brass pin front
Finish: Color case-hardened frame, hammer loading lever, plunger and latch; blue barrel, wedge, cylinder, trigger guard and backstrap. Varnished one-piece grips.
Price: $250.73

COLT

1862 POCKET POLICE

SPECIFICATIONS:
Caliber: 36
Barrel: 5½" round, 7 groove, left-hand twist
Weight: 25 oz.
Cylinder: 5 chambers, rebated, fluted
Sights: Brass front
Finish: Color case-hardened frame, hammer, loading lever, plunger and latch. Blue barrel, wedge, cylinder, trigger and screws. Silver-plated trigger guard and backstrap, Varnished one-piece walnut grips.
Price: $250.73

COLT WALKER

SPECIFICATIONS:
Caliber: 44
Barrel: 9", 7 groove, right-hand twist
Weight: 73 oz.
Cylinder: 6 chambers, 1 safety lock pin, scene of soldiers fighting Indians.
Sight: German silver
Finish: Color case-hardened frame, hammer, loading lever and plunger. Blue barrel, cylinder, backstrap, trigger and wedge. Polished-brass trigger guard and oil finish grip.
Price: $357.30

1ST MODEL DRAGOON

SPECIFICATIONS:
Caliber: 44
Barrel: 7½", part round, part octagonal, 7 grooves, left-hand twist
Weight: 66 oz.
Cylinder: 6 Chambers, ranger-Indian scene
Sights: German silver
Finish: Color case-hardened frame, loading lever, plunger; blue barrel, cylinder, trigger and wedge. Polished-brass backstrap and trigger guard; one-piece oil finish walnut stocks.

Price:		
1st Model Dragoon		$285.38
2nd Model Dragoon		285.38
3rd Model Dragoon		285.38

1860 ARMY REVOLVER

SPECIFICATIONS:
Caliber: 44
Barrel: 8"
Overall Length: 13¾"
Weight: 8 lbs.
Sight Radius: 10½"
Finish: Colt blue, color case-hardened frame, hammer loading lever, plunger.
Price: $273.81

CVA

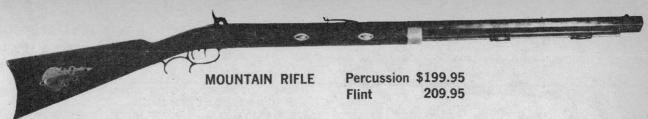

MOUNTAIN RIFLE

Percussion $199.95
Flint   209.95

SPECIFICATIONS:
Ignition: Engraved percussion color case-hardened lock with adjustable sear engagement, fly and bridle, authentic V-type mainspring.
Caliber: 45 and 50 percussion and flintlock.
Barrel: 32", custom rifled, octagon, hooked breech with two barrel tenons.
Overall Length: 48".
Weight: 8 lbs.

Finish: Brown steel, German silver patch box and wedge plates, pewter-type nose cap.
Triggers: Double set, will fire both set and unset.
Sights: German silver blade front, screw adjustable dovetail rear.
Stock: American maple with fully formed cheek piece.
Accessories: Stainless steel nipple, hardwood ramrod, cleaning jag.

FRONTIER RIFLE
45 and 50 Caliber Percussion $169.95

SPECIFICATIONS:
Lock: Color case-hardened, engraved percussion-style, bridle with fly and tumbler; screw-adjustable, sear engagement; authentic V-type mainspring.
Barrel: 28" octagon; $^{15}/_{16}$" across the flats; barrel tenon, hooked breech, round brass thimbles, deep-grooved.
Overall Length: 44".

Weight: 6 lbs. 14 oz.
Stock: American hardwood.
Sights: Brass blade front sight; screw-adjustable, dovetailed rear.
Finish: Blue steel; brass wedge plates; brass nose cap; trigger guard and butt plate.
Accessories: Stainless steel nipple, hardwood ramrod with brass tips, cleaning jag.

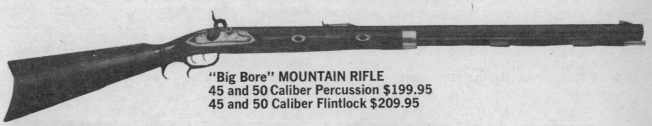

"Big Bore" MOUNTAIN RIFLE
45 and 50 Caliber Percussion $199.95
45 and 50 Caliber Flintlock $209.95

SPECIFICATIONS:
Lock: Color case-hardened, engraved percussion and flint lock style; adjustable sear engagement; bridle and fly in tumbler; authentic V-type mainspring.
Barrel: 32" octagon; $^{15}/_{16}$" across the flats; hooked breech with two barrel tenons; rifled 1 turn 66" for patch ball accuracy; authentic round thimbles; especially smooth rifling for fast break-in.

Overall Length: 48"
Weight: 7 lbs. 14 oz.
Stock: American maple with fully-formed cheekpiece.
Sights: German silver front sight; screw-adjustable dovetail rear.
Finish: Rich browned steel and wedge plates; authentic pewter-type nose cap.
Accessories: Stainless-steel nipple; hardwood ramrod with brass-tips; cleaning jag.

KENTUCKY RIFLE

Percussion $129.95
Flintlock   137.95

SPECIFICATIONS:
Ignition: Engraved flint or percussion lock.
Caliber: 45 (451 bore)
Barrel: 32", rifled, octagon.
Overall Length: 50".
Weight: 7 lbs.

Finish: Deep-luster blue, polished brass hardware.
Sights: Kentucky-style front and rear.
Stock: Dark, walnut tone.
Accessories: Brass-tipped, hardwood ramrod, stainless steel nipple.

CVA

MOUNTAIN PISTOL

MOUNTAIN PISTOL
45 and 50 Caliber Percussion $89.95

SPECIFICATIONS:
Ignition: Engraved percussion color case-hardened lock with adjustable sear engagement, fly and bridle.
Caliber: 45 or 50
Barrel: 9" octagon, 15/16" across the flats, hooked breech, custom rifling.
Overall Length: 15".
Weight: 43 oz.
Finish: Brown steel, German silver wedge plates.
Trigger: Early style.
Sights: German silver blade front, fixed primitive rear.
Stock: American maple.
Accessories: Stainless steel nipple, hardwood ramrod, belt hook.

TOWER PISTOL
45 Caliber Percussion $69.95

SPECIFICATIONS:
Ignition: Engraved percussion lock on finished pistol.
Caliber: 45 (451 bore).
Barrel: 8¼", round, smoothbore.
Overall Length: 14¼".
Weight: 39 oz.
Finish: Case-hardened lock, blued barrel, brass hardware.
Stock: Dark-grained walnut tone.
Accessories: Steel ramrod, stainless steel nipple.

KENTUCKY PISTOL
45 Caliber Percussion $72.95

SPECIFICATIONS:
Ignition: Engraved percussion lock on finished pistol, adjustable sear.
Caliber: 45 (451 bore).
Barrel: 10¼", rifled, octagon.
Overall Length: 15¼".
Weight: 40 oz.
Finish: Case-hardened lock, blued barrel, brass hardware.
Sights: Dovetailed Kentucky front and rear.
Accessories: Brass-tipped, hardwood ramrod.

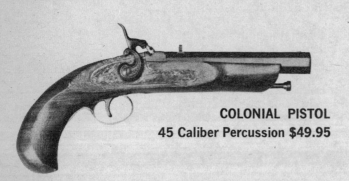

COLONIAL PISTOL
45 Caliber Percussion $49.95

SPECIFICATIONS:
Ignition: Engraved percussion lock on finished pistol.
Caliber: 45 (451 bore).
Barrel: 6½", rifled, octagon.
Overall Length: 12".
Weight: 30 oz.
Finish: Case-hardened lock, blued barrel, brass hardware.
Sights: Dovetail rear, brass blade front.
Stock: Dark, walnut tone.
Accessories: Steel ramrod, stainless steel nipple.

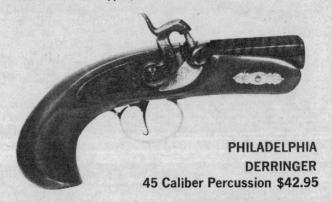

PHILADELPHIA DERRINGER
45 Caliber Percussion $42.95

SPECIFICATIONS:
Ignition: Percussion, coil-spring back-action lock.
Caliber: 45.
Barrel: 3⅛", rifled.
Overall Length: 7⅛".
Weight: 14 oz.
Finish: Case hardened with brass hardware, blued barrel.
Stock: Walnut toned.
Accessories: Stainless steel nipple.

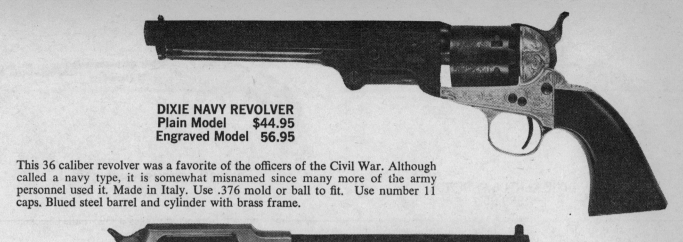

DIXIE NAVY REVOLVER
Plain Model $44.95
Engraved Model   56.95

This 36 caliber revolver was a favorite of the officers of the Civil War. Although called a navy type, it is somewhat misnamed since many more of the army personnel used it. Made in Italy. Use .376 mold or ball to fit. Use number 11 caps. Blued steel barrel and cylinder with brass frame.

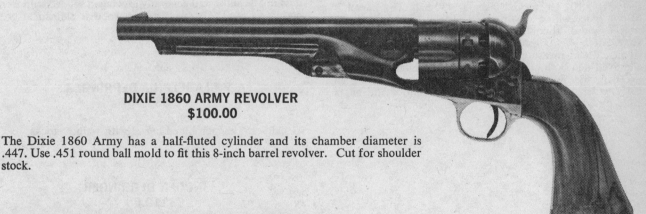

SPILLER & BURR 36 CALIBER BRASS FRAME REVOLVER
$69.95

The 36 caliber octagon barrel on this revolver is 7 inches long. The cylinder chambers mike .378. The cylinder is a six shot and the hammer engages a slot between the nipples on the cylinder as an added safety device. It has a solid brass trigger guard and frame with backstrap cast integral with the frame, two-piece walnut grips and Whitney-type case-hardened loading lever.

DIXIE 1860 ARMY REVOLVER
$100.00

The Dixie 1860 Army has a half-fluted cylinder and its chamber diameter is .447. Use .451 round ball mold to fit this 8-inch barrel revolver. Cut for shoulder stock.

THE TROPHY WINNER 44 SINGLE SHOT PISTOL
$79.95

The Trophy Winner 44 has a smooth bore shotgun pistol barrel that will interchange with the rifle barrel that is on the pistol. The gun is equipped with a 10-inch blued octagon barrel and has 7 grooves and 7 lands of equal width. Groove to groove diameter mikes .445, land to land diameter mikes .442. It has a fixed ramp front sight and adjustable rear sight. Overall length 12¾". Weight 42 oz. **SHOTGUN PISTOL BARREL:** 28-gauge blued octagon smooth bore barrel, 10 inches long, brass front sight. . . . . .
$12.95

"WYATT EARP" REVOLVER
$62.50

12" octagon rifled barrel; cylinder is rebated and is 44 caliber. Highly polished brass frame, backstrap and trigger guard. The barrel and cylinder have a deep blue lustre finish. Hammer, trigger, and loading lever are case-hardened. Walnut grips. Recommended ball size is .451.

Shoulder stock for Dixie's "Wyatt Earp" Revolver....**$40.00**

DIXIE

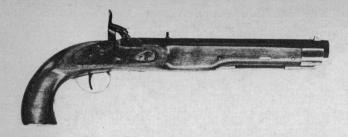

DIXIE KENTUCKY PISTOL
$89.95

Percussion model. 45 caliber single-shot pistol with 9-inch barrel. Brass furniture, Kentucky-type rifling, Kentucky-type sights, dark cherry-stained maple stock. Thimbles, trigger guard and eagle head type butt plate are of brass.

DIXIE PENNSYLVANIA PISTOL

Percussion $75.00
Flintlock   85.00

Available in percussion or flint. Barrels have a bright lustre blue finish, 7⁄8″ octagon, rifled, 44 caliber, brass front and rear sight, 10″ length and takes a .430 ball. The barrel is held in place with a steel wedge and tang screw. The brass trigger guard, thimbles, nosecap, wedge plates and side plates are highly polished. Locks are fine quality with early styling. Plates measure 4¾″ x 7⁄8″. Percussion hammer is engraved and both plates are left in the white. Flint is an excellent style lock with the gooseneck hammer having an early wide thumb piece. Stock is walnut stained and has a wide bird head type grip.

MX 3 OVERCOAT PISTOL
$26.95

39 caliber with 4-inch smooth bore barrel. The breech plug and engraved lock have a burnished-steel finish and the octagon barrel and guard are blued.

MX 3S OVERCOAT PISTOL

Same as MX 3 but with engraved barrel, lock, trigger guard and breech plug. **$34.50**

SPANISH PERCUSSION PISTOL
$45.00

40 caliber smooth bore which takes a .395 ball. Checkered grip and steel fittings with ramrod.

BRASS MOUNTED FLINT TOWER PISTOL
$42.50

Sometimes called a pirate pistol it has a 9½-inch steel barrel with a bore size of .670.

DIXIE DUELING PISTOL
$79.95

This 9-inch smooth bore barreled pistol will vary from about a 44 to 50 caliber and generally is octagon shaped with front-action locks. The rubbed maple wood is stained assorted shades and the grips are checkered.

PHILADELPHIA DERRINGER
$39.95

41 caliber, 3½-inch blued barrel with walnut stocks.

LINCOLN DERRINGER
$110.00

41 caliber, 2-inch browned barrel with 8 lands and 8 grooves and will shoot a .400 patch ball.

DIXIE BRASS FRAMED "HIDEOUT" DERRINGER
Plain $32.50
Engraved   37.50

Made with brass frame and walnut grips and fires a .395 round ball.

DIXIE

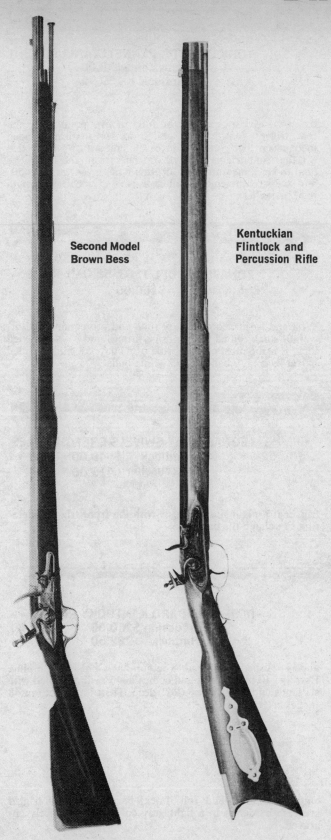

Second Model Brown Bess

Kentuckian Flintlock and Percussion Rifle

SECOND MODEL BROWN BESS MUSKET
$250.00

74 caliber with a 41¾-inch smooth bore barrel which takes a .715 round ball. In keeping with the traditional musket it has brass furniture on a walnut-stained stock. The lock is marked "Tower" and has the crown with the "GR" underneath. Barrel, lock and ramrod are left bright.

1st MODEL BROWN BESS MUSKET
$450.00

75 caliber with a 42-inch smooth bore barrel. Overall length 59″. The lock is marked "Grice 1762" and has the crown with the "GR" underneath it. The barrel, lock and ramrod are left bright; and in keeping with the traditional musket, they have used brass furniture on a walnut-stained stock.

DIXIE HAWKEN PERCUSSION RIFLE
$175.00

45 and 50 caliber with 28-inch blued barrel. Overall length 45½ inches. Recommended round ball size is .445 for 45 caliber, .495 for 50 caliber. Double set triggers, blade front sight, adjustable rear sight and case-hardened bar-style percussion lock.

THE KENTUCKIAN FLINTLOCK AND PERCUSSION RIFLE
$145.00

This rifle has a 33½-inch octagon blued barrel which is 13/16 inches across the flats. The rifle comes in 45 caliber only. The bore is rifled with 6 lands and grooves of equal width and about .006 inch deep. Land to land diameter is .453 and groove to groove diameter is .465. You will need a ball size .445 to .448. The rifle has a brass blade front sight and a steel open rear sight. Overall length of the rifle is 48 inches. The Kentuckian is furnished with brass butt plate, trigger guard, patch box, side plate, thimbles and nose cap. It has a case-hardened and engraved lock plate. Weight is about 6¼ pounds. Has a highly polished and finely finished stock in European walnut.

SINGLE BARREL PERCUSSION SHOTGUNS
$59.95

Spanish–made percussion shotgun, 28 ga. with a 32-inch blued barrel. Most will have steel furniture with cap-box.

DIXIE

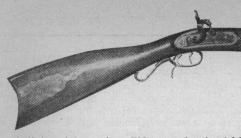

YORK COUNTY, PENNSYLVANIA RIFLE
Percussion $150.00
Flintlock   159.95

A lightweight at just 7½ pounds, the 36-inch blued rifle barrel is fitted with a standard open-type brass Kentucky rifle rear sight and front blade. The maple one-piece stock is stained a medium darkness that contrasts with the polished brass butt plate, toe plate, patchbox, side plate, trigger guard, thimbles and nose cap. Featuring double-set triggers, the rifle can be fired by pulling only the front trigger, which has a normal trigger pull of four to five pounds; or the rear trigger can first be pulled to set a spring loaded mechanism that greatly reduces the amount of pull needed for the front trigger to kick off the sear in the lock. The land-to-land measurement of the bore is an exact .450 and the recommended ball size is .445 . Overall length is 51½ inches.

ZOUAVE, MODEL 1863, 58 CAL. RIFLE
$150.00

The Zouave is a copy of an original Remington Zouave rifle which saw service in the Civil War and was acknowledged to be the most accurate military rifle of its day. In the hands of many a Civil War veteran, it helped open the West and furnished necessary food and protection. With its walnut stock, blued barrel, brass fittings and case-hardened lock, it is the most colorful rifle of its day. 58 caliber, rifled barrel. Use .570 ball or .575 Minie bullet.

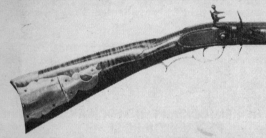

LEONARD DAY SWIVELS BREECH RIFLES
Flintlock $540.00
Percussion   415.00

These rifles have a standard .450 land to land caliber that take a .435 ball. The ramrod fits on the right hand side of the 32-inch browned octagonal wood panelled barrels. The trigger is a plain single trigger with the front trigger operating to unlatch the barrel.

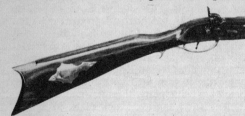

DIXIE STANDARD KENTUCKY RIFLE
Percussion $260.00
Flintlock   282.50

The Dixie Kentucky rifles have single set triggers; the stock is of hard plain straight-grain maple with a Tennessee-style cheek piece. Regular Kentucky rifle sights, and a "candy-stripe" ramrod. The barrel is made of Siemens-Martin steel, and is polished and blued. The gun has a bolster-type plug. Barrel is 40 inches long and comes in 45 caliber. Rifled with six lands and six grooves .007" deep. Twist is one turn in 48 inches.

DIXIE DOUBLE BARREL
MUZZLE LOADING SHOTGUN
$175.00

A high-quality double-barrel percussion shotgun with browned barrels that are 30 inches long and a full 12 ga. Will take the plastic shot cups for better patterns. Bores are choked modified and full. Lock, barrel tang and trigger are case hardened in a light gray color and are nicely engraved.

DIXIE

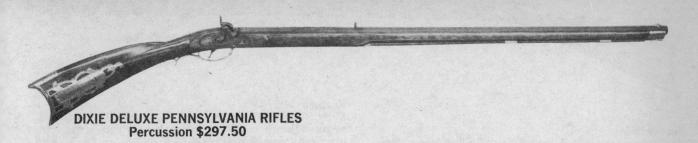

DIXIE DELUXE PENNSYLVANIA RIFLES
Percussion $297.50

These rifles have the same parts as the Dixie Kentucky Rifle. The great difference is in the styling of the buttstocks and the addition of the brass patch box and extra wide butt plate. The barrel is 45 caliber, 40 inches long, 13/16 inch across flats and overall length of rifle is 55 inches. Lock is case-hardened; barrel is blued and the rest of the furniture is brass. Rear sight is the typical Kentucky open type with a Kentucky brass blade front sight. Stock is chestnut colored and of plain straight grain maple wood.
Also available in Deluxe Engraved Model **$315.00**

WINCHESTER '73 CARBINE
$250.00
ENGRAVED WINCHESTER '73 RIFLE
$295.00

44-40 caliber which may use modern or black powder cartridges. Overall length is 39 inches with the round barrel being 20 inches long. Its full tubular magazine will hold 11 shots. The walnut forearm and buttstock complement the high-lustre bluing of the all steel parts such as the frame, barrel, magazine, loading lever and butt plate. Comes with the trap door in the butt for the cleaning rod. It comes with the leaf rear sight and blade front sight. This carbine is marked "Model 1873" on the tang and caliber "44-40" on the brass carrier block.

DIXIE TENNESSEE MOUNTAIN RIFLE
Percussion $195.00
Flint   195.00

50 caliber rifle. Length, 41½". Width, ⅞". Finish brown. 6 lands and 6 grooves. Double set triggers with adjustable set screw.

KENTUCKIAN FLINTLOCK & PERCUSSION CARBINE
Flintlock $135.00
Percussion   135.00

This carbine is made exactly like the Kentuckian Rifle with the exception that it has a 27½" long barrel and the gun is 43" in length overall. Comes in 45 caliber only. Land-to-land diameter is .453 and groove-to-groove diameter is .465 and will take a .445 to .448 ball. Weight: 5½ lbs.

FIE

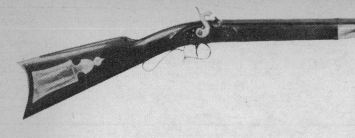

Kentucky Rifle

Zouave Rifle
Remington Zouave rifle replica 58 cal. rifled barrel, case-hardened hammer and lock, polished brass fittings. Weight 9 lbs. **$116.95**

Berdan Rifle
Muzzle-loading 45 cal. percussion rifle. Adjustable sights, double-set adjustable trigger, solid brass patch box and fittings. Overall length: 42¾". Weight: 7 lbs. **$97.95**

Kentucky Rifle
Muzzle-loading Kentucky rifle. 45 cal. rifled 35" octagonal barrel—polished solid-brass patch box, trigger guard, butt plate and stock fittings. Weight 7 lbs. .... **$ 94.95**
Engraved model **104.95**
Flintlock model **106.95**
Flintlock engraved model **114.95**

Navy Revolver
1851 Model Navy 36 cal. cap and ball revolver, 7½" octagonal barrel, polished-brass frame, one-piece walnut grip. Weight 40 oz. **$52.95**
Also available in engraved model **59.95**

Baby Dragoon Revolver
Baby Dragoon 31 cal. revolver replica engraved cylinder 4" or 6" octagonal barrel, polished-brass frame, square back trigger guard, one-piece walnut grip.
Weight 23 oz.—4"; 26 oz.—6" **$54.95**
Also available in engraved model **60.95**

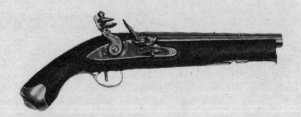

Navy Revolver
1851 Model Navy 44 cal. cap and ball revolver, 7½" octagonal barrel, polished-brass frame, one-piece walnut grip. Weight 40 oz. **$54.95**
Also available in engraved model **54.95**

Remington Revolver
New Army Remington replica 44 cal. Revolver model 1858 with polished-brass frame, 7½" blued octagonal barrel, walnut grips. Weight 42 oz. **$60.95**
Also available in engraved model **71.95**
Also available in 36 caliber **60.95**
36 caliber engraved model **65.95**

Tower Flintlock Pistol
Tower Flintlock pistol 69 cal. smooth bore, cherrywood stock with solid-brass trim, ramrod 9" barrel, 15½" long. Weight 48 oz. **$47.95**

Percussion Pistol Deluxe
Handcrafted 44 cal. percussion pistol with heavy rifled octagonal barrel, polished-brass fittings, fine Walnut stock, 15½" long, engraved lock. Weight 34 oz. **$62.95**

Model HAW50 Hawken $156.95
50 caliber percussion or flintlock. Oil finished European walnut stock. Highly polished brass furniture, double triggers, sights fully adjustable for windage and elevation.

MODEL ML GALLYON $161.95

Model ML Gallyon
A recreation of an old English fowling piece. 12 gauge. The unchoked barrel is 32″ long. Hand-rubbed walnut stock, deep blue receiver.

H&R MUZZLE LOADERS

MODEL 175
Calibers: 45; 58

A traditional cap lock sporting rifle with action design reminiscent of the famous Springfield rifles of the Civil War period . . . featuring modern steel construction for improved accuracy, performance and reliability. The perfect rifle for primitive weapon big game hunting.

SPECIFICATIONS
Calibers: 45 caliber
        58 caliber
Stock: American Walnut
Barrel Length: 28″
Sights: Modern open hunting sights adjustable for windage and elevation. Solid blade front sight.
Weight: 45 caliber—7½ lbs.
       58 caliber—7½ lbs.
Overall Length: 43″
Metal Finish: Blue-Black
Nipple Size: #11 percussion cap
Accessories Supplied with Rifle: Solid wood ramrod with hard wood handle, spare nipple and nipple wrench.

Model 175 — 45 caliber	**$210.00**
Model 175 — 58 caliber	**210.00**

H&R MUZZLE LOADER

Calibers: 45 & 58
$350.00

MODEL 175 DELUXE

SPECIFICATIONS

Calibers: 45 caliber, 58 caliber
Stock: American Walnut, hand checkered
Barrel Length: 28"

Sights: Modern open hunting sights adjustable for windage and elevation. Solid blade front sight.
Weight: 45 caliber—7½ lbs.
         58 caliber—7½ lbs.

Overall Length: 43"
Metal Finish: Blue-Black
Nipple Size: #11 percussion cap
Accessories Supplied with Rifle: Solid wood ramrod with hard wood handle, spare nipple and nipple wrench.

HOPKINS & ALLEN

THE BUGGY DELUXE
MUZZLE LOADING CARBINE $199.95
Calibers: 45

The Buggy Deluxe Muzzle Loading Carbine is equipped with American walnut stock and forend, 15/16th octagon 20" 8 grooved barrel, and is available in 36 or 45 caliber. It weighs 6 lbs.

MODEL 7087AE KENTUCKY RIFLE
Flint   **$144.95**
Percussion $139.95

SPECIFICATIONS:
Caliber: 45
Stock: 2-piece beech, walnut finish
Barrel: 34$^{15}/_{16}$" octagon blued

Sights: Fixed, notched rear, blade front
Fixtures: Brass
Length: 50"
Weight: 8 lbs.

PENNSYLVANIA
HALF-STOCK RIFLE

Calibers: 45 & 50
Flint **$279.95**
Percussion **267.95**

SPECIFICATIONS

Here's an exact reproduction of the famous Pennsylvania Half-Stock Rifle. The half-stock's design, fine handling characteristics, and superb accuracy made it popular with early frontiersmen who came to rely heavily on these guns for food and protection.

The Lock Mechanism: The famous Hopkins & Allen lock mechanism is just like the favorite Pennsylvania Half-Stock Rifle action. You may choose either flintlock or percussion. **The Stock:** The traditional stock is of fine walnut, hand rubbed and finished to a rich luster just like it was originally. **The Furniture:** The traditional beauty of this rifle is high-lighted by highly polished brass furniture. **The Barrel:** The beautifully blued barrel is 32" long and is available in 45 or 50 caliber: either smoothbore or with the famous Hopkins & Allen precision rifling. **Sights:** With sights like the originals, these guns are authentic in every way. **Weight:** 9 lbs.

BOOT PISTOL

The "Boot Pistol" is available in 45 caliber and comes with a sculptured walnut pistol grip and a full 6" octagonal barrel. It measures 13" over-all in length. The 15/16" octagon barrel is fitted with open sights—post type front sight and open rear sight with step elevator. The H&A "Boot Pistol" features a rich blueblack finish and is equipped with a match trigger.

Calibers: 45
$69.95

HOPKINS & ALLEN

The muzzle loading gun blazed a great era in the pages of history. It is the turning point of weapons design and perhaps the very apex of basic fundamentals which started the renaissance of firearms design and improvement in which we are living. "Charcoal burning" as it is affectionately called by its advocates, is a rapidly-growing sport and its devotees are increasing in number daily. It is truly a rewarding pastime and one of the finest new shooting sports in existence. Muzzle loading clubs are springing up all over the nation and their very existence have caused some states to open up special seasons for hunting game with muzzle loaders.

Hopkins and Allen offers the black powder shooter an **entirely American-made,** black powder rifle, featuring both the traditional "Kentucky Type" Minuteman rifle and the American Hopkins & Allen "underhammer" guns.

The Hopkins & Allen underhammer guns are the only truly American designed percussion rifles, dating back to the early 1830's when the design became popular for its simplicity and well known reliability.

OVER/UNDER MUZZLE LOADING RIFLE

45 caliber only $199.95

Now the black powder muzzle loader can have a 2-shot capability. The special swivel breech allows the second shot to be fired in only seconds by merely rotating the barrels. Positive and precise sighting for each barrel is assured by a complete set of sights on each barrel, making this rifle a true hunting gun.

The Lock Mechanism: The lock is specially designed to accommodate a swivel breech and still provide long-lasting, dependable ignition.

The Stock: Fine American gunsmiths crafted this rich American walnut stock with pride.

The Furniture: A classic Crescent butt plate in gleaming brass highlights the traditional stock.

The Barrels: Two famous Hopkins & Allen precision rifled barrels mounted to a rugged swivel breech.

Sights: Each barrel carries its own set of quick-aligning rifle sights.

Weight: 8½ lbs.

THE MINUTEMAN RIFLE

45 or 50 caliber

Flint	$289.95
Percussion	274.95

The Lock Mechanism: Authentic in every way, the famous Hopkins and Allen Minuteman action is exactly like the lock mechanisms of the era of these rifles. You may choose either flintlock or percussion.

The Stock: Shaped in the classic Kentucky style, this beautifully figured maple stock is a full 55" long and features a rich oil finish.

The Furniture: The gleaming brass patch box, butt plate and trigger guard tastefully complement the beautiful lines of this classic rifle.

The Barrel: A full 15/16" across the flats, this richly blued 39" long octagonal barrel is available in 45 or 50 caliber. The 8-groove twist rifling—.45 uniform twist one turn in 56"—offers unparalleled muzzle loading accuracy.

Sights: Traditional in every way, the famous "Silver Blade" front sight and notched "Kentucky" rear sight offer the same precise aim that the original rifles were famous for.

Weight: 45 caliber—9 lbs.

INTERARMS

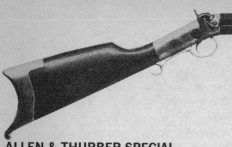

REPLICA

ALLEN & THURBER SPECIAL
$239.00

Caliber: 50, 54, 58
Barrel Length: 32"
Overall Length: 48"
Weight: 10 lbs.
Features: Ideal for both offhand and bench shooting. Of same design as original Allen & Thurber except for walnut forend. 1" diameter, octagon barrel is blued to fine finish. Machined sights are open, adjustable for windage. Highly polished Inco brass furniture.

ALLEN & THURBER REPLICA
$229.00

Caliber: 50, 54, 58
Barrel Length: 32"
Overall Length: 48"
Rifling: 8 grooves with a twist of 1 in 60"
Weight: 10 lbs.
Features: Manufactured using only American materials and craftsmanship. Is individually and carefully hand-crafted with cut rifling, hand-formed lines and each part is individually fitted. Stock is made of rich walnut and has a hand-rubbed finish.

THE MOWREY HAWK

THE MOWREY HAWK
$249.00

Caliber: 45, 54, 58
Overall Length: 49"
Weight: 9½ lbs.
Features: Hand-crafted "sporter" type butt stock w/cheek piece and **Hawken-type** butt plate. 1" diameter octagon barrel polished and blued.

Overall Length: 48"
Weight: 7½ lbs.
Stock: Maple, oil finish, brass furniture
Sights: Bead front and middle sights

ALLEN & THURBER BICENTENNIAL
$249.00

Gauge: 50

ALLEN & THURBER MUZZLE LOADING SHOTGUN
$219.00

Gauge: 12 gauge only
Barrel Length: 32" octagon

THE GEORGIA TREE GUN
$239.00

Caliber: 45, 50, 54, 58
Overall Length: 38"
Weight: 7½ lbs.
Features: Identical to the Allen & Thurber special, except for the shorter length of the barrel.

KASSNAR

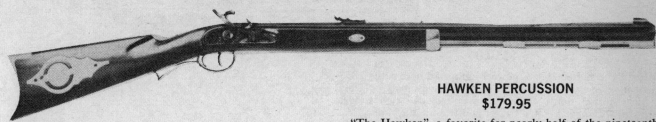

HAWKEN PERCUSSION
$179.95

"The Hawken", a favorite for nearly half of the nineteenth century, as well as playing an important part in the shaping of American history, has once again emerged as a favorite among muzzle-loading enthusiasts. Available in 45, 50, 54 and 58 caliber in flintlock or percussion.

KENTUCKY PERCUSSION
$129.95

Allowing freedom to ring in the Colonies was the Kentucky rifle's purpose and it successfully stood the test. Available in 45 caliber only in flintlock or percussion.

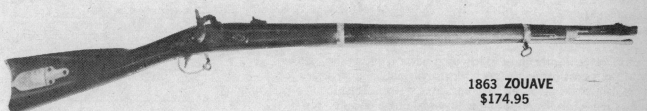

1863 ZOUAVE
$174.95

"The Zouave," the 1863 58 caliber Zouave was designed to meet the needs of a nation at war with itself. Its dreaded mini-ball resulted in heavy tolls north and south of the Mason-Dixon line. Available in 58 caliber only and featuring a polished-brass patch box, case-hardened lock and adapter for bayonet.

KASSNAR

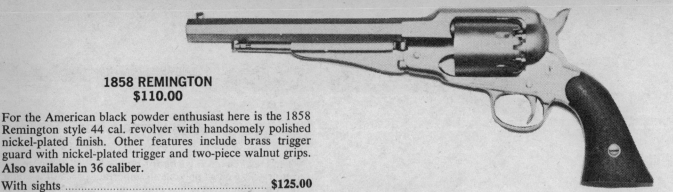

1858 REMINGTON
$110.00

For the American black powder enthusiast here is the 1858 Remington style 44 cal. revolver with handsomely polished nickel-plated finish. Other features include brass trigger guard with nickel-plated trigger and two-piece walnut grips. **Also available in 36 caliber.**

With sights **$125.00**

LYMAN RIFLES

PLAINS RIFLE
Percussion $199.95
Flintlock   209.95

The Lyman Plains Rifle is patterned after the reliable and accurate guns used by the early plainsmen who opened the West and Northwest. Traditionally styled, this black-powder firearm features a double-set trigger and fully adjustable sight. In addition, its hooked breech makes takedown and cleaning a breeze. The handsome European walnut stock is highlighted by a gleaming brass trigger guard, buttplate, and a distinctive, easy-to-open patch box. Available in 45, 50, 54 or 58 caliber; barrel length: 28″; overall length: 45″; weight: 8¾ lbs. Percussion style is available in 45, 50, 54 or 58 caliber. Flintlock style is available in 50 or 54 caliber.

GREAT PLAINS RIFLE $224.95

The Great Plains Rifle has a 32″ deep-grooved barrel and 1 in 66″ twist to shoot patched round balls. Browned steel furniture including the thick steel wedge plates and steel toe plate; correct lock and hammer styling with coil spring dependability; and a walnut stock without a patch box. A Hawken-style trigger guard protects double set triggers. Steel front sight and authentic buckhorn styling in an adjustable rear sight. Available in 50 or 54 caliber.

LYMAN REVOLVERS

1860 ARMY 44
$119.95

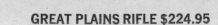

This revolver was the most widely used sidearm during the Civil War. Both sides prized the 1860 for its reliability and advanced features such as the "creeping" loading lever system. This, the last U.S. military percussion revolver, was the most advanced of the open-top revolvers. After the War, this gun went West and helped the pioneers survive and settle. Lyman's 1860 Army 44 is patterned exactly after the original and features one-piece walnut grips, color case-hardened frame, hammer and loading lever. The barrel and rebated engraved cylinder are polished blued steel while the backstrap and trigger guard are **nickel-plated** brass. The four-screw frame is cut for a shoulder stock.
Available in 44 caliber; barrel length: 8″; overall length: 13⅝″; weight: 2 lbs. 9 oz.

LYMAN REVOLVERS

NEW MODEL ARMY 44
$119.95

This rugged replica of Remington's 1858 New Model Army 44 has been the favorite of target shooters and other experienced muzzle loaders. The sturdy top strap, besides strengthening the basic frame design, provides an excellent platform for installation of an adjustable rear sight. Features include a deep-blue finish on the machined steel frame, barrel, cylinder and loading lever. The trigger and hammer are color case-hardened. The trigger guard is polished brass and the two-piece grips are well-finished European walnut. Available in 44 caliber; barrel length: 8"; overall length: 13½"; weight: 2 lbs. 9 oz.

1851 SQUAREBACK NAVY 36
$114.95

This 36 caliber replica is patterned after what may be the most famous percussion revolver ever made. Its classic lines and historic appeal make it as popular today as it was when Sam Colt was turning out the originals. Like the Remingtons, this replica of the second model 1851 (about 5,000 made) is made of quality material. The revolver features a color case-hardened steel frame, hammer and loading lever. The blued cylinder is engraved with the same naval battle scene as were the originals. The nickel-plated backstrap, square-back trigger guard and one-piece walnut grips combine to make Lyman's 1851 a real classic. Available in 36 caliber; barrel length: 7½"; overall length: 13"; weight: 2 lbs. 9 oz.

NEW MODEL NAVY 36
$119.95

The same features found in the New Model Army 44 replica can be found in its smaller naval version. Many of these revolvers are fitted with target sights and provide years of reliable service. The reduced length of this pistol makes it a handy belt gun which, when properly loaded, performs comparably to the 38 Special. Features include a deep-blue finish on the machined steel frame, barrel, cylinder and loading lever. The trigger and hammer are color case-hardened while the trigger guard is of polished brass. Grips are well-finished European walnut. Available in 36 caliber; barrel length: 6½"; overall length: 12¼"; weight: 2 lbs. 10 oz.

NAVY ARMS REPLICAS

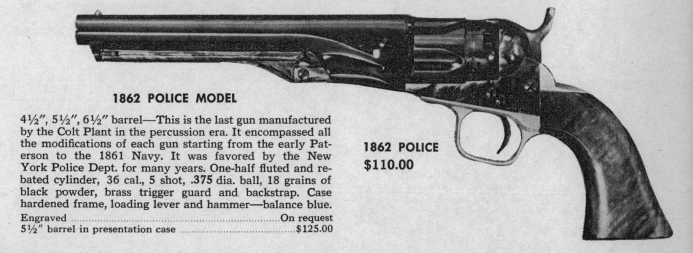

1862 POLICE MODEL

4½", 5½", 6½" barrel—This is the last gun manufactured by the Colt Plant in the percussion era. It encompassed all the modifications of each gun starting from the early Paterson to the 1861 Navy. It was favored by the New York Police Dept. for many years. One-half fluted and rebated cylinder, 36 cal., 5 shot, .375 dia. ball, 18 grains of black powder, brass trigger guard and backstrap. Case hardened frame, loading lever and hammer—balance blue.

Engraved ....On request
5½" barrel in presentation case $125.00

1862 POLICE
$110.00

NAVY ARMS REPLICAS

SPILLER & BURR REVOLVER

A brass-frame copy of the Whitney revolvers made in the Confederacy. Available in 36 caliber only with 7" full-octagon barrel. Weight 2½ lbs., overall length 12½".

SPILLER & BURR
$85.00

36 CALIBER 1861 NAVY

The Officer model 1861 Navy Replica comes in 36 caliber with a 7½" barrel and may be had with a 6-shot round or fluted cylinder and choice of brass or iron straps. The model with iron straps is also available with a square back guard. Features include: case hardened frame, lever, and hammer; balance of gun is blued. The 1861 Navy comes cut for a shoulder stock.

1861 NAVY
$110.00

COLT WALKER 1847

The 1847 Walker replica comes in 44 caliber with a 9" barrel.   The full size Walker 44 weighs 4 lbs. 8 oz. and is well suited for the collector as well as the black powder shooter. Features include: rolled cylinder scene; blue and case hardened finish; and brass guard. Proof tested.

Engraved with gold bands at muzzle $250.00

COLT WALKER 1847
$145.00

SPECIFICATIONS:
Weight:	2 lbs. 9 oz.
Barrel length:	8"
Over-all length:	13½"
Caliber:	36 & 44

REMINGTON MODEL ARMY REVOLVER

The most advanced design of the time, the Remington was considered the most accurate cap & ball revolver. A rugged, dependable, battle-proven Civil War veteran. With its top strap and rugged frame these guns are considered the magnum of C. W. revolvers and are ideally suited for the heavy 44 charges.
New Model Army Revolver, blue: **$100.00**; nickel: **$125.00**

NAVY ARMS REPLICAS

REB MODEL 1860

SPECIFICATIONS: 36 caliber—Weight: 2 lbs. 11 oz. Barrel Length: 7¼". Overall Length: 13". 44 caliber—Weight: 2 lbs. 10 oz. Barrel Length: 7¼". Overall Length: 13". Finish: Brass Frame, back strap & trigger guard, round barrel hinged rammer and on the 44 cal. rebated cylinder.

A modern replica of the confederate Griswold & Gunnison percussion Army revolver. In 36 or 44 caliber, rendered with a polished brass frame and a rifled steel barrel finished in a high luster blue with genuine walnut grips. **All Army Model 60's** are completely proof-tested by the Italian Government to the most exacting standards. **$65.00**

Matching Shoulder Stock **$45.00**

LEECH & RIGDON

SPECIFICATIONS—Weight: 2 lbs. 10 oz. Barrel Length: 7¼". Overall Length: 13". Caliber: 36. Finish: Steel Case hardened frame. Round barrel, hinged rammer.

A modern version of the famous Leech & Rigdon Army Revolver. Manufactured during the Civil War in Augusta, Georgia and furnished to many of the Georgia Cavalry units. It is basically a copy of the Colt Navy Revolver, but with a round Dragoon type barrel. **$110.00**

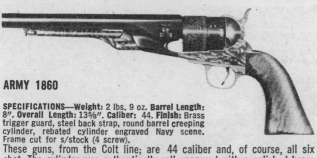

ARMY 1860

SPECIFICATIONS—Weight: 2 lbs. 9 oz. Barrel Length: 8". Overall Length: 13⅝". Caliber: 44. Finish: Brass trigger guard, steel back strap, round barrel creeping cylinder, rebated cylinder engraved Navy scene. Frame cut for s/stock (4 screw).

These guns, from the Colt line; are 44 caliber and, of course, all six shot. The cylinder was authentically roll engraved with a polished brass trigger guard and steel back strap cut for shoulder stock. The frame, loading lever and hammer are finished in high luster color case hardening. Walnut grips complement the high quality craftsmanship metal work. **$110.00**

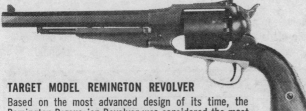

TARGET MODEL REMINGTON REVOLVER

Based on the most advanced design of its time, the Remington Percussion Revolver was considered the most accurate and dependable of all the cap and ball of its era. With its top strap and frame these guns are considered the magnum of Civil War revolvers and are ideally suited for the heavy 44 caliber charges. We are now offering our popular Army Model as a Target gun with target sights for the serious target shooter who desires to control the accuracy of his shooting with a more definite set of sights. Ruggedly built from modern steel and proof tested. Also available in 36 caliber **$125.00**

NAVY CALIBER POCKET MODEL

MODEL 1853

SPECIFICATIONS: Weight, 1 lb. 9 oz.; Barrel Lengths: 4½", 5½", 6½"; Caliber: 36; Number of Shots: 5.

One of the rarer Colt firearms, the Navy Caliber Pocket Model, made in .36 caliber so that they could employ the same conical balls used in the standard Navy Pistol. **$105.00**

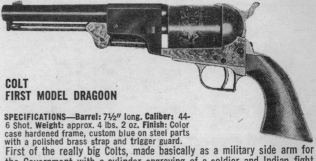

COLT FIRST MODEL DRAGOON

SPECIFICATIONS—Barrel: 7½" long. Caliber: 44-6 Shot. Weight: approx. 4 lbs. 2 oz. Finish: Color case hardened frame, custom blue on steel parts with a polished brass strap and trigger guard.

First of the really big Colts, made basically as a military side arm for the Government with a cylinder engraving of a soldier and Indian fight scene. It retained the old cylinder locking slots and square back guard housing of its predecessors. The grip abuts the frame and guard squarely. **$137.50**

SECOND MODEL 44 DRAGOON

SPECIFICATIONS—Weight: 4 lbs. Barrel Length: 7½". Overall Length: 14". Caliber: 44. Finish: Steel case hardened frame, Round barrel, hinged Navy type rammer.

The cylinder is fully roll engraved and finished in a deep, blue with contrasting color hardened frame and loading lever. The barrel is manufactured from precision rifled modern ordnance steel and each gun is proof fired and tested. **$137.50**

THIRD MODEL DRAGOON

SPECIFICATIONS—Barrel: 7½" long. Caliber: 44-6 Shot. Weight: 4 lbs. 2 oz. Finish: Color case hardened frame and loading lever with contrasting custom blue on the remaining steel parts. Polished brass trigger guard.

Sam Colt's favorite, of the Dragoon models. The third model Dragoon varied from its predecessors by having provisions for a shoulder stock, and a three leaf sight. First Dragoon model that had a rounded trigger guard. **$143.00**

Third Model Dragoon with Shoulder Stock **$225.00**
Buntline model with Shoulder Stock and 18" barrel **245.00**

"YANK" REVOLVER 36 CAL.

One of the most famous guns in all American history. During the Civil War it served both the North and South. Later, when the rush to open the west began, it became "standard equipment" for every man who ventured on a horse or rode a covered wagon to the virgin lands of wheat, cattle and gold. Due to its light recoil and lightning-fast action, it is still selected by many quick draw artists as the fastest single-action revolver in the world.

Cylinder roll engraved with classic naval battle scene. Back Strap and trigger guard are polished brass $110.00

SPECIFICATIONS:
Weight:	2 lbs. 9 oz.
Barrel Length:	7½"
Overall length:	13"
Caliber:	36

Finish: Polished Brass back strap and trigger guard. Engraved cylinder, Navy scene. Case hardened frame hammer and loading lever.

ENGRAVED "YANK"

Just for that special spot in a collection. Hand-engraved to your specifications with gold inlay. Special grips of pearl, ivory and ebony plastic available.

Engraving type "A"	....	Price Not Set
type "B"	....	Price Not Set
type "C"	....	Price Not Set

ENGRAVED ARMY

Engraving type "A"	....	Price Not Set
type "B"	....	Price Not Set
type "C"	....	Price Not Set

NEW MODEL NAVY REVOLVER

CIVILIAN MODEL "YANK" NAVY 36 CAL. (not shown)
Cylinder roll engraved with classic naval battle scene. Backstrap and trigger guard silverplated. $115.00

REVOLVING CARBINES

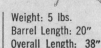

REVOLVING CARBINE
357 MAGNUM AND 45 Long Colt

A Revolving Carbine Rifle based on the famous and popular Remington pattern. It features a precision rifled ordnance steel barrel complemented by color case hardened frame and a high polished brass trigger guard and butt plate complementing the richly grained walnut stock. This is an ideal lightweight brush gun for the average white-tailed deer fan. It is available in 357 magnum and the popular 44/40 & 45 Long Colt $190.00

Weight: 5 lbs.
Barrel Length: 20"
Overall Length: 38"

PERCUSSION REVOLVING CARBINE—REMINGTON STYLE

An additional carbine model to be a companion piece to the Army Revolver. In matching 44 caliber with 20" barrel. Finished in a beautiful high-luster blue with buckhorn rear sight and adjustable blade front sight. A beautiful, light, handy six-shot repeating carbine which affected the design stimulus of the automatic weapon $185.00

SPECIFICATIONS:
Weight	.... 5 lbs.
Barrel length	.... 20"
Overall length	.... 38"
Caliber	 44

Finish: Walnut Stock, Brass Mounts, Solid Frame with Top Strap.

NAVY ARMS REPLICAS

1875 REMINGTON
357 Magnum, 44/40
& 45 Long Colt
Blue $165.00
Nickel 190.00

Replica Arms first cartridge gun—copy of the 1875 Remington that was used by the James boys and Butch Cassidy. Available in 357 Magnum, 44/40 and 45 Long Colt. Two-piece **walnut grips**, all blue, frame-case hardened, 7½" barrel.

ROLLING BLOCK MAGNUM SINGLE SHOT PISTOL

This pistol is an exact copy of the famous Number Three Remington Rolling Block Pistol.
It has a precision rifled ordnance steel barrel in the traditional half-round, half-octagonal pattern, finished in a high-luster custom blue. The authentically reproduced action is finished in a rich color-case hardening. The stocks are genuine walnut with a deep oil finish. Available in the popular 357 magnum caliber. **$135.00**
Additional calibers available: 22LR.

SHERIFF'S MODEL 1863

SPECIFICATIONS—Weight: 2 lbs. 7 oz. **Barrel length:** 5". **Over-all length:** 10½". **Caliber:** .36. **Finish:** Polished brass back strap and trigger guard. Engraved Navy scene. Case hardened frame, hammer and loading lever.

These shortened versions of the Navy Revolvers were favored by both sides of the law in the old west. With their reduced barrel length they are ideal for quick draw and as a personal protection weapon. .... **Price $110.00**

THIRD MODEL DRAGOON SHOULDER STOCKS

An interesting, practical accessory to enhance the value of your favorite Dragoon. Third Model Dragoon Shoulder Stocks are so authentically reproduced that they will fit all original as well as replica Colts. Colt was the first to patent the detachable stock. An adjustable folding leaf sight also became standard equipment on this type of revolver.... **$195.00**

DELUXE UPLAND 12 GAUGE SHOTGUN

The gun is classic in design with the styling reminiscent of the early English & French doubles. It is a Rabbit Ear sidelock configuration with a forward locking pin holding the barrels. A lightweight, fast handling beauty with traditionally hand-checkered wooden stock, walnut in color, and browned barrels.
Careful attention has been paid to the most minute detail including a limited covering of delicate scroll graving. Weight of the gun is just about 6 lbs. and the barrels are choked in IC and MOD. **$195.00**
SPECIFICATIONS: Weight approx. 6¼ lbs. Length of barrel 30". Choking, Improved cylinder and modified. Length of pull, 14" Overall-length, 45". Finish: Oil-finished, hand-rubbed walnut stock tastefully hand checkered. Barrels are browned with the remaining metal parts engraved with delicate scroll and polished.

12-GA. MAGNUM DELUXE SHOTGUN DOUBLE-BARREL PERCUSSION

This gun is classic in design with the styling reminiscent of the early English and French doubles. It is a rabbit ear side-lock configuration with a forward-locking pin holding the barrels. A fast handling beauty with traditionally hand-checkered walnut stock, blued barrels, and color case-hardened locks and fittings. Careful attention has been paid to the most minute detail, including a limited covering of delicate scroll engraving. Weight of the gun is just about 7½ pounds, and the barrels are choked in IC and MOD in 28" length, modified and full in 30" length. This Magnum will shoot all 12, 10 and light 8-gauge equivalent percussion loads. Patent breech with removable breech plugs. **$225.00**

NAVY ARMS REPLICAS
MISSISSIPPI RIFLE Model 1841

Model 1841 Mississippi Rifle
—The historic percussion lock weapon that gained its name as a result of its performance in the hands of Jefferson Davis' Mississippi Regiment during the heroic stand at the Battle of Buena Vista. Also known as the "Yager" (a misspelling of the German **Jaeger**) this was the last rifle adopted by Army Ordnance to fire the traditional round ball. In 58 caliber, the Mississippi is handsomely furnished in brass including patch box for tools and spare parts. This rifle is an authentic addition to Navy Arms' growing line of historic replica arms. **Price $176.00**

SPECIFICATIONS:
Weight ....9½ lbs.
Barrel length ....32½"
Overall length ....48½"
Caliber 58
Finish: Walnut Finish stock, Brass mounted.

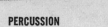

HARPERS FERRY RIFLE—58 CALIBER

Navy Arms is now proud to offer the ever popular and most-sought-after Harpers Ferry Rifle. The most authentic replica rendition ever offered to the Amercan shooter. Available in limited quantities. A historically significant weapon complete with precision rifled 58 caliber browned barrel with attractive highly polished brass furniture. $200.00

KENTUCKY PISTOLS

PERCUSSION

FLINTLOCK

The Kentucky Pistol is truly a historical American gun ... carried during the Revolution by the Minutemen ... the sidearm of "Andy" Jackson in the Battle of New Orleans. Now Navy Arms Company has gone through great research to manufacture a pistol truly representative of its kind and with the balance and handle of the original for which it became famous.

Flint $95.00
Percussion 90.00
Flint 110.00
Brass-barrel models ....**Percussion** 100.00

SPECIFICATIONS—Weight: 2 lbs. Barrel length: 10⅛". Overall length: 15½". Caliber: 44. Finish: Walnut stock, brass mounted, case hardened lock, blued barrel.

HARPER'S FERRY PISTOLS

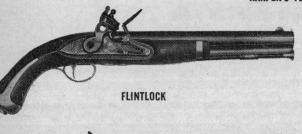

FLINTLOCK

PERCUSSION

HARPER'S FERRY

Of all the early American martial pistols, Harper's Ferry is one of the best known. They were carried by both the Army and the Navy. **NAVY ARMS COMPANY** has authentically reproduced the Harper's Ferry to the last minute detail. Well balanced and well made. $115.00

SPECIFICATIONS:
Weight: 2 lb. 9 oz. **Barrel length:** 10". **Over-all length:** 16". **Caliber:** 58 smoothbore. **Finish:** Walnut stock, case hardened lock, brass mounted browned barrel.

HARPER'S FERRY
MODEL 1855 DRAGOON PISTOL

Developed at Harpers Ferry Arsenal as a holster pistol for the U.S. mounted rifles, this pistol was later fitted with a shoulder stock and designated the Springfield Pistol Carbine Model 1855. In .58 cal., this pistol fires the standard 500 gr. minie ball and is the most powerful pistol ever made. Issued in pairs and designed to be carried in saddle holsters $125.00
Shoulder stock (not illus.) 40.00

NAVY ARMS REPLICAS

MARTINI TARGET RIFLE $250.00

This gun is available with 26" or 30" precision rifled pre-straightened ordnance steel barrels. The action is completely finished in deep rich color case hardening, and the simplicity of the Martini system will allow the shooter to achieve a closely timed shot string if used as a hunting rifle. Available full octagonal or half round in 45-70 caliber.

THE BUNTLINE FRONTIER TARGET $231.00

This model features a detachable shoulder stock and 16½" barrel. Available in 45 Long Colt and 357 Magnum.

ARMY 60 SHERIFF'S MODEL $65.00

A shortened version of the Army Model 60 Revolver. The Sheriff's model version became popular because the shortened barrel was fast out of the leather. This is actually the original snub nose. The predecessor of the detective specials or belly guns designed for quick-draw use. A piece of traditional Americana, the Sheriff's model was adopted by many local police departments. Available in 36 and 44 calibers.

STAINLESS STEEL 1858 REMINGTON $165.00

Exactly like the standard 1858 Remington except that every part with the exception of the grips and trigger guard is manufactured from corrosion-resistant stainless steel. This gun has all the style and feel of its ancestor with all of the conveniences of stainless steel. 44 Caliber.

PATTERSON COLT

The first successful revolver in the beginning of the Colt dynasty. This famous arm saw service in the Mexican and Indian wars and is the most sought after of all the Colt weapons by collectors. Reproduced in a limited edition of 500 units. Deluxe limited edition (illustrated) of 50 units to be made with original styled engraving on special order only.

Specifications: Caliber: 36. Barrel Length: 9". Overall Length: 14".

Weight: 2½" lbs.	$175.00
Engraved Model	500.00

PATTERSON COLT

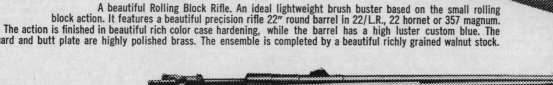

ROLLING BLOCK BABY CARBINE
22 LR $145.00
357 Mag.   160.00

A beautiful Rolling Block Rifle. An ideal lightweight brush buster based on the small rolling block action. It features a beautiful precision rifle 22" round barrel in 22/L.R., 22 hornet or 357 magnum. The action is finished in beautiful rich color case hardening, while the barrel has a high luster custom blue. The trigger guard and butt plate are highly polished brass. The ensemble is completed by a beautiful richly grained walnut stock.

45-70 MAUSER CARBINE $165.00

A short, fast-handling carbine with the western-style stock. Ideal for saddle scabbard or car gun. Barrel length is 18". Complete with hand-checkered walnut stock.

45-70 MAUSER RIFLE $165.00

45-70 bolt-action rifle based on the famous '98 Mauser action. Complete with checkered American walnut stock. Capacity 4 rds. (3 in magazine). Available in 24" and 26" barrels.

NAVY ARMS REPLICAS

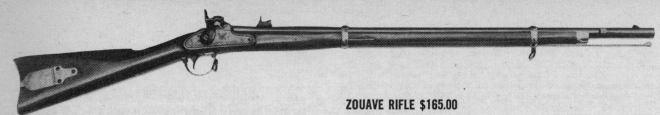

ZOUAVE RIFLE $165.00

A 58 caliber military percussion, it features a walnut-toned stock, deep-blued barrel, case hardened lock, brass fitting and patch box. The precision rifled barrel is 32½" with an overall length of 48½".

THE YELLOWBOY CARBINE

A copy of the most popular variation—the Saddle Ring Carbine with 19" barrel.

38 spl $210.00
44-40 .... 210.00

THE NAVY ARMS YELLOWBOY RIFLE

An exact copy of an all-time classic-brass buttplate and nose cap. 24" octagonal barrel and rifle-type sights.

38 spl $275.00
44-40 .... 275.00

THE YELLOWBOY TRAPPER

The shortest and lightest Yellowboy. All fittings are the same as the carbine except for its 16" barrel.

38 spl $210.00
44-40 .... 210.00

ZOUAVE MODEL 1864 CARBINE $165.00

The Zouave Carbine in 58 caliber . . . the design considered by many as one of the most thoroughly perfected percussion rifles. The carbine is an ideal fast-handling brush-busting percussion carbine with precision rifled 22" ordnance steel barrel, finished in a deep luster blue which handsomely contrasts with the color case-hardened lock.

ZOUAVE SHOTGUN 12 GAUGE $165.00

The famous Zouave Rifle fitted with a 12 ga. cylinder choked barrel. Weight 7½ lbs.

PARKER-HALE 2 BAND RIFLE—MODEL 1858
Barrel: 33", Overall length: 40¼", Weight: 7½ lbs. $245.00

PARKER-HALE MUSKETOON—MODEL 1861
Barrel: 24", Overall length: 40¼", Weight: 7½ lbs. $245.00

PARKER-HALE 3 BAND MUSKET—MODEL 1853
Barrel: 39", Overall length: 55", Weight: 9 lbs. $295.00

THE STANDARD FRONTIER

THE STANDARD FRONTIER $159.50

A standard model is available with a 4½", 5½" and 7½" barrel and combines modern materials and old-world craftsmanship in a competitively priced single-action revolver. It comes with a blued chromoly steel barrel and cylinder, case-hardened frame and walnut-finished one-piece grips. The Frontier is available in 22 Long Rifle, 22 Winchester Magnum, 357 Magnum and 45 Long Colt, and on special order — 30 MI Carbine, 38-40 Winchester, 44-40 Winchester and 9mm Luger.
Available in Target Model $165.00

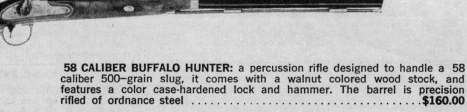

58 CALIBER BUFFALO HUNTER: a percussion rifle designed to handle a 58 caliber 500—grain slug, it comes with a walnut colored wood stock, and features a color case-hardened lock and hammer. The barrel is precision rifled of ordnance steel $160.00

NAVY ARMS REPLICAS

A Hawken Rifle designed for the hunter and serious target shooter. In the past, all Hawken-type rifles have relied on the round–ball projectile . . . but now Navy Arms offers a Hawken designed to handle hollow base mini–type bullets. This is the most advanced muzzle–loading rifle ever offered to the sportsman with match accuracy and a new positive magnum ignition system.

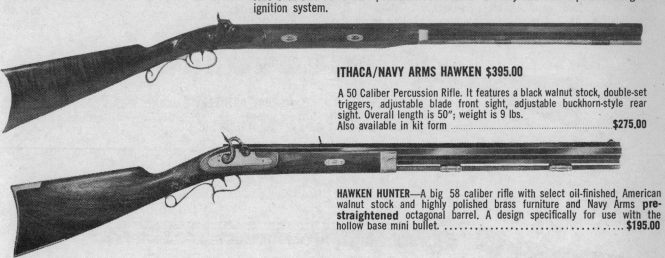

ITHACA/NAVY ARMS HAWKEN $395.00

A 50 Caliber Percussion Rifle. It features a black walnut stock, double-set triggers, adjustable blade front sight, adjustable buckhorn-style rear sight. Overall length is 50"; weight is 9 lbs.
Also available in kit form **$275.00**

HAWKEN HUNTER—A big 58 caliber rifle with select oil-finished, American walnut stock and highly polished brass furniture and Navy Arms **pre-straightened** octagonal barrel. A design specifically for use with the hollow base mini bullet. **$195.00**

HAWKEN HURRICANE—Designed specifically for the hollow base mini bullet with a choice of 45 or 50 caliber featuring Navy's famous precision rifled, **pre-straightened** octagonal barrel and polished brass furniture............ **$195.00**

REMINGTON ROLLING BLOCK BUFFALO RIFLE & CARBINE
45/70 AND 50-70 CALIBER

Navy Arms is proud to introduce the creation of the famous Remington Rolling—Block Action. Authentically reproduced in modern steels to the very finest detail. Each rifle is barreled with a famous octagonal Numrich Arms Corp. barrel featuring the famous hook rifling which is a process that every groove is singularly cut. The actions are case hardened complemented by a solid highly polished brass trigger guard and walnut colored stock. There are four models available. A Standard model with a full-length octagonal barrel for both rifle and carbine, a Creedmoor model which features half-round, half-octagonal barrel in both rifle and carbine model. All models are available in 45/70 or **50-70** caliber: 18" & 26".......... **$175.00**   30".......... **$185.00**   30" Creedmoor.......... **$200.00**

NAVY ARMS REPLICAS

HENRY CARBINE

This arm first utilized by the Kentucky Cavalry. Available in either original 44 rimfire caliber or in 44/40 caliber. Oil stained American walnut stock, blued finish with brass frame. Also available in a limited deluxe edition of only 50 engraved models to be made complete with deluxe American walnut stock, original styled engraving and silver plated frames.

Specifications: Caliber: 44 rimfire & 44/40. Barrel Length: 23⅝".
Overall Length: 45". **$500.00**
Engraved Model **1500.00**

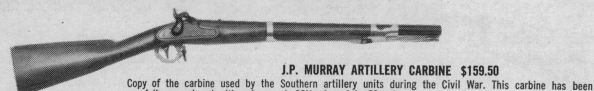

J.P. MURRAY ARTILLERY CARBINE $159.50

Copy of the carbine used by the Southern artillery units during the Civil War. This carbine has been carefully reproduced with a browned, 23½" barrel in 58 cal.

MORSE/NAVY
SINGLE BARREL PERCUSSION 12 GAUGE SHOTGUN

The Morse/Navy single barrel 12-gauge Muzzle-Loading Shotgun is a well-balanced, American-made replica featuring a highly polished brass receiver with select American walnut stock. Navy Arms has improved upon the old Morse design to modernize this into a contemporary and exciting muzzle-loading configuration. **$125.00**

KENTUCKY RIFLE — 45 CALIBER PERCUSSION $175.00   FLINT $185.00

No weapon, before or since, has been so imbued with Americana as the Kentucky Rifle. The Kentucky was the wilderness weapon, Pennsylvania-born and universally used along the frontier. First called simply the long rifle, it was designated "the Kentucky" by gun lovers after the Civil War because Daniel Boone used it most effectively in opening up the Kentucky territory. In the hands of those who know how to use it, the Kentucky still can give many modern rifles a run for the money. The frontiersman could, with ease, pot a squirrel high in an oak tree or drop a deer at 100 yards. Barrel length is 35". Available in flint or percussion.

MORSE MUZZLE—LOADING RIFLE

Improved production techniques and modern engineering have produced this traditionally styled, muzzle-loading rifle. Quality plus custom craftsmanship is evident throughout this rifle with careful attention being paid to the most minute detail. It features Navy Arms "pre-straightened" precision rifled ordnance steel barrel. 45, 50 or 58 caliber. **$110.00**
Also available in 12-gauge. **125.00**

PARKER-HALE

Whitworth Military Target Rifle

1861 Enfield Musketoon

1853 Enfield Rifle Musket

1858 Enfield Rifle

1861 ENFIELD MUSKETOON $250.00

The 1861 Enfield Musketoon is a Limited Collector's edition, individually serial numbered with certificate of authenticity. Supplied complete with many extras: Facsimile 1859 "Instructions of Musketry" Handbook. Replica 8-part Combination Tool.

SPECIFICATIONS:
Caliber: 577
Barrel length(s): 24″
Weight: 7 lbs. 8 oz.
Overall length: 40.25″
Sights: Fixed front; graduated rear
Rifling: 5 groove; cold forged
Stock: Seasoned walnut with solid brass furniture

1853 ENFIELD RIFLE MUSKET $275.00

The Enfield Rifle Musket marked the zenith in design and manufacture of the military percussion rifle and this perfection has been reproduced by Parker-Hale with reference to the original 120-year-old gauges. This, and the other Enfield muzzle loaders reproduced by Parker-Hale, were the most coveted rifles of the Civil War, treasured by Union and Confederate troops alike for their fine quality and deadly accuracy.

SPECIFICATIONS:
Caliber: 577
Barrel length(s): 39″
Weight: 9 lbs.
Overall length: 55″
Sights: Fixed front; graduated rear
Rifling: 3 groove; cold forged
Stock: Seasoned walnut with solid brass furniture

1858 ENFIELD RIFLE $250.00

In the late 1850's the British Admiralty, after extensive experiments, settled on a pattern of rifle which had a 5-groove barrel of heavy construction, sighted to 1100 yards, and this was designated the Naval rifle, Pattern 1858. In the recreation of this famous rifle Parker-Hale has referred to the original 1858 Enfield Rifle in the Tower of London and has closely followed the specification even to the progressive depth rifling.

SPECIFICATIONS:
Caliber: 577
Barrel length(s): 33″
Weight: 8 lbs. 8 oz.
Overall length: 48.5″
Sights: Fixed front; graduated rear
Rifling: 5 groove; cold forged
Stock: Seasoned walnut with solid brass furniture

WHITWORTH MILITARY TARGET RIFLE $495.00

Sir Joseph Whitworth was an Enfield engineer, who turning his attention to the problem of improving long range accuracy in muzzle loading rifles, developed during the late 1850's and early 1860's the most deadly sniper and target weapon of its era. The barrel is cold forged from ordnance steel and has a patent breech, a device developed for small-bore target and hunting rifles.

SPECIFICATIONS:
Caliber: 451
Sights: Globe front adjustable for windage; open military target rifle rear sight.
Stock: Hand checkered walnut

RUGER BLACK POWDER REVOLVER

Ruger Old Army cap
and ball revolver. 44 caliber,
7½ in. barrel, 46 ounces, American
Walnut grips, adjustable rear sight, stainless steel nipples. Made to same best quality
standard as the Ruger cartridge revolvers.
Note: Use with lead ball or conical bullet of .457 diameter.

OLD ARMY...$148.50
OLD ARMY—STAINLESS STEEL...$194.00

SPECIFICATIONS of the OLD ARMY

Frame, Cylinder, and other **Working Components** are of heat-treated chrome-
    moly steel.
Caliber: 44. Bore .443 in., groove .451 in.
Weight: 2 pounds 14 ounces (46 ounces).
Barrel: 7½ in. Six grooves, right twist, 1 in 16 in.
Sights: Target rear (adjustable for elevation and windage) and ramp front.
Nipples: Stainless steel for standard caps.
Grips: American Walnut.
Finish: Polished all over;   blued and anodized.
The Lockwork is the same as that in the original Ruger Super Blackhawk. All
    Springs are coil, made from the highest quality steel music wire.

SHILOH

MODEL 1874 MILITARY RIFLE
$450.00

45-70 and 50-70 calibers. 30" round barrel. Blade front and Lawrence-style
sights. Military style forend with 3 barrel bands and 1¼" swivels. Receiver
group, butt plate and barrel bands case-colored, barrel—dark blue, wood—oil
finish. 8 lbs. 12 oz.

MODEL 1874 MILITARY CARBINE
$389.00

45-70 and 50-70 calibers. 22" round barrel. Blade and Lawrence-style sights.
Military forend with one barrel band, saddle ring and slide bar—"left side".
Same as Military Rifle. 8 lbs.

SHILOH

MODEL 1874 HUNTERS RIFLE
$417.00

45-70 caliber. 26″ round barrel. Single trigger, blade front and sporting rear sight, butt stock straight grip, steel rifle butt plate, forend sporting Schnabble style. Case-colored receiver group and butt plate, barrel—dark blue, wood—oil finish. 8 lbs. 4 oz.

MODEL 1874 BUSINESS RIFLE
$435.00

45-70, 45-90, 45-120, 50-70, 50-90 and 50-140 calibers. 28″ heavy-tapered round barrel, double set triggers adjustable set, sights, blade front and sporting rear with leaf. Butt stock is straight grip rifle butt plate, forend sporting Schnabble style. Receiver group and butt plate case-colored, barrel—dark blue, wood—American Walnut oil finished. 9 lbs. 8 oz.

MODEL 1874 SPORTING RIFLE NO. 3
OLD RELIABLE
$489.00

45-70, 45-90, 45-120, 50-70, 50-90 and 50-140 calibers. 28″ or 30″ tapered octagon barrel. Double-set triggers with adjustable set, blade front sight, sporting rear with elevation leaf and sporting tang sight adjustable for elevation and windage. Butt stock is straight grip with rifle butt plate, sporting forend Schnabble style. Receiver group and butt plate case colored, barrel—high finish blue-black, wood—American Walnut oil finish. 9 lbs. 8 oz.

MODEL 1874 SPORTING RIFLE NO. 2
$527.00

45-70, 45-90, 45-120, 50-70, 50-90 and 50-140 calibers. 28″ or 30″ tapered octagon barrel, double set triggers with adjustable set, blade front sight, sporting rear with elevation leaf and sporting tang sight adjustable for elevation and windage. Butt stock is pistol grip with rifle butt plate, trigger plate is curved and checkered to match pistol grip. Forend is sporting Schnabble style. Receiver group and butt plate is case colored, barrel—high finish blu-black, wood—American Walnut oil finished. 9 lbs. 12 oz.

NEW MODEL 1863 MILITARY RIFLE
$425.00

54 caliber (Calibers 45 and 50—Special Order). 30″ round barrel with blade front sight. Lawrence rear sight with elevation leaf. Forend 24″ in length with steel nose cap, 3 barrel bands, 1¼″ sling swivels. Butt stock straight grip Military-style, steel butt plate and patch box. 8 lbs. 12 oz.

SHILOH

NEW MODEL 1863 CAVALRY CARBINE
$375.00

54 caliber (Calibers 45 and 50—Special Order). 22″ round barrel with blade front and Lawrence rear sight with elevation leaf. Military forend with barrel band butt stock Military-style straight grip. Walnut finish. 7 lbs. 8 oz.

NEW MODEL 1859 CAVALRY CARBINE
$409.00

54 caliber (Calibers 45 and 50—Special Order). Same as 1863 carbine except steel patch box added to right side of butt stock. 7 lbs. 10 oz.

ROBINSON 1862 CONFEDERATE CAVALRY CARBINE
$399.00

54 caliber. A replica of the original 21½″ round barrel with fixed sights, forend with single brass barrel band. Military straight grip butt stock, brass butt plate, saddle barr and ring. Case-colored and hardened receiver group and blued barrel. 8 lbs. 8 oz.

MODEL 1863 SPORTING RIFLE NO. 3
$448.00

54 caliber. 30″ round barrel, blade front sight, sporting rear with elevation leaf, sporting Tang sight adjustable for elevation and windage, double set triggers adjustable set. Straight grip butt stock, steel butt plate, forend Schnabble style. Powder charge approximately 100 grains.

MODEL 1863 SPORTING RIFLE NO. 2
$489.00

54 caliber. 30″ round barrel, blade front sight, sporting rear with elevation leaf, sporting Tang sight adjustable for elevation and windage, double set triggers with adjustable set. Curved and checkered trigger plate, pistol grip butt stock with steel butt plate, forend Schnabble style. Powder capacity 100 grains. 9 lbs.

THOMPSON/CENTER

CONTENDER

Ventilated Rib/Internal Choke Models:

Featuring a raised ventilated (7/16″ wide) rib, this new Contender model is available in either 357 or 44 Magnum caliber. Its rear leaf sight folds down to provide an unobstructed sighting plane when the pistol is used with Hot Shot Cartridges. A patented detachable choke (1⅞″ long) screws into the muzzle (internally). Overall barrel length 10″.
$200.00

Bull Barrel Models:

Two "Wildcat Calibers" 30 Herrett and 357 Herrett are offered in this heavy 10″ Bull Barrel model. Bull Barrel models are available either with iron sights or less sights (drilled and tapped for scope mount).
With Iron Sights **$190.00**
Less Iron Sights **185.00**

Standard Models:

This Contender may be purchased with a standard barrel of your choice, in any of the standard calibers listed. Barrels are available in either 10″ or 8¾″ length (see asterisk following barrel listing). 357 or 44 Magnum calibers are available either with or without patented choke. All standard barrels are supplied with iron sights; however, the rear sight may be removed for scope mounting. 357 and 44 Magnum calibers are available with the Thompson/Center patented detachable choke for use with the Hot Shot Cartridge. When the choke is removed, standard factory ammo may be fired from the same barrel without accuracy loss. **$190.00**

22 Long Rifle*, 22 Win. Mag.*, 5mm Rem.*, 22 Hornet*, 22 K Hornet*, 22 Rem. Jet*, 218 Bee*, 221 Fireball*, 222 Rem.*, 256 Win. Mag.*, 25-35*, 30/30 Win.*, 38 Special*, 357 Mag. with choke**, 357 Mag. less choke*, 45 ACP*, 45 Colt with choke**, 45 Colt less choke*, 44 Mag. with choke**, 44 Mag. less choke*, 41 Mag.

** with choke   * less choke

THE PATRIOT
45 caliber

Featuring a hooked breech, double-set triggers, first-grade American walnut stock, adjustable (patridge-type) target sights, solid-brass trim, beautifully decorated and color case-hardened lock with a small dolphin-shaped hammer, the Patriot weighs approximately 36 ounces. Inspired by traditional gallery and dueling-type pistols, its carefully selected features retain the full flavor of antiquity, yet modern metals and manufacturing methods have been used to ensure its shooting qualities.

Patriot Pistol 45 caliber **$145.00**
Patriot Pistol 45 caliber with accessory pack......................... **177.00**

THOMPSON/CENTER

Super "14" Models

Chambered in seven calibers (30 Herrett, 30/30 Winchester, 357 Herrett, 35 Remington, 41 mag., 44 mag. and 45 Win. mag.), this gun is equipped with a 14″ bull barrel, fully adjustable target rear sight and brass insert ramped front sight (Patridge style). It offers a sight radius of 13½″, beavertail forend and grips designed by Steve Herrett. Overall length is 18¼″; weight is 3½ lbs. **$210.00**

THE RENEGADE
54 caliber

Available in 54 or 56 caliber percussion, the Renegade was designed to provide maximum accuracy and maximum shocking power. Constructed from superior modern steel with investment cast parts carefully fitted to an American walnut stock, the rifle features a precision-rifled (26″ carbine-type) octagon barrel, hooked-breech system, coil spring lock, double-set triggers, adjustable hunting sights and steel trim.

Renegade 54 caliber Caplock and 56 caliber smoothbore **$180.00**
Renegade 54 caliber Caplock with accessory pack **195.90**
Renegade 54 caliber Flintlock **185.00**
Renegade 54 caliber Flintlock with accessory pack **200.90**

THE SENECA
36 & 45 caliber

Available in either 36 or 45 caliber percussion, the Seneca rifle is patterned on the style of an early New England hunting rifle. Six pounds light, this graceful little half-stock features a hooked breech, double-set triggers, first-grade American walnut, adjustable hunting sights, solid-brass trim, coil mainspring and finely patterned color case-hardened lock.

Seneca 36 or 45 caliber Caplock **$225.00**
Seneca 36 or 45 caliber Caplock with accessory pack **257.00**

THE HAWKEN
45 & 50 caliber

Similar to the famous Rocky Mountain rifles made during the early eighteen hundreds, the Hawken is intended for serious shooting. Button-rifled for ultimate precision, the Hawken is available in 45 or 50 caliber, flint or percussion. Featuring a hooked breech, double-set triggers, first-grade American walnut, adjustable hunting sights, solid-brass trim, beautifully decorated and color case-hardened lock.

Hawken 45 or 50 caliber Caplock **$220.00**
Hawken 45 or 50 caliber Flintlock **230.00**

Air Guns

AIR RIFLE HEADQUARTERS

SPECIFICATIONS:
Caliber: 177
Barrel Length(s): 6¼"
Weight: 2 lbs. 6 oz.
Overall Length: 12¾"
Sights: Front sight is a post enclosed within a tunnel system; rear sight is square notched
Safety: Auto-safety engages during loading; barrel may be tilted back to rearrange

**WEIHRAUCH
HW 70
$79.50**

SPECIFICATIONS:
Caliber: 177
Barrel Length(s): 18½"
Weight: 7¾ lbs. with 9½ oz. match sight installed
Overall Length: 43½"
Safety: Mainspring may be uncocked without firing
Stock: Walnut with checkering, soft curved rubber butt plate

**WEIHRAUCH
HW 55
TYROLEAN
$340.00**

SPECIFICATIONS:
Caliber: 177
Barrel Length(s): 7½"
Weight: 2 lbs., 10 oz.
Overall Length: 14.9"
Sights: Slotted front sight; adjustable rear sight

**FEINWERKBAU
F-65 MKI
$399.50**

SPECIFICATIONS:
Caliber: 177
Barrel Length(s): 18¼"
Weight: 7 lbs. 6 oz.
Overall Length: 43½"
Sights: Hooded ramp front sight; open rear sight

**FEINWERKBAU
F-124 DELUXE
$209.50**

SPECIFICATIONS:
Caliber: 177
Barrel Length(s): 7"
Weight: 2 lbs. 2 oz.
Overall Length: 15¾"
Sights: Hooded front sight; all steel rear sight with windage provision and micro-click adjusted elevation adjustment

**WISCHO
CUSTOM MATCH
$112.50**

AIR RIFLE HEADQUARTERS

WISCHO 70 DX
$386.00

SPECIFICATIONS:
Caliber: 177
Barrel: 19", rifled, hinged type.
Length: 44 inches overall. **Weight:** 7 lbs., 10 oz.
Power: Spring air, single-stroke barrel cocking.
Stock: Walnut-finished hardwood with cheekpiece, pistol-grip checkering, elaborate forearm checkering, and rubber buttplate with trim.
Sights: 2x-6x 1-inch tube, widefield scope included.

Features: Equipped with 1" sling, detachable swivels, filler screws, trigger shoe, and total internal accurization for optimum performance.

FEINWERKBAU F300S RBT
(RT) $595.00

SPECIFICATIONS:
Caliber: 177
Barrel: 20", rifled, fixed solid with receiver.
Length: 43 inches overall. **Weight:** 10 lbs., 4 oz.
Power: Single-stroke sidelever, spring piston.
Stock: Adapted for fixed and moving target use. Walnut with adjustable buttplate, pistol-grip cap.
Sights: Shipped without sights; scope optional.

Features: Recoilless, vibration free. Permanent lubrication and seals. Barrel stabilizer weight included. Single-stage trigger.

FEINWERKBAU F-124 SCX
$284.50

SPECIFICATIONS:
Caliber: 177
Barrel: 18¼-inches, rifled, hinged type.
Length: 43½ inches overall. **Weight:** 8 lbs., 14 oz.
Power: Spring air, single-stroke barrel cocking.
Stock: Walnut-finished hardwood.
Sights: 3x-7x ⅞-inch tube widefield scope included.

Features: Equipped with 1-inch sling, detachable swivels, filler screws, and internal accurization for optimum velocity and accuracy.

FEINWERKBAU F-12 CX
$386.50

SPECIFICATIONS:
Caliber: 177
Barrel: 18¼", rifled, hinged type.
Length: 43½ inches overall. **Weight:** 8 lbs., 14 oz.
Power: Spring air, single-stroke barrel cocking.
Stock: Walnut-finished hardwood with curved rubber buttplate, pistol-grip cap with spacer, hand-cut checkering, Monte Carlo cheekpiece.

Sights: 2x-6x 1-inch tube, widefield scope included.
Features: Equipped with 1-inch sling, detachable swivels, filler screws, trigger shoe. Internally accurized for exceptional velocity.

BEEMAN AIR GUNS

BEEMAN/WEBLEY TEMPEST AIR PISTOL
$79.95

The **Tempest** is available in 177 caliber for target shooting or 22 caliber for field work. Both feature an adjustable rear sight and trigger pull; steel piston in steel liner for maximum performance. Weight 2 lbs. Length 9".

BEEMAN/WEBLEY OSPREY AIR RIFLE
$179.95

The Osprey Air Rifle with a fixed barrel and side lever loading in 22 and 177 caliber has these features: Easy to load side lever; side lever ratchet for extra safety; trigger pull adjustment from 8 lbs. to 3 lbs.; micro-click adjustable rear sight; manual safety catch.

Also available in supertarget model with heavier barrel, walnut stock, and Anschutz micrometer sights **$388.00**

BEEMAN MODEL 100
$129.50

The 177 caliber Model 100 has adjustable trigger and walnut-finished hardwood stock. Barrel length: 18.7". Overall length: 42". Weight: 6 lbs.

BEEMAN/FEINWERKBAU MODEL 80 MATCH PISTOL

Available in 177 caliber. Spring piston, single stroke side-lever cocking. Interchangeable blade front; adjustable rear sights. Features two-stage trigger adjustable for finger length, pull, and release. Weight: 2.8-3.2 lbs. Barrel: 7.5", twelve-grooved rifled steel. Length: 16.4" overall.

BEEMAN/FEINWERKBAU MODEL 80 MATCH PISTOL
$495.00-$515.00

BEEMAN/WEBLEY HAWK MARK III AIR RIFLE
$99.95

The Mark III features a fixed barrel in either 177 or 22 caliber. It has non-metallic piston rings that are self-lubricated for long life. The stock has a full cheekpiece with Monte Carlo comb and no-slip rubber buttplate. Weight: 6.5 lbs. Length: 41".

BEEMAN AIR GUNS

BEEMAN MODEL 200
$159.50

The Model 200 is 177 caliber with walnut-stained beech stock, cheekpiece, Monte Carlo comb, embossed checkering on the pistol grip, and rubber buttplate. Weight: 7.1 lbs. Length: 44.3"

BEEMAN MODEL 400
$475.00

The Model 400 features recoilless operation with double-piston construction, fixed barrel and side-cocking lever. The sights are micrometer peepsight. The stock is oil-polished walnut with adjustable curved butt pad. Weight: 10.8 lbs. Barrel: Cal. 177, 4.5mm rifled—length 480mm with barrel sleeve and detachable weight 100 g. Length: 1130mm.

BEEMAN/FEINWERKBAU MAGNUM AIR RIFLE
Model 124D 177 caliber $209.50
Model 127D 22 caliber   214.50

BEEMAN/WEBLEY HURRICANE
$89.95

Available in 177 and 22 caliber. Features an adjustable rear sight and trigger pull, manual safety and scope mount. Weight: 2.4 lbs.; 11½" overall; 8" barrel

BEEMAN MODEL 900 MATCH PISTOL
$375.00
(w/tools and attache case)
$345.00
(w/o attache case)

BEEMAN MODEL 800 DELUXE RECOILLESS AIR PISTOL
$149.50

BEEMAN MODEL 700 STANDARD AIR PISTOL
$97.50

BEEMAN AIR GUNS

BEEMAN MODEL 850 AIR PISTOL

Available in 177 caliber. Features advanced recoilless action; rotating barrel-housing for easier cocking. 7″ rifled steel barrel. Weight: 3.2 lbs. Length: 16″ overall. Available in left-hand model for $184.95.

**BEEMAN MODEL 850 AIR PISTOL
$179.95**

BEEMAN/WEIHRAUCH HW 50M SPORT/TARGET AIR RIFLE $159.95

Available in 177 Caliber. Barrel-cocking, spring piston mechanism. May be uncocked. Adjustable 2-stage, cast and grooved trigger. Monte Carlo comb and rubber buttplate. Barrel: 18.3″. Overall length: 43.1″. Weight: 7.1 lbs.

**BEEMAN/FEINWERKBAU 300S RIFLES
300S RUNNING TARGET AIR RIFLE: $695.00**

Both available in 177, single-shot calibers, with 19.9″ barrel lengths and overall lengths of 43.3″. Weight: 300S Running Target Model, 10.9 lbs.; 300S Universal Model, 10.8 lbs.

BEEMAN/FEINWERKBAU 300S UNIVERSAL AIR RIFLE: $635.00-$685.00

BEEMAN/WEIHRAUCH HW 35L AIR RIFLE $189.50

Available in 177 caliber. Adjustable heavy-duty match trigger. Walnut stock with cheekpiece and checkered grip. Weight: 8 lbs. Barrel: 19.6″. Length: 44.7″ overall.

BENJAMIN AIR RIFLE

MODELS 3100, 3120: Benjamin Super Repeater Air Rifles with Monte Carlo stock. Cal. BB or 22 .. **$69.45**

MODELS NO. 340, 342, 347: Benjamin Super Single Shot Air Rifle with Monte Carlo stock. Cal. BB or 177 or 22 has new rugged square top ramp-type front sight **$69.45**

No. 273 Detachable Rear Peep

Sight. Adjustable. For Models 340 - 342 - 347 - 310 - 312 - 317 - 720 - BENJAMIN AIR RIFLES. Advise Model. Each **$4.30**
Extra Discs; Small, Medium, Large. Each................... **$2.15**

BAR-O Detachable Rear Peep

Sight. Adjustable. For all Models Benjamin Rifles with BAR-V Sight. Advise Model. Each **$1.90**

Extra Discs; Small, Medium, Large. Each.............. **$ .95**

Benjamin BAR-V Rear

Sight. It Rotates! Provides Quick, Sensitive Adjustment of Elevation and Windage. Each...... **$1.90**

BENJAMIN H-C LEAD PELLETS
"Sized and Lubricated"

	Per Can
Benjamin H-C Lead Pellets Cal. 177 (250)	**$1.32**
Benjamin H-C Lead Pellets Cal. 177 (500)	**2.42**
Benjamin H-C Lead Pellets Cal. 22 (250)	**1.71**
Benjamin H-C Lead Pellets Cal. 22 (500)	**3.15**

BENJAMIN ROUND BALL SHOT

Benjamin Steel Air Rifle Shot—BB 500	**$ .82**
Benjamin Steel Air Rifle Shot—BB 1 lb.	**1.70**
Benjamin Lead Air Rifle Shot—BB 500	**2.59**
Benjamin Lead Air Rifle Shot—BB—4.5 mm	
1 lb.	**$4.00**
Benjamin Round Lead Shot—Cal. 22—5.5 mm.	
1 lb.	**$4.00**

MODELS 130, 132, 137 Single Shot Air Pistol Cal. BB or 177 or 22 $56.40

STANDARD SIZE JET KING CO₂ CARTRIDGE

For use in Benjamin Super Gas Rifles and Pistols. 10 in a box. **$3.40**
Size 2⅝" x 47/64". 8.5 Gram.

CROSMAN AIR & GAS PISTOLS

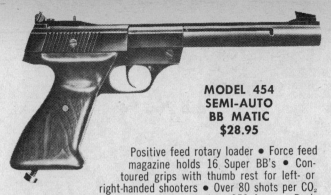

MODEL 454 SEMI-AUTO BB MATIC
$28.95

Positive feed rotary loader • Force feed magazine holds 16 Super BB's • Contoured grips with thumb rest for left- or right-handed shooters • Over 80 shots per CO_2 Powerlet • Average muzzle velocity—350 f.p.s. • Positive slide-action safety • Rear sights adjustable for windage and elevation • Barrel length—7¾" • Overall length—11⅜" • Weight —29 Oz.

MARK 1 & MARK II
$44.95

Single-shot CO_2 target pistol • Steel construction • Rifled barrel • Safety • Adjustable power and sights • Mark I 22 cal. pellet • Mark II 177 pellet or BB • Wt. 43 oz. • Length 11⅛". (Left-hand grips available.)

MODELS 1322 & 1377
$39.95

MODEL 1322: Single-shot 22 caliber pump pistol. Heavy duty pump link with sure grip checkered forearm. Selective pump power. Fully adjustable sights. Cross-bolt safety. Button rifled solid steel barrel. Gun blued steel parts.

MODEL 1377: Single-shot 177 caliber pump pistol. Heavy duty pump link with sure grip checkered forearm. Selective pump power. Fully adjustable sights. Cross-bolt safety. Button rifled, solid steel barrel. Gun blued steel parts.

MODEL 38-T
$39.95

MODEL 38-C: Combat. CO_2 177 Pellet Revolver. Holds six 177 caliber Pells. Single and Double action and revolving cylinder. Length 9½". Weight 3½ ozs. 10 lands R.H. twist. 3¼" barrel. **$39.95**

MODEL 38-T: CO_2 177 Pellet Revolver. For Target shooting. Length 11¾". Weight 42 ozs. Rifling: 10 lands R.H. twist, 1 turn in 16", button rifled. 6" barrel. **$39.95**

MODEL 44 PEACEMAKER
$23.95

6-shot single action, 177 cal. Pellet Revolver • Long spur hammer for fast fanning • 6 shot positive stop revolving cylinder • Walnut finished grips • Post front sight • Button rifled • All steel barrel • Blue-black finish on solid zinc receiver • Powered by one CO_2 Powerlet • Weight 34 oz., length 10⅜".

MODEL 1600 POWERMATIC
$23.95

MODEL 1600 POWERMATIC

Automatic firing 16-shot BB repeater • Leakproof CO_2 powered • Length 11⅜" • Weight 29 oz.

CROSMAN AIR & GAS RIFLES

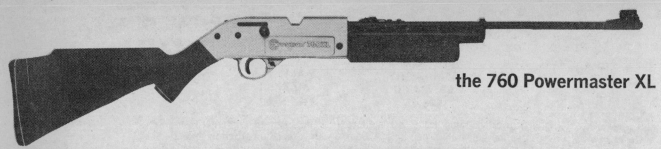

the 760 Powermaster XL

- Monte Carlo stock, contoured and checkered. High-impact plastic
- Gold-finished receiver for added elegance and greater durability
- Button-rifled, heavy-duty solid steel barrel
- Improved, adjustable rear sight for pinpoint accuracy
- Hooded front sight
- Receiver grooved for scope

- Solid steel trigger
- Reservoir holds over 180 Super BB's
- Also shoots 177 cal. Super Pells®
- Cross-bolt safety
- Butt-plate with white line spacer
- Improved bolt for better action
- Barrel length 19" O/A length 36". Weight 4¾ lbs.
- Price without scope **$42.95**

MODEL 73: 16 shot BB repeater. CO_2 powered. Solid steel barrel. Positive lever safety. Also shoots 177 caliber pellets. Length: 34¾". Weight: 3 lbs. 4 oz. Average muzzle velocity: BB—425 fps; Pellet—400 fps. **$24.95**

MODEL 760: 180-shot BB repeater, pump action. Shoots 177 or BB Caliber. BB's from storage chamber are metered into visual loading magazine. **$36.95**

MODEL 788 BB SCOUT: Starter gun with selective pump-up power with gravity-feed magazine, open rear sights adjustable for windage and elevation, positive bolt action, butt plate on stock and a solid-steel barrel and cross-bolt safety. Magazine holds 22 BBs and one BB in chamber. Overall length is 31". **$21.95**

MODEL 2200 MAGNUM: Bolt action, single shot 22 caliber pellet pneumatic rifle with a contoured pistol-grip stock, pumping mechanism with selective power; fixed blade front sight; butt plate with white line spacer with metal rear sights that are adjustable for windage and elevation. Weight is 5 lbs. 1 oz. Overall length is 39¾". **$49.00**

$49.95

CROSMAN RIFLES & ACCESSORIES

**MODEL 70
BOLT-ACTION
$49.95**

The Model 70 features a rifled steel barrel and hand-rubbed hardwood stock. 177 caliber pellet, CO_2 powered. Velocity 600 ft. per sec. 40 shots per CO_2 Powerlet. Length 41". Weight 5 lbs. Open sights, fully adjustable. Cross-bolt safety. Cam action piercing assembly.

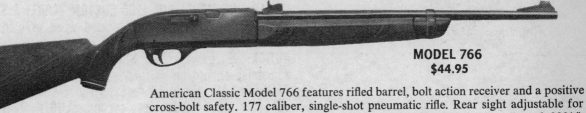

**MODEL 766
$44.95**

American Classic Model 766 features rifled barrel, bolt action receiver and a positive cross-bolt safety. 177 caliber, single-shot pneumatic rifle. Rear sight adjustable for windage and elevation with a fixed blade front sight. Weight 5 lbs. 9 oz. Length 39¾"

CROSMAN SUPER BB's

- Perfect-round, copper-plated steel shot.
- Top accuracy.

Model 717—50 packs of 200 BBs to a carton ..... **$ .19** per pack
Model 727—25 packs of 400 BBs to a carton ...... **.39** per pack
Model 737—12 packs of 1500 BBs to a carton .... **1.49** per pack
Model 747—12 packs of 2500 BBs to a carton .... **2.49** per pack
Model 757—6 packs of 5000 BBs to a carton .... **4.69** per pack

CROSMAN POWERLETS

CO_2 cartridges with Perma-Lok caps assure positive seal, and are clean piercing. Zinc-chromium plating, no rust, scale or grease. Box of 5-Model 321/5. 8.5 grams; box of 5 (for all other guns other than Crosman) Model 238/5.

DAISY AIR GUNS

**MODEL 179
$15.50**

DAISY 179 SIX GUN The "Spittin' Image" of the famed Colt Peacemaker in style and action. Forced-feed 12-shot repeating action. Single-action cocking hammer. Blued barrel, receiver; wood-grained molded grips. 11½" length.

DAISY AIR GUNS

POWER LINE CO₂ 1200 CUSTOM TARGET PISTOL
$33.95

POWER LINE MODEL CO₂ 1200 CUSTOM TARGET PISTOL.
GRIP: Contoured, checkered, molded wood grained.
BARREL: Smoothbore, heavy wall, seamless.
ACTION: CO₂ gas operated. **SIGHTS:** Blade and ramp front, fully adjustable square notch rear.
CALIBER: 177 Caliber BB repeater, 60 BB shot reservoir.
VELOCITY: 420/450 feet per second. **LENGTH:** 12⅛".

MODELS 717 & 722
$43.00

• **MATCH QUALITY PNEUMATIC AIR PELLET PISTOLS. CALIBER:** Model 717, 177 cal.; Model 722, 22 cal. **OVERALL LENGTH:** 13½". **ACTION:** Single pump pneumatic, side-operating pump lever. **MUZZLE VELOCITY:** Model 717, 360 feet-per-second (109.7 mps); Model 722, 290 feet-per-second (88.3 mps). **SIGHTS:** Blade and front ramp, match grade fully adjustable notch rear with micrometer adjustments. **GRIPS:** Super-strength molded, woodgraining and checkering; contoured with thumb rest. Left-hand grips available.

MODEL 188 B·B/PELLET PISTOL
$15.50

• **SPRING ACTION AIR PISTOL. CALIBER:** 177 cal. **OVERALL LENGTH:** 12". **MUZZLE VELOCITY:** B·B's, 215 feet-per-second (65.5 mps); pellets, 180 feet-per-second (55 mps). **ACTION:** Under barrel cocking lever. **SIGHTS:** Blade and ramp front, notched rear. **GRIPS:** Checkered and contoured with thumb rest. **FEED:** Gravity, easy-loading port, 24 B·B shot capacity or single shot pellet.

DAISY AIR GUNS

POWER LINE MODEL 880 PUMP-UP
B·B REPEATER & SINGLE SHOT PELLET
$41.50

POWER LINE MODEL 880 PUMP-UP B·B REPEATER AND SINGLE SHOT PELLET GUN IN ONE. Great for shooters 14 and over. Pneumatic pump-up for variable power (velocity and range) increasing with pump strokes. Only 10 strokes required for maximum power. 100-shot capacity B•B magazine. Single-shot 177 caliber pellets. Ramp front and open rear sights. Scope mount. Monte Carlo design, molded stock with cheek piece and molded fore-arm. Cross bolt safety with red indicator and positive cocking valve safety prevents hang-fires. Length: 37¾".

POWER LINE MODEL 1880 PUMP-UP
B·B REPEATER & SINGLE SHOT PELLET
$55.95

Power Line Model 1880 Pump-Up B•B Repeater and Single Shot Pellet Gun in One.
Same as Model 880 with Daisy Model 808 4x scope which is adjustable for windage and elevation. Cross hair reticle. Sure and easy pump action rapidly achieves maximum velocity and range limits with 10 quick strokes. Custom gun design loaded with quality extras sport shooters want: pump handle is easy to grasp and operate; man-size; perfectly weighted and balanced for shooting comfort; constant trigger pull through entire pumping range; longer sights radius makes for greater accuracy.

POWER-LINE
MODEL 881
$49.00

POWER LINE MODEL 881 PNEUMATIC PUMP-UP AIR GUN. Burnished receiver. Molded Monte Carlo stock with cheek piece and white spacer before the butt plate and grip cap. Checkered, molded forearm. It's a B•B repeater and a single-shot pellet gun in one. With pneumatic pump-up for variable power (velocity and range) increasing with pump strokes. Only 10 strokes for maximum power. Shoots 177 caliber pellets. 100 B•B shot capacity magazine. Ramp front sight and open rear sight. Cross bolt trigger safety with red indicator and positive cocking valve. Length: 37¾".

POWER LINE MODEL 1881 PNEUMATIC PUMP-UP AIR GUN CRAFTED BY DAISY.
Same as Power Line Model 881 with Model 808 detachable, 4-power scope. **$63.50**

DAISY AIR GUNS

MODELS 1922, 917 & 1917

MODELS 1922, 917 & 1917
CLIP FED PNEUMATIC PUMP-UP AIR RIFLES

MODEL 1922: $69.95

MODEL 917: $53.50

MODEL 1917: $69.95

Models 1922 and 1917 are equipped with 808 4-power scope.

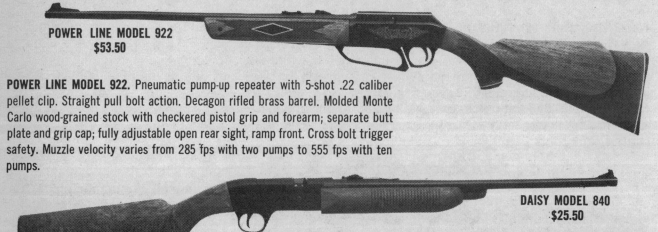

DAISY MODEL 1938
RED RYDER COMMEMORATIVE
$28.95

DAISY MODEL 1938 RED RYDER COMMEMORATIVE. The B•B gun Dads remember. Wood stock burned with Red Ryder lariat signature, wood forearm, saddle ring with leather thong. Lever cocking, 700-shot repeating action. Post front, adjustable V-slot, rear sights. Length: 35".

POWER LINE MODEL 922
$53.50

POWER LINE MODEL 922. Pneumatic pump-up repeater with 5-shot .22 caliber pellet clip. Straight pull bolt action. Decagon rifled brass barrel. Molded Monte Carlo wood-grained stock with checkered pistol grip and forearm; separate butt plate and grip cap; fully adjustable open rear sight, ramp front. Cross bolt trigger safety. Muzzle velocity varies from 285 fps with two pumps to 555 fps with ten pumps.

DAISY MODEL 840
$25.50

DAISY MODEL 840. Single pump pneumatic rifle with straight pull bolt action. Single shot .155 caliber pellet or 350-shot BB repeater. Molded wood-grained stock and forearm; steel butt plate. Forearm forms pump lever. Adjustable open rear sight, ramp front. Cross bolt trigger safety. Muzzle velocity: BBs 310 fps; pellets 270 fps.

DAISY AIR GUNS

DAISY MODEL 99
$36.00

DAISY 99 CHAMPION. Approved for NRA, Jaycee, Scout, 4-H training programs. Full seasoned wood Monte Carlo stock, modified forearm. Target features include controlled velocity, forced-feed 50-shot action, hooded front sight with 4 inserts, deluxe rear peep sight. New army sling. Special stock medallion. Length: 36¼".

DAISY MODEL 95
$23.95

DAISY 95 WOODSTOCK. Modern sporter style with real gun heft and feel. Full Seasoned wood stock, sporter forearm. Gravity-feed 700-shot repeating action. Controlled velocity. Ramp front, adjustable "V" slot rear sights. Length: 35".

DAISY MODEL 111
$19.95

DAISY 111 WESTERN CARBINE. Lever-cocking western carbine style with under-barrel rapid-loading port. Famed Daisy gravity-feed 700-shot repeating action with controlled velocity. Post front, adjustable "V" slot rear sights. Simulated gold receiver engraving. Length 35".

DAISY MODEL 1894
$33.50

DAISY 1894 SPITTIN' IMAGE B·B GUN. The "Spittin' Image" of the famed "carbine that won the West." 2-way lever cocking, side-loading port. 40-shot controlled-velocity repeated. 38".

DAISY MODEL 105
$15.50

DAISY PAL 105. Lever action with automatic trigger block safety. Post front sight, open rear sight. Extra strength molded stock. Gravity feed, 350 shot. 260' controlled velocity. Length: 30½".

HEALTHWAYS AIR GUNS

PLAINSMAN
MODEL 9401
CO_2 POWERED

**PLAINSMAN
$32.95**

SPECIFICATIONS:
Caliber: 177 BB shot
Capacity: 100 rds.
Barrel Length(s): 5⅞″
Weight: 1 ¾ lbs.
Sights: Sport blade front; fixed notched rear
Action: Double-action trigger pull
Safety: Thumb
Finish: Durable black epoxy with walnut wood-grain plastic grips

TOPSCORE
MODEL 9100
SPRING POWERED

**TOPSCORE
$22.95**

SPECIFICATIONS:
Caliber: 177 BB shot
Capacity: 50 rds.
Barrel Length(s): 6½″
Weight: 1 ¾ lbs.
Sights: Sport blade front; fixed notch rear
Action: Single-action trigger pull
Safety: Thumb, on right side of frame
Finish: Durable black epoxy and checkered integral with frame

HY-SCORE

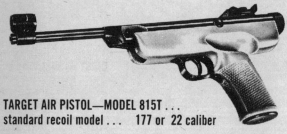

TARGET AIR PISTOL—MODEL 815T . . .
standard recoil model . . .   177 or 22 caliber

This pistol features unusual target grip design which will help even the beginning shooter improve his accuracy. Its penetrating power comes from simple one-break loading. Match trigger is fully adjustable. The 4-way rear sight has micro-click adjustment for windage and elevation combined with hooded target front sight. **Barrel length 7″; overall length 15¾″; muzzle velocity— 177 caliber: 410 f p s ; weight 48 oz. $69.95**

TARGET MATCH AIR PISTOL—MODEL 819M . . . recoilless target match model . . . 177 caliber

Adjustable oil-polished walnut pistol grip. Barrel length 180mm; overall length 410mm; muzzle velocity 177 caliber: 460 fps; weight 1.5 kilos. $314.95

MATCH AIR RIFLE—MODEL 811M

match recoilless model
177 caliber

Oil-polished walnut stock with adjustable butt plate. Adjustable sight hood. Barrel length 460mm; overall length 1100mm; weight 5000g; 177 caliber; muzzle velocity 575 fps. $349.95

HY-SCORE

CARBINE MODEL 808 . . . for 177 caliber pellets, darts and BB. "THREE GUNS IN ONE"

Shoots pellets, darts and BB's. By employing modern jet-age production techniques, HY-SCORE can now offer this "triple threat" quality air gun with power and accuracy. **Barrel length 12"; overall length 33"; weight 3 lbs.; 177 caliber; muzzle velocity 410 f p s $19.95**

STANDARD MODEL 805 . . . for 177 caliber pellets darts and BB. "THREE GUNS IN ONE"

This handsome junior model is furnished with full stock—see illustration. It has the same shooting capabilities, length, weight and velocity as Model 808, above. **$29.95**

MARK I—MODEL 813 . . . 177 or 22 caliber

Increased velocity combines with rifled steel barrel and ramp front sight to bring to the shooter pleasure and fun. Handsome walnut-finished wood stock . . . a deluxe custom feature exclusive with HY-SCORE. **Barrel rifled; length 14½; overall length 36½"; weight 4 lbs.; muzzle velocity— 177 caliber models: 450 f p s; range 125 ft. with genuine HY-SCORE pellets.** **$39.95**

MARK V—MODEL 809 . . . 177 or 22 caliber . . . the most powerful

Ideal choice for target work or pest control. Regular firearm-size stock has rubber butt and checkered pistol grip. Match trigger and hooded 4 aperture front sight. Accepts riflescopes. Model 809 is also available as a target gun, Model 809M with added target sight **Barrel rifled; length 19"; overall length 44"; weight 7 lbs.; muzzle velocity— 177 caliber model: 725 f p s; range 200 ft. with genuine HY-SCORE Pellets.**

Model 809 . . . .$124.95
Model 809M $159.95

TARGET AIR PISTOL—MODEL 816M . . . recoilless match model . . . accurized . . . 177 caliber

Fully recoilless target air pistol designed for the most discriminating pistol shooter. It has the balance and feel of a real precision target firearm. The match trigger is fully adjustable to satisfy the shooter's personal requirements. The accurizing greatly increases the weapon's capability to shoot with pinpoint accuracy. Rear sight has 4 adjustable click sights. The shooter is urged to use HY-SCORE No. 215 wadcutter pellets. **Barrel length 7"; overall length 16"; muzzle velocity 410 f p s; weight 50 oz.**
Price **$124.95**

CHAMPION MODEL 801 . . . 177 or 22 caliber

A big, powerful, handsomely stocked airgun with true rifle feel. The precision rifled barrel has hooded front sight. Powerful and accurate enough to command respect. Will accept riflescopes. **Barrel rifled; length 15¾"; overall length 39"; weight 5½ lbs.; muzzle velocity— 177 caliber model: 550 f p s; range 175 ft. with genuine HY-SCORE pellets.** **$84.95**

HY-SCORE

MARK III—MODEL 870 ... 177 caliber

This model, with a longer barrel, is designed for target training. It is a break-loading system with a locking device, coupling the barrel and housing solidly together. Walnut colored stock with checkered pistol grip. Advanced trigger mechanism is locked when barrel is opened. Not illustrated. **Barrel rifled; length 18"; overall length 42½"; weight 5½ lbs.; 177 caliber; muzzle velocity 550 f p s**
Price. $34.95

MATCH AIR RIFLE—MODEL 820 SM ...177 caliber

Recoilless operation on the proved double piston construction. Fixed barrel and side-cocking lever. Full-ring foresight with index—less adjustment from 3.8 to 4.8mm. Oil-polished walnut stock and adjustable, curved butt pad. Stocks available for right- and left-handed shooters. **Barrel rifled; barrel length 480mm; overall length 1130mm; muzzle velocity 525 fps; weight 5 kilos** $399.95

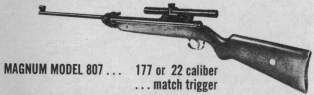

MAGNUM MODEL 807 ... 177 or 22 caliber ... match trigger

In caliber 177, suitable for target work; in caliber 22, for pest control. Built-in super-silent power is instantly yours. Maximum power obtained with trouble-free, one break loading. Simply break barrel, load, and fire like expensive over and under shotguns. Accepts any standard riflescope. **Barrel rifled; length 17⅜"; overall length 42"; weight 6 lbs.; muzzle velocity— 177 caliber 600 f p s; range 185 ft.** $94.95

HY-SCORE LEVER ACTION AIR RIFLE—MODEL 894 ... with barrel weight ... 22 caliber

Combination target and pest control air rifle with easy-handling side lever. The removable barrel weight stabilizer provides greater accuracy. Receiver is grooved for standard riflescope mount. Furnished with WILLIAMS detachable swivel and HUNTER military sling. **Barrel length 18½; overall length 43¾"; muzzle velocity 650 fps; weight 8½ lbs.** $74.95

HY-SCORE LEVER ACTION AIR RIFLE—MODEL 821 ... standard ... 22 caliber

HY-SCORE'S lowest-priced, high power, lever action model. Easy lever action, with one movement, delivers 650 f.p.s. with HY-SCORE lowest-priced, high power, lever action model. Easy lever action, with one movement, delivers 775 f.p.s. with HY-SCORE 177 caliber penetrating pellets.   Walnut-colored Monte Carlo stock has cheek piece. Furnished with WILLIAMS detachable swivel and HUNTER military sling. **Barrel length 18½"; overall length 43¾"; weight 7½ lbs.** $69.95

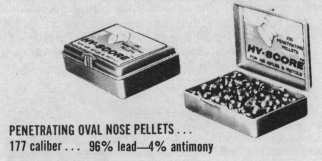

PENETRATING OVAL NOSE PELLETS ... 177 caliber ... 96% lead—4% antimony

Low weight 7¾ grain pellet for increased velocity and higher penetration. Packed in attractive, re-usable plastic boxes, with lock, of 250. .... **$1.00 per box**

STEEL DARTS—ASSORTED COLORS ... 177 caliber

ITEM No. 221. Darts, packed in envelopes containing one dozen, may be re-used. 6 displays, containing 12 envelopes each, per case.
Price per box **$1.00**

PENETRATING OVAL NOSE PELLETS ... 22 caliber ... 96% lead—4% antimony

Pellet weight 14 grains. Same packing and specifications as 177 caliber.
.... **$1.90 per box**

WADCUTTER MATCH FLAT NOSE PELLETS ... .177 caliber ... 100% pure lead

ITEM No. 215. Flat nose for accurate shooting. Low pellet weight only 8 grains. Pellets are packed individually to prevent rattling in boxes of 200. 6 counter displays per case, each containing 12 boxes.
Price per box **$2.50**

ITHACA-BSA AIR GUNS

ITHACA-BSA AIRSPORTER
Calibers: 177 & 22
Price Not Set

Sighting equipment comprises adjustable bead/blade foresight and tangent type rearsight with click adjustment for windage and elevation and reversible "V" and "U" element. The Airsporter's cylinder is dovetailed to accept any of the four BSA telescopes. Stock with sculptured Monte Carlo cheek piece and ventilated rubber recoil pad. Underlever loading system with barrel and cylinder permanently in line.

SPECIFICATIONS:
Calibers: 177 and 22
Overall Length: 44.2"
Barrel Length: 18.5"
Weight: 8 lb.
Sight Base (open sights): 17.3"
Muzzle Velocity: 700 fps and 550 fps
Bead Foresight Width: 0.080"
Blade Foresight Width: 0.120"
Trigger Pull: 4-6 lbs.
Range: 50 yd and 60 yd

ITHACA-BSA BUCCANEER
Calibers: 177 & 22
Price Not Set

Developed for the younger shooter, features full pistol grip and thumb-hole stock. Spring-loaded hammer, nonautomatic safety catch. Aperture rearsight with click adjustment for windage. Bead or blade foresight. Polyurethane stock.

SPECIFICATIONS:
Calibers: 177 and 22
Overall Length: 35.5"
Barrel Length: 18.5"
Weight: 6 lbs.
Sight Base: 25.0"
Muzzle Velocity: 510 fps and 400 fps
Trigger Pull: 2-5 lbs.
Range: 40 yds. and 45 yds.

ITHACA-BSA SCORPION
Calibers: 177 & 22
Price Not Set

Power enough for plinking or varmint shooting. Single shot. Precision rifled barrel of ordnance steel. One-piece, molded-nylon stock. Removable rear sight, hooded front sight protector. Features a 15¾" sight base, grooved for scope mounting. Trigger is adjustable for pull. Barrel extender cocking aid comes with each Scorpion. Packed with pellets, targets, target holder, lubricating oil and gun's specific inspection certificate.

ITHACA-BSA METEOR
Price Not Set

The barrel-breakdown loading system features the patented barrel-stop which ensures positive relocation from shot to shot. The double-link cocking system and fully adjustable trigger mechanism provide smoother loading and crisp let-off. Broad-ribbed trigger. Forsight can swivel to become either a bead sight or a blade front sight. Tangent rear sight has a click adjustment for windage and elevation. Cylinder dovetailed to accept any scope.

SPECIFICATIONS:
Calibers: 177
Overall Length: 42"
Barrel Length: 18½"
Weight: 6 lbs.
Muzzle Velocity: 500 fps.

MARKSMAN AIR GUNS & ACCESSORIES

MARKSMAN AIR PISTOL 1010
$14.95

1010 Repeater Air Pistol: 20-shot, 177 caliber BB, 177 caliber pellet or 177 darts. Black finish. Also available, Model 1020 Air Pistol, shoots BB's only

MODEL 740
177 caliber
$29.50

The 740, 100 plus BB repeater requires only one "break" for full-shooting force because of its "Break-Action" cocking. It has an adjustable rear sight and hooded front sight. One-piece walnut finished stock. Barrel length: 15½". Overall length: 36½". Also available in 177 caliber pellet and darts. Approx. 450 fps.

MODEL 742
$23.95

The 742 shoots BBs with a 100 load capacity magazine and also fires .177 (4.5mm) pellets and darts loaded one at a time. "Break" action cocking and automatic safety. Barrel length: 15½". Overall length: 36½". Approx. 400 fps.

MARKSMAN SHOOTING GALLERY

For indoor or outdoor shooting. For use with most 177 and 22 cal. air pistols and air rifles. Improve skill by shooting at moving ducks, spinning targets, and Ring-the-Bell Bull's-Eye. Electrically operated. Set includes Shooting Gallery with a supply of replacement paper Moving Duck Targets—Spinning Targets—Ring-the-Bell Bulls-Eye Targets and assembly instructions. **$36.95**

SHERIDAN AIR GUNS

Model EB-CO2 Pistol **$43.50**

SPECIFICATIONS:
- Turn bolt-single action.
- 5mm (.20 cal.).
- 6½" rifled rust proof barrel.
- Blade front—fully adjustable rear sight.
- 9" overall length.
- Checkered simulated walnut grips.
- Durable blue finish.
- Weighs 27 oz.
- Powered by 12 gram CO_2 cylinders.

PNEUMATIC RIFLES

Blue Streak Model CB   **Single Shot: 5 MM.**

Silver Streak Model C

A rifle for target or small game shooters. Full-length Mannlicher stock is made of genuine hand rubbed walnut. All working parts are precision engineered to assure accuracy and dependability.
- Controlled velocity. Pump action permits the shooter to determine the exact amount of velocity required for each shot. Improved valving mechanism assures long, trouble-free, high-quality performance.
- "Over and under" design with precision-rifled rigid mount barrel.
- Take-down walnut stock is readily removable.
- Single shot, bolt action design.
- Manual safety, mounted for easy thumb control.
- Choice of blue (BLUE STREAK) or satin-silver (SILVER STREAK) finish.
- Overall length: 37 in. Weight: 5¼ lbs.

MODELS AVAILABLE

MODEL	DESCRIPTION	PRICE
	With Standard Open Sight	
CB	Blue Streak	$73.75
C	Silver Streak	76.75
	With Receiver Sight	
CBW	Blue Streak	86.00
CW	Silver Streak	89.00
	With Scope Sight	
CBS	Blue Streak	102.95
CS	Silver Streak	105.95

GAS-POWERED CO2 RIFLES

Blue Streak Model FB   **Single Shot: 5MM**

Silver Streak Model F

35 Power Packed Shots

The Gas-Powered CO_2 Rifle is a companion line to the Pneumatics for those who enjoy or need faster shooting or who can't or just don't like to pump an air rifle.
- Blade type front sight.
- 5mm (20 cal.) precision-rifled rust proof barrel.
- Lightweight (6 lbs.).
- Compact length (37 in.).
- Over and under type construction with rigid mount barrel.
- Open sight easily adjustable for windage and elevation.
- Choice of blue or durable silver-satin plated finish.
- Bolt action (single shot).
- "Fireproof" safety.
- Sturdy valving mechanism with "locked in" charge.
- Easy takedown design.
- Full sporter length walnut stock.

Note—All rifles listed on this page are available in left hand versions at the same price. Add "LH" to above

MODELS AVAILABLE

MODEL	DESCRIPTION	PRICE
	With Standard Open Sight	
FB	Blue Streak	$73.75
F	Silver Streak	76.75
	With Receiver Sight	
FBW	Blue Streak	86.00
FW	Silver Streak	89.00
	With Scope Sight	
FBS	Blue Streak	102.95
FS	Silver Streak	105.95

SHERIDAN ACCESSORIES

SHERIDAN INTERMOUNT

The Sheridan Intermount will accept any scope and mount made to fit the ⅜ in. standard dove tail. We can of course also furnish an excellent low-priced scope sight that we feel best suited to the needs of Sheridan owners. Prices are shown below.

Each
No. 61—Wt. each 3 oz. $8.95

SHERIDAN INTERMOUNT AND SCOPE
Supplied with Weaver D4 scope.

Each
No. 62—Wt. each 2 lbs. $26.70

PELLETRAP

Sheridan's new Pelletrap is a compact, inexpensive, versatile target holder and backstop for air rifle practice. Wall hanger and flat base permit use most anywhere, indoors or out.

Each
No. 22—Weight each 6 lbs. $13.95

Pelletrap Target Faces
No. 24—Per 100 .... $1.95

LOW COST SHERIDAN AMMUNITION

The 5mm (20 caliber) ammo is solid-nosed, bullet-shaped, super-penetrating, matched to the precision-rifled Sheridan barrels for proper sectional density and best ballistic coefficient. New plastic, reusable pellet box holds 500 rounds. Inset, hinged dispenser permits removal of pellets, one at a time.

Per box
No. 50—500 in a box $3.75

Power, penetration, and accuracy depend on ammunition as well as on a precision barrel and bullet fit. Velocities high enough for true gyroscopic stability in flight are, of course, also of prime importance. The Sheridan has all three: (1) a correct bullet, (2) a proper barrel fit, and (3) velocity to spare.
No. 51–500 in a
box .... $3.75 a box

SHERIDAN CO₂ CARTRIDGES

Standard 12.5 gram size and may be used in any CO_2 Rifle or Pistol calling for a 12.5 gram cartridge.

Per box
No. 63–5 in a
box $2.60

No. 66 .... $8.95

Genuine leather holster for Sheridan CO_2 pistol. Features snap buttons on belt loop and safety snap.

No. 41 .... $4.00

Cleaning rod for Sheridan products.

SMITH & WESSON AIR GUNS

MODEL 80G BB RIFLE
$43.50

Features . . . • Top Tang Safety • Rich Walnut colored, checkered stock with a wood grain finish • S & W imprinted and contoured recoil butt plate • Ramp style front sight • Fully adjustable rear sight • Grooved receiver for scope mounting • Fast CO_2 cartridge loading—just cycle the S & W CO_2 loading cam lever • Simplified BB loading—through the contoured loading funnel built into the stock • Conserve gas—an automatic gas cut-off is actuated when the last shot in the 50 shot tubular magazine is fired • Have a safe rifle—empty the magazine when you've finished shooting. The Model 80 maga-

zine can be emptied with a charged CO_2 cartridge in place. **SPECIFICATIONS—ACTION:** Autoloading. **FEED SYSTEM:** Tubular, 50 shot spring forced. **CALIBER:** 177 BB **SAFETY:** Manual, top tang type. **FRONT SIGHT:** Ramp style with fixed post. **REAR SIGHT:** Fully adjustable. **SIGHT RADIUS:** 18¾". **BARREL:** 22" Smooth Bore, steel. **POWER SYSTEM:** S & W 12.5 Gram CO_2 cartridge. **STOCK:** Monte Carlo style, walnut finished, checkered with contoured butt plate. **RECEIVER:** Gun blued, grooved for scope mounting. **OVER-ALL LENGTH:** 39". **WEIGHT:** 3.25 lbs.

MODEL 78G CO_2 PISTOL 22 CAL.
MODEL 79G CO_2 PISTOL 177 CAL.
$47.50

Features include a rifled steel barrel, and fully adjustable rear sight. It's a natural for target practice or handgun training.

You don't have to pump this one up. It uses economical **S&W** CO_2 cartridges. Set it for high power and you get 65 shots from each cartridge, or change to low power for up to 125 shots. Adjustable power means that you can use this pellet gun anywhere—indoors or out.

Each pistol features a cross-bolt safety. If you are left handed, you won't need special stocks like you do with other pistols. These checkered target stocks comfortably fit both left and right hands.

Each CO_2 Pistol is packed with a can of **Smith & Wesson Pellets** and **Smith & Wesson** CO_2 cartridges.

SPECIFICATIONS—ACTION: Pull Bolt—single shot. **CALIBER:** 22 cal. Pellet (78G) or 177 cal. Pellet (79G). **SIGHTS:** Patridge Front; Fully Adjustable Rear with Micrometer Click Windage Adjustment. **SIGHT RADIUS:** 10". **SAFETY:** Cross-bolt safety. **BARREL:** 8½" long. Rifled Steel (10 lands, right hand twist). **POWER:** Smith & Wesson 12.5 gram CO_2 cartridge, High-Low Power Adjustment. **STOCKS:** Simulated walnut. Checkered. Fits left and right hands. **FINISH:** Gun Blue. **WEIGHT:** 42 oz.

SMITH & WESSON PELLETS AND CO_2 CARTRIDGES

Smith & Wesson CO_2 Cartridges are made for use in any CO_2 gun calling for a 12.5 gram cartridge. With the **Smith & Wesson Model 78G** or **Model 79G Pistol** you can get up to 125 shots from each bottle. **Smith & Wesson's** extra-tight top keeps the cartridge full until you are ready to use it. Packet in boxes of 5 . . . . **$2.42**

Smith & Wesson Pellets are precision-made. Available in 22 caliber and 177 caliber, they complement the quality of **Smith & Wesson Pellet Guns.** In fact they'll help bring out the best in you no matter what kind of pellet gun you shoot. Packed 250 to a can.
22 cal. . . . .**$1.80** per can, 177 cal. . . . .**$1.50** per can.

WALTHER AIR GUNS

SPECIFICATIONS:
Caliber: 177
Capacity: Single shot
Barrel Length(s): 9⅜"
Weight: 45.8 oz.
Overall Length: 13³⁄₁₆"
Sights: Micro-click rear sight, adjustable for windage and elevation
Action: Lever
Features: Power is compressed air. Recoilless operation, cocking in grip frame. 4-way adjustable trigger. Plastic thumbrest grips

WALTHER MODEL LP3
$390.00

WALTHER MODEL LP3 MATCH $490.00
SPECIFICATIONS:
Same as Model LP3 except with improved target grips with adjustable hand shelf

WALTHER MODEL LP53 $225.00
SPECIFICATIONS:
Caliber: 177
Capacity: Single shot
Barrel Length(s): 9⅜"
Weight: 40.5 oz.
Overall Length: 12⅜"
Sights: Micrometer rear sight; interchangeable rear sight blades
Features: Power is spring air. Target grips. Optional equipment includes barrel weight for improved balance

WALTHER LGR MATCH AIR RIFLE
$740.00

SPECIFICATIONS:
Caliber: 4.5mm (177)
Barrel Length: 19½
Overall Length: 44¼"
Weight: 10 lbs. 2 oz.

Stock: Same as LGR Air with exception of a high comb stock.
Sights: Same as LGR Air with the exception that sights are mounted on riser blocks.
Features: Same as LGR Air Rifle.

WALTHER MODEL LGR
$660.00

SPECIFICATIONS:
Caliber: 4.5mm (177)
Barrel Length(s): 19½"
Weight: 10 lbs. 2 oz.
Overall Length: 44¼"
Sights: Globe front sight; fully adjustable micrometer rear sight
Stock: Heavy walnut target stock with adjustable butt plate and adjustable muzzle weight
Features: Lever cocking, static pressure system provides constant velocity, shot after shot. Recoilless and vibration free. Adjustable trigger

WALTHER MODEL LGV SPECIAL
$540.00

SPECIFICATIONS:
Caliber: 4.5mm (177)
Capacity: Single shot
Barrel Length(s): 16"
Weight: 10 lbs. 4 oz.
Overall Length: 41⅜"
Sights: Globe front sight; micrometer adjustable rear sight
Trigger: Adjustable
Stock: Heavy walnut target stock matches styling and weight of the Walther small-bore target rifles, with fully adjustable butt plate

Sights, Scopes & Mounts

BUEHLER SCOPE MOUNTS

BUEHLER TELESCOPIC SIGHT MOUNTS: By using one of the five basic styles of mount bases, you may position the scope of your choice in the best possible location. The best location is the one that positions the scope in such a way as to give a full field of view when the shooter's face is nestled in a comfortable, natural position against the stock. Scopes vary in eye relief from 3 to 5 inches. Sight adjustment turrets are in different locations. The amount of space available on the scope for the mount varies. Most important of all is the difference in shooters and in the way each one holds a rifle. One of the five styles of mounts will locate your scope in the best position for you. A good gunsmith or experienced sporting goods dealer is a great help in making this choice. All Buehler mount rings fit and are interchangeable with all Buehler bases.

4 AND 5-INCH BASES

SHORT ONE-PIECE BASES

The short one-piece base locates the front ring over the top of the receiver ring about 1 inch aft of the long one-piece base. The rear ring is in about the same location. Thus, ring spacing averages 4 inches. The short base is recommended for shorter scopes, scopes with large and long objective bells, and scopes with turrets near the center of the tube.

LONG ONE-PIECE BASES

This base is made to fit most of the rifles in common use. In most models it has the rings spaced about 5 inches apart with the front ring located *ahead* of the receiver on all bolt action rifles. The long base gives the greatest possible support to the scope and the longest amount of eye relief. It is recommended for long scopes and scopes with adjustment turrets located ahead of center.

One Piece Scope Mount base, 4" or 5" $17.75

TWO-PIECE BASES

Two-piece bases locate the front ring over the receiver ring in the same place as the short one-piece base. The rear ring, however, is over the bridge on bolt action rifles, not ahead of it as is the case with the one-piece bases. The ring spacing averages 4½ inches. Will accommodate scopes described under the *short* one-piece bases. The eye relief is shorter than either one-piece base but adequate for the average installation.

Two-Piece Scope Mount Base. $17.75

ENGRAVED SPLIT RINGS
Beautiful fully engraved one-inch Split Rings. Available in Codes 6,7,8.
Per Set $58.00

BUEHLER RINGS FOR BOTH ONE- AND TWO-PIECE MOUNTS

SOLID RINGS   **SPLIT RINGS**

A double split type ring with the added beauty of a smoothly rounded "ball turret top." The steel spacer at the top of each ring not only fills up an unsightly gap, but is made of 16 laminations .002 thick which may be peeled off one or more at a time, thus accurately fitting all scopes up to .010 smaller in size than the normal dimension of the ring.

BUEHLER RINGS AND HEIGHTS:

CODE	SOLID RINGS	Height
3	¾" Solid	.040
6	1" Split (Standard) (Low)	.075
7	1" High Split (Medium)	.136
8	1" Extra High Split (High)	2.12
10	26 mm. (Standard)	.125
11	26 mm. High	.200
16	28 mm.	.181

SOLID & DOUBLE RING

Solid rings, per set $15.00
Double split rings, codes 6, 7 & 8 . . . . 23.25
Double split rings, codes 5, 10 thru 16 . . . . 30.00

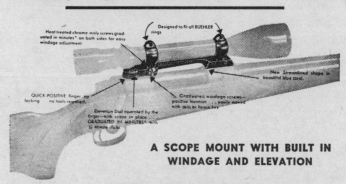

A SCOPE MOUNT WITH BUILT IN WINDAGE AND ELEVATION

MICRO DIAL MOUNT

Both windage and elevation features are built in. A twist of the fingers dials the elevation desired on a dial clearly marked in minutes (one inch at 100 yards). With ¼ minute clicks. Another twist on the lock wheel directly below the dial securely locks the setting. The windage screws also are calibrated in minutes on both sides. The Micro Dial is designed primarily for all scopes with internal adjustments, such as the Balvar 2½ to 8 (use Code 7 Rings for Balvar), but can be used to advantage with many other scopes—the reticule can always be perfectly centered. The Micro Dial also makes it possible to switch scopes between rifles. The ring spacing is 4 inches.

Micro-Dial Base Only $27.50
Solid Rings Only, per set 15.00
Split Rings Only, per set, codes 6, 7 & 8 . . . . 23.25
Special Rings Only, per set, codes 5, 10 thru 16 . . . . 30.00

BUEHLER SAFETY & GUN SCREWS

BUEHLER LOW-SCOPE SAFETY

The Buehler Safety operates on the same mechanical principles as the manufacturer's original safety. In the "ON" position, pressure of the striker spring locks it securely. It will not cam over into firing position. Safety holds BOTH BOLT and STRIKER in locked position.

This safety operates on the right side of the action, rotating through an arc of 70 degrees with definite stops in the OFF and ON positions. It can be used equally well with or without a scope, and will be found to be faster and more convenient than the original safety. Complete with instructions for installation.

For following models:
MAUSER (M98, F.N.), KRAG, SPRINGFIELD WINCHESTER M54, 1891 ARGENTINE MAUSER

M93 (Fits most small ring Mauser actions which cock on closing such as M93, M95 and M96 Spanish, Mexican, Swedish) M94
Price each $12.25

FILLISTER HEAD & PLUG SCREWS

	Prices
6x48 SCREWS (1/8, 1/4, 5/16, 1/2" Mixed) 12-	$1.50
6x48 PLUG SCREWS 3/32" . 12-	1.50
8x40 SCREWS (1/4 & 3/8" Mixed) 12-	1.50
8x40 PLUG SCREWS 3/32". 12-	1.50
10x32 PLUG SCREWS 3/32". 12-	1.50

GUARD SCREWS:

	Prices
UNIVERSAL	1.50 Ea.
ENFIELD GUARD SCREW SCREWS UNIVERSAL	1.50 Ea.
SPRINGFIELD (KRAG) GD. MAUSER GUARD SCREWS Set	3.50

RIFLE ACTION CHART—TOP MOUNT BASES

Mount bases listed by Code.

No. 34	Micro Dial	Long 1-Piece Base	Short 1-Piece Base	2-Piece Base
MAUSER				
M98 Military. Com. (1.4-1.42 dia.)	FI-U ④	FM	FI-S	98
Small Ring (1.3 dia.) M91-M98 etc.	HV-U ④		SR-S	95
1891 Argentine	HV-U ④		91-S	
F.N. & Mark X Actions	FI-U	FM	FI-S	F
Mauser 3000 R.H., L.H. Models				M3
BRNO Mauser Commercial				
Flat Top	BLU-WCC ②	5/16 BBWCC ②		B2 ②
Round Rec. Ring	HV-U ④		SR-S	H2 ①
BROWNING				
F.N. Action .264 thru .458	FI-U	FM	FI-S	F
Automatic Rifle (All Grades)				BA-2
Lever Action High Power				BL-2
B.S.A. Monarch Round Receiver				U9
COLT SAUER				CS
ENFIELD Remington 30 Conversion		E	E-S	
Bridge flat up to .075 low	E-U		E7-S	
Bridge shaped like M70	70-U			W ③
Bridge shaped like R721	21-U ③	21 ③	21-S ③	R ③
GOLDEN EAGLE			GE	
HARRINGTON & RICHARDSON, 22s				S2 ②
H&R 300 Ultra Bolt F.N. Action	FI-U	FM	FI-S	F
H&R 300, 301, Sako cal. .270 up				HS
HERTERS J9				F
HIGGINS — SEARS ROEBUCK				
50 & 51 1/2" Bridge Hole Spacing	FI-U	FM	FI-S	F
51L, 51C, 52C	HV-U			H2
53C	70-U			W
237C, 238C		70	70-S	
29, 31, 33			36	
			60	
HUSQVARNA				
HVA crown grade rifles	HV-U		SR-S	H2
8000 & 9000 Series				8-9
HVA-Carl Gustaf				8-9
JAPANESE ARISAKA		E ④	E-S ④	
KLEINGUENTHER				
K-14 & Shikar M2130 Voere			K1	KV
MARLIN				
336			36	
455	FI-U	FM	FI-S	F
39A, 56, 57, 62			36 ⑥	
80, 81, 88, 89, 98				S2
MOSSBERGS — Most Models .22 Cal.				S2 ②
M800				M8
M810 & 812				81
PARKER-HALE Super 1200 Series ⑥	FI-U	FM	FI-S	F

	Micro Dial	Long 1-Piece Base	Short 1-Piece Base	2-Piece Base
REMINGTON				
M600 & XP-100, M660			6XP	
M700, 721, 725 long actions	21-U	21	21-S	R
M700, 722, 725 short actions			6XP	R
M700 L.H. short or long action				R
760, 740, 742			60	
M788				78
37				T2
510, 511, 512, 513, 514, 521, 550, 560				S2
12, 121, 552, 572, 24, 241			60 ②	
40X, 40XB				R
RUGER 44 CARBINE				RC2
M77 Round Receiver Long Act.	21-U	21	21-S	R
No. 3 Carbine Single Shot				R3
10/22 Carbine				R1
SAVAGE				
99 — All Models		99		
110 R.H., L.H. short or long				V2
110 R.H. long action only	10-U			V2
SPRINGFIELD				
1906-03, A1	S-U	S	S-S	
A3	A-U		A3-S	
SCHULTZ & LARSEN 54, 60, 64, 65, 68				L2
SHILEN DGA Single Shot				SH
STEYR-MANNLICHER Mod. L, SL (metric screws)				SL
Models M, S, ST (metric screws)				SM
Mannlicher-Schonauer M72 All models (metric screws)				72
THOMPSON HAWKEN			HK	
WEATHERBY F.N. Actions	FI-U	FM	FI-S	F
Mark V R.H., L.H. long action				R
Mark V R.H., long action only	21-U	21	21-S	R
Mark V Varmintmaster .224, .22/250				MV
Vanguard (all calibers)	21-U	21	21-S	R
WINCHESTER				
M70 Std. ⑤ M670, 770	70-U	70	70-S	W
M70 Prewar (WW II) M54	54-U			W4
M70 Mag. H&H .300, .375 & N.M.	70-U			W
M70 Mag. .375 (Ser. No. 700,000 UP)	70-U			
M88, M100			88	
69, 72, 75, 74				S2
M52				T2
07, 61, 63, 77			60 ②	
BLANK BASES, flat on bottom for special installations	BL-U	5/16, 3/8, 7/16, 1/2 Full Blanks		B-2 ⑨
	BL-UWCC			

SPECIALS: We can fit many rifles and actions that do not warrant a production run of bases at a premium of only $7.25. Champlin, Steyr Mannlicher, Brevex Mag. and Omega are just a few. Special slotted bases to cover dovetail receivers, such as Sako (installed with screws) makes a nice neat installation. Write your needs.

FOOTNOTES (indicated by circled numbers above)
① If clip lips and hump are removed.
② Mounted with screws.
③ Rear screw hole matches hole in bridge.
④ File small flat at top of clip lips.
⑤ Serial numbers above 66,350, incl. Win. Magnums.
⑥ May be adapted with minor changes.
⑨ 2 piece available flat on the bottom 3/8" thick.
⑩ Drill and tap two additional holes.

BUSHNELL RIFLE SCOPES

CUSTOM 22

3X-7X All Purpose $41.95
w/ BDC 43.95

4X All Purpose $33.95
w/ BDC 35.95

Custom 3x-7x 22 Variable

Magnifications:	3x	4x	5x	6x	7x
Field at 100 yards (ft.):	33	23	17	15	13.6
Exit pupil (mm):	6	4	3.2	2.7	2.6

Overall length: 10"; overall weight: 6½ oz.; clear aperture of objective lens: 18mm; outside diameter, eyepiece end: 1⅛"; outside diameter, objective end: ⅞"; eye relief: 2¼"-2½"; adjustment scale graduations equal: 1" at 100 yds.

Custom 4x 22

Field at 100 yards (ft.): 28.4; exit pupil:4.5mm·overall length: 10⁵⁄₁₆"; overall weight: 5¼ oz.; clear aperture of objective lens: 18mm; outside diameter, eyepiece end: 1"; outside diameter, objective end: ⅞"; eye relief: 2½"; adjustment scale graduations equals: 1" at 100 yds.

SCOPECHIEF VI

SCOPECHIEF® VI WITH MULTI-X® RETICLE

With its MULTI-X RETICLE, Bushnell brings to the shooter in one reticle the advantage of the popular crosshairs, plus — post and crosshair, and rangefinding reticles.

The heavier portions of the new reticle lead the eye to the center aiming point providing improved accuracy under dawn and dusk shooting conditions. At the same time, the crosshairs at the center offer superior accuracy under normal shooting conditions for even the small target.

The ScopeChief VI Riflescope also comes with the Bullet Drop Compensator feature (BDC) and provides two scopes in one. BDC's whole purpose is to take the guesswork out of hold-over. Range still has to be estimated as it would with any scope. But BDC gives the hunter a choice: he can simply dial the estimated distance to the target and aim dead-on. Or he can preset it at the distance at which he zeroed in and allow for hold-over as he would with a regular scope. Scopes equipped with BDC come with three calibrated dials to cover normal factory loads. Additionally, there's a fourth dial for wildcat loads.

SCOPECHIEF VI 1.5x-4.5x $134.95
w/ BDC 139.95

SCOPECHIEF VI 2.5x-8x $139.95
w/ BDC 144.95

SCOPECHIEF VI SPECIFICATION CHART

Click adjustment equals ⅓" @ 100 yards.
Scale equals 1" @ 100 yards. Tube diameter: 1".

	VARIABLE POWERS			FIXED POWER
Magnification	3x-9x	2.5x-8x	1.5x-4.5x	4x
Objective Lens Aperture (mm)	40	32	20	32
Field of View @ 100 yards (ft)	3x-35 9x-12.6	2.5x-45 8x-14	1.5x-73.7 4.5x-24.5	29
Weight (oz)	14.3	12.1	9.5	9.3
Length (in)	12.6	11.2	9.6	12
Eye Relief (in)	3x-3.5 9x-3.3	2.5x-3.7 8x-3.3	1.5x-3.5 4.5x-3.5	3.5
Exit Pupil (mm)	3x-13.3 9x-4.4	2.5x-12.8 8x-4	15x-13.3 4.5x-4.4	8
Relative Light Efficiency	3x-267 9x-30	2.5x-247 8x-96	1.5x-267 4.5x-30	96
MX Center CH Width @ 100 yards	3x-.67 9x-.22	2.5x-.8 8x-.25	1.5x-1.3 4.5x-.44	.5
MX Distance Post Tip to Post Tip (in) @ 100 yards	3x-24 9x-8	2.5x-28.8 8x-9	1.5x-48 4.5x-16	18
Graduation @ 100 yards (in)	.75 .5	1.5	1	1

SCOPECHIEF VI 3x-9x ...$164.95
w/ BDC 169.95
w/ BDC and PRF 199.95

SCOPECHIEF VI 4x ... $ 99.95
w/ BDC 104.95

BUSHNELL RIFLE SCOPES

1.3X BUSHNELL MAGNUM PHANTOM

The Phantom increases clarity of sight picture and permits accurate holding on the target because the crosshair and target are on the same plane. The scope has micrometer reticle adjustments, and is made in crosshair reticle only.

This scope was designed specifically for handguns, and has an eye-relief of 7" thru 21" which takes the shooter easily from "two hand" varmint to "arms length," target position. All optics are hard coated.

1.3x all purpose game & target $63.50
2.5x varmint & long range 67.50

BANNER RIFLESCOPES

Banner riflescopes feature the Multi-X reticle and are available with the Bullet Drop Compensator. The neoprene eye guard combines with the long eye relief to give that extra margin of safety (except in wide angles).

Fixed Powers

BANNER 10X 40mm Long Range
(MX) $124.95
w/BDC 129.95

BANNER 6X 32mm Open Country
(MX) $94.95
w/BDC 99.95

BANNER 4X 40mm Wide Angle General-purpose
(MX) $114.95
w/BDC 119.95

BANNER 4X 32mm General-purpose
(MX) $84.95
w/BDC 89.95

BANNER 2.5X Short Range
(MX) $74.95

BUSHNELL RIFLE SCOPES

Variable Power

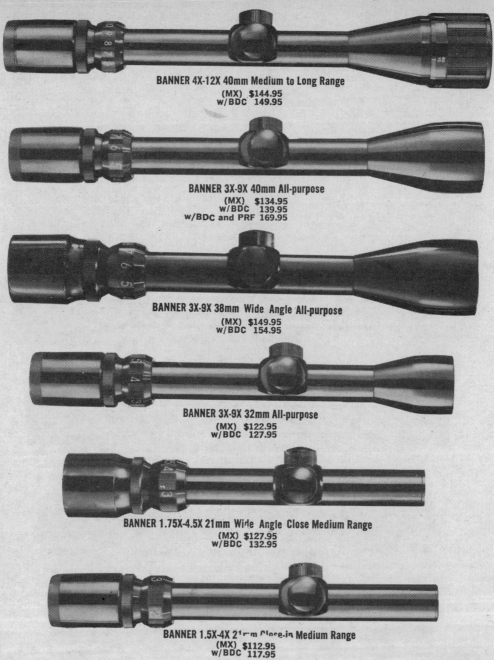

BANNER 4X-12X 40mm Medium to Long Range
(MX) $144.95
w/BDC   149.95

BANNER 3X-9X 40mm All-purpose
(MX) $134.95
w/BDC   139.95
w/BDC and PRF   169.95

BANNER 3X-9X 38mm Wide Angle All-purpose
(MX) $149.95
w/BDC   154.95

BANNER 3X-9X 32mm All-purpose
(MX) $122.95
w/BDC   127.95

BANNER 1.75X-4.5X 21mm Wide Angle Close Medium Range
(MX) $127.95
w/BDC   132.95

BANNER 1.5X-4X 21mm Close-in Medium Range
(MX) $112.95
w/BDC   117.95

PRISMATIC RANGEFINDER

The Prismatic Rangefinder measures the distance to the game. The hunter rotates the power selection ring and the distance in yards appears at the top of the field of view.

Scopechief $199.95
Banner 169.95

BUSHNELL RIFLE SCOPES

Magnification	RANGE-MASTER	Field of view at 100 yds. (ft.)	Weight (oz.)	Length (inches)	Eye distance (inches)	Entrance pupil (mm)	Exit pupil (mm)	Relative Light Efficiency	MX center CH width at 100 yds. (inches)	MX distance post tip to post tip (inches)	Graduation at 100 yds. (inches)
4x-12x 40mm	BDC	29 at 4x 10 at 12x	15.5	13.5	3.2	40	10 at 4x 3.3 at 12x	150 17	0.5 .167	18 6	.5
3x-9x 40mm	BDC	35 at 3x 12.6 at 9x	13	13	3.5	40	13.3 at 3x 4.4 at 9x	267 30	.66 .22	24.0 8.0	.5
3x-9x 38mm	BDC	43 at 3x WIDE ANGLE 14.6 at 9x	14	12	3	38	12.7 at 3x 4.2 at 9x	241 26.5	.66 .22	24.0 8.0	.6
3x-9x 32mm	BDC	39 at 3x 13 at 9x	11	11.5	3.5	32	10.7 at 3x 3.6 at 9x	171 19	.66 .22	24.0 8.0	1.0
1.75x-4.5x 21mm	BDC	71 at 1.75x WIDE ANGLE 27 at 4.5x	11.5	10.2	2.9	21	12 at 1.75x 4.7 at 4.5x	216 33	1.18 .44	45.7 17.8	1.0
1.5x-4x 21mm	BDC	63 at 1.5x 28 at 4x	10.3	10.5	3.5	21	14 at 1.5x 5 at 4x	294 41	1.3 0.5	48 18	.9
10x 40mm	BDC	12	14.6	14.5	3	40	4	24	0.2	7.2	.5
6x 32mm	BDC	19.5	10.5	13.5	3	32	5.3	42	0.3	12.0	.75
4x 40mm	BDC	37.3 WIDE ANGLE	12	12.3	3	40	10	150	0.6	21	1.5
4x 32mm	BDC	29	10	12.0	3.5	32	8	96	0.5	18	1.0
2.5x 20mm		45	8	10.9	3.5	20	8	96	0.8	28.8	1.5

TRU SCOPE POCKET BORE SIGHTER

This pocket-size bore sighter gives you the flexibility to carry it in your shirt or hunting jacket pocket. Rugged plastic case; comes complete with weatherproof cap and adjustable arbor. Fits any bore from 243 to 308 caliber.

Tru Scope will work on all scopes and most rifles, excluding rifles with magazines, full stocks or extra wide barrels (bull barrels). **Color—Gray; Weight 3.6 oz.; Size 3½" x 2¾" x 1⅛"** **$24.95**

FEATHERLIGHT

7 power, 50mm with INSTA-FOCUS Traditional Navy style, ideal when image brightness is more important than size or weight.
Field at 1000 yards: 375'
Exit pupil: 7.1mm
Height: 7⅜"
Weight: 39 oz.
Deluxe case and straps included **$194.50**

GRIFFIN & HOWE

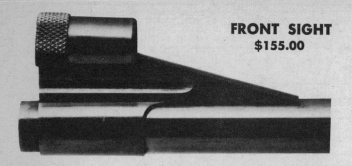

FRONT SIGHT
$155.00

The Griffin & Howe type matted ramp front sight is hand-fitted to the barrel by means of a band. When fitted with a gold or ivory bead front sight and removable front sight cover, this sight gives a pleasing appearance and maximum efficiency. Available only on an installed basis.

BARREL BAND
$50.00

The forward swing swivel may be attached by a barrel band in front of the forearm or a barrel band through the forearm. Available only on an installed basis.

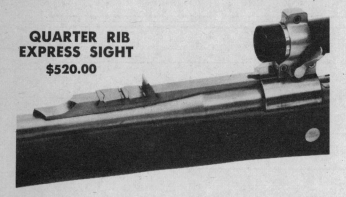

QUARTER RIB
EXPRESS SIGHT
$520.00

This sight may be made with fixed standing bar and folding leaves sighted in for any range desired. All leaves are marked for distance; the surface is matted with a gold directional line extending down from a wide V. Available only on an installed basis.

Top Ejection Mount   Standard Double-Lever Side Mount

TELESCOPE MOUNT

This mount has a locking cam action and is available for all models of rifles and is obtainable with 1″ or 26mm brackets, there are models to fit both domestic and imported telescopes. The mount holds the scope immovable in its split ring brackets. It can be mounted either low or high enough to enable using the iron sights when the telescope is mounted. It is readily detachable and, when replaced, it will always return to its original position with no scope mount adjustment necessary. It comes in the following models:

Side Mount	$ 85.00
Side Mount, installed	155.00
Top Mount*	200.00

*Available only on an installed basis.

Standard double-lever side mount with split rings, for telescopes with built in elevation and windage adjustment; Top ejection mount, for rifles similar to the Winchester 94, where the fired cases extract upwards. This mount, of necessity, has to be fitted in the off-set position; Garand mount, designed for use on the Garand and new M-14 military rifles, is mounted on the left side of the receiver to permit clip loading and top ejection.

JAEGER MOUNTS & ACCESSORIES

JAEGER QUICK DETACHABLE SIDE MOUNT

The Jaeger mount permits removing and attaching scope within a few seconds without the use of any coins or tools. The construction combines light weight with great rigidity. The unique clamping device locks the slide to the base securely, and insures return to zero. All mounts have windage adjustment at the rear ring.

Made for most bolt action rifles as well as Remington 740 & 760, Savage 99, Winchester 88 and other lever action rifles.

Especially well suited for Mannlicher Schoenauer rifles. $80.00

All mounts have split rings and are made in the following ring sizes and heights:

Mod. 20—1" low
Mod. 21—1" medium
Mod. 22—1" high

Low rings for most scopes in low position, medium height rings for large objective scopes in low position, high rings for use of iron sights below scope.

JAEGER
M2 SAFETY

For low mounted scope. Available in two models: For Springfield and Mauser.
$11.00

LEUPOLD RIFLE SCOPES

M8-2X (2-Power)

This scope is specially designed for a non-critical (10" to 24") eye relief, permitting mounting ahead of the receiver opening. It is primarily intended for the Winchester 94, and other rifles where a rear-mounted scope would interfere with top ejection. Also used on handguns, such as the popular Thompson Center single-shot pistol. Adjustable eyepiece. $108.50   M8-2.5X Compact $108.50

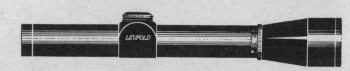

M8-3X (3-Power)

This light, compact scope combines an extra-wide field-of-view for getting on game quickly in heavy cover, with adequate magnification to make it usable up to normal hunting ranges for big game. A good choice for timbered country. Widely used on 375's and 458's for hunting dangerous African game. $122.50

M8-4X (4-Power)

Light, compact and modestly priced, this scope has what many big-game hunters consider to be the optimum combination of a generous field-of-view and magnification. In fact, the M8-4X is by far the most popular of all Leupold fixed-power scopes. $130.50   M8-4X E.E.R. $122.50

M8-6X (6-Power)

Only slightly larger than our 4X, and very close to the same external dimensions of many other 4-powers, if offers a little better resolution (because of the extra magnification) and therefore can be considered an improved long-range, big-game scope. Also excellent for light varmint rifles. $139.50

M8-8X AO (8-Power)

The scope has both the magnification and excellent resolution needed for hunting mountain sheep and goats. It could be excellent for antelope, as well as a fine varmint scope, too. The AO (Adjustable Objective) provides precise focusing and eliminates parallax error at any distance from less than 50 yards to infinity. $186.50

M8-10X AO (10-Power) and
M8-10X (10-Power Silhouette)
M8-12X AO (12-Power)

All of these scopes offer superb resolution for precision shooting at extended ranges, thus are naturals for long-range varmint hunting. The M8-10X is 1½" shorter than the M8-12X, for those who prefer a more compact scope. The AO (Adjustable Objective) provides precise focusing and eliminates parallax error at any distance from less than 50 yards to infinity.

10X AO	$186.50
10X Silhouette	217.50
12X AO	190.50

Dot reticles available at extra cost

Leupold Target Scopes

Today, target matches are being won with 5-shot groups measuring as small as .100", at 100 yards. It takes sights designed and manufactured for extreme accuracy to accomplish this. Leupold target scopes provide the resolution to clearly see bullet imprints at 100 or 200 yards. Changing conditions, such as wind or mirage movements also can be readily seen. Their compact 15" length and generous eye relief permit taking advantage of all the benefits of receiver mounting. Weight has been pared down to a minimum to allow for maximum rifle weight. They are excellent target scopes and the M8-16X also can be used for long-range varmint shooting. Its more modest 16X power, which doesn't magnify minor movements as much, sometimes can be desirable.

M8-16X* (16-Power)
M8-20X* (20-Power)
M8-24X* (24-Power)

A 2½" long screw-on sunshade is included as standard equipment with Leupold target scopes. Target scopes available with Crosshair $263.00 Conventional Dots $280.50

*With Adjustable Objective

LEUPOLD RIFLE SCOPES

The "GOLD-MEDALLION" Vari-X III Series

The introduction of Leupold's newest series, the Vari-X III scopes, advances the state-of-the-art of scope technology another step. In scientific terms, these scopes feature a new "Anastigmat" power-changing system that is similar to the sophisticated lens systems in today's finest cameras. Some of the improvements are subtle, such as the extremely accurate internal control system which is the result of both design and time-consuming hand matching of critical mating parts. Others —the sharp, superb-contrast sight picture and the "flatness" of field—are obvious. The total result is a series of tough, dependable scopes that are superior in optical and mechanical quality . . . particularly pleasing to the discriminating sportsman who really appreciates the true value of such quality. Reticles are same apparent size throughout power range, stay centered during elevation and windage adjustments. Fog free, of course.

VARI-X III 1.5x5 (1½ to 5- Power)

This scope's 1.5X-power setting is particularly helpful for hunting whitetail deer, since they often are taken in fairly heavy cover. Also, because a large field-of-view makes it easier to get on target fast, this magnification is often used when hunting dangerous game. **$191.50**

VARI-X III 2.5x8 (2½ to 8-Power)

This scope is excellent for all types of big game and varmint hunting. It offers a versatile range of magnifications—in a compact package (approximately the same size as a Leupold M8-6X). **$216.50**

VARI-X III 3.5x10 AO (3½ to 10-Power)

The extra power and Adjustable Objective feature makes this scope the optimum choice for the year-round shooter who enjoys every phase of shooting, from big game and varmint hunting to target shooting. **$248.50**

VARI-X III 3.5x10 (3½ to 10-Power)
Without Adjustable Objective **$225.00**

The PERFORMANCE-PROVED Vari-X II Series

VARI-X II 1x4 (1 to 4-Power)

This is a good magnification range for a variety of hunting. At the low end, the larger field-of-view makes it easier to make close-in shots on fast-moving game. At the high end, many hunters feel the 4X power is the optimum magnification for big-game hunting. **$160.50**

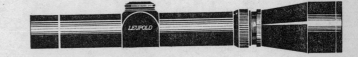

VARI-X II 2x7 (2 to 7-Power)

A compact scope, no larger than the Leupold M8-4X offering a wide range of power. It can be set at 2X for close ranges in heavy cover, or zoomed to maximum power for shooting or identifying game at longer ranges. **$176.50**

VARI-X II 3x9 and VARI-X II 3x9 AO
(3 to 9-Power)

A wide selection of powers lets you choose the right combination of field-of-view and magnification to fit the particular conditions you are hunting at the time. Many hunters use the 3x9 at the 3X or 4X setting most of the time, cranking up to 9X for positive identification of game or for extremely long shots. The AO (Adjustable Objective) eliminates parallax and permits precise focusing on any object from less than 50 yards to infinity, for extra-sharp definition. **3x9** . . **$189.50** **3x9 AO** . . . **$212.50**

Dot reticles available at extra cost

Leupold Scope Specifications

Scope	M8													Vari-X II						Vari-X III					
	2X[3]	4X[3]	2.5X[4]	4X[4]	3X	4X	6X	8X[5]	10X[5]	12X[5]	16X[5]	20X[5]	24X[5]	1 x 4		2 x 7		3 x 9 & 3 x 9[5]		1.5 x 5		2.5 x 8		3.5 x 10[5]	
														1X	4X	2X	7X	3X	9X	1.5X	5X	2.5X	8X	3.5X	10X
Actual Magnification	1.8	3.5	2.3	3.6	2.7	4.1	5.9	7.8	10.1	12.2	16.3	19.6	23.6	1.6	4.2	2.5	6.6	3.5	9.0	1.5	4.6	2.7	7.9	3.4	9.9
Field Feet[2]	22.0	7.7	42	26.5	43.0	30.0	18.0	14.5	10.3	9.0	6.6	5.4	4.5	70.5	28.5	42.0	18.0	30.5	13.0	64.0	23.0	36.0	12.7	29.5	10.5
Meter[2]	7.3	2.6	14	8.83	14.3	10.0	6.0	4.8	3.3	3.0	2.2	1.8	1.5	24.3	9.5	14.0	6.0	10.2	4.3	21.3	7.7	12.0	4.2	9.8	3.5
Optimum inch	10	24	4.3	4.1	3.9	3.9	3.9	3.6	3.5	3.5	3.5	3.5	3.5	4.3	3.4	4.1	3.7	4.1	3.5	4.7	3.5	4.2	3.4	3.9	3.4
Eye Relief mm	254	610	109	104	99	99	99	91	89	89	89	89	89	109	86	104	94	104	89	119	89	107	86	99	86
Length inch	8.1	8.4	8.5	10.3	10.3	11.9	11.7	12.9	12.9	14.3	15.2	15.2	15.2	9.5		10.9		12.6		9.7		11.6		12.8	
mm	206	213	216	262	262	302	297	328	328	363	386	386	386	241		277		320		246		295		325	
Weight oz.	6.8	7.6	7.4	8.5	8.7	9.3	10.4	13.5	14.0	14.4	16.0	16.0	16.0	9.5		10.9		13.6 15.0		9.8		11.5		14.9	
gram	193	215	210	241	247	264	295	383	397	408	454	454	454	269		309		386 425		278		326		422	
Adj. Scale mins. Div. Equal angle	1	1	1	1	1	1	1	1	1	½	1[6]	1[6]	1[6]	1		½		½		1		1		½	
Max. Adj. inch[2]	100	75	100	100	100	80	70	68	60	60	60	60	60	50		36		26		80		60		44	
Elev. & Wind cm[2]	278	208	278	278	278	222	194	189	167	167	167	167	167	139		100		72		222		167		122	

Available with these reticles.

	2X[3]	4X[3]	2.5X[4]	4X[4]	3X	4X	6X	8X[5]	10X[5]	12X[5]	16X[5]	20X[5]	24X[5]	1x4	2x7	3x9	1.5x5	2.5x8	3.5x10
Duplex	✓	✓	✓	✓	✓	✓	✓	✓	✓	✓	—	—	—	✓	✓	✓	✓	✓	✓
CPC	—	—	—	—	✓	✓	✓	✓	✓	✓	—	—	—	✓	✓	✓	✓	✓	✓
Crosshair	—	—	—	—	—	—	—	—	—	—	✓	✓	✓	—	—	—	—	—	—
Dot	—	—	—	—	—	—	—	—	✓	✓	5	6	7	✓	✓	✓	✓	✓	✓

(1) European No. 4 Style.
(2) @ 100 Yards/Meters.
(3) Extended Eye Relief.
(4) Compact.
(5) With Adjustable Objective.
(6) Target scopes have 1-Min. scale divisions, with ¼-Min. "clicks."

(7) 3/16 Min. = 0.19″ (5.3 mm); 3/8 Min. = 0.38″ (10.6 mm).
(8) 5/32 Min. = 0.16″ (4.4 mm); 5/16 Min. = 0.31″ (8.6 mm).
(9) 1/8 Min. = 0.13″ (3.6 mm); 1/4 Min. = 0.25″ (6.9 mm).

NOTES: A. All Leupold Scopes have self-centered, non-magnifying reticles. B. Windage and Elevation adjustments are internal. C. Diameter of all scope tubes is 1″. D. We reserve the right to make design modifications and other improvements without prior notice. E. Leupold Scopes are manufactured under one or more of the following patents: No. 3,058,391; No. 3,161,716; No. 3,286,352; No. 3,297,389; No. 3,918,791 (Foreign Patents Pending).

Leupold "STD" Standard Mount

...the perfect companion to your Leupold "Golden Ring®" Scope

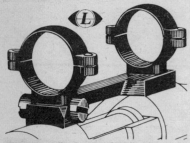

The new Leupold "STD" Mount is carefully machined from cold-rolled bar-stock steel to provide the ultimate in strength and rugged dependability. Featuring generous windage adjustments, precision-fitted dovetail and handsome, streamlined rings, the "STD" offers a firm, slip-free mount for any 1″-tube-diameter scope. Permits quick removal and return of scope. Available for the majority of popular rifles. *Note: "STD" Mount Bases and Rings interchange with Redfield "JR" and "SR" components.*

Rings furnished with conventional slotted-head and socket-head cap screws, wrench included.

Leupold "STD" Mount Bases fit these popular models:

Model	Firearm Model
STD BA	Browning Automatic Rifle, all calibers
STD BLA	Browning Lever Action
STD FN	FN Mauser and other rifles using this basic long action .
STD HC	Husqvarna Crown Grade, J. C. Higgins (after 1955), Smith & Wesson and HVA-Carl Gustaf
STD 336R	Marlin 36 and 336 Models and Western Field M/740
STD M	Mauser 95 and 98*
STD 700RH-LA	Remington 700, 721, 725 (long actions); Ruger M/77 (round receiver); and Weatherby Mark V
STD 700LH-LA	Remington 700 (left hand, long action)
STD 700RH-SA	Remington 700, 722, 725 and 40X (short actions)
STD 700SA-Spec	Long base for Remington Short Action 700
STD 760	Remington 740, 742, 760
STD 788	Remington 788 (long and extra long actions)
STD RBH	Ruger Black Hawk and other Ruger revolvers having adjustable rear sight*
STD 1022	Ruger 1022 Rimfire
STD R77	Ruger Model 77 (short or long action) w/Dovetail receiver*
STD 99R	Savage 99 Lever Action
STD 110RL	Savage 110, 110C, 111 (long action)
STD S&W-K	Smith & Wesson K-frame Revolver*
STD S	Springfield 1903*
STD S-Spec	Springfield 1903A3*
STD T/C-C	Thompson/Center Contender
STD T/C-H	Thompson/Center Hawken Rifle
STD 70A	All Winchester Model 70's above #66,350, not including .300 H&H and .375 H&H Magnums
STD W94	Winchester Model 94 Carbine*

*Drilling and tapping required.

Leupold Reticles

Specifications chart above shows reticles available in each Leupold scope.

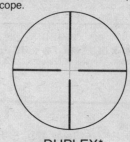

DUPLEX*

CPC

Dot

*Our most popular reticle by far.

CHOICE OF 3 RING HEIGHTS

.650″ 1″ LOW Rings
.770″ 1″ MEDIUM Rings
.900″ 1″ HIGH Rings

Leupold Extension Ring Sets

Reversible extended front ring, regular rear ring, in Low or Medium heights.

Special Colt .45 "Gold Cup" Ring Mount

Permits mounting of an M8-2X or M8-4X EXTENDED E.R. scope on a colt .45 "Gold Cup" National Match. Cross slots must be cut by a vertical mill.

LONDON GUN SIGHTS

DOVETAIL BASE FOR EXPRESS SIGHT

Available in large and small sizes.   **$19.95**

BRITISH STYLE EXPRESS SIGHT

Features one standing sight with three folding leaves. Made of steel.   **$49.95**

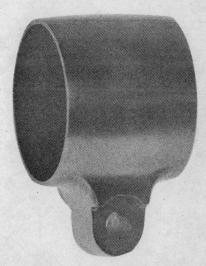

SCOPE MOUNT

Quick-detachable claw-style scope mount for Mauser 98 with 1″ rings. Scope pivots to rear to detach.   **$150.00**

BARREL BAND FOR QUICK-DETACHABLE SWIVELS

Available in three styles: standard quick-detachable swivels (SD), old-style Winchester quick-detachable swivels (W), and hook-style swivels (H). Twelve sizes available from .630 through .905; all made of steel.

SD & W	**$15.95**
H	**20.95**

LYMAN RIFLE SCOPES

A scope should be selected on the basis of power, or magnification. The lower powers will give the widest fields of view, excellent for snapshots of running game, or deer-stalking in dense woods. The higher powers with their narrow fields come into their own for long-range big-game hunting, and varmint shooting in particular.

There is no hard-and-fast rule when it comes to scope power. Four power scopes are generally considered best for all-around hunting, but many shooters prefer the pano-ramic view and easier holding of the lower powers. And other shooters will swear by the superb accuracy they derive from the high magnification of their scopes—even though the range is moderate anad the game fair-sized.

All Lyman scopes are made in standard crosshair, tap-ered post & crosshair, and tapered post reticles.

Various sizes of dot reticles are also availabale (at $10.00 additional) as follows:

½ MINUTE DOT in 8X and 10X model;
1 MINUTE DOT in 6X, 8X and 10X models;
2 MINUTE DOT in all models;
3 MINUTE DOT in 2½, 4, and 6X models;
4 MINUTE DOT in 2½ and 4X models.

Lyman 2½X . . . for big game, close-in brush country where wide field-of-view (43') at 100 yards permits easy "off-hand" shots at fast-moving targets. **$99.95**

Lyman 4X . . preferred for forest-and-plains shooting at big game. Ideal for distances of 75 - 300 yards and beyond, most often selected as "all-round" sight. **$124.95**

Lyman 6X . perfect for small game at long range, small game and varmints to 300 yds., and where most shooting is done from rest or prone. **$129.95**

Lyman 8 and 10X . . strictly long-range shooting, finest for varmints like crows, woodchucks, predator and other small animals where extremely accurate, pinpoint shooting is an absolute requirement.

8X **$169.95**
10X **179.95**

LYMAN RIFLE SCOPES

Lyman rifle scopes are made in 2½, 3, 4, 6, 8 and 10 power; all models are equipped with their new Perma-center reticule.

Specifications are shown below; descriptions and prices may be found on the following page.

SPECIFICATIONS OF LYMAN TELESCOPIC SIGHTS

Power	Length (Inches)	Weight (Ounces)	Tube Diameter (Inches)	Windage and Elevation Adjustment Click Values In Inches at 100 Yds.	Field of View in Feet at 100 Yards	Eye Distance or Relief Optimum (Inches)	Factory Pre-Set Parallax Corrected Range Optimum
2½ x	10½″	8¾ oz.	1 Inch	1 Inch or Minute of Angle	43 Feet	3¼″	100 Yds. To Infinity
4 x	12″	10¼ oz.	1 Inch	¾ Inch	36 Feet	3″	100 Yds. To Infinity
6 x	12¾″	11 oz.	1 Inch	½ Inch	24 Feet	3″	150 Yds. To Infinity
8 x	14⅝″	13 oz.	1 Inch	⅓ Inch	14 Feet	3¼″	Adjustable for Parallax Correction
10 x	15⅜″	13½ oz.	1 Inch	3/10 Inch	12 Feet	3¼″	Adjustable for Parallax Correction

2½

4x

LYMAN RIFLE SCOPES

LYMAN 1.75-5X VARIABLE SCOPE

$129.95

1.75-5X VARIABLE Specifications
LENGTH: 12¼", WEIGHT: 11⅓ oz.,
OUTSIDE DIAMETER, OBJECTIVE:
1.490", OUTSIDE DIAMETER,
EYEPIECE: 1.540", EYE RELIEF: 3",
FIELD OF VIEW (1.75X): 48' at 100 yds.,
FIELD OF VIEW (5X): 18' at 100 yds.,

1.75-5X

#7 Standard Crosswire	4 Center-range
Wires Cover	Center Wire Covers
2" (1.75X) at 100 yds.	2" (1.75X) at 100 yds.
1¼" (5X) at 100 yds.	1" (5X) at 100 yds.
4011707	4011704

LYMAN 2-7X VARIABLE SCOPE

$139.95

2-7X VARIABLE Specifications
LENGTH: 11⅝", WEIGHT: 10½ oz.,
OUTSIDE DIAMETER, OBJECTIVE:
1.500", OUTSIDE DIAMETER,
EYEPIECE: 1.570", EYE RELIEF: 3¼",
FIELD OF VIEW (2X): 49' at 100 yds.,
FIELD OF VIEW (7X): 19' at 100 yds.,

2-7X

#7 Standard Crosswire	4 Center-range
Wires Cover	Center Wire Covers
2" (2X) at 100 yds.	2" (2X) at 100 yds.
1¼" (7X) at 100 yds.	1" (7X) at 100 yds.
4233004	4233003

LYMAN 3-9X VARIABLE SCOPE

$149.95

#7 Standard Crosswire	4 Center-range
(3 X 9 Scope only)	
Center Wires Cover	Center Covers
1½" at 100 yds.	¼" at 100 yds.
½" at 100 yds.	¾" at 100 yds.

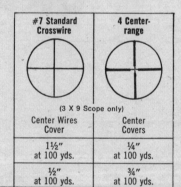

3-9 VARIABLE Specifications

Length	12½"
Weight	12 oz.
Tube Dia.	1"
Click Values	½" at 100 yds.
Field of View (3x)	39' at 100 yds.
Field of View (9x)	13' at 100 yds.
Eye Relief (3x)	3½"
Eye Relief (9x)	3½"

FEATURES
• Full magnification at all power settings. • Full field of view.
• Non-magnifying, constantly centered reticle • Finest quality, fully coated optical system to provide top light transmission.
• Ultra durable anodized exterior surface. • Matted interior surfaces to reduce stray light reflection. • Smooth control power ring, free of projections which could snag on clothing or straps.

LYMAN RIFLE SCOPES

The L.W.B.R. series rifle scopes have been designed to fulfill the demanding needs of today's benchrest, high-power, and small-bore rifleman. They are hand-assembled for dependable performance on the range.

SPECIFICATIONS:

20x L.W.B.R.
Length: .... 17″
Weight: .... 16 oz.
Tube Diameter: ....1″
Click Values: .... ⅛″ at 100 yds.
Field of View: ....5′6″ at 100 yds.
Eye Relief: ....3¼″
Price with standard reticle $259.95

SPECIFICATIONS:

25x L.W.B.R.
Length: .... 17″
Weight: .... 19 oz.
Tube Diameter: ....1″
Click Value: .... ⅛″ at 100 yds.
Field of View: ....4′8″
Eye Relief: ....3″
Price with standard reticle $289.95

SILHOUETTE

These scopes are designed for metallic silhouette competition and have been carefully constructed to withstand the punishment of adverse hunting conditions, while delivering the unexcelled performance inherent in Lyman's LWBR Target Rifle Scopes. They feature Lyman's exclusive hand-fit optical/mechanical system, parallax-adjustable objective lens with positive recoil-proof locking, Lyman hand-lapped, zero-repeat, windage and elevation systems, and external adjustment controls with zero reset, a feature allowing each user to preselect the zero reference point for his guns and loads.

SPECIFICATIONS:

6X—SL
Length: ....13⅞″
Weight: ....14¼ oz.
Tube Diameter: ....1″
Click Value : .... ½″ at 100 yds.

Field of View: ....20′ at 100 yds.
Price with external adjustments: $169.95

8X—SL
Length: ....14⅝″
Weight: ....15¼ oz.

Tube Diameter: ....1″
Click Values: .... ⅓″ at 100 yds.

Field of View: ....14′ at 100 yds.
Price with external adjustments: $179.95

10X—SL
Length: ....15⅜″
Weight: ....15¼ oz.
Tube Diameter: ....1″
Click Values: .... ⅓″ at 100 yds.

Field of View: ....12′ at 100 yds.
Price with external adjustments: $189.95

LYMAN RECEIVER SIGHTS

LYMAN 57 RECEIVER SIGHT: An unobtrusive micrometer receiver sight for hunting or target shooting with sporter, target or military rifle.

This sight is equipped with a push-button quick-release slide that makes it ideal for alternating use on a scope-equipped rifle.

Fully adjustable with audible ¼-minute clicks for windage and elevation. Choice of coin-slotted stayset knobs for hunting or finger operated target knobs.

Slide adjustments are equipped with precision scales to aid in pre-setting sights for specific ranges or wind conditions. Slide furnished with elevation stop screw that facilitates return to "zero" if removed and re-attached.

Slide operates in dovetail channel.

No. 57 Receiver Sight, complete **$28.00**

LYMAN 66 RECEIVER SIGHT: Similar in design and construction to the No. 57 receiver sight, the model 66 was designed specifically for autoloading, pump-action and lever-action rifles. Ideally suited for use on the new Ruger .44 Carbine.

Features include ¼-minute click adjustments for windage and elevation, quick release slide, and elevation stop screw for return to "zero" if detached.

Push button release features of slide facilitates speedy removal and re-attachment.

May be had with choice of coin-slotted stayset hunting knobs or target knobs.

Like the model 48 and 57 this sight is furnished with settings scales for easy reference.

No. 66 Receiver Sight, complete **$28.00**

NO. 57 SIGHT

NO. 66 SIGHT

TARGET FRONT SIGHTS

SIGHT HEIGHT*

17AHB	.360"	17AMI	.445"	17AUG	.532"
17AHI	.360"	17ASF	.500"		

*From bottom of dovetail to center of aperture.

SERIES 17A TARGET FRONTS

Teamed with a Lyman receiver sight, these low silhouette front sights provide precise, X-ring accuracy on the range. Designed for use with dovetail slot mounting, they are supplied with seven interchangeable inserts (see descriptions below) that are locked into place with a threaded cap.

Price:
Series 17A Target Front Sight
Complete with Inserts....$12.00

INSERTS FOR USE WITH SERIES 17A SIGHTS

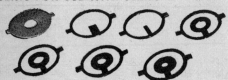

Set includes: two post type inserts (.100" and .050" wide), five aperture type inserts (1 plastic .120" hole insert and four steel inserts with .070", .093", .110", and .120" holes).

Price: Complete Set of Inserts for Series 17A or 77 Sights............. **$4.00**

424

Despite the exceptionally sharp definition provided by a fine aperture receiver sight, an equally fine front sight is necessary for consistently accurate shooting—particularly in extreme glare and overcast in the field. Lyman ivory bead front sights are the ideal field front sights. They present a flat optical surface that's equally illuminated by bright or dull light, and they keep their "color" under all light conditions. The Lyman ivory bead front sight is the perfect teammate for your favorite Lyman receiver sight, and will give you a reliable, sharply defined, glareless aiming surface, even under the worst conditions. You can fit a readily adaptable Lyman bead front sight to your rifle in minutes.

These illustrations show the size and appearance difference between the two standard base widths. In general, the outside diameter of the barrel determines the width of the base to be used. "A" width is used with most ramps.

DOVETAIL TYPE FRONT SIGHTS (first letter following number of sight gives the height, the second letter the width)

DOVETAIL FRONTS

No. 31
O 1/16" BEAD

No. 37
O 3/32" BEAD

NO. 31 AND NO. 37 FRONT SIGHTS . . . Identical except for bead size, these sights are designed to be used on ramps. Standard 3/8" dovetail. Choice of ivory or gold bead. See Sight Selection Chart.

Price: No. 31 or No. 37 Front Sight . . . $5.50

No. 3
O 1/16" BEAD

No. 28
O 3/32" BEAD

NO. 3 AND NO. 28 FRONT SIGHTS . . . Identical except for bead size, these sights are mounted directly in the barrel dovetail. 3/8" dovetail is standard but the sights are also available for narrow Mauser, Enfield, or Mannlicher-Schoenauer dovetail. Choice of ivory, silver, gold, or red bead. See Sight Selection Chart.

Price: No. 3 or No. 28 Front Sight $5.50

MODELS SUPPLIED		Height Inches	Width Inches
1/16" bead	3/32" bead		
31BA	37BA	.240	11/32
31CA	37CA	.290	11/32
3CF	28CF	.290	17/32
31FA	37FA	.330	11/32
		.330	7/16
3FF	28FF	.330	17/32
31GA	37GA	.345	11/32
		.345	7/16
3GF	28GF	.345	17/32
31HA	37HA	.360	11/32
		.360	7/16
3HF	28HF	.360	17/32
31JA	37JA	.390	11/32
		.390	7/16
3JF	28JF	.390	17/32
31KA	37KA	.410	11/32
		.410	7/16
3KF	28KF	.410	17/32
31MA	37MA	.445	11/32
		.445	7/16
3MF	28MF	.445	17/32
31SA	37SA	.500	11/32
		.500	7/16
3SF	28SF	.500	17/32
31VA	37A	.560	11/32
		.560	7/16
3VF	28VF	.560	17/32

RAMP FRONT SIGHTS

18E

18A

18C

NO. 18 SCREW-ON TYPE RAMP . . . The screw-on ramp is designed to be secured with a heavy 8-40 screw (it may be brazed on if desired). Screw-on ramps are ruggedly built and extremely versatile. They use A width front sights, and are available in the following heights:

18A — Low Ramp: .100" from top of barrel to bottom of dovetail.

18C — Medium Ramp: .250" from top of barrel to bottom of dovetail.

18E — High Ramp: .350" from top of barrel to bottom of dovetail.

Price:
No. 18 Screw-On Ramp Complete With Sight $13.00
No. 18 Screw-On Ramp Less Sight 7.50

LYMAN SIGHTS

LEAF SIGHTS

NO. 16 FOLDING LEAF SIGHT... Designed primarily as open rear sights with adjustable elevation, leaf sights make excellent auxiliary sights for scope-mounted rifles. They fold close to the barrel when not in use, and they can be installed and left on the rifle without interfering with scope or mount. Two lock screws hold the elevation blade adjustments firmly in place. A sight of this type could save the day if the scope becomes damaged through rough handling. Leaf sights are available in the following heights:

16A —.400" high; elevates to .500".
16B —.345" high; elevates to .445".
16C —.500" high; elevates to .600".

For installation on rifles without a dovetail slot, use Lyman No. 25 Base.

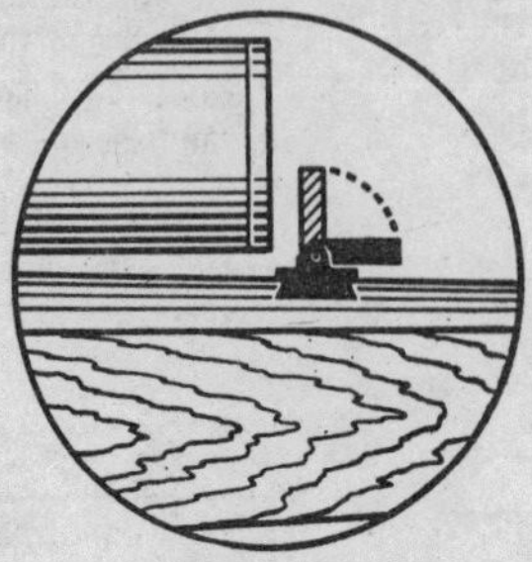

SIGHT FOLDS TO CLEAR SCOPE

GRADUATED BLADE ELEVATES BY SLIDING IN ELONGATED SCREW HOLES

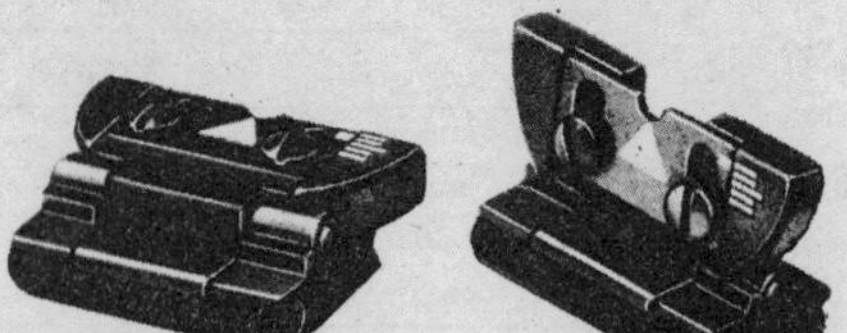

A "Patridge" type blade for the No. 16A Folding Leaf Sight is offered as an auxiliary blade.

Price:
No. 16 Folding Leaf Sight...... **$6.50**

BASES

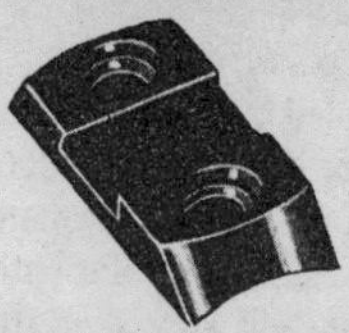

NO. 25 BASES

Permit the installation of dovetail rear sights such as Lyman 16 leaf sight on rifles that do not have dovetail cut in barrel. They also supply a higher line of sight when needed. The No. 25 Base is mounted by drilling and tapping the barrel for two 6-48 screws. Screws are supplied with base.

Price: No. 25 Base **$5.50**

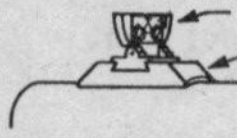

STANDARD BASES	HEIGHT FROM TOP OF BARREL to BOTTOM of DOVETAIL	BARREL RADIUS
25A-Base (Low)	.025—	.875 or larger
25C-Base (High)	.125—	.875 or larger
SPECIAL BASES		
25B-Base Fits factory screw holes on Remington 740, 742, 760, 725 & replaces factory rear	.125—	.875 or larger
25D-Base For small diameter barrels, Note Radius	.025—	For Barrels under .875 dia.

NOTE: For gunsmith use — 25A, C and D bases are also available in the white (unblued), and without screw holes. Heights and radii as above. **Price: $1.25**

NO. 12 SLOT BLANKS

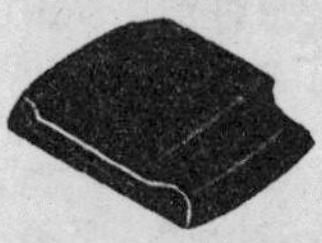

These Blanks fill the standard 3/8" rear barrel dovetail when a receiver sight is installed. They are also available for front sight dovetails and ramps when a scope is being used. Three lengths are available, all fit standard 3/8" dovetails.

No. 12S (3/8" x 5/8" long) for standard rear barrel slots.
No. 12SS (3/8" x 9/16" long) for standard front sight slots and some rear slots in narrow barrels.
No. 12SF (3/8" x 11/32" long) this blank has square ends and is intended for use in ramps.

Price: (all sizes) **$2.00**

SHOTGUN SIGHTS

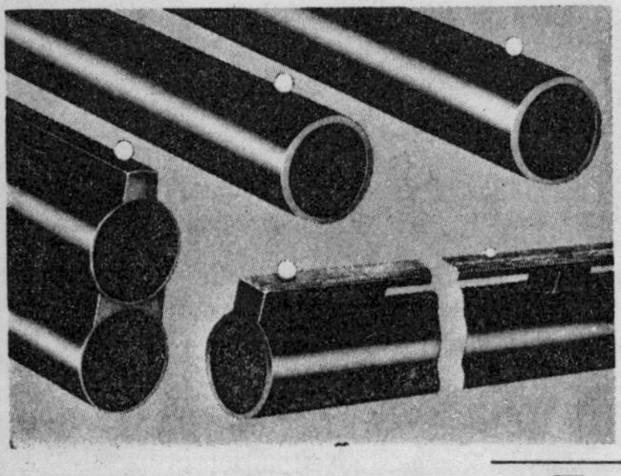

SHOTGUN SIGHTS .... Lyman shotgun sights are available for all shotguns. Equipped with oversized ivory beads that give perfect definition on either bright, or dull days, they are easy to see under any light conditions. They quickly catch your eye on fast upland targets, and point out the lead on long passing shots. Lyman shotgun sights are available with WHITE or RED bead, and can be fitted to your gun in minutes.

NO. 10 FRONT SIGHT (Press Fit) for use on double barrel, or ribbed single barrel guns. Sight **$2.00**

NO. 10D FRONT SIGHT (Screw Fit) for use on non-ribbed single barrel guns. These sights are supplied with a wrench. Sight & Wrench **$2.50**

NO. 11 MIDDLE SIGHT (Press Fit) This small middle sight is intended for use on double barrel and ribbed single barrel guns. Sight **$2.00**

NO. 9 SET — This set consists of both the No. 10 and No. 11 sight listed above. Set **$4.00**

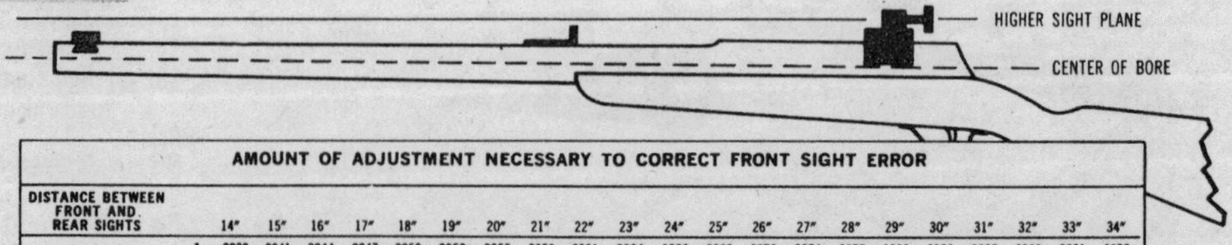

When you replace an open rear sight with a receiver sight, it is usually necessary to install a higher front sight, to compensate for the higher plane of the new receiver sight. The table below shows the increase in front sight height that's required to compensate for a given error at 100 yards.

AMOUNT OF ADJUSTMENT NECESSARY TO CORRECT FRONT SIGHT ERROR

DISTANCE BETWEEN FRONT AND REAR SIGHTS		14"	15"	16"	17"	18"	19"	20"	21"	22"	23"	24"	25"	26"	27"	28"	29"	30"	31"	32"	33"	34"
Amount of Error at 100 Yards Given in Inches	1	.0038	.0041	.0044	.0047	.0050	.0053	.0055	.0058	.0061	.0064	.0066	.0069	.0072	.0074	.0077	.0080	.0082	.0085	.0088	.0091	.0093
	2	.0078	.0083	.0089	.0094	.0100	.0105	.0111	.0116	.0122	.0127	.0133	.0138	.0144	.0149	.0155	.0160	.0156	.0171	.0177	.0182	.0188
	3	.0117	.0125	.0133	.0142	.0150	.0159	.0167	.0175	.0184	.0192	.0201	.0209	.0217	.0226	.0234	.0243	.0251	.0259	.0268	.0276	.0285
	4	.0155	.0167	.0178	.0189	.0200	.0211	.0222	.0234	.0244	.0255	.0266	.0278	.0289	.0300	.0311	.0322	.0333	.0344	.0355	.0366	.0377
	5	.0194	.0208	.0222	.0236	.0250	.0264	.0278	.0292	.0306	.0319	.0333	.0347	.0361	.0375	.0389	.0403	.0417	.0431	.0445	.0458	.0472
	6	.0233	.0250	.0267	.0283	.0300	.0317	.0333	.0350	.0367	.0384	.0400	.0417	.0434	.0450	.0467	.0484	.0500	.0517	.0534	.0551	.0567

EXAMPLE: Suppose your rifle has a 27 inch sight radius, and shoots 4 inches high at 100 yards, with the receiver sight adjusted as low as possible. The 27 inch column shows that the correction for a 4 inch error is .0300 inch. This correction is added to the over-all height of the front sight (including dovetail). Use a micrometer or similar accurate device to measure sight height. Thus, if your original sight measured .360 inch, it should be replaced with a sight .390 inch high, such as a J height sight.

MERIT SHOOTING AIDS

MERIT IRIS SHUTTER MASTER TARGET DISC

WITH
FLEXIBLE NEOPRENE LIGHT SHIELD

May be cut to size

Particularly adapted for use with extension, telescope height and tang sights . . .

PATENT PENDING

• The 1½" in diameter flexible neoprene light shield is permanently attached to the eye cup which is replaceable by removing three screws. The shield is concentrically ribbed on its concave face for cutting to suitable size. It is more advantageous than a large metal disc since it protects the sighting equipment in case the disc is accidentally bumped.

• The Master Target Disc may be used on all sights having clearance for a disc 7/16" thick and 3/4" or larger in diameter.

Master Disc . . .	$30.00
MERIT DELUX Master Disc . . .	37.00
Replacement Shield	5.50
Delux Replacement Shield and Steel Cup	6.50

THE MERIT LENS DISC is made with any of the No. 3 Series shanks. The body of the Standard Lens Disc is 7/16" thick . . . the Master Target Lens Disc is ¾" thick . . . Outside diameters are the same as shown for No. 3 Series and Master Target Discs. The Merit Lens Disc is properly cushioned to absorb recoil shock.

MERIT DELUX No. 3 Lens Disc	$37.00
MERIT DELUX Master Lens Disc . . .	43.75

MERIT No. 4SS—Outside diameter of disc ½". Shank 5/16" long. Disc thickness ¼". **$24.00**

MERIT No. 4LS—Outside diameter of disc ½". Shank 11/32" long. Disc thickness ¼". **24.00**

MERIT No. 4ELS—Outside diameter of disc ½". Shank ½" long. Disc thickness ¼". **24.00**

SIGHT CHART

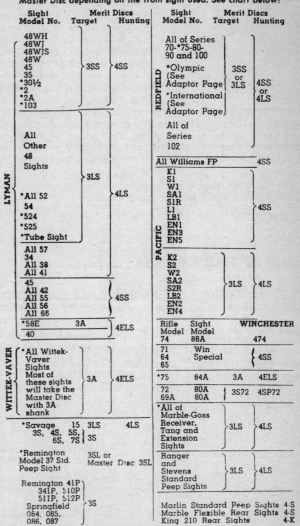

Popular Peep Sights and the proper Merit Discs to fit them. The Merit Master Target Disc may be had with any of the No. 3 series shanks. All of the sights marked ★ will take the Master Disc depending on the front sight used. See chart below:

LYMAN

Sight Model No.	Target	Hunting
48WH, 48WJ, 48WJS, 48W, 45, 35, *30½, *2, *2A, *103	3SS	4SS
All Other 48 Sights	3LS	
*All 52, 54, *524, *525, *Tube Sight		4LS
All 57, 34, All 38, All 41		
45, All 42, All 55, All 56, All 66		4SS
*58E	3A	4ELS
40		

WITTEK-VAVER

Sight Model No.	Target	Hunting
*All Wittek-Vaver Sights. Most of these sights will take the Master Disc with 3A shank	3A	4ELS
*Savage 15, 3S, 4S, 5S, 6S, 7S	3LS / 3S	4LS
*Remington Model 37 Std. Peep Sight	3SL or Master Disc 3SL	
Remington 41P, 341P, 510P, 511P, 512P, Springfield 084, 085, 086, 087	3S	

REDFIELD

Sight Model No.	Target	Hunting
All of Series 70-*75-80-90 and 100	3SS	4SS
*Olympic (See Adaptor Page)	3SS or 3LS	4SS or 4LS
*International (See Adaptor Page)		
All of Series 102		
All Williams FP		4SS

PACIFIC

Sight Model No.	Target	Hunting
K1, S1, W1, SA1, S1R, L1, LB1, EN1, EN3, EN5		4SS
K2, S2, W2, SA2, S2R, LB2, EN2, EN4	3LS	4LS

WINCHESTER

Rifle Model	Sight Model	WINCHESTER
74	88A	474
71, 64, 65	Win Special	4SS
*75	84A	3A 4ELS
72, 69A	80A, 80A	3S72 4SP72

Sight Model No.	Target	Hunting
*All of Marble-Goss Receiver, Tang and Extension Sights	3LS	4LS
Ranger and Stevens Standard Peep Sights	3LS	4LS

Marlin Standard Peep Sights 4-S
Marble Flexible Rear Sights 4-S
King 210 Rear Sights 4-K

THE MERIT OPTICAL ATTACHMENT WITH APERTURE IS THE ANSWER TO A SHOOTER'S PROBLEM WHEN THE EYESIGHT IS IMPAIRED.

(1) concentrates and sharpens the vision by increasing the focal depth of the eye, making pistol or rifle sights stand out sharp and clear; (2) Cuts out objectionable side lights; (3) Helps the shooter to take the same position for each shot. (This is a very vital factor in accurate shooting;) (4) Gives instant and easy choice of just the right aperture suiting your own eye and particular conditions at time of shooting.

Delux Optical Attachment Price: **$29.40**
The Delux model has swinging arm feature so that the shooter can swing the aperture from the line of vision when not shooting.

Replacement suction cup—Price **$4.50**

MICRO SIGHTS FOR HANDGUNS

The Micro Sight is small and compact. The sight is attached to models with dovetail slot for rear and removable front sights in the same manner as the factory sight. The rear sight has positive self-locking click adjustments in both windage and elevation. Each click changes point of impact ½" at twenty-five yards. Once set—the sight is constant and will not move from recoil. The sighting radius is raised, allowing for a deep notch in the rear aperture. This added depth gives the shooter sharper definition and eliminates glare. It is necessary to install a higher front sight to conform with the rear.

Front sight blades are available in : ⅛"
The styles are plain post or quick-draw.

ADJUSTABLE REAR SIGHTS with BLADE FRONT SIGHTS
for the following:

IP Standard Adj. sights for Colt 45 ACP & 45 Commander; and Star Model "B" 9m/m	
2P Standard Adj. sights for Colt 38 Super, 9 MM & 38 Commander	
3P Low Mount Adj. sights for Colt 45 ACP and 45 Commander	
4P Low Mount Adj. sights for Colt 38 Super, 9 MM & 38 Commander	
5P Low Mount Adj. sights for Colt 22 Service Ace & 22/45 Conversion unit	
15P Colt M. T. Woodsman, Postwar	
16P Colt Target Woodsman, Postwar	
17P Colt M. T. Woodsman, Prewar	$22.00
19P Colt 22 Officers Model Match & Officers Model Special	
20P Colt 38 Officers Model Match & Officers Model Special	
23P Ruger 22 Standard Sport Model	
25P High Standard Sport King, 102 Series	
26P Browning 9m/m Hi-Power	
27P Browning 9MM Hi-Power LOW MT	

Adjustable Micro Rear only	$18.00
Micro Front Blade only	4.00
MICRO front ramp only—less blade	5.00
MICRO blade only for front ramp	4.00
MICRO-TITE barrel bushing for Colt 45 Govt Model	7.50
MICRO barrel bushing wrench	1.25
MICRO insert only for rear sight	1.25

TYPES OF MICRO FRONT BLADE SIGHTS

Quick Draw   Plain Post

WIDTH OF FRONT BLADES ⎕ 1/8"

INTERCHANGEABILITY OF MICRO ADJUSTABLE REAR SIGHTS

Group #1—IP 2P QR RR 28P 3R 4R 5R 7R 29P
Group #2—3P 4P 5P 16P 17P 19P 20P 27P 25P
Group #3—6P 13P 14P SR
Group #4—7P 18P TR
Group #5—8P 21P
Group #6—BR CR DR ER FR GR HR IR JR KR LR MR NR OR PR ZR 8R 9R
Group #7—VR WR
Group #8—UR YR 6R
Group #9—XR 25P

INTERCHANGEABILITY OF MICRO FRONT SIGHTS

Group #4—15P 20P
Group #6—BR FR
Group #7—ER HR
Group #8—JR MR
Group #9—KR NR OR PR
Group #10—LR QR 3R

ADJUSTABLE REAR SIGHTS with RAMP FRONT SIGHTS
for the following:

AR	Ruger Single Six	$26.00
BR	Smith & Wesson 38 Military Police	26.00
CR	Colt 38 Official Police	26.00
DR	Colt 22 Official Police	26.00
ER	Smith & Wesson 1917 45 Revolver	26.00
FR	Smith & Wesson 38/44	26.00
GR	Smith & Wesson 44 Special	26.00
HR	Smith & Wesson 1950 45	26.00
IR	Colt Single Action 22	26.00
JR	Colt Single Action 38	26.00
KR	Colt Single Action 45	26.00
LR	Great Western 22	26.00
MR	Great Western 38	26.00
NR	Great Western 45	26.00
OR	Colt New Service 38	26.00
PR	Colt New Service 45	26.00
QR	Colt Challenger 22	26.00
RR	Colt Sport Model Woodsman (Prewar)	26.00
VR	Supermatic Trophy & Citation	26.00
WR	Supermatic Tournament	26.00
XR	102 Series Sport King & Duramatic	26.00
ZR	Colt Scout 22	26.00
2R	Browning 9MM Hi-Power	26.00
3R	Colt Huntsman	26.00
4R	Colt Targetsman	26.00
5R	Colt Navy Cap & Ball	26.00
6R	Hawes 44 Rem Cap & Ball	26.00
7R	Navy Arms 44 Rem Cap & Ball	26.00
8R	Hy Hunter Six Shooter 357	26.00

(RAMP STYLE NOT MADE FOR 45 GOVT)

PACHMAYR SCOPE MOUNTS

(FOR 1-INCH & 26 M/M SCOPES)

PACHMAYR LO-SWING® SCOPE MOUNT

Combines two important advantages in one mount. Provides instant use of open sights and a scope mounted as low as possible on your rifle. Don't let fogged lenses or a damaged scope spoil your chance for a kill. Guaranteed to maintain zero alignment no matter how many times removed or swung to the side. Side mount $30.00 top mount $35.00

Exploded view of Lo-Swing Top Mount showing exclusive Pachmayr spherical eccentric bearing windage & elevation adjustment principle.

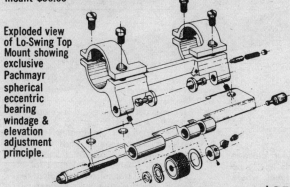

TOP MOUNTS   Available for: $35.00

MAKE OF GUN	GUN MODELS	MOUNT NO.
Remington	700, 721, 725 (long actions)	R700 RT
	700, 722, 725 (short actions)	R700 RT
	700 L.H. (long action)	R700 L.H. RT
	700 L.H. (short action)	R700 L.H. ST
	720, 30	R30T
	600	R600T
	(**660)	R600T
	740	
	742 Ser. 184, 499 & below	R7 40T
	742 Ser. 184, 500 & up	R742BDLT
	760 Ser. 443, 499 & below	R740T
	760 Ser. 443, 500 & up	R742 BDLT
	788 short action	R788S-T
	788 long action	R788L-T
	788 extra long action	R788X-T
	141	R141-T
Winchester		
	Win. 70 - 670, 770 All calibers, except .300 & .375 H&H Mag., above Serial No. 66,350	W 70T
	Win. 70 .300 / .375 H&H Mag., above Serial No. 700,000	W70MT
	Win. 70 Target	W70 TGT
	Win. 70 .300 & .375 H&H Mag., between Serial Nos. 66,350 and 700,000	W70 TGT
	Win. 70 All Cals. except .300 & .375 H&H Mag., below Serial No. 66,350	W70 T
	Win. 70 .300 & .375 H&H Mag., below Serial No. 66,350	W70 TGT
	88 & 100	W-88T
Savage	99	S-99T
	110 R.H. Long Action	S-110 RHT
	110 L.H. Long Action	S-110 LHT
	110 short action R.H.	S-110 RHST
	110 short action L.H.	S-110 LHST
	**24V	S-24VT
Sako	Finnbear	SK-FIT
	Forester	SK-FOT
	Vixen	SK-VT
Marlin	**336, 1895, 44	M-336T
	**1894	M-1894T
Mauser	98 (large ring long action)	MR-T
	Yugoslav 1924 (lrg. Rg. sht. act.)	YU-T
	Kar 98 (sm. ring, long action)	KA-T
	Mexican (sm. ring, short action)	Mex-T
	FN (std. FN action)	FN-T
	Santa Fe (FN action spec. hole spacing)	MSF-T
	66 (dovetail receiver)	MR66T
	2000	MR2000T
	4000	M-4000T

**Due to special stop pin lengths, these bases should be ordered only with matching loop.

Mossberg	800	MO-800T
	810	MO-810T
	472	MO-472T
Krico	Varmint	KRICO-T
Husqvarna	Short action (small ring)	HV-SRT
	Long action (large ring)	HV-T
Springfield	03-06	SPR-03T
	03/A3	SPR-A3T
Enfield	Eddystone	EN-T
Schultz & Larsen	Regular	SLR-T
	Magnum	SLM-T
Ruger	44	R-44T
	10/22	R-22T
	M-77 RS long (dovetail)	R77-RS-LT
	M-77 RS short (dovetail)	R77-RS-ST
	M-77 ST long (round)	R77-ST-LT
	No. 1	R. No. 1T
Browning Sako	222, 222 Magnum	B469-T
	243. 308, 22-250	B479-T
Browning	Safari	FN-T
	Short Action	BRO-S-T
	Semi-auto. rifle	BRO-SAT
	Lever action	BRO-LAT
BSA Monarch	Dovetail rec. long action	BSA-TR
	Dovetail rec. short action	BSA-TS
	Round Receiver Long Action	R 700 RT
	Round Receiver Short Action	R 700 ST
Weatherby	Mark V, left hand Vangard, LH	WLH-T
	Mark V, Vangard, RH	R700 RT
Parker Hale Harrington	1200 & P1200	FN-T
Richardson	300 & 301	FN-T
Smith & Wesson	A, B, C, D, E	HV-SRT
Ranger Arms	Texas Maverick	RA-TMV
	Texas Magnum 458	RA-458-T
	Texas Magnum 375	RA-375-T
Interarms	Mark X	FN-T
Voere Shikar		VST

SIDE MOUNTS   Available for: $30.00

MAKE OF GUN	GUN MODELS	MOUNT NO.
Winchester	54, 70	W-70
	64, 94, Rem. 121, 241	W-94
	Model 12 shotgun	W-12
	88, 100	W-88
Remington	Enfield 30S, R720	Enf
	8, 81	R-81
	141, 14	R-14
	721, 722, 725 and 700 series	R-721
	740, 760, 742	R-740
	Shotgun 1100	R-1100
	870	R-1100
Savage	40, 45 and Ariska, Husqvarna Cr., Swedish Mauser	S-40
	20, Japanese 25	S-20
	99	S-99
	340, 342, Sako .222	S-340
	24 DL	S-24 DL
Springfield	1903, A3, 1922, Sedley-Newton	Spr.
Stevens	325C, 322 Sako L 46	S-325C
Marlin	36A, 336	M-36
	39A	M-39
Mauser	93	S-40
	98	MR
	FN 1949 Auto	FN 49A
	All FN Bolt Actions	MR
Mauser Carbine	Carbine Brno	MC
Mannlicher-Schoenauer	1950 or later	MS
Krag..		K
Garand Brng. Std. - Rem. 11	Military auto 30/06, 308	M-1
	Shotguns	B-R
Military	*Carbine 30M1	M-1 Carbine
Lee Enfield	SMLE No. 1, Mk. 1, 2, 3.	L-Enf A
	SMLE No. 4 Mk.1	L-Enf B
Ithaca	37	W-12
Ruger	Mini. 14	Ru-14

*Due to near vertical shell ejection, it is recommended that these bases be used with a left hand loop and a crosshair reticle scope.

REDFIELD SCOPES

Traditional
Fixed Power

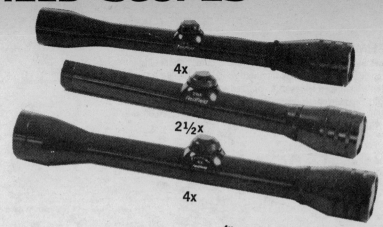

4x

The Traditional's ¾" tube, at 6½ ozs. and a compact 9½" long, is the perfect complement to a .22 or other small caliber rifle. This scope is hermetically sealed to prevent fogging. The Traditional features precision-ground coated glass lenses throughout for precise resolution. This tough scope is designed and tested to withstand the recoil of magnum caliber rifles.

4x
¾" Tube Diameter

Reticle	Price
4-Plex	$49.75

Lens Covers	Price
Storm Queen	$7.70

6X

This traditional 6x eyepiece gives extra magnification for longer ranges. Has all the famous Redfield features including tough aluminum alloy construction, coated lenses. Hermetically sealed, 1" tube diameter.

Reticle	Price
4-Plex	$124.95

2½x

Provides a 43' field of view for close-in type brush hunting. Complements any "slug gun package" for use on shotguns where slugs are used for deer hunting. All the features of the 4x.

2½x
1" Tube Diameter

Reticle	Price
4-Plex	$93.75
PCH	93.75

4x

Efficient performance at a moderate price for hunters who prefer a medium power scope. All the quality Redfield features: unscratchable, hard anodized finish. Magnum proof. Streamlined Redfield look. Coated glass lenses for increased light transmission. Brilliant distortion-free resolution. Hermetically sealed with O-rings to prevent fogging.

4x
1" Tube Diameter

Reticle	Price
4-Plex	$109.40

Lens Covers	Price
Storm Queen	$7.70

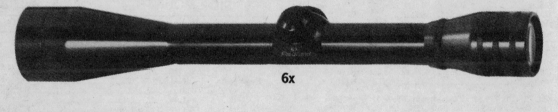

6x

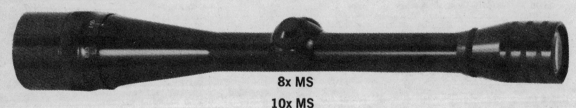

8x MS
10x MS
12x MS

Metallic Silhouette Scopes: Designed to furnish precise point of impact change at all ranges. Adjustable objective lens assembly eliminates parallax/focus error at ranges from 50 feet to infinity. Marked in yards and meters, including 385 for turkey. Also useful as a varmint scope.

8x MS

1" Tube Diameter	Price
Reticle	$191.00
4-Plex	191.00

10x MS

1" Tube Diameter	Price
Reticle	$205.30
4-Plex	205.30

12x MS

1" Tube Diameter	Price
Reticle	$221.35
4-Plex	221.35

Traditional

Variable Power

2x-7x

3x-9x

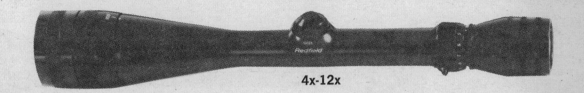

4x-12x

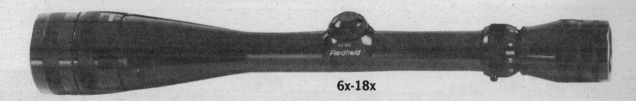

6x-18x

2x-7x

This model of the Traditional line gives the same advantages of the 4x Traditional, but with the added benefit of a popular variable power range.

2x-7x
1" Tube Diameter

Reticle	Price
4-Plex	$147.35
PCH	117.90
AT 4-Plex	174.15

Lens Covers	Price
Storm Queen	$7.70

3x-9x

Actually works like three scopes in one. At 3x, it's perfect for close-in woods and brush hunting. At 4x-6x, it handles normal open range hunting. And at 9x, it's ideal for long range spotting and shooting.

3x-9x
1" Tube Diameter

Reticle	Price
4-Plex	$177.70
3x9x Accu-Range Variable	
AT 4-Plex	$204.50

Lens Covers	Price
Storm Queen	$7.70

3x-9x ROYAL

A rifle scope made specially for heavy recoil magnum rifles. Offers you an extra ½" eye relief for high recoil magnum rifles. One piece tube construction. Anodized finished.

3x-9x Royal

Reticle	Price
4-Plex	$196.35

3x-9x Royal Accu-Range Variable

Reticle	Price
AT 4-Plex	$223.15

4x-12x

Power to go after everything from varmints to big game. Parallax-Focus (from 50 yards to infinity) on the objective bell is clearly marked and easy to adjust . . . an important feature for varmint and bench-rest shooters to whom the higher power range is vital. Positive stops prevent over-turning of the parallax adjusting sleeve.

4x-12x Variable
1" Tube Diameter

Reticle	Price
CH	$249.95
4-Plex	249.95
AT 4-Plex	276.75

Lens Covers	Price
Storm Queen	$7.70

6x-18x

A favored scope of higher power for varmint hunting and bench-rest shooting. Excellent field of view at all power settings with Parallax-Focus adjustment from 50 yards to infinity. Stops at either end prevent over-turning of this adjustment.

6x-18x Variable
1" Tube Diameter

Reticle	Price
CH	$276.75
4-Plex	276.75
AT 4-Plex	303.55

Lens Covers	Price
Storm Queen	$7.70

Widefield

**Low Profile
Fixed Power**

2¾ x LP

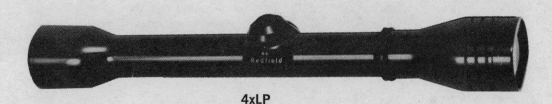

4xLP

6x LP

2¾ x LP

A rugged and efficient lower magnification scope with a 55.5′ field of view at 100 yards. For comparatively short range brush and/or slug gun hunting. Even in poor light, dawn or dusk, moving targets are easy to locate.

2¾ x LP
1″ Tube Diameter

Reticle	Price
PCH	$124.95
4-Plex	124.95

Lens Covers	Price
Storm Queen	$7.70

4x LP

The most popular fixed-power member of the Widefield LP family. Outstanding field of view in an all-purpose, all-around scope with the flexibility to handle close-in shots or those at moderately long range.

4x LP
1″ Tube Diameter

Reticle	Price

4x LP
1″ Tube Diameter

Reticle	Price
PCH	$142.80
4-Plex	142.80

Lens Covers	Price
Storm Queen	$7.70

6x LP

A scope for long ranges in wide open spaces or big mountain country. The combination of 6x magnification and 30% extra field of view has caused many hunters to switch from lower-powered scopes. A proven complement to all-around, flat-shooting sporting rifles for medium to long range varmint hunting.

6x LP
1″ Tube Diameter

Reticle		Price
4-Plex		$157.10

Lens Covers		Price
Storm Queen	022	$7.70

REDFIELD SCOPES

widefield
Low Profile
Variable Power

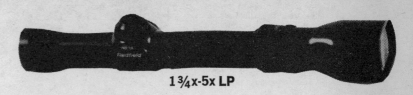

1¾x-5x LP

2x-7x LP

3x-9xLP

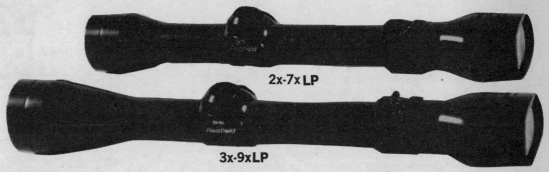

1¾x-5x LP

Ideal for fast, accurate close-in brush and slug shooting . . . the field of view at 100 yards at 1¾x is an outstanding 70 feet. Ample magnification is provided at 5x for longer ranges.

1¾x-5x Variable LP
1" Tube Diameter

Reticle	Price
PCH	$160.65
4-Plex	160.65

Lens Covers	Price
Storm Queen	$7.70

2x-7x LP

For the all-purpose hunter . . . smaller than the 3x-9x for conventional scabbards, tough enough to handle most any hunting situation or range.

2x-7x Variable LP
1" Tube Diameter

Reticle	Price
PCH	$178.50
4-Plex	178.50
2x-7x Accu-Trac Variable	
AT 4-Plex	205.30

Lens Covers	Price
Storm Queen	$7.70

3x-9x LP

All the versatility and rugged dependability for big game and varmint hunting are built into this model. It fulfills a variety of purposes from long-range, peak-to-peak spotting and shooting to shorter ranges in wooded situations and poor light conditions.

3x-9x Variable LP
1" Tube Diameter

Reticle	Price
PCH	$214.35
4-Plex	214.35
3x-9x Accu-Trac Variable	
AT 4-Plex	241.10

Lens Covers	Price
Storm Queen	$7.70

SPECIFICATIONS:

Power	2½x	1½x
Field @ 100 yds. (m)	9' (2.7m)	14' (4.3m)
Eye relief	14"-24"	19"-32"
	(35-60cm)	(48-81cm)
Overall length	Both 9.82" (24.9cm)	
Diameter of tube	Both 1" (2.54cm)	
Outside diameter of objective end	Both 1" (2.54cm)	
Outside diameter of eyepiece	Both 1.515" (3.8cm)	
Clear aperture of objective lens	Both .725" (1.84cm)	
Weight	Both 10.5 oz. (297g)	
Internal adjustment graduation (in @ 100 yds.) (cm @ 100m)	Both 1" (2.54cm)	
Maximum internal adjustment (in. @ 100 yds.) (m @ 100m)	Both 120" (3m)	
Reticle adjustment	Internal	Internal
Finish	Anodize H.C.	Anodize H.C.
Exit pupil	8mm	13mm
Reticles available	4-Plex	4-Plex

REDFIELD PISTOL SCOPE

1½x Traditional Fixed Power

1½x PS 4-Plex	$108.95

2½x Traditional Fixed Power

2½x PS 4-Plex	$114.30

REDFIELD SCOPES

Accu-Trac™ Variables

Combines Accu-Range® feature with 3 trajectory compensating dials: one of which will fit any popular bullet weight and caliber. Tells you the distance to your target, then, by dialing that distance in the window of the elevation dial, hold zero-on target without holdover. Eliminates holdover guesswork at any range out to 600 yards. Blank dial available for special handloaded cartridges. Available on all Redfield Variables except the 1¾x-5x LP Wildefield.

The RM 6400 16x, 20x and 24x target scopes are offered with FCH reticles. These scopes combine the outstanding optical quality of the 3200 and allow the additional feature of receiver of barrel mounting.

RM target scopes weigh only 18 ounces and are only 17 inches long. The Model RM 6400 offers a 25% wider field of view than the Model 3200. For example, in 16x it's 6.5 feet at 100 yards against 5.2 feet for the Model 3200. Either ⅛ MOA or ¼ MOA click (accuracy to ± 1/32 MOA) adjustment knobs are provided. This permits immediate adjustment with pinpoint accuracy for serious target and varmint shooters. Packaged in a handsome high-styrene carrying case.

RETICLE		PRICE
16X FCH		$265.20
20X FCH		$274.15
24X FCH		$283.10

RM 6400

RETICLE		PRICE
16X FCH		$296.50
20X FCH		$296.50
24X FCH		$296.50

⅛' and ⅜' dots are available at additional cost

The 3200 Target Scope, available in 16x, 20x, and 24x powers, is the first sealed target scope with internal adjustments. Precision machining and the use of spring-loaded, hardened steel clicker balls, give the Redfield 3200 crisp consistent ¼-minute adjustments capable of obtaining an accurate ± 1/32 MOA with every positive click.

3200 TARGET SCOPE

REDFIELD RECEIVER SIGHTS

PALMA METALLIC TARGET RECEIVER SIGHT

Replaces the International Match and Olympic receiver sights used by competitive shooters. Elevation staff and sighting disc block feature dovetail construction for precise, stable travel and provide a means for the shooter to correct for longtime wear. Insert in sighting disc block accepts either American or European thread. Adapter for front of sighting disc block. Optional to accept European light filters, etc. forward of the sighting disc block. Windage and elevation adjustments are ¼ MOA and can be adjusted for either a hard or soft feel by the shoulder. Repeatability error is limited to .001″ per click (.012 MOA, or ⅛″ @ 100 yards). Averages between .0002″ to .0004″.

Palma Metallic Target Receiver Sight **$144.30**

REDFIELD SURE-X DISC

SURE-X DISC

Selective aperture sizes from .028″ to .042″ in increments of .002″. Each size is clearly stamped on the aperture wheel. Selection of the proper aperture for the prevailing light conditions provides an optimum sight picture with good contrast and crisp, round front sight aperture.

Sure-X Disc $13.20

REDFIELD RINGS AND BASES

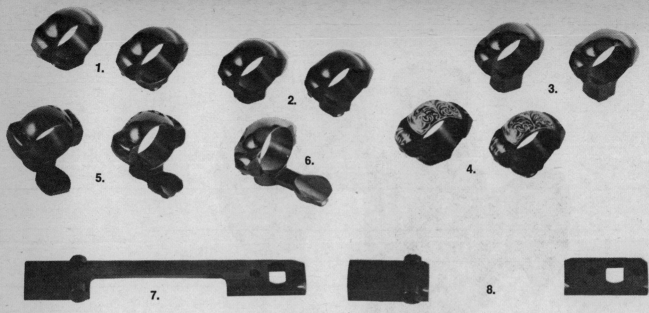

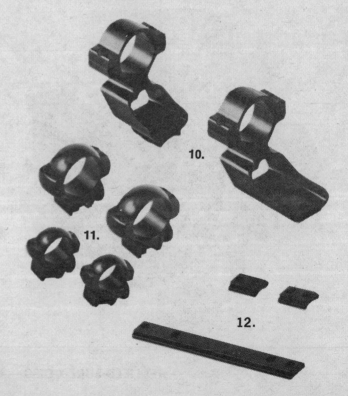

1. **Low.** For scopes up to 1.6″ objective diameter. Height 0.152″ **$21.50**
2. **Medium.** For scopes with 1.6″ to 1.9″ objective diameter. Height 0.272″ **$21.50**
3. **High.** For scopes over 1.9″ objective diameter. Height 0.402″ **$21.50**
4. **Engraved Rings.** Come in two heights: Low, **$40.70**; Medium, **$40.70**
5. **Extension front** .625″ (low, medium and high). **$29.40**
6. **Long Extension front** 1.150″ (medium height only) **$31.70**
7. **JR Bases** (one piece) **$14.50**
8. **SR Bases** (two piece) **$14.50-$25.50**
9. **Colt Sauer SR Base** (two piece) **$25.50**
10. **FR See-Thru Mounts** **$17.50** a pair
11. **Ring Mounts for Rimfire Rifles**
    Same as FRontier but fit mounting grooves on most 22's. (¾″ **$13.20**) (1″ **$15.80**)
12. **22 Adapter Bases**
    For 22 rifles without dovetail receiver.

Rifle	Item No.	Price
Model 39A Marlin	614002	$4.20
Model 57 Marlin	614003	4.20
Model 10/22 Ruger	614004	4.20
Browning Auto. 22	614009	8.20

INTERNATIONAL SMALLBORE FRONT

This improved model of an old favorite allows for easy drop-in insertion of eared Skeleton (Polycarbonate) inserts, with inner sleeve which eliminates possibility of light leakage. Round, optically clear, plastic inserts accommodated with speed and ease **$32.40**

GLOBE FRONT SIGHTS

1" long, ½" diam. Inserts held firmly by simple locking sleeve, which loosens but doesn't have to be removed when changing inserts.

GLOBE NO.	HEIGHT "A"	BASE	PRICE W/INSERTS
63	.483"	Uses Standard Front Base (Separate $2.95)	**$15.90**
64	.733"	Standard Front Base (separate $2.95)	**15.90**
65	.316"	Integral male dovetail	**12.00**
65NB	.316"	base drives into dovetail	**12.00**
66	.595"	on barrel 66 for Spring	**12.00**
68	.441"	field dovetail 65, 68 for	**12.00**
Extra inserts for Globe Front Set			**3.20**

INTERNATIONAL BIG BORE FRONT

For .30 caliber shooting, same as small bore except tube shortened to approximately 2", eyepiece same size as tube to provide greatest possible rapid fire visibility. **$32.40**
All Big Bore Fronts are within I.S.U. maximum dimension limits.

Target Sight Bases and Accessories

Redfield offers you a complete line of bases and accessories to complement the target sights shown on the previous pages. All are manufactured to the most exacting of specifications in order to provide you with the most professional and dependable sighting equipment available.

Index of Receiver Sight Bases

Receiver Sight Bases

#75

Olympic and International

This base provides a series of threaded attachment holes to permit rear sight mounting locations for any shooting position.

Index of Front Sight Bases

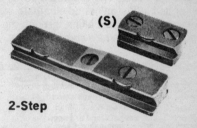

(S)

2-Step

Special base for Small Bore shooting. Height given is for the lower or 100 yard step. 50 yard step is .054" higher. Fast, convenient, saves wear on your Receiver Sight.

OLYMPIC DETACHABLE FRONT

Admits a greater volume of light, perfectly controlled by shading flanges. Set of 10 easy-change inserts includes five steel apertures, one post, four transparent apertures. Transparent available in clear, green or amber, with or without crosslines. Amber with crosslines will be furnished unless otherwise requested.
Olympic Front w/Inserts
(no base) **$22.60**
Extra Set Olympic Inserts **6.00**

REDFIELD SPOTTING SCOPES

Spotting Scopes and Accessories

The new Regal variable power spotting scopes are also available in 15X-45X or 15X-60X variables. These fog-proof spotting scopes assure constant focus as power is changed. And the clicker or detent positions give you "clicks" you can feel as you change power. The separated power and focus rings offer one-handed adjustment and eliminate confusion when changing power or focus while looking through the scope. Both Regal scopes come with a new sighting device.

ITEM	PRICE
15X-45X Regal Spotting Scope	$317.00
15X-60X Regal Spotting Scope	351.65
Redfield Tripod Stand	
Redfield Bipod Stand	
Scope/Bipod or Tripod Combination Case	55.00

15X-45X

Like the 15X-60X, this scope gives you the same rugged construction, brilliant optical system and features and is finished in the same handsome crackletone "Redfield red" enamel. The only difference is the power range and the price.

15X-60X

This veteran performer features long eye relief, a large objective lens system for gathering the extra light needed for good resolution at high powers, a retractable eye shield and a built-in sunshade.

Regal Spotting Scope Specifications

	15X-45X		15X-60X	
	AT 15X	AT 45X	AT 15X	AT 60X
Actual magnification	15.0X	45.0X	15.0X	60.0X
Clear aperture of objective lens	2.362''	2.362''	2.362''	2.362''
Exit pupil	3,45mm	1,24mm	3,45mm	0,97mm
Field of view at 100 yds.	16.1'	5.4'	16.1'	4.0'
Eye relief	1''	1''	1''	1''
Overall length	18''	18''	18''	18''
Weight	49 ozs.	49 ozs.	49 ozs.	49 ozs.

SAKO SCOPE MOUNTS

Peep Sight

The scope mounting system on Sako Scopes is among the strongest in the world. Instead of using separate bases, a tapered dovetail is milled right into the reciever, to which the scope rings are mounted. A beautifully simple system that's been proven by over twenty years of use. Available in low (2½- 3-power); medium (4-power), and high (6-power). Either 1-inch or 26mm rings.

Low	$48.95
Medium	48.95
High	48.95
Peep Sight	16.95

WEATHERBY PREMIER SCOPES

CHOICE OF RETICLES

Standard Model

"LUMI-PLEX" with luminous reticle   **Open Dot**   **Cross Hair**   **Tapered Post and Cross Hair**

Not Available In Wide angle Model

Wide Angle Model

3 TO 9 POWER

The most desirable variable for every kind of shooting from target to long range big game. Outstanding light-gathering power. Fast, convenient focusing adjustment.

4 POWER

This is a fixed power scope for big game and varmint hunting. Bright, clear image. "Never-wear" coated lenses for maximum luminosity under adverse conditions. 31-foot field of view at 100 yards.

2¾ POWER— AVAILABLE IN STANDARD MODEL ONLY

One of the widest fields of view on any scope . . . 45 feet at 100 yards. Ideal for big game because of its clear, bright image. Ruggedly built to withstand even the pounding of our .460 Magnum.

WEATHERBY PREMIER SCOPES

WIDE ANGLE FIELD OF VIEW. Now, a twenty-five per cent wider field! Great for holding running game in full view.

As every hunter knows, one of his most difficult problems is keeping running game in the field of view of his scope.

Once lost, precious seconds fade away trying to find the animal in the scope again. Too much time wasted means the ultimate frustration. No second shot. Or no shot at all.

The Weatherby Wide Angle helps you surmount the problem by increasing your field of view by a full 25%!

FEATURES

OPTICAL EXCELLENCE—NOW PROTECTED WITH NEW "NEVER-WEAR" ANTI-GLARE COATING. ● FOG FREE AND WATERPROOF CONSTRUCTION. ● CONSTANTLY SELF CENTERED RETICLES. ● NON-MAGNIFYING RETICLE. ● FINGER TIP ¼" CLICK ADJUSTMENTS. ● QUICK VARIABLE POWER CHANGE. ● UNIQUE LUMINOUS RETICLE. ● LIFETIME NEOPRENE EYEPIECE. ● EXCLUSIVE BINOCULAR TYPE SPEED FOCUSING. ● RUGGED SCORE TUBE CONSTRUCTION.

SPECIFICATIONS FOR WEATHERBY PREMIER SCOPES

	STANDARD LENS			WIDE ANGLE LENS	
	2¾X40	4X40	3X - 9X40	4X40	3X - 9X40
Field of view	45' 0"	31' 0"	40' - 12'	35' 8"	43' 7" - 14' 8"
Clear aperture of objective lens	40mm	40mm	40mm	40mm	40mm
Diameter of exit pupil	14.56mm	10.0mm	13.3 - 4.4mm	10mm	13.3 - 4.4mm
Relative brightness	211.99	100.0	176.9 - 19.3	100.0	176.9 - 19.3
Eye relief	3.5"	3.5"	3.5"	3.0"	3.4" - 3.0"
Overall length	11.8"	12.7"	12.2"	11.8"	12.1"
Diameter of tube	1"	1"	1"	1"	1"
O.D. of objective end	1.85"	1.85"	1.85"	1.85"	1.85"
O.D. of ocular end	1.53"	1.53"	1.53"	1.71"	1.71"
Weight	12.3 oz.	12.3 oz.	13.7 oz.	14.1 oz.	14.8 oz.
Internal adjustment graduation	¼" clicks 1" calibration marks			¼" clicks 1" calibration marks	
Price and reticle:					
CH or TP&CH	$126.95	$137.95	$142.95	$159.95	$169.95
Lumi-Plex	131.95	142.95	153.95	164.95	179.95
Open Dot	131.95	142.95	153.95	Not Available	

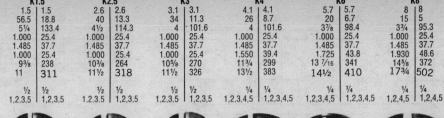

Model	K1.5		K2.5		K3		K4		K6		K8	
Actual Magnification*	1.5	1.5	2.6	2.6	3.1	3.1	4.1	4.1	5.7	5.7	8	8
Field of View* at 100 yds (ft) at 100 m (m)	56.5	18.8	40	13.3	34	11.3	26	8.7	20	6.7	15	5
Eye Distance* (inches) (mm)	5¼	133.4	4½	114.3	4	101.6	4	101.6	3⅞	98.4	3¾	95.3
Tube Diameter (inches) (mm)	1.000	25.4	1.000	25.4	1.000	25.4	1.000	25.4	1.000	25.4	1.000	25.4
Eyepiece Diameter (inches) (mm)	1.485	37.7	1.485	37.7	1.485	37.7	1.485	37.7	1.485	37.7	1.485	37.7
Front End Diameter (inches) (mm)	1.000	25.4	1.000	25.4	1.000	25.4	1.550	39.4	1.725	43.8	1.930	48.6
Length (inches) (mm)	9⅜	238	10⅜	264	10⅝	270	11¾	299	13 7/16	341	14⅝	372
Weight (ounces) (grams)	11	311	11½	318	11½	326	13½	383	14½	410	17¾	502
Graduated Adjustments (change in inches at 100 yards, or minute of angle)	½	½	½	½	½	½	¼	¼	¼	¼	¼	¼
Reticles** Available	1,2,3,5	1,2,3,5	1,2,3,5	1,2,3,5	1,2,3,5	1,2,3,5	1,2,3,4,5	1,2,3,4,5	1,2,3,4,5	1,2,3,4,5	1,2,4,5	1,2,4,5

*Weaver-Scopes offer carefully balanced magnification, field of view, eye relief, and diaphragming to provide hunters with maximum efficiency, safety, and clarity.

**RETICLES 1 Crosshair 2 Dual X 3 Post and Crosshair 4 Range-Finder 5 Dot
Reticles available as indicated: 1, 2, 3 and 4 at no extra cost. 5 at extra cost.

FOCUS Eyepiece of all scopes adjusts to user's vision.

K MODELS

1.

CROSSHAIR

2.

DUAL X®

3.

POST AND CROSSHAIR

4.

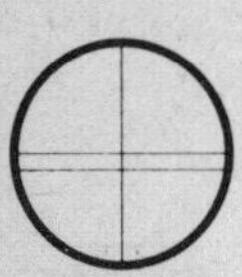

RANGE-FINDER®

5.

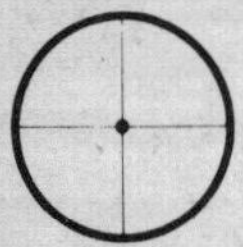

DOT
(at extra cost)

Model K1.5	$ 59.50
Model K2.5	71.00
Model K3	76.00
Model K4	88.00
Model K6	99.00
Model K8	113.00
Model K-10F	118.00
Model K-12F	130.00
Dot Reticle, extra	13.30

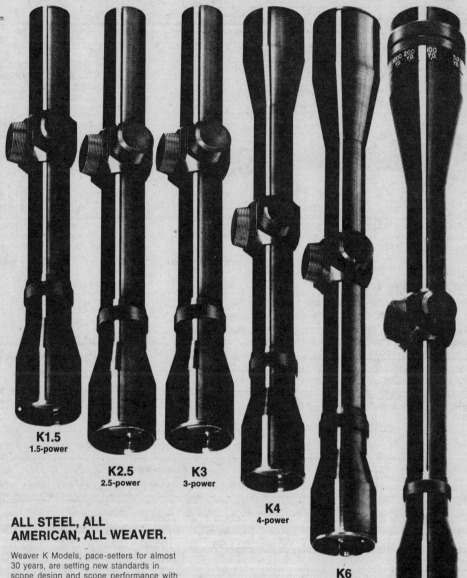

K1.5
1.5-power

K2.5
2.5-power

K3
3-power

K4
4-power

K6
6-power

K8
8-power

ALL STEEL, ALL AMERICAN, ALL WEAVER.

Weaver K Models, pace-setters for almost 30 years, are setting new standards in scope design and scope performance with the All-Steel Scope. Truly the Great American Scope.

Unique, one-piece steel tube. The sharp, clean-cut shape is machine-tooled and hand-polished to make it a fine match for the finest of rifles. And highest quality steel provides the best possible protection for the superior optics.

The K Models feature Weaver's micro-adjustable windage and elevation settings for super-accuracy. They're vacuumized, filled with dry nitrogen gas, and super-sealed with a patented process.

Models K8, K10 and K12 feature compact Weaver Range Focus for precision in long-range shooting.

All five reticle styles are available in most K Models (post and crosshair not offered in K8, K10, K12; Range-Finder not offered in K1.5, K2.5, K3).

WEAVER "K" & "V" MODEL SCOPES

Model	K10		K12		V4.5		V7		V9		V12	
Actual Magnification*	10	10	12	12	1.5-4.2	1.5-4.2	2.4-6.6	2.4-6.6	3-8.3	3-8.3	4-12	4-12
Field of View* at 100 yds (ft) at 100 m (m)	12	4	10	3.3	62-24	20.7-8	40-15	13.3-5	33-12	11-4	24-9	8-3
Eye Distance* (inches) (mm)	3⅝	92	3⅝	92	4½-4	114.3-101.6	4-3⅞	101.6-98.4	3¾-3¾	95.3-95.3	3⅞-4¼	98.4-108
Tube Diameter (inches) (mm)	1.000	25.4	1.000	25.4	1.000	25.4	1.000	25.4	1.000	25.4	1.000	25.4
Eyepiece Diameter (inches) (mm)	1.485	37.7	1.485	37.7	1.485	37.7	1.485	37.7	1.485	37.7	1.485	37.7
Front End Diameter (inches) (mm)	1.930	48.6	1.930	48.6	1.000	25.4	1.550	39.4	1.930	48.6	1.930	48.6
Length (inches) (mm)	15½	394	15¾	400	10⅜	264	12⅜	314	13¾	349	13¾	349
Weight (ounces) (grams)	18½	523	18¾	530	15½	439	17½	503	22	624	22	624
Graduated Adjustments (change in inches at 100 yards, or minute of angle)	¼	¼	¼	¼	½	½	¼	¼	¼	¼	¼	¼
Reticles** Available	1,2,4,5	1,2,4,5	1,2,4,5	1,2,4,5	1,2,3,4,5	1,2,3,4,5	1,2,3,4,5	1,2,3,4,5	1,2,3,4,5	1,2,3,4,5	1,2,3,4,5	1,2,3,4,5

*Weaver-Scopes offer carefully balanced magnification, field of view, eye relief, and diaphragming to provide hunters with maximum efficiency, safety, and clarity.

**RETICLES 1 Crosshair 2 Dual X 3 Post and Crosshair 4 Range-Finder 5 Dot
Reticles available as indicated: 1, 2, 3, and 4 at no extra cost. 5 at extra cost.
FOCUS Eyepiece of all scopes adjusts to user's vision.

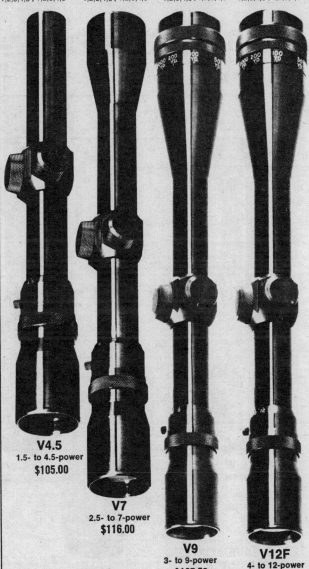

V MODELS

1.
CROSSHAIR

2.
DUAL X®

3.
POST AND CROSSHAIR

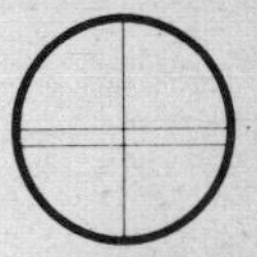

4.
RANGE-FINDER®

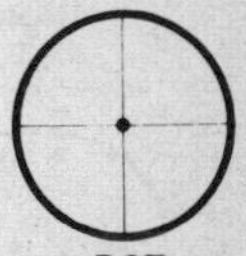

5.
DOT
(at extra cost)

V4.5
1.5- to 4.5-power
$105.00

V7
2.5- to 7-power
$116.00

V9
3- to 9-power
$127.50

V12F
4- to 12-power
$139.00

K10F
10-power
$118.00

K12F
12-power
$130.00

THE ALL-STEEL VARIABLES. MORE RUGGED, MORE DEPENDABLE THAN EVER.

Now Weaver offers important advances in its V Model design: All steel, one-piece tube construction with machine-tooled, handcrafted quality.

Vacuumized, nitrogen processed, and super-sealed with a patented process — to guarantee fogproofing for the life of the scope. Micro-adjustable elevation and windage settings.

Focus and point of impact are the same at all powers. Reticle remains constantly centered.

Precision optics are magnesium fluoride coated. Long eye relief is safe at all magnifications. Models V9 and V12 have Weaver Range Focus. All five reticle styles are offered.

Weaver "K-W" & "V-W" Model Scopes

Model	K3-W		K4-W		K6-W		V4.5-W		V7-W		V9-W	
Actual Magnification*	2.9	2.9	3.9	3.9	5.8	5.8	1.6-4.2	1.6-4.2	2.5-6.7	2.5-6.7	3.2-8.6	3.2-8.6
Field of View* at 100 yds (ft) at 100 m (m)	50	16.7	36	12	25	8.3	75-29	25-9.7	45-18	15-6	36-14	12-4.7
Eye Distance* (inches) (mm)	3⅝	92	3⅝	92	3⅝	92	4⅜-3¾	111-95	3⅞-3⅞	98-98	3⅝-3⅝	92-92
Tube Diameter (inches) (mm)	1.000	25.4	1.000	25.4	1.000	25.4	1.000	25.4	1.000	25.4	1.000	25.4
Eyepiece Diameter (inches) (mm)	1.710	43.4	1.710	43.4	1.710	43.4	1.710	43.4	1.710	43.4	1.710	43.4
Front End Diameter (inches) (mm)	x1.425	x36.2	x1.425	x36.2	x1.425	x36.2	x1.425	x36.2	x1.425	x36.2	x1.425	x36.2
	1.000	25.4	1.000	25.4	1.725	43.8	1.000	25.4	1.550	39.4	1.930	48.6
Length (inches) (mm)	11	279	11 13/16	300	13¼	337	10⅜	263	12⅜	314	13¾	349
Weight (ounces) (grams)	12¼	346	13¾	389	15¾	445	15¾	447	18	515	22½	637
Graduated Adjustments (change in inches at 100 yards, or minute of angle)	½	½	¼	¼	¼	¼	½	½	¼	¼	¼	¼
Reticles** Available	1,2,3,5	1,2,3,5	1,2,3,4,5	1,2,3,4,5	1,2,3,4,5	1,2,3,4,5	1,2,3,4,5	1,2,3,4,5	1,2,3,4,5	1,2,3,4,5	1,2,3,4,5	1,2,3,4,5

*Weaver-Scopes offer carefully balanced magnification, field of view, eye relief, and diaphragming to provide hunters with maximum efficiency, safety, and clarity.

**RETICLES 1 Crosshair 2 Dual X 3 Post and Crosshair 4 Range-Finder 5 Dot
Reticles available as indicated: 1, 2, 3, and 4 at no extra cost. 5 at extra cost.
FOCUS Eyepiece of all scopes adjusts to user's vision.

K-W & V-W MODELS

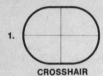

1.
CROSSHAIR

2. 
DUAL X®

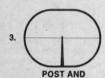

3.
POST AND CROSSHAIR
On Wider-View V-W Models, post does not extend above crosshair.

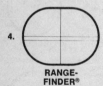

4.
RANGE-FINDER®

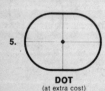

5.
DOT
(at extra cost)

Model K3-W	$102.00
Model K4-W	113.50
Model K6-W	124.50
Model V4.5-W	130.50
Model V7-W	142.00
Model V9-W	153.50
Model V9-WF	165.00
Dot Reticle, extra	13.30

K3-W
3-power

K4-W
4-power

K6-W
6-power

V4.5-W
1.5- to 4.5-power

V7-W
2.5- to 7-power

V9-W
3- to 9-power

You see what might be out of the picture with a standard scope.

WEAVER OFFERS THE POPULAR WIDER-VIEW WITH A PICTURE THAT'S UP TO 40% WIDER.

The Great American Scope line features six handsome Wider-View Models. A beautifully-shaped rectangular eyepiece gives a wider view than a standard scope of the same power — as much as 40% wider on the V4.5-W at highest power. And there's no sacrifice in superior quality and outstanding performance.

Wider-View is an All-Steel Scope, designed by Weaver engineers to include all the proven features that have made K and V Models America's leading scopes: one-piece, machine-tooled steel tube. Micro-adjustable windage and elevation settings. Vacuumized, nitrogen-processed, and super-sealed for absolute fogproofing. Bright, crisp, distortion-free optics. Long, safe eye relief.

Range Focus offered on the V9-W. All five reticle styles available (except Range-Finder not offered on K3-W).

Model	D4		D6		V22	
Actual Magnification*	4.2	4.2	6.2	6.2	3-5.8	3-5.8
Field of View* at 100 yds (ft) at 100 m (m)	29	9.7	19.75	6.6	31-16.25	10.3-5.4
Eye Distance* (inches) (mm)	2¼	57	2¼	57	1⅝-2¼	41.3-57
Tube Diameter (inches) (mm)	.875	22.2	.875	22.2	.875	22.2
Eyepiece Diameter (inches) (mm)	1.310	33.3	1.310	33.3	1.310	33.3
Front End Diameter (inches) (mm)	.875	22.2	.875	22.2	.875	22.2
Length (inches) (mm)	11⅞	302	12 5/16	313	12⅜	314
Weight (ounces) (grams)	5.5	155.9	5.5	155.9	7	198.4
Graduated Adjustments (change in inches at 100 yards, or minute of angle)	1	1	1	1	1	1
Reticles ** Available	1 only	1 only	1 only	1 only	1,2	1,2

*Weaver-Scopes offer carefully balanced magnification, field of view, eye relief, and diaphragming to provide hunters with maximum efficiency, safety, and clarity.
**RETICLES 1 Crosshair 2 Dual X
Reticles available as indicated: 1 at no extra cost. 2 at extra cost (on V22 only).
†Weight without mount 4 ounces; with mount 5 ounces.
FOCUS Eyepiece of all scopes adjusts to user's vision.

D4
4-power

D6
6-power

V22
3- to 6-power

22 MODELS

1.
CROSSHAIR

2.
DUAL X®
(at extra cost, on V22 only)

Model D4 with Crosshair Reticle $18.50
Model D4 with Dual X Reticle 20.50
Model D6 with Crosshair Reticle 20.50
Model D6 with Dual X Reticle 22.50
Model V22 with Crosshair Reticle 24.50
Model V22 with Dual X Reticle 27.00

WITH THE BIG SCOPE FEATURES.

Advanced D Models and V22 have outstanding features usually found only in more expensive scopes: large ⅞" tubes, matching turret of modern design, improved optics with larger eyepiece. Lighter and stronger than ever, they are made of finest materials by skilled American craftsmen.

Weaver's constantly-centered reticle permits unusual speed and ease of aim. Use is limited to light recoil rifles only because of relatively short eye relief.

Factory-equipped with Tip-Off or N Mount at no extra cost.

Crosshair reticle is standard in all three scopes; Dual X is optional in the V22 at extra cost.

WEAVER LENS CAPS

Transparent windows allow the scope to be used quickly with the caps in position in emergency. Durable and snug fitting, Weaver Lens Caps provide attractive, inexpensive protection for the scope's optics. Made in eleven sizes:

D4, D6, V22   V9, V12
K1.5   K3-W, V4.5-W
K2.5, K3, V4.5   K4-W, V7-W
K4, V7   K6-W
K6   V9-W
K8, K10, K12

WEAVER PARTS KIT

A handy, comprehensive collection of useful, everyday replacement parts and screws for all Weaver-Scopes and Weaver-Mounts. Includes such often-needed items as turret caps and base screws. Complete set is arranged in a dozen compartments in an attractive, durable plastic box.

WEAVER SIGHTS & MOUNTS

QWIK-POINT®

QUICKEST WAY TO IMPROVE SHOTGUN AND SHORT-RANGE RIFLE SHOOTING.

S-1
for
shotguns

S-1100
for
Remington
1100 and
870
shotguns

R-1
for
center-
fire
rifles

R-22
for 22
rifles

Keep your eye on the target. The blaze-orange dot is OUT THERE where your target is.

Dot is bright blaze-orange, even in dim light or heavy cover.

Weaver's amazing Qwik-Point is a completely different sighting concept. It can quickly improve natural shooting skills with shotgun, center-fire rifle, or 22.

With one or both eyes open, simply look at the target, move the blaze-orange dot to the target, and fire. The dot is focused to infinity, so it will automatically appear where eyes are focused.

Dot and target are seen simultaneously in clear, sharp focus. No changing point of focus from sight to target.

On shotguns, Qwik-Point is an effective short-cut to becoming an accomplished wingshot. Makes "swing" and "lead" easy to see, understand, and follow. Helps the expert detect where and why he missed.

Qwik-Point is shockproof, weatherproof, foolproof. Made of lightweight aluminum with durable jet-black anodizing. Easily sighted in like a scope.

Specifications:
Weight:
S-1, 7¾ ounces
S-1100, 7¾ ounces
R-1, 8¾ ounces
R-22, 7½ ounces
Length:
S-1, 6 inches
S-1100, 6 inches
R-1, 6¼ inches
R-22, 6¾ inches
Adjustments:
¼" click at 40 yards
Eye Relief: Infinite
Focus: Universal

Mounting:
Model S-1 for shotguns:
Complete with mount and base (8A) for most pumps and automatics.

Model S-1100 for Remington 1100 and 870 shotguns: Complete with side mount and bolts; installed in minutes without special tools.

Model R-1 for center fire rifles: Built-in mount attaches to Weaver Top Mount bases (bases extra). Special bases (77, 78) available for Model 94 Winchester.

Model R-22 for 22's: Complete with mount which fits factory-grooved receivers.

WEAVER TIP-OFF® MOUNTS

Weaver 1" Tip-Off Mount for K Models and other 1" scopes

Weaver ⅞" Tip-Off Mount for D Models, V22, and other ⅞" scopes

Tip-Off Mounts are made for use on 22 rifles with ⅜" dovetail receiver grooves. No bases required. They clamp into the rifle receiver grooves. No tools needed. Clamping screws tighten easily with a coin.

1" Tip-Off Mounts, a pair of split rings, are designed to mount K Models and other 1" scopes.

⅞" Tip-Off Mounts, a pair of solid rings, are designed to mount Weaver D Models, V22, and other ⅞" scopes. Also available in ¾" rings to fit ¾" scopes.

These rifles have ⅜" receiver grooves:
Anschutz 141, 153, Mark 10
Browning T-Bolt, BL-22
CIL 68, 121, 125, 167, 180, 190S, 212, 227, 300, 310, 470
Colt "Colteer"
Cooey 64
Glenfield 10, 20, 60, 70
H&R 422, 750, 751, 755, 760, 800, 865, 866
High Standard 22 Sport-King
Ithaca X5 Lightning
Kodiak 260
Lee-Enfield requires adapter TO-1 at extra cost; must be drilled, tapped
Marlin 49, 56, 57, 80, 81, 88, 89, 98, 99, 101, 122, 780, 781, 782, 783, 980, 989
Mossberg 142, 144, 146, 151, 152, 300 Series, 400, 402, 430, 432, 620, 640
Noble 235, 275, 285, 835, 875, 885
Remington 10, 11, 12, 66, 76, 77, 510, 511, 512, 513S, 521T, 540X, 541, 550, 552, 572, 580, 581, 582, 590M, 591M, 592M
Ruger 10/22 with T9 base
Savage 4, 5, 6, 24, 29, 54, 60, 63, 65, 88, 90, 164, 184, 219
Stevens 34, 46, 73, 84, 85, 86, 87
Weatherby XXII
Winchester 61, 69, 72, 74, 75S, 77, 121, 131, 135, 141, 145, 150, 190, 250, 255, 270, 275, 290, 310, 320, 325, 9422 (T10 adapter base available for 9422)

Model R-1 for rifles ... $56.50
Model R-22 for 22 rifles 56.50
Model S-1 for shotguns 56.50
Model S-1100 for Remington 1100 and 870 shotguns, and other Remington shotguns and rifles 56.50
Tip-off Mount Solid Rings (pair) in ¾", ⅞" diameters.. 6.25
Tip-Off Mount Split Rings (pair) in 1" diameter...... 14.50
Tip-Off Adapter Base TO-1 for Lee Enfield.......... 4.20

WEAVER SIGHTS & MOUNTS

WEAVER-DETACHABLE MOUNTS

Detachable Top Mount made in ⅞", 1", and 1.023" (26mm) diameters; Hi-Style made in 1" diameter only $14.50

Detachable Side Mount made in 1" diameters $14.50

WEAVER-PIVOT MOUNTS

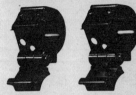

Pivot Mount open

Extension Top Mount made in 1" diameter only $16.75

Detachable Long Side Mount in 1" diameter for Winchester 94 and other short-action rifles $16.75

Pivot Mount closed $17.75

Light, compact and finely finished, Weaver-Detachable Mounts can be used with complete assurance on rifles of heaviest recoil and under roughest hunting use. Installation is easy since most rifle receivers are factory drilled and tapped specifically for Weaver-Mounts.

Hi-Style Top Mounts, made in 1" diameter only, are designed to provide adequate barrel and iron sight clearance for most scopes having objective diameters greater than 1¾". Scopes of this size (1¾") can be mounted on some rifles using regular Top Mounts.

Use Hi-Style Top Mounts when installing K6, K6-W, K8, K10, K12, V9, V9-W, V12 on Remington 600, 660, 788, Marlin 336, 444, Savage 99; K6, K6-W, V9, V9-W, V12, on Remington 740, 742, 760; V9, V9-W and V12 on Remington 700, 721, 722, 725.

On some bolt-action rifles, it is necessary to use Hi-Style Top Mounts when installing K-W and V-W Models to prevent bolt interference.

Extension Top Mounts allow the scope to be positioned ¾" further forward for improved eye relief.

Weaver Detachable Side Mounts are especially suitable for shorter scopes, and are made with split rings in 1" diameter

Detachable Long Side Mounts are made in 1" diameter with split rings, and are designed for Winchester 94 and other short-action rifles.

WEAVER N MOUNTS

Type N Mounts (side bracket design) are pressed from tough alloy steel. They are rigid, sturdy, and suitable for use on high-power rifles and 22's. Made in ⅞" diameter for D Models and V22.

The dependability of the inexpensive N Mount has been proved under all conditions and on large caliber rifles. **$6.50**

Weaver-Pivot Mounts permit choice of scope or iron sights. Top mounting gives wide spacing of mount rings, rigidity, low scope position, easy installation and removal. Replacement is accurate, alignment exact and fully dependable. Made for ¾" and 1" scopes.

Hi-Style Pivot Mounts are available in 1" diameter only. The high rings position the scope ¼" higher than the standard ring, and provide adequate barrel and iron sight clearance for scopes with objective diameters greater than 1¾". Use Hi-Style Pivot Mounts when installing K6, K6-W, K8, K10, K12, V9, V9-W, and V12 scopes on these rifles: Remington 700, 742, 760, 600, 660; Marlin 336, 444; and Savage 99.

WEAVER MOUNTS AND BASES

Make, Model of Rifle	Bases for Detachable Mounts			Bases for Pivot Mounts		Bases for All-Steel Mounts	N Mounts Made for 7/8" dia. Scopes
	Top Mount Rear	Top Mount Front	Side Mount	Rear	Front		
ANSCHUTZ 153 Deluxe, 1530, 1532, 1534	19	19	....	119	119		
1568	61	46	1	161	146	6146L	....
BROWNING 22 Auto (base attaches to barrel extending back over receiver)		60	....	.....	......		
243, 308, 22-250, 222, and 222 Magnum (all in Sako actions)	72	71	....	.....	......		
Bolt Action, High-Power, other calibers	45	46	5	145	146	4546	
Semi-Automatic, High-Power	54	54	....	154	154	5454	
BLR	25	25	....	......	......		
BSA Monarch Medium Action 222, 243, 308	36	40A	....	136	140		
Monarch Long Action 7mm, 270, 30-06	36	35	....	136	135		
Other high-powers	28	28	....	......	......		
CIL 830			1				
871		62	....		162		
900	19	19	....	119	119		
950, 950C	61	46	1	161	146		
972-C	45	46	....	145	146		
COLT Coltsman in 223, 243, 308 calibers (round receivers)	25	25	....				
Coltsman in 264, 30-06 calibers (round receivers)	54	54	....				
Coltsman in 223 (Sako action)	67	66	....				
Coltsman other cal (Sako action)	67	65	....				
Sauer	35	35	....	135	135		
57	45	46	....	145	146	4546	
COOEY 60, 600			2				N3
71	47	46	1	147	146		
ENFIELD receiver cut down like: Remington 30	11	11	1				
Winchester 70†	47	46	....	147	146		
Remington 721†	36	35	....	136	135		
GARCIA 73		53	....		153		
74	67	66	....				
H&R 300, 301, 330, 370 prior to '73	45	46	5	145	146	4546	
300, 301 short action for 1973 and after (22-250, 243, 308)	83	84	....				
300, 301 long action for 1973 and after (270, 30-06, 7mm, 300 Win)	54	46	....	154	146		
360, 361		81	....				
317, 322	11	35	....				
317 prior to 1975 model	67	66	....				
Topper 30, 22 Jet, 158 prior to 1973		60	....				
Topper 158C for 1973 and after		82	....				
65, 165, 150, 151 (Auto)	18	18	2				N3
264, 265, 365, 250, 251, 450, 550	18	16	2				N3
700		87	....				
HERTERS U9 BSA Action (requires drilling, tapping)	28	28	....				
U9 round receiver	36	35	....	136	135		
U9	45	46	5	145	146		
HIGH STANDARD Hi-Power	55	46	1				
ITHACA LSA-55, LSA-65	61	61	....				
JAPANESE 6.5mm*†, 7.7mm*†		70	1		170		
KRAG (offset to left for easy ejection)			2				
LEE-ENFIELD (Use TO-1 Adapter Base and Tip-Off Mount)							
MARLIN 36, 336		63A	....		163A	0063	
62, 93, 444, 1893, 1895, Glenfield 30, Zane Grey		63A	....		163A		
1894		63A	....		163A	0063A	
455	45	46	5			4546	
57 Magnum		58	....				
MAUSER FN including former Husqvarna (with receiver ring about 1.410" dia.)*	45	46	5	145	146	4546	
98, 95	45	46	5	145	146	4546A	
Mark X	55	20A	....				
HVA, Lightweight Husqvarna (with receiver ring about 1.300" diameter)*	55	46	1	155	146	5546	
ZB 8mm*, 7mm*, 6.5mm* with round receivers	55	46	1	155	146	5546	
Bauer 3000, 4000	68	46	....	168	146		
MOSSBERG 800	55	55	....	155	155	5555	
810	25	11	....			2511	
25, 26, 42, 46M, 140, 142, 146. Also late Models 45, 46 with 3/4" dia. bbls.	12	13	2				N3
43, 44, 144, 46BT, 35. Also early Models 45, 46, 46A, 46B with 13/16" dia. bbls.	12	16	2				N3
40	16	21	2				N3
400	20A	42	....				
472		80	....				
500AS shotgun		88	....				
MUSGRAVE Mark I, Mark II	54	46	....	154	146		
Mark III, Mark IV	45	46	....	145	146	4546	
PARKER-HALE 1000, 1000C, 1100, 1700	45	46	....	145	146		
1200	45	46	....	145	146	4546	
REMINGTON 700 in 270, 280, 25-06, 30-06, 7mm Magnum, 300 Winchester Magnum, 264, 375, 458, 40X-L; 721; 725 in 280, 270, 30-06, 375 calibers	36	35	1	136	135	3635	
700 in 17, 222, 222 Mag., 22-250, 243, 6mm, 308; 722, 40X-S; 725 in 222, 244, 243 calibers	36	40A	1	136	140	3640	
740, 742, 760		62	....		162	0062	
660, 600		70	1		170	0070	
788 long action 222, 22/250, 30/30	76	75	....			7675L	
788 extra long 243, 6mm, 308	76	75	....			7675X	
30	11	11	1			1111	
14, 141	20A	27	....				
12A, 121 with 3/4" dia. bbls.	18	13	2				
121 with 13/16" diameter barrels	18	17	2				
12C octagon barrel	18	31	....				N5
24, 241 (#60 1-pc. base attaches to bbl., extends back over receiver; 1" scopes only)		60	1				N5
25	18	21	2				N5
REMINGTON continued							
10, 11, 12, 521T, 34*, 341*	43	42	2				N3
513S, 513T	43	44	2				N3
514	16	11	2				N3
541S	15	15	....				
33*	17	13	2				N3
41*	17	17	2				N3
XP-100		70	....				
RUGER 44 Magnum Deerstalker	47	68	....	147	168		
10/22		TO-9					
77ST round top	79	35	....				
3	85	86	....				
Mini-14			9				
SAKO Vixen (requires no drilling)	67	66	....				
Forester, Finnbear (no drilling)	67	65	....				
Finnwolf		53	....		153		
SAVAGE 99	14	19	....	114	119	1419	
1895	14	19	....	114	119		
110 short action RH**	61	46	1	161	146	6146S	
110, 111, 112 long action RH**	61	46	1	161	146	6146L	
54 Anschutz, 1422, 1424	15	15	....				
24V		74	....				
20*, 340, 342			1				
40, 45	11	11	2				
3	16	21	2				N3
7	12	12	2				N3
19, 23	15	15	2				N3
219	12	30	2				N3
25 octagon barrel	19	31	....				N5
170		62	....		162		
2400	67	66	....				
SCHULTZ & LARSEN 50, 51	54	46	1	154	146		
SEARS 50, 51	45	46	5	145	146	4546	
51L	55	46	1	155	146		
53	47	46	1	147	146		
54, 100			3B				
SMITH & WESSON Mauser actions with small receiver ring	55	46	1	155	146	5546	
SPRINGFIELD '03*†	54	55	1	154	155	5455	
'03-A3*†	59	45	....	159	145	5945	
STEVENS 26	22	22	2				N3
27 octagon	31	31	....				N5
53	16	21	2				
56, 66	12	13	2				N3
57, 76, 417½, 762	12	12	2				N3
416	18	17	2				
417	15	15	2				N3
418, 418½	16	16	2				N3
325, 322			1				
STEVENS-SPRINGFIELD 83	16	21	2				
872	12	12	2				N3
840			1				
U. S. CARBINE Cal. 30 M1			M				
VOERE 2150, 2165/1, 2165/2, 2165/3, 2165/4	45	46	....	145	146	4546	
2130 (must be drilled, tapped)	28	28	....				
WEATHERBY Mark V	36	35	....	136	135	3635	
Vanguard	36	35	....	136	135	3635	
Mark V 22-250, 224	36	46	....	136	146		
Models with FN Mauser actions	45	46	5	145	146	4546	
WESTERNFIELD 730	25	11	....				
740		63A	....		163A	0063	
750	67	65	....				
770	55	20A	....				
772		80	....				
775, 780	55	55	....	155	155	5555	
WINCHESTER 70 postwar models: 300 H&H, 375 H&H Magnum Calibers prior to 1964	49A	46	1	149	146	4946	
375 H&H Magnum 1964 model	49A	46	1	139	146		
300 Win Mag; all other cal	47	46	1	147	146	4746	
54*, early Model 70	48	46	1	148	146	4846	
670, 770	47	46	1	147	146	4746	
88, 100		53	....		153	0053	
94			3B				
53, 55, 64, 65, 66, 71, 86, 92, 95		3A					
07, 05, 10	20A	17	....				
43	18	18	....				
03, 63	19	22	2				
06, 62, 62A, 90 octagon barrel	32	32	....				N5
61 round barrel	19	13	2				
61 octagon barrel	25	32	....				N5
60*, 67*, 68*	21	21	....			2121	N3
57, 69	12	13	2			2121	N3
69A, 72, 47	12	17	2				N3
74	12	12	2				
77	15	32	2				N3
75 Sporter	15	30	2				N3
75 Target	15	16	2				N3
52*	25	57	2				N3
9422		TO-10					
ZB 22	28	24	2				N3
Hornet, 218 Bee	39	24	....				
SHOTGUNS Pump shotguns except Winchester 42			8				
Winchester 42			2				
Auto shotguns EXCEPT Remington 11-48, 1100, Sportsman 48, 58, Winchester 50, Browning Double Auto, High Standard Auto			7				
Remington Auto 11-48, 1100, Sportsman 48, 58, Winchester 50, High Standard Auto			8				

NOTE: Top Mounts with No. 50 (long, one-piece) base can be used on double and single barrel shotguns with ribs thick enough for base screws.

QWIK-POINT and **ACCU-POINT:** Installation information packed with product.

*Rifles so marked (and older guns in some other models) require bolt handle alteration.

**Due to wide ring spacing, V7, V7-W, V9, V9-W, and V12 Models cannot be installed on Savage 110, 111, and 112 with Pivot Mount rings.

†Enfield, Japanese, and Springfield: Pivot Mount usable only on sporterized guns with suitable front and middle sights.

D4, D6, and V22 Scopes (like other makes designed for 22 rifles) have short eye relief, and for this reason should not be used on high-power rifles.

W. R. Weaver Company / El Paso, Texas 79915

WILLIAMS APERTURES & BASES

TWILIGHT APERTURE $2.40

REGULAR SERIES $1.75

SHOTGUN BIG GAME APERTURE $3.30

5D

FP

TWILIGHT APERTURES are designed for shooting under poor light conditions, early morning, late evening and other inclement conditions. They create a sharp contrast that gives quick definition to the aperture hole, and they eliminate the "fuzz" with which many shooters have trouble.

These new apertures are perhaps the greatest development in metallic sights in the last three decades. Positive sighting when the light is poor but the hunting best.

Williams Twilight Apertures will accommodate Redfield, Lyman, etc.

TW-⅜—.093	⅜" O.D. with .093 inner hole
TW-⅜—.125	⅜" O.D. with .125 inner hole
TW-½—.093	½" O.D. with .093 inner hole

SHOTGUN BIG GAME APERTURE

All Williams receiver sights can now be equipped with the new shotgun aperture. This new aperture has amazing light gathering ability. Permits clear shooting even when the light is poor. Designed for aerial shooting, slug shooting and for big game rifles. PROVIDES THE FASTEST, MOST ACCURATE SIGHTING YOU CAN HAVE!

REGULAR SERIES Buckbuster Standard

We have always felt that a disc with a small outer diameter and a large inner hole is best for hunting. For this reason, we have made the ⅜" O.D. disc with a .093 inner hole as standard equipment. Other sizes are optional.

For the shooter who wants the FASTEST sighting aperture, we can now supply our BUCKBUSTER model which has a ⅜" O.D. and a large .125 inner hole. Our special target aperture has a ⅝" O.D. with a small .050 inner hole. Williams discs are standard thread size and will accommodate Redfield, Lyman, etc.

R-⅜—.050	⅜" O.D. with .050 inner hole
R-⅜—.093	⅜" O.D. with .093 inner hole (STANDARD, unless otherwise specified)
R-⅜—.125	⅜" O.D. with .125 inner hole— BUCKBUSTER
R-½—.093	½" O.D. with .093 inner hole
R-½—.125	½" O.D. with .125 inner hole

GOLD OR SILVER METAL SHOTGUN SIGHTS

Nos. 1 & 2 Front

No. 3 Front

$1.50

No. 4 Rear

Model	Thread	Bead Dia.	Shank Length
No. 1	6-48	.175	⅛"
No. 2	3-56	.175	⅛"
No. 3	3-56	.130	⅛"
No. 4	3-56	.067	³⁄₃₂"

GARAND CLIP $6.00

For hunting, most states limit the magazine capacity to five shot.

5 Shot Garand

SMLE EXTRACTOR SPRINGS

New, and specially made from tempered spring steel. Easily fitted. Only a punch is needed.

$3.20

NUMBER 1   NUMBER 4 & 5

GUNSMITH'S DRILL AND TAP SETS

3-56 Tap ($2.50)   Carbon

6-48 Tap (2.50)   Carbon

8-40 Tap (2.50)   Carbon

6-48 H.S. Tap — #31 H.S. Drill $6.50

8-40 H.S. Tap — #28 H.S. Drill   6.50

10-32 H.S. Tap — #21 H.S. Drill   6.50

SLOT BLANK $1.85

For appearance sake—use this slot blank after removing iron sight. It will also cover up most burr marks.

Standard ⅜" (left) for Winchester, Stevens, Marlin, Remington, Savage, and other rifles.

OPEN FOLDING SIGHT BASE

$3.15

For Military and Standard Rifles. Will accommodate standard folding sights such as Marble 69, 70, 69H. 70H, Lyman 16A or 16B and Redfield 46, 47 and 48. Base furnished with 6-48 screws. Acts as a riser to give open rear sight necessary height to align properly with ramp front sights or to use with scoped rifles.

WILLIAMS TWILIGHT SCOPES

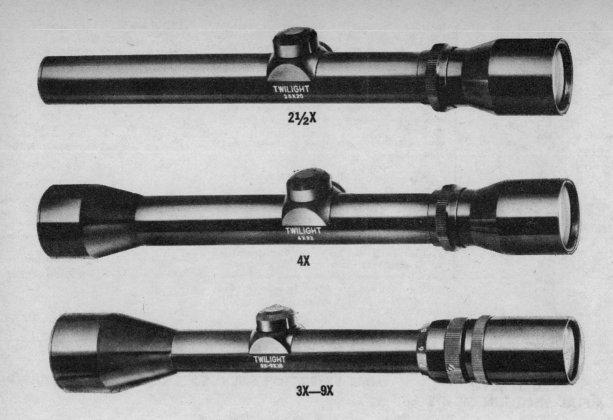

2½X

4X

3X—9X

The 'Twilight' series of scopes was introduced to accommodate those shooters who want a high-quality scope in the medium-priced field. The 'Twilight' scopes are the best value on the market. They are waterproof and shockproof, have coated lenses and are nitrogen filled. Resolution is sharp and clear — actually much superior to the optics of several other more expensive makes. All 'Twilight' scopes have a highly polished, rich-black, hard-anodized finish.

There are four models available — the 2½X, the 4X, the 2X-6X, and the 3X-9X. They are available in two styles of reticles — the plain crosshair and our T-N-T (which stands for thick and thin.)

TWILIGHT SPECIFICATIONS

OPTICAL SPECIFICATIONS	2.5X	4X	2X-6X At 2X	2X-6X At 6X	3X-9X At 3X	3X-9X At 9X
Clear aperture of objective lens	20mm	32mm	32mm	Same	38mm	Same
Clear aperture of ocular lens	32mm	32mm	32mm	Same	32mm	Same
Exit Pupil	8mm	8mm	16mm	5.3mm	12.7mm	4.2mm
Relative Brightness	64	64	256	28	161.2	17.6
Field of view (degree of angle)	12°20'	5°30'	8°30"	3°10'	7°	2°20'
Field of view at 100 yards	32'	29'	45½'	16¾'	36½'	12¾'
Eye Relief	3.7"	3.6"	3"	3"	3.1"	2.9"
Parallax Correction (at)	50 yds.	100 yds.	100 yds.	Same	100 yds.	Same
Lens Construction	9	9	11	Same	11	Same
MECHANICAL SPECIFICATIONS						
Outside diameter of objective end	1.00"	1.525"	1.525"	Same	1.850"	1.850"
Outside diameter of ocular end	1.455"	1.455"	1.455"	Same	1.455"	Same
Outside diameter of tube	1"	1"	1"	Same	1"	Same
Internal adjustment graduation	½ min.	½ min.	½ min.	Same	½ min.	Same
Minimum internal adjustment	75 min.	75 min.	75 min.	Same	60 min.	Same
Finish	Glossy Hard Black Anodized					
Length	11¼"	11¾"	11½"	11½"	12¾"	12¾"
Weight	8½ oz.	9½ oz.	11½ oz.	Same	13½ oz.	Same

Power	Reticle	Price
2½X	Crosshair	$62.00
2½X	T-N-T	69.00

Power	Reticle	Price
4X	Crosshair	$68.00
4X	T-N-T	74.00

Power	Reticle	Price
2X-6X	Crosshair	$ 94.00
2X-6X	T-N-T	100.00

Power	Reticle	Price
3X-9X	Crosshair	$ 99.00
3X-9X	T-N-T	105.00

NEW SIGHT-THRU* MOUNT

INSTANT DUAL SIGHTING — SCOPE ABOVE, IRON SIGHTS BELOW

MODEL 742 REM. WITH SIGHT-THRU MOUNT

- One-piece construction
- Large field of view for Iron Sights right under the scope
- Available for a wide assortment of factory drilled rifles
- All parts are precision machined
- Lightweight
- Hard black anodized finish
- Fast accurate sighting under all field conditions

The Williams Sight-Thru Mount provides instant use of scope, above, or iron sights below. Easily installed. Uses existing holes on top of receiver. No drilling or tapping necessary. The Sight-Thru is compact and lightweight — will not alter balance of the rifle. The high tensile strength alloy will never rust. All parts are precision machined. Completely rigid. Shockproof. The attractive streamlined appearance is further enhanced by a beautiful, hard black anodized finish.

Rings are 1" in size

⅞" Sleeves available at $1.00 per set.

Sight-Thru Mount complete (includes front and rear mount, rings, screws **$15.70**

One Ring complete with Sight-Thru base **7.85**

Sub Block, when required **1.80

*Patent Pending

MODELS	Front	Rear
Winchester Models 88 and 100; Sako Finnwolf; Ithaca 37†	A	A
Remington Models 760-740-742; Savage Model 170; Remington 870† and 1100†	A	B
Winchester Models 70 Standard, 670 and 770 . .	D	C
Remington Models 700 R.H. and L.H., 721, 722, 725; Weatherby MK-V and Vanguard; BSA round top receivers; Ruger 77ST	D	E
Savage Models 110, 111 and 112V	D	F
Browning High Power Auto and lever action; Mossberg 800; Remington 541S†. Will also fit Ward's Western Field Model 72 and Mossberg Model 472 lever action. *See note below	G	G
Late Models Marlin 336 and 44 Magnum	H	H
FN Mauser; Browning Bolt Action; J. C. Higgins 50-51; Interarms Mark X Mauser	D	I
Savage 99 (New Style)	J	K**
Schultz & Larsen	A	G
1917 Enfield	J	J
Ruger 10/22	L	M
Ruger 44	O	M
Ruger 77R and RS Series†	H	P

* When ordering 'G' bases for Western Field Model 72 and Mossberg Model 472, please specify that .360 screws must be furnished.
** Requires Sub Block   † Drilling and Tapping Required

SIGHT-THRU MOUNT FOR 22s

These new mounts are precision made. They are designed to fasten on the dovetails of all current 22's. For those 22's not having dovetails available are mounting plates to attach to receiver that creates the dovetails. Base of mount can be installed in a very low position with an unobstructed, clear view right down to the top of receiver—yet scope can still be elevated approximately ¼" additional.

These WST-D22 Sight-Thru mounts are recommended for 22's only and are available in ¾", ⅞" and 1" tube diameters. Specify tube diameter when ordering—

WST-D22 ¾"	. . . .	**$7.15**
WST-D22 ⅞"	. . . .	**7.75**
WST-D22 1"	. . . .	**8.35**

This Remington model 552 is equipped with a WST-D22-1" mount and a Williams 4X Twilight scope. This sighting system is much more than just a plinking piece of equipment. It is accurate and dependable for target work and excellent for shooting running game.

WILLIAMS SCOPE MOUNTS

WILLIAMS QC SIDE MOUNTS

HCO Rings place scope overbore.

The Williams QC Side Mounts permit the shooter to have both scope and receiver sight always available for instant use. From the same base, shooter has his choice of rings that place scope directly over the bore or in the offset position.

Williams Side Mounts have positive locks. Using these locks, the mount becomes a "one piece" mount. Used optionally, the mount is quickly detached. Williams QC Mounts are provided with a limited amount of windage in the base to insure you of a good mounting job.

QC Side Mount Base	$14.75
QC Side Mount Complete, with split or extension rings	26.20
QC Side Mount Complete with HCO rings	31.85

Regular Rings place scope offset.

THE QUICK CONVERTIBLE SIDE MOUNT — WITH REGULAR OR HCO RINGS

SM 94 SIDE MOUNT ON 94 WINCHESTER

Mounting plate for the 30-M1 carbine **$7.75**
(Attach with 8-40 fillister screws). Use the Williams SM-740 side mount base with this mounting plate. Scope can be offset or high overbore.

Mounting plate for SMLE No. 1 .... **$3.85**
(Attach with 8-40 fillister head mounting screws). This mounting plate is supplied with long 8-40 fillister head screws to replace SM-70 short screws. Use the QC SM-70 base. Mount can be installed offset or central overbore.

Mounting plate for M1 Garand rifle **$7.75**
The mounting screws for this mounting plate are 8-40 x .475 Fillister head. Use the Williams QC SM-740 (4 holes) side mount with this mounting plate.

Mounting Plate for Norwegian Krag **$7.75**
(Attach with 8-40 fillister head screws.) Use the Williams SM-88 side mount base with the above mounting plate. Scope should not be installed central overbore because of top ejection of cartridge.

SM-70	Fits 70, 770, 670, 54 Winchesters; 600, 660, 700 R.H. and L.H., 721, 722 Remingtons; Mossberg 800 and 3000; Weatherby; Mauser; Enfield; Springfield; Jap; 40-45, 322-325 and 340-343 Savages; S&W and Mark X rifles; Stevens; round receivered SMLE's; Husqvarna; 7x61 S&H; Swiss 1911; 7.5; BSA; Savage 110 R.H.; and 91-93-95 small ring Mausers. (Also fits 98 Mauser large ring and 1917 Enfield large ring -- request shim packs with mount.)
SM-71	Fits 36, 336, 93, 444, 44 Magnum, and 95 Marlins; 71* and 86* Winchesters; Remington 14 and 141; 7.62 Russian; and flat receivered SMLE's.
SM-88	Fits 88 and 100 Winchesters; Ruger 44 and 10/22; Winchester 150, 190, 250, 270, and 290; Weatherby 22; Browning lever action; Marlin 1894; Sako Finnwolf; and Norwegian Krag with mounting plate.
SM-94/36	Fits 64, 65, 66, and 94 Winchesters. No drilling or tapping. On 36 and 336 Marlins drill and tap just one hole. NOTE: If mount is to be used with FP or 5D receiver sight, then use the SM-71 mount equipped with proper 94 screws.
SM-99	Fits 99 Savage.
SM-110LH	For the Savage 110 left hand model (fastens on right side of receiver) and fits both short or long actions; and Weatherby Mark 5 L.H.
SM-760/40/42	For 760-740-742 Remingtons. Regular mount base with four mounting holes. Also fits 30-M1 Garand and Carbine with mounting plate; Browning A.R.; Winchester 1200 and 1400; flat receivered shotguns such as Model 12; and flat receivered .22's such as 572 and 552.
SM-MS-52/56	For Mannlicher-Schoenauer of the modified version imported by Stoeger in 1952 and altered in 1956. Also for 1903 Greek Mannlicher modified receiver, like the 52-56.
SM-Krag	For Krag* and Remington 788 right and left hand. Also, for Remington 870 and 1100.
SM-Mini-14	Fits old style Ruger Mini-14 .223 rifle with flat sided receiver. Does not fit new receiver produced since mid-1977.
SM-Mini-14(NS)	(New Style) Fits Ruger Mini-14 .223 rifle with new style receiver.

* Will not accommodate central overbore rings.

QC SIDE MOUNT, BASES ONLY	$14.75
QC SIDE MOUNT, COMPLETE WITH SPLIT, OR EXTENSION RINGS	$26.20
QC SIDE MOUNT, COMPLETE WITH HCO (HIGH CENTRAL OVERBORE) RINGS	$31.85

WILLIAMS DOVETAIL OPEN SIGHT

A precision sight made of lightweight high tensile strength alloy. Has steel screws and locks. Fits the standard ⅜" dovetail. Anodized black finish. Rustproof.

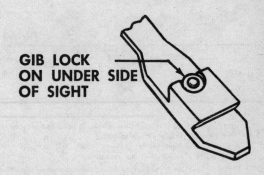

GIB LOCK ON UNDER SIDE OF SIGHT

The revolutionary design of the W.D.O.S. means **no more driving or hammering an open sight into the dovetail** of the rifle. The dovetail of the W.D.O.S. simply slides into the dovetail slot in the rifle barrel with just finger tip pressure as you tighten the locking screw it pulls the steel gib lock up snug against the dovetail on the rifle barrel and locks the sight in place.

Available in four heights with four different styles of blades — the same blades as used in the famous Williams Guide Open Sight — the U, V, SQ, and Britisher type notches.

WINDAGE ADJUSTMENT — Windage Adjustment is obtained by simply loosening the screw to unlock the steel gib lock and then the Williams Open Sight Blade can be moved either to the right or the left. In extreme cases, a double amount of windage can be obtained by getting windage in the dovetail of the barrel as well as with the blade.

ELEVATION — Elevation is obtained simply by an elevation set screw that can be turned in a full 1/16". Since the sight blades are also 1/16" from one model to another, you can get a wide range of adjustment from .281 up to .531. The .281 height is adjustable up to .345 — the .345 height is adjustable up to .406 — the .406 height is adjustable up to .468 — and the .468 height is adjustable up to .531.

Model numbers are:

WDOS—281   WDOS—406
WDOS—345   WDOS—468

TYPES OF BLADES

"SQ"   "U"   "V"   "B"

Sight blades are available in four styles and four heights. The "U", The "V", and "SQ" and the "B" in 3/16", ¼" 5/16" and ⅜".
EXTRA BLADES, each ----------------------------------- $2.35

BLADES

The "U" style is widely used by big game hunters and the "V" has almost as many advocates. The square notch is very popular with target shooters. However, many hunters prefer the square notch blade particularly when using a flat bladed front sight. "B" Britisher blade is exceedingly popular among African big game hunters.

Sight blades are interchangeable and may be quickly removed. Simply loosen the gib lock screw and change to any style or height of blade desired.

Extra sighting blades are just $1.95 each so that an assortment is inexpensive and will provide the shooter with a wide range of heights and styles to suit his taste or requirements.

Price with blade **$6.90**

WILLIAMS GUIDE OPEN SIGHT

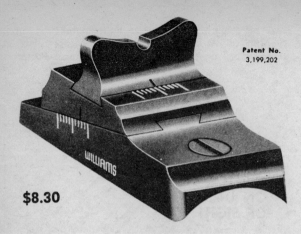

Patent No.
3,199,202

$8.30

The new Guide Open Sight was designed, engineered and field tested by the Williams. It advances a new concept in sighting. It is compact, lightweight, and has a neat streamlined appearance. Both windage and elevation adjustments have positive locks — and various base and blade sizes permit the fitting of most any military or sporting rifle barrel in the greatest range of heights. Also used on rifles when you want iron sights high enough so that sighting plane is above a scope base on the receiver or when you want iron sights close to the height of scope sights.

Fast - the contour of the sighting blade is designed to give the shooter the greatest speed

- Made from high tensile strength metal. Will not rust.
- All parts are .nilled — no stampings.
- Streamlined and lightweight with tough anodized finish.
- Dovetailed windage and elevation — Adjustments quickly made by loosening one screw.
- Positive locks for windage and elevation.
- Hardened gib locks assure positive retention of zeroing.
- Fits all military and sporting rifles with ramp front sights.

- Easily installed. No dovetailing of barrel necessary. Simply fasten to barrel with two 6-48 screws.
- Interchangeable sighting blades of four different heights and four styles of notches.
- Fits the Drilling and Tapping on the 760, 740, 742, 700, 725 Remington, late 70 Win. etc. (9/16" distance center to center on mounting screws.)

SIMPLE WAY TO DESIGNATE SIGHT DESIRED

1) SPECIFY TYPE OF SIGHT —

"WGOS" means
Williams Guide Open Sight

2) SPECIFY RADIUS OF BASE DESIRED S-M-L or FLAT
   (Small - Medium - Large or Flat)

Small: for barrels .660 to .730
Medium: for barrels .730 to .830
Large: for barrels .830 to .930

SPECIAL high base is available for the model 70 Winchester with high line of sights for bbls .730 to .830.

3) SPECIFY OVERALL HEIGHT DESIRED

HEIGHT

The WGOS with 3/16" blade is adjustable in height from .369 to .431.
The WGOS with 1/4" blade is adjustable in height from .431 to .493.
The WGOS with 5/16" blade is adjustable in height from .493 to .555.
The WGOS with 3/8" blade is adjustable in height from .555 to .617.
The WGOS with flat base is .050 higher than the above standard models.
The WGOS-Special in extra large radius is .100 higher than any of the above models.
The WGOS flat base with peep sight aperture is adjustable from .481 to .543.

4) SPECIFY STYLE OF BLADE DESIRED

"SQ" - or - "U" - or - "V" or "B"

EXTRA BLADES — $2.10 each

The most popular blade is the 'U' type notch. Because of this, our WGOS are listed by models, all with the 'U' type notch blade fitted in them. You may want the other style notches as extra or as optional equipment. The following are the basic model numbers.

WGOS S 3/16" 'U'		WGOS M 3/16" 'U'	
WGOS S 1/4" 'U'		WGOS M 1/4" 'U'	
WGOS S 5/16" 'U'		WGOS M 5/16" 'U'	
WGOS S 3/8" 'U'		WGOS M 3/8" 'U'	

WGOS L 3/16" 'U'
WGOS L 1/4" 'U'
WGOS L 5/16" 'U'
WGOS L 3/8" 'U'

The WGOS can be ordered with other style blades or with the Flat bases instead of the Small (S), Medium (M) or Large (L) radii—or in the WGOS Special.

WILLIAMS SIGHT COMBINATION CHART

Ramp Height	Height from Base to Dovetail	Height of Williams Bead	From Top of Barrel to Top of Bead
1/8"	.035	.250	.285
1/8"	.035	.290	.325
1/8"	.035	.312	.347
3/16"	.0975	.250	.3475
1/8"	.035	.343	.378
3/16"	.0975	.290	.3875
3/16"	.0975	.312	.4095
1/8"	.035	.375	.410
3/16"	.0975	.343	.4405
1/8"	.035	.406	.441
9/32"	.191	.250	.441
9/32"	.191	.290	.481
3/16"	.0975	.375	.4725
5/16"	.2225	.250	.4725
1/8"	.035	.450	.485
9/32"	.191	.312	.503
3/16"	.0975	.406	.5035
5/16"	.2225	.290	.5125
9/32"	.191	.343	.534
5/16"	.2225	.312	.5345
3/8"	.285	.250	.535
3/16"	.0975	.450	.5475
5/16"	.2225	.343	.5655
9/32"	.191	.375	.566
3/8"	.285	.290	.575
9/32"	.191	.406	.597

Ramp Height	Height from Base to Dovetail	Height of Williams Bead	From Top of Barrel to Top of Bead
3/8"	.285	.312	.597
5/16"	.2225	.375	.5975
7/16"	.3475	.250	.5975
3/8"	.285	.343	.628
5/16"	.2225	.406	.6285
7/16"	.3475	.290	.6375
9/32"	.191	.450	.641
7/16"	.3475	.312	.6595
3/8"	.285	.375	.660
5/16"	.2225	.450	.6725
7/16"	.3475	.343	.6905
3/8"	.285	.406	.691
3/8"	.285	.450	.735
7/16"	.3475	.375	.7225
9/16"	.4725	.250	.7225
7/16"	.3475	.406	.7535
9/16"	.4725	.290	.7625
9/16"	.4725	.312	.7845
7/16"	.3475	.450	.7975
9/16"	.4725	.343	.8155
9/16"	.4725	.375	.8475
9/16"	.4725	.406	.8785
9/16"	.4725	.450	.9225

AMOUNT OF ADJUSTMENT NECESSARY TO CORRECT FRONT SIGHT ERROR

DISTANCE BETWEEN FRONT AND REAR SIGHTS	14"	15"	16"	17"	18"	19"	20"	21"	22"	23"	24"	25"	26"	27"	28"	29"	30"	31"	32"	33"	34"
Amount of 1	.0038	.0041	.0044	.0047	.0050	.0053	.0055	.0058	.0061	.0064	.0066	.0069	.0072	.0074	.0077	.0080	.0082	.0085	.0088	.0091	.0093
Error 2	.0078	.0083	.0089	.0094	.0100	.0105	.0111	.0116	.0122	.0127	.0133	.0138	.0144	.0149	.0155	.0160	.0156	.0171	.0177	.0182	.0188
at 3	.0117	.0125	.0133	.0142	.0150	.0159	.0167	.0175	.0184	.0192	.0201	.0209	.0217	.0226	.0234	.0243	.0251	.0259	.0268	.0276	.0285
100 Yards 4	.0155	.0167	.0178	.0189	.0200	.0211	.0222	.0234	.0244	.0255	.0266	.0278	.0289	.0300	.0311	.0322	.0333	.0344	.0355	.0366	.0377
Given in 5	.0194	.0208	.0222	.0236	.0250	.0264	.0278	.0292	.0306	.0319	.0333	.0347	.0361	.0375	.0389	.0403	.0417	.0431	.0445	.0458	.0472
Inches 6	.0233	.0250	.0267	.0283	.0300	.0317	.0333	.0350	.0367	.0384	.0400	.0417	.0434	.0450	.0467	.0484	.0500	.0517	.0534	.0551	.0567

When you replace an open rear sight with a receiver sight, it is usually necessary to install a higher front sight, to compensate for the higher plane of the new receiver sight. The table above shows the increase in front sight height that's required to compensate for a given error at 100 yards. Suppose your rifle has a 19 inch sight radius, and shoots 6 inches high at 100 yards, with the receiver sight adjusted as low as possible. The 19 inch column shows that the correction for a 6 inch error is .0317 inch. This correction is added to the over-all height of the front sight (including dovetail). Use a micrometer or similar accurate device to measure sight height. Thus, if your original sight measured .250 inch, it should be replaced with a sight .290 inch high.

WILLIAMS FRONT SIGHT PUSHER

$23.85

In the past there was only one accepted way to install a front sight in a ramp—pound it in with a hammer from the side. This method frequently marred a beautiful finish and loosened or damaged the ramp.

The Williams Front Sight Pusher provides the easiest and best way to install a front sight in a ramp. By equalizing the pressure on ramp and sight, it permits installation without marring or damaging, and eliminates excessive pressure on the ramp itself. Sight is smoothly and accurately moved into exact position.

The Front Sight Pusher is a precision tool for neat precision work.

WILLIAMS GUIDE RECEIVER SIGHTS

$11.95

In most cases these sights utilize dovetail or existing screws on top of receiver for installation. They are made from an aluminum alloy that is stronger than many steels. Light. Rustproof. Williams quality throughout.

WGRS-37 — For Ithaca 37 pump shotgun.

WGRS-44 — For Ruger 44. Similar to the WGRS-RU22, but not interchangeable. Usually requires a higher front sight — .500 to .560.

WGRS-54 — For Savage-Anschutz 54, 64, 141, 141M, 153, 153S. Also Remington 541S, 552BDL, 572BDL, and Winchester 310 and 320. This is a very versatile sight in that it can be fitted on most of the dovetails on the receivers of .22 rifles. These dovetails have quite a wide tolerance and in many cases will require some hand fitting of the WGRS-54, but this can be easily accomplished by filing the bottom of the sight slightly to increase the width of the dovetail and then it is just a matter of slipping the sight on. Because most .22's do not have ramp front sights, a higher front sight is required. Use of the Williams Shorty or Streamlined ramp and a Williams beaded front sight should solve any of these problems.

WGRS-70 — For all post war Model 70 Winchesters. Will also fit the Model 670 and 770.

- Compact Low Profile
- Lightweight, Strong, Rustproof
- Positive Windage and Elevation Locks

WGRS-70 — For all post war Model 70 Winchesters. Will also fit the Model 670 and 770.

WGRS-100 — For Winchester 88 lever action and 100 automatic. (Higher front sight needed — .406 height.) Also for Sako Finnwolf.

WGRS-700 — For Remington 700, 721 and 722.

WGRS-742 — For Remington 760 and 742. Early models will require a higher front sight. For the BDL's, use the FP-740AP.

WGRS-BAR — For Browning High Power Auto rifle and lever action sporting version.

WGRS-FN — Will fit any FN type action with ½'' hole spacing including the Mauser FN, S&W, Crown Grade Husqvarna (CGH), and the Browning high power bolt action, and Mark X.

WGRS-M1 CAR. — For the 30 M1 Carbine. Fits dovetail.

WGRS-M/L — For Thompson/Center Hawken and most black powder rifles with octagon barrels.

WGRS-RU-22 — Fits Ruger 10/22 without drilling or tapping. A higher front sight is normally required, usually .500 to .560.

WGRS-WR — For late Winchester and Remington slide action and autoloading shotguns. Also will fit Hopkins & Allen muzzleloaders.

OPEN SIGHT BLADES
FOR THE GUIDE OPEN SIGHT

Many shooters wish to make open sights out of receiver sights. This can be done since the blades from our Guide Open Sights are interchangeable with the apertures of the receiver sights. Any Guide Receiver Sight can be ordered special with a Guide Open Sight blade in the SQ, U, V, or B. Normally the 3/16'' blade is used since it is the approximate same height as the regular peep sight aperture.

WILLIAMS STREAMLINED TOP MOUNT

SHOWN ON MODEL 70A WIN.

- AVAILABLE FOR WIDE ASSORTMENT OF FACTORY DRILLED RIFLES
- PRECISION MACHINED — LIGHTWEIGHT
- SOLID CONSTRUCTION
- ELIMINATES NEED FOR EXTENSION RINGS — ALLOWS USE OF VIRTUALLY ALL 1" SCOPES

- THE BASES ARE THE RINGS
- HARD BLACK ANODIZED FINISH

Streamline two-piece Top Mount complete **$15.00**
Streamline front or rear base only **7.50**
Streamline sub-blocks for Hawken ML (per pair) **5.30**

WILLIAMS SIGHTS & ACCESSORIES

Patent No. 2578386

THE FOOLPROOF

One of the reasons the Foolproof is so popular is that it is free from knobs and other obstructions that impair and blot-out much of the shooter's field of vision.

Internal micrometer adjustments have positive internal locks — there is nothing — no exterior knobs or posts — that could be accidentally jarred or moved to throw the sight out of adjustment.

The Foolproof is strong, rugged, dependable. The alloy used to manufacture this sight has a tensile strength of 85,000 lbs. Yet the Foolproof is light and compact, weighing only 1½ ounces.

$21.10

with Twilight Aperture—
$22.75

with Target Knobs = $26.20
with Target Knobs and Twilight
Aperture = $26.85

FOOLPROOF RECEIVER SIGHT WITH TARGET KNOBS

The FP-TK has audible micrometer click adjustments. Target knobs allow quick positive windage and elevation adjustments without the use of a screwdriver. Positive internal locks.

These Models Fit More Than 100 Guns

FP-12/37	For Winchester 12, 1200, 1400, 150, 190, 250, 255, 270 275 and 290; Ithaca 37; Remington Sportsman 48, 58, 11-48, 1100, 870* and most flat receivered pumps and autoloaders.
FP-14	For Remington 14 and 141.
FP-17	For Enfield, Remington Express and British Pattern 14.
FP-30 Car.	For Government 30 Carbine.
FP-39	For Marlin 39A lever action.
FP-52	For Win. 52 Sporter or other round receivered 52 models.
FP-70	For 70 and 54 Winchesters; 721, 722, 725 Remingtons; Mossberg 800.
FP-70AP	For new Model 70, 670 and 770 with high sight line; Remington 700; Mossberg 800 and 3000; and BSA.
FP-71	For Win. 71, 86, 05, 07, and 10.
FP-88/100	For Win. 88 lever action; Win. 100 auto; Marlin 56, 57, 62, 99 auto-loading; and Sako Finnwolf.
FP-94/36	For Winchester Models 94, 55, 63, 64, 65, and 9422; Marlin Models 36, 336, 444, 44 Magnum, and 93; Sears and Browning centerfire lever actions.
FP-95	For 95 Winchester lever action.
FP-98	For military Mauser, Husqvarna, Weatherby Mark V, right and left, and BRNO without dovetailed receiver.
FP-98AP	For Browning high power bolt with high line of sights; also for Rem. 700 left hand.
FP-99	For Savage 99 lever action.
FP-99S	For late Savage 99 with top tang safety.
FP-110	For Savage 110 bolt action, right and left.
FP-121	For Remington 12 and 121.
FP-340	For 322-325-340-342 Stevens-Savage.

FP-600	For Remington 600, 660 bolt action.
FP-740AP	For all 742 Remingtons and for the late 760-740 Remingtons with high comb (all purpose stock) and high iron sights. Also for the higher sight models of the 740 in the 30-06 and 280 calibers above serial number 207,200 and the 308 caliber above serial number 200,000. Also for Remington 572BDL and 552BDL and Savage 170.
FP-788	For Remington 788 bolt action.
FP-788LH	For Remington 788 left hand action.
FP-A3	For 03/A3 and 03 Springfields.
FP-BAR	For Browning auto-loading high power rifle.
FP-BR	For .22 Browning Auto and 24-241 Remingtons.
FP-CGH	For Crown Grade Husqvarna and S&W rifle.
FP-FN	For factory drilled and tapped FN and Dumoulin, Mark X, Daisy 99 and 299.
FP-Hawken	For Thompson/Center Hawken and Renegade M/L rifles.
FP-JAP	For Jap .25 and .31 caliber rifles.
FP-Krag	For American Krag and Norwegian Krag.
FP-RU	For 44 Mag. Ruger carbine and .22 L.R. 10/22 all models.
FP-RU-77	For Ruger Model 77 bolt action.
FP-S&L	For Schultz & Larsen 54J, Model 60 and 65DL.
FP-SMLE	For British Short Magazine Lee Enfields.
FP-SSM	For square sterned auto shotguns. Also fits 8-81 Rem.
FP-SW	For 1911, Swiss 7.5.
FP-T/C	For Thompson/Center Contender Pistol.

NOTE: Add 'TK' to model number if target knobs are desired.

WILLIAMS SIGHTS & ACCESSORIES

5D-12-37

5D-22-410

5D-94-36

5D-JEMS

The Williams 5D receiver sight is made for big game rifles, shotguns, and 22 Caliber rifles. It is well made of the finest materials with positive windage and elevation adjustments. Standard thread sizes permit use of a wide range of apertures for all sighting conditions. This high-grade alloy is finished with an anodize in a deep blue-black that adds even further to the strength of the sight by creating an extra hard surface **$12.50**

FOR FOLLOWING MODELS

5D-12/37* Winchester 1200, 1400, 12-25, 150, 190, 250, 255, 270, 275, and 290; Remington 1100, '58, 11-48, Spt's. 48, 870, and 31; Stevens 620; Ithaca 37; and other shotguns with flat-sided receivers.

5D-22/410 For the .22-410, 20, etc. over and under Savage or Stevens.

5D-39A Marlin 39A lever action. No drilling or tapping necessary.

5D-49 For the Ithaca 49 Saddlegun .22 cal.

5D-56/989 For Marlin Levermatic 56, 57, 62, 99 Auto, Marlin 989 and 99's; Sako Finnwolf; Winchester 88 and 100.

5D-70 For Winchester 70, 54, 670, 770, and 74 .22 Auto; Remington 700, 721, 722, and 725; Mossberg 800 and 3000.

5D-74 For Winchester Model 74 .22 Auto.

5D-77 For Winchester 77 .22 Auto.

5D-81 For Marlin 80, 81 and A1 rifles (factory drilled and tapped).

5D-94/36 For Winchester 94, 64, 9422; Marlin 36, 336, 1894, .44 Magnum.

5D-510 For Remington 510, 511, 512, and 513 (some factory drilled and tapped), Nylon 12 tubular loading, Nylon 11 box magazine.

5D-550 For Remington 550 auto (it will also fit some of the Stevens-Savage .22's that are not drilled and tapped).

5D-572 For Remington 572, 572BDL, 552BDL .22 slide action; Kodiak 260.

5D-760N–740–742 For the Remington 760 with serial numbers above 154,965 and 740's above serial number 64,046. Also for Remington Nylon 66; Winchester new series 250, 255, 270, 275, and 290 with ramp; and Savage 170.

5D-CR-160 For Crosman air rifles model 160.

5D-JEMS For Jap, Enfield, Mauser, and Springfield 03; Remington 700 L.H.; Daisy 99 and 299.

5D-Krag For American Krag.

5D-03/A3 For 1903-A3 Springfield.

5D-RU For 44 Ruger Carbine and 10/22 (all models).

5D-SH For Sheridan Model 'C'; Benjamin 340, 342, 347. (The Benjamin needs a higher front sight).

5D-SMLE For British Short Magazine Lee Enfield, Nos. 1, 4, & 5.

5D-SSM* For square stern models of Remington, Browning and Savage auto shotguns. Also fits Rem. 8-81 autoloaders.

*Special shotgun aperture optional. Extra shotgun apertures $2.95
3/8'' OD Aperture with 093 inner hole furnished unless otherwise specified.

Some of the Higgins guns are made by Marlin. Usually if the model number 103 is on a Higgins gun— then it's made by Marlin. Consequently, some of the sights we have designed for Marlin will fit a few models of the Higgins.

AVAILABLE IN IVORY, RED, GOLD
Available in Ivory, Red, Gold

WILLIAMS "GUIDE BEAD" SHOTGUN SIGHTS
$2.65

Fits all shotguns. Large ⅛'' jewel finish bead has exceptional light gathering ability. Gets you on target fast. Easily installed. Screws into existing sight hole. Two thread sizes: 6-48 and 3-56, and two shank lengths, ³⁄₃₂'' and ⁵⁄₃₂''.

WILLIAMS SCOPE MOUNTS

WILLIAMS QUICK CONVERTIBLE TOP MOUNT

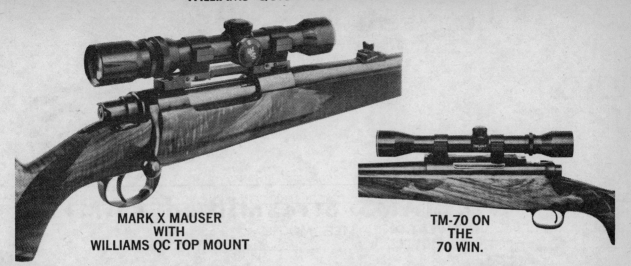

**MARK X MAUSER
WITH
WILLIAMS QC TOP MOUNT**

**TM-70 ON
THE
70 WIN.**

TM-03	For 03 Springfield.
TM-03/A3	For 03/A3 Springfield.
*TM-7x61 (54)	For Sharpe & Hart 7x61, 54 bolt action.
*TM-7x61 (60)	For Sharpe & Hart 7x61, 60 bolt action.
*TM-14	For Remington Model 14 slide action.
TM-17	For 1917 Enfield and 30 Express and 720 Remingtons. On the Enfield grind the receiver to the same height and radius in the rear as in the front.
TM-17 Special	For 1917 Enfield. There is enough stock left at the rear of mount base so the Model 17's not cut to standard specifications may be fitted.
TM-22 RU	For Ruger 10/22 Auto rifle.
*TM-30	For J. C. Higgins Model 30.
*TM-43N	For new Model 43 factory drilled and tapped.
*TM-50	For early versions of J. C. Higgins Model 50.
*TM-52	Fits late Winchester Model 52 Sporter and Target. (Older models are not drilled and tapped.)
*TM-63/121	For Win. 63 Auto and Rem. 121 slide action.
TM-70	For all factory drilled 70's and 670's, 770's except 300 H&H and 375 H&H. Rear hole spacing—center to center—.860.
*TM-77	For Winchester 77 .22 Auto.
TM-88	For Winchester 88 lever action, fitting factory drilling and tapping.
TM-93/95	For Mexican or Spanish Mausers (short action). It is necessary to flatten the top of receiver where the 5-shot clip enters receiver if the gun is not going to be reblued. If it is to be reblued, grind this lobe off entirely. Also for 91 Argentine Mauser, 94 Swedish Mauser.
TM-98	For 98 Mauser and standard Husqvarna. It is necessary to flatten the top of receiver where the 5-shot clip enters receiver if the gun is not going to be reblued. If it is to be reblued, grind this lobe off.
TM-99	For all 99's without tang safety.
TM-99S	For the 99 Savages 99DL and F models with tang type safety.
TM-100	For Model 100 Winchester Auto, Sako Finnwolf.
*TM-110-L	For Savage Model 110's, 30-06, 270, 7mm, 264, and 338 Magnum with longer action.
*TM-110-LS	For Savage left hand, short actions, 243 and 308.
*TM-110-S	For Savage Model 110, 243 and 308 short actions.

TM-336N	Fits late 336 Marlins that are factory drilled and tapped. Mounting screw holes are 8-40. Earlier models must be drilled and tapped. Includes the 444's.
TM-600	For Rem. 600, 660 bolt action, 40X and XP100 pistol.
TM-721-MK5	Fits factory drilled and tapped 721, 725, 700 (long action) Remingtons and Weatherby Mark 5, BSA.
TM-722	Fits factory drilled and tapped 722 and 700 short action Remingtons.
TM-760	Fits 760, 740, 742 Remingtons. Most of these rifles are drilled and tapped on top for this mount. Also fits Savage 170.
*TM-788	For Remington R.H. and L.H. 788. The .222, 30-30 and 22-250 require no drilling or tapping. The 44 Magnum requires drilling and tapping rear hole.
*TM-800	For Mossberg 800.
TM-B22-241	For Browning .22 Auto and Rem. 241 with mount fastening on barrel and extending back over receiver.
TM-BAR	For Browning High Power Auto rifle and lever action.
*TM-BRS	For short action 243 Browning, FN Browning short action.
TM-CGH	For Crown Grade Husqvarna. Fits factory drilling and tapping. Also for Smith & Wesson rifle.
TM-FNA	For F.N. actions. Fits FN actions, Weatherby, and late J. C. Higgins Models 50 and 51, Browning High Power rifles. (Except short FN actions.)
*TM-L-57	For Sako medium action 243, 308, etc. Necessary to drill and tap.
TM-MK5-LH	For Weatherby Mark V L.H. and Rem. 700 L.H.
*TM-RU	For Ruger .44 Magnum carbine. Fits old style factory drilling and tapping with all 4 holes on receiver.
TM-SW Mauser	For Mauser Mark X.
TM-VOERE	For Voere Mauser.
TM-WBY-VM	Varmint Master, Weatherby 224 and 22/250 calibers.
TM-AR-15	For Colt AR-15 .223. (Also M-16)

QC Top Mount, Bases only **$14.75**

QC Top Mount, Complete **26.20**

* Discontinued — Subject To Stock On Hand.

WILLIAMS RAMPS

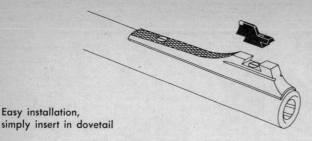

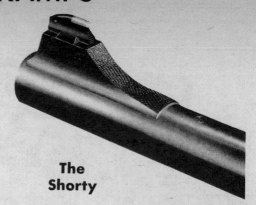

Easy installation, simply insert in dovetail

The Streamlined

The Shorty

WILLIAMS Streamlined RAMPS

SWEAT-ON MODEL   STEEL MODELS

SCREW-ON MODEL

WITH HOOD $9.30
LESS HOOD   7.75

The STREAMLINED

Available in heights of: 9/16", 7/16", ⅜", 5/16", 3/16".

WILLIAMS SHORTY RAMP — Steel —

MAY BE SWEATED ON

INSTALL WITH DOVETAIL LOCK

SCREW ON
IN LOW ⅛" Model

ATTACH WITH ONE SCREW

A SHORTENED VERSION OF THE POPULAR STREAMLINED RAMP

The new Shorty ramp is the companion to the popular Streamlined ramp. It is much shorter, being designed especially for handguns, .22s and some of the big game rifles. The Shorty is easily installed. It can be sweated on or screwed on a Special locking device that fits the standard 3/8" dovetail cut and a 6:48 screw is also furnished. The single screw firmly locks ramp snugly to barrel for a neat perfect fit.
Four heights available: 1/8", 3/16", 9/32" and 3/8".

$5.95
HOODLESS ONLY

WILLIAMS RIFLE SIGHT ASSORTMENT KIT $145.20

Front sights available in eight heights with a 1/16" bead. Also 3/32" bead on special order. Half of the sights have a base width of .250 for the Streamlined and Shorty ramp and the other sights have a wide .340 base for the 99 Savage, 94 Winchester, 336 Marlin, etc.

Dovetail open sights available in four heights — from .281 to .468 with a "U" type notch unless otherwise specified.

4 Front Sights .250 high—Gold and White—Two Widths
4 Front Sights .281 high—Gold and White—Two Widths
4 Front Sights .312 high—Gold and White—Two Widths
4 Front Sights .343 high—Gold and White—Two Widths
4 Front Sights .375 high—Gold and White—Two Widths
4 Front Sights .406 high—Gold and White—Two Widths
4 Front Sights .437 high—Gold and White—Two Widths
4 Front Sights .468 high—Gold and White—Two Widths
4 Willaims Dovetail Open Sights—Four Heights

Ammunition

REMINGTON RIM-FIRE AMMUNITION
with "KLEANBORE" PRIMING

22 Win. Automatic

No.	Bullet weight and style	Wt. case, lbs.	Per box
7522	45 gr., Lead	52	$5.25

50 in a box, 5,000 in a case.

"HIGH VELOCITY" CARTRIDGES
with "Golden" Bullets

22 Short

No.	Bullet weight and style	Wt. case, lbs.	Per box
1022	29 gr., Lead	29	$1.47
1122	27 gr., Lead, Hollow Point	28	1.57

50 in a box, 5,000 in a case.

22 Long

No.	Bullet weight and style	Wt. case, lbs.	Per box
1322	29 gr., Lead	31	$1.57

50 in a box, 5,000 in a case.

22 Long Rifle

No.	Bullet weight and style	Wt. case, lbs.	Per box
1522	40 gr., Lead	40	$1.65
1622	36 gr., Lead, Hollow Point	38	1.81

50 in a box, 5,000 in a case.

100 Pack

1500	40 gr., Lead	40	$3.30
1600	36 gr., Lead, Hollow Point	38	3.62

100 in a box, 5,000 in a case.

22 W.R.F. (Remington Special)

No.	Bullet weight and style	Wt. case, lbs.	Per box
1822	45 gr., Lead	48	4.79

50 in a box, 5,000 in a case.

★ **New**

"TARGET" STANDARD VELOCITY CARTRIDGES

22 Short

No.	Bullet weight and style	Wt. case, lbs.	Per box
5522	29 gr., Lead	29	$1.47

50 in a box, 5,000 in a case.

22 Short Gallery

No.	Bullet weight and style	Wt. case, lbs.	Per box
5722*	29 gr., Lead	57	$6.90
6722*	15 gr., Special Composition	37	6.90

250 in a box, 10,000 in a case.

* New Improved—not for Revolvers.

22 Long Rifle

No.	Bullet weight and style	Wt. case, lbs.	Per box
6122	40 gr., Lead	40	$1.65

50 in a box, 5,000 in a case.

.22 Long Rifle, Target
100 pack.

No.	Bullet weight and style	Wt. case, lbs.	Per box
6100	40 gr., Lead	40	$3.30

100 in a box, 5,000 in a case.

5mm Remington Magnum

No.	Bullet weight and style	Wt. case, lbs.	Per box
1050	38 gr., "Power Lokt" H.P.	21	$8.21

50 in a box, 2,000 in a case.

Prices Subject to Change Without Notice.

"YELLOW JACKET" CARTRIDGES
Hyper-Velocity

22 Long Rifle

No.	Bullet weight and style	Wt. case, lbs.	Per box
★1722	33 gr. Truncated Cone, Hollow Point	36	$2.00

50 in a box, 5,000 in a case.

MATCH CARTRIDGES

Rifle Match 22 Long Rifle
100 pack.

No.	Bullet weight and style	Wt. case, lbs.	Per box
6600	40 gr., Lead	39	$5.51

100 in a box, 5,000 in a case.

Pistol Match 22 Long Rifle

No.	Bullet weight and style	Wt. case, lbs.	Per box
6800	40 gr., Lead	39	$5.51

100 in a box, 5,000 in a case.

SHOT

22 Long Rifle Hi-Speed

No.	Wt. case, lbs.	Per box
9322	33	$3.41

50 in a box, 5,000 in a case.

BLANK

22 Short

No.	Wt. case, lbs.	Per box
9022	7	$9.46

250 in a box, 5,000 in a case.

PETERS RIM-FIRE AMMUNITION
with "KLEANBORE" PRIMING

"HIGH VELOCITY" with "Golden" Bullets

22 Short

No.	Bullet weight and style
2267	29 gr., Lead
2268	27 gr., Lead, Hollow Point

50 in a box

22 Long

No.	Bullet weight and style
2269	29 gr., Lead

50 in a box

"HIGH VELOCITY" with "Golden" Bullets

22 Long Rifle

No.	Bullet weight and style	Wt. case, lbs.	Per box
2283	40 gr., Lead	40	$1.33
2284	36 gr., Hollow Point	38	1.47

50 in a box, 5,000 in a case.

STANDARD "TARGET" VELOCITY

22 Long Rifle "High Velocity"

No.
2299

50 in a box

"VICTOR" HI-SPEED 22

22 Long Rifle

No.	Bullet weight and style
PR 22	40 gr., Lead

50 in a box.

FEDERAL RIM-FIRE AMMUNITION

HI-POWER 22's with copper-plated bullets. A high velocity load for that extra-hard blow you need when hunting small game or pests. Their flat trajectory and accuracy provide an advantage at normal ranges. All have a non-corrosive, non-mercuric priming mixture that has long-term stability and will not cause barrel rust. Packed 50 per box except where noted.

NO.	CALIBER	WT. GRS.	BULLET STYLE	PER BOX
701	22 Short Hi-Power	29	Lead, Solid	$1.47
703	22 Short Hi-Power Hollow Point	29	Lead, HP	1.57
706	22 Long Hi-Power	29	Lead, Solid	1.57
710	22 Long Rifle Hi-Power	40	Lead, Solid	1.65
712	22 Long Rifle Hi-Power Hollow Point	38	Lead, HP	1.81
716	22 Long Rifle Hi-Power Shot	25	No. 12 Shot	3.41
810	22 Long Rifle Hi-Power (100 pack)	40	Lead, Solid	3.30
812	22 Long Rifle Hi-Power Hollow Point (100 pack)	38	Lead, HP	3.62
510	22 Long Rifle Power-Flite (unplated)	40	Lead, Solid	1.36
514	22 Long Rifle Semi-Hollow Point	40	Lead, SHP	1.43

CHAMPION standard velocity 22's. A standard velocity load with a lubricated lead bullet for plinking, short range hunting, and informal target shooting where consistent accuracy is needed. All have non-corrosive, non-mercuric priming mixture which will not cause barrel rust. Packed 50 per box except where noted.

NO.	CALIBER	WT. GRS.	BULLET STYLE	PER BOX
702	22 Short	29	Lead, Solid	$1.47
711	22 Long Rifle	40	Lead, Solid	1.65
811	22 Long Rifle (100 pack)	40	Lead, Solid	3.30

WINCHESTER AND WESTERN RIM-FIRE AMMUNITION

Rim Fire— Staynless Non-Corrosive Priming. All Rim Fire Ammunition packed 5,000 per case

Super-X 22 Rim Fire Cartridges—High Velocity

WESTERN SYMBOL	WINCHESTER SYMBOL	CARTRIDGE	BULLET OR SHOT WT. GRS.	BULLET TYPE	SUGGESTED RETAIL PRICE PER BOX
SX22S	WSX22S	22 Short, Super-X	29	L—K	$1.47
SX22SH	WSX22SH	22 Short, H.P., Super-X	27	L—K	1.57
SX22L	WSX22L	22 Long, Super-X	29	L—K	1.57
WWSX22X	WWSX22X	22 Long Rifle, Super-X Xpediter	29	L	2.27
SX22LR	WSX22LR	22 Long Rifle, Super-X	40	L—K	1.66
SX22LR1	WSX22LR1	22 Long Rifle, Super-X	40	L—K	3.31
SX22LRD	WSX22LRD	22 Long Rifle DYNAPOINT Super-X (Semi-H.P.)	40	L—K	1.81
SX22LRH	WSX22LRH	22 Long Rifle, H.P., Super-X	37	L—K	1.82
SX22LRH1	WSX22LRH1	22 Long Rifle, H.P., Super-X	37	L—K	3.64
SX22LRS	WSX22LRS	22 Long Rifle Shot, Super-X	25	No. 12 Shot	3.41

L=Western Lubaloy   K=Winchester Kopperklad   H.P.=Hollow Point

Super-X 22 Winchester Magnum Rim Fire Cartridges

SX22WMR	WSX22WMR	22 Winchester Magnum, Super-X	40	J.H.P.	4.52
SX22MR1	WSX22MR1	22 Winchester Magnum, Super-X	40	F.M.C.	4.52

J.H.P.=Jacketed Hollow Point   F.M.C.=Full Metal Case

T 22 Rim Fire Cartridges—Standard Velocity Target and Sporting

T22S	WT22S	22 Short	29	Lead	1.47
T22LR	WT22LR	22 Long Rifle	40	Lead	1.65

Super-Match Rim Fire Cartridges

SM22LR	†	22 Long Rifle SUPER-MATCH MARK III	40	Lead	3.33
SM22LR4	†	22 Long Rifle SUPER-MATCH MARK IV Pistol	40	Lead	3.59

Super-Match Gold Rim Fire Cartridges

SM22G	†	22 Long Rifle SUPER-MATCH GOLD	40	Lead	4.45

SUPER-MATCH cartridges are especially recommended for the highest degree of accuracy in all match shooting with rifles and pistols.

Other Winchester Rim Fire Cartridges

†	W22BL	22 Short Blank (Black Powder)	—	—		1.91
WW22CBS2	WW22CBS2	22 Short C.B.	29	Lead	250	7.31

FIOCCHI
22 Rimfire Cartridges

CALIBER	BULLET WEIGHT IN GRAINS	BULLET TYPE	CALIBER	BULLET WEIGHT IN GRAINS	BULLET TYPE	CALIBER	BULLET WEIGHT IN GRAINS	BULLET TYPE
22 SHORT TRAINING	29	Lead	22 SHORT "Z"	29	Lead	22 L.R. ULTRASONIC	40	Lead
22 SHORT NOMALE	29	Lead	22 LONG	28	Lead	22 L.R. EXPANSIVE	37	Lead
22 SHORT OLIMPIONICO	31	Lead	22 LONG "Z"	29	Lead	22 L.R. COMPETIZIONE	40	Lead
22 SHORT V 50	28	Lead	22 LONG L.R. MAXAC	40	Lead	22 L.R. PISTOLA LIBERA	40	Lead
22 SHORT EXPANSIVE	28	Lead	22 L.R. CARB. BERETTA	40	Lead	22 EXTRA LONG	40	Lead

Short

Short H.P.

Short Spatterpruf

Long Rifle

Long Rifle H.P.

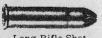
Long Rifle Shot

Long Rifle Match

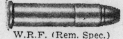
W.R.F. (Rem. Spec.)

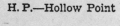
Winchester Magnum

H. P.—Hollow Point   **LUB.—Lubricated**   **L. V.—Low Velocity**

AMMUNITION

CCI 22 RIMFIRE

Part No.		Description	Retail per box	Qty. per Case	lbs. per Case
Plastic 100 PAK					
0030	P22HS	Mini-Mag Long Rifle	$3.30	5000	47
0031	P22HP	Mini-Mag Long Rifle (HP)	3.63	5000	45
0032	P22SV	Mini-Group Long Rifle	3.30	5000	47
0029	P22L	Mini-Mag Long	3.12	5000	39
0027	P22S	Mini-Mag Short	2.93	5000	37
0028	P22SHP	Mini-Mag Short (HP)	3.12	5000	37
0037	P22ST	Mini-Group Short Target	3.08	5000	37
0038	P22CBL	Mini-Cap Long	2.92	5000	38
0026	P22CB	Mini-Cap CB	2.92	5000	38
0039*	P22SS	Mini-Mag (Shotshell)	1.71	2000	18
Paper 50 PAK					
0034	22HS	Mini-Mag Long Rifle	1.44	5000	40
Plastic 50 PAK					
0050	STINGER	Penta-Point (LRHP)	2.26	5000	44
0023	WMR22HS	Maxi-Mag (Solid)	4.52	5000	58
0024	WMR22HP	Maxi-Mag (HP)	4.52	5000	58
0025*	WMR22SS	Maxi-Mag (Shotshell)	2.78	2000	26

CCI-SPEER LAWMAN CENTERFIRE

Plastic 50 PAK

Part No.		Description	Retail per box	Qty. per Case	lbs. per Case
380 AUTO					
3605	88 gr. JHP	Reserve	$11.45	1000	22
9mm LUGER					
3610	100 gr. JHP	Marshal	13.95	1000	27
3620	125 gr. JSP	M-P	13.95	1000	31
38 SPECIAL					
3710	110 gr. JHP	Special Agent	13.45	1000	30
3720	125 gr. JHP+P	Detective	13.45	1000	32
3725	125 gr. JSP+P	Patrolman	13.45	1000	32
3740	140 gr. JHP+P	Deputy	13.45	1000	34
3748	148 gr. HBWC	Match	11.05	1000	35
3752	158 gr. SWC L	Service	10.85	1000	37
3758	158 gr. RN L	Service	10.85	1000	37
3759	158 gr. JSP+P	Trooper	13.45	1000	37
3760	158 gr. JHP+P	S.W.A.T	13.45	1000	37
3708	#9 SHOTSHELL		14.10	1000	31
3709**	#9 SHOTSHELL	(10-PAK)	3.50	1000	33
357 MAGNUM					
3910	110 gr. JHP	Special Agent	14.75	1000	35
3920	125 gr. JHP	Detective	14.75	1000	36
3925	125 gr. JSP	Patrolman	14.75	1000	36
3940	140 gr. JHP	Deputy	14.75	1000	38
3959	158 gr. JSP	Trooper	14.75	1000	39
3960	158 gr. JHP	S.W.A.T.	14.75	1000	39
Plastic 25 PAK					
44 MAGNUM					
3972	200 gr. JHP	Sheriff	9.60	500	30
3974	240 gr. JSP	Sheriff	9.60	500	30
3978	#9 SHOTSHELL		10.48	500	30
3979**	#9 SHOTSHELL	(10-PAK)	4.68	1000	50
45 AUTO					
3965	200 gr. JHP	Inspector	7.93	500	29

* - 10 Rounds per Box - 10 Boxes per Carton - 10 Cartons per Shipper

CENTERFIRE RIFLE CARTRIDGES

No.	MAKE	WT. GRS.	BULLET STYLE	PER BOX OF	

17 REMINGTON: (.172" dia.)

No.	MAKE	WT. GRS.	BULLET STYLE	PER BOX OF	
R17REM	Rem.	25	Hollow Point, Power Lokt	20	**$8.70**
P17REM	Peters	25	Hollow Point, Power Lokt	20	

218 BEE: (.224" dia.)

W218B	Win.	46	Hollow Point	50	**$23.30**
218B	West.	46	Hollow Point	50	

22 HORNET: (.224" dia.)

R22HN1	Rem.	45	Pointed Soft Point	50	
R22HN2	Rem.	45	Hollow Point	50	
W22H1	Win.	45	Soft Point	50	**$16.05**
W22H2	Win.	46	Hollow Point	50	
22H1	West.	45	Soft Point	50	
22H2	West.	46	Hollow Point	50	

222 REMINGTON: (.224" dia.)

R222R1	Rem.	50	Pointed Soft Point	20	
R222R2	Rem.	50	Metal Case	20	
R222R3	Rem.	50	Hollow Point, Power-Lokt	20	
P22441	Peters	50	Pointed Soft Point	20	**$6.85**
W222R	Win.	50	Pointed Soft Point	20	
222R	West.	50	Pointed Soft Point	20	
222R1	West.	55	Full Metal Case, Oil-Proof	20	

222 REMINGTON MAGNUM: (.224" dia.)

R222M1	Rem.	55	Pointed Soft Point	20	**$7.75**
R222M2	Rem.	55	Hollow Point, Power-Lokt	20	**8.30**

22-250 REMINGTON: (.224" dia.)

R22501	Rem.	55	Pointed Soft Point	20	**$7.50**
R22502	Rem.	55	Hollow Point, Power-Lokt	20	**8.05**
P22501	Peters	55	Pointed Soft Point	20	
W222501	Win.	55	Pointed Soft Point	20	**7.50**
222501	West.	55	Pointed Soft Point	20	

223 REMINGTON (5.56mm): (.224" dia.)

R223R1	Rem.	55	Pointed Soft Point	20	**$7.50**
R223R2	Rem.	55	Hollow Point, Power-Lokt	20	**8.05**
P223R1	Peters	55	Pointed Soft Point	20	
W223R	Win.	55	Pointed Soft Point	20	**7.50**
223R	West.	55	Pointed Soft Point	20	
233R1	West.	55	Full Metal Case, Oil-Proof	20	

225 WINCHESTER: (.224" dia.)

W2251	Win.	55	Pointed Soft Point	20	**$8.05**
2251	West.	55	Pointed Soft Point	20	

6MM REMINGTON: (.243" dia.)

R6MM1	Rem.	80	Pointed Soft Point	20	**$9.35**
R6MM2	Rem.	80	Hollow Point, Power-Lokt	20	**9.95**
R6MM3	Rem.	90	Pointed Soft Point	20	
R6MM4	Rem.	100	Pointed Soft Point, Core-Lokt	20	**9.35**
P6MM2	Peters	80	Hollow Point, Power-Lokt	20	
P6MM4	Peters	100	Pointed Soft Point, Core-Lokt	20	
6MMR1	West.	80	Pointed Soft Point	20	**9.35**
6MMR2	West.	100	Pointed Soft Point	20	

243 WINCHESTER: (.243" dia.)

R243W1	Rem.	80	Pointed Soft Point	20	**$9.35**
R243W2	Rem.	80	Hollow Point, Power-Lokt	20	**9.95**
R243W3	Rem.	100	Pointed Soft Point, Core-Lokt	20	**9.35**
P243W1	Peters	80	Pointed Soft Point	20	
P243W3	Peters	100	Pointed Soft Point, Core-Lokt	20	
W2431	Win.	80	Pointed Soft Point	20	
W2432	Win.	100	Power-Point, Soft Point	20	**9.35**
2431	West.	80	Pointed Soft Point	20	
2432	West.	100	Power-Point, Soft Point	20	

25-06 REMINGTON:

R25061	Rem.	87	Hollow Point, Power-Lokt	20	
R25062	Rem.	100	Pointed Soft Point, Core-Lokt	20	
R25063	Rem.	120	Pointed Soft Point, Core-Lokt	20	
P25062	Peters	100	Pointed Soft Point, Core-Lokt	20	**$10.20**
P25063	Peters	120	Pointed Soft Point, Core-Lokt	20	
W25061	Win.	90	Positive Expanding Point	20	
W25062	Win.	120	Positive Expanding Point	20	
25061	West.	90	Positive Expanding Point	20	
25062	West.	120	Positive Expanding Point	20	

25-20 WINCHESTER: (.257" dia.)

R25202	Rem.	86	Soft Point	50	
W25201	Win.	86	Lead	50	
W25202	Win.	86	Soft Point	50	**$15.20**
25201	West.	86	Lead	50	
25202	West.	86	Soft Point	50	

25-35 WINCHESTER: (.257" dia.)

R2535W	Rem.	117	Soft Point, Core-Lokt	20	**$10.40**
W2535	Win.	117	Soft Point	20	
2535	West.	117	Soft Point	20	

250 SAVAGE: (.257" dia.)

R250SV	Rem.	100	Pointed Soft Point	20	**$9.50**
W2501	Win.	87	Pointed Soft Point	20	**9.50**
W2503	Win.	100	Silvertip Expanding	20	**9.50**
2501	West.	87	Pointed Soft Point	20	
2503	West.	100	Silvertip Expanding	20	**10.00**

256 WINCHESTER MAGNUM: (.257" dia.)

2561P	West.	60	Hollow Point	50	**$18.65**

257 ROBERTS: (.257" dia.)

R257	Rem.	117	Soft Point, Core-Lokt	20	**$10.50**
2572	West.	100	Silvertip Expanding	20	**11.05**
2573	West.	117	Power-Point, Soft Point	20	**10.50**

6.5 REMINGTON MAGNUM: (.264" dia.)

R65MM2	Rem.	120	Pointed Soft Point, Core-Lokt	20	**$15.20**

CENTERFIRE RIFLE CARTRIDGES

No.	MAKE	WT. GRS.	BULLET STYLE	PER BOX OF	
264 WINCHESTER MAGNUM: (.264" dia.)					
R264W1	Rem.	100	Pointed Soft Point, Core-Lokt	20	
R264W2	Rem.	140	Pointed Soft Point, Core-Lokt	20	
P264W2	Peters	140	Pointed Soft Point, Core-Lokt	20	$13.10
W2641	Win.	100	Pointed Soft Point	20	
W2642	Win.	140	Power-Point, Soft Point	20	
2641	West.	100	Pointed Soft Point	20	
2642	West.	140	Power-Point, Soft Point	20	
270 WINCHESTER: (.277" dia.)					
R270W1	Rem.	100	Pointed Soft Point	20	$10.20
R270W2	Rem.	130	Pointed Soft Point, Core-Lokt	20	10.75
R270W3	Rem.	130	Bronze Point	20	10.20
R270W4	Rem.	150	Soft Point, Core-Lokt	20	8.75
P270W2	Peters	130	Pointed Soft Point, Core Lokt	20	
P270W4	Peters	150	Soft Point, Core-Lokt	20	
W2701	Win.	100	Pointed Soft Point	20	
W2705	Win.	130	Power-Point, Soft Point	20	10.20
W2703	Win.	130	Silvertip Expanding	20	
W2704	Win.	150	Power-Point, Soft Point	20	
2701	West.	100	Pointed Soft Point	20	
2703	West.	130	Silvertip Expanding	20	10.75
2705	West.	130	Power-Point, Soft Point	20	10.20
2704	West.	150	Power-Point, Soft Point	20	
280 REMINGTON: (.284" dia.)					
R280R1	Rem.	150	Pointed Soft Point, Core-Lokt	20	$10.55
R280R2	Rem.	165	Soft Point, Core-Lokt	20	
284 WINCHESTER: (.284" dia.)					
W2841	Win.	125	Power-Point, Soft Point	20	
W2842	Win.	150	Power-Point, Soft Point	20	$11.55
2841	West.	125	Power-Point, Soft Point	20	
2842	West.	150	Power-Point, Soft Point	20	
7MM MAUSER (7x57): (.284" dia.)					
R7MSR	Rem.	175	Soft Point	20	
P7MSR	Peters	175	Soft Point	20	$10.35
W7MM	Win.	175	Soft Point	20	
7MM	West.	175	Soft Point	20	
7MM REMINGTON MAGNUM: (.284" dia.)					
R7MM1	Rem.	125	Pointed Soft Point, Core-Lokt	20	
R7MM2	Rem.	150	Pointed Soft Point, Core-Lokt	20	
R7MM3	Rem.	175	Pointed Soft Point, Core-Lokt	20	
P7MM2	Peters	150	Pointed Soft Point, Core-Lokt	20	$12.60
P7MM3	Peters	175	Pointed Soft Point, Core-Lokt	20	
7MMR1	West.	150	Power-Point, Soft Point	20	
7MMR2	West.	175	Power-Point, Soft Point	20	
7MMR3	West.	125	Power-Point, Soft Point	20	

No.	MAKE	WT. GRS.	BULLET STYLE	PER BOX OF	
30 CARBINE: (.308" dia.)					
R30CAR	Rem.	110	Soft Point	50	
P30CAR	Peters	110	Soft Point	50	$16.35
W30M1	Win.	110	Hollow Soft Point	50	
W30M2	Win.	110	Full Metal Case	50	
Wells Fargo & Co. Commemorative (with Nickel-plated case)					
30-30 Winchester SUPER-X: (.308" dia.)					
W3030 WF	Win.	150	Silvertip Expanding	20	$8.70
30-30 WINCHESTER: (.308" dia.)					
R30301	Rem.	150	Soft Point, Core-Lokt	20	$8.00
R30302	Rem.	170	Soft Point, Core-Lokt	20	
R30303	Rem.	170	Hollow Point, Core-Lokt	20	
P30301	Peters	150	Soft Point, Core-Lokt	20	
P30302	Peters	170	Soft Point, Core-Lokt	20	
W30301	Win.	150	Hollow Point	20	
W30302	Win.	150	Silvertip Expanding	20	8.00
W30303	Win.	170	Power-Point, Soft Point	20	
W30304	Win.	170	Silvertip Expanding	20	8.40
W30306	Win.	150	Power-Point, Soft Point	20	
30301	West.	150	Open Point Expanding	20	
30302	West.	150	Silvertip Expanding	20	8.00
30303	West.	170	Power-Point, Soft Point	20	
30304	West.	170	Silvertip Expanding	20	8.40
30306	West.	150	Power-Point, Soft Point	20	
7MM EXPRESS REMINGTON:					
R7M061	Rem.	150	Pointed Soft Point, Core-Lokt	20	$10.55
30 REMINGTON: (.308" dia.)					
R30REM	Rem.	170	Soft Point, Core-Lokt	20	$10.25
300 SAVAGE: (.308" dia.)					
R30SV1	Rem.	150	Soft Point, Core-Lokt	20	
R30SV2	Rem.	150	Pointed Soft Point, Core-Lokt	20	
R30SV3	Rem.	180	Soft Point, Core-Lokt	20	$10.25
R30SV4	Rem.	180	Pointed Soft Point, Core-Lokt	20	
P30SV2	Peters	150	Pointed Soft Point, Core-Lokt	20	
P30SV3	Peters	180	Soft Point, Core-Lokt	20	
P30SV4	Peters	180	Pointed Soft Point, Core-Lokt	20	
W3001	Win.	150	Power-Point, Soft Point	20	10.25
W3003	Win.	150	Silvertip Expanding	20	10.80
W3004	Win.	180	Power-Point, Soft Point	20	10.25
W3005	Win.	180	Silvertip Expanding	20	10.80
3001	West.	150	Power-Point, Soft Point	20	10.25
3003	West.	150	Silvertip Expanding	20	10.80
3004	West.	180	Power-Point, Soft Point	20	10.25
3005	West.	180	Silvertip Expanding	20	10.80
30-40 KRAG: (.308" dia.)					
R30401	Rem.	180	Soft Point, Core-Lokt	20	$10.70
R30402	Rem.	180	Pointed Soft Point, Core-Lokt	20	
30401	West.	180	Power-Point, Soft Point	20	10.70
30403	West.	180	Silvertip Expanding	20	11.30

CENTERFIRE RIFLE CARTRIDGES

No.	Make	Wt. Grs.	Bullet Style	Box Of	Per
30-06 SPRINGFIELD: (.308″ dia.)					
R30061	Rem.	125	Pointed Soft Point	20	$10.20
R30062	Rem.	150	Pointed Soft Point, Core-Lokt	20	10.20
R30063	Rem.	150	Bronze Point	20	10.75
R30064	Rem.	180	Soft Point, Core-Lokt	20	10.20
R30065	Rem.	180	Pointed Soft Point, Core-Lokt	20	10.20
R30066	Rem.	180	Bronze Point	20	10.75
R30067	Rem.	220	Soft Point, Core-Lokt	20	10.20
P30061	Peters	125	Pointed Soft Point	20	
P30062	Peters	150	Pointed Soft Point	20	
P30064	Peters	180	Soft Point, Core-Lokt	20	
P30065	Peters	180	Pointed Soft Point, Core-Lokt	20	
P30067	Peters	220	Soft Point, Core-Lokt	20	
W30060	Win.	110	Pointed Soft Point	20	10.20
W30062	Win.	125	Pointed Soft Point	20	10.20
W30061	Win.	150	Power-Point, Soft Point	20	10.20
W30063	Win.	150	Silvertip Expanding	20	10.75
W30064	Win.	180	Power-Point, Soft Point	20	10.20
W30066	Win.	180	Silvertip Expanding	20	10.75
W30069	Win.	220	Silvertip Expanding	20	10.20
30060	West.	110	Pointed Soft Point	20	10.20
30062	West.	125	Pointed Soft Point	20	10.20
30061	West.	150	Power-Point, Soft Point	20	10.20
30063	West.	150	Silvertip Expanding	20	
30064	West.	180	Power-Point, Soft Point	20	
30066	West.	180	Silvertip Expanding	20	
30068	West.	220	Power-Point, Soft Point	20	
30069	West.	220	Silvertip Expanding	20	
30-06 Accelerator: (.224″ dia.)					
R30069	Rem.	55	Pointed Soft Point	20	$11.30
R30069	Peters	55	Pointed Soft Point		
300 H&H MAGNUM: (.308″ dia.)					
R300HH	Rem.	180	Pointed Soft Point, Core-Lokt	20	$13.65
W300H2	Win.	180	Silvertip Expanding	20	13.65
W300H3	Win.	220	Silvertip Expanding	20	14.35
300 WINCHESTER MAGNUM: (.308″ dia.)					
R300W1	Rem.	150	Pointed Soft Point, Core-Lokt	20	$13.30
R300W2	Rem.	180	Pointed Soft Point, Core-Lokt	20	13.30
P300W1	Peters	150	Pointed Soft Point, Core-Lokt	20	
P300W2	Peters	180	Pointed Soft Point, Core-Lokt	20	
W30WM1	Win.	150	Power-Point, Soft Point	20	13.30
W30WM2	Win.	180	Power-Point, Soft Point	20	13.30
W30WM3	Win.	220	Silvertip Expanding	20	14.00
30WM1	West.	150	Power-Point, Soft Point	20	
30WM2	West.	180	Power-Point, Soft Point	20	
30WM3	West.	220	Silvertip Expanding	20	
303 SAVAGE: (.308″ dia.)					
W3032	West.	190	Silvertip Expanding	20	$11.90
303 BRITISH: (.311″ dia.)					
R303B1	Rem.	180	Soft Point, Core-Lokt	20	$10.45
P303B1	Peters	180	Soft Point, Core-Lokt	20	
W303B1	Win.	180	Power-Point, Soft Point	20	10.45
308 WINCHESTER: (.308″ dia.)					
R308W1	Rem.	150	Pointed Soft Point, Core-Lokt	20	$10.20
R308W2	Rem.	180	Soft Point, Core-Lokt	20	10.20
R308W3	Rem.	180	Pointed Soft Point, Core-Lokt	20	9.45
P308W1	Peters	150	Pointed Soft Point, Core-Lokt	20	9.45
P308W2	Peters	180	Soft Point, Core-Lokt	20	9.45
P308W3	Peters	180	Pointed Soft Point, Core-Lokt	20	10.20
W3081	Win.	110	Pointed Soft Point	20	10.20
W3087	Win.	125	Pointed Soft Point	20	10.20
W3082	Win.	150	Silvertip Expanding	20	10.75
W3085	Win.	150	Power-Point, Soft Point	20	10.75
W3083	Win.	180	Silvertip Expanding	20	10.20
W3086	Win.	180	Power-Point, Soft Point	20	10.75
W3084	Win.	200	Silvertip Expanding	20	10.20
3081	West.	110	Pointed Soft Point	20	10.20
3087	West.	125	Pointed Soft Point	20	10.75
3082	West.	150	Silvertip Expanding	20	10.20
3085	West.	150	Power-Point, Soft Point	20	10.75
3083	West.	180	Silvertip Expanding	20	10.20
3086	West.	180	Power-Point, Soft Point	20	10.75
3084	West.	200	Silvertip Expanding	20	
8MM. (7.9 MM.) MAUSER: (.322″ dia.)					
R8MSR	Rem.	170	Soft Point, Core-Lokt	20	$10.50
P8MSR	Peters	170	Soft Point, Core-Lokt	20	10.50
W8MM	Win.	170	Power-Point, Soft Point	20	10.50
8mm Remington Magnum: (.323″ dia.)					
R8mm1	Rem.	185	Pointed Soft Point, Core-Lokt	20	$14.90
R8mm2	Rem.	220	Pointed Soft Point, Core-Lokt	20	14.90
32-20 WINCHESTER: (.310″ dia.)					
R32201	Rem.	100	Lead	50	$12.30
R32202	Rem.	100	Soft Point	50	15.20
W32201	Win.	100	Lead, Oil-Proof	50	12.30
W32202	Win.	100	Soft Point, Oil-Proof	50	15.20
32201	West.	100	Lead, Oil-Proof	50	12.30
32202	West.	100	Soft Point, Oil-Proof	50	15.20
32 WINCHESTER SPECIAL: (.320″ dia.)					
R32WS2	Rem.	170	Soft Point, Core-Lokt	20	$8.50
P32WS2	Peters	170	Soft Point, Core-Lokt	20	
W32WS2	Win.	170	Power-Point, Soft Point	20	8.50
W32WS3	Win.	170	Silvertip Expanding	20	9.00
32WS2	West.	170	Power-Point, Soft Point	20	8.50
32WS3	West.	170	Silvertip Expanding	20	9.00

No.	MAKE	WT. GRS.	BULLET STYLE		PER BOX OF

338 WINCHESTER MAGNUM: (.338″ dia.)

No.	MAKE	WT. GRS.	BULLET STYLE		PER BOX OF
W3381	Win.	200	Power-Point, Soft Point	20	$15.95
W3382	Win.	250	Silvertip Expanding	20	16.80
3381	West.	200	Power-Point, Soft Point	20	15.95
3382	West.	250	Silvertip Expanding	20	16.80

348 WINCHESTER: (.348″ dia.)

No.	MAKE	WT. GRS.	BULLET STYLE		PER BOX OF
W3482	Win.	200	Silvertip Expanding	20	$19.00

35 REMINGTON: (.358″ dia.)

No.	MAKE	WT. GRS.	BULLET STYLE		PER BOX OF
R35R1	Rem.	150	Pointed Soft Point, Core-Lokt	20	$ 9.40
R35R2	Rem.	200	Soft Point, Core-Lokt	20	9.40
P35R1	Peters	150	Pointed Soft Point, Core-Lokt	20	
P35R2	Peters	200	Soft Point, Core-Lokt	20	
W35R1	Win.	200	Power-Point, Soft Point	20	9.40
W35R3	Win.	200	Silvertip Expanding	20	10.25
35R1	West.	200	Power-Point, Soft Point	20	9.40
35R3	West.	200	Silvertip Expanding	20	10.25

350 REMINGTON MAGNUM: (.358″ dia.)

No.	MAKE	WT. GRS.	BULLET STYLE		PER BOX OF
R350M1	Rem.	200	Pointed Soft Point, Core-Lokt	20	$14.65

351 WINCHESTER SELF-LOADING: (.351″ dia.)

No.	MAKE	WT. GRS.	BULLET STYLE		PER BOX OF
W351SL2	Win.	180	Soft Point, Oil-Proof	50	$25.55

358 WINCHESTER (8.8 MM): (.358″ dia.)

No.	MAKE	WT. GRS.	BULLET STYLE		PER BOX OF
W3581	Win.	200	Silvertip Expanding	20	$14.85

375 H&H MAGNUM: (.375″ dia.)

No.	MAKE	WT. GRS.	BULLET STYLE		PER BOX OF
R375M1	Rem.	270	Soft Point	20	$15.80
R375M2	Rem.	300	Metal Case	20	15.80
W375H1	Win.	270	Power-Point, Soft Point	20	15.80
W375H2	Win.	300	Silvertip Expanding	20	16.65
W375H3	Win.	300	Full Metal Case	20	15.80
375H1	West.	270	Power-Point, Soft Point	20	15.80
375H2	West.	300	Silvertip Expanding	20	16.65

38-40 WINCHESTER: (.400″ dia.)

No.	MAKE	WT. GRS.	BULLET STYLE		PER BOX OF
R3840W	Rem.	180	Soft Point	50	
W3840	Win.	180	Soft Point, Oil-Proof	50	$19.25
3840	West.	180	Soft Point, Oil-Proof	50	

44-40 WINCHESTER: (.425″ dia.)

No.	MAKE	WT. GRS.	BULLET STYLE		PER BOX OF
R4440W	Rem.	200	Soft Point	50	
W4440	Win.	200	Soft Point, Oil-Proof	50	$20.35
4440	West.	200	Soft Point, Oil-Proof	50	

444 MARLIN: (.430″ dia.)

No.	MAKE	WT. GRS.	BULLET STYLE		PER BOX OF
R444M	Rem.	240	Soft Point	20	$10.95
P444M	Peters	240	Soft Point	20	

44 REMINGTON MAGNUM: (.430″ dia.)

No.	MAKE	WT. GRS.	BULLET STYLE		PER BOX OF
R44MG2	Rem.	240	Soft Point	20	$ 7.00
P44MG1	Peters	240	Lead, Gas-Check	50	
P44MG2	Peters	240	Soft Point	20	
P44MG3	Peters	240	Semi-Jacketed, Hollow Point	20	
44MP	West.	240	Lead, Gas-Check	50	18.80
44MHSP	West.	240	Hollow Soft Point	20	7.70

45-70 GOVERNMENT: (.457″ dia.)

No.	MAKE	WT. GRS.	BULLET STYLE		PER BOX OF
R4570G	Rem.	405	Soft Point	20	
P4570G	Peters	405	Soft Point	20	$11.55
W4570	Win.	405	Soft Point	20	

458 WINCHESTER MAGNUM: (.458″ dia.)

No.	MAKE	WT. GRS.	BULLET STYLE		PER BOX OF
R458W1	Rem.	500	Metal Case	20	$32.25
R458W2	Rem.	510	Soft Point	20	21.30
W4580	Win.	500	Full Metal Case	20	32.35
W4581	Win.	510	Soft Point	20	21.30

SHOT PATTERNS AND CHOKE

The amount of constriction in a gun's muzzle is referred to as the "choke." Different amounts of constriction give different sized patterns to a shot charge. For example, a "full choke" forces the shot charge closer together as it leaves the gun, delaying the tendency of the shot to spread. As a result, a "full choke" pattern is effective at greater distances. At close range, however, a "full choke" pattern may be too small to insure being on target, or so dense that the game is ruined.

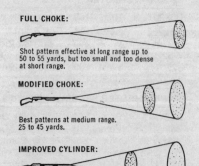

FULL CHOKE:
Shot pattern effective at long range up to 50 to 55 yards, but too small and too dense at short range.

MODIFIED CHOKE:
Best patterns at medium range. 25 to 45 yards.

IMPROVED CYLINDER:
Excellent for short range up to 30 to 35 yards, but pattern may be too thin at long range to insure enough hits.

NO.	9	8½	8	7½	6	5	4	2	1	BB
SHOT SIZES Diameter in inches	.08	.085	.09	.095	.11	.12	.13	.15	.16	.18

	No. 4	No. 3	No. 2	No. 1	No. 0	No. 00
BUCKSHOT Diameter in inches	.24	.25	.27	.30	.32	.33

LEAD SHOT PELLETS PER OUNCE (Approximate) Shot shells are loaded by weight, so small shot means more pellets in the load.

Size	Pellets	Size	Pellets	Size	Pellets
9	585	7½	350	4	135
8½	490	6	225	2	87
8	410	5	170	BB	50

Federal

NORMA RIFLE AMMUNITION

NO.	WT. GRAINS	BULLET STYLE	PER BOX OF 20
220 SWIFT:			
15701	50	Soft Point Semi Pointed	$11.50
222 REMINGTON:			
15711	50	Soft Point Semi Pointed	7.00
15712	50	Spire Point Soft Point	7.00
15714	53	Soft Point Semi Pointed Match Spitzer	7.30
22-250			
15733	53	Soft Point Semi Pointed Match Spitzer	9.25
22 SAVAGE HIGH POWER: (5.6x52 R):			
15604	71	Soft Point Semi Pointed	16.80
15605	71	Full Jacketed Semi Pointed	16.80
243 WINCHESTER:			
16002	100	Full Jacketed Semi Pointed	9.30
16003	100	Soft Point Semi Pointed	9.30
6.5 JAP:			
16531	139	Soft Point Semi Pointed Boat Tail	15.30
16532	156	Soft Point Round Nose	15.30
6.5 x 55:			
16550	77	Soft Point Semi Pointed	15.30
16557	139	Plastic Pointed "Dual-Core"	15.30
16552	156	Soft Point Round Nose	15.30
6.5 CARCANO:			
16535	156	Soft Point Round Nose	15.30
16536	139	Plastic Pointed "Dual-Core"	15.30
270 WINCHESTER:			
16902	130	Soft Point Semi Pointed Boat Tail	10.15
16903	150	Soft Point Semi Pointed Boat Tail	10.15
7 x 57:			
17002	150	Soft Point Semi Pointed Boat Tail	10.40
7 x 57 R:			
17005	150	Soft Point Semi Pointed Boat Tail	16.80
17006	150	Full Jacketed Pointed Boat Tail	16.80
SUPER 7 x 61:			
17012	150	Soft Point Boat Tail	14.80
7MM REM. MAGNUM:			
17021	150	Soft Point Semi Pointed Boat Tail	12.60
7 x 64:			
17013	150	Soft Point Semi Pointed Boat Tail	16.80
17015	175	Soft Point Nosler	16.80

NO.	WT. GRAINS	BULLET STYLE	PER BOX OF 20
280 REMINGTON:			
17050	150	Soft Point Semi Pointed Boat Tail	$10.45
7.5 x 55 SWISS:			
17511	180	Soft Point Semi Pointed Boat Tail	15.65
30 U.S. CARBINE:			
17621	110	Soft Point Round Nose	6.30
7.62 RUSSIAN:			
17634	180	Soft Point Semi Pointed Boat Tail	15.80
30-06 SPRINGFIELD:			
17640	130	Soft Point Semi Pointed Boat Tail	10.15
17643	150	Soft Point Semi Pointed Boat Tail	10.15
17648	180	Soft Point Round Nose	10.15
17653	180	Plastic Pointed "Dual-Core"	10.15
17656	180	Plastic Pointed "Dual-Core"	5.30
30-30 WINCHESTER:			
17630	150	Soft Point Flat Nose	9.80
17631	170	Soft Point Flat Nose	9.80
308 WINCHESTER:			
17623	130	Soft Point Semi Pointed Boat Tail	10.20
17624	150	Soft Point Semi Pointed Boat Tail	10.20
17628	180	Plastic Pointed "Dual-Core"	10.20
308 NORMA MAGNUM:			
17638	180	Plastic Pointed "Dual-Core"	20.60
7.65 ARGENTINE:			
17701	150	Soft Point Semi Pointed	15.30
303 BRITISH:			
17712	150	Soft Point Semi Pointed	10.45
17713	180	Soft Point Semi Pointed Boat Tail	10.45
7.7 JAP:			
17721	130	Soft Point Semi Pointed	15.65
17722	180	Soft Point Semi Pointed Boat Tail	15.65
8 x 57 J:			
18007	196	Plastic Pointed "Dual-Core"	10.45
8x57 JS:			
18003	196	Soft Point Round Nose	10.45
358 NORMA MAGNUM:			
19001	250	Soft Point	20.60
9.3 x 57:			
19302	286	Plastic Pointed "Dual-Core"	19.80
9.3 x 62:			
19314	286	Plastic Pointed "Dual-Core"	19.80
25 ACP:			
16401	50	Full Jacketed Round Nose	9.65[1]

NORMA PISTOL AMMUNITION

NO.	WT. GRAINS	BULLET STYLE	PER BOX OF 20
30 LUGER:			
17612	93	Full Jacketed Round Nose	$19.95
32 ACP:			
17614	77	Full Jacketed Round Nose	12.45
9MM LUGER:			
19021	115	Hollow Point	15.60
19022	116	Full Jacketed Round Nose	15.60
19026	116	Soft Point Flat Nose	15.60
38 SPECIAL:			
19114	158	Full Jacketed Semi-Wad Cutter	18.30
19119	110	Hollow Point	15.95
19110	148	Lead Wad Cutter	12.65
19112	158	Lead Round Nose	12.45

NO.	WT. GRAINS	BULLET STYLE	PER BOX OF 20
38 SPECIAL:			
19124	158	Soft Point Flat Nose	$14.95
19125	158	Hollow Point	14.95
357 MAGNUM:			
19101	158	Hollow Point	16.60
19106	158	Full Jacketed Semi-Wad Cutter	19.80
19107	158	Soft Point Flat Nose	16.60
38 S & W:			
19131	146	Lead Round Nose	11.20
44 MAGNUM:			
11101	236	Hollow Point	20.70
11103	240	Power Cavity	10.65
44 AUTO MAGNUM:			
11105	240	Full Point	14.15

FEDERAL PISTOL AMMUNITION

25AP 32AP 357A 357B 357D 357C 9AP 9BP 380AP 38B 38D 38C 38G 38E 38F 45A 45B

INDEX NO.	CALIBER	WT. GRS.	BULLET STYLE	PRIMER NO.	BOX OF 50
25 AP	25 Auto Pistol (6.35mm)	50	Metal Case	100	$ 9.80
32AP	32 Auto Pistol (7.65mm)	71	Metal Case	100	11.20
380AP	380 Auto Pistol	95	Metal Case	100	11.45
380BP	380 Auto Pistol	90	Jacketed Hollow Point	100	11.45
9AP	9mm Luger Auto Pistol	123	Metal Case	100	13.95
9BP	9mm Luger Auto Pistol	115	Jacketed Hollow Point	100	13.95
38A	38 Special (Match)	148	Lead Wadcutter	100	11.05
38B	38 Special	158	Lead Round Nose	100	10.60
38C	38 Special	158	Lead Semi-Wadcutter	100	10.85
38D	38 Special (High Vel + P)	158	Lead Round Nose	200	11.75
38E	38 Special (High Vel + P)	125	Jacketed Hollow Point	200	13.45
38F	38 Special (High Vel + P)	110	Jacketed Hollow Point	200	13.45
38G	38 Special (High Vel + P)	158	Lead Semi-Wad Cutter Hollow Point	200	13.20
38J	38 Special (High Vel + P)	125	Jacketed Soft Point	200	13.45
38H	38 Special (High Vel + P)	158	Lead Semi-Wadcutter	200	10.85
357A	357 Magnum	158	Jacketed Soft Point	200	14.75
357B	357 Magnum	125	Jacketed Hollow Point	200	12.50
357C	357 Magnum	158	Lead Semi-Wadcutter	200	14.75
357D	357 Magnum	110	Jacketed Hollow Point	200	14.75
44A	44 Rem. Magnum	240	Jacketed Hollow Soft Point	150	7.70
44B	44 Remington Magnum	180	Jacketed Hollow Point	150	17.50
45A	45 Automatic (Match)	230	Metal Case	150	15.35
45B	45 Automatic (Match)	185	Metal Case S.W.C.	150	15.85
45C	45 Automatic	185	Jacketed Hollow Point	150	15.85
45LCA	45 Colt	225	Lead Semi-Wad Cutter Hollow Point	150	14.20

FEDERAL RIFLE AMMUNITION
CENTER FIRE RIFLE CARTRIDGES

NO.	CALIBER	WT. GRS.	BULLET STYLE	FACTORY PRIMER NO.	BOX OF 20
222A	222 Remington	50	Soft Point	205	$6.85
22250A	22-250 Remington	55	Soft Point	210	7.50
223A	223 Remington (5.56mm)	55	Soft Point	205	7.50
223B	223 Remington (5.56mm)	55	Metal Case Boat-tail	205	7.50
6A	6mm Remington	80	Soft Point	210	9.35
6B	6mm Remington	100	Hi-Shok Soft Point	210	9.35
243A	243 Winchester	80	Soft Point	210	9.35
243B	243 Winchester	100	Hi-Shok Soft Point	210	9.35
2506A	25-06 Remington	90	Hollow Point	210	10.20
2506B	25-06 Remington	117	Hi-Shok Soft Point	210	10.20
270A	270 Winchester	130	Hi-Shok Soft Point	210	10.20
270B	270 Winchester	150	Hi-Shok Soft Point	210	10.20
7A	7mm Mauser	175	Hi-Shok Soft Point	210	10.35
7B	7mm Mauser	139	Hi-Shok Soft Point	210	10.35
7RA	7mm Remington Magnum	150	Hi-Shok Soft Point	215	12.60
7RB	7mm Remington Magnum	175	Hi-Shok Soft Point	215	12.60
30CA	30 Carbine	110	Soft Point	200	6.55
30CB	30 Carbine	110	Metal Case	200	6.55
3030A	30-30 Winchester	150	Hi-Shok Soft Point	210	8.00
3030B	30-30 Winchester	170	Hi-Shok Soft Point	210	8.00
3006A	30-06 Springfield	150	Hi-Shok Soft Point	210	10.20
3006B	30-06 Springfield	180	Hi-Shok Soft Point	210	10.20
3006C	30-06 Springfield	125	Soft Point	210	10.20
3006D	30-06 Springfield	165	Soft Point Boat-tail	210	10.60
3006E	30-06 Springfield	200	Soft Point Boat-tail	210	10.60
300A	300 Savage	150	Hi-Shok Soft Point	210	10.25
300B	300 Savage	180	Hi-Shok Soft Point	210	10.25
300WA	300 Winchester Magnum	150	Hi-Shok Soft Point	215	13.30
300WB	300 Winchester Magnum	180	Hi-Shok Soft Point	215	13.30
308A	308 Winchester	150	Hi-Shok Soft Point	210	10.20
308B	308 Winchester	180	Hi-Shok Soft Point	210	10.20
8A	8mm Mauser	170	Hi-Shok Soft Point	210	10.50
32A	32 Winchester Special	170	Hi-Shok Soft Point	210	8.50
35A	35 Remington	200	Hi-Shok Soft Point	210	9.40
44A	44 Remington Magnum	240	Hollow Soft Point	150	7.70
4570A	45-70 Government	300	Hollow Soft Point	210	11.55
3030C	30-30 Winchester	125	Hollow Point	210	8.00

WEATHERBY RIFLE AMMUNITION
CENTER FIRE RIFLE CARTRIDGES

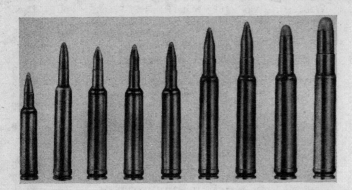

Weatherby Magnum Cartridges: Left to Right—.224 W.M., .240 W.M., .257 W.M., .270 W.M., 7mm W.M., .300 W.M., .340 W.M., .378 W.M., and .460 W.M.

Cartridge	Ammunition 20 per box	Unprimed Cases 20 per box
224—50 or 55 gr.	$17.95	$10.40
240—70, 87 or 100 gr.	17.95	10.40
—85 or 100 gr. Nosler	23.65	
257—87, 100 or 117 gr.	18.95	10.40
—100 or 117 gr. Nosler	24.75	
270—100, 130 or 150 gr.	18.95	10.40
—130 or 150 gr. Nosler	24.75	
7mm—139,154 or 175 gr.	18.95	10.40
—140, 160 or 175 gr. Nosler	24.95	
300—110, 150, 180 or 220 gr.	18.95	10.40
—150, 180 or 200 gr. Nosler	25.85	
340—200 or 250 gr.	19.95	10.40
—210 or 250 gr. Nosler	29.15	
378—270, or 300 RN	31.95	19.75
—300 gr. FMJ	35.95	
—270 or 300 gr. Nosler	42.35	
460—500 RN	34.95	
—500 RMJ	39.95	

PISTOL & REVOLVER CARTRIDGES

No.	MAKE	WT. GRS.	BULLET STYLE	PER BOX OF	
22 REMINGTON "JET" MAGNUM: (Adapted to Smith & Wesson revolvers)					
R22JET	Rem.	40	Soft Point	40	**$16.85**
221 REMINGTON "FIREBALL": (Adapted to Remington XP-100 pistol)					
R221F	Rem.	50	Pointed Soft Point	20	**$7.65**
25 (6.35 MM.) AUTOMATIC PISTOL: (Adapted to Colt, Browning, Mauser, Llama, other automatic pistols.)					
R25AP	Rem.	50	Metal Case	50	
P25AP	Peters	50	Metal Case	50	**$9.80**
W25AP	Win.	50	Full Metal Case, Oil-Proof	50	
25AP	West.	50	Full Metal Case, Oil-Proof	50	
256 WINCHESTER MAGNUM: (Adapted to Ruger Hawkeye revolver.)					
2561P	West.	60	Point	50	**$18.65**
30 (7.65 MM.) LUGER AUTOMATIC PISTOL: (Adapted to Luger automatic pistol; cannot be used in Luger Carbine.)					
R30LUG	Rem.	93	Metal Case	50	
W30LP	Win.	93	Full Metal Case, Oil-Proof	50	**$15.75**
30LP	West.	93	Full Metal Case, Oil-Proof	50	
32 SHORT COLT: (Adapted to Colt, Webley, other revolvers; Marlin 1892 repeating rifles; not adapted to revolvers chambered for 32 Smith & Wesson cartridge.)					
R32SC	Rem.	80	Lead	50	**$9.10**
32SCP	West.	80	Lead, Oil-Proof	50	
32 LONG COLT: (Adapted to Colt, Webley, other revolvers; Marlin 1892 repeating rifles; not adapted to revolvers chambered for 32 Smith & Wesson Long cartridges.)					
R32LC	Rem.	82	Lead	50	**$9.50**
32LCP	West.	82	Lead, Oil-Proof	50	
32 COLT NEW POLICE: (See 32 Smith & Wesson Long)					
32 (7.65 MM.) AUTOMATIC PISTOL: (Adapted to Browning, Colt, Mauser; Remington, Savage, Llama, Smith & Wesson, other automatic pistols.)					
R32AP	Rem.	71	Metal Case	50	
P32AP	Peters	71	Metal Case	50	**$11.20**
W32AP	Win.	71	Full Metal Case, Oil-Proof	50	
32AP	West.	71	Full Metal Case, Oil-Proof	50	

No.	MAKE	WT. GRS.	BULLET STYLE	PER BOX OF	
32 SMITH & WESSON:					
R32SW	Rem.	88	Lead	50	
P32SW	Peters	88	Lead	50	**$9.20**
W32SWP	Win.	85	Lead, Oil-Proof	50	
32SWP	West.	85	Lead, Oil-Proof	50	
32 SMITH & WESSON LONG:					
R32SWL	Rem.	98	Lead	50	
P32SWL	Peters	98	Lead	50	**$9.50**
W32SWLP	Win.	98	Lead, Oil-Proof	50	
32SWLP	West.	98	Lead, Oil-Proof	50	
32-20 WINCHESTER: (Adapted to Colt, Smith & Wesson revolvers; use cartridge with 100 grain all lead bullet only.) Note: 32-20 Winchester "Hi-Speed" cartridge is for use in rifles only and should not be used in revolvers. See Center Fire Rifle section.					
R32201	Rem.	100	Lead	50	**$11.45**
W32201	Win.	100	Lead, Oil-Proof	50	**12.30**
W32202	Win.	100	Soft Point, Oil-Proof	50	**15.20**
32201	West.	100	Lead, Oil-Proof	50	**12.30**
32202	West.	100	Soft Point, Oil-Proof	50	**15.20**
38 SPECIAL:					
R38S1	Rem.	95	Semi-Jacketed, Hollow Point, High Pressure	50	**$13.45**
R38S2	Rem.	125	Semi-Jacketed, Hollow Point, High Pressure	50	**13.45**
R38S5	Rem.	158	Lead	50	**10.60**
R38S6	Rem.	158	Lead, Semi-Wadcutter	50	**10.85**
R38S7	Rem.	158	Metal Point	50	**13.45**
R38S8	Rem.	158	Lead, High Pressure	50	**11.75**
R38S9	Rem.	200	Lead	50	**11.35**
P38S2	Peters	125	Semi-Jacketed, Hollow-Point, High Pressure	50	
P38SA	Peters	158	Lead, High Pressure	50	
P38S4	Peters	158	Targetmaster, Lead, Round Nose	50	
P38S5	Peters	158	Lead	50	
P38S7	Peters	158	Metal Point	50	
W387PH	Win.	125	Jacketed Hollow Point, High Pressure	50	**12.25**
W38S1P	Win.	158	Lead, Oil-Proof	50	**10.60**
W38S2P	Win.	158	Metal Point, Oil-Proof	50	**13.45**
W38SPD	Win.	158	Hollow Point, Oil-Proof, High Pressure	50	**12.25**
W38WCP	Win.	158	Semi-Wadcutter, Oil-Proof, High Pressure	50	**10.10**
W38S3P	Win.	200	Lead, Oil-Proof	50	**11.35**
38S6PH	West.	110	Jacketed Hollow Point, High Pressure	50	**12.25**
38S4P	West.	150	Lead, Oil-Proof	50	**10.70**
38S5P	West.	150	Metal Piercing, Oil-Proof, High Pressure	50	**12.70**
38S1P	West.	158	Lead, Oil-Proof	50	**10.60**
38S2P	West.	158	Metal Point, Oil-Proof	50	**13.45**
38S3P	West.	200	Lead, Oil-Proof	50	**11.35**

PISTOL & REVOLVER CARTRIDGES

No.	MAKE	WT. GRS.	BULLET STYLE	PER	BOX OF

38 SPECIAL MATCH AMMUNITION:

No.	MAKE	WT. GRS.	BULLET STYLE		PER BOX OF
R38S3	Rem.	148	Targetmaster, Lead Wadcutter	50	$11.05
R38S4	Rem.	158	Targetmaster, Lead, Round Nose	50	10.85
P38S3	Peters	148	Targetmaster, Lead, Wadcutter	50	
W38SMRP	Win.	148	Lead, Mid-Range, Oil-Proof	50	11.05
38SMRP	West.	148	Lead, Mid-Range, Oil-Proof	50	
38SMP	West.	158	Lead, Oil-Proof	50	10.85

38 SHORT COLT: (Adapted to Colt revolvers.)

No.	MAKE	WT. GRS.	BULLET STYLE		PER BOX OF
R38SC	Rem.	125	Lead	50	$10.35
38SCP	West.	130	Lead, Oil-Proof	50	

38 LONG COLT: (Adapted to Colt, Smith & Wesson revolvers.)

No.	MAKE	WT. GRS.	BULLET STYLE		PER BOX OF
38LCP	West.	150	Lead, Oil-Proof	50	$15.25

38-40 WINCHESTER: (Adapted to Colt revolvers—"Hi-Speed" cartridges are for use in rifles only and should not be used in revolvers.)

No.	MAKE	WT. GRS.	BULLET STYLE		PER BOX OF
R3840W	Rem.	180	Soft Point	50	$19.25
W3840	Win.	180	Soft Point, Oil-Proof	50	
3840	West.	180	Soft Point, Oil-Proof	50	

357 MAGNUM HI-SPEED: (Adapted to Smith & Wesson and other revolvers originally chambered for this cartridge.)

No.	MAKE	WT. GRS.	BULLET STYLE		PER BOX OF
R357M1	Rem.	125	Semi-Jacketed, Hollow Point	50	$14.75
R357M2	Rem.	158	Semi-Jacketed, Hollow Point	50	
R357M3	Rem.	158	Soft Point	50	
R357M4	Rem.	158	Metal Point	50	14.55
R357M5	Rem.	158	Lead	50	12.50
3576P	West.	125	Jacketed Hollow Point	50	14.75
P357M3	Peters	158	Soft Point	50	
P357M5	Peters	158	Lead	50	
3573P	West.	110	Jacketed, Hollow Point	50	14.75
3571P	West.	158	Lead, Oil-Proof	50	12.50
3572P	West.	158	Metal Piercing, Oil-Proof	50	14.55
3574P	West.	158	Jacketed Hollow Point	50	14.75
3575P	West.	158	Jacketed Soft Point	50	

9 MM. LUGER AUTOMATIC PISTOL: (Adapted to Smith & Wesson, Colt and other semi-automatic pistols.)

(PARABELLUM)

No.	MAKE	WT. GRS.	BULLET STYLE		PER BOX OF
R9MM1	Rem.	115	Jacketed Hollow Point	50	$13.95
R9MM2	Rem.	124	Metal Case	50	
P9MM1	Peters	115	Jacketed Hollow Point	50	
P9MM2	Peters	124	Metal Case	50	
W9MMJSP	Win.	95	Jacketed Soft Point	50	
W9MMPP	Win.	100	Power-Point, Oil-Proof	50	
W9MMJHP	Win.	100	Jacketed Hollow Point, Oil-Proof	50	
W9LP	Win.	115	Full Metal Case, Oil-Proof	50	

38 SMITH & WESSON: (Adapted to Smith & Wesson, Colt, other revolvers.)

No.	MAKE	WT. GRS.	BULLET STYLE		PER BOX OF
R38SW	Rem.	146	Lead	50	$10.55
P38SW	Peters	146	Lead	50	
W38SWP	Win.	145	Lead, Oil-Proof	50	
38SWP	West.	145	Lead, Oil-Proof	50	

38 SUPER AUTOMATIC COLT PISTOL: (Adapted to Colt Super 38 Automatic, Colt Commander and Llama automatic pistols only.)

No.	MAKE	WT. GRS.	BULLET STYLE		PER BOX OF
R38SUP	Rem.	130	Metal Case, High Pressure	50	$12.15
P38SUP	Peters	130	Metal Case	50	
W38A3P	Win.	125	Jacketed Hollow Point, Oil-Proof	50	12.60
W38A1P	Win.	130	Full Metal Case, Oil-Proof, High Pressure	50	12.15
38A3P	West.	125	Jacketed Hollow Point, Oil-Proof	50	12.60
38A1P	West.	130	Full Metal Case, Oil-Proof, High Pressure	50	12.15

38 AUTOMATIC COLT PISTOL: (Adapted only for 38 Colt Sporting, Military and Pocket Model Automatic pistols. These pistols were discontinued after 1928.)

No.	MAKE	WT. GRS.	BULLET STYLE		PER BOX OF
R38ACP	Rem.	130	Metal Case	50	$12.35
W38A2P	Win.	130	Full Metal Case, Oil-Proof, High Pressure	50	
38A2P	West.	130	Full Metal Case, Oil-Proof, High Pressure	50	

380 AUTOMATIC PISTOL: (Adapted to Browning, Colt, Remington, Llama, Savage, Walther, other automatic pistols.)

No.	MAKE	WT. GRS.	BULLET STYLE		PER BOX OF
R380AP	Rem.	95	Metal Case	50	$11.45
P38AOP	Peters	95	Metal Case	50	
W380AP	Win.	95	Full Metal Case, Oil-Proof	50	11.45
380AP	West.	95	Full Metal Case, Oil-Proof	50	

41 MAGNUM: (Adapted to Smith & Wesson 41 Magnum revolver.)

No.	MAKE	WT. GRS.	BULLET STYLE		PER BOX OF
R41MG1	Rem.	210	Soft Point	50	$19.40
R41MG2	Rem.	210	Lead	50	16.55
P41MG1	Peters	210	Soft Point	50	

44 SMITH & WESSON SPECIAL: (Adapted to Smith & Wesson, Colt revolvers.)

No.	MAKE	WT. GRS.	BULLET STYLE		PER BOX OF
R44SW	Rem.	246	Lead	50	$14.85
W44SP	Win.	246	Lead, Oil-Proof	50	

44 REMINGTON MAGNUM:

No.	MAKE	WT. GRS.	BULLET STYLE		PER BOX OF
R44MG1	Rem.	240	Lead, Gas-Check	50	$18.80
R44MG2	Rem.	240	Soft Point	20	7.70
R44MG3	Rem.	240	Semi-Jacketed Hollow Point	20	

PISTOL & REVOLVER CARTRIDGES

No.	MAKE	WT. GRS.	BULLET STYLE	PER BOX OF	
44 REMINGTON MAGNUM:					
P44MG1	Peters	240	Lead, Gas-Check	50	
P44MG2	Peters	240	Soft Point	20	
P44MG3	Peters	240	Semi-Jacketed Hollow Point	20	
44MP	West.	240	Lead, Gas-Check	50	$18.80
44MHSP	West.	240	Hollow Soft Point	20	7.70

44-40 WINCHESTER: (Adapted to Colt revolvers—Hi-Speed cartridges are for use in rifles only and should not be used in revolvers.)

No.	MAKE	WT. GRS.	BULLET STYLE	PER BOX OF	
R4440W	Rem.	200	Soft Point	50	$18.90
W4440	Win.	200	Soft Point, Oil-Proof	50	20.35
4440	West.	200	Soft Point, Oil-Proof	50	20.35

45 COLT:

No.	MAKE	WT. GRS.	BULLET STYLE	PER BOX OF	
R45C	Rem.	250	Lead	50	
P45C	Peters	250	Lead	50	$15.05
W45CP	Win.	255	Lead, Oil-Proof	50	
45CP	West.	255	Lead, Oil-Proof	50	

45 AUTOMATIC: (Adapted to Colt Automatic Pistol, Llama 45 Automatic Pistol, Thompson Sub-Machine-gun, Colt 1917 revolver with clips, Smith & Wesson 1917 revolver with clips, Smith & Wesson 1950 & 1955 revolvers.)

No.	MAKE	WT. GRS.	BULLET STYLE	PER BOX OF	
R45AP2	Rem.	185	Jacketed, Hollow Point	50	
R45AP4	Rem.	230	Metal Case	50	
P45AP2	Peters	185	Jacketed, Hollow Point	50	$15.85
P45AP4	Peters	230	Metal Case	50	
W24A1P	Win.	230	Full Metal Case, Oil-Proof	50	
45A1P	West.	230	Full Metal Case, Oil-Proof	50	

45 AUTOMATIC MATCH AMMUNITION:

No.	MAKE	WT. GRS.	BULLET STYLE	PER BOX OF	
R45AP1	Rem.	185	Targetmaster, Wadcutter, Metal Case	50	
R45AP3	Rem.	230	Targetmaster, Metal Case	50	$15.85
P45AP1	Peters	185	Targetmaster, Metal Case, Wadcutter	50	
45AWCP	West.	185	Full Metal Case	50	

45 AUTOMATIC RIM: (Adapted to Colt 1917 revolver, Smith & Wesson 1917 revolver, Smith & Wesson 1950 & 1955 revolvers.)

No.	MAKE	WT. GRS.	BULLET STYLE	PER BOX OF	
R45AR	Rem.	230	Lead	50	$16.40

RECOMMENDED SPECIFICATIONS FOR VARIOUS GAME

GAME	SHOT SIZE	GAUGE	OUNCES OF SHOT[1] (Load)	CHOKE	BARREL LENGTH
Turkey, Geese, Fox	BB, 2, 4	12, 16 / 20	1¼ / 1³/₁₆	Mod. or Full	28″ to 32″
Ducks (Pass Shooting)	4, 5	12, 16 / 20	1¼ / 1³/₁₆	Mod. or Full	30″ or 32″
Ducks (Over Decoys)	6, 7½	12 / 16, 20	1⅛ / 1	Mod.	26″ or 28″
Pheasants	6	12 / 16, 20, 28	1⅛ / 1	Mod. or Imp. Cyl.	26″ or 28″
Sage Grouse, Prairie Chicken	6, 7½	12 / 16, 20, 28	1⅛ / 1	Mod. or Imp. Cyl.	26″ or 28″
Squirrel, Rabbit	5, 6	12, 16 / 20, 28, .410	1 / ¾	Mod.	28″ or 30″
Partridge, Grouse	6, 7½	12, 16 / 20, 28, .410	1 / ¾	Mod. or Imp. Cyl.	26″ or 28″
Quail, Doves	7½, 8	12, 16 / 20, 28, .410	1 / ¾	Mod. or Imp. Cyl.	26″ or 28″
Woodcock, Jacksnipe, Rail	7½, 8, 9	12, 16 / 20, 28 / .410	1 / ¾ / ½	Imp. Cyl.	26″
Trap	7½, 8	12	1⅛	Full, Imp., Mod. or Mod.	30″ to 34″
Skeet	9	12, 20, 28, .410	½	Skeet	26″ or 28″
Deer	Rifled Slug or 00 Buck Shot	12 / 16 / 20	1 / ⅞ / ⅝	Mod., Imp. Cyl. or Special[2]	26″ to 32″

[1]Minimum load recommended. In most cases, heavier loads are available.

Browning

HORNADY FRONTIER CARTRIDGES

Brand-new brass cases loaded with famous Hornady bullets.

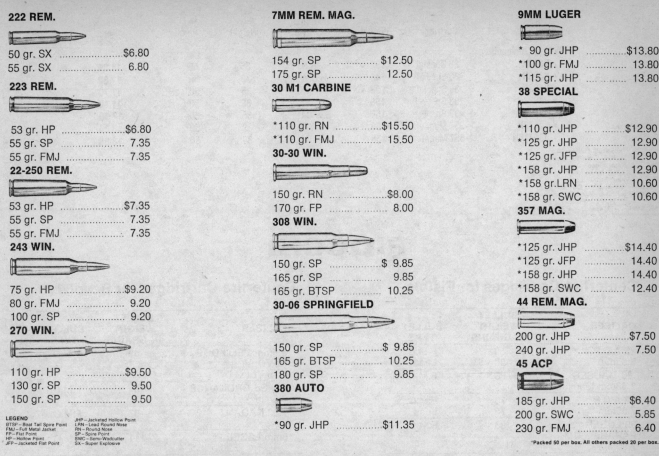

222 REM.
50 gr. SX	$6.80
55 gr. SX	6.80

223 REM.
53 gr. HP	$6.80
55 gr. SP	7.35
55 gr. FMJ	7.35

22-250 REM.
53 gr. HP	$7.35
55 gr. SP	7.35
55 gr. FMJ	7.35

243 WIN.
75 gr. HP	$9.20
80 gr. FMJ	9.20
100 gr. SP	9.20

270 WIN.
110 gr. HP	$9.50
130 gr. SP	9.50
150 gr. SP	9.50

7MM REM. MAG.
154 gr. SP	$12.50
175 gr. SP	12.50

30 M1 CARBINE
*110 gr. RN	$15.50
*110 gr. FMJ	15.50

30-30 WIN.
150 gr. RN	$8.00
170 gr. FP	8.00

308 WIN.
150 gr. SP	$9.85
165 gr. SP	9.85
165 gr. BTSP	10.25

30-06 SPRINGFIELD
150 gr. SP	$9.85
165 gr. BTSP	10.25
180 gr. SP	9.85

380 AUTO
*90 gr. JHP	$11.35

9MM LUGER
* 90 gr. JHP	$13.80
*100 gr. FMJ	13.80
*115 gr. JHP	13.80

38 SPECIAL
*110 gr. JHP	$12.90
*125 gr. JHP	12.90
*125 gr. JFP	12.90
*158 gr. JHP	12.90
*158 gr. LRN	10.60
*158 gr. SWC	10.60

357 MAG.
*125 gr. JHP	$14.40
*125 gr. JFP	14.40
*158 gr. JHP	14.40
*158 gr. SWC	12.40

44 REM. MAG.
200 gr. JHP	$7.50
240 gr. JHP	7.50

45 ACP
185 gr. JHP	$6.40
200 gr. SWC	5.85
230 gr. FMJ	6.40

*Packed 50 per box. All others packed 20 per box.

LEGEND
BTSP – Boat Tail Spire Point
FMJ – Full Metal Jacket
FP – Flat Point
HP – Hollow Point
JFP – Jacketed Flat Point
JHP – Jacketed Hollow Point
LRN – Lead Round Nose
RN – Round Nose
SP – Spire Point
SWC – Semi-Wadcutter
SX – Super Explosive

S & W Center Fire Pistol and Revolver Cartridges

Symbol Number	Cartridge	Bullet Weight	Bullet Style		Ave. Case Weight	Rnds. Per Box	Price Per Box
• S44M1	44 Magnum	240	J.H.P.		29	20	$ 7.70
• S45A1	45 Automatic	185	M.C.S.W.C.		43	50	15.85
• S357M1	357 Magnum	90	J.S.P.		28	50	
• S357M5	357 Magnum	110	J.H.P.		33	50	
• S357M7	357 Magnum	125	J.S.P.		34	50	14.75
• S357M6	357 Magnum	125	J.H.P.		34	50	
• S357M8	357 Magnum	158	J.H.P.		39	50	
• S357M9	357 Magnum	158	J.S.P.		39	50	
• S357M3	357 Magnum	158	S.W.C.		39	50	12.50
• S357M10	357 Magnum	158	S.W.C.H.P.		39	50	13.10
• S38S2	38 Special	158	R.N.		35	50	10.60
• S38S4	38 Special	148	W.C.		33	50	11.05
• S38+P1	38 Sp. +P	90	J.S.P.		26	50	
• S38+P5	38 Sp. +P	110	J.H.P.		28	50	
• S38+P6	38 Sp. +P	125	J.H.P.		32	50	13.45
• S38+P7	38 Sp. +P	125	J.S.P.		32	50	
• S38+P8	38 Sp. +P	158	J.H.P.		35	50	
• S38+P9	38 Sp. +P	158	J.S.P.		35	50	
• S38+P3	38 Sp. +P	158	S.W.C.		35	50	10.85
• S38+P10	38 Sp. +P	158	S.W.C.H.P.	Small Pistol	35	50	11.45
• S9MM4	9 mm	100	F.M.C.		25	50	
• S9MM5	9 mm	115	F.M.C.		27	50	13.95
• S9MM3	9 mm	115	J.H.P.		27	50	
• S9MM6	9 mm	115	M.C.S.W.C.		27	50	
• S380AP1	380 Auto	84	J.H.P.		21	50	11.45
• S380AP2	380 Auto	95	F.M.C.		23	50	11.45

S & W Center Fire Pistol and Revolver Cartridges

Symbol Number	Cartridge	Bullet Weight	Bullet Style	Ave. Case Weight	Rnds. Per Box	Price Per Box
NYCLAD Ammunition						
• N382N	38 Special	158	R.N.	35	50	11.35
• N386N	38 Special	148	H.B.W.C.	33	50	11.80
• N383N	38 Special	158	S.W.C.	35	50	11.70
• N38P3N	38 Sp. + P	158	S.W.C.	35	50	11.70
• N38P10N	38 Sp. + P	158	S.W.C.H.P.	35	50	12.30
• N3573N	357 Magnum	158	S.W.C.	39	50	13.30
• N35710N	357 Magnum	158	S.W.C.H.P.	39	50	13.90

JHP — Jacketed Hollow Point
JSP — Jacketed Soft Point
MC — Metal Case
RN — Round Nose-Lead
WC — Wad Cutter-Lead
SWC — Semi-Wad Cutter-Lead
SWCHP — Semi-Wad Cutter-Lead
      Hollow Point
MCSWC — Metal Case Semi-Wad Cutter

FIOCCHI

Centerfire Cartridges for Pistols

CALIBER	BULLET WEIGHT IN GRAINS	BULLET TYPE
25 A.C.P.	50	F.M.C.
6.35mm	50	Lead
.30 MAUSER 7.63mm Mauser	88	F.M.C.
32 A.C.P.	73	F.M.C.
7.65mm	75	Lead
30 LUGER PARABELLUM 7.65mm	93	F.M.C.
ROTH-STEYR 8mm	113	F.M.C.
380 A.C.P. 9mm (short M34)	93	F.M.C.
9mm LUGER 9mm (long M38)	115	F.M.C.
9mm GLISENTI	123	F.M.C.
9mm LUGER PARABELLUM	123	F.M.C.
9mm STEYR	115	F.M.C.
30 MI CARBINE	111	F.M.C.
38 A.C.P. 38	129	F.M.C.
45 A.C.P. 45	230	F.M.C.

Centerfire Cartridges for Revolvers

CALIBER	BULLET WEIGHT IN GRAINS	BULLET TYPE
5.5mm VELO DOG REVOLVER 5.75 VELO DOG	43	F.M.C.
SWISS ORDNANCE 7.5mm	107	F.M.C.
7.62 NAGANT	97	F.M.C.
8mm LEBEL	111	F.M.C.
8mm GASSER	126	F.M.C.
ITALIAN ORDNANCE 10.4mm	177	F.M.C.
32 SMITH & WESSON SHORT	85	F.M.C.
	85	Lead
32 SMITH & WESSON LONG	98	F.M.C.
	98	Lead
320 SHORT	82	F.M.C.
	82	Lead
320 LONG	82	F.M.C.
	82	Lead
38 SMITH & WESSON SHORT	145	F.M.C.
	145	Lead
38 SPECIAL	158	F.M.C.
	158	Lead
38 SPECIAL WAD CUTTER	148	Lead
380 SHORT	125	F.M.C.
	125	Lead
380 LONG	125	F.M.C.
	125	Lead
44 SMITH & WESSON RUSSIAN	247	Lead
450 SHORT	226	Lead
455 MK II	262	Lead
357 MAGNUM	158	J.S.P.

LOADS AND SHOT SIZES

THE SHOTSHELL SELECTOR
Lead Shot Unless Indicated "Steel"

	Type of Shell	Size
DUCKS	Magnum or Hi-Power	4, 5, 6
	Steel 2, 4	
GEESE	Magnum or Hi-Power	BB, 2, 4
	Steel 1, 2,	
PHEASANTS	Magnum or Hi-Power	5, 6, 7½
QUAIL	Hi-Power or Field Load	7½, 8, 9
RUFFED GROUSE & HUNGARIAN PARTRIDGE	Hi-Power or Field Load	6, 7½, 8
OTHER GROUSE CHUKAR PARTRIDGE	Hi-Power or Field Load	5, 6, 7½

DOVES & PIGEONS	Hi-Power or Field Load	6, 7½, 8, 9
RABBITS	Hi-Power or Field Load	4, 5, 6, 7½
WOODCOCK, SNIPE, RAIL	Field Load	7½, 8, 9
SQUIRRELS	Hi-Power or Field Load	4, 5, 6
WILD TURKEY	Magnum or Hi-Power	BB, 2, 4, 5, 6
CROWS	Hi-Power or Field Load	5, 6, 7½
FOX	Magnum or Hi-Power	BB, 2, 4

Federal

SHOT AND ITS MANUFACTURE

The forerunner of modern shot is the old grape shot of the middle ages which is mentioned as far back as 1420. By the year 1510 this was employed in the earliest handguns. Actual manufacture in the form of balls dates back to the British Patent No. 725 of the year 1758 whereby the shot was poured and then polished in drums. Manufacture of shot is based on the British Patent 1347 of the year 1782. The first shot tower was constructed in Austria in 1818. The exact composition of shot varies but is principally of lead with some arsenic added which has the property of not only making the lead harder but to make it flow more readily. The arsenic content in the small size shot may run approximately .2% and in larger shot sizes nearly twice that amount. This alloy is made up into blocks which are then used for shot manufacture which is usually carried out in one of two manners.

No. 1—The melted alloy is poured through a sieve-like container from which the ball shape drops fall from a considerable height into a tank of cold water. In the course of the fall the shot becomes rounded and the size depends upon the sieve. For very small sizes the drop is usually 100 ft. and for larger sizes as much as 100 yards.

Above: Remington "Power Piston" plastic shotshell.

No. 2—The melted alloy falls upon a quickly rotating metal disc from which the pellets are thrown by centrifugal force against an apron and then dropped into water. The size of the shot depends upon the speed of the revolving disc. The sorting of the shot for sizes is accomplished by rolling them down a surface with various size openings. The shot which have thus been sorted are mixed with very finely ground graphite and placed in revolving drums. This completely rounds the shot and covers them with a coat of graphite which protects them from oxidation. Hard shot contains in addition to the arsenic about 2% antimony. Such shot retain their form better than soft shot and consequently are less apt to stray away from the central shot mass and thus give better pattern with greater penetration. The most essential point is that the shot be round which is much more important than exact sizes. The characteristic of hard shot is enhanced by copper plating but this adds considerably to the cost and relatively little to performance.

Standard Shot Chart — Diameter in inches

No. 12	11	10	9	8½	8	7½*	6*	5*	4*	2*	BB	No. 4 Buck	No. 3 Buck	No. 1 Buck	No. 0 Buck	No. 00
•	•	•	•	•	•	•	●	●	●	●	●	●	●	●	●	●
.05	.06	.07	.08	.085	.09	.095	.11	.12	.13	.15	.18	.24	.25	.30	.32	.33
APPROXIMATE NUMBER OF PELLETS TO THE OUNCE												APPROXIMATE NUMBER TO THE POUND				
2385	1380	870	585	485	410	350	225	170	135	90	50	340	300	175	145	130

* Also Available in Lubaloy (copper plated) shot.

Winchester-Western

REMINGTON PLASTIC SHOTSHELLS

REMINGTON "EXPRESS" HIGH BASE PLASTIC SHELLS
with "POWER-PISTON" WADS and "KLEANBORE" PRIMING

- Packed 5 per box—250 per case.
  25 in a box, 500 in a case.
  Prices Subject to Change Without Notice
  ★ **New**

	No.	Gauge	Length shell, in.	Powder equiv. drams	Shot, oz.	Size shot	Wt. case, lbs.	Per box
"EXPRESS" LONG RANGE LOADS	SP10	10	2⅞	4¾	1⅝	4	74	$10.20
	SP12	12	2¾	3¾	1¼	BB 2 4 5 6 7½ 9	58	7.40
	SP16	16	2¾	3¼	1⅛	4 5 6 7½ 9	52	7.10
	SP20	20	2¾	2¾	1	4 5 6 7½ 9	46	6.50
	SP28	28	2¾	2¼	¾	6 7½	37	6.60
	SP410	410	2½	Max.	½	4 6 7½	22	5.25
	SP4103	410	3	Max.	11⁄16	4 5 6 7½ 9	31	6.15

‡ 28 ga. and 2½", 410 bore No. 9 shot marked "Skeet Load."

	No.	Gauge	Length shell, in.	Powder equiv. drams	Shot, oz.	Size shot	Wt. case, lbs.	Per box
"NITRO MAG" HIGH PERFORMANCE MAGNUM LOADS	SP12SNM	12	2¾	Max.	1½	2 4	66	$10.20
	SP12NM	12	3	4	1⅝	2 4	70	11.15

	No.	Gauge	Length shell, in.	Powder equiv. drams	Shot, oz.	Size shot	Wt. case, lbs.	Per box
"EXPRESS" MAGNUM LOADS	SP10Mag	10	3½	Max.	2	BB 2 4 (Mag.)	89	$17.30
	SP12Mag	12	3	4	1⅝	2 4 6 (Mag.)	70	10.75
	SP12SMag	12	2¾	Max.	1½	2 4 5 6 (Mag.)	66	9.65
	SP12HMag	12	3	Max.	1⅞	BB 2 4 (Mag.)	77	11.60
	SP16CMag	16	2¾	Max.	1¼	2 4 6 (Mag.)	56	9.10
	SP20SMag	20	2¾	Max.	1⅛	4 6 7½ (Mag.)	50	7.75
	SP20HMag	20	3	Max.	1¼	2 4 6 7½ (Mag.)	55	**8.75**

	No.	Gauge	Length shell, in.	Powder equiv. drams	Shot, oz.	Size shot	Wt. case, lbs.	Per box
STEEL SHOT WATER FOWL LOADS New! Magnum	STL12	12	2¾	Max.	1⅛	1 2 4	55	$10.55
	★STL12Mag	12	3	Max.	1¼	1 2 4	60	13.20

	No.	Gauge	Length shell, in.	Powder equiv. drams	Shot, oz.	Size shot	Wt. case, lbs.	Per box
RIFLED SLUG LOADS	SP12RS-25PK	12	2¾	3¾	⅞	Rifled Slug	51	$12.20
	SP12RS-5PK●	12	2¾	3¾	⅞	Rifled Slug	26	2.44
	SP16RS-5PK●	16	2¾	3	⅘	Rifled Slug	24	2.44
	SP20RS-5PK●	20	2¾	2¾	⅝	Rifled Slug	19	2.20
	SP410RS-5PK●	410	2½	Max.	⅕	Rifled Slug	8	2.10

	No.	Gauge	Length shell, in.	Powder equiv. drams	Shot, oz.	Size shot	Wt. case, lbs.	Per box
"Power Pakt" "EXPRESS" BUCKSHOT LOADS	★SP12BK-5PK●	12	2¾	3¾	...	000 Buck— 8 Pellets	26	$ 2.10
	SP12BK	12	2¾	3¾	...	00 Buck— 9 Pellets	55	10.50
	SP12BK-5PK●	12	2¾	3¾	...	00 Buck— 9 Pellets	29	2.10
	SP12BK	12	2¾	3¾	...	0 Buck—12 Pellets	63	10.50
	SP12BK-5PK●	12	2¾	3¾	...	0 Buck—12 Pellets	32	2.10
	SP12BK	12	2¾	3¾	...	1 Buck—16 Pellets	63	10.50
	SP12BK-5PK●	12	2¾	3¾	...	1 Buck—16 Pellets	33	2.10
	SP12BK	12	2¾	3¾	...	4 Buck—27 Pellets	60	10.50
	SP12BK-5PK●	12	2¾	3¾	...	4 Buck—27 Pellets	31	2.10
	SP16BK-5PK●	16	2¾	3	...	1 Buck—12 Pellets	26	2.10
	SP20BK-5PK●	20	2¾	2¾	...	3 Buck—20 Pellets	24	2.10

	No.	Gauge	Length shell, in.	Powder equiv. drams	Shot, oz.	Size shot	Wt. case, lbs.	Per box
"Power Pakt" "EXPRESS" MAGNUM BUCKSHOT LOADS	SP12SMagBK	12	2¾	4	...	00 Buck—12 Pellets	72	$11.75
	SP12SMagBK-5PK●	12	2¾	4	...	00 Buck—12 Pellets	34	2.35
	SP12SMagBK	12	2¾	4	...	1 Buck—20 Pellets	72	11.75
	SP12SMagBK-5PK●	12	2¾	4	...	1 Buck—20 Pellets	34	2.35
	SP12HMagBK	12	3	4½	...	00 Buck—15 Pellets	79	13.45
	SP12HMagBK-5PK●	12	3	4½	...	00 Buck—15 Pellets	40	2.70
	SP12HMagBK	12	3	4½	...	1 Buck—24 Pellets	79	13.45
	SP12HMagBK-5PK●	12	3	4½	...	1 Buck—24 Pellets	40	2.70
	SP12HMagBK	12	3	4½	...	4 Buck—41 Pellets	81	13.45
	SP12HMagBK-5PK●	12	3	4½	...	4 Buck—41 Pellets	42	2.70

REMINGTON PLASTIC SHOTSHELLS

REMINGTON "SHURSHOT" LOW BASE PLASTIC SHELLS AND REMINGTON TARGET LOADS
with "POWER-PISTON" WADS and "KLEANBORE" PRIMING

Sectional Cut-Away
RXP Target Load

Prices Subject to Change Without Notice

25 in a box, 500 in a case.

REMINGTON FIELD LOADS

	No.	Gauge	Length shell, in.	Powder equiv. drams	Size, oz.	Size shot			Wt. case, lbs.	Per box
"SHUR SHOT"	R12L	12	2¾	3¼	1	4 5 6	8		48	$5.90
PLASTIC FIELD	R12H	12	2¾	3¼	1⅛	4 5 6 7½	8 9		51	6.30
LOADS	RP12H	12	2¾	3¼	1¼	7½	8		58	6.60
With "Power	R16	16	2¾	2½	1	6	8		47	5.90
Piston" Wad	R16H	16	2¾	2¾	1⅛	4 5 6 7½	8 9		51	6.30
	R20	20	2¾	2½	⅞	6	8		41	5.30
	R20M	20	2¾	2½	1	4 5 6 7½	8 9		45	5.70
"SHUR SHOT" PLASTIC SCATTER LOADS With Special Wad Column	RSL12	12	2¾	3	1⅛	8			51	$6.70

REMINGTON TARGET LOADS

	No.	Gauge	Length shell, in.	Power equiv. drams	Size, oz.	Size shot			Wt. case, lbs.	Per box
"RXP" PLASTIC	XR12M	12	2¾	3	1⅛	7½ 8		9	54	$6.10
TRAP & SKEET LOADS	XR12L	12	2¾	2¾	1⅛	7½ 8 8½		9	54	6.10
With "Power Piston" Wad	XR20	20	2¾	2½	⅞			9	41	5.30
12 GAUGE "EXPRESS" INTERNATIONAL	SP12H	12	2¾	3¼	1⅛	7½ 8			58	$6.65
TARGET LOADS With "Power Piston" Wad	NSP12H	12	2¾	3¼	1⅛	7½ 8 (nickel)			58	7.80
"EXPRESS" PLASTIC	SP28	28	2¾	2	¾			9	37	$6.40
TARGET LOADS	SP410	410	2½	Max.	½			9	22	5.25

PETERS PLASTIC SHOTSHELLS
with "KLEANBORE" PRIMING

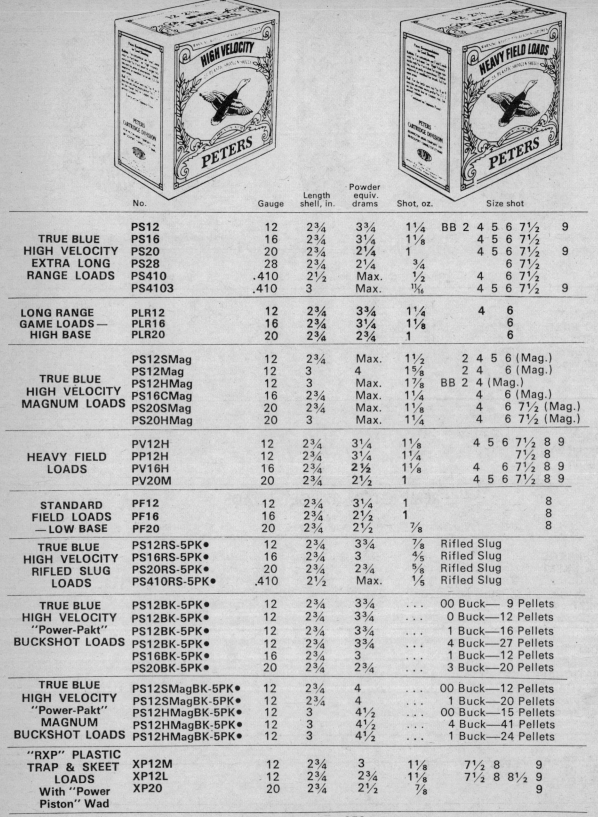

	No.	Gauge	Length shell, in.	Powder equiv. drams	Shot, oz.	Size shot
TRUE BLUE HIGH VELOCITY EXTRA LONG RANGE LOADS	PS12	12	2¾	3¾	1¼	BB 2 4 5 6 7½ 9
	PS16	16	2¾	3¼	1⅛	4 5 6 7½
	PS20	20	2¾	2¼	1	4 5 6 7½ 9
	PS28	28	2¾	2¼	¾	6 7½
	PS410	.410	2½	Max.	½	4 6 7½
	PS4103	.410	3	Max.	11⁄16	4 5 6 7½ 9
LONG RANGE GAME LOADS — HIGH BASE	PLR12	12	2¾	3¾	1¼	4 6
	PLR16	16	2¾	3¼	1⅛	6
	PLR20	20	2¾	2¾	1	6
TRUE BLUE HIGH VELOCITY MAGNUM LOADS	PS12SMag	12	2¾	Max.	1½	2 4 5 6 (Mag.)
	PS12Mag	12	3	4	1⅝	2 4 6 (Mag.)
	PS12HMag	12	3	Max.	1⅞	BB 2 4 (Mag.)
	PS16CMag	16	2¾	Max.	1¼	4 6 (Mag.)
	PS20SMag	20	2¾	Max.	1⅛	4 6 7½ (Mag.)
	PS20HMag	20	3	Max.	1¼	4 6 7½ (Mag.)
HEAVY FIELD LOADS	PV12H	12	2¾	3¼	1⅛	4 5 6 7½ 8 9
	PP12H	12	2¾	3¼	1¼	7½ 8
	PV16H	16	2¾	2½	1⅛	4 6 7½ 8 9
	PV20M	20	2¾	2½	1	4 5 6 7½ 8 9
STANDARD FIELD LOADS — LOW BASE	PF12	12	2¾	3¼	1	8
	PF16	16	2¾	2½	1	8
	PF20	20	2¾	2½	⅞	8
TRUE BLUE HIGH VELOCITY RIFLED SLUG LOADS	PS12RS-5PK●	12	2¾	3¾	⅞	Rifled Slug
	PS16RS-5PK●	16	2¾	3	⅘	Rifled Slug
	PS20RS-5PK●	20	2¾	2¾	⅝	Rifled Slug
	PS410RS-5PK●	.410	2½	Max.	⅕	Rifled Slug
TRUE BLUE HIGH VELOCITY "Power-Pakt" BUCKSHOT LOADS	PS12BK-5PK●	12	2¾	3¾	. . .	00 Buck— 9 Pellets
	PS12BK-5PK●	12	2¾	3¾	. . .	0 Buck—12 Pellets
	PS12BK-5PK●	12	2¾	3¾	. . .	1 Buck—16 Pellets
	PS12BK-5PK●	12	2¾	3¾	. . .	4 Buck—27 Pellets
	PS16BK-5PK●	16	2¾	3	. . .	1 Buck—12 Pellets
	PS20BK-5PK●	20	2¾	2¾	. . .	3 Buck—20 Pellets
TRUE BLUE HIGH VELOCITY "Power-Pakt" MAGNUM BUCKSHOT LOADS	PS12SMagBK-5PK●	12	2¾	4	. . .	00 Buck—12 Pellets
	PS12SMagBK-5PK●	12	2¾	4	. . .	1 Buck—20 Pellets
	PS12HMagBK-5PK●	12	3	4½	. . .	00 Buck—15 Pellets
	PS12HMagBK-5PK●	12	3	4½	. . .	4 Buck—41 Pellets
	PS12HMagBK-5PK●	12	3	4½	. . .	1 Buck—24 Pellets
"RXP" PLASTIC TRAP & SKEET LOADS With "Power Piston" Wad	XP12M	12	2¾	3	1⅛	7½ 8 9
	XP12L	12	2¾	2¾	1⅛	7½ 8 8½ 9
	XP20	20	2¾	2½	⅞	9

● Packed 5 per box—250 per case

WINCHESTER-WESTERN SHOTSHELLS

Staynless Non-Corrosive Priming.　　Packed 25 per Box. 500 per Case unless otherwise noted.

Super-X—Mark 5—Long Range—Short Shot String

WESTERN SYMBOL	WINCHESTER SYMBOL	GAUGE	LENGTH OF SHELL INCHES	POWDER DRAM EQUIV.	OZ. SHOT	SHOT SIZES	CASE WT. LBS.	CASES PER PALLET	NET WEIGHT PER PALLET	SUGGESTED RETAIL PRICE PER BOX
□SX10	*□WSX10	10	2⅞	Max.	1⅝	4	36	48	1728	$10.20
SX12P	WSX12P	12	2¾	Max.	1¼	BB. 2. 4. 5. 6. 7½. 9	56	60	3360	7.40
SX16PH	WSX16PH	16	2¾	Max.	1⅛	4. 5. 6. 7½. 9	49	64	3136	7.10
SX20P	WSX20P	20	2¾	Max.	1	4. 5. 6. 7½. 9	44	80	3520	6.50
SX28	WSX28	28	2¾	Max.	¾	6. 7½	35	90	3150	6.60
SX41	WSX41	410	2½	Max.	½	4. 6. 7½	23	161	3703	5.25
SX413	WSX413	410	3	Max.	11⁄16	4. 5. 6. 7½. 9	29	108	3132	6.15

Super-X—Mark 5—Long Range—Short Shot String—Magnum Loads

WESTERN SYMBOL	WINCHESTER SYMBOL	GAUGE	LENGTH OF SHELL INCHES	POWDER DRAM EQUIV.	OZ. SHOT	SHOT SIZES	CASE WT. LBS.	CASES PER PALLET	NET WEIGHT PER PALLET	SUGGESTED RETAIL PRICE PER BOX
□SX10M	†	10	3½ Mag.	Max.	2	2	44	40	1760	17.30
SX12PH	WSX12PH	12	2¾ Mag.	Max.	1½	2. 4. 5. 6	63	45	2835	9.65
§SX12PJ	§WSX12PJ	12	3 Mag.	Max.	1⅜	2. 4. 6	61	48	2928	8.95
SX12PM	WSX12PM	12	3 Mag.	Max.	1⅝	2. 4. 6	69	48	3312	10.75
SX123P	WSX123P	12	3 Mag.	Max.	1⅞	BB. 2. 4	75	48	3600	11.60
SX16PM	WSX16PM	16	2¾ Mag.	Max.	1¼	2. 4. 6	52	64	3328	9.10
SX20PH	WSX20PH	20	2¾ Mag.	Max.	1⅛	4. 6. 7½	48	64	3072	7.75
SX20PM	WSX20PM	20	3 Mag.	Max.	1¼	4. 6. 7½	52	48	2496	8.75

Super-X—Mark 5 Double X Magnum

WESTERN SYMBOL	WINCHESTER SYMBOL	GAUGE	LENGTH OF SHELL INCHES	POWDER DRAM EQUIV.	OZ. SHOT	SHOT SIZES	CASE WT. LBS.	CASES PER PALLET	NET WEIGHT PER PALLET	SUGGESTED RETAIL PRICE PER BOX
□SX103X	†	10	3½ Mag.	Max.	2¼	BB. 2. 4	48	40	1920	18.40
SX12X	WSX12X	12	2¾ Mag.	Max.	1½	2. 4. 6	66	45	2970	10.20
SX123X	WSX123X	12	3 Mag.	Max.	1⅞	BB. 2. 4	77	48	3696	12.00
SX203X	WSX203X	20	3 Mag.	Max.	1¼	2. 4. 6	54	48	2592	9.65

Steel Shot—Super-X

WESTERN SYMBOL	WINCHESTER SYMBOL	GAUGE	LENGTH OF SHELL INCHES	POWDER DRAM EQUIV.	OZ. SHOT	SHOT SIZES	CASE WT. LBS.	CASES PER PALLET	NET WEIGHT PER PALLET	SUGGESTED RETAIL PRICE PER BOX
SX12SSF	WSX12SSF	12	2¾	Max.	1¼	1. 2. 4	58	60	3480	12.65
SX12SSM	WSX12SSM	12	3	Max.	1½	1. 2. 4	62	48	2976	15.50

Super-X With Lubaloy [Copperized] Shot

WESTERN SYMBOL	WINCHESTER SYMBOL	GAUGE	LENGTH OF SHELL INCHES	POWDER DRAM EQUIV.	OZ. SHOT	SHOT SIZES	CASE WT. LBS.	CASES PER PALLET	NET WEIGHT PER PALLET	SUGGESTED RETAIL PRICE PER BOX
§L12P	†	12	2¾	Max.	1¼	2. 4. 5. 6. 7½	56	60	3360	7.60
§L20P	†	20	2¾	Max.	1	5. 6. 7½	44	80	3520	6.60

Super-X With Lubaloy [Copperized] Shot—Magnum Loads

WESTERN SYMBOL	WINCHESTER SYMBOL	GAUGE	LENGTH OF SHELL INCHES	POWDER DRAM EQUIV.	OZ. SHOT	SHOT SIZES	CASE WT. LBS.	CASES PER PALLET	NET WEIGHT PER PALLET	SUGGESTED RETAIL PRICE PER BOX
§L12PJ	†	12	3 Mag.	Max.	1⅜	2. 4. 6	62	48	2976	9.35
§L12PM	†	12	3 Mag.	Max.	1⅝	2. 4. 6	67	48	3216	10.75
§L20PMH	†	20	3 Mag.	Max.	1³⁄₁₆	4	51	48	2448	10.30

BUCKSHOT LOADS

Super-X Mark 5 Super Buckshot Loads—25 Round Box

WESTERN SYMBOL	WINCHESTER SYMBOL	GAUGE	LENGTH OF SHELL INCHES	PELLETS	SHOT SIZES	CASE WT. LBS.	CASES PER PALLET	NET WEIGHT PER PALLET	SUGGESTED RETAIL PRICE PER BOX
SX12PRB	WSX12PRB	12	2¾	9 Pellets	00 Buck	52	60	3120	10.55
▪SX12P0B	▪WSX12P0B	12	2¾	12 Pellets	0 Buck	61	45	2745	10.55
▪SX12P1B	▪WSX12P1B	12	2¾	16 Pellets	1 Buck	64	45	2880	9.75
SX12P4B	WSX12P4B	12	2¾	27 Pellets	4 Buck	56	60	3360	10.55
▪SX16PB	▪WSX16PB	16	2¾	12 Pellets	1 Buck	50	64	3200	10.55

Super-X Mark 5 Super Buckshot Loads—5 Round Pack—Packed 250 Rounds per Case

WESTERN SYMBOL	WINCHESTER SYMBOL	GAUGE	LENGTH OF SHELL INCHES	PELLETS	SHOT SIZES	CASE WT. LBS.	CASES PER PALLET	NET WEIGHT PER PALLET	SUGGESTED RETAIL PRICE PER BOX
SX12RB5PK	WSX12RB5PK	12	2¾	9 Pellets	00 Buck	27	63	1701	2.11
SX120B5PK	WSX120B5PK	12	2¾	12 Pellets	0 Buck	32	54	1728	2.11
SX121B5PK	WSX121B5PK	12	2¾	16 Pellets	1 Buck	33	54	1782	2.11
SX124B5PK	WSX124B5PK	12	2¾	27 Pellets	4 Buck	29	54	1566	2.11
SX16B5PK	WSX16B5PK	16	2¾	12 Pellets	1 Buck	26	91	2366	2.11
SX20B5PK	WSX20B5PK	20	2¾	20 Pellets	3 Buck	24	104	2496	2.08

Super-X Magnum Mark 5 Super Buckshot Loads—25 Round Box

WESTERN SYMBOL	WINCHESTER SYMBOL	GAUGE	LENGTH OF SHELL INCHES	PELLETS	SHOT SIZES	CASE WT. LBS.	CASES PER PALLET	NET WEIGHT PER PALLET	SUGGESTED RETAIL PRICE PER BOX
▪SX12PB	▪WSX12PB	12	2¾ Mag.	12 Pellets	00 Buck	63	45	2835	11.75
▪SX123PB	▪WSX123PB	12	3 Mag.	15 Pellets	00 Buck	75	48	3600	13.40
▪SX12MB	†	12	2¾ Mag.	20 Pellets	1 Buck	75	45	3375	11.75
SX1231B	†	12	3 Mag.	24 Pellets	1 Buck	86	36	3096	13.40
SX12PMB	WSX12PMB	12	3 Mag.	41 Pellets	4 Buck	76	48	3648	13.40

Super-X Magnum Mark 5 Super Buckshot Loads—5 Round Pack—Packed 250 Rounds per Case

WESTERN SYMBOL	WINCHESTER SYMBOL	GAUGE	LENGTH OF SHELL INCHES	PELLETS	SHOT SIZES	CASE WT. LBS.	CASES PER PALLET	NET WEIGHT PER PALLET	SUGGESTED RETAIL PRICE PER BOX
SX12B5PK	WSX12B5PK	12	2¾ Mag.	12 Pellets	00 Buck	33	54	1782	2.35
SX123B5PK	WSX123B5PK	12	3 Mag.	15 Pellets	00 Buck	39	45	1755	2.68
SX12M1B5PK	†	12	2¾ Mag.	20 Pellets	1 Buck	38	45	1710	2.35
SX1231B5PK	†	12	3 Mag.	24 Pellets	1 Buck	44	45	1980	2.68
SX12MB5PK	WSX12MB5PK	12	3 Mag.	41 Pellets	4 Buck	39	45	1755	2.68

11% Excise tax included
†See adjoining column for available brand symbol

▪25 Round Box Discontinued - Will supply 5 round boxes when 25 round stock is depleted
□Packed 25 Rounds per Carton. 250 Rounds per Case

*Will be furnished in Western Brand when Winchester inventory is depleted
§Discontinued stock - Offered subject to prior sale

WINCHESTER-WESTERN SHOTSHELLS

Staynless Non-Corrosive Priming.   Packed 25 per Box. 500 per Case unless otherwise noted.

RIFLED SLUG LOADS

Super-X Rifled Slug Loads—25 Round Box

WESTERN SYMBOL	WINCHESTER SYMBOL	GAUGE	LENGTH OF SHELL INCHES	POWDER DRAM EQUIV.	SLUG WT. OZ.	SHOT SIZES	CASE WT. LBS.	CASES PER PALLET	NET WEIGHT PER PALLET	SUGGESTED RETAIL PRICE PER BOX
■SX16PRS	■WSX16PRS	16	2¾	Max.	⅘	Rifled Slug	39	64	2496	12.20
■SX20PRS	■WSX20PRS	20	2¾	Max.	⅝	Rifled Slug	34	80	2720	11.05
■SX41RS	■WSX41RS	410	2½	Max.	⅕	Rifled Slug	15	161	2415	10.55

Super-X Rifled Slug Loads—5 Round Pack—Packed 250 Rounds per Case

WESTERN SYMBOL	WINCHESTER SYMBOL	GAUGE	LENGTH OF SHELL INCHES	POWDER DRAM EQUIV.	SLUG WT. OZ.	SHOT SIZES	CASE WT. LBS.	CASES PER PALLET	NET WEIGHT PER PALLET	SUGGESTED RETAIL PRICE PER BOX
SX12RS5PK	WSX12RS5PK	12	2¾	Max.	⅞	Rifled Slug	24	63	1512	2.44
SX16RS5PK	WSX16RS5PK	16	2¾	Max.	⅘	Rifled Slug	21	117	2457	2.44
SX20RS5PK	WSX20RS5PK	20	2¾	Max.	⅝	Rifled Slug	18	117	2106	2.21
SX41RS5PK	WSX41RS5PK	410	2½	Max.	⅕	Rifled Slug	8	198	1584	2.11

UPLAND—MARK 5 FIELD LOADS

WESTERN SYMBOL	WINCHESTER SYMBOL	GAUGE	LENGTH OF SHELL INCHES	POWDER DRAM EQUIV.	OZ. SHOT	STANDARD SHOT SIZES	CASE WT. LBS.	CASES PER PALLET	NET WEIGHT PER PALLET	SUGGESTED RETAIL PRICE PER BOX
†	WU10BL	10	2⅞	8	—	‡Blank	32	48	1536	12.30
U12	WU12	12	2¾	3¼	1	4. 5. 6. 8	47	60	2820	5.90
U12H	WU12H	12	2¾	3¼	1⅛	4. 5. 6. 7½. 8. 9	51	60	3060	6.30
U12P	WU12P	12	2¾	3¼	1¼	6. 7½. 8	54	60	3240	6.60
†	WU12BL	12	2¾	6	—	‡Blank	28	48	1344	9.40
U16	WU16	16	2¾	2½	1	6. 8	44	64	2816	5.90
#△U16H	#△WU16H	16	2¾	2¾	1⅛	4. 5. 6. 7½. 8. 9	49	64	3136	6.30
U20	WU20	20	2¾	2½	⅞	6. 8	40	80	3200	5.30
△U20H	△WU20H	20	2¾	2½	1	4. 5. 6. 7½. 8. 9	43	80	3440	5.70

WESTERN FIELD TRIAL POPPER LOAD

WESTERN SYMBOL	WINCHESTER SYMBOL	GAUGE	LENGTH OF SHELL INCHES	POWDER DRAM EQUIV.	OZ. SHOT	STANDARD SHOT SIZES	CASE WT. LBS.	CASES PER PALLET	NET WEIGHT PER PALLET	SUGGESTED RETAIL PRICE PER BOX
XP12FBL	†	12	2¾	—	—	Blank	21	60	1260	4.70

UPLAND BRUSH LOAD

WESTERN SYMBOL	WINCHESTER SYMBOL	GAUGE	LENGTH OF SHELL INCHES	POWDER DRAM EQUIV.	OZ. SHOT	STANDARD SHOT SIZES	CASE WT. LBS.	CASES PER PALLET	NET WEIGHT PER PALLET	SUGGESTED RETAIL PRICE PER BOX
§U12BR	§WU12BR	12	2¾	3	1⅛	8	51	60	3060	5.80

WINCHESTER—WESTERN TRAP AND SKEET LOADS

Double A Trap Loads

WW12AA	WW12AA	12	2¾	2¾	1⅛	7½. 8. 8½	50	60	3000	6.25
WW12MAA	WW12MAA	12	2¾	3	1⅛	7½. 8. 8½	50	60	3000	6.25

Double A Handicap Trap Loads

WW12AAX	WW12AAX	12	2¾	3	1⅛	7½. 8	51	60	3060	6.25

Double A International Trap Load

WWIN12AH	WWIN12AH	12	2¾	3¼	1⅛	7½. 8 (Nic. Pl. Shot) ·	51	60	3060	8.00
WWIN12A	WWIN12A	12	2¾	3¼	1⅛	7½. 8	51	60	3060	6.80

Double A International Skeet Load (No shot protectors)

WWAA12IS	WWAA12IS	12	2¾	3½	1⅛	9	50	60	3000	6.80

Double A Skeet Loads

WW12AA	WW12AA	12	2¾	2¾	1⅛	9	51	60	3060	6.25
WW12MAA	WW12MAA	12	2¾	3	1⅛	9	51	60	3060	6.25
WW20AA	WW20AA	20	2¾	2½	⅞	9	40	80	3200	5.45
WW28AA	WW28AA	28	2¾	2	¾	9	35	90	3150	6.55
WW41AA	WW41AA	410	2½	Max.	½	9	23	161	3703	5.35

Double A SPECIAL Skeet Loads (No shot protectors)

§WW12AAS	§WW12AAS	12	2¾	2¾	1⅛	9	50	60	3000	5.30
§WW12MAAS	§WW12MAAS	12	2¾	3	1⅛	9	50	60	3000	5.30

Super Target Loads (Paper not Plastic)

WW12	WW12	12	2¾	2¾	1⅛	8. 9	53	60	3180	6.25
WW12M	WW12M	12	2¾	3	1⅛	7½. 8. 9	53	60	3180	6.25

Super Pigeon Target Loads

WW12SP	WW12SP	12	2¾	3¼	1¼	7½. 8	54	60	3120	7.60

11% Excise tax included
§Discontinued stock —Offered subject to prior sale
‡Black Powder

∗Less than Carload Orders add 4%
†See adjoining column for available brand symbol
△Loads with 7½ or 8 Shot recommended for Trapshooting

#9 Shot recommended for Skeet
■25 Round Box Discontinued — Will supply 5 round boxes when 25 round stock is depleted

FEDERAL SHOTSHELLS

Gauge	Load No.	Shell Length Inches	Dram Equiv.	Shot Charge Oz.	Shot Sizes	Per Box
FEDERAL HI-POWER MAGNUM LOADS						
10	F103	3½	4½	2	BB,2,4	$15.75
12	F131	3	4	1⅞	BB,2,4	11.60
12	F129	3	4	1⅝	2,4,6	10.75
12	F130	2¾	3¾	1½	BB,2,4,5,6	9.65
16	F165	2¾	3¼	1¼	2,4,6	9.10
20	F207	3	3	1¼	2,4,6,7½	8.75
20	F205	2¾	2¾	1⅛	4,6,7½	7.75
FEDERAL HI-POWER LOADS						
12	F127	2¾	3¾	1¼	BB,2,4,5,6,7½,8,9	7.40
16	F164	2¾	3¼	1⅛	4,5,6,7½,9	7.10
20	F203	2¾	2¾	1	4,5,6,7½,8,9	6.50
28	F283	2¾	2¼	⅞	6,7½,8	6.60
.410	F413	3	Max.	11/16	4,5,6,7½,8,9	6.15
.410	F412	2½	Max.	½	6,7½	5.25
FEDERAL WATERFOWL STEEL SHOT LOADS						
12	W147	2¾	3¾	1⅛	1,2,4 Steel	10.55
12	W148	2¾	Max.	1¼	1,2,4 Steel	12.65
12	W149	3	Max.	1⅜	BB1,2,4 Steel	14.10
FEDERAL FIELD LOADS						
12	F124	2¾	3¼	1¼	7½,8,9	6.65
12	F123	2¾	3¼	1⅛	4,5,6,7½,8,9	6.30
16	F162	2¾	2¾	1⅛	4,5,6,7½,8,9	6.15
20	F202	2¾	2½	1	4,5,6,7½,8,9	5.70
FEDERAL GAME LOADS						
12	F121	2¾	3¼	1	6,7½,8	5.80
16	F160	2¾	2½	1	6,7½,8	5.60
20	F200	2¾	2½	⅞	6,7½,8	5.30
FEDERAL DUCK & PHEASANT LOADS						
12	F126	2¾	3¾	1¼	4,5,6,7½	6.45
16	F163	2¾	3¼	1⅛	4,6,7½	6.45
20	F204	2¾	2¾	1	4,6,7½	6.10
FEDERAL RIFLED SLUG LOADS (5 PER BOX)						
12	F127	2¾	Max.	⅞	Rifled Slug	2.44
16	F164	2¾	Max.	4/5	Rifled Slug	2.44
20	F203	2¾	Max.	⅝	Rifled Slug	2.20
.410	F412	2½	Max.	1/5	Rifled Slug	2.10

Gauge	Load No.	Shell Length Inches	Dram Equiv.	Shot Charge Oz.	Shot Sizes	Per Box
FEDERAL TARGET LOADS						
12	K117	2¾	2¾	1⅛	7½,8,9	$6.10
12	K118	2¾	3	1⅛	7½,8,9	6.10
12	C117	2¾	2¾	1⅛	7½,8,8½,9	5.95
12	C118	2¾	3	1⅛	7½,8,8½,9	5.95
12	F119	2¾	2¾	1⅛	8,9	5.70
12	F122	2¾	3	1⅛	7½,8,9	5.70
12	T122	2¾	3	1⅛	7½,8,9	6.10
12	T123	2¾	3½	1⅛	10	6.20
16	F167	2¾	2¾	1⅛	7½,8,9	6.10
20	F206	2¾	2½	⅞	8,9	5.30
20	S206	2¾	2½	⅞	8,9	5.30
28	F280	2¾	2	¾	9	6.40
.410	F412	2½	Max.	½	9	5.25

FEDERAL HI-POWER BUCKSHOT LOADS (5 per box)

Gauge	Load No.	Shell Length Inches	Dram Equiv.	Shot Sizes	Per Box
10	G108	3½	Sup.Mag.	No. 4 Buck-54 Pellets	3.52+
12	F131	3	Sup.Mag.	00 Buck-15 Pellets	2.70
12	F131	3	Sup.Mag.	No.1 Buck-24 Pellets	2.70
12	F131	3	Sup.Mag.	No.4 Buck-41 Pellets	2.70
12	A131	3	Sup.Mag.	No.4 Buck-41 Pellets	13.50*
12	F130	2¾	Mag.	00 Buck-12 Pellets	2.35
12	F130	2¾	Mag.	No.1 Buck-20 Pellets	2.35
12	F130	2¾	Mag.	No.4 Buck-34 Pellets	2.35
12	A130	2¾	Mag.	No.4 Buck-34 Pellets	11.75*
12	G127	2¾	Max.	00 Buck-9 Pellets	2.10+
12	F127	2¾	Max.	00 Buck-9 Pellets	2.10
12	F127	2¾	Max.	0 Buck-12 Pellets	2.10
12	F127	2¾	Max.	No. 1 Buck-16 Pellets	2.10
12	F127	2¾	Max.	No. 4 Buck-27 Pellets	2.10
16	F164	2¾	Max.	No. 1 Buck-12 Pellets	2.10
20	F207	3	Mag.	No. 2 Buck-18 Pellets	2.35
20	F203	2¾	Max.	No. 3 Buck-20 Pellets	2.10

*25 per box.
+With granulated plastic filler.

FIOCCHI BALLISTICS

Centerfire Cartridges for Pistols

CALIBER	BULLET WEIGHT IN GRAINS	VELOCITY IN FT./SEC. MV	VELOCITY IN FT./SEC. 50 YDS.	ENERGY IN FOOT LBS. MV	ENERGY IN FOOT LBS. 50 YDS.	BARREL LENGTH INCHES
25 A.C.P.	50	754.6	698.8	62.2	53.5	2⅜"
6.35mm	50	656.2	607.00	47.00	40.5	2⅜"
.30 MAUSER 7.63mm Mauser	88	1443.6	1253.3	400.00	301.6	5½"
32 A.C.P.	73	951.5	879.3	147.6	125.9	3⅜"
7.65mm	75	885.8	826.8	130.2	113.6	3⅜"
30 LUGER PARABELLUM 7.65mm	93	1181.1	1066.3	287.2	233.6	4 17/32"
ROTH-STEYR 8mm	113	1082.7	1010.5	293.7	255.3	5"
380 A.C.P. 9mm (short M34)	93	984.3	876.00	199.6	157.7	3⅜"
9mm LUGER 9mm (long M38)	115	1345.2	1158.2	462.2	342.8	7⅞"
9mm GLISENTI	123	1230.3	1072.9	415.2	315.4	7⅞"
9mm LUGER PARABELLUM	123	1312.4	1122.1	472.3	345.00	7⅞"
9mm STEYR	115	1181.1	1000.7	356.6	256.1	5"
30 MI CARBINE	111	1968.5	1804.5	956.2	803.6	20"
38 A.C.P. 38	129	1148.3	1004.00	377.6	288.6	6 1/32
45 A.C.P. 45	230	820.2	777.6	343.6	308.9	5"

Centerfire Cartridges for Revolvers

CALIBER	BULLET WEIGHT IN GRAINS	VELOCITY IN FT./SEC. MV	VELOCITY IN FT./SEC. 50 YDS.	ENERGY IN FOOT LBS. MV	ENERGY IN FOOT LBS. 50 YDS.	BARREL LENGTH INCHES
5.5mm VELO DOG REVOLVER	43	853.00	777.6	70.2	57.9	3¾"
SWISS ORDNANCE 7.5mm	107	1115.5	997.4	296.6	237.2	5"
7.62 NAGANT	97	1049.9	987.6	238.00	210.5	6"
8mm LEBEL	111	885.8	839.9	193.8	174.3	5"
8mm GASSER	126	885.8	856.3	219.2	204.7	4¾"
ITALIAN ORDNANCE 10.4mm	177	951.5	895.7	356.6	316.1	5"
32 SMITH &	85	738.2	708.7	102.7	94.8	5"
WESSON SHORT	85	721.8	639.8	98.4	77.4	5"
32 SMITH &	98	836.6	784.1	151.2	133.1	5"
WESSON LONG	98	820.2	771.00	145.4	128.7	5"
320 SHORT	82	820.2	790.7	122.2	113.6	5"
	82	787.4	744.8	112.8	100.5	5"

FIOCCHI BALLISTICS

Centerfire Cartridges for Revolvers

CALIBER	BULLET WEIGHT IN GRAINS	VELOCITY IN FT./SEC. MV	50 YDS.	ENERGY IN FOOT LBS. MV	50 YDS.	BARREL LENGTH INCHES
320 LONG	82	853.00	803.8	132.4	117.2	3⅜″
	82	820.2	764.4	122.2	106.3	3⅜″
38 SMITH & WESSON SHORT	145	754.6	721.8	183.7	167.8	5″
	145	721.8	682.4	167.8	149.7	5″
38 SPECIAL	158	918.7	876.00	296.6	269.8	6″
	158	685.8	820.2	275.6	236.5	6″
38 SPECIAL WAD CUTTER	148	787.4	669.3	203.3	146.8	6″
380 SHORT	125	820.2	790.7	186.6	173.6	5″
	125	787.4	734.9	172.1	149.7	5″
380 LONG	125	853.00	800.5	201.8	177.9	7⅞″
	125	820.2	761.2	186.6	160.6	7⅞″
44 SMITH & WESSON RUSSIAN	247	820.2	790.7	368.9	342.8	6½″
450 SHORT	226	853.00	813.7	365.3	332.7	7½″
455 MK II	262	853.00	816.9	423.9	389.1	7½″
357 MAGNUM	158	1378.00		667.6		7⅝″

22 Rimfire Cartridges Short-Long-Long Rifle-Extra Long

CALIBER	BULLET WEIGHT IN GRAINS	VELOCITY IN FT./SEC. MV	50 YDS.	ENERGY IN FOOT LBS. MV	50 YDS.	BARREL LENGTH INCHES
22 SHORT TRAINING	29	1049.9	948.2	71.6	58.6	22″
22 SHORT NORMALE	29	951.5	849.5	59.3	47.00	22″
22 SHORT OLIMPIONICO	31	787.4	702.1	42.7	34.00	5″
22 SHORT V 50	28	1181.1	987.6	86.1	60.00	22″
22 SHORT EXPANSIVE	28	1181.1	931.8	86.1	53.5	22″
22 SHORT "Z"	29	853.00	764.4	47.7	38.8	22″
22 LONG	28	1246.7	1013.8	96.2	63.7	27¼″
22 LONG "Z"	29	820.2	748.00	44.1	36.9	27¼″
22 LONG L.R. MAXAC	40	1148.3	1063.00	117.9	100.5	27¼″
22 L.R. CARB. BERETTA	40	1099.1	1033.5	107.8	95.5	27¼″
22 L.R. ULTRASONIC	40	1328.8	1197.5	157.7	128.00	27¼″
22 L.R. EXPANSIVE	37	1345.2	1210.7	149.00	120.8	27¼″
22 L.R. COMPETIZIONE	40	1082.7	1023.6	104.2	93.3	27¼″
22 L.R. PISTOLA LIBERA	40	1049.9	1013.8	98.4	91.9	9″
22 EXTRA LONG	40	1410.8	1325.5	177.2	157.00	27¼″

All specifications are nominal. Individual guns may vary from test barrel figures.

NORMA BALLISTICS

Cartr. index no.	Cartr. length inch.	Norma primer	Norma powder	grains	Velocity – Feet per sec. Muzzle	100 yards	200 yards	300 yards	Energy – Foot pounds Muzzle	100 yards	200 yards	300 yards	Press. psi	Sight at yards	25 yards	50 yards	100 yards	150 yards	200 yards	300 yards
15701	2.62	LR	203	40.9	4110	3611	3133	2681	1877	1448	1090	799	53700	100	-0.9	-0.5	0	-0.2	-1.2	-5.9
	Special load		203	39.2	3910									180	-0.8	-0.3	+0.4	+0.4	-0.4	-4.7
	Special load		203	37.8	3710									200	-0.8	-0.2	+0.6	+0.7	0	-4.1
15711	2.11	SR	200	21.0	3200	2650	2170	1750	1137	780	520	340	46400	100	-0.8	-0.3	0	-0.9	-3.2	-12.9
	Special load		200	20.2	3000									180	-0.5	+0.3	+1.2	+0.8	-0.9	-9.4
	Special load		200	18.5	2800									200	-0.4	+0.5	+1.6	+1.5	0	-8.2
15712	2.11	SR	200	21.0	3200	2610	2080	1630	1137	756	480	295	46400	100	-0.7	-0.2	0	-1.1	-3.7	-15.7
	Special load		200	20.2	3000									180	-0.4	+0.5	+1.4	+1.0	-1.0	-11.6
	Special load		200	18.5	2800									200	-0.3	+0.7	+1.9	+1.7	0	-10.1
15713	2.11	SR	200	17.7	2789	2235	1755	1390	863	554	341	214	46400	100	-0.6	±0.0	0	-1.7	-5.8	-23.4
														180	-0.1	+1.0	+2.1	+1.5	-1.5	-17.1
														200	+0.1	+1.4	+2.9	+2.6	0	-14.8
15604	2.50	LR	201	25.1	2788	2296	1886	1558	1226	831	561	383	42100	100	-0.6	-0.1	0	-1.5	-4.8	-18.6
														180	-0.2	+0.8	+1.8	+1.2	-1.2	-13.2
														200	±0.0	+1.1	+2.4	+2.1	0	11.4
15605	2.50	LR	201	25.1	2788	2296	1886	1558	1226	831	561	383	42100	100	-0.6	-0.1	0	-1.5	-4.8	-18.6
														180	-0.2	+0.8	+1.8	+1.2	-1.2	-13.2
														200	±0.0	+1.1	+2.4	+2.1	0	-11.4
16003	2.62	LR	204	45.1	3070	2790	2540	2320	2090	1730	1430	1190	52200	100	-0.7	-0.2	0	-0.9	-2.9	-10.6
	Special load		204	43.8	2870									180	-0.5	+0.3	+1.1	+0.7	-0.7	-7.4
	Special load		204	42.0	2670									200	-0.4	+0.5	+1.4	+1.3	0	-6.3
16002	2.62	LR	204	45.1	3070	2790	2540	2320	2090	1730	1430	1190	52200	100	-0.7	-0.2	0	-0.9	-2.9	-10.6
	Special load		204	43.8	2870									180	-0.5	+0.3	+1.1	+0.7	-0.7	-7.4
	Special load		204	42.0	2670									200	-0.4	+0.5	+1.4	+1.3	0	-6.3
16531	2.82	LR	203	32.8	2428	2280	2130	1990	1820	1605	1401	1223	32200	100	-0.5	±0.0	0	-1.8	-5.4	-18.8
	Special load		201	28.2	2228									130	-0.4	+0.4	+0.6	-0.8	-4.1	-16.9
	Special load		200	24.0	2028									200	+0.1	+1.4	+2.7	+2.3	0	-10.8
16532	2.89	LR	203	29.3	2067	1871	1692	1529	1481	1213	992	810	32200	100	-0.3	+0.4	0	-2.9	-8.5	-29.2
	Special load		201	24.7	1867									130	±0.0	+0.9	+1.1	-1.2	-6.3	-26.0
	Special load		200	20.5	1667									200	+0.8	+2.5	+4.3	+3.5	0	-16.4
16550	2.62	LR	200	33.2	2725	2362	2030	1811	1271	956	706	562	45000	100	-0.6	-0.1	0	-1.5	-4.8	-18.1
	Special load		200	37.8	3116									180	-0.2	+0.8	+1.8	+1.2	-1.2	-12.7
	Special load		200	34.1	2916									200	±0.0	+1.1	+2.4	+2.1	0	-10.9
16557	2.99	LR	204	46.6	2788	2630	2470	2320	2402	2136	1883	1662	45000	100	-0.7	-0.2	0	-1.1	-3.7	-13.3
	Special load		203	39.5	2588									180	-0.3	+0.5	+1.4	+0.9	-0.9	-9.2
	Special load		203	36.5	2388									200	-0.2	+0.8	+1.8	+1.6	0	-7.8
16552	3.07	LR	204	44.2	2493	2271	2062	1867	2153	1787	1473	1208	45000	100	-0.6	+0.2	0	-1.7	-5.3	-18.8
	Special load		204	42.5	2293									180	±0.0	+1.0	+2.0	+1.3	-1.3	-12.7
	Special load		204	39.8	2093									200	+0.1	+1.3	+2.6	+2.2	0	-10.9
16535	2.97	LR	200	27.5	2000	1810	1640	1485	1386	1135	932	764	37700	100	-0.2	+0.4	0	-3.1	-9.1	-31.2
	Special load		200	25.2	1800									130	+0.1	+1.0	+1.2	-1.3	-6.8	-27.6
	Special load		200	23.0	1600									200	+0.9	+2.8	+4.6	+3.7	0	-17.5
16902	3.15	LR	204	57.0	3140	2884	2639	2404	2847	2401	2011	1669	52200	100	-0.8	-0.3	0	-0.8	-4.1	-10.7
	Special load		204	55.0	2940									180	-0.5	+0.2	+1.0	+0.7	-0.7	-7.7
	Special load		204	52.0	2740									200	-0.4	+0.4	+1.4	+1.3	0	-6.6
16903	3.23	LR	204	52.4	2800	2616	2436	2262	2616	2280	1977	1705	52200	100	-0.7	-0.2	0	-1.1	-3.6	-13.1
	Special load		204	50.5	2600									180	-0.3	+0.5	+1.4	+0.9	-0.9	-9.0
	Special load		204	46.7	2400									200	-0.2	+0.7	+1.8	+1.6	0	-7.7
17002	3.05	LR	203	44.1	2756	2539	2331	2133	2530	2148	1810	1516	49300	100	-0.7	-0.1	0	-1.2	-3.9	-14.3
	Special load		201	40.0	2556									180	-0.3	+0.6	+1.5	+1.0	-1.0	-9.8
	Special load		201	36.5	2356									200	-0.2	+0.9	+2.0	+1.7	0	-8.4
17005	3.05	LR	203	43.0	2690	2476	2270	2077	2411	2042	1717	1437	43500	100	-0.6	-0.1	0	-1.3	-4.2	-15.2
	Special load		203	42.0	2490									180	-0.2	+0.7	+1.6	+1.1	-1.0	-10.4
	Special load		201	36.3	2290									200	-0.1	+1.0	+2.1	+1.8	0	-8.9
17006	3.05	LR	203	43.0	2690	2476	2270	2077	2411	2042	1717	1437	43500	100	-0.6	-0.1	0	-1.3	-4.2	-15.2
	Special load		203	42.0	2490									180	-0.2	+0.7	+1.6	+1.1	-1.0	-10.4
	Special load		201	36.3	2290									200	-0.1	+1.0	+2.1	+1.8	0	-8.9
17012	3.19	LR MRP	67.4		3165	2881	2619	2375	3337	2765	2285	1879	55100	100	-0.8	-0.3	0	-0.8	-2.7	-10.6
	Special load		204	58.5	2950									180	-0.5	+0.2	+1.0	+0.7	-0.7	-7.6
	Special load		204	55.3	2750									200	-0.4	+0.4	+1.4	+1.3	0	-6.5
17021	3.29	LR MRP	71.4		3250	2960	2690	2440	3519	2919	2411	1983	55100	100	-0.8	-0.3	0	-0.7	-2.4	-9.5
	Special load		204	66.6	3060									180	-0.6	+0.1	+0.9	+0.6	+0.6	-6.8
	Special load		204	62.4	2860									200	-0.5	+0.3	+1.2	+1.1	0	-5.8
17013	2.13	LR	204	57.1	2888	2598	2329	2113	2779	2449	1807	1487	52200	100	-0.7	-0.2	0	-1.0	-3.3	-12.5
	Special load		204	52.9	2687									180	-0.4	+0.4	+1.2	+0.9	-0.8	-8.8
	Special load		204	49.5	2487									200	-0.3	+0.6	+1.7	+1.5	0	-7.5
17014	2.13	LR MRP	56.6		2724	2516	2339	2198	2884	2460	2126	1878	52200	100	-0.7	-0.1	0	-1.2	-3.6	-12.7
	Special load		MRP	51.7	2474									180	-0.3	+0.6	+1.4	+0.9	-0.9	-8.5
	Special load		MRP	48.3	2274									200	-0.2	+0.8	+1.8	+1.6	0	-7.2
17511	2.91	LR	204	52.2	2650	2441	2248	2056	3060	2380	2020	1690	45000	100	-0.6	-0.1	0	-1.4	-4.3	.15.3
	Special load		204	54.0	2690									180	-0.2	+0.7	+1.6	+1.1	-1.0	-10.4
														200	-0.1	+1.0	+2.1	+1.8	0	-8.9

Loading data in light print are factory loads. Loading data in **bold print** are given as service to the handloaders.

NORMA BALLISTICS

Cartr. index no.	Cartr. length inch.	Norma primer	Norma powder grains	Velocity – Feet per sec. Muzzle	100 yards	200 yards	300 yards	Energy – Foot pounds Muzzle	100 yards	200 yards	300 yards	Press. psi	Sight at yards	25 yards	50 yards	100 yards	150 yards	200 yards	300 yards
17621	1.67	SR	–	1970	1595	1300	1090	948	622	413	290	46400	100	-0.1	+0.6	0	-4.1	-12.4	-45.7
			–										130	+0.3	+1.4	+1.5	-1.8	-9.3	-41.1
													200	+1.4	+3.7	+6.2	+5.2	0	-27.0
17634	2.82	LR	203 45.2	2624	2415	2222	2030	2749	2326	1970	1644	47900	100	-0.6	-0.1	0	-1.4	-4.4	-15.7
	Special load		203 42.8	2424									180	-0.2	+0.8	+1.7	+1.1	-1.1	-10.7
	Special load		201 37.2	2224									200	-0.1	+1.0	+2.2	+1.9	0	-9.1
17640	3.11	LR	203 57.5	3280	2951	2636	2338	3108	2514	2006	1578	50800	100	-0.8	-0.3	0	-0.7	-3.9	-10.1
	Special load		203 56.0	3080									180	-0.6	+0.2	+0.9	+0.7	-0.7	-7.4
	Special load		203 52.5	2880									200	-0.5	+0.3	+1.3	+1.2	0	-6.3
17643	3.13	LR	203 54.7	2970	2680	2402	2141	2943	2393	1922	1527	50800	100	-0.7	-0.2	0	-1.0	-3.4	-12.9
	Special load		203 53.0	2770									180	-0.4	+0.4	+1.3	+0.9	-0.9	-9.1
	Special load		203 50.3	2570									200	-0.3	+0.6	+1.7	+1.5	0	-7.8
17653	3.17	LR	203 50.0	2700	2494	2296	2109	2914	2487	2107	1778	50800	100	-0.6	-0.1	0	-1.3	-4.1	-14.8
	Special load		203 47.0	2500									180	-0.3	+0.7	+1.5	+1.0	-1.0	-10.2
	Special load		201 41.6	2300									200	-0.1	+0.9	+2.0	+1.8	0	-8.7
17649	3.21	LR	203 50.0	2700	2494	2296	2109	2914	2487	2107	1778	50800	100	-0.6	-0.1	0	-1.3	-4.1	-14.8
	Special load		203 47.0	2500									180	-0.3	+0.7	+1.5	+1.0	-1.0	-10.2
	Special load		201 41.6	2300									200	-0.1	+0.9	+2.0	+1.8	0	-8.7
17648	3.15	LR	203 50.0	2700	2477	2261	2109	2893	2430	2025	1525	50800	100	-0.6	-0.1	0	-1.3	-4.1	-14.9
	Special load		203 47.0	2500									180	-0.3	+0.7	+1.6	+1.0	-1.7	-10.2
	Special load		201 41.6	2300									200	-0.1	+0.9	+2.1	+1.8	0	-8.7
17630	2.50	LR	201 35.5	2410	2075	1790	1550	1934	1433	1066	799	43500	100	-0.5	+0.1	0	-2.2	-7.0	-26.1
	Special load		201 32.5	2210									130	-0.3	+0.6	+0.8	-1.0	-5.4	-23.6
	Special load		200 26.1	2010									200	+0.4	+1.9	+3.5	+3.0	0	-15.6
17631	2.50	LR	201 32.4	2220	1890	1630	1410	1860	1350	1000	750	43500	100	-0.4	+0.3	0	-2.7	-8.1	-29.2
	Special load		200 28.3	2020									130	-0.1	+0.8	+1.0	-1.2	-6.1	-26.3
	Special load		200 23.3	1820									200	+0.6	+2.3	+4.0	+3.4	0	-17.1
17623	2.62	LR	200 40.6	2900	2590	2300	2030	2428	1937	1527	1190	52200	100	-0.7	-0.2	0	-1.1	-3.7	-14.2
	Special load		200 38.2	2700									180	-0.4	+0.5	+1.4	+1.0	-0.9	-10.0
	Special load		200 35.1	2500									200	-0.2	+0.8	+1.9	+1.7	0	-8.6
17624	2.65	LR	201 45.5	2860	2570	2300	2050	2725	2200	1760	1400	52200	100	-0.7	-0.2	0	-1.2	-3.8	-14.2
	Special load		201 43.3	2660									180	-0.3	+0.6	+1.4	+1.0	-1.0	-10.0
	Special load		201 40.6	2460									200	-0.2	+0.8	+1.9	+1.7	0	-8.5
17628	2.70	LR	203 44.3	2610	2400	2210	2020	2725	2303	1952	1631	52200	100	-0.6	-0.1	0	-1.4	-4.5	-16.2
	Special load		203 41.1	2410									180	-0.2	+0.8	+1.7	+1.1	-1.1	-11.0
	Special load		203 38.0	2210									200	±0.0	+1.1	+2.3	+1.9	0	-9.4
17638	3.25	LR MRP	74.3	3020	2798	2585	2382	3646	3130	2671	2268	55100	100	-0.8	-0.3	0	-0.8	-2.6	-10.1
	Special load		204 71.8	2900									180	-0.5	+0.2	+1.0	+0.7	-0.7	-7.1
	Special load		204 70.0	2700									200	-0.4	+0.4	+1.3	+1.2	0	-6.1
17701	2.85	LR	201 47.8	2920	2630	2355	2105	2841	2304	1848	1476	49300	100	-0.7	-0.2	0	-1.0	-3.6	-12.9
	Special load		201 44.0	2720									180	-0.4	+0.5	+1.3	+0.9	-0.9	-9.1
	Special load		201 42.5	2720									200	-0.3	+0.7	+1.7	+1.5	0	-7.8
17712	2.95	LR	201 44.6	2720	2440	2170	1930	2465	1983	1569	1241	46400	100	-0.6	-0.1	0	-1.4	-4.4	-16.3
	Special load		201 41.4	2520									180	-0.2	+0.7	+1.7	+1.1	-1.1	-11.3
	Special load		200 33.9	2320									200	-0.1	+1.0	+2.2	+1.9	0	-9.7
17713	2.97	LR	203 43.7	2540	2340	2147	1965	2579	2189	1843	1544	46400	100	-0.6	±0.0	0	-1.6	-4.9	-17.3
	Special load		203 40.5	2340									130	-0.4	+0.3	+0.6	-0.7	-3.7	-15.6
	Special load		201 36.2	2140									200	±0.0	+1.2	+2.4	+2.1	0	-10.0
17721	2.84	LR	203 50.0	2952	2635	2340	2065	2513	2004	1581	1231	39200	100	-0.7	-0.2	0	-1.1	-3.5	-13.5
	Special load		203 48.0	2752									180	-0.4	+0.5	+1.3	+0.9	-0.9	-9.5
	Special load		203 46.0	2552									200	-0.3	+0.7	+1.8	+1.6	0	-8.2
17722	3.03	LR	203 45.2	2493	2292	2101	1922	2484	2100	1765	1477	39200	100	-0.6	±0.0	0	-1.7	-5.2	-18.1
	Special load		203 43.8	2293									130	-0.4	+0.3	+0.6	-0.8	-3.9	-16.3
	Special load		203 39.7	2093									200	+0.1	+1.3	+2.6	+2.2	0	-10.4
18003	2.95	LR	203 48.3	2526	2195	1894	1627	2778	2097	1562	1152	49300	100	-0.6	±0.0	0	-1.8	-5.8	-21.4
	Special load		203 45.4	2326									130	-0.4	+0.4	+0.7	-0.8	-4.4	-19.3
	Special load		200 36.4	2126									200	+0.2	+1.5	+2.9	+2.5	0	-12.7
18007	2.97	LR	203 48.3	2526	2195	1894	1627	2778	2097	1562	1152	49300	100	-0.6	±0.0	0	-1.8	-5.8	-21.4
	Special load		203 45.4	2326									130	-0.4	+0.4	+0.7	-0.8	-4.4	-19.3
	Special load		200 36.4	2126									200	+0.2	+1.5	+2.9	+2.5	0	-12.7
19001	3.23	LR	203 70.2	2800	2493	2231	2001	4322	3451	2764	2223	53400	100	-0.7	-0.1	0	-1.2	-4.0	-14.3
	Special load		203 65.7	2600									180	-0.3	+0.6	+1.5	+1.0	-1.0	-9.8
	Special load		201 57.0	2400									200	-0.2	+0.9	+2.0	+1.7	0	-8.3
19302	3.01	LR	201 44.6	2067	1818	1595	1404	2714	2099	1616	1252	36300	100	-0.3	+0.4	0	-3.1	-9.1	-32.0
	Special load		201 40.6	1867									130	±0.0	+1.0	+1.1	-1.3	-6.8	-28.5
	Special load		200 34.2	1667									200	+0.9	+2.7	+4.6	+3.8	0	-18.3
19314	3.23	LR	201 54.7	2362	2088	1815	1592	3544	2769	2092	1700	49300	100	-0.5	+0.1	0	+2.1	-6.5	-23.5
	Special load		201 51.2	2162									180	+0.1	+1.4	+2.5	+1.6	-1.6	-16.0
	Special load		200 44.0	1962									200	+0.3	+1.8	+3.3	+2.8	0	-13.7

The breech pressures shown are the maximum permitted for the caliber in question according to international agreements. Where such agreement does not yet exist, the table shows the maximum permitted breech pressure according to our own standards. The breech pressure of our factory loaded ammunition is normally 10 to 20 % below the maximum level. Loading data in light print are factory loads. Loading data in bold print are given as service to the handloaders.

REMINGTON BALLISTICS

CALIBER

CARTRIDGE

17 REM.

22 HORNET

222 REM.

222 REM. MAG.

22-250 REM.

223 REM. (5.56mm)

6mm REM.

243 WIN.

25-06 REM.

25-20 WIN.

25-35 WIN.

250 SAV.

6.5mm REM. MAG.

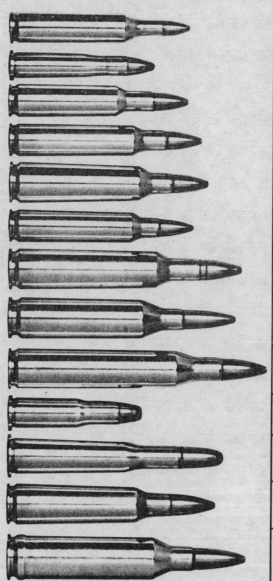

Remington Center Fire Rifle

REMINGTON	BULLET		Primer No.
	Wt.-Grs.	Style	
R17REM	25*	Hollow Point Power-Lokt	7½
R22HN1	45*	Soft Point	6½
R22HN2	45	Hollow Point	6½
R222R3	50	Hollow Point Power-Lokt	7½
R222R1	50*	Pointed Soft Point	7½
R222R2	50	Metal Case	7½
R222M2	55	Hollow Point Power-Lokt	7½
R222M1	55*	Pointed Soft Point	7½
R22502	55	Hollow Point Power-Lokt	9½
R22501	55*	Pointed Soft Point	9½
R223R2	55	Hollow Point Power-Lokt	7½
R223R1	55*	Pointed Soft Point	7½
R6MM1	80**	Pointed Soft Point	9½
R6MM2	80**	Hollow Point Power-Lokt	9½
R6MM3	90**	Pointed Soft Point Core-Lokt	9½
R6MM4	100*	Pointed Soft Point Core-Lokt	9½
R243W1	80	Pointed Soft Point	9½
R243W2	80	Hollow Point Power-Lokt	9½
R243W3	100*	Pointed Soft Point Core-Lokt	9½
R25061	87*	Hollow Point Power-Lokt	9½
R25062	100	Pointed Soft Point Core-Lokt	9½
R25063	120	Pointed Soft Point Core-Lokt	9½
R25202	86*	Soft Point	6½
R2535W	117*	Soft Point Core-Lokt	9½
R250SV	100*	Pointed Soft Point	9½
R65MM2	120*	Pointed Soft Point Core-Lokt	9½M

*Illustrated
**Interchangeable in 244 Rem.

"Power-Lokt®" and "Core-Lokt®" are trademarks registered in the United States Patent and Trademark Office by Remington Arms Company, Inc.

REMINGTON BALLISTICS

| Cartridges. | | | | | | | | | | | | | TRAJECTORY† (+) Indicates yardage at which rifle is sighted in. | | | | | | | | | | | | | |
| | VELOCITY—FEET PER SECOND | | | | | | ENERGY—FOOT POUNDS | | | | | | Short Range (Bullet does not rise more than one inch above line of sight from muzzle to sighting-in range.) | | | | | | Long Range (Bullet does not rise more than three inches above line of sight from muzzle to sighting-in range.) | | | | | | | BARREL |
	Muzzle	100 Yds.	200 Yds.	300 Yds.	400 Yds.	500 Yds.	Muzzle	100 Yds.	200 Yds.	300 Yds.	400 Yds.	500 Yds.	50 Yds.	100 Yds.	150 Yds.	200 Yds.	250 Yds.	300 Yds.	100 Yds.	150 Yds.	200 Yds.	250 Yds.	300 Yds.	400 Yds.	500 Yds.	
	4040	3284	2644	2086	1606	1235	906	599	388	242	143	85	0.1	0.5	(+)	-1.5	-4.2	-8.5	2.1	2.5	1.9	(+)	-3.5	-17.0	-44.3	24"
	2690	2042	1502	1128	947	840	723	417	225	127	90	70	0.3	(+)	-2.4	-7.7	-16.9	-31.3	1.6	(+)	-4.5	-12.8	-26.4	-75.6	-163.4	24"
	2690	2042	1502	1128	947	840	723	417	225	127	90	70	0.3	(+)	-2.4	-7.7	-16.9	-31.3	1.6	(+)	-4.5	-12.8	-26.4	-75.6	-163.4	
	3140	2635	2182	1777	1432	1172	1094	771	529	351	228	152	0.5	0.9	(+)	-2.4	-6.6	-13.1	2.1	1.8	(+)	-3.6	-9.5	-30.2	-68.1	24"
	3140	2602	2123	1700	1350	1107	1094	752	500	321	202	136	0.5	0.9	(+)	-2.5	-6.9	-13.7	2.2	1.9	(+)	-3.8	-10.0	-32.3	-73.8	
	3140	2602	2123	1700	1350	1107	1094	752	500	321	202	136	0.5	0.9	(+)	-2.5	-6.9	-13.7	2.2	1.9	(+)	-3.8	-10.0	-32.3	-73.8	
	3240	2773	2352	1969	1627	1341	1282	939	675	473	323	220	0.4	0.8	(+)	-2.1	-5.8	-11.4	1.8	1.6	(+)	-3.2	-8.2	-25.5	-56.0	24"
	3240	2748	2305	1906	1556	1272	1282	922	649	444	296	198	0.4	0.8	(+)	-2.2	-6.0	-11.8	1.9	1.6	(+)	-3.3	-8.5	-26.7	-59.5	
	3730	3253	2826	2436	2079	1755	1699	1292	975	725	528	376	0.2	0.5	(+)	-1.4	-4.0	-7.7	2.1	2.4	1.7	(+)	-3.0	-13.6	-32.4	24"
	3730	3180	2695	2257	1863	1519	1699	1235	887	622	424	282	0.2	0.5	(+)	-1.5	-4.3	-8.4	2.2	2.6	1.9	(+)	-3.3	-15.4	-37.7	
	3240	2773	2352	1969	1627	1341	1282	939	675	473	323	220	0.4	0.8	(+)	-2.1	-5.8	-11.4	1.8	1.6	(+)	-3.2	-8.2	-25.5	-56.0	24"
	3240	2748	2305	1906	1556	1272	1282	922	649	444	296	198	0.4	0.8	(+)	-2.2	-6.0	-11.8	1.9	1.6	(+)	-3.3	-8.5	-26.7		
	3470	3064	2694	2352	2036	1747	2139	1667	1289	982	736	542	0.3	0.6	(+)	-1.6	-4.5	-8.7	2.4	2.7	1.9	(+)	-3.3	-14.9	-35.0	24"
	3470	3064	2694	2352	2036	1747	2139	1667	1289	982	736	542	0.3	0.6	(+)	-1.6	-4.5	-8.7	2.4	2.7	1.9	(+)	-3.3	-14.9	-35.0	
	3260	2927	2618	2330	2060	1809	2123	1712	1369	1085	848	654	0.3	0.7	(+)	-1.8	-4.9	-9.4	2.6	2.9	2.1	(+)	-3.5	-15.6	-35.9	
	3130	2857	2600	2357	2127	1911	2175	1812	1501	1233	1004	811	0.4	0.7	(+)	-1.9	-5.1	-9.7	1.7	1.4	(+)	-2.7	-6.8	-20.0	-40.8	
	3420	3019	2652	2313	2000	1715	2077	1619	1249	950	710	522	0.3	0.6	(+)	-1.7	-4.6	-9.0	2.5	2.8	2.0	(+)	-3.4	-15.4	-36.2	24"
	3420	3019	2652	2313	2000	1715	2077	1619	1249	950	710	522	0.3	0.6	(+)	-1.7	-4.6	-9.0	2.5	2.8	2.0	(+)	-3.4	-15.4	-36.2	
	2960	2697	2449	2215	1993	1786	1945	1615	1332	1089	882	708	0.5	0.9	(+)	-2.2	-5.8	-11.0	1.9	1.6	(+)	-3.1	-7.8	-22.6	-46.3	
	3440	2995	2591	2222	1884	1583	2286	1733	1297	954	686	484	0.3	0.6	(+)	-1.7	-4.8	-9.3	2.5	2.9	2.1	(+)	-3.6	-16.4	-39.1	24"
	3230	2893	2580	2287	2014	1762	2316	1858	1478	1161	901	689	0.4	0.7	(+)	-1.9	-5.0	-9.7	1.6	1.4	(+)	-2.7	-6.9	-20.5	-42.7	
	3050	2786	2538	2302	2079	1870	2478	2068	1716	1412	1151	932	0.5	0.8	(+)	-2.0	-5.4	-10.2	1.8	1.5	(+)	-2.9	-7.2	-21.0	-42.9	
	1460	1194	1030	931	858	797	407	272	203	165	141	121	(+)	-4.1	-14.4	-31.8	-57.3	-92.0	(+)	-8.2	-23.5	-47.0	-79.6	-175.9	-319.4	24"
	2270	1942	1645	1390	1188	1053	1338	980	703	502	367	288	0.5	(+)	-2.8	-8.4	-17.2	-29.8	1.9	(+)	-4.6	-12.5	-24.1	-61.7	-123.9	24"
	2820	2504	2210	1936	1684	1461	1765	1392	1084	832	630	474	0.2	(+)	-1.6	-4.7	-9.6	-16.5	2.3	2.0	(+)	-3.7	-9.5	-28.3	-59.5	24"
	3210	2905	2621	2353	2102	1867	2745	2248	1830	1475	1177	929	0.4	0.7	(+)	-1.8	-4.9	-9.5	2.7	3.0	2.1	(+)	-3.5	-15.5	-35.3	24"

†Inches above (+) or below (–) line of sight   Hold low for (+) figures, high for (–) figures.

"Specifications are nominal." Ballistics figures established in test barrels. Individual guns may vary from test barrel specifications.

REMINGTON BALLISTICS

Remington Center Fire Rifle

CALIBER	CARTRIDGE	REMINGTON Order No.	BULLET Wt.-Grs.	BULLET Style	Primer No.
257 ROBERTS		R257	117*	Soft Point Core-Lokt®	9½
264 WIN. MAG.		R264W1	100	Pointed Soft Point Core-Lokt	9½M
		R264W2	140*	Pointed Soft Point Core-Lokt	9½M
270 WIN.		R270W1	100	Pointed Soft Point	9½
		R270W4	150	Soft Point Core-Lokt	9½
		R270W2	130	Bronze Point	9½
		R270W3	130*	Pointed Soft Point Core-Lokt	9½
280 REM.		R280R1	150*	Pointed Soft Point Core-Lokt	9½
		R280R2	165	Soft Point Core-Lokt	9½
7mm REM. MAG.		R7MM1	125	Pointed Soft Point Core-Lokt	9½M
		R7MM2	150*	Pointed Soft Point Core-Lokt	9½M
		R7MM3	175	Pointed Soft Point Core-Lokt	9½M
7mm MAUSER		R7MSR	175*	Soft Point	9½
30 CARBINE		R30CAR	110*	Soft Point	6½
30-30 WIN.		R30303	170	Hollow Point Core-Lokt	9½
		R30302	170	Soft Point Core-Lokt	9½
		R30301	150*	Soft Point Core-Lokt	9½
30 REM.		R30REM	170*	Soft Point Core-Lokt	9½
30-40 KRAG		R30401	180*	Soft Point Core-Lokt	9½
		R30402	180	Pointed Soft Point Core-Lokt	9½
30-06 SPRINGFIELD		R30067	220	Soft Point Core-Lokt	9½
		R30062	150	Pointed Soft Point Core-Lokt	9½
		R30063	150	Bronze Point	9½
		R30066	180	Bronze Point	9½
		R30061	125	Pointed Soft Point	9½
		R30064	180	Soft Point Core-Lokt	9½
		R30065	180*	Pointed Soft Point Core-Lokt	9½
30-06 "ACCELERATOR™"		R30069	55*	Pointed Soft Point	9½
300 SAV.		R30SV3	180*	Soft Point Core-Lokt	9½
		R30SV4	180	Pointed Soft Point Core-Lokt	9½
		R30SV1	150	Soft Point Core-Lokt	9½
		R30SV2	150	Pointed Soft Point Core-Lokt	9½
300 H. & H. MAG.		R300HH	180*	Pointed Soft Point Core-Lokt	9½M
300 WIN. MAG.		R300W1	150	Pointed Soft Point Core-Lokt	9½M
		R300W2	180*	Pointed Soft Point Core-Lokt	9½M

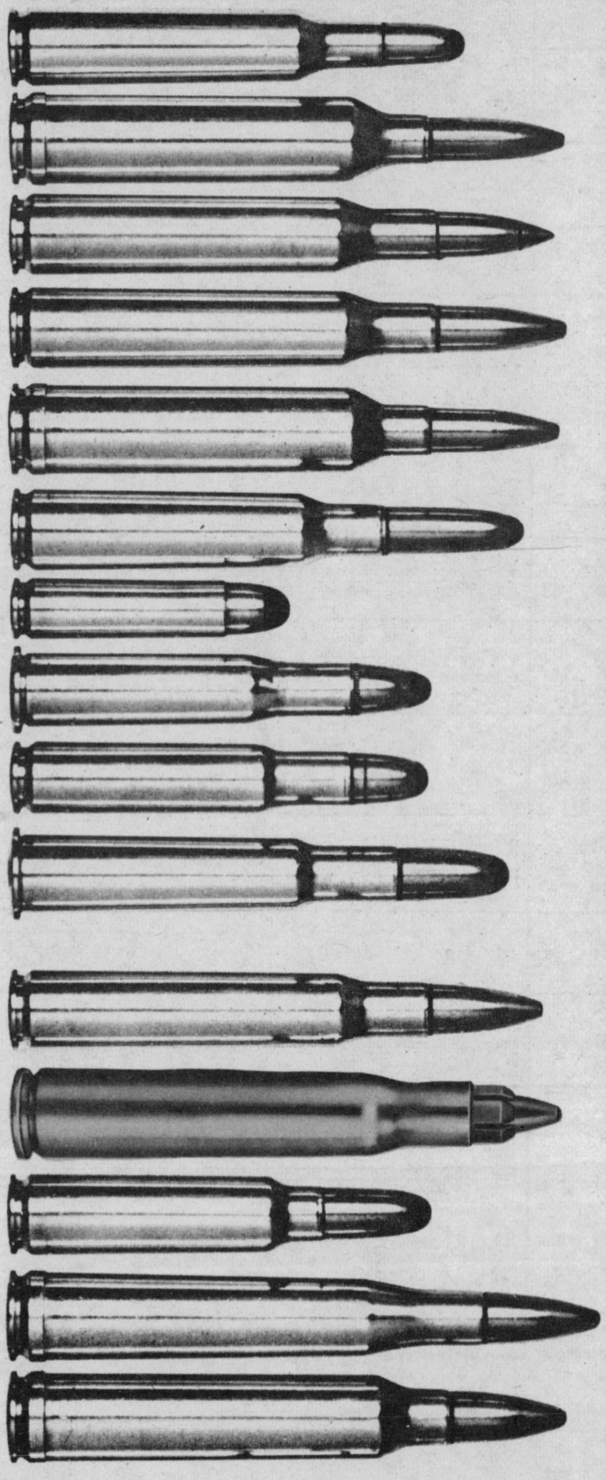

*Illustrated

"Power-Lokt®" and "Core-Lokt®" are trademarks registered in the United States Patent and Trade-mark Office by Remington Arms Company, Inc.

REMINGTON BALLISTICS

Cartridges.

| VELOCITY—FEET PER SECOND | | | | | | ENERGY—FOOT POUNDS | | | | | | TRAJECTORY† (+) Indicates yardage at which rifle is sighted in. | | | | | | | | | | | | | BARREL |
| | | | | | | | | | | | | Short Range — Bullet does not rise more than one inch above line of sight from muzzle to sighting-in range. | | | | | | Long Range — Bullet does not rise more than three inches above line of sight from muzzle to sighting-in range. | | | | | | | |
Muzzle	100 Yds.	200 Yds.	300 Yds.	400 Yds.	500 Yds.	Muzzle	100 Yds.	200 Yds.	300 Yds.	400 Yds.	500 Yds.	50 Yds.	100 Yds.	150 Yds.	200 Yds.	250 Yds.	300 Yds.	100 Yds.	150 Yds.	200 Yds.	250 Yds.	300 Yds.	400 Yds.	500 Yds.	
2650	2291	1961	1663	1404	1199	1824	1363	999	718	512	373	0.3	(+)	−1.9	−5.8	−11.9	−20.7	2.9	2.4	(+)	−4.7	−12.0	−36.7	−79.2	24″
3620	3198	2814	2462	2136	1836	2909	2271	1758	1346	1013	748	0.2	0.5	(+)	−1.5	−4.1	−7.9	2.1	2.4	1.8	(+)	−3.0	−13.6	−31.9	24″
3140	2886	2647	2419	2203	1998	3064	2589	2178	1819	1508	1241	0.4	0.7	(+)	−1.9	−4.9	−9.4	2.7	3.0	2.1	(+)	−3.5	−15.0	−33.7	
3480	3067	2690	2343	2023	1730	2689	2088	1606	1219	909	664	0.3	0.6	(+)	−1.6	−4.5	−8.7	2.4	2.7	1.9	(+)	−3.3	−15.0	−35.2	24″
2900	2550	2225	1926	1653	1415	2801	2165	1649	1235	910	667	0.6	1.0	(+)	−2.5	−6.8	−13.1	2.2	1.9	(+)	−3.6	−9.3	−28.1	−59.7	
3110	2823	2554	2300	2061	1837	2791	2300	1883	1527	1226	974	0.4	0.8	(+)	−2.0	−5.3	−10.0	1.7	1.5	(+)	−2.8	−7.1	−20.8	−42.7	
3110	2849	2604	2371	2150	1941	2791	2343	1957	1622	1334	1087	0.4	0.7	(+)	−1.9	−5.1	−9.7	1.7	1.4	(+)	−2.7	−6.8	−19.9	−40.5	
2890	2624	2373	2135	1912	1705	2781	2293	1875	1518	1217	968	0.6	0.9	(+)	−2.3	−6.2	−11.8	2.1	1.7	(+)	−3.3	−8.3	−24.2	−49.7	24″
2820	2510	2220	1950	1701	1479	2913	2308	1805	1393	1060	801	0.2	(+)	−1.5	−4.6	−9.5	−16.4	2.3	1.9	(+)	−3.7	−9.4	−28.1	−58.8	
3310	2966	2647	2350	2073	1815	3040	2441	1944	1533	1193	914	0.3	0.7	(+)	−1.8	−4.8	−9.2	2.6	2.9	2.0	(+)	−3.4	−15.3	−35.2	24″
3110	2830	2568	2320	2085	1866	3221	2667	2196	1792	1448	1160	0.4	0.8	(+)	−1.9	−5.2	−9.9	1.7	1.5	(+)	−2.8	−7.0	−20.5	−42.1	
2860	2645	2440	2244	2057	1879	3178	2718	2313	1956	1644	1372	0.6	0.9	(+)	−2.3	−6.0	−11.3	2.0	1.7	(+)	−3.2	−7.9	−22.7	−45.8	
2470	2165	1883	1626	1402	1218	2370	1821	1378	1027	764	576	0.4	(+)	−2.2	−6.6	−13.4	−23.0	1.5	(+)	−3.6	−9.7	−18.6	−46.8	−92.8	24″
1990	1567	1236	1035	922	842	967	600	373	262	208	173	0.9	(+)	−4.5	−13.5	−28.3	−49.9	(+)	−4.5	−13.5	−28.3	−49.9	−118.6	−228.1	20″
2200	1895	1619	1381	1191	1061	1827	1355	989	720	535	425	0.6	(+)	−3.0	−8.9	−18.0	−31.1	2.0	(+)	−4.8	−13.0	−25.1	−63.6	−126.7	24″
2200	1895	1619	1381	1191	1061	1827	1355	989	720	535	425	0.6	(+)	−3.0	−8.9	−18.0	−31.1	2.0	(+)	−4.8	−13.0	−25.1	−63.6	−126.7	
2390	1973	1605	1303	1095	973	1902	1296	858	565	399	315	0.5	(+)	−2.7	−8.2	−17.0	−30.0	1.8	(+)	−4.6	−12.5	−24.6	−65.3	−134.9	
2120	1822	1555	1328	1153	1036	1696	1253	913	666	502	405	0.7	(+)	−3.3	−9.7	−19.6	−33.8	2.2	(+)	−5.3	−14.1	−27.2	−69.0	−136.9	24″
2430	2098	1795	1525	1298	1128	2360	1759	1288	929	673	508	0.4	(+)	−2.4	−7.1	−14.5	−25.0	1.6	(+)	−3.9	−10.5	−20.3	−51.7	−103.9	24″
2430	2213	2007	1813	1632	1468	2360	1957	1610	1314	1064	861	0.4	(+)	−2.1	−6.2	−12.5	−21.1	1.4	(+)	−3.4	−8.9	−16.8	−40.9	−78.1	
2410	2130	1870	1632	1422	1246	2837	2216	1708	1301	988	758	0.4	(+)	−2.3	−6.8	−13.8	−23.6	1.5	(+)	−3.7	−9.9	−19.0	−47.4	−93.1	24″
2910	2617	2342	2083	1843	1622	2820	2281	1827	1445	1131	876	0.6	0.9	(+)	−2.3	−6.3	−12.0	2.1	1.8	(+)	−3.3	−8.5	−25.0	−51.8	
2910	2656	2416	2189	1974	1773	2820	2349	1944	1596	1298	1047	0.6	0.9	(+)	−2.2	−6.0	−11.4	2.0	1.7	(+)	−3.2	−8.0	−23.3	−47.5	
2700	2485	2280	2084	1899	1725	2913	2468	2077	1736	1441	1189	0.2	(+)	−1.6	−4.7	−9.6	−16.2	2.4	2.0	(+)	−3.6	−9.1	−26.2	−53.0	
3140	2780	2447	2138	1853	1595	2736	2145	1662	1269	953	706	0.4	0.8	(+)	−2.1	−5.6	−10.7	1.8	1.5	(+)	−3.0	−7.7	−23.0	−48.5	
2700	2348	2023	1727	1466	1251	2913	2203	1635	1192	859	625	0.2	(+)	−1.8	−5.5	−11.2	−19.5	2.7	2.3	(+)	−4.4	−11.3	−34.4	−73.7	
2700	2469	2250	2042	1846	1663	2913	2436	2023	1666	1362	1105	0.2	(+)	−1.6	−4.8	−9.7	−16.5	2.4	2.0	(+)	−3.7	−9.3	−27.0	−54.9	
4080	3485	2965	2502	2083	1709	2033	1983	1074	764	530	356	0.4	1.0	0.9	(+)	−1.9	−5.0	1.8	2.1	1.5	(+)	−2.7	−12.5	−30.5	24″
2350	2025	1728	1467	1252	1098	2207	1639	1193	860	626	482	0.5	(+)	−2.6	−7.7	−15.6	−27.1	1.7	(+)	−4.2	−11.3	−21.9	−55.8	−112.0	24″
2350	2137	1935	1745	1570	1413	2207	1825	1496	1217	985	798	0.4	(+)	−2.3	−6.7	−13.5	−22.8	1.5	(+)	−3.6	−9.6	−18.2	−44.1	−84.2	
2630	2247	1897	1585	1324	1131	2303	1681	1198	837	584	426	0.3	(+)	−2.0	−6.1	−12.5	−21.9	1.3	(+)	−3.4	−9.2	−17.9	−46.3	−94.8	
2630	2354	2095	1853	1631	1433	2303	1845	1462	1143	886	684	0.3	(+)	−1.8	−5.4	−11.0	−18.8	2.7	2.2	(+)	−4.2	−10.7	−31.5	−65.5	
2880	2640	2412	2196	1990	1798	3315	2785	2325	1927	1583	1292	0.6	0.9	(+)	−2.3	−6.0	−11.5	2.1	1.7	(+)	−3.2	−8.0	−23.3	−47.4	24″
3290	2951	2636	2342	2068	1813	3605	2900	2314	1827	1424	1095	0.3	0.7	(+)	−1.8	−4.8	−9.3	2.6	2.9	2.1	(+)	−3.5	−15.4	−35.5	24″
3000	2783	2577	2379	2190	2010	3597	3095	2654	2262	1917	1614	0.5	0.8	(+)	−2.0	−5.3	−10.1	1.8	1.5	(+)	−2.8	−7.0	−20.2	−40.7	

REMINGTON BALLISTICS

CALIBER	CARTRIDGE
303 BRITISH	
308 WIN.	
32 WIN. SPECIAL	
32-20 WIN.	
35 REM.	
350 REM. MAG.	
375 H. & H. MAG.	
38-40 WIN.	
444 MAR.	
44-40 WIN.	
44 REM. MAG.	
45-70 GOVERNMENT	
458 WIN. MAG.	

Remington Center Fire Rifle

REMINGTON Order No.	BULLET Wt.-Grs.	BULLET Style	Primer No.
R303B1	180	Soft Point Core-Lokt	9½
R308W1	150*	Pointed Soft Point Core-Lokt	9½
R308W3	180	Pointed Soft Point Core-Lokt	9½
R308W2	180	Soft Point Core-Lokt	9½
R32WS2	170*	Soft Point Core-Lokt	9½
R32201	100*	Lead	6½
R32202	100	Soft Point	6½
R35R1	150	Pointed Soft Point Core-Lokt	9½
R35R2	200*	Soft Point Core-Lokt	9½
R350M1	200	Pointed Soft Point Core-Lokt	9½M
R375M1	270*	Soft Point	9½M
R375M2	300	Metal Case	9½M
R3840W	180*	Soft Point	2½
R444M	240*	Soft Point	9½
R4440W	200*	Soft Point	2½
R44MG2	240*	Soft Point	2½
R4570G	405*	Soft Point	9½
R458W2	510*	Soft Point	9½M
R458W1	500	Metal Case	9½M

*Illustrated

REMINGTON BALLISTICS

Cartridges.

TRAJECTORY† [+] Indicates yardage at which rifle is sighted in.

Short Range: Bullet does not rise more than one inch above line of sight from muzzle to sighting-in range.

Long Range: Bullet does not rise more than three inches above line of sight from muzzle to sighting-in range.

VELOCITY—FEET PER SECOND						ENERGY—FOOT POUNDS						Short Range						Long Range							BARREL
Muzzle	100 Yds.	200 Yds.	300 Yds.	400 Yds.	500 Yds.	Muzzle	100 Yds.	200 Yds.	300 Yds.	400 Yds.	500 Yds.	50 Yds.	100 Yds.	150 Yds.	200 Yds.	250 Yds.	300 Yds.	100 Yds.	150 Yds.	200 Yds.	250 Yds.	300 Yds.	400 Yds.	500 Yds.	
2520	2180	1867	1587	1347	1162	2538	1899	1393	1006	725	540	0.3	(+)	-2.2	-6.5	-13.3	-23.0	1.4	(+)	-3.6	-9.7	-18.7	-47.7	-96.0	24″
2820	2533	2263	2009	1774	1560	2648	2137	1705	1344	1048	810	0.2	(+)	-1.5	-4.5	-9.3	-15.9	2.3	1.9	(+)	-3.6	-9.1	-26.9	-55.7	24″
2620	2393	2178	1974	1782	1604	2743	2288	1896	1557	1269	1028	0.2	(+)	-1.8	-5.2	-10.4	-17.7	2.6	2.1	(+)	-4.0	-9.9	-28.9	-58.8	
2620	2274	1955	1666	1414	1212	2743	2066	1527	1109	799	587	0.3	(+)	-2.0	-5.9	-12.1	-20.9	2.9	2.4	(+)	-4.7	-12.1	-36.9	-79.1	
2250	1921	1626	1372	1174	1044	1911	1393	998	710	520	411	0.6	(+)	-2.9	-8.6	-17.6	-30.5	1.9	(+)	-4.7	-12.7	-24.7	-63.2	-126.9	24″
1290	1063	940	855	786	727	369	251	196	162	137	117	(+)	-5.6	-18.8	-40.8	-72.7	-115.4	(+)	-10.5	-29.7	-58.8	-98.7	-215.2	-388.1	24″
1290	1063	940	855	786	727	369	251	196	162	137	117	(+)	-5.6	-18.8	-40.8	-72.7	-115.4	(+)	-10.5	-29.7	-58.8	-98.7	-215.2	-388.1	
2390	1954	1573	1267	1066	952	1902	1271	824	535	378	302	0.5	(+)	-2.8	-8.4	-17.5	-31.0	1.8	(+)	-4.7	-12.9	-25.5	-68.0	-141.0	24″
2080	1698	1376	1140	1001	911	1921	1280	841	577	445	368	0.8	(+)	-3.8	-11.3	-23.5	-41.2	2.5	(+)	-6.3	-17.1	-33.6	-87.7	-176.3	
2710	2410	2130	1870	1631	1421	3261	2579	2014	1553	1181	897	0.2	(+)	-1.7	-5.1	-10.4	-17.9	2.6	2.1	(+)	-4.0	-10.3	-30.5	-64.0	20″
2690	2420	2166	1928	1707	1507	4337	3510	2812	2228	1747	1361	0.2	(+)	-1.7	-5.1	-10.3	-17.6	2.5	2.1	(+)	-3.9	-10.0	-29.4	-60.7	24″
2530	2171	1843	1551	1307	1126	4263	3139	2262	1602	1138	844	0.3	(+)	-2.2	-6.5	-13.5	-23.4	1.5	(+)	-3.6	-9.8	-19.1	-49.1	-99.5	
1330	1091	960	872	803	743	707	476	368	304	258	221	(+)	-5.2	-17.7	-38.6	-68.9	-109.6	(+)	-9.9	-28.2	-55.9	-94.0	-205.5	-371.0	24″
2350	1815	1377	1087	941	845	2942	1755	1010	630	472	380	0.6	(+)	-3.2	-9.9	-21.3	-38.5	2.1	(+)	-5.6	-15.9	-32.1	-87.8	-182.7	24″
1310	1069	940	852	782	721	762	507	392	322	272	231	(+)	-5.4	-18.5	-40.3	-71.9	-114.4	(+)	-10.3	-29.4	-58.3	-98.1	-214.7	-388.1	24″
1760	1380	1114	970	878	805	1650	1015	661	501	411	345	(+)	-2.7	-10.0	-23.0	-43.0	-71.2	(+)	-5.9	-17.6	-36.3	-63.1	-145.4	-273.0	20″
1330	1168	1055	977	917	868	1590	1227	1001	858	756	677	(+)	-4.7	-15.8	-34.0	-60.0	-94.5	(+)	-8.7	-24.6	-48.2	-80.3	-172.4	-305.9	24″
2110	1834	1583	1366	1192	1069	5041	3808	2837	2113	1609	1294	0.7	(+)	-3.3	-9.5	-19.2	-33.0	2.2	(+)	-5.2	-13.8	-26.5	-66.5	-131.0	24″
2120	1898	1691	1503	1338	1202	4989	3999	3174	2508	1987	1604	0.6	(+)	-3.0	-8.8	-17.6	-29.8	2.0	(+)	-4.7	-12.5	-23.7	-58.1	-112.0	

†Inches above (+) or below (−) line of sight. Hold low for (+) figures, high for (−) figures.

NO. 71, 1980 EDITION

493

REMINGTON BALLISTICS

Remington Center Fire Pistol and Revolver Cartridges

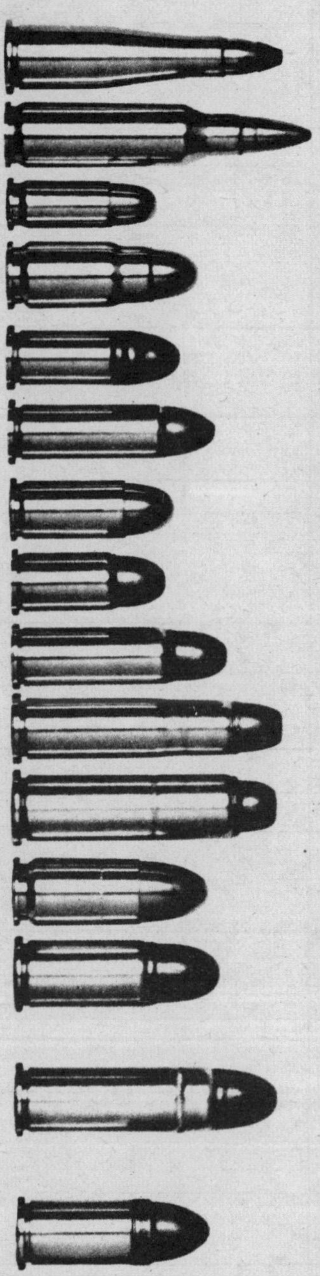

CALIBER	CARTRIDGE
22 REM. "JET" MAG.	
221 REM. "FIRE BALL"	
25 (6.35mm) AUTO. PISTOL	
30 (7.65mm) LUGER AUTO. PISTOL	
32 SHORT COLT	
32 LONG COLT	
32 (7.65mm) AUTO. PISTOL	
32 S. & W.	
32 S. & W. LONG	
32-20 WIN.	
357 MAG.	
9mm LUGER AUTO. PISTOL	
38 S. & W.	
38 SPECIAL	
38 SHORT COLT	

REM-INGTON	BULLET			VELOCITY—FEET PER SECOND			ENERGY—FOOT POUNDS			MID-RANGE TRAJECTORY		BARREL
	Primer No.	Wt.-Grs.	Style	Muzzle	50 Yds.	100 Yds.	Muzzle	50 Yds.	100 Yds.	50 Yds.	100 Yds.	
R22JET	6½	40*	Soft Point	2100	1790	1510	390	285	200	0.3"	1.4"	8⅜"
R221F	7½	50*	Pointed Soft Point	2650	2380	2130	780	630	505	0.2"	0.8"	10½"
R25AP	1½	50*	Metal Case	810	775	700	73	63	54	1.8"	7.7"	2"
R30LUG	1½	93*	Metal Case	1220	1110	1040	305	255	225	0.9"	3.5"	4½"
R32SC	1½	80*	Lead	745	665	590	100	79	62	2.2"	9.9"	4"
R32LC	1½	82*	Lead	755	715	675	100	93	83	2.0"	8.7"	4"
R32AP	1½	71*	Metal Case	960	905	850	145	130	115	1.3"	5.4"	4"
R32SW	5½	88*	Lead	680	645	610	90	81	73	2.5"	10.5"	3"
R32SWL	1½	98*	Lead	705	670	635	115	98	88	2.3"	10.5"	4"
R32201	6½	100*	Lead	1030	970	920	271	209	188	1.2"	4.4"	6"
R357M7	5½	110	Semi-Jacketed H.P.	1295	1094	975	410	292	232	0.8"	3.5"	4"
R357M1	5½	125	Semi-Jacketed H.P.	1450	1240	1090	583	427	330	0.6"	2.8"	4"
R357M2	5½	158	Semi-Jacketed H.P.	1235	1104	1015	535	428	361	0.8"	3.5"	4"
R357M3	5½	158	Soft Point	1235	1104	1015	535	428	361	0.8"	3.5"	4"
R357M4	5½	158	Metal Point	1235	1104	1015	535	428	361	0.8"	3.5"	4"
R357M5	5½	158*	Lead	1235	1104	1015	535	428	361	0.8"	3.5"	4"
R357M6	5½	158	Lead (Brass case)	1235	1104	1015	535	428	361	0.8"	3.5"	4"
R9MM2	1½	124*	Metal Case	1120	1030	965	345	290	255	1.0"	4.1"	4"
R9MM1	1½	115	Jacketed H.P.	1160	1060	990	345	285	250	0.9"	3.8"	4"
R38SW	1½	146*	Lead	685	650	620	150	135	125	2.4"	10.0"	4"
R38S4	1½	158	"Targetmaster" Lead Round Nose	755	723	692	200	183	168	2.0"	8.3"	4"
R38S5	1½	158*	Lead	755	723	692	200	183	168	2.0"	8.3"	4"
R38S6	1½	158	Semi-Wadcutter	755	723	692	200	183	168	2.0"	8.3"	4"
R38S7	1½	158	Metal Point	755	723	692	200	183	168	2.0"	8.3"	4"
R38S8	1½	158	Lead (+P)	915	878	844	294	270	250	1.4"	5.6"	4"
R38S12	1½	158	Lead H.P. (+P)	915	878	844	294	270	250	1.4"	5.6"	4"
R38S9	1½	200	Lead	635	614	594	179	168	157	2.8"	11.5"	4"
			See Note B									
R38SC	1½	125*	Lead	730	685	645	150	130	115	2.2"	9.4"	6"

*Illustrated   "JET", "FIRE BALL", and "Targetmaster" are trademarks registered in the United States Patent and Trademark Office by Remington Arms Company, Inc.

Note B: Ammunition with (+P) on the case headstamp is loaded to higher pressure. Use only in firearms designated for this cartridge and so recommended by the gun manufacturer.

REMINGTON BALLISTICS

Remington Center Fire Pistol and Revolver Cartridges

CALIBER	CARTRIDGE	REMINGTON	BULLET Primer No.	BULLET Wt.-Grs.	BULLET Style	VELOCITY—FEET PER SECOND Muzzle	VELOCITY 50 Yds.	VELOCITY 100 Yds.	ENERGY—FOOT POUNDS Muzzle	ENERGY 50 Yds.	ENERGY 100 Yds.	MID-RANGE TRAJECTORY 50 Yds.	MID-RANGE TRAJECTORY 100 Yds.	BARREL
38-40 WIN.	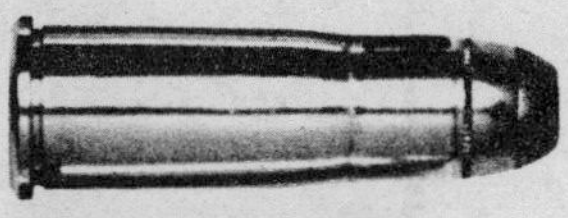	R3840W	2½	180*	Soft Point	975	920	870	380	338	302	1.5"	5.4"	5"
38 SUPER AUTO. COLT PISTOL		R38SUP	1½	130*	Metal Case (+P)	1280	1140	1050	475	375	320	0.8"	3.4"	5"
38 AUTO. COLT PISTOL		R38ACP	1½	130*	Metal Case	1040	980	925	310	275	245	1.0"	4.7"	4½"
380 AUTO. PISTOL	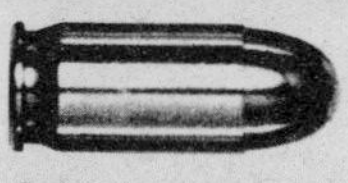	R380AP	1½	95*	Metal Case	955	865	785	190	160	130	1.4"	5.9"	3¾"
41 MAG.		R41MG2 R41MG1	2½ 2½	210 210*	Lead Soft Point	1050 1500	985 1350	930 1220	515 1050	450 850	405 695	1.0" 0.5"	4.4" 2.6"	8⅜" 8⅜"
44 S. & W. SPECIAL	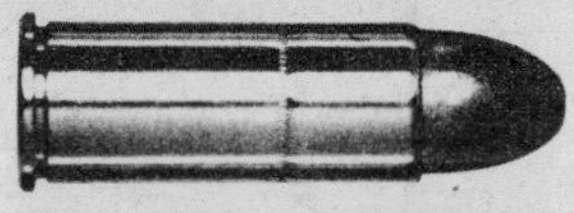	R44SW	2½	246*	Lead	755	725	695	310	285	265	2.0"	8.3"	6½"
44 REM. MAG.		R44MG1 R44MG2 R44MG3 R44MG4	2½ 2½ 2½ 2½	240* 240 240 240	Lead Gas Check Soft Point Semi-Jacketed H.P. Lead (Med. Vel.)	1350 1180 1180 1000	1186 1081 1081 947	1069 1010 1010 902	971 741 741 533	749 623 623 477	608 543 543 433	0.7" 0.9" 0.9" 1.1"	3.1" 3.7" 3.7" 4.8"	4" 4" 4" 6½"
44-40 WIN.	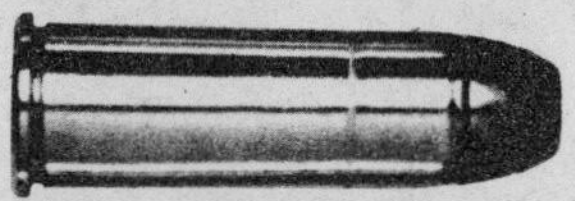	R4440W	2½	200*	Soft Point	975	920	865	420	376	332	0.5"	5.7"	7½"
45 COLT		R45C	2½	250*	Lead	860	820	780	410	375	340	1.6"	6.6"	5½"
45 AUTO.	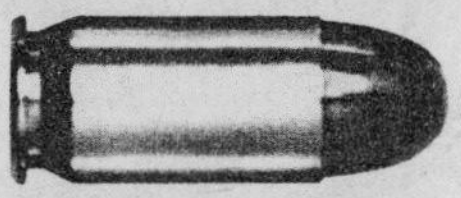	R45AP4 R45AP1 R45AP3 R45AP2	2½ 2½ 2½ 2½	230* 185 230 185	Metal Case Metal Case Wad Cutter Metal Case, Targetmaster Jacketed H.P.	850 775 850 950	810 695 810 900	775 625 775 860	370 245 370 370	335 200 335 335	305 160 305 305	1.6" 2.0" 1.6" 1.3"	6.5" 9.0" 6.5" 5.3"	5" 5" 5" 5"
45 AUTO. RIM	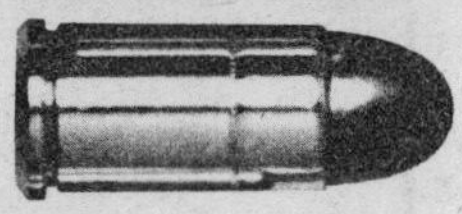	R45AR	2½	230*	Lead	810	770	730	335	305	270	1.8"	7.4"	5½"

"Specifications are nominal." Ballistics figures established in handguns. Individual guns may vary in cylinder gap, chamber and bore dimensions, etc.

PETERS BALLISTICS

PETERS CENTERFIRE PISTOL AND REVOLVER CARTRIDGES

CALIBER	Primer No.	BULLET Wt.-Grs.	BULLET Style	VELOCITY—FEET PER SECOND Muzzle	50 Yds.	100 Yds.	ENERGY—FOOT POUNDS Muzzle	50 Yds.	100 Yds.	MID-RANGE TRAJECTORY 50 Yds.	100 Yds.	BARREL
25 (6.35mm) AUTO. PISTOL	1½	50	Metal Case	810	775	700	73	63	54	1.8″	7.7″	2″
32 (7.65mm) AUTO. PISTOL	1½	71	Metal Case	960	905	850	145	130	115	1.3″	5.4″	4″
32 S. & W.	5½	88	Lead	680	645	610	90	81	73	2.5″	10.5″	3″
32 S. & W. LONG	1½	98	Lead	705	670	635	115	98	88	2.3″	10.5″	4″
357 MAG. CONVEN-TIONAL	5½	125	Semi-Jacketed H.P.	1675	1420	1215	780	560	410	0.5″	2.2″	8⅜″
	5½	158	Semi-Jacketed H.P.	1550	1350	1190	845	640	490	0.5″	2.4″	8⅜″
	5½	158	Soft Point	1550	1380	1230	845	665	530	0.5″	2.5″	8⅜″
	5½	158	Lead	1410	1240	1120	695	540	440	0.6″	2.8″	8⅜″
9mm LUGER AUTO. PISTOL †	1½	115	Jacketed H.P.	1110	1030	971	339	292	259	1.0″	4.1″	4″
	1½	124	Metal Case	1155	1047	971	341	230	241	0.9″	3.9″	4″
38 S. & W.	1½	146	Lead	685	650	620	150	135	125	2.4″	10.0″	4″
38 SPECIAL CONVENTIONAL	1½	125	Semi-Jacketed H.P. (+P)	1210	1100	1020	405	335	290	0.8″	3.6″	6″
	1½	148	Targetmaster, Lead W.C.	770	655	560	195	140	105	2.1″	10.0″	6″
	1½	158	Targetmaster, Lead	855	820	790	255	235	220	1.6″	6.5″	6″
	1½	158	Lead	855	820	790	255	235	220	1.6″	6.5″	6″
	1½	158	Metal Point	855	820	790	255	235	220	1.6″	6.5″	6″
	1½	158	Lead (+P)	1090	1030	980	415	370	335	1.0″	4.2″	6″
			See Note									
38 SUPER AUTO. COLT PISTOL	1½	130	Metal Case (+P)	1280	1140	1050	475	375	320	0.8″	3.4″	5″
380 AUTO. PISTOL	1½	95	Metal Case	955	865	785	190	160	130	1.4″	5.9″	3¾″
41 MAG. CONVENTIONAL	2½	210	Soft Point	1500	1350	1220	1050	850	695	0.5″	2.6″	8⅜″
44 REM. MAG. CONVENTIONAL	2½	240	Lead, Gas-Check	1470	1280	1120	1150	875	670	0.6″	2.7″	6½″
	2½	240	Soft Point	1470	1300	1170	1150	900	730	0.6″	2.5″	6½″
	2½	240	Semi-Jacketed H.P.	1470	1290	1150	1150	885	705	0.6″	2.6″	6½″
45 COLT	2½	250	Lead	860	820	780	410	375	340	1.6″	6.6″	5½″
45 AUTO. †	2½	185	Metal Case Wad Cutter	770	707	650	244	205	174	2.0″	8.7″	5″
	2½	185	Jacketed H.P.	940	890	846	363	325	294	1.3″	5.5″	5″
	2½	230	Metal Case	810	776	745	335	308	284	1.7″	7.2″	5″

Note: Ammunition with (+P) on the case headstamp is loaded to higher pressure. Use only in firearms designated for this cartridge and so recommended by the gun manufacturer.   †New ballistic data based on horizontal powder orientation, solid test barrel.

PETERS CENTERFIRE RIFLE CARTRIDGES

	BULLET Wt.-Grs.	Primer No.
17 REM.	25	7½
222 REM.	50	7½
22-250 REM.	55	9½
223 REM. (5.56mm)	55	7½
6mm REM.	80	9½
	100	9½
243 WIN.	80	9½
	100	9½
25-06 REM.	100	9½
	120	9½
264 WIN. MAG.	140	9½ M
270 WIN.	130	9½
	150	9½
7mm REM. MAG.	150	9½ M
	175	9½ M
30-06 SPRINGFIELD	125	9½
	150	9½
	180	9½
	180	9½
	220	9½
30-06 Accelerator	55	9½
300 WIN. MAG.	150	9½ M
	180	9½ M
308 WIN.	150	9½
	180	9½
	180	9½

PETERS CENTERFIRE RIFLE CARTRIDGES

TRAJECTORY†
(+) Indicates yardage at which rifle is sighted in.

SHORT RANGE — Bullet does not use more than one inch above line of sight from muzzle to sighting in range

LONG RANGE — Bullet does not rise more than three inches above line of sight from muzzle to sighting in range

Velocity—Feet Per Second Muzzle	100 Yds.	200 Yds.	300 Yds.	400 Yds.	500 Yds.	Energy—Foot Pounds Muzzle	100 Yds.	200 Yds.	300 Yds.	400 Yds.	500 Yds.	Short Range 50 Yds.	100 Yds.	150 Yds.	200 Yds.	250 Yds.	300 Yds.	Long Range 100 Yds.	150 Yds.	200 Yds.	250 Yds.	300 Yds.	400 Yds.	500 Yds.	Barrel
4040	3284	2644	2086	1606	1235	906	599	388	242	143	85	0.1	0.5	(+)	−.15	−4.2	−8.5	2.1	2.5	1.9	(+)	−3.5	−17.0	−44.3	24″
3140	2602	2123	1700	1350	1107	1094	752	500	321	202	136	0.5	0.9	(+)	−2.5	−6.9	−13.7	2.2	1.9	(+)	−3.8	−10.0	−32.3	−73.8	24″
3730	3180	2695	2257	1863	1519	1699	1235	887	622	424	282	0.2	0.5	(+)	−1.5	−4.3	−8.4	2.2	2.6	1.9	(+)	−3.3	−15.4	−37.7	24″
3240	2748	2305	1906	1556	1272	1282	922	649	444	296	198	0.4	0.8	(+)	−2.2	−6.0	−11.8	1.9	1.6	(+)	−3.3	−8.5	−26.7	−59.5	24″
3470	3064	2644	2352	2036	1747	2139	1667	1289	982	736	542	0.3	0.6	(+)	−1.6	−4.5	−8.7	2.4	2.7	1.9	(+)	−3.3	−14.9	−35.0	24″
3130	2857	2600	2357	2127	1911	2175	1812	1501	1233	1004	811	0.4	0.7	(+)	−1.9	−5.1	−9.7	1.7	1.4	(+)	−2.7	−6.8	−20.0	−40.8	
3420	3019	2652	2313	2000	1715	2077	1619	1249	950	710	522	0.3	0.6	(+)	−1.7	−4.6	−9.0	2.5	2.8	2.0	(+)	−3.4	−15.4	−36.2	24″
2960	2697	2449	2215	1993	1786	1945	1615	1332	1089	882	708	0.5	0.9	(+)	−2.2	−5.8	−11.0	1.9	1.6	(+)	−3.1	−7.8	−22.6	−46.3	
3230	2893	2580	2287	2014	1762	2316	1858	1478	1161	901	689	0.4	0.7	(+)	−1.9	−5.0	−9.7	1.6	1.4	(+)	−2.7	−6.9	−20.5	−42.7	24″
3050	2786	2538	2302	2079	1870	2478	2068	1716	1412	1151	932	0.5	0.8	(+)	−2.0	−5.4	−10.2	1.8	1.5	(+)	−2.9	−7.2	−21.0	−42.9	
3140	2886	2646	2419	2203	1998	3064	2589	2176	1819	1508	1241	0.4	0.7	(+)	−1.9	−4.9	−9.4	2.7	3.0	2.1	(+)	−3.5	−15.0	−33.7	24″
3110	2823	2554	2300	2061	1837	2791	2300	1883	1527	1226	974	0.4	0.8	(+)	−2.0	−5.3	−10.0	1.7	1.5	(+)	−2.8	−7.1	−20.8	−42.7	24″
2900	2550	2225	1926	1653	1415	2801	2165	1649	1235	910	667	0.6	1.0	(+)	−2.5	−6.8	−13.1	2.2	1.9	(+)	−3.6	9.3	−28.1	−59.7	
3110	2830	2568	2320	2085	1866	3221	2667	2196	1792	1448	1160	0.4	0.8	(+)	−1.9	−5.2	−9.9	1.7	1.5	(+)	−2.8	−7.0	−20.5	−42.1	24″
2860	2645	2440	2244	2057	1879	3178	2718	2313	1956	1644	1372	0.6	0.9	(+)	−2.3	−6.0	−11.3	2.0	1.7	(+)	−3.2	−7.9	−22.7	−45.8	
3140	2780	2447	2138	1853	1595	2736	2145	1662	1269	953	706	0.4	0.8	(+)	−2.1	−5.6	−10.7	1.8	1.5	(+)	−3.0	−7.7	−23.0	−48.5	
2910	2617	2342	2083	1843	1622	2820	2281	1827	1445	1131	876	0.6	0.9	(+)	−2.3	−6.3	−12.0	2.1	1.8	(+)	−3.3	−8.5	−25.0	−51.8	
2700	2348	2023	1727	1466	1251	2913	2203	1635	1192	859	625	0.2	(+)	−1.8	−5.5	−11.2	−19.5	2.7	2.3	(+)	−4.4	−11.3	−34.4	−73.7	24″
2700	2469	2250	2042	1846	1663	2913	2436	2023	1666	1362	1105	0.2	(+)	−1.6	−4.8	−9.7	−16.5	2.4	2.0	(+)	−3.7	−9.3	−27.0	−54.9	
2410	2130	1870	1632	1422	1246	2837	2216	1708	1301	988	758	0.4	(+)	−2.3	−6.8	−13.8	−23.6	1.5	(+)	−3.7	−9.9	−19.0	−47.4	−93.1	
4080	3485	2965	2302	2083	1709	2033	1483	1074	764	530	356	0.4	1.0	0.9	(+)	−1.9	−5.0	1.8	2.1	1.5	(+)	−2.7	−12.5	−34.5	24″
3290	2951	2636	2342	2068	1813	3605	2900	2314	1827	1424	1095	0.3	0.7	(+)	−1.8	−4.8	−9.3	2.6	2.9	2.1	(+)	−3.5	−15.4	−35.5	24″
3000	2783	2577	2379	2190	2010	3597	3095	2654	2262	1917	1614	0.5	0.8	(+)	−2.0	−5.3	−10.1	1.8	1.5	(+)	−2.8	−7.0	−20.2	−40.7	
2820	2532	2263	2009	1774	1560	2648	2135	1705	1344	1048	810	0.2	(+)	−1.5	−4.5	−9.3	−15.9	2.3	1.9	(+)	−3.6	−9.1	−26.9	−55.7	
2620	2274	1955	1666	1414	1212	2743	2066	1527	1109	799	587	0.3	(+)	−2.0	−5.9	−12.1	−20.9	2.9	2.4	(+)	−4.7	−12.1	−36.9	−79.1	24″
2620	2393	2178	1974	1782	1604	2743	2288	1896	1557	1269	1028	0.2	(+)	−1.8	−5.2	−10.4	−17.7	2.6	2.1	(+)	−4.0	−9.9	−28.9	−58.8	

"Power-Lokt" and "Core-Lokt" are trademarks registered in the United States Patent and Trademark Office by Remington Arms Company, Inc. Specifications are nominal. Ballistics figures established in test barrels. Individual guns may vary from test barrel specifications.

† Inches above (+) or below (−) line of sight.   Hold low for (+) figures, high for (−) figures.

WEATHERBY BALLISTICS

7MM WEATHERBY MAGNUM

Primer: Federal #215   Overall cartridge length: 3¼"

Charge	Powder	Bullet	Muzzle Velocity in 26" Barrel	Avg. Breech Pressure	Muzzle Energy in Foot-Pounds
68 grs	4350	139 gr	3250	51,930	3254
69 grs	4350	139 gr	3308	54,310	3375
70 grs	4350	139 gr	3373	57,960	3500
72 grs	4831	139 gr	3147	45,990	3047
73 grs	4831	139 gr	3233	49,700	3223
74 grs	4831	139 gr	3291	52,570	3335
75 grs	4831	139 gr	3328	54,520	3417
76 grs	4831	139 gr	3382	57,190	3520
68.5 grs	Norma 205	139 gr	3110	38,400	2986
70.5 grs	Norma 205	139 gr	3220	43,500	3201
72.5 grs	Norma 205	139 gr	3300	50,300	3362
66 grs	4350	154 gr	3055	49,960	3191
67 grs	4350	154 gr	3141	54,500	3365
68 grs	4350	154 gr	3175	55,210	3439
70 grs	4831	154 gr	3013	46,940	3109
71 grs	4831	154 gr	3066	49,160	3212
72 grs	4831	154 gr	3151	53,010	3387
73 grs	4831	154 gr	3183	54,910	3462
74 grs	4831	154 gr	3227	57,400	3548
66.5 grs	Norma 205	154 gr	2910	39,200	2896
68.5 grs	Norma 205	154 gr	3045	43,200	3171
70.5 grs	Norma 205	154 gr	3155	50,500	3405
63 grs	4350	*175 gr	2828	46,900	3112
65 grs	4350	*175 gr	2946	53,830	3369
68 grs	4831	*175 gr	2852	49,470	3157
69 grs	4831	*175 gr	2885	49,930	3234
70 grs	4831	*175 gr	2924	52,680	3323
71 grs	4831	*175 gr	2975	55,800	3439
67 grs	Norma 205	*175 gr	2890	43,650	3246
69 grs	Norma 205	*175 gr	2980	48,700	3452
71 grs	Norma 205	*175 gr	3050	53,350	3616

*The 175 grain bullet is recommended for use only in 7mm W.M. rifles having 1 in 10" twist barrels.

.257 WEATHERBY MAGNUM

Primer: Federal #215   Overall cartridge length: 3¼"

Charge	Powder	Bullet	Muzzle Velocity in 26" barrel	Avg. Breech Pressure	Muzzle Energy in Foot-Pounds
68 grs	4350	87 gr	3698	51,790	2644
69 grs	4350	87 gr	3715	53,270	2666
70 grs	4350	87 gr	3831	56,120	2835
69 grs	4831	87 gr	3521	44,750	2390
71 grs	4831	87 gr	3617	48,140	2532
73 grs	4831	87 gr	3751	52,470	2717
75 grs	4831	87 gr	3876	57,910	2901
67 grs	Norma 205	87 gr	3390	37,500	2216
70 grs	Norma 205	87 gr	3530	43,000	2404
73 grs	Norma 205	87 gr	3750	50,700	2716
65 grs	4350	100 gr	3450	52,860	2638
66 grs	4350	100 gr	3520	54,860	2747
67 grs	4350	100 gr	3588	57,130	2857
66 grs	4831	100 gr	3315	43,640	2435
68 grs	4831	100 gr	3418	48,190	2593
70 grs	4831	100 gr	3543	53,410	2786
71 grs	4831	100 gr	3573	55,690	2833
67 grs	Norma 205	100 gr	3280	44,200	2391
69 grs	Norma 205	100 gr	3380	47,400	2535
71 grs	Norma 205	100 gr	3530	51,400	2766
62 grs	4350	117 gr	3152	50,020	2573
64 grs	4350	117 gr	3262	54,860	2755
63 grs	4831	117 gr	3152	46,650	2573
65 grs	4831	117 gr	3213	48,520	2679
67 grs	4831	117 gr	3326	53,930	2867
63 grs	Norma 205	117 gr	3110	43,000	2512
66 grs	Norma 205	117 gr	3190	48,100	2645
69 grs	Norma 205	117 gr	3350	55,400	2912

WEATHERBY BALLISTICS

.270 WEATHERBY MAGNUM

Primer: Federal #215   Overall cartridge length: 3¼"

Charge		Powder	Bullet	Muzzle Velocity in 26" Barrel	Avg. Breech Pressure	Muzzle Energy in Foot-Pounds
70	grs	4350	100 gr	3636	49,550	2934
72	grs	4350	100 gr	3764	54,540	3148
74	grs	4350	100 gr	3885	58,200	3353
74	grs	4831	100 gr	3492	43,800	2700
76	grs	4831	100 gr	3594	47,790	2865
77	grs	4831	100 gr	3654	50,940	2966
78	grs	4831	100 gr	3705	52,890	3048
74	grs	Norma 205	100 gr	3610	43,200	2895
76	grs	Norma 205	100 gr	3690	50,100	3023
77	grs	Norma 205	100 gr	3770	54,300	3154
65	grs	4350	130 gr	3184	46,780	2922
66	grs	4350	130 gr	3228	49,130	3006
67	grs	4350	130 gr	3286	52,120	3108
68	grs	4350	130 gr	3345	55,210	3224
68	grs	4831	130 gr	3076	43,320	2730
70	grs	4831	130 gr	3178	47,600	2913
71	grs	4831	130 gr	3242	51,150	3024
72	grs	4831	130 gr	3301	52,980	3138
73	grs	4831	130 gr	3335	54,350	3206
74	grs	4831	130 gr	3375	56,520	3283
69	grs	Norma 205	130 gr	3190	45,400	2942
71	grs	Norma 205	130 gr	3300	47,800	3144
73	grs	Norma 205	130 gr	3390	51,000	3317
65	grs	4350	150 gr	3085	52,120	3167
67	grs	4350	150 gr	3150	57,560	3299
66	grs	4831	150 gr	2920	46,470	2840
67	grs	4831	150 gr	2971	48,380	2939
68	grs	4831	150 gr	3014	50,580	3027
69	grs	4831	150 gr	3069	53,720	3140
70	grs	4831	150 gr	3124	56,960	3246
65	grs	Norma 205	150 gr	2910	43,300	2819
67	grs	Norma 205	150 gr	3020	47,800	3040
69	grs	Norma 205	150 gr	3130	53,400	3260

.340 WEATHERBY MAGNUM

Primer: Federal #215   Overall cartridge length: 3-9/16"

Charge		Powder	Bullet	Muzzle Velocity in 26" Barrel	Avg. Breech Pressures	Muzzle Energy in Foot-Pounds
80	grs	4350	200 gr	3075	48,290	4200
82	grs	4350	200 gr	3151	53,180	4398
84	grs	4350	200 gr	3210	54,970	4566
84	grs	4831	200 gr	2933	43,240	3824
86	grs	4831	200 gr	3004	45,940	4012
88	grs	4831	200 gr	3066	48,400	4172
90	grs	4831	200 gr	3137	52,730	4356
87	grs	Norma 205	200 gr	3015	41,100	4038
89	grs	Norma 205	200 gr	3120	46,050	4324
91	grs	Norma 205	200 gr	3210	50,200	4577
74	grs	4350	250 gr	2741	49,240	4168
76	grs	4350	250 gr	2800	51,370	4353
78	grs	4350	250 gr	2862	55,490	4540
80	grs	4831	250 gr	2686	44,970	4005
82	grs	4831	250 gr	2764	49,180	4243
84	grs	4831	250 gr	2835	53,370	4460
85	grs	4831	250 gr	2860	54,400	4540
86	grs	4831	250 gr	2879	55,500	4605
87	grs	4831	250 gr	2886	56,270	4623
79.5	grs	Norma 205	250 gr	2650	39,500	3899
81.5	grs	Norma 205	250 gr	2760	45,250	4230
83.5	grs	Norma 205	250 gr	2850	49,650	4510

WEATHERBY BALLISTICS

.300 WEATHERBY MAGNUM

Primer: Federal #215   Overall cartridge length: 3-9/16"

Charge	Powder	Bullet	Muzzle Velocity in 26" Barrel	Avg. Breech Pressure	Muzzle Energy in Foot-Pounds
84 grs	4350	110 gr	3620	45,790	3201
86 grs	4350	110 gr	3726	48,950	3390
88 grs	4350	110 gr	3798	51,180	3528
90 grs	4350	110 gr	3863	53,460	3649
76 grs	Norma 203	110 gr	3570	46,300	3114
78 grs	Norma 203	110 gr	3725	48,900	3390
80 grs	Norma 203	110 gr	3880	52,500	3678
80 grs	4350	130 gr	3404	46,580	3341
82 grs	4350	130 gr	3488	49,540	3510
84 grs	4350	130 gr	3567	52,570	3663
86 grs	4350	130 gr	3627	54,730	3793
79 grs	4350	150 gr	3225	43,230	3458
80 grs	4350	150 gr	3343	48,000	3710
82 grs	4350	150 gr	3458	52,380	3981
84 grs	4350	150 gr	3538	56,230	4167
84 grs	4831	150 gr	3305	47,620	3632
86 grs	4831	150 gr	3394	51,990	3831
88 grs	4831	150 gr	3470	54,570	4004
85.5 grs	Norma 205	150 gr	3395	48,400	3840
87.5 grs	Norma 205	150 gr	3470	51,200	4011
89.5 grs	Norma 205	150 gr	3550	53,900	4199
75 grs	4350	180 gr	2952	45,020	3478
77 grs	4350	180 gr	3066	50,830	3755
78 grs	4350	180 gr	3110	53,130	3857
79 grs	4350	180 gr	3145	53,610	3946
80 grs	4350	180 gr	3226	57,620	4149
78 grs	4831	180 gr	2969	46,100	3526
80 grs	4831	180 gr	3060	50,240	3742
82 grs	4831	180 gr	3145	54,310	3946
84 grs	4831	180 gr	3223	57,370	4147
78 grs	Norma 205	180 gr	2980	44,700	3550
80 grs	Norma 205	180 gr	3050	48,000	3719
82 grs	Norma 205	180 gr	3130	51,300	3917
73 grs	4350	220 gr	2878	54,890	4052
75 grs	4350	220 gr	2926	56,510	4180
74 grs	4831	220 gr	2740	47,920	3667
76 grs	4831	220 gr	2800	51,060	3830
78 grs	4831	220 gr	2881	55,760	4052
74.5 grs	Norma 205	220 gr	2665	46,900	3470
76.5 grs	Norma 205	220 gr	2795	49,900	3817
78.5 grs	Norma 205	220 gr	2900	52,900	4109

WEATHERBY BALLISTICS

.224 WEATHERBY MAGNUM VARMINTMASTER

Primer: Federal #210   Overall cartridge length: 2-5/16"

Charge	Powder	Bullet	Muzzle Velocity in 26" Barrel	Avg. Breech Pressure	Muzzle Energy in Foot-Pounds
29.5 grs	IMR-3031	50 gr	3500	45,700	1360
30.0 grs	IMR-3031	50 gr	3560	47,500	1410
30.5 grs	IMR-3031	50 gr	3620	50,000	1455
31.0 grs	IMR-3031	50 gr	3670	52,000	1495
31.5 grs	IMR-3031	50 gr	3695	52,600	1515
32.0 grs	IMR-3031	50 gr	3740	55,200	1550
28.5 grs	Norma 201	50 gr	3360	32,300	1253
29.5 grs	Norma 201	50 gr	3460	34,200	1330
30.5 grs	Norma 201	50 gr	3570	37,100	1415
31.5 grs	Norma 201	50 gr	3660	42,000	1488
32.5 grs	Norma 201	50 gr	3720	48,200	1538
33.0 grs	Norma 201	50 gr	3750	52,300	1560
29.0 grs	IMR-3031	55 gr	3390	46,700	1405
29.5 grs	IMR-3031	55 gr	3450	48,000	1455
30.0 grs	IMR-3031	55 gr	3470	49,100	1470
30.5 grs	IMR-3031	55 gr	3525	53,200	1520
31.0 grs	IMR-3031	55 gr	3580	56,200	1570
28.5 grs	Norma 201	55 gr	3310	33,000	1340
29.5 grs	Norma 201	55 gr	3420	37,400	1432
30.5 grs	Norma 201	55 gr	3530	42,000	1523
31.5 grs	Norma 201	55 gr	3610	48,200	1597
32.5 grs	Norma 201	55 gr	3670	56,800	1648

.378 WEATHERBY MAGNUM

Primer: Federal #215   Overall cartridge length: 3-11/16"

Caution: Use only the #215 primer in reloading the .378 W. M.

Charge	Powder	Bullet	Muzzle Velocity in 26" Barrel	Avg. Breech Pressure	Muzzle Energy in Foot-Pounds
106 grs	4350	270 gr	3015	44,800	5446
107 grs	4350	270 gr	3090	49,700	5713
108 grs	4350	270 gr	3112	54,620	5786
116 grs	4831	270 gr	3080	50,190	5689
117 grs	4831	270 gr	3102	50,930	5748
118 grs	4831	270 gr	3128	51,930	5862
101 grs	4350	300 gr	2831	49,500	5334
103 grs	4350	300 gr	2922	54,300	5679
110 grs	4831	300 gr	2897	51,050	5583
111 grs	4831	300 gr	2933	52,270	5736
112 grs	4831	300 gr	2958	53,410	5835

.460 WEATHERBY MAGNUM

Primer: Federal #215   Overall cartridge length: 3¾"

Caution: Use only the #215 primer in reloading the .460 W. M.

Charge	Powder	Bullet	Muzzle Velocity in 26" Barrel	Avg. Breech Pressure	Muzzle Energy in Foot-Pounds
115 grs	4350	500 gr	2513	44,400	6995
118 grs	4350	500 gr	2577	47,460	7390
120 grs	4350	500 gr	2601	48,330	7505
122 grs	4350	500 gr	2632	50,370	7680
124 grs	4350	500 gr	2678	52,980	7980
126 grs	4350	500 gr	2707	55,130	8155
102 grs	4064	500 gr	2486	49,000	6860
104 grs	4064	500 gr	2521	51,340	7050
106 grs	4064	500 gr	2553	53,280	7220
92 grs	3031	500 gr	2405	49,530	6420
94 grs	3031	500 gr	2426	50,170	6525
96 grs	3031	500 gr	2470	53,560	6775

WINCHESTER-WESTERN PISTOL & REVOLVER CENTERFIRE BALLISTICS

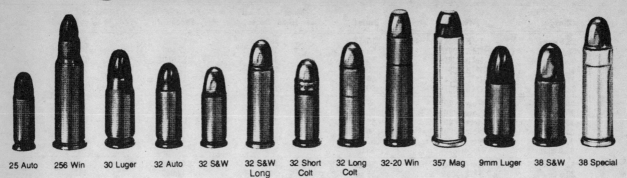

| 25 Auto | 256 Win | 30 Luger | 32 Auto | 32 S&W | 32 S&W Long | 32 Short Colt | 32 Long Colt | 32-20 Win | 357 Mag | 9mm Luger | 38 S&W | 38 Special |

CALIBER	WT. GRS.	TYPE	WINCHESTER	WESTERN	PRIMER
25 Automatic (6.35mm) (Oilproof)	50	FMC	W25AP	25AP	1½-108
256 Winchester Magnum Super-X	60	OPE (HP)	—	2561P	6½-116
30 Luger (7.65mm) (Oilproof)	93	FMC	W30LP	30LP	1½-108
32 Automatic (Oilproof)	71	FMC	W32AP	32AP	1½-108
32 Smith & Wesson (Oilproof) (inside lubricated)	85	Lead	W32SWP	32 SWP	1½-108
32 Smith & Wesson Long (Oilproof) (inside lubricated)	98	Lead	W32SWLP	32SWLP	1½-108
32 Short Colt (Oilproof) (greased)	80	Lead	—	32SCP	1½-108
32 Long Colt (Oilproof) (inside lubricated)	82	Lead	—	32LCP	1½-108
32-20 Winchester (Oilproof) (inside lubricated)	100	Lead	W32201	32201	6½-116
32-20 Winchester (Oilproof)	100	SP	W32202	32202	6½-116
357 Magnum Jacketed Hollow Point Super-X (Oilproof)	110	JHP	—	3573P	1½-108
357 Magnum Jacketed Hollow Point Super-X (Oilproof)	125	JHP	—	3576P	1½-108
357 Magnum Super-X (Oilproof) (inside lubricated)	158	Lead	—	3571P	1½-108
357 Magnum Jacket Hollow Point Super-X (Oilproof)	158	JHP	—	3574P	1½-108
357 Magnum Jacketed Soft Point Super-X (Oilproof)	158	JSP	—	3575P	1½-108
357 Magnum Metal Piercing Super-X (Oilproof) (inside lubricated, lead bearing)	158	Met. Pierc.	—	3572P	1½-108
9mm Luger (Parabellum)	95	JSP	W9MMJSP	—	1½-108
9mm Luger (Parabellum) (Oilproof)	100	PP	W9MMPP	—	1½-108
9mm Luger (Parabellum) (Oilproof)	100	JHP	W9MMJHP	—	1½-108
9mm Luger (Parabellum) (Oilproof)	115	FMC	W9LP	—	1½-108
38 Smith & Wesson (Oilproof) (inside lubricated)	145	Lead	W38SWP	38SWP	1½-108
38 Special (Oilproof) (inside lubricated)	158	Lead	W38SIP	38SIP	1½-108
38 Special Metal Point (Oilproof) (inside lubricated, lead bearing)	158	Met. Pt.	W38S2P	38S2P	1½-108
38 Special Super Police (Oilproof) (inside lubricated)	200	Lead	W38S3P	38S3P	1½-108
38 Special Super-X Jacketed Hollow Point (Oilproof) +P	110	JHP	—	38S6PH	1½-108
38 Special Super-X Jacketed Hollow Point (Oilproof) +P	125	JHP	W38S7PH	—	1½-108
38 Special Super-X +P	130	FMC	—	38S8P	1½-108
38 Special Super-X (Oilproof) (inside lubricated) +P	150	Lead	—	38S4P	1½-108
38 Special Metal Piercing Super-X (Oilproof) (inside lubricated, lead bearing) +P	150	Met. Pierce	—	38S5P	1½-108
38 Special Super-X (Oilproof) (inside lubricated) +P	158	Lead H.P.	W38SPD	—	1½-108
38 Special Super-X Semi-Wad Cutter (Oilproof) (inside lubricated) +P	158	Lead-SWC	W38WCP	—	1½-108
38 Special Super-Match and Match Mid-Range Clean Cutting (Oilproof) (inside lubricated)	148	LEAD-WC	W38SMRP	38SMRP	1½-108
38 Special Super-Match (Oilproof) (inside lubricated)	158	Lead	—	38SMP	1½-108
38 Short Colt (Oilproof) (greased)	130	Lead	—	38SCP	1½-108
38 Long Colt (Oilproof) (inside lubricated)	150	Lead	—	38LCP	1½-108
38 Automatic Super-X (Oilproof) +P (For use only in 38 Colt Super and Colt Commander Automatic Pistols)	125	JHP	W38A3P	38A3P	1½-108
38 Automatic Super-X (Oilproof) +P (For use only in 38 Colt Super and Colt Commander Automatic Pistols)	130	FMC	W38A1P	38A1P	1½-108
38 Automatic (Oilproof) (For all 38 Colt Automatic Pistols)	130	FMC	W38A2P	38A2P	1½-108
380 Automatic (Oilproof)	95	FMC	W380AP	380AP	1½-108
38-40 Winchester (Oilproof)	180	SP	W3840	3840	7-111
41 Remington Magnum Super-X (Oilproof) (inside lubricant)	210	Lead	W41MP	—	7-111F
41 Remington Magnum Super-X Jacketed Soft Point (Oilproof)	210	JSP	W41MJSP	—	7-111F
44 Smith & Wesson Special (Oilproof) (inside lubricated)	246	Lead	W44SP	—	7-111
44 Remington Magnum Super-X (Oilproof) (inside lubricated)	240	Lead	—	44MP	7-111F
44-40 Winchester (Oilproof)	200	SP	W4440	4440	7-111
45 Colt (Oilproof) (inside lubricated)	255	Lead	W45CP	45CP	7-111
45 Automatic	185	STHP	—	45ASHP	7-111
45 Automatic (Oilproof)	230	FMC	W45A1P	45A1P	7-111
45 Automatic Super-Match Clean Cutting	185	FMC-WC	—	45AWCP	7-111
45 Winchester Magnum	230	FMC	W45WM		7-111

Test barrels are used to determine ballistics figures. Individual firearms may differ from these test barrel statistics.

+P Ammunition with (+P) on the case head stamp is loaded to higher pressure. Use only in firearms designated for this cartridge and so recommended by the gun manufacturer.

WINCHESTER-WESTERN PISTOL & REVOLVER CENTERFIRE BALLISTICS

| 38 Special S.M. | 38 Short Colt | 38 Long Colt | 38 Auto | 380 Auto | 38-40 Win | 41 Rem. Mag. | 44 S&W | 44 Rem. Mag. | 44-40 Win | 45 Colt | 45 Auto | 45 Auto S.M. |

VELOCITY-FPS			ENERGY FT./LBS.			MID RANGE TRAJECTORY INCHES		BARREL LENGTH INCHES
MUZZLE	50 YDS.	100 YDS.	MUZZLE	50 YDS.	100 YDS.	50 YDS.	100 YDS.	
810	755	700	73	63	54	1.8	7.7	2
2350	2030	1760	735	550	415	0.3	1.1	8½
1220	1110	1040	305	255	225	0.9	3.5	4½
905	855	810	130	115	97	1.4	5.8	4
680	645	610	90	81	73	2.5	10.5	3
705	670	635	115	98	88	2.3	10.5	4
745	665	590	100	79	62	2.2	9.9	4
755	715	675	100	93	83	2.0	8.7	4
1030	970	920	270	210	190	1.2	4.4	6
1030	970	920	270	210	190	1.2	4.4	6
1295	1094	975	410	292	232	0.8	3.5	4V
1450	1240	1090	583	427	330	0.6	2.8	4V
1235	1104	1015	535	428	361	0.8	3.5	4V
1235	1104	1015	535	428	361	0.8	3.5	4V
1235	1104	1015	535	428	361	0.8	3.5	4V
1235	1104	1015	535	428	361	0.8	3.5	4V
1355	1140	1008	387	274	214	0.7	3.3	4V
1320	1114	991	387	275	218	0.7	3.4	4V
1320	1114	991	387	275	218	0.7	3.4	4V
1155	1047	971	341	280	241	0.9	3.9	4V
685	650	620	150	135	125	2.4	10.0	4
755	723	693	200	183	168	2.0	8.3	4V
755	723	693	200	183	168	2.0	8.3	4V
635	614	594	179	168	157	2.8	11.5	4V
1020	945	887	254	218	192	1.1	4.8	4V
945	898	858	248	224	204	1.3	5.4	4V
950	910	880	260	240	225	1.3	5.2	4V
910	870	835	276	252	232	1.4	5.7	4V
910	870	835	276	252	232	1.4	5.7	4V
915	878	844	294	270	250	1.4	5.6	4V
915	878	844	294	270	250	1.4	5.6	4V
710	634	566	166	132	105	2.4	10.8	4V
755	723	693	200	183	168	2.0	8.3	4V
730	685	645	150	130	115	2.2	9.4	6
730	700	670	175	165	150	2.1	8.8	6
1245	1105	1010	430	340	285	0.8	3.6	5
1245	1120	1035	450	365	310	0.8	3.4	5
1040	980	925	310	275	245	1.0	4.7	4½
955	865	785	190	160	130	1.4	5.9	3¾
975	920	870	380	340	300	1.5	5.4	5
965	898	842	434	376	331	1.3	5.4	4V
1300	1162	1062	778	630	526	0.7	3.2	4V
755	725	695	310	285	265	2.0	8.3	6½
1350	1186	1069	971	749	608	0.7	3.1	4V
975	920	865	420	375	330	0.5	5.7	7½
860	820	780	410	375	340	1.6	6.6	5½
1000	938	888	411	362	324	1.2	4.9	5
810	776	745	335	308	284	1.7	7.2	5
770	707	650	244	205	174	2.0	8.7	5
1400	1232	1107	1001	775	636	0.6	2.8	5

Met Pierc—Metal Piercing   FMC—Full Metal Case   SP—Soft Point   JHP—Jacketed Hollow Point   JSP—Jacketed Soft Point   Met Pt—Metal Point
OPE—Open Point Expanding   HP—Hollow Point   PP—Power Point   WC—Wad Cutter   SWC—Semi Wad Cutter
V—Data is based on velocity obtained from 4″ vented barrels for revolver cartridges (38 Special, 357 Magnum, 41 Rem. Mag.
  and 44 Rem. Mag.) and unvented (solid) test barrels of the length specified for 9mm and 45 auto pistols.

WINCHESTER-WESTERN CENTERFIRE RIFLE BALLISTICS

218 Bee   22 Hornet   22-250 Rem   222 Rem   223 Rem   225 Win   243 Win   6 MM Rem   25-06 Rem   25-20 Win   25-35 Win   250 Savage

CARTRIDGE	BULLET WT. GRS.	TYPE	SYMBOL WINCHESTER	WESTERN	PRIMER	BARREL LENGTH INCHES	MUZZLE	100	200	300	400	500
218 Bee Super-X	46	OPE(HP)	W218B	218B	6½-116	24	2760	2102	1550	1156	961	850
22 Hornet Super-X	45	SP	W22H1	22H1	6½-116	24	2690	2042	1502	1128	948	840
22 Hornet Super-X	46	OPE(HP)	W22H2	22H2	6½-116	24	2690	2042	1502	1128	948	841
22-250 Remington Super-X	55	PSP	W222501	222501	8½-120	24	3730	3180	2695	2257	1863	1519
222 Remington Super-X	50	PSP	W222R	222R	6½-116	24	3140	2602	2123	1700	1350	1107
222 Remington Super-X	55	FMC	—	222R1	6½-116	24	3020	2675	2355	2057	1783	1537
223 Remington Super-X	55	PSP	W223R	223R	6½-116	24	3240	2747	2304	1905	1554	1270
223 Remington Super-X	55	FMC	—	223R1	6½-116	24	3240	2877	2543	2231	1943	1679
225 Winchester Super-X	55	PSP	W2251	2251	8½-120	24	3570	3066	2616	2208	1838	1514
243 Winchester Super-X	80	PSP	W2431	2431	8½-120	24	3420	3019	2652	2313	2000	1715
243 Winchester Super-X	100	PP(SP)	W2432	2432	8½-120	24	2960	2697	2449	2215	1993	1786
6 MM Remington Super-X	80	PSP	—	6MMR1	8½-120	24	3470	3064	2694	2352	2036	1747
6 MM Remington Super-X	100	PP(SP)	—	6MMR2	8½-120	24	3130	2857	2600	2357	2127	1911
25-06 Remington Super-X	90	PEP	W25061	25061	8½-120	24	3440	3043	2680	2344	2034	1749
25-06 Remington Super-X	120	PEP	W25062	25062	8½-120	24	3050	2786	2538	2302	2080	1870
25-20 Winchester	86	SP	W25202	25202	6½-116	24	1460	1194	1030	931	858	798
25-20 Winchester	86	Lead	W25201	25201	6½-116	24	1460	1194	1030	931	858	798
25-35 Winchester Super-X	117	SP	W2535	2535	8½-120	24	2270	1902	1576	1306	1112	994
250 Savage Super-X	87	PSP	W2501	2501	8½-120	24	3030	2673	2342	2036	1755	1504
250 Savage Super-X	100	ST	W2503	2503	8½-120	24	2820	2467	2140	1839	1569	1339
256 Winchester Mag. Super-X	60	OPE(HP)	—	2561P	6½-116	24	2760	2097	1542	1149	957	846
257 Roberts Super-X	100	ST	—	2572	8½-120	24	2900	2541	2210	1904	1627	1387
257 Roberts Super-X	117	PP(SP)	—	2573	8½-120	24	2650	2291	1961	1663	1404	1199
264 Winchester Mag. Super-X	100	PSP	W2641	2641	8½-120	24	3620	3198	2814	2462	2136	1836
264 Winchester Mag. Super-X	140	PP(SP)	W2642	2642	8½-120	24	3140	2886	2646	2419	2203	1998
270 Winchester Super-X	100	PSP	W2701	2701	8½-120	24	3480	3067	2690	2343	2023	1730
270 Winchester Super-X	130	PP(SP)	W2705	2705	8½-120	24	3110	2849	2604	2371	2150	1941
270 Winchester Super-X	130	ST	W2703	2703	8½-120	24	3110	2823	2554	2300	2061	1837
270 Winchester Super-X	150	PP(SP)	W2704	2704	8½-120	24	2900	2632	2380	2142	1918	1709
284 Winchester Super-X	125	PP(SP)	W2841	2841	8½-120	24	3140	2829	2538	2265	2010	1772
284 Winchester Super-X	150	PP(SP)	W2842	2842	8½-120	24	2860	2595	2344	2108	1886	1680
7 MM Mauser (7 × 57) Super-X	175	SP	W7MM	7MM	8½-120	24	2470	2165	1883	1626	1402	1219
7 MM Remington Mag. Super-X	125	PP(SP)	—	7MMR3	8½-120	24	3310	2976	2666	2376	2105	1852
7 MM Remington Mag. Super-X	150	PP(SP)	—	7MMR1	8½-120	24	3110	2830	2568	2320	2085	1866
7 MM Remington Mag. Super-X	175	PP(SP)	—	7MMR2	8½-120	24	2860	2528	2219	1933	1671	1440
30 Carbine	110	HSP	W30M1	—	6½-116	20	1990	1567	1236	1035	923	842
30 Carbine	110	FMC	W30M2	—	6½-116	20	1990	1596	1278	1070	952	870
30-30 Winchester Super-X	150	OPE	W30301	30301	8½-120	24	2390	2018	1684	1398	1177	1036
30-30 Winchester Super-X	150	PP	W30306	30306	8½-120	24	2390	2018	1684	1398	1177	1036
30-30 Winchester Super-X	150	ST	W30302	30302	8½-120	24	2390	2018	1684	1398	1177	1036
30-30 Winchester Super-X	170	PP(SP)	W30303	30303	8½-120	24	2200	1895	1619	1381	1191	1061
30-30 Winchester Super-X	170	ST	W30304	30304	8½-120	24	2200	1895	1619	1381	1191	1061
30 Remington Super-X	170	ST	—	30R2	8½-120	24	2120	1822	1555	1328	1153	1036
30-06 Springfield Super-X	110	PSP	W30060	30060	8½-120	24	3380	2843	2365	1936	1561	1261
30-06 Springfield Super-X	125	PSP	W30062	30062	8½-120	24	3140	2780	2447	2138	1853	1595
30-06 Springfield Super-X	150	PP(SP)	W30061	30061	8½-120	24	2920	2580	2265	1972	1704	1466
30-06 Springfield Super-X	150	ST	W30063	30063	8½-120	24	2910	2617	2342	2083	1843	1622
30-06 Springfield Super-X	180	PP(SP)	W30064	30064	8½-120	24	2700	2348	2023	1727	1466	1251
30-06 Springfield Super-X	180	ST	W30066	30066	8½-120	24	2700	2469	2250	2042	1846	1663
30-06 Springfield Super-X	220	PP(SP)	—	30068	8½-120	24	2410	2130	1870	1632	1422	1246
30-06 Springfield Super-X	220	ST	W30069	30069	8½-120	24	2410	2192	1985	1791	1611	1448

PEP—Positive Expanding Point   HSP—Hollow Soft Point   PP(SP)—Power-Point Soft Point   HP—Hollow Point   PSP—Pointed Soft Point   ST(Exp)—Silvertip Expanding

WINCHESTER-WESTERN CENTERFIRE RIFLE BALLISTICS

256 Win   257 Roberts   264 Win   270 Win   284 Win   7 MM Mauser   7 MM Rem Mag.   30 Carbine   30-30 Win   30 Rem   30-06 Springfield

TRAJECTORY Inches above (+) or below (−) line of sight   0 = indicates yardage at which rifle is sighted in.

| ENERGY IN FOOT POUNDS | | | | | | SHORT RANGE | | | | | | LONG RANGE | | | | | | |
MUZZLE	100	200	300 (YARDS)	400	500	50	100	150 (YARDS)	200	250	300	100	150	200	250 (YARDS)	300	400	500
778	451	245	136	94	74	0.3	0	−2.3	−7.2	−15.8	−29.4	1.5	0	−4.2	−12.0	−24.8	−71.4	−155.6
723	417	225	127	90	70	0.3	0	−2.4	−7.7	−16.9	−31.3	1.6	0	−4.5	−12.8	−26.4	−75.6	−163.4
739	426	230	130	92	72	0.3	0	−2.4	−7.7	−16.9	−31.3	1.6	0	−4.5	−12.8	−26.4	−75.5	−163.3
1699	1235	887	622	424	282	0.2	0.5	0	−1.5	−4.3	−8.4	2.2	2.6	1.9	0	−3.3	−15.4	−37.7
1094	752	500	321	202	136	0.5	0.9	0	−2.5	−6.9	−13.7	2.2	1.9	0	−3.8	−10.0	−32.3	−73.8
1114	874	677	517	388	288	0.5	0.9	0	−2.2	−6.1	−11.7	2.0	1.7	0	−3.3	−8.3	−24.9	−52.5
1282	921	648	443	295	197	0.4	0.8	0	−2.2	−6.0	−11.8	1.9	1.6	0	−3.3	−8.5	−26.7	−59.6
1282	1011	790	608	461	344	0.4	0.7	0	−1.9	−5.1	−9.9	1.7	1.4	0	−2.8	−7.1	−21.2	−44.6
1556	1148	836	595	412	280	0.2	0.6	0	−1.7	−4.6	−9.0	2.4	2.8	2.0	0	−3.5	−16.3	−39.5
2077	1619	1249	950	710	522	0.3	0.6	0	−1.7	−4.6	−9.0	2.5	2.8	2.0	0	−3.4	−15.4	−36.2
1945	1615	1332	1089	882	708	0.5	0.9	0	−2.2	−5.8	−11.0	1.9	1.6	0	−3.1	−7.8	−22.6	−46.3
2139	1667	1289	982	736	542	0.3	0.6	0	−1.6	−4.5	−8.7	2.4	2.7	1.9	0	−3.3	−14.9	−35.0
2175	1812	1501	1233	1004	811	0.4	0.7	0	−1.9	−5.1	−9.7	1.7	1.4	0	−2.7	−6.8	−20.0	−40.8
2364	1850	1435	1098	827	611	0.3	0.6	0	−1.7	−4.5	−8.8	2.4	2.7	2.0	0	−3.4	−15.0	−35.2
2478	2068	1716	1412	1153	932	0.5	0.8	0	−2.0	−5.4	−10.2	1.8	1.5	0	−2.9	−7.2	−21.0	−42.9
407	272	203	165	141	122	0	−4.1	−14.4	−31.8	−57.3	−92.0	0	−8.2	−23.5	−47.0	−79.6	−175.9	−319.4
407	272	203	165	141	122	0	−4.1	−14.4	−31.8	−57.3	−92.0	0	−8.2	−23.5	−47.0	−79.6	−175.9	−319.4
1338	940	645	443	321	257	0.6	0	−3.0	−8.8	−18.2	−31.8	2.0	0	−4.9	−13.3	−25.9	−67.4	−136.9
1773	1380	1059	801	595	437	0.5	0.9	0	−2.3	−6.1	−11.8	2.0	1.7	0	−3.3	−8.4	−25.2	−53.4
1765	1351	1017	751	547	398	0.2	0	−1.6	−4.9	−10.0	−17.4	2.4	2.0	0	−3.9	−10.1	−30.5	−65.2
1015	586	317	176	122	95	0.3	0	−2.3	−7.3	−15.9	−29.6	1.5	0	−4.2	−12.1	−25.0	−72.1	−157.2
1867	1433	1084	805	588	427	0.6	1.0	0	−2.5	−6.9	−13.2	2.3	1.9	0	−3.7	−9.4	−28.6	−60.9
1824	1363	999	718	512	373	.	0	−1.9	−5.8	−11.9	−20.7	2.9	2.4	0	−4.7	−12.0	−36.7	−79.2
2909	2271	1758	1346	1013	748	0.2	.5	0	−1.5	−4.1	−7.9	2.1	2.4	1.8	0	−3.0	−13.6	−31.9
3064	2589	2176	1819	1508	1241	0.4	0.7	0	−1.9	−4.9	−9.4	2.7	3.0	2.1	0	−3.5	−15.0	−33.7
2689	2088	1606	1219	909	664	0.3	0.6	0	−1.6	−4.5	−8.7	2.4	2.7	1.9	0	−3.3	−15.0	−35.2
2791	2343	1957	1622	1334	1087	0.4	0.7	0	−1.9	−5.1	−9.7	1.7	1.4	0	−2.7	−6.8	−19.9	−40.5
2791	2300	1883	1527	1226	974	0.4	0.8	0	−2.0	−5.3	−10.0	1.7	1.5	0	−2.8	−7.1	−20.8	−42.7
2801	2307	1886	1528	1225	973	0.6	0.9	0	−2.3	−6.1	−11.7	2.1	1.7	0	−3.3	−8.2	−24.1	−49.4
2736	2221	1788	1424	1121	871	0.4	0.8	0	−2.0	−5.3	−10.1	1.7	1.5	0	−2.8	−7.2	−21.1	−43.7
2724	2243	1830	1480	1185	940	0.6	1.0	0	−2.4	−6.3	−12.1	2.1	1.8	0	−3.4	−8.5	−24.8	−51.0
2370	1821	1378	1027	764	577	0.4	0	−2.2	−6.6	−13.4	−23.0	1.5	0	−3.6	−9.7	−18.6	−46.8	−92.8
3040	2458	1972	1567	1230	952	0.3	0.6	0	−1.7	−4.7	−9.1	2.5	2.8	2.0	0	−3.4	−15.0	−34.5
3221	2667	2196	1792	1448	1160	0.4	0.8	0	−1.9	−5.2	−9.9	1.7	1.5	0	−2.8	−7.0	−20.5	−42.1
3178	2483	1913	1452	1085	806	0.2	0	−1.5	−4.6	−9.4	−16.3	2.3	1.9	0	−3.7	−9.4	−28.2	−59.5
967	600	373	262	208	173	0.9	0	−4.5	−13.5	−28.3	−49.9	0	−4.5	−13.5	−28.3	−49.9	−118.6	−228.1
967	622	399	280	221	185	0.9	0	−4.3	−13.0	−26.9	−47.4	2.9	0	−7.2	−19.7	−38.7	−100.4	−200.5
1902	1356	944	651	461	357	0.5	0	−2.6	−7.7	−16.0	−27.9	1.7	0	−4.3	−11.6	−22.7	−59.1	−120.5
1902	1356	944	651	461	357	0.5	0	−2.6	−7.7	−16.0	−27.9	1.7	0	−4.3	−11.6	−22.7	−59.1	−120.5
1902	1356	944	651	461	357	0.5	0	−2.6	−7.7	−16.0	−27.9	1.7	0	−4.3	−11.6	−22.7	−59.1	−120.5
1827	1355	989	720	535	425	0.6	0	−3.0	−8.9	−18.0	−31.1	2.0	0	−4.8	−13.0	−25.1	−63.6	−126.7
1827	1355	989	720	535	425	0.6	0	−3.0	−8.9	−18.0	−31.1	2.0	0	−4.8	−13.0	−25.1	−63.6	−126.7
2790	1974	1366	915	595	388	0.4	0.7	0	−2.0	−5.6	−11.1	1.7	1.5	0	−3.1	−8.0	−25.5	−57.4
2790	1974	1366	915	595	388	0.4	0.7	0	−2.0	−5.6	−11.1	1.7	1.5	0	−3.1	−8.0	−25.5	−57.4
2736	2145	1662	1269	953	706	0.4	0.8	0	−2.1	−5.6	−10.7	1.8	1.5	0	−3.0	−7.7	−23.0	−48.5
2839	2217	1708	1295	967	716	0.6	1.0	0	−2.4	−6.6	−12.7	2.2	1.8	0	−3.5	−9.0	−27.0	−57.1
2820	2281	1827	1445	1131	876	0.6	0.9	0	−2.3	−6.3	−12.0	2.1	1.8	0	−3.3	−8.5	−25.0	−51.8
2913	2203	1635	1192	859	625	0.2	0	−1.8	−5.5	−11.2	−19.5	2.7	2.3	0	−4.4	−11.3	−34.4	−73.7
2913	2436	2023	1666	1362	1105	0.2	0	−1.6	−4.8	−9.7	−16.5	2.4	2.0	0	−3.7	−9.3	−27.0	−54.9
2837	2216	1708	1301	988	758	0.4	0	−2.3	−6.8	−13.8	−23.6	1.5	0	−3.7	−9.9	−19.0	−47.4	−93.1
2837	2347	1924	1567	1268	1024	0.4	0	−2.2	−6.4	−12.7	−21.6	1.5	0	−3.5	−9.1	−17.2	−41.8	−79.9

OPE—Open Point Expanding   SP—Soft Point   FMC—Full Metal Case

WINCHESTER-WESTERN CENTERFIRE RIFLE BALLISTICS

30-40 Krag   300 Win Mag.   300 H.&H. Mag.   300 Savage   303 Savage   303 British   308 Win   32 Win. Special   32 Rem   32-20 Win   8 MM Mauser

CARTRIDGE	BULLET WT. GRS.	TYPE	SYMBOL WINCHESTER	WESTERN	PRIMER	BARREL LENGTH INCHES	MUZZLE	100	200	300 YARDS	400	500
30-40 Krag Super-X	180	PP(SP)	—	30401	8½-120	24	2430	2099	1795	1525	1298	1128
30-40 Krag Super-X	180	ST	—	30403	8½-120	24	2430	2213	2007	1813	1632	1468
300 Winchester Mag. Super-X	150	PP(SP)	W30WM1	30WM1	8½-120	24	3290	2951	2636	2342	2068	1813
300 Winchester Mag. Super-X	180	PP(SP)	W30WM2	30WM2	8½-120	24	3000	2783	2577	2379	2190	2010
300 Winchester Mag. Super-X	220	ST	W30WM3	30WM3	8½-120	24	2680	2448	2228	2020	1823	1640
300 H.&H. Magnum Super-X	180	ST	W300H2	—	8½-120	24	2880	2640	2412	2196	1991	1798
300 H.&H. Magnum Super-X	220	ST	W300H3	—	8½-120	24	2580	2341	2114	1901	1702	1520
300 H.&H. Magnum Super-X	220	ST	W300H3	—	8½-120	24	2580	2341	2114	1901	1702	1520
300 Savage Super-X	150	PP(SP)	W3001	3001	8½-120	24	2630	2311	2015	1743	1500	1295
300 Savage Super-X	150	ST	W3003	3003	8½-120	24	2630	2354	2095	1853	1632	1434
300 Savage Super-X	180	PP(SP)	W3004	3004	8½-120	24	2350	2025	1728	1467	1252	1098
300 Savage Super-X	180	ST	W3005	3005	8½-120	24	2350	2137	1935	1745	1571	1413
303 Savage Super-X	190	ST	—	3032	8½-120	24	1940	1657	1410	1211	1073	982
303 British Super-X	180	PP(SP)	W303B1	—	8½-120	24	2520	2290	2072	1867	1675	1501
308 Winchester Super-X	110	PSP	W3081	3081	8½-120	24	3280	2755	2286	1866	1502	1218
308 Winchester Super-X	125	PSP	W3087	3087	8½-120	24	3100	2743	2413	2107	1824	1569
308 Winchester Super-X	150	PP(SP)	W3085	3085	8½-120	24	2820	2488	2179	1893	1633	1405
308 Winchester Super-X	150	ST	W3082	3082	8½-120	24	2820	2533	2263	2009	1774	1560
308 Winchester Super-X	180	PP(SP)	W3086	3086	8½-120	24	2620	2274	1955	1666	1414	1212
308 Winchester Super-X	180	ST	W3083	3083	8½-120	24	2620	2393	2178	1974	1782	1604
308 Winchester Super-X	200	ST	W3084	3084	8½-120	24	2450	2208	1980	1767	1572	1397
32 Win. Special Super-X	170	PP(SP)	W32WS2	32WS2	8½-120	24	2250	1870	1537	1267	1082	972
32 Win. Special Super-X	170	ST	W32WS3	32WS3	8½-120	24	2250	1870	1537	1267	1082	972
32 Remington Super-X	170	ST	—	32R2	8½-120	24	2140	1785	1475	1228	1064	963
32-20 Winchester	100	SP	W32202	32202	6½-116	24	1290	1063	940	855	787	728
32-20 Winchester	100	Lead	W32201	32201	6½-116	24	1290	1063	940	855	787	728
8 MM Mauser (8 × 57) Super-X	170	PP(SP)	W8MM	—	8½-120	24	2510	2105	1741	1429	1188	1035
338 Winchester Mag. Super-X	200	PP(SP)	W3381	3381	8½-120	24	2960	2658	2375	2110	1862	1635
338 Winchester Mag. Super-X	250	ST	W3382	3382	8½-120	24	2660	2395	2145	1910	1693	1497
338 Winchester Mag. Super-X	300	PP(SP)	W3383	3383	8½-120	24	2430	2152	1893	1655	1443	1265
348 Winchester Super-X	200	ST	W3482	—	8½-120	24	2520	2215	1931	1672	1443	1253
35 Remington Super-X	200	PP(SP)	W35R1	35R1	8½-120	24	2080	1698	1376	1140	1001	912
35 Remington Super-X	200	ST	W35R3	35R3	8½-120	24	2080	1698	1376	1140	1001	912
351 Winchester S.L.	180	SP	W351SL2	—	6½-116	20	1850	1556	1310	1128	1012	934
358 Winchester Super-X	200	ST	W3581	—	8½-120	24	2490	2171	1876	1610	1379	1194
358 Winchester Super-X	250	ST	W3582	—	8½-120	24	2230	1988	1763	1557	1375	1224
375 H.&H. Magnum Super-X	270	PP(SP)	W375H1	375H1	8½-120	24	2690	2420	2166	1928	1707	1507
375 H.&H. Magnum Super-X	300	ST	W375H2	375H2	8½-120	24	2530	2268	2022	1793	1584	1397
375 H.&H. Magnum Super-X	300	FMC	W375H3	—	8½-120	24	2530	2171	1843	1552	1307	1126
38-40 Winchester	180	SP	W3840	3840	7-111	24	1330	1091	960	873	804	745
44 Remington Magnum Super-X	240	HSP	—	44MHSP	7M-111F	20	1760	1362	1094	953	861	789
44-40 Winchester	200	SP	W4440	4440	7-111	24	1310	1069	940	853	783	722
45-70 Government	405	SP	W4570	—	8½-120	24	1330	1168	1055	977	918	869
458 Winchester Mag. Super-X	500	FMC	W4580	—	8½-120	24	2120	1898	1691	1503	1338	1202
458 Winchester Mag. Super-X	510	SP	W4581	—	8½-120	24	2110	1834	1583	1366	1192	1070

HSP—Hollow Soft Point   PEP—Positive Expanding Point   PSP—Pointed Soft Point   PP(SP)—Power-Point Soft Point   FMC—Full Metal Case   SP—Soft Point   HP—Hollow Point

WINCHESTER-WESTERN CENTERFIRE RIFLE BALLISTICS

338 Win Mag.   348 Win   35 Rem   351 Win S.L.   358 Win   375 H.&H. Mag.   38-40 Win   44 Rem. Mag.   44-40 Win   45-70 Government   458 Win Mag.

TRAJECTORY Inches above (+) or below (−) line of sight 0 = Indicates yardage at which rifle is sighted in.

| ENERGY IN FOOT POUNDS | | | | | | SHORT RANGE | | | | | | LONG RANGE | | | | | | |
MUZZLE	100	200	300	400	500	50	100	150	200	250	300	100	150	200	250	300	400	500
2360	1761	1288	929	673	508	0.4	0	−2.4	−7.1	−14.5	−25.0	1.6	0	−3.9	−10.5	−20.3	−51.7	−103.9
2360	1957	1610	1314	1064	861	0.4	0	−2.1	−6.2	−12.5	−21.1	1.4	0	−3.4	−8.9	−16.8	−40.9	−78.1
3605	2900	2314	1827	1424	1095	0.3	0.7	0	−1.8	−4.8	−9.3	2.6	2.9	2.1	0	−3.5	−15.4	−35.5
3597	3095	2654	2262	1917	1614	0.5	0.8	0	−2.0	−5.3	−10.1	1.8	1.5	0	−2.8	−7.0	−20.2	−40.7
3508	2927	2424	1993	1623	1314	0.2	0	−1.7	−4.9	−9.9	−16.9	2.5	2.0	0	−3.8	−9.5	−27.5	−56.1
3315	2785	2325	1927	1584	1292	0.6	0.9	0	−2.3	−6.0	−11.5	2.1	1.7	0	−3.2	−8.0	−23.3	−47.4
3251	2677	2183	1765	1415	1128	0.3	0	−1.9	−5.5	−11.0	−18.7	2.7	2.2	0	−4.2	−10.5	−30.7	−63.0
3251	2677	2183	1765	1415	1128	0.3	0	−1.9	−5.5	−11.0	−18.7	2.7	2.2	0	−4.2	−10.5	−30.7	−63.0
2303	1779	1352	1012	749	558	0.3	0	−1.9	−5.7	−11.6	−19.9	2.8	2.3	0	−4.5	−11.5	−34.4	−73.0
2303	1845	1462	1143	887	685	0.3	0	−1.8	−5.4	−11.0	−18.8	2.7	2.2	0	−4.2	−10.7	−31.5	−65.5
2207	1639	1193	860	626	482	0.5	0	−2.6	−7.7	−15.6	−27.1	1.7	0	−4.2	−11.3	−21.9	−55.8	−112.0
2207	1825	1496	1217	986	798	0.4	0	−2.3	−6.7	−13.5	−22.8	1.5	0	−3.6	−9.6	−18.2	−44.1	−84.2
1588	1158	839	619	486	407	0.9	0	−4.1	−11.9	−24.1	−41.4	2.7	0	−6.4	−17.3	−33.2	−83.7	−164.3
2538	2096	1716	1393	1121	900	0.3	0	−2.0	−5.8	−11.6	−19.6	2.9	2.4	0	−4.4	−11.0	−32.0	−65.5
2627	1854	1276	850	551	362	0.4	0.8	0	−2.2	−6.0	−11.9	1.9	1.6	0	−3.3	−8.6	−27.4	−61.8
2667	2088	1616	1232	923	683	0.5	0.8	0	−2.1	−5.7	−11.1	1.9	1.6	0	−3.1	−7.9	−23.7	−50.0
2648	2061	1581	1193	888	657	0.2	0	−1.6	−4.8	−9.8	−16.9	2.4	2.0	0	−3.8	−9.8	−29.3	−62.0
2648	2137	1705	1344	1048	810	0.2	0	−1.5	−4.5	−9.3	−15.9	2.3	1.9	0	−3.6	−9.1	−26.9	−55.7
2743	2066	1527	1109	799	587	0.3	0	−2.0	−5.9	−12.1	−20.9	2.9	2.4	0	−4.7	−12.1	−36.9	−79.1
2743	2288	1896	1557	1269	1028	0.2	0	−1.8	−5.2	−10.4	−17.7	2.6	2.1	0	−4.0	−9.9	−28.9	−58.8
2665	2165	1741	1386	1097	867	0.3	0	−2.1	−6.3	−12.6	−21.4	1.4	0	−3.4	−9.0	−17.2	−42.1	−81.1
1911	1320	892	606	442	357	0.6	0	−3.1	−9.2	−19.0	−33.2	2.0	0	−5.1	−13.8	−27.1	−70.9	−144.3
1911	1320	892	606	442	357	0.6	0	−3.1	−9.2	−19.0	−33.2	2.0	0	−5.1	−13.8	−27.1	−70.9	−144.3
1728	1203	821	569	427	350	0.7	0	−3.4	−10.2	−20.9	−36.5	2.3	0	−5.6	−15.2	−29.6	−76.7	−154.5
369	251	196	162	138	118	0	−5.6	−18.8	−40.8	−72.7	−115.4	0	−10.5	−29.7	−58.8	−98.7	−215.2	−388.1
369	251	196	162	138	118	0	−5.6	−18.8	−40.8	−72.7	−115.4	0	−10.5	−29.7	−58.8	−98.7	−215.2	−388.1
2378	1672	1144	771	533	404	0.4	0	−2.3	−7.0	−14.6	−25.7	−1.6	0	−3.9	−10.7	−21.0	−55.4	−114.3
3890	3137	2505	1977	1539	1187	0.5	0.9	0	−2.3	−6.1	−11.6	2.0	1.7	0	−3.2	−8.2	−24.3	−50.4
3927	3184	2554	2025	1591	1244	0.2	0	−1.7	−5.2	−10.5	−18.0	2.6	2.1	0	−4.0	−10.2	−30.0	−61.9
3933	3084	2387	1824	1387	1066	0.4	0	−2.3	−6.7	−13.5	−23.1	1.5	0	−3.6	−9.7	−18.6	−46.2	−90.7
2820	2178	1656	1241	925	697	0.3	0	−2.1	−6.2	−12.7	−21.9	1.4	0	−3.4	−9.2	−17.7	−44.4	−87.9
1921	1280	841	577	445	369	0.8	0	−3.8	−11.3	−23.5	−41.2	2.5	0	−6.3	−17.1	−33.6	−87.7	−176.3
1921	1280	841	577	445	369	0.8	0	−3.8	−11.3	−23.5	−41.2	2.5	0	−6.3	−17.1	−33.6	−87.7	−176.3
1368	968	686	508	409	349	0	−2.1	−7.8	−17.8	−32.9	−53.9	0	−4.7	−13.6	−27.6	−47.5	−108.8	−203.9
2753	2093	1563	1151	844	633	0.4	0	−2.2	−6.5	−13.3	−23.0	1.5	0	−3.6	−9.7	−18.6	−47.2	−94.1
2760	2194	1725	1346	1049	832	0.5	0	−2.7	−7.9	−16.0	−27.1	1.8	0	−4.3	−11.4	−21.7	−53.5	−103.7
4337	3510	2812	2228	1747	1361	0.2	0	−1.7	−5.1	−10.3	−17.6	2.5	2.1	0	−3.9	−10.0	−29.4	−60.7
4263	3426	2723	2141	1671	1300	0.3	0	−2.0	−5.9	−11.9	−20.3	2.9	2.4	0	−4.5	−11.5	−33.8	−70.1
4263	3139	2262	1604	1138	844	0.3	0	−2.2	−6.5	−13.5	−23.4	1.5	0	−3.6	−9.8	−19.1	−49.1	−99.5
707	476	368	305	258	222	0	−5.2	−17.7	−38.6	−68.9	−109.6	0	−9.9	−28.2	−55.9	−94.0	−205.5	−371.0
1650	988	638	484	395	332	0	−2.7	−10.2	−23.6	−44.2	−73.3	0	−6.1	−18.1	−37.4	−65.1	−150.3	−282.5
762	507	392	323	272	231	0	−5.4	−18.5	−40.3	−71.9	−114.4	0	−10.3	−29.4	−58.3	−98.1	−214.7	−388.1
1590	1227	1001	858	758	679	0	−4.7	−15.8	−34.0	−60.0	−94.5	0	−8.7	−24.6	−48.2	−80.3	−172.4	−305.9
4989	3999	3174	2508	1987	1604	0.6	0	−3.0	−8.8	−17.6	−29.8	2.0	0	−4.7	−12.5	−23.7	−58.1	−112.0
5041	3808	2837	2113	1609	1296	0.7	0	−3.3	−9.5	−19.2	−33.0	2.2	0	−5.2	−13.8	−26.5	−66.5	−131.0

OPE— Open Point Expanding   ST(Exp)—Silvertip Expanding

FEDERAL BALLISTICS

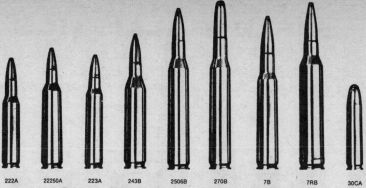

222A   22250A   223A   243B   2506B   270B   7B   7RB   30CA

Centerfire Rifle Cartridge Ballistics

Federal Load No.	Caliber	Bullet Wgt. in Grains	Bullet Style	Factory Primer	Velocity In Feet Per Second						Energy In Foot Pounds					
					Muzzle	100 yds	200 yds	300 yds	400 yds	500 yds	Muzzle	100 yds	200 yds	300 yds	400 yds	500 yds
222A	222 Remington	50	Soft Point	205	3140	2600	2120	1700	1350	1110	1090	750	500	320	200	135
22250A	22-250 Remington	55	Soft Point	210	3730	3180	2700	2260	1860	1520	1700	1240	885	620	425	280
223A	223 Remington	55	Soft Point	205	3240	2750	2300	1910	1550	1270	1280	920	650	445	295	195
6A	6mm Remington	80	Soft Point	210	3470	3060	2690	2350	2040	1750	2140	1670	1290	980	740	540
6B		100	Hi-Shok S.P.	210	3130	2860	2600	2360	2130	1910	2180	1810	1500	1230	1000	810
243A	243 Winchester	80	Soft Point	210	3420	3020	2650	2310	2000	1720	2080	1620	1250	950	710	520
243B		100	Hi-Shok S.P.	210	2960	2700	2450	2220	1990	1790	1950	1620	1330	1090	880	710
2506A	25-'06 Remington	90	Hollow Point	210	3440	3040	2680	2340	2030	1750	2360	1850	1440	1100	825	610
2506B		117	Hi-Shok S.P.	210	3060	2790	2530	2280	2050	1840	2430	2020	1660	1360	1100	875
270A	270 Winchester	130	Hi-Shok S.P.	210	3110	2850	2600	2370	2150	1940	2790	2340	1960	1620	1330	1090
270B		150	Hi-Shok S.P.	210	2900	2550	2230	1930	1650	1420	2800	2170	1650	1240	910	665
7A	7mm Mauser	175	Hi-Shok S.P.	210	2470	2170	1880	1630	1400	1220	2370	1820	1380	1030	765	575
7B		139	Hi-Shok S.P.	210	2660	2400	2150	1910	1690	1500	2180	1770	1420	1130	885	690
7RA	7mm Remington Magnum	150	Hi-Shok S.P.	215	3110	2830	2570	2320	2090	1870	3220	2670	2200	1790	1450	1160
7RB		175	Hi-Shok S.P.	215	2860	2650	2440	2240	2060	1880	3180	2720	2310	1960	1640	1370
*†30CA	30 Carbine	110	Soft Point	200	1990	1570	1240	1040	920	840	965	600	375	260	210	175
3030A	30-30 Winchester	150	Hi-Shok S.P.	210	2390	2020	1680	1400	1180	1040	1900	1360	945	650	460	355
3030B		170	Hi-Shok S.P.	210	2200	1900	1620	1380	1190	1060	1830	1360	990	720	535	425
3030C		125	Hollow Point	210	2570	2090	1660	1320	1080	960	1830	1210	770	480	320	260
3006A	30-'06 Springfield	150	Hi-Shok S.P.	210	2910	2620	2340	2080	1840	1620	2820	2280	1830	1450	1130	875
3006B		180	Hi-Shok S.P.	210	2700	2470	2250	2040	1850	1660	2910	2440	2020	1670	1360	1110
3006C		125	Soft Point	210	3140	2780	2450	2140	1850	1600	2740	2150	1660	1270	955	705
3006D		165	Boat Tail S.P.	210	2800	2610	2420	2240	2070	1910	2870	2490	2150	1840	1580	1340
3006E		200	Boat Tail S.P.	210	2550	2400	2260	2120	1990	1860	2890	2560	2270	2000	1760	1540
300WA	300 Winchester Magnum	150	Hi-Shok S.P.	215	3290	2950	2640	2340	2070	1810	3610	2900	2310	1830	1420	1100
300WB		180	Hi-Shok S.P.	215	3000	2780	2580	2380	2190	2010	3600	3100	2650	2260	1920	1640
300A	300 Savage	150	Hi-Shok S.P.	210	2630	2350	2100	1850	1630	1430	2300	1850	1460	1140	885	685
300B		180	Hi-Shok S.P.	210	2350	2140	1940	1750	1570	1410	2210	1830	1500	1220	985	800
308A	308 Winchester	150	Hi-Shok S.P.	210	2820	2530	2260	2010	1770	1560	2650	2140	1710	1340	1050	810
308B		180	Hi-Shok S.P.	210	2620	2390	2180	1970	1780	1600	2740	2290	1900	1560	1270	1030
**8A	8mm Mauser	170	Hi-Shok S.P.	210	2510	2110	1740	1430	1190	1040	2380	1670	1140	770	530	400
32A	32 Winchester Special	170	Hi-Shok S.P.	210	2250	1920	1630	1370	1170	1040	1910	1390	1000	710	520	410
35A	35 Remington	200	Hi-Shok S.P.	210	2080	1700	1380	1140	1000	910	1920	1280	840	575	445	370
*††44A	44 Remington Magnum	240	Hollow S.P.	150	1760	1360	1090	950	860	790	1650	990	640	485	395	330
*4570A	45-'70 Government	300	Hollow S.P.	210	1810	1410	1120	970	875	NA	2180	1320	840	630	510	NA

Unless otherwise noted, ballistic specifications were derived from test barrels 24 inches in length.

†Test Barrel Length 18 Inches.   ††Test Barrel Length 20 Inches.
*Without Cartridge Carrier.

**Only for use in barrels intended for .323 inch diameter bullets. Do not use in 8mm Commission Rifles (M1888) or sporting arms of similar bore diameter.

FEDERAL BALLISTICS

3030B · 3006B · 300WB · 300B · 308B · 8A · 32A · 35A · 44A

Centerfire Rifle Cartridge Ballistics

Bullet Drop In Inches From Bore Line

Drift In Inches In 10 mph Crosswind

Height of Trajectory

Inches above line of sight if sighted in at ⊕ yards. For sights .9″ above bore.
Trajectory figures show the height of bullet impact above or below the line of sight at the indicated yardages. Aim low indicated amount for + figures and high for − figures. Zero ranges indicated by circled crosses.

Bullet Drop 100	200	300	400	500	Drift 100	200	300	400	500	Height 50	100	150	200	250	300	Height 100	150	200	250	300	400	500
2.0	9.2	24.3	51.6	98.2	1.7	7.3	18.3	36.4	63.1	+0.5	+0.9	⊕	−2.5	−6.9	−13.7	+2.2	+1.9	⊕	−3.8	−10.0	−32.3	−73.8
1.4	6.2	16.0	32.6	59.4	1.2	5.1	12.3	23.9	41.2	+0.2	+0.5	⊕	−1.5	−4.3	−8.4	+2.2	+2.6	+1.9	⊕	−3.3	−15.4	−37.7
1.8	8.4	21.5	44.4	81.8	1.4	6.1	15.0	29.4	50.8	+0.4	+0.8	⊕	−2.2	−6.0	−11.8	+1.9	+1.6	⊕	−3.3	−8.5	−26.7	−59.6
1.6	6.9	17.0	33.4	58.3	1.0	4.1	9.9	18.8	31.6	+0.3	+0.6	⊕	−1.6	−4.5	−8.7	+2.4	+2.7	+1.9	⊕	−3.3	−14.9	−35.0
1.9	8.0	19.4	37.0	62.3	0.8	3.3	7.8	14.5	23.8	+0.4	+0.7	⊕	−1.9	−5.1	−9.7	+1.7	+1.4	⊕	−2.7	−6.8	−20.0	−40.8
1.6	7.1	17.5	34.5	60.2	1.0	4.2	10.1	19.2	32.3	+0.3	+0.6	⊕	−1.7	−4.6	−9.0	+2.5	+2.8	+2.0	⊕	−3.4	−15.4	−36.2
2.1	9.0	21.7	41.6	70.2	0.9	3.6	8.4	15.7	25.8	+0.5	+0.9	⊕	−2.2	−5.8	−11.0	+1.9	+1.6	⊕	−3.1	−7.8	−22.6	−46.3
1.6	7.0	17.2	33.8	58.9	1.0	4.1	9.8	18.7	31.3	+0.3	+0.6	⊕	−1.7	−4.5	−8.8	+2.4	+2.7	+2.0	⊕	−3.4	−15.0	−35.2
2.0	8.4	20.4	39.0	65.9	0.8	3.5	8.2	15.3	25.2	+0.5	+0.8	⊕	−2.0	−5.4	−10.3	+1.8	+1.5	⊕	−2.9	−7.3	−21.2	−43.4
1.9	8.1	19.4	37.0	62.1	0.8	3.2	7.4	13.9	22.7	+0.4	+0.7	⊕	−1.9	−5.1	−9.7	+1.7	+1.4	⊕	−2.7	−6.8	−19.9	−40.5
2.2	9.9	24.6	48.8	85.4	1.2	5.2	12.5	23.9	40.2	+0.6	+1.0	⊕	−2.5	−6.8	−13.1	+2.2	+1.9	⊕	−3.6	−9.3	−28.1	−59.7
3.1	13.7	34.1	67.8	119.3	1.5	6.2	15.0	28.7	47.8	+0.4	⊕	−2.2	−6.6	−13.4	−23.0	+1.5	⊕	−3.6	−9.7	−18.6	−46.8	−92.8
2.6	11.4	27.7	53.5	91.6	1.1	4.5	10.7	20.2	33.6	+0.2	⊕	−1.7	−5.2	−10.5	−18.0	+2.6	+2.1	⊕	−4.0	−10.2	−29.9	−61.8
1.9	8.2	19.7	37.8	63.9	0.8	3.4	8.1	15.1	24.9	+0.4	+0.8	⊕	−1.9	−5.2	−9.9	+1.7	+1.5	⊕	−2.8	−7.0	−20.5	−42.1
2.2	9.5	22.5	42.5	70.8	0.7	3.1	7.2	13.3	21.7	+0.6	+0.9	⊕	−2.3	−6.0	−11.3	+2.0	+1.7	⊕	−3.2	−7.9	−22.7	−45.8
5.2	24.8	67.2	142.0	257.6	3.4	15.0	35.5	63.2	96.7	+0.9	⊕	−4.5	−13.5	−28.3	−49.9	⊕	−4.5	−13.5	−28.3	−49.9	−118.6	−228.1
3.4	15.4	39.9	82.3	149.8	2.0	8.5	20.9	40.1	66.1	+0.5	⊕	−2.6	−7.7	−16.0	−27.9	+1.7	⊕	−4.3	−11.6	−22.7	−59.1	−120.5
4.0	17.7	44.8	90.3	160.2	1.9	8.0	19.4	36.7	59.8	+0.6	⊕	−3.0	−8.9	−18.0	−31.1	+2.0	⊕	−4.8	−13.0	−25.1	−63.6	−126.7
3.0	14.2	38.0	81.0	148.7	2.2	10.1	25.4	49.4	81.6	+0.1	⊕	−2.0	−7.3	−15.8	−28.1	+3.2	+2.4	⊕	−5.5	−15.8	−51.7	−112.2
2.2	9.5	23.2	44.9	76.9	1.0	4.2	9.9	18.7	31.2	+0.6	+0.9	⊕	−2.3	−6.3	−12.0	+2.1	+1.8	⊕	−3.3	−8.5	−25.0	−51.8
2.5	10.8	25.9	49.4	83.2	0.9	3.7	8.8	16.5	27.1	+0.5	⊕	−1.6	−4.8	−9.7	−16.5	+2.4	+2.0	⊕	−3.7	−9.3	−27.0	−54.9
1.9	8.3	20.6	40.6	70.7	1.1	4.5	10.8	20.5	34.4	+0.4	+0.8	⊕	−2.1	−5.6	−10.7	+1.8	+1.5	⊕	−3.0	−7.7	−23.0	−48.5
2.2	9.5	22.7	42.8	71.0	0.7	2.8	6.6	12.3	19.9	+0.5	⊕	−1.1	−4.2	−8.8	−14.3	+2.1	+1.8	⊕	−3.0	−8.0	−22.9	−45.9
2.6	11.2	26.6	59.7	81.6	0.6	2.6	6.0	11.0	17.7	+0.6	⊕	−2.7	−6.0	−12.4	−18.8	+2.3	+1.8	⊕	−4.1	−9.0	−25.8	−51.3
1.7	7.5	18.2	35.4	60.7	0.9	3.8	9.0	16.9	28.2	+0.3	+0.7	⊕	−1.8	−4.8	−9.3	+2.6	+2.9	+2.1	⊕	−3.5	−15.4	−35.5
2.6	11.0	26.4	50.3	84.8	0.7	2.8	6.5	12.0	19.6	+0.5	+0.8	⊕	−2.0	−5.3	−10.1	+1.8	+1.5	⊕	−2.8	−7.0	−20.2	−40.7
2.7	11.7	28.7	55.8	96.1	1.1	4.8	11.6	21.9	36.3	+0.3	⊕	−1.8	−5.4	−11.0	−18.8	+2.7	+2.2	⊕	−4.2	−10.7	−31.5	−65.5
3.4	14.3	34.7	66.4	112.3	1.1	4.6	10.9	20.3	33.3	+0.4	⊕	−2.3	−6.7	−13.5	−22.8	+1.7	⊕	−3.6	−9.6	−18.2	−44.1	−84.2
2.3	10.1	24.8	48.0	82.4	1.0	4.4	10.4	19.7	32.7	+0.2	⊕	−1.5	−4.5	−9.3	−15.9	+2.3	+1.9	⊕	−3.6	−9.1	−26.9	−55.7
2.7	11.5	27.6	52.7	88.8	0.9	3.9	9.2	17.2	28.3	+0.2	⊕	−1.8	−5.2	−10.4	−17.7	+2.6	+2.1	⊕	−4.0	−9.9	−28.9	−58.8
3.1	14.2	36.8	76.7	141.2	1.9	8.5	21.0	40.6	67.5	+0.4	⊕	−2.3	−7.0	−14.6	−25.7	+1.6	⊕	−3.9	−10.7	−21.0	−55.4	−114.3
3.8	17.1	43.7	88.9	159.3	1.9	8.4	20.3	38.6	63.0	+0.6	⊕	−2.9	−8.6	−17.6	−30.5	+1.9	⊕	−4.7	−12.7	−24.7	−63.2	−126.9
4.6	21.5	56.9	118.9	215.6	2.7	12.0	29.0	53.3	83.3	+0.8	⊕	−3.8	−11.3	−23.5	−41.2	+2.5	⊕	−6.3	−17.1	−33.6	−87.7	−176.3
6.7	32.4	87.0	179.8	319.6	4.2	17.8	39.8	68.3	102.5	⊕	−2.7	−10.2	−23.6	−44.2	−73.3	⊕	−6.1	−18.1	−37.4	−65.1	−150.3	−282.5
6.2	30.3	81.9	170.0	NA	4.0	17.2	38.9	67.2	NA	⊕	−2.5	−9.5	−22.0	−41.5	−69.0	⊕	−5.7	−17.0	−35.2	−61.4	−142.5	NA

NOTE: These trajectory tables were calculated by computer and are given here unaltered. The computer used a standard modern scientific technique to predict trajectories from the best available data for each round. Each trajectory is expected to be reasonably representative of the behavior of the ammunition at sea level conditions, but the shooter is cautioned that trajectories differ because of variations in ammunition, rifles, and atmospheric conditions.

FEDERAL BALLISTICS

25AP 32AP 357A 357B 357C 357D 9AP 9BP 380AP 38B 38C 38E 45A 45B

Centerfire Pistol Cartridge Ballistics

(Approximate)

Federal Load No.	Caliber	Bullet Style	Bullet Wt. in Grains	Factory Primer Number	Case Finish	Velocity Ft. Per Sec. Muzzle	Velocity Ft. Per Sec. 50 yds	Energy in ft./lbs. Muzzle	Energy in ft./lbs. 50 yds	Mid-Range Trajectory 50 yds	Test Barrel Length
25AP	25 Auto Pistol (6.35mm)	Metal Case	50	100	Brass	810	775	73	63	1.8"	2"
32AP	32 Auto Pistol (7.65mm)	Metal Case	71	100	Brass	905	855	129	115	1.4"	4"
380AP	380 Auto Pistol	Metal Case	95	100	Brass	955	865	190	160	1.4"	3¾"
380BP	380 Auto Pistol	Jacketed Hollow Point	90	100	Brass	1000	890	200	160	1.4"	3¾'
9AP	9mm Luger Auto Pistol	Metal Case	123	100	Brass	1120	1030	345	290	1.0"	4"
9BP	9mm Luger Auto Pistol	Jacketed Hollow Point	115	100	Brass	1160	1060	345	285	0.9"	4"
38A	38 Special (Match)	Lead Wadcutter	148			710	634	166	132	2.4"	4"
38B	38 Special	Lead Round Nose	158			755	723	200	183	2.0"	4"
38C	38 Special	Lead Semi-Wadcutter	158			755	723	200	183	2.0"	4"
*38D	38 Special (High Velocity + P)	Lead Round Nose	158			915	878	294	270	1.4"	4"
*38E	38 Special (High Velocity + P)	Jacketed Hollow Point	125			945	898	248	224	1.3"	4"
*38F	38 Special (High Velocity + P)	Jacketed Hollow Point	110			1020	945	254	218	1.1"	4"
*38G	38 Special (High Velocity + P)	Lead, Semi-Wadcutter Hollow Point	158			915	878	294	270	1.4"	4"
*38H	38 Special (High Velocity + P)	Lead Semi-Wadcutter	158			915	878	294	270	1.4"	4"
38J	38 Special (High Velocity + P)	Jacketed Soft Point	125			945	898	248	224	1.3"	4"
357A	357 Magnum	Jacketed Soft Point	158			1235	1104	535	428	0.8"	4"
357B	357 Magnum	Jacketed Hollow Point	125			1450	1240	583	427	0.6"	4"
357C	357 Magnum	Lead Semi-Wadcutter	158			1235	1104	535	428	0.8"	4"
357D	357 Magnum	Jacketed Hollow Point	110			1295	1094	410	292	0.8"	4"
357E	357 Magnum	Jacketed Hollow Point	158			1235	1104	535	428	0.8"	4"
44A	44 Rem. Magnum	Jacketed Hollow Point	240			1180	1081	741	623	0.9"	4"
44B	44 Rem. Magnum	Jacketed Hollow Point	180			1610	1365	1045	750	0.5"	4"
45LCA	45 Colt	Semi-Wadcutter Hollow Point	225			900†	860	405	369	1.5"	5½"

*This ammunition is loaded to a higher pressure, as indicated by the "+P" marking on the case headstamp, to achieve higher velocity. Use only in firearms especially designed for this cartridge and so recommended by the manufacturer.

22 Caliber Rimfire Cartridges

	Federal Load Number	Cartridges Per Box	Cartridge	Bullet Type	Bullet Wt. in Grains	Velocity in Ft. Per Sec. Muzzle	Velocity in Ft. Per Sec. 100 yds	Energy in Foot/lbs. Muzzle	Energy in Foot/lbs. 100 yds	Bullet Drop In Inches at 100 yds	Drift In 10 mph Cross-wind 100 yds	Height of Trajectory 50 yds	Height of Trajectory 100 yds	Height of Trajectory 150 yds	Height of Trajectory 50 yds	Height of Trajectory 100 yds	Height of Trajectory 150 yds
HI Power	701	50	22 Short	Solid	29	1095	905	77	53	16.8	5.3"	⊕	−8.0	−26.8	+4.0	⊕	−14.7
	703	50	22 Short	Hollow Point	29	1120	905	81	53	16.4	5.9"	⊕	−7.9	−26.4	+3.9	⊕	−14.6
	706	50	22 Long	Solid	29	1240	960	99	60	14.1	6.9"	⊕	−6.8	−23.0	+3.4	⊕	−12.8
	710	50	22 Long Rifle	Solid	40	1255	1015	140	92	13.2	5.5"	⊕	−6.2	−20.8	+3.1	⊕	−11.5
	712	50	22 Long Rifle	Hollow Point	38	1280	1020	138	88	12.9	5.9"	⊕	−6.1	−20.6	+3.1	⊕	−11.4
	716	50	22 Long Rifle	No. 12 Shot	25	—	—	—	—	—	—	—	—	—	—	—	—
100 Pack	810	100	22 Long Rifle	Solid	40	1255	1015	140	92	13.2	5.5"	⊕	−6.2	−20.8	+3.1	⊕	−11.5
	812	100	22 Long Rifle	Hollow Point	38	1280	1020	138	88	12.9	5.9"	⊕	−6.1	−20.6	+3.1	⊕	−11.4
Champion Standard Velocity	702	50	22 Short	Solid	29	1045	870	70	49	18.1	5.0"	⊕	−8.7	−28.9	+4.4	⊕	−15.8
	711	50	22 Long Rifle	Solid	40	1150	975	117	85	15.0	4.4"	⊕	−7.0	−23.2	+3.5	⊕	−12.6
	811	100	22 Long Rifle	Solid	40	1150	975	117	85	15.0	4.4"	⊕	−7.0	−23.2	+3.5	⊕	−12.6

Unless otherwise noted, these ballistic specifications were derived from test barrels 24 inches in length.
All specifications are nominal; individual guns may vary from test barrel figures.

Reloading

DUPONT SMOKELESS POWDERS

SHOTSHELL POWDER

Hi-Skor 700-X Double-Base Shotshell Powder. Specifically designed for today's 12-gauge components. Developed to give optimum ballistics at minimum charge weight (means more reloads per pound of powder). 700-X is dense, easy to load, clean to handle and loads uniformly.

PB Shotshell Powder. Produces exceptional 20- and 28-gauge skeet reloads; preferred by many in 12-gauge target loads,

it gives 3-dram equivalent velocity at relatively low chamber pressures.

SR-4756 Powder. Great all-around powder for target and field loads.

SR-7625 Powder. A fast growing "favorite" for reloading target as well as light and heavy field loads in 4 gauges. Excellent velocity-chamber pressure.

IMR-4227 Powder. Can be used effectively for reloading .410-gauge shotshell ammunition.

RIFLE POWDER

IMR-3031 Rifle Powder. Specifically recommended for medium-capacity cartridges.

IMR-4064 Rifle Powder. Has exceptionally uniform burning qualities when used in medium- and large-capacity cartridges.

IMR-4198. Made the Remington 222 cartridge famous. Developed for small- and medium-capacity cartridges.

IMR-4227 Rifle Powder. Fastest burning of the IMR Series. Specifically designed for the 22 Hornet class of cartridges.

SR-4759. Brought back by shooter demand. Available for Cast bullet loads.

IMR-4320. Recommended for high-velocity cartridges.

IMR-4350 Rifle Powder. Gives unusually uniform results when loaded in magnum cartridges. Slowest burning powder of the IMR series.

IMR-4831. Produced as a canister-grade handloading powder. Packaged in 1 lb. canister, 8 lb. caddy and 20 lb. kegs.

IMR-4895 Rifle Powder. The time-tested standard for caliber 30 military ammunition is now being manufactured again. Slightly faster than IMR-4320. Loads uniformly in all powder measures. One of the country's favorite powders.

PISTOL POWDER

PB Powder. Another powder for reloading a wide variety of center-fire handgun ammunition.

IMR-4227 Powder. Can be used effectively for reloading "magnum" handgun ammunition.

"Hi-Skor" 700-X Powder. The same qualities that make it a superior shotshell powder contribute to its excellent

performance in all the popular handguns.

SR-7625 Powder. For reloading a wide variety of center-fire handgun ammunition.

SR-4756, IMR-3031 and IMR-4198. Three more powders in a good selection—all clean burning and with uniform performance.

SMOKELESS SPORTING POWDERS FOR RELOADING

Eight types of Hercules smokeless sporting powders are available to the handloader. These have been selected from the wide range of powders produced for factory loading to provide at least one type that can be used efficiently and economically for each type of ammunition. These include:

RELODER® 7

Outstanding accuracy in small-capacity center-fire rifle cartridges used in bench rest shooting. Produces high velocity with minimum charge weights for optimum performance. Available in 1-pound containers.

RED DOT®

The preferred powder for light-to-medium shotshell use; specifically designed for 12-gauge target loads. Available in 1-, 4-, 8-, and 15-pound containers.

HERCO®

A coarse-grained shotshell powder for use in heavy 12-gauge shotshells and medium-small-gauge shotshell loads. Available in 1-, 4-, 8-, and 15-pound containers.

BULLSEYE®

A high-energy, quick-burning powder designed for pistol and revolver use. Available in 1-, 4-, 8-, and 15-pound containers.

GREEN DOT®

Designed for use in 12-gauge medium shotshell loads. Outstanding in 20-gauge skeet loads. Available in 1-, 4-, 8-, and 15-pound containers.

UNIQUE®

The all-around powder. Performs well in pistol and revolver, shotshell, and rifle gallery loads. Available in 1-, 4-, 8-, and 15-pound containers.

BLUE DOT®

Blue Dot is specifically designed for magnum waterfowl shotshells. Available in 1-pound containers and in 5-pound kegs.

HERCULES 2400®

A fine-grained powder intended for small-capacity rifle cartridges and/or reduced loads in larger capacity rifle cartridges. Outstanding with cast bullets. Available in 1-, 4-, 8-, and 15-pound containers.

HODGDON SMOKELESS POWDER

RIFLE POWDER

H4227 and H4198

H4227 is the fastest burning of the IMR series. Well adapted to Hornet, light bullets in 222 and all bullets in 357 and 44 magnum pistols. Cuts leading with lead bullets. H4198 was developed especially for small and medium capacity cartridges.

1 lb. can $8.45; 8 lb. keg $62.50

H322

A new extruded bench-rest powder which has proved to be capable of producing fine accuracy in the .22 and .308 Bench-rest guns. This powder fills the gap between H4198 and BL-C(2). Performs best in small to medium capacity cases.

1 lb. can $5.95; 8 lb. keg $42.50

SPHERICAL BL-C®, Lot No. 2

A highly popular favorite of the Bench-rest shooters. Best performance is in the 222, and in other cases smaller than 30/06.

1 lb. can $8.45; 8 lb. keg $62.50

SPHERICAL H335®

Similar to BL-C(2), H335 is popular for its performance in medium capacity cases, especially in 222 and 308 Winchester.

1 lb. can $4.95

4895®

4895 may well be considered the most versatile of all propellants. It gives desirable performance in almost all cases from 222 Rem. to 458 Win. Reduced loads, to as low as ³/₅ of maximum, still give target accuracy.

1 lb. can $8.45; 8 lb. keg $62.50

SPHERICAL H380®

This number fills a gap between 4320 and 4350. It is excellent in 22/250, 220 Swift, the 6mm's, 257 and 30/06.

1 lb. can $8.40; 8 lb. keg $62.50

SPHERICAL H414®

A new development in spherical powder. In many popular medium to medium-large calibers, pressure velocity relationship is better.

1 lb. can $8.45; 8 lb. keg $62.50

H205

A specialized extruded powder which gives outstanding performance in medium to large capacity .30 caliber cartridges. It will give good results in most medium to large capacity cases. Use our data only with this powder.

1 lb. can $8.45; 8 lb. keg $62.50

SPHERICAL H450®

A powder well adapted to maximum loads in most cartridges. Gives excellent performance in 30/06.

1 lb. can $8.45; 8 lb. keg $62.50

H4831® — NEWLY MANUFACTURED

Here is a new batch of the original 4831. The most popular of all powders. Use same loading data as our original surplus powder. Outstanding performance with medium and heavy bullets in the 6mm's, 25/06, 270 and magnum calibers.

1 lb. can $8.45; 8 lb. keg $62.50

SPHERICAL H870®

Very slow burning rate adaptable to over-bore capacity magnum cases such as 257, 264, 270 and 300 mags with heavy bullets.

1 lb. can $4.95; 8 lb. keg $30.19

SHOTGUN AND PISTOL POWDER

HP38

A fast pistol powder for most pistol loading. Especially recommended for mid-range 38 special.

12 oz. can $6.25; 8 lb. keg $58.50

TRAP 100

Trap 100 is a spherical trap and light field load powder, also excellent for target loads in centerfire pistol. Mild recoil.

8 oz. can $4.00; 8 lb. keg $54.25

HS-5, HS-6 and HS-7

HS-5 for heavy field and HS-6 and HS-7 for magnum field loads are unsurpassed since they do not pack in the measure. They deliver uniform charges and are dense so allow sufficient wad column for best patterns.

HS-5, HS-6 1 lb. can $7.50; 8 lb. keg $53.95
HS-7 1 lb. can $7.75; 8 lb. keg $56.50

H110

A spherical powder made especially for the 30 M1 carbine. H110 also does very well in 357, 44 Spec., 44 Mag. or 410 ga. Shotshell. Magnum primers are recommended for consistent ignition.

1 lb. can $7.25; 8 lb keg $53.50

NORMA SMOKELESS POWDER

RIFLE POWDERS

NORMA 200

A fast-burning powder, for small capacity cartridge cases as the 222, but also for use with light bullets and/or light loads in larger calibers. **400 g. canister $12.60**

NORMA 201

Slower than the 200, used with lighter bullets in medium-size cases, or with big-caliber cartridges where a large bore volume is to be filled up quickly by expanding gases.
400 g. canister $12.60

NORMA 202

A rifle powder of medium-burning rate that makes it the right choice for cartridges in the 6. 5mm-7mm—30-06 caliber range of regular case capacity. **400 g. canister $12.60**

NORMA 204

A slow-burning powder, adapted for cartridges with a large case capacity and/or using heavy bullets in relation to the caliber.
400 g. canister $12.60

NORMA MAGNUM RIFLE POWDER

Exceptionally slow-burning, high-energy powder for highest velocity with large capacity cases. A must for Magnums. **400 g. canister $12.60**

HANDGUN POWDERS

NORMA POWDER R-1

Is a fast-burning, easily-ignited powder especially adapted for revolver cartridges with lead bullets, such as 38 Special target loads. It is clean burning, and the granules are of such size and shape that they flow easily in the powder measure and without binding the cylinder. It also handles very easily in the spoon or powder trickler for shooters who prefer weighing their loads. **275 g. canister $14.95**

NORMA POWDER R-123

Is a slow-burning handgun powder for heavier loads in cartridges such as 357 and 44 Magnum, especially when using jacketed bullets. This powder gives a lower breech pressure and the charge weight can therefore be increased for higher bullet velocities.
400 g. canister $19.95

NORMA RELOADING

Rifle Powders/Pulver für Büchsenpatronen

Caliber	Bullet index no	Bullet weight (grains)	Max Cartridge length (inch.)	(mm)	Norma primer	Norma powder	Load (grains)	(grams)	Muzzle vel Feet per sec	Meter per sec	Pressure¹) (psi)	(bar)
220 Swift	65701	50	2.62	66.5	LR	202	39.3	2.55	3980	1213	53700	3700
222 Rem	65701 +65702	50	2.11	53.5	SR	200	21.0	1.36	3200	975	46400	3200
						200	20.2	1.31	3000	914	46400	3200
						200	17.7	1.15	2790	850	46400	3200
	65704	53	2.16	55.0	SR	200	20.8	1.35	3115	950	46400	3200
22-250	65704	53	2.38	60.5	LR	202	36.6	2.37	3710	1130	53700	3700
5.6x52 R	65604	71	2.50	63.5	LR	202	27.0	1.75	2835	864	42100	2900
	65605	71	2.50	63.5	LR	202	27.0	1.75	2835	864	42100	2900
243 Win	66002 +66003	100	2.62	66.5	LR	204	45.1	2.92	3070	936	52200	3600
						204	43.8	2.84	2870	875	52200	3600
						204	42.0	2.72	2670	814	52200	3600
6.5 Jap.	66531	139	2.82	71.5	LR	202	30.9	2.00	2270	692	32200	2220
						201	28.2	1.83	2230	680	32200	2220
						200	24.0	1.55	2030	618	32200	2220
	66532	156	2.89	73.5	LR	202	28.2	1.83	2035	620	32200	2220
						201	24.7	1.60	1865	568	32200	2220
						200	20.5	1.33	1665	508	32200	2220
6.5x55	66551	77	2.62	66.5	LR	200	33.2	2.15	2725	830	45000	3100
						200	37.8	2.45	3115	950	45000	3100
						200	34.1	2.21	2915	889	45000	3100
	66512	139	2.99	76.0	LR	204	46.6	3.02	2790	850	45000	3100
						MRP	49.4	3.20	2815	858	45000	3100
						MRP	47.8	3.10	2740	835	45000	3100
	66532	156	3.07	78.0	LR	204	44.2	2.86	2495	760	45000	3100
						204	42.5	2.75	2295	700	45000	3100
						204	39.8	2.58	2095	639	45000	3100
6.5 Carc.	66532	156	2.97	75.5	LR	202	35.5	2.30	2340	713	37700	2600
						200	25.2	1.63	1800	549	37700	2600
270 Win.	66902	130	3.15	80.0	LR	204	57.0	3.69	3140	957	52200	3600
						204	55.0	3.56	2940	896	52200	3600
						204	52.0	3.37	2740	835	52200	3600
	66903	150	3.23	82.0	LR	204	52.4	3.39	2800	853	52200	3600
						204	50.5	3.27	2600	792	52200	3600
						204	46.7	3.02	2400	731	52200	3600
7x57	67002	150	3.05	77.5	LR	202	44.0	2.85	2690	820	49300	3400
						201	40.0	2.59	2555	779	49300	3400
						201	36.5	2.36	2355	718	49300	3400
7x57 R	67002 +67003	150	3.02	76.7	LR	202	42.9	2.78	2620	799	43500	3000
						201	36.3	2.35	2290	698	43500	3000
Super 7x61	67002	150	3.19	81.0	LR	MRP	67.4	4.37	3165	965	55100	3800
						204	58.5	3.79	2950	899	55100	3800
						204	55.3	3.58	2750	838	55100	3800
7 mm Rem. M.	67002	150	3.25	82.5	LR	MRP	71.4	4.63	3250	990	55100	3800
						204	66.6	4.31	3060	933	55100	3800
						204	62.4	4.04	2860	872	55100	3800
7x64	67002	150	2.13	84.0	LR	204	57.1	3.70	2890	880	52200	3600
						204	52.9	3.43	2690	819	52200	3600
						204	49.5	3.21	2490	758	52200	3600
	67036	175	2.13	84.0	LR	MRP	56.6	3.67	2725	830	52200	3600
						MRP	51.7	3.35	2475	754	52200	3600
						MRP	48.3	3.13	2275	693	52200	3600
280 Rem.	67002	150	3.29	83.5	LR	MRP	59.4	3.85	2980	910	50800	3500
7.5x55 Swiss	67625	180	2.91	74.0	LR	204	52.2	3.38	2650	808	45000	3100
						204	54.0	3.50	2690	820	45000	3100
7.62 Russ.	67623	130	2.66	67.5	LR	201	51.4	3.33	3100	945	47900	3300
	67624	150	2.75	70.0	LR	201	47.8	3.10	2800	853	47900	3300
	67625	180	2.82	71.5	LR	202	47.1	3.05	2595	791	47900	3300
						201	37.2	2.41	2225	678	47900	3300

Caliber	Bullet index no	Bullet weight (grains)	Max Cartridge length (inch.)	(mm)	Norma primer	Norma powder	Load (grains)	(grams)	Muzzle vel Feet per sec	Meter per sec	Pressure¹) (psi)	(bar)
30 US Carb.	67621	110	1.67	42.5	SR	–	–	–	1970	600	46400	3200
30-06	67621	110	2.87	73.0	LR	201	54.5	3.53	3280	1000	50800	3500
	67623	130	3.11	79.0	LR	202	56.3	3.65	3205	977	50800	3500
	67624	150	3.13	79.5	LR	202	52.5	3.40	2955	901	50800	3500
						MRP	62.4	4.04	2820	860	50800	3500
	67628	180	3.17	80.5	LR	204	56.3	3.65	2700	823	50800	3500
						202	48.5	3.14	2645	806	50800	3500
						201	41.6	2.69	2300	701	50800	3500
	67648	180	3.15	80.0	LR	204	56.3	3.65	2700	823	50800	3500
						202	48.5	3.14	2645	806	50800	3500
						201	41.6	2.69	2300	701	50800	3500
30-30 Win	67630	150	2.50	63.5	LR	201	35.5	2.30	2410	735	43500	3000
						201	32.5	2.10	2210	674	43500	3000
						200	26.1	1.69	2010	613	43500	3000
	67631	170	2.50	63.5	LR	201	32.4	2.10	2220	677	43500	3000
						200	26.3	1.70	2020	616	43500	3000
						200	23.3	1.51	1820	555	43500	3000
308 Win.	67621	110	2.38	60.5	LR	200	40.1	2.60	2740	835	52200	3600
	67623	130	2.62	66.5	LR	200	40.6	2.63	2900	884	52200	3600
						200	38.2	2.47	2700	823	52200	3600
						200	35.1	2.27	2500	762	52200	3600
	67624	150	2.65	67.5	LR	201	45.5	2.95	2860	872	52200	3600
						201	43.3	2.80	2660	811	52200	3600
						201	40.6	2.63	2460	750	52200	3600
	67628	180	2.70	68.5	LR	202	42.1	2.73	2525	770	52200	3600
308 Norma M.	67623	130	3.17	80.5	LR	204	78.4	5.08	3545	1080	55100	3800
	67624	150	3.21	81.5	LR	204	76.7	4.97	3330	1015	55100	3800
	67628	180	3.25	82.5	LR	MRP	74.3	4.81	3020	920	55100	3800
						204	71.8	4.65	2900	884	55100	3800
						204	70.0	4.53	2700	823	55100	3800
7.65 Arg	67701	150	2.85	72.5	LR	201	47.8	3.10	2920	890	49300	3400
						201	44.0	2.85	2720	829	49300	3400
						201	42.5	2.75	2520	768	49300	3400
303 British	67701	150	2.95	75.0	LR	201	44.6	2.89	2720	829	46400	3200
						201	41.4	2.68	2520	768	46400	3200
						200	33.9	2.19	2320	707	46400	3200
	67713	180	2.97	75.5	LR	202	43.0	2.79	2540	774	46400	3200
						202	43.5	2.82	2600	792	46400	3200
						201	36.2	2.34	2140	652	46400	3200
7.7 Jap.	67711	130	2.84	72.0	LR	202	51.7	3.35	3005	916	39200	2700
	67713	180	3.03	77.0	LR	202	46.0	2.98	2515	767	39200	2700
8x57 J	67901	196	2.97	75.5	LR	202	48.0	3.11	2485	757	48500	3300
						201	39.8	2.58	2125	648	48500	3300
8x57 JS	68003	196	2.95	75.0	LR	202	48.3	3.13	2485	757	49300	3400
						200	36.4	2.36	2125	648	49300	3400
	68007	196	2.97	75.5	LR	202	48.3	3.13	2485	757	49300	3400
						200	36.4	2.36	2125	648	49300	3400
358 Norma M.	69001	250	3.23	82.0	LR	202	66.3	4.30	2710	826	53400	3700
						201	57.0	3.69	2400	731	53400	3700
9.3x57	69303	286	3.01	76.5	LR	201	44.6	2.89	2065	630	36300	2500
						201	40.6	2.63	1865	569	36300	2500
						200	34.2	2.22	1665	508	36300	2500
9.3x62	69303	286	3.23	82.0	LR	201	54.7	3.54	2360	720	49300	3400
						201	51.2	3.32	2160	659	49300	3400
						200	44.0	2.85	1960	598	49300	3400

NORMA RELOADING

MRP/Magnum Rifle Powder

An exceptionally slow burning, high-energy powder for highest velocity with large capacity cases. Replaces the famous Norma 205 powder. A must for magnums.

Caliber	Bullet index no.	Bullet weight grains	Max Cartridge length inch.	mm	Norma primer	Norma powder	Load grains	grams	Muzzle vel. Feet per sec.	Meter per sec.	Pressure [1] psi	bar
243 Win.	–	80	2.54	64.5	LR	MRP	50.6	3.28	3347	1020	52200	3600
243 Win.	66003	100	2.62	66.5	LR	MRP	49.2	3.19	3199	975	52200	3600
6 mm Rem.	66003	100	2.82	71.6	LR	MRP	46.4	3.01	3117	950	54400	3750
6 mm Rem.	66003	100	2.82	71.6	LR	MRP	48.2	3.12	3248	990	54400	3750
6.5 Carc.	66551	77	2.52	64.0	LR	MRP	46.5	3.01	2965	904	37700	2600
6.5 Carc.	66522	80	2.50	63.5	LR	MRP	46.6	3.02	2950	899	37700	2600
6.5 Carc.	66512	139	2.85	72.5	LR	MRP	43.2	2.80	2570	783	37700	2600
6.5 Carc.	66510	144	2.95	75.0	LR	MRP	43.2	280	2550	777	37700	2600
6.5 Carc.	66532	156	2.95	75.0	LR	MPR	42.4	2.75	2435	744	37700	2600
6.5 Jap.	66512	139	2.81	71.5	LR	MRP	37.7	2.44	2335	712	37700	2600
6.5 Jap.	66532	156	2.89	73.3	LR	MRP	38.1	2.47	2310	704	37700	2600
6.5x55	66531	139	2.99	76.0	LR	MRP	47.8	3.10	2740	835	45000	3100
6.5x55	66512	139	2.99	76.0	LR	MRP	49.4	3.20	2815	858	49300	3400[2]
6.5x55	66510	144	3.05	77.5	LR	MRP	48.6	3.15	2780	847	49300	3400[2]
6.5x55	66532	156	3.07	78.0	LR	MRP	48.0	3.11	2645	806	49300	3400[2]
270 Win.	–	110	3.15	80.0	LR	MRP	61.5	3.98	3166	965	52200	3600
270 Win.	66902	130	3.15	80.0	LR	MRP	60.9	3.95	3133	955	52200	3600
270 Win.	66903	150	3.23	82.0	LR	MRP	58.4	3.78	2969	905	52200	3600
7x57	67002	150	3.03	77.0	LR	MRP	50.9	3.30	2615	797	49300	3400
7x57 R	67002	150	3.02	76.7	LR	MRP	51.3	3.32	2690	820	43500	3000
7x57 R	–	160	3.06	77.7	LR	MRP	50.4	3.27	2608	795	43500	3000
7x61 Super	–	160	3.19	81.0	LR	MRP	66.5	4.31	3100	945	55100	3800
7x61 Super	–	175	3.19	81.0	LR	MRP	64.8	4.20	2904	885	55100	3800
7x64	67002	150	3.27	83.0	LR	MRP	59.6	3.86	2960	902	52200	3600
7 mm Rem.	–	160	3.19	81.0	LR	MRP	70.2	4.55	3166	965	55100	3800
7 mm Rem.	–	175	3.21	81.5	LR	MRP	68.0	4.41	2986	910	55100	3800
7.5x55	67621	110	2.56	65.0	LR	MRP	60.9	3.95	3085	940	45000	3100
7.5x55	67623	130	2.80	71.0	LR	MRP	60.2	3.90	3060	933	45000	3100
7.5x55	67602	146	2.81	71.5	LR	MRP	57.1	3.70	2920	890	45000	3100
7.5x55	67624	150	2.80	71.0	LR	MRP	57.1	3.70	2890	881	45000	3100
7.5x55	67625	180	2.80	71.0	LR	MRP	55.6	3.60	2730	832	45000	3100
30—06	67624	150	3.13	79.5	LR	MRP	62.4	4.04	2822	860	50800	3500
30—06	67628	180	3.17	80.5	LR	MRP	60.1	3.89	2658	810	50800	3500
30—06	–	200	3.23	82.0	LR	MRP	59.4	3.85	2608	795	50800	3500
30—06	67628	180	3.17	80.5	–	MRP	61.7	4.00	2790	850	50800	3500

Loading data for Weatherby Magnums/Ladedata für Weatherby Magnum Patronen

Caliber	Bullet index no.	Bullet weight grains	Max Cartridge length inch.	mm	Norma primer	Norma powder	Load grains	grams	Muzzle vel. Feet per sec.	Meter per sec.	Pressure [1] psi	bar
240 WM	–	70	3.15	80.0	–	MRP	59.4	3.85	3838	1170	55100	3800
240 WM	–	85	3.15	80.0	–	MRP	54.9	3.56	3497	1066	55100	3800
240 WM	–	87	3.15	80.0	–	MRP	54.5	3.53	3497	1066	55100	3800
240 WM	–	100	3.15	80.0	–	MRP	54.0	3.50	3395	1035	55100	3800
257 WM	–	87	3.42	87.0	–	MRP	74.1	4.80	3757	1145	55100	3800
257 WM	–	100	3.42	87.0	–	MRP	71.3	4.62	3555	1084	55100	3800
257 WM	–	117	3.42	87.0	–	MRP	67.1	4.35	3300	1006	55100	3800
270 WM	–	100	3.42	87.0	–	MRP	77.2	5.00	3760	1146	55100	3800
270 WM	–	130	3.42	87.0	–	MRP	73.3	4.75	3375	1029	55100	3800
270 WM	–	150	3.42	87.0	–	MRP	71.7	4.65	3245	990	55100	3800
7 mm WM	–	139	3.42	87.0	–	MRP	74.1	4.80	3300	1006	55100	3800
7 mm WM	–	154	3.42	87.0	–	MRP	72.8	4.72	3160	963	55100	3800
7 mm WM	–	160	3.42	87.0	–	MRP	72.5	4.70	3150	960	55100	3800
7 mm WM	–	175	3.42	87.0	–	MRP	71.0	4.60	3070	935	55100	3800
300 WM	–	110	3.58	91.0	–	MRP	81.0	5.25	3900	1189	55100	3800
300 WM	–	150	3.58	91.0	–	MRP	88.0	5.70	3545	1081	55100	3800
300 WM	–	180	3.58	91.0	–	MRP	83.3	5.40	3245	990	55100	3800
300 WM	–	200	3.58	91.0	–	MRP	78.7	5.10	3000	914	55100	3800
300 WM	–	220	3.58	91.0	–	MRP	79.2	5.13	2905	885	55100	3800
340 WM	–	200	3.70	94.0	–	MRP	91.0	5.90	3210	978	55100	3800
340 WM	–	210	3.70	94.0	–	MRP	91.0	5.90	3180	969	55100	3800
340 WM	–	250	3.70	94.0	–	MRP	85.2	5.52	2850	869	55100	3800
378 WM	–	270	3.70	94.0	–	MRP	115.5	7.48	3180	969	58785	4055
378 WM	–	300	3.70	94.0	–	MRP	111.8	7.20	2925	892	58785	4055

Handgun Powders

Caliber	Bullet index no.	Bullet weight grains	Max Cartridge length inch.	mm	Norma primer	Norma powder	Load grains	grams	Muzzle velocity Feet per sec.	Meter per sec.	Pressure[1] psi	bar
9 mm Luger	69010	116	1.16	29.5	SP	R-1	3.8	0.246	1115	340	36300	2500
38 Special	69110	148	1.16	29.5	SP	R-1	2.5	0.162	800	244	17000	1170
	69112	158	1.50	38.0	SP	R-1	3.5	0.227	870	265	20000	1380
	69107	158	1.48	37.5	SP	R-1	4.2	0.272	900	274	20000	1380
	69101	158	1.46	37.0	SP	R-1	4.2	0.272	900	274	20000	1380
357 Mag.	69101	158	1.59	40.5	SP	R-123	13.9	0.900	1450	442	40600	2800
	69107	158	1.59	40.5	SP	R-123	13.9	0.900	1450	442	40600	2800
38 S & W		146	1.16	29.5	SP	R-1	2.0	0.130	730	222	13800	950
44 Mag.	61103	240	1.61	41.0	LP	R-123	19.1	1.240	1675	511	40600	2800

Hornady Bullets

RIFLE BULLETS

17 CALIBER (.172)
		Retail
25 gr. HP	#1710	$ 5.90

22 CALIBER (.222)
40 gr. Jet	#2210	$ 5.00

22 CALIBER (.223)
45 gr. Hornet	#2220	$ 5.00

22 CALIBER (.224)
45 gr. Hornet	#2230	$ 5.00
50 gr. SPSX	#2240	$ 5.10
50 gr. SP	#2245	$ 5.10

■ 22 CALIBER MATCH
53 gr. HP	#2250	$ 6.00
55 gr. SPSX	#2260	$ 5.15
55 gr. SP	#2265	$ 5.15
55 gr. FMJ	#2267	$ 5.50
60 gr. SP	#2270	$ 5.50
60 gr. HP	#2275	$ 6.10

■ 22 CALIBER (.227)
70 gr. SP	#2280	$ 6.75

■ 6MM CALIBER (.243)
70 gr. SP	#2410	$ 6.55
75 gr. HP	#2420	$ 6.60
80 gr. FMJ	#2430	$ 7.15
87 gr. SP	#2440	$ 6.85
I 100 gr. SP	#2450	$ 7.15
100 gr. RN	#2455	$ 7.25

■ 25 CALIBER (.257)
60 gr. FP	#2510	$ 6.50
75 gr. HP	#2520	$ 6.80

		Retail
I 175 gr. RN	#2855	$ 9.00

■ 30 CALIBER (.308)
100 gr. SJ	#3005	$ 5.00
110 gr. SP	#3010	$ 7.25
110 gr. RN	#3015	$ 6.20
110 gr. FMJ	#3017	$ 6.20
130 gr. SP	#3020	$ 7.85
I 150 gr. SP	#3031	$ 8.00
I 150 gr. RN (30-30)	#3035	$ 8.00
150 gr. FMJ-BT	#3037	NEW $ 9.00
I 165 gr. SP	#3040	$ 8.35
I 165 gr. BTSP	#3045	$ 8.65

■ 30 CALIBER NEW NATIONAL MATCH
168 gr. BTHP	#3050	$10.15
I 170 gr. FP (30-30)	#3060	$ 8.35
I 180 gr. SP	#3070	$ 8.50
180 gr. RN	#3075	$ 8.50

■ 30 CALIBER MATCH
190 gr. BTHP	#3080	$11.00
I 220 gr. RN	#3090	$ 9.50
220 gr. RN-FMJ	#3097	$24.85

■ 303 CAL. and 7.7 JAP (.312)
150 gr. SP	#3120	$ 8.50
174 gr. RN	#3130	$ 8.85

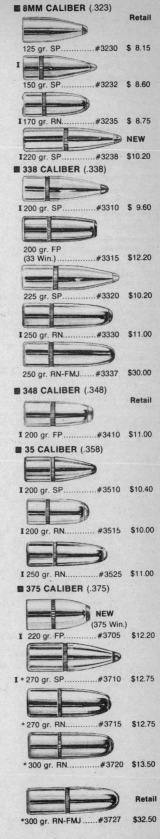

■ 32 SPECIAL (.321)
170 gr. FP	#3210	$ 8.50

		Retail
87 gr. SP	#2530	$ 7.00
100 gr. SP	#2540	$ 7.25
117 gr. RN	#2550	$ 7.70
120 gr. HP	#2560	$ 7.85

■ 6.5MM CALIBER (.264)
100 gr. SP	#2610	$ 7.70
129 gr. SP	#2620	$ 8.30
I 140 gr. SP	#2630	$ 8.50
140 gr. RN	#2635	$ 8.65
I 160 gr. RN	#2640	$ 9.20

■ 270 CALIBER (.277)
100 gr. SP	#2710	$ 7.50
110 gr. HP	#2720	$ 7.65
I 130 gr. SP	#2730	$ 8.10
I 150 gr. SP	#2740	$ 8.50
I 150 gr. RN	#2745	$ 8.50

■ 7MM CALIBER (.284)
120 gr. SP	#2810	$ 7.75
120 gr. HP	#2815	$ 7.80
I 139 gr. SP	#2820	$ 8.10
I 154 gr. SP	#2830	$ 8.65
I 154 gr. RN	#2835	$ 8.80

■ 7MM MATCH
162 gr. BTHP	#2840	$10.15
I 175 gr. SP	#2850	$ 8.95

■ 8MM CALIBER (.323)
		Retail
125 gr. SP	#3230	$ 8.15
I 150 gr. SP	#3232	$ 8.60
I 170 gr. RN	#3235	$ 8.75
I 220 gr. SP	#3238	NEW $10.20

■ 338 CALIBER (.338)
I 200 gr. SP	#3310	$ 9.60
200 gr. FP (33 Win.)	#3315	$12.20
225 gr. SP	#3320	$10.20
I 250 gr. RN	#3330	$11.00
250 gr. RN-FMJ	#3337	$30.00

■ 348 CALIBER (.348)
		Retail
I 200 gr. FP	#3410	$11.00

■ 35 CALIBER (.358)
I 200 gr. SP	#3510	$10.40
I 200 gr. RN	#3515	$10.00
I 250 gr. RN	#3525	$11.00

■ 375 CALIBER (.375)
I 220 gr. FP	#3705	NEW (375 Win.) $12.20
I * 270 gr. SP	#3710	$12.75
* 270 gr. RN	#3715	$12.75
* 300 gr. RN	#3720	$13.50
		Retail
*300 gr. RN-FMJ	#3727	$32.50

Hornady

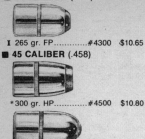

44 CALIBER (.430)

I 265 gr. FP............#4300 $10.65

45 CALIBER (.458)

* 300 gr. HP............#4500 $10.80

* 350 gr. RN............#4502 $18.00

* 500 gr. RN............#4504 $23.00

*500 gr. RN-FMJ......#4507 $40.00

*Packed 50 per box
ALL BULLETS PRICED PER 100
LEGEND

BBWC—Bevel Base Wadcutter	HP—Hollow Point
BT—Boat Tail	RN—Round Nose
DEWC—Double End Wadcutter	SJ—Short Jacket
FMJ—Full Metal Jacket	SP—Spire Point
FP—Flat Point	SWC—Semi-Wadcutter
HBWC—Hollow Base Wadcutter	SX—Super Explosive

"I" denotes Interlock bullets.

(All prices subject to change without notice.)

JACKETED PISTOL BULLETS

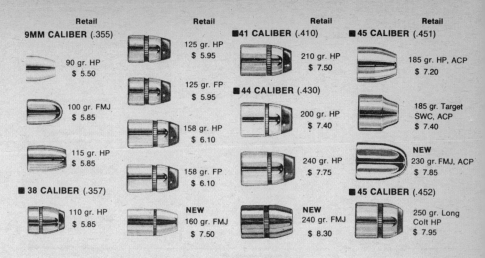

9MM CALIBER (.355)

90 gr. HP $ 5.50

100 gr. FMJ $ 5.85

115 gr. HP $ 5.85

38 CALIBER (.357)

110 gr. HP $ 5.85

41 CALIBER (.410)

210 gr. HP $ 7.50

44 CALIBER (.430)

200 gr. HP $ 7.40

240 gr. HP $ 7.75

NEW
160 gr. FMJ $ 7.50

NEW
240 gr. FMJ $ 8.30

45 CALIBER (.451)

185 gr. HP, ACP $ 7.20

185 gr. Target SWC, ACP $ 7.40

NEW
230 gr. FMJ, ACP $ 7.85

45 CALIBER (.452)

250 gr. Long Colt HP $ 7.95

LEAD PISTOL BULLETS

Boxed Price Per 100
Bulk Price Per 1000

Retail

38 cal. (.358)
148 gr. ....#3580 $ 4.60
BBWC ....*#3581   35.65

38 cal. (.358)
148 gr. ....#3582 $ 4.60
HBWC ....*#3583   35.65

NEW
38 cal. (.358)
148 gr. ....(Bulk only)
DEWC ....*#3585 $35.65

38 cal. (.358)   #3586 $ 4.80
158 gr. RN ......*#3587   38.20

38 cal. (.358)   #3588 $ 4.80
158 gr. SWC ....*#3589   38.20

44 cal. (.430)   #4430 $ 6.85
240 gr. SWC ....*#4431   56.00

45 cal. (.452)   #4526 $ 6.00
200 gr. SWC ....*#4527   51.72

*500 Per Box except 44, 400 Per Box

Hornady Crimp-on Gas Checks

Designed with open edges thicker than sidewalls. Size die crimp assures tight fit to the bullet. They're permanent.

Before sizing on bullets

After sizing on bullets

	Per 1000 Retail			Per 1000 Retail	
22 cal. ....#7010	$ 7.50	____	32 cal. (8mm) ....#7080	$ 7.50	____
6mm cal. ....#7020	$ 7.50	____	338 cal. ....#7090	$ 8.75	____
25 cal. ....#7030	$ 7.50	____	348 cal. ....#7100	$ 8.75	____
6.5mm cal. ....#7040	$ 7.50	____	35 cal. ....#7110	$ 7.50	____
270 cal. ....#7050	$ 7.50	____	375 cal. ....#7120	$ 8.75	____
7mm cal. ....#7060	$ 7.50	____	44 cal. ....#7130	$ 8.75	____
30 cal. ....#7070	$ 7.50	____	45 cal. ....#7140	$ 8.75	____

DOMESTIC PRIMERS

MAKE	PRIMER NUMBER	TYPE	DIA.	DESCRIPTION	CALIBERS			Per 1,000
For Small Pistol Cartridges								
Remington	1½	Small Pistol	.175"	Brass. Nickel-plated. For centerfire Pistol and Revolver cartridges.	25 Automatic	32 Colt New Police	38 Long Colt	$10.50
Peters	1½	Small Pistol	.175"		30 Luger Auto	357 Magnum	38 Colt New Police	
Winchester Western	1½-108	Small Pistol	.175"		32 Automatic	9mm Luger Automatic	38 Super-Auto Colt	$10.50
					32 S&W		38 Automatic	
					32 S&W Long	38 S&W	38 Automatic Colt	
CCI	500	Small Pistol	.175"		32 Short Colt	38 Special	380 Automatic	$10.40
CCI	550	Mag. Sm. Pistol	.175"	Brass. Nickel-plated. For centerfire Revolver cartridges.	32 S&W			$11.90
Winchester Western	1½M-108	Mag. Sm. Pistol	.175"		357 Magnum			$12.15
For Large Pistol Cartridges								
Remington	5½	Large Pistol	.210"	Brass. Nickel-plated. For centerfire Rifle, Pistol and Revolver cartridges, also Brass Shot Shells except .410 gauge.	38-40 Winchester	45 Auto Rim		$10.50
Remington	2½	Large Pistol	.210"		41 Magnum	45 Automatic		
Peters	2½	Large Pistol	.210"		44 S&W Special			
Winchester Western	7-111	Large Pistol	.210"		44 Magnum			$10.50
					44-40 Winchester			
CCI	300	Large Pistol	.210"		45 Colt			$10.40
CCI	350	Mag. Lg. Pistol	.210"					$11.90
Winchester Western	7M-111F	Mag. Lg. Pistol	.210"					$12.15
For Small Rifle Cartridges								
Remington	6½	Small Rifle	.175"	Brass. Nickel-plated. For centerfire Rifle and Revolver cartridges.	22 Remington "Jet" Magnum	256 Winchester Magnum		$10.50
Peters	6½	Small Rifle	.175"		218 Bee	30 Carbine		$10.50
Remington	6½-116	Small Rifle	.175"		22 Hornet	32-20 Winchester		$10.50
Winchester	6½-116	Small Rifle	.175"		25-20 Winchester			$10.40
CCI	400	Small Rifle	.175"					
CCI	BR-4	Small Rifle	.175"					$15.50
Remington	7½	Small Rifle	.175"	Brass. Copper plated. For centerfire Rifle and XP-100 Pistol cartridges.	221 Remington "Fireball"	222 Remington Mag.	17 Remington	$12.15
CCI	450	Mag. Sm. Rifle	.175"		222 Remington	223 Remington (5.56 mm)		$11.90
For Large Rifle Cartridges								
Remington	9½	Large Rifle	.210"		220 Swift	7mm Remington Magnum	32 Remington	$10.55
Peters	9½	Large Rifle	.210"		22-250 Remington	30-30 Winchester	32-40 Winchester	
Winchester Western	8½-120	Large Rifle	.210"		25-06 Remington	30 Remington	8mm Mauser	$10.50
CCI	200	Large Rifle	.210"		243 Winchester	30-06 Springfield	338 Winchester Magnum	$10.40
CCI	BR-2	Large Rifle	.210"		6mm Remington	30-40 Krag	348 Winchester	$15.50
CCI	250 Mag.	Large Rifle	.210"		225 Winchester	300 Winchester Magnum	35 Remington	$11.90
					25-35 Winchester	300 Savage	358 Winchester	
					250 Savage	300 H&H Magnum	375 H&H Magnum	
					257 Roberts	300 Savage	38-55 Winchester	
					264 Winchester Magnum	303 Savage	444 Marlin	
					270 Winchester	303 British	45-70 Government	
					280 Remington	308 Winchester	458 Winchester Magnum	
					284 Winchester	32 Winchester Special		
					7mm Mauser			
Remington	9½M	Large Rifle	.210"	Brass. Nickel-plated. For centerfire belted Magnum Rifle.	264 Winchester Magnum	350 Remington Magnum		$12.15
					6.5mm Remington Magnum	375 H&H Magnum		
					7mm Remington Magnum	8mm Remington Magnum		
CCI	250	Mag. Lg. Rifle	.210"		300 H&H Magnum	458 Winchester Magnum		$11.90

For Shotgun Shells (Battery Cup Type)

MAKE	No.	DESCRIPTION	Per 1,000	MAKE	No.	DESCRIPTION	Per 1,000
Remington	97 (209 Size)	Battery Cup. Used in Remington and Peters 12- and 20-gauge target loads and all 28-gauge loads with plastic base wad.	$18.80	Winchester Western	209	Battery Cup. Used in 10, 12, 16, 20, 28 and .410 gauge.	$18.80
Remington	57	Battery Cup. Used in all Remington and Peters 10-, 12-, 16-, 20- and 28-gauge shells (except 12 and 20 plastic target loads and all 28-gauge shells with plastic base wad.)	$18.80	CCI	109	Battery Cup. (Winchester Size).	$19.60
				CCI	157	Battery Cup. (Remington Size).	$19.60
Remington	97-4	Battery Cup. Used in 410 Gauge, 2½ and 3" plastic shotshells with solid plastic base wad.	$18.80	CCI	209	Trap and Skeet	$18.40

UNPRIMED CASES FOR RELOADERS

WINCHESTER CENTERFIRE RIFLE CARTRIDGE CASES
(Packed 20 per Box)

Cartridge Case Caliber & Symbol	Per 100
*218 Bee	
U218B Unprimed	$14.05
*22 Hornet	
U22H Unprimed	14.05
22-250 U22250 Unprimed	24.10
220 Swift	
U220S Unprimed	25.55
222 Remington	
U222R Unprimed	16.80
223 Remington	
U223R	19.80
225 Winchester	
U225 Unprimed	20.60
243 Winchester	
U243 Unprimed	24.10
6mm Rem.	
U6MMR	24.10
*25-20 Winchester	
U2520 Unprimed	16.30
*256 Winchester Magnum	
U256P	17.35
250 Savage	
U250 Unprimed	25.95
25-06 Remington	
U2506 Unprimed	25.40
257 Roberts	
U257 Unprimed	25.95
264 Winchester Magnum	
U264 Unprimed	31.60

Cartridge Case Caliber & Symbol	Per 100
270 Winchester	
U270 Unprimed	$25.40
284 Winchester	
U284 Unprimed	29.30
7 mm Mauser	
U7MM Unprimed	27.35
7 mm Remington Magnum	
U7 Mag. Unprimed	31.60
*30 Carbine	
UW30M1 Unprimed	14.60
30-30 Winchester	
U30C Unprimed	21.85
30-06 Springfield	
U3006 Unprimed	25.40
30-40 Krag	
U3040 Unprimed	27.35
300 Winchester Magnum	
U30WM Unprimed	31.60
300 H & H Magnum	
U300H Unprimed	34.80
300 Savage	
U300	25.95
303 British	
UW303B Unprimed	27.35

*Packed 50 to the box—all others 20 per box.

Cartridge Case Caliber & Symbol	Per 100
308 Winchester	
U308 Unprimed	$24.10
32 Winchester Special	
U32W Unprimed	23.50
*32-20 Winchester	
U3220 Unprimed	16.25
8 mm Mauser	
U8MM Unprimed	27.35
338 Winchester Magnum	
U338 Unprimed	31.60
348 Winchester	
U348 Unprimed	37.05
35 Remington	
U35R Unprimed	25.95
358 Winchester	
U358 Unprimed	26.45
375 H & H Magnum	
U375H Unprimed	37.20
*38-40 Winchester	
U3840 Unprimed	16.30
*44-40 Winchester	
U4440 Unprimed	16.30
*44 Remington Magnum	
U44M	14.90
45-70 Government	
U4570 Unprimed	23.40
458 Winchester Magnum	
U458 Unprimed	37.20
38-55 Winchester	30.75

WINCHESTER PISTOL & REVOLVER CARTRIDGE CASES
(Packed 50 per Box)

Cartridge Case Caliber & Symbol	Per 100
25 Automatic	
U25A Unprimed	$ 9.80
256 Winchester Magnum	
U256 Unprimed	17.35
32 Automatic	
U32A Unprimed	9.60
32 S & W	
U32SW Unprimed	8.55
32 S & W Long	
U32SWL Unprimed	
(32 Colt New Police)	8.55

Cartridge Case Caliber & Symbol	Per 100
357 Magnum (nickel-plated)	
U357 Unprimed	$11.00
U9 mm Luger	
Unprimed	14.05
38 S & W (38 Colt New Police)	
U38SW Unprimed	9.60
38 Special	
U38S Unprimed	9.95

Cartridge Case Caliber & Symbol	Per 100
38 Automatic (& 38 Super)	
U38A Unprimed	$11.55
380 Automatic	
U380A Unprimed	9.60
41 Remington Magnum	
U41M	14.50
44 S & W	
UW44S Unprimed	12.40
44 Magnum	
U44M Unprimed	14.90
45 Colt	
U45C Unprimed	14.90
45 Automatic	
U45A Unprimed	14.05

NORMA EMPTY UNPRIMED RIFLE CASES

Caliber	Box 20
220 Swift	$5.60
222 Remington	3.95
22 SAV High Power	5.85
243 Winchester	5.15
6.5 Jap	6.00
6.5 Norma (6.5x55)	6.00
6.5 Carcano	6.00
270 Winchester	5.45
7mm Mauser	5.45
7x57 R (Rimmed)	7.50
Super 7x61 Belted Magnum	7.20
7mm Rem. Mag.	7.35
7x64	7.90
7.5x55 (7.5 Swiss)	6.45

Caliber	Box 20
30 U.S. Carbine	$3.40
7.62 Russian	6.45
30-06 Springfield	5.45
22-250 Rem.	5.50
280 Rem.	5.90
30-30 WIN	5.30
308 Winchester	5.45
308 Norma Belted Magnum	7.90
7.65 Argentine Mauser	6.45
303 British	5.45
7.7mm Jap	6.45
8x57J (.318 dia.)	6.00
8mm Mauser (.323 dia.)	5.45

Caliber	Box 20
358 Norma Belted Magnum	$7.95
358 Winchester	4.01
9.3x57 Dual Core	7.95
9.3x62 Dual Core	7.95

NORMA EMPTY UNPRIMED PISTOL CASES

	Box 50
9mm Luger	$9.25
38 Special	6.50
357 Magnum	9.55
38 S & W	7.60
44 Magnum	10.10

FEDERAL UNPRIMED CASES

RIFLE—Unprimed

Code Number	Caliber	No. Per Box	Recommended Federal Primer Number for Handloads	Per Box
222 UP	222 Remington	20	200 or 205	$3.20
223 UP	223 Remington	20	200 or 205	3.95
22250 UP	22-250 Remington	20	210	4.60
243 UP	243 Winchester	20	210	4.60
2506 UP	25-06 Remington	20	210	4.85
270 UP	270 Winchester	20	210	4.85
7 UP	7mm Mauser	20	210	5.20
7R UP	7mm Rem. Magnum	20	215	6.05
30C UP	30 Carbine	20*	200	2.80
3030 UP	30-30 Winchester	20	210	4.15
3006 UP	30-06 Springfield	20	210	4.85
300W UP	300 Win. Magnum	20	215	6.05
308 UP	308 Winchester	20	210	4.60
8 UP	8mm Mauser	20	210	5.20
222M UP	222 Rem. Match†	20*	205M	3.90
308M UP	308 Win. Match†	20*	210M	5.30
647M UP	6x4 7mm Match†	20	205M	5.30

*Packed in partitioned carton, without plastic "Cartridge Carrier pack.
†Nickel-plated case.

PISTOL—Unprimed

Code Number	Caliber	No. Per Box	Recommended Federal Primer Number for Handloads	Per Box
380 UP	380 Auto Pistol	50	100	$4.60
9 UP	9mm Luger Auto Pistol	50	200	6.70
38 UP	38 Special	50	100*	4.75
357 UP	357 Magnum	50	200	5.25
44 UP	44 Rem. Magnum	50	150	7.10
45 UP	45 Automatic	50	150	6.70

Packed 50 per box, 20 boxes per case of 1000.
*For standard velocity loads only. No. 200 recommended for high velocity loads.

FEDERAL PRIMERS

Code Number	Type	Use	Nominal Diameter in Inches	Color Coding	Per 1000
100	Small Pistol	Standard velocity pistol and revolver loads.	.175	Green	$10.50
150	Large Pistol	Standard velocity and magnum pistol and revolver loads.	.210	Green	10.50
200	Small Rifle	Rifle; high velocity and magnum pistol and revolver loads.	.175	Red	10.50
205	Small Rifle	Thick cup design especially for 17 Rem. and 22 centerfire loads.	.175	Purple	10.50
210	Large Rifle	Standard rifle loads.	.210	Red	10.50
215	Large Magnum Rifle	Magnum rifle loads.	.210	Purple	12.15
205M	Small Rifle Match	Match version of No. 205.	.175	Purple	14.70
210M	Large Rifle Match	Match version of No. 210.	.210	Red	14.70
209	Shotshell	Standard and magnum loads in 12, 16 and 20 gauge.	.243		18.80
399	Shotshell	Alternate for 12- and 20-gauge target loads, especially Champion II hull.	.243		18.80
410	Shotshell	For .410 and 28-gauge loads.	.243		18.80

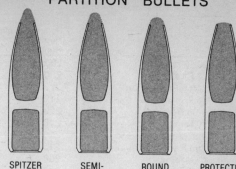

PARTITION™ BULLETS

| SPITZER | SEMI-SPITZER | ROUND NOSE | PROTECTED POINT |

While Nosler bullets resemble traditional bullet styles outwardly, the cutaway drawings illustrate some basic inside design features that put these bullets in a class of their own.

The Partition bullet, easily recognized by the lead core visible in the base end, is a unique concept in hunting bullet design. This lead core, held in position by the integral partition, retains more than half the bullet weight, providing controlled expansion and deeper penetration and game-stopping power on heavy game.

The Solid Base bullet, featuring a thick copper base, is a superbly accurate bullet for all types of shooting.

Both bullet styles are manufactured by a special impact-extrusion process which allows absolute control over wall thickness, weight distribution and concentricity for better radial and axial balance.

SOLID BASE BOAT TAIL BULLETS

| SPITZER BOAT TAIL | HOLLOW POINT |

CAL.	DIAMETER	BULLET WEIGHT AND STYLE	100 PER BOX
	.224	50 Gr. Spitzer	$5.65
	.224	50 Gr. Hollow-Point	5.70
	.224	50 Gr. Hollow-Point, Match	7.35
22	.224	52 Gr. Hollow-Point	6.75
	.224	52 Gr. Hollow-Point, Match	7.90
	.224	55 Gr. Spitzer	6.00
	.224	60 Gr. Spitzer	6.20
	.243	70 Gr. Hollow-Point	7.70
6MM	.243	70 Gr. Hollow-Point, Match	10.00
	.243	85 Gr. Spitzer	7.90
	.243	100 Gr. Spitzer	8.30
25	.257	100 Gr. Spitzer	8.45
	.257	120 Gr. Spitzer	9.00
6.5 mm	.264	120 Gr. Spitzer	9.30
270	.277	100 Gr. Spitzer	8.55
	.277	130 Gr. Spitzer	9.50
	.277	150 Gr. Spitzer	9.90
7MM	.284	120 Gr. Spitzer	9.00
	.284	140 Gr. Spitzer	9.55
	.284	150 Gr. Spitzer	9.85
	.308	150 Gr. Flat Point	9.65
	.308	150 Gr. Spitzer	9.65
	.308	150 Gr. Hollow-Point	9.65
	.308	150 Gr. Hollow-Point, Match	12.10
30	.308	165 Gr. Spitzer	9.95
	.308	168 Gr. Hollow-Point	10.80
	.308	168 Gr. Hollow-Point, Match	12.60
	.308	170 Gr. Flat Point	9.95
	.308	180 Gr. Spitzer	10.25

CAL.	DIAMETER	BULLET WEIGHT AND STYLE	50 PER BOX
6MM	.243	85 Gr. Semi-Spitzer	$9.05
	.243	95 Gr. Spitzer	9.15
	.243	100 Gr. Semi-Spitzer	9.30
25	.257	100 Gr. Spitzer	9.30
	.257	115 Gr. Spitzer	9.65
	.257	117 Gr. Semi-Spitzer	9.65
6.5MM	.264	125 Gr. Spitzer	9.95
	.264	140 Gr. Spitzer	10.35
270	.277	130 Gr. Spitzer	10.10
	.277	150 Gr. Spitzer	10.55
	.277	160 Gr. Semi-Spitzer	10.75
7MM	.284	140 Gr. Spitzer	10.35
	.284	150 Gr. Spitzer	10.55
	.284	160 Gr. Spitzer	10.80
	.284	175 Gr. Semi-Spitzer	11.10
30	.308	150 Gr. Spitzer	10.50
	.308	150 Gr. Protected Point	10.50
	.308	165 Gr. Spitzer	10.80
	.308	165 Gr. Protected Point	10.80
	.308	180 Gr. Spitzer	11.25
	.308	180 Gr. Protected Point	11.25
	.308	200 Gr. Round Nose	11.50
338	.338	210 Gr. Spitzer	14.50
	.338	250 Gr. Round Nose	15.45

Sierra Bullets

JACKETED RIFLE BULLETS

	RETAIL
.22 CALIBER .223 Diameter Hornet	
40 gr. Hornet	5.50
45 gr. Hornet	5.50
.22 CALIBER .224 Diameter Hornet	
40 gr. Hornet	5.50
45 gr. Hornet	5.50
.22 CALIBER .224 Diameter High Velocity	
45 gr. Semi-pointed	5.75
45 gr. Spitzer	5.75
50 gr. Semi-pointed	5.75
50 gr. Spitzer	5.75
50 gr. Blitz	5.75
55 gr. Semi-pointed	5.90
55 gr. Spitzer	5.90
63 gr. Semi-pointed	5.90
.22 CALIBER .224 Diameter Bench Rest	
53 gr. Hollow Point	7.05
52 gr. Hollow Point B.T.	7.20
6MM .243 Diameter	
60 gr. Hollow Point	7.15
70 gr. Hollow Point B.T.	7.95
75 gr. Hollow Point	7.55
85 gr. Spitzer	7.70
85 gr. Hollow Point B.T.	7.90
100 gr. Spitzer	8.15
100 gr. Semi-pointed	8.15
100 gr. Spitzer B.T.	8.45
.25 CALIBER .257 Diameter	
75 gr. Hollow Point	7.65
87 gr. Spitzer	7.95
90 gr. Hollow Point B.T.	8.05
100 gr. Spitzer	8.25
117 gr. Spitzer Boat Tail	8.90
117 gr. Spitzer Flat Base	8.85
120 gr. Hollow Point B.T.	8.90
6.5MM .264 Diameter	
85 gr. Hollow Point	7.95
100 gr. Hollow Point	8.45
120 gr. Spitzer	8.90
140 gr. Spitzer Boat Tail	9.50
140 gr. Matchking H.P.	10.25
.270 CALIBER .277 Diameter	RETAIL
90 gr. Hollow Point	8.45
110 gr. Spitzer	8.65
130 gr. Spitzer Boat Tail	9.55

	RETAIL
130 gr. Spitzer Flat Base	9.15
150 gr. Spitzer Boat Tail	10.00
150 gr. Round Nose	9.35
7MM .284 Diameter	
120 gr. Spitzer	8.70
140 gr. Spitzer	9.25
160 gr. Spitzer Boat Tail	10.15
168 gr. Matchking H.P.	10.80
175 gr. Spitzer Boat Tail	10.75
170 gr. Round Nose	9.90
.30 CALIBER .307 Diameter	
150 gr. Flat Nose 30-30	9.30
170 gr. Flat Nose 30-30	9.60
125 gr. Hollow Point Flat Nose 30-30	8.95
.30 CALIBER .308 Diameter	
110 gr. Rd. Nose Carbine	6.85
110 gr. Hollow Point	8.30
125 gr. Spitzer	8.85
150 gr. Spitzer	9.20
150 gr. Round Nose	9.20
165 gr. Hollow Point B.T.	10.00
165 gr. Spitzer Boat Tail	10.00
180 gr. Spitzer Flat Base	10.10
180 gr. Spitzer Boat Tail	10.30
200 gr. Spitzer Boat Tail	11.40
180 gr. Round Nose	9.80
220 gr. Round Nose	10.70
.30 CALIBER Competition	
168 gr. International H.P.	11.65
190 gr. Matchking H.P.	12.00
180 gr. Matchking H.P.	11.75
200 gr. Matchking H.P.	12.20
220 gr. Matchking H.P.	13.75

JACKETED RIFLE BULLETS

	RETAIL
.303 CALIBER .311 Diameter	
150 gr. Spitzer	9.70
180 gr. Spitzer	10.00
8MM .323 Diameter	
150 gr. Spitzer	9.80
175 gr. Spitzer	10.10

	RETAIL
220 gr. Spitzer B.T.	6.90*
.338 CALIBER	
250 gr. Spitzer Boat Tail	7.25
.35 CALIBER	
200 gr. Round Nose	5.50*
.375 CALIBER	
.375 Cal. 300 gr. Spitzer Boat Tail	9.25*
.45-70 CALIBER	
.45-70 Gov't 300 gr. Flat Nose	6.15*

JACKETED PISTOL BULLETS

.38 CALIBER .357 Diameter	
110 gr. Jacketed Hollow Cavity	6.65
125 gr. Jacketed Soft Point	6.85
125 gr. Jacketed Hollow Cavity	6.85
150 gr. Jacketed Hollow Cavity	6.95
158 gr. Jacketed Soft Point	6.95
170 gr. Silhouette F.M.J.	8.35
9MM .355 Diameter	RETAIL
90 gr. Jacketed Hollow Cavity	6.65
115 gr. Jacketed Hollow Cavity	6.85
.41 CALIBER .410 Diameter	
170 gr. Jacketed Hollow Cavity	8.60
210 gr. Jacketed Hollow Cavity	8.75
44 MAGNUM .4295 Diameter	
180 gr. Jacketed Hollow Cavity	8.65
240 gr. Jacketed Hollow Cavity	8.85
.45 CALIBER .4515 Diameter	
185 gr. ACP Jacketed Hollow Cavity	8.70
185 gr. Match	8.90
240 gr. Jacketed Hollow Cavity Long Colt	8.85

*Box of 50 Bullets

SPEER BULLETS

Jacketed Pistol Bullets
(Packed 100 Per Box)

9mm CALIBER (.355)

88 grain Hollow Point, #4000
No Photo Available $5.50

100 grain Hollow Point, #3983 5.50

125 grain Soft Point, #4005 6.25

38 CALIBER (.357)

110 grain Hollow Point, #4007 5.90

125 grain Hollow Point, #4013 6.00

125 grain Soft Point, #4011 6.00

140 grain Hollow Point, #4203 6.30

146 grain Hollow Point, #4205 6.00

158 grain JHP, #4211 6.10

158 grain Soft Point, #4217 6.10

160 grain Soft Point, #4223 6.10

41 CALIBER (.410)

200 grain Hollow Point, #4405 7.50

220 grain Soft Point, #4417 7.75

44 CALIBER (.429)

200 grain Magnum HP, #4425 7.40

225 grain Hollow Point, #4435 7.65

240 grain Soft Point, #4447 7.95

240 grain Magnum HP, #4453 $7.75

240 grain Magnum SP, #4457 7.75

45 CALIBER (.451)

200 grain HP, #4477 8.10

225 grain Magnum HP, #4479 8.15
260 grain Hollow Point, #4481 8.00

Lead Pistol Bullets
(Packed 100 Per Box)

9mm CALIBER (.356)

125 grain RN, #4601
#4602 4.55

38 CALIBER (.358)

148 grain BBWC, #4605
#4606 4.60

148 grain HBWC, #4617
#4618 4.60

158 grain Semi-Wadcutter, #4623
#4624 4.80

158 grain Round Nose, #4647
#4648 4.80

44 CALIBER (.430)

240 grain SWC, #4660
#4661 6.85

45 CALIBER (.452)

200 grain SWC, #4677
#4678 6.05

230 grain Round Nose, #4690
#4691 6.95

250 grain SWC, #4683
#4684 $7.35 *:

Rifle Bullets
(Packed 100 per box)

22 CALIBER (.223)

40 grain Spire Point #1005 5.05   45 grain Spitzer #1011 5.05

22 CALIBER (.224)

40 grain Spire Point #1017 5.05   45 grain Spitzer #1023 5.05

50 grain Spitzer, #1029 5.15

52 grain Hollow Point, #1035 6.00

52 grain GOLD MATCH, #1039 8.90

55 grain Full Metal Jacket, #1045 5.50

55 grain Spitzer, #1047 5.20

70 grain Semi-Spitzer, #1053 6.60

22 CALIBER (.228)

70 grain Semi-Spitzer, #1057 6.70

6mm CALIBER (.243)

75 grain Hollow Point, #1205 6.65

80 grain Spitzer, #1211 6.95

90 grain Full Metal Jacket, #1215 7.60

90 grain Spitzer, #1217 6.85

105 grain Round Nose, #1223 7.30

105 grain Spitzer, #1229 7.20

25 CALIBER (.257)

87 grain Spitzer, #1241 7.05

100 grain Hollow Point, #1407 7.55

Bullets priced per 100

100 grain Spitzer, #1405 $7.30

120 grain Spitzer, #1411 7.90

6.5mm CALIBER (.263)

120 grain Spitzer, #1435 8.05

140 grain Spitzer, #1441 8.55

270 CALIBER (.277)

100 grain Hollow Point, #1447 7.70

100 grain Spitzer, #1453 7.55

130 grain Spitzer, #1459 8.15

130 grain Grand Slam, #1465 *10.80

150 grain Spitzer, #1605 8.50

150 grain Grand Slam, #1608 *11.35

7mm CALIBER (.284)

115 grain Hollow Point, #1617 7.85

130 grain Spitzer, #1623 8.15

145 grain Spitzer, #1629 8.70

160 grain Spitzer, #1635 8.70

160 grain Grand Slam, #1638 *11.90

HOT-COR BULLETS

* Packed 50 per box
** Packed 500 per box

SPEER BULLETS

160 grain Magnum *MAG-TIP*, #1637 $10.30

175 grain Magnum *MAG-TIP*, #1641   10.80

175 grain Grand Slam, #1643   *12.20

30 CALIBER (.308)

100 grain PLINKER,® #1805   5.10

110 grain HP VARMINTER, #1835   5.90

110 grain Round Nose, #1845   6.20

110 grain Spire Point, #1855   7.30

130 grain Hollow Point, #2005   7.90

150 grain Flat Nose, #2011   8.10

150 grain Round Nose, #2017   8.10

150 grain Spitzer, #2023   8.10

---

150 grain Magnum *MAG-TIP*, #2025 $9.70

165 grain Round Nose, #2029   8.85

165 grain Spitzer, #2035   8.35

165 grain Grand Slam, #2038   *12.50

170 grain Flat Nose, #2041   8.35

180 grain Round Nose, #2047   8.55

180 grain Spitzer, #2053   8.50

180 grain Magnum *MAG-TIP*, #2059   10.95

180 grain Grand Slam, #2063   *12.80

200 grain Spitzer, #2211   *4.90

303 CALIBER (.311)

150 grain Spitzer, #2217   8.55

180 grain Round Nose, #2223   8.90

---

32 CALIBER (.321)

170 grain Flat Nose, #2259 $8.55

8mm CALIBER (.323)

150 grain Spitzer, #2277   8.65

170 grain Semi-Spitzer, #2283   8.80

338 CALIBER (.338)

200 grain Spitzer, #2405   *4.80

275 grain Semi-Spitzer, #2411   6.25

35 CALIBER (.358)

180 grain Flat Nose, #2435   9.85

250 grain Spitzer, #2453   *5.65

375 CALIBER (.375)

235 grain Semi-Spitzer, #2471   *5.55

45 CALIBER (.458)

400 grain Flat Nose, #2479   *6.85

HOT-COR BULLETS
* Packed 50 per box
** Packed 500 per box

BEAR RELOADING TOOLS

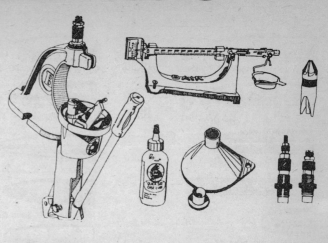

GRIZZLY BEAR

The Grizzly Bear "C" Press combines strength, quality and ease of operation for all reloading operations including bullet swaging. Precision alignment, hardened and ground pins, universal primer arm and ram that is designed to accept interchangeable shell holder heads assure you of the very most for your money. Standard ⅞ x 14 thread accepts Bear Cub and similar size die sets.

130-100 Grizzly Bear C Press with ram and primer arm $62.40
322-000 Primer catcher 3.75
130-110 Grizzly Bear C Press, removable shell holder head, primer arm and one set of precision dies. Everything to load one caliber...... 81.12
130-013 Universal C-Press Ram, for removable shell holder head 8.75
310-000 Removable shell holder head. 3.75

SPORTSMAN SPECIAL

A complete kit of matched precision tools and accessories. Obtain additional savings by purchasing the complete kit. Consists of: Grizzly Bear "C" Micro Measure, Magna Damp Scale, Primer Catcher, Case Lubricant, Shell Holder Head, Chamfer and Deburring Tool, Set of Bear Cub Dies.

130-200 Sportsman Special $181.15

BEAR CUB DIE SETS
(3 Die Pistol Set, 2 Die Rifle Set)

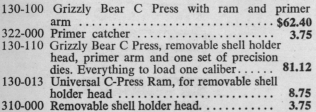

Bear Cub metallic cartridge reloading dies are made in over 80 popular rifle and pistol calibers. All Bear Cub dies are reamed and honed to minimum SAAMI standards, hardened by a special carbon nitrate process then polished to ultra smooth finish. Die bodies receive a special chrome plating to eliminate rust and corrosion, other parts are finished using Bear Company's special gun blue finish. All rifle caliber seating dies have adjustable crimper, pistol caliber seating dies have built in crimper. Every Bear Cub Set is packaged in a durable plastic storage box.

223-000 2 Die Rifle Set .... $$22.50
224-000 3 Die Rifle Set 35.62
　Includes Neck Sizes. Full Length Size and Seater Dies
210-000 Full Length Size Die Only .. 11.25
230-000 Neck Size Die Only 13.12
220-000 Seating Die Only 10.00
240-000 File Type Trim Die 11.90
256-000 3 Die Pistol Set 22.50
250-000 Pistol Size Die Only 8.75
260-000 Pistol Expander Die Only ... 8.75
270-000 Pistol Seating Die Only 8.75
210-101 Plastic Die Box
　　(for 2 or 3 Die Set) Only 1.25

HUNTER'S SPECIAL

Save money with this economical Kit of Bear essentials with everything needed for you to start reloading your favorite rifle or pistol ammunition. Included is the Black Bear "C" Press and primer arm, set of Bear Cub dies, magna Damp Powder Scale, Shell holder head, camfer and deburring tool, case lubricant, Speer reloading manual and powder funnel. **$122.40**

BEAR CAT II

The Bear Cat II is a simple and positive operation. Every case is full length resized, including head and rim.

"Plastic-Glas" crimp stations provide a fresh shell, crimped in original creases, locked and tapered to properly function in the tightest automatic, pump action, double or single barrel shotgun.

Floating crimp starter, self aligns with original crimp.

By making a simple adjustment and changing the final crimp die, 3" mag. shells can be loaded. **$77.50**

BEAR RELOADING TOOLS

HONEY BEAR

The Honey Bear is the addition to the Bear line of shotshell reloaders. The Honey Bear features compact large capacity hoppers with built in shut off, crimp-easy crimp die requiring 30% less crimping pressure, built in primer catcher, maximum leverage for ease of operation and precision alignment. Interchangeable charge bar bushings, die sets and powder and shot hoppers make changing gauges or loads quick and easy. Paper or plastic cases may be loaded without die change.

405-110 Honey Bear Loader Complete—
    For 12M, 12, 20M or 20 gauge **$125.00**
    For 16, 28, 410M or 410 gauge **131.25**

405-2 Conversion kit—12M, 12, 20M or 20 gauge. **37.50**
    16, 28, 410M or 410 gauge **43.75**

HONEY BEAR WITH AUTOMATIC PRIMER FEED

All New Automatic Priming System. Primer is transferred from tubular magazine to primer seating base automatically. No handling of primer or extra movements required. Includes 308-000 primer tube filler as standard equipment.

405-210 Honey Bear Reloader as described above with Automatic Primer Feed and primer tube filler. 12M, 12, 20M, or 20 gauge . **$141.25**
    16, 28, 410M or 410 gauge **147.50**

405-200 Kit to convert 405-110 to Automatic Primer Feed **24.38**

GLACIER BEAR

The Glacier Bear offers maintenance free precision, speed and ease of operation. "H" type construction, maximum leverage, built in primer catcher, large capacity hoppers and floating crimp starter die. Interchangeable die sets, which allow loading of all types of cases both paper and plastic, allow convenient conversion to other gauges. May be converted to load 3″ cases by changing only the crimp die. Up to 250 precision reloads per hour.

500-110 Glacier Bear Loader Complete—
    12M, 12, 20M, or 20 gauge **$174.88**
    16, 28, 410M or 410 gauge **181.13**

500-1 Conversion kit for
    12M, 12, 20M or 20 gauge **40.00**
    16, 28, 410M or 410 gauge **46.25**

BROWN BEAR III

The Brown Bear III "H" type press offers speed and convenience. Three station design allows loading of either pistol or rifle cartridges without die change. Special built in automatic priming system which includes both large and small tubes, feeds primers and operates primer arm without additional effort or attention of operator. Primer seating depth is completely adjustable. Exceptional leverage and strength allow for swift, easy performance of all reloading operations.

#160-100 Brown Bear III, with automatic primer feeding system **$174.88**
#160-110 Brown Bear III, with automatic primer feeding system, set of Bear Cub precision engineered dies and shell holders **$199.88**

POLAR BEAR

The Polar Bear features reloading at a popular price. Compare the features offered by the Polar Bear. Each pull of the lever produces a completed, factory like reload, up to 600 per hour. Built in provision for complete case resizing including head and rim. New "Crimp-easy" crimp die that requires 30% less effort for crimping. New swing away wad guide greatly speeds operation. Floating, self aligning crimp starter die. Positive cam actuated charge bar. Interchangeable charge bar bushings and die sets for all popular gauges except .410. Includes automatic primer feed and primer tube filler.

600-210 Polar Bear Loader Complete—
    For 12 or 20 gauge **$281.13**
    For 16 or 28 gauge **287.38**
600-2 Conversion kit for 12 or 20 gauge **61.13**
    For 16 or 28 gauge **67.38**
    Kits do not include brushings.

BLACK BEAR

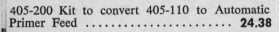

This Bear has found a home on many reloading benches across the country by introducing sportsmen to the economy and enjoyment of Metallic Shell Reloading.
Reduces shooting costs 60 per cent.
• Heavy annealed cast-iron frame. • Accepts standard dies—7 x 14 thread and interchangeable shell-holder heads. • Fully automatic primer feed optional.
Black Bear **$56.13**

BEAR RELOADING TOOLS

PISTOL POWDER MEASURE

The measure is fitted with a visible powder tube. Its cone shaped nozzle will accommodate all case sizes. Wing nut fastens the measure securely to bench mounted base plate. Detached easily for removing powder. Equipped with fixed charge rotor.

#315-000 Pistol Measure
(With rotor, state charge)

$22.38

#315-200 Extra Rotor (state powder drop desired)   **$5.00**

Bear Pistol Powder Measure Rotors are available in the following charges: Bullseye: 2, 2.5, 2.7, 3, 3.5, 4, 4.5, and 5 grain

Unique: 6, 8, and 10 grain   2400: 12, 14 and 16 grain.

Blank rotors are available for those who wish to make up rotors for other charges.

MICRO-MEASURE

BEAR'S micro-measure features micrometer adjusting screw to permit operator to record settings for future reference. A built-in baffle equalizes pressure of powder entering measuring housing. A wing-nut fastens measure securely to bench mounted base plate. Easily detachable for emptying powder. Allows fast, accurate measurement of all powder types up to 100 grains per charge. All parts are precision finished for lifetime accuracy. Equipped with two clear plastic drop tubes (.22 - .30 caliber and .30 - .45 caliber).

#316-000 Micro-Measure   **$43.63**

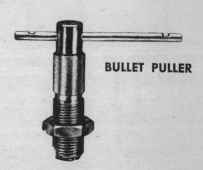

BULLET PULLER

MAGNA DAMP SCALE

The Bear Magna Damp Scale is designed to quickly bring under control unwanted oscillation of scale beam. Magnetic dampening cannot impair the accuracy of the scale. Precision ground and hardened knife bearings, 500 grain capacity, three counterpoise adjustment, tenth grain over and under scale, adjustable leveling screw and clearly marked anodized scale beam.

#317-100
Magna Damp Scale **$31.13**

Here is a chrome plated bullet puller to fit all basic tools. A new collet design maintains an even pressure on the bullet. It will not mar or scratch. The fast action of the collet promptly releases the bullet when tension is off. Puller comes equipped with standard ⅞ x 14 thread.
#320-000 Bullet Puller and Collet **$15.63**

BONANZA RELOADING TOOLS

CO-AX PRESS

MODEL 68 PRESS

CO-AX PRESS
Snap-in and snap-out die change, positive spent primer catcher, automatic self-acting shell holder, floating guide rods, perfect alignment of die and case is assured, good for right- or left-handed operators, uses standard ⅞ x 14 dies.

MODEL 68 PRESS
No obstructions to visibility of operator, open working space, upright mounting, equal thrust distribution, simple in construction, heavy duty, constructed of automotive-type casting, ram is machined and fitted.

BONANZA MODEL 68 PRESS $46.00
BONANZA CO-AX PRESS (B-1) less dies 89.95
EXTRA SET JAWS for Co-Ax .... set 12.00

PISTOL DIES

CO-AX RIFLE DIES

BONANZA PISTOL DIES are three-die sets. **The .38 Spl. & .357 Mag., and the .44 Spl. & .44 Mag. are so designed that each set may be used to load the two calibers.** You need not buy extra dies to load the magnums. The Bonanza Cross Bolt Lock Ring is standard on all Bonanza Dies. A special taper crimp die is available for .45 ACP and 38-357.
Bonanza Three-Die Pistol Set $19.50
Bonanza Taper Crimp Die 9.50
All Bonanza Dies are made with ⅞ x 14 threads and

can be used on various other makes of presses. The CO-AX SEATER can be adjusted to crimp or not to crimp. All calibers crimp except .22 caliber. The Sizer, with **elevated expander button,** is the same as is supplied with the Bench Rest Dies. This "E-Z" OUT expander button is drawn through the case neck while the operator uses the full mechanical advantage of the press.
Bonanza CO-AX Die Set $18.95
Bonanza CO-AX Seating Dies only 8.95
Bonanza CO-AX Sizing Die only 13.60
Bonanza Three-Die Rifle Set 19.50

BONANZA RELOADING TOOLS

CO-AX INDICATOR

CASE TRIMMER MODEL "66"

Gives a reading of how closely the axis of the bullet corresponds with the axis of the cartridge case. Spring-loaded plunger holds against cartridges **a recessed, adjustable rod** supported in a "V" block.

BONANZA CO-AX INDICATOR, less Indicator Dial $16.50

Indicator Dial only 23.50

Neck case pilot eliminates the need for a collet and shell holder. Reversible mandrell and four-blade case-mouth trimmer. Dull cutter is exchanged for a sharpened cutter.

BONANZA CASE TRIMMER, complete with Pilot (state caliber) $16.95
extra Pilots (state caliber) 1.00
extra Cutter 2.50
Cutter Sharpening "Exchange" 1.75

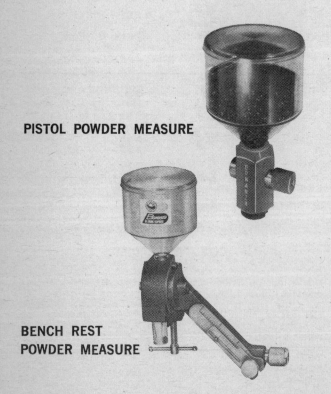

PISTOL POWDER MEASURE

BENCH REST POWDER MEASURE

BONANZA BULLS-EYE PISTOL POWDER MEASURE

Measure has fixed-charge rotor. Supplied with a quick detachable bracket for use on a bench, or it can be held by hand.
Bonanza Pistol Powder Measure and One Rotor .. $21.50
Extra Rotor or Blank Rotor 3.75

BONANZA BENCH REST POWDER MEASURE

Powder is metered from the charge arm.
Measure will throw uniform charges from 2½-grains bulls-eye to 95-grains 4320.
Measure empties by removing charge bar from charge arm, letting contents flow through charge arm into powder container.
BBRPM BONANZA BENCH REST POWDER MEASURE $31.00

BONANZA RELOADING TOOLS

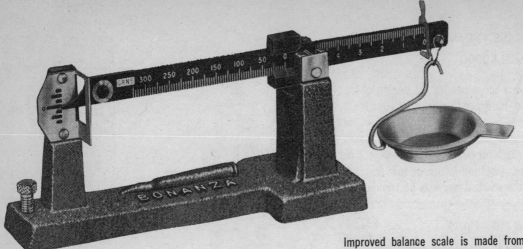

**BONANZA
POWDER
AND
BULLET
SCALE
MODEL "C"**

Improved balance scale is made from "Marlon-Lexon," an inert, non-magnetic material. Allows greater sensitivity, precision alignment and bearing, eliminates static electricity, accuracy guaranteed to 1/10 grain.
Bonanza Powder and Bullet Scale Model "C" **$22.50**

**BONANZA
"M" MAGNETIC
DAMPENED
SCALE**

505 grain capacity, tempered stainless steel right hand poise, diamond polished agate "V" bearings, non-glare white markings, three point suspension base, strengthened beam at pivot points, powder pan for right or left pouring, guaranteed accurate to 1/10 grain.

Bonanza "M" Magnetic Dampened Scale **$28.75**

BONANZA CO-AX PRIMER SEATER

The Bonanza Primer Seater is designed so that primers are seated Co-Axially (primer in line with primer pocket). Mechanical leverage allows primers to be seated fully without crushing. With the addition of one extra set of Disc Shell Holders and one extra Primer Unit, all modern cases, rim or rimless, from .222 up to .458 Magnum can be primed. Shell Holders are easily adjusted to any case by rotating to contact rim or cannelure of the case.

Bonanza Primer Seater **$26.50**
Primer Tube **2.10**

BONANZA RELOADING TOOLS

CO-AX CASE TRIMMER
Model 80000

The cutter shaft rides within a honed bearing for turning of the crank handle when trimming. Hardened and ground cutter teeth remove excess brass. Case to be trimmed is locked in a collet case holder, case is seated against the collet then locked, cases are trimmed to the same length regardless of rim thickness or head diameter. For accuracy of setting to proper trim length a collar stop is provided on the shaft. Cases may be trimmed to a tolerance of .001" or less.

Case Trimmer with one collet and one pilot	$23.00
Case Trimmer less collet and pilot	19.50
Case Trimmer Pilot 8009 (give caliber)	1.00
Case Trimmer Collet 0102-(No. 1, 2, or 3)	3.30
Case Trimmer Cutter Shaft 0107 (Standard)	6.00
Case Trimmer Cutter Shaft 0107 — .17 caliber	6.00
Case Trimmer Pilot for .17 caliber	1.00
(Above two items are accessories and not offered with a trimmer. Not interchangeable with standard shaft.)	
Short Base 0104-S	4.75
Long Base 0104-L	4.75

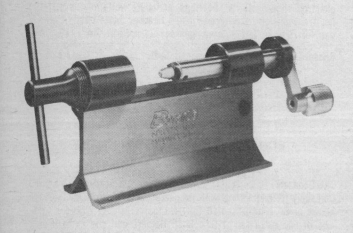

CO-AX BENCH REST
RIFLE DIES

BONANZA BENCH REST DIES are glass hard for long wear and minimum friction. Interiors are polished mirror smooth. Special attention is given to headspace, tapers and diameters so that brass will not be overworked when resized. Our sizing die has an elevated expander button which is drawn through the neck of the case at the moment of the greatest mechanical advantage of the press. Since most of the case neck is still in the die when expanding begins, better alignment of case and neck is obtained. **Our Bench Rest Seating Die** is of the chamber type. The bullet is held in alignment in a close fitting channel. The case is held in a tight fitting chamber. Both bullet and case are held in alignment all the while the bullet is being seated. These dies represent the first improvement in design since 1924. The set costs less than some are charging for a straight line seater alone. As a bonus you get our cross bolt lock ring.

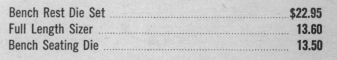

Bench Rest Die Set	$22.95
Full Length Sizer	13.60
Bench Seating Die	13.50

C-H RELOADING TOOLS

C-H RELOADING DIES

C-H reloading dies are available in all popular calibers. The outside has a non-glare satin finish. The outside threads are ⅞x14 and will fit all standard presses. C-H die lock rings feature a nylon ball lock inside the set screw to prevent damage to the threads and facilitate readjustment.

Standard Caliber Die Sets:

Series 'A' Full Length Sizer and Seater Die ..	$17.95
Series 'B' Sizer, Expander-Decapper and Seater Die	17.95
Series 'C' Sizer-Decapper, Expander and Seater Die	17.95
Series 'D' Neck Sizer and Seater Die	17.95
Series 'E' Full Length Sizer, Neck Sizer and Seater Die	23.50
Series 'F' Sizer, Expander-Decapper and Speed Seater Die	19.50
Series 'G' Carbide Sizer, Expander-Decapper and Seater Die	34.50
Series 'H' Carbide Sizer, Expander-Decapper and Speed Seater Die	35.50
Decapping Pin, Specify caliber (standard or heavy duty) pkg. of 5	1.00

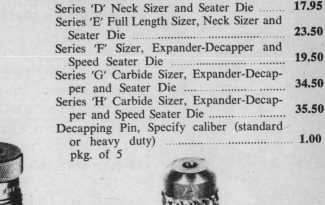

C-H TUNGSTEN CARBIDE EXPANDER BALLS

C-H TRIM DIES

By using these C-H Trim Dies you can shorten the neck of your cases with a file or a fine-tooth hacksaw. Dies are hardened and will not be effected by the filing. Available in the following calibers: 222 Rem., 22-250, 225 Win., 243 Win., 6mm R, 257 Robts., 25-06, 257 Wea., 6.5x55, 270 Win., 7x57 Mauser, 7mm Rem. Mag., 7mm Wea., 308 Win., 30-06, 300 Win. Mag., 300 Wea., 8x57.
File Trim Die **$9.00**

Now available as an accessory, the C-H Tungsten Carbide Expander Ball eliminates the need for lubricating the inside of the case neck.
Available in the following calibers: 22, 243, 25, 270, 7mm, 30, 320, 322. Calibers 7mm and larger have 10-32 inside threads, 243 to 270 have 8-32 inside threads and 22 has 6-32 inside threads. (270 will not fit RCBS)
C-H Carbide Expander Ball . . **$5.50**
For the RCBS 22 expander unit we can provide a complete rod with carbide expander that will fit their die body.
C-H Carbide Expander Ball to fit 22 cal. RCBS die **$6.50**

C-H CHAMPION PRESS

Compound leverage press for all phases of re-loading. Heavyweight (26#) C-Hampion comes complete with primer arm, ⅞x14 bushing for use with all reloading dies. Spent primers fall through back of press into waste basket. 'O' frame design will not spring under any conditions. Ideal press for swaging bullets. Top of frame bored 1¼x18 for use with special dies and shot-shell dies.
$99.50

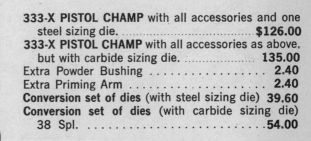

PISTOL CHAMP

333-X PISTOL CHAMP with all accessories and one steel sizing die. **$126.00**
333-X PISTOL CHAMP with all accessories as above, but with carbide sizing die. 135.00
Extra Powder Bushing 2.40
Extra Priming Arm 2.40
Conversion set of dies (with steel sizing die) 39.60
Conversion set of dies (with carbide sizing die) 38 Spl. 54.00

Conversion kit includes priming post, sizing die, powder bushing, expander die, speed seater die, and 3 shell holders.

C-H RELOADING TOOLS

CHAMPION Jr. RELOADING PRESS

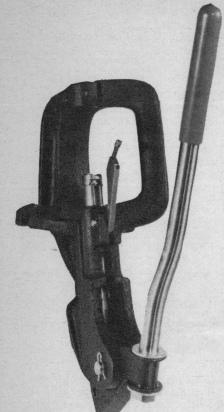

CHAMPION Jr. Heavy Duty Reloading Press—semi steel (cast iron) "O" press offset so the opening is 210 degrees for better access. Solid steel handle is offset to match opening.

Positioning of toggle pin provides maximum leverage—so powerful that a 30/06 case can be forced into a 250 full length resizing die. In addition to usual 2 bolt fastening we put a 3rd bolt so the "big" jobs using maximum power won't break off your bench.

Weight 13½ lbs.

Uses standard detachable shell holders.

Price complete w/primer arm and 1 shell holder $52.50

Price complete with 1 die set $68.50

BULLET SWAGING DIE EJECTOR

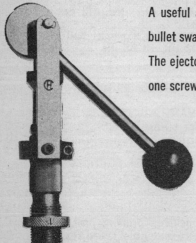

A useful accessory for use with the new C-H jacketed bullet swaging dies.

The ejector attaches easily to the swaging die body with one screw. Can be used with either the core seating die or the swage die. Ejects the seated core or finished bullet with ease. No more tapping the top of the die.

Price $14.95

C-H DIE BOX

Protect your dies from dust and damage with a C-H 3-compartment plastic Die Box. High-impact plastic—will not break. Easy to label and stack.
No. 700 C-H Die Box ...... .75¢

FROM C-H 3/4 JACKETED PISTOL BULLET SWAGING DIES

- Any bullet weight from 110 gr. to 250 gr. with same set of dies
- Can be used in any good ⅞ x 14 loading tool
- Absolutely no leading
- Complete — no extras to buy
- Increased velocity
- Solid Nose or hollow point (hollow point $2.50 extra)
- Available in 38/357, 41 S & W 44 Mag. and 45 colt calibers

PRICE
$29.95

FROM C-H NEW SOLID STEEL CANNELURE TOOL

PRICE
$21.95

- Will work on all sizes of bullets, from 17 to 45
- Completely adjustable for depth and height
- One set will process thousands of bullets
- Necessary for rolling in grooves on bullets prior to crimping
- Hardened cutting wheel, precision machined throughout.

C-H RELOADING TOOLS

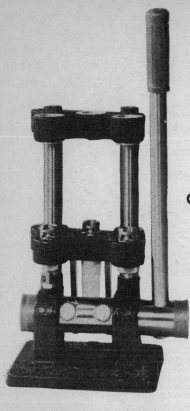

**NO. 333
C-H UNIVERSAL
3 STATION
"H" PRESS**

The C-H Universal is a unique H press because it has 3 stations, instead of the usual two. When reloading for pistol using a 3-die set it is possible to mount all three dies simultaneously easily, in this tool. When reloading for rifle, with conventional two-die rifle set, it is possible to mount the C-H powder measure in the third (open) station.

This is a heavy duty production press designed for speedy, easy reloading. The manufacturer claims that it is possible with this tool to full length size three cartridge cases simultaneously.

All components are precision made from heavy duty tool steel. Except for the bearing surfaces, exterior finish is black crinkle.

The main drive bar—to which is connected the operating lever—is equipped with two power levers which activate the moving shell holder base. More than adequate leverage and power is provided by this system.

No. 333 PRESS—Complete for one caliber (rifle).

No. 333 Press w/3 Rams and 3 shell holders and one Primer Arm	$79.50
No. 408 Shell Holder Head (3 @ 3.00)	9.00
No. 407 Shell Holder Ram (3 @ 3.00)	9.00
No. 333 Primer Arm, large or small	2.40
No. 333 Press complete for one caliber (pistol)	93.50

ACCESSORIES FOR C-H UNIVERSAL 3-STATION "H" PRESS

No. 402 C-H Bullet Puller complete w/one collet	$5.95

**NO. 204
C-H CAST IRON
"C" PRESS**
Up and Down Stroke

**FITS ALL STANDARD
AND UNIVERSAL SHELL
HOLDERS, SHELL HOLDER
RAMS AND PRIMING ARMS**

Press, with handle, toggle, Universal shell holder ram, one shell holder, Universal priming arm and full sized bottle of C-H lube $49.95
Complete with one set of dies (⅞"x14) 65.95

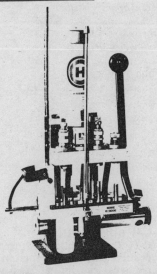

**AUTO-
CHAMPION MARK III**

PRESENTLY AVAILABLE FOR 38 SPECIAL, 357 & 45 ACP

**PRICE COMPLETE
$579.50**

• Truly progressive Loading • Complete! No extras to buy • One completed round with each pull of the handle. Our timed tests show we can load a box of 50 in less than 3 minutes • Case feeder and Automatic Positive Indexing at no extra cost • Uses Standard ⅞" sizing and seating Dies (Bell-Expanding Die altered to allow powder to drop) • Tungsten Carbide Sizing die at no extra cost! • Interchangeable powder bushings • Automatic indexing makes double powder charge impossible • Seating stems for any type of bullet • Exclusive "Speed Seater" die included. • Conversion kit to switch from 38/357 to 45 ACP ...**$99.00**

C-H RELOADING ACCESSORIES

NO. 725 POWDER and BULLET SCALE

Chrome plated, brass beam. Graduated in 10 gr., 1 gr. and 1/10th gr. increments. Convenient pouring spout on pan. Leveling screw on base. All metal construction. 360 gr. capacity. **Price** **$19.95**

C-H POWDER MEASURE

The new steel drum is designed so the handle can be placed on either the right or left side, and the charge can be dropped on either the up or down stroke. Or reverse for use with micrometer either front or back. Base threads are ⅞ x 14. The rifle micrometer adjusts precisely and permits up to 100 grains of 4831. The Pistol micrometer permits up to 12 grains of Bullseye.

A baffle plate is supplied with the optional 10″ production hopper.

No. 502 Powder Measure *Specify Rifle or Pistol* **$28.50**
No. 502-1 Stand ⅞″ *thread* **4.50**
No. 502-2 Micrometer *Specify Rifle or Pistol* **8.50**
No. 592-3 10″ Production Hopper (*with baffle*) **4.95**

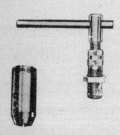

C-H BULLET PULLER

C-H Bullet Puller features positive die-locking action, removes the bullet easily without any damage to housing or bullet. The detachable handle is constructed of ⅜″ stock and adjusts to any position. The hex nut for crescent wrench adjustment locks the die into firm position. Extra long internal thread for extra locking leeway.

No. 402 with Collet . **$8.50**
No. 402-1 Extra Collet **2.50**

C-H CARTRIDGE RACK TRAY

Holds 60 cartridges. Comes in black, white or red. It is handy for the reloader who works up cases for different loads, etc. Holes are 15/16″ deep which is too deep for 38 Spl. Holes are not large enough for 45/70 or 348 but hold all sizes up to 375 H&H.
No. 403 Cartridge Rack Tray **$1.20**

C-H CASE TRIMMER
No. 301

This design features a unique clamp to lock case holder in position. Ensures perfect uniformity from 22 cal. thru 45 cal. whether rifle or pistol cases. Complete including hardened case holder . . . **$17.95**
Extra case holders (hardened & hand-lapped) . . . **$2.50**

C-H UNIVERSAL PRIMING ARMS

Accommodates all standard rifle and pistol primers. Made of fine metal—not a stamping, for extra strength and dimensional stability. Packaged in clear acetate tube.

No. 414 C-H Universal "C" Priming Arm . . **$4.25**

C-H UNIVERSAL SHELL HOLDERS

Up to now, shell holders came in one piece and you had to have as many shell holders as the calibers you wished to reload. However, with the C-H Universal Shell Holder all the reloader needs is the Shell Holder ram and then get the heads for the calibers desired.

No. 408 C-H Universal "C" or "H" Shell Holder Head **$3.00**
No. 407 C-H Universal "H" Shell Holder Ram **4.25**
No. 412 C-H Universal "C" Shell Holder Ram **4.95**

LYMAN RELOADING TOOLS

FOR RIFLE OR PISTOL CARTRIDGES

The 310 Tool is a compact, portable reloading kit that can be used anywhere—home, hunting camp, in the field, on the range. Using the 310 Tool, the novice can start reloading with a small investment. The 310 Tool performs all the operations required for reloading metallic cartridges for handguns and rifles. It removes the old primer, resizes the cartridge neck, it inserts a new primer, and seats the new bullet. A practiced reloader can load, fire, adjust and reload his charge right on the range, test firing until he determines his best load.

310 Tool Complete with one set of dies **$35.00**
310 Tool Handles Only (large or small) **16.00**

310 Dies (rifle or handgun)—Set consists of five pieces: Neck Resizing and Decapping Die, Priming Chamber, Neck Expanding Chamber, Bullet Seating Chamber and an Adapter Die **$19.00**

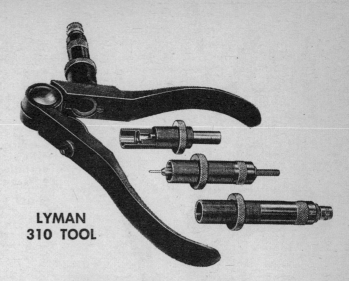

LYMAN 310 TOOL

LYMAN ALL-AMERICAN TURRET PRESS

The All-American Turret Press (uses standard 7/8" x 14 dies or Lyman Ideal Dies with 7/8" x 14 adapter) makes it possible to completely reload any cartridge without removing it from the shell holder. The four-station turret mounts three dies and a powder measure in reloading operation sequence. As the turret is revolved, dies remain in place, and positioned directly over the shell holder with a positive-locking, audible-click action at each of the four turret stations. The Lyman 55 Powder Measure and the push-button primer feed are optional. The press can be used in either up or down-stroke (left or right-hand) operation.

All-American Turret Press only **$129.95**
Push-Button Primer Feed (rifle & pistol only) **24.95**
Shell Holder (J-type) **5.00**
Priming Punch (T-type) **4.50**
Shell Holder Adapter (use w/spec. T.) **3.50**
"Special" Priming Punch **4.50**

The second edition of the Lyman Shotshell Handbook features an authoritative study devoted exclusively to shotshell reloading—a reloading handbook which covers every aspect of modern shotshell reloading. Dealing with the latest components it is an indispensable reference book which belongs on every reloading bench. Complete "How To Reload" section on choosing a load, factory velocities, assembling shotshells, etc. Reference section covers up-to-date pressure information, four color case identification chapter, plus chapters on wads, patterns, powder and primers. Over 1000 tested loads covering all gauges 10, 12, 16, 20, 28 and 410. Contains suggested reloads using modern components from all of the major manufacturers **$7.95**

LYMAN RELOADING TOOLS
FOR RIFLE OR PISTOL CARTRIDGES

LYMAN SPAR-T TURRET PRESS

The Lyman Spar-T Press combines the maximum speed of turret loading with the operating ease, and strength of the ever popular C Frame Press. It's massive frame, and 6 station Turret, are ruggedly constructed of high-silicone, iron-steel castings (not aluminum alloy). It's Verti-Lock Turret is firmly secured to the frame by a heavy duty ¾" steel stud. Positive stop, audible click action insures foolproof cartridge to die alignment and rapid operation. Uses standard ⅞ x 14 dies.

Features : ● Lock nut rigidly locks turret in one position for swaging. ● Powerful toggle-link leverage (25 to 1) ● UP or DOWN STROKE operation. ● Alignment ramp positions Shell Holder at top of stroke. ● Uses standard Spartan accessories.

Spar-T Press with ram and primer arm **$67.95**

SPAR-T SET: Consists of Spar-T Press, Spar-T Auto-Primer Feed, Spartan Primer Arm, Spartan Ram, Spartan Shell Holder Head, Complete set of All-American Dies. **$82.95**

SPARTAN SET: Consists of Spartan Press, Spartan Ram, Spartan Shell Holder Head, Spartan Primer Arm, Complete set of All American Dies (standard ⅞" by 14). Spartan Primer Catcher. **$59.95**

SPARTAN SPAR–T ACCESSORIES

PRIMER CATCHER: Made of heavy-duty plastic, this unit may be used on either the Spartan or Spart-T Press. Locks securely to press, yet allows for easy removal when emptying primers. **$4.00**

RAM: Designed for perfect alignment. Fits Lyman Spartan press. Pacific Standard, RCBS, Jr., C & H Super C. **$5.00**

DETACHABLE SHELL HOLDER: Precision cut and hardened to ensure perfect case fit. Used with the Spartan Ram on the Spartan Press and on many other presses. **$3.50**

UNIVERSAL PRIMING ARM: Seats all sizes and types of primers. Supplied with two priming sleeves (large and small) two flat priming punches (large and small), and two round priming punches (large and small). **$4.95**

AUTO-PRIMER FEED: Eliminates handling of primer with oily fingers, speeds loading. Supplied with two tubes (large and small) Spartan and O-Mag.
$9.95
Spar-t **9.95**

LYMAN SPARTAN RELOADING PRESS

The Lyman Spartan Press is a massive, 11 lb. heavy-duty iron frame press which reloads all rifle and pistol cases quickly, accurately and easily. Its powerful toggle-link mechanism multiplies the force applied to the handle 25 times and takes the hard work out of full-length resizing and case forming, and is even rugged enough for bullet swaging.
● Uses Lyman All-American (standard ⅞" x 14) dies ● Simple changeover to either up- or down-stroke ● Alignment ramp positions shell holder at top of each stroke ● Precision bored frame ensures perfect alignment ● Maximum serviceability at extremely low cost.
Spartan Press With ram and priming arm. **$46.95**

LYMAN SHOTSHELL PRESS

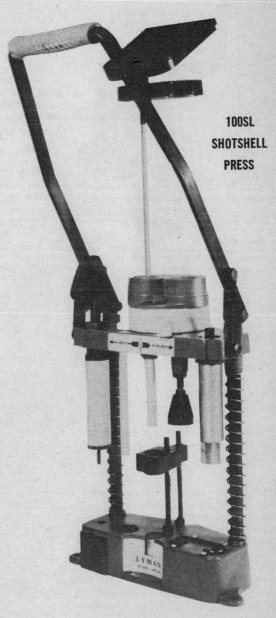

The cost of shotgun shells, like other costs, has been rapidly rising over the last several years. When a box of shells that you could once buy for $1.25, costs as much as $3.75, most shotgun enthusiasts can't afford to shoot as much as they would like to. The hunter who fires a shell, ejects it, and leaves the empty case behind in the field is throwing away half the cost of each round. This cost can be turned into an investment by reloading. The basic steps in shotshell reloading, decapping, priming, loading the powder, wad and shot, are steps to real shooting economy.

ROLL CRIMPER HEAD ... with drill press adapter. For roll crimping shotshells. This head also works on rifled slugs; mounts in any drill press. Specify 12 or 20 gauge.   **$10.00**

• Full length sizing, hi or low brass, 2¾ or 3" shell smooth cam ejection of all sizes without adjustment. • Auto Primer Feed—the Primer is automatically placed each complete cycle of the press. • Floating wad guide automatically positions itself on the case mouth during wad insertion. • Clear view wad pressure indicator clearly indicates wad pressure at a glance.
• Floating crimp starter aligns itself on case mouth folds and applies the exact amount of fold required for a uniformly tight crimp. • Crimping die applies a uniformly tight crimp to each shell assuring durability in the field and smooth functioning through the gun action. • Quick-dump reservoirs are emptied by activating a dump valve. The 100SL
Available in either 12 or 20 gauge $94.50
Conversion kits:
12 to 20 gauge 20.00
20 to 12 gauge 20.00

100SL SHOTSHELL PRESS

LYMAN BULLET SIZING EQUIPMENT

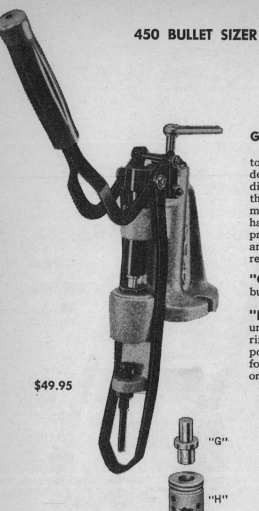

450 BULLET SIZER

$49.95

The 450 Bullet Sizer and Lubricator sizes the bullet to the correct diameter, forces lubricant under pressure into the bullet grooves, and will seat gas checks, if required—all in one rapid, accurate operation. Adaptable to all bullets by changing "G" and bullet sizing assembly "H & I". Use with Ideal Bullet Lubricant..... **$49.95**

G, H & I DIES "WITH SWAGING ACTION":

Cast bullets as much as ten thousandths oversize can be easily formed to size by the use of these dies. Lyman bullet sizing dies have been newly designed to supply a swaging rather than shearing action in reducing bullet diameters. The mouth of the "H" die contains a gentle taper which allows the gas check and bullet to start into the die easily. This tapering of the mouth combined with the exact tolerance and ultra-smoothness of the hardened inner chamber, completely eliminates shearing of lead and produces a perfectly cylindrical bullet. As this swaging action compresses and work hardens the alloy, a tougher, smoother, and more accurate bullet results.

"G" TOP PUNCH: Top Punches are designed to fit the contour of the bullet point. **$2.75**

"H & I" SIZING DIE ASSEMBLY: H & I Dies should be supplied as one unit. Their diameter should correspond to the groove diameter of your rifle, or pistol. The listing below shows the basic groove diameter for many popular calibers. A complete listing of all available sizes is also shown for the shooter who wishes to experiment with different bullet diameters or for those who have rifles with worn or non-standard bores **$7.95**

"G"

"H"

"I"

BASIC GROOVE DIAMETER FOR RIFLES

Caliber	Groove Dia.	Caliber	Groove Dia.
All 22 cal. (except 22 Hi-power)	.224	338 Win. & 33 Win.	.338
.22 Hi-Power	.226	348 Win.	.348
.243, .244, 6 M/M	.243	35 Win. S. L. & 351 S. L.	.352
.256 Win. & All 25 cals.	.257	9 x 56 M/M & 9 x 57 M/M	.354
.264 Win., 6.5 M/M	.264	35 cal.	.358
.270 Win.	.277	375 H & H Mag.	.375
7 M/M, .280 Rem., .284 Win.	.284	38/55	.379
7.35 Carcano	.299	38/40	.400
30 cals.	.308	401 S.L.	.406
7.62 Russian	.310	405 Win.	.412
32/20 Win.	.311	44/40 Win. Rifles	.428
7.65 Mauser	.311	44/40 Rem. Rifles	.425
.303 British, 7.7 M/M Jap.	.313	444 Marlin	.430
8 M/M Mauser (J.Bore)	.318	11 Mauser	.439
8 M/M Mauser (S Bore)	.323	45/70 & 458 Win.	.457
32 Win. Spec. 32 S. L. & 32 Rem.	.321		

BASIC GROOVE DIAMETER FOR PISTOLS

Caliber	Groove Dia.	Caliber	Groove Dia.
22 Jet	.222	38/40	.400
30 Mauser	.309	41 Colt	.406
30 Luger	.310	41 S & W Mag.	.410
32 Auto	.311	44/40 (revolver)	.425
32/20	.312	44 S & W Spec. & 44 Russian	.429
32 S&W & 32 Colt N.P.	.314	44 Mag. (S & W & Ruger)	.430
9 M/M Luger	.354	45 A.C.P.	.450
38 Special & 357 Mag. (Colt), 38 A.C.P. & 380 Auto	.355	45 Auto Rim	.451
38 Special & 357 Mag. (S & W)	.357	45 Colt (post-war)	.451
38 S&W	.360	45 Colt (pre-war)	.454
		.455 Webley	.457

COMPLETE LIST OF H & I DIAMETERS

.222	.223	.224	.225	.228	.243	.244	.245	.257	.258	.259	.263	.264
.266	.277	.278	.280	.284	.285	.287	.299	.301	.308	.309	.310	.311
.312	.313	.314	.315	.316	.318	.319	.320	.321	.322	.323	.325	.338
.340	.348	.350	.352	.354	.355	.356	.357	.358	.359	.360	.366	.375
.377	.378	.379	.380	.386	.400	.401	.403	.406	.410	.412	.414	.419
.424	.425	.427	.428	.429	.430	.431	.434	.439	.446	.450	.451	.452
.454	.456	.457	.459	.509	.512	.515	.580 (lub. only)					

IDEAL BULLET LUBRICANT . . . Special grease developed especially for use as a cast bullet lubricant. One stick lubricates 2500 small of 500 large bullets.

Ideal Bullet Lubricant **$1.95**

Highest Quality Graphite Lubricant **$2.45**

LYMAN RELOADING ACCESSORIES

PRIMER POCKET REAMER

Cleans and removes rough metal edges from a primer pocket. This tool is a must for military type primers. Available in large or small—see priming punch size in cartridge table.

Price $5.00

POWDER FUNNEL

This plastic powder funnel is designed to fill cases from 22 Hornet through 45-70 without inserts or adjustments.

Price: $1.50

Powder Dribbler $5.45

THE NO. 55 POWDER MEASURE

This Powder Measure and dispensing device charges any number of cases with black, or smokeless, powder loads that are consistent within a fraction of a grain. Its three-slide micrometer adjustable cavity adjusts the load accurately, and locks in place to provide accurate charging. The 2400 grain capacity plastic reservoir gives a clear view of the powder level. The reservoir is fabricated from blue-tinted polyvinylchloride plastic that resists chemical action of double base powders, and filters out light rays that would damage powders. An optional 7000 grain reservoir is available. The measure clamps securely to the loading bench, or mounts directly to any turret press by means of threaded drop tubes (supplied with measure). A knocker mounted on the side of the measure insures complete discharge of powder directly into the cartridge case. No funnel is required.

No. 55 POWDER MEASURE $36.95
Optional 7000 grain capacity reservoir .. 6.00
⅞" x 14 Adapter for Turret Mounting 1.50

The unique three-slide micrometer adjustable cavity is the key to the unfailing accuracy of the 55 Powder Measure. Micrometer adjustments for both width and depth provide a dependable, consistent measure that minimizes cutting of coarse powder.

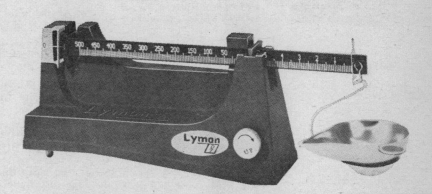

LYMAN D-7 SCALE

Dial markings are white on jet black for easy reading. The pointer, and dial, are placed on the same plane to eliminate parallax error. Its high capacity of up to 505 grains, permits the heaviest charges and even bullets to be weighed. Features magnetic damping. Genuine agate bearings guarantee one tenth of a grain of sensitivity. **Lyman D-7 Scale** $32.95

LYMAN RELOADING DIES

The All-American Dies shown on this page are designed for use with the Lyman Spartan, Spar-T, AA Turret, and all other reloading presses having 7/8" x 14" thread die stations. AA die sets are offered in either 2 or 3 die combinations, depending on shape of cartridge case, and type of bullet to be loaded.

Outer surfaces of all dies are chrome-plated. All bullet seating dies are adjustable to crimp or not crimp the bullet. Sizing dies for bottleneck cartridges are vented to prevent air traps.

TWO-DIE RIFLE SET

These sets consist of two dies. The first die full-length resizes, decaps, and expands, while the second die seats the bullet and crimps when desired. Two die sets are specifically designed for loading bottleneck shape cartridge cases using jacketed bullets. These sets are not offered for straight-taper shape cases. They should not be used with cast bullets unless in conjunction with an "M" die (see below).

Two-die rifle set (complete with wrench) $19.45

THREE-DIE RIFLE SET

Required to load straight-taper cartridge cases, and all other cartridges when using cast bullets.

This set consists of: full-length resizing and decapping die, a 2-step neck expanding die, and a bullet seating and crimping die. The added advantage of the three-die set is in the use of the 2-step neck expanding die which allows the bullet to enter the case freely, without cutting or marring lead. This method of neck-expanding insures precise case neck tension on seated bullet.

Standard Three-die rifle set
(complete with wrench) $19.45

THREE-DIE PISTOL SET

Available for pistol calibers 38 S & W, 38ACP, 38 Super, 38 Special, 357 Magnum, 41 Magnum, 44 Special, 44 Magnum, 45 ACP, 45 Colt. Set consists of a Lyman T-C (Tungsten Carbide) Full-Length Resizing and Decapping Die, plus a 2-Step Neck Expanding Die and a Bullet Seating and Crimping Die.

Deluxe Three-Die Pistol Set (complete with wrench) . . **$37.95**

THREE-DIE PISTOL SETS

Available for all pistol calibers this set can be used with either cast of jacketed bullets.

Set consists of: full-length resizing and decapping die, a 2-step neck expanding die, and a bullet seating and crimping die. Available for various bullet styles.

Standard Three-die pistol set
(complete with wrench) $19.45

TWO-STEP "M" NECK-EXPANDING DIE
FOR CAST RIFLE BULLETS

Available for all rifle cases this die is required when loading cast bullets, and will also improve the accuracy of jacketed bullet reloads. The first step expands the neck of the cartridge to slightly under bullet diameter. The second step expands the first 1/16" of the neck to slightly over bullet diameter, allowing the bullet to enter the case freely, without cutting lead. This die insures precise case neck tension on seated bullet. **$8.00**

LYMAN RELOADING DIES

T-C* PISTOL DIE

*Tungsten Carbide Resizing & Decapping Die for handgun cartridges.

A lifetime of reloads, some 200,000 rounds can be pushed through this Full-Length Sizing and Decapping Die without a sign of wear. Its diamond-like sizing surface of polished tungsten carbide creates far less friction (75% less) than steel dies. With the Lyman T-C Die, cases need not be lubricated and even dirty cases come out of the die with a polished burnished appearance. T-C Dies are available for the following pistol cartridges.

38 S & W (also fits 38 ACP & 38 Super)	44 Special (also fits 44 Magnum)
38 Special (also fits 357 Magnum)	45 ACP
	45 Colt
41 Magnum	

T-C Pistol Die $24.95

P-A* RIFLE DIE

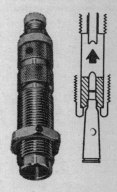

*Precision Alignment seating die for bottleneck rifle cartridges.

This bullet seating and crimping die is uniquely designed to give maximum alignment to bullets when seating them in bottleneck cases. The illustration shows how the cartridge neck and bullet are immediately centered by the sliding inner sleeve. As the case is pushed further into the die, the sleeve moves upwards, holding the bullet and case neck in alignment. These dies can also be adjusted to crimp the bullet in place, if desired. P-A Dies are available for all bottleneck rifle cartridges. $15.00

Both the bullet, and case neck, are trapped and aligned by the sliding inner sleeve. As the case is pushed into the die, the sleeve moves upwards holding the bullet and neck in alignment throughout the seating operation. The base of the cartridge case is centered by the lower portion of the die body. This die insures alignment of base, neck and bullet.

AA DIE ACCESSORIES

HEX NUTS (7/8 x 14 Thread)
These heavy duty steel check nuts are supplied as standard equipment with All-American Dies. They must be used on other brands of 7/8" x 14 thread dies when used on the Spar-T Press. **Price (each) .50**

DIE WRENCH
Supplied as standard equipment with All-American Die Sets — this handy adjustment wrench fits the various sizes of hex nuts used on A-A Dies.
Price: $2.00

EXTRA DECAPPING PINS
(package of ten)
$1.00

"T" PRIMING PUNCH
Designed for use with the All-American Turret and Tru-Line Jr. Press, these punches are available in two sizes (large or small). See page 372 for correct size. **Price: $4.50**

"J" SHELL HOLDER
Designed for use with the All-American Turret and Tru-Line Jr. Press, see complete listing of Shell Holders on page 372. **Price: $5.00**

7/8 x 14 ADAPTERS
These dies are used to adapt the smaller diameter True-Line Die to 7/8 x 14 thread. One Adapter is required for each reloading die.
Price (each) $1.50

LYMAN BULLET MOULDS

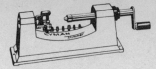

UNIVERSAL TRIMMER

MOULD MASTER XX

Lyman's Mould Master XX electric casting furnace features greatly increased capacity with lighter overall weight. It operates on household current. The thermostat housing has been relocated to one side allowing the caster a better view of the bottom-pour spout. Furthermore, access to the pot for ladle casting has been improved by replacing the over-arm stop with a metering thumbscrew in the lever hinge. Other features include:

- 20 lb. pot capacity.
- Calibrated thermostat permits controlled heat throughout the casting spectrum.
- Available in 115V A.C.

Furnace alone .... **$ 99.95**
Furnace w/mould guide **106.95**

MOULD MASTER BULLET CASTING FURNACE—
Heavy-duty, 11 lb. capacity furnace. Operates on standard household power—115 volts, A.C. or D.C., 1000 Watts. Calibrated dial control heats from 450° to 850° F. within 20°. Discharge spout is controlled by a lever operated valve.
Mould Master Furnace complete with Ingot
Mould and Mould Guide **$91.95**
Extra Ingot Mould **5.00**
Mould Guide **11.00**

DEBURRING TOOL—
Lyman's deburring tool can be used for chamfering or deburring of cases up to 45 caliber. For precise bullet seating, use the pointed end of the tool to bevel the inside of new or trimmed cases. To remove burrs left by trimming, place the other end of the deburring tool over the mouth of the case and twist. The tool's centering pin will keep the case aligned **$5.50**

LYMAN SINGLE CAVITY MOULD

Blocks are interchangeable with handles. Permits use of blocks for casting different bullets with the same set of handles. Attaching screws are concealed and handles give a cool comfortable grip. Group A— **$19.95** Hollow Base **$24.95** or Hollow Point— **$26.95** B— **$21.00** Hollow Base or Hollow Point— **$25.00** Group C— **$24.00** Hollow Base or Hollow Point—Not Available; Handles— **$7.00**

LYMAN DOUBLE CAVITY MOULD

The Ideal Double Cavity Mould has blocks which are interchangeable in handles adapted for large size blocks. Double-Cavity Mold Block only Group A— **$19.95** Group B— **$21.00**; Handles— **$7.00**

LYMAN FOUR CAVITY MOULD

Mould blocks and handles can be supplied as separate units. If you already have a pair of handles you need only order a set of blocks as these can be used on the same handles.
Group A— **$40.00** Handles— **$11.00**

LEAD DIPPER—
Dipper with cast iron head. Spout is shaped for easy, accurate pouring that prevents air pockets in the finished bullet. **$5.00**

INERTIA BULLET PULLER
Quickly and easily removes bullets from cartridges. **$14.95**

UNIVERSAL TRIMMER
This trimmer with patented chuck head accepts all metallic rifle or pistol cases, regardless of rim thickness. To change calibers, simply change the case head pilot. Other features include coarse and fine cutter adjustments, an oil-impregnated bronze bearing, and a rugged cast base assures precision alignment and years of service.
Trimmer less pilot **$34.95**
Trimmer and 1 pilot (state caliber) **36.45**
Extra pilot (state caliber) **1.50**
Replacement cutter head **2.00**

UNIVERSAL DRILL PRESS TRIMMER
This universal chuck head bolts to your drill press. By mounting the cutter head and case head pilot to your drill chuck, you have a fast, accurate method of processing large quantities of cases.
Trimmer (state caliber) **$27.50**

PILOTS ARE AVAILABLE IN THE FOLLOWING SIZES, STATE SIZE WHEN ORDERING **$1.50**

17	All 17 caliber rifle cases
22	All 22 caliber rifle cases
24	All 6 M M rifle cases
25A	25 ACP pistol cases
25	All 25 caliber rifle cases
26	All 6.5 M M and 264 caliber rifle cases
27	All 270 caliber rifle cases
28	All 7 M M and 284 caliber rifle cases
29	7.35 M M Italian rifle cases
30	All 30 caliber rifle plus 30 Mauser, 30 Luger and 32 Auto pistol cases
31	303 British, 7.65 M M Argentine, 7.7 M M Japanese, 32 20 rifle, plus 32 Colt and 32 S & W pistol cases
32	All 32 caliber rifle cases
8MM	8M M rifle (.323" dia.) cases
33	All 33 caliber rifle cases
9MM	9M M Luger, 38 ACP, 38 Super, 380 Auto pistol cases
34	348 Winchester rifle cases
35A	351 Winchester rifle cases
35	All 35 caliber rifle cases plus 38 Special 357, Magnum, 38 Colt and 38 S & W pistol cases
37	375 H & H, 378 Weatherby Mag., 38 55 rifle plus 41 Long Colt pistol cases
39	38 40, 301 Winchester rifle cases
41	41 S & W Magnum pistol plus 405 Winchester rifle cases
44A	44 40 rifle and pistol cases
44	44 Special, 44 Magnum pistol plus 444 Marlin and 43 Spanish rifle cases
45A	45 ACP, 45 A.R., 45 Colt, 455 Webley pistol, plus 11 M M Mauser rifle cases
45	45 70, 458 Winchester Mag., 460 Weatherby Mag. rifle cases

GAS CHECKS—
Gas checks are gilding metal caps which fit to the base of cast bullets. These caps protect the bullet base from the burning effect of hot powder gases and permit higher velocities. Easily seated during the bullet sizing operation, only Lyman gas checks should be used with Lyman cast bullets.
22 through 45 caliber (per 1000)
Note: .38 Special same as 35 caliber. **$10.00**
Also available in 45 caliber **12.00**

LEAD POT
Cast iron pot and holder for melting lead alloy using any source of heat. Pot capacity is 10 pounds of alloy. Holder keeps pot secure and level, prevents lead from splashing on stove or burner.
Lead Pot **$5.00**

LYMAN RELOADING
DIE REFERENCE CHART

PISTOL CARTRIDGE	Die Group	Shell Holder Number	Primer Punch & Sleeve	Case Trimmer Pilot Number	Bullet Puller Collet Number
22 Remington Jet	VII	1	small	22	22
221 Remington Fireball	VII	26	small	22	22
25ACP	NA	NA	small	25A	25
30 Luger (7.65mm Parabellum)	VII	12	small	30	30
30 Mauser (7.63mm Mauser)	VII	12	small	30	30
32 Auto (32 ACP, 7.65mm Browning)	VII	23	small	30	30
32 Smith and Wesson (also loads 32 S&W Long, 32 Colt New Police)	VII	9	small	31	32
9mm Luger (9mm Parabellum)	VII, X	12	small	9mm	38
38 Special — 357 Magnum (also loads 38 Colt, 38 Long Colt)	VII, IX	1	small	35	38
38 Super Auto (38 Auto, 38 ACP)	VII, X	12	small	9mm	38
38 Smith and Wesson (38 Colt New Police, 380 MK1)	VII, IX	21	small	35	38
380 Auto (9mm Corto, 9mm Short)	VII, X	26	small	9mm	38
38-40 Winchester (38 WCF)	VII	14B	large	39	40
41 Long Colt	VII	41LC	large	37	40
41 Magnum	VII, IX	30	small	41	41
44 Magnum — 44 Special	VII, IX	7	large	44	44
44-40 Winchester (44 WCF)	VII	14B	large	44A	44
45 Auto (45 ACP)	VII, IX, X	2	large	45A	45
45 Auto (also loads 45 Auto Rim)	VII, IX, X	14A	large	45A	45
45 Colt	VII, IX	11	large	45A	45
455 Webley	VII	13	large	45A	45

RIFLE CARTRIDGE	Die Group	Shell Holder Number	Primer Punch & Sleeve	Case Trimmer Pilot Number	Bullet Puller Collet Number
218 Bee	I	10	small	22	22
219 Zipper	I	6	large	22	22
219 Wasp	I	6	large	22	22
22 Spitfire (MMJ-5.7mm)	I	19	small	22	22
22 Hornet (5.6 x 35Rmm)	I, VI	4	small	22	22
22 K Hornet	I	4	small	22	22
22 Savage Hi-Power	I	6	large	22	22
22 PPC	V	12	small	22	22
22-250 (22 Varminter)	I, V	2	large	22	22
220 Swift	I, V	5	large	22	22
222 Remington	I, V, VI	26	small	22	22
222 Remington Magnum	I, V	26	small	22	22
223 Remington (5.56mm)	I, V	26	small	22	22
224 Weatherby Magnum	I	3	large	22	22
225 Winchester	I	5	large	22	22
240 Weatherby Magnum	I	2	large	24	24
243 Winchester	I, V, VI	2	large	24	24
6mm Remington (244 Rem.)	I, V	2	large	24	24
6mm PPC	V	12	small	24	24
6 x 47mm	V	26	small	24	24
25 Remington	I	15 or 3	large	25	25
25-06	I	2	large	25	25
25-20 Winchester (25 WCF)	I, VI	10	small	25	25
25-35 Winchester (6.5 x 52Rmm)	I	6	large	25	25
250-3000 Savage	I, VI	2	large	25	25
256 Winchester	I	1	small	25	25

RIFLE CARTRIDGE	Die Group	Shell Holder Number	Primer Punch & Sleeve	Case Trimmer Pilot Number	Bullet Puller Collet Number
257 Roberts	I, VI	2 or 8	large	25	25
257 Weatherby Magnum	I	13	large	25	25
6.5mm Remington Magnum	I	13	large	26	26
6.5 x 50mm Jap. Arisaka		5	large	26	26
6.5 x 52mm Italian Mann. Carc.	I	28	large	26	26
6.5 x 54mm Mann. Schoe. (also loads 5 x 53mm M.S.)	I	28	large	26	26
6.5 x 54mm Mann. Schoe. (for loading 6.5 x 54Rmm)	I	13	large	26	26
6.5 x 55mm Swedish Mauser	I	27	large	26	26
6.5 x 57mm	I	2	large	26	26
6.5 x 257 (Jap. Roberts)	I	2 or 8	large	26	26
264 Winchester Magnum	I	13	large	26	26
270 Winchester	I, V, VI	2	large	27	27
270 Weatherby Magnum	I	13	large	27	27
7mm Remington Magnum	I, V	13	large	28	28
7mm Weatherby Magnum	I	13	large	28	28
7mm Mauser (7 x 57mm)	I, V, VI	2	large	28	28
7mm Mauser (also loads 7 x 57R)	I, V, VI	13	large	28	28
7 x 61mm Sharpe & Hart	I	13	large	28	28
7 x 64mm	I	2	large	28	28
7 x 65Rmm	I	14B	large	28	28
280 Remington	I	2	large	28	28
284 Winchester	I	2	large	28	28
7.35mm Italian (Terni)	I	28	large	29	30
30 Remington	I, VI	15 or 3	large	30	30
30 M1 Carbine	III	19	small	30	30
30-06 (7.62 x 63mm)	I, V, VI	2	large	30	30
30-30 Winchester (30 WCF)	I, VI	6	large	30	30
30-40 Krag	I, VI	7	large	30	30
300 Savage	I, VI	2	large	30	30
300 Winchester Magnum	I, V, VI	13	large	30	30
300 Weatherby Magnum	I	13	large	30	30
300 H&H Magnum (7.63 x 72mm)	I	13	large	30	30
303 Savage	I, VI	7	large	30	30
308 Norma Magnum	I	13	large	30	30
308 Winchester (7.62 x 51mm Nato)	I, V, VI	2	large	30	30
7.62mm Russian (7.62 x 54Rmm)	I	17	large	30	30
303 British	I, VI	7	large	31	30
7.65mm Argentine Mauser (7.65 x 53mm)	I	2	large	31	30
7.7mm Jap. (7.7 x 58mm Arisaka)	I	2	large	31	30
32 Remington	I, VI	15 or 3	large	32	32
32 Winchester Special	I, VI	6	large	32	32
32-20 Winchester (32 WCF)	VI	10	small	32	32
32-40	VI	6	large	32	32
8mm Remington Magnum	I	13	large	8mm	32
8mm Lebel (8 x 50Rmm)	I	18S	large	8mm	32
8mm Mauser (8 x 57mm, 8 x 57JSmm, 7.9 x 57mm)	I, VI	2	large	8mm	32
8mm Mauser (also loads 8 x 57JRSmm)	I, VI	14B	large	8mm	32
33 Winchester	I	17	large	33	33
338 Winchester Magnum	I	13	large	33	33
340 Weatherby Magnum	I	13	large	33	33

LYMAN RELOADING
DIE REFERENCE CHART

RIFLE CARTRIDGE	Die Group	Shell Holder Number	Primer Punch & Sleeve	Case Trimmer Pilot Number	Bullet Puller Collet Number
348 Winchester	I	18	large	34	34
35 Remington	I, VI	8 or 2	large	35	35
350 Remington Magnum	I	13	large	35	35
351 Winchester	III	15	large	35A	35
358 Winchester (8.8mm)	I	2	large	35	35
358 Norma Magnum	I	13	large	35	35
9mm Mauser (9 x 57mm, also loads 9 x 57R)	I	13	large	35	35
375 Winchester	III	6	large	37	37
375 H&H Magnum	I	13	large	37	37
375 Weatherby Magnum	I	13	large	37	37
378 Weatherby Magnum	I	17	large	37	37
38-40 Winchester (38 WCF)	VII	14B	large	37	40
38-55 Winchester	III	6	large	37	37
401 Winchester	III	2	large	39	40
405 Winchester	III	7	large	41	40
11mm Mauser (43 Mauser, 11.15 x 60Rmm)	III	20	large	45A	45
43 Spanish (11.15 x 58Rmm)	III	20	large	44	44
44-40 Winchester (44 WCF)	VII	14B	large	44A	44
444 Marlin	III	14B	large	44	44
45-70 Government	III	17	large	45	45
458 Winchester Magnum (11.5 x 63mm)	III	13	large	45	45
460 Weatherby Magnum	I	17	large	45	45
50-70 Government	III	31	large	NA	50

AA Cast Bullet 3-Die Sets   Price: (1 lb. 8 oz.) $22.95

All of Lyman's cast bullet expertise has gone into building this three die set. The set consists of a full length resizing die with decapping stem, a bullet seating die, and our special AA Two-Step Neck Expanding (M) Die. This is the only die set specifically designed for cast bullet reloading. These die sets may also be used for jacketed bullets with superb results.

Cartridge	Die Set Number	Neck-Expanding (M) Die
22 Hornet	7468581	7349058
222 Remington	7462325	7342097
243 Winchester	7462324	7349007
25-20 Winchester (25 WCF)	7469042	7342089
250-3000 Savage	7464981	7349010
257 Roberts	7469021	7349006
270 Winchester	7462293	7349009
7mm Mauser (7 x 57mm)	7469033	7349011
30 Remington	7469082	7348194
30-06 (7.62 x 63mm)	7460498	7349002
30-30 Winchester (30 WCF)	7462318	7349003
30-40 Krag	7467113	7340851
300 Savage	7469039	7340808
300 Winchester Magnum	7461884	7349012
303 Savage	7468205	7349055
308 Winchester (7.62 x 51mm Nato)	7464934	7349050
303 British	7469040	7349005
32 Remington	7460510	7341814
32 Winchester Special	7469070	7342073
32-20 (32 WCF)	7460484	7349054
32-40	7460525	7349020
8mm Mauser	7467143	7349018
35 Remington	7464922	7340809

LYMAN RELOADING

AA Bench Rest 2-Die Sets
(for jacketed bullets)

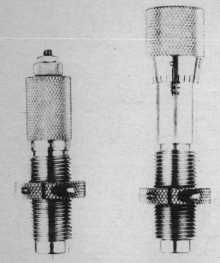

Match grade performance through the use of proven bench rest techniques. The set consists of a neck sizing die and our AA Micro-Seat Die. This combination enables you to get neck sizing and truly precise bullet seating from a traditional reloading press.

Cartridge	Die Set Number	Micrometer Seating Die	Neck Sizing Die
22 PPC	7690122	7161122	7135122
22-250 (22 Varminter)	7690012	7161012	7135012
220 Swift	7690013	7161013	7135013
222 Remington	7690005	7161005	7135005
222 Remington Magnum	7690007	7161007	7135007
223 Remington (5.56mm)	7690006	7161006	7135006
243 Winchester	7690015	7161015	7135015
6mm Remington (244 Rem.)	7690016	7161016	7135016
6mm PPC	7690123	7161123	7135123
6 x 47mm	7690124	7161124	7135124
25-06	7690024	7161024	7135024
270 Winchester	7690033	7161033	7135033
7mm Remington Magnum	7690039	7161039	7135039
7mm Mauser (7 x 57mm)	7690035	7161035	7135035
30-06 (7.62 x 63mm)	7690049	7161049	7135049
300 Winchester Magnum	7690051	7161051	7135051
308 Winchester (7.62 x 51mm Nato)	7690047	7161047	7135047
Price:	$29.95	$18.95	$12.00

SNAP CAPS

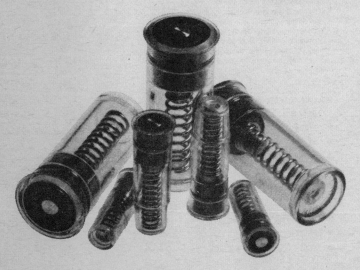

SNAP CAPS FOR GUN MAINTENANCE AND SAFETY

Snap caps help keep handguns and shotguns in perfect working order. Placed in the chamber of your gun, they protect the firing pin when dry firing, testing or cleaning, and let you check firing-pin alignment. They also eliminate the possibility of loading and accidentally misfiring live ammunition. No gun owner should be without them.

Available in 12, 20, & 28 gauge and .410 bore .. $ 9.95
Available in 38 Spec/ 357 Mag., ... 14.95
44 Mag., 45 Colt, and 22 L.R. 19.95

PRICE PER CARD

MEC RELOADING

GRABBER 76

The Grabber grabs and squeezes the shell to dimensions well within commercial tolerances for new shells. Grabber resizing completely reforms the metal portion of the fired shotgun shell to factory standards in **all** respects. (Low brass 2¾″ shells.) Resizing is done as an integral part of the reloading sequence and without undue agitation that might affect the uniformity of the charges. The measure assembly has been designed for strength and safety. Large capacity shot container holds 17+ pounds.

- AUTOMATIC PRIMER FEED
- GRABBER RESIZING
- EXCLUSIVE CHARGE BAR WINDOW
- FLIP TYPE MEASURE
- EXCLUSIVE PRIMER SEATING
- LARGE CAPACITY SHOT CONTAINER

12, 16, 20, 28 gauge and .410 bore

price complete
$253.00

HUSTLER 76

The Grabber with its revolutionary resize chamber, combined with the MEC hydraulic system, becomes the Hustler. It gives you your own miniature reloading factory, but one that resizes to under industry standards for minimum chamber. The motor operates on regular 110 volt household current and the pump supplies instant, constant pressure. The entire downstroke and upstroke functions are utilized and synchronized to allow continuous action. Every stroke of the cylinder piston is positive and performs all operations at six reloading stations. Every downstroke of the reloader produces one finished shell.
Reloader less pump and hose... $322.96

- ALL THE FINE FEATURES OF THE GRABBER PLUS HYDRAULIC POWER

12, 16, 20, 28 gauge and .410 bore

price complete
$679.80

600 JR.
THE PLASTIC MASTER

Any MEC reloader can be used for reloading plastic shells, but the "600 jr." positively masters the process. The PLASTIC MASTER is a single stage tool, but is designed to permit rapid, progressive operation. Every step from fired shell to the fresh-crimped product is performed with a minimum of motion. An exclusive shell holder positions and holds the shell at each station. No transfer die is required . . . resizing dies at reconditioning and crimping stations give your shell its proper form.

- CAM-ACTUATED RECONDITIONING STATION
- SPINDEX STAR CRIMP HEAD
- ADJUSTA-GUIDE WAD FEED
- CAM-LOCK CRIMP
- HARDENED CHARGING BAR
- TOGGLE LINKAGE
- FLIP-TYPE MEASURE
- ALL STEEL CONSTRUCTION
- PRIMER CATCHER

Choice of 10, 12, 16, 20, 28 or .410 gauges—fitted in beautiful lifetime chrome.

price complete
$87.73

700
VERSAMEC
THE SINGLE STAGE ULTIMATE

The exclusive Platform Cam which provides the longer ejection stroke necessary to eject existing field shells at the resize station. No adjustments or part changes are required, regardless of brass length. The Pro-Check, which programs the charge bar and wad guide. This ingenious device programs the measure assembly to position the charge bar in the correct sequence. Even the hunter who reloads once or twice a year cannot err . . . the Pro-Check eliminates mistakes . . . automatically. The paper crimp starter which assembles into the Spindex Crimper. Only seconds are required to change from the 6 or 8 point plastic crimp spinner to the smooth cone for fired paper shells.

- CAM-ACTUATED RECONDITIONING STATION
- PRO-CHECK
- SPINDEX STAR CRIMP HEAD
- ADJUSTA-GUIDE WAD FEED
- CAM LOCK CRIMP
- HARDENED CHARGING BAR
- TOGGLE LINKAGE
- FLIP TYPE MEASURE
- PRIMER CATCHER
- ALL STEEL CONSTRUCTION

Choice of 12, 16, 20, 28 or .410 gauges—fitted in beautiful lifetime chrome.

price complete
$100.43

MEC RELOADING

650
THE RELOADER WITH A MEMORY

Up to 12 operations on 6 individual shells are performed simultaneously with one stroke of the press handle. Outstanding features of the 650 include a revolutionary Star Crimp Head, Automatic Primer feeding, exclusive Resize-Deprime apparatus, Toggle linkage, cam operated crimping die and Auto-Cycle charging sequence. The Auto-Cycle charging sequence automatically maintains the correct operating sequence of the charge bar. The charge bar can be actuated only when a shell is properly located to receive the powder. The MEC 650 can even handle the 3 inch shells . . . high-base, low base and light or heavy plastics. It's all steel with an extra heavy base-column. Tool comes completely assembled, tested and ready to use . . . without adjustment.

- AUTOMATIC PRIMER FEED.
- AUTOMATIC POWDER AND SHOT CHARGING
- FLIP-TYPE MEASURE
- HARDENED CHARGING BAR
- OPEN BASE
- PRIMER CATCHER
- EXCLUSIVE CAM-OPERATED CRIMP
- EXCLUSIVE RESIZE-DEPRIME APPARATUS
- 12 OPERATIONS WITH 1 STROKE
- SPINDEX STAR CRIMP HEAD
- AUTO-CYCLE

Choice of 12, 16, 20, 28 or .410 gauges — fitted in beautiful lifetime chrome

price complete

$184.64

THE MINIATURE RELOADING FACTORY

Take the 650 or the Super 600 reloader and marry it to a hydraulic system . . . the result is the hydraMEC, today's most advanced concept in high-volume reloaders. The hydraulic system is compact, lightweight and designed for long, trouble-free service. The motor operates on regular 110 volt household current and the pump supplies instant, constant pressure . . . no slowdown, no misses. The entire downstroke and upstroke functions are utilized and synchronized to allow continuous action. Every stroke of the cylinder piston is positive and performs up to 12 operations on six reloading stations. Every downstroke of the reloader produces one finished shell. The operator inserts empty shells and wads . . . the hydraMEC does the rest . . . automatically.

Tool linked for hydraulic operation to include base and cylinder.

hydraMEC 650 . . . . $252.36

HYDRAULIC UNIT ONLY—Hydraulic unit to include pump, motor, cylinder, controls, base, links and bolts required to attach to reloader with instructions. **$443.10**

650 HYDRAMEC

- AUTOMATIC PRIMER FEED
- AUTOMATIC POWDER & SHOT CHARGING
- FLIP-TYPE MEASURE
- HARDENED CHARGING BAR
- PRIMER CATCHER
- EXCLUSIVE CAM-OPERATED CRIMP
- EXCLUSIVE RESIZE-DEPRIME APPARATUS
- TOGGLE LINKAGE
- FOOL PROOF HYDRAULIC SYSTEM
- 12 OPERATIONS WITH 1 STROKE

$611.77

Choice of 12, 16, 20, 28 or .410 gauges — fitted in beautiful lifetime chrome

---

ACCESSORY EQUIPMENT
MEC E-Z PRIME "V" & "S"

COMPLETELY AUTOMATIC PRIMER FEED

SPINDEX STAR CRIMP HEAD

The SPINDEX STAR CRIMP HEAD is a revolutionary crimp starter that prepares plastic shells for a perfect crimp . . . everytime. The SPINDEX automatically engages the original folds of each shell. No prior indexing of the shell is required . . . even on some of the earlier, unskived plastics that show no impressions of the original crimp folds. Because it employs a pressed metal part that spins into alignment with the original folds, the SPINDEX starts every crimp perfectly. And even better . . . you have a choice of an 8-segment, 6-segment, or smooth crimp starter, depending on the shells you are reloading.

FROM CARTON TO SHELL WITH SECURITY, IT PROVIDES SAFE, CONVENIENT PRIMER POSITIONING AND INCREASES RATE OF PRODUCTION. REDUCES BENCH CLUTTER, ALLOWING MORE FREE AREA FOR WADS AND SHELLS.

- PRIMERS TRANSFER DIRECTLY FROM CARTON TO RELOADER — ELIMINATING TUBES AND TUBE FILLERS.
- POSITIVE MECHANICAL FEED (NOT DEPENDENT UPON AGITATION OF PRESS)
- VISIBLE SUPPLY
- AUTOMATIC — ELIMINATES HAND MOTION
- LESS SUSCEPTIBLE TO DAMAGE
- ADAPTS TO ALL DOMESTIC AND MOST FOREIGN PRIMERS WITH ADJUSTMENT OF THE COVER
- MAY BE PURCHASED SEPARATELY TO REPLACE TUBE TYPE PRIMER FEED OR TO UPDATE YOUR PRESENT RELOADER.

E-Z PRIME "V"
For 600 Jr.
700 Versamec
Sizemaster 77

$22.00

E-Z PRIME "S"
For 650

$22.00

SPINDEX STAR CRIMP HEAD
SPINDEX STAR CRIMP HEAD 234-434-534 (specify gauge and model) $5.45
* 634P INSERT FOR PRE—CRIMPING (CONING) PAPER SHELLS 2.66
453P FINGERS (specify gauges) . . . . .73 ea.
30IL — 13x CONTAINER . . . . 1.09 ea.

MEC E-Z PAK   IT'S ALL STEEL! IT'S TILTED!

Here's how to pack shot shell reloads the easy way. As each shell is reloaded, they're placed in E-Z PAK, exactly as if they were being placed in the box. After each 25 shells, original box is slipped over E-Z PAK, which is then inverted, and removed. Nothing easier — nothing neater. Available in all gauges.

$2.66

MEC E-Z WAD DISPENSER

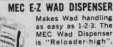

Makes Wad handling as easy as 1-2-3: The MEC Wad Dispenser is "Reloader-high", making your wadding operation faster . . . neater . . . more convenient.

$13.31

MEC SIZEMASTER 7.7

- SINGLE-STAGE
- PRECISION SHELL HOLDER
- EXCLUSIVE RESIZING CHAMBER
- AUTOMATIC PRIMER FEED
- POSITIVE REPRIMING
- CHARGE BAR WINDOW
- PRO-CHECK
- ADJUSTA-GUIDE WAD FEED
- WAD PRESSURE GAUGE
- WAD HEIGHT GAUGE
- EXTRA CAPACITY SHOT CONTAINER
- SPINDEX CRIMP STARTER
- CAM-ACTUATED CRIMPING STATION

FOR THE MEC 600 JR.	
MEC DIE SETS—(12-16-20-28-.410)	$30.25
(10 gauge)	33.88
PRO-CHECK	2.66
FOR THE VERSAMEC 700	
741V DIE SET—(10-12-16-20-28- 410) specify gauge	$33.88

Size Master 77 (includes Primer Feed) **$140.80**
77 Die Set 12, 16, 20, 28 and .410 . . . . **50.60**
77-10 10 guage Die Set **59.40**

MTM

CASE-GARD 50 SERIES RIFLE AMMO CASES

Features include
- versatility - cases for every caliber from 222 to 458 Win.
- durability - material doesn't warp, crack, chip, peel, expand, or contract.
- each case rests in its own individual compartment.
- unique hinge is designed to keep the cover in the open position when reloading.
- Snap-lok latch protects contents from inadvertent spilling.
- each CASE-GARD 50 ammo box is supplied with a form for recording load and sight data.

Available in Red or MTM Green

RS-50 (Small Rifle)	222 to 222 Mag	$2.50
RM-50 (Medium Rifle)	22-250 to 308 Win	2.50
RL-50 (Large Rifle)	220 Swift to 458 Win	2.50
RS-S-50	22 Hornet, 22 & 6mm PPC's, 22 & 6mm Rem. BR's, 7.62x39	2.50

CASE-GARD H50 SERIES DELUXE AMMO CASE

Features include:
- handle for ease of carrying.
- scuff resistant, texturized finish.
- extra space between rounds to facilitate removal when wearing gloves.
- design that allows belted magnums to be carried rim up or down.

Available in Red or MTM Green

H50-RS	17 Rem. to 223 Rem.	$3.69
H50-RM	22-250 to 308 Win.	3.69
H50-RL	6mm Rem. to 30-06	3.69
H50-R MAG	264 Win. Mag to 470 KYNOCH	3.69

CASE-GARD 22 MATCH AMMO BOX

CASE-GARD® 22 Match Ammo Box— For the Small Bore Competitor. Precision molded body designed to hold 30 rounds - 3 strings - projectile-down for easy handling; plus box of ammo and loose rounds, if desired. Inside of lid equipped with supports for stop watch. The lid holds the watch at a 40° angle, for ease of reading by shooter. The Case-Gard 22 Match Ammo Box features Snap-lok latch, virtually indestructible integral hinge, and leather-like textured finish.

Available in Red and MTM Green

SB-22	$3.99

CASE-GARD 9 AMMO WALLET

CASE-GARD 9 Ammo Wallet™ ammunition carrier holds 9 rounds in pocket or saddlebag. Provides absolute protection for ammunition.

Available in Dark Brown

W-9 SM	22-250 to 30-30	$2.39
W-9 LM	22-250 to 375 Mag	2.39

CASE-GARD 50 SERIES HANDGUN AMMO CASES

Features include:
- versatility - cases for every caliber from 9mm to 44 Mag.
- durability - virtually indestructible material doesn't warp, crack, chip, peel, expand or contract.
- each round rests in its own individual compartment.
- unique hinge designed to keep the cover in the open position when reloading.
- Snap-lok latch protects contents from inadvertent spilling.

Available in Dark Green or MTM Green

50-9	9mm	$1.25
PS-3	38 to 357 Mag.	1.25
PL-4	45, 41, and 44 Mag.	1.25

CASE-GARD MAGAZINE WALLET AMMO CARRIER

Features include:
- Snap-lok latch that won't open until you want it open, even if dropped on a hard surface.
- integral hinge.
- textured finish assures secure handling, even when wet.
- precision molded of space-age material that doesn't warp, chip, crack, peel, expand or contract.

Available in Dark Brown

Caliber Capacity	380 Auto & 9mm	38 & 357 Mag.	41 Mag.	44 Mag.	45 Auto
6 Round	W6-9 $1.99	W6-38 $1.99	W6-41 $1.99	W6-44 $1.99	W6-45 $1.99
12 Round	W12-9 $2.19	W12-38 $2.19	W12-41 $2.19	W12-44 $2.19	W12-45 $2.19
18 Round	18-9 $2.39	18-38 $2.39	18-41 $2.39	18-44 $2.39	18-45 $2.39

MTM

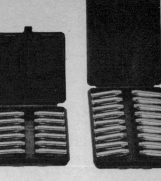

CASE-GARD AMMO WALLET
CASE-GARD 6, 12 AND 18

MTM offers 3 different models of varying capacity. All share common design features:

- textured finish looks like leather, and provides good gripping surface, even when wet.
- Snap-lok latch protects contents from damage, even if unit is dropped.
- integral hinge.
- contents are protected from dust and moisture.
- each round is carried securely in its own individual **rattleproof** recess.

CALIBER→ CAPACITY↓	380 Auto & 9mm	38 & 357 Mag	41 Mag	44 Mag	45 Auto
6 Round	W6-9 $1.99	W6-38 $1.99	W6-41 $1.99	W6-44 $1.99	W6-45 $1.99
12 Round	W12-9 $2.19	W12-38 $2.19	W12-41 $2.19	W12-44 $2.19	W12-45 $2.19
18 Round	18-9 $2.39	18.38 $2.39	18-41 $2.39	18-44 $2.39	18-45 $2.39

CASE-GARD AMMO WALLET FOR 22's

Special **CASE-GARD Ammo Wallet** carrier holds 30 rounds, 22 Longs or 22 Mags . . . a convenient way to carry ammo to the range or field. Design features are:

- leather-like finish.
- Snap-lok latch protects case against inadvertent opening, even if dropped.
- each round is carried securely in its own recess.
- virtually indestructible hinge.

Available in Dark Brown
30-22M $2.95

MTM HANDLOADER'S LOG

MTM Handloader's Log. Space provided for 1,000 entries covering date, range, group size or score, components, and conditions. Book is heavy duty vinyl, reinforced 3-ring binder.
HL-74 .... $6.99
HL-50 extra pages 3.99

CASE-GARD 100 AMMO CARRIER FOR SKEET AND TRAP

THE MTM^{T.M.} CASE-GARD® 100 Round Shotshell Case carries 100 rounds in 2 trays; or 50 rounds, plus 2 boxes of factory ammo; or 50 rounds plus sandwiches and insulated liquid container; or 50 rounds, with room left for fired hulls.

And check these features:

- stainless steel hinge pin
- center balanced handles facilitate carrying and can be padlocked for security
- high-impact material supports 300 pounds, and will not warp, split, expand or contract
- dustproof and rainproof

Each **CASE-GARD 100** Shotshell case is supplied with 2 50-round trays.

Available in Textured Black
S100-12 .... 12 gauge $9.49
S100-16 .... 16 gauge 9.49
S100-20 .... 20 gauge 9.49

FUNNELS

Color coded ABS funnels designed specifically for the benchrest shooter. One fits 222 and 243 cases only; the other 7mm and 308 cases. Both can be used with pharmaceutical vials popular with benchrest competitors for storage of pre-weighed charges. Funnel design prevents their rolling off the bench.

BF-2 .... $1.89

PACIFIC

105 Shotshell Reloader

- All the features of expensive reloaders . . . without sacrificing quality.
- Crimps shells perfectly. Floating crimp starter automatically aligns with original crimp folds. Final crimp die is fully adjustable.
- Seats wads easily with built-in wad guide.
- Eliminates guesswork . . . all operations end on positive stop.

105 SHOTSHELL RELOADER   **$75.00**
Complete with charge bushings.

105 DIE SET   **$30.00**
For quick-change conversion to different gauge.

105 MAGNUM CONVERSION SET   **$15.00**
Converts 2¾" dies to load 3" shells of same gauge, or vice versa.

105 CRIMP STARTER   **$ 2.00**
(8-point crimp starter standard equipment with loader and with Die Sets),

EXTRA CHARGE BUSHINGS ....$ 2.00

POWER 'C'®

"C" Type Metallic Cartridge Reloading Tool

- Pacific's patented primer system for convenient and positive primer seating.
- Pacific's patented automatic primer feed easily attached.
- Convenient offset handle for maximum leverage. Handle locks out of the way in "up" position when not in use.
- All bearing surfaces hardened and precision ground.

POWER 'C' complete press (does not include dies, primer catcher or shell holder). **$54.50**

POWER 'C' PACKAGE (Series I & II full-length die sets only). Includes Power 'C' press, complete set of Durachrome dies, primer catcher and removable shell holder **$77.25**

POWER 'C' PACKAGE with carbide sizing die. (Series II only). **$106.50**

MULTI-POWER 'C'®

Smooth, precise operation. More power with minimum effort for all reloading jobs including bullet swaging.

- Pacific's patented primer system for convenient and positive primer seating.
- Pacific's patented automatic primer feed easily attached.
- "O" frame of high-density annealed cast iron insures perfect alignment of die and shell holder. Impossible for frame to spring even when swaging large caliber bullets.
- Swinging toggle multiplies leverage for easy operation when resizing and case forming.
- Steel links for maximum strength.
- All bearing surfaces hardened and precision ground.

MULTI-POWER 'C' complete press (does not include dies, primer catcher or shell holder). **$81.50**

MULTI-POWER 'C' PACKAGE (Series I & II full-length die sets only). Includes Multi-Power 'C' press, complete set of Durachrome dies, primer catcher and removable head shell holder. **$99.50**

MULTI-POWER 'C' PACKAGE with carbide sizing die. (Series II only). **$129.50**

PACIFIC

155 SHOTSHELL RELOADER

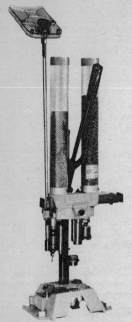

The 155 resizes entire length of the shell including head and rim. Spring-loaded finish die produces perfect tapered crimp. 113 interchangeable shot and powder bushings and handles both plastic and paper shells. Quick-change die sets let you load everything from 3-inch 12-gauge shells to 2½-inch .410 gauge shells. Dies are polished steel with deep blued finish. All operations end on a positive stop, including fully adjustable wad seating.

155 SHOTSHELL RELOADER 12 & 20 Ga.
...........$123.50

155 SHOTSHELL RELOADER 16, 28 & .410 Ga...............$128.50
Complete with standard charge bushings. (Does not include automatic primer feed.)

155 APF SHOTSHELL RELOADER 12 & 20 Ga..................$135.00

155 APF SHOTSHELL RELOADER 16, 28 & .410 Ga..................$139.00
Complete with standard charge bushings.

155/155 APF DIE SET 12 & 20 Ga. $40.50
155/155 APF DIE SET 16, 28 & .410 Ga.
$43.50

155/155 APF MAGNUM CONVERSION SET
$18.50
Converts 2¾" dies to load 3" shells of same gauge, or vice versa.

AUTOMATIC PRIMER FEED CONVERSION UNIT $25.50

EXTRA CRIMP STARTERS 2.00
EXTRA CHARGE BUSHINGS 2.00

266 SHOTSHELL RELOADER

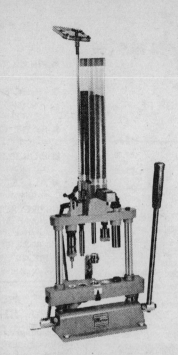

The most advanced loader in its price range. Right or left-hand operation to suit the operator. New wad guide with unbreakable spring fingers prevents wad tipping. Two-way adjustable crimper assures precise crimp depth and taper. Automatic primer feed automatically drops primer when preceding shell is powder charged.

SAFE AND CONVENIENT — Charging assembly constructed for no-spark safety. Shot and powder assembly removes completely for fast, easy load change.

266 SHOTSHELL RELOADER
Complete with charge bushings.
12 & 20 ga. **$189.00**; 16, 28 & .410 ga. **$195.00**
266 DIE SET
For conversion to different gauge.
12 & 20 ga. **$45.00** 16, 28 & .410 ga. **$50.50**
266 MAGNUM CONVERSION SET $18.50
Converts 2¾" dies to load 3" shells of same gauge, or vice versa.
EXTRA CRIMP STARTER ...... $ 2.00
EXTRA CHARGE BUSHINGS 2.00

366-AUTO SHOTSHELL RELOADER

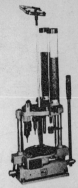

The 366-Auto features full-length resizing with each stroke, automatic primer feed, swing-out wad guide, three stage crimping featuring Taper-Loc for factory tapered crimp, automatic advance to the next station and automatic ejection. The turntable holds 8 shells for 8 operations with each stroke. The primer tube filler is fast; automatic charge bar loads shot and powder; right or left hand operation; interchangeable charge bushings, die sets and magnum dies and crimp starters for 6 point, 8 point and paper crimps.

366-AUTO SHOTSHELL RELOADER 12, 16, 20 or 28 gauge $373.00
Complete with standard charge bushings.

366—AUTO ● ADVANCE $39.50
The Auto ● Advance automatically advances the shells to the next station. It is standard equipment on 366 loaders manufactured after November 1, 1975 and it can be added to any earlier models.
366—SHELL DROP $44.50
Makes it unnecessary to manually remove loaded shells from the shell plate. Standard on 366-Auto loaders manufactured after February 1, 1976. The shell drop can be installed on earlier models; please return your 366 to Pacific postpaid for factory installation (specify gauge).
366—SWING-OUT WAD GUIDE AND SHELL DROP COMBO $100.00
Return your 366 to Pacific postpaid (specify gauge).
366—SWING-OUT WAD GUIDE $69.50
Makes insertion of the wad easier. Return 366 to Pacific postpaid for installation.
366—SHOT/POWDER SHUTOFF $25.00
Now standard on Pacific's 366 loaders, the unit fits any 366 loader and can be purchased separately.

366-AUTO DIE SET 12 & 20 Ga. $69.50
366-AUTO DIE SET 16 & 28 Ga. 75.00
366-AUTO MAGNUM CONVERSION SET
$18.50
Converts 2¾" dies to load 3" shells of same gauge, or vice versa.
EXTRA CRIMP STARTERS $2.00
EXTRA CHARGE BUSHINGS 2.00

PACIFIC
DURACHROME® DIES

GUARANTEED FOR LIFE
For All Popular Rifle & Pistol Calibers

- ■ **LIFETIME DURACHROME FINISH** — satin-hard chrome protection that keeps dies looking and working like new. Guaranteed never to chip, crack or peel.

- ■ **HEXAGON SPINDLE HEADS** — for easy removal of stuck cases and more positive adjustment.

- ■ **PRECISION-ROLLED** 7/8 x 14 threads held to perfect size and pitch. Fits most other tools because this pioneer Pacific development has been widely copied.

- ■ **FAST CONVENIENT ADJUSTMENT** is made possible by Pacific's all-steel lock rings.

- ■ **BUILT IN PROVISION FOR CRIMPING** provided on all bullet seating dies.

- ■ **ALL STEEL CONSTRUCTION** — no inexpensive substitute metals.

- ■ **PRECISE DIMENSIONS** — minimum tolerances maintained throughout. After chambering, dies are hardened for lifetime wear, then polished to insure perfect dimensions and smooth interior surfaces.

- ■ **HEAVY DUTY STORAGE BOX,** sample of Pacific Die Lube and spare decap pin are included with each set.

2 DIE SETS
(for bottleneck cases)

Full-length sizing set (Series 1)	$18.50
Full-length sizing set (Series III)	22.50
Neck sizing set (Series I)	18.50
Neck sizing set (Series III)	22.50
Set with Carbide Expander (Series 1 only)	27.50

3 DIE SETS
(for straight sided cases)

Standard 3 die set (Series II)	$19.50
Standard 3 die set (Series IV)	23.50
Carbide 3 die set (Series II only)	45.00
Carbide sizing set (Series II only)	34.00

DELUXE FILE TYPE TRIM DIE

Uses a fine grade file to insure precision case length. The most inexpensive and practical way to trim and form rifle cases.

- ■ Made of finest steel with lifetime Durachrome finish.
- ■ Available in most rifle calibers.

Deluxe FILE TYPE TRIM DIE $10.75

#1 CARBIDE SIZE DIES For 3 Die Sets
The ideal answer for large volume reloading. Diamond-hard finish won't scratch cases, no lubrication needed. Cases need not be cleaned.

Removable Head SHELL HOLDER
Precision machined from hardened steel then heat treated to prevent wear and give lifetime operation. Each Shell Holder is specifically designed for case to assure accurate alignment and eliminate tipping and side movement. Fits all tools using Pacific "C" design. $4.25

CALIBER LIST

Caliber	Number Of Dies	Neck Dies	File Trim Dies	Shell Holder
218 Bee	2	no	no	7
219 Zipper	2	no	yes	2
22 Hornet	2	no	no	3
22K Hornet	2	no	no	3
22 RCFM (Jet)	2	no	no	6
17-222	2	yes	yes	16
17-223	2	yes	no	16
221 Remington-(Fireball)	2	no	no	16
222 Remington	2	yes	yes	16
222 Remington Magnum	2	yes	yes	16
223 Remington	2	yes	yes	16
224 Weatherby	2	yes	yes	17
225 Winchester	2	yes	yes	18
22-250	2	yes	yes	1
220 Swift	2	yes	yes	4
22 Savage H. P.	2	no	no	2
243 Winchester	2	yes	yes	1
244-6mm Remington	2	yes	yes	1
6mm Internationl	2	yes	yes	1
6mm-284	2	yes	yes	1
6 x 47 Remington	2	yes	no	16
25-20 Winchester	2	no	no	7
250 Savage	2	no	yes	1
25 Remington	2	no	no	12
25-35 Winchester	2	no	yes	2
25-06	2	yes	yes	1
256 Winchester	2	no	no	6
257 Roberts	2	yes	yes	1
257 Weatherby	2	yes	yes	5
25-284	2	yes	yes	1
6.5 x 55	2	no	yes	19
6.5-06	2	yes	yes	1
6.5 Remington Magnum	2	yes	yes	5
6.5 Mannlicher	2	no	yes	20
6.5 Carcano	2	no	yes	21
6.5 Jap	2	no	yes	34
264 Winchester Magnum	2	yes	yes	5
270 Winchester	2	yes	yes	1
270 Weatherby	2	yes	yes	5
7mm Mauser	2	yes	yes	1
7x61 Sharpe & Hart	2	yes	yes	35
7mm Remington Magnum	2	yes	yes	5
7mm Weatherby	2	yes	yes	5
7x57 Rim	2	no	yes	13
280 Remington	2	yes	yes	1
284 Winchester	2	yes	yes	1
30 M1	3	no	no	22
30-30 Winchester	2	no	yes	2
300 Savage	2	yes	yes	1
303 Savage	2	no	no	33
303 British	2	yes	yes	11
308 Winchester	2	yes	yes	1
30-40	2	no	no	11
308 Norma Magnum	2	yes	yes	5
7.35 Carcano	2	no	no	21
7.62 Russian	2	no	no	23
7.65 Belgium	2	no	no	24
7.7 Jap	2	no	no	1
30-06	2	yes	yes	1
300 H&H Magnum	2	yes	yes	5
300 Weatherby	2	yes	yes	5
300 Winchester Magnum	2	yes	yes	5
30 Luger	2	no	no	8
32-20	2	no	no	7
32-40	2	no	no	2
32 Winchester Special	2	no	yes	2
32 Remington	2	no	no	12
33 Winchester	2	no	no	14
8mm Mauser	2	yes	yes	1
8x57 Rim	2	yes	yes	13
8mm-06	2	yes	yes	1
8mm-06 Improved	2	no	no	1
30-338	2	yes	yes	5
338 Winchester	2	yes	yes	5
348 Winchester	2	no	no	25
35 Remington	2	yes	yes	26
350 Remington Magnum	2	yes	yes	5
358 Norma Magnum	2	yes	no	5
375 H&H Magnum	2	yes	yes	5
358 Winchester	2	no	no	1
9mm Luger	3	no	no	8
38 Super Auto	3	no	no	8
38 S & W	3	no	no	28
38 Special	3	no	no	6
38-40	3	no	no	9
357 Magnum	3	no	no	6
41 Magnum	3	no	no	29
44 Special	3	no	no	30
44 Magnum	3	no	no	30
444 Marlin	3	no	no	27
44-40	3	no	no	9
45 ACP	3	no	no	1
45 Colt	3	no	no	32
45-70	3	no	no	14
458 Winchester	3	no	no	5

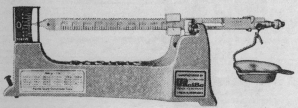
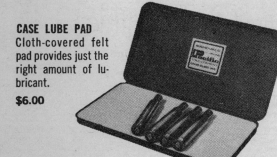

PONSNESS-WARREN SHOTSHELL RELOADING TOOLS

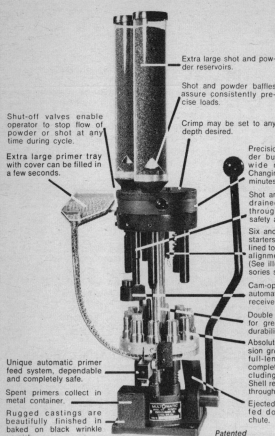

Extra large shot and powder reservoirs.

Shot and powder baffles assure consistently precise loads.

Crimp may be set to any depth desired.

Shut-off valves enable operator to stop flow of powder or shot at any time during cycle.

Extra large primer tray with cover can be filled in a few seconds.

Precision shot and powder bushings provide a wide range of loads. Changing takes but a few minutes.

Shot and powder may be drained out completely through drop tube for safety and convenience.

Six and eight point crimp starters are ball bearing lined to give perfect crimp alignment every time. (See illustration in Accessories section.)

Cam-operated wad carrier automatically tips out to receive all types of wads.

Double post construction for greater leverage and durability.

Absolute resizing — precision ground and polished full-length sizing dies completely resize case including brass and rim. Shell remains in sizing die through entire operation.

Ejected shells are gravity fed down handy shell chute.

Unique automatic primer feed system, dependable and completely safe.

Spent primers collect in metal container.

Rugged castings are beautifully finished in baked on black wrinkle varnish.

Patented

Large shot and powder reservoirs.

Shot and powder baffles assure consistently precise loads.

Bushing access plug allows instant inspection or changing of bushings and also provides a direct shot drop for loading buck shot or granulated plastic.

Charging ring has positive lock to prevent accidental flow of powder.

Tool head can hold two gauges simultaneously.

Six and eight point crimp starters are ball bearing lined to give perfect crimp alignment every time.

Shot and powder may be drained out completely through shot and powder drop tube.

Trouble-free tip-out wad guide.

Double post construction for greater leverage and wear.

Absolute resizing, shell stays in full length sizing die through entire operation.

Sizing die is centered at each station by spring-loaded ball check.

Handy, removable spent-primer box.

Photo shows Du-O-Matic with 12 and 20 gauge tooling attached.

Patented.

Mult-O-Matic*
New Model 600B

Du-O-Matic*
Model 375

Mult-O-Matic 600B Complete (with 6 or 8 point crimp starter) 12, 16, 20, 28 or 410 gauge $389.50
The 28 and 410 gauge 600's are designed primarily to load plastic casings using one piece plastic wads.

Accessories:

600B Additional Tooling Set Complete (with 6 or 8 point crimp starter) 12, 16, 20, 28 or 410 gauge	$129.50
600B 3" Conversion Kit (12 and 20 gauge only)	$124.50
(For 20 gauge, brand of ammunition to be loaded should be specified)	
600B Crimp Starter Complete (6 or 8 point)	$ 14.00
Crimp Starter Head Only (6 or 8 point)	$ 7.00
Special Paper Crimp Assembly (12 or 20 gauge only) . .	$ 11.50

Du-O-Matic 375, One gauge complete; 12, 16, 20, 28 or 410 gauge, (with 6 or 8 point crimp starter) $189.50
NOTE: 10 gauge available as accessory tooling set only.

Accessories:

375 Additional Tooling Set 12, 16, 20, 28 or 410 gauge . .	$ 59.50
(Crimp starter or head extra)	
375 Special 10 gauge (3½") magnum additional tooling set	$ 99.50
(Includes tool head, tooling and 6 point crimp starter)	
375 Crimp Starter Complete (6 or 8 point)	$ 14.00
Crimp Starter Head Only (6 or 8 point)	$ 7.00
375 3" Conversion Kit (12, 20 or 410 gauge)	$ 10.50
(For 20 gauge, brand of ammunition to be loaded should be specified)	
375 2½", 12 gauge conversion kit	$ 24.50
(for international 65/67.5mm 12 gauge shells only)	
375 Tool head (No tooling included)	$ 24.50
Special Paper Crimp Assembly	$ 11.50

PONSNESS-WARREN
SHOTSHELL RELOADING TOOLS

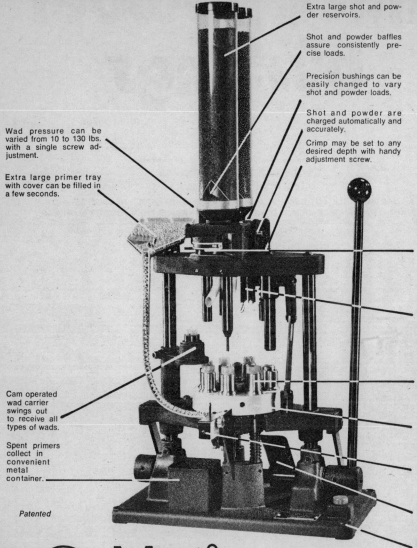

Extra large shot and powder reservoirs.

Shot and powder baffles assure consistently precise loads.

Precision bushings can be easily changed to vary shot and powder loads.

Shot and powder are charged automatically and accurately.

Crimp may be set to any desired depth with handy adjustment screw.

Wad pressure can be varied from 10 to 130 lbs. with a single screw adjustment.

Extra large primer tray with cover can be filled in a few seconds.

Shut off switches enable operator to stop flow of powder or shot at any time during cycle. Switches include a drain feature which permits complete draining of reservoirs.

Six and eight point crimp starters are ball bearing lined to assure perfect crimp alignment automatically.

Absolute resizing. Shell remains in full length, precision die through the entire operation, eliminating feeding and chambering problems and assuring increased case life.

Cam operated wad carrier swings out to receive all types of wads.

Spent primers collect in convenient metal container.

Cylinder indexes automatically. A factory perfect shell is produced with every pull of the handle.

Unique automatic primer feed system is dependable and completely safe.

Finished shell is automatically ejected by knock out rod down convenient shell chute at rear.

Rugged aluminum castings are finished in a handsome baked-on black wrinkle varnish.

Patented

Size-O-Matic

Model 800B

This is the ultimate shotshell reloader, the tool for the shooter who demands the finest in all the world—unequaled performance. It is an incredibly efficient machine. One reasonably experienced operator can load shells at a rate of 700 rounds per hour; two operators, 1200 rounds; three operators, as many as 1800 rounds per hour. Individual rates will vary slightly according to the experience and dexterity of the operator or operators. The Size-O-Matic has an ingenious automatic primer feed system with no tubes to fill and primers always in full view of the operator. A full box of 100 primers loads in just seconds. Each shell is held in a full-length sizing die through the entire loading operation, affording consistently perfect reloads, guaranteed to feed and

chamber into any firearm. All tooling is ground to exacting specifications, then polished or richly blued. Nylon liners virtually eliminate wear. The Size-O-Matic will handle paper or plastic shells, either high or low base, with unmatched ease and speed.

*No separate case resizer or conditioner needed

Pricing data

Size-O-Matic 800B Complete (with 6 or 8 point crimp
starter) 12, 20, 28 or 410 gauge $649.50
The 28 and 410 gauge 800B's are designed primarily to load plastic
casings using one piece plastic wads.

Accessories:

800B Crimp Starter Complete (6 or 8 point)	$ 14.00
Crimp Starter Head only (6 or 8 point)	$ 7.00
Special Paper Crimp Assembly (12 or 20 gauge only) ...	$ 11.50
Additional Shot or Powder Bushings	$ 2.50
Additional Wad Guide Fingers	$ 1.25

PONSNESS-WARREN
shot & powder bushings

SHOT BUSHINGS

1 – 1/2 oz.	4 – 7/8 oz.	7 – 1-1/4 oz.	10 – 1-5/8 oz.	13 – 2 oz.
2 – 5/8 oz.	5 – 1 oz.	8 – 1-3/8 oz.	11 – 1-3/4 oz.	14 – 2¼ oz.
3 – 3/4 oz.	6 – 1-1/8 oz.	9 – 1-1/2 oz.	12 – 1-7/8 oz.	

(All shot bushings meet N.S.S.A. and A.T.A. requirements)

POWDER BUSHINGS
(UNITS SHOWN IN GRAINS)

THIS IS NOT A LOADING TABLE, BUT RATHER A CHART BASED ON RELATIVE HOLE SIZES, SHOWING THE APPROXIMATE NUMBER OF GRAINS DROPPED BY PONSNESS-WARREN POWDER BUSHINGS.

	DU PONT					HERCULES						WINCHESTER					HODGDON			ALCAN		
	700-X	PB	SR 7625	SR 4756	IMR 4227	RED DOT	GREEN DOT	BLUE DOT	HERCO	UNIQUE	2400	296	452AA	473AA	540	571	HS-5	HS-6	H-110	AL-5	AL-7	AL-8
1A					12.1					12.1		13.7		—					13.7			
2A					12.6					12.6		14.8							14.8			
3A					14.0						13.9	15.6		15.3					15.6			
A	8.8	9.3	10.0	10.5	15.9	8.0	8.0		10.0	11.3	15.8	17.5			16.8	17.1	18.2	16.8	17.5	13.2	13.2	
B	9.5	9.7	11.0	11.0	16.8	8.5	8.5		10.6	12.1	16.7	18.8			17.6	18.2	19.5	17.7	18.8	14.1	14.1	
C	10.0	10.3	11.5	12.0	17.8	9.3	9.3		11.3	12.7	17.7	20.0			18.5	18.8	20.7	18.8	20.0	14.6	14.6	
C1	10.3	10.4	11.9	12.4	18.2	9.5	9.5		11.7	13.2	18.0				19.6	20.1	21.1	19.2	20.6	14.9	14.9	
D	10.8	11.1	12.5	13.0	19.1	9.8	9.8		12.1	13.8	19.2				20.4	21.0	22.3	20.5	21.5	16.0	16.0	
D1	11.4	12.3	13.6	13.7	19.9	10.7	10.7		13.2	14.5	20.0		15.5		21.3	22.4	23.4	21.9		16.8	16.8	
E	12.4	13.1	15.0	15.0	22.6	11.5	11.5		14.6	16.2	22.5		16.8		23.5	24.2	25.5	24.2		18.7	18.7	
E1	12.9	13.8	15.6	15.8	23.9	12.1	12.1	19.1	15.3	17.0	23.7		17.1		24.0	24.7	28.3	25.5		19.7	19.7	
E2	13.6	14.5	16.8	16.6	25.2	12.8	12.8	21.7	16.0	17.9	25.3		15.0	18.0	26.1	26.5	28.9	26.8		20.8	20.8	
F	14.5	15.3	18.0	17.5	26.5	13.5	13.5	22.0	16.7	18.8	26.3		15.6	19.6	27.5	28.5	30.4	28.0		21.9	21.9	17.8
F1	15.0	16.1	19.2	18.4	27.9	14.1	14.1	22.4	17.7	19.7	27.7		16.4	20.1	28.3	29.3	31.5	29.4		23.0	23.0	18.6
G	16.3	17.0	20.5	19.5	29.3	14.7	14.7	24.5	18.6	20.6	29.0		18.3	22.7	31.2	32.3	33.6	30.7		24.1	24.1	19.5
G1	17.0	18.4	21.7	21.1	31.5	15.9	15.9	26.2	19.9	22.6	31.4		19.0	23.0	32.7	33.4	36.4	33.1		26.1	26.1	21.4
H	17.9	18.8	22.0	21.5	32.1	16.5	16.5	27.0	20.2	23.1	32.1		19.9	24.1	34.0	34.8	37.0	33.6		26.7	26.7	21.9
I	18.5	19.2	22.5	22.0	33.0	17.0	17.0	27.8	20.7	23.5	33.0		20.3	24.7	34.4	36.5	38.3	35.0		27.3	27.3	22.4
J	19.0	19.7	23.0	22.5	34.0	17.2	17.2	28.2	21.5	24.4	34.0		21.5	25.4	35.5	37.1	39.5	36.2		28.2	28.2	23.2
J1	19.6	20.3	24.2	23.2	35.4	17.7	17.9	29.3	22.2	25.4	35.4		22.3	26.8	36.9	38.8	40.7	37.2		29.1	29.1	23.7
K	20.0	20.9	24.5	24.0	35.9	18.2	18.2	29.5	22.7	25.8	36.0		22.5	27.0	37.1	39.0	41.9	38.3		29.9	29.9	24.2
L	21.0	21.7	26.3	25.5	37.4	19.0	19.0	31.3	24.2	27.3	37.5		23.4		39.5	41.1	43.8	39.4		31.0	31.0	25.3
M	22.0	23.0	27.3	26.5	39.6	19.9	19.9	32.7	25.3	28.1	39.5		24.0		41.2	42.8	45.9	41.8		32.9	32.9	26.8
N	23.5	24.5	28.8	28.0	42.0	21.2	21.2	35.0	26.4	30.3	42.5		26.5			46.4	48.7	44.6		34.8	34.8	28.5
O	24.0	24.7	29.3	28.5	42.4	21.5	21.5	35.5	26.8	30.5	42.5						49.4	45.3		35.4	35.4	28.7
P	24.5	25.8	30.3	29.5	43.8	22.0	22.0	36.0	27.1	30.9	43.8						49.9	45.5		36.0	36.0	29.5
Q	25.0	26.2	30.8	30.0	44.8	22.8	22.8	37.5	28.1	32.2	45.0						52.4	47.6		37.4	37.4	30.3
R	25.5	26.6	31.3	30.5	45.4	23.3	23.3	38.5	29.3	32.8	45.5						53.0	49.5		38.3	38.3	31.0
S	26.5	27.7	32.8	32.0		23.8	23.8	39.2	29.9	33.8	47.2						54.7	49.9		38.9	38.9	32.2
T	28.0	29.2	33.8	33.5		25.2	25.2	42.0	31.6	36.1	49.9						57.8	52.6		41.7	41.7	33.8
U	29.5	30.9	36.3	36.5		26.7	26.7	45.1	32.7	38.1	52.8						61.4	56.9		43.8	43.8	35.8
V	30.5	31.9	36.8	36.5		27.5	27.5	46.3	33.7	38.9	54.5						63.0	57.4		45.0	45.0	37.1
W	32.5	33.7	39.3	39.0		28.9	28.9	48.1	35.9	41.8	57.5						66.8	61.2		47.8	47.8	39.3
X	33.0	34.1	39.8	39.5		29.4	29.4	48.7	36.4	42.1	58.1									48.5	48.5	39.6
Y	34.0	35.7	41.3	41.0		30.8	30.8	50.3	37.9	43.7	60.6									50.5	50.5	41.3
Z	38.0	39.3	45.8	45.5		33.9	33.9	56.3	42.8	48.2	67.2									55.5	55.5	46.1
AA	41.0	42.2	49.3	49.0		37.1	37.1	60.6	46.0	52.2	72.4									60.4	60.4	49.6

All Ponsness-Warren reloaders and additional tooling sets come with one shot bushing and one powder bushing included. If you have need to vary your loads, additional bushings are $2 each.

Drops from powder bushings will vary slightly depending on the model of tool, the stability of the loading bench and the individual operator as well as for the reasons stated below. *We recommend that you weigh a powder charge prior to each reloading session so that you can be assured of the exact powder drop you are getting.*

The above data has been obtained by methods and from sources that are normally reliable. Since Ponsness-Warren has no control over the actual loading, choice or condition of firearms and components, no responsibility for any use of this data is assumed or implied. It is wise to weigh a few charges of powder before each loading session. Powder charges can be affected by a number of factors, the most important being humidity. With some particularly hygroscopic powders, charges may vary as much as 5%. Other factors are oil or residue on drop tubes and bushings, varying density between powder lots and inconsistent operation.

PONSNESS-WARREN

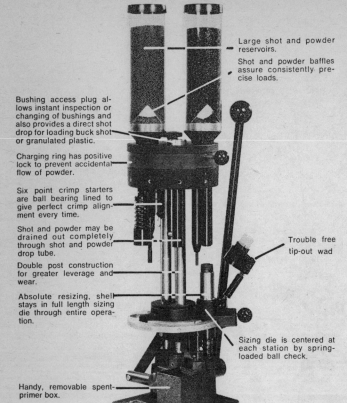

Large shot and powder reservoirs.

Shot and powder baffles assure consistently precise loads.

Bushing access plug allows instant inspection or changing of bushings and also provides a direct shot drop for loading buck shot or granulated plastic.

Charging ring has positive lock to prevent accidental flow of powder.

Six point crimp starters are ball bearing lined to give perfect crimp alignment every time.

Shot and powder may be drained out completely through shot and powder drop tube.

Double post construction for greater leverage and wear.

Absolute resizing, shell stays in full length sizing die through entire operation.

Handy, removable spent-primer box.

Trouble free tip-out wad

Sizing die is centered at each station by spring-loaded ball check.

Patented

Magn-O-Matic 10*

Special 10 gauge shotshell reloader

The Big 10 is here! Because of the growing interest in 10 gauge reloading, we have redesigned our popular Du-O-Matic into a special 10 gauge reloader, the Magn-O-Matic 10. It has all the features of its twin, the Du-O-Matic, with the exception of being convertible to other gauges. The Magn-O-Matic 10 is an exclusive 10 gauge tool for 3½ inch magnum shells. A special shot drop tube allows up to BB shot to be loaded easily, without bridging in the drop tube, while a special bushing access plug allows direct shot drop for even larger sizes. New shot and powder bushings will accommodate all 10 gauge loads up to 2¼ ounces. The Magn-O-Matic 10 possesses all of Ponsness-Warren's exclusive features. Factory-perfect reloads are made consistently by moving a shell encased in a full-length sizing die around the five station loading plate. The full length siz-

ing die and tooling are precision ground, then polished or richly blued. All castings are of the finest grade aluminum, precision machined and handsomely finished in baked-on, black wrinkle varnish. The Magn-O-Matic 10 will handle all types of 10-gauge 3½" shells at a rate of 4 to 6 boxes of shells per hour.

*No separate case resizer or conditioner needed

Pricing data

S.T.O.S. Lubricant

This special lubricant, besides being ideal for our reloading tools, for all firearms and as a case sizing lubricant, is also excellent for any bearing, gear or caming surface—wherever friction-free performance is required.

Shot and Powder bushings

Our bushings are manufactured with extreme care to assure absolute accuracy and consistent performance. Shot and powder bushings are of different diameters to eliminate any possibility of their being reversed. Aluminum powder bushings absolutely eliminate sparking. All bushings are clearly and permanently marked.

Crimp starters

Our six and eight point crimp starters are ball bearing lined and have sensitive automatic pick-up fingers to assure perfect crimp alignment every time. The crimp heads are interchangeable, so to broaden the loading capabilities of the tools, additional crimp heads can be attached to the original crimp starter housing.

Special paper crimp assembly

This paper crimp conversion kit is intended for shooters who reload paper shells predominately. The crimp assembly which is standard on all Ponsness-Warren tools is designed primarily for plastic shells, and while paper shells can be loaded adequately, this special paper crimp assembly provides optimum appearance for paper shells. Installation can be accomplished easily in just a few minutes.

Wad guide fingers

Our engineers, taking advantage of recent developments in the plastics industry, have developed a wad guide finger with longer life and greater spring action than any available before. Our wad guide fingers handle all types of wad and are adaptable to most shotshell reloading tools. They are available in 10, 12, 16, 20, 28 and 410 gauge.

PONSNESS-WARREN

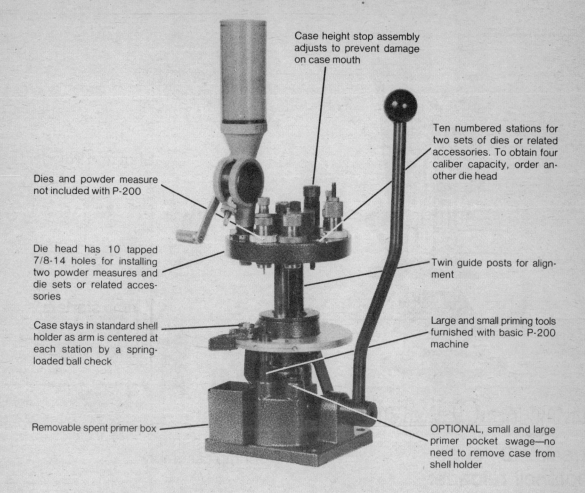

Case height stop assembly adjusts to prevent damage on case mouth

Ten numbered stations for two sets of dies or related accessories. To obtain four caliber capacity, order another die head

Dies and powder measure not included with P-200

Die head has 10 tapped 7/8-14 holes for installing two powder measures and die sets or related accessories

Case stays in standard shell holder as arm is centered at each station by a spring-loaded ball check

Removable spent primer box

Twin guide posts for alignment

Large and small priming tools furnished with basic P-200 machine

OPTIONAL, small and large primer pocket swage—no need to remove case from shell holder

Metal-Matic P-200

Straight-wall case loader

The Metal-Matic P-200 has been designed to hold two calibers at one time. Conversion from one caliber to another is accomplished in less than five minutes. The P-200 uses standard 7/8-14 die sets and powder measure. Castings are heavy die cast aluminum coated with a silver vein black plastic applied with electrostatics and baked on for durability. Under normal conditions a person can load 200 rounds per hour, with some exceeding this average. The P-200 is designed for straight-wall cartridges.

Pricing data

Metal-Matic P-200 Complete (with small and large primer seating tools, less dies and powder measure)............ $225.00

Accessories:

Extra die head	$ 27.50
Large primer pocket swaging tool....	$ 15.00
Small primer pocket swaging tool....	$ 15.00
Case height stop assembly	$ 15.00

RCBS
RELOADING EQUIPMENT

RCBS AUTOMATIC PRIMING TOOL

Precision-engineered to provide fast, accurate and uniform seating of primers in one simple step. Single-stage leverage system is so sensitive it enables you to actually "feel" the primer being seated to the bottom of the primer pocket. This priming tool permits you to visually check each primer pocket before seating the primer; thus eliminating wasted motion or slowing down the reloading process.

Primers are released one at a time through the RCBS automatic primer feed, eliminating contamination caused by handling primers with oily fingers.

Both primer rod assemblies furnished with this tool will handle all large and small American-made Boxer-type rifle and pistol primers.

ECONOMY FEATURES: If you already have RCBS automatic primer feed tubes, and RCBS shell holders, they will fit this RCBS Priming Tool—thus eliminating the need to buy extras.

BERDAN PRIMER ROD ASSEMBLIES

Optional Berdan Primer Rod Assemblies are available in the three sizes shown below, and are interchangeable with the American Boxer-type Primer Rod Assemblies, furnished with the Priming Tool.

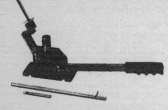

PART NO.	DESCRIPTION	PRICE
09460	Priming Tool (less Shell Holder)	$32.00

RCBS AUTOMATIC PRIMER FEED

Stop misfires — greasy hands never need to touch primers. Automatically drops primers one at a time into the Primer Plug and Sleeve of the Primer Arm. Adjustable Primer Stop Pin eliminates jamming found in other Automatic Primer Feeds. Easily mounted on RCBS and most "C" type Presses. The Primer Tubes for large and small primers are completely interchangeable with the Body.

PART NO.	AUTO. PRIMER FEED	PRICE
09589	Combo for large and small primers	$9.20
09592	Tube for large primers	2.80
09593	Tube for small primers	2.80
09594	Body only	5.70

RCBS PRIMER POCKET SWAGER

For fast, precision removal of primer pocket crimp from military cases. Leaves primer pocket perfectly rounded and with correct dimensions for seating of American Boxer-type primers. Will not leave oval-shaped primer pocket that reaming produces. Swager Head Assemblies furnished for large and small primer pockets — no need to buy a complete unit for each primer size. For use with all presses with standard 7/8"-14 top thread, except RCBS "A-3" Press. The RCBS "A-2" Press requires the optional Case Stripper Washer.

PART NO.	POCKET SWAGER	PRICE
09495	Combo for large and small primers	$10.80

RCBS UNIVERSAL PRIMER ARM

ONE PRIMER ARM HANDLES ALL PRIMERS

RCBS Primer Arms are designed for fast, accurate seating of primers. Interchangeable Primer Plugs and Sleeves eliminate necessity of having to buy a complete new Primer Arm for each primer size. Primer Plugs and Sleeves furnished for large and small primers. Body cast of rust-resistant zinc alloy. The Universal Primer Arm is designed for use with RCBS Rock Chucker and J.R. as well as most "C" type Presses.

PART NO.	UNIVERSAL PRIMER ARM	PRICE
09500	For large and small primers	$4.60
09502	Plug and Sleeve for large primers	1.50
09503	Plug and Sleeve for small primers	1.50

RCBS PRIMER TRAY

For fast, easy handling of primers and loading Automatic Primer Feed Tubes, place primers in this tray, shake tray horizontally, and primers will automatically position themselves anvil side up. Sturdy plastic case.

PART NO.	PRIMER TRAY	PRICE
09475	Single Tray	$1.40

RCBS PRIMER POCKET BRUSH

A slight twist of this tool thoroughly cleans residue out of primer pockets. Interchangeable stainless steel brushes, for large and small primer pockets, attaches easily to Accessory Handle.

PART NO.	PRIMER POCKET BRUSH	PRICE
09574	Complete, Combo	$6.80
09577	Brush Only, Large	3.00
09578	Brush Only, Small	3.00

RCBS RELOADING TOOLS

RCBS CASE LUBE KIT

Everything you need for proper case lubrication! Kit contains RCBS Case Lube Pad, 2 ounce tube RCBS Resizing Lubricant and RCBS Accessory Handle with .22 and .30 caliber Case Neck Brushes. See descriptions of items below.

PART NO.	DESCRIPTION	PRICE
09335	Case Lube Kit	$7.50

RCBS RESIZING LUBRICANT

A must for proper lubrication of cases before sizing or forming. Easily applied to cases with an RCBS Case Lube Pad. Packaged in convenient 2 ounce tube.

PART NO.	RESIZING LUBRICANT	PRICE
09300	Single Tube	$1.00

RCBS CASE NECK BRUSH

A handy tool for removing dirt and powder residue, and for lightly lubricating the insides of case necks to ease neck expanding operation. Accessory Handle accepts interchangeable nylon bristle Case Neck Brushes in the calibers shown below. Order Accessory Handle, and Brush in caliber of your choice.

SMALL	.22-.25 caliber	$1.00
MEDIUM	.270-.30 caliber	1.00
LARGE	.35-.45 caliber	1.00

RCBS CASE LUBE PAD

This companion to RCBS Resizing Lubricant is ideal for lubricating cases before sizing or forming. Cases rolled lightly across Pad pick up just the right amount of lubricant. Plastic cover to protect pad.

PART NO	CASE LUBE PAD	PRICE
09305	1 Pad	$3.80

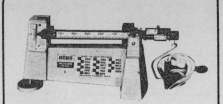

RCBS MODEL 5-10 SCALE

A major improvement in reloading scales. Gives fast, accurate weighings of powder charges and cartridge components, from 1/10th to 510 grains. **NEW Micrometer Poise** permits fast precision adjustments from 1/10th to 10 grains by merely rotating micrometer-type cylinder. **NEW Approach-to-Weight** Feature visually tells reloader when he is approaching the pre-set weight. **Easy-to-read scale beam** is graduated in 1/10th grain increments; has conventional large poise and extra-deep notches. **Magnetic Damper** eliminates beam oscillation. All-metal base and extra-large leveling foot reduce tipping. Weighted, anti-tip pan hanger, and pan platform accommodate long cartridges and components.

PART NO.	DESCRIPTION	PRICE
09070	Reloading Scale	$45.00
09072	Metric	52.00

RCBS POWDER TRICKLER

For fast, easy balancing of scales with precision powder charges. Merely twist knob and powder trickles into the scale pan a kernel at a time. Has large capacity powder reservoir. Extra large base minimizes tipping.

PART NO.	DESCRIPTION	PRICE
09094	Powder Trickler	$5.60

RCBS POWDER MEASURE STAND

Now more height — a full seven inches from the reloading bench to the bottom of the threads! The ideal accessory for raising Powder Measure to proper working height. Permits placing of Reloading Scale or cases in loading block under Powder Measure Drop Tube. Easily bolts to loading bench. For all Powder Measures with standard ⅞" - 14 thread.

PART NO.	DESCRIPTION	PRICE
09030	Powder Measure Stand	$11.40

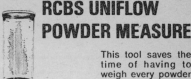

RCBS UNIFLOW POWDER MEASURE

This tool saves the time of having to weigh every powder charge when reloading a quantity of cases. With it you will be able to throw consistently accurate and uniform powder charges directly into cases. RCBS Precisioneered Measuring Cylinder pours powder into case to eliminate clogging that occurs in powder measures that "dump" charges. Adjusts quickly and easily from one charge to another without emptying powder hopper. Powder level visible at all times. Includes stand plate for mounting on press or bench, and two drop tubes to fit from .22 to .45 caliber cases. Optional .17 caliber drop tube also available. Choice of large measuring cylinder for rifle cases, or small measuring cylinder for bench rest or pistol cases.

PART NO.	POWDER MEASURE	PRICE
09001	With Large Measuring Cylinder	$32.50
09002	With Small Measuring Cylinder	32.50
09000	Combo with Large & Small Measuring Cylinders	39.50
09003	Large Measuring Cylinder Assembly*	9.20
09004	Small Measuring Cylinder Assembly*	9.20
09028	Drop Tube .17 caliber	3.50

*Consists of Measuring Cylinder and Measuring Screw.

RCBS POWDER FUNNEL

For powder charging just a few cases at a time. Large, easy-to-use, plastic Powder Funnel in two sizes: .22 to .45 calibers, and .17 caliber. Specially designed drop tube prevents powder spills around case mouths. Antistatic treatment prevents powder from sticking. Square lip stops Funnel from rolling.

PART NO.	POWDER FUNNEL	PRICE
09090	.22-.45 calibers	$1.60
09088	.17 caliber	1.60

RCBS RELOADING TOOLS

RELOADER SPECIAL
RCBS R.S. PRESS COMBINATION OFFER

Costs less than 9 boxes of .30-06 cartridges

This RCBS J.R. Press is the ideal setup to get started reloading your own rifle and pistol ammo — from the largest Magnums down to .22 Hornets. This Press develops ample leverage and pressure to perform all reloading tasks including (1) resizing cases their full length, (2) forming cases from one caliber into another, (3) making bullets. Rugged Block "O" Frame, designed by RCBS, prevents Press from springing out of alignment — even under tons of pressure. Extra-long ram-bearing surface minimizes wobble and side play. Comfort grip handle. Converts to up or down stroke in minutes. Standard 7/8"-14 thread accepts all popular dies and reloading accessories. Price includes: PRIMER CATCHER, to collect ejected primers; RCBS UNIVERSAL PRIMER ARM with large and small primer plugs and sleeves; RCBS SHELL HOLDER; one set of RCBS DIES in choice of calibers shown below.

PART NO.	R.S. PRESS, LESS DIES	PRICE
09356	Less Shell Holder	$49.00

$65.00

ROCK CHUCKER "COMBO"
RCBS R.C. PRESS COMBINATION OFFER

For Heavy-Duty Reloading

U.S. Pat. No. 2,847,895

The Rock Chucker Press, with Patented RCBS Compound Leverage System, delivers up to 200% more leverage than most presses for heavy-duty reloading of even the largest rifle and pistol cases. Rugged, Block "O" Frame prevents Press from springing out of alignment — even under the most strenuous operations. It case-forms as easily as most presses full-length size; it full-length sizes and makes bullets with equal ease. Shell Holders snap into sturdy, all-purpose shell holder ram. Non-slip handle with convenient grip. Operates on down-stroke for increased leverage. Standard 7/8"-14 thread. Price includes: PRIMER CATCHER to collect spent primers; RCBS UNIVERSAL PRIMER ARM with large and small primer plugs and sleeves; one RCBS SHELL HOLDER; one set of RCBS DIES in choice of calibers shown below.

PART NO.	ROCK CHUCKER PRESS, LESS DIES	PRICE
09366	Less Shell Holder	$77.00

$94.00

RCBS DIE CHART

RIFLE CALIBERS	ROCK CHUCKER COMBO PART NO.	RIFLE CALIBERS	ROCK CHUCKER COMBO PART NO.	PISTOL CALIBERS	ROCK CHUCKER COMBO PART NO.
.17 Remington	17281	7.7mmx58 Japanese Arisaka	14481	.22 Remington Jet	10481
.218 Bee	10081	.30 M1 Carbine	18081	.221 Remington Fire Ball	10881
.22 Hornet	10281	.30-30 Winchester	14681	.25 ACP (.25 Automatic)	21084
.22 Remington Jet	10481	.30-40 Krag	14781	.32 ACP (7.65mm Auto)	20084
.22 Savage High Power	10581	.30-06 Springfield	14881	.32 Smith & Wesson Long (RN)	20184
.22-250 (.22 Varminter)	10681	.300 H&H Magnum	15081	.32 Smith & Wesson Long (WC)	20187
.220 Swift	10781	.300 Savage	15181	.32-20 Winchester	18181
.221 Remington Fire Ball	10881	.300 Weatherby Magnum	15281	.357 Magnum (RN)	18285
.222 Remington	10981	.300 Winchester Magnum	15381	.357 Magnum (SWC)	18286
.222 Remington Magnum	11081	.303 British	15481	.357 Magnum (WC)	18287
.223 Remington (5.56mm)	11181	.308 Winchester	15581	.38 Colt Super Automatic	20284
.225 Winchester	11381	.308 Norma Magnum	15681	.38 Smith & Wesson	20384
.243 Winchester	11481	.32 Winchester Special	15781	.38 Special (RN)	18385
6mm Remington (.244 Rem.)	11581	8x57 Mauser (8mm Mauser)	15981	.38 Special (SWC)	18386
.25-20 Winchester	11881	8mm Remington Magnum	16081	.38 Special (WC)	18387
.25-06	12081	.338 Winchester Magnum	16381	.380 Auto Pistol	20484
.25-35 Winchester	12181	.35 Remington	16581	9mm Luger	20584
.250 Savage (.250-3000 Sav.)	12281	.375 H&H Magnum	16981	.41 Magnum (RN)	18585
.257 Roberts	12581	.444 Marlin	20784	.41 Magnum (SWC)	18586
.257 Weatherby Magnum	12681	.458 Winchester Magnum	20884	.41 Magnum (WC)	18587
.264 Winchester Magnum	12781	.45-70 US Government	20984	.44 Magnum (RN)	18685
6.5mmx55 Swedish Mauser	13281			.44 Magnum (SWC)	18686
.270 Weatherby Magnum	13481	NOTE: The following abbreviations are used to indicate bullet seater plug types (RN) Round Nose, (SWC) Semi-Wadcutter, (WC) Wadcutter.		.44 Magnum (WC)	18687
.270 Winchester	13581			.44 Special	18786
7mm Remington Magnum	13681			.44-40 Win. (.44 Win.) (RN)	18885
7mm Weatherby Magnum	13781			.45 Auto (.45 ACP) (RN)	18985
7x57 Mauser (7mm Mauser)	13881			.45 Auto (.45 ACP) (SWC)	18986
7mmx64 Brenneke	17381			.45 Auto (.45 ACP) (WC)	18987
.280 Remington	14081			.45 Colt (RN)	19185
.284 Winchester	14181			.45 Colt (SWC)	19186
7.65x53mm Mauser (Belgian)	14381				

RCBS RELOADING TOOLS

IMPORTANT
Before checking these tables for the Die Set you require, refer to Die Reference Table. When you find the caliber you want, note the letter in Die Group column. This letter tells you which Group your caliber will be listed under in this section (Group A, B, C, etc.).

Each of these Full Length Die Sets includes a Full Length Sizer Die with Expander-Decapping Assembly and a Seater Die with built-in crimper.

GROUP A — $20.50 — Full Length Die Set 1½ lbs.

.17 Remington	17201
.218 Bee	10001
.22 Hornet	10201
.22 Remington Jet	10401
.22 Savage High Power	10501
.22-250 (.22 Varminter)	10601
.220 Swift	10701
.221 Remington Fire Ball	10801
.222 Remington	10901
.222 Remington Magnum	11001
.223 Remington (5.56mm)	11101
.225 Winchester	11301
.243 Winchester	11401
6mm Remington (.244 Remington)	11501
.25-06	12001
.25-20 Winchester	11801
.25-35 Winchester	12101
.250 Savage (.250-3000 Savage)	12201
.257 Roberts	12501
.257 Weatherby Magnum	12601
.264 Winchester Magnum	12701
6.5mmx55 Swedish Mauser	13201
.270 Weatherby Magnum	13401
.270 Winchester	13501
7mm Remington Magnum	13601
7mm Weatherby Magnum	13701
7mmx57 Mauser (7mm Mauser)	13801
7mmx57R Mauser	13801
7mmx64 Brenneke	17301
.280 Remington	14001
.284 Winchester	14101
7.65mmx53 Mauser (Belgian)	14301
7.7mmx58 Japanese Arisaka	14401
.30-30 Winchester	14601
.30-40 Krag	14701
.30-06 Springfield	14801
.300 Holland & Holland Magnum	15001
.300 Savage	15101
.300 Weatherby Magnum	15201
.300 Winchester Magnum	15301
.303 British	15401
.308 Winchester	15501
.308 Norma Magnum	15601
.32 Winchester Special	15701
8mmx57 Mauser (8mm Mauser)	15901
8mm Remington Magnum	16001
.338 Winchester Magnum	16301
.35 Remington	16501
.375 Holland & Holland Magnum	16901

GROUP B — $20.50 — 3-Die Set 1½ lbs.

.30 M1 Carbine (RN)	18005
.32-20 Winchester (RN)	18105
.357 Magnum (RN)	18205
.357 Magnum (SWC)	18206
.357 Magnum (WC)	18207
.38 Special (RN)	18305
.38 Special (SWC)	18306
.38 Special (WC)	18307
.41 Magnum (RN)	18505
.41 Magnum (SWC)	18506
.41 Magnum (WC)	18507
.44 Magnum (RN)	18605
.44 Magnum (SWC)	18606
.44 Magnum (WC)	18607
.44 Special (SWC)	18706
.44-40 Winchester (.44 Win.) (RN)	18805
.45 Automatic (.45 ACP) (RN)	18905
.45 Automatic (.45 ACP) (SWC)	18906
.45 Automatic (.45 ACP) (WC)	18907
.45 Colt (RN)	19105
.45 Colt (SWC)	19106

(RN) — Roundnose, (SWC) — Semi-Wadcutter, (WC) — Wadcutter.

GROUP D — $24.50 — Full Length Die Set 1½ lbs.

.219 Zipper	26001
.22 K-Hornet	26201
.224 Weatherby Magnum	32301
.240 Weatherby Magnum	33201
.256 Winchester Magnum	33301
.257 Improved (40°)	32221
6.5mm Remington Magnum	33401
6.5mm-06	27801
6.5mmx50 Japanese Arisaka	32401
6.5mmx52 Carcano	27601
6.5mmx54 Mannlicher-Schoenauer	27701
6.5mmx57	32801
7mmx65 Rimmed	33001
7.5mm Schmidt-Rubin	33501
7.62mm Russian	29001
7.62mmx39	32901
.30 Herrett	33101
.30 Remington	29201
.30-338 Winchester Magnum	29401
.303 Savage	29601
.32-40 Winchester	32501
8mm-06	32601
.33 Winchester	30501
.340 Weatherby Magnum	30601
.348 Winchester	33601
.35 Whelen	30701
.350 Remington Magnum	33701
.358 Norma Magnum	31001
.358 Winchester	32701
.30 Luger (7.65mm Luger)	25001
.30 Mauser (7.63mm Mauser)	25101

These 3-Die Sets include a Sizer Die with Decapping Unit, Expander Die with Expander and Seater Die with built-in Crimper.

GROUP C — $24.50 — 3-Die Set 1½ lbs.

.444 Marlin	20704
.458 Winchester Magnum	20804
.45-70 U.S. Government	20904
.25ACP (.25 Automatic)	21004
.32 ACP (7.65mm Automatic)	20004
.32 Smith & Wesson, Long (RN)	20104
.32 Smith & Wesson, Long (WC)	20107
.38 Colt Super Automatic	20204
.38 Smith & Wesson	20304
.380 Auto Pistol	20404
9mm Luger	20504

GROUP F — $26.50 — 3-Die Set 1½ lbs.

.38-55 Winchester & Ballard	36504
.50-70 U.S. Government	38704
8mm Nambu	36404

RCBS originated 3-Die (and 4-Die) sets for straight wall rifle and pistol cases to avoid "overworking" of the brass case. Sizing is done in one Die, expanding in another, and seating in the final die.

The 3-Die Sets include a Sizer Die, Expander Die with Expander-Decapping Assembly and Seater Die with built-in crimper.

GROUP E — $24.50 — 3-Die Set 1½ lbs.

.357 Auto Magnum	35505
.38-40 Winchester (RN)*	35605
.45 Auto Rim (RN)	35705

*Jacketed bullets only —
others on Special Order at extra cost.

RCBS RELOADING TOOLS

SMALL BASE DIES
GROUP A

A must for sizing small base cases to minimum dimensions, thereby ensuring smooth functioning in the actions of automatic, pump, slide and some lever action rifles. Each Small Base Die Set includes a Small Base Sizer Die with Expander-Decapping Assembly and a Seater Die with built-in crimper.

For bottle-neck rifle
& pistol cases

GROUP A Caliber	Small Base Die Set 1 ½ lbs. **$20.50**	Small Base Sizer Die ¾ lb. **$10.50**
.223 Remington (5.6mm) (SB)	11103	11131
.243 Winchester (SB)	11403	11431
6mm Remington (.244 Remington) (SB)	11503	11531
.270 Winchester (SB)	13503	13531
.280 Remington (SB)	14003	14031
.284 Winchester (SB)	14103	14131
.30-06 Springfield (SB)	14803	14831
.300 Savage (SB)	15103	15131
.308 Winchester (SB)	15503	15531

NECK DIES
GROUP A

These Dies size only the neck of the case, not the shoulder or body, just enough to grip the bullet. Each Neck Die Set includes a Neck Sizer Die with Expander-Decapping Assembly and a Seater Die with built-in crimper.

GROUP A Caliber	Neck Die Set 1 ½ lbs. **$20.50**	Neck Sizer Die ¾ lb. **$10.50**
.22-250 (.22 Varminter)	10602	10630
.222 Remington	10902	10930
.222 Remington Magnum	11002	11030
.223 Remington (5.56mm)	11102	11130
.243 Winchester	11402	11430
6mm Remington (.244 Remington)	11502	11530
.25-06	12002	12030
.270 Winchester	13502	13530
7mm Remington Magnum	13602	13630
7mmx57 Mauser (7mm Mauser)	13802	13830
.30-06 Springfield	14802	14830
.300 Winchester Magnum	15302	15330
.308 Winchester	15502	15530

ULTRA SMALL BASE DIES
GROUP A

These are required for sizing case bases and shoulders smaller than is possible with standard Sizer Dies. Each Ultra Small Base Die Set includes an Ultra Small Base Sizer Die with Expander-Decapping Assembly and a Seater Die with built-in crimper.

GROUP A Caliber	Ultra Small Base Die Set 1 ½ lbs.	Ultra Small Base Sizer Die ¾ lb.
.243 Winchester (USB)	11404	11433
.308 Winchester (USB)	15504	15533

BROWNING AUTOMATIC RIFLE DIES
GROUP A

Features shorter headspace than standard Sizer Dies, which is necessary for proper chambering in Browning Automatic Rifles. Each B.A.R. Die Set includes a B.A.R. Sizer Die with Expander-Decapping Assembly and a Seater Die with built-in crimper.

GROUP A Caliber	B.A.R. Die Set 1 ½ lbs.	B.A.R. Sizer Die ¾ lb.
7mm Remington Magnum (BAR)	13605	13640
.300 Winchester Magnum (BAR)	15305	15340

Note: Browning Automatic Rifles in .243 Winchester, .270 Winchester, .30-06 and .308 Winchester calibers require *Small Base Dies* shown above. The .338 caliber rifle requires *Standard Dies.*

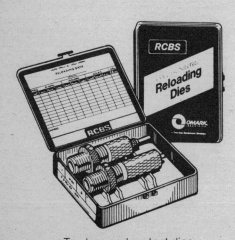

To store and protect dies.

TUNGSTEN CARBIDE DIES
GROUP B

The most extravagant Dies made, these are for the perfectionist who loads large quantities on a regular basis and wants to eliminate the need for lubing cases. Each 3-Die Carbide Set, 4-Die Carbide Set and 4-Die Carbide Set with Tamper Crimp includes a Carbide Sizer Die, Expander Die with Expander-Decapping Assembly. The 3-Die Carbide Set has Seater Die with built-in crimper, while the 4-Die Carbide Sets have a Seater Die without crimper and therefore a separate roll Crimper Die. Either roll or taper. The 4-Die Carbide Sets with Taper Crimp have a Seater Die without crimper and a Taper Crimp Die.

GROUP B

Caliber	Carbide Sizer Die ½ lb.	3-Die Carbide Set 1½ lbs.	4-Die Carbide Set 1½ lbs.	4-Die Carbide Set With Taper Crimp 1½ lbs.	Taper Crimp Die ½ lb.
.30 M-1 Carbine (RN)	18037	18009	—	—	—
.357 Magnum (RN)	18237	18209	18217	18221	18264
.357 Magnum (SWC)	18237	18210	18218	18222	18264
.357 Magnum (WC)	18237	18211	18219	18223	18264
.38 Special (RN)	18237	18309	18317	18321	18264
.38 Special (SWC)	18237	18310	18318	18322	18264
.38 Special (WC)	18237	18311	18319	18323	18264
.41 Magnum (RN)	18537	18509	18517	—	—
.41 Magnum (SWC)	18537	18510	18518	—	—
.41 Magnum (WC)	18537	18511	18519	—	—
.44 Auto Magnum (SWC)	—	—	—	19226*	19264
.44 Auto Magnum (WC)	—	—	—	19227*	19264
.44 Magnum (RN)	18637	18609	18617	—	—
.44 Magnum (SWC)	18637	18610	18618	—	—
.44 Magnum (WC)	18637	18611	18619	—	—
.44 Special (SWC)	18637	18710	18718	—	—
.45 Automatic (RN)	18937	18909	18917	18921	18964
.45 Automatic (SWC)	18937	18910	18918	18922	18964
.45 Automatic (WC)	18937	18911	18919	18923	18964
.45 Colt (RN)	19137	19109	19117	—	—
.45 Colt (SWC)	19137	19110	19118	—	—

*Set includes regular Sizer Die. Tungsten Carbide Sizer Die not available in this caliber.

TUNGSTEN CARBIDE DIES
GROUP C

Identical to above Carbide Dies but for Group C calibers, Each 3-Die Carbide Set and 4-Die Carbide Set with Taper Crimper includes a Carbide Sizer Die with Decapping Assembly and Expander Die with Expander. The 3-Die Carbide Set has Seater Die with built-in crimper. The 4-Die Carbide Set with Taper Crimper has a Seater Die without crimper and a separate Taper Crimp Die.

GROUP C

Caliber	Carbide Sizer Die ½ lb.	3-Die Carbide Set 1½ lbs.	4-Die Carbide Set With Taper Crimp 1½ lbs.	Taper Crimp Die ½ lb.
.32 ACP (7.65mm Automatic)	20037	20009	—	—
.32 Smith & Wesson Long (RN)	20137	20109	20121	20164
.32 Smith & Wesson Long (WC)	20137	20111	20123	20164
.38 Colt Super Automatic	20237	20209	—	—
.380 Auto Pistol	20437	20409	20421	20464
9mm Luger	20537	20509	20521	20564

Note: Browning Automatic Rifles in .243 Winchester, .270 Winchester, .30-06 and .308 Winchester calibers require *Small Base Dies* shown above. The .338 caliber rifle requires *Standard Dies*.

(RN) = Roundnose, (SWC) = Semi-Wadcutter, (WC) = Wadcutter.

RCBS TRIM DIE
TO CUT CASES DOWN TO SIZE.

A sure way of checking and adjusting case lengths. Insert a case into this Trim Die and if it sticks out above the top it's too long. So simply file case down until it is flush with Die top. Don't worry about ruining Die with file – it's been specially heat treated to withstand a file bearing against the top.

After filing, just remove the burrs from outside of case and bevel the inside with an RCBS Burring Tool.

These Dies have precision-machined Sizer Die Chambers, but with slightly larger necks, to guarantee accuracy in gauging case lengths. Headspace is kept to minimum tolerances to avoid accidentally changing the case length when it's run into the Trim Die.

RCBS Trim Dies are available in all calibers for nearly all lengths of cases. For extra short cases, overall length of 1.700" to 0.875", the Trim Die must be used with the Extended Shell Holder. All dies come in plastic storage box.

Trim Die 1/2 lb.	
Caliber	Part No.
GROUP A	
.22 Hornet	10265
.22-250 (.22 Varminter)	10665
.220 Swift	10765
.222 Remington	10965
.223 Remington (5.56mm)	11165
.243 Winchester	11465
6mm Remington (.244 Remington)	11565
.25-06	12065
.257 Roberts	12565
.270 Winchester	13565
7mm Remington Magnum	13665
7x57 Mauser (7mm Mauser)	13865
7.65mmx53 Mauser (Belgian)	14365
.30-30 Winchester	14665
.30-06 Springfield	14865
.300 Weatherby Magnum	15265
.300 Winchester Magnum	15365
.308 Winchester	15565
8x57 Mauser (8mm Mauser)	15965
8mm Remington Magnum	16065
GROUP D	
.30 Herrett	33165
GROUP B	
.30 M-1 Carbine (RN)	18065
.357 Magnum (RN, SWC, WC)	18265
.38 Special (RN, SWC, WC)	18365
.44 Magnum (RN, SWC, WC)	18665
.45 Automatic (.45 ACP) (RN, SWC, WC)	18965
GROUP C	
.45-70 U.S. Government	20965

RCBS RELOADING TOOLS

MODEL 304

Here's a laboratory quality balance scale designed for the advanced reloader. Features include direct reading dial in values from 0.1 to 10 grains, twin tiered beams (10 to 100 grains on one and 100 to 1000 grains on the other) with center reading poises, magnetic dampener and agate bearings. Guaranteed sensitivity 0.1 grain. Includes platform for holding powder trickler.

Model 304 Scale	09074	4¾ lbs.

MODEL 5-0-5

This 511 grain capacity scale has a three poise system with widely spaced, deep beam notches to keep them in place. Two smaller poises on right side adjust from 0.1 to 10 grains, larger one on left side adjusts in full 10 grain steps. The first scale to use magnetic dampening to eliminate beam oscillation, the 5-0-5 also has a sturdy die cast base with large leveling legs for stability. Self-aligning agate bearings support the hardened steel beam pivots for a guaranteed sensitivity to 0.1 grains.

Model 5-0-5 Scale	09071	1½ lbs.

MODEL 5-10

The model number has changed but this is the same scale that reloaders have been using for years. Weighs powder, bullets or complete cartridges up to 510 grains instantly and accurately thanks to a micrometer poise, an approach-to-weight indicator system, large easy-to-read graduations, magnetic dampening, agate bearings and an anti-tip pan. Guaranteed to 0.1 grain sensitivity. Also available in metric readings.

Model 5-10 Scale	09070	2 lbs.
Model 5-10 Metric Scale	09072	2 lbs.

A smart investment to protect the model 5-0-5 or 5-10 scale when not in use. Soft, vinyl dust cover folds easily to stow away, or has loop for hanging up.

Scale Cover	09075	1/8 lb.

Model 505	$34.50
Model 5-10	$45.00
Model 5-10 Metric	$52.00
Model 10-10	$54.00
Model 304	$136.00

Du-O-Measure, 5-0-5 and 10-10 are Registered Trademarks of Ohaus Scale Corporation.

MODEL 10-10

UP TO 1010 GRAIN CAPACITY.

Normal capacity is 510 grains, which can be increased, without loss in sensitivity, by attaching the included extra weight.

Features include micrometer poise for quick, precise weighing, special approach-to-weight indicator, easy-to-read graduations, magnetic dampener, agate bearings anti-tip pan, and dustproof lid snaps on to cover scale for storage. Sensitivity is guaranteed to 0.1 grains.

Model 10-10 Scale	09073	3 lbs.

RCBS ROTARY CASE TRIMMER $30.00
PRECISIONEERED®
09369 CASE TRIMMER WITHOUT COLLET OR PILOT $27.00

CASE TRIMMER PILOT $1.40			
PART NO.	PILOT CAL.	PART NO.	PILOT CAL.
09377	.17	09387	.33
09378	.22	09388	.34
09379	.24	09390	.36
09380	.25	09391	.37
09381	.26	09392	.40
09382	.27	09393	.41
09383	.28	09394	.44
09384	.30	09395	.45
09385	.31	09396	.45-R
09386	.32		

This tool is used to (1) trim to standard length those cases which have stretched after repeated firings; (2) to trim a quantity of cases to the same length for uniform bullet seating; (3) to correct uneven case mouths.

The RCBS Rotary Case Trimmer works just like a lathe. To trim a brass case to the desired length — quickly, easily, and accurately — you lock the case into the trimmer collet. Then adjust the cutting blade to the length you wish case trimmed . . . turn the handle a few times . . . and your case is trimmed. Neatly and accurately. Bevel and deburr the trimmed case mouth with an RCBS Burring Tool and you're ready to reload it!

Interchangeable quick-release collets, available for all popular calibers (.17 to .45), lock cases securely into place for trimming. Trimmer Pilots are Precisioneered to the exact dimension of the case mouth, and lock into the cutter with a setscrew. This eliminates wobbling and ensures perfect vertical and horizontal alignment of case. Pilots are inter-

CASE TRIMMER COLLET $4.00			
PART NO.	COLLET NO.	PART NO.	COLLET NO.
09371	1	09373	3
09372	2	09374	4

changeable and available in twenty sizes to fit from .17 to .45 caliber cases.

Double lock rings on the cutting assembly permit any quantity of cases to be trimmed to the same length with a single adjustment. Cutter blades are made of hardened mill-type steel for extended service life, and removable for sharpening.

The RCBS Case Trimmer is 100 percent metal — no wood or plastic. Has slots for holding extra collets and pilots. Base can be secured to bench with screws.

RCBS RELOADING TOOLS

MODEL 304 SCALE

PART NO.	DESCRIPTION	SHPG. WT.	PRICE
09074	Model 304 Scale	4¾ lbs.	$136.00

The 304 is a laboratory-quality scale offering an easy-to-set **direct reading** dial in values from 0.1 to 10 grains. Instead of the usual single beam, it has **two** tiered beams (10 to 100 grains and 100 to 1000 grains). Both beams have center-reading poises. The magnetic damper, plus agate bearings, provide both speed of operation and accuracy. Guaranteed sensitivity 0.1 grain. Includes platform for holding powder trickler.

RCBS STUCK CASE REMOVER

Removes stuck cases from Sizer Dies quickly and efficiently. To use, back Die Expander-Decapping unit away from case head, drill case head and tap. Then place RCBS Stuck Case Remover on top of case head and turn hexhead screw until stuck case pulls free!

PART NO.	DESCRIPTION	PRICE
09340	STUCK CASE REMOVER	$6.00

RCBS BULLET PULLER

A valuable tool for pulling bullets from cases that have wrong powder charges, or for salvaging bullets from old ammo. Pulls bullets of any length or shape without damaging or marking them. Soft lead bullets may distort. Interchangeable Bullet Puller Collets work like a draw collet on a lathe, securely holding the bullet as the case is pulled away. Each Collet is precision-machined internally to the exact bullet diameter. Fits all reloading presses with standard ⅞"-14 thread. Order Bullet Puller plus one Collet in caliber of your choice from chart below.

PART NO.	DESCRIPTION	PRICE
09440	BULLET PULLER (less Collet)	$5.40
	BULLET PULLER COLLETS	4.00

PART NO.	CALIBER	PART NO.	CALIBER
09419	.17	09428	.32/8mm
09420	.22	09429	.348
09421	6mm	09430	.35/.38 Spec.
09422	.25	09431	.375
09423	6.5mm	09432	.40
09424	.270	09433	.41
09425	7mm	09435	.44/11mm
09426	.30/7.35 Carc	09436	.45
09427	.338		

RCBS BURRING TOOL

For beveling and removing burrs from case mouths of new factory cases, newly formed and trimmed cases. To bevel, insert pointed end of tool into case mouth and twist slightly. To remove burrs, place other end of tool over case mouth and twist. Centering pin keeps case aligned during deburring. Precision-machined and hardened for years of usage. Knurled for use by hand or in lathe. For .17 to .45 calibers.

PART NO.	DESCRIPTION	PRICE
09349	Burring Tool	$6.00

RCBS SETSCREW WRENCH

Here's a handy item for every reloading bench. The convenient hexagonal plastic handle will not roll off bench. Size is stamped in large easy-to-read numbers for quick identification. Available in two sizes to fit all popular RCBS products as shown below:

3/32" Dies/Trim Dies/Case Forming Dies/Automatic Primer Feed attaching screws, bullet molds.

5/64" Universal Primer Arm (new), Case Trimmer

PART NO.	SETSCREW WRENCH	PRICE
09646	Combo	$3.25

RCBS RELOADING GUIDE

Discover how safe and easy reloading actually is. Shows step by step with illustrations, how to reload rifle and pistol ammunition. Contains articles by famous gun writers and instructions by renowned experts and manufacturers. Lists tools you need to start reloading and a beginner's table of powder loads.

PART NO.	RELOADING GUIDE	PRICE
09298	Each	$ 2.00

RCBS RELOADING TOOLS

LUBE-A-MATIC Lubricator

The Lube-A-Matic frame, housing, and lubricant reservoir are cast in one piece—from sturdy cast iron—for strength, rigidity, and simplicity. The ram-bearing surface, and the Die housing, are drilled and reamed straight through, in one operation. This guarantees perfect alignment of the Top Punch with the Bullet Sizer Die below. The construction, combined with the link-leverage system, permits the largest cast bullets to be swaged in one short, continuous stroke, without strain on the sizer-lubricator.

Lube-A-Matic Bullet Sizer Dies—available in many different bullet diameters—lock firmly into the Die housing with a hexagonal Locking Cap.

Intercangeable Top Punches are available to fit the nose of any bullet design, and lock rigidly into the steel ram with an Allen set-screw.

The Lube-A-Matic Bullet Sizer-Lubricator is available completely equipped as shown. Lube-A-Matic Bullet Sizer Dies and Top Punches available separately—are listed below.

Lubricator

PART NO.	DESCRIPTION	SHPG. WT.	PRICE
80060	Lube-A-Matic—less Sizer Die and Top Punch	8 lbs.	$55.00

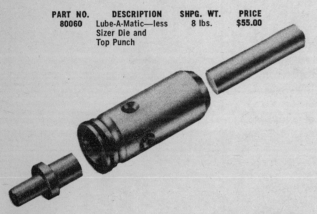

LUBE-A-MATIC TOP PUNCHES

These Top Punches are designed for use in the RCBS Lube-A-Matic Bullet Sizer-Lubricator or with most other popular sizer-lubricators. Each Top Punch is precision machined for a perfect fit to the contour of the bullet nose. Locks into Bullet Sizer-Lubricator ram with Allen setscrew.

LUBE-A-MATIC TOP PUNCH
SHPG. WT. ⅛ lb. $3.00

Part No.	Top Punch	Part No.	Top Punch	Part No.	Top Punch	Part No.	Top Punch
82504	#115	82534	#460	85535	#535	85585	#585
82506	#190	82536	#465	85540	#540	85590	#590
82513	#311	82541	#495	85546	#546	85595	#595
82515	#344	82500	#500	85550	#550	85600	#600
82519	#374	85505	#505	85555	#555	85605	#605
82522	#402	85510	#510	85560	#560	82544	#610
82527	#421	85516	#516	85565	#565	85615	#615
82528	#424	85520	#520	85570	#570	85620	#620
82529	#429	85525	#525	85575	#575	82545	#680
82543	#445	85530	#530	85580	#580		

LUBE-A-MATIC BULLET SIZER DIES

Lube-A-Matic Sizer Dies are designed to swage bullets—with or without gas checks—to their correct diameters without shaving lead. This swaging action work-hardens the alloy through compression and produces a perfectly cylindrical bullet of increased strength, smoothness and accuracy.

BULLET SIZER DIE
SHPG. WT. ¼ lb. $9.00

Part No.	Sizer Die	Part No.	Sizer Die
82200	.224"	82222	.357"
82236	.228"	82223	.358"
82201	.243"	82224	.375"
82203	.257"	82225	.400"
82204	.264"	82238	.406"
82205	.277"	82226	.410"
82208	.284"	82227	.427"
82211	.308"	82228	.429"
82212	.309"	82230	.439"
82213	.310"	82239	.446"
82217	.321"	82231	.450"
82237	.323"	82232	.451"
82218	.338"	82233	.452"
82219	.354"	82234	.454"
82220	.355"	82235	.457"
82221	.356"	82240	.512"

45 BASIC BRASS CASES

45 Basic Brass is ideal for the reloader who wants to produce unusual calibers of cartridges, or calibers that are no longer available from the factory. They can be formed into many different calibers with RCBS Case Forming Dies. With proper reloading, each case can be reloaded up to 20 times.

PART NO.	DESCRIPTION	SHPG. WT.	PRICE
79001	45 Basic Brass Cases	1 lb.	$17.20

REDDING RELOADING TOOLS

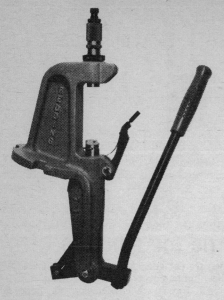

IMPROVED "C" PRESS
MODEL No. 7

New improvements include: Stronger frame (ASTM 30 alloy) for the heaviest reloading task; extremely shallow throat eliminates deflection; stronger (alloy steel) lower linkage; added rear mounting lug—prevents springing and "bench splitting;" snap-in shell holder may be rotated to any position; accepts all standard ⅞-14 threaded dies and all universal shell holders. Press includes primer arm for seating both large and small primers.

No. 7 "C" Press, complete	$48.00
No. 7K Kit includes press, shell holder, and one set of dies .	64.95
No. 19 Automatic Primer Feeder	10.95
No. 20 Primer Catcher	4.00

SUPER 32
SHOTSHELL RELOADER

Turret-type press capable of producing up to 300 reloads/hr. All operations are performed at one station without shell handling. Will handle high or low brass cases from 2½″ to 3″ without complicated adjustments or conversion kits. Quick change—pull pin die head allows user to change to a different gauge in about 60-90 seconds without die adjustments. Press comes complete with all necessary bushings, dies, etc. for one gauge.

CONVERSION KIT FOR SUPER 32

All the parts necessary to change from one gauge to another.
Includes complete die head assembly, dies, crimp starter, shellholder, bushings and quick release pin.

Conversion Kit Super 32, 12 or 20 ga.	$ 44.50
16, 28 or 410 ga.	49.50
Super 32, complete, 12 or 20 ga.	124.95
16, 28 or .410 ga.	129.95

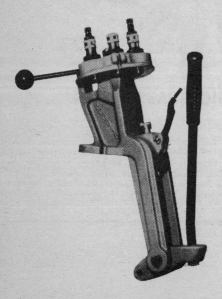

TURRET RELOADING PRESS
MODEL 25:

Extremely rugged, ideal for production reloading. Choice of four or six Station Turrets. No need to move shell, just rotate turret head to positive alignment. Ram accepts any standard snap-in shell holder. Includes primer arm for seating both small and large primers.

No. 25 Press, complete	$124.95
No. 25K Kit, includes press, shell holder, and one set of dies.	$142.00
No. 25T Extra Turret (4 or 6 Station)	28.00
No. 19T Automatic Primer Feeder	12.00

REDDING RELOADING TOOLS

MASTER CASE TRIMMER, MODEL 14

A unique spindle design permits all operations to be done with the handle of the tool: After insertion of case, a one-quarter turn clockwise of handle locks the case; handle is then advanced toward cutter and rotated clockwise to cut; handle is withdrawn to remove case neck from pilot; handle is turned about one-quarter turn counter-clockwise to release case. The handle is provided with a large knurled and rounded knob that rotates freely under pressure.

Supplied with two cutting blades.

No. 14 Case Trimmer $28.95
No. 15 Pilot.......................... $1.75 each.

MASTER CASE TRIMMER MODEL No. 14K

This unit features a universal collet that accepts all rifle and pistol cases. This trimmer is also unique in that it chamfers and deburrs the case neck at the same time it is trimmed to length. The frame is solid cast iron with storage holes in the base for extra pilots. Both coarse and fine adjustments are provided for case length.

The case-neck cleaning brush and primer pocket cleaners attached to the frame of this tool make it a very handy addition to the reloading bench.

Trimmer comes complete with the following:
* * Two cutting blades (one cuts straight, one chamfers while cutting)
* * Two pilots (.22 cal. and .30 cal.)
* * Universal collet
* * Two neck cleaning brushes (.22 thru .30 cal.)
* * Two primer pocket cleaners (Large and Small)

No. 14K Master Case Trimmer complete. $34.50
No. 15 Pilots. 1.75

MASTER POWDER MEASURE MODEL 3

Universal- or pistol-metering chambers interchange in seconds. Measures charges from ½ to 100 grains. Unit fitted with lock ring for fast dump with large "clear" plastic reservoir. "See-thru" Drop Tube accepts all calibers from .22 to .600. Precision-fitted rotating drum, critically honed to prevent powder escape. Knife-edged powder chamber shears coarse-grained powders with ease, ensuring accurate charges.

No. 3 Master Powder Measure, (Specify Universal- or Pistol-Metering chamber) $39.95
No. 3K Kit Form, includes both Universal and Pistol chambers. . . $47.50
No. 3-12 Universal or Pistol chamber. $9.50

POWDER TRICKLER MODEL No. 5

Brings underweight charges up to accurate reading, adding powder to scale pan a granule or two at a time by rotating knob. Speeds weighing of each charge. Solid steel, low center of gravity. "Companion" height to all reloading scales; weighs a full pound.
No. 5 Powder Trickler. $7.95

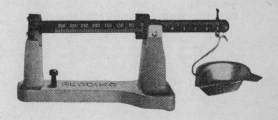

STANDARD POWDER AND BULLET SCALE
Model No. 1

For the beginner or veteran reloader. Only two counterpoises need to be moved to obtain the full capacity range of 1/10 grain to 380 grains. Clearly graduated with white numerals and lines on a black background. Total capacity of this scale is 380 grains. An over and under plate graduate in 10th grains allows checking of variations in powder charges or bullets without further adjustments.
Model No. 1 ....$24.95

REDDING RELOADING TOOLS

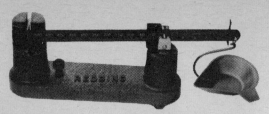

MASTER POWDER AND BULLET SCALE
MODEL No. 2

Guaranteed accurate to less than 1/10 grain. Master model has magnetic dampening for fast readings. 1/10 grain graduated over/under plate permits checking powder charge variations without moving counterpoises. Features also include: 505-grain capacity; high-visibility graduated beam; pour-spout pan; stable cast base; large convenient leveling screw; hardened and honed, self-aligning beam bearings for lifetime accuracy.

No. 2 Scale $32.95

RELOADING DIES
MODEL No. 10

Redding dies are made from alloy steels heat treated and hand polished. All Redding dies are lifetime guaranteed and use no aluminum parts or plating. Standard ⅞-14 thread to fit most presses. Available in 2 Or 3 die rifle sets, 3 die pistol sets and 4 die pistol sets with taper crimp.

Series A $19.50
Series B 22.95

All Redding dies are packaged in the combination plastic storage box/loading block.

Neck sizing dies are available in most bottleneck calibers for those who wish to resize only the necks for longer case life and better accuracy.

Custom made dies are available on special order.

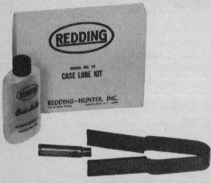

CASE LUBE KIT
MODEL No. 12

New Case Lube Tongs simplify and increase speed of case lubrication. Conforms to all cartridge cases, especially useful to ensure proper case neck lubrication. Eliminates stuck cases and pulled rims. Prolongs life of dies and simplifies case reforming. Includes 2 oz. plastic bottle of Redding case lube.

No. 12 Case Lube Kit $5.95
No. 21 Case Lube only, 2 oz. Bottle 2.00

"SUPERCHARGER"
POWDER MEASURE KITS
MODEL No. 101 AND 102

Supercharger Kit No. 101

Contains: Model No. 1 Standard Powder and Bullet Scale, Model No. 3 Master Powder Measure, Model No. 5 Powder Trickler and Model No. 6 Bench Stand.

No. 101 .... $74.50

Supercharger Kit No. 102

Contains: Model No. 2 Master Powder and Bullet Scale, Model No. 3 Powder Measure, Model No. 5 Powder Trickler and Model No. 6 Bench Stand.

No. 102 .... $81.75

TITANIUM CARBIDE PISTOL Dies
Model No. 10-TIC

Titanium carbide has the highest hardness of any readily available carbide yet is not as brittle. Its smooth, rounded micrograins present a slippery, nongalling surface, unattainable with other carbides. Lubrication is a thing of the past and the inserts are tapered, to prevent belts or shoulders on your cases.

No. 10-TIC Pistol Die Sets $42.50
  (9mm Luger approximately 25 percent higher)
No. 10-TIC Sizing Die Complete 32.50
  (9mm Luger approximately 25 percent higher)
No. 1021 R Decapping Rod Assembly 4.00

SELF-INDEXING STAR
CRIMP STARTER
MODEL 23

In reloading some plastic and new paper cases, a good folded crimp can only be obtained by use of a Star Crimp Starter. The Redding Self-indexing Star Crimp Starter attaches to the No. 32 Shotshell Reloader and is available in 6 or 8 point star. Fired cases must be recrimped with the same number of folds as in the original for best results. Available in 12, 16, 20 Ga., 6 & 8 point—28 & .410 Ga., 6 point only.

Model No. 23 Crimp Starter, 6 or 8 point.......... $6.00

CASE PREPARATION KIT MODEL NO. 18

All the tools you need in one package for removing dirt and powder residue from the inside of case necks and primer pockets. Kit comes complete with accessory handle, large and small primer pocket cleaners and three case neck brushes to handle all cartridges from 22 thru 45 caliber.

$5.95

TEXAN RELOADING TOOLS

MODEL RT 6 STATION

The Model RT6 Station with adjustable wad pressure has the Texan split bar arrangement, self-aligning nylon crimp starter, all steel crimper for Texan Taper Crimp, double-link leverage. It features an indexing turret, primer catcher box right in front. It is designed for high speed production of shotgun shells and is ideally suited for skeet and trap shooters' high volume requirements.

12 and 20 gauge only $189.95

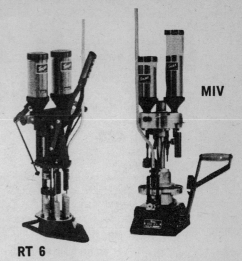

MIV

MODEL MIV

The MIV has a smooth self-indexing action which moves cases through all stations to produce a completed shell for each pull of the handle. The automatic priming system functions only if there is a case in position to be reprimed. It features a wad guide, which prevents deformed cases, easy to adjust and read wad pressure system, shell retention system, self-aligning crimp starter. It includes 6- and 8-point* crimp starters, shell ejector, cam, shell catcher, primer catcher, automatic primer feed and shot and powder bushings for both target and field loads.

RT 6

M-V	New Loader with Brass Resizing station plus all features of MIV Complete with primer feed, shell ejector and catcher and automatic index. 12, 16, 20, 28 410 gauges $459.95
M-IV	Loader 12, 16, 20, 28, 410 gauges with primer feed, shell ejector, and catcher $359.95
M-IV	Loader - "Basic" without primer feed, ejector or shell catcher 12, 16, 20, 28, 410 ga. $269.95
MIV-CS	Crimp Starter. (Specify gauge and number of points) ....$ 5.95

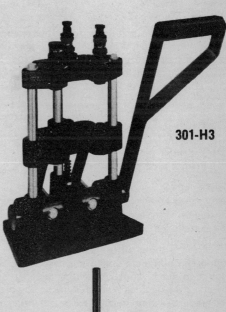

301-H3

MODIFICATIONS

Modernize the Texan Models M-II or MIIA to include several of the new systems from the MIV. The following systems may be installed without drilling, reaming or othewise modifying the basic tool.

MIV-APF*	Complete Priming System ....$ 49.95 *Red Model M requires additional deprime punch for Primer Feed conversion .... $ 2.95
MIV-WG	Complete Self Lowering Wad Guide System, including Nylon Wad Guide Finger ....$ 9.95 (Specify Gauge)
MIV-WP	Complete Wad Pressure System ....$ 9.95 (Specify Gauge)
MIV-STAGE	with Plate, Springs and E.C. Cam ....$ 45.00
MII, MIIA/MIV	Change Over Package (Specify Gauge) Complete— Includes Priming, Wad Guide, Wad Pressure, and Stage .... $ 99.95
M-V	New Sizer Package to fit Models MIIA and MIV (Press Head, Measure Cam holder, and All sizer parts) $100.00

101-T-11

Factory Overhaul of any Model M, MII, MIIA, MIV, or MV for parts, transportation, and $25.00 flat rate labor.

TEXAN RELOADING TOOLS

SHELLHOLDER

Texan Shellholder heads and rams are made of high quality steel. The No. 214 Universal Shellholder Head is interchangeable between both No. 214 C-type and No. 214 H-type Shellholder Rams.

The No. 214 C-type fits Texan Model "C" and other "C" presses. No. 214 H-type fits Texan Model 101-T-II, 301-H3 and other make H-type presses. When ordering rams, specify No. 214-C or No. 214-H type.

No. 214	Universal Head (specify number)	....$2.95
No. 214-H	Universal Ram, H-Type	3.95
No. 214-C	Universal Ram, C-Type	3.95

NO. 214 SHELLHOLDER HEAD GROUP NUMBERS

GROUP NO. 1		GROUP NO. 2	30 Remington	8mm - 338	44 Magnum	357 Magnum	GROUP NO. 16
225 Win.	7mm - 270	219 Zipper	32 Remington	338 Winchester	44 Russian	38 Special	9 MM Luger
22/250 (22 Var.)	280 Remington	219 Donaldson	351 Winchester	35 Newton	.444 Marlin	38 Long Colt	GROUP NO. 17
243 Winchester	7.7 Jap	22 Sav. Hi-Power		358 Norma Mag.	GROUP NO. 9	GROUP NO. 13	41 Mag.
243 Rockchucker	30 - 06	25-35	GROUP NO. 6	375 Wea. Mag.	38 - 40	6.5 x 55	GROUP NO. 18
244 Remington	300 Savage	30-30	257 Wea. Mag.	375 H & H Mag.	44 - 40	7.65 Belgian Mauser	45 Auto Rim.
6mm Remington	308 Winchester	32 Special	264 Winchester	11mm Mauser	GROUP NO. 10	GROUP NO. 14	SPECIALS
228 Ack. Mag.	7.9 Mauser	32 - 40	264 - 270	458 Winchester	32 Long Colt	.35 Rem.	45 Long Colt
257 Roberts	8mm Mann. Sch.	38 - 55	270 Wea. Mag.	ALL Ack. Sh. Mag.	32 S & W	6.5 Carcano	30 M1 or 32 ACP
250/3000 (250 Sav.)	8mm Mauser	GROUP NO. 3	275 H & H Mag.	6.5 Rem. Mag.	GROUP NO. 11	7.35 Italian	
250 Donaldson	8 x 51	218 Bee	276 Dubiel	350 Rem. Mag.	30 Luger	GROUP NO. 15	
25/06	8 x 60	25 - 20 Repeater	7 x 61 Sharpe & Hart	GROUP NO. 7	30 Mauser	221	
6.5 x 57	8mm - 06	32 - 20	7mm Wea. Mag.	8 x 57 Rimmed	38 Super Auto	222 Rem.	
6.5 x 06	333 OKH	GROUP NO. 4	7 mm Rem. Mag.	GROUP NO. 8	GROUP NO. 12	222 Rem. Mag.	
6mm - 06	35 Whelen	220 Swift	300 Wea. Mag.	25 - 303	22 Super Jet	223 Rem.	
256 Newton	358 Winchester	220 Rocket	300 H & H Mag.	30 - 40 Krag	22 Rem. Jet	380 Auto	
270 WCF	9mm Mauser	240 Cobra	300 Winchester	303 British	256 Win. Mag.	9 MM Short	
7mm Mauser	9mm Mann. Sch.	GROUP NO. 5	300 Norma Mag.	35 WCF	All other shellholder heads must be ordered by caliber as		
7 x 57	9.3 x 72	25 Remington	30 - 338	44 Special	they are not interchangeable with this group of calibers.		
7 x 64	45 ACP		30 Newton				

MODEL 101-T-11

The 101T11 is a seven-station turret-type press that provides space for three two-die rifle sets or two three-die pistol sets plus one station for powder measure or other accessory. All stations threaded 7/8 -14 to accept all popular rifle and pistol die sets. Interchangeable universal shell holder heads allow fast easy caliber changes. Rugged cast iron base and powerful leverage plus rigid two-post construction to insure ease of operation. Optional primer feed eliminates handling of primers and speeds up reloading operation.

101-T-II Press with primer feed	$149.95
101-T-II Press without primer feed	134.95
191 Primer feed complete	22.95
101-T Primer post, large or small	1.95
191 Primer feed post, large or small	1.95

MODEL FW

The FW features rugged aluminum castings and two column design plus double, toggle-action linkage. Cam action ejects high or low brass cases from resize die without adjustment. Repriming is positive with full base wad support to eliminate concaving case head. Shell mouth spreader opens shell mouth to aid in effortless seating of all types of wads through the self-lowering wad guide. Wad pressure is completely adjustable for all type wads. Self-aligning crimp starter seeks out original folds and final crimp die produces "Taper Crimp." Swivel top allows easy draining of powder or shot and convenient changing of powder or shot bushings. Unique base design allows operation without being bolted to bench or table. Conversion to other gauges is simple. All parts, including shot and powder, are included in kit.

FW Loader 12, 16, 20, 28, 410 gauge	$89.95
FW Loader, 12, 20, or 410 gauge 3"	89.95
FW Loader with Primer Feed Installed	99.95
12, 16, 20, 28 not available in 410 gauge	
FW-CK Conversion Kit 12, 16, 20, 28, 410 gauge	$34.95
FW-SPL-CK Conversion Kit—Special 3" 2¾" to 3"	19.95
12, 20, or 410 gauge	
FW-CK 3" Conversion Kit 12, 20, or 410 ga. 3" regular	$39.95
FW-APF Automatic Primer Feed	14.95
FW-CS Crimp Starter (Specify gauge and number of points)	5.95

The FW crimp starter may be used on Texan RT and FW loaders.

MODEL 256 DOUBLE C PRESS

The Model 256 double C press is a heavy duty press with a rugged malleable cast frame. Precise alignment of the die and ram is insured by precision broaching. Threaded 7/8 -14 to accept all popular dies. Universal primer arm includes cups and punches to seat both large and small primers. Equipped with universal shell holder ram and primer arm.

Model 256 C Press	$44.95
(with primer arm and ram)	

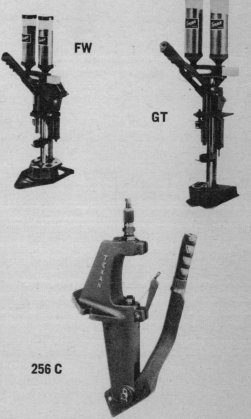

FW

GT

256 C

TEXAN RELOADING TOOLS

MODEL R-1 SHOTSHELL RECONDITIONER

Recommended for use in conjunction with the Texan models M-IV and other automatic reloaders. Reconditions both plastic and paper cases to fit all makes of shotguns. One pull of the handle resizes, deprimes, flattens bulged or concaved case head and reseats base wad. Makes possible reloads that look and perform like new.

Model R1 12 & 20 gauge $34.95
Model R1 12, 16, 20, 28 or 410 guage $29.95
Model R1-CK Conversion Kit 12, 16, 20, 28 or
   410 gauge ....$ 9.95

POWDER SCALE

With magnetic or oil damped beam. Tenth grain to 500 grain graduation. Hardened knife-edged fulcrum points, three counterpoises, large pan with pouring spout and leveling screw. Rugged cast base.

No. 304 with magnetic damped beam $24.95

POWDER FUNNEL/FUNNEL HOLDER

Aids in filling all size cartridges. Attachable to Texan powder scales. Non-clog tapered funnel of bright luminescent yellow plastic. Steel holder.

No. 305110 Funnel Small (for calibers .264 and
   under) ....$ .75
No. 305120 Funnel Large (for calibers .270 and
   over) ....$ .75

RELOADING ACCESSORIES

DEBURRING TOOL. Chamfers or deburrs mouth of cartridge cases to clean, smooth edge.
No. 259 ....$3.50

TEXAN DIE LUBE. Specially formulated lubricant. Exacting companion to Texan Micro-Bore dies.
2 oz. $1.00

BULLET PULLER. Will not mar or scratch bullet. Standard 7/8-14 thread.
No. 302 Bullet Puller without collet $4.50
No. 302 Collet of Special Caliber (specify) 2.00

CASE TRIMMER. Collets and pilots for all size cases. Accurate precision trimming.
No. 303 Case Trimmer without Collet and Pilot $14.50
No. 303 Collet 2.75
No. 303 Pilot (specify caliber) .... .60

CASE LUBE PAD. The fast, easy way to lubricate. Eliminates dents caused by excess lube.
Use with Texan die lube $2.95

"C" TYPE PRIMER ARM. For Texan No. 156 and No. 256 "C" presses. Fits most standard "C" presses or other makes.
No. 255 ....$3.95

ACCESSORIES INCLUDED WITH "C" TYPE PRIMER ARM. Large primer pin, concave; large primer pin, flat; small primer pin, concave; small primer pin, large sleeve and small sleeve $1.50

MICRO-BORE PISTOL AND RIFLE DIES

Texan two-die sets, for bottle neck cases, and three-die sets for straight wall cases are constructed from special alloy steel, micro-bored and polished to rigid specifications. Each die body is treated inside and out, for protection against wear, rust or corrosion. Precision dies that feature the hex body design and double hex lock rings for secure, mar-free wrench adjustment. Every set packaged in attractive plastic display and storage box.

2 Die Rifle Set $19.50
   Sizer Complete 10.00
   Seater Complete 10.00
3 Die Pistol Set 19.50
   Sizing Die Complete 8.00
   Expander Die Complete 7.00
Plastic Die Storage Box Only 1.00

Caliber Available	No. Dies in Set	Shell Holder	Caliber Available	No. Dies in Set	Shell Holder	Caliber Available	No. Dies in Set	Shell Holder
222 Rem.	2	15	280 Rem.	2	1	350 Rem. Mag.	2	6
222 Rem. Mag.	2	15	284 Win.	2	1	38 S&W	3	SPL
223 Rem. (AR)	2	15	7MM Rem. Mag.	2	6	38 Super Auto.	3	11
22-250 Rem.	2	1	30 M1. Car.	3	SPL 30 M1	380 Auto.	3	15
243 Win.	2	1	30-30 Win.	2	2	9MM Luger	3	16
244 Rem.	2	1	300 Savage	2	1	38 Special	3	12
6MM Rem.	2	1	308 Win.	2	1	357 Mag.	3	12
257 Roberts	2	1	30-06	2	1	41 Mag.	3	17
25-06 Rem.	2	1	300 Win. Mag.	2	6	44 Special	3	8
264 Win.	2	6	303 British	2	8	44 Mag.	3	8
6.5 Rem. Mag.	2	6	8MM Mauser (8 x 57)	2	1	45 Auto. Rim.	3	18
270 Win.	2	1	338 Win. Mag.	2	6	45 A.C.P.	3	1
7MM Mauser (7 x 57)	2	1	35 Rem.	2	14	45 Long Colt	3	SPL 45 LC

MODEL 301-H3

Uses 3-die pistol or 2-die rifle sets in one press without changing dies during the reloading operation. Stations are threaded 7/8-14 to accept all standard rifle and pistol dies. Uses H-type Universal rams and Universal shellholder heads. Three-column design maintains positive alignment for exacting reloading and smooth operation. Includes both large and small primer seating posts and three Universal H-type rams. Heavy-duty cast metal brass drilled for bench mounting.

Press with handle, 3 Universal H-type Shellholder
   Rams, large and small primer seating posts $79.95
H-3 Primer Posts, large or small 1.95

Index

A collection of early SHOOTER'S BIBLE pages has been reproduced on the inside front and back covers to capture the flavor of a past which is gone but not forgotten.